W9-DIR-196

West's Law School
Advisory Board

JESSE H. CHOPER
Professor of Law,
University of California, Berkeley

DAVID P. CURRIE
Professor of Law, University of Chicago

YALE KAMISAR
Professor of Law, University of Michigan
Professor of Law, University of San Diego

MARY KAY KANE
Chancellor, Dean and Distinguished Professor of Law,
University of California,
Hastings College of the Law

WAYNE R. LaFAVE
Professor of Law, University of Illinois

ARTHUR R. MILLER
Professor of Law, Harvard University

GRANT S. NELSON
Professor of Law,
University of California, Los Angeles

JAMES J. WHITE
Professor of Law, University of Michigan

LAW AND RELIGION, A READER: CASES, CONCEPTS, AND THEORY

By

Frank S. Ravitch
Associate Professor of Law
Michigan State University College of Law

AMERICAN CASEBOOK SERIES®

THOMSON
WEST

Mat # 40105564

West, a Thomson business, has created this publication to provide you with accurate and authoritative information concerning the subject matter covered. However, this publication was not necessarily prepared by persons licensed to practice law in a particular jurisdiction. West is not engaged in rendering legal or other professional advice, and this publication is not a substitute for the advice of an attorney. If you require legal or other expert advice, you should seek the services of a competent attorney or other professional.

American Casebook Series and West Group are trademarks registered in the U.S. Patent and Trademark Office.

© 2004 West, a Thomson business
    610 Opperman Drive
    P.O. Box 64526
    St. Paul, MN 55164–0526
    1–800–328–9352

ISBN 0–314–14413–7

TEXT IS PRINTED ON 10% POST CONSUMER RECYCLED PAPER

This book is dedicated to my wife Jamie, and to
my daughters Elysha and Ariana, whose
love and support add perspective
to everything I do

*

Preface

This book focuses on Law and Religion. The book covers two general topics: 1) Church/State Law (issues relating to the First Amendment to the United States Constitution); and 2) Religious Law (the role and substance of law in various religious traditions). Most books in this field have little or no material on the latter topic. While the bulk of this book is devoted to Church/State Law, the book also provides an overview of Jewish Law (Halakha), Islamic Law (Shari'ah), Catholic Canon Law, Protestant conceptions of law, and Buddhist conceptions of law. The discussion of Church/State law integrates cases, narrative, and excerpts from leading articles and books to provide an in-depth understanding of the Religion Clauses of the United States Constitution.

This book includes a brief narrative discussion of each topic included, followed by the relevant cases and articles, and then notes and questions. The goal of the narrative is to provide students with context (the forest) so that they can grapple with the many complex issues that are raised in law and religion cases/articles (the trees). The sections on religious law will follow a similar format, especially for the sections on Jewish Law, Islamic Law, and Canon Law, which are more formalized legal systems.

Most of the cases and articles in this book have been edited. I have attempted not to over-edit cases so that students will have as much context as possible for each decision, but naturally some cases have been edited more than others given considerations of space. Deletions from the original document are denoted with three ellipses (***). Deleted citations (of which there are many) and footnotes, however, are not denoted. Footnotes that have not been deleted retain the note number assigned by the court/author. I have included lengthy excerpts from concurring and dissenting opinions in a number of cases. I have done so because concurring and dissenting opinions in Religion Clause cases often make significant points that are important for a full understanding of the underlying debates or that later become the law.

Acknowledgments

There are many people I would like to thank for their support and advice during the writing and production of this book. First, my wife Jamie, for her love and support, and for always serving as an excellent sounding board and reader for my work. My daughters Elysha and Ariana, whose smiles and unconditional love make every day brighter and add balance to everything I do. My parents, Carl and Arline Ravitch, who are a source of constant support and love, and who are an inspiration for all three of their children. To my late Bubby and Pop Pop, who are always close to my heart, and who embodied all that is best in religion and in law, without being lawyers or overtly religious. To my in-laws, Barbara and

v

Gerry Grosslicht, my sisters Sharon and Elizabeth and their families, my Uncle Gary and Aunt Mindy, and my Aunt Jackie and Uncle Ken, who have been exceptionally supportive of all my work, and who each in their own way have an interest in law and/or religion.

I am grateful to Dean Terence Blackburn and the Michigan State University College of Law, which supported some of my work on this book with a summer research grant, and to Charles Ten Brink, Hildur Hannah, Jane Edwards, and the staff of the Michigan State University College of Law Library for their help and support. I would also like to thank Sarah Belzer for her excellent research assistance and Jacklyn Beard for her excellent secretarial support. I am also grateful to my Spring 2004 Law & Religion class at MSU for their helpful input, and for serving as wonderful "Guinea Pigs" for this book, which will inure to the benefit of every class that uses the book in the future. This project would have never come into being without the support of Louis Higgins at West, to whom I am grateful for seeing the potential of this book, and Roxy Birkel at West, who did a tremendous job getting this book to press.

Summary of Contents

Table of Contents

Table of Cases

The principal cases are in bold type. Cases cited or discussed in the text are roman type. References are to pages. Cases cited in principal cases and within other quoted materials are not included.

*

LAW AND RELIGION, A READER: CASES, CONCEPTS, AND THEORY

*

SECTION ONE: RELIGION IN THE U.S. LEGAL SYSTEM

INTRODUCTION

A.   THE RELIGION CLAUSES: AN OVERVIEW

The First Amendment to the United States Constitution reads as follows:

> Congress shall make no law respecting an establishment of religion, or prohibiting the free exercise thereof; or abridging the freedom of speech, or of the press; or the right of the people peaceably to assemble, and to petition the Government for a redress of grievances.

The two Religion Clauses contained in the First Amendment are commonly referred to as the Establishment Clause and the Free Exercise Clause, respectively. The only other mention of religion in the United States Constitution is the prohibition against religious tests "as a qualification to any office or public trust under the United States," which is contained in Article VI. As you will see, much attention has been paid to the Religion Clauses of the First Amendment, particularly since the early part of the Twentieth Century. The next seven chapters of this book are devoted primarily to understanding the Establishment Clause and the Free Exercise Clause.

Both the Free Exercise Clause and the Establishment Clause have been incorporated via the Fourteenth Amendment, and thus state and local governments as well as the federal government are bound by the religion clauses. *See Everson v. Bd. of Educ.*, 330 U.S. 1, 67 S.Ct. 504, 91 L.Ed. 711 (1947) (incorporation of the Establishment Clause); *Cantwell v. Connecticut*, 310 U.S. 296, 60 S.Ct. 900, 84 L.Ed. 1213 (1940) (incorporation of the Free Exercise Clause). Prior to incorporation the religion clauses only applied to the federal government. Therefore, it should come as no surprise that the number of Religion Clause cases increased dramatically after incorporation; although there are demographic and social reasons for the increase as well.

The relationship between the two clauses, and between each and the Free Speech Clause also contained in the First Amendment, is a complex one. The role of the Free Speech Clause, especially in relation to Establishment Clause issues, will be discussed in later chapters. Yet it is essential to point out the potential tension between the two religion clauses even at this early juncture in your study of the subject matter. You will have an opportunity in later chapters to decide for yourself

1

whether the tension between the two clauses is real or imagined, significant or insignificant. For now, it is important to note that when government seeks to avoid an establishment of religion by altering its relations with private citizens and entities the Free Exercise Clause could potentially be implicated. Similarly, when government seeks to accommodate the free exercise of religion the Establishment Clause could potentially be implicated. This will become more clear as you learn the various approaches to issues that arise under the religion clauses.

The tension between the two clauses may be, in part, the result of the principles that are said to undergird the clauses. Principles such as separation of church and state and accommodation of religion can coexist in some contexts, but this is not always so. Moreover, the nature of the two clauses may be different in ways that will become clear as you learn about each clause. For now, it is useful to note that the Establishment Clause generally focuses upon the government's relationship to religion, and some have argued it is not an individual right in the same way that free exercise or free speech are, while the Free Exercise Clause focuses upon an individual's right to practice her religion free from unconstitutional government interference.

B. ORGANIZATION OF THIS SECTION

This section begins with a discussion of the Establishment Clause. That discussion will be broken into five chapters. Chapter One will provide a discussion of the early development of the Establishment Clause from *Everson* to the 1960's. As will be seen this material is not just a matter of historical curiosity as it continues to effect analysis of Establishment Clause issues. Chapter Two will focus on public religious exercises and expression. This discussion will include public school prayer, public school curricular decisions, ceremonial deism, and legislative prayer. Chapter Three will focus on public displays, religious symbolism, and access to government owned facilities. Issues such as holiday displays and the display of other religious symbols such as the Ten Commandments will be addressed in this chapter. Moreover, the chapter will explore the distinction between government sponsored displays and privately sponsored displays on government property that has been opened for expressive activity. Chapter Four will focus on aid to religiously affiliated institutions. This chapter will address issues such as financial and other support for religious schools, school vouchers, tax exemptions for religious institutions, financial support for other religiously affiliated institutions, access by religious groups to various types of public funding, and charitable choice. Chapter Five will explore the conceptual framework said to undergird the Establishment Clause. This chapter will explore questions such as: 1. what is neutrality and does it exist?; and 2. how should principles such as separation and accommodation function in various situations, and can they be consistently applied? The material in this chapter is especially important if one wants to consider in which direction Establishment Clause jurisprudence might go in the future, or if one be able to critically analyze current or earlier doctrines developed by the courts.

Following the discussion of the Establishment Clause will be an analysis of the Free Exercise Clause. That discussion will be broken into two chapters. Chapter Six will address the historical evolution of Free Exercise Clause doctrine, the doctrine applicable to Free Exercise Clause "exemption" cases and the response to that doctrine, and the analysis of intentional discrimination by government entities under the Free Exercise Clause. Chapter Seven will provide several perspectives on the Free Exercise Clause. Each of these perspectives is grounded in current theoretical approaches to Free Exercise Clause questions, and each will enable students to better understand and question the various doctrines that have evolved under the Free Exercise Clause. The discussion of the Free Exercise Clause will include a discussion of legislative measures that have been passed in response to the Court's treatment of free exercise issues. Chapter Seven will be followed by Section Two, where the focus will shift to the role of law in various religious systems.

Chapter One

THE EARLY DEVELOPMENT OF ESTABLISHMENT CLAUSE DOCTRINE

A. *EVERSON* AND THE "HIGH AND IMPREGNABLE WALL" (WITH A GATE FOR SCHOOL BUSES)

When people discuss issues that arise under the Establishment Clause there is a tendency, at least in common parlance, to refer to the "separation of church and state." Indeed the phrase "a wall of separation between church and state" was invoked in the first modern Establishment Clause case, and the principle of separationism was a guiding principle in the Court's early attempts to grapple with the Establishment Clause. It remains a relevant principle in many areas of Establishment Clause analysis today, but the "wall" is currently neither high nor impregnable. Our discussion of Establishment Clause doctrine will start in 1947, the beginning of the modern era of Establishment Clause analysis. In that year the U.S. Supreme Court decided *Everson v. Board of Educ.*, 330 U.S. 1, 67 S.Ct. 504, 91 L.Ed. 711 (1947). *Everson* is important for a number of reasons. First, it addresses the incorporation of the Establishment Clause through the Fourteenth Amendment. Second, it is the first modern decision by the Court to attempt to define a standard governing Establishment Clause issues. Finally, both the development of that standard and the disagreement among the Justices over its application portended the complex and winding path Establishment Clause analysis has taken since *Everson*. Justices have frequently disagreed over the principles and tests that govern in Establishment Clause cases, and even when Justices have agreed, there have been vast disagreements over the application of those principles and tests to various situations.

The tension between competing principles and the debate over the role and application of principles evidenced in the early cases, remain today. While the Court no longer relies on strict separationism as the hallmark principle for Establishment Clause claims, *see infra*, Chapters Two–Five, debate continues over the role and application of separationism and other principles that arise in one or more of the cases that follow. Thus, while these cases are historical, they are not merely historical. Aspects of each decision remain today, and none of the following cases has been overturned; although as you will see later, they have been distinguished. In order to understand the materials presented in later chapters it is important to study *Everson* and it's progeny.

EVERSON v. BOARD OF EDUCATION OF EWING TP.

United States Supreme Court, 1947.
330 U.S. 1, 67 S.Ct. 504, 91 L.Ed. 711.

MR. JUSTICE BLACK delivered the opinion of the Court.

A New Jersey statute authorizes its local school districts to make rules and contracts for the transportation of children to and from schools. The appellee, a township board of education, acting pursuant to this statute authorized reimbursement to parents of money expended by them for the bus transportation of their children on regular busses operated by the public transportation system. Part of this money was for the payment of transportation of some children in the community to Catholic parochial schools. These church schools give their students, in addition to secular education, regular religious instruction conforming to the religious tenets and modes of worship of the Catholic Faith. The superintendent of these schools is a Catholic priest.

The appellant, in his capacity as a district taxpayer, filed suit in a State court challenging the right of the Board to reimburse parents of parochial school students. * * *

* * *

The only contention here is that the State statute and the resolution, in so far as they authorized reimbursement to parents of children attending parochial schools, violate the Federal Constitution * * *. * * * The statute and the resolution forced inhabitants to pay taxes to help support and maintain schools which are dedicated to, and which regularly teach, the Catholic Faith. This is alleged to be a use of State power to support church schools contrary to the prohibition of the First Amendment which the Fourteenth Amendment made applicable to the states.

* * *

* * * The New Jersey statute is challenged as a "law respecting an establishment of religion." The First Amendment, as made applicable to the states by the Fourteenth, commands that a state "shall make no law respecting an establishment of religion, or prohibiting the free exercise thereof." These words of the First Amendment reflected in the minds of early Americans a vivid mental picture of conditions and practices which they fervently wished to stamp out in order to preserve liberty for themselves and for their posterity. Doubtless their goal has not been

entirely reached; but so far has the Nation moved toward it that the expression "law respecting an establishment of religion," probably does not so vividly remind present-day Americans of the evils, fears, and political problems that caused that expression to be written into our Bill of Rights. Whether this New Jersey law is one respecting the "establishment of religion" requires an understanding of the meaning of that language, particularly with respect to the imposition of taxes. Once again, therefore, it is not inappropriate briefly to review the background and environment of the period in which that constitutional language was fashioned and adopted.

A large proportion of the early settlers of this country came here from Europe to escape the bondage of laws which compelled them to support and attend government favored churches. The centuries immediately before and contemporaneous with the colonization of America had been filled with turmoil, civil strife, and persecutions, generated in large part by established sects determined to maintain their absolute political and religious supremacy. With the power of government supporting them, at various times and places, Catholics had persecuted Protestants, Protestants had persecuted Catholics, Protestant sects had persecuted other Protestant sects, Catholics of one shade of belief had persecuted Catholics of another shade of belief, and all of these had from time to time persecuted Jews. In efforts to force loyalty to whatever religious group happened to be on top and in league with the government of a particular time and place, men and women had been fined, cast in jail, cruelly tortured, and killed. Among the offenses for which these punishments had been inflicted were such things as speaking disrespectfully of the views of ministers of government-established churches, nonattendance at those churches, expressions of non-belief in their doctrines, and failure to pay taxes and tithes to support them.

These practices of the old world were transplanted to and began to thrive in the soil of the new America. The very charters granted by the English Crown to the individuals and companies designated to make the laws which would control the destinies of the colonials authorized these individuals and companies to erect religious establishments which all, whether believers or non-believers, would be required to support and attend. An exercise of this authority was accompanied by a repetition of many of the old world practices and persecutions. Catholics found themselves hounded and proscribed because of their faith; Quakers who followed their conscience went to jail; Baptists were peculiarly obnoxious to certain dominant Protestant sects; men and women of varied faiths who happened to be in a minority in a particular locality were persecuted because they steadfastly persisted in worshipping God only as their own consciences dictated. And all of these dissenters were compelled to pay tithes and taxes to support government-sponsored churches whose ministers preached inflammatory sermons designed to strengthen and consolidate the established faith by generating a burning hatred against dissenters.

These practices became so commonplace as to shock the freedom-loving colonials into a feeling of abhorrence.[9] The imposition of taxes to pay ministers' salaries and to build and maintain churches and church property aroused their indignation. It was these feelings which found expression in the First Amendment. No one locality and no one group throughout the Colonies can rightly be given entire credit for having aroused the sentiment that culminated in adoption of the Bill of Rights' provisions embracing religious liberty. But Virginia, where the established church had achieved a dominant influence in political affairs and where many excesses attracted wide public attention, provided a great stimulus and able leadership for the movement. The people there, as elsewhere, reached the conviction that individual religious liberty could be achieved best under a government which was stripped of all power to tax, to support, or otherwise to assist any or all religions, or to interfere with the beliefs of any religious individual or group.

The movement toward this end reached its dramatic climax in Virginia in 1785–86 when the Virginia legislative body was about to renew Virginia's tax levy for the support of the established church. Thomas Jefferson and James Madison led the fight against this tax. Madison wrote his great Memorial and Remonstrance against the law. In it, he eloquently argued that a true religion did not need the support of law; that no person, either believer or non-believer, should be taxed to support a religious institution of any kind; that the best interest of a society required that the minds of men always be wholly free; and that cruel persecutions were the inevitable result of government-established religions. Madison's Remonstrance received strong support throughout Virginia,[12] and the Assembly postponed consideration of the proposed tax measure until its next session. When the proposal came up for consideration at that session, it not only died in committee, but the Assembly enacted the famous "Virginia Bill for Religious Liberty" originally written by Thomas Jefferson. The preamble to that Bill stated among other things that:

> "Almighty God hath created the mind free; that all attempts to influence it by temporal punishments, or burthens, or by civil incapacitations, tend only to beget habits of hypocrisy and meanness, and are a departure from the plan of the Holy author of our

---

9. Madison wrote to a friend in 1774: "That diabolical, hell-conceived principle of persecution rages among some. * * * This vexes me the worst of anything whatever. There are at this time in the adjacent country not less than five or six well-meaning men in close jail for publishing their religious sentiments, which in the main are very orthodox. I have neither patience to hear, talk, or think of anything relative to this matter; for I have squabbled and scolded, abused and ridiculed, so long about it to little purpose, that I am without common patience. So I must beg you to pity me, and pray for liberty of conscience to all." I Writings of James Madison (1900) 18, 21.

12. In a recently discovered collection of Madison's papers, Madison recollected that his Remonstrance "met with the approbation of the Baptists, the Presbyterians, the Quakers, and the few Roman Catholics, universally; of the Methodists in part; and even of not a few of the Sect formerly established by law." Madison, Monopolies, Perpetuities, Corporations, Ecclesiastical Endowments, in Fleet, Madison's "Detached Memorandum," 3 William and Mary Q. (1946) 534, 551, 555.

religion who being Lord both of body and mind, yet chose not to propagate it by coercions on either . . . ; that to compel a man to furnish contributions of money for the propagation of opinions which he disbelieves, is sinful and tyrannical; that even the forcing him to support this or that teacher of his own religious persuasion, is depriving him of the comfortable liberty of giving his contributions to the particular pastor, whose morals he would make his pattern. * * * "

And the statute itself enacted:

"That no man shall be compelled to frequent or support any religious worship, place, or ministry whatsoever, nor shall be enforced, restrained, molested, or burthened, in his body or goods, nor shall otherwise suffer on account of his religious opinions or belief. . . ."[14]

This Court has previously recognized that the provisions of the First Amendment, in the drafting and adoption of which Madison and Jefferson played such leading roles, had the same objective and were intended to provide the same protection against governmental intrusion on religious liberty as the Virginia statute. Prior to the adoption of the Fourteenth Amendment, the First Amendment did not apply as a restraint against the states. Most of them did soon provide similar constitutional protections for religious liberty. But some states persisted for about half a century in imposing restraints upon the free exercise of religion and in discriminating against particular religious groups.[17] * * *

The meaning and scope of the First Amendment, preventing establishment of religion or prohibiting the free exercise thereof, in the light of its history and the evils it was designed forever to suppress, have been several times elaborated by the decisions of this Court prior to the application of the First Amendment to the states by the Fourteenth. The broad meaning given the Amendment by these earlier cases has been accepted by this Court in its decisions concerning an individual's religious freedom rendered since the Fourteenth Amendment was interpreted to make the prohibitions of the First applicable to state action abridging religious freedom.[22] There is every reason to give the same application and broad interpretation to the "establishment of religion" clause. * * *

14. 12 Hening, Statutes of Virginia (1823) 84; Commager, Documents of American History (1944) 125.

17. Test provisions forbade office holders to "deny * * * the truth of the Protestant religion," e.g. Constitution of North Carolina 1776, s XXXII, II Poore, supra, 1413. Maryland permitted taxation for support of the Christian religion and limited civil office to Christians until 1818, Id., I, 819, 820, 832.

22. Cantwell v. State of Conn., 310 U.S. 296, 60 S.Ct. 900, 84 L.Ed. 1213, 128 A.L.R.

1352; Jamison v. State of Texas, 318 U.S. 413, 63 S.Ct. 669, 87 L.Ed. 869; Largent v. State of Texas, 318 U.S. 418, 63 S.Ct. 667, 87 L.Ed. 873; Murdock v. Commonwealth of Pennsylvania, supra; West Virginia State Board of Education v. Barnette, 319 U.S. 624, 63 S.Ct. 1178, 87 L.Ed. 1628, 147 A.L.R. 674; Follett v. Town of McCormick, 321 U.S. 573, 64 S.Ct. 717, 88 L.Ed. 938, 152 A.L.R. 317; Marsh v. State of Alabama, 326 U.S. 501, 66 S.Ct. 276; Cf. Bradfield v. Roberts, 175 U.S. 291, 20 S.Ct. 121, 44 L.Ed. 168.

The "establishment of religion" clause of the First Amendment means at least this: Neither a state nor the Federal Government can set up a church. Neither can pass laws which aid one religion, aid all religions, or prefer one religion over another. Neither can force nor influence a person to go to or to remain away from church against his will or force him to profess a belief or disbelief in any religion. No person can be punished for entertaining or professing religious beliefs or disbeliefs, for church attendance or non-attendance. No tax in any amount, large or small, can be levied to support any religious activities or institutions, whatever they may be called, or whatever from they may adopt to teach or practice religion. Neither a state nor the Federal Government can, openly or secretly, participate in the affairs of any religious organizations or groups and vice versa. In the words of Jefferson, the clause against establishment of religion by law was intended to erect "a wall of separation between Church and State." Reynolds v. United States, supra, 98 U.S. at page 164, 25 L.Ed. 244.

We must consider the New Jersey statute in accordance with the foregoing limitations imposed by the First Amendment. But we must not strike that state statute down if it is within the state's constitutional power even though it approaches the verge of that power. New Jersey cannot consistently with the "establishment of religion" clause of the First Amendment contribute tax-raised funds to the support of an institution which teaches the tenets and faith of any church. On the other hand, other language of the amendment commands that New Jersey cannot hamper its citizens in the free exercise of their own religion. Consequently, it cannot exclude individual Catholics, Lutherans, Mohammedans, Baptists, Jews, Methodists, Non-believers, Presbyterians, or the members of any other faith, because of their faith, or lack of it, from receiving the benefits of public welfare legislation. While we do not mean to intimate that a state could not provide transportation only to children attending public schools, we must be careful, in protecting the citizens of New Jersey against state-established churches, to be sure that we do not inadvertently prohibit New Jersey from extending its general State law benefits to all its citizens without regard to their religious belief.

Measured by these standards, we cannot say that the First Amendment prohibits New Jersey from spending taxraised funds to pay the bus fares of parochial school pupils as a part of a general program under which it pays the fares of pupils attending public and other schools. It is undoubtedly true that children are helped to get to church schools. There is even a possibility that some of the children might not be sent to the church schools if the parents were compelled to pay their children's bus fares out of their own pockets when transportation to a public school would have been paid for by the State. The same possibility exists where the state requires a local transit company to provide reduced fares to school children including those attending parochial schools, or where a municipally owned transportation system undertakes to carry all school children free of charge. Moreover, state-paid policemen, detailed to protect children going to and from church schools from the very real hazards of traffic, would serve much the same purpose and accomplish much the same result as state provisions intended to guarantee free transportation of a kind which the state deems to be best for the school children's welfare. And parents might refuse to risk their children to the serious danger of traffic accidents going to and from parochial schools, the approaches to which were not protected by policemen. Similarly, parents might be reluctant to permit their children to attend schools which the state had cut off from such general government services as ordinary police and fire protection, connections for sewage disposal, public highways and sidewalks. Of course, cutting off church schools from these services, so separate and so indisputably marked off from the religious function, would make it far more difficult for the schools to operate. But such is obviously not the purpose of the First Amendment. That Amendment requires the state to be a neutral in its relations with groups of religious believers and non-believers; it does not require the state to be their adversary. State power is no more to be used so as to handicap religions, than it is to favor them.

* * *

The First Amendment has erected a wall between church and state. That wall must be kept high and impregnable. We could not approve the slightest breach. New Jersey has not breached it here.

Affirmed.

MR. JUSTICE JACKSON, joined by MR. JUSTICE FRANKFURTER, dissenting.

I find myself, contrary to first impressions, unable to join in this decision. I have a sympathy, though it is not ideological, with Catholic citizens who are compelled by law to pay taxes for public schools, and also feel constrained by conscience and discipline to support other schools for their own children. Such relief to them as this case involves is not in itself a serious burden to taxpayers and I had assumed it to be as little serious in principle. Study of this case convinces me otherwise. The Court's opinion marshals every argument in favor of state aid and puts the case in its most favorable light, but much of its reasoning confirms my conclusions that there are no good grounds upon which to support the present legislation. In fact, the undertones of the opinion, advocating complete and uncompromising separation of Church from State, seem utterly discordant with its conclusion yielding support to their commingling in educational matters. The case which irresistibly comes to mind as the most fitting precedent is that of Julia who, according to Byron's reports, "whispering 'I will ne'er consent,'—consented."

I.

The Court sustains this legislation by assuming two deviations from the facts of this particular case; first, it assumes a state of facts the record does not support, and secondly, it refuses to consider facts which are inescapable on the record.

The Court concludes that this "legislation, as applied, does no more than provide a general program to help parents get their children, regardless of their religion, safely and expeditiously to and from accredited schools," and it draws a comparison between "state provisions intended to guarantee free transportation" for school children with services such as police and fire protection, and implies that we are here dealing with "laws authorizing new types of public services * * * " This hypothesis permeates the opinion. The facts will not bear that construction.

The Township of Ewing is not furnishing transportation to the children in any form; it is not operating school busses itself or contracting for their operation; and it is not performing any public service of any kind with this taxpayer's money. All school children are left to ride as ordinary paying passengers on the regular busses operated by the public transportation system. What the Township does, and what the taxpayer complains of, is at stated intervals to reimburse parents for the fares paid, provided the children attend either public schools or Catholic Church schools. This expenditure of tax funds has no possible effect on the child's safety or expedition in transit. As passengers on the public busses they travel as fast and no faster, and are as safe and no safer, since their parents are reimbursed as before.

In addition to thus assuming a type of service that does not exist, the Court also insists that we must close our eyes to a discrimination which does exist. The resolution which authorizes disbursement of this taxpayer's money limits reimbursement to those who attend public schools and Catholic schools. That is the way the Act is applied to this taxpayer.

The New Jersey Act in question makes the character of the school, not the needs of the children determine the eligibility of parents to reimbursement. The Act permits payment for transportation to parochial schools or public schools but prohibits it to private schools operated in whole or in part for profit. * * * Thus, under the Act and resolution brought to us by this case children are classified according to the schools they attend and are to be aided if they attend the public schools or private Catholic schools, and they are not allowed to be aided if they attend private secular schools or private religious schools of other faiths.

* * * [This case] is one of a taxpayer urging that he is being taxed for an unconstitutional purpose. I think he is entitled to have us consider the Act just as it is written. The statement by the New Jersey court that it holds the Legislature may authorize use of local funds "for the transportation of pupils to any school," in view of the other constitutional views expressed, is not a holding that this Act authorizes transportation of all pupils to all schools. * * *

If we are to decide this case on the facts before us, our question is simply this: Is it constitutional to tax this complainant to pay the cost of carrying pupils to Church schools of one specified denomination?

II.

Whether the taxpayer constitutionally can be made to contribute aid to parents of students because of their attendance at parochial schools depends upon the nature of those schools and their relation to the Church. The Constitution says nothing of education. It lays no obligation on the states to provide schools and does not undertake to regulate state systems of education if they see fit to maintain them. But they cannot, through school policy any more than through other means, invade rights secured to citizens by the Constitution of the United States. One of our basic rights is to be free of taxation to support a transgression of the constitutional command that the authorities "shall make no law respecting an establishment of religion, or prohibiting the free exercise thereof."

The function of the Church school is a subject on which this record is meager. It shows only that the schools are under superintendence of a priest and that "religion is taught as part of the curriculum." But we know that such schools are parochial only in name—they, in fact, represent a worldwide and age-old policy of the Roman Catholic Church. * * *

* * *

It is no exaggeration to say that the whole historic conflict in temporal policy between the Catholic Church and non-Catholics comes to a focus in their respective school policies. The Roman Catholic Church, counseled by experience in many ages and many lands and with all sorts and conditions of men, takes what, from the viewpoint of its own progress and the success of its mission, is a wise estimate of the importance of education to religion. It does not leave the individual to pick up religion by chance. It relies on early and indelible indoctrination in the faith and order of the Church by the word and example of persons consecrated to the task.

* * *

I should be surprised if any Catholic would deny that the parochial school is a vital, if not the most vital, part of the Roman Catholic Church. If put to the choice, that venerable institution, I should expect, would forego its whole service for mature persons before it would give up education of the young, and it would be a wise choice. Its growth and cohesion, discipline and loyalty, spring from its schools. Catholic education is the rock on which the whole structure rests, and to render tax aid to its Church school is indistinguishable to me from rendering the same aid to the Church itself.

III.

It is of no importance in this situation whether the beneficiary of this expenditure of tax-raised funds is primarily the parochial school and incidentally the pupil, or whether the aid is directly bestowed on the pupil with indirect benefits to the school. The state cannot maintain a

Church and it can no more tax its citizens to furnish free carriage to those who attend a Church. The prohibition against establishment of religion cannot be circumvented by a subsidy, bonus or reimbursement of expense to individuals for receiving religious instruction and indoctrination.

* * * Of course, the state may pay out tax-raised funds to relieve pauperism, but it may not under our Constitution do so to induce or reward piety. It may spend funds to secure old age against want, but it may not spend funds to secure religion against skepticism. It may compensate individuals for loss of employment, but it cannot compensate them for adherence to a creed.

It seems to me that the basic fallacy in the Court's reasoning, which accounts for its failure to apply the principles it avows, is in ignoring the essentially religious test by which beneficiaries of this expenditure are selected. A policeman protects a Catholic, of course—but not because he is a Catholic; it is because he is a man and a member of our society. The fireman protects the Church school—but not because it is a Church school; it is because it is property, part of the assets of our society. Neither the fireman nor the policeman has to ask before he renders aid 'Is this man or building identified with the Catholic Church.' But before these school authorities draw a check to reimburse for a student's fare they must ask just that question, and if the school is a Catholic one they may render aid because it is such, while if it is of any other faith or is run for profit, the help must be withheld. To consider the converse of the Court's reasoning will best disclose its fallacy. That there is no parallel between police and fire protection and this plan of reimbursement is apparent from the incongruity of the limitation of this Act if applied to police and fire service. Could we sustain an Act that said police shall protect pupils on the way to or from public schools and Catholic schools but not while going to and coming from other schools, and firemen shall extinguish a blaze in public or Catholic school buildings but shall not put out a blaze in Protestant Church schools or private schools operated for profit? That is the true analogy to the case we have before us and I should think it pretty plain that such a scheme would not be valid.

* * * [T]he effect of the religious freedom Amendment to our Constitution was to take every form of propagation of religion out of the realm of things which could directly or indirectly be made public business and thereby be supported in whole or in part at taxpayers' expense. That is a difference which the Constitution sets up between religion and almost every other subject matter of legislation, a difference which goes to the very root of religious freedom and which the Court is overlooking today. This freedom was first in the Bill of Rights because it was first in the forefathers' minds; it was set forth in absolute terms, and its strength is its rigidity. It was intended not only to keep the states' hands out of religion, but to keep religion's hands off the state, and above all, to keep bitter religious controversy out of public life by denying to every denomination any advantage from getting control of public policy or the

public purse. Those great ends I cannot but think are immeasurably compromised by today's decision.

* * *

* * * If these principles seem harsh in prohibiting aid to Catholic education, it must not be forgotten that it is the same Constitution that alone assures Catholics the right to maintain these schools at all when predominant local sentiment would forbid them. Pierce v. Society of Sisters, 268 U.S. 510, 45 S.Ct. 571, 69 L.Ed. 1070, 39 A.L.R. 468. Nor should I think that those who have done so well without this aid would want to see this separation between Church and State broken down. If the state may aid these religious schools, it may therefore regulate them. Many groups have sought aid from tax funds only to find that it carried political controls with it. * * *

But in any event, the great purposes of the Constitution do not depend on the approval or convenience of those they restrain. I cannot read the history of the struggle to separate political from ecclesiastical affairs, well summarized in the opinion of Mr. Justice Rutledge in which I generally concur, without a conviction that the Court today is unconsciously giving the clock's hands a backward turn.

MR. JUSTICE RUTLEDGE, with whom MR. JUSTICE FRANKFURTER, MR. JUSTICE JACKSON and MR. JUSTICE BURTON agree, dissenting.

* * *

I.

Not simply an established church, but any law respecting an establishment of religion is forbidden. The [First] Amendment was broadly but not loosely phrased. It is the compact and exact summation of its author's views formed during his long struggle for religious freedom. In Madison's own words characterizing Jefferson's Bill for Establishing Religious Freedom, the guaranty he put in our national charter, like the bill he piloted through the Virginia Assembly, was "a Model of technical precision, and perspicuous brevity." Madison could not have confused "church" and "religion," or "an established church" and "an establishment of religion."

The Amendment's purpose was not to strike merely at the official establishment of a single sect, creed or religion, outlawing only a formal relation such as had prevailed in England and some of the colonies. Necessarily it was to uproot all such relationships. But the object was broader than separating church and state in this narrow sense. It was to create a complete and permanent separation of the spheres of religious activity and civil authority by comprehensively forbidding every form of public aid or support for religion. * * *

"Religion" appears only once in the Amendment. But the word governs two prohibitions and governs them alike. It does not have two meanings, one narrow to forbid "an establishment" and another, much broader, for securing "the free exercise thereof." "Thereof" brings down "religion" with its entire and exact content, no more and no less, from the first into the second guaranty, so that Congress and now the states are as broadly restricted concerning the one as they are regarding the other.

* * *

* * * [D]aily religious education commingled with secular is "religion" within the guaranty's comprehensive scope. So are religious training and teaching in whatever form. The word connotes the broadest content, determined not by the form or formality of the teaching or where it occurs, but by its essential nature regardless of those details.

* * *

II.

* * *

For Madison, as also for Jefferson, religious freedom was the crux of the struggle for freedom in general. Madison was coauthor with George Mason of the religious clause in Virginia's great Declaration of Rights of 1776. He is credited with changing it from a mere statement of the principle of tolerance to the first official legislative pronouncement that freedom of conscience and religion are inherent rights of the individual. * * *

[Justice Rutledge next discusses the role Madison and Jefferson played in the battle over religious assessments in Virginia, and asserts a connection between the experience in Virginia and the development of the First Amendment].

* * *

[The Memorial and Remonstrance Against Religious Assessments] is Madison's complete, though not his only, interpretation of religious liberty. It is a broadside attack upon all forms of "establishment" of religion, both general and particular, nondiscriminatory or selective. * * * [T]he Remonstrance is at once the most concise and the most accurate statement of the views of the First Amendment's author concerning what is "an establishment of religion." * * *

* * * Madison was certain in his own mind that under the Constitution "there is not a shadow of right in the general government to intermeddle with religion" and that "this subject is, for the honor of America, perfectly free and unshackled. The Government has no jurisdiction over it. . . ." Nevertheless he pledged that he would work for a Bill of Rights, including a specific guaranty of religious freedom, and Virginia, with other states, ratified the Constitution on this assurance.

Ratification thus accomplished, Madison was sent to the first Congress. There he went at once about performing his pledge to establish freedom for the nation as he had done in Virginia. Within a little more than three years from his legislative victory at home he had proposed and secured the submission and ratification of the First Amendment as the first article of our Bill of Rights.[27]

* * *

As the Remonstrance discloses throughout, Madison opposed every form and degree of official relation between religion and civil authority. For him religion was a wholly private matter beyond the scope of civil power either to restrain or to support. Denial or abridgment of religious freedom was a violation of rights both of conscience and of natural equality. State aid was no less obnoxious or destructive to freedom and to religion itself than other forms of state interference. "Establishment" and "free exercise" were correlative and coextensive ideas, representing only different facets of the single great and fundamental freedom. The Remonstrance, following the Virginia statute's example, referred to the history of religious conflicts and the effects of all sorts of establishments, current and historical, to suppress religion's free exercise. With Jefferson, Madison believed that to tolerate any fragment of establishment would be by so much to perpetuate restraint upon that freedom. * * *

In no phase was he more unrelentingly absolute than in opposing state support or aid by taxation. Not even "three pence" contribution was thus to be exacted from any citizen for such a purpose. Remonstrance, Par. 3. Tithes had been the life blood of establishment before and after other compulsions disappeared. Madison and his coworkers made no exceptions or abridgments to the complete separation they created. Their objection was not to small tithes. It was to any tithes whatsoever. * * * Not the amount but "the principle of assessment was wrong." And the principle was as much to prevent "the interference of law in religion" as to restrain religious intervention in political matters. In this field the authors of our freedom would not tolerate "the first experiment on our liberties" or "wait till usurped power had strengthened itself by exercise, and entangled the question in precedents." Remonstrance, Par. 3. Nor should we.

In view of this history no further proof is needed that the Amendment forbids any appropriation, large or small, from public funds to aid or support any and all religious exercises. But if more were called for, the debates in the First Congress and this Court's consistent expressions, whenever it has touched on the matter directly, supply it.

By contrast with the Virginia history, the congressional debates on consideration of the Amendment reveal only sparse discussion, reflecting the fact that the essential issues had been settled. Indeed the matter had become so well understood as to have been taken for granted in all but formal phrasing. Hence, the only enlightening reference shows concern,

---

27. The amendment with respect to religious liberties read, as Madison introduced it: "The civil rights of none shall be abridged on account of religious belief or worship, nor shall any national religion be established, nor shall the full and equal rights of conscience be in any manner, or on any pretext, infringed." 1 Annals of Congress 434. In the process of debate this was modified to its present form. See especially 1 Annals of Congress 729–731, 765 * * *.

not to preserve any power to use public funds in aid of religion, but to prevent the Amendment from outlawing private gifts inadvertently by virtue of the breadth of its wording. In the margin are noted also the principal decisions in which expressions of this Court confirm the Amendment's broad prohibition.[35]

III.

* * * [T]oday, apart from efforts to inject religious training or exercises and sectarian issues into the public schools, the only serious surviving threat to maintaining that complete and permanent separation of religion and civil power which the First Amendment commands is through use of the taxing power to support religion, religious establishments, or establishments having a religious foundation whatever their form or special religious function.

Does New Jersey's action furnish support for religion by use of the taxing power? Certainly it does, if the test remains undiluted as Jefferson and Madison made it, that money taken by taxation from one is not to be used or given to support another's religious training or belief, or indeed one's own. * * *

* * *

Now, as in Madison's time, not the amount but the principle of assessment is wrong.

IV.

But we are told that the New Jersey statute is valid in its present application because the appropriation is for a public, not a private purpose, namely, the promotion of education, and the majority accept this idea in the conclusion that all we have here is "public welfare legislation." If that is true and the Amendment's force can be thus destroyed, what has been said becomes all the more pertinent. For then there could be no possible objection to more extensive support of religious education by New Jersey.

* * *

35. The decision most closely touching the question, where it was squarely raised, is Quick Bear v. Leupp, 210 U.S. 50, 28 S.Ct. 690, 52 L.Ed. 954. The Court distinguished sharply between appropriations from public funds for the support of religious education and appropriations from funds held in trust by the Government essentially as trustee for private individuals, Indian wards, as beneficial owners. The ruling was that the latter could be disbursed to private, religious schools at the designation of those patrons for paying the cost of their education. But it was stated also that such a use of public moneys would violate both the First Amendment and the specific statutory declaration involved, namely, that "it is hereby declared to be the settled policy of the government to hereafter make no appropriation whatever for education in any sectarian school." 210 U.S. at page 79, 28 S.Ct. at page 697, 52 L.Ed. 954. Cf. Ponce v. Roman Catholic Apostolic Church, 210 U.S. 296, 322, 28 S.Ct. 737, 747, 52 L.Ed. 1068. And see Bradfield v. Roberts, 175 U.S. 291, 20 S.Ct. 121, 44 L.Ed. 168, an instance of highly artificial grounding to support a decision sustaining an appropriation for the care of indigent patients pursuant to a contract with a private hospital.

The reasons underlying the Amendment's policy have not vanished with time or diminished in force. Now as when it was adopted the price of religious freedom is double. It is that the church and religion shall live both within and upon that freedom. There cannot be freedom of religion, safeguarded by the state, and intervention by the church or its agencies in the state's domain or dependency on its largesse. The great condition of religious liberty is that it be maintained free from sustenance, as also from other interferences, by the state. For when it comes to rest upon that secular foundation it vanishes with the resting. Public money devoted to payment of religious costs, educational or other, brings the quest for more. It brings too the struggle of sect against sect for the larger share or for any. * * * It is the very thing Jefferson and Madison experienced and sought to guard against, whether in its blunt or in its more screened forms. The end of such strife cannot be other than to destroy the cherished liberty. * * *

* * *

This is not therefore just a little case over bus fares. In paraphrase of Madison, distant as it may be in its present form from a complete establishment of religion, it differs from it only in degree; and is the first step in that direction. Today as in his time "the same authority which can force a citizen to contribute three pence only * * * for the support of any one religious establishment, may force him" to pay more; or "to conform to any other establishment in all cases whatsoever." * * *

* * *

VI.

* * *

Two great drives are constantly in motion to abridge, in the name of education, the complete division of religion and civil authority which our forefathers made. One is to introduce religious education and observances into the public schools. The other, to obtain public funds for the aid and support of various private religious schools. In my opinion both avenues were closed by the Constitution. Neither should be opened by this Court. The matter is not one of quantity, to be measured by the amount of money expended. Now as in Madison's day it is one of principle * * *.

The judgment should be reversed.

Notes and Questions

1. *The meaning of separation.* All of the Justices on the *Everson* Court seem to agree that the standard for evaluating Establishment Clause cases should be one based on a "wall of separation between church and state," but the majority and the dissents disagree over the meaning of that term as well as its application to the facts. If the opinions all agree that the Framers intended a "high and impregnable" wall between church and state, how do their interpreta-

tions of that term differ? Which opinion do you think best captures the separation principle given the history the Court relies upon?

2. *The case from history and the intent of the framers.* Consider the possibility that the Court overplayed the historical hand, by attributing to the "founders" generally (which would include both those who drafted and those who ratified the Constitution), a view that *may* have only animated the drafters of the First Amendment. *See* PHILIP HAMBURGER, THE SEPARATION OF CHURCH AND STATE (Harvard Univ. Press 2002). If the Amendment was drafted and ratified by people who did not all share one view of its meaning or application to concrete cases, is it a good or bad idea to place so much weight on the intent of the Amendment's initial drafters? Does it make a difference that, as the Court notes, Madison and Jefferson would have never conceived of the modern role of government, and thus it is impossible to know how they might answer the question of whether providing funds for transportation to parochial schools automatically violates the Constitution? Since *Everson* makes the Establishment Clause applicable to the states through the Fourteenth Amendment shouldn't the Court also carefully analyzed the meaning of that Amendment and the views of those who drafted and ratified it? *See generally* Akhil Reed Amar, THE BILL OF RIGHTS (Yale Univ. Press 1998).

3. *Incorporation of the Establishment Clause through the Fourteenth Amendment.* In *Everson* the Court incorporated the Establishment Clause, thus making it applicable to state and local governments. The Court did so by extending the rationale it used in earlier cases to incorporate the other provisions of the First Amendment, including the Free Exercise Clause. How might the Establishment Clause differ from the Free Exercise and Free Speech Clauses? Should the differences between the clauses have played a more prominent role in any discussion of incorporation? Does the fact that all the Justices agreed the Establishment Clause should be incorporated affect your analysis? Some have argued that the Establishment Clause should not have been incorporated because it is quite different from the Free Exercise and Free Speech Clauses. This view, however, has never commanded great support among the Justices. *But see*, Zelman v. Simmons–Harris, 536 U.S. 639, 677–80, 122 S.Ct. 2460, 2480–82, 153 L.Ed.2d 604 (2002) (Thomas, J., concurring) (suggesting that the Establishment Clause should be applied differently to the states than the federal government).

4. *Was the Court influenced by animus?* There are several references in the various opinions to anti-Catholic tracts, and some have argued quite persuasively that *Everson* and its progeny were highly influenced by anti-Catholic animus. *See* PHILIP HAMBURGER, THE SEPARATION OF CHURCH AND STATE (Harvard Univ. Press 2002); Paul Salamanca, *Choice Programs and Market–Based Separationism*, 50 BUFF. L. REV. 931 (2002). Should this make a difference in assessing the viability of the separationist principle? Does it make a difference that many supporters of separation have pointed to several viable and non-invidious reasons for separationism despite the taint of anti-Catholic animus? Is your answer effected by the fact that even the Justices who harbored anti-Catholic bigotry may have been motivated by other considerations as well? Is it ever appropriate to utilize a doctrine that was motivated by bigotry, even if it could be justified by non-bigoted considerations? If so, what would be required to validate the doctrine?

5. *Government regulation of religious entities, religious divisiveness, and sectarian conflict.* The Court points to the strife that can occur when various religious sects compete for public funds or approval and to the fact that with government funds may come government regulation. How should these considerations effect the development of Establishment Clause doctrine? Does the history

of religious persecution and strife between religious sects that have or seek government approval provide independent support for the Court's position? Does it support that position only if the Framers were motivated by such concerns? Consider that Madison was concerned about factionalism generally, and that he specifically mentioned the tendency of religious factions to "vex and oppress" each other in the famous Federalist #10. James Madison, "FEDERALIST NO. 10," *in* THE FEDERALIST PAPERS (Clinton Rossiter ed., Penguin Books 1961). Does this give further support to the Court's historical argument? Or does it simply represent the views of one framer, albeit an especially important framer in the First Amendment context? Is the potential battle between religions over the proverbial economic pie of government subsidies a valid animating concern in interpreting the Establishment Clause? What about the issue of government regulation—does it matter that the government may attach strings to any funding religious institutions receive, and that such strings could effect religious doctrine by tempting religious organizations to compromise doctrine or alter the nature of the services they provide (even if religious doctrine is unaffected)? Is the latter concern—over altering services rather than doctrine—relevant under the Establishment Clause?

6. *Neutrality*. At the end of Justice Black's opinion for the court, he writes that the First Amendment:

> requires the state to be a neutral in its relations with groups of religious believers and non-believers; it does not require the state to be their adversary. State power is no more to be used so as to handicap religions, than it is to favor them.

What does this mean? How can a government entity be neutral when it comes to an issue like funding? If the court had denied funding wouldn't it be handicapping religion? Conversely, by granting the funding didn't the Court favor religious schools over nonreligious private schools, most of which operate for profit? Doesn't this favor private educational venues for "believers" of the more dominant faiths in a given area over private educational venues where "nonbelievers" and those whose faiths do not have enough adherents in a given area to support separate schools are likely send their children? We will spend a great deal of time on the question of neutrality throughout the rest of this book. For now it useful to begin considering these questions as well as the general question of what neutrality may mean in the context of the Religion Clauses.

7. *Taxing citizens to fund religious entities they do not support*. The Court and the dissents both point out that parochial school transportation is being subsidized through tax revenue paid by adherents and non adherents alike. What difference should this make to the analysis of the constitutionality of such funding? How do the various opinions address this concern? Is the majority's position that this argument is problematic if taken to its logical extreme because it could be used to deny tax dollars for the support of basic services, such as fire and police protection, persuasive? How do Justices Jackson and Rutledge respond to this argument in their dissenting opinions? Would it make a difference if citizens' tax dollars were used only to fund transportation to parochial schools whose religious tenets they agree with? Should it make a difference?

B. EARLY ATTEMPTS TO APPLY THE PRINCIPLE OF SEPARATION: *McCOLLUM* AND *ZORACH*

After *Everson* was decided it was unclear how high the wall of separation extended in practice because the result in that case seemed to betray the Court's forceful description of the separationist principle as a wall of separation that should remain "high and impregnable." Two cases decided in the years shortly after *Everson* reflect the disagreement that remained over the application of the principle of separation, a disagreement that was obvious in the various opinions in *Everson*. As you read about these cases in the following pages, ask yourself which is more consistent with the separation principle as expounded in *Everson*, and whether the two opinions can be reconciled with each other.

In *People of State of Illinois ex rel. McCollum v. Board of Education of School Dist. No. 71*, 333 U.S. 203, 68 S.Ct. 461, 92 L.Ed. 649 (1948), the Court struck down a "released time" program in which public school students in Champaign, Illinois were released from secular classes to attend religious classes taught by teachers paid for by private religious groups on public school premises. Students who did not attend the religious classes were not released from school, but rather had to leave their regular classrooms and go elsewhere in the building to engage in their "secular studies." Attendance was taken for both the religious and secular classes, and students were required to be at one or the other.

Justice Black wrote for the majority:

> The foregoing facts, without reference to others that appear in the record, show the use of tax-supported property for religious instruction and the close cooperation between the school authorities and the religious council in promoting religious education. The operation of the state's compulsory education system thus assists and is integrated with the program of religious instruction carried on by separate religious sects. Pupils compelled by law to go to school for secular education are released in part from their legal duty upon the condition that they attend the religious classes. This is beyond all question a utilization of the tax-established and tax-supported public school system to aid religious groups to spread their faith. And it falls squarely under the ban of the First Amendment (made applicable to the States by the Fourteenth) as we interpreted it in Everson v. Board of Education. * * * The majority in the Everson case, and the [dissents] * * *, agreed that the First Amendment's language, properly interpreted, had erected a wall of separation between Church and State. They disagreed as to the facts shown by the record and as to the proper application of the First Amendment's language to those facts.

> * * *

> To hold that a state cannot consistently with the First and Fourteenth Amendments utilize its public school system to aid any

or all religious faiths or sects in the dissemination of their doctrines and ideals does not, as counsel urge, manifest a governmental hostility to religion or religious teachings. A manifestation of such hostility would be at war with our national tradition as embodied in the First Amendment's guaranty of the free exercise of religion. For the First Amendment rests upon the premise that both religion and government can best work to achieve their lofty aims if each is left free from the other within its respective sphere. Or, as we said in the Everson case, the First Amendment had erected a wall between Church and State which must be kept high and impregnable.

Here not only are the state's tax supported public school buildings used for the dissemination of religious doctrines. The State also affords sectarian groups an invaluable aid in that it helps to provide pupils for their religious classes through use of the state's compulsory public school machinery. This is not separation of Church and State.

Justice Frankfurter wrote a concurring opinion that was joined by Justices Jackson, Rutledge and Burton. Justice Frankfurter's opinion stressed that the "wall of separation" principle should be defined as it is applied from "case to case." He argued that the separation principle should have led to a different outcome in *Everson*, and that while the released time program at issue in *McCollum* was unconstitutional, not all released time programs are inherently unconstitutional.

He wrote:

The case, in the light of the Everson decision, demonstrates anew that the mere formulation of a relevant Constitutional principle is the beginning of the solution of a problem, not its answer. This is so because the meaning of a spacious conception like that of the separation of Church from State is unfolded as appeal is made to the principle from case to case. We are all agreed that the First and the Fourteenth Amendments have a secular reach far more penetrating in the conduct of Government than merely to forbid an 'established church.' But agreement, in the abstract, that the First Amendment was designed to erect a 'wall of separation between Church and State,' does not preclude a clash of views as to what the wall separates. Involved is not only the Constitutional principle but the implications of judicial review in its enforcement. Accommodation of legislative freedom and Constitutional limitations upon that freedom cannot be achieved by a mere phrase. We cannot illuminatingly apply the 'wall-of-separation' metaphor until we have considered the relevant history of religious education in America, the place of the 'released time' movement in that history, and its precise manifestation in the case before us.

* * *

* * * The Champaign arrangement * * * presents powerful elements of inherent pressure by the school system in the interest of religious sects. The fact that this power has not been used to discriminate is beside the point. Separation is a requirement to abstain from fusing functions of Government and of religious sects, not merely to treat them all equally. That a child is offered an alternative may reduce the constraint; it does not eliminate the operation of influence by the school in matters sacred to conscience and outside the school's domain. The law of imitation operates, and nonconformity is not an outstanding characteristic of children. The result is an obvious pressure upon children to attend. Again, while the Champaign school population represents only a fraction of the more than two hundred and fifty sects of the nation, not even all the practicing sects in Champaign are willing or able to provide religious instruction. The children belonging to these non-participating sects will thus have inculcated in them a feeling of separatism when the school should be the training ground for habits of community, or they will have religious instruction in a faith which is not that of their parents. As a result, the public school system of Champaign actively furthers inculcation in the religious tenets of some faiths, and in the process sharpens the consciousness of religious differences at least among some of the children committed to its care. These are consequences not amenable to statistics. But they are precisely the consequences against which the Constitution was directed when it prohibited the Government common to all from becoming embroiled, however innocently, in the destructive religious conflicts of which the history of even this country records some dark pages.

* * *

We do not consider, as indeed we could not, school programs not before us which, though colloquially characterized as 'released time,' present situations differing in aspects that may well be constitutionally crucial. Different forms which 'released time' has taken during more than thirty years of growth include programs which, like that before us, could not withstand the test of the Constitution; others may be found unexceptionable. We do not now attempt to weigh in the Constitutional scale every separate detail or various combination of factors which may establish a valid 'released time' program. * * *

Separation means separation, not something less. Jefferson's metaphor in describing the relation between Church and State speaks of a 'wall of separation,' not of a fine line easily overstepped. The public school is at once the symbol of our democracy and the most pervasive means for promoting our common destiny. In no activity of the State is it more vital to keep out divisive forces than in its schools, to avoid confusing, not to say fusing, what the Constitution sought to keep strictly apart. 'The great American principle of eternal separation'—Elihu Root's phrase bears repetition—is one of the vital reliances of our Constitutional system for assuring unities among our people stronger than our diversities. It is the Court's duty to enforce this principle in its full integrity.

We renew our conviction that 'we have staked the very existence of our country on the faith that complete separation between the state and religion is best for the state and best for religion.' Everson v. Board of Education. If nowhere else, in the relation between Church and State, 'good fences make good neighbors.'

Justice Jackson filed a concurring opinion in which he questioned the breadth of the writ of mandamus sought by the plaintiffs/appellees. He noted the writ went beyond the Court's holding that the released time program was unconstitutional, and also asked that all religious teaching and content be removed from the public schools in Champaign. In this regard Justice Jackson noted:

> While we may and should end such formal and explicit instruction as the Champaign plan and can at all times prohibit teaching of creed and catechism and ceremonial and can forbid forthright proselytizing in the schools, I think it remains to be demonstrated whether it is possible, even if desirable, to comply with such demands as plaintiff's completely to isolate and cast out of secular education all that some people may reasonably regard as religious instruction * * *.

> * * * Perhaps subjects such as mathematics, physics or chemistry are, or can be, completely secularized. But it would not seem practical to teach either practice or appreciation of the arts if we are to forbid exposure of youth to any religious influences. Music without sacred music, architecture minus the cathedral, or painting without the scriptural themes would be eccentric and incomplete, even from a secular point of view. Yet the inspirational appeal of religion in these guises is often stronger than in forthright sermon. Even such a 'science' as biology raises the issue between evolution and creation as an explanation of our presence on this planet. Certainly a course in English literature that omitted the Bible and other powerful uses of our mother tongue for religious ends would be pretty barren. And I should suppose it is a proper, if not an indispensable, part of preparation for a worldly life to know the roles that religion and religions have played in the tragic story of mankind. The fact is that, for good or for ill, nearly everything in our culture worth transmitting, everything which gives meaning to life, is saturated with religious influences, derived from paganism, Judaism, Christianity—both Catholic and Protestant—and other faiths accepted by a large part of the world's peoples. One can hardly respect a system of education that would leave the student wholly ignorant of the currents of religious thought that move the world society for a part in which he is being prepared.

> But how one can teach, with satisfaction or even with justice to all faiths, such subjects as the story of the Reformation, the Inquisition, or even the New England effort to found 'a Church without a

Bishop and a State without a King,' is more than I know. It is too much to expect that mortals will teach subjects about which their contemporaries have passionate controversies with the detachment they may summon to teaching about remote subjects such as Confucius or Mohamet. When instruction turns to proselytizing and imparting knowledge becomes evangelism is, except in the crudest cases, a subtle inquiry.

The opinions in this case show that public educational authorities have evolved a considerable variety of practices in dealing with the religious problem. Neighborhoods differ in racial, religious and cultural compositions. It must be expected that they will adopt different customs which will give emphasis to different values and will induce different experiments. And it must be expected that, no matter what practice prevails, there will be many discontented and possibly belligerent minorities. We must leave some flexibility to meet local conditions, some chance to progress by trial and error. While I agree that the religious classes involved here go beyond permissible limits, I also think the complaint demands more than plaintiff is entitled to have granted. * * *

* * *

It is idle to pretend that this task is one for which we can find in the Constitution one word to help us as judges to decide where the secular ends and the sectarian begins in education. Nor can we find guidance in any other legal source. It is a matter on which we can find no law but our own prepossessions. If with no surer legal guidance we are to take up and decide every variation of this controversy, raised by persons not subject to penalty or tax but who are dissatisfied with the way schools are dealing with the problem, we are likely to have much business of the sort. And, more importantly, we are likely to make the legal "wall of separation between church and state" as winding as the famous serpentine wall designed by Mr. Jefferson for the University he founded.

Justice Reed filed a strongly worded dissent, suggesting that the separation concept was historically flawed and that there was a great deal of historical information contrary to the Court's use of history to support the separation concept. His argument is later echoed in Justice Rehnquist's dissent in *Wallace v. Jaffree*, 472 U.S. 38, 105 S.Ct. 2479, 86 L.Ed.2d 29 (1985), a case involving an Alabama "moment of silence" law. *See infra.* at Chapter Two. The debate over the historical support for the separation concept will be addressed in several other cases and in other materials later in this chapter and elsewhere in the book. In *McCollum*, Justice Reed was the lone dissenting Justice and the only Justice besides Justice Jackson to question the notion of strict separation.

Four years after deciding *McCollum*, the Court again confronted a released time program, this time with quite different results. In *Zorach v. Clauson*, 343 U.S. 306, 72 S.Ct. 679, 96 L.Ed. 954 (1952), the Court upheld a released time program in New York City that was quite similar to the one in Champaign, but which did have several differences, differences upon which the Court relied to uphold the program. Justice Douglas delivered the opinion of the Court, in which he distinguished the program found unconstitutional in *McCollum*. He noted that the New York City program did not involve religious classes on school property, but rather the district released students to attend religious classes at various "religious centers." Students who were not released remained at school, and the churches and other religious institutions reported each week which children released from school did not report "for religious instruction." He then added:

> This 'released time' program involves neither religious instruction in public school classrooms nor the expenditure of public funds. All costs * * * are paid by the religious organizations. The case is therefore unlike McCollum v. Board of Education * * *. In that case the classrooms were turned over to religious instructors. We accordingly held that the program violated the First Amendment * * *.

The majority rejected the argument that the released time program coerced public school students to attend religious classes, and in reasoning that was arguably strained in light of *McCollum*, upheld the program as consistent with the separation principle. The opinion stated:

> * * * [W]e do not see how New York by this type of 'released time' program has made a law respecting an establishment of religion within the meaning of the First Amendment. There is much talk of the separation of Church and State in the history of the Bill of Rights and in the decisions clustering around the First Amendment. There cannot be the slightest doubt that the First Amendment reflects the philosophy that Church and State should be separated. And so far as interference with the 'free exercise' of religion and an 'establishment' of religion are concerned, the separation must be complete and unequivocal. The First Amendment within the scope of its coverage permits no exception; the prohibition is absolute. The First Amendment, however, does not say that in every and all respects there shall be a separation of Church and State. Rather, it studiously defines the manner, the specific ways, in which there shall be no concert or union or dependency one on the other. That is the common sense of the matter. Otherwise the state and religion would be aliens to each other—hostile, suspicious, and even unfriendly. * * *

> We would have to press the concept of separation of Church and State to these extremes [in a preceding part of the opinion Justice Douglas listed a parade of horribles that might occur if government were not able to accommodate or interact at all with religion and religious institutions] to condemn the present law on constitutional grounds. The nullification of this law would have wide and profound effects. * * *

> We are a religious people whose institutions presuppose a Supreme Being. We guarantee the freedom to worship as one chooses.

We make room for as wide a variety of beliefs and creeds as the spiritual needs of man deem necessary. We sponsor an attitude on the part of government that shows no partiality to any one group and that lets each flourish according to the zeal of its adherents and the appeal of its dogma. When the state encourages religious instruction or cooperates with religious authorities by adjusting the schedule of public events to sectarian needs, it follows the best of our traditions. For it then respects the religious nature of our people and accommodates the public service to their spiritual needs. To hold that it may not would be to find in the Constitution a requirement that the government show a callous indifference to religious groups. That would be preferring those who believe in no religion over those who do believe. Government may not finance religious groups nor undertake religious instruction nor blend secular and sectarian education nor use secular institutions to force one or some religion on any person. * * * The government must be neutral when it comes to competition between sects. It may not thrust any sect on any person. It may not make a religious observance compulsory. It may not coerce anyone to attend church, to observe a religious holiday, or to take religious instruction. But it can close its doors or suspend its operations as to those who want to repair to their religious sanctuary for worship or instruction. No more than that is undertaken here.

* * *

In the McCollum case the classrooms were used for religious instruction and the force of the public school was used to promote that instruction. Here, as we have said, the public schools do no more than accommodate their schedules to a program of outside religious instruction. We follow the McCollum case. But we cannot expand it to cover the present released time program unless separation of Church and State means that public institutions can make no adjustments of their schedules to accommodate the religious needs of the people. We cannot read into the Bill of Rights such a philosophy of hostility to religion.

Justices Black, Frankfurter and Jackson each filed a dissenting opinion. Justice Black argued that McCollum dictated that the New York City program be found unconstitutional and that separation does not allow for the kind of "cooperative" arrangement between government and religious institutions involved in the program. He wrote in part:

I see no significant difference between the invalid Illinois system and that of New York here sustained. Except for the use of the school buildings in Illinois, there is no difference between the systems which I consider even worthy of mention. In the New York program, as in that of Illinois, the school authorities release some of the children on the condition that they attend the religious classes, get reports on whether they attend, and hold the other children in the school building until the religious hour is over. As we attempted to make categorically clear, the McCollum decision would have been the same if the religious classes had not been held in the school buildings. We said:

> "Here not only are the state's tax-supported public school buildings used for the dissemination of religious doctrines. The State also affords sectarian groups an invaluable aid in that it helps to provide pupils for their religious classes through use of the state's compulsory public school machinery. This is not separation of Church and State." (Emphasis supplied.) McCollum v. Board of Education.

McCollum thus held that Illinois could not constitutionally manipulate the compelled classroom hours of its compulsory school machinery so as to channel children into sectarian classes. Yet that is exactly what the Court holds New York can do.

* * *

* * * Here the sole question is whether New York can use its compulsory education laws to help religious sects get attendants presumably too unenthusiastic to go unless moved to do so by the pressure of this state machinery. That this is the plan, purpose, design and consequence of the New York program cannot be denied. The state thus makes religious sects beneficiaries of its power to compel children to attend secular schools. Any use of such coercive power by the state to help or hinder some religious sects or to prefer all religious sects over nonbelievers or vice versa is just what I think the First Amendment forbids. In considering whether a state has entered this forbidden field the question is not whether it has entered too far but whether it has entered at all. * * *

The Court's validation of the New York system rests in part on its statement that Americans are 'a religious people whose institutions presuppose a Supreme Being.' This was at least as true when the First Amendment was adopted; and it was just as true when eight Justices of this Court invalidated the released time system in McCollum on the premise that a state can no more 'aid all religions' than it can aid one. * * * [I]t is only by wholly isolating the state from the religious sphere and compelling it to be completely neutral, that the freedom of each and every denomination and of all nonbelievers can be maintained. It is this neutrality the Court abandons today when it treats New York's coercive system as a program which merely 'encourages religious instruction or cooperates with religious authorities.' The abandonment is all the more dangerous to liberty because of the Court's legal exaltation of the orthodox and its derogation of unbelievers.

* * *

State help to religion injects political and party prejudices into a holy field. It too often substitutes force for prayer, hate for love, and persecution for persuasion. Government should not be allowed, under cover of the soft euphemism of 'co-operation,' to steal into the sacred area of religious choice.

Justice Frankfurter also dissented. He generally agreed with Justice Jackson's dissent (excerpted below), but he added several concerns regarding the functioning and purpose of the program because students who did not attend the religious classes were compelled to remain at school while their fellow students were released for religious classes. He wrote in part:

> The pith of the case is that formalized religious instruction is substituted for other school activity which those who do not participate in the released-time program are compelled to attend. The school system is very much in operation during this kind of released time. If its doors are closed, they are closed upon those students who do not attend the religious instruction, in order to keep them within the school. That is the very thing which raises the constitutional issue. It is not met by disregarding it. Failure to discuss this issue does not take it out of the case.

* * *

> When constitutional issues turn on facts, it is a strange procedure indeed not to permit the facts to be established. * * * I cannot see how a finding that coercion was absent, deemed critical by this Court in sustaining the practice, can be made here, when appellants were prevented from making a timely showing of coercion because the courts below thought it irrelevant.

> The result in the McCollum case, was based on principles that received unanimous acceptance by this Court, barring only a single vote. I agree with Mr. Justice Black that those principles are disregarded in reaching the result in this case. Happily they are not disavowed by the Court. From this I draw the hope that in future variations of the problem which are bound to come here, these principles may again be honored in the observance.

> The deeply divisive controversy aroused by the attempts to secure public school pupils for sectarian instruction would promptly end if the advocates of such instruction were content to have the school 'close its doors or suspend its operations'—that is, dismiss classes in their entirety, without discrimination—instead of seeking to use the public schools as the instrument for securing attendance at denominational classes. The unwillingness of the promoters of this movement to dispense with such use of the public schools betrays a surprising want of confidence in the inherent power of the various faiths to draw children to outside sectarian classes—an attitude that hardly reflects the faith of the greatest religious spirits.

Justice Jackson also dissented, arguing that the plan was coercive and thus unconstitutional. He also criticized the Majority's attempt to distinguish McCollum, as reflected in the following quote from his dissenting opinion:

* * * A reading of the Court's opinion in [*McCollum*] along with its opinion in this case will show such difference of overtones and undertones as to make clear that the McCollum case has passed like a storm in a teacup. The wall which the Court was professing to erect between Church and State has become even more warped and twisted than I expected. Today's judgment will be more interesting to students of psychology and of the judicial processes than to students of constitutional law.

Regarding the coercive nature of released time programs, Justice Jackson wrote:

This released time program is founded upon a use of the State's power of coercion, which, for me, determines its unconstitutionality. Stripped to its essentials, the plan has two stages, first, that the State compel each student to yield a large part of his time for public secular education and, second, that some of it be 'released' to him on condition that he devote it to sectarian religious purposes.

No one suggests that the Constitution would permit the State directly to require this 'released' time to be spent 'under the control of a duly constituted religious body.' This program accomplishes that forbidden result by indirection. If public education were taking so much of the pupils' time as to injure the public or the students' welfare by encroaching upon their religious opportunity, simply shortening everyone's school day would facilitate voluntary and optional attendance at Church classes. But that suggestion is rejected upon the ground that if they are made free many students will not go to the Church. Hence, they must be deprived of freedom for this period, with Church attendance put to them as one of the two permissible ways of using it.

* * *

As one whose children, as a matter of free choice, have been sent to privately supported Church schools, I may challenge the Court's suggestion that opposition to this plan can only be antireligious, atheistic, or agnostic. My evangelistic brethren confuse an objection to compulsion with an objection to religion. It is possible to hold a faith with enough confidence to believe that what should be rendered to God does not need to be decided and collected by Caesar.

Within five years of *Everson* the wall of separation concept, whether of the "high and impregnable" variation or not, was quite malleable depending on the programs it was applied to and which Justices made up the majority applying it. Yet all the Justices, except perhaps Justice Reed, seemed to believe the "wall of separation" was the appropriate governing concept.

Notes and Questions

1. *A tale of two cases.* Can *McCollum* and *Zorach* be reconciled with each other? What do you think of Justice Douglas' suggestion in *Zorach* that the difference between the Champaign, Illinois and New York plans was that the former utilized school buildings for instruction while the latter did not? Does this distinction answer the dissenting Justices' concern about the use of the state's compulsory education machinery to support religious education?

2. *Why not just release everyone?* As the dissenters in *Zorach* point out, the schools could simply release all students and let the students and their parents decide whether they should go for religious instruction. Why do you think the school boards did not choose this option? We could assume that the board in McCollum may have failed to do so because it had no reason to believe its program was unconstitutional, but what about the New York school board? Wouldn't the failure to use this option suggest that the result in *McCollum* is more consistent with the principle of separation espoused in *Everson, McCollum,* and *Zorach?* Interestingly, under modern doctrine, if the school chose to release everyone and made its facilities open to a variety of non-curriculum related student activities during this non-instructional time, religious activities could be held on campus so long as the school in no way favored the religious activities over nonreligious activities. *See Lamb's Chapel v. Center Moriches Union Free School District,* 508 U.S. 384, 113 S.Ct. 2141, 124 L.Ed.2d 352 (1993); *Good News Club v. Milford Central School,* 533 U.S. 98, 121 S.Ct. 2093, 150 L.Ed.2d 151 (2001), infra. at Chapter Three (providing a detailed discussion of "equal access" issues). Should this affect the analysis in *McCollum* or *Zorach?* If so, which case should it affect?

3. *Coercion.* To what extent do the dissenting Justices in *Zorach* rely on coercion? Is there coercion under the New York plan? Under the Champaign plan? Is coercion an appropriate standard for analyzing whether state action breaches the "high and impregnable" wall between church and state? This issue will be discussed further in Chapter Two.

4. *Neutrality.* Both the majority and Justice Black's dissenting opinion in *Zorach* claim to be furthering neutrality. How can this be so? Is one approach neutral and the other not? What standards might help you decide this? Is neutrality simply impossible in this area? If so, why would the Court and the dissenters claim to be acting neutrally? *See infra.* at Chapters Four and Five.

C. OTHER EARLY "AID" CASES: *WALZ* AND *ALLEN*

As will be seen in Chapter Four questions regarding government aid to religious entities, both financial and other forms, are still being answered today. Disagreement persists among the Justices and among scholars over the proper role of government in such situations. Chapter Four will explore the evolution of this issue from the famous decision in *Lemon v. Kurtzman,* 403 U.S. 602, 91 S.Ct. 2105, 29 L.Ed.2d 745 (1971), to the Court's recent decision in *Zelman v. Simmons–Harris,* 536 U.S. 639, 122 S.Ct. 2460, 153 L.Ed.2d 604 (2002) (the voucher case). There are two additional Pre-*Lemon* cases that are worth exploring, however, and this section will provide a brief overview of both.

In *Board of Education of Central School Dist. No. 1 v. Allen*, 392 U.S. 236, 88 S.Ct. 1923, 20 L.Ed.2d 1060 (1968), the Court upheld the loan of text books to students attending religious and other private secondary schools. The textbooks were the same as those approved by school authorities for use in secular subjects in the public schools. The Court held the program had the secular purpose of promoting education, and because the books were given to the children and not the school, it was the children and their parents that received the government subsidized benefit, not the religious institutions. Moreover, the Court held that religious schools serve both a secular and religious function, and that such schools had done an "acceptable job of providing secular education to their students." The Court argued that the "processes of secular and religious training [in religious schools are not] so intertwined that secular textbooks furnished to students by the public are . . . instrumental in the teaching of religion." Is this true? Might not at least some religious schools view even secular subjects through a religious lens? Does the Court create an artificial dichotomy between the secular and religious that may not be real for many religious individuals and institutions? Are the textbooks akin to the aid the Court upheld in *Everson*? Would not allowing the loan of textbooks help facilitate student attendance at religious schools by lowering the cost at those schools? Won't it save the religious schools money by sparing them from subsidizing the textbooks? What about the alternative; wouldn't excluding only religious schools from the program put them at a disadvantage, at least when compared to nonreligious private schools that would still be eligible to receive the books?

In *Walz v. Tax Commission*, 397 U.S. 664, 90 S.Ct. 1409, 25 L.Ed.2d 697 (1970), the Court upheld property tax exemptions for religious organization in part because it did not consider tax exemptions to be a form of subsidization of religion—i.e., it was not "aid" in the sense of a monetary subsidy. *Walz* is also an important case because it stands for the proposition that exempting religious organizations from taxes is acceptable if other charitable or educational organizations are exempted as well. The *Walz* Court suggested its holding reflected a "benevolent neutrality," and that such tax exemptions are a longstanding permissible accommodation of religion. In fact, the Court suggested that tax exemptions may be preferable to taxing religious institutions, because it creates less entanglement between government and religious organizations.

The Court analyzed the inclusive nature of the exemption in *Walz* as follows:

> The legislative purpose of a property tax exemption is neither the advancement nor the inhibition of religion; it is neither sponsorship nor hostility. New York, in common with the other States, has determined that certain entities that exist in a harmonious relationship to the community at large, and that foster its 'moral or mental improvement,' should not be inhibited in their activities by property taxation or the hazard of loss of those properties for nonpayment of taxes. It has not singled out one particular church or religious group

or even churches as such; rather, it has granted exemption to all houses of religious worship within a broad class of property owned by nonprofit, quasi-public corporations which include hospitals, libraries, playgrounds, scientific, professional, historical, and patriotic groups. The State has an affirmative policy that considers these groups as beneficial and stabilizing influences in community life and finds this classification useful, desirable, and in the public interest. Qualification for tax exemption is not perpetual or immutable; some tax-exempt groups lose that status when their activities take them outside the classification and new entities can come into being and qualify for exemption.

Governments have not always been tolerant of religious activity, and hostility toward religion has taken many shapes and forms—economic, political, and sometimes harshly oppressive. Grants of exemption historically reflect the concern of authors of constitutions and statutes as to the latent dangers inherent in the imposition of property taxes; exemption constitutes a reasonable and balanced attempt to guard against those dangers. The limits of permissible state accommodation to religion are by no means co-extensive with the noninterference mandated by the Free Exercise Clause. * * * We cannot read New York's statute as attempting to establish religion; it is simply sparing the exercise of religion from the burden of property taxation levied on private profit institutions.

The Court discussed the difference between a subsidy and an exemption in several places. For example, it stated:

Granting tax exemptions to churches necessarily operates to afford an indirect economic benefit and also gives rise to some, but yet a lesser, involvement than taxing them. In analyzing either alternative the questions are whether the involvement is excessive, and whether it is a continuing one calling for official and continuing surveillance leading to an impermissible degree of entanglement. Obviously a direct money subsidy would be a relationship pregnant with involvement and, as with most governmental grant programs, could encompass sustained and detailed administrative relationships for enforcement of statutory or administrative standards, but that is not this case. The hazards of churches supporting government are hardly less in their potential than the hazards of government supporting churches; each relationship carries some involvement rather than the desired insulation and separation. We cannot ignore the instances in history when church support of government led to the kind of involvement we seek to avoid.

The notion that when a broad group of charitable or educational entities receive a tax exemption religious organizations can also receive an exemption makes some sense. Consider a system where all charities or non-profits are eligible for tax exemptions except religious ones. This would appear hostile to religion. Yet, the Court's suggestion that an exemption is not really a subsidy or aid in the traditional sense makes little sense. How can a tax exemption, which might save a religious institution thousands of dollars and take an equal amount from government coffers not be government aid to religion? If the answer is that an exemption is different from a subsidy, can this be justified in the real world given the holdings in *Everson* and *McCollum*? Is it anything more than a purely formalistic distinction? Perhaps, however, the first idea makes the second more plausible (or even unnecessary?).

Both *Allen* and *Walz* were decided after the cases set forth in the next section. The cases in the next section deal with religious exercises, such as prayer, in the public schools. As you read the cases in the following section consider how they might relate to the aid cases, whether they help add coherence to Establishment Clause doctrine and the separation principle, and whether they mesh with some of the aid cases more than others (if so, which ones and why?).

D. REENFORCING THE WALL? THE EARLY SCHOOL PRAYER CASES

As should be obvious by now, the Court's use of the principles of separation and neutrality from *Everson* to *Zorach* were hardly consistent. The cases studied thus far have all dealt with government "aid" to religion, either financial or institutional (in the released time cases). In the early 1960's the Court for the first time addressed questions of government supported religious exercises, such as school prayer. The results in these cases were more consistent, and have remained so to this day. *See Infra.* at Chapter Two. However, the "school prayer" cases, as they have come to be known in common parlance, raised a firestorm of controversy. As you read the following cases consider what they have in common with the "aid" cases and what is different about them. Should the same rules apply to both situations? The same principles? Did the Court apply the same rules? The same principles?

ENGEL v. VITALE

Supreme Court of the United States, 1962.
370 U.S. 421, 82 S.Ct. 1261, 8 L.Ed.2d 601.

Mr. Justice Black delivered the opinion of the Court.

The respondent Board of Education of Union Free School District No. 9, New Hyde Park, New York, acting in its official capacity under state law, directed the School District's principal to cause the following prayer to be said aloud by each class in the presence of a teacher at the beginning of each school day:

> 'Almighty God, we acknowledge our dependence upon Thee, and we beg Thy blessings upon us, our parents, our teachers and our Country.'

This daily procedure was adopted on the recommendation of the State Board of Regents, a governmental agency created by the State

Constitution to which the New York Legislature has granted broad supervisory, executive, and legislative powers over the State's public school system. These state officials composed the prayer which they recommended and published as a part of their "Statement on Moral and Spiritual Training in the Schools," saying: "We believe that this Statement will be subscribed to by all men and women of good will, and we call upon all of them to aid in giving life to our program."

Shortly after the practice of reciting the Regents' prayer was adopted by the School District, the parents of ten pupils brought this action in a New York State Court insisting that use of this official prayer in the public schools was contrary to the beliefs, religions, or religious practices of both themselves and their children. * * *

We think that by using its public school system to encourage recitation of the Regents' prayer, the State of New York has adopted a practice wholly inconsistent with the Establishment Clause. There can, of course, be no doubt that New York's program of daily classroom invocation of God's blessings as prescribed in the Regents' prayer is a religious activity. It is a solemn avowal of divine faith and supplication for the blessings of the Almighty. The nature of such a prayer has always been religious, none of the respondents has denied this and the trial court expressly so found * * *.

The petitioners contend among other things that the state laws requiring or permitting use of the Regents' prayer must be struck down as a violation of the Establishment Clause because that prayer was composed by governmental officials as a part of a governmental program to further religious beliefs. For this reason, petitioners argue, the State's use of the Regents' prayer in its public school system breaches the constitutional wall of separation between Church and State. We agree with that contention since we think that the constitutional prohibition against laws respecting an establishment of religion must at least mean that in this country it is no part of the business of government to compose official prayers for any group of the American people to recite as a part of a religious program carried on by government.

It is a matter of history that this very practice of establishing governmentally composed prayers for religious services was one of the reasons which caused many of our early colonists to leave England and seek religious freedom in America. The Book of Common Prayer, which was created under governmental direction and which was approved by Acts of Parliament in 1548 and 1549, set out in minute detail the accepted form and content of prayer and other religious ceremonies to be used in the established, tax-supported Church of England. The controversies over the Book and what should be its content repeatedly threatened to disrupt the peace of that country as the accepted forms of prayer in the established church changed with the views of the particular ruler that happened to be in control at the time. Powerful groups representing some of the varying religious views of the people struggled among themselves to impress their particular views upon the Government and obtain amendments of the Book more suitable to their respective notions of how religious services should be conducted in order that the official religious establishment would advance their particular religious beliefs. Other groups, lacking the necessary political power to influence the Government on the matter, decided to leave England and its established church and seek freedom in America from England's governmentally ordained and supported religion.

It is an unfortunate fact of history that when some of the very groups which had most strenuously opposed the established Church of England found themselves sufficiently in control of colonial governments in this country to write their own prayers into law, they passed laws making their own religion the official religion of their respective colonies. Indeed, as late as the time of the Revolutionary War, there were established churches in at least eight of the thirteen former colonies and established religions in at least four of the other five. But the successful Revolution against English political domination was shortly followed by intense opposition to the practice of establishing religion by law. * * *

By the time of the adoption of the Constitution, our history shows that there was a widespread awareness among many Americans of the dangers of a union of Church and State. These people knew, some of them from bitter personal experience, that one of the greatest dangers to the freedom of the individual to worship in his own way lay in the Government's placing its official stamp of approval upon one particular kind of prayer or one particular form of religious services. They knew the anguish, hardship and bitter strife that could come when zealous religious groups struggled with one another to obtain the Government's stamp of approval from each King, Queen, or Protector that came to temporary power. * * * The First Amendment was added to the Constitution to stand as a guarantee that neither the power nor the prestige of the Federal Government would be used to control, support or influence the kinds of prayer the American people can say—that the people's religions must not be subjected to the pressures of government for change each time a new political administration is elected to office. Under that Amendment's prohibition against governmental establishment of religion, as reinforced by the provisions of the Fourteenth Amendment, government in this country, be it state or federal, is without power to prescribe by law any particular form of prayer which is to be used as an official prayer in carrying on any program of governmentally sponsored religious activity.

There can be no doubt that New York's state prayer program officially establishes the religious beliefs embodied in the Regents' prayer. The respondents' argument to the contrary, which is largely based upon the contention that the Regents' prayer is "nondenominational" and the fact that the program, as modified and approved by state courts, does not require all pupils to recite the prayer but permits those who wish to do so to remain silent or be excused from the room, ignores the essential nature of the program's constitutional defects. Neither the fact that the prayer may be denominationally neutral nor the fact that its observance on the part of the students is voluntary can serve to free it from the limitations of the Establishment Clause, as it might from the Free Exercise Clause, of the First Amendment, both of which are operative against the States by virtue of the Fourteenth Amendment. Although these two clauses may in certain instances overlap, they forbid two quite different kinds of governmental encroachment upon religious freedom. The Establishment Clause, unlike the Free Exercise Clause, does not depend upon any showing of direct governmental compulsion and is violated by the enactment of laws which establish an official religion whether those laws operate directly to coerce nonobserving individuals or not. This is not to say, of course, that laws officially prescribing a particular form of religious worship do not involve coercion of such individuals. When the power, prestige and financial support of government is placed behind a particular religious belief, the indirect coercive pressure upon religious minorities to conform to the prevailing officially approved religion is plain. But the purposes underlying the Establishment Clause go much further than that. Its first and most immediate purpose rested on the belief that a union of government and religion tends to destroy government and to degrade religion. The history of governmentally established religion, both in England and in this country, showed that whenever government had allied itself with one particular form of religion, the inevitable result had been that it had incurred the hatred, disrespect and even contempt of those who held contrary beliefs. That same history showed that many people had lost their respect for any religion that had relied upon the support for government to spread its faith. The Establishment Clause thus stands as an expression of principle on the part of the Founders of our Constitution that religion is too personal, too sacred, too holy, to permit its "unhallowed perversion" by a civil magistrate. Another purpose of the Establishment Clause rested upon an awareness of the historical fact that governmentally established religions and religious persecutions go hand in hand. The Founders knew that only a few years after the Book of Common Prayer became the only accepted form of religious services in the established Church of England, an Act of Uniformity was passed to compel all Englishmen to attend those services and to make it a criminal offense to conduct or attend religious gatherings of any other kind—a law which was consistently flouted by dissenting religious groups in England * * * And they knew that similar persecutions had received the sanction of law in several of the colonies in this country soon after the establishment of official religions in those colonies. It was in large part to get completely away from this sort of systematic religious persecution that the Founders brought into being our Nation, our Constitution, and our Bill of Rights with its prohibition against any governmental establishment of religion. The New York laws officially prescribing the Regents' prayer are inconsistent both with the purposes of the Establishment Clause and with the Establishment Clause itself.

It has been argued that to apply the Constitution in such a way as to prohibit state laws respecting an establishment of religious services in public schools is to indicate a hostility toward religion or toward prayer. Nothing, or course, could be more wrong. The history of man is inseparable from the history of religion. And perhaps it is not too much to say that since the beginning of that history many people have devoutly believed that "More things are wrought by prayer than this world dreams of." It was doubtless largely due to men who believed this that there grew up a sentiment that caused men to leave the cross-currents of officially established state religions and religious persecution in Europe and come to this country filled with the hope that they could find a place in which they could pray when they pleased to the God of their faith in the language they chose.[20] And there were men of this same faith in the power of prayer who led the fight for adoption of our Constitution and also for our Bill of Rights with the very guarantees of religious freedom that forbid the sort of governmental activity which New York has attempted here. These men knew that the First Amendment, which tried to put an end to governmental control of religion and of prayer, was not written to destroy either. They knew rather that it was written to quiet well-justified fears which nearly all of them felt arising out of an awareness that governments of the past had shackled men's tongues to make them speak only the religious thoughts that government wanted them to speak and to pray only to the God that government wanted them to pray to. It is neither sacrilegious nor antireligious to say that each separate government in this country should stay out of the business of writing or sanctioning official prayers and leave that purely religious function to the people themselves and to those the people choose to look to for religious guidance.[21]

20. Perhaps the best example of the sort of men who came to this country for precisely that reason is Roger Williams, the founder of Rhode Island, who has been described as "the truest Christian amongst many who sincerely desired to be Christian." Parrington, Main Currents in American Thought (1930), Vol. 1, at p. 74. Williams, who was one of the earliest exponents of the doctrine of separation of church and state, believed that separation was necessary in order to protect the church from the danger of destruction which he thought inevitably flowed from control by even the best-intentioned civil authorities: "The unknowing zeale of Constantine and other Emperours, did more hurt to Christ Jesus his Crowne and Kingdome, then the raging fury of the most bloody Neroes. In the persecutions of the later, Christians were sweet and fragrant, like spice pounded and beaten in morters: But those good Emperours, persecuting some erroneous persons, Arrius, & c. and advancing the professours of some Truths of Christ (for there was no small number of Truths lost in those times) and maintaining their Religion by the materiall Sword, I say by this meanes Christianity was ecclipsed,

and the Professors of it fell asleep * * *." Williams, The Bloudy Tenent, of Persecution, for cause of Conscience, discussed in A Conference betweene Truth and Peace (London, 1644), reprinted in Narragansett Club Publications, Vol. III, p. 184. To Williams, it was no part of the business or competence of a civil magistrate to interfere in religious matters: "(W)hat imprudence and indiscretion is it in the most common affaires of Life, to conceive that Emperours, Kings and Rulers of the earth must not only be qualified with politicall and state abilities to make and execute such Civill Lawes which may concerne the common rights, peace and safety (which is worke and businesse, load and burthen enough for the ablest shoulders in the Commonweal) but also furnished with such Spirituall and heavenly abilities to governe the Spirituall and Christian Commonweale * * *." Id., at 366. See also id., at 136—137.

21. There is of course nothing in the decision reached here that is inconsistent with the fact that school children and others are officially encouraged to express love for our country by reciting historical documents such as the Declaration of Indepen-

It is true that New York's establishment of its Regents' prayer as an officially approved religious doctrine of that State does not amount to a total establishment of one particular religious sect to the exclusion of all others—that, indeed, the governmental endorsement of that prayer seems relatively insignificant when compared to the governmental encroachments upon religion which were commonplace 200 years ago. To those who may subscribe to the view that because the Regents' official prayer is so brief and general there can be no danger to religious freedom in its governmental establishment, however, it may be appropriate to say in the words of James Madison, the author of the First Amendment:

> '(I)t is proper to take alarm at the first experiment on our liberties. * * * Who does not see that the same authority which can establish Christianity, in exclusion of all other Religions, may establish with the same ease any particular sect of Christians, in exclusion of all other Sects? That the same authority which can force a citizen to contribute three pence only of his property for the support of any one establishment, may force him to conform to any other establishment in all cases whatsoever?'[22]

The judgment of the Court of Appeals of New York is reversed and the cause remanded for further proceedings not inconsistent with this opinion.

Reversed and remanded.

MR. JUSTICE FRANKFURTER took no part in the decision of this case.

MR. JUSTICE WHITE took no part in the consideration or decision of this case.

MR. JUSTICE DOUGLAS, concurring.

It is customary in deciding a constitutional question to treat it in its narrowest form. Yet at times the setting of the question gives it a form and content which no abstract treatment could give. The point for decision is whether the Government can constitutionally finance a religious exercise. Our system at the federal and state levels is presently honeycombed with such financing. Nevertheless, I think it is an unconstitutional undertaking whatever form it takes.

First, a word as to what this case does not involve. Plainly, our Bill of Rights would not permit a State or the Federal Government to adopt an official prayer and penalize anyone who would not utter it. This, however, is not that case, for there is no element of compulsion or coercion in New York's regulation * * *.

dence which contain references to the Deity or by singing officially espoused anthems which include the composer's professions of faith in a Supreme Being, or with the fact that there are many manifestations in our public life of belief in God. Such patriotic or ceremonial occasions bear no true resemblance to the unquestioned religious exercise that the State of New York has sponsored in this instance.

22. Memorial and Remonstrance against Religious Assessments, II Writings of Madison 183, at 185–186.

The prayer is said upon the commencement of the school day, immediately following the pledge of allegiance to the flag. The prayer is said aloud in the presence of a teacher, who either leads the recitation or selects a student to do so. No student, however, is compelled to take part. The respondents have adopted a regulation which provides that "Neither teachers nor any school authority shall comment on participation or non-participation * * * nor suggest or request that any posture or language be used or dress be worn or be not used or not worn." Provision is also made for excusing children, upon written request of a parent or guardian, from the saying of the prayer or from the room in which the prayer is said. * * *

In short, the only one who need utter the prayer is the teacher; and no teacher is complaining of it. Students can stand mute or even leave the classroom, if they desire.

* * *

The question presented by this case is * * * whether New York oversteps the bounds when it finances a religious exercise.

What New York does on the opening of its public schools is what we do when we open court. Our Crier has from the beginning announced the convening of the Court and then added "God save the United States and this Honorable Court." That utterance is a supplication, a prayer in which we, the judges, are free to join, but which we need not recite any more than the students need recite the New York prayer.

* * *

In New York the teacher who leads in prayer is on the public payroll; and the time she takes seems minuscule as compared with the salaries appropriated by state legislatures and Congress for chaplains to conduct prayers in the legislative halls. Only a bare fraction of the teacher's time is given to reciting this short 22–word prayer, about the same amount of time that our Crier spends announcing the opening of our sessions and offering a prayer for this Court. Yet for me the principle is the same, no matter how briefly the prayer is said, for in each of the instances given the person praying is a public official on the public payroll, performing a religious exercise in a governmental institution. It is said that the element of coercion is inherent in the giving of this prayer. If that is true here, it is also true of the prayer with which this Court is convened, and of those that open the Congress. Few adults, let alone children, would leave our courtroom or the Senate or the House while those prayers are being given. Every such audience is in a sense a "captive" audience.

At the same time I cannot say that to authorize this prayer is to establish a religion in the strictly historic meaning of those words. A religion is not established in the usual sense merely by letting those who choose to do so say the prayer that the public school teacher leads. Yet once government finances a religious exercise it inserts a divisive influence into our communities. The New York Court said that the prayer given does not conform to all of the tenets of the Jewish, Unitarian, and Ethical Culture groups. One of the petitioners is an agnostic.

* * * By reason of the First Amendment government is commanded "to have no interest in theology or ritual", for on those matters "government must be neutral." The First Amendment leaves the Government in a position not of hostility to religion but of neutrality. The philosophy is that the atheist or agnostic—the nonbeliever—is entitled to go his own way. The philosophy is that if government interferes in matters spiritual, it will be a divisive force. The First Amendment teaches that a government neutral in the field of religion better serves all religious interests.

My problem today would be uncomplicated but for Everson v. Board of Education, which allowed taxpayers' money to be used to pay "the bus fares of parochial school pupils as a part of a general program under which" the fares of pupils attending public and other schools were also paid. The Everson case seems in retrospect to be out of line with the First Amendment. Its result is appealing, as it allows aid to be given to needy children. Yet by the same token, public funds could be used to satisfy other needs of children in parochial schools—lunches, books, and tuition being obvious examples. Mr. Justice Rutledge stated in dissent what I think is durable First Amendment philosophy:

'The reasons underlying the Amendment's policy have not vanished with time or diminished in force. Now as when it was adopted the price of religious freedom is double. It is that the church and religion shall live both within and upon that freedom. There cannot be freedom of religion, safeguarded by the state, and intervention by the church or its agencies in the state's domain or dependency on its largesse. Madison's Remonstrance, Par. 6, 8. The great condition of religious liberty is that it be maintained free from sustenance, as also from other interferences, by the state. For when it comes to rest upon that secular foundation it vanishes with the resting. Id., Par. 7, 8. Public money devoted to payment of religious costs, educational or other, brings the quest for more. It brings too the struggle of sect against sect for the larger share or for any. Here one by numbers alone will benefit most, there another. That is precisely the history of societies which have had an established religion and dissident groups. Id., Par. 8, 11. It is the very thing Jefferson and Madison experienced and sought to guard against, whether in its blunt or in its more screened forms. Ibid. The end of such strife cannot be other than to destroy the cherished liberty. The dominating group will achieve the dominate benefit; or all will embroil the state in their dissensions. Id., Par. 11.'

What New York does with this prayer is a break with that tradition. I therefore join the Court in reversing the judgment below.

Mr. Justice Stewart, dissenting.

A local school board in New York has provided that those pupils who wish to do so may join in a brief prayer at the beginning of each school day, acknowledging their dependence upon God and asking His blessing upon them and upon their parents, their teachers, and their country. The Court today decides that in permitting this brief non-denominational prayer the school board has violated the Constitution of the United States. I think this decision is wrong.

* * *

With all respect, I think the Court has misapplied a great constitutional principle. I cannot see how an "official religion" is established by letting those who want to say a prayer say it. On the contrary, I think that to deny the wish of these school children to join in reciting this prayer is to deny them the opportunity of sharing in the spiritual heritage of our Nation.

The Court's historical review of the quarrels over the Book of Common Prayer in England throws no light for me on the issue before us in this case. England had then and has now an established church. Equally unenlightening, I think, is the history of the early establishment and later rejection of an official church in our own States. For we deal here not with the establishment of a state church, which would, of course, be constitutionally impermissible, but with whether school children who want to begin their day by joining in prayer must be prohibited from doing so. Moreover, I think that the Court's task, in this as in all areas of constitutional adjudication, is not responsibly aided by the uncritical invocation of metaphors like the "wall of separation," a phrase nowhere to be found in the Constitution. What is relevant to the issue here is not the history of an established church in sixteenth century England or in eighteenth century America, but the history of the religious traditions of our people, reflected in countless practices of the institutions and officials of our government.

At the opening of each day's Session of this Court we stand, while one of our officials invokes the protection of God. Since the days of John Marshall our Crier has said, "God save the United States and this Honorable Court." Both the Senate and the House of Representatives open their daily Sessions with prayer. Each of our Presidents, from George Washington to John F. Kennedy, has upon assuming his Office asked the protection and help of God. [Justice Stewart included a footnote containing quotes to this effect from a number of Presidents, including James Madison].

* * *

In 1954 Congress added a phrase to the Pledge of Allegiance to the Flag so that it now contains the words "one Nation under God, indivisible, with liberty and justice for all." In 1952 Congress enacted legislation calling upon the President each year to proclaim a National Day of Prayer. Since 1865 the words "IN GOD WE TRUST" have been impressed on our coins.

Countless similar examples could be listed, but there is no need to belabor the obvious. It was all summed up by this Court just ten years ago in a single sentence: "We are a religious people whose institutions presuppose a Supreme Being." Zorach v. Clauson.

I do not believe that this Court, or the Congress, or the President has by the actions and practices I have mentioned established an "official religion" in violation of the Constitution. And I do not believe the State of New York has done so in this case. What each has done has been to recognize and to follow the deeply entrenched and highly cherished spiritual traditions of our Nation—traditions which come down to us from those who almost two hundred years ago avowed their "firm Reliance on the Protection of divine Providence" when they proclaimed the freedom and independence of this brave new world.

I dissent.

SCHOOL DISTRICT OF ABINGTON TOWNSHIP v. SCHEMPP

Supreme Court of the United States, 1963.
374 U.S. 203, 83 S.Ct. 1560, 10 L.Ed.2d 844.

Mr. Justice Clark delivered the opinion of the Court.

Once again we are called upon to consider the scope of the provision of the First Amendment to the United States Constitution which declares that "Congress shall make no law respecting an establishment of religion, or prohibiting the free exercise thereof * * *." These companion cases* present the issues in the context of state action requiring that schools begin each day with readings from the Bible. While raising the basic questions under slightly different factual situations, the cases permit of joint treatment. In light of the history of the First Amendment and of our cases interpreting and applying its requirements, we hold that the practices at issue and the laws requiring them are unconstitutional under the Establishment Clause, as applied to the States through the Fourteenth Amendment.

I.

The Facts in Each Case: No. 142. The Commonwealth of Pennsylvania by law, requires that "At least ten verses from the Holy Bible shall be read, without comment, at the opening of each public school on each school day. Any child shall be excused from such Bible reading, or attending such Bible reading, upon the written request of his parent or guardian." The Schempp family, husband and wife and two of their three children, brought suit to * * * enjoin the appellant school district, wherein the Schempp children attend school, and its officers and the Superintendent of Public Instruction of the Commonwealth from continuing to conduct such readings and recitation of the Lord's Prayer in the public schools of the district pursuant to the statute. * * *

---

* [Author's footnote—This opinion addresses two cases, one from Abington Township, PA and the other from Balti- more, MD. The facts of each are set forth separately within the Court's opinion].

The appellees Edward Lewis Schempp, his wife Sidney, and their children, Roger and Donna, are of the Unitarian faith and are members of the Unitarian Church in Germantown, Philadelphia, Pennsylvania, where they, as well as another son, Ellory, regularly attend religious services. * * * The * * * children attend the Abington Senior High School, which is a public school operated by appellant district.

On each school day at the Abington Senior High School between 8:15 and 8:30 a.m., while the pupils are attending their home rooms or advisory sections, opening exercises are conducted pursuant to the statute. The exercises are broadcast into each room in the school building through an intercommunications system and are conducted under the supervision of a teacher by students attending the school's radio and television workshop. Selected students from this course gather each morning in the school's workshop studio for the exercises, which include readings by one of the students of 10 verses of the Holy Bible, broadcast to each room in the building. This is followed by the recitation of the Lord's Prayer, likewise over the intercommunications system, but also by the students in the various classrooms, who are asked to stand and join in repeating the prayer in unison. The exercises are closed with the flag salute and such pertinent announcements as are of interest to the students. Participation in the opening exercises, as directed by the statute, is voluntary. The student reading the verses from the Bible may select the passages and read from any version he chooses, although the only copies furnished by the school are the King James version, copies of which were circulated to each teacher by the school district. During the period in which the exercises have been conducted the King James, the Douay and the Revised Standard versions of the Bible have been used, as well as the Jewish Holy Scriptures. There are no prefatory statements, no questions asked or solicited, no comments or explanations made and no interpretations given at or during the exercises. The students and parents are advised that the student may absent himself from the classroom or, should he elect to remain, not participate in the exercises.

It appears from the record that in schools not having an intercommunications system the Bible reading and the recitation of the Lord's Prayer were conducted by the home-room teacher * * *.

At the first trial Edward Schempp and the children testified as to specific religious doctrines purveyed by a literal reading of the Bible "which were contrary to the religious beliefs which they held and to their familial teaching." The children testified that all of the doctrines to which they referred were read to them at various times as part of the exercises. Edward Schempp testified at the second trial that he had considered having Roger and Donna excused from attendance at the exercises but decided against it for several reasons, including his belief that the children's relationships with their teachers and classmates would be adversely affected.[3]

---

3. The trial court summarized his testimony as follows:

"Edward Schempp, the children's father, testified that after careful consideration

Expert testimony was introduced by both appellants and appellees at the first trial, which testimony was summarized by the trial court as follows:

"Dr. Solomon Grayzel testified that there were marked differences between the Jewish Holy Scriptures and the Christian Holy Bible, the most obvious of which was the absence of the New Testament in the Jewish Holy Scriptures. Dr. Grayzel testified that portions of the New Testament were offensive to Jewish tradition and that, from the standpoint of Jewish faith, the concept of Jesus Christ as the Son of God was 'practically blasphemous'. He cited instances in the New Testament which, assertedly, were not only sectarian in nature but tended to bring the Jews into ridicule or scorn. Dr. Grayzel gave as his expert opinion that such material from the New Testament could be explained to Jewish children in such a way as to do no harm to them. But if portions of the New Testament were read without explanation, they could be, and in his specific experience with children Dr. Grayzel observed, had been, psychologically harmful to the child and had caused a divisive force within the social media of the school."

"Dr. Grayzel also testified that there was significant difference in attitude with regard to the respective Books of the Jewish and Christian Religions in that Judaism attaches no special significance to the reading of the Bible per se and that the Jewish Holy Scriptures are source materials to be studied. But Dr. Grayzel did state that many portions of the New, as well as of the Old, Testament contained passages of great literary and moral value."

"Dr. Luther A. Weigle, an expert witness for the defense, testified in some detail as to the reasons for and the methods employed in developing the King James and the Revised Standard Versions of the Bible. On direct examination, Dr. Weigle stated that the Bible was non-sectarian. He later stated that the phrase 'non-sectarian' meant to him non-sectarian within the Christian faiths. Dr. Weigle stated that his definition of the Holy Bible would include the Jewish Holy Scriptures, but also stated that the 'Holy Bible' would not be complete without the New Testament. He stated that the New Testament 'conveyed the message of Christians.' In his opinion,

he had decided that he should not have Roger or Donna excused from attendance at these morning ceremonies. Among his reasons were the following. He said that he thought his children would be 'labeled as odd balls' before their teachers and classmates every school day; that children, like Roger's and Donna's classmates, were liable to lump all particular religious difference(s) or religious objections (together) as atheism and that to-day the word 'atheism' is often connected with 'atheistic communism', and has 'very bad' connotations, such as 'un-American' or 'anti-Red', with overtones of possible immorality. Mr. Schempp pointed out that due to the events of the morning exercises following in rapid succession, the Bible reading, the Lord's Prayer, the Flag Salute, and the announcements, excusing his children from the Bible reading would mean that probably they would miss hearing the announcements so important to children. He testified also that if Roger and Donna were excused from Bible reading they would have to stand in the hall outside their 'homeroom' and that this carried with it the imputation of punishment for bad conduct."

reading of the Holy Scriptures to the exclusion of the New Testament would be a sectarian practice. Dr. Weigle stated that the Bible was of great moral, historical and literary value. This is conceded by all the parties and is also the view of the court."

The trial court, in striking down the practices and the statute requiring them, made specific findings of fact that the children's attendance at Abington Senior High School is compulsory and that the practice of reading 10 verses from the Bible is also compelled by law. It also found that:

'The reading of the verses, even without comment, possesses a devotional and religious character and constitutes in effect a religious observance. The devotional and religious nature of the morning exercises is made all the more apparent by the fact that the Bible reading is followed immediately by a recital in unison by the pupils of the Lord's Prayer. The fact that some pupils, or theoretically all pupils, might be excused from attendance at the exercises does not mitigate the obligatory nature of the ceremony * * * The record demonstrates that it was the intention of * * * the Commonwealth * * * to introduce a religious ceremony into the public schools of the Commonwealth.'

No. 119. In 1905 the Board of School Commissioners of Baltimore City adopted a rule [that] * * * provided for the holding of opening exercises in the schools of the city, consisting primarily of the "reading, without comment, of a chapter in the Holy Bible and/or the use of the Lord's Prayer." The petitioners, Mrs. Madalyn Murray and her son, William J. Murray III, are both professed atheists. Following unsuccessful attempts to have the respondent school board rescind the rule, this suit was filed for mandamus to compel its rescission and cancellation. It was alleged that William was a student in a public school of the city and Mrs. Murray, his mother, was a taxpayer therein; that it was the practice under the rule to have a reading on each school morning from the King James version of the Bible; that at petitioners' insistence the rule was amended to permit children to be excused from the exercise on request of the parent and that William had been excused pursuant thereto; that nevertheless the rule as amended was in violation of the petitioners' rights 'to freedom of religion under the First and Fourteenth Amendments' and in violation of "the principle of separation between church and state, contained therein. * * *" The petition particularized the petitioners' atheistic beliefs and stated that the rule, as practiced, violated their rights

'in that it threatens their religious liberty by placing a premium on belief as against non-belief and subjects their freedom of conscience to the rule of the majority; it pronounces belief in God as the source of all moral and spiritual values, equating these values with religious values, and thereby renders sinister, alien and suspect the beliefs and ideals of your Petitioners, promoting doubt and question of their morality, good citizenship and good faith.'

* * *

II.

It is true that religion has been closely identified with our history and government. As we said in Engel v. Vitale, The history of man is inseparable from the history of religion. And * * * since the beginning of that history many people have devoutly believed that "More things are wrought by prayer than this world dreams of." In Zorach v. Clauson, we gave specific recognition to the proposition that "(w)e are a religious people whose institutions presuppose a Supreme Being." The fact that the Founding Fathers believed devotedly that there was a God and that the unalienable rights of man were rooted in Him is clearly evidenced in their writings, from the Mayflower Compact to the Constitution itself. This background is evidenced today in our public life through the continuance in our oaths of office from the Presidency to the Alderman of the final supplication, "So help me God." Likewise each House of the Congress provides through its Chaplain an opening prayer, and the sessions of this Court are declared open by the crier in a short ceremony, the final phrase of which invokes the grace of God. Again, there are such manifestations in our military forces, where those of our citizens who are under the restrictions of military service wish to engage in voluntary worship. Indeed, only last year an official survey of the country indicated that 64% of our people have church membership, while less than 3% profess no religion whatever. It can be truly said, therefore, that today, as in the beginning, our national life reflects a religious people * * *.

This is not to say, however, that religion has been so identified with our history and government that religious freedom is not likewise as strongly imbedded in our public and private life. Nothing but the most telling of personal experiences in religious persecution suffered by our forebarers, see Everson v. Board of Education, could have planted our belief in liberty of religious opinion any more deeply in our heritage. It is true that this liberty frequently was not realized by the colonists, but this is readily accountable by their close ties to the Mother Country. However, the views of Madison and Jefferson, preceded by Roger Williams, came to be incorporated not only in the Federal Constitution but likewise in those of most of our States. This freedom to worship was indispensable in a country whose people came from the four quarters of the earth and brought with them a diversity of religious opinion. Today authorities list 83 separate religious bodies, each with membership exceeding 50,000, existing among our people, as well as innumerable smaller groups.

III.

Almost a hundred years ago in Minor v. Board of Education of Cincinnati, Judge Alphonso Taft, father of the revered Chief Justice, in an unpublished opinion stated the ideal of our people as to religious freedom as one of "absolute equality before the law, of all religious opinions and sects * * *."

'The government is neutral, and, while protecting all, it prefers none, and it disparages none.'

* * *

* * * [T]his Court has rejected unequivocally the contention that the Establishment Clause forbids only governmental preference of one religion over another. Almost 20 years ago in Everson, the Court said that "(n)either a state nor the Federal Government can set up a church. Neither can pass laws which aid one religion, aid all religions, or prefer one religion over another." * * *

* * *

The same conclusion has been firmly maintained ever since that time, see Illinois ex rel. McCollum, and we reaffirm it now.

While none of the parties to either of these cases has questioned these basic conclusions of the Court, both of which have been long established, recognized and consistently reaffirmed, others continue to question their history, logic and efficacy. Such contentions, in the light of the consistent interpretation in cases of this Court, seem entirely untenable and of value only as academic exercises.

IV.

* * *

* * * [I]n Engel v. Vitale, only last year, these principles were so universally recognized that the Court, without the citation of a single case and over the sole dissent of Mr. Justice Stewart, reaffirmed them. * * *

* * *

V.

The wholesome "neutrality" of which this Court's cases speak thus stems from a recognition of the teachings of history that powerful sects or groups might bring about a fusion of governmental and religious functions or a concert or dependency of one upon the other to the end that official support of the State or Federal Government would be placed behind the tenets of one or of all orthodoxies. This the Establishment Clause prohibits. And a further reason for neutrality is found in the Free Exercise Clause, which recognizes the value of religious training, teaching and observance and, more particularly, the right of every person to freely choose his own course with reference thereto, free of any compulsion from the state. This the Free Exercise Clause guarantees. Thus, as we have seen, the two clauses may overlap. As we have indicated, the Establishment Clause has been directly considered by this Court eight times in the past score of years and, with only one Justice dissenting on the point, it has consistently held that the clause withdrew all legislative power respecting religious belief or the expression thereof. The test may be stated as follows: what are the purpose and the primary effect of the enactment? If either is the advancement or inhibition of religion then the enactment exceeds the scope of legislative power as circumscribed by the Constitution. That is to say that to withstand the strictures of the Establishment Clause there must be a secular legislative purpose and a primary effect that neither advances nor inhibits religion. Everson v. Board of Education; McGowan v. Maryland. The Free Exercise Clause, likewise considered many times here, withdraws from legislative power, state and federal, the exertion of any restraint on the free exercise of religion. * * * The distinction between the two clauses is apparent—a violation of the Free Exercise Clause is predicated on coercion while the Establishment Clause violation need not be so attended.

Applying the Establishment Clause principles to the cases at bar we find that the States are requiring the selection and reading at the opening of the school day of verses from the Holy Bible and the recitation of the Lord's Prayer by the students in unison. These exercises are prescribed as part of the curricular activities of students who are required by law to attend school. They are held in the school buildings under the supervision and with the participation of teachers employed in those schools. None of these factors, other than compulsory school attendance, was present in the program upheld in Zorach v. Clauson. The trial court in No. 142 has found that such an opening exercise is a religious ceremony and was intended by the State to be so. We agree with the trial court's finding as to the religious character of the exercises. Given that finding, the exercises and the law requiring them are in violation of the Establishment Clause.

There is no such specific finding as to the religious character of the exercises in No. 119, and the State contends (as does the State in No. 142) that the program is an effort to extend its benefits to all public school children without regard to their religious belief. Included within its secular purposes, it says, are the promotion of moral values, the contradiction to the materialistic trends of our times, the perpetuation of our institutions and the teaching of literature. * * * [E]ven if its purpose is not strictly religious, it is sought to be accomplished through readings, without comment, from the Bible. Surely the place of the Bible as an instrument of religion cannot be gainsaid, and the State's recognition of the pervading religious character of the ceremony is evident from the rule's specific permission of the alternative use of the Catholic Douay version as well as the recent amendment permitting nonattendance at the exercises. None of these factors is consistent with the contention that the Bible is here used either as an instrument for nonreligious moral inspiration or as a reference for the teaching of secular subjects.

The conclusion follows that in both cases the laws require religious exercises and such exercises are being conducted in direct violation of the rights of the appellees and petitioners. Nor are these required exercises mitigated by the fact that individual students may absent themselves upon parental request, for that fact furnishes no defense to a claim of unconstitutionality under the Establishment Clause. Further, it is no defense to urge that the religious practices here may be relatively minor encroachments on the First Amendment. The breach of neutrality that is today a trickling stream may all too soon become a raging torrent and, in the words of Madison, "it is proper to take alarm at the first experiment on our liberties." Memorial and Remonstrance Against Religious Assessments, quoted in Everson.

It is insisted that unless these religious exercises are permitted a "religion of secularism" is established in the schools. We agree of course that the State may not establish a "religion of secularism" in the sense of affirmatively opposing or showing hostility to religion, thus "preferring those who believe in no religion over those who do believe." Zorach v. Clauson. We do not agree, however, that this decision in any sense has that effect. In addition, it might well be said that one's education is not complete without a study of comparative religion or the history of religion and its relationship to the advancement of civilization. It certainly may be said that the Bible is worthy of study for its literary and historic qualities. Nothing we have said here indicates that such study of the Bible or of religion, when presented objectively as part of a secular program of education, may not be effected consistently with the First Amendment. But the exercises here do not fall into those categories. They are religious exercises, required by the States in violation of the command of the First Amendment that the Government maintain strict neutrality, neither aiding nor opposing religion.

Finally, we cannot accept that the concept of neutrality, which does not permit a State to require a religious exercise even with the consent of the majority of those affected, collides with the majority's right to free exercise of religion. While the Free Exercise Clause clearly prohibits the use of state action to deny the rights of free exercise to anyone, it has never meant that a majority could use the machinery of the State to practice its beliefs. Such a contention was effectively answered by Mr. Justice Jackson for the Court in West Virginia Board of Education v. Barnette, 319 U.S. 624, 628, 63 S.Ct. 1178, 1185, 87 L.Ed. 1628 (1943):

'The very purpose of a Bill of Rights was to withdraw certain subjects from the vicissitudes of political controversy, to place them beyond the reach of majorities and officials and to establish them as legal principles to be applied by the courts. One's right to * * * freedom of worship * * * and other fundamental rights may not be submitted to vote; they depend on the outcome of no elections.'

The place of religion in our society is an exalted one, achieved through a long tradition of reliance on the home, the church and the inviolable citadel of the individual heart and mind. We have come to recognize through bitter experience that it is not within the power of government to invade that citadel, whether its purpose or effect be to aid or oppose, to advance or retard. In the relationship between man and religion, the State is firmly committed to a position of neutrality. Though the application of that rule requires interpretation of a delicate sort, the rule itself is clearly and concisely stated in the words of the First Amendment. Applying that rule to the facts of these cases, we affirm the judgment in No. 142. In No. 119, the judgment is reversed and the cause remanded to the Maryland Court of Appeals for further proceedings consistent with this opinion.

It is so ordered.

MR. JUSTICE DOUGLAS, concurring.

I join the opinion of the Court and add a few words in explanation.

While the Free Exercise Clause of the First Amendment is written in terms of what the State may not require of the individual, the Establishment Clause, serving the same goal of individual religious freedom, is written in different terms.

Establishment of a religion can be achieved in several ways. The church and state can be one; the church may control the state or the state may control the church; or the relationship may take one of several possible forms of a working arrangement between the two bodies. * * *

The vice of all such arrangements under the Establishment Clause is that the state is lending its assistance to a church's efforts to gain and keep adherents. Under the First Amendment it is strictly a matter for the individual and his church as to what church he will belong to and how much support, in the way of belief, time, activity or money, he will give to it. * * *

In these cases we have no coercive religious exercise aimed at making the students conform. The prayers announced are not compulsory, though some may think they have that indirect effect because the nonconformist student may be induced to participate for fear of being called an "oddball." But that coercion, if it be present, has not been shown; so the vices of the present regimes are different.

These regimes violate the Establishment Clause in two different ways. In each case the State is conducting a religious exercise; and, as the Court holds, that cannot be done without violating the 'neutrality' required of the State by the balance of power between individual, church and state that has been struck by the First Amendment. But the Establishment Clause is not limited to precluding the State itself from conducting religious exercises. It also forbids the State to employ its facilities or funds in a way that gives any church, or all churches, greater strength in our society than it would have by relying on its members alone. Thus, the present regimes must fall under that clause for the additional reason that public funds, though small in amount, are being used to promote a religious exercise. Through the mechanism of the State, all of the people are being required to finance a religious exercise that only some of the people want and that violates the sensibilities of others.

The most effective way to establish any institution is to finance it; and this truth is reflected in the appeals by church groups for public funds to finance their religious schools. Financing a church either in its strictly religious activities or in its other activities is equally unconstitutional, as I understand the Establishment Clause. * * *

* * * It is not the amount of public funds expended; as this case illustrates, it is the use to which public funds are put that is controlling. For the First Amendment does not say that some forms of establishment are allowed; it says that "no law respecting an establishment of religion" shall be made. What may not be done directly may not be done indirectly lest the Establishment Clause become a mockery.

Mr. Justice Brennan, concurring [considerations of space have led the author of this book to delete large portions of Justice Brennan's opinion, which is quite long, but worth reading in full].

Almost a century and a half ago, John Marshall, In M'Culloch v. Maryland, enjoined: " * * * we must never forget, that it is a constitution we are expounding." The Court's historic duty to expound the meaning of the Constitution has encountered few issues more intricate or more demanding than that of the relationship between religion and the public schools. Since undoubtedly we are "a religious people whose institutions presuppose a Supreme Being," Zorach v. Clauson, deep feelings are aroused when aspects of that relationship are claimed to violate the injunction of the First Amendment that government may make "no law respecting an establishment of religion, or prohibiting the free exercise thereof * * *." Americans regard the public schools as a most vital civic institution for the preservation of a democratic system of government. It is therefore understandable that the constitutional prohibitions encounter their severest test when they are sought to be applied in the school classroom. Nevertheless it is this Court's inescapable duty to declare whether exercises in the public schools of the States, such as those of Pennsylvania and Maryland questioned here, are involvements of religion in public institutions of a kind which offends the First and Fourteenth Amendments.

When John Locke ventured in 1689, "I esteem it above all things necessary to distinguish exactly the business of civil government from that of religion and to settle the just bounds that lie between the one and the other,"[1] he anticipated the necessity which would be thought by the Framers to require adoption of a First Amendment, but not the difficulty that would be experienced in defining those "just bounds." The fact is that the line which separates the secular from the sectarian in American life is elusive. The difficulty of defining the boundary with precision inheres in a paradox central to our scheme of liberty. While our institutions reflect a firm conviction that we are a religious people, those institutions by solemn constitutional injunction may not officially in-

---

1. Locke, A Letter Concerning Toleration, in 35 Great Books of the Western World (Hutchins ed. 1952), 2.

volve religion in such a way as to prefer, discriminate against, or oppress, a particular sect or religion. Equally the Constitution enjoins those involvements of religious with secular institutions which (a) serve the essentially religious activities of religious institutions; (b) employ the organs of government for essentially religious purposes; or (c) use essentially religious means to serve governmental ends where secular means would suffice. The constitutional mandate expresses a deliberate and considered judgment that such matters are to be left to the conscience of the citizen * * *.

I join fully in the opinion and the judgment of the Court. I see no escape from the conclusion that the exercises called in question in these two cases violate the constitutional mandate. * * * It should be unnecessary to observe that our holding does not declare that the First Amendment manifests hostility to the practice or teaching of religion, but only applies prohibitions incorporated in the Bill of Rights in recognition of historic needs shared by Church and State alike. While it is my view that not every involvement of religion in public life is unconstitutional, I consider the exercises at bar a form of involvement which clearly violates the Establishment Clause.

* * *

I.

* * *

[A]n awareness of history and an appreciation of the aims of the Founding Fathers do not always resolve concrete problems. The specific question before us has, for example, aroused vigorous dispute whether the architects of the First Amendment—James Madison and Thomas Jefferson particularly—understood the prohibition against any "law respecting an establishment of religion" to reach devotional exercises in the public schools. It may be that Jefferson and Madison would have held such exercises to be permissible—although even in Jefferson's case serious doubt is suggested by his admonition against 'putting the Bible and Testament into the hands of the children at an age when their judgments are not sufficiently matured for religious inquiries. * * *' But I doubt that their view, even if perfectly clear one way or the other, would supply a dispositive answer to the question presented by these cases. A more fruitful inquiry, it seems to me, is whether the practices here challenged threaten those consequences which the Framers deeply feared; whether, in short, they tend to promote that type of interdependence between religion and state which the First Amendment was designed to prevent. Our task is to translate "the majestic generalities of the Bill of Rights, conceived as part of the pattern of liberal government in the eighteenth century, into concrete restraints on officials dealing with the problems of the twentieth century * * *." West Virginia State Board of Education v. Barnette, 319 U.S. 624, 639, 63 S.Ct. 1178, 1186, 87 L.Ed. 1628.

A too literal quest for the advice of the Founding Fathers upon the issues of these cases seems to me futile and misdirected for several reasons: First, on our precise problem the historical record is at best ambiguous, and statements can readily be found to support either side of the proposition. The ambiguity of history is understandable if we recall the nature of the problems uppermost in the thinking of the statesmen who fashioned the religious guarantees; they were concerned with far more flagrant intrusions of government into the realm of religion than any that our century has witnessed. While it is clear to me that the Framers meant the Establishment Clause to prohibit more than the creation of an established federal church such as existed in England, I have no doubt that, in their preoccupation with the imminent question of established churches, they gave no distinct consideration to the particular question whether the clause also forbade devotional exercises in public institutions.

Second, the structure of American education has greatly changed since the First Amendment was adopted. In the context of our modern emphasis upon public education available to all citizens, any views of the eighteenth century as to whether the exercises at bar are an "establishment" offer little aid to decision. * * *

Third, our religious composition makes us a vastly more diverse people than were our forefathers. They knew differences chiefly among Protestant sects. Today the Nation is far more heterogeneous religiously, including as it does substantial minorities not only of Catholics and Jews but as well of those who worship according to no version of the Bible and those who worship no God at all. * * * In the face of such profound changes, practices which may have been objectionable to no one in the time of Jefferson and Madison may today be highly offensive to many persons, the deeply devout and the nonbelievers alike.

Whatever Jefferson or Madison would have thought of Bible reading or the recital of the Lord's Prayer in what few public schools existed in their day, our use of the history of their time must limit itself to broad purposes, not specific practices. By such a standard, I am persuaded, as is the Court, that the devotional exercises carried on in the Baltimore and Abington schools offend the First Amendment because they sufficiently threaten in our day those substantive evils the fear of which called forth the Establishment Clause of the First Amendment. It is "a constitution we are expounding," and our interpretation of the First Amendment must necessarily be responsive to the much more highly charged nature of religious questions in contemporary society.

Fourth, the American experiment in free public education available to all children has been guided in large measure by the dramatic evolution of the religious diversity among the population which our public schools serve. The interaction of these two important forces in our national life has placed in bold relief certain positive values in the consistent application to public institutions generally, and public schools particularly, of the constitutional decree against official involvements of religion which might produce the evils the Framers meant the Establishment Clause to forestall. * * *

* * *

IV.

I turn now to the cases before us. The religious nature of the exercises here challenged seems plain. * * *

* * *

The last quarter of the nineteenth century found the courts beginning to question the constitutionality of public school religious exercises. The legal context was still, of course, that of the state constitutions, since the First Amendment had not yet been held applicable to state action. And the state constitutional prohibitions against church-state cooperation or governmental aid to religion were generally less rigorous than the Establishment Clause of the First Amendment. It is therefore remarkable that the courts of a half dozen States found compulsory religious exercises in the public schools in violation of their respective state constitutions. These courts attributed much significance to the clearly religious origins and content of the challenged practices, and to the impossibility of avoiding sectarian controversy in their conduct. The Illinois Supreme Court expressed in 1910 the principles which characterized these decisions:

> 'The public school is supported by the taxes which each citizen, regardless of his religion or his lack of it, is compelled to pay. The school, like the government, is simply a civil institution. It is secular, and not religious, in its purposes. The truths of the Bible are the truths of religion, which do not come within the province of the public school. * * * No one denies that they should be taught to the youth of the State. The constitution and the law do not interfere with such teaching, but they do banish theological polemics from the schools and the school districts. This is done, not from any hostility to religion, but because it is no part of the duty of the State to teach religion,—to take the money of all and apply it to teaching the children of all the religion of a part, only. Instruction in religion must be voluntary.' People ex rel. Ring v. Board of Education of Dist. No. 24, 245 Ill. 334, 349, 92 N.E. 251, 256 (1910).

* * *

A.

* * * [I]t is argued that however clearly religious may have been the origins and early nature of daily prayer and Bible reading, these practices today serve so clearly secular educational purposes that their religious attributes may be overlooked. I do not doubt, for example, that morning devotional exercises may foster better discipline in the classroom, and elevate the spiritual level on which the school day opens. * * *

It is not the business of this Court to gainsay the judgments of experts on matters of pedagogy. Such decisions must be left to the discretion of those administrators charged with the supervision of the Nation's public schools. The limited province of the courts is to determine whether the means which the educators have chosen to achieve legitimate pedagogical ends infringe the constitutional freedoms of the First Amendment. The secular purposes which devotional exercises are said to serve fall into two categories—those which depend upon an immediately religious experience shared by the participating children; and those which appear sufficiently divorced from the religious content of the devotional material that they can be served equally by nonreligious materials. With respect to the first objective, much has been written about the moral and spiritual values of infusing some religious influence or instruction into the public school classroom. To the extent that only religious materials will serve this purpose, it seems to me that the purpose as well as the means is so plainly religious that the exercise is necessarily forbidden by the Establishment Clause. The fact that purely secular benefits may eventually result does not seem to me to justify the exercises, for similar indirect nonreligious benefits could no doubt have been claimed for the released time program invalidated in McCollum.

The second justification assumes that religious exercises at the start of the school day may directly serve solely secular ends—for example, by fostering harmony and tolerance among the pupils, enhancing the authority of the teacher, and inspiring better discipline. To the extent that such benefits result not from the content of the readings and recitation, but simply from the holding of such a solemn exercise at the opening assembly or the first class of the day, it would seem that less sensitive materials might equally well serve the same purpose. * * * Such substitutes would, I think, be unsatisfactory or inadequate only to the extent that the present activities do in fact serve religious goals. * * * [T]he State acts unconstitutionally if it either sets about to attain even indirectly religious ends by religious means, or if it uses religious means to serve secular ends where secular means would suffice.

B.

* * * [I]t is argued that the particular practices involved in the two cases before us are unobjectionable because they prefer no particular sect or sects at the expense of others. Both the Baltimore and Abington procedures permit, for example, the reading of any of several versions of the Bible, and this flexibility is said to ensure neutrality sufficiently to avoid the constitutional prohibition. One answer, which might be dispositive, is that any version of the Bible is inherently sectarian, else there would be no need to offer a system of rotation or alternation of versions in the first place, that is, to allow different sectarian versions to be used on different days. The sectarian character of the Holy Bible has been at the core of the whole controversy over religious practices in the public schools throughout its long and often bitter history. To vary the version

as the Abington and Baltimore schools have done may well be less offensive than to read from the King James version every day, as once was the practice. But the result even of this relatively benign procedure is that majority sects are preferred in approximate proportion to their representation in the community and in the student body, while the smaller sects suffer commensurate discrimination. So long as the subject matter of the exercise is sectarian in character, these consequences cannot be avoided.

The argument contains, however, a more basic flaw. There are persons in every community—often deeply devout—to whom any version of the Judaeo–Christian Bible is offensive. There are others whose reverence for the Holy Scriptures demands private study or reflection and to whom public reading or recitation is sacrilegious, as one of the expert witnesses at the trial of the Schempp case explained. To such persons it is not the fact of using the Bible in the public schools, nor the content of any particular version, that is offensive, but only the manner in which it is used. For such persons, the anathema of public communion is even more pronounced when prayer is involved. Many deeply devout persons have always regarded prayer as a necessarily private experience. * * *

* * *

C.

A third element which is said to absolve the practices involved in these cases from the ban of the religious guarantees of the Constitution is the provision to excuse or exempt students who wish not to participate. Insofar as these practices are claimed to violate the Establishment Clause, I find the answer which the District Court gave after our remand of Schempp to be altogether dispositive:

'The fact that some pupils, or theoretically all pupils, might be excused from attendance at the exercises does not mitigate the obligatory nature of the ceremony * * *. The exercises are held in the school buildings and perforce are conducted by and under the authority of the local school authorities and during school sessions. Since the statute requires the reading of the "Holy Bible", a Christian document, the practice, as we said in our first opinion, prefers the Christian religion. The record demonstrates that it was the intention of the General Assembly of the Commonwealth of Pennsylvania to introduce a religious ceremony into the public schools of the Commonwealth.'

Thus the short, and to me sufficient, answer is that the availability of excusal or exemption simply has no relevance to the establishment question * * *.

* * *

Also apposite is the answer given more than 70 years ago by the Supreme Court of Wisconsin to the argument that an excusal provision saved a public school devotional exercise from constitutional invalidation:

> '* * * * the excluded pupil loses caste with his fellows, and is liable to be regarded with aversion, and subjected to reproach and insult. But it is a sufficient refutation of the argument that the practice in question tends to destroy the equality of the pupils which the constitution seeks to establish and protect, and puts a portion of them to serious disadvantage in many ways with respect to the others.' State ex rel. Weiss v. District Board of School District No. 8, 76 Wis. 177, 200, 44 N.W. 967, 975, 7 L.R.A. 330.

* * *

To summarize my views concerning the merits of these two cases: The history, the purpose and the operation of the daily prayer recital and Bible reading leave no doubt that these practices standing by themselves constitute an impermissible breach of the Establishment Clause. Such devotional exercises may well serve legitimate nonreligious purposes. To the extent, however, that such purposes are really without religious significance, it has never been demonstrated that secular means would not suffice. Indeed, I would suggest that patriotic or other nonreligious materials might provide adequate substitutes—inadequate only to the extent that the purposes now served are indeed directly or indirectly religious. Under such circumstances, the States may not employ religious means to reach a secular goal unless secular means are wholly unavailing. I therefore agree with the Court that the judgment in Schempp, No. 142, must be affirmed, and that in Murray, No. 119, must be reversed.

V.

These considerations bring me to a final contention of the school officials in these cases: that the invalidation of the exercises at bar permits this Court no alternative but to declare unconstitutional every vestige, however slight, of cooperation or accommodation between religion and government. I cannot accept that contention. While it is not, of course, appropriate for this Court to decide questions not presently before it, I venture to suggest that religious exercises in the public schools present a unique problem. For not every involvement of religion in public life violates the Establishment Clause. Our decision in these cases does not clearly forecast anything about the constitutionality of other types of interdependence between religious and other public institutions.

* * *

The principles which we reaffirm and apply today can hardly be thought novel or radical. They are, in truth, as old as the Republic itself, and have always been as integral a part of the First Amendment as the very words of that charter of religious liberty. No less applicable today than they were when first pronounced a century ago, one year after the very first court decision involving religious exercises in the public schools, are the words of a distinguished Chief Justice of the Commonwealth of Pennsylvania, Jeremiah S. Black:

> 'The manifest object of the men who framed the institutions of this country, was to have a State without religion, and a Church without politics—that is to say, they meant that one should never be used as an engine for any purpose of the other, and that no man's rights in one should be tested by his opinions about the other. As the Church takes no note of men's political differences, so the State looks with equal eye on all the modes of religious faith. * * * Our fathers seem to have been perfectly sincere in their belief that the members of the Church would be more patriotic, and the citizens of the State more religious, by keeping their respective functions entirely separate.' Essay on Religious Liberty, in Black, ed., Essays and Speeches of Jeremiah S. Black (1866), 53.

MR. JUSTICE GOLDBERG, with whom MR. JUSTICE HARLAN joins, concurring.

As is apparent from the opinions filed today, delineation of the constitutionally permissible relationship between religion and government is a most difficult and sensitive task, calling for the careful exercise of both judicial and public judgment and restraint. The considerations which lead the Court today to interdict the clearly religious practices presented in these cases are to me wholly compelling; I have no doubt as to the propriety of the decision and therefore join the opinion and judgment of the Court. The singular sensitivity and concern which surround both the legal and practical judgments involved impel me, however, to add a few words in further explication, while at the same time avoiding repetition of the carefully and ably framed examination of history and authority by my Brethren.

The First Amendment's guarantees, as applied to the States through the Fourteenth Amendment, foreclose not only laws "respecting an establishment of religion" but also those "prohibiting the free exercise thereof." These two proscriptions are to be read together, and in light of the single end which they are designed to serve. The basic purpose of the religion clause of the First Amendment is to promote and assure the fullest possible scope of religious liberty and tolerance for all and to nurture the conditions which secure the best hope of attainment of that end.

The fullest realization of true religious liberty requires that government neither engage in nor compel religious practices, that it effect no favoritism among sects or between religion and nonreligion, and that it work deterrence of no religious belief. But devotion even to these simply stated objectives presents no easy course, for the unavoidable accommodations necessary to achieve the maximum enjoyment of each and all of them are often difficult of discernment. There is for me no simple and clear measure which by precise application can readily and invariably demark the permissible from the impermissible.

It is said, and I agree, that the attitude of government toward religion must be one of neutrality. But untutored devotion to the concept of neutrality can lead to invocation or approval of results which partake not simply of that noninterference and noninvolvement with the religious which the Constitution commands, but of a brooding and pervasive devotion to the secular and a passive, or even active, hostility to the religious. Such results are not only not compelled by the Constitution, but, it seems to me, are prohibited by it.

Neither government nor this Court can or should ignore the significance of the fact that a vast portion of our people believe in and worship God and that many of our legal, political and personal values derive historically from religious teachings. Government must inevitably take cognizance of the existence of religion and, indeed, under certain circumstances the First Amendment may require that it do so. * * *

The practices here involved do not fall within any sensible or acceptable concept of compelled or permitted accommodation and involve the state so significantly and directly in the realm of the sectarian as to give rise to those very divisive influences and inhibitions of freedom which both religion clauses of the First Amendment preclude. The state has ordained and has utilized its facilities to engage in unmistakably religious exercises—the devotional reading and recitation of the Holy Bible—in a manner having substantial and significant import and impact. * * * The pervasive religiosity and direct governmental involvement inhering in the prescription of prayer and Bible reading in the public schools, during and as part of the curricular day, involving young impressionable children whose school attendance is statutorily compelled, and utilizing the prestige, power, and influence of school administration, staff, and authority, cannot realistically be termed simply accommodation, and must fall within the interdiction of the First Amendment. * * *

The First Amendment does not prohibit practices which by any realistic measure create none of the dangers which it is designed to prevent and which do not so directly or substantially involve the state in religious exercises or in the favoring of religion as to have meaningful and practical impact. It is of course true that great consequences can grow from small beginnings, but the measure of constitutional adjudication is the ability and willingness to distinguish between real threat and mere shadow.

Mr. Justice Stewart, dissenting.

I think the records in the two cases before us are so fundamentally deficient as to make impossible an informed or responsible determination of the constitutional issues presented. Specifically, I cannot agree that on these records we can say that the Establishment Clause has necessarily been violated. But I think there exist serious questions under both that provision and the Free Exercise Clause—insofar as each is imbedded in the Fourteenth Amendment—which require the remand of these cases for the taking of additional evidence.

I.

The First Amendment declares that "Congress shall make no law respecting an establishment of religion, or prohibiting the free exercise thereof * * *." It is, I think, a fallacious oversimplification to regard these two provisions as establishing a single constitutional standard of "separation of church and state," which can be mechanically applied in every case to delineate the required boundaries between government and religion. We err in the first place if we do not recognize, as a matter of history and as a matter of the imperatives of our free society, that religion and government must necessarily interact in countless ways. Secondly, the fact is that while in many contexts the Establishment Clause and the Free Exercise Clause fully complement each other, there are areas in which a doctrinaire reading of the Establishment Clause leads to irreconcilable conflict with the Free Exercise Clause.

* * * The short of the matter is simply that the two relevant clauses of the First Amendment cannot accurately be reflected in a sterile metaphor which by its very nature may distort rather than illumine the problems involved in a particular case.

II.

As a matter of history, the First Amendment was adopted solely as a limitation upon the newly created National Government. The events leading to its adoption strongly suggest that the Establishment Clause was primarily an attempt to insure that Congress not only would be powerless to establish a national church, but would also be unable to interfere with existing state establishments. Each State was left free to go its own way and pursue its own policy with respect to religion. Thus Virginia from the beginning pursued a policy of disestablishmentarianism. Massachusetts, by contrast, had an established church until well into the nineteenth century.

* * *

I accept without question that the liberty guaranteed by the Fourteenth Amendment against impairment by the States embraces in full the right of free exercise of religion protected by the First Amendment, and I yield to no one in my conception of the breadth of that freedom. I accept too the proposition that the Fourteenth Amendment has somehow absorbed the Establishment Clause, although it is not without irony that a constitutional provision evidently designed to leave the States free to go their own way should now have become a restriction upon their autonomy. But I cannot agree with what seems to me the insensitive definition of the Establishment Clause contained in the Court's opinion, nor with the different but, I think, equally mechanistic definitions contained in the separate opinions which have been filed.

III.

Since the Cantwell pronouncement in 1940, this Court has only twice held invalid state laws on the ground that they were laws "respecting an establishment of religion" in violation of the Fourteenth Amendment. Illinois ex rel. McCollum v. Board of Education; Engel v. Vitale. On the other hand, the Court has upheld against such a challenge laws establishing Sunday as a compulsory day of rest, McGowan v. Maryland, 366 U.S. 420, 81 S.Ct. 1101, 6 L.Ed.2d 393, and a law authorizing reimbursement from public funds for the transportation of parochial school pupils. Everson v. Board of Education.

Unlike other First Amendment guarantees, there is an inherent limitation upon the applicability of the Establishment Clause's ban on state support to religion. That limitation was succinctly put in Everson v. Board of Education: "State power is no more to be used so as to handicap religions, than it is to favor them." And in a later case, this Court recognized that the limitation was one which was itself compelled by the free exercise guarantee. "To hold that a state cannot consistently with the First and Fourteenth Amendments utilize its public school system to aid any or all religious faiths or sects in the dissemination of their doctrines and ideals does not * * * manifest a governmental hostility to religion or religious teachings. A manifestation of such hostility would be at war with our national tradition as embodied in the First Amendment's guaranty of the free exercise of religion." Illinois ex rel. McCollum v. Board of Education.

That the central value embodied in the First Amendment—and, more particularly, in the guarantee of "liberty" contained in the Fourteenth—is the safeguarding of an individual's right to free exercise of his religion has been consistently recognized. * * *

It is this concept of constitutional protection embodied in our decisions which makes the cases before us such difficult ones for me. For there is involved in these cases a substantial free exercise claim on the part of those who affirmatively desire to have their children's school day open with the reading of passages from the Bible.

* * * It might be argued here that parents who wanted their children to be exposed to religious influences in school could, * * * send their children to private or parochial schools. But the consideration which renders this contention too facile to be determinative has already been recognized by the Court: "Freedom of speech, freedom of the press, freedom of religion are available to all, not merely to those who can pay their own way." Murdock v. Commonwealth of Pennsylvania, 319 U.S. 105, 111, 63 S.Ct. 870, 874, 87 L.Ed. 1292.

It might also be argued that parents who want their children exposed to religious influences can adequately fulfill that wish off school property and outside school time. With all its surface persuasiveness, however, this argument seriously misconceives the basic constitutional justification for permitting the exercises at issue in these cases. For a compulsory state educational system so structures a child's life that if religious exercises are held to be an impermissible activity in schools, religion is placed at an artificial and state-created disadvantage. Viewed in this light, permission of such exercises for those who want them is necessary if the schools are truly to be neutral in the matter of religion. And a refusal to permit religious exercises thus is seen, not as the realization of state neutrality, but rather as the establishment of a religion of secularism, or at the least, as government support of the beliefs of those who think that religious exercises should be conducted only in private.

What seems to me to be of paramount importance, then, is recognition of the fact that the claim advanced here in favor of Bible reading is sufficiently substantial to make simple reference to the constitutional phrase "establishment of religion" as inadequate an analysis of the cases before us as the ritualistic invocation of the nonconstitutional phrase "separation of church and state." What these cases compel, rather, is an analysis of just what the "neutrality" is which is required by the interplay of the Establishment and Free Exercise Clauses of the First Amendment, as imbedded in the Fourteenth.

IV.

Our decisions make clear that there is no constitutional bar to the use of government property for religious purposes. On the contrary, this Court has consistently held that the discriminatory barring of religious groups from public property is itself a violation of First and Fourteenth Amendment guarantees. A different standard has been applied to public school property, because of the coercive effect which the use by religious sects of a compulsory school system would necessarily have upon the children involved. Illinois ex rel. McCollum v. Board of Education. But insofar as the McCollum decision rests on the Establishment rather than the Free Exercise Clause, it is clear that its effect is limited to religious instruction—to government support of proselytizing activities of religious sects by throwing the weight of secular authority behind the dissemination of religious tenets.

The dangers both to government and to religion inherent in official support of instruction in the tenets of various religious sects are absent in the present cases, which involve only a reading from the Bible unaccompanied by comments which might otherwise constitute instruction. * * *

In the absence of evidence that the legislature or school board intended to prohibit local schools from substituting a different set of readings where parents requested such a change, we should not assume that the provisions before us—as actually administered—may not be construed simply as authorizing religious exercises, nor that the designations may not be treated simply as indications of the promulgating body's view as to the community's preference. We are under a duty to interpret these provisions so as to render them constitutional if reasonably possible. * * *

* * * In the absence of coercion upon those who do not wish to participate—because they hold less strong beliefs, other beliefs, or no beliefs at all—such provisions cannot, in my view, be held to represent

the type of support of religion barred by the Establishment Clause. For the only support which such rules provide for religion is the withholding of state hostility—a simple acknowledgment on the part of secular authorities that the Constitution does not require extirpation of all expression of religious belief.

V.

* * *

It is clear that the dangers of coercion involved in the holding of religious exercises in a schoolroom differ qualitatively from those presented by the use of similar exercises or affirmations in ceremonies attended by adults. Even as to children, however, the duty laid upon government in connection with religious exercises in the public schools is that of refraining from so structuring the school environment as to put any kind of pressure on a child to participate in those exercises; it is not that of providing an atmosphere in which children are kept scrupulously insulated from any awareness that some of their fellows may want to open the school day with prayer, or of the fact that there exist in our pluralistic society differences of religious belief.

* * *

The governmental neutrality which the First and Fourteenth Amendments require in the cases before us, in other words, is the extension of evenhanded treatment to all who believe, doubt, or disbelieve—a refusal on the part of the State to weight the scales of private choice. In these cases, therefore, what is involved is not state action based on impermissible categories, but rather an attempt by the State to accommodate those differences which the existence in our society of a variety of religious beliefs makes inevitable. The Constitution requires that such efforts be struck down only if they are proven to entail the use of the secular authority of government to coerce a preference among such beliefs.

* * *

VI.

Viewed in this light, it seems to me clear that the records in both of the cases before us are wholly inadequate to support an informed or responsible decision. Both cases involve provisions which explicitly permit any student who wishes, to be excused from participation in the exercises. There is no evidence in either case as to whether there would exist any coercion of any kind upon a student who did not want to participate. No evidence at all was adduced in the Murray case, because it was decided upon a demurrer. All that we have in that case, therefore, is the conclusory language of a pleading. While such conclusory allegations are acceptable for procedural purposes, I think that the nature of the constitutional problem involved here clearly demands that no decision be made except upon evidence. * * *

What our Constitution indispensably protects is the freedom of each of us, be he Jew or Agnostic, Christian or Atheist, Buddhist or Freethinker, to believe or disbelieve, to worship or not worship, to pray or keep silent, according to his own conscience, uncoerced and unrestrained by government. It is conceivable that these school boards, or even all school boards, might eventually find it impossible to administer a system of religious exercises during school hours in such a way as to meet this constitutional standard—in such a way as completely to free from any kind of official coercion those who do not affirmatively want to participate. But I think we must not assume that school boards so lack the qualities of inventiveness and good will as to make impossible the achievement of that goal.

I would remand both cases for further hearing.

Notes and Questions

1. *From principle to legal test.* Were the holdings in *Engel* and *Abington* the result of the same legal test? Did the *Engel* Court specify how one knows when a given religious exercise crosses the line to become unconstitutional behavior? Did the *Abington* Court answer this question by specifying a test? If so, what was that test and from where was it derived? Was it clearly delineated in earlier opinions?

2. *Neutrality and separation.* Both *Engel* and *Abington* rely on the principles of separation and neutrality, suggesting that the two concepts are linked. Is this so? Can a separationist approach be neutral? If so, what about the argument that strict separationism would be hostile to religion? Yet, could a system without some form of separation between church and state be neutral? Does the problem lie with the principle of separation or with the principle of neutrality? Are either or both of these principles appropriate actuating principles under the Establishment Clause? Recent decisions by the Supreme Court have increased the tension between the two principles. *See infra.* at Chapters Four and Five. For excellent discussion about the relationship between separation and neutrality in light of more recent developments, *see* Douglas Laycock, *The Underlying Unity of Separation and Neutrality*, 46 EMORY L.J. 43 (1997); Frederick Mark Gedicks, *A Two Track Theory of the Establishment Clause*, 43 B.C. L. REV. 1071 (2002).

3. *Coercion.* The majority in *Abington* rejects the notion that coercion is necessary for an Establishment Clause violation but Justice Stewart disagrees. Why does Justice Stewart argue coercion is necessary in the school prayer context? How does Justice Clark respond? Justice Brennan? Which position do you find more persuasive? How would you define coercion? Is a student who does not participate in a religious exercise and is picked on, harassed, or ostracized by other students as a result, coerced? Should it matter whether the harassment or ostracism is the result of the school policy supporting religious activity? For a discussion of the harassment and discrimination issue, see Frank S. Ravitch, SCHOOL PRAYER AND DISCRIMINATION: THE CIVIL RIGHTS OF RELIGIOUS MINORITIES AND DISSENTERS (Northeastern Univ. Press 1999).

4. *What do the decisions govern?* After *Engel* and *Abington*, it is clear that private prayer by students is allowed. Thus, a student can quietly say grace before meals or say a silent prayer during class time. Moreover, it is clear that

schools may teach about religion in secular subjects so long as the discussion of religion is in an appropriate secular context. Thus, the bible can be studied as an important piece of historic literature, the role of Christianity in the history of Europe can be taught, and even courses in comparative religion that teach about the various religions in an objective fashion would seemingly be allowed. What is prevented? Is it only organized prayer that occurs during curricular time? If so, doesn't this result make sense as a balance between the two religion clauses? Why did Justice Stewart see it differently? Would organized student initiated prayer during curricular time or during school activities be allowed under the holdings in *Engel* and *Abington*? *See Infra.* at Chapter Two (discussing this issue).

E. FROM SCHOOL PRAYER TO THE EVOLUTION/CREATIONISM DEBATE: *EPPERSON v. ARKANSAS*

Given the reasoning in *Engel* and *Abington*, it would seem that public schools can not impose religious exercises or teachings on students, but that they can include religious texts in an appropriate secular course. Thus, a teacher could use the bible in a course on literature so long as it was not taught as religious truth (or historical truth) and was treated and questioned like any other work of literature. What then was the constitutional status of the teaching of creationism after *Engel* and *Abington*? It was likely unconstitutional because it involved teaching religious doctrine as historical and scientific fact (at least when the issue is traditional creationism—modern "intelligent design theory" raises similar concerns, but will be addressed later in this book. *See infra.* at Chapter Two).

In *Epperson v. Arkansas*, 393 U.S. 97, 89 S.Ct. 266, 21 L.Ed.2d 228 (1968), the Court struck down an Arkansas law that made it a crime (a misdemeanor) to teach evolution in any state supported school or university. Any teacher who did so was also subject to dismissal from his or her position under the law. The school administration for the Little Rock school district decided to adopt a textbook that contained a chapter on evolution for high school biology classes beginning in the 1965–66 academic year. Of course this placed teachers like Susan Epperson in a tough position. She could either follow her district's suggested curriculum with which she apparently agreed and be subject to prosecution and possible dismissal from her job under the statute, or she could refuse to use the book or skip the chapter on evolution—a result which she may not have believed to be educationally sound—and face possible discipline for not following the district's prescribed curriculum.

It is important to note that the Arkansas law did not prescribe that any account of human origins be taught, only that evolution may not be taught. Thus, there was no requirement that creationism be taught; although it could be, and if it were, evolution could not be taught as an alternative or even complimentary theory. The Court was not presented with a case where a religious theory was required to be taught in the public schools, but rather with a situation where a scientific theory that was at odds with some peoples' religious beliefs could not be taught while religious theories could be at the discretion of the various schools and teachers.

The Court held that the Arkansas law did not have a secular purpose and thus violated the Establishment Clause. The law was designed to prevent a view that was antithetical to a particular religion—and only that view—from being taught in the public schools. The Court stated:

> ' * * * there can be no doubt that Arkansas has sought to prevent its teachers from discussing the theory of evolution because it is contrary to the belief of some that the Book of Genesis must be the exclusive source of doctrine as to the origin of man. No suggestion has been made that Arkansas' law may be justified by considerations of state policy other than the religious views of some of its citizens.'

The Court further held that the law can not be defended as neutral because it only excluded discussion of evolution and not all discussion of human origins.

Interestingly, forty years before *Epperson*, in the famous "Scopes Monkey Trial" case, the Tennessee Supreme Court held that a similar Tennessee statute did not violate the state constitution because it did not mandate that anything be taught, but rather simply prohibited the teaching of evolution. *Scopes v. State*, 154 Tenn. 105, 289 S.W. 363 (1927). This was reflected in Justice Black's concurring opinion in *Epperson*, where he suggested that a secular purpose behind the statute may have been to take the "emotional and controversial" subject of human origins out of the schools since the law did not mandate that anything be taught on the subject. Justice Black also argued by requiring state's to permit the teaching of evolution, which some might see as an "anti-religious" theory, the Court's decision might lead to infringement of the religious freedom of those who consider evolution to be an anti-religious theory. Justice Black concurred, however, because he believed the law was unconstitutionally vague.

F.   WHAT DOES HISTORY TELL US ABOUT THE ESTABLISHMENT CLAUSE?

As the cases above (and many of the cases throughout the rest of this book) demonstrate, the Court has often used history to support its Establishment Clause decisions and the principles underlying them. Yet the Justices often seem to disagree over the meaning and relevant aspects of that history, and scholars have had similar disagreements. The differences among the Justices regarding the history of the religion clauses will become a common theme in the cases excerpted in later Chapters. For now it is useful to look at two somewhat conflicting views of the history of the Establishment Clause (and the meaning of that history) presented by two leading legal historians.

It is not an overstatement to say that the two books excerpted below are major contributions to the field. Philip Hamburger's book is quite new but has already become an exceptionally important book on the history of the religion clauses, and Leonard Levy's book is a classic in the field. Space concerns necessitate that the excerpts be relatively short, but of course they are part of much larger works. For example, the Levy excerpts below contain a large number of quotes from historical documents and it might be assumed that there is not much commentary in the broader book, but that would be untrue. Conversely, the excerpt from Hamburger's book involves more commentary and an overview of some of the history, and thus it might be assumed that he doesn't utilize as many historical documents as Levy, yet this too would be untrue.

The following excerpts are just a taste of what scholars have to say about the history the Court has so often relied upon. As you read the following material consider whether the various Justices' use of history in the opinions contained in this chapter was consistent with either or both of the stories sketched out below? Are the views of the relevant history expressed below necessarily opposed to each other? On what do the two authors agree? On what do they disagree (keep in mind that each book deals with issues addressed by the other in places not excerpted here)? How much weight, if any, should be placed on history when evaluating claims under the Establishment Clause? If some weight should be placed on history, what history should count? That of the framers of the Constitution, the framer's of the 14th Amendment through which it was incorporated, both, or the entire history of the nation?

FROM THE ESTABLISHMENT CLAUSE: RELIGION AND THE FIRST AMENDMENT
by Leonard W. Levy at 94–111, 146–150, 226–228, 234–250.
Copyright © 1994 by the University of North Carolina Press.
Used by permission of publisher.

AT THE FIRST session of the First Congress, Representative Madison on June 8, 1789, proposed for House approval a series of amendments to the Constitution. He accompanied his presentation with a lengthy speech explaining his action and defending the value of a bill of rights, but he did not discuss the proposal relating to an establishment of religion. The section on religion read: "The civil rights of none shall be abridged on account of religious belief or worship, nor shall any national religion be established, nor shall the full and equal rights of conscience be in any manner, or on any pretext, infringed."

The term "national religion" has ambiguous connotations. It might have meant quite narrowly a nationwide preference for one denomination over others or, more broadly, preference for Christianity, that is, for all Christian denominations over non-Christian religions. Proponents of a narrow interpretation of the establishment clause see in the word "national" proof of their contention that nothing more was intended than a prohibition against the preference for one church or religion over others. Madison did not, at this time or when the proposal was debated, explain what he meant by the clause, "nor shall any national religion be established."

Taken in the context of Madison's recommended amendments it seems likely that "national" in this case signified action by the national government, because his next recommendation proposed a restriction upon the powers of the states: "No State shall violate the equal rights of conscience, or the freedom of the press, or the trial by jury in criminal cases."

In other words, the term "national" signified that the prohibition against an establishment of religion—whatever that meant—applied to Congress only and not to the states. That is, Congress had no power to enact an establishment of religion or to interfere with state establishments. Perhaps the word "national" was superfluous, but Madison aimed at allaying apprehensions on the part of those states that maintained their own establishments of religion. In any case, if there is any validity to the argument that "national" signified the intention to prohibit only the establishment of a single religion or sect, the fact remains that the word "national" was deleted and does not appear in the final version of the amendment, thereby indicating that Congress rejected that intention and meant something broader by its ban on an establishment of religion.

Without debate, Madison's recommendations for amendments were referred for consideration to a select committee of the House, composed of one member from each state, including Madison. Although we know nothing of the committee's deliberations, which took one week, its report to the House shows that Madison was the dominating figure because his proposed amendments remained intact with but slight changes in phraseology in the interest of brevity. From the proposal on religion the committee deleted the clause on civil rights and the word "national." The proposed amendment then read: "No religion shall be established by law, nor shall the equal rights of conscience be infringed." The report of the select committee to the House merely recommended a redrafting of the original proposals; no explanation of the changes was included.

The House, sitting as a Committee of the Whole, began and ended its debate on the amendment on August 15. Our only account of the debate, in the *Annals of Congress,* is more in the nature of a condensed and paraphrased version than it is a verbatim report. The account is brief enough to be given here in full:

* * *

The House again went into a Committee of the Whole on the proposed amendments to the constitution, Mr. Boudinot in the chair.

The fourth proposition being under consideration, as follows:

Article I. Section 9. Between paragraphs two and three insert "no religion shall be established by law, nor shall the equal rights of conscience be infringed."

Mr. Sylvester had some doubts of the propriety of the mode of expression used in this paragraph. He apprehended that it was liable to a construction different from what had been made by the committee. He feared it might be thought to have a tendency to abolish religion altogether.

Mr. Vining suggested the propriety of transposing the two members of the sentence.

Mr. Gerry said it would read better if it was, that no religious doctrine shall be established by law.

Mr. Sherman thought the amendment altogether unnecessary, inasmuch as Congress had no authority whatever delegated to them by the constitution to make religious establishments; he would, therefore, move to have it struck out.

Mr. Carroll–As the rights of conscience are, in their nature, of peculiar delicacy, and will little bear the gentlest touch of governmental hand; and as many sects have concurred in opinion that they are not well secured under the present constitution, he said he was much in favor of adopting the words. He thought it would tend more towards conciliating the minds of the people to the government than almost any other amendment he had heard proposed. He would not contend with gentlemen about the phraseology, his object was to secure the substance in such a manner as to satisfy the wishes of the honest part of the community.

Mr. Madison said, he apprehended the meaning of the words to be, that Congress should not establish a religion, and enforce the legal observation of it by law, nor compel men to worship God in any manner contrary to their conscience. Whether the words are necessary or not, he did not mean to say, but they had been required by some of the State Conventions, who seemed to entertain an opinion that under the clause of the constitution, which gave power to Congress to make all laws necessary and proper to carry into execution the constitution, and the laws made under it, enabled them to make laws of such a nature as might infringe the rights of conscience, and establish a national religion; to prevent these effects he presumed the amendment was intended, and he thought it as well expressed as the nature of the language would admit.

Mr. Huntington said that he feared, with the gentleman first up on this subject, that the words might be taken in such latitude as to be extremely harmful to the cause of religion. He understood the amendment to mean what had been expressed by the gentleman from Virginia; but others might find it convenient to put another construction upon it. The ministers of their congregations to the Eastward were maintained by the contributions of those who belonged to their society; the expense of building meeting-houses was contributed in the same manner. These things were regulated by by-laws. If an action was brought before a Federal Court on any of these cases, the person who had neglected to perform his engagements could not be compelled to do it; for a support of ministers, or building of places of worship might be construed into a religious establishment.

By the charter of Rhode Island, no religion could be established by law; he could give a history of the effects of such a regulation; indeed the people were now enjoying the blessed fruits of it [intended as irony]. He hoped, therefore, the amendment would be made in such a way as to secure the rights of conscience, and a free exercise of the rights of religion, but not to patronize those who professed no religion at all.

Mr. Madison thought, if the word national was inserted before religion, it would satisfy the minds of honorable gentlemen. He believed that the people feared one sect might obtain a preeminence, or two combine together, and establish a religion to which they would compel others to conform. He thought if the word national was introduced, it would point the amendment directly to the object it was intended to prevent.

Mr. Livermore was not satisfied with that amendment; but he did not wish them to dwell long on the subject. He thought it would be better if it was altered, and made to read in this manner, that Congress shall make no laws touching religion, or infringing the rights of conscience.

Mr. Gerry did not like the term national, proposed by the gentleman from Virginia, and he hoped it would not be adopted by the House. It brought to his mind some observations that had taken place in the conventions at the time they were considering the present constitution. It had been insisted upon by those who were called antifederalists, that this form of Government consolidated the Union; the honorable gentleman's motion shows that he considers it in the same light. Those who were called antifederalists at that time complained that they had injustice done them by the title, because they were in favor of a Federal Government, and the others were in favor of a national one; the federalists were for ratifying the constitution as it stood, and the others not until amendments were made. Their names then ought not to have been distinguished by federalists and antifederalists, but rats and antirats.

Mr. Madison withdrew his motion, but observed that the words "no national religion shall be established by law," did not imply that the Government was a national one; the question was then taken on Mr. Livermore's motion, and passed in the affirmative, thirty-one for, and twenty against it.

The debate as unreliably reported was sometimes irrelevant, usually apathetic and unclear. Ambiguity, brevity, and imprecision in thought and expression characterize the comments of the few members who spoke. That the House understood the debate, cared deeply, about its outcome, or shared a common understanding of the finished amendment seems doubtful. Only a few members participated.

Not even Madison himself, dutifully carrying out his pledge to secure amendments, seems to have troubled to do more than was necessary to get something adopted in order to satisfy the popular clamor for a bill of rights and deflate Anti–Federalist charges that the new national government imperiled liberty. Indeed, Madison agreed with Roger Sherman's statement that the amendment was "altogether unnecessary, inasmuch as Congress had no authority whatever delegated to them by the constitution to make religious establishments." The difficulty, however, lies in the fact that neither Sherman, Madison, nor anyone else except Benjamin Huntington took the trouble to define what he was talking about. What were "religious establishments"? Huntington of Connecticut understood that government support of ministers or of places of worship came within the meaning of the term. But what did the select committee on amendments intend by recommending that "no religion shall be established by, law"? Madison's statement that the words meant "that Congress should not establish a religion" hardly showed the clarity for which we might have hoped.

On two occasions, however, he commented in such a way as to give some force to the arguments of those who defend a narrow interpretation of the establishment clause. In his answer to Sherman, made after Daniel Carroll's comment, Madison declared that the amendment was intended to satisfy "some of the State Conventions" which feared that Congress "might infringe the rights of conscience, and establish a national religion. . . ." At the time he spoke he had the recommendations from four states. That of New Hampshire, drafted by the same Samuel Livermore who was present in Congress and took an essential part in the debate, was very much in line with his own thinking. But the recommendations from Virginia, New York, and North Carolina used the language of no preference. If Madison's intent was merely to yield to their requests, whatever may have been his own ideas on the subject, he might have meant by "national religion" that Congress should not prefer one denomination over others.

* * * Yet we know from other evidence (reviewed later) that Madison himself did not regard the element of preference as indispensable to the idea of an establishment of religion. If *all* denominations combined together or if the government supported all, giving preference to none, the result would in his mind have been an establishment.

* * *

Livermore's motion for a change of wording apparently expressed what Madison meant by his use of the word "national" and satisfied the Committee of the Whole. The proposed amendment, adopted by a vote of 31 to 20, then read: "Congress shall make no laws touching religion, or infringing the rights of conscience." But a few days later, on August 20, when the House took up the report of the Committee of the Whole and voted clause by clause on the proposed amendment, an additional change was made. Fisher Ames of Massachusetts moved that the amendment read: "Congress shall make no law establishing religion, or to prevent the free exercise thereof, or to infringe the rights of conscience.'' Without debate the House adopted Ames's motion by the necessary two-thirds vote. Apparently the House believed that the draft of the clause based on Livermore's motion might not satisfy the demands of those who wanted something said specifically against establishments of religion. The amendment as submitted to the Senate reflected a stylistic change that gave it the following reading: ''Congress shall make no law establishing religion, or prohibiting the free exercise thereof, nor shall the rights of conscience be infringed.''

The Senate began debate on the House amendments on September 3 and continued through September 9. The debate was conducted in secrecy and no record exists but the bare account of motions and votes in the *Senate Journal.* According to the record of September 3, three motions of special interest here were defeated on that day. These motions restricted the ban in the proposed amendment to establishments preferring one sect above others, The first motion would have made the clause in the amendment read: ''Congress shall make no law establishing one religious sect or society in preference to others.'' After the failure of this motion and of another to kill the amendment, a new motion was made to change it to read: ''Congress shall not make any law infringing the rights of conscience, or establishing any religious sect or society,'' The final defeated motion restated the same thought differently: ''Congress shall make no law establishing any particular denomination of religion in preference to another.'' The Senate then adopted the language of the House: ''Congress shall make no law establishing religion.''

The failure of these three motions, each of which seemed to express a narrow intent, and the Senate's adoption of the House version prove that the Senate intended something broader than merely a ban on preference to one sect. Yet, if anything is really clear about the problem of ''meaning'' and ''intent'' it is that little is clear; when the Senate returned to the clause six days later, it altered the House amendment to read: ''Congress shall make no law establishing articles of faith or a mode of worship, or prohibiting the free exercise of religion.'' Like the three previously defeated motions, this one had the unmistakable meaning of limiting the ban to acts that prefer one denomination over others or that, to put it simply, establish a single state church.

Appearances can be deceiving, however. A Baptist memorial of 1774 had used similar language: ''. . . the magistrate's power extends not to the establishing any articles of faith or forms of worship, by force of laws.'' Yet the Baptists, who advocated separation of government and religion, opposed nondiscriminatory government aid to all sects—proving once again how misleading language can be. To Baptists, if law did not extend to articles of faith, no establishment of religion was possible. And, as the 1780 returns from Massachusetts towns showed, people who endorsed the principle that no denomination should be subordinated to any other or that no denomination should have preference of any kind favored separation of church and state. In short, nonpreferentialism could signify voluntarism or the private support of religion.

The Senate's wording provoked the House to take action that made *its* intent clear, as the next step in the drafting of the amendment revealed. In voting on the Senate's proposed amendments, the House accepted some and rejected others, including the Senate's article on religion. To resolve the disagreement between the two branches, the House proposed a joint conference committee. The Senate refused to recede from its position but agreed to the proposal. for a conference committee. The committee, a strong and distinguished one, consisted of Madison as chairman of the House conferees, joined by Sherman and Vining, and Ellsworth as chairman of the Senate conferees, joined by Paterson and Carroll. Four of the six men had been influential members of the Constitutional Convention. The House members of the conference flatly refused to accept the Senate's version of the amendment on religion, indicating that the House would not be satisfied with merely a ban on preference of one sect or religion over others. The Senate conferees abandoned the Senate's version, and the amendment was redrafted to give it its present phraseology. On September 24, Ellsworth reported to the Senate that the House would accept the Senate's version of the other amendments provided that the amendment on religion "shall read as follows: Congress shall make no laws respecting an establishment of religion, or prohibiting the free exercise thereof." On the same day, the House sent a message to the Senate verifying Ellsworth's report. On the next day, September 25, the Senate by a two-thirds vote accepted the condition laid down by the House. Congress had passed the establishment clause.

The one fact that stands out is that Congress very carefully considered and rejected the wording that seems to imply the narrow interpretation. The House's rejection of the Senate's version of the amendment shows that the House did not intend to frame an amendment that banned only congressional support of one sect, church, denomination, or religion. The Senate three times defeated versions of the amendment embodying that narrow interpretation, on a fourth vote adopted such a version, and finally abandoned it in the face of uncompromising hostility by the House. The amendment's framers definitely intended something broader than the narrow interpretation which some judges and scholars have given it. The amendment reflected the fundamental fact that the framers of the Constitution had not empowered Congress to act in the field of religion. The "great object" of the Bill of Rights, as Madison explicitly said when introducing his draft of amendments to the House, was to "limit and qualify the powers of Government" for the purpose of making certain that the powers granted could not be exercised in forbidden fields, such as religion.

* * *

Little or no new light on the meaning of the establishment clause derives from the deliberations of the state legislatures to which the amendments to the Constitution were submitted for ratification. Records of state debates are nonexistent; private correspondence, newspapers, and tracts provide no help.

* * *

[However], [t]he circumstances surrounding ratification in Virginia are of particular interest. The state senate held up ratification for nearly two years while Anti–Federalists attacked the amendment as inadequate. The eight state senators who opposed it explained their vote publicly in these words:

> The 3rd amendment [the First Amendment] recommended by Congress does not prohibit the rights of conscience from being violated or infringed: and although it goes to restrain Congress from passing laws establishing any national religion, they might, notwithstanding, levy taxes to any amount, for the support of religion or its preachers; and any particular denomination of [C]hristians might be so favored and supported by the General Government, as to give it a decided advantage over others, and in process of time render it as powerful and dangerous as if it was established as the national religion of the country.... This amendment then, when considered as it relates to any of the rights it is pretended to secure, will be found totally inadequate, and betrays an unreasonable, unjustifiable, but a studied departure from the amendment proposed by Virginia.

Taken out of context and used uncritically, this statement by the eight Virginia state senators supposedly proves that the establishment clause had only the narrowest intent of nonpreferentialism, that the Virginia legislators so understood it, and that the state eventually approved of it with only that narrow intent attached. The conclusion is drawn that the amendment did not purport to ban government aid to religion generally or to all denominations without discrimination. However, examination of the intricate party maneuverings and complex motives in the Virginia ratification dispute sheds a different light on the senators' statement.

Virginia's Anti–Federalists, led by Patrick Henry and U. S. Senators Richard Henry Lee and William Grayson, had opposed the ratification of the Constitution for a variety of reasons. Chief among these was the belief that the Constitution established too strong a central government at the expense of the states. For example, the Anti–Federalists wanted amendments to the Constitution that would restrict Congress's commerce and tax powers. The same people led the movement for amendments that would protect personal liberties, but many cried out against the absence of a bill of rights more for the purpose of defeating the Constitution than of actually getting such a bill of rights.

When Congress had considered amending the Constitution, the Anti–Federalists sought to secure amendments that would aggrandize state powers, but in this effort they failed. In the ratification controversy, therefore, the strategy of Virginia's Anti–Federalists hinged on the defeat of the proposed Bill of Rights in order to force Congress to reconsider the whole subject of amendments. The Federalists, on the other hand, eagerly supported the Bill of Rights in order to prevent additional amendments that might hamstring the national government.

On November 30, 1789, Virginia's lower house, dominated by the Federalists, quickly passed all the amendments proposed by Congress "without debate of any consequence." But the opposition party controlled the state senate. "That body," reported Edmund Randolph to Washington, "will attempt to postpone them [the amendments]; for a majority is unfriendly to the government." As a member of the Virginia lower house reported to Madison, the state senate was inclined to reject the amendments not from dissatisfaction with them but from apprehension "that the adoption of them at this time will be an obstacle to the chief objection of their pursuit, the amendment on the subject of direct taxation." As Randolph had predicted, the senate, by a vote of 8–to–7, did decide to postpone final action on what are now the First, Sixth, Ninth, and Tenth Amendments until the next session of the legislature, thereby allowing time for the electorate to express itself. It was on this occasion that the eight senators in question made their statement on the allegedly weak Bill of Rights by presenting themselves as champions of religious liberty and advocates of separation between government and religion.

Madison remained unworried by this tactic, confidently predicting that the action of the senators would boomerang against them. "The miscarriage of the third article [the First Amendment], particularly, will have this effect," he wrote to George Washington. His confidence is explainable on several counts. First, he knew that the First Amendment had the support of the Baptists, the one group most insistent upon demanding a thorough separation between government and religion. Second, he knew that the eight senators did not come before the electorate with clean hands. Like Henry and Lee, who laid down their strategy for them, they had consistently voted against religious liberty and in favor of taxes for religion. Their legislative record on this score was well known. By contrast, the seven senators who favored ratification of the First Amendment had stood with Jefferson and Madison in the fight between 1784 and 1786 against a state establishment of religion and for religious liberty. Finally, Madison reasoned that the statement by the eight senators was an inept piece of propaganda with little chance of convincing anyone because it was so obviously misleading and inaccurate. The eight senators alleged that "any particular denomination of Christians might be so favored and supported by the general government, as to give it a decided advantage over others"—a construction of the First Amendment that not even proponents of the narrow interpretation would accept—and they also asserted that the amendment "does not prohibit the rights of conscience from being violated or infringed"— despite the positive statement in the amendment that Congress shall not abridge the free exercise of religion.* * * Moreover, the amendment proposed by Congress banned a law even *respecting* an establishment; the amendment proposed by Virginia and endorsed by the eight senators was framed in nonpreferentialist language—no preference to one sect over others, and was therefore not nearly as protective in its text as the amendment proposed by Congress.

In the end, Madison's confidence proved justified. On December 15, 1791, after a session of inaction on the Bill of Rights, the state senate finally ratified without a recorded vote. In the context of Anti–Federalist maneuverings, there is every reason to believe that Virginia supported the First Amendment with the understanding that it had been misrepresented by the eight senators. There is no reason exists to believe that Virginia ratified with the understanding that the amendment permitted any government aid to religion.

What conclusions can one come to, then, in connection with ratification of the First Amendment by the states? In Virginia, the one state for which there is some evidence, we can arrive only at a negative conclusion: the narrow interpretation of the establishment clause is insupportable. In nine other states there was perfunctory ratification, with no record of the debates, and in the remaining three states there was inaction. Therefore, it is impossible to state on the basis of ratification alone the general understanding of the establishment clause. But the legislative history of the framing of the clause demonstrates that Congress rejected a narrow or nonpreferentialist intent. And that history, seen in the context of the drive to add a bill of rights to the Constitution in order to restrict the powers of the national government, proves that the framers of the establishment clause meant to make explicit a point on which the entire nation agreed: the United States had no power to legislate on the subject of religion.

* * *

* * * Most of the framers of [the First Amendment] very probably meant that government should not promote, sponsor, or subsidize religion because it is best left to private voluntary support for the sake of religion itself as well as for government, and above all for the sake of the individual. Some of the framers undoubtedly believed that government should maintain a close relationship with religion, that is, with Protestantism, and that people should support taxes for the benefit of their own churches and ministers. The framers who came from Massachusetts and Connecticut certainly believed this, as did the representatives of New Hampshire, but New Hampshire was the only one of these New England states that ratified the First Amendment. Of the eleven states that ratified the First Amendment, New Hampshire and Vermont were probably the only ones in which a majority of the people believed that the government should support religion. In all the other ratifying states, a majority very probably opposed such support. But whether those who framed and ratified the First Amendment believed in government aid to religion or in its private voluntary support, the fact is that no framer believed that the United States had or should have power to legislate on the subject of religion, and no state supported that power either.

Those who framed and ratified the First Amendment meant that the establishment clause, like the rest of the Bill of Rights, should apply to the national government only. After all, the First Amendment explicitly levies a ban on Congress, in contrast to the later Fourteenth Amendment, which expressly limits the states. James Madison in 1789 proposed an amendment to the Constitution prohibiting the states from violating certain rights, including freedom of religion. Had that amendment been adopted, the federal courts could easily have construed it to prohibit the states from maintaining establishments of religion. Except, perhaps, for Congregational New England, most of the nation believed that an establishment of religion violated religious liberty. The House approved of Madison's proposal but the Senate voted it down. The fact that Congress considered an amendment limiting the states shows that the establishment clause, which limited Congress, could not have been meant to apply to the states. The fact that Congress considered and rejected a prohibition on the states showed, further, that so far as the U.S. Constitution was concerned, the states were free to recreate the Inquisition or to erect and maintain exclusive establishments of religion, at least until ratification of the Fourteenth Amendment in 1868.

According to the Fourteenth Amendment, no state may deprive any person of liberty without due process of law. Is a state law respecting an establishment of religion a deprivation of liberty? Does the word "liberty" include within its meaning right to be free from a law respecting an establishment of religion? There is a difference between the intent of the amendments framers and the language that they used. The preponderance of evidence suggests that the framers of the Fourteenth Amendment intended its provisions neither to incorporate any part of the Bill of Rights nor to impose on the states the same limitations previously imposed on the United States only. * * *

* * * In 1940, when the Supreme Court incorporated the free-exercise clause into the Fourteenth Amendment, the Court assumed that the establishment clause imposed upon the states the same restraints as upon the United States. In the 1947 *Everson* case that *obiter dictum* became a holding of constitutional law. The Court unanimously agreed that the Fourteenth Amendment incorporated the establishment clause. Consequently the principle embodied in the First Amendment separated government and religion throughout the land, outlawing government support of religion, or, rather, outlawing laws respecting an establishment of religion. But what constitutes an establishment or prohibited support, according to the Supreme Court?

In the *Everson* case the Court laid down principles for interpreting the establishment clause that it has never abandoned, despite its frequently perplexing application of those principles. One such principle is that an establishment of religion includes "aid to all religions" as well as aid to just one in preference to others; another principle is that no tax in any amount can be used "to support any religious activities or institutions." These principles express, in part, the broad interpretation of what the framers of the First Amendment intended by the establishment clause. * * *

* * *

To expect the Supreme Court to turn back the clock by scrapping the entire incorporation doctrine is so unrealistic as not to warrant consideration. Numerous reactionaries including former attorney general Edwin Meese, Professor James McClellan, Robert Cord, Charles Rice, and Daniel Dreisbach, indulge their emotions when denouncing the Court for six decades of decisions based on a doctrine that has "shaky" foundations or for pursuing its "revolutionary course" in making the First Amendment applicable to the states. Poor historians that they are, the nonpreferentialists think that the incorporation doctrine originated in cases beginning with *Gitlow v. New York* in 1925 and that the Court "arbitrarily" assumed that religious liberty and freedom from establishments of religion came within the meaning of the "liberty" of the Fourteenth Amendment's due process clause. But such extravagance of language by the nonpreferentialists persuades no one who remembers that the revolutionists were led not by Chief Justice Earl Warren but by Justice Edward T. Sanford, joined by fellow conservatives on the Supreme Court, including Justices James C. McReynolds, George Sutherland, Pierce Butler, Joseph McKenna, Willis Vandevanter, and William Howard Taft, among others; and the *Gitlow* Court was unanimous as to the incorporation doctrine. In 1940 the *Cantwell* Court, which incorporated the free exercise clause and, by obiter dictum, the establishment clause, spoke unanimously through Owen Roberts, one-time nemesis of the New Deal. And, in 1947 the Court was unanimous on the incorporation issue.

* * * In fact, as early as the late nineteenth century the Court used the incorporation doctrine to protect property rights; in 1894 the Court read the equal protection clause of the Fourteenth Amendment to include or incorporate the eminent domain or takings clause of the Fifth Amendment in order to strike down rate regulation, and then in 1897 the Court crammed the eminent domain clause into the Fourteenth's due process clause to achieve the same end. Protecting First Amendment freedoms from state abridgment seems no more radical or arbitrary than protecting property rights. Moreover, the incorporation doctrine has a history so fixed that overthrowing it is as likely as bagging snarks on the roof of the Court's building. Of all the amendments constituting the Bill of Rights, the First Amendment is the least likely to be thrown out of its nesting place within the word "liberty" of the Fourteenth. The Hughes Court unanimously awarded the First Amendment the laurels of uttermost fundamentality: no freedoms are more precious or more basic than those protected by the First Amendment.

* * *

Although Congress has no constitutional authority to legislate on religion as such or make it the beneficiary of legislation or other government action, the blunt fact is that regardless of what the framers intended and regardless of the absence of a power to legislate on religion, the United States does possess constitutional powers to benefit or burden religion as an indirect result of the exercise of delegated powers. For example, the First Congress, in the course of debating the amendments that became the Bill of Rights, recommended the presidential proclamation of a day of national thanksgiving and prayer, and it also reenacted the Northwest Ordinance. Passed in 1787 by the Congress of the Confederation, the Northwest Ordinance included a clause providing that schools and the means of education should be encouraged because religion, like morality and knowledge, is "necessary to good government and the happiness of mankind." And without doubt, religion (Protestantism) constituted an important part of the curriculum at that time. In 1789 Congress extended the statute by adapting it to the new Constitution but not to the First Amendment, which had not yet been recommended to the states by Congress. * * * "The vast majority of Americans," as Thomas Curry wrote, "assumed that theirs was a Christian, i.e. Protestant country, and they automatically expected that government would uphold the commonly agreed on Protestant ethos and morality. In many instances, they had not come to grips with the implications their belief in the powerlessness of government in religious matters held for a society in which the values, customs and forms of Protestant Christianity thoroughly permeated civil and political life."

When the Congress that adopted the First Amendment promoted religion in the Northwest Ordinance by urging a national day of prayer, it surely acted unconstitutionally–by later standards. * * *

* * *

[Significantly,] [t]he same authority that can indirectly benefit religion by the exercise of legitimate powers may also injure religion. A power to help is also a power to hinder or harm. Congress could draft conscientious objectors or tax church property, for example. That it does not do so is a matter of politics, not the result of constitutional power. Those who clamor for additional government support of religion should beware of the risks to religion from government entanglements. Those damaging risks are possible.* * *

From a constitutional standpoint, government can go too far in implementing a spirit of "benevolent neutrality," to use a phrase of Chief Justice Warren Burger, by purportedly serving religious needs. Benign "accommodation" is one thing; its purpose should be to protect religious freedom. If that is not its purpose, it should be held unconstitutional. An implicit alliance with religion or state encouragement or sponsorship of religion is not a legitimate accommodation.

* * *

The establishment clause is over two centuries old. At the time the First Amendment was framed, government and religion were much closer than they are today, but nothing was clearer than the fact that financial aid to religion or religious establishments constituted an establishment of religion. On the point the founding generation had given systematic thought to the meaning of an establishment of religion; it had scarcely thought at all about government chaplains, fast days, or the many other aids to religion that were taken pretty much for granted. The establishment clause should be far broader in meaning now than it was when adopted. The nation was relatively homogeneous in religion then; it is astoundingly heterogeneous today and is growing even more religiously pluralistic. * * *

We should not want the ban on establishments of religion to mean only what it meant in 1789 or only what its framers intended. Oliver Wendell Holmes said, "Historical continuity with the past is not a duty, it is only a necessity." That delphic statement can be construed to mean that we cannot escape history because it has shaped us and guides our policies, but we are not obliged to remain static. Two hundred years of expanding the meaning of democracy should have some constitutional impact. We are not bound by the wisdom of the Framers; we are bound only to consider whether the purposes they had in mind still merit political respect and constitutional obedience. History can only be a guide, not a controlling factor. If we followed the framers of the Constitution blindly, we would be duplicating the method of the *Dred Scott* decision by freezing the meaning of words at the time they became part of the Constitution. * * *

The broad purpose of the establishment clause should not be the only thing kept in mind. A little common sense helps too in the constitutional politics of its interpretation, and that common sense should come from public-interest lawyers and counsel representing defense organizations, such as the ACLU and the Rutherford Institute, as well as from courts. Those who profess to be broad separationists ought to understand that popular government will continue to aid religion and show respect for it, and that not every accommodation with religion, deriving from incidental assistance, is necessarily unconstitutional. Indeed, separationists ought to understand that even if they profoundly believe that a practice is unconstitutional, wisdom sometimes dictates against pressing a suit. Trying to ensure that the wall of separation is really impregnable might be futile and dangerously counterproductive. Indeed, the cracks in the wall might be more numerous than at present without seriously harming it or the values that it protects. * * *

Accommodationists seem insatiable and use every exception as precedents for still more exceptions. The moral majority does not compromise. Consequently passionate separationists who see every exception as a disaster tend to run around, like Chicken Little, screaming, "The wall is falling, the wall is falling." It really is not and will not, so long as it leaks just a little at the seams. If it did not leak a little, pressure on the wall might generate enough force to break it. The *de minimis* principle has some value, as Madison understood and as the Supreme Court occasionally has understood too; it has referred to "ceremonial deism" as a way of sweeping under the rug theistic practices like the invocation "God save this honorable Court" or "In God We Trust." * * *

* * *

The establishment clause may not be self-defining, but it embodies a policy that time has proved to be best. Despite continuing complaints about the wall of separation between government and religion, that is the policy embodied by the establishment clause. The Constitution erected that wall. If the fact that it is the policy of the Constitution does not satisfy, history helps validate it. A page of history is supposed to be worth a volume of logic, so let us consider a page from Tocqueville. Slightly more than half a century after independence he wrote that "the religious atmosphere of the country was the first thing that struck me on my arrival in the United States." He expressed "astonishment" because in Europe religion and freedom marched in "opposite directions." Questioning the "faithful of all communions," including clergymen, especially Roman Catholic priests, he found that "they all agreed with each other except about details; all thought that the main reason for the quiet sway of religion over their country was the *complete separation of church and state*. I have no hesitation in stating that throughout my stay in America I met nobody, lay or cleric, who did not agree about that."

* * * In a famous letter to the Baptist Association of Danbury, Connecticut, President Jefferson spoke of the "wall of separation." After declaring that religion belonged "solely between man and his God," Jefferson added: "I contemplate with sovereign reverence that act of the whole American people which declared that their legislature should 'make no law respecting an establishment of religion, or prohibiting the free exercise thereof,' thus building a wall of separation between church and state." The usual interpretation of Jefferson's Danbury Baptist letter by those who seek to weaken its force is either to minimize it or to argue that he was here concerned only with the rights of conscience, and that these would "never be endangered by treating all religions *equally* in regard to support" by the government. Neither interpretation is valid.

The rights-of-conscience argument ignores the fact that Jefferson quoted the establishment clause in the very sentence in which he spoke of a wall of separation, indicating that he was concerned with more than protection of the free exercise of religion. In any case, Jefferson most assuredly did believe that government support of all religions violated the rights of conscience. His Statute of Religious Freedom expressly asserts that "even forcing him [any man] to support this or that teacher of his own religious persuasion, is depriving him of the comfortable liberty of giving his contributions.... [No] man shall be compelled to frequent or support any religious worship, place, or ministry whatsoever."

The second technique of robbing the Danbury letter of its clear intent to oppose any government support of religion belittles it as a "little address of courtesy" containing a "figure of speech ... a metaphor," Or, as Edward S, Corwin suggested, the letter was scarcely "deliberate" or "carefully considered"; it was rather "not improbably motivated by an impish desire to heave a brick at the Congregationalist–Federalist hierarchy of Connecticut." Jefferson, however, had powerful convictions on the subject of establishment and religious freedom, and he approached discussion of it with great solemnity. Indeed, on the occasion of writing this letter he was so concerned with the necessity of expressing himself with deliberation and precision that he went out of his way to get the approval of the attorney general of the United States. Sending him the letter before dispatching it to Danbury, Jefferson asked his advice as to its contents and explained:

> 'Adverse to receive addresses, yet unable to prevent them, I have generally endeavored to turn them to some account, by making them the occasion, by way of answer, so sowing useful truths and principles among the people, which might germinate and become rooted among their political tenets. The Baptist address, now enclosed, admits of a condemnation of the alliance between Church and State, under the authority of the Constitution. It furnished an occasion, too, which I have long wished to find, of saying why I do not proclaim fast and thanksgiving days, as my predecessors did.'

On the matter of proclaiming fast and thanksgiving days, President Jefferson departed from the precedents of Washington and Adams, and went further even than Madison, by utterly refusing on any occasion to recommend or designate a day for worship, citing as a reason, among others, the clause against establishments of religion.

However, even Jefferson was not wholly consistent when it came to an establishment of religion. * * *

* * *

* * * Government and religion in America are mutually independent of each other, much as Jefferson and Madison hoped they would be. Government maintains a benign neutrality toward religion without promoting or serving religion's interests in any significant way except, perhaps, for the policy of tax exemption. To be sure, government's involvement with religion takes many forms. The joint chiefs of staff supposedly begin their meetings with prayer, as do our legislatures. The incantation, "God save the United States and this honorable Court" and the motto "In God We Trust" and its relatives are of trifling significance in the sense that they have little genuine religious content. Caesar exploits, secularizes, and degrades or trivializes, religion in such instances, but leaves organized religion alone. Free of government influence, organized religion in turn does not use government for religious ends.

Thus, history has made the wall of separation real. The wall is not just a metaphor. It has constitutional existence. * * * Despite its detractors and despite its leaks, cracks, and its archways, the wall ranks as one of the mightiest monuments of constitutional government in this nation. * * *

Reprinted by permission of the publisher from SEPARATION OF CHURCH AND STATE by Philip Hamburger at 481–492, Cambridge, Mass.: Harvard University Press, Copyright © 2002 by the President and Fellows of Harvard College. All Rights Reserved.

Constitutional Authority

As should be clear from the contrast between separation and the religious liberty guaranteed by the First Amendment, the constitutional authority for separation is without historical foundation. True, Thomas Jefferson, in his letter to the Danbury Baptist Association, wrote that the First Amendment built a wall of separation between church and state. The Baptists, however, do not seem to have agreed. Later, when anti-Catholic nativists and the Liberals popularized separation, few of them argued that the U.S. Constitution had already guaranteed a separation of church and state. Instead, they suggested that separation was a political principle underlying the Constitution. While Liberals sought an amendment to remedy the Constitution's imperfect guarantees of separation, and while President Grant and other appealed to nativists with an amendment proposal declaring church and state separate, Americans had little reason to develop historical or interpretive claims for separation. Gradually, however, as it became clear that hopes for an amendment to the U.S. Constitution were unrealistic, advocates of separation easily persuaded themselves and others that separation was the religious liberty already guaranteed by the First Amendment.

To modern lawyers and judges anxious for legal authority and unfamiliar with the history examined here, Jefferson's role has often seemed profoundly important. In fact, in the history of separation, Jefferson is but a passing figure, less important for what he wrote than for the significance later attributed to it. Ironically, the pope did more than Jefferson to popularize the idea of separation of church and state in America, for by condemning separation among French Catholics, the pope made it all the more attractive to American Protestants. Nonetheless, Jefferson's participation is revealing. It is no coincidence that the separation he endorsed was contrary to what Baptists and other dissenters sought. Nor is it mere happenstance that Jefferson's principle has been incompatible with the lives of many Americans or that it has simplified and impoverished discussions of religious liberty in ways that have obscured the necessarily complex and textured relationships between civil and religious societies. Although Jefferson took justifiable pleasure in his contribution to religious liberty, he was indifferent to the religion of most of his countrymen and downright hostile to their religious institutions. Not until he came under scrutiny as president did he publicly suggest that he considered religion essential to the preservation of liberty. Even then, unlike many of his contemporaries, he certainly did not consider American religious groups and their clergy valuable for this purpose. On the contrary, traditional religious organizations and their clergy, even if purely voluntary, seemed to Jefferson a threat to religious and civil freedom. Indeed, Jefferson hoped to revolutionize Americans into a citizenry of republican individuals unbounded by the customs, hierarchies, and superstitions that might divert them from their rational pursuit of equal freedom under government. Only since the mid-twentieth century, when large numbers of Americans were able to take this sort of society for granted, and when courts began to enforce it, has Jefferson's letter to the Danbury Baptist Association come to seem widely attractive as authority for the constitutional imposition of a separation of church and state.

In an era in which Americans often assume they have a living constitution—a constitution that evolves in response to their prevailing needs and ideals—the fig leaf of Jefferson's letter should not obscure the development of the First Amendment's religious liberty. Like so much legal change, this evolution occurred under the cover of an historical myth that conveniently allowed Americans to avoid perceiving the changing character of their constitutional law. Yet, once the fig leaf is stripped away, it becomes clear that the constitutional religious freedom of Americans developed in accord with popular expectations—that minority rights were redefined to satisfy majority perceptions of them. This supple response of the Constitution conformed (in all but its historical cover) to the increasingly popular conception of constitutional law as flexible. Yet whether it preserved religious freedom—for unpopular religious minorities or even most other religious groups—may be doubted.

Of course, the principle of separation between church and state may be valuable even though it lacks an historical foundation in the Constitution. If only as a matter of prudence, churches and their clergy often have good reason to separate themselves from partisan politics. Moreover, separation may offer a plausible legal solution to a wide range of issues, including clerical authority and hierarchy, church property and power, religious speech and influence, foreign claims of authority, and divided loyalties. Nonetheless, in discussions of these and other issues, separation ought not to be assumed to have any special legitimacy as an early American and thus Constitutional idea. On the contrary, precisely because of its history—both its lack of constitutional authority and its development in response to prejudice—the idea of separation should, at best, be viewed with suspicion.

Diminished Freedom

The separation of church and state not only departed from the religious liberty guaranteed by the U.S. Constitution but also undermined this freedom. In the election of 1800 Republicans used the idea of separation to limit the speech of clergymen in political matters. Beginning in the mid-nineteenth century, Protestants repeatedly relied upon the concept to deny Catholics equal rights in publicly funded schools and to discourage Catholic political activity. In the 1870s the National Liberal League attempted to use the idea of separation of church and state to limit the political participation of religious groups and to challenge otherwise secular laws that benefitted these groups, that were influenced by them, or that coincided with their distinctive moral obligations.

Today, many Americans still sometimes draw such conclusions from separation. For example, on the basis of this principle, many Americans question the right of others to bring their distinct religious views to bear on politics, and some courts limit the rights of religious organizations to receive government benefits distributed on entirely secular grounds. Put more generally, separation has barred otherwise constitutional connections between church and state. It even has discriminated among religions, for it has placed especially severe limitations upon persons whose religion is that of a "church" or religious group rather than a mere individual religiosity. In all of these ways, the First Amendment, which was written to limit government, has been interpreted directly to constrain religion.

Separation protected not so much individual liberty as the liberty of individuals who were understood to be independent of a church. At first, therefore, few Americans advocated separation. In the seventeenth century the sole advocate of what might be considered a sort of separation, Roger Williams, had been a minority of one with so refined a fear of impurity as to be unwilling to remain even in his own tiny Baptist congregation for more than a few months. Eventually, however, politicians and even political majorities adopted visions of citizenship in which individuals were expected to put aside any group loyalty that might compete with that to the state. Accordingly, in the nineteenth and twentieth centuries the advocates of separation usually were self-proclaimed defenders of "American" liberty, who conceived of themselves as intellectually independent and who held profoundly coercive expectations that others should conform to their ideals. Thus separation became part of a majority's oddly conformist demands for individual independence and strangely dogmatic rejections of authority.

That American majorities used the separation of church and state to impose their vision of their religion and their Americanism upon religious minorities is a sober reminder that as religious liberty becomes more individualistic, it does not necessarily increase individual liberty. Particularly if, as was true of separation, a concept of religious liberty directly limits religious groups, it can impose substantial costs upon members of religious minorities who refuse to abandon their distinctive identity, affiliation, and sense of authority. It can even place burdens on members of the majority, who have not always been as independent of religious groups as they have sometimes perceived themselves to be.

Looming at the edges of the dispute over separation have been two conflicting visions of liberty and its relationship to religious groups. The traditional perspective of numerous eighteenth-century Americans— most vocally, establishment ministers but also many dissenters—remains familiar in the version presented by Alexis de Tocqueville when he observed the role of religion in the United States. By inculcating morals, by encouraging mutual love and forgiveness, and by directing ambitions toward another world, religion could diminish injurious behavior, dissension, and distrust. Accordingly, it could reduce the necessity of civil coercion—a necessity that might otherwise lead a people to desire harsh or even tyrannical government. Religion could also establish a lasting foundation in public opinion for the various rights that seemed particularly vulnerable to fluctuations in popular sentiments. It thereby could temper the selfish passions and oppression to which republics were all too prone. Thus religion—specifically, the Christianity inherited and shared by a community—seemed essential for the preservation of liberty.

Increasingly, however, this perspective coexisted with another, very different, point of view, drawn from European experiences and fears—a perspective that survives most prominently in the writings of Thomas Jefferson. Together with expanding numbers of other Americans, Jefferson feared that clergymen, creeds, and therefore most churches undermine the inclination and ability of individuals to think for themselves. He worried that individuals would defer to their church's clergy and creed in a way that would render them subservient to a hierarchy and would deprive them of intellectual independence. In such ways, the clerical and creedal religion of most churches appeared to threaten the individual equality and mental freedom that Jefferson increasingly understood to be essential for the citizens of a republic.

As such fears about the influence of religious groups became increasingly widespread, many Americans began to depart from the Jeffersonian precept that there was time enough for government to interfere "when principles break out into overt acts against peace and good order." Numerous Americans, including Jeffersonians, Jacksonians, theological liberals, and nativists, feared assertions of clerical authority. Increasingly, Americans worried in particular about the claims of the Catholic Church and concluded that the adherents of Rome ought not have all of the secular rights enjoyed by Americans who held more popular, individualistic conceptions of their faith. Undoubtedly, it was imprudent for any religious minority to enter the political fray with principles not shared by other Americans. Perhaps, moreover, the doctrines believed by some Christian groups were more irrational and dangerous than those espoused by others. Nonetheless, to deny secular rights on the basis of religious beliefs was a violation of the liberty that, in the eighteenth century, both Jefferson and most evangelical dissenters had so carefully sought to protect.

A Simple Metaphor

Separation of church and state is an attractively simple metaphor. Like so many beguiling metaphors, however, it is an oversimplification, and on account of its appeal, it has gradually rendered Americans ever less inclined to appreciate the more measured positions advanced by eighteenth-century evangelical dissenters.

Separation has increasingly come to seem the only alternative to another metaphor, the union of church and state. If Americans were to avoid a union of church and state, had they any option except to maintain a separation between the two? Of course, union and separation were not the only possible alternatives, as revealed by the Baptists and other dissenters whose struggle for religious freedom led to the adoption of the First Amendment. They no more wanted a separation of church and state than they wanted an establishment. Yet, with each decade since the Republican campaign for separation in 1800, growing numbers of Americans have forgotten that there are myriad connections between religion and government that do not amount to an establishment, let alone a full union of church and state. Accordingly, they have mistakenly assumed that such connections infringe upon their constitutional freedom. They have come to believe that even nonestablishment connections between religious organizations and government amount to a union of church and state and that anything less than a complete separation of church and state is, in effect, a union of these institutions. On this basis, they have often leapt to the conclusion that persons who question separation desire an establishment, as if the rejection of separation were a renunciation of freedom and disestablishment. Happily, some commentators have noticed that union and separation are overgeneralizations between which lies much middle ground. These principles are, in fact, extremes along a continuum very different than that between establishment and disestablishment. In a society, however, in which many are willing to view their surroundings in seductively simplistic terms, the distinction between union and separation has distracted most Americans from other conceptions of their religious liberty.

Unfortunately, opponents of separation have often lent credence to the belief that separation is the only alternative to a union of church and state. In the nineteenth century, many Protestant critics of separation speculated about a Christian nation without indicating whether they meant a voluntary or an established Christianity. Some proposed laws clearly unconstitutional under the First Amendment. Others naively sought a Christian amendment to the Constitution. Even more dramatically, many Catholic priests and intellectuals, following the pope, claimed for their church a power superior to secular authority. In so doing, these various Christians gave the impression that the alternative to separation was an establishment or "union of church and state." Presented with this alternative, most Americans preferred separation.

Contributing to the appeal of this simplistic vision and the abandonment of more sophisticated, traditional conceptions of religious liberty has been the association of separation with Americanism. Following a pattern set by mid-nineteenth-century nativists, those advocating separation, including theological and political liberals, have long presented this ideal as an American freedom. Even today they work through organizations with names such as "People for the American Way" or "Americans United for the Separation of Church and State." In defense of separation, its advocates, both religious and secular, have recited its development in tones suggestive of sacred history. Whether striving for the "purity" of church and state, defending the "altar" of American freedom, or staking the existence of the nation on their "faith" in separation, they have often depicted separation in the image of religion and have sometimes denounced dissent from their creed as an almost heretical deviation from Americanism and its principles of freedom. Even the nineteenth-century Liberals, who, at least until 1885, were so endearingly honest as to draw attention to the difference between their separationist principles and the realities of the U.S. Constitution, declared in that year that "[a]ny sect, church, or 'religion' that militates against these principles openly or covertly, directly or indirectly, is the enemy of American liberty and of the American people"—an aggressive demand for conformity little less strongly felt than in a theocracy.

* * *

Etching this metaphor on the minds of Americans with particular vividness has been the mental image of a wall of separation. By reducing the complexity of religion and its place among nations to a bold visual construct—by allowing Americans to see in tangible terms the abstractions they might otherwise have to cogitate—the wall of separation has achieved much popularity. Yet this and other visual metaphors—whether the candle, the dark lantern, the prostate cross draped with the American flag, the Mary who was mother of George, or the fiery cross—have encouraged Americans to see their world with more clarity than accuracy. While allowing a broad populace to perceive richly delicate questions with ease, such images have all too often encouraged learned and unlearned alike to envision these matters in sharp contrasts of light and dark—a chiaroscuro more dramatic than revealing. Indeed, the inaccuracy of such depictions makes them poor guides for conduct. The image of the candle—whether in the wilderness or the garden—is profoundly appealing. Yet no one sees a light or reads the Bible in an entirely individuated, independent way, without the knowledge, experience, and preconceptions acquired in society and its groups. It is difficult to conceive how any religion, as an institution, could exist among a people so individuated as never to acknowledge or defer to communal beliefs. Similarly, the image of a wall of separation between church and state is appealing. Yet no state or church can develop its laws and beliefs in a cultural vacuum, separate from the other institutions in society. Churches are distinct from states but are not entirely separate from states, and it is difficult to understand how they could be fully separated, unless either churches or states were to be completely abandoned. Thus the stark image of separation, especially that of a wall of separation, lends itself to demands for a purity not possible in this world. As a result, the metaphor bodes ill for actual churches and states, which must function as institutions and must coexist in a far more metaphorical realm. In particular, separation and all the barriers it creates portend ill for individuals who value their participation in religious as well as civil associations and who hope to flourish and even, perhaps, find some truth in each.

Separations in Society

Of course, the history of the separation of church and state cannot be confined to an account of religious liberty, for this separation developed amid broader separations in American society. At the very least, the idea of separation between church and state seems to have been part of a reconceptualization of religious liberty that had particular appeal for Americans who conceived of themselves as independent of clerical and ecclesiastical claims of authority. Whereas eighteenth-century demands for disestablishment were often made by dissenters who were unified in their desire to limit the power of government, the nineteenth-and twentieth-century demands for separation were made by those who sought to limit religious groups as much as government. Separation was especially attractive for Americans who feared churches that emphasized the authority of their creeds and clergies. In such churches, it seemed, individuals were unlikely to remain free or to become independent citizens, loyal to the United States and devoted to its civil and religious liberty. Most fundamentally, Catholics who "submitted" to the clergy or creed of their church seemed incapable of the intellectual independence needed in Americans. Viewed as a challenge to individual freedom, a claim of clerical or church authority was, by extension, also frequently perceived as a threat to the state and the majority that lay not far behind it * * *. Gradually, in response to their fears of church authority, especially Catholic Church authority, Americans reconceptualized their religion, their citizenship, and their sense of themselves in highly individualistic ways, and, concomitantly, they redefined their religious liberty to protect themselves from the groups they feared, making separation of church and state part of their broader reconception of their individual, religious, and national identity.

More generally, as Jefferson himself suggested, the separation of church and state has been attractive in a modern world of specialization—in a world in which people divide their knowledge and their lives into specialized fields, such as medicine, law, politics, and religion. Engaged in very different activities and idealizing their sense of independence, Americans have expected to be free to attend to their specialized professions, interests, and activities without interference from persons focused upon other fields, and even without much obligation to reconcile their own conduct in different areas of endeavor. In this specialized world, Americans found that the sort of religion that once had harmonized them now seemed oppressive and divisive. Accordingly, Americans increasingly insisted upon pursuing their various secular activities, including politics, without complaint or instruction from churches and clergymen. Like the cigar-loving members of the American Secular Union who had difficulty finding a cigar on a Sunday and therefore gave generously to defeat Sunday laws, many Americans, even if not hostile to Christianity, did not want it to intrude upon areas of their lives in which they sought freedom. In this sense "[e]very open violator of the Sabbath is to be counted in their ranks. Every railroad corporation that runs its trains on the Sabbath is a part of their forces." Americans resented demands that they should integrate religion with the rest of their already specialized lives, and therefore they eagerly reduced not only their professions but also politics and even religion to specialized activities. In this spirit, they increasingly supported a separation of religion from other worldly activities, especially a separation of church and state.

Ironically, even as religion has been separated from politics, politics has become, in a sense, religious. Although this peculiar development has had many causes, including a general secularization, it surely is not coincidence that many of the very groups that have sought to exclude churches from politics have pursued their political goals by appealing to religious passions and aspirations—to the intense feelings and improbable hopes, including aspirations for purity and transcendence, that have, traditionally, seemed unlikely to be satisfied in this world. Perhaps the powerful emotions and desires associated with religion are unavoidable and, if not channeled through conventional religious institutions, are likely to find other outlets. Certainly, advocates of separation participated in the transformation of politics into a venue for aspirations and feelings once more typically focused on another world. Indeed, some spoke of their hopes for an "absolute" or "total" separation or for a state "purified" of clerical influence in almost religious tones. This displacement of religious feelings from the organized communal channels of denominational fellowship, identity, and expression has affected not only politics but also other activities. In diverse areas of life, ranging from the most personal to the most public, many Americans candidly describe feelings of intensity and transcendence akin to the religious. Perhaps there is no earthly reason to regret that Americans have concentrated with almost religious zeal upon secular, worldly aspirations. Yet it remains unclear whether powerful yearnings for purity and transcendence are less dangerous when focused on this world than on another.

In the end, these various separations and the associated displacement of passions suggests that the history of the separation between church and state cannot be understood simply as the history of religious liberty and its protection by American institutions. On the contrary, separation needs to be recognized as part of much broader social and cultural developments. In particular, separation became a popular vision of religious liberty in response to deeply felt fears of ecclesiastical and especially Catholic authority. These anxieties intensified as Americans increasingly identified with their specialized roles and worried about the failure of minorities to conform to what were elevated as Protestant and American ideals of individual independence. In the transfiguring light of their fears, Americans saw their religious liberty anew, no longer merely as a limitation on government, but also as a means of separating themselves and their government from threatening claims of ecclesiastical authority. Americans thereby gradually forgot the character of their older, antiestablishment religious liberty and eventually came to understand their religious freedom as a separation of church and state.

Chapter Two

PUBLIC RELIGIOUS EXERCISES

A. ORGANIZED "RELIGIOUS" EXERCISES IN THE PUBLIC SCHOOLS

In *Engel v. Vitale* and *Abington Tp. v. Schempp*, the Court held that schools could not sponsor religious exercises such as prayer or bible reading during the school day, but questions remained. Could such exercises be held during school functions such as graduations? Would it make a difference if the students, rather than the state, decided to have the religious exercise? By 1992, the year the Court next confronted the school prayer issue, an additional question had arisen. What test should be applied in determining the constitutionality of religious exercises in the public schools? *Schempp* had used a test that was essentially the same as the first two prongs of the famous *Lemon* test. *See infra.* Chapter Four. Thus, in *Schempp* the Court looked at whether the religious exercise had a secular purpose and whether it had the primary effect of either advancing or inhibiting religion. An activity is unconstitutional under this standard if it fails either prong of the test.

By the time the Court decided *Lee v. Weisman* (the next principle case), however, both the *Lemon* test and the newer Endorsement test—which arguably works within the first two prongs of the *Lemon* test—were in use, as was the "tradition" test used in a case you will read later in this Chapter. *See Marsh v. Chambers, infra.* at Section B. As you read the cases in this Chapter, consider which of these tests works best (you will see all of them used by one Justice or another). In addition, *Lee* introduces another major test—the coercion test. In this and the following Chapters you will learn more about these tests as you study the elements of each test and how the tests function in the various contexts to which they are applied. In the Court's most recent school prayer decision, *Santa Fe Independent School Dist. v. Doe*, included below at Section A.2., the majority applies all three of the major tests (i.e. the endorsement, coercion and *Lemon* tests). The various opinions in *Lee v. Weisman* address all of the potential tests, although as you will see, there is disagreement among the various opinions regarding which test should apply.

LEE v. WEISMAN

Supreme Court of the United States, 1992.
505 U.S. 577, 112 S.Ct. 2649, 120 L.Ed.2d 467.

JUSTICE KENNEDY delivered the opinion of the Court.

School principals in the public school system of the city of Providence, Rhode Island, are permitted to invite members of the clergy to offer invocation and benediction prayers as part of the formal graduation ceremonies for middle schools and for high schools. The question before us is whether including clerical members who offer prayers as part of the official school graduation ceremony is consistent with the Religion Clauses of the First Amendment, provisions the Fourteenth Amendment makes applicable with full force to the States and their school districts.

I

A

Deborah Weisman graduated from Nathan Bishop Middle School, a public school in Providence, at a formal ceremony in June 1989. She was about 14 years old. For many years it has been the policy of the Providence School Committee and the Superintendent of Schools to permit principals to invite members of the clergy to give invocations and benedictions at middle school and high school graduations. Many, but not all, of the principals elected to include prayers as part of the graduation ceremonies. Acting for himself and his daughter, Deborah's father, Daniel Weisman, objected to any prayers at Deborah's middle school graduation, but to no avail. The school principal, petitioner Robert E. Lee, invited a rabbi to deliver prayers at the graduation exercises for Deborah's class. * * *

It has been the custom of Providence school officials to provide invited clergy with a pamphlet entitled "Guidelines for Civic Occasions," prepared by the National Conference of Christians and Jews. The Guidelines recommend that public prayers at nonsectarian civic ceremonies be composed with "inclusiveness and sensitivity," though they acknowledge that "[p]rayer of any kind may be inappropriate on some civic occasions." The principal gave Rabbi Gutterman the pamphlet before the graduation and advised him the invocation and benediction should be nonsectarian.

Rabbi Gutterman's prayers were as follows:

"INVOCATION

"God of the Free, Hope of the Brave:

"For the legacy of America where diversity is celebrated and the rights of minorities are protected, we thank You. May these young men and women grow up to enrich it.

"For the liberty of America, we thank You. May these new graduates grow up to guard it.

"For the political process of America in which all its citizens may participate, for its court system where all may seek justice we thank You. May those we honor this morning always turn to it in trust.

"For the destiny of America we thank You. May the graduates of Nathan Bishop Middle School so live that they might help to share it.

"May our aspirations for our country and for these young people, who are our hope for the future, be richly fulfilled. AMEN"

"BENEDICTION

"O God, we are grateful to You for having endowed us with the capacity for learning which we have celebrated on this joyous commencement.

"Happy families give thanks for seeing their children achieve an important milestone. Send Your blessings upon the teachers and administrators who helped prepare them.

"The graduates now need strength and guidance for the future, help them to understand that we are not complete with academic knowledge alone. We must each strive to fulfill what You require of us all: To do justly, to love mercy, to walk humbly.

"We give thanks to You, Lord, for keeping us alive, sustaining us and allowing us to reach this special, happy occasion. AMEN"

* * * [W]e are unfamiliar with any fixed custom or practice at middle school graduations, referred to by the school district as "promotional exercises." We are not so constrained with reference to high schools, however. High school graduations are such an integral part of American cultural life that we can with confidence describe their customary features, confirmed by aspects of the record and by the parties' representations at oral argument. In the Providence school system, most high school graduation ceremonies are conducted away from the school, while most middle school ceremonies are held on school premises. * * * The graduating students enter as a group in a processional, subject to the direction of teachers and school officials, and sit together, apart from their families. We assume the clergy's participation in any high school graduation exercise would be about what it was at Deborah's middle school ceremony. There the students stood for the Pledge of Allegiance and remained standing during the rabbi's prayers. Even on the assumption that there was a respectful moment of silence both before and after the prayers, the rabbi's two presentations must not have extended much beyond a minute each, if that. * * *

* * *

B

Deborah's graduation was held on the premises of Nathan Bishop Middle School on June 29, 1989. Four days before the ceremony, Daniel Weisman, in his individual capacity as a Providence taxpayer and as next friend of Deborah, sought a temporary restraining order in the United States District Court for the District of Rhode Island to prohibit school officials from including an invocation or benediction in the graduation ceremony. The court denied the motion for lack of adequate time to consider it. Deborah and her family attended the graduation, where the prayers were recited. In July 1989, Daniel Weisman filed an amended complaint seeking a permanent injunction barring petitioners, various officials of the Providence public schools, from inviting the clergy to deliver invocations and benedictions at future graduations. * * *

* * *

II

These dominant facts mark and control the confines of our decision: State officials direct the performance of a formal religious exercise at promotional and graduation ceremonies for secondary schools. Even for those students who object to the religious exercise, their attendance and participation in the state-sponsored religious activity are in a fair and real sense obligatory, though the school district does not require attendance as a condition for receipt of the diploma.

* * * [T]he controlling precedents as they relate to prayer and religious exercise in primary and secondary public schools compel the holding here that the policy of the city of Providence is an unconstitutional one. We can decide the case without reconsidering the general constitutional framework by which public schools' efforts to accommodate religion are measured. * * * The government involvement with religious activity in this case is pervasive, to the point of creating a state-sponsored and state-directed religious exercise in a public school. Conducting this formal religious observance conflicts with settled rules pertaining to prayer exercises for students, and that suffices to determine the question before us.

The principle that government may accommodate the free exercise of religion does not supersede the fundamental limitations imposed by the Establishment Clause. It is beyond dispute that, at a minimum, the Constitution guarantees that government may not coerce anyone to support or participate in religion or its exercise, or otherwise act in a way which "establishes a [state] religion or religious faith, or tends to do so." *Lynch v. Donnelly*. The State's involvement in the school prayers challenged today violates these central principles.

That involvement is as troubling as it is undenied. A school official, the principal, decided that an invocation and a benediction should be given; this is a choice attributable to the State, and from a constitutional perspective it is as if a state statute decreed that the prayers must occur.

The principal chose the religious participant, here a rabbi, and that choice is also attributable to the State. The reason for the choice of a rabbi is not disclosed by the record, but the potential for divisiveness over the choice of a particular member of the clergy to conduct the ceremony is apparent.

Divisiveness, of course, can attend any state decision respecting religions, and neither its existence nor its potential necessarily invalidates the State's attempts to accommodate religion in all cases. The potential for divisiveness is of particular relevance here though, because it centers around an overt religious exercise in a secondary school environment where, as we discuss below, subtle coercive pressures exist and where the student had no real alternative which would have allowed her to avoid the fact or appearance of participation.

The State's role did not end with the decision to include a prayer and with the choice of a clergyman. Principal Lee provided Rabbi Gutterman with a copy of the "Guidelines for Civic Occasions," and advised him that his prayers should be nonsectarian. Through these means the principal directed and controlled the content of the prayers. Even if the only sanction for ignoring the instructions were that the rabbi would not be invited back, we think no religious representative who valued his or her continued reputation and effectiveness in the community would incur the State's displeasure in this regard. It is a cornerstone principle of our Establishment Clause jurisprudence that "it is no part of the business of government to compose official prayers for any group of the American people to recite as a part of a religious program carried on by government," *Engel v. Vitale,* and that is what the school officials attempted to do.

Petitioners argue, and we find nothing in the case to refute it, that the directions for the content of the prayers were a good-faith attempt by the school to ensure that the sectarianism which is so often the flashpoint for religious animosity be removed from the graduation ceremony. The concern is understandable, as a prayer which uses ideas or images identified with a particular religion may foster a different sort of sectarian rivalry than an invocation or benediction in terms more neutral. The school's explanation, however, does not resolve the dilemma caused by its participation. The question is not the good faith of the school in attempting to make the prayer acceptable to most persons, but the legitimacy of its undertaking that enterprise at all when the object is to produce a prayer to be used in a formal religious exercise which students, for all practical purposes, are obliged to attend.

We are asked to recognize the existence of a practice of nonsectarian prayer, prayer within the embrace of what is known as the Judeo–Christian tradition, prayer which is more acceptable than one which, for example, makes explicit references to the God of Israel, or to Jesus Christ, or to a patron saint. There may be some support, as an empirical observation, to the statement * * * that there has emerged in this country a civic religion, one which is tolerated when sectarian exercises are not. If common ground can be defined which permits once conflicting faiths to express the shared conviction that there is an ethic and a morality which transcend human invention, the sense of community and purpose sought by all decent societies might be advanced. But though the First Amendment does not allow the government to stifle prayers which aspire to these ends, neither does it permit the government to undertake that task for itself.

The First Amendment's Religion Clauses mean that religious beliefs and religious expression are too precious to be either proscribed or prescribed by the State. The design of the Constitution is that preservation and transmission of religious beliefs and worship is a responsibility and a choice committed to the private sphere, which itself is promised freedom to pursue that mission. * * *

These concerns have particular application in the case of school officials, whose effort to monitor prayer will be perceived by the students as inducing a participation they might otherwise reject. Though the efforts of the school officials in this case to find common ground appear to have been a good-faith attempt to recognize the common aspects of religions and not the divisive ones, our precedents do not permit school officials to assist in composing prayers as an incident to a formal exercise for their students. And these same precedents caution us to measure the idea of a civic religion against the central meaning of the Religion Clauses of the First Amendment, which is that all creeds must be tolerated and none favored. The suggestion that government may establish an official or civic religion as a means of avoiding the establishment of a religion with more specific creeds strikes us as a contradiction that cannot be accepted.

The degree of school involvement here made it clear that the graduation prayers bore the imprint of the State and thus put school-age children who objected in an untenable position. We turn our attention now to consider the position of the students, both those who desired the prayer and she who did not.

To endure the speech of false ideas or offensive content and then to counter it is part of learning how to live in a pluralistic society, a society which insists upon open discourse towards the end of a tolerant citizenry. And tolerance presupposes some mutuality of obligation. It is argued that our constitutional vision of a free society requires confidence in our own ability to accept or reject ideas of which we do not approve, and that prayer at a high school graduation does nothing more than offer a choice. By the time they are seniors, high school students no doubt have been required to attend classes and assemblies and to complete assignments exposing them to ideas they find distasteful or immoral or absurd or all of these. Against this background, students may consider it an odd measure of justice to be subjected during the course of their educations to ideas deemed offensive and irreligious, but to be denied a brief, formal prayer ceremony that the school offers in return. This argument cannot prevail, however. It overlooks a fundamental dynamic of the Constitution.

The First Amendment protects speech and religion by quite different mechanisms. Speech is protected by ensuring its full expression even when the government participates, for the very object of some of our most important speech is to persuade the government to adopt an idea as its own. The method for protecting freedom of worship and freedom of conscience in religious matters is quite the reverse. In religious debate or expression the government is not a prime participant, for the Framers deemed religious establishment antithetical to the freedom of all. The Free Exercise Clause embraces a freedom of conscience and worship that has close parallels in the speech provisions of the First Amendment, but the Establishment Clause is a specific prohibition on forms of state intervention in religious affairs with no precise counterpart in the speech provisions. The explanation lies in the lesson of history that was and is the inspiration for the Establishment Clause, the lesson that in the hands of government what might begin as a tolerant expression of religious views may end in a policy to indoctrinate and coerce. A state-created orthodoxy puts at grave risk that freedom of belief and conscience which are the sole assurance that religious faith is real, not imposed.

* * *

As we have observed before, there are heightened concerns with protecting freedom of conscience from subtle coercive pressure in the elementary and secondary public schools. Our decisions in *Engel v. Vitale*, and *School Dist. of Abington,* recognize, among other things, that prayer exercises in public schools carry a particular risk of indirect coercion. The concern may not be limited to the context of schools, but it is most pronounced there. What to most believers may seem nothing more than a reasonable request that the nonbeliever respect their religious practices, in a school context may appear to the nonbeliever or dissenter to be an attempt to employ the machinery of the State to enforce a religious orthodoxy.

We need not look beyond the circumstances of this case to see the phenomenon at work. The undeniable fact is that the school district's supervision and control of a high school graduation ceremony places public pressure, as well as peer pressure, on attending students to stand as a group or, at least, maintain respectful silence during the invocation and benediction. This pressure, though subtle and indirect, can be as real as any overt compulsion. Of course, in our culture standing or remaining silent can signify adherence to a view or simple respect for the views of others. And no doubt some persons who have no desire to join a prayer have little objection to standing as a sign of respect for those who do. But for the dissenter of high school age, who has a reasonable perception that she is being forced by the State to pray in a manner her conscience will not allow, the injury is no less real. There can be no doubt that for many, if not most, of the students at the graduation, the act of standing or remaining silent was an expression of participation in the rabbi's prayer. That was the very point of the religious exercise. It is of little comfort to a dissenter, then, to be told that for her the act of standing or remaining in silence signifies mere respect, rather than participation. What matters is that, given our social conventions, a reasonable dissenter in this milieu could believe that the group exercise signified her own participation or approval of it.

Finding no violation under these circumstances would place objectors in the dilemma of participating, with all that implies, or protesting. We do not address whether that choice is acceptable if the affected citizens are mature adults, but we think the State may not, consistent with the Establishment Clause, place primary and secondary school children in this position. Research in psychology supports the common assumption that adolescents are often susceptible to pressure from their peers towards conformity, and that the influence is strongest in matters of social convention. To recognize that the choice imposed by the State constitutes an unacceptable constraint only acknowledges that the government may no more use social pressure to enforce orthodoxy than it may use more direct means.

* * * [T]he embarrassment and the intrusion of the religious exercise cannot be refuted by arguing that these prayers, and similar ones to be said in the future, are of a *de minimis* character. To do so would be an affront to the rabbi who offered them and to all those for whom the prayers were an essential and profound recognition of divine authority. And for the same reason, we think that the intrusion is greater than the two minutes or so of time consumed for prayers like these. Assuming, as we must, that the prayers were offensive to the student and the parent who now object, the intrusion was both real and, in the context of a secondary school, a violation of the objectors' rights. That the intrusion was in the course of promulgating religion that sought to be civic or nonsectarian rather than pertaining to one sect does not lessen the offense or isolation to the objectors. At best it narrows their number, at worst increases their sense of isolation and affront.

There was a stipulation in the District Court that attendance at graduation and promotional ceremonies is voluntary. * * * [T]o say a teenage student has a real choice not to attend her high school graduation is formalistic in the extreme. True, Deborah could elect not to attend commencement without renouncing her diploma; but we shall not allow the case to turn on this point. Everyone knows that in our society and in our culture high school graduation is one of life's most significant occasions. A school rule which excuses attendance is beside the point. Attendance may not be required by official decree, yet it is apparent that a student is not free to absent herself from the graduation exercise in any real sense of the term "voluntary," for absence would require forfeiture of those intangible benefits which have motivated the student through youth and all her high school years. * * *

The importance of the event is the point the school district and the United States rely upon to argue that a formal prayer ought to be permitted, but it becomes one of the principal reasons why their argument must fail. Their contention, one of considerable force were it not for the constitutional constraints applied to state action, is that the prayers are an essential part of these ceremonies because for many persons an occasion of this significance lacks meaning if there is no recognition, however brief, that human achievements cannot be understood apart from their spiritual essence. We think the Government's position that this interest suffices to force students to choose between compliance or forfeiture demonstrates fundamental inconsistency in its argumentation. It fails to acknowledge that what for many of Deborah's classmates and their parents was a spiritual imperative was for Daniel and Deborah Weisman religious conformance compelled by the State. While in some societies the wishes of the majority might prevail, the Establishment Clause of the First Amendment is addressed to this contingency and rejects the balance urged upon us. The Constitution forbids the State to exact religious conformity from a student as the price of attending her own high school graduation. * * *

* * *

We do not hold that every state action implicating religion is invalid if one or a few citizens find it offensive. People may take offense at all manner of religious as well as nonreligious messages, but offense alone does not in every case show a violation. We know too that sometimes to endure social isolation or even anger may be the price of conscience or nonconformity. But, by any reading of our cases, the conformity required of the student in this case was too high an exaction to withstand the test of the Establishment Clause. The prayer exercises in this case are especially improper because the State has in every practical sense compelled attendance and participation in an explicit religious exercise at an event of singular importance to every student, one the objecting student had no real alternative to avoid.

* * *

Our society would be less than true to its heritage if it lacked abiding concern for the values of its young people, and we acknowledge the profound belief of adherents to many faiths that there must be a place in the student's life for precepts of a morality higher even than the law we today enforce. We express no hostility to those aspirations, nor would our oath permit us to do so. A relentless and all-pervasive attempt to exclude religion from every aspect of public life could itself become inconsistent with the Constitution. We recognize that, at graduation time and throughout the course of the educational process, there will be instances when religious values, religious practices, and religious persons will have some interaction with the public schools and their students. But these matters, often questions of accommodation of religion, are not before us. * * *

For the reasons we have stated, the judgment of the Court of Appeals is *Affirmed.*

JUSTICE BLACKMUN, with whom JUSTICE STEVENS and JUSTICE O'CONNOR join, concurring.

Nearly half a century of review and refinement of Establishment Clause jurisprudence has distilled one clear understanding: Government may neither promote nor affiliate itself with any religious doctrine or organization, nor may it obtrude itself in the internal affairs of any religious institution. The application of these principles to the present case mandates the decision reached today by the Court.

I

This Court first reviewed a challenge to state law under the Establishment Clause in *Everson v. Board of Ed. of Ewing.* Relying on the history of the Clause, and the Court's prior analysis, Justice Black outlined the considerations that have become the touchstone of Establishment Clause jurisprudence: Neither a State nor the Federal Government can pass laws which aid one religion, aid all religions, or prefer one religion over another. Neither a State nor the Federal Government, openly or secretly, can participate in the affairs of any religious organization and vice versa. "In the words of Jefferson, the clause against establishment of religion by law was intended to erect 'a wall of separation between church and State.' " *Everson.* * * *

* * *

* * * In [*Abington Township v.*] *Schempp,* the school day for Baltimore, Maryland, and Abington Township, Pennsylvania, students began with a reading from the Bible, or a recitation of the Lord's Prayer, or both. After a thorough review of the Court's prior Establishment Clause cases, the Court concluded:

> "[T]he Establishment Clause has been directly considered by this Court eight times in the past score of years and, with only one Justice dissenting on the point, it has consistently held that the clause withdrew all legislative power respecting religious belief or the expression thereof. The test may be stated as follows: what are the purpose and the primary effect of the enactment? If either is the advancement or inhibition of religion, then the enactment exceeds the scope of legislative power as circumscribed by the Constitution."

Because the schools' opening exercises were government-sponsored religious ceremonies, the Court found that the primary effect was the advancement of religion and held, therefore, that the activity violated the Establishment Clause.

* * *

In 1971, Chief Justice Burger reviewed the Court's past decisions and found: "Three . . . tests may be gleaned from our cases." *Lemon v. Kurtzman,* 403 U.S. 602, 612, 91 S.Ct. 2105, 2111. In order for a statute to survive an Establishment Clause challenge, "[f]irst, the statute must have a secular legislative purpose; second, its principal or primary effect must be one that neither advances nor inhibits religion; finally the statute must not foster an excessive government entanglement with religion." *Id.,* at 612–613, 91 S.Ct., at 2111 (internal quotation marks and citations omitted).[3] After *Lemon,* the Court continued to rely on these basic principles in resolving Establishment Clause disputes.

Application of these principles to the facts of this case is straightforward. There can be "no doubt" that the "invocation of God's blessings" delivered at Nathan Bishop Middle School "is a religious activity." *Engel.* * * * The question then is whether the government has "plac[ed] its official stamp of approval" on the prayer. As the Court ably demonstrates, when the government "compose[s] official prayers," selects the member of the clergy to deliver the prayer, has the prayer delivered at a public school event that is planned, supervised and given by school officials, and pressures students to attend and participate in the prayer, there can be no doubt that the government is advancing and promoting religion. As our prior decisions teach us, it is this that the Constitution prohibits.

II

I join the Court's opinion today because I find nothing in it inconsistent with the essential precepts of the Establishment Clause developed in our precedents. The Court holds that the graduation prayer is unconstitutional because the State "in effect required participation in a religious exercise." Although our precedents make clear that proof of government coercion is not necessary to prove an Establishment Clause violation, it is sufficient. Government pressure to participate in a religious activity is an obvious indication that the government is endorsing or promoting religion.

But it is not enough that the government restrain from compelling religious practices: It must not engage in them either. The Court repeatedly has recognized that a violation of the Establishment Clause is not predicated on coercion. The Establishment Clause proscribes public schools from "conveying or attempting to convey a message that religion or a particular religious belief is *favored* or *preferred,*" *County of Allegheny v. American Civil Liberties Union, Greater Pittsburgh Chapter,* 492 U.S. 573, 593, 109 S.Ct. 3086, 3101, 106 L.Ed.2d 472 (1989), even if the schools do not actually "impos[e] pressure upon a student to participate in a religious activity." *Board of Ed. of Westside Community Schools (Dist. 66) v. Mergens,* 496 U.S. 226, 261, 110 S.Ct. 2356, 2378, 110

3. The final prong, excessive entanglement, was a focus of *Walz v. Tax Comm'n of New York City,* 397 U.S. 664, 674, 90 S.Ct. 1409, 1414, 25 L.Ed.2d 697 (1970), but harkens back to the final example in *Everson:* "Neither a state nor the Federal Government can, openly or secretly, participate in the affairs of any religious organizations or groups and *vice versa.*" *Everson,* 330 U.S., at 16, 67 S.Ct., at 511. The discussion in *Everson* reflected the Madisonian concern that secular and religious authorities must not interfere with each other's respective spheres of choice and influence. See generally The Complete Madison 298–312 (S. Padover ed. 1953).

L.Ed.2d 191 (1990) (Kennedy, J., concurring in part and concurring in judgment).

* * *

The mixing of government and religion can be a threat to free government, even if no one is forced to participate. When the government puts its *imprimatur* on a particular religion, it conveys a message of exclusion to all those who do not adhere to the favored beliefs.[9] A government cannot be premised on the belief that all persons are created equal when it asserts that God prefers some. * * *

When the government arrogates to itself a role in religious affairs, it abandons its obligation as guarantor of democracy. Democracy requires the nourishment of dialog and dissent, while religious faith puts its trust in an ultimate divine authority above all human deliberation. When the government appropriates religious truth, it "transforms rational debate into theological decree." Nuechterlein, Note, The Free Exercise Boundaries of Permissible Accommodation Under the Establishment Clause, 99 Yale L.J. 1127, 1131 (1990). Those who disagree no longer are questioning the policy judgment of the elected but the rules of a higher authority who is beyond reproach.

* * *

* * * We have believed that religious freedom cannot exist in the absence of a free democratic government, and that such a government cannot endure when there is fusion between religion and the political regime. We have believed that religious freedom cannot thrive in the absence of a vibrant religious community and that such a community cannot prosper when it is bound to the secular. And we have believed that these were the animating principles behind the adoption of the Establishment Clause. To that end, our cases have prohibited government endorsement of religion, its sponsorship, and active involvement in religion, whether or not citizens were coerced to conform.

I remain convinced that our jurisprudence is not misguided, and that it requires the decision reached by the Court today. Accordingly, I join the Court in affirming the judgment of the Court of Appeals.

[JUSTICE SOUTER's concurring opinion, which was joined by JUSTICE STEVENS and JUSTICE O'CONNOR is omitted].

JUSTICE SCALIA, with Whom the CHIEF JUSTICE, JUSTICE WHITE, and JUSTICE THOMAS join, dissenting.

* * *

9. "[T]he Establishment Clause is infringed when the government makes adherence to religion relevant to a person's standing in the political community. Direct government action endorsing religion or a particular religious practice is invalid under this approach because it sends a message to nonadherents that they are outsiders, not full members of the political community, and an accompanying message to adherents that they are insiders, favored members of the political community." *Wallace v. Jaffree,* 472 U.S., at 69, 105 S.Ct., at 2496 (O'Connor, J., concurring in judgment) (internal quotation marks omitted).

* * * In holding that the Establishment Clause prohibits invocations and benedictions at public-school graduation ceremonies, the Court—with nary a mention that it is doing so—lays waste a tradition that is as old as public-school graduation ceremonies themselves, and that is a component of an even more longstanding American tradition of nonsectarian prayer to God at public celebrations generally. As its instrument of destruction, the bulldozer of its social engineering, the Court invents a boundless, and boundlessly manipulable, test of psychological coercion * * *. Today's opinion shows more forcefully than volumes of argumentation why our Nation's protection, that fortress which is our Constitution, cannot possibly rest upon the changeable philosophical predilections of the Justices of this Court, but must have deep foundations in the historic practices of our people.

I

* * * As we have recognized, our interpretation of the Establishment Clause should "compor[t] with what history reveals was the contemporaneous understanding of its guarantees." *Lynch v. Donnelly,* 465 U.S. 668, 673, 104 S.Ct. 1355, 1359, 79 L.Ed.2d 604 (1984). "[T]he line we must draw between the permissible and the impermissible is one which accords with history and faithfully reflects the understanding of the Founding Fathers." *School Dist. of Abington v. Schempp* (Brennan, J., concurring). "[H]istorical evidence sheds light not only on what the draftsmen intended the Establishment Clause to mean, but also on how they thought that Clause applied" to contemporaneous practices. *Marsh v. Chambers,* 463 U.S. 783, 790, 103 S.Ct. 3330, 3335, 77 L.Ed.2d 1019 (1983). Thus, "[t]he existence from the beginning of the Nation's life of a practice, [while] not conclusive of its constitutionality . . . [,] is a fact of considerable import in the interpretation" of the Establishment Clause. *Walz v. Tax Comm'n of New York City,* 397 U.S. 664, 681, 90 S.Ct. 1409, 1417–1418, 25 L.Ed.2d 697 (1970) (Brennan, J., concurring).

The history and tradition of our Nation are replete with public ceremonies featuring prayers of thanksgiving and petition. Illustrations of this point have been amply provided in our prior opinions * * *.

* * *

In addition to this general tradition of prayer at public ceremonies, there exists a more specific tradition of invocations and benedictions at public school graduation exercises. By one account, the first public high school graduation ceremony took place in Connecticut in July 1868—the very month, as it happens, that the Fourteenth Amendment (the vehicle by which the Establishment Clause has been applied against the States) was ratified—when "15 seniors from the Norwich Free Academy marched in their best Sunday suits and dresses into a church hall and waited through majestic music and long prayers." Brodinsky, Commencement Rites Obsolete? Not At All, A 10–Week Study Shows, 10 Updating School Board Policies, No. 4, p. 3 (Apr. 1979). As the Court obliquely acknowledges in describing the "customary features" of high school graduations, and as respondents do not contest, the invocation and benediction have long been recognized to be "as traditional as any other parts of the [school] graduation program and are widely established." H. McKown, Commencement Activities 56 (1931); see also Brodinsky, *supra,* at 5.

II

The Court presumably would separate graduation invocations and benedictions from other instances of public "preservation and transmission of religious beliefs" on the ground that they involve "psychological coercion." * * * A few citations of "[r]esearch in psychology" that have no particular bearing upon the precise issue here, cannot disguise the fact that the Court has gone beyond the realm where judges know what they are doing. The Court's argument that state officials have "coerced" students to take part in the invocation and benediction at graduation ceremonies is, not to put too fine a point on it, incoherent.

The Court identifies two "dominant facts" that it says dictate its ruling that invocations and benedictions at public school graduation ceremonies violate the Establishment Clause. Neither of them is in any relevant sense true.

A

The Court declares that students' "attendance and participation in the [invocation and benediction] are in a fair and real sense obligatory." But what exactly is this "fair and real sense"? According to the Court, students at graduation who want "to avoid the fact or appearance of participation," in the invocation and benediction are *psychologically* obligated by "public pressure, as well as peer pressure, . . . to stand as a group or, at least, maintain respectful silence" during those prayers. This assertion—*the very linchpin of the Court's opinion*—is almost as intriguing for what it does not say as for what it says. It does not say, for example, that students are psychologically coerced to bow their heads, place their hands in a Dürer-like prayer position, pay attention to the prayers, utter "Amen," or in fact pray. (Perhaps further intensive psychological research remains to be done on these matters.) It claims only that students are psychologically coerced "to stand . . . *or,* at least, maintain respectful silence." * * *

* * * The Court's notion that a student who simply *sits* in "respectful silence" during the invocation and benediction (when all others are standing) has somehow joined—or would somehow be perceived as having joined—in the prayers is nothing short of ludicrous. We indeed live in a vulgar age. But surely "our social conventions," have not coarsened to the point that anyone who does not stand on his chair and shout obscenities can reasonably be deemed to have assented to everything said in his presence. * * *

But let us assume the very worst, that the nonparticipating graduate is "subtly coerced" . . . to stand! * * * The Court acknowledges that "in our culture standing . . . can signify adherence to a view or simple respect for the views of others." * * * But if it is a permissible inference that one who is standing is doing so simply out of respect for the prayers of others that are in progress, then how can it possibly be said that a "reasonable dissenter . . . could believe that the group exercise signified her own participation or approval"? Quite obviously, it cannot. * * *

* * *

B

The other "dominant fac[t]" identified by the Court is that "[s]tate officials direct the performance of a formal religious exercise" at school graduation ceremonies. "Direct[ing] the performance of a formal religious exercise" has a sound of liturgy to it, summoning up images of the principal directing acolytes where to carry the cross, or showing the rabbi where to unroll the Torah. * * * All the record shows is that principals of the Providence public schools, acting within their delegated authority, have invited clergy to deliver invocations and benedictions at graduations; and that Principal Lee invited Rabbi Gutterman, provided him a two-page pamphlet, prepared by the National Conference of Christians and Jews, giving general advice on inclusive prayer for civic occasions, and advised him that his prayers at graduation should be nonsectarian. How these facts can fairly be transformed into the charges that Principal Lee "directed and controlled the content of [Rabbi Gutterman's] prayer," that school officials "monitor prayer," and attempted to " 'compose official prayers,' " and that the "government involvement with religious activity in this case is pervasive," is difficult to fathom. * * *

* * *

III

The deeper flaw in the Court's opinion does not lie in its wrong answer to the question whether there was state-induced "peer-pressure" coercion; it lies, rather, in the Court's making violation of the Establishment Clause hinge on such a precious question. The coercion that was a hallmark of historical establishments of religion was coercion of religious orthodoxy and of financial support *by force of law and threat of penalty*. Typically, attendance at the state church was required; only clergy of the official church could lawfully perform sacraments; and dissenters, if tolerated, faced an array of civil disabilities. * * *

The Establishment Clause was adopted to prohibit such an establishment of religion at the federal level (and to protect state establishments of religion from federal interference). I will further acknowledge for the sake of argument that, as some scholars have argued, by 1790 the term "establishment" had acquired an additional meaning—"financial support of religion generally, by public taxation"—that reflected the development of "general or multiple" establishments, not limited to a single church. But that would still be an establishment coerced *by force* *of law*. And I will further concede that our constitutional tradition * * * rule[s] out of order government-sponsored endorsement of religion— even when no legal coercion is present, and indeed even when no ersatz, "peer-pressure" psycho-coercion is present—where the endorsement is sectarian, in the sense of specifying details upon which men and women who believe in a benevolent, omnipotent Creator and Ruler of the world are known to differ (for example, the divinity of Christ). But there is simply no support for the proposition that the officially sponsored nondenominational invocation and benediction read by Rabbi Gutter- man—with no one legally coerced to recite them—violated the Constitu- tion of the United States. To the contrary, they are so characteristically American they could have come from the pen of George Washington or Abraham Lincoln himself.

Thus, while I have no quarrel with the Court's general proposition that the Establishment Clause "guarantees that government may not coerce anyone to support or participate in religion or its exercise," I see no warrant for expanding the concept of coercion beyond acts backed by threat of penalty * * *.

* * *

IV

* * *

The reader has been told much in this case about the personal interest of Mr. Weisman and his daughter, and very little about the personal interests on the other side. They are not inconsequential. Church and state would not be such a difficult subject if religion were, as the Court apparently thinks it to be, some purely personal avocation that can be indulged entirely in secret, like pornography, in the privacy of one's room. For most believers it is *not* that, and has never been. Religious men and women of almost all denominations have felt it necessary to acknowledge and beseech the blessing of God as a people, and not just as individuals, because they believe in the "protection of divine Providence," as the Declaration of Independence put it, not just for individuals but for societies * * *. One can believe in the effective- ness of such public worship, or one can deprecate and deride it. But the longstanding American tradition of prayer at official ceremonies displays with unmistakable clarity that the Establishment Clause does not forbid the government to accommodate it.

* * *

I must add one final observation: The Founders of our Republic knew the fearsome potential of sectarian religious belief to generate civil dissension and civil strife. And they also knew that nothing, absolutely nothing, is so inclined to foster among religious believers of various faiths a toleration—no, an affection—for one another than voluntarily joining in prayer together, to the God whom they all worship and seek. Needless to say, no one should be compelled to do that, but it is a shame to deprive our public culture of the opportunity, and indeed the encouragement, for people to do it voluntarily. The Baptist or Catholic who heard and joined in the simple and inspiring prayers of Rabbi Gutterman on this official and patriotic occasion was inoculated from religious bigotry and prejudice in a manner that cannot be replicated. To deprive our society of that important unifying mechanism, in order to spare the nonbeliever what seems to me the minimal inconvenience of standing or even sitting in respectful nonparticipation, is as senseless in policy as it is unsupported in law.

For the foregoing reasons, I dissent.

Notes and Questions

1. *Tests, Tests, and More Tests.* Which test(s) should lower courts apply to school prayer cases after *Lee*? Does a majority of the Court support exclusive use of the coercion test? If not, what other tests might be used? How many Justices at the time of *Lee* would appear to support each of the alternative tests? How does the majority opinion treat the *Lemon* test? The Endorsement test? The "Tradition" test? Can a lower court avoid applying each test after *Lee* (other than the "Tradition" test which was rejected by a majority of the Court in the graduation prayer context)?

2. *What is Coercion?* Justice Kennedy's opinion for the Court and Justice Scalia's dissenting opinion are at odds over the meaning of "coercion." What does Justice Kennedy mean by the term coercion? It clearly is more than forced religious observance, but how far might the indirect coercion analysis go? Would indirect coercion result from a private baccalaureate ceremony held off school premises, but advertised within the school and attended by most students, teachers, and school administrators (Justice Souter suggested in his concurring opinion in *Lee* that a privately sponsored baccalaureate ceremony would be constitutional)? Is peer pressure required for indirect coercion, or is it simply one of the factors that makes such coercion more likely? Is the indirect coercion advocated by Justice Kennedy best understood as coercion, or would it make more sense to follow the lead of the concurrences and treat it as an endorsement of religion? Would it make sense to analyze it as an action that advances religion under the *Lemon* test? Justice Scalia suggests that it would be best to allow graduation prayer, in part, because it is a longstanding tradition. Should the Court only find actionable coercion under the circumstances where Justice Scalia would do so? What types of government supported or endorsed activities would be precluded under Justice Scalia's approach? How would *Schempp* and *Engel v. Vitale* be analyzed under Justice Scalia's approach? Which opinion(s) in *Lee* do you agree with most and why?

3. *Bad Psychology?* The Majority opinion relies on psychological studies on peer pressure to support its holding. Should the Court rely on such studies in a case like this? It is interesting to note that the Court may have over relied on and/or misapplied the psychological studies it used. See, e.g., Landon Summers, *The Justices and Psychological Research: But Is It Really Science?*, 21 LAW & PSYCH. REV. 93 (1997)(suggesting that the Court misused social science research in *Lee*, even if it ultimately made the right legal decision despite the misuse of the studies); Scott Vaughn Carroll, *Note, Lee v. Weisman: Amateur Psychology or an Accurate Representation of Adolescent Development, How Should Courts Evaluate Psychological Evidence?*,10 J. OF CONTEMP. HEALTH LAW & POLICY 513

(1993)(same, but implying oversimplification rather than misuse). Additionally, there is a strong argument that Courts often misconstrue or oversimplify social scientific data when they use it. *Cf. id.*; *See also* Gregory Mitchell, *Taking Behavioralism Seriously? The Unwarranted Pessimism of the New Behavioral Analysis of Law*, 43 WILLIAM & MARY L. REV. 1907 (2002)(noting, among other things, that legal scholars often misuse empirical research). Ironically, the Court's concerns may have been supported by an even broader array of social science data upon which it did not rely. *See* FRANK S. RAVITCH, SCHOOL PRAYER AND DISCRIMINATION: THE CIVIL RIGHTS OF RELIGIOUS MINORITIES AND DISSENTERS (Northeastern Univ. Press 1999) at 74–87. Does this support the use of such data in Establishment Clause cases or does it militate against it? *See id.* (implying that it supports the use of such data, but only if the data is carefully analyzed with an understanding of its complex nature and relevant disagreements within the social scientific community).

4. *What Does School Sponsored Mean*? The Court relies heavily upon the fact that the school sponsored the graduation ceremony, invited the clergy member to deliver the invocation and benediction, and gave him guidelines for prayers at graduation ceremonies. How important were each of these factors? Would only one of these factors have been enough to find the graduation prayer unconstitutional? If so, which one(s)? The Court acknowledges that, at the very least, the Establishment Clause prohibits the type of coercion at issue in *Lee*, but this suggests that more may be prohibited. How would the various opinions analyze a situation where the school allowed students to select the person giving the prayer without advising the speaker about what to say? What if the speaker selected is a student? Can either of these factors make a difference if the prayer occurs at a school sponsored activity of "singular importance" in the lives of graduating seniors? How might the person giving the prayer be selected by students? What message might be sent to those in the religious minority if the students vote on the speaker? Could a majority of citizens vote to have a cross installed in a state capital or to have a prayer service included at all state sponsored activities? Does this suggest that the most important factor is government sponsorship of the graduation ceremony? These questions will be answered in the following sections. As you read the following sections consider which decisions/opinions you agree with and why.

1. The Aftermath of Lee

Shortly after *Lee* was decided the question of "voluntary student-initiated" prayer at graduation ceremonies came to the fore. The term describes a situation where prayer occurs at graduation ceremonies, but school officials do not invite or advise the speaker who gives the prayer. Rather, the school leaves it up to students to determine if a prayer(s) is to be delivered and by whom. Most commonly this is done through a voting process. Such practices would seem to run afoul of *Lee* because the prayer occurs at ceremonies sponsored and overseen by schools, and the students are only able to vote on the prayer speaker as a result of school policies allowing them to do so. Still, courts disagreed over the constitutionality of such prayer. Moreover, there have been a variety of relevant differences in the way such prayers come to be offered. It is useful at the outset to note that if a speaker delivers a prayer, but is selected to speak at a graduation ceremony without regard to the likelihood that he/she would offer the prayer—for example a valedictorian or class president—there is likely no constitutional violation unless there is some reason to believe that the school somehow encouraged the selection of the student because he/she was likely to offer a prayer. Thus, the cases in this section are not concerned with what might be called "unexpected spontaneous prayer by a graduating student."

The following two cases, which are both heavily edited, demonstrate the disagreements among the lower courts over the "voluntary student-initiated prayer" issue after *Lee*. As you will see, the issue is tied closely to free speech arguments, which make the issue more complex. As you will see later in this Chapter, the Supreme Court answered the question in part in 2000, see *Santa Fe Independent School Dist. v. Doe*, infra. Doe suggests that the reasoning of the panel of the Federal Court of Appeals for the 5th Circuit in the following case (*Jones v. Clear Creek*) was flawed (later cases in the 5th Circuit hinted at this as well), but that the reasoning in the majority decision for the Federal Court of Appeals for the 3rd Circuit, sitting en banc in the *Black Horse Pike* case (following *Jones*), was close to the mark. Yet *Jones* is an important opinion because it helped keep the graduation prayer issue alive after *Lee*, and demonstrated the tenacity and creativity of those attempting to keep the issue alive. Interestingly, even after *Santa Fe Independent School Dist. v. Doe*, a panel of the Federal Court of Appeals for the 11th Circuit has suggested that student-initiated graduation prayer might still be constitutional in certain circumstances, although the reasoning in that decision is highly questionable. *Compare Chandler v. Siegelman*, 230 F.3d 1313 (11th Cir.2000), *with Santa Fe Independent School Dist. v. Doe*, *infra*.

JONES v. CLEAR CREEK INDEPENDENT SCHOOL DISTRICT

United States Court of Appeals, Fifth Circuit, 1992.
977 F.2d 963.

REAVLEY, CIRCUIT JUDGE.

In *Jones v. Clear Creek Independent School Dist.*, 930 F.2d 416 (5th Cir.1991) (*Jones I*), *vacated*, 505 U.S. 1215, 112 S.Ct. 3020, 120 L.Ed.2d 892 (1992), we held that Clear Creek Independent School District's Resolution[10] permitting public high school seniors to choose student volunteers to deliver nonsectarian, nonproselytizing invocations at their

---

10. 1. The use of an invocation and/or benediction at high school graduation exercise shall rest within the discretion of the graduating senior class, with the advice and counsel of the senior class principal;

2. The invocation and benediction, if used, shall be given by a student volunteer; and

3. Consistent with the principle of equal liberty of conscience, the invocation and benediction shall be nonsectarian and nonproselytizing in nature.

graduation ceremonies does not violate the Constitution's Establishment Clause. * * *

Then, in *Lee v. Weisman*, the Supreme Court held that Robert E. Lee, a public-school principal acting in accord with the policy of his Providence, Rhode Island school district, violated the Establishment Clause by inviting a local clergy member, Rabbi Leslie Gutterman, to deliver a nonsectarian, nonproselytizing invocation at his school's graduation ceremony. The Court reasoned that Lee's actions represent governmental coercion to participate in religious activities, a paradigmatic establishment of religion. The Court then granted certiorari in this case, vacated our judgment, and remanded it to us for further consideration in light of *Lee*. Upon reconsideration, we hold that *Lee* does not render Clear Creek's invocation policy unconstitutional * * *.

I.   The Supreme Court Tells This Court What the Establishment Clause Means

* * * Although the Supreme Court's doctrinally-centered manner of resolving Establishment Clause disputes may be credited with accommodating a society of remarkable religious diversity, it requires considerable micromanagement of government's relationship to religion as the Court decides each case by distilling fact-sensitive rules from its precedents.

* * *

The Court has repeatedly held that the Establishment Clause forbids the imposition of religion through public education. That leads to difficulty because of public schools' responsibility to develop pupils' character and decision making skills, a responsibility more important in a society suffering from parental failure. If religion be the foundation, or at least relevant to these functions and to the education of the young, as is widely believed, it follows that religious thought should not be excluded as irrelevant to public education. * * *

Nevertheless, it is neither our object nor our place to opine whether the Court's Establishment Clause jurisprudence is good, fair, or useful. What the Establishment Clause finally means in a specific case is what the Court says it means. We sit only to apply the analytical methods sanctioned by the Court in accord with its precedent.

II.   From *Lemon* to *Lee*

* * *

[I]n the time between *Lemon* and *Lee,* the Court has used five tests to determine whether public schools' involvement with religion violates the Establishment Clause. To fully reconsider this case in light of *Lee,* we reanalyze the Resolution under all five tests that the Court has stated are relevant. * * *

A. Secular Purpose

Nothing in *Lee* abrogates our conclusion that the Resolution has a secular purpose of solemnization, and thus satisfies *Lemon's* first requirement. The Resolution represents Clear Creek's judgment that society benefits if people attach importance to graduation. A meaningful graduation ceremony can provide encouragement to finish school and the inspiration and self-assurance necessary to achieve after graduation, which are secular objectives.

* * *

B. Primary Effect

In *Jones I,* we held that the Resolution's *primary* effect was to solemnize graduation ceremonies, not to "advance religion" in contravention of *Lemon's* second requirement. * * *

The Resolution can only advance religion by increasing religious conviction among graduation attendees, which means attracting new believers or increasing the faith of the faithful. Its requirement that any invocation be nonsectarian and nonproselytizing minimizes any such advancement of religion. * * *

The fact that *Lemon* only condemns government action that has the *primary* effect of advancing religion, requires us to compare the Resolution's secular and religious effect. The Resolution may or may not have any religious effect. The students may or may not employ the name of any deity; heads may or may not be bowed; indeed, an invocation may or may not appear on the program. If the students choose a nonproselytizing, nonsectarian prayer, the effect may well marshall attendees' extant religiosity for the secular purpose of solemnization; but no one would likely expect the advancement of religion by the initiation or increase of religious faith through these prayers. The Resolution's primary effect is secular.

C. Entanglement

We held in *Jones I* that the Resolution's proscription of sectarianism does not, of itself, excessively entangle government with religion. We know of no authority that holds yearly review of unsolicited material for sectarianism and proselytization to constitute excessive entanglement. * * * Moreover, nothing in *Lee* abrogates our reading of the Court's entanglement precedent to limit violative entanglement to *institutional* entanglement. * * *

D. Endorsement

Like *Lemon's* advancement test, the Court's endorsement analysis focuses on the *effect* of a challenged governmental action. * * *

From the Court's various pronouncements, we understand government to unconstitutionally endorse religion when a reasonable person would view the challenged government action as a disapproval of her contrary religious choices. * * *

* * *

* * * Unlike the policy at issue in *Lee,* [the Clear Creek policy] does not mandate a prayer. The Resolution does not even mandate an invocation; it merely permits one if the seniors so choose. Moreover, the students present Clear Creek with *their* proposed invocation under the Resolution, while in *Lee* the school explained its idea for an invocation to a member of an organized religion and directed him to deliver it. The Resolution is passive compared to the governmental overture toward religion at issue in *Lee.*

* * * [A] graduating high school senior *who participates in the decision as to whether her graduation will include an invocation by a fellow student volunteer* will understand that any religious references are the result of student, not government, choice. * * *

We think that Clear Creek does not unconstitutionally endorse religion if it submits the decision of graduation invocation content, if any, to the majority vote of the senior class. Clear Creek is legitimately concerned with solemnizing its graduation ceremonies, and the Resolution simply permits each senior class to decide how this can best be done. School districts commonly provide similarly secular criteria for the selection of other student graduation speakers, and no court has held that their religious speech at graduation represents government endorsement of religion. After participating in a student determination of what kind of invocation their graduation will contain, we do not believe that students will perceive * * * government endorsement of religion * * *. Clear Creek students certainly perceive a less-direct relationship between state and religion under the Resolution than Providence students did before *Lee.* We find no unconstitutional endorsement.

E.   Coercion

Instead of directly considering any of the tests that we have previously discussed, the *Lee* Court invalidated the Providence school district's policy on its evaluation of the coercive effect of Lee's actions. The Court held that Lee *coerced* graduation attendees to join in a formal religious exercise. * * *

* * * *Lee* identifies unconstitutional coercion when (1) the government directs (2) a formal religious exercise (3) in such a way as to oblige the participation of objectors. * * * Upon considering this case in light of *Lee's* coercion analysis, we find that the Resolution does not succumb to one, let alone all three, of the elements of unconstitutional coercion, and thus survives the analysis that felled graduation prayer in *Lee.*

1.   Direction

Throughout *Lee's* entire coercion analysis, the Court repeatedly stresses the government's direct and complete control over the graduation prayers there at issue as determinative of the establishment question. * * *

The Court deplored three instances of government involvement in graduation prayer in *Lee,* none of which is tolerated, let alone prescribed, by the [Clear Creek] Resolution. First, the Court found that Lee "decided that an invocation and benediction should be given; this is a choice attributable to the State, and from a constitutional perspective it is as if a state statute decreed that the prayers must occur." The Resolution requires that the state *not* decide whether an invocation will occur; it respects the graduating class's choice on the matter. The Resolution acknowledges that a school official may offer "advice and counsel" to the senior class in deciding whether to include invocations at graduation, and officials could exploit this clause to impose their will on the students. But, again, in evaluating the Resolution's facial constitutionality, we are only concerned with whether the Resolution necessarily charges government with the decision of whether to include invocations. * * *

Second, the Court was critical of the fact that "[t]he principal chose the religious participant, here a rabbi, and that choice is also attributable to the State." In contrast, the Resolution explicitly precludes anyone but a student volunteer from delivering Clear Creek's invocations. Moreover, the Resolution says nothing of government involvement in the selection of the person who delivers any invocation. That the government can remain detached from this selection consistent with the Resolution maintains the Resolution's facial constitutionality.

The Court recognized that Lee completed his control over the invocation at his school's graduation ceremonies when he "provided Rabbi Gutterman with a copy of the 'Guidelines for Civic Occasions,' and advised him that his prayers should be nonsectarian." In three respects, Clear Creek exercises significantly less control over the content of invocations at its schools. Clear Creek does not solicit invocations; the Resolution only forbids Clear Creek schools from *accepting* sectarian or proselytizing invocations. Moreover, because a graduating senior drafts proposed invocations each year under the Resolution, the same person will never repeatedly propose an invocation. Finally, the Resolution imposes two one-word restrictions "nonsectarian and nonproselytizing" which enhance solemnization and minimize advancement of religion, instead of a pamphlet full of invocation suggestions.

We conclude that Clear Creek does not direct prayer presentations at its graduation ceremonies.

2. Religiosity

Lee directed Rabbi Gutterman to pray, and the Court characterized this as a "formal religious observance." By contrast, the Resolution tolerates nonsectarian, nonproselytizing prayer, but does not require or favor it.

3. *Participation*

The *Lee* Court held that government-mandated prayer at graduation places a constitutionally impermissible amount of psychological pressure upon students to participate in religious exercises. We think that the graduation prayers permitted by the Resolution place less psychological pressure on students than the prayers at issue in *Lee* because all students, *after having participated in the decision of whether prayers will be given,* are aware that any prayers represent the will of their peers, who are less able to coerce participation than an authority figure from the state or clergy.

We also consider the age of the graduating seniors relevant to the determination of whether prayers under the Resolution can coerce these young people into participating in a religious exercise. *Lee* explains that *the state-initiated clergy prayers there at issue* have a coercive effect on public-school students regardless of age, but it nowhere compromises the Court's previous recognition that graduating seniors "are less impressionable than younger students." *Mergens,* 496 U.S. at 235–37, 110 S.Ct. at 2364–65 * * *.

Accordingly, we think that the coercive effect of any prayer permitted by the Resolution is more analogous to the innocuous "God save the United States and this Honorable Court" stated *by and to* adults than the government-mandated message delivered to young people from religious authority that the Court considered in *Lee.*

None of *Lee's* three elements of coercive effect exist here. Prayers allowed under the Resolution do not unconstitutionally coerce objectors into participation.

III.   FROM SEA TO SHINING SEA, GREAT GOD OUR KING[14]

The practical result of our decision, viewed in light of *Lee,* is that a majority of students can do what the State acting on its own cannot do to incorporate prayer in public high school graduation ceremonies. In *Lee,* the Court forbade schools from exacting participation in a religious exercise as the price for attending what many consider to be one of life's most important events. This case requires us to consider *why* so many people attach importance to graduation ceremonies. If they only seek government's recognition of student achievement, diplomas suffice. If they only seek God's recognition, a privately-sponsored baccalaureate will do. But to experience the *community's* recognition of student achievement, they must attend the public ceremony that other interested community members also hold so dear. By attending graduation to experience and participate in the community's display of support for the

---

14. America! America!

God shed His grace on thee,

And crown thy good with brotherhood

From sea to shining sea.

America the Beautiful

Long may our land be bright. With freedom's holy light;

Protect us by Thy might,

Great God, our King.

America

graduates, people should not be surprised to find the event affected by community standards. The Constitution requires nothing different.

We again affirm the district court's judgment denying injunctive and declaratory relief from the Resolution.

AMERICAN CIVIL LIBERTIES UNION OF NEW JERSEY v. BLACK HORSE PIKE REGIONAL BOARD OF EDUCATION

United States Court of Appeals, Third Circuit, 1996.
84 F.3d 1471 (en banc).

McKEE, CIRCUIT JUDGE.

We are asked to decide whether a policy adopted by the Black Horse Pike Regional Board of Education that allows a vote of the senior class to determine if prayer will be included in high school graduation ceremonies is constitutional. For the reasons that follow we hold that this policy is inconsistent with the First Amendment of the United States Constitution. * * *

I.   FACTUAL BACKGROUND

The Black Horse Pike Regional Board of Education (the "School Board" or "Board") has had a longstanding tradition of including a nonsectarian invocation and benediction in high school graduation ceremonies. These prayers have historically been delivered by local clergy on a rotating basis in an attempt to afford different denominations the opportunity to be represented.

In May of 1993, the School Board decided to reconsider this policy because of the Supreme Court's decision in *Lee v. Weisman* * * *. As part of the Board's reexamination, the Superintendent of Schools tendered a policy entitled "Religion at Graduation Exercises" ("Version A") for the Board's consideration. Version A prohibited all prayer at graduation ceremonies. The Board rejected that policy and directed the school administration to prepare a second version that would parallel the holding of *Jones v. Clear Creek Indep. Sch. Dist.* * * *

Two policies were presented to the Board at its May 23, 1993 meeting. One version allowed graduating students to decide whether prayer would be included in the graduation ceremony as well as the nature of any such prayer ("Version D"). The other proposal would not have allowed "prayer" but would have allowed a "moment of reflection, during which pupils and parents [could] be asked to think silently about what has been and what is to come for each graduate." * * * At the conclusion of the meeting, the Board unanimously adopted Version D. That policy, as finally adopted, allowed the senior class officers to conduct a poll of the graduating class to determine whether seniors wanted "prayer, a moment of reflection, or nothing at all" to be included in their graduation ceremony.

* * * Version D * * *further required that printed programs for the graduation include a disclaimer explaining that any presentation that may be given at commencement did not reflect the views of the School Board, the School District, administrators, staff, or other students.

On June 3, 1993, Principal Frank Palatucci of the Highland Regional High School explained the Board's decision to the students during the morning announcements over the school public address system. After he explained the policy, he introduced the senior class president who explained that a poll would be taken of the senior class, and how the balloting would be conducted. The vote was taken the next day and produced the following results: 128 students voted for prayer, 120 for reflection/moment of silence, and 20 voted to have neither. Students then volunteered to deliver the graduation prayer, and the senior class officers selected the senior class recording secretary from among those volunteers.

On June 9, Edward Ross, a member of the senior class, approached Principal Palatucci and requested that a representative from the ACLU also be permitted to speak at the graduation to discuss safe sex and condom distribution. Principal Palatucci denied Ross' request explaining that the time constraints of the ceremony would not permit a keynote speaker, and that the topic requested was not generally one discussed at graduation ceremonies.

II. PROCEDURAL HISTORY

On June 18, 1993, the ACLU and Edward Ross filed a Complaint in the District Court for the District of New Jersey, in which they asked the court to enjoin any student-led prayer at graduation. * * *

* * *

IV. DISCUSSION

A. *The Free Speech Rights of Students*

The Board relies upon the student referendum in an attempt to define the instant controversy as one impacting upon the students' right of free speech as opposed to a dispute over the constitutionality of prayer at a public high school graduation. Version D * * * does state: "[i]n the spirit of protected free speech, the pupils in attendance must choose to have prayer conducted." However, Version D allowed the 128 seniors who wanted verbal prayer at their graduation to impose their will upon 140 of their fellow classmates who did not. The Board's position would have us recognize a right in that plurality to do so, and ignore the right of others to worship in a different manner, or in no manner at all. This we can not do because "the individual freedom of conscience protected by the First Amendment embraces the right to select any religious faith or none at all." *Wallace v. Jaffree*, 472 U.S. 38, 52, 105 S.Ct. 2479, 2487, 86 L.Ed.2d 29 (1985). Therefore, the Board's emphasis on voting majorities is misplaced. "While in some societies the wishes of the majority might prevail, the Establishment Clause of the First Amendment is addressed to this contingency and rejects the balance urged upon us." *Lee.* * * *

An impermissible practice can not be transformed into a constitutionally acceptable one by putting a democratic process to an improper use. There should be no question "that the electorate as a whole, whether by referendum or otherwise, could not order [governmental] action violative of the [Constitution], and the [government] may not avoid the strictures of [the Constitution] by deferring to the wishes or objections of some fraction of the body politic." *City of Cleburne v. Cleburne Living Center,* 473 U.S. 432, 448, 105 S.Ct. 3249, 3258, 87 L.Ed.2d 313 (1985) (citation omitted). A policy that does this can not be legitimized by arguing that it promotes the free speech of the majority.

* * * "The very purpose of a Bill of Rights was to withdraw certain subjects from the vicissitudes of political controversy, to place them beyond the reach of majorities and officials and to establish them as legal principles to be applied by the courts. One's ... fundamental rights may not be submitted to vote; they depend on the outcome of no elections." *Board of Educ. v. Barnette,* 319 U.S. 624, 638, 63 S.Ct. 1178, 1185, 87 L.Ed. 1628 (1943).

High school graduation ceremonies have not been regarded, either by law or tradition, as public fora where a multiplicity of views on any given topic, secular or religious, can be expressed and exchanged. School officials at Highland did not allow a representative of the ACLU to speak about "safe sex" and condom distribution at graduation, as requested by one of the graduating seniors. The question was not submitted to referendum of the graduating seniors because the principal understandably determined that the proposed topic was not suitable for graduation. We do not suggest that the school's response to this request was inappropriate. However, we do note that the response illustrates the degree of control the administration retained over student speech at graduation. * * *

* * *

B. Lee v. Weisman

The degree of control that school officials retained over the speech that would be permitted at graduation is also relevant under *Lee v. Weisman.* * * *

In ruling the prayer unconstitutional, the Supreme Court emphasized:

These dominant facts mark and control the confines of our decision: [1] State officials direct the performance of a formal religious exercise at promotional and graduation ceremonies for secondary schools. [2] Even for those students who object to the religious exercise, their attendance and participation in the state sponsored religious activity are in a fair and real sense obligatory, though the school district does not require attendance as a condition for receipt of the diploma.

Accordingly, we must examine (1) the state's control of the graduation ceremony, and (2) the students' coerced participation in the ceremony here.

(1)

The School Board argues that the student referendum here significantly distinguishes this case from *Lee*. We disagree. It is, of course, true that the state's entanglement with the graduation prayer in *Lee* was more obvious, pronounced, and intrusive than the School District's involvement here. * * *

Although the state's involvement here is certainly less evident, the student referendum does not erase the state's imprint from this graduation prayer. Graduation at Highland Regional High School, like graduation at nearly any other school, is a school sponsored event. School officials decide the sequence of events and the order of speakers on the program, and ceremonies are typically held on school property at no cost to the students. The atmosphere at Highland's graduations is characterized by order and uniformity. * * * The district court carefully questioned the principal about what he would do if a majority of the student body, without administrative approval, voted to have a speaker who would not be included in the program but would be introduced by the valedictorian and allowed to give a one minute speech. The principal responded: "I couldn't allow that to happen.... If I have a police officer, I have her arrested." Thus, the school officials' involvement and control is not as limited, unintrusive, or neutral as the School Board suggests.

Delegation of one aspect of the ceremony to a plurality of students does not constitute the absence of school officials' control over the graduation. Students decided the question of prayer at graduation only because school officials agreed to let them decide that one question. Although the delegation here may appear to many to be no more than a neutral means of deciding whether prayer should be included in the graduation, it does not insulate the School Board from the reach of the First Amendment. * * *

Furthermore, the text of Version D affirms that it was adopted in response to *Lee*. The Board's avowed purpose in reexamining its policy was to provide an option that might allow the "longstanding tradition" of graduation prayer to survive the prohibitions of that Supreme Court decision. We believe that the control exercised by state officials here, though different in degree than was present in *Lee,* is not sufficiently distinct to require a different result under the "first dominant fact" of *Lee.*

(2)

* * * We find no difference whatsoever between the coercion in *Lee* and the coercion here. * * *

"The fact that attendance at the graduation ceremonies is voluntary in a legal sense does not save the religious exercise." *Lee.* The objector's presence at his or her graduation compels participation in the religious observance decreed by the results of the poll that is sanctioned under Version D. This, the Constitution does not allow. * * *

Here, the hypothetical dissenter in *Lee* is replaced by 140 students who voted not to have a formal prayer at their public high school graduation. The Board's policy would have required each of those 140 students to participate (or at the very least maintain respectful silence) as others engaged in student-led worship. "It is beyond dispute that, at a minimum, the Constitution guarantees that government may not coerce anyone to support or participate in religion or its exercise." Here, as in *Lee,* "[t]he prayer exercises . . . are especially improper because the State has in every practical sense compelled attendance and participation in an explicit religious exercise at an event of singular importance to every student, one the objecting student had no real alternative to avoid." Students at Highland had to either conform to the model of worship commanded by the plurality or absent themselves from graduation and thereby forego one of the most important events in their lives. That is an improper choice to force upon dissenting students. * * *

* * *

The disclaimer required under Version D does help to recapture some of the separation between church and state that has been obscured by the state's control over the graduation. However, the Board cannot sanction coerced participation in a religious observance merely by disclaiming responsibility for the content of the ceremony. * * *

We recognize that the Court of Appeals for the Fifth Circuit has reached a result contrary to the one we reach today. *See Jones v. Clear Creek Indep. Sch. Dist.* * * * We are not, however, persuaded by that court's analysis. *Jones* also involved a challenge to a policy that allowed students to decide if they wanted prayer at a public school's graduation ceremony. The *Jones* court upheld the policy while acknowledging that "the practical result of [its] decision, viewed in light of *Lee,* is that a majority of students can do what the State acting on its own cannot do to incorporate prayer in public high school graduation ceremonies."

[The Court addressed the *Jones* Court's holding that "student initiated" prayer is allowed where government initiated prayer is not because of the solemn nature of the "once in a lifetime" event, and that Court's holding that high school age children are not as impressionable as younger children]: * * * *Lee* clearly established that the "once-in-a-lifetime event" [graduation] does not justify allowing a public school to authorize collective prayer * * *. To the contrary, the significance of that "once-in-a-lifetime" event weighed heavily in favor of invalidating the prayer. It was precisely because graduation was a "once-in-a-life-time" event that students were denied the option of foregoing the ceremony to avoid compromising their religious scruples. Similarly, the Court in *Lee* was not convinced that the maturity level of high school students immunized them from the coercion endemic in coerced participation. Indeed, few would doubt the influence of peer pressure upon children in high school. Furthermore, we are not inclined to alter our analysis merely because Version D does not expressly allow proselytization.

* * *

C. *Lemon v. Kurtzman*

In *Lemon v. Kurtzman*, the Supreme Court announced a three part test to determine if a government practice offends the Establishment Clause. Under *Lemon,* a government practice regarding religion will not offend the Establishment Clause if: (1) it has a secular purpose; (2) its principal or primary effect neither advances nor inhibits religion; and (3) it does not create an excessive entanglement of the government with religion. * * *

The *Lemon* test has been the subject of critical debate in recent years, and its continuing vitality has been called into question by members of the Supreme Court and by its noticeable absence from the analysis in some of the Court's recent decisions (including *Lee*). Nevertheless, *Lemon* remains the law of the land, and we are obligated to consider it until instructed otherwise by a majority of the Supreme Court.

(1) A Secular Purpose

The Board argues that Version D has the secular purpose of recognizing the students' rights to free speech and their desire to solemnize the occasion. * * *

* * * We have already explained why the Board's assertion of the secular purpose of free speech does not control. " 'Graduation ceremonies have never served as forums for public debate or discussions, or as a forum through which to allow varying groups to voice their views.' " *Brody v. Spang,* 957 F.2d 1108, 1118 (3d Cir.1992) (citation omitted). * * *

* * *

In addition, Version D permits a student to give a sectarian, proselytizing address. If a student were to decide to give such an address after a student referendum "authorized" verbal prayer, the administration could not halt it without violating its own policy. If this were to occur, a proselytizing prayer (perhaps even degrading other religions) would be delivered in a forum controlled by the School Board. * * *

The Board also argues that the inclusion of prayer solemnizes the graduation, but we are unable to understand why graduation would be any less solemn if students were not permitted to vote for prayer, a moment of silence or no observance at graduation. Surely students who graduate in a year where students may chose to have no prayer at all would think their graduation to be a solemn event, and it is doubtful that the Board would disagree with that assessment. * * *

Furthermore, assuming *arguendo* that Version D serves the secular purpose of solemnizing one's graduation, we believe it does so in a constitutionally impermissible manner. Students who are devoutly religious may feel that prayer is not something that should be put to a vote. Such students may even have a religious objection to such a vote and may, therefore, refuse to vote out of religious conviction. Version D puts such students on the horns of an impossible dilemma by forcing them to chose between doing violence to their own religious beliefs and voting, or abstaining and thereby risking that their forbearance may provide the margin of victory for those with a different religious preference. * * * Such a Hobson's choice "sends a message to nonadherents that they are outsiders, not full members of the political community. . . . " *Lynch,* 465 U.S. at 688, 104 S.Ct. at 1367 (O'Connor, J., concurring). * * *

(2) The Endorsement of Religion

Under the second prong of *Lemon,* a government practice can neither advance, nor inhibit religion. This means that a challenged practice must "not have the effect of communicating a message of government endorsement or disapproval of religion." *Lynch,* 465 U.S. at 692. This endorsement test has at times been characterized as part and parcel of the *Lemon* test, and at other times as separate and apart from it. Whether "the endorsement test" is part of the inquiry under *Lemon* or a separate inquiry apart from it, the import of the test is the same. We must determine whether, under the totality of the circumstances, the challenged practice conveys a message favoring or disfavoring religion. "The question under endorsement analysis, in short, is whether a reasonable observer would view such longstanding practices as a disapproval of his or her particular religious choices. . . . " *Allegheny,* 492 U.S. at 631, 109 S.Ct. at 3121 (O'Connor, J., concurring). * * *

* * *

Although it is true that Version D does not require the view that prevails in any given year to prevail in subsequent years, it is nonetheless true that the effect of the particular prayer that is offered in any given year will be to advance religion and coerce dissenting students. The Constitution's "prohibition against governmental endorsement of religion 'preclude[s] government from conveying or attempting to convey a message that religion or a particular religious belief is favored or preferred.' "

* * *

* * * The Supreme Court has never countenanced a practice that requires some members of a community to subordinate their religious preferences to those of a majority. Rather, "[t]he Establishment Clause, at the very least, prohibits government from appearing to take a position on questions of religious belief or from 'making adherence to a religion

relevant in any way to a person's standing in the political community.' " *Allegheny,* 492 U.S. at 593–94, 109 S.Ct. at 3101 (quoting *Lynch,* 465 U.S. at 687, 104 S.Ct. at 1367 (O'Connor, J., concurring)).

* * *

(3) Excessive Entanglement With Religion

The third prong of the *Lemon* test—no excessive entanglement of government with religion—is a much closer question. * * * However, because we find that Version D violates the first two prongs *Lemon,* we need not determine if it also violates the third prong.

V. Conclusion

In closing, we emphasize the difficulty posed by the issue that we confront here and the intensity and sincerity of persons on both sides. Issues of religion touch litigants and interested observers of the law as few other issues can. For example, one of the students who opposed Version D testified before the district court that he received threatening letters in his school locker and threatening telephone calls at home after coming forward in this case.

References to, and images of, religion are to be found throughout this society. Yet, the prevalence of religious beliefs and imagery cannot erode the state's obligation to protect the entire spectrum of religious preferences from the most pious worshiper to the most committed atheist. Those preferences are the business of the individual, not the state nor the public schools it maintains. The First Amendment does not allow the state to erect a policy that only respects religious views that are popular because the largest majority can not be licensed to impose its religious preferences upon the smallest minority.

* * * [W]e affirm the judgment of the district court.

[The dissenting opinion of JUDGE MANSMANN is omitted].

2. The Supreme Court's Treatment of the Organized "Student–Initiated Prayer" Concept

As you can see from the cases in the previous section, the "student-initiated prayer" concept raises a lot of questions. The Supreme Court answered some of those questions in 2000. Interestingly, the case that addresses these issues involved prayer at football games rather than graduation ceremonies.

The case as initially filed also involved graduation prayer (as well as other religious activities), but the Supreme Court granted *certiorari* only on the football game prayer issue.

SANTA FE INDEPENDENT SCHOOL DISTRICT v. DOE

Supreme Court of the United States, 2000.
530 U.S. 290, 120 S.Ct. 2266, 147 L.Ed.2d 295.

JUSTICE STEVENS delivered the opinion of the Court.

Prior to 1995, the Santa Fe High School student who occupied the school's elective office of student council chaplain delivered a prayer over the public address system before each varsity football game for the entire season. This practice, along with others, was challenged in District Court as a violation of the Establishment Clause of the First Amendment. While these proceedings were pending in the District Court, the school district adopted a different policy that permits, but does not require, prayer initiated and led by a student at all home games. The District Court entered an order modifying that policy to permit only nonsectarian, nonproselytizing prayer. The Court of Appeals held that, even as modified by the District Court, the football prayer policy was invalid. We granted the school district's petition for certiorari to review that holding.

I

The Santa Fe Independent School District (District) is a political subdivision of the State of Texas, responsible for the education of more than 4,000 students in a small community in the southern part of the State. * * * Respondents are two sets of current or former students and their respective mothers. One family is Mormon and the other is Catholic. The District Court permitted respondents (Does) to litigate anonymously to protect them from intimidation or harassment.[1]

Respondents commenced this action in April 1995 * * *. In their complaint the Does alleged that the District had engaged in several proselytizing practices, such as promoting attendance at a Baptist revival meeting, encouraging membership in religious clubs, chastising children who held minority religious beliefs, and distributing Gideon Bibles on school premises. They also alleged that the District allowed students to read Christian invocations and benedictions from the stage at graduation

---

1. A decision, the Fifth Circuit Court of Appeals noted, that many District officials "apparently neither agreed with nor particularly respected." 168 F.3d 806, 809, n. 1 (C.A.5 1999). About a month after the complaint was filed, the District Court entered an order that provided, in part:

"[A]ny further attempt on the part of District or school administration, officials, counsellors, teachers, employees or servants of the School District, parents, students or anyone else, overtly or covertly to ferret out the identities of the Plaintiffs in this cause, by means of bogus petitions, questionnaires, individual interrogation, or downright 'snooping', will cease immediately. ANYONE TAKING ANY ACTION ON SCHOOL PROPERTY, DURING SCHOOL HOURS, OR WITH SCHOOL RESOURCES OR APPROVAL FOR PURPOSES OF ATTEMPTING TO ELICIT THE NAMES OR IDENTITIES OF THE PLAINTIFFS IN THIS CAUSE OF ACTION, BY OR ON BEHALF OF ANY OF THESE INDIVIDUALS, WILL FACE THE HARSHEST POSSIBLE CONTEMPT SANCTIONS FROM THIS COURT, AND MAY ADDITIONALLY FACE CRIMINAL LIABILITY. The Court wants these proceedings addressed on their merits, and not on the basis of intimidation or harassment of the participants on either side."

ceremonies,[2] and to deliver overtly Christian prayers over the public address system at home football games.

On May 10, 1995, the District Court entered an interim order addressing a number of different issues.[3] With respect to the impending graduation, the order provided that "non-denominational prayer" consisting of "an invocation and/or benediction" could be presented by a senior student or students selected by members of the graduating class. The text of the prayer was to be determined by the students, without scrutiny or preapproval by school officials. References to particular religious figures "such as Mohammed, Jesus, Buddha, or the like" would be permitted "as long as the general thrust of the prayer is non-proselytizing."

In response to that portion of the order, the District adopted a series of policies over several months dealing with prayer at school functions. The policies enacted in May and July for graduation ceremonies provided the format for the August and October policies for football games. The May policy provided:

> " 'The board has chosen to permit the graduating senior class, with the advice and counsel of the senior class principal or designee, to elect by secret ballot to choose whether an invocation and benediction shall be part of the graduation exercise. If so chosen the class shall elect by secret ballot, from a list of student volunteers, students to deliver nonsectarian, nonproselytizing invocations and benedictions for the purpose of solemnizing their graduation ceremonies.' " 168 F.3d 806, 811 (C.A.5 1999) (emphasis deleted).

The parties stipulated that after this policy was adopted, "the senior class held an election to determine whether to have an invocation and benediction at the commencement [and that the] class voted, by secret

---

2. At the 1994 graduation ceremony the senior class president delivered this invocation:

"Please bow your heads.

"Dear heavenly Father, thank you for allowing us to gather here safely tonight. We thank you for the wonderful year you have allowed us to spend together as students of Santa Fe. We thank you for our teachers who have devoted many hours to each of us. Thank you, Lord, for our parents and may each one receive the special blessing. We pray also for a blessing and guidance as each student moves forward in the future. Lord, bless this ceremony and give us all a safe journey home. In Jesus' name we pray."

3. For example, it prohibited school officials from endorsing or participating in the baccalaureate ceremony sponsored by the Santa Fe Ministerial Alliance, and ordered the District to establish policies to deal with:

"manifest First Amendment infractions of teachers, counsellors, or other District or school officials or personnel, such as ridiculing, berating or holding up for inappropriate scrutiny or examination the beliefs of any individual students. Similarly, the School District will establish or clarify existing procedures for excluding overt or covert sectarian and proselytizing religious teaching, such as the use of blatantly denominational religious terms in spelling lessons, denominational religious songs and poems in English or choir classes, denominational religious stories and parables in grammar lessons and the like, while at the same time allowing for frank and open discussion of moral, religious, and societal views and beliefs, which are non-denominational and non-judgmental."

ballot, to include prayer at the high school graduation." In a second vote the class elected two seniors to deliver the invocation and benediction.[4]

In July, the District enacted another policy eliminating the requirement that invocations and benedictions be "nonsectarian and nonproselytising," but also providing that if the District were to be enjoined from enforcing that policy, the May policy would automatically become effective.

The August policy, which was titled "Prayer at Football Games," was similar to the July policy for graduations. It also authorized two student elections, the first to determine whether "invocations" should be delivered, and the second to select the spokesperson to deliver them. Like the July policy, it contained two parts, an initial statement that omitted any requirement that the content of the invocation be "nonsectarian and nonproselytising," and a fallback provision that automatically added that limitation if the preferred policy should be enjoined. On August 31, 1995, according to the parties' stipulation: "[T]he district's high school students voted to determine whether a student would deliver prayer at varsity football games. . . . The students chose to allow a student to say a prayer at football games." A week later, in a separate election, they selected a student "to deliver the prayer at varsity football games."

The final policy (October policy) is essentially the same as the August policy, though it omits the word "prayer" from its title, and refers to "messages" and "statements" as well as "invocations."[5] It is the validity of that policy that is before us.[6]

* * *

4. The student giving the invocation thanked the Lord for keeping the class safe through 12 years of school and for gracing their lives with two special people and closed: "Lord, we ask that You keep Your hand upon us during this ceremony and to help us keep You in our hearts through the rest of our lives. In God's name we pray. Amen." The student benediction was similar in content and closed: "Lord, we ask for Your protection as we depart to our next destination and watch over us as we go our separate ways. Grant each of us a safe trip and keep us secure throughout the night. In Your name we pray. Amen."

5. Despite these changes, the school did not conduct another election, under the October policy, to supersede the results of the August policy election.

6. It provides:

"STUDENT ACTIVITIES:

"PRE–GAME CEREMONIES AT FOOTBALL GAMES

"The board has chosen to permit students to deliver a brief invocation and/or message to be delivered during the pregame ceremonies of home varsity football games to solemnize the event, to promote good sportsmanship and student safety, and to establish the appropriate environment for the competition.

"Upon advice and direction of the high school principal, each spring, the high school student council shall conduct an election, by the high school student body, by secret ballot, to determine whether such a statement or invocation will be a part of the pre-game ceremonies and if so, shall elect a student, from a list of student volunteers, to deliver the statement or invocation. The student volunteer who is selected by his or her classmates may decide what message and/or invocation to deliver, consistent with the goals and purposes of this policy.

"If the District is enjoined by a court order from the enforcement of this policy, then and only then will the following policy automatically become the applicable policy of the school district.

We granted the District's petition for certiorari, limited to the following question: "Whether petitioner's policy permitting student-led, student-initiated prayer at football games violates the Establishment Clause." We conclude, as did the Court of Appeals, that it does.

II

* * * In *Lee v. Weisman,* we held that a prayer delivered by a rabbi at a middle school graduation ceremony violated that Clause. Although this case involves student prayer at a different type of school function, our analysis is properly guided by the principles that we endorsed in *Lee.*

As we held in that case:

"The principle that government may accommodate the free exercise of religion does not supersede the fundamental limitations imposed by the Establishment Clause. It is beyond dispute that, at a minimum, the Constitution guarantees that government may not coerce anyone to support or participate in religion or its exercise, or otherwise act in a way which 'establishes a [state] religion or religious faith, or tends to do so.' " *Id.* (citations omitted) (quoting *Lynch v. Donnelly,* 465 U.S. 668, 678, 104 S.Ct. 1355, 79 L.Ed.2d 604 (1984)).

In this case the District first argues that this principle is inapplicable to its October policy because the messages are private student speech, not public speech. It reminds us that "there is a crucial difference between *government* speech endorsing religion, which the Establishment Clause forbids, and *private* speech endorsing religion, which the Free Speech and Free Exercise Clauses protect." *Board of Ed. of Westside Community Schools (Dist.66) v. Mergens,* 496 U.S. 226, 250, 110 S.Ct. 2356, 110 L.Ed.2d 191 (1990) (opinion of O'Connor, J.). We certainly agree with that distinction, but we are not persuaded that the pregame invocations should be regarded as "private speech."

These invocations are authorized by a government policy and take place on government property at government-sponsored school-related events. Of course, not every message delivered under such circumstances is the government's own. We have held, for example, that an individual's contribution to a government-created forum was not government speech. See *Rosenberger v. Rector and Visitors of Univ. of Va.,* 515 U.S. 819, 115

"The board has chosen to permit students to deliver a brief invocation and/or message to be delivered during the pregame ceremonies of home varsity football games to solemnize the event, to promote good sportsmanship and student safety, and to establish the appropriate environment for the competition.

"Upon advice and direction of the high school principal, each spring, the high school student council shall conduct an election, by the high school student body, by secret ballot, to determine whether such a message or invocation will be a part of the pre-game ceremonies and if so, shall elect a student, from a list of student volunteers, to deliver the statement or invocation. The student volunteer who is selected by his or her classmates may decide what statement or invocation to deliver, consistent with the goals and purposes of this policy. Any message and/or invocation delivered by a student must be nonsectarian and nonproselytizing."

S.Ct. 2510, 132 L.Ed.2d 700 (1995). Although the District relies heavily on *Rosenberger* and similar cases involving such forums, it is clear that the pregame ceremony is not the type of forum discussed in those cases.[13] The Santa Fe school officials simply do not "evince either 'by policy or by practice,' any intent to open the [pregame ceremony] to 'indiscriminate use,' . . . by the student body generally." *Hazelwood School Dist. v. Kuhlmeier,* 484 U.S. 260, 270, 108 S.Ct. 562, 98 L.Ed.2d 592 (1988) * * *. Rather, the school allows only one student, the same student for the entire season, to give the invocation. The statement or invocation, moreover, is subject to particular regulations that confine the content and topic of the student's message. * * *

Granting only one student access to the stage at a time does not, of course, necessarily preclude a finding that a school has created a limited public forum. Here, however, Santa Fe's student election system ensures that only those messages deemed "appropriate" under the District's policy may be delivered. That is, the majoritarian process implemented by the District guarantees, by definition, that minority candidates will never prevail and that their views will be effectively silenced.

* * *

[T]his student election does nothing to protect minority views but rather places the students who hold such views at the mercy of the majority.[15] Because "fundamental rights may not be submitted to vote; they depend on the outcome of no elections," *West Virginia Bd. of Ed. v. Barnette,* 319 U.S. 624, 638, 63 S.Ct. 1178, 87 L.Ed. 1628 (1943), the District's elections are insufficient safeguards of diverse student speech.

* * *

Moreover, the District has failed to divorce itself from the religious content in the invocations. It has not succeeded in doing so, either by claiming that its policy is " 'one of neutrality rather than endorsement' " or by characterizing the individual student as the "circuit-breaker" in the process. Contrary to the District's repeated assertions that it has adopted a "hands-off" approach to the pregame invocation, the realities of the situation plainly reveal that its policy involves both perceived and actual endorsement of religion. In this case, as we found in *Lee,* the "degree of school involvement" makes it clear that the pregame prayers

13. A conclusion that the District had created a public forum would help shed light on whether the resulting speech is public or private, but we also note that we have never held the mere creation of a public forum shields the government entity from scrutiny under the Establishment Clause. * * *

15. If instead of a choice between an invocation and no pregame message, the first election determined whether a political speech should be made, and the second election determined whether the speaker should be a Democrat or a Republican, it would be rather clear that the public address system was being used to deliver a partisan message reflecting the viewpoint of the majority rather than a random statement by a private individual.

The fact that the District's policy provides for the election of the speaker only after the majority has voted on her message identifies an obvious distinction between this case and the typical election of a "student body president, or even a newly elected prom king or queen."

bear "the imprint of the State and thus put school-age children who objected in an untenable position."

The District has attempted to disentangle itself from the religious messages by developing the two-step student election process. The text of the October policy, however, exposes the extent of the school's entanglement. The elections take place at all only because the school "board *has chosen to permit* students to deliver a brief invocation and/or message." The elections thus "shall" be conducted "by the high school student council" and "[u]pon advice and direction of the high school principal." The decision whether to deliver a message is first made by majority vote of the entire student body, followed by a choice of the speaker in a separate, similar majority election. Even though the particular words used by the speaker are not determined by those votes, the policy mandates that the "statement or invocation" be "consistent with the goals and purposes of this policy," which are "to solemnize the event, to promote good sportsmanship and student safety, and to establish the appropriate environment for the competition."

In addition to involving the school in the selection of the speaker, the policy, by its terms, invites and encourages religious messages. The policy itself states that the purpose of the message is "to solemnize the event." A religious message is the most obvious method of solemnizing an event. Moreover, the requirements that the message "promote good sportsmanship" and "establish the appropriate environment for competition" further narrow the types of message deemed appropriate, suggesting that a solemn, yet nonreligious, message, such as commentary on United States foreign policy, would be prohibited. Indeed, the only type of message that is expressly endorsed in the text is an "invocation"—a term that primarily describes an appeal for divine assistance. In fact, as used in the past at Santa Fe High School, an "invocation" has always entailed a focused religious message. Thus, the expressed purposes of the policy encourage the selection of a religious message, and that is precisely how the students understand the policy. The results of the elections described in the parties' stipulation make it clear that the students understood that the central question before them was whether prayer should be a part of the pregame ceremony. * * *

The actual or perceived endorsement of the message, moreover, is established by factors beyond just the text of the policy. Once the student speaker is selected and the message composed, the invocation is then delivered to a large audience assembled as part of a regularly scheduled, school-sponsored function conducted on school property. The message is broadcast over the school's public address system, which remains subject to the control of school officials. It is fair to assume that the pregame ceremony is clothed in the traditional indicia of school sporting events, which generally include not just the team, but also cheerleaders and band members dressed in uniforms sporting the school name and mascot. The school's name is likely written in large print across the field and on banners and flags. The crowd will certainly include many who display the school colors and insignia on their school

T-shirts, jackets, or hats and who may also be waving signs displaying the school name. It is in a setting such as this that "[t]he board has chosen to permit" the elected student to rise and give the "statement or invocation."

In this context the members of the listening audience must perceive the pregame message as a public expression of the views of the majority of the student body delivered with the approval of the school administration. In cases involving state participation in a religious activity, one of the relevant questions is "whether an objective observer, acquainted with the text, legislative history, and implementation of the statute, would perceive it as a state endorsement of prayer in public schools." *Wallace,* 472 U.S., at 73, 76, 105 S.Ct. 2479 (O'Connor, J., concurring in judgment) * * *. Regardless of the listener's support for, or objection to, the message, an objective Santa Fe High School student will unquestionably perceive the inevitable pregame prayer as stamped with her school's seal of approval.

The text and history of this policy, moreover, reinforce our objective student's perception that the prayer is, in actuality, encouraged by the school. When a governmental entity professes a secular purpose for an arguably religious policy, the government's characterization is, of course, entitled to some deference. But it is nonetheless the duty of the courts to "distinguis[h] a sham secular purpose from a sincere one."

According to the District, the secular purposes of the policy are to "foste[r] free expression of private persons . . . as well [as to] solemniz[e] sporting events, promot[e] good sportsmanship and student safety, and establis[h] an appropriate environment for competition." We note, however, that the District's approval of only one specific kind of message, an "invocation," is not necessary to further any of these purposes. Additionally, the fact that only one student is permitted to give a content-limited message suggests that this policy does little to "foste[r] free expression." Furthermore, regardless of whether one considers a sporting event an appropriate occasion for solemnity, the use of an invocation to foster such solemnity is impermissible when, in actuality, it constitutes prayer sponsored by the school. And it is unclear what type of message would be both appropriately "solemnizing" under the District's policy and yet nonreligious.

Most striking to us is the evolution of the current policy from the long-sanctioned office of "Student Chaplain" to the candidly titled "Prayer at Football Games" regulation. This history indicates that the District intended to preserve the practice of prayer before football games. The conclusion that the District viewed the October policy simply as a continuation of the previous policies is dramatically illustrated by the fact that the school did not conduct a new election, pursuant to the current policy, to replace the results of the previous election, which occurred under the former policy. Given these observations, and in light of the school's history of regular delivery of a student-led prayer at athletic events, it is reasonable to infer that the specific purpose of the policy was to preserve a popular "state-sponsored religious practice."

School sponsorship of a religious message is impermissible because it sends the ancillary message to members of the audience who are nonadherents "that they are outsiders, not full members of the political community, and an accompanying message to adherents that they are insiders, favored members of the political community." *Lynch,* 465 U.S., at 688, 104 S.Ct. 1355 (O'Connor, J., concurring). The delivery of such a message—over the school's public address system, by a speaker representing the student body, under the supervision of school faculty, and pursuant to a school policy that explicitly and implicitly encourages public prayer—is not properly characterized as "private" speech.

III

The District next argues that its football policy is distinguishable from the graduation prayer in *Lee* because it does not coerce students to participate in religious observances. Its argument has two parts: first, that there is no impermissible government coercion because the pregame messages are the product of student choices; and second, that there is really no coercion at all because attendance at an extracurricular event, unlike a graduation ceremony, is voluntary.

The reasons just discussed explaining why the alleged "circuit-breaker" mechanism of the dual elections and student speaker do not turn public speech into private speech also demonstrate why these mechanisms do not insulate the school from the coercive element of the final message. In fact, this aspect of the District's argument exposes anew the concerns that are created by the majoritarian election system. The parties' stipulation clearly states that the issue resolved in the first election was "whether a student would deliver prayer at varsity football games," and the controversy in this case demonstrates that the views of the students are not unanimous on that issue.

One of the purposes served by the Establishment Clause is to remove debate over this kind of issue from governmental supervision or control. We explained in *Lee* that the "preservation and transmission of religious beliefs and worship is a responsibility and a choice committed to the private sphere." The two student elections authorized by the policy, coupled with the debates that presumably must precede each, impermissibly invade that private sphere. The election mechanism, when considered in light of the history in which the policy in question evolved, reflects a device the District put in place that determines whether religious messages will be delivered at home football games. The mechanism encourages divisiveness along religious lines in a public school setting, a result at odds with the Establishment Clause. Although it is true that the ultimate choice of student speaker is "attributable to the students," the District's decision to hold the constitutionally problematic election is clearly "a choice attributable to the State," *Lee,* 505 U.S., at 587, 112 S.Ct. 2649.

The District further argues that attendance at the commencement ceremonies at issue in *Lee* "differs dramatically" from attendance at high school football games, which it contends "are of no more than passing interest to many students" and are "decidedly extracurricular," thus dissipating any coercion. Attendance at a high school football game, unlike showing up for class, is certainly not required in order to receive a diploma. * * *

There are some students, however, such as cheerleaders, members of the band, and, of course, the team members themselves, for whom seasonal commitments mandate their attendance, sometimes for class credit. The District also minimizes the importance to many students of attending and participating in extracurricular activities as part of a complete educational experience. As we noted in *Lee*, "[l]aw reaches past formalism." To assert that high school students do not feel immense social pressure, or have a truly genuine desire, to be involved in the extracurricular event that is American high school football is "formalistic in the extreme." We stressed in *Lee* the obvious observation that "adolescents are often susceptible to pressure from their peers towards conformity, and that the influence is strongest in matters of social convention." High school home football games are traditional gatherings of a school community; they bring together students and faculty as well as friends and family from years present and past to root for a common cause. Undoubtedly, the games are not important to some students, and they voluntarily choose not to attend. For many others, however, the choice between attending these games and avoiding personally offensive religious rituals is in no practical sense an easy one. The Constitution, moreover, demands that the school may not force this difficult choice upon these students for "[i]t is a tenet of the First Amendment that the State cannot require one of its citizens to forfeit his or her rights and benefits as the price of resisting conformance to state-sponsored religious practice."

Even if we regard every high school student's decision to attend a home football game as purely voluntary, we are nevertheless persuaded that the delivery of a pregame prayer has the improper effect of coercing those present to participate in an act of religious worship. For "the government may no more use social pressure to enforce orthodoxy than it may use more direct means." * * *

The Religion Clauses of the First Amendment prevent the government from making any law respecting the establishment of religion or prohibiting the free exercise thereof. By no means do these commands impose a prohibition on all religious activity in our public schools. Indeed, the common purpose of the Religion Clauses "is to secure religious liberty." Thus, nothing in the Constitution as interpreted by this Court prohibits any public school student from voluntarily praying at any time before, during, or after the schoolday. But the religious liberty protected by the Constitution is abridged when the State affirmatively sponsors the particular religious practice of prayer.

IV

Finally, the District argues repeatedly that the Does have made a premature facial challenge to the October policy that necessarily must fail. The District emphasizes, quite correctly, that until a student actually delivers a solemnizing message under the latest version of the policy, there can be no certainty that any of the statements or invocations will be religious. Thus, it concludes, the October policy necessarily survives a facial challenge.

This argument, however, assumes that we are concerned only with the serious constitutional injury that occurs when a student is forced to participate in an act of religious worship because she chooses to attend a school event. But the Constitution also requires that we keep in mind "the myriad, subtle ways in which Establishment Clause values can be eroded," *Lynch,* 465 U.S., at 694, 104 S.Ct. 1355 (O'Connor, J., concurring), and that we guard against other different, yet equally important, constitutional injuries. One is the mere passage by the District of a policy that has the purpose and perception of government establishment of religion. Another is the implementation of a governmental electoral process that subjects the issue of prayer to a majoritarian vote.

The District argues that the facial challenge must fail because "Santa Fe's Football Policy cannot be invalidated on the basis of some 'possibility or even likelihood' of an unconstitutional application." Our Establishment Clause cases involving facial challenges, however, have not focused solely on the possible applications of the statute, but rather have considered whether the statute has an unconstitutional purpose. * * * [In the context of facial challenges] we assess the constitutionality of an enactment by reference to the three factors first articulated in *Lemon v. Kurtzman,* 403 U.S. 602, 612, 91 S.Ct. 2105, 29 L.Ed.2d 745 (1971) * * *. Under the *Lemon* standard, a court must invalidate a statute if it lacks "a secular legislative purpose." It is therefore proper, as part of this facial challenge, for us to examine the purpose of the October policy.

As discussed, the text of the October policy alone reveals that it has an unconstitutional purpose. The plain language of the policy clearly spells out the extent of school involvement in both the election of the speaker and the content of the message. Additionally, the text of the October policy specifies only one, clearly preferred message—that of Santa Fe's traditional religious "invocation." Finally, the extremely selective access of the policy and other content restrictions confirm that it is not a content-neutral regulation that creates a limited public forum for the expression of student speech. * * *

* * *

The District, nevertheless, asks us to pretend that we do not recognize what every Santa Fe High School student understands clearly—that this policy is about prayer. The District further asks us to accept what is obviously untrue: that these messages are necessary to "solemnize" a football game and that this single-student, year-long position is essential to the protection of student speech. We refuse to turn a blind eye to the context in which this policy arose, and that context quells any doubt that this policy was implemented with the purpose of endorsing school prayer.

Therefore, the simple enactment of this policy, with the purpose and perception of school endorsement of student prayer, was a constitutional violation. We need not wait for the inevitable to confirm and magnify the constitutional injury. * * * Government efforts to endorse religion cannot evade constitutional reproach based solely on the remote possibility that those attempts may fail.

This policy likewise does not survive a facial challenge because it impermissibly imposes upon the student body a majoritarian election on the issue of prayer. Through its election scheme, the District has established a governmental electoral mechanism that turns the school into a forum for religious debate. It further empowers the student body majority with the authority to subject students of minority views to constitutionally improper messages. The award of that power alone, regardless of the students' ultimate use of it, is not acceptable.[23] * * * Such a system encourages divisiveness along religious lines and threatens the imposition of coercion upon those students not desiring to participate in a religious exercise. Simply by establishing this school-related procedure, which entrusts the inherently nongovernmental subject of religion to a majoritarian vote, a constitutional violation has occurred. No further injury is required for the policy to fail a facial challenge.

* * * The policy is invalid on its face because it establishes an improper majoritarian election on religion, and unquestionably has the purpose and creates the perception of encouraging the delivery of prayer at a series of important school events.

The judgment of the Court of Appeals is, accordingly, affirmed.

CHIEF JUSTICE REHNQUIST, with whom JUSTICE SCALIA and JUSTICE THOMAS join, dissenting.

The Court distorts existing precedent to conclude that the school district's student-message program is invalid on its face under the Establishment Clause. But even more disturbing than its holding is the tone of the Court's opinion; it bristles with hostility to all things religious in public life. Neither the holding nor the tone of the opinion is faithful to the meaning of the Establishment Clause * * *.

We do not learn until late in the Court's opinion that respondents in this case challenged the district's student-message program at football

---

23. The Chief Justice accuses us of "essentially invalidat[ing] all student elections." This is obvious hyperbole. We have concluded that the resulting religious message under this policy would be attributable to the school, not just the student. For this reason, we now hold only that the District's decision to allow the student majority to control whether students of minority views are subjected to a school-sponsored prayer violates the Establishment Clause.

games before it had been put into practice. * * * Therefore, the question is not whether the district's policy *may be* applied in violation of the Establishment Clause, but whether it inevitably will be.

The Court, venturing into the realm of prophecy, decides that it "need not wait for the inevitable" and invalidates the district's policy on its face. To do so, it applies the most rigid version of the oft-criticized test of *Lemon v. Kurtzman*.

Lemon has had a checkered career in the decisional law of this Court. * * * [I]n *Lee v. Weisman*, an opinion upon which the Court relies heavily today, we mentioned, but did not feel compelled to apply, the *Lemon* test.

Even if it were appropriate to apply the *Lemon* test here, the district's student-message policy should not be invalidated on its face. The Court applies *Lemon* and holds that the "policy is invalid on its face because it establishes an improper majoritarian election on religion, and unquestionably has the purpose and creates the perception of encouraging the delivery of prayer at a series of important school events." The Court's reliance on each of these conclusions misses the mark.

First, the Court misconstrues the nature of the "majoritarian election" permitted by the policy as being an election on "prayer" and "religion." To the contrary, the election permitted by the policy is a two-fold process whereby students vote first on whether to have a student speaker before football games at all, and second, if the students vote to have such a speaker, on who that speaker will be. It is conceivable that the election could become one in which student candidates campaign on platforms that focus on whether or not they will pray if elected. It is also conceivable that the election could lead to a Christian prayer before 90 percent of the football games. If, upon implementation, the policy operated in this fashion, we would have a record before us to review whether the policy, as applied, violated the Establishment Clause or unduly suppressed minority viewpoints. But it is possible that the students might vote not to have a pregame speaker, in which case there would be no threat of a constitutional violation. It is also possible that the election would not focus on prayer, but on public speaking ability or social popularity. And if student campaigning did begin to focus on prayer, the school might decide to implement reasonable campaign restrictions.

But the Court ignores these possibilities by holding that merely granting the student body the power to elect a speaker that may choose to pray, "regardless of the students' ultimate use of it, is not acceptable." The Court so holds despite that any speech that may occur as a result of the election process here would be *private,* not *government,* speech. The elected student, not the government, would choose what to say. Support for the Court's holding cannot be found in any of our cases. And it essentially invalidates all student elections. A newly elected student body president, or even a newly elected prom king or queen, could use opportunities for public speaking to say prayers. Under the Court's view, the mere grant of power to the students to vote for such offices, in light of the fear that those elected might publicly pray, violates the Establishment Clause.

Second, with respect to the policy's purpose, the Court holds that "the simple enactment of this policy, with the purpose and perception of school endorsement of student prayer, was a constitutional violation." But the policy itself has plausible secular purposes: "[T]o solemnize the event, to promote good sportsmanship and student safety, and to establish the appropriate environment for the competition." Where a governmental body "expresses a plausible secular purpose" for an enactment, "courts should generally defer to that stated intent." The Court grants no deference to—and appears openly hostile toward—the policy's stated purposes, and wastes no time in concluding that they are a sham.

For example, the Court dismisses the secular purpose of solemnization by claiming that it "invites and encourages religious messages." The Court so concludes based on its rather strange view that a "religious message is the most obvious means of solemnizing an event." But it is easy to think of solemn messages that are not religious in nature, for example urging that a game be fought fairly. * * * Although the Court apparently believes that solemnizing football games is an illegitimate purpose, the voters in the school district seem to disagree. Nothing in the Establishment Clause prevents them from making this choice.

The Court bases its conclusion that the true purpose of the policy is to endorse student prayer on its view of the school district's history of Establishment Clause violations and the context in which the policy was written, that is, as "the latest step in developing litigation brought as a challenge to institutional practices that unquestionably violated the Establishment Clause." But the context—attempted compliance with a District Court order—actually demonstrates that the school district was acting diligently to come within the governing constitutional law. * * * Thus, the policy cannot be viewed as having a sectarian purpose.

The Court also relies on our decision in *Lee v. Weisman*, to support its conclusion. In *Lee,* we concluded that the content of the speech at issue * * * was "directed and controlled" by a school official. In other words, at issue in *Lee* was *government* speech. Here, by contrast, the potential speech at issue, if the policy had been allowed to proceed, would be a message or invocation selected or created by a student. That is, if there were speech at issue here, it would be *private* speech. The "crucial difference between *government* speech endorsing religion, which the Establishment Clause forbids, and *private* speech endorsing religion, which the Free Speech and Free Exercise Clauses protect," applies with particular force to the question of endorsement.

* * *

Finally, the Court seems to demand that a government policy be completely neutral as to content or be considered one that endorses religion. This is undoubtedly a new requirement, as our Establishment Clause jurisprudence simply does not mandate "content neutrality."

That concept is found in our First Amendment *speech* cases and is used as a guide for determining when we apply strict scrutiny. * * *

* * * [E]ven our speech jurisprudence would not require that all public school actions with respect to student speech be content neutral. Schools do not violate the First Amendment every time they restrict student speech to certain categories. * * *

The policy at issue here may be applied in an unconstitutional manner, but it will be time enough to invalidate it if that is found to be the case. I would reverse the judgment of the Court of Appeals.

Notes and Questions

1. *Free Speech or Endorsement?* The Court rejected the school district's free speech arguments. Did the Court do so on free speech grounds or establishment grounds? It would seem that the Court considered both, although the Court was not explicit regarding the connection. The Court notes that football games are not generally public fora or limited public fora for speech (and neither is the time allotted for prayer before games), and thus there is no real opportunity for counterspeech. If this is so the prayer is occurring in a closed forum for speech purposes, and the likelihood that the "private" speech will be attributed to the government or that the government will be perceived as endorsing the speech is much greater. Thus, when one considers public forum doctrine in regard to "student-initiated prayer" at school sponsored or endorsed events, it would seem that the free speech rationale for such prayer becomes much weaker. In fact, under policies like Santa Fe's, only the majority's speech interests will be protected in any given year. This places the district in a lose-lose situation because if the football game or prayer slot were a public forum or limited public forum, the school might be favoring the speech of the majority of students and squelching the speech rights of those who disagree—a seemingly obvious free speech violation, and if it is a closed forum the possibility that the school is endorsing or even sponsoring the prayer raises serious concerns under the Establishment Clause.

2. *Tests, Tests, and More Tests.* The Majority utilizes the endorsement, coercion, and *Lemon* tests in various parts of the opinion. Does this mean that all three tests must be applied in the school prayer context? Should they be? Is there any distinction between the contexts in which the various tests were applied?

3. *Lemon or Lemonade?* As you will see in Chapter Four, the Supreme Court has dramatically altered the *Lemon* test in the government funding context. In *Agostini v. Felton*, the Court rolled the entanglement prong of *Lemon* into the effects prong and eliminated the divisiveness factor. In later cases, such as *Zelman v. Simmons–Harris*, the Court essentially used a test of facial neutrality plus private choice (explained in Chapter Four) that minimizes the effects analysis under the *Lemon* test in situations where the government is not providing "direct aid" to religious organizations. Yet in *Santa Fe*, the majority opinion suggests that all three prongs of the *Lemon* test are applicable when there is a facial challenge to a government policy. Is it possible that *Lemon* is essentially dead in the aid context, but that it still applies, at least to facial challenges, in cases involving government supported religious exercises? If so, what, if anything, is the distinction that justifies this differing treatment in the two contexts?

4. *Endorsement and Coercion.* The Majority applies both the endorsement and indirect coercion tests and much of the analysis under one test supports the conclusion under the other. What is the practical distinction between the two approaches in school prayer cases? Is there any distinction other than the surface differences between the tests? Would the choice of test make a difference in religious exercise cases other than school prayer cases?

5. *Is Clear Creek justifiable?* After reading *Lee*, *Santa Fe*, and *Black Horse Pike* can the *Jones v. Clear Creek* decision be justified as anything other than judicial activism? Would it make a difference if the *Jones* court made a reasonable point as a matter of first principles? Is there any merit to the free speech and solemnization arguments in *Clear Creek*? If the *Jones* court felt that the relevant Supreme Court precedent was itself activist and/or confusing, how should it have proceeded? Would your answers be the same if other panels of the 5th Circuit Court of Appeals tried to distinguish and limit the *Jones* decision? The 5th Circuit Court of Appeals panel that decided *Santa Fe* did so. *See Doe v. Santa Fe Independent School Dist.*, 168 F.3d 806 (5th Cir.1999).

6. *The de minimis argument.* What is the harm in having a brief non-proselytizing nonsectarian prayer delivered by a student at a graduation ceremony or football game? Would the harm from such a religious exercise be only *de minimis*? Can a constitutional violation ever be *de minimis*?

7. *The "tradition" argument.* The dissenting opinions in *Santa Fe* and *Lee* argue that graduation prayer is part of a long tradition of ceremonial deism in American public life, a tradition that was alive and well at the time of the framers of the Constitution and the framers of the 14th Amendment. Thus, to find such activities unconstitutional is to misread the meaning of the Establishment Clause. Does the longstanding nature of a tradition that is alleged to be unconstitutional suggest that it is in fact constitutional? If so, what about the longstanding tradition of segregation? Or is there something different about school prayer? Does the fact that the tradition of school prayer is connected to a broader tradition of ceremonial deism make a difference? Or is it simply that until there were an adequate number of religious minorities and dissenters to object to such "traditions," the will of the majority maintained them? Can the will of a majority dictate constitutional rights? Should it?

8. *Other Religious Exercises.* What do the cases in this section and the preceding section suggest about the constitutionality of moment of silence laws? State laws requiring the recitation of the Pledge of Allegiance in public school classrooms? These issues will be explored in greater detail in the following sections, but for now consider how the Court might decide such issues in light of the school prayer decisions.

3. Moments of Silence

There are numerous "moment of silence" laws around the country. Naturally, the question arises as to whether they are constitutional. In 1985, the Supreme Court addressed this issue and held that such laws can be constitutional, but that the Alabama law in question was not. Read on to find out why.

WALLACE v. JAFFREE

Supreme Court of the United States, 1985.
472 U.S. 38, 105 S.Ct. 2479, 86 L.Ed.2d 29.

JUSTICE STEVENS delivered the opinion of the Court.

At an early stage of this litigation, the constitutionality of three Alabama statutes was questioned: (1) § 16–1–20, enacted in 1978, which authorized a 1–minute period of silence in all public schools "for meditation"; (2) § 16–1–20.1, enacted in 1981, which authorized a period of silence "for meditation or voluntary prayer";[2] and (3) § 16–1–20.2, enacted in 1982, which authorized teachers to lead "willing students" in a prescribed prayer to "Almighty God ... the Creator and Supreme Judge of the world."

* * *

* * * [T]he narrow question for decision is whether § 16–1–20.1, which authorizes a period of silence for "meditation or voluntary prayer," is a law respecting the establishment of religion within the meaning of the First Amendment.

I

Appellee Ishmael Jaffree is a resident of Mobile County, Alabama. On May 28, 1982, he filed a complaint on behalf of three of his minor children; two of them were second-grade students and the third was then in kindergarten. * * * [The plaintiffs sought] a declaratory judgment and an injunction restraining the Defendants * * * from maintaining or allowing the maintenance of regular religious prayer services or other forms of religious observances in the Mobile County Public Schools in violation of the First Amendment * * *.

* * *

On August 2, 1982, the District Court held an evidentiary hearing on appellees' motion for a preliminary injunction. At that hearing, State Senator Donald G. Holmes testified that he was the "prime sponsor" of the bill that was enacted in 1981 as § 16–1–20.1. He explained that the bill was an "effort to return voluntary prayer to our public schools ... it is a beginning and a step in the right direction." Apart from the purpose to return voluntary prayer to public school, Senator Holmes unequivocally testified that he had "no other purpose in mind." * * *

* * *

2. Alabama Code § 16–1–20.1 (Supp. 1984) provides:

"At the commencement of the first class of each day in all grades in all public schools the teacher in charge of the room in which each class is held may announce that a period of silence not to exceed one minute in duration shall be observed for meditation or voluntary prayer, and during any such period no other activities shall be engaged in."

* * * The District Court found that during that academic year each of the minor plaintiffs' teachers had led classes in prayer activities, even after being informed of appellees' objections to these activities.

In its lengthy conclusions of law, the District Court reviewed a number of opinions of this Court interpreting the Establishment Clause of the First Amendment, and then embarked on a fresh examination of the question whether the First Amendment imposes any barrier to the establishment of an official religion by the State of Alabama. After reviewing at length what it perceived to be newly discovered historical evidence, the District Court concluded that "the establishment clause of the first amendment to the United States Constitution does not prohibit the state from establishing a religion." * * *

The Court of Appeals * * * reversed. The Court of Appeals noted that this Court had considered and had rejected the historical arguments that the District Court found persuasive, and that the District Court had misapplied the doctrine of *stare decisis.* * * *

II

Our unanimous affirmance of the Court of Appeals' judgment concerning § 16–1–20.2 [See *Wallace v. Jaffree,* 466 U.S. 924, 104 S.Ct. 1704, 80 L.Ed.2d 178 (1984)] makes it unnecessary to comment at length on the District Court's remarkable conclusion that the Federal Constitution imposes no obstacle to Alabama's establishment of a state religion. * * *

* * *

* * * [W]hen the Constitution was amended to prohibit any State from depriving any person of liberty without due process of law, that Amendment imposed the same substantive limitations on the States' power to legislate that the First Amendment had always imposed on the Congress' power. This Court has confirmed and endorsed this elementary proposition of law time and time again.

* * *

The State of Alabama, no less than the Congress of the United States, must respect that basic truth.

III

When the Court has been called upon to construe the breadth of the Establishment Clause, it has examined the criteria developed over a period of many years. Thus, in *Lemon v. Kurtzman*, we wrote:

"Every analysis in this area must begin with consideration of the cumulative criteria developed by the Court over many years. Three such tests may be gleaned from our cases. First, the statute must have a secular legislative purpose; second, its principal or primary effect must be one that neither advances nor inhibits religion, finally, the statute must not foster an excessive government entanglement with religion."

It is the first of these three criteria that is most plainly implicated by this case. As the District Court correctly recognized, no consideration of the second or third criteria is necessary if a statute does not have a clearly secular purpose. For even though a statute that is motivated in part by a religious purpose may satisfy the first criterion, the First Amendment requires that a statute must be invalidated if it is entirely motivated by a purpose to advance religion.

In applying the purpose test, it is appropriate to ask "whether government's actual purpose is to endorse or disapprove of religion." In this case, the answer to that question is dispositive. For the record not only provides us with an unambiguous affirmative answer, but it also reveals that the enactment of § 16–1–20.1 was not motivated by any clearly secular purpose—indeed, the statute had *no* secular purpose.

IV

The sponsor of the bill that became § 16–1–20.1, Senator Donald Holmes, inserted into the legislative record—apparently without dissent—a statement indicating that the legislation was an "effort to return voluntary prayer" to the public schools.[43] Later Senator Holmes confirmed this purpose before the District Court. In response to the question whether he had any purpose for the legislation other than returning voluntary prayer to public schools, he stated: "No, I did not have no other purpose in mind."[44] The State did not present evidence of *any* secular purpose.[45]

---

43. The statement indicated, in pertinent part:

"Gentlemen, by passage of this bill by the Alabama Legislature our children in this state will have the opportunity of sharing in the spiritual heritage of this state and this country. The United States as well as the State of Alabama was founded by people who believe in God. *I believe this effort to return voluntary prayer* to our public schools for its return to us to the original position of the writers of the Constitution, this local philosophies and beliefs hundreds of Alabamians have urged my continuous support for permitting school prayer. Since coming to the Alabama Senate I have worked hard *on this legislation to accomplish the return of voluntary prayer in our public schools and return to the basic moral fiber.*"

44. The District Court and the Court of Appeals agreed that the purpose of § 16–1–20.1 was "an effort on the part of the State of Alabama to encourage a religious activity." *Jaffree v. James,* 544 F.Supp., at 732; 705 F.2d, at 1535. The evidence presented to the District Court elaborated on the ex-

press admission of the Governor of Alabama (then Fob James) that the enactment of § 16–1–20.1 was intended to "clarify [the State's] intent to have prayer as part of the daily classroom activity," and that the "expressed legislative purpose in enacting Section 16–1–20.1 (1981) was to 'return voluntary prayer to public schools.'" * * *

45. Appellant Governor George C. Wallace now argues that § 16–1–20.1 "is best understood as a permissible accommodation of religion" and that viewed even in terms of the *Lemon* test, the "statute conforms to acceptable constitutional criteria." These arguments seem to be based on the theory that the free exercise of religion of some of the State's citizens was burdened before the statute was enacted. The United States, appearing as *amicus curiae* in support of the appellants, candidly acknowledges that "it is unlikely that in most contexts a strong Free Exercise claim could be made that time for personal prayer must be set aside during the school day." There is no basis for the suggestion that § 16–1–20.1 "is a means for accommodating the religious and meditative needs of students

The unrebutted evidence of legislative intent contained in the legislative record and in the testimony of the sponsor of § 16–1–20.1 is confirmed by a consideration of the relationship between this statute and the two other measures that were considered in this case. The District Court found that the 1981 statute and its 1982 sequel had a common, nonsecular purpose. The wholly religious character of the later enactment is plainly evident from its text. When the differences between § 16–1–20.1 and its 1978 predecessor, § 16–1–20, are examined, it is equally clear that the 1981 statute has the same wholly religious character.

There are only three textual differences between § 16–1–20.1 and § 16–1–20: (1) the earlier statute applies only to grades one through six, whereas § 16–1–20.1 applies to all grades; (2) the earlier statute uses the word "shall" whereas § 16–1–20.1 uses the word "may"; (3) the earlier statute refers only to "meditation" whereas § 16–1–20.1 refers to "meditation or voluntary prayer." The first difference is of no relevance in this litigation because the minor appellees were in kindergarten or second grade during the 1981–1982 academic year. The second difference would also have no impact on this litigation because the mandatory language of § 16–1–20 continued to apply to grades one through six. Thus, the only significant textual difference is the addition of the words "or voluntary prayer."

The legislative intent to return prayer to the public schools is, of course, quite different from merely protecting every student's right to engage in voluntary prayer during an appropriate moment of silence during the schoolday. The 1978 statute already protected that right, containing nothing that prevented any student from engaging in voluntary prayer during a silent minute of meditation. Appellants have not identified any secular purpose that was not fully served by § 16–1–20 before the enactment of § 16–1–20.1. Thus, only two conclusions are consistent with the text of § 16–1–20.1: (1) the statute was enacted to convey a message of state endorsement and promotion of prayer; or (2) the statute was enacted for no purpose. No one suggests that the statute was nothing but a meaningless or irrational act.

We must, therefore, conclude that the Alabama Legislature intended to change existing law and that it was motivated by the same purpose that the Governor's answer to the second amended complaint expressly admitted; that the statement inserted in the legislative history revealed; and that Senator Holmes' testimony frankly described. The legislature enacted § 16–1–20.1, despite the existence of § 16–1–20 for the sole

without in any way diminishing the school's own neutrality or secular atmosphere." In this case, it is undisputed that at the time of the enactment of § 16–1–20.1 there was no governmental practice impeding students from silently praying for one minute at the beginning of each schoolday; thus, there was no need to "accommodate" or to exempt individuals from any general gov-ernmental requirement because of the dictates of our cases interpreting the Free Exercise Clause. * * * What was missing in the appellants' eyes at the time of the enactment of § 16–1–20.1—and therefore what is precisely the aspect that makes the statute unconstitutional—was the State's endorsement and promotion of religion and a particular religious practice.

purpose of expressing the State's endorsement of prayer activities for one minute at the beginning of each schoolday. The addition of "or voluntary prayer" indicates that the State intended to characterize prayer as a favored practice. Such an endorsement is not consistent with the established principle that the government must pursue a course of complete neutrality toward religion.

The importance of that principle does not permit us to treat this as an inconsequential case involving nothing more than a few words of symbolic speech on behalf of the political majority. For whenever the State itself speaks on a religious subject, one of the questions that we must ask is "whether the government intends to convey a message of endorsement or disapproval of religion." The well-supported concurrent findings of the District Court and the Court of Appeals—that § 16–1–20.1 was intended to convey a message of state approval of prayer activities in the public schools—make it unnecessary, and indeed inappropriate, to evaluate the practical significance of the addition of the words "or voluntary prayer" to the statute. Keeping in mind, as we must, "both the fundamental place held by the Establishment Clause in our constitutional scheme and the myriad, subtle ways in which Establishment Clause values can be eroded," we conclude that § 16–1–20.1 violates the First Amendment.

The judgment of the Court of Appeals is affirmed.

JUSTICE POWELL, concurring.

I concur in the Court's opinion and judgment that Ala.Code § 16–1–20.1 violates the Establishment Clause of the First Amendment. My concurrence is prompted by Alabama's persistence in attempting to institute state-sponsored prayer in the public schools by enacting three successive statutes. I agree fully with Justice O'Connor's assertion that some moment-of-silence statutes may be constitutional, a suggestion set forth in the Court's opinion as well.

I write separately to express additional views and to respond to criticism of the three-pronged *Lemon* test. *Lemon v. Kurtzman*, identifies standards that have proved useful in analyzing case after case both in our decisions and in those of other courts. It is the only coherent test a majority of the Court has ever adopted. Only once since our decision in *Lemon,* have we addressed an Establishment Clause issue without resort to its three-pronged test. See *Marsh v. Chambers*, 463 U.S. 783, 103 S.Ct. 3330, 77 L.Ed.2d 1019 (1983). *Lemon,* has not been overruled or its test modified. Yet, continued criticism of it could encourage other courts to feel free to decide Establishment Clause cases on an ad hoc basis.

* * *

I would vote to uphold the Alabama statute if it also had a clear secular purpose. * * * Nothing in the record before us, however, identifies a clear secular purpose, and the State also has failed to identify any nonreligious reason for the statute's enactment. Under these circumstances, the Court is required by our precedents to hold that the statute fails the first prong of the *Lemon* test and therefore violates the Establishment Clause.

Although we do not reach the other two prongs of the *Lemon* test, I note that the "effect" of a straightforward moment-of-silence statute is unlikely to "advanc[e] or inhibi[t] religion." Nor would such a statute "foster 'an excessive government entanglement with religion.' "

I join the opinion and judgment of the Court.

JUSTICE O'CONNOR, concurring in the judgment.

Nothing in the United States Constitution as interpreted by this Court or in the laws of the State of Alabama prohibits public school students from voluntarily praying at any time before, during, or after the school day. Alabama has facilitated voluntary silent prayers of students who are so inclined by enacting Ala.Code § 16–1–20, which provides a moment of silence in appellees' schools each day. The parties to these proceedings concede the validity of this enactment. At issue in these appeals is the constitutional validity of an additional and subsequent Alabama statute, Ala.Code § 16–1–20.1, which both the District Court and the Court of Appeals concluded was enacted solely to officially encourage prayer during the moment of silence. I agree with the judgment of the Court that, in light of the findings of the courts below and the history of its enactment, § 16–1–20.1 of the Alabama Code violates the Establishment Clause of the First Amendment. In my view, there can be little doubt that the purpose and likely effect of this subsequent enactment is to endorse and sponsor voluntary prayer in the public schools. I write separately to identify the peculiar features of the Alabama law that render it invalid, and to explain why moment of silence laws in other States do not necessarily manifest the same infirmity. * * *

I

* * *

* * * "[I]t is far easier to agree on the purpose that underlies the First Amendment's Establishment and Free Exercise Clauses than to obtain agreement on the standards that should govern their application." *Walz v. Tax Comm'n*, 397 U.S. 664, 694, 90 S.Ct. 1409, 1424, 25 L.Ed.2d 697 (1970) (opinion of Harlan, J.). It once appeared that the Court had developed a workable standard by which to identify impermissible government establishments of religion. Under the now familiar *Lemon* test, statutes must have both a secular legislative purpose and a principal or primary effect that neither advances nor inhibits religion, and in addition they must not foster excessive government entanglement with religion. Despite its initial promise, the *Lemon* test has proved problematic. * * *

Perhaps because I am new to the struggle, I am not ready to abandon all aspects of the *Lemon* test. I do believe, however, that the standards announced in *Lemon* should be reexamined and refined in order to make them more useful in achieving the underlying purpose of the First Amendment. * * * [O]ur goal should be "to frame a principle for constitutional adjudication that is not only grounded in the history and language of the first amendment, but one that is also capable of consistent application to the relevant problems." Choper, Religion in the Public Schools: A Proposed Constitutional Standard, 47 Minn.L.Rev. 329, 332–333 (1963) (footnotes omitted). Last Term, I proposed a refinement of the *Lemon* test with this goal in mind. *Lynch v. Donnelly*, 465 U.S., at 687–689, 104 S.Ct., at 1366–1367 (concurring opinion).

The *Lynch* concurrence suggested that the religious liberty protected by the Establishment Clause is infringed when the government makes adherence to religion relevant to a person's standing in the political community. Direct government action endorsing religion or a particular religious practice is invalid under this approach because it "sends a message to nonadherents that they are outsiders, not full members of the political community, and an accompanying message to adherents that they are insiders, favored members of the political community." Under this view, *Lemon*'s inquiry as to the purpose and effect of a statute requires courts to examine whether government's purpose is to endorse religion and whether the statute actually conveys a message of endorsement.

* * *

The endorsement test does not preclude government from acknowledging religion or from taking religion into account in making law and policy. It does preclude government from conveying or attempting to convey a message that religion or a particular religious belief is favored or preferred. Such an endorsement infringes the religious liberty of the nonadherent, for "[w]hen the power, prestige and financial support of government is placed behind a particular religious belief, the indirect coercive pressure upon religious minorities to conform to the prevailing officially approved religion is plain." *Engel v. Vitale*. At issue today is whether state moment of silence statutes in general, and Alabama's moment of silence statute in particular, embody an impermissible endorsement of prayer in public schools.

A

Twenty-five states permit or require public school teachers to have students observe a moment of silence in their classrooms. * * * Federal trial courts have divided on the constitutionality of these moment of silence laws. Relying on this Court's decisions disapproving vocal prayer and Bible reading in the public schools, the courts that have struck down the moment of silence statutes generally conclude that their purpose and effect are to encourage prayer in public schools.

The *Engel* and *Abington* decisions are not dispositive on the constitutionality of moment of silence laws. In those cases, public school teachers and students led their classes in devotional exercises. * * * [A] student who did not share the religious beliefs expressed in the course of the exercise was left with the choice of participating, thereby compromising the nonadherent's beliefs, or withdrawing, thereby calling attention to his or her nonconformity. The decisions acknowledged the coercion implicit under the statutory schemes, but they expressly turned only on the fact that the government was sponsoring a manifestly religious exercise.

A state-sponsored moment of silence in the public schools is different from state-sponsored vocal prayer or Bible reading. First, a moment of silence is not inherently religious. Silence, unlike prayer or Bible reading, need not be associated with a religious exercise. Second, a pupil who participates in a moment of silence need not compromise his or her beliefs. During a moment of silence, a student who objects to prayer is left to his or her own thoughts, and is not compelled to listen to the prayers or thoughts of others. For these simple reasons, a moment of silence statute does not stand or fall under the Establishment Clause according to how the Court regards vocal prayer or Bible reading. * * * It is difficult to discern a serious threat to religious liberty from a room of silent, thoughtful schoolchildren.

By mandating a moment of silence, a State does not necessarily endorse any activity that might occur during the period. Even if a statute specifies that a student may choose to pray silently during a quiet moment, the State has not thereby encouraged prayer over other specified alternatives. Nonetheless, it is also possible that a moment of silence statute, either as drafted or as actually implemented, could effectively favor the child who prays over the child who does not.

For example, the message of endorsement would seem inescapable if the teacher exhorts children to use the designated time to pray. Similarly, the face of the statute or its legislative history may clearly establish that it seeks to encourage or promote voluntary prayer over other alternatives, rather than merely provide a quiet moment that may be dedicated to prayer by those so inclined. The crucial question is whether the State has conveyed or attempted to convey the message that children should use the moment of silence for prayer. This question cannot be answered in the abstract, but instead requires courts to examine the history, language, and administration of a particular statute to determine whether it operates as an endorsement of religion.

Before reviewing Alabama's moment of silence law to determine whether it endorses prayer, some general observations on the proper scope of the inquiry are in order. First, the inquiry into the purpose of the legislature in enacting a moment of silence law should be deferential and limited. In determining whether the government intends a moment of silence statute to convey a message of endorsement or disapproval of religion, a court has no license to psychoanalyze the legislators. If a legislature expresses a plausible secular purpose for a moment of silence statute in either the text or the legislative history, or if the statute disclaims an intent to encourage prayer over alternatives during a moment of silence, then courts should generally defer to that stated intent. It is particularly troublesome to denigrate an expressed secular purpose due to postenactment testimony by particular legislators or by interested persons who witnessed the drafting of the statute. Even if the text and official history of a statute express no secular purpose, the statute should be held to have an improper purpose only if it is beyond purview that endorsement of religion or a religious belief "was and is the law's reason for existence." Since there is arguably a secular pedagogical value to a moment of silence in public schools, courts should find an improper purpose behind such a statute only if the statute on its face, in its official legislative history, or in its interpretation by a responsible administrative agency suggests it has the primary purpose of endorsing prayer.

* * * It is of course possible that a legislature will enunciate a sham secular purpose for a statute. I have little doubt that our courts are capable of distinguishing a sham secular purpose from a sincere one * * *.

* * *

The relevant issue is whether an objective observer, acquainted with the text, legislative history, and implementation of the statute, would perceive it as a state endorsement of prayer in public schools. * * * A moment of silence law that is clearly drafted and implemented so as to permit prayer, meditation, and reflection within the prescribed period, without endorsing one alternative over the others, should pass this test.

B

The analysis above suggests that moment of silence laws in many States should pass Establishment Clause scrutiny because they do not favor the child who chooses to pray during a moment of silence over the child who chooses to meditate or reflect. Alabama Code § 16–1–20.1 does not stand on the same footing. However deferentially one examines its text and legislative history, however objectively one views the message attempted to be conveyed to the public, the conclusion is unavoidable that the purpose of the statute is to endorse prayer in public schools. * * *

* * *

* * * Alabama Code § 16–1–20.1 does more than permit prayer to occur during a moment of silence "without interference." It endorses the decision to pray during a moment of silence, and accordingly sponsors a religious exercise. For that reason, I concur in the judgment of the Court.

II

In his dissenting opinion, Justice Rehnquist reviews the text and history of the First Amendment Religion Clauses. His opinion suggests that a long line of this Court's decisions are inconsistent with the intent of the drafters of the Bill of Rights. He urges the Court to correct the historical inaccuracies in its past decisions by embracing a far more restricted interpretation of the Establishment Clause, an interpretation that presumably would permit vocal group prayer in public schools.

* * *

Justice Rehnquist does not assert, however, that the drafters of the First Amendment expressed a preference for prayer in public schools, or that the practice of prayer in public schools enjoyed uninterrupted government endorsement from the time of enactment of the Bill of Rights to the present era. The simple truth is that free public education was virtually nonexistent in the late 18th century. Since there then existed few government-run schools, it is unlikely that the persons who drafted the First Amendment, or the state legislators who ratified it, anticipated the problems of interaction of church and state in the public schools. Even at the time of adoption of the Fourteenth Amendment, education in Southern States was still primarily in private hands, and the movement toward free public schools supported by general taxation had not taken hold.

This uncertainty as to the intent of the Framers of the Bill of Rights does not mean we should ignore history for guidance on the role of religion in public education. * * * When the intent of the Framers is unclear, I believe we must employ both history and reason in our analysis. * * * This Court's decisions have recognized a distinction when government-sponsored religious exercises are directed at impressionable children who are required to attend school, for then government endorsement is much more likely to result in coerced religious beliefs. * * *

* * *

III

The Court does not hold that the Establishment Clause is so hostile to religion that it precludes the States from affording schoolchildren an opportunity for voluntary silent prayer. To the contrary, the moment of silence statutes of many States should satisfy the Establishment Clause standard we have here applied. The Court holds only that Alabama has intentionally crossed the line between creating a quiet moment during which those so inclined may pray, and affirmatively endorsing the particular religious practice of prayer. This line may be a fine one, but our precedents and the principles of religious liberty require that we draw it. In my view, the judgment of the Court of Appeals must be affirmed.

CHIEF JUSTICE BURGER, dissenting.

Some who trouble to read the opinions in these cases will find it ironic—perhaps even bizarre—that on the very day we heard arguments in the cases, the Court's session opened with an invocation for Divine protection. Across the park a few hundred yards away, the House of Representatives and the Senate regularly open each session with a prayer. These legislative prayers are not just one minute in duration, but are extended, thoughtful invocations and prayers for Divine guidance. They are given, as they have been since 1789, by clergy appointed as official chaplains and paid from the Treasury of the United States. Congress has also provided chapels in the Capitol, at public expense, where Members and others may pause for prayer, meditation—or a moment of silence.

* * *

I make several points about today's curious holding.

(a) It makes no sense to say that Alabama has "endorsed prayer" by merely enacting a new statute "to specify expressly that voluntary prayer is *one* of the authorized activities during a moment of silence." To suggest that a moment-of-silence statute that includes the word "prayer" unconstitutionally endorses religion, while one that simply provides for a moment of silence does not, manifests not neutrality but hostility toward religion. For decades our opinions have stated that hostility toward any religion or toward all religions is as much forbidden by the Constitution as is an official establishment of religion. * * *

(b) The inexplicable aspect of the foregoing opinions, however, is what they advance as support for the holding concerning the purpose of the Alabama Legislature. Rather than determining legislative purpose from the face of the statute as a whole, the opinions rely on three factors in concluding that the Alabama Legislature had a "wholly religious" purpose for enacting the statute under review, Ala.Code § 16–1–20.1 (Supp.1984): (i) statements of the statute's sponsor, (ii) admissions in Governor James' answer to the second amended complaint, and (iii) the difference between § 16–1–20.1 and its predecessor statute.

Curiously, the opinions do not mention that *all* of the sponsor's statements relied upon—including the statement "inserted" into the Senate Journal—were made *after* the legislature had passed the statute * * *. As even the appellees concede, there is not a shred of evidence that the legislature as a whole shared the sponsor's motive or that a majority in either house was even aware of the sponsor's view of the bill when it was passed. The sole relevance of the sponsor's statements, therefore, is that they reflect the personal, subjective motives of a single legislator. No case in the 195–year history of this Court supports the disconcerting idea that post-enactment statements by individual legislators are relevant in determining the constitutionality of legislation.

* * *

The several preceding opinions conclude that the principal difference between § 16–1–20.1 and its predecessor statute proves that the sole purpose behind the inclusion of the phrase "or voluntary prayer" in § 16–1–20.1 was to endorse and promote prayer. This reasoning is simply a subtle way of focusing exclusively on the religious component of the statute rather than examining the statute as a whole. * * * [Even if] the Court's method [were] correct, the inclusion of the words "or voluntary prayer" in § 16–1–20.1 is wholly consistent with the clearly permissible purpose of clarifying that silent, voluntary prayer is not *forbidden* in the public school building.

(c) The Court's extended treatment of the "test" of *Lemon v. Kurtzman*, suggests a naive preoccupation with an easy, bright-line approach for addressing constitutional issues. We have repeatedly cautioned that *Lemon* did not establish a rigid caliper capable of resolving every Establishment Clause issue, but that it sought only to provide "signposts." "In each [Establishment Clause] case, the inquiry calls for line-drawing; no fixed, *per se* rule can be framed." In any event, our responsibility is not to apply tidy formulas by rote; our duty is to determine whether the statute or practice at issue is a step toward establishing a state religion. * * *

(d) The notion that the Alabama statute is a step toward creating an established church borders on, if it does not trespass into, the ridiculous. The statute does not remotely threaten religious liberty; it affirmatively furthers the values of religious freedom and tolerance that the Establishment Clause was designed to protect. * * *

The Court today has ignored the wise admonition of Justice Goldberg that "the measure of constitutional adjudication is the ability and willingness to distinguish between real threat and mere shadow." * * *

JUSTICE WHITE, dissenting.

For the most part agreeing with the opinion of The Chief Justice, I dissent from the Court's judgment invalidating Ala.Code § 16–1–20.1. Because I do, it is apparent that in my view the First Amendment does not proscribe either (1) statutes authorizing or requiring in so many words a moment of silence before classes begin or (2) a statute that provides, when it is initially passed, for a moment of silence for meditation or prayer. As I read the filed opinions, a majority of the Court would approve statutes that provided for a moment of silence but did not mention prayer. But if a student asked whether he could pray during that moment, it is difficult to believe that the teacher could not answer in the affirmative. If that is the case, I would not invalidate a statute that at the outset provided the legislative answer to the question "May I pray?" * * *

* * *

JUSTICE REHNQUIST, dissenting.

Thirty-eight years ago this Court, in *Everson v. Board of Education*, summarized its exegesis of Establishment Clause doctrine thus:

> "In the words of Jefferson, the clause against establishment of religion by law was intended to erect 'a wall of separation between church and State.' *Reynolds v. United States*, [98 U.S. 145, 164, 25 L.Ed. 244 (1879)]."

* * *

It is impossible to build sound constitutional doctrine upon a mistaken understanding of constitutional history, but unfortunately the Establishment Clause has been expressly freighted with Jefferson's misleading metaphor for nearly 40 years. Thomas Jefferson was of course in France at the time the constitutional Amendments known as the Bill of Rights were passed by Congress and ratified by the States. His letter to the Danbury Baptist Association was a short note of courtesy, written 14 years after the Amendments were passed by Congress. He would seem to any detached observer as a less than ideal source of contemporary history as to the meaning of the Religion Clauses of the First Amendment.

Jefferson's fellow Virginian, James Madison, with whom he was joined in the battle for the enactment of the Virginia Statute of Religious Liberty of 1786, did play as large a part as anyone in the drafting of the Bill of Rights. He had two advantages over Jefferson in this regard: he was present in the United States, and he was a leading Member of the First Congress. But when we turn to the record of the proceedings in the First Congress leading up to the adoption of the Establishment Clause of the Constitution, including Madison's significant contributions thereto, we see a far different picture of its purpose than the highly simplified "wall of separation between church and State."

* * *

On June 8, 1789, James Madison rose in the House of Representatives and "reminded the House that this was the day that he had heretofore named for bringing forward amendments to the Constitution." Madison's subsequent remarks in urging the House to adopt his drafts of the proposed amendments were less those of a dedicated advocate of the wisdom of such measures than those of a prudent statesman seeking the enactment of measures sought by a number of his fellow citizens which could surely do no harm and might do a great deal of good. * * *

* * *

[Justice Rehnquist sets forth the evolution of the religion clauses in Congress and some of the discussion between Congressmen over the proposed clauses].

* * *

It seems indisputable from these glimpses of Madison's thinking, as reflected by actions on the floor of the House in 1789, that he saw the Amendment as designed to prohibit the establishment of a national religion, and perhaps to prevent discrimination among sects. He did not see it as requiring neutrality on the part of government between religion and irreligion. Thus the Court's opinion in *Everson*—while correct in bracketing Madison and Jefferson together in their exertions in their home State leading to the enactment of the Virginia Statute of Religious Liberty—is totally incorrect in suggesting that Madison carried these views onto the floor of the United States House of Representatives when he proposed the language which would ultimately become the Bill of Rights.

The repetition of this error in the Court's opinion in *Illinois ex rel. McCollum v. Board of Education*, and, *inter alia, Engel v. Vitale*, does not make it any sounder historically. * * * [S]*tare decisis* may bind courts as to matters of law, but it cannot bind them as to matters of history.

* * *

[JUSTICE REHNQUIST next discussed a number of historical practices from the time of the Framers or shortly thereafter, such as the history of Thanksgiving Proclamations, the reenactment of the Northwest Ordinance in 1789 (which included provisions supporting the Christian proselytization of Native Americans in the territories), and the granting of funds to Indian Tribes for the support of proselytization and churches, to support his argument].

* * *

Joseph Story, a Member of this Court from 1811 to 1845 * * * published by far the most comprehensive treatise on the United States Constitution that had then appeared. Volume 2 of Story's Commentaries on the Constitution of the United States discussed the meaning of the Establishment Clause of the First Amendment this way:

* * *

"The real object of the [First] [A]mendment was not to countenance, much less to advance, Mahometanism, or Judaism, or infidelity, by prostrating Christianity; but to exclude all rivalry among Christian sects, and to prevent any national ecclesiastical establishment which should give to a hierarchy the exclusive patronage of the national government. It thus cut off the means of religious persecution (the vice and pest of former ages), and of the subversion of the rights of conscience in matters of religion, which had been trampled upon almost from the days of the Apostles to the present age...." (Footnotes omitted.)

* * *

It would seem from this evidence that the Establishment Clause of the First Amendment had acquired a well-accepted meaning: it forbade establishment of a national religion, and forbade preference among religious sects or denominations. * * * The Establishment Clause did not require government neutrality between religion and irreligion nor did it prohibit the Federal Government from providing nondiscriminatory aid to religion. There is simply no historical foundation for the proposition that the Framers intended to build the "wall of separation" that was constitutionalized in *Everson*.

Notwithstanding the absence of a historical basis for this theory of rigid separation, the wall idea might well have served as a useful albeit misguided analytical concept, had it led this Court to unified and principled results in Establishment Clause cases. The opposite, unfortunately, has been true; in the 38 years since *Everson* our Establishment Clause cases have been neither principled nor unified. * * *

* * *

But the greatest injury of the "wall" notion is its mischievous diversion of judges from the actual intentions of the drafters of the Bill of Rights. The "crucible of litigation," is well adapted to adjudicating factual disputes on the basis of testimony presented in court, but no amount of repetition of historical errors in judicial opinions can make the errors true. The "wall of separation between church and State" is a metaphor based on bad history, a metaphor which has proved useless as a guide to judging. It should be frankly and explicitly abandoned.

The Court has more recently attempted to add some mortar to *Everson*'s wall through the three-part test of *Lemon v. Kurtzman*, which served at first to offer a more useful test for purposes of the Establishment Clause than did the "wall" metaphor. Generally stated, the *Lemon* test proscribes state action that has a sectarian purpose or effect, or causes an impermissible governmental entanglement with religion.

Lemon cited *Board of Education v. Allen,* 392 U.S. 236, 243, 88 S.Ct. 1923, 1926, 20 L.Ed.2d 1060 (1968), as the source of the "purpose" and "effect" prongs of the three-part test. The *Allen* opinion explains, however, how it inherited the purpose and effect elements from *Schempp* and *Everson,* both of which contain the historical errors described above. Thus the purpose and effect prongs have the same historical deficiencies as the wall concept itself: they are in no way based on either the language or intent of the drafters.

The secular purpose prong has proven mercurial in application because it has never been fully defined, and we have never fully stated how the test is to operate. If the purpose prong is intended to void those aids to sectarian institutions accompanied by a stated legislative purpose to aid religion, the prong will condemn nothing so long as the legislature utters a secular purpose and says nothing about aiding religion. Thus the constitutionality of a statute may depend upon what the legislators put into the legislative history and, more importantly, what they leave out. * * *

* * *

These difficulties arise because the *Lemon* test has no more grounding in the history of the First Amendment than does the wall theory upon which it rests. The three-part test represents a determined effort to craft a workable rule from a historically faulty doctrine; but the rule can only be as sound as the doctrine it attempts to service. The three-part test has simply not provided adequate standards for deciding Establishment Clause cases, as this Court has slowly come to realize. Even worse, the *Lemon* test has caused this Court to fracture into unworkable plurality opinions, depending upon how each of the three factors applies to a certain state action. * * *

[Justice Rehnquist sets forth the seemingly conflicting holdings of the school funding and aid cases up to the time *Wallace* was decided, *see infra.* at Chapter Four].

* * *

* * * It is not surprising in the light of this record that our most recent opinions have expressed doubt on the usefulness of the *Lemon* test.

* * *

The true meaning of the Establishment Clause can only be seen in its history. As drafters of our Bill of Rights, the Framers inscribed the principles that control today. Any deviation from their intentions frustrates the permanence of that Charter and will only lead to the type of unprincipled decisionmaking that has plagued our Establishment Clause cases since *Everson*.

* * *

The Court strikes down the Alabama statute because the State wished to "characterize prayer as a favored practice." It would come as much of a shock to those who drafted the Bill of Rights as it will to a large number of thoughtful Americans today to learn that the Constitution, as construed by the majority, prohibits the Alabama Legislature from "endorsing" prayer. George Washington himself, at the request of the very Congress which passed the Bill of Rights, proclaimed a day of "public thanksgiving and prayer, to be observed by acknowledging with grateful hearts the many and signal favors of Almighty God." History must judge whether it was the Father of his Country in 1789, or a majority of the Court today, which has strayed from the meaning of the Establishment Clause.

The State surely has a secular interest in regulating the manner in which public schools are conducted. Nothing in the Establishment Clause of the First Amendment, properly understood, prohibits any such generalized "endorsement" of prayer. I would therefore reverse the judgment of the Court of Appeals.

Notes and Questions

1. *Determining Legislative Purpose.* In *Wallace v. Jaffree*, the Court held the statute had no secular purpose. This conclusion was based on the statements of the bill's sponsor, those of other government officials, and the language of the three statutes relating to moments of silence. The wording of the statute in question might raise concerns about its purpose, but does the wording demonstrate by itself that there was no secular purpose? Wouldn't it be easier to consider the effect of such a law in light of the earlier statutes—i.e. it basically

just adds prayer—without trying to speculate about the purpose? What about the evidence of purpose gleaned from the statements by state officials? As the dissent points out, one might question whether it is appropriate to determine the purpose of a legislative body based on the statements of a few of its members. Or is relying on purpose a good thing because it puts legislators on notice that they should have publically accessible reasons for their decisions—reasons not motivated solely by factional religious views or views on religion, but rather reasons that those without a given religious view can understand, even if they don't agree? If so, would inquiring about legislative purpose further the goal or would it simply cause legislators to hide their religious motivations under sham secular arguments that may or may not be transparent?

2. *"As Applied" Versus Facial Challenges*. In *Wallace*, the court struck down the Alabama statute on its face. Arguments that a law is unconstitutional on its face are called facial challenges. Such challenges declare a law to be unconstitutional based on its language, history, function and/or structure. Most of the cases in this book are the result of facial challenges to the laws/policies involved. Laws and policies can be subject to "as applied" challenges as well. An as applied challenge alleges that a law which may be constitutional on its face has been applied in an unconstitutional fashion. There is language in *Wallace* suggesting that moment of silence laws that are constitutional under the Court's analysis may nonetheless be subject to as applied challenges if they are applied in a manner that promotes or endorses prayer. For an especially interesting case upholding such a challenge and finding that a state moment of silence law is unconstitutional as applied, *see Walter v. West Virginia Bd. of Education*, 610 F.Supp. 1169 (D.W.Va.1985).

3. *The Constitutional Status of Moment of Silence Laws*. As the Court suggests in *Wallace*, moment of silence laws that (unlike the Alabama law) have a secular purpose are likely to be constitutional unless they are applied in a manner that favors or promotes religion. Most moment of silence laws and policies around the country—and there are a number of them—are constitutional.

4. *Are Moments of Silence Religious Exercises*? If a moment of silence law has a secular purpose and is not applied so as to promote prayer can the resulting moments of silence really be considered religious exercises? After all, the government is essentially saying, "here is a moment to silently reflect on whatever you want or on nothing at all." The Court has consistently recognized the right of students to privately pray anytime at school as long as such prayer does not interfere with school activities or cause disruption. To the extent a properly enacted and applied moment of silence law leads to prayer would that prayer be the type of private prayer the Court would allow?

4. Ceremonial Deism

You have seen repeated references to "ceremonial deism," which may be described as public recognition of G-d that is considered to be ceremonial or traditional. This has been argued to minimize its religious impact. Such activity seems to be considered de minimis by some Justices and beyond the reach of the Establishment Clause by others. Defining ceremonial deism is not an easy task, and a majority of the Court has never specifically defined it. Various Justices have discussed it, however, and Justice Brennan attempted to define it in a famous passage that is referenced in the following material. Oft cited examples of ceremonial deism are "In God We Trust" on currency, references to G-d in patriotic songs, the reference to G-d made by court officers when calling courts into session (including the Supreme Court), and the reference to G-d in the Pledge of Allegiance. As you will see, however, the history of how the reference to G-d was added to the pledge and the nature of a "pledge" may make the pledge different from other forms of ceremonial deism. At least a panel of the 9th Circuit Court of Appeals thought so in the following case, which is currently scheduled to be heard by the U.S. Supreme Court. As you read the following case and the material that follows it consider whether there should be an exception under the Establishment Clause for ceremonial deism, and if so, what the basis of that exception is. Also consider whether the Pledge of Allegiance as amended in 1954 to add the words "under God" is a form of ceremonial deism. If you think so, why? If not, why not?

NEWDOW v. U.S. CONGRESS*

United States Court of Appeals, Ninth Circuit, 2002.
292 F.3d 597.

GOODWIN, CIRCUIT JUDGE:

Michael Newdow appeals a judgment dismissing his challenge to the constitutionality of the words "under God" in the Pledge of Allegiance to the Flag. Newdow argues that the addition of these words by a 1954 federal statute to the previous version of the Pledge of Allegiance (which made no reference to God) and the daily recitation in the classroom of the Pledge of Allegiance, with the added words included, by his daughter's public school teacher are violations of the Establishment Clause of the First Amendment to the United States Constitution.

FACTUAL AND PROCEDURAL BACKGROUND

Newdow is an atheist whose daughter attends public elementary school in the Elk Grove Unified School District ("EGUSD") in California. In accordance with state law and a school district rule, EGUSD teachers begin each school day by leading their students in a recitation of the Pledge of Allegiance ("the Pledge"). The California Education Code requires that public schools begin each school day with "appropriate patriotic exercises" and that "[t]he giving of the Pledge of Allegiance to the Flag of the United States of America shall satisfy" this requirement. Cal. Educ.Code § 52720 (1989) (hereinafter "California statute"). To implement the California statute, the school district that Newdow's

---

* This case has a somewhat confusing procedural history. The opinion included herein was amended and superseded by, *Newdow v. U.S. Congress*, 328 F.3d 466 (9th Cir. 2003), which includes an amended version of the partial concurrence and dissent in this opinion, and opinions by several judges resulting from the denial of rehearing en banc, including an opinion by Judge Reinhart who was a member of the panel

that issued the current opinion. The Supreme Court recently granted *certiorari* in the case, *Elk Grove Unified School Dist. v. Newdow*, 71 U.S.L.W. 3724 (2003). One of the issues on which the Court granted *cert.* was whether Mr. Newdow had standing to sue on behalf of his daughter, and thus the Supreme Court may or may not reach the merits of the case.

daughter attends has promulgated a policy that states, in pertinent part: "Each elementary school class [shall] recite the pledge of allegiance to the flag once each day."

The classmates of Newdow's daughter in the EGUSD are led by their teacher in reciting the Pledge codified in federal law. On June 22, 1942, Congress first codified the Pledge as "I pledge allegiance to the flag of the United States of America and to the Republic for which it stands, one Nation indivisible, with liberty and justice for all." On June 14, 1954, Congress amended Section 1972 to add the words "under God" after the word "Nation." Pub.L. No. 396, Ch. 297, 68 Stat. 249 (1954) ("1954 Act"). The Pledge is currently codified as "I pledge allegiance to the Flag of the United States of America, and to the Republic for which it stands, one nation under God, indivisible, with liberty and justice for all."

Newdow does not allege that his daughter's teacher or school district requires his daughter to participate in reciting the Pledge.[3] Rather, he claims that his daughter is injured when she is compelled to "watch and listen as her state-employed teacher in her state-run school leads her classmates in a ritual proclaiming that there is a God, and that our's [sic] is 'one nation under God.'"

* * *

DISCUSSION

* * *

D. Establishment Clause

* * * Over the last three decades, the Supreme Court has used three interrelated tests to analyze alleged violations of the Establishment Clause in the realm of public education: the three-prong test set forth in *Lemon v. Kurtzman*; the "endorsement" test, first articulated by Justice O'Connor in her concurring opinion in *Lynch,* and later adopted by a majority of the Court in *County of Allegheny v. ACLU,* 492 U.S. 573, 109 S.Ct. 3086, 106 L.Ed.2d 472 (1989); and the "coercion" test first used by the Court in *Lee.*

* * * To survive the *"Lemon* test," the government conduct in question (1) must have a secular purpose, (2) must have a principal or primary effect that neither advances nor inhibits religion, and (3) must not foster an excessive government entanglement with religion. The Supreme Court applied the *Lemon* test to every Establishment case it

---

3. Compelling students to recite the Pledge was held to be a First Amendment violation in *West Virginia State Board of Education v. Barnette,* 319 U.S. 624, 642, 63 S.Ct. 1178, 87 L.Ed. 1628 (1943) ("[T]he action of the local authorities in compelling the flag salute and pledge transcends con- stitutional limitations on their power and invades the sphere of intellect and spirit which it is the purpose of the First Amend- ment to our Constitution to reserve from all official control."). *Barnette* was decided be- fore the 1954 Act added the words "under God" to the Pledge.

decided between 1971 and 1984, with the exception of *Marsh v. Chambers*, 463 U.S. 783, 103 S.Ct. 3330, 77 L.Ed.2d 1019 (1983), the case upholding legislative prayer.

In the 1984 *Lynch* case, which upheld the inclusion of a nativity scene in a city's Christmas display, Justice O'Connor wrote a concurring opinion in order to suggest a "clarification" of Establishment Clause jurisprudence. Justice O'Connor's "endorsement" test effectively collapsed the first two prongs of the *Lemon* test:

> The Establishment Clause prohibits government from making adherence to a religion relevant in any way to a person's standing in the political community. Government can run afoul of that prohibition in two principal ways. One is excessive entanglement with religious institutions.... The second and more direct infringement is government endorsement or disapproval of religion. Endorsement sends a message to nonadherents that they are outsiders, not full members of the political community, and an accompanying message to adherents that they are insiders, favored members of the political community.

* * * Declining to reconsider the validity of the *Lemon* test, the Court in *Lee* found it unnecessary to apply the *Lemon* test to find the challenged practices unconstitutional. Rather, it relied on the principle that "at a minimum, the Constitution guarantees that government may not coerce anyone to support or participate in religion or its exercise, or otherwise to act in a way which establishes a state religion or religious faith, or tends to do so." * * * The Court concluded that primary and secondary school children may not be placed in the dilemma of either participating in a religious ceremony or protesting.

Finally, in its most recent school prayer case, the Supreme Court applied the *Lemon* test, the endorsement test, and the coercion test to strike down a school district's policy of permitting student-led "invocations" before high school football games. *See Santa Fe*, 530 U.S. at 310–16, 120 S.Ct. 2266. * * *

We are free to apply any or all of the three tests, and to invalidate any measure that fails any one of them. * * * [W]e will analyze the school district policy and the 1954 Act under all three tests.

We first consider whether the 1954 Act and the EGUSD's policy of teacher-led Pledge recitation survive the endorsement test. The magistrate judge found that "the ceremonial reference to God in the pledge does not convey endorsement of particular religious beliefs." Supreme Court precedent does not support that conclusion.

In the context of the Pledge, the statement that the United States is a nation "under God" is an endorsement of religion. It is a profession of a religious belief, namely, a belief in monotheism. The recitation that ours is a nation "under God" is not a mere acknowledgment that many Americans believe in a deity. Nor is it merely descriptive of the undeniable historical significance of religion in the founding of the Republic.

Rather, the phrase "one nation under God" in the context of the Pledge is normative. To recite the Pledge is not to describe the United States; instead, it is to swear allegiance to the values for which the flag stands: unity, indivisibility, liberty, justice, and—since 1954—monotheism. The text of the official Pledge, codified in federal law, impermissibly takes a position with respect to the purely religious question of the existence and identity of God. A profession that we are a nation "under God" is identical, for Establishment Clause purposes, to a profession that we are a nation "under Jesus," a nation "under Vishnu," a nation "under Zeus," or a nation "under no god," because none of these professions can be neutral with respect to religion. "[T]he government must pursue a course of complete neutrality toward religion." *Wallace.* Furthermore, the school district's practice of teacher-led recitation of the Pledge aims to inculcate in students a respect for the ideals set forth in the Pledge, and thus amounts to state endorsement of these ideals. Although students cannot be forced to participate in recitation of the Pledge, the school district is nonetheless conveying a message of state endorsement of a religious belief when it requires public school teachers to recite, and lead the recitation of, the current form of the Pledge.

The Supreme Court recognized the normative and ideological nature of the Pledge in *Barnette,* 319 U.S. 624, 63 S.Ct. 1178, 87 L.Ed. 1628. There, the Court held unconstitutional a school district's wartime policy of punishing students who refused to recite the Pledge and salute the flag. The Court noted that the school district was compelling the students "to declare a belief," and "requir[ing] the individual to communicate by word and sign his acceptance of the political ideas [the flag] . . . bespeaks." "[T]he compulsory flag salute and pledge requires affirmation of a belief and an attitude of mind." The Court emphasized that the political concepts articulated in the Pledge[6] were idealistic, not descriptive: " '[L]iberty and justice for all,' if it must be accepted as descriptive of the present order rather than an ideal, might to some seem an overstatement." The Court concluded that: "If there is any fixed star in our constitutional constellation, it is that no official, high or petty, can prescribe what shall be orthodox in politics, nationalism, religion, or other matters of opinion or force citizens to confess by word or act their faith therein."

The Pledge, as currently codified, is an impermissible government endorsement of religion because it sends a message to unbelievers "that they are outsiders, not full members of the political community, and an accompanying message to adherents that they are insiders, favored members of the political community." * * *
Consequently, the policy and the Act fail the endorsement test.

Similarly, the policy and the Act fail the coercion test. Just as in *Lee,* the policy and the Act place students in the untenable position of choosing between participating in an exercise with religious content or

---

6. *Barnette* was decided before "under God" was added, and thus the Court's discussion was limited to the political ideals contained in the Pledge.

protesting. * * * Although the defendants argue that the religious content of "one nation under God" is minimal, to an atheist or a believer in certain non-Judeo-Christian religions or philosophies, it may reasonably appear to be an attempt to enforce a "religious orthodoxy" of monotheism, and is therefore impermissible. The coercive effect of this policy is particularly pronounced in the school setting given the age and impressionability of schoolchildren, and their understanding that they are required to adhere to the norms set by their school, their teacher and their fellow students. Furthermore, under *Lee,* the fact that students are not required to participate is no basis for distinguishing *Barnette* from the case at bar because, even without a recitation requirement for each child, the mere fact that a pupil is required to listen every day to the statement "one nation under God" has a coercive effect. The coercive effect of the Act is apparent from its context and legislative history, which indicate that the Act was designed to result in the daily recitation of the words "under God" in school classrooms. President Eisenhower, during the Act's signing ceremony, stated: "From this day forward, the millions of our school children will daily proclaim in every city and town, every village and rural schoolhouse, the dedication of our Nation and our people to the Almighty." Therefore, the policy and the Act fail the coercion test.[10]

Finally we turn to the *Lemon* test, the first prong of which asks if the challenged policy has a secular purpose. Historically, the primary purpose of the 1954 Act was to advance religion, in conflict with the first prong of the *Lemon* test. The federal defendants "do not dispute that the words 'under God' were intended" "to recognize a Supreme Being," at a time when the government was publicly inveighing against atheistic communism. Nonetheless, the federal defendants argue that the Pledge must be considered as a whole when assessing whether it has a secular purpose. They claim that the Pledge has the secular purpose of "solemnizing public occasions, expressing confidence in the future, and encouraging the recognition of what is worthy of appreciation in society." *Lynch,* 465 U.S. at 693, 104 S.Ct. 1355.

The flaw in defendants' argument is that it looks at the text of the Pledge "as a whole," and glosses over the 1954 Act. The problem with this approach is apparent when one considers the Court's analysis in *Wallace.* There, the Court struck down Alabama's statute mandating a moment of silence for "meditation or voluntary prayer" not because the final version "as a whole" lacked a primary secular purpose, but because the state legislature had amended the statute specifically and solely to add the words "or voluntary prayer."

10. In *Aronow v. United States,* 432 F.2d 242 (9th Cir.1970), this court, without reaching the question of standing, upheld the inscription of the phrase "In God We Trust" on our coins and currency. * * * *Aronow* is distinguishable in many ways from the present case. The most important distinction is that school children are not coerced into reciting or otherwise actively led to participating in an endorsement of the markings on the money in circulation.

By analogy to *Wallace,* we apply the purpose prong of the *Lemon* test to the amendment that added the words "under God" to the Pledge, not to the Pledge in its final version. As was the case with the amendment to the Alabama statute in *Wallace,* the legislative history of the 1954 Act reveals that the Act's *sole* purpose was to advance religion, in order to differentiate the United States from nations under communist rule. "[T]he First Amendment requires that a statute must be invalidated if it is entirely motivated by a purpose to advance religion." As the legislative history of the 1954 Act sets forth:

> At this moment of our history the principles underlying our American Government and the American way of life are under attack by a system whose philosophy is at direct odds with our own. Our American Government is founded on the concept of the individuality and the dignity of the human being. Underlying this concept is the belief that the human person is important because he was created by God and endowed by Him with certain inalienable rights which no civil authority may usurp. The inclusion of God in our pledge therefore would further acknowledge the dependence of our people and our Government upon the moral directions of the Creator. At the same time it would serve to deny the atheistic and materialistic concepts of communism with its attendant subservience of the individual.

H.R.Rep. No. 83–1693, at 1–2 (1954), *reprinted in* 1954 U.S.C.C.A.N. 2339, 2340. This language reveals that the purpose of the 1954 Act was to take a position on the question of theism, namely, to support the existence and moral authority of God, while "deny[ing] ... atheistic and materialistic concepts." Such a purpose runs counter to the Establishment Clause, which prohibits the government's endorsement or advancement not only of one particular religion at the expense of other religions, but also of religion at the expense of atheism.

* * *

In language that attempts to prevent future constitutional challenges, the sponsors of the 1954 Act expressly disclaimed a religious purpose. "This is not an act establishing a religion.... A distinction must be made between the existence of a religion as an institution and a belief in the sovereignty of God. The phrase 'under God' recognizes only the guidance of God in our national affairs." H.R.Rep. No. 83–1693, at 3 (1954), *reprinted in* 1954 U.S.C.C.A.N. 2339, 2341–42. This alleged distinction is irrelevant for constitutional purposes. The Act's affirmation of "a belief in the sovereignty of God" and its recognition of "the guidance of God" are endorsements by the government of religious beliefs. The Establishment Clause is not limited to "religion as an institution"; this is clear from cases such as *Santa Fe,* where the Court struck down student-initiated and student-led prayer at high school football games. The Establishment Clause guards not only against the establishment of "religion as an institution," but also against the endorsement of religious ideology by the government. Because the Act fails the purpose prong of *Lemon,* we need not examine the other prongs.

Similarly, the school district policy also fails the *Lemon* test. Although it survives the first prong of *Lemon* because, as even Newdow concedes, the school district had the secular purpose of fostering patriotism in enacting the policy, the policy fails the second prong. * * * [T]he second *Lemon* prong asks "whether the challenged government action is sufficiently likely to be perceived by adherents of the controlling denominations as an endorsement, and by the nonadherents as a disapproval, of their individual religious choices." [School District of Grand Rapids v.] *Ball,* 473 U.S. at 390, 105 S.Ct. 3216. Given the age and impressionability of schoolchildren, as discussed above, particularly within the confined environment of the classroom, the policy is highly likely to convey an impermissible message of endorsement to some and disapproval to others of their beliefs regarding the existence of a monotheistic God. Therefore the policy fails the effects prong of *Lemon,* and fails the *Lemon* test. In sum, both the policy and the Act fail the *Lemon* test as well as the endorsement and coercion tests.[12]

In conclusion, we hold that (1) the 1954 Act adding the words "under God" to the Pledge, and (2) EGUSD's policy and practice of teacher-led recitation of the Pledge, with the added words included, violate the Establishment Clause. The judgment of dismissal is vacated

---

12. We recognize that the Supreme Court has occasionally commented in dicta that the presence of "one nation under God" in the Pledge of Allegiance is constitutional. However, the Court has never been presented with the question directly, and has always clearly refrained from deciding it. Accordingly, it has never applied any of the three tests to the Act or to any school policy regarding the recitation of the Pledge. That task falls to us, although the final word, as always, remains with the Supreme Court.

The only other United States Court of Appeals to consider the issue is the Seventh Circuit, which held in *Sherman v. Community Consolidated School District 21,* 980 F.2d 437 (7th Cir.1992), that a policy similar to the one before us regarding the recitation of the Pledge of Allegiance containing the words "one nation under God" was constitutional.

The *Sherman* court first stated that:

If as *Barnette* holds no state may require anyone to recite the Pledge, and if as the prayer cases hold the recitation by a teacher or rabbi of unwelcome words is coercion, then the Pledge of Allegiance becomes unconstitutional under all circumstances, just as no school may read from a holy scripture at the start of class.

It then concludes, however, that this reasoning is flawed because the First Amendment "[does] not establish general rules about speech or schools; [it] call[s] for religion to be treated differently." We have some difficulty understanding this statement; we do not believe that the Constitution prohibits compulsory patriotism as in *Barnette,* but permits compulsory religion as in this case. If government-endorsed religion is to be treated differently from government-endorsed patriotism, the treatment must be less favorable, not more.

The Seventh Circuit makes an even more serious error, however. It not only refuses to apply the *Lemon* test because of the Supreme Court's criticism of that test in *Lee,* but it also fails to apply the coercion test from *Lee* or the endorsement test from *Lynch.* Circuit courts are not free to ignore Supreme Court precedent in this manner.

* * *

* * * Our application of *all* of the tests compels the conclusion that the policy and the Act challenged here violate the Establishment Clause of the Constitution. Thus, we must respectfully differ from the Seventh Circuit.

with respect to these two claims, and the cause is remanded for further proceedings consistent with our holding. * * *

FERNANDEZ, CIRCUIT JUDGE, concurring and dissenting (this is JUDGE FERNANDEZ' original opinion, which was later amended and superseded. *See*, *Newdow v. U.S. Congress*, 328 F.3d 466 (9th Cir.2003)):

I concur in parts A, B and C [these parts dealt with jurisdiction and standing]of the majority opinion, but dissent as to part D.

We are asked to hold that inclusion of the phrase "under God" in this nation's Pledge of Allegiance violates the religion clauses of the Constitution of the United States. We should do no such thing. We should, instead, recognize that those clauses were not designed to drive religious expression out of public thought; they were written to avoid discrimination.

We can run through the litany of tests and concepts which have floated to the surface from time to time. Were we to do so, the one that appeals most to me, the one I think to be correct, is the concept that what the religion clauses of the First Amendment require is neutrality; that those clauses are, in effect, an early kind of equal protection provision and assure that government will neither discriminate for nor discriminate against a religion or religions. But, legal world abstractions and ruminations aside, when all is said and done, the danger that "under God" in our Pledge of Allegiance will tend to bring about a theocracy or suppress somebody's beliefs is so minuscule as to be de minimis. The danger that phrase presents to our First Amendment freedoms is picayune at most.

Judges, including Supreme Court Justices, have recognized the lack of danger in that and similar expressions for decades, if not for centuries, as have presidents and members of our Congress. * * * In *County of Allegheny*, the Supreme Court had this to say: "Our previous opinions have considered in dicta the motto and the pledge, characterizing them as consistent with the proposition that government may not communicate an endorsement of religious belief." The Seventh Circuit, reacting in part to that statement, has wisely expressed the following thought:

> Plaintiffs observe that the Court sometimes changes its tune when it confronts a subject directly. True enough, but an inferior court had best respect what the majority says rather than read between the lines. If the Court proclaims that a practice is consistent with the establishment clause, we take its assurances seriously. If the Justices are just pulling our leg, let them say so.

Sherman, 980 F.2d at 448.

Some, who rather choke on the notion of de minimis, have resorted to the euphemism "ceremonial deism." But whatever it is called (I care not), it comes to this: such phrases as "In God We Trust," or "under God" have no tendency to establish a religion in this country or to suppress anyone's exercise, or non-exercise, of religion, except in the fevered eye of persons who most fervently would like to drive all tincture of religion out of the public life of our polity. * * * I recognize that some people may not feel good about hearing the phrases recited in their presence, but, then, others might not feel good if they are omitted. At any rate, the Constitution is a practical and balanced charter for the just governance of a free people in a vast territory. Thus, although we do feel good when we contemplate the effects of its inspiring phrasing and majestic promises, it is not primarily a feel-good prescription. * * *

My reading of the stelliscript suggests that upon Newdow's theory of our Constitution, accepted by my colleagues today, we will soon find ourselves prohibited from using our album of patriotic songs in many public settings. "God Bless America" and "America the Beautiful" will be gone for sure, and while use of the first three stanzas of "The Star Spangled Banner" will still be permissible, we will be precluded from straying into the fourth. And currency beware! Judges can accept those results if they limit themselves to elements and tests, while failing to look at the good sense and principles that animated those tests in the first place. But they do so at the price of removing a vestige of the awe we all must feel at the immenseness of the universe and our own small place within it, as well as the wonder we must feel at the good fortune of our country. That will cool the febrile nerves of a few at the cost of removing the healthy glow conferred upon many citizens when the forbidden verses, or phrases, are uttered, read, or seen.

In short, I cannot accept the eliding of the simple phrase "under God" from our Pledge of Allegiance, when it is obvious that its tendency to establish religion in this country or to interfere with the free exercise (or non-exercise) of religion is de minimis.[9]

Thus, I respectfully concur in part and dissent in part.

What is Ceremonial Deism

Ceremonial deism raises some complex problems for the courts. Of course, one explanation for the pledge case is that the addition of "under God" to the pledge in 1954 is not an example of ceremonial deism because of the legislative purpose behind, and obvious effect of, the addition. Yet, even if the pledge is not a good case for analyzing whether ceremonial deism is constitutional, the issue arises in other contexts such as "in God we trust" on money and other similar practices. The following article excerpt argues that ceremonial deism is generally unconstitutional, and that the Court contradicts itself when it strikes down some of the practices it has found unconstitutional while allowing various forms of ceremonial deism to survive. The article also tries to define ceremonial deism. As you read the article consider the following questions. Is the author correct in assuming that to maintain consistency the Court must strike down most forms of ceremonial deism, or is it equally plausible that to maintain consistency the Court should uphold

---

9. Lest I be misunderstood, I must emphasize that to decide this case it is not necessary to say, and I do not say, that there is such a thing as a de minimis constitutional violation. What I do say is that the de minimis tendency of the Pledge to establish a religion or to interfere with its free exercise is no constitutional violation at all.

some of the practices it has struck down? Do you agree with the author's arguments regarding original intent? If you do, what implications does this have for the original intent arguments undergirding Establishment Clause jurisprudence generally? If you do not, what about segregation and anti-miscegenation laws that would seemingly have been acceptable to the framers of the Constitution and the framers of the 14th Amendment to the Constitution? Should the longstanding tradition of a practice be an adequate basis for holding that it is constitutional? If not, could a longstanding tradition serve as *evidence* that a practice is Constitutional? Or is tradition simply evidence that the majority has had its way for a long time? Do you agree with the author's definition of ceremonial deism? Which of the practices raised by the author would you consider ceremonial deism?

STEVEN B. EPSTEIN, RETHINKING THE CONSTITUTIONALITY OF CEREMONIAL DEISM

96 Columbia Law Review 2083 (1996).

INTRODUCTION[a]

The year is 2096. Due to radically altered immigration and birth patterns over the past century, Muslims now comprise seventy percent of the American population, while Christians and Jews comprise only twenty-five percent collectively. Elementary school students in most public school systems begin each day with the Pledge of Allegiance in which they dutifully recite that America is one nation "under Allah;" our national currency—both coins and paper—contains the inscription codified as our national motto, "In Allah We Trust;" witnesses in court proceedings and public officials are sworn in by government officials asking them to place one hand on the Koran and to conclude "so help me Allah;" presidential addresses are laced with appeals to Allah; federal and state legislative proceedings begin with a formal prayer typically delivered by a Muslim chaplain in which supplications to Allah are unabashed; state and federal judicial proceedings—including proceedings before the United States Supreme Court—begin with the invocation "Allah save this Honorable Court;" and, pursuant to federal and state law, only Muslim holy days are officially celebrated as national holidays. Surely this scenario could not be squared with the First Amendment to the United States Constitution. Surely any court addressing these practices would conclude that the federal and state governments behind them have impermissibly sought to "establish" the religion of Islam. Right? Not necessarily. To date, every court that has analyzed these types of governmental appeals to the deity, albeit in Christian or Judeo–

---

a [Authors Note: The hypothetical in this introduction should not be read to suggest that Islam is totally alien to Christian and/or Jewish traditions. *See infra* at Chapter Eight (addressing religious law). Rather it is likely Professor Epstein was simply using the example to point out how members of larger religions in the United States would feel if their preferences were no longer "privileged," and other faiths' preferences were.]

Christian form rather than Muslim form, has assumed as axiomatic that they do not encroach upon the Establishment Clause of the First Amendment. * * * [T]he Supreme Court has either held explicitly, or implied in dicta, that the forms of "ceremonial deism" described above are immune from constitutional scrutiny. Yet the prevailing current of United States Supreme Court jurisprudence is that, at its core, the Establishment Clause "preclude[s] government from conveying or attempting to convey a message that religion or a particular religious belief is favored or preferred" and prohibits government expressions of religion which result in American citizens feeling like outsiders in their own country. In sponsoring the practices described in the opening paragraph, is the government not conveying a message that religion generally, and the Islamic religion in particular, is favored or preferred? Would the average Christian or Jew seriously contend that this America of 2096 would not make them feel like outsiders in their own country? How then can Christians and Jews reconcile this feeling of exclusion with approval of a state of affairs in 1996 in which non-Christians, non-Jews, and nonreligionists have no constitutional basis for attacking "ceremonial" Christian or Judeo–Christian forms of government expression? More to the point, how can the Supreme Court continue to countenance these practices? The implications of ceremonial deism are far-reaching because courts frequently employ this amorphous concept as a springboard from which to hold that other challenged practices do not violate the Establishment Clause. After all, the argument typically goes, if practices such as the Pledge of Allegiance to a nation "under God," legislative prayer, the invocation to God prior to court proceedings, and the Christmas holiday are permissible notwithstanding the Establishment Clause, then surely the practice at hand (be it a nativity scene, commencement invocation, or some other governmental practice)—which does not advance religion "any more than" these accepted practices—must also pass muster under the Establishment Clause * * *.

This syllogistic reasoning has been aptly named the "any more than" test. Its central flaw is that no court has ever squarely and faithfully probed the validity of the major premise under the Supreme Court's long-standing Establishment Clause jurisprudence. If the major premise is invalid, a court may not properly conclude that a challenged practice is permissible merely because it advances religion no more than the long-standing practices embraced by that premise. Not surprisingly, the "any more than" approach has yielded an ever expanding sphere of activities courts have found to be permissible forms of ceremonial deism. Each step in the process is valuable ammunition for the next. * * * [I]t is increasingly apparent that two distinct and incompatible doctrines are driving Establishment Clause jurisprudence, one purporting to invalidate practices in which the government endorses religion and the other validating the exact same practices if they fit within the above syllogism. As the latter doctrine expands its coverage, the former necessarily contracts. Consequently, one must seriously consider how long it will be until the latter eviscerates the former altogether, if it has not done so already. Despite its increasing significance in Establishment Clause litigation, the concept of ceremonial deism has received only scant scholarly attention. Like the courts, most scholars have assumed that the majority of practices constituting ceremonial deism are innocuous and inconsequential in the grand constitutional scheme. No commentator has systematically analyzed the constitutionality of the various practices constituting ceremonial deism to determine whether the major premise to the syllogism authorizing an expanding universe of governmental religious activity is valid or flawed. That is what I seek to do in this Article. * * *

I. WHAT IS CEREMONIAL DEISM?

A. *Background*

The phrase "ceremonial deism" was coined by former Yale Law School Dean Walter Rostow in a 1962 lecture he delivered at Brown University. As reported by Professor Arthur Sutherland in 1964, Rostow reconciled the Establishment Clause with a "class of public activity, which ... c[ould] be accepted as so conventional and uncontroversial as to be constitutional." Rostow labeled this class of public activity "ceremonial deism." Deism in America was a product of French intellectual thought in the eighteenth century and had among its fundamental principles the existence of a Supreme Deity, worthy of adoration, and the necessity of religious liberty. It also eschewed theological and ecclesiastical extremes. One of deism's most ardent American proponents was Thomas Paine. According to Paine, "[d]eism, from the Latin word Deus, God, is the belief of a God, and this belief is the first article of every man's creed." Dean Rostow's combination of "ceremonial" with "deism" was probably intended to refer to expressions of and to God in ceremonial, as opposed to theological, settings. Yet this literal definition gets us only so far. It is more helpful to examine the Supreme Court's use of the phrase. The phrase has explicitly appeared in only two Supreme Court opinions, the nativity scene cases of Lynch v. Donnelly and County of Allegheny v. ACLU. In his dissent in Lynch, Justice Brennan suggested that practices like "the designation of 'In God We Trust' as our national motto, or the references to God contained in the Pledge of Allegiance to the flag can best be understood, in Dean Rostow's apt phrase, as [ ] form[s of] 'ceremonial deism,' protected from Establishment Clause scrutiny chiefly because they have lost through rote repetition any significant religious content." Justice Brennan stated that these practices are "uniquely suited to serve such wholly secular purposes as solemnizing public occasions, or inspiring commitment to meet some national challenge in a manner that simply could not be fully served in our culture if government were limited to purely nonreligious phrases." He opined that such practices are "probably necessary to serve certain secular functions, and that necessity, coupled with their long history, gives those practices an essentially secular meaning." Similarly, in Allegheny, the plurality opinion referred to legislative prayer, the Court's own invocation, and the inclusion of God in the national motto

and Pledge of Allegiance as examples of "ceremonial deism," "a form of acknowledgment of religion that 'serve[s], in the only wa[y] reasonably possible in our culture, the legitimate secular purposes of solemnizing public occasions, expressing confidence in the future, and encouraging the recognition of what is worthy of appreciation in society.'" The plurality observed that such practices "'are not understood as conveying government approval of particular religious beliefs.'" Justice O'Connor embraced the same theme in her concurrence, suggesting that such practices are permissible due to their long-standing existence and non-sectarian nature, and because they are today "generally understood as a celebration of patriotic values rather than particular religious beliefs."
* * *

* * * The defining moment for ceremonial deism came in Lynch v. Donnelly. In his majority opinion, Chief Justice Burger justified a city's inclusion of a nativity scene in a holiday display by referring to "an unbroken history of official acknowledgment by all three branches of government of the role of religion in American life from at least 1789" and the fact that "[o]ur history is replete with official references to the value and invocation of Divine guidance in deliberations and pronounce-ments of the Founding Fathers and contemporary leaders." In no fewer than five pages of the United States Reports, Justice Burger rattled off a comprehensive litany of government practices embracing religion, includ-ing the Thanksgiving and Christmas holidays, congressional and military chaplains and the congressional prayer room, the motto, the Pledge of Allegiance, and presidential proclamations for a National Day of Prayer, implying that all of these practices are permissible notwithstanding the Establishment Clause. Similar implicit references to the concept of ceremonial deism have been commonplace in the Court's recent Estab-lishment Clause jurisprudence.

B. Definition

As the above discussion illustrates, the Supreme Court has utilized the concept of ceremonial deism to immunize a certain class of activities from Establishment Clause scrutiny. This class of activities seems to have or is perceived to have certain defining characteristics supporting a definition of ceremonial deism that would include all practices involving:

1) actual, symbolic, or ritualistic;

2) prayer, invocation, benediction, supplication, appeal, reverent reference to, or embrace of, a general or particular deity;

3) created, delivered, sponsored, or encouraged by government offi-cials;

4) during governmental functions or ceremonies, in the form of patriotic expressions, or associated with holiday observances;

5) which, in and of themselves, are unlikely to indoctrinate or proselytize their audience;

6) which are not specifically designed to accommodate the free religious exercise of a particular group of citizens; and

7) which, as of this date, are deeply rooted in the nation's history and traditions.

Practices which fit this definition can be divided into two categories, the first of which I label "core" ceremonial deism, and the second, "fringe" ceremonial deism. "Core" ceremonial deism includes practices which have been noncontroversial, have resulted in very little litigation, and have never been held unconstitutional by any court. Core ceremonial deism consists of the types of practices that are usually employed in the major premise of the "any more than" syllogism. The bulk of the practices referred to in the Supreme Court opinions discussed above fall into this category, including: (1) legislative prayers and prayer rooms; (2) prayers at presidential inaugurations; (3) presidential addresses invoking the name of God; (4) the invocation "God save the United States and this Honorable Court" prior to judicial proceedings; (5) oaths of public officers, court witnesses, and jurors and the use of the Bible to administer such oaths; (6) the use of "in the year of our Lord" to date public documents; (7) the Thanksgiving and Christmas holidays; (8) the National Day of Prayer; (9) the addition of the words "under God" to the Pledge of Allegiance; and (10) the national motto "In God We Trust." I classify other practices that fit this definition as "fringe" ceremonial deism. Compared to practices which constitute "core" ceremonial deism, these have been more controversial and have resulted in significantly more litigation and occasional findings of unconstitutionality. Fringe ceremonial deism consists of those practices that are usually employed in the minor premise of the "any more than" syllogism, such as: (1) commencement prayers; (2) governmental displays of nativity scenes; (3) religious symbols on government property or embedded in government seals; and (4) the public holiday of Good Friday. Because the focus of this Article is to probe the validity of the major premise of the "any more than" syllogism, the remainder of this Article concentrates on core, rather than fringe, ceremonial deism.

* * *

II.   WHERE DID CORE CEREMONIAL DEISM COME FROM?

According to the definition outlined above, one of the distinguishing features of practices which can be labeled "ceremonial deism" is their deeply rooted origin in the nation's history and traditions. In attempting to assess the constitutional implications of ceremonial deism, therefore, it will be helpful to have in mind a basic understanding of how these practices became so deeply rooted and the continuing role such practices play in modern American society. * * *

A.   Religion in Early America

The citizens of colonial America were "virtually all Christians," the "overwhelming majority" of whom were Protestants. Not surprisingly, therefore, "the values, customs, and forms of Protestant Christianity thoroughly permeated civil and political life." As is widely known, many American colonists came to America to flee religious persecution in Europe. What is perhaps less well known is the extent to which these same colonists made religion an integral part of public life in America. By the time of the American Revolution, there were established churches in ten of the thirteen colonies * * *. Blasphemy was a crime in most jurisdictions; in Vermont it was punishable by death. Sunday Sabbath laws went hand-in-hand with the established European churches America inherited. * * * The religious purpose of these laws was manifest. * * * Although many of the colonists fled Europe specifically to escape religious test oaths, these same colonists were "perfectly willing, when they had the power to do so, to force dissenters from their faith to take test oaths in conformity with that faith." * * * In all, eleven of the thirteen states restricted office holding to Protestants or Christians. * * * Religion was also part of the fabric of the federal government from its very first days. The Declaration of Independence of 1776 "appeal[ed] to the Supreme Judge of the world for the rectitude of our intentions" and avowed "a firm reliance on the protection of a divine Providence." The Articles of Confederation of 1781 paid tribute to the "Great Governor of the World." The Continental Congress authorized mass production of an American edition of the Bible, the accuracy of which was attested to by its chaplains. The First Congress enacted legislation providing for chaplains for the military establishment. * * * Although public schools did not exist in the colonies, it is noteworthy that religious instruction occurred in almost all colonial schools. * * * As formal religious instruction later began to recede, Bible reading, hymns, prayers, and opening and closing religious exercises remained. All seventeen state colleges and universities that existed prior to 1860 "considered themselves Christian and required students to attend religious services." Religion even found its way into early American judicial opinions. Several state courts faced with challenges to Sunday Sabbath legislation gushed about the religious nature of the public and polity. * * *

* * *

B.   The Origin of Core Ceremonial Deism and Its Continuing Significance in Modern American Society

1.   Legislative Prayers and Prayer Rooms.—Legislative prayer was a natural and uncontroversial offshoot of established colonial churches and occurred in colonial legislatures both before and after disestablishment. Prayer continues to be commonplace in modern state legislatures. * * * Although the use of the Capitol for formal worship services eventually ceased, in 1953 the House of Representatives voted to establish a prayer room in the Capitol both to allow legislators to pray while in the Capitol Building and to provide a symbol to the nation and the world that Congress practiced what it preached. The resolution's sponsor

stated that the legislation's purpose was to "provide a place of retreat as an encouragement to prayer. . . . "

* * *

2. Prayers at Presidential Inaugurations.—Formal prayers by Christian ministers have been associated with presidential inaugurations since the inauguration of George Washington. Those who organized President Washington's inauguration took their cue from the analogous practice with which they were most familiar: the English coronation ceremony. The coronation service consisted of both the "crowning" by the Archbishop of Canterbury and the recitation of prayers. The organizers of Washington's inauguration chose to borrow the latter practice despite its foundation in the established Church of England. * * * Although the venue of inaugural prayers * * * moved from the church to the Capitol, the Christian nature of the prayers has remained to this day. * * * The ministers delivering these prayers have sometimes requested the audience to join in them by standing, bowing their heads, and/or praying. * * *

3. Presidential Addresses Invoking the Name of God.—Every President has included reverent references to the deity in his inaugural address to the nation. In his first inaugural address, President Washington offered his "fervent supplications to that Almighty Being who rules over the universe, who presides in the councils of nations, and whose providential aids can supply every human defect." * * * More recently, Presidents Eisenhower, Reagan, and Bush have asked their audiences to join them in prayer. On January 20, 1993, Bill Clinton became the forty-second President to season his inaugural address with an appeal to the deity: " 'We have changed the guard. And now—each in our own way, and with God's help—we must answer the call. Thank you, and God bless you all.' "

4. The Invocation "God save the United States and this Honorable Court" Prior to Judicial Proceedings.—Like the practice of inaugural prayers, the invocation of the Supreme Court, and most lower federal courts, was inherited from England. * * * The invocation "God save the United States and this Honorable Court" has been used to convene Supreme Court sessions since the time John Marshall was Chief Justice and continues today as standard practice in federal courts.

5. Oaths of Public Officers, Court Witnesses, and Jurors and the Use of the Bible to Administer Such Oaths.—Oaths to God to assume public office and in judicial proceedings were inherited from England as well. Anyone who wanted to assume public office in England or to testify in a court proceeding was required to do so in the presence of Almighty God, according to the teachings of the Holy Evangelists, and to kiss the Bible. According to one English scholar, the purpose of the oath was to provide the "highest possible security which men in general can give for the truth of their statements."

Although the oath of office specified in the Constitution for the President and other federal officers does not include a reference to God, Presidents have appealed to the deity in their oaths since the inauguration of George Washington. * * * [U]nder English common law, no one but a believer in God and in a future state of rewards and punishments could serve on a jury or testify as a witness. The oath was taken on a Christian Bible, in effect disqualifying non-Christians. * * *

* * * [A]s late as 1939, five states and the District of Columbia excluded the testimony of those professing a disbelief in God, and, in a dozen or so additional states, the testimony of nonbelievers was subject to attack on the ground that one's credibility was impaired by irreligion or a lack of belief in a deity. Oaths on the Bible are still standard fare in American courtrooms today; witnesses, grand jurors, prospective petit jurors, and interpreters are all asked to swear to tell the truth, "so help me God."

6. The Use of "in the year of our Lord" to Date Public Documents.—Public documents throughout the Christian world have been dated with reference to the birth of Jesus Christ for many centuries. In fact, the American Constitution is dated "the Seventeenth Day of September in the Year of our Lord one thousand seven hundred and Eighty seven." Governmental documents from presidential proclamations to state law licenses to educational diplomas often employ such language. * * *

7. The Thanksgiving and Christmas Holidays.—The Thanksgiving holiday has its origin in the Plymouth colony in 1620. The Continental Congress issued several Thanksgiving Day proclamations between 1775 and 1787. * * * President Washington proclaimed November 26, 1789 the first official American Thanksgiving holiday. His Thanksgiving day proclamation urged all Americans to "unite in most humbly offering our prayers and supplications to the great Lord and Ruler of Nations, and beseech Him to pardon our national and other transgressions." Presidents Adams and Madison also issued Thanksgiving proclamations, as have most Presidents since. These proclamations typically recognize the religious origins and overtones of the holiday. * * * Congress declared Thanksgiving a permanent holiday in the District of Columbia in 1870 and for per diem federal employees in 1885. In 1941, Congress enacted legislation making Thanksgiving a permanent national holiday.

Congress first declared Christmas an official holiday for the District of Columbia in 1870 and for per diem federal employees in 1885, and then made it a national holiday in 1894. Presidents typically make formal Christmas statements to the nation. * * *

8. The National Day of Prayer.—The National Day of Prayer was first proclaimed by the Continental Congress in 1775. * * * It was not until * * * [the Twentieth Century], however, that the "National Day of Prayer" became a permanent, statutory day of observation. In 1952, the Reverend Billy Graham, delivering an evangelical sermon from the east steps of the Capitol, suggested that Congress call on the President to

proclaim an official national day of prayer. A congressional resolution was introduced the following day. The House sponsor, acknowledging the legislation's genesis "by the great spiritual leader, Billy Graham," asserted that "the national interest would be much better served if we turn aside for a full day to pray for spiritual help and guidance from the Almighty during these turbulent times." He also expressed his "hope that all denominations, Catholics, Jewish, and Protestants, will join in this day of prayer.... " * * * The prayer resolution's Senate sponsor stressed a need for divine guidance at this particular time due to threats "at home and abroad by the corrosive forces of communism which seek simultaneously to destroy our democratic way of life and the faith in an Almighty God on which it is based." * * * The enacted legislation calls on the President to "set aside and proclaim the first Thursday in May in each year as a National Day of Prayer, on which the people of the United States may turn to God in prayer and meditation at churches, in groups, and as individuals." Since 1952, every President has issued such a proclamation. * * *

9. The Addition of the Words "under God" to the Pledge of Allegiance.—Few Americans under the age of forty realize that the Pledge of Allegiance has not always contained the words "under God." From its first utterance at a national public school conference in 1892 through its codification as federal law in 1945, the Pledge of Allegiance did not contain any reference to the deity. It was not until June 1954, at the height of the Cold War with the Soviet Union, that this reference to God was added. That change was precipitated by a sermon delivered by the Reverend George M. Docherty at the New York Avenue Presbyterian Church in Washington, with President Eisenhower and several Senators and Representatives in attendance.

* * * This sermon was so powerful that in its wake no fewer than seventeen bills were introduced to incorporate God into the Pledge of Allegiance and portions of it were reprinted in the Senate Report on the final version of the legislation. The fervor that began with this sermon soon infected the public, which responded to Reverend Docherty's proposal and the congressional legislation with overwhelming support. Several themes pervaded the debate to add God to the Pledge of Allegiance. First * * * there was the conclusion that something was needed to distinguish America from its atheistic Cold War rival. Representatives and Senators making this distinction referred to atheism as being amoral, evil, and certainly un-American. Second, repeated reference was made to America as a religious, and to some, a Christian, nation, which was morally compelled to incorporate that spirituality into its national pledge. The symbolism of placing the words " 'under God' on millions of lips" was likened to "running up the believer's flag as the witness of a great nation's faith" to forcefully remind "those who deny the sacred sanctities which it symbolizes" that, like it or not, theirs is a nation that believes devoutly in God. Third, some elected officials fervently believed that America needed to redirect its moral compass to God and, in the opinion of at least one representative, to Jesus Christ. To those legisla-

tors, inserting God into the Pledge of Allegiance was an important symbolic step in that direction. The most pronounced theme running throughout the debate involved the upbringing of America's youth. In floor speech after floor speech, Representatives and Senators asserted that American schoolchildren needed to be indoctrinated with the belief that America is a nation under God. * * *

* * * In view of the legislative history of the enactment of the Pledge of Allegiance, it is hardly surprising that in the same month that the Pledge resolution was enacted, the Senate Judiciary Subcommittee on Constitutional Amendments held hearings on a proposal by Senator Ralph Flanders of Vermont to amend the Constitution "to recognize the authority and law of Jesus Christ."

10. The National Motto "In God We Trust."—Use of slogans recognizing a national trust in God has a wartime lineage dating back to the War of 1812. In September of 1814, fearing for the fate of his country while watching the British bombardment of Fort McHenry in Baltimore, Francis Scott Key composed the poem the "Star Spangled Banner," of which one line in the final stanza is "And this be our motto—'In God is our trust.'" In 1861, in the early days of the Civil War, the Reverend M.R. Watkinson of Pennsylvania wrote to then Secretary of the Treasury Salmon P. Chase, suggesting that a motto signifying America's trust in God be stamped on American coins * * * Soon thereafter, Chase, who would later become Chief Justice of the Supreme Court, wrote the following in a letter to the Director of the Mint: " 'No nation can be strong except in the strength of God, or safe except in His defense. The trust of our people in God should be declared on our national coins.' " * * * * * * [T]he patterns for the half dollar and half eagle submitted in 1862 contained the inscription "God our Trust," and a pattern for a two-cent piece in 1863 included a bust of Washington with the legend "God and our Country." In 1864, the motto "In God We Trust" appeared on the two-cent piece. In 1865, Congress enacted legislation authorizing the phrase to be placed on certain coins. President Theodore Roosevelt ordered the motto removed in 1907, believing that stamping the phrase on coins came " 'dangerously close to sacrilege' " and that there was " 'no legal warrant to place the motto on coins.' " The very next year, Congress responded by mandating the inscription of the phrase on all coins on which it had appeared before Roosevelt's action; Roosevelt acquiesced and signed the legislation.

However, it was not until the height of the Cold War in 1955, in the wake of the Pledge of Allegiance fervor described above, that Congress mandated the inscription of "In God We Trust" on all coins and paper currency. * * *

The following year, Congress codified "In God We Trust" as our national motto. * * *

III. DOES CORE CEREMONIAL DEISM VIOLATE THE ESTABLISHMENT CLAUSE?

With a complete understanding of the origin and current significance of core ceremonial deism in hand, we can now examine the constitutionality of such practices under the Supreme Court's prevailing Establishment Clause jurisprudence. Part III first outlines the Court's Establishment Clause doctrine and principles and then employs this outline in a systematic analysis of the constitutionality of all ten practices of core ceremonial deism. This analysis will answer the questions raised in the Introduction—namely, whether ceremonial deism is compatible with the Court's Establishment Clause doctrine, whether the initial premise of the "any more than" syllogism is valid, and whether the ever-expanding list of practices authorized by that syllogism is justified.

* * *

B. Application of Establishment Clause Jurisprudence to Core Ceremonial Deism

1. Legislative Prayers and Prayer Rooms.—In Congress, each legislative day typically begins with an ordained, appropriately attired, Christian minister delivering a formal prayer to God (and often, to Jesus Christ). That these prayers have the official Congressional stamp of approval is evidenced by (1) Congress's selection and employment of the chaplains; (2) Congress's invitation to these chaplains to deliver prayers from the floor of the House and Senate; and (3) the printing of these prayers in the official transcript of Congress, the Congressional Record. Moreover, these prayers are not delivered merely to a private audience affirmatively seeking spiritual guidance, as might be the case in the military, prisons, or hospitals. Because Congress is a public body, the gallery is typically filled with spectators including ordinary citizens, and, quite frequently, schoolchildren who are brought to Capitol Hill to learn more about the inner workings of their government. Perhaps even more significantly, the daily proceedings of both the House and the Senate are now televised live on cable television, gavel to gavel. The potential viewing audience is, therefore, unlimited and is likely to include children assigned to watch the coverage for school assignments. Legislative prayer consists of "solemn avowal of divine faith and supplication for the blessings of the Almighty. The nature of such a prayer has always been religious. . . . " Furthermore, its sectarian nature cannot be ignored. Every Chaplain selected by Congress in the more than two hundred years of its existence has been Christian. Americans who regularly observe congressional proceedings quickly ascertain that these prayers embrace them only if they happen to be Christian. How else could a non-Christian interpret a prayer that our civilization " 'can be saved only by becoming permeated with the spirit of Christ' " and prayers of similar substance? * * * Analyzing legislative prayer through the endorsement test lens reveals that this practice does not pass constitutional muster. Leaving the obvious purpose of this practice aside, there can be no doubt that legislative prayer sends a message to non-Christians and nonbelievers that "they are outsiders, not full members of the political community, and an accompanying message to [Christians and believers] that they are insiders, favored members of the political community." Legislative

prayer "infringes the religious liberty of the nonadherent" by placing " 'the power, prestige and financial support of government' " behind the religious message embodied by the prayers. The objective, reasonable observer, no matter how well informed about the "history and context" of the practice, could scarcely escape such a conclusion. * * *

2. Prayers at Presidential Inaugurations.—There is perhaps no more of a defining moment in the American democracy than the inauguration of a new President. Inaugural prayers are quite different from legislative prayers in that they are patently intended for all Americans, the thousands in attendance, and millions—including school children in their public classrooms—watching the proceedings live on television. The world and national leaders in attendance and the pomp and circumstance of the event lend the government's stamp of approval to every item on the official inaugural agenda. And the first and last such item on the agenda is typically a prayer by a Christian minister. Just like legislative prayers, inaugural prayers are typically devoutly religious and usually contain Christian references. Inaugural prayer violates the endorsement test's effect prong for the very same reasons legislative prayer does because it too endorses religion over nonreligion and Christianity over other religions. If the purpose of inaugural prayer is to solemnize the seriousness of the occasion, surely this function can be achieved equally effectively through nonreligious means. Consequently, inaugural prayer is unconstitutional.

3. Presidential Addresses Invoking the Name of God.—The practice of presidents invoking the name of God during official addresses presents a different problem than that posed by legislative and inaugural prayers. First, such a practice does not involve selection of a member of a clergy to perform a religious function on behalf of the government. Second, this practice typically does not involve a formal prayer. Third, and most significant, when the President speaks, it is very difficult to draw the line between the individual and the office; to the extent that the individual is perceived to be speaking, a reasonable, objective observer would not view the President's references to God as governmental endorsement of religion. The objective observer would understand that the President does not surrender his First Amendment right to speak freely upon taking the oath of office. * * * As a purely prudential matter, however, presidents should refrain from wrapping their speeches in religious imagery, for in doing so they certainly can make Americans feel like outsiders in their own political community. * * *

4. The Invocation "God save the United States and this Honorable Court" Prior to Judicial Proceedings.—Although brief, this judicial invocation "is a supplication, a prayer." This prayer is similar to legislative and inaugural prayers in that it occurs just prior to official government business and is imbued with the same sort of governmental approval. However, unlike those prayers, it is typically delivered by a bailiff or crier, rather than a minister. Moreover, although the public is invited to attend, the audience is typically much smaller—consisting only of those in attendance in the courtroom. Further, the prayer is static and,

therefore, never sectarian. Nevertheless, the intended audience is significantly more captive than those to whom legislative and inaugural prayers are addressed, since most people present in the courtroom are there to conduct official business. The judicial invocation violates the endorsement test's effect prong. Just like the nonsectarian prayer at issue in Engel, which also referred to God just once, the judicial invocation "convey[s] a message that religion or a particular religious belief is favored or preferred" and "sends a message to nonadherents that they are outsiders, not full members of the political community, and an accompanying message to adherents that they are insiders, favored members of the political community." That this message is nonsectarian does not lessen the endorsement. Those who are required to be in court to conduct official business must listen to the government's endorsement of a transcendent, monotheistic, Judeo–Christian God. * * *

5. Oaths of Public Officers, Court Witnesses, and Jurors and the Use of the Bible to Administer Such Oaths.—As was the case with Sunday Sabbath laws, there can be little dispute that the purpose of public officer and courtroom oaths was initially religious: namely, to employ the fear of eternal damnation to assure that public officers were worthy of the public's trust and that witnesses and jurors would tell the truth. Thus, the key question is whether the religious purpose behind asking public officials, witnesses, and jurors to tell the truth "so help me God" has disappeared. The only logical answer to this question is that it has not; otherwise, the phrase "so help me God" would serve no purpose at all. Moreover, the effect of such oaths is to endorse religion because they send an inescapable message to nonadherents that they are outsiders in the American political community. * * * It is difficult to understand why Torcaso v. Watkins does not compel the conclusion that this practice violates the Establishment Clause. In that case, the State of Maryland permitted elected and appointed officials to take office only upon a declaration that they believed in God. The Court invalidated this requirement on Establishment Clause—not Free Exercise Clause—grounds. * * *[B]ecause the Court chose to ground its opinion on the Establishment Clause, which relates to the purpose and effect of the government's conduct, Torcaso stands for the broader proposition that government officials' involvement in accepting an oath to God offends the First Amendment whether that oath is compelled or not. In language foreshadowing the endorsement test, the Court in Torcaso ruled that the requirement did not pass muster because "[t]he power and authority of the State of Maryland thus is put on the side of one particular sort of believers—those who are willing to say they believe in 'the existence of God.'" The same could be said when government agents ask public officials to swear their oaths "so help me God." That officials can decline to do so does not change the fact that a government agent has placed a Bible in front of them and asked them to do so, thereby placing governmental "power and authority . . . on the side of one particular sort of believers—those who are willing to say they believe in the existence of God." The courtroom oath similarly violates the endorse-

ment test's effect prong. Indispensable to that oath and to the administration of justice is the Christian Bible, which is typically left in open view in American trial courtrooms * * *. By using a Christian Bible to administer the courtroom oath, courts embrace the Bible every bit as much as the school system in Stone embraced the Ten Commandments and the county in Allegheny embraced the nativity scene. * * * A witness or juror who does not believe in the Christian Bible, in swearing to God, or in the God envisioned in the oath, must publicly declare her disbelief in front of (and with the likely perception of disapproval of) a judge and her fellow citizens. If the government is forbidden from coercing a statement of belief, it should be equally forbidden from coercing a confession of nonbelief. * * * [T]he courtroom oath can be said to involve actual coercion of witnesses and jurors to say "I do" even if they do not. The public officer's oath and courtroom oath are classic examples of the government using religious means to accomplish wholly secular goals. * * *

6. The Use of "in the year of our Lord" to Date Public Documents.—The use of the phrase "in the year of our Lord" on public documents implies that Jesus Christ is the official Lord of the governmental entity issuing the document. As the Court concluded in Allegheny with respect to a county creche display, "praise to God in Christian terms is indisputably religious—indeed sectarian—just as it is when said in the Gospel or in a church service." No one viewing a governmental document so dated could reasonably conclude that the phrase had been included on the document, as the creche in Allegheny had stood on the staircase of the county government building, "without the support and approval of the government, [and this] sends an unmistakable message that [the government] supports and promotes the Christian praise to God that is the [phrase's] religious message." * * * [T]he phrase "in the year of our Lord" refers to more than historical fact like "B.C.," "Before Christ." Rather, the phrase "in the year of our Lord" suggests that Jesus Christ is the Lord of both the issuer and the recipient of the document—if not the public generally—whether this is true or not. * * *

7. The Thanksgiving and Christmas Holidays.—Government holidays like Thanksgiving and Christmas are official governmental endorsements of those holidays: by definition, they are selected from the 365–day calendar for special governmental recognition. The question regarding these holidays is whether the governmental endorsement includes an endorsement of religion. The Thanksgiving holiday was unquestionably a religious holiday both at Plymouth Rock and when George Washington proclaimed the first American Thanksgiving to acknowledge the many signal favors of Almighty God. Many would argue that these religious roots have given way to some other, nonreligious meaning and would point to the abundance of secular activities which have become associated with this holiday, including travel, family reunions, turkey and stuffing, professional football games, and the like. Nevertheless, alongside of these secular aspects of Thanksgiving, the religious aspect—as well as the government's endorsement of that aspect—endures. When

the President uses the occasion of Thanksgiving to urge Americans to read the Holy Scriptures, as President Roosevelt did, or to "acknowledge the bounty and mercy of Divine Providence" by gathering in their places of worship, as President Clinton did, it cannot be doubted that the "holiday has not lost its theme of expressing thanks for Divine aid . . . . " As Justice Kennedy stated in Allegheny, "[i]t requires little imagination to conclude that these [Thanksgiving] proclamations would cause non-adherents to feel excluded . . . . " Thus, although the endorsing effect of the Thanksgiving holiday is not as pronounced as the endorsing effect of legislative and inaugural prayer, the Thanksgiving holiday is nonetheless an unconstitutional endorsement of religion. The Christmas holiday is an even clearer violation of the endorsement test. Although, like Thanksgiving, secular elements have attached to this holiday over the years, the religious purpose and effect of this holiday remain unmistakable. The holiday is, after all, the celebration of the birth of the lord and savior of a particular religion, Christianity. * * *

8. The National Day of Prayer.—As was demonstrated above, the National Day of Prayer was a national response to an evangelical sermon by the Reverend Billy Graham. Its explicit purpose was and is to set aside a day for Americans to turn to God in prayer * * *. * * * If the State of Alabama in Wallace violated the Establishment Clause by enacting moment-of-silence legislation with an implicit purpose of "convey[ing] a message of state endorsement and promotion of prayer," then the federal government has even more clearly violated the Clause by enacting legislation in which that purpose is explicit.

9. The Addition of the Words "under God" to the Pledge of Allegiance.—The addition of the words "under God" to the Pledge of Allegiance does, and was intended to, have the effect of endorsing religion. The legislative history of the Pledge amendment mirrors the legislative history behind the moment-of-silence law in Wallace and the anti-evolution statute in Epperson. * * * As the sponsor of the Pledge amendment stated, the legislation was intended to contrast America's embrace of Almighty God with Communist Russia's embrace of atheism. Indeed, like the National Day of Prayer, the genesis of the Pledge amendment occurred not in Congress, but in the pulpit. Although the effect of including the words "under God" in the Pledge of Allegiance may be less pronounced than the effect of the prayers at issue in Engel, Schempp, and Lee, the daily recitation of the amended Pledge of Allegiance nevertheless sends a message to students who do not believe in a monotheistic god "that they are outsiders, not full members of the political community" and instills in them a perception of "disapproval[ ] of their individual religious choices." That this message is nonsectarian does not lessen the endorsement. Finally, like the constitutionally infirm practices at issue in those cases, the Pledge of Allegiance is customarily recited in public schools, where impressionable children are a captive audience. * * *

10. The National Motto "In God We Trust."—It would take an exceptionally creative argument to suggest that a national motto is not a

government endorsement of the content of the motto or that the phrase "In God We Trust" does not embrace religion and a monotheistic god. The legislative history of the various statutes spawning the motto merely serves to underscore its obvious purpose * * *. Although, like the Pledge of Allegiance, the effect of "In God We Trust" is not as pronounced as other endorsements, its pervasiveness on currency serves as a daily reminder to those who do not believe in a monotheistic god "that they are outsiders, not full members of the political community" and instills in them a perception of "disapproval[ ] of their individual religious choices." That this message is non-coercive and nonsectarian does not lessen the endorsement.

IV.   DO ARGUMENTS IN FAVOR OF PRESERVING CORE CEREMONIAL DEISM HAVE MERIT?

Having concluded that all but one of the various forms of core ceremonial deism I have addressed in this Article violate the Establishment Clause, I pause now to consider whether any valid arguments can nevertheless be constructed to defend these practices from constitutional invalidation. Judges and commentators have formulated several such arguments, many of which blend into one another and embody similar themes. * * *

A.   Original Intent

I readily concede that the arguments advanced above fly in the face of the original intent of the Framers of the First Amendment. Chief Justice Burger's statement in Marsh that, in the case of legislative prayer, "historical evidence sheds light not only on what the draftsmen intended the Establishment Clause to mean, but also on how they thought that Clause applied" is highly persuasive. The same argument can be employed to defend most of the practices I have chronicled above. I seriously doubt that any of the Framers would have found these practices troubling, notwithstanding the First Amendment. But unless we are prepared to return to the days when presidential inaugurations include church services, when the House and Senate chambers are used for regular Sunday church services, when Congress may charter a religious institution, when our military institutions can compel those in service to attend religious worship service, and when the Supreme Court can refer to America as a Christian nation, we cannot * * * let an originalist analysis end the inquiry. The Supreme Court has recognized time and time again, in myriad contexts, that the Constitution is not a static document frozen in time and constricted by the predilections of those who framed it. Were it otherwise, African–Americans would still be subjected to Jim Crow laws, segregated schools, and miscegenation statutes; women would not be entitled to the protections of the Equal Protection Clause * * *. The key question is not what the Constitution meant in 1789 or 1791, but what it should mean today. The religious composition and habits of contemporary America are so radically different from those at the time of the founding that using the founding as a baseline is a non sequitur. At the time of the founding, nearly one hundred percent of the nation's citizens were Christian, and most of them were Protestant. Established churches existed in ten of the thirteen colonies, four of which continued those establishments well beyond the adoption of the First Amendment; blasphemy and Sabbath laws were in place everywhere. * * * The America of 1996 is one in which the endorsement test, not originalism, asks the right questions. If there is to be freedom of religion in this country today of the type the Framers contemplated 220 years ago, some practices that seemed perfectly permissible then cannot be perfectly permissible now. * * *

B.   *Solemnization/Acknowledgment*

The argument most frequently advanced by contemporary Supreme Court Justices to justify ceremonial deism, and the one advanced by Justice O'Connor, the endorsement test's founder, is that ceremonial deism serve[s], in the only ways reasonably possible in our culture, the legitimate secular purposes of solemnizing public occasions, expressing confidence in the future, and encouraging the recognition of what is worthy of appreciation in society. For that reason, and because of their history and ubiquity, those practices are not understood as conveying government approval of particular religious beliefs. * * * Boiled down to its essence, this rationale suggests that the practices I have labeled as ceremonial deism are constitutionally permissible because they are (1) necessary to set some governmental events and actions apart from others as being truly important, serious, or special (solemnization); and (2) so ingrained in our history and traditions that the public has come to expect government to embrace religion where it has customarily done so * * *. As was demonstrated in Part III, there are nonreligious means available which are equally, if not more, effective than religious means for "solemnizing public occasions" and "inspiring commitment to meet some national challenge." * * * Moreover, if religious means can be justified by this solemnization function, despite their incompatibility with the governing normative Establishment Clause test, why should constitutional permissibility end with ceremonial deism? Why not permit formal church services during all public events? Why not permit school prayer? * * * The acknowledgment aspect of this argument is flawed for the same reason the original intent justification is flawed: that a practice was embraced by the Founders, and/or has endured for decades or centuries, does not immunize it from constitutional scrutiny. If history and tradition were sufficient to validate long-standing practices against constitutional attack, discrimination against people of color and women, both of which persisted at and long after the enactment of the Fourteenth Amendment, would be constitutionally permissible. In its wisdom, the Court has looked beyond history to recognize that discriminatory practices cannot be squared with the Fourteenth Amendment. * * * * * * [E]ven the seemingly innocuous practices that constitute ceremonial deism cannot be justified by history and tradition, for doing so would validate the very historical discrimination that the Court has stated should play no part in Establishment Clause jurisprudence. * * * Finally, rather than insulating ceremonial deism from constitutional attack, the longevity of the practices at issue makes their affront to religious minorities even more acute than would otherwise be the case. Not only must religious outsiders tolerate these practices now, but they must also do so with the awareness that those who share their religious beliefs have endured these practices for generations. This is one reason why slavery and racial discrimination can still be such painful subjects for African–Americans today. * * *

C. Loss of Religious Significance

Another popular argument used to justify the constitutional permissibility of ceremonial deism is that through rote repetition, transformations which have occurred over time, and the emergence of secular and patriotic traditions associated with religious holidays, these practices have lost whatever religious significance they may once have had. * * * This argument is flawed for three reasons. First, it is squarely at odds with the solemnization argument just discussed. * * * Second, this argument is inconsistent with the abundant supply of cases that have used ceremonial deism in the major premise of the "any more than" syllogism as a springboard from which to hold a religious practice constitutional. To make this syllogism work, ceremonial deism must have a significant religious element; otherwise, the syllogism would break down at the minor premise because the challenged practice would advance religion more than the practices inserted into the major (ceremonial deism) premise, rather than vice versa as intended. * * * Finally, and most significantly, under any honest appraisal of modern American society, the practices constituting ceremonial deism have not lost their religious significance. For instance, it would probably come as a great surprise to most Christians that religion is no longer a significant component of the Christmas holiday. It would likely be equally surprising to the ministers delivering sermons on the floors of Congress and during presidential inaugurations that their actions, over time, have lost religious significance. And although oaths, the judicial invocation, "under God" in the Pledge of Allegiance, and the national motto seem fairly innocuous at first blush, they pack a powerful religious punch to both the most and the least devout members of the American population. * * *

D. De Minimis Endorsement

A fourth justification for leaving ceremonial deism undisturbed despite technical incompatibility with the Establishment Clause hinges on the view that the resulting violation of the Clause is de minimis, and not worthy of judicial action. This argument posits that these practices are so innocuous even to religious minorities, agnostics, and atheists that they cause too little harm to be a real threat to religious liberty. * * * This argument is flawed for several reasons. First and foremost, the Supreme Court has stated several times that "it is no defense to urge that the religious practices here may be relatively minor encroachments on the First Amendment. The breach of neutrality that is today a trickling stream may all too soon become a raging torrent.... " This slippery slope concern is particularly warranted in the case of ceremonial deism because of its use in the "any more than" syllogism to authorize an ever-expanding sphere of activities which are held constitutionally permissible because they do not advance religion "any more than" the practices embodying ceremonial deism. * * * Second, whether a violation of the Establishment Clause is "de minimis" cannot be reduced to normative inquiry; it is rather a matter of perspective. It is all too simple for those in the religious mainstream to argue that pledging allegiance to a nation "under God," whose motto is "In God We Trust," produces at most a de minimis endorsement. The magnitude of the endorsement, however, is enhanced significantly for those for whom "God" has either no meaning or a meaning wholly inconsistent with strongly held religious beliefs. Those in the religious mainstream can better appreciate this reality by substituting "Allah" for God in these examples and the ones recounted in the opening paragraph in this Article. If the examples embracing Allah appear to be more than de minimis violations of the Establishment Clause to those in the religious mainstream, merely substituting "God" for "Allah" should not alter that constitutional reality. Third, even when the message embodied by ceremonial deism is watered down into its most nonsectarian formulation, its effect is more than de minimis on religious outsiders. The watered-down, "nonsectarian" religious content "amplifies the message of exclusion to those left out. Because such prayers are carefully orchestrated not to offend anyone who counts in the community, the message to those who are offended is that they do not count—that they are not important enough to avoid offending." * * *

E. Societal Acceptance

A closely related argument is that despite technical incompatibility with the Establishment Clause, ceremonial deism should be left alone because American citizens—even nonbelievers and religious minorities—overwhelmingly accept these practices. This rationale infers societal acceptance from the dearth of complaints and litigation over ceremonial deism. It would be a huge leap to deduce from the paucity of challenges to these practices that they have been warmly embraced by the American citizenry. As history has poignantly made clear, the price of challenging unconstitutional establishments of religion can be exacting. The president of the American Civil Liberties Union recently wrote that "[o]ften these victims of religious liberty violations do not want even to file a claim in court, even when we assure them they would win, because of the hostility, enmity, persecution, and attacks they would face." As an example, she recounted the startling facts surrounding a case involving a public elementary and junior high school in Oklahoma which sponsored organized student prayer meetings at the beginning of the school day until the 1980s. Plaintiff children were harassed and insulted by teachers and students for not attending the meetings. After suit was filed, upside-down crosses were taped to their school lockers and the prize-winning goat of one of the children had its throat slit; their mother was attacked by a school employee, who repeatedly bashed her head against a car door and threatened to kill her; and, eventually, the family's home was burned to the ground while the mother attended her son's football game. Violent responses to litigation challenging governmental endorsements of religion are not simply a product of the violent times in which we live. They result from the intensity with which religious believers savor and cling to governmental endorsement. * * * Simply stated, the ostracism that befalls plaintiffs who challenge cherished governmental endorsements of religion is so extreme that most who are offended by these practices bite their tongues and go about their lives. Moreover, in view of the dicta in Supreme Court and lower court cases suggesting that ceremonial deism passes constitutional muster, those who might be inclined to file suit must consider not only the hatred and violence that their litigation will engender, but also the dismal prospect that suffering through such harassment will be worth their while. * * * In addition, there is a disturbing veneer to the societal acceptance argument that majority acceptance equates with constitutional validity. The purpose of the Constitution generally, and the Establishment Clause specifically, is to protect minorities from raw majoritarian impulses. * * * Using majority acceptance of ceremonial deism to justify its constitutionality stands the Constitution on its head.

F. Accommodation

Still another argument that has been used to justify ceremonial deism is that these practices merely serve to accommodate the religious practices of most American citizens and, thus, should not be viewed as unconstitutional endorsement. This rationale has been used most frequently to justify the Christmas holiday * * *. * * *

This argument is flawed for two reasons. First, when the government sets aside the Christmas day as a national holiday, its true motive is to recognize the religious meaning of the day, rather than to accommodate the religious practices of American citizens. The sectarian Christmas messages delivered by our last three Presidents on Christmas day make this point amply clear. Second, accommodation is permissible under the First Amendment only if it "lift[s] a discernible burden on the free exercise of religion." Just as "[t]he display of a creche in a courthouse does not remove any burden on the free exercise of Christianity," governmental declaration of the holiday itself removes no burdens because none exist. Even if the government did not declare Christmas a holiday, Christians would still be able to exercise their religion on that day just as freely as they do on Christian holidays not recognized by the federal and state governments, such as Good Friday, and just as Muslims, Hindus, and other religious minorities do on their non governmentally endorsed religious holidays. To be sure, as is the case with the display of a creche in a courthouse, prohibiting the governmental declaration of the Christmas holiday also "deprives Christians of the satisfaction of seeing the government adopt their religious message as their own; but this kind of government affiliation with particular religious messages is precisely what the Establishment Clause precludes." * * *

CONCLUSION

Since the emergence of its Establishment Clause jurisprudence nearly fifty years ago, the Supreme Court has struggled mightily to explain why ceremonial deism is permitted in our constitutional framework while other practices the Court has invalidated are not. The normative vision embraced by the endorsement test is blurred beyond recognition if practices such as legislative prayer, the National Day of Prayer, a Pledge of Allegiance to a nation "under God," and the like are permitted to persist. Any explanation of why these practices survive constitutional scrutiny under this test, while school prayer and other practices invalidated by the Court do not, is hopelessly inadequate. As Justice Kennedy noted in his Allegheny dissent, "[e]ither the endorsement test must invalidate scores of traditional practices . . . or it must be twisted and stretched to avoid inconsistency with practices we know to have been permitted in the past." Equally, if not more problematic, the Court's embrace of the "any more than" syllogism, coupled with its acceptance of ceremonial deism, has created a slippery slope that will likely erode the endorsement test significantly in the years ahead. If, however, the Court means what it says when it espouses the principle that government may not, consistent with the Establishment Clause, endorse religion and send messages to citizens that cause them to feel like outsiders in the political community, the Court should have the intellectual honesty and fortitude to recognize that ceremonial deism violates a core purpose of the Establishment Clause. Undoubtedly, such a decision will be very unpopular in an America in which the religious majority has grown all too accustomed to seeing its practices and traditions endorsed by the government. But the Court has in the past had the courage to make and enforce unpopular decisions in the areas of segregation, school prayer, criminal procedure, and abortion. Just as society has, in large measure, grown to accept these decisions, American citizens can certainly learn to accept a decision that will ensure that their grandchildren and great-grandchildren, no matter what America's religious composition is in their time, will never be made to feel like outsiders.

Notes and Questions

1. *Defending Ceremonial Deism.* Epstein's article represents one side of the debate over ceremonial deism. The other side is reflected in a number of judicial opinions throughout this book, including *Marsh v. Chambers*, the next principle case. Daniel O. Conkle, a leading scholar in the Law & Religion field, has noted:

Under a political-moral analysis, government action designed to favor religion is less troublesome when it is supported by tradition, and the judicial invalidation of such action carries significant costs of its own. As a result, the Supreme Court's subtheme, recognizing exceptions to the usual doctrine of Everson and Lemon [in the context of ceremonial deism], is at least partially defensible. In particular, the Court properly may uphold traditional symbolic support for religion, and it may permit certain types of traditional financial support as well.

Daniel O. Conkle, *Toward a General Theory of the Establishment Clause*, 82 Nw. U. L. Rev. 1113, 1186–87 (1988).

However, Conkle suggests that the Pledge of Allegiance issue might require a different analysis than other forms of traditional government acknowledgment of religion:

The reference to God in the Pledge of Allegiance * * * is considerably more problematic. In many settings, such as the public schools, the pledge is likely to be used in a manner that is directly coercive. Even in the absence of direct coercion, moreover, this practice, dating back only to 1954, may not be sufficiently long-standing to qualify as 'traditional' under the analysis I have suggested. * * *

Id. at 1185 n. 283. What do you think of Conkle's suggestion that upholding practices that are supported by a long tradition is less problematic because of that tradition? Isn't Conkle almost certainly correct when he asserts that invalidating such practices can carry a "significant" cost? Think about the public and Congressional response to the *Newdow* case. Should this matter to the Court? Can strong public and political approval validate an allegedly unconstitutional practice? Can it *help* to validate such a practice? Or should it be irrelevant to the constitutionality of a challenged practice?

2. *Defining Ceremonial Deism.* After reading the materials in this section, how would you define ceremonial deism? Should the definition allow for expansion or will this simply lead to an enveloping syllogism as suggested in Epstein's article? Is there any point to defining ceremonial deism? If so, what purpose does it serve? If not, how would you address the motto "In God We Trust" on U.S. currency and similar phenomena?

3. *Is the pledge different?* If there is a viable category of ceremonial deism, the question remains whether the Pledge of Allegiance, or more specifically the 1954 amendment to the pledge that added the words "Under God," is Constitutional. Does the history of the 1954 amendment to the pledge take the pledge out of the realm of ceremonial deism? If so, can the history of other practices included under the rubric of ceremonial deism take those practices out of the category of ceremonial deism? Does the relatively recent time of the 1954 amendment make a difference in analyzing the constitutionality of the pledge? If so, how recent must a practice be to fall outside the category of longstanding tradition?

4. *Legislative Prayer.* One of the issues mentioned in the Epstein article, and often referred to by proponents and opponents of giving ceremonial deism special status, is the issue of legislative prayer. As you will see in the next section, the Supreme Court has specifically addressed this issue. Before reading the next section, consider whether you think such prayer should be Constitutional under the Court's existing Establishment Clause precedent. What factors might be relevant to your analysis and what would you want to know about the legislative prayer in question?

B. ORGANIZED RELIGIOUS EXERCISES IN CONTEXTS OTHER THAN PUBLIC SCHOOLS

One of the most common examples of religious exercises at government sponsored events is legislative prayer. Legislative prayer has often been characterized as a form of ceremonial deism (including in the above materials). Unlike prayer in the public schools, legislative prayer dates back to the time of the Framers both in federal and state governments. At the time of the framing public schools did not generally exist, so the prayer in school issue was not even on the radar screen for the framers. However, legislative prayer and legislative chaplains did exist. What should this mean for the practice? Does it make a difference that there is generally only one legislative chaplain at a time in a given legislature and that Protestant ministers have dominated most state, and until recently, the federal chaplaincies? Recently, Congress approved the first Catholic chaplain, but even that decision was fraught with disagreements along religious lines. Yet, there has been a legislative chaplain since the time of the first Congress, which ratified the First Amendment. What should this mean for legislative chaplaincy and legislative prayer? Would the prayer be more acceptable if there was not an official chaplain? How would legislative prayer and legislative chaplaincies be analyzed under the *Lemon* test—the prevailing test at the time the following case was decided? How would legislative chaplaincies or legislative prayer be analyzed under the Court's other tests? Read on and you will see how the Court and the dissenting Justices addressed this issue.

MARSH v. CHAMBERS

Supreme Court of the United States, 1983.
463 U.S. 783, 103 S.Ct. 3330, 77 L.Ed.2d 1019.

CHIEF JUSTICE BURGER delivered the opinion of the Court.

The question presented is whether the Nebraska Legislature's practice of opening each legislative day with a prayer by a chaplain paid by the State violates the Establishment Clause of the First Amendment.

I

The Nebraska Legislature begins each of its sessions with a prayer offered by a chaplain who is chosen biennially by the Executive Board of the Legislative Council and paid out of public funds. Robert E. Palmer, a Presbyterian minister, has served as chaplain since 1965 at a salary of $319.75 per month for each month the legislature is in session.

Ernest Chambers is a member of the Nebraska Legislature and a taxpayer of Nebraska. Claiming that the Nebraska Legislature's chaplaincy practice violates the Establishment Clause of the First Amendment, he brought this action under 42 U.S.C. § 1983, seeking to enjoin enforcement of the practice. * * *

* * *

We granted certiorari limited to the challenge to the practice of opening sessions with prayers by a State-employed clergyman * * *.

II

The opening of sessions of legislative and other deliberative public bodies with prayer is deeply embedded in the history and tradition of this country. From colonial times through the founding of the Republic and ever since, the practice of legislative prayer has coexisted with the principles of disestablishment and religious freedom. In the very courtrooms in which the United States District Judge and later three Circuit Judges heard and decided this case, the proceedings opened with an announcement that concluded, "God save the United States and this Honorable Court." The same invocation occurs at all sessions of this Court.

The tradition in many of the colonies was, of course, linked to an established church, but the Continental Congress, beginning in 1774, adopted the traditional procedure of opening its sessions with a prayer offered by a paid chaplain. Although prayers were not offered during the Constitutional Convention, the First Congress, as one of its early items of business, adopted the policy of selecting a chaplain to open each session with prayer. Thus, on April 7, 1789, the Senate appointed a committee "to take under consideration the manner of electing Chaplains." On April 9, 1789, a similar committee was appointed by the House of Representatives. On April 25, 1789, the Senate elected its first chaplain; the House followed suit on May 1, 1789. A statute providing for the payment of these chaplains was enacted into law on Sept. 22, 1789.[8]

On Sept. 25, 1789, three days after Congress authorized the appointment of paid chaplains, final agreement was reached on the language of the Bill of Rights. Clearly the men who wrote the First Amendment Religion Clause did not view paid legislative chaplains and opening prayers as a violation of that Amendment, for the practice of opening sessions with prayer has continued without interruption ever since that early session of Congress.[10] It has also been followed consistently in most of the states, including Nebraska, where the institution of opening

8. It bears note that James Madison, one of the principal advocates of religious freedom in the colonies and a drafter of the Establishment Clause, was one of those appointed to undertake this task by the House of Representatives, and voted for the bill authorizing payment of the chaplains.

10. The chaplaincy was challenged in the 1850's by "sundry petitions praying Congress to abolish the office of chaplain." After consideration by the Senate Committee on the Judiciary, the Senate decided that the practice did not violate the Establishment Clause, reasoning that a rule permitting Congress to elect chaplains is not a law establishing a national church and that the chaplaincy was no different from Sunday Closing Laws, which the Senate thought clearly constitutional. In addition, the Senate reasoned that since prayer was said by the very Congress that adopted the Bill of Rights, the Founding Fathers could not have intended the First Amendment to forbid legislative prayer or viewed prayer as a step toward an established church. In any event, the 35th Congress abandoned the practice of electing chaplains in favor of inviting local clergy to officiate. Elected chaplains were reinstituted by the 36th Congress.

legislative sessions with prayer was adopted even before the State attained statehood.

Standing alone, historical patterns cannot justify contemporary violations of constitutional guarantees, but there is far more here than simply historical patterns. In this context, historical evidence sheds light not only on what the draftsmen intended the Establishment Clause to mean, but also on how they thought that Clause applied to the practice authorized by the First Congress—their actions reveal their intent. * * *

In *Walz v. Tax Comm'n*, we considered the weight to be accorded to history:

> "It is obviously correct that no one acquires a vested or protected right in violation of the Constitution by long use, even when that span of time covers our entire national existence and indeed predates it. Yet an unbroken practice . . . is not something to be lightly cast aside."

No more is Nebraska's practice of over a century, consistent with two centuries of national practice, to be cast aside. It can hardly be thought that in the same week Members of the First Congress voted to appoint and to pay a Chaplain for each House and also voted to approve the draft of the First Amendment for submission to the States, they intended the Establishment Clause of the Amendment to forbid what they had just declared acceptable. In applying the First Amendment to the states through the Fourteenth Amendment, it would be incongruous to interpret that clause as imposing more stringent First Amendment limits on the States than the draftsmen imposed on the Federal Government.

This unique history leads us to accept the interpretation of the First Amendment draftsmen who saw no real threat to the Establishment Clause arising from a practice of prayer similar to that now challenged. * * *

Respondent cites Justice Brennan's concurring opinion in *Abington School Dist. v. Schempp*, and argues that we should not rely too heavily on "the advice of the Founding Fathers" because the messages of history often tend to be ambiguous and not relevant to a society far more heterogeneous than that of the Framers. Respondent also points out that John Jay and John Rutledge opposed the motion to begin the first session of the Continental Congress with prayer.

We do not agree that evidence of opposition to a measure weakens the force of the historical argument; indeed it infuses it with power by demonstrating that the subject was considered carefully and the action not taken thoughtlessly, by force of long tradition and without regard to the problems posed by a pluralistic society. Jay and Rutledge specifically grounded their objection on the fact that the delegates to the Congress "were so divided in religious sentiments . . . that [they] could not join in the same act of worship." Their objection was met by Samuel Adams, who stated that "he was no bigot, and could hear a prayer from a gentleman of piety and virtue, who was at the same time a friend to his country."

This interchange emphasizes that the delegates did not consider opening prayers as a proselytizing activity or as symbolically placing the government's "official seal of approval on one religious view." * * * The Establishment Clause does not always bar a state from regulating conduct simply because it "harmonizes with religious canons." Here, the individual claiming injury by the practice is an adult, presumably not readily susceptible to "religious indoctrination," or peer pressure.

In light of the unambiguous and unbroken history of more than 200 years, there can be no doubt that the practice of opening legislative sessions with prayer has become part of the fabric of our society. To invoke Divine guidance on a public body entrusted with making the laws is not, in these circumstances, an "establishment" of religion or a step toward establishment; it is simply a tolerable acknowledgment of beliefs widely held among the people of this country. As Justice Douglas observed, "[w]e are a religious people whose institutions presuppose a Supreme Being." *Zorach v. Clauson*.

III

We turn then to the question of whether any features of the Nebraska practice violate the Establishment Clause. Beyond the bare fact that a prayer is offered, three points have been made: first, that a clergyman of only one denomination—Presbyterian—has been selected for 16 years; second, that the chaplain is paid at public expense; and third, that the prayers are in the Judeo–Christian tradition.[14] Weighed against the historical background, these factors do not serve to invalidate Nebraska's practice.

The Court of Appeals was concerned that Palmer's long tenure has the effect of giving preference to his religious views. We, no more than Members of the Congresses of this century, can perceive any suggestion that choosing a clergyman of one denomination advances the beliefs of a particular church. To the contrary, the evidence indicates that Palmer was reappointed because his performance and personal qualities were acceptable to the body appointing him. Palmer was not the only clergyman heard by the Legislature; guest chaplains have officiated at the request of various legislators and as substitutes during Palmer's absences. Absent proof that the chaplain's reappointment stemmed from an impermissible motive, we conclude that his long tenure does not in itself conflict with the Establishment Clause.[17]

---

14. Palmer characterizes his prayers as "nonsectarian," "Judeo Christian," and with "elements of the American civil religion." Although some of his earlier prayers were often explicitly Christian, Palmer removed all references to Christ after a 1980 complaint from a Jewish legislator.

17. We note that Dr. Edward L.R. Elson served as Chaplain of the Senate of the United States from January 1969 to February 1981, a period of 12 years; Dr. Frederick Brown Harris served from February 1949 to January 1969, a period of 20 years.

Nor is the compensation of the chaplain from public funds a reason to invalidate the Nebraska Legislature's chaplaincy; remuneration is grounded in historic practice initiated, as we noted earlier, by the same Congress that adopted the Establishment Clause of the First Amendment. The Continental Congress paid its chaplain, as did some of the states. Currently, many state legislatures and the United States Congress provide compensation for their chaplains. * * * The content of the prayer is not of concern to judges where, as here, there is no indication that the prayer opportunity has been exploited to proselytize or advance any one, or to disparage any other, faith or belief. That being so, it is not for us to embark on a sensitive evaluation or to parse the content of a particular prayer.

We do not doubt the sincerity of those, who like respondent, believe that to have prayer in this context risks the beginning of the establishment the Founding Fathers feared. But this concern is not well founded * * *.

The judgment of the Court of Appeals is *Reversed.*

JUSTICE BRENNAN, with whom JUSTICE MARSHALL joins, dissenting.

The Court today has written a narrow and, on the whole, careful opinion. In effect, the Court holds that officially sponsored legislative prayer, primarily on account of its "unique history," is generally exempted from the First Amendment's prohibition against "the establishment of religion." The Court's opinion is consistent with dictum in at least one of our prior decisions, and its limited rationale should pose little threat to the overall fate of the Establishment Clause. Moreover, disagreement with the Court requires that I confront the fact that some twenty years ago, in a concurring opinion in one of the cases striking down official prayer and ceremonial Bible reading in the public schools, I came very close to endorsing essentially the result reached by the Court today. Nevertheless, after much reflection, I have come to the conclusion that I was wrong then and that the Court is wrong today. I now believe that the practice of official invocational prayer, as it exists in Nebraska and most other State Legislatures, is unconstitutional. It is contrary to the doctrine as well the underlying purposes of the Establishment Clause, and it is not saved either by its history or by any of the other considerations suggested in the Court's opinion. * * *

I

The Court makes no pretense of subjecting Nebraska's practice of legislative prayer to any of the formal "tests" that have traditionally structured our inquiry under the Establishment Clause. That it fails to do so is, in a sense, a good thing, for it simply confirms that the Court is carving out an exception to the Establishment Clause rather than reshaping Establishment Clause doctrine to accommodate legislative prayer. For my purposes, however, I must begin by demonstrating what should be obvious: that, if the Court were to judge legislative prayer through the unsentimental eye of our settled doctrine, it would have to strike it down as a clear violation of the Establishment Clause.

* * *

That the "purpose" of legislative prayer is preeminently religious rather than secular seems to me to be self-evident. "To invoke Divine guidance on a public body entrusted with making the laws," is nothing but a religious act. Moreover, whatever secular functions legislative prayer might play—formally opening the legislative session, getting the members of the body to quiet down, and imbuing them with a sense of seriousness and high purpose—could so plainly be performed in a purely nonreligious fashion that to claim a secular purpose for the prayer is an insult to the perfectly honorable individuals who instituted and continue the practice.

The "primary effect" of legislative prayer is also clearly religious. As we said in the context of officially sponsored prayers in the public schools, "prescribing a particular form of religious worship," even if the individuals involved have the choice not to participate, places "indirect coercive pressure upon religious minorities to conform to the prevailing officially approved religion.... " *Engel v. Vitale*.[5] More importantly, invocations in Nebraska's legislative halls explicitly link religious belief and observance to the power and prestige of the State. * * *

Finally, there can be no doubt that the practice of legislative prayer leads to excessive "entanglement" between the State and religion. *Lemon* pointed out that "entanglement" can take two forms: First, a state statute or program might involve the state impermissibly in monitoring and overseeing religious affairs. In the case of legislative prayer, the process of choosing a "suitable" chaplain, whether on a permanent or rotating basis, and insuring that the chaplain limits himself or herself to "suitable" prayers, involves precisely the sort of supervision that agencies of government should if at all possible avoid.

Second, excessive "entanglement" might arise out of "the divisive political potential" of a state statute or program. * * * In this case, this second aspect of entanglement is also clear. The controversy between Senator Chambers and his colleagues, which had reached the stage of difficulty and rancor long before this lawsuit was brought, has split the Nebraska Legislature precisely on issues of religion and religious conformity. The record in this case also reports a series of instances, involving legislators other than Senator Chambers, in which invocations by Reverend Palmer and others led to controversy along religious lines. And in general, the history of legislative prayer has been far more

---

5. * * * The Court argues that legislators are adults, "presumably not readily susceptible to ... peer pressure." I made a similar observation in my concurring opinion in *Schempp*. Quite apart from the debatable constitutional significance of this argument, I am now most uncertain as to whether it is even factually correct: Legislators, by virtue of their instinct for political survival, are often loath to assert in public religious views that their constituents might perceive as hostile or non-conforming. See generally P. Blanshard, God and Man in Washington 94–106 (1960).

eventful—and divisive—than a hasty reading of the Court's opinion might indicate.[10]

In sum, I have no doubt that, if any group of law students were asked to apply the principles of *Lemon* to the question of legislative prayer, they would nearly unanimously find the practice to be unconstitutional.

II

The path of formal doctrine, however, can only imperfectly capture the nature and importance of the issues at stake in this case. A more adequate analysis must therefore take into account the underlying function of the Establishment Clause, and the forces that have shaped its doctrine.

A

Most of the provisions of the Bill of Rights, even if they are not generally enforceable in the absence of state action, nevertheless arise out of moral intuitions applicable to individuals as well as governments. The Establishment Clause, however, is quite different. It is, to its core, nothing less and nothing more than a statement about the proper role of *government* in the society that we have shaped for ourselves in this land.

The Establishment Clause embodies a judgment, born of a long and turbulent history, that, in our society, religion "must be a private matter for the individual, the family, and the institutions of private choice.... " *Lemon v. Kurtzman.* * * *

The principles of "separation" and "neutrality" implicit in the Establishment Clause serve many purposes. Four of these are particularly relevant here.

The first, which is most closely related to the more general conceptions of liberty found in the remainder of the First Amendment, is to guarantee the individual right to conscience. The right to conscience, in

---

10. As the Court points out, the practice of legislative prayers in Congress gave rise to serious controversy at points in the 19th century. Opposition to the practice in that period arose "both on the part of certain radicals and of some rather extreme Protestant sects. These have been inspired by very different motives but have united in opposing government chaplaincies as breaking down the line of demarcation between Church and State. The sectarians felt that religion had nothing to do with the State, while the radicals felt that the State had nothing to do with religion." 3 A. Stokes, Church and State in the United States 130 (1950) (hereinafter Stokes). Similar controversies arose in the States.

In more recent years, particular prayers and particular chaplains in the state legislatures have periodically led to serious politi-cal divisiveness along religious lines. See, *e.g.,* The Oregonian, Apr. 1, 1983, p. C8 ("Despite protests from at least one representative, a follower of an Indian guru was allowed to give the prayer at the start of Thursday's [Oregon] House [of Representatives] session. Shortly before Ma Anand Sheela began the invocation, about a half-dozen representatives walked off the House floor in apparent protest of the prayer."); California Senate Journal, 37th Sess., 171–173, 307–308 (1907) (discussing request by a State Senator that State Senate Chaplain not use the name of Christ in legislative prayer, and response by one local clergyman claiming that the legislator who made the request had committed a "crowning infamy" and that his "words were those of an irreverent and godless man").

the religious sphere, is not only implicated when the government engages in direct or indirect coercion. It is also implicated when the government requires individuals to support the practices of a faith with which they do not agree. * * *

The second purpose of separation and neutrality is to keep the state from interfering in the essential autonomy of religious life, either by taking upon itself the decision of religious issues, or by unduly involving itself in the supervision of religious institutions or officials.

The third purpose of separation and neutrality is to prevent the trivialization and degradation of religion by too close an attachment to the organs of government. The Establishment Clause "stands as an expression of principle on the part of the Founders of our Constitution that religion is too personal, too sacred, too holy to permit its 'unhallowed perversion' by a civil magistrate." *Engel v. Vitale*, quoting Memorial and Remonstrance against Religious Assessments.

Finally, the principles of separation and neutrality help assure that essentially religious issues, precisely because of their importance and sensitivity, not become the occasion for battle in the political arena. With regard to most issues, the Government may be influenced by partisan argument and may act as a partisan itself. In each case, there will be winners and losers in the political battle, and the losers' most common recourse is the right to dissent and the right to fight the battle again another day. With regard to matters that are essentially religious, however, the Establishment Clause seeks that there should be no political battles, and that no American should at any point feel alienated from his government because that government has declared or acted upon some "official" or "authorized" point of view on a matter of religion.[17]

B

The imperatives of separation and neutrality are not limited to the relationship of government to religious institutions or denominations, but extend as well to the relationship of government to religious beliefs and practices. * * * As we said in *Engel*, "[i]t is neither sacrilegious nor anti-religious to say that each separate government in this country should stay out of the business of writing or sanctioning official prayers and leave that purely religious function to the people themselves and to those the people choose to look to for religious guidance."

Nor should it be thought that this view of the Establishment Clause is a recent concoction of an overreaching judiciary. Even before the First Amendment was written, the Framers of the Constitution broke with the practice of the Articles of Confederation and many state constitutions,

---

17. It is sometimes argued that to apply the Establishment Clause alienates those who wish to see a tighter bond between religion and state. This is obviously true. (I would vigorously deny, however, any claim that the Establishment Clause disfavors the much broader class of persons for whom religion is a necessary and important part of life.) But I would submit that even this dissatisfaction is tempered by the knowledge that society is adhering to a fixed rule of neutrality rather than rejecting a particular expression of religious belief.

and did not invoke the name of God in the document. This "omission of a reference to the Deity was not inadvertent; nor did it remain unnoticed." Moreover, Thomas Jefferson and Andrew Jackson, during their respective terms as President, both refused on Establishment Clause grounds to declare national days of thanksgiving or fasting. And James Madison, writing subsequent to his own Presidency on essentially the very issue we face today, stated:

> "Is the appointment of Chaplains to the two Houses of Congress consistent with the Constitution, and with the pure principle of religious freedom?
>
> In strictness, the answer on both points must be in the negative. The Constitution of the U.S. forbids everything like an establishment of a national religion. The law appointing Chaplains establishes a religious worship for the national representatives, to be performed by Ministers of religion, elected by a majority of them; and these are to be paid out of the national taxes. Does not this involve the principle of a national establishment, applicable to a provision for a religious worship for the Constituent as well as of the representative Body, approved by the majority, and conducted by Ministers of religion paid by the entire nation." Fleet, Madison's "Detached Memoranda," 3 Wm. & Mary Quarterly 534, 558 (1946).

C

Legislative prayer clearly violates the principles of neutrality and separation that are embedded within the Establishment Clause. It is contrary to the fundamental message of *Engel* and *Schempp*. It intrudes on the right to conscience by forcing some legislators either to participate in a "prayer opportunity," with which they are in basic disagreement, or to make their disagreement a matter of public comment by declining to participate. It forces all residents of the State to support a religious exercise that may be contrary to their own beliefs. It requires the State to commit itself on fundamental theological issues. It has the potential for degrading religion by allowing a religious call to worship to be intermeshed with a secular call to order. And it injects religion into the political sphere by creating the potential that each and every selection of a chaplain, or consideration of a particular prayer, or even reconsideration of the practice itself, will provoke a political battle along religious lines and ultimately alienate some religiously identified group of citizens.

* * *

III

* * * I sympathize with the Court's reluctance to strike down a practice so prevalent and so ingrained as legislative prayer. I am, however, unconvinced by the Court's arguments, and cannot shake my conviction that legislative prayer violates both the letter and the spirit of the Establishment Clause.

A

The Court's main argument for carving out an exception sustaining legislative prayer is historical. The Court cannot—and does not—purport to find a pattern of "undeviating acceptance," of legislative prayer. It also disclaims exclusive reliance on the mere longevity of legislative prayer. The Court does, however, point out that, only three days before the First Congress reached agreement on the final wording of the Bill of Rights, it authorized the appointment of paid chaplains for its own proceedings, and the Court argues that in light of this "unique history," the actions of Congress reveal its intent as to the meaning of the Establishment Clause. I agree that historical practice is "of considerable import in the interpretation of abstract constitutional language." This is a case, however, in which—absent the Court's invocation of history— there would be no question that the practice at issue was unconstitutional. And despite the surface appeal of the Court's argument, there are at least three reasons why specific historical practice should not in this case override that clear constitutional imperative.[30]

First, it is significant that the Court's historical argument does not rely on the legislative history of the Establishment Clause itself. * * * Rather, the Court assumes that the Framers of the Establishment Clause would not have themselves authorized a practice that they thought violated the guarantees contained in the clause. This assumption, however, is questionable. Legislators, influenced by the passions and exigencies of the moment, the pressure of constituents and colleagues, and the press of business, do not always pass sober constitutional judgment on every piece of legislation they enact, and this must be assumed to be as true of the members of the First Congress as any other. Indeed, the fact that James Madison, who voted for the bill authorizing the payment of the first congressional chaplains, later expressed the view that the practice was unconstitutional, is instructive on precisely this point. * * *

Second, the Court's analysis treats the First Amendment simply as an Act of Congress, as to whose meaning the intent of Congress is the single touchstone. Both the Constitution and its amendments, however, became supreme law only by virtue of their ratification by the States, and the understanding of the States should be as relevant to our analysis as the understanding of Congress. This observation is especially compelling in considering the meaning of the Bill of Rights. The first 10 Amendments were not enacted because the members of the First Congress came up with a bright idea one morning; rather, their enactment was forced upon Congress by a number of the States as a condition for

---

30. Indeed, the sort of historical argument made by the Court should be advanced with some hesitation in light of certain other skeletons in the congressional closet. See, *e.g.,* An Act for the Punishment of certain Crimes against the United States, § 16, 1 Stat. 116 (1790) (enacted by the First Congress and requiring that persons convicted of certain theft offenses "be publicly whipped, not exceeding thirty-nine stripes"); Act of July 23, 1866, 14 Stat. 216 (reaffirming the racial segregation of the public schools in the District of Columbia; enacted exactly one week after Congress proposed Fourteenth Amendment to the States).

their ratification of the original Constitution. To treat any practice authorized by the First Congress as presumptively consistent with the Bill of Rights is therefore somewhat akin to treating any action of a party to a contract as presumptively consistent with the terms of the contract. * * *

Finally, and most importantly, the argument tendered by the Court is misguided because the Constitution is not a static document whose meaning on every detail is fixed for all time by the life experience of the Framers. We have recognized in a wide variety of constitutional contexts that the practices that were in place at the time any particular guarantee was enacted into the Constitution do not necessarily fix forever the meaning of that guarantee. To be truly faithful to the Framers, "our use of the history of their time must limit itself to broad purposes, not specific practices." *Abington School Dist. v. Schempp,* 374 U.S., at 241, 83 S.Ct., at 1581 (Brennan, J., concurring). * * *

The inherent adaptability of the Constitution and its amendments is particularly important with respect to the Establishment Clause. "[O]ur religious composition makes us a vastly more diverse people than were our forefathers.... In the face of such profound changes, practices which may have been objectionable to no one in the time of Jefferson and Madison may today be highly offensive to many persons, the deeply devout and the nonbelievers alike." *Schempp,* 374 U.S., at 240–241, 83 S.Ct., at 1581 (Brennan, J., concurring). President John Adams issued during his Presidency a number of official proclamations calling on all Americans to engage in Christian prayer. Justice Story, in his treatise on the Constitution, contended that the "real object" of the First Amendment "was, not to countenance, much less to advance Mahometanism, Judaism, or infidelity, by prostrating Christianity; but to exclude all rivalry among Christian sects.... " Whatever deference Adams' actions and Story's views might once have deserved in this Court, the Establishment Clause must now be read in a very different light. Similarly, the members of the First Congress should be treated, not as sacred figures whose every action must be emulated, but as the authors of a document meant to last for the ages. Indeed, a proper respect for the Framers themselves forbids us to give so static and lifeless a meaning to their work. To my mind, the Court's focus here on a narrow piece of history is, in a fundamental sense, a betrayal of the lessons of history.

B

Of course, the Court does not rely entirely on the practice of the First Congress in order to validate legislative prayer. There is another theme which, although implicit, also pervades the Court's opinion. It is exemplified by the Court's comparison of legislative prayer with the formulaic recitation of "God save the United States and this Honorable Court." * * * Simply put, the Court seems to regard legislative prayer as at most a *de minimis* violation, somehow unworthy of our attention. I frankly do not know what should be the proper disposition of features of our public life such as "God save the United States and this Honorable

Court," "In God We Trust," "One Nation Under God," and the like. I might well adhere to the view expressed in *Schempp* that such mottos are consistent with the Establishment Clause, not because their import is *de minimis,* but because they have lost any true religious significance. 374 U.S., at 203–204, 83 S.Ct., at 1560–1562 (Brennan, J., concurring). Legislative invocations, however, are very different.

First of all, as Justice Stevens' dissent so effectively highlights, legislative prayer, unlike mottos with fixed wordings, can easily turn narrowly and obviously sectarian. I agree with the Court that the federal judiciary should not sit as a board of censors on individual prayers, but to my mind the better way of avoiding that task is by striking down all official legislative invocations.

More fundamentally, however, *any* practice of legislative prayer, even if it might look "non-sectarian" to nine Justices of the Supreme Court, will inevitably and continuously involve the state in one or another religious debate. Prayer is serious business—serious theological business—and it is not a mere "acknowledgment of beliefs widely held among the people of this country" for the State to immerse itself in that business. Some religious individuals or groups find it theologically pro- blematic to engage in joint religious exercises predominantly influenced by faiths not their own. Some might object even to the attempt to fashion a "non-sectarian" prayer. Some would find it impossible to participate in any "prayer opportunity," marked by Trinitarian refer- ences. Some would find a prayer *not* invoking the name of Christ to represent a flawed view of the relationship between human beings and God. Some might find any petitionary prayer to be improper. Some might find any prayer that lacked a petitionary element to be deficient. Some might be troubled by what they consider shallow public prayer, or non-spontaneous prayer, or prayer without adequate spiritual prepara- tion or concentration. Some might, of course, have *theological* objections to any prayer sponsored by an organ of government. Some might object on theological grounds to the level of political neutrality generally expected of government-sponsored invocational prayer. And some might object on theological grounds to the Court's requirement, that prayer, even though religious, not be proselytizing. * * * [I]n this case, we are faced with potential religious objections to an activity at the very center of religious life, and it is simply beyond the competence of government, and inconsistent with our conceptions of liberty, for the state to take upon itself the role of ecclesiastical arbiter.

IV

The argument is made occasionally that a strict separation of religion and state robs the nation of its spiritual identity. I believe quite the contrary. It may be true that individuals cannot be "neutral" on the question of religion. But the judgment of the Establishment Clause is that neutrality by the organs of *government* on questions of religion is both possible and imperative. Alexis de Tocqueville wrote the following concerning his travels through this land in the early 1830s:

"The religious atmosphere of the country was the first thing that struck me on arrival in the United States. . . .

In France I had seen the spirits of religion and of freedom almost always marching in opposite directions. In America I found them intimately linked together in joint reign over the same land.

My longing to understand the reason for this phenomenon increased daily.

To find this out, I questioned the faithful of all communions; I particularly sought the society of clergymen, who are the depsitaries of the various creeds and have a personal interest in their survival. . . . I expressed my astonishment and revealed my doubts to each of them; I found that they all agreed with each other except about details; all thought that the main reason for the quiet sway of religion over the country was the complete separation of church and state. I have no hesitation in stating that throughout my stay in America I met nobody, lay or cleric, who did not agree about that." Democracy in America 295 (G. Lawrence, trans., J. Mayer, ed., 1969).

More recent history has only confirmed de Tocqueville's observations. If the Court had struck down legislative prayer today, it would likely have stimulated a furious reaction. But it would also, I am convinced, have invigorated both the "spirit of religion" and the "spirit of freedom."

I respectfully dissent.

JUSTICE STEVENS, dissenting.

In a democratically elected legislature, the religious beliefs of the chaplain tend to reflect the faith of the majority of the lawmakers' constituents. Prayers may be said by a Catholic priest in the Massachusetts Legislature and by a Presbyterian minister in the Nebraska Legislature, but I would not expect to find a Jehovah's Witness or a disciple of Mary Baker Eddy or the Reverend Moon serving as the official chaplain in any state legislature. Regardless of the motivation of the majority that exercises the power to appoint the chaplain, it seems plain to me that the designation of a member of one religious faith to serve as the sole official chaplain of a state legislature for a period of 16 years constitutes the preference of one faith over another in violation of the Establishment Clause of the First Amendment.

The Court declines to "embark on a sensitive evaluation or to parse the content of a particular prayer." Perhaps it does so because it would be unable to explain away the clearly sectarian content of some of the prayers given by Nebraska's chaplain.[2] Or perhaps the Court is unwilling

---

2. On March 20, 1978, for example, Chaplain Palmer gave the following invocation:

"Father in heaven, the suffering and death of your son brought life to the whole world moving our hearts to praise your glory. The power of the cross reveals your concern for the world and the wonder of Christ crucified.

to acknowledge that the tenure of the chaplain must inevitably be conditioned on the acceptability of that content to the silent majority.

I would affirm the judgment of the Court of Appeals.

Notes and Questions

1. *Ignoring Lemon.* Are the dissenting Justices correct when they assert that the legislative prayer in Nebraska could not survive the *Lemon* test? It seems that they are almost certainly correct. If this is so, why did the Court not rely on *Lemon*? The Court suggests that it is the longstanding tradition of legislative prayer, including at the time of the framers, that validates it. Couldn't this be said of a number of practices at the time of the framers that today would be said to violate some part of the Constitution? If so, why not apply the prevailing test under the Establishment Clause to test the constitutionality of the practice? Is the answer that this is an example of ceremonial deism or longstanding tradition that has never been struck down, and is therefore exempt from analysis under *Lemon*? If so, what other practices might fall into this category? Does the fact that the framers allowed legislative prayer suggest that it would be inappropriate to apply the *Lemon* test to it because the focus on purpose and effect under that test would undervalue the practices accepted at the time of the framers?

2. *Endorsement and Coercion?* The endorsement and coercion tests had not been created when *Marsh* was decided. Assume for present purposes that they were. How could legislative prayer like that in Nebraska not be an endorsement of religion, where the legislative chaplain has always been Protestant and most of the prayers are Christian even when guest Chaplains deliver them? Does the fact that the legislators and public would know the history of such prayer lessen or increase the endorsement under the endorsement test—i.e would it make religious minorities and nonbelievers more or less likely to feel like outsiders, not full members of the political community, and those in the religious majority feel like insiders? Legislators can come and go at any time during the legislative session, and they are not as likely as school aged children to be influenced by peer pressure. Would legislative prayer violate the coercion test given these points? What if a legislator who does not agree with the prayer or finds it offensive represents a community with strong religious beliefs, and her failure to remain for the prayer is used to hurt her chances at reelection? To stimulate prejudice against her as a nonbeliever?

"The days of his life-giving death and glorious resurrection are approaching. This is the hour when he triumped over Satan's pride; the time when we celebrate the great event of our redemption.

"We are reminded of the price he paid when we pray with the Psalmist:

"My God, my God, why have you forsaken me, far from my prayer, from the words of my cry?

"O my God, I cry out by day, and you answer not; by night, and there is no relief for me.

"Yet you are enthroned in the Holy Place, O glory of Israel!

"In you our fathers trusted; they trusted, and you delivered them.

"To you they cried, and they escaped; in you they trusted, and they were not put to shame.

"But I am a worm, not a man; the scorn of men, despised by the people.

"All who see me scoff at me; they mock me with parted lips, they wag their heads:

"He relied on the Lord; let Him deliver him, let Him rescue him, if He loves him. Amen."

3. *Can't Have it Both Ways*. How can legislative prayer be upheld, but school prayer be struck down? While there are plausible differences, those differences are not very meaningful under the *Lemon* and endorsement tests. If the decisions are inconsistent, is the answer to overturn *Marsh* or the cases that would seem to conflict with it? What if as a matter of first principles the *Marsh* decision could be justified based on the history of the practice (and by analogy so might school prayer)? Does *stare decisis* by itself justify striking down practices that might otherwise be found constitutional? Does this suggest that the Court should question its espoused first principles, or only that the Court should not rely on *stare decisis* when a ubiquitous practice like legislative prayer is involved as opposed to more recently developed practices such as school prayer? Do you agree with either suggestion?

4. *Legislative Prayer and Ceremonial Deism*. The Court seems to imply that legislative prayer is just another form of ceremonial deism, albeit one with a strong historical pedigree. Is this an accurate characterization? Was the prayer at the Nebraska legislature only ceremonial? Was it nonsectarian? If it wasn't an example of ceremonial deism might it be constitutional simply based on the longstanding practice, or is that analysis reserved only for ceremonial deism?

C. THE CREATIONISM/EVOLUTION DEBATE RE-VISITED

In Chapter One you read about the *Epperson* case. In the following case, decided 19 years after *Epperson*, the Court again confronted the creationism/evolution question, but in a somewhat different form.

EDWARDS v. AGUILLARD

Supreme Court of the United States, 1987.
482 U.S. 578, 107 S.Ct. 2573, 96 L.Ed.2d 510.

JUSTICE BRENNAN delivered the opinion of the Court.*

The question for decision is whether Louisiana's "Balanced Treatment for Creation–Science and Evolution–Science in Public School Instruction" Act (Creationism Act), is facially invalid as violative of the Establishment Clause of the First Amendment.

I

The Creationism Act forbids the teaching of the theory of evolution in public schools unless accompanied by instruction in "creation science." No school is required to teach evolution or creation science. If either is taught, however, the other must also be taught. The theories of evolution and creation science are statutorily defined as "the scientific evidences for [creation or evolution] and inferences from those scientific evidences."

Appellees, who include parents of children attending Louisiana public schools, Louisiana teachers, and religious leaders, challenged the constitutionality of the Act in District Court * * *. Appellants, Louisiana

* Justice O'Connor joins all but Part II of
this opinion.

officials charged with implementing the Act, defended on the ground that the purpose of the Act is to protect a legitimate secular interest, namely, academic freedom. * * *

* * *

II

The Establishment Clause forbids the enactment of any law "respecting an establishment of religion." The Court has applied a three-pronged test to determine whether legislation comports with the Establishment Clause. First, the legislature must have adopted the law with a secular purpose. Second, the statute's principal or primary effect must be one that neither advances nor inhibits religion. Third, the statute must not result in an excessive entanglement of government with religion. *Lemon v. Kurtzman.* State action violates the Establishment Clause if it fails to satisfy any of these prongs.

In this case, the Court must determine whether the Establishment Clause was violated in the special context of the public elementary and secondary school system. States and local school boards are generally afforded considerable discretion in operating public schools. "At the same time ... we have necessarily recognized that the discretion of the States and local school boards in matters of education must be exercised in a manner that comports with the transcendent imperatives of the First Amendment." *Board of Education, Island Trees Union Free School Dist. No. 26 v. Pico,* 457 U.S. 853, 864, 102 S.Ct. 2799, 2806, 73 L.Ed.2d 435 (1982).

The Court has been particularly vigilant in monitoring compliance with the Establishment Clause in elementary and secondary schools. Families entrust public schools with the education of their children, but condition their trust on the understanding that the classroom will not purposely be used to advance religious views that may conflict with the private beliefs of the student and his or her family. Students in such institutions are impressionable and their attendance is involuntary. The State exerts great authority and coercive power through mandatory attendance requirements, and because of the students' emulation of teachers as role models and the children's susceptibility to peer pressure. * * *

* * *

Therefore, in employing the three-pronged *Lemon* test, we must do so mindful of the particular concerns that arise in the context of public elementary and secondary schools. We now turn to the evaluation of the Act under the *Lemon* test.

III

Lemon's first prong focuses on the purpose that animated adoption of the Act. "The purpose prong of the *Lemon* test asks whether government's actual purpose is to endorse or disapprove of religion." *Lynch v.*

Donnelly, 465 U.S. 668, 690, 104 S.Ct. 1355, 1368, 79 L.Ed.2d 604 (1984) (O'Connor, J., concurring). A governmental intention to promote religion is clear when the State enacts a law to serve a religious purpose. This intention may be evidenced by promotion of religion in general, or by advancement of a particular religious belief. If the law was enacted for the purpose of endorsing religion, "no consideration of the second or third criteria [of *Lemon*] is necessary." *Wallace v. Jaffree, supra,* 472 U.S., at 56, 105 S.Ct., at 2489. In this case, appellants have identified no clear secular purpose for the Louisiana Act.

True, the Act's stated purpose is to protect academic freedom. This phrase might, in common parlance, be understood as referring to enhancing the freedom of teachers to teach what they will. The Court of Appeals, however, correctly concluded that the Act was not designed to further that goal. We find no merit in the State's argument that the "legislature may not [have] use[d] the terms 'academic freedom' in the correct legal sense. They might have [had] in mind, instead, a basic concept of fairness; teaching all of the evidence." Even if "academic freedom" is read to mean "teaching all of the evidence" with respect to the origin of human beings, the Act does not further this purpose. The goal of providing a more comprehensive science curriculum is not furthered either by outlawing the teaching of evolution or by requiring the teaching of creation science.

A

While the Court is normally deferential to a State's articulation of a secular purpose, it is required that the statement of such purpose be sincere and not a sham. * * *

It is clear from the legislative history that the purpose of the legislative sponsor, Senator Bill Keith, was to narrow the science curriculum. During the legislative hearings, Senator Keith stated: "My preference would be that neither [creationism nor evolution] be taught." Such a ban on teaching does not promote—indeed, it undermines—the provision of a comprehensive scientific education.

It is equally clear that requiring schools to teach creation science with evolution does not advance academic freedom. The Act does not grant teachers a flexibility that they did not already possess to supplant the present science curriculum with the presentation of theories, besides evolution, about the origin of life. Indeed, the Court of Appeals found that no law prohibited Louisiana public school teachers from teaching any scientific theory. As the president of the Louisiana Science Teachers Association testified, "[a]ny scientific concept that's based on established fact can be included in our curriculum already, and no legislation allowing this is necessary." The Act provides Louisiana school teachers with no new authority. Thus the stated purpose is not furthered by it.

* * *

Furthermore, the goal of basic "fairness" is hardly furthered by the Act's discriminatory preference for the teaching of creation science and against the teaching of evolution. While requiring that curriculum guides be developed for creation science, the Act says nothing of comparable guides for evolution. Similarly, resource services are supplied for creation science but not for evolution. Only "creation scientists" can serve on the panel that supplies the resource services. The Act forbids school boards to discriminate against anyone who "chooses to be a creation-scientist" or to teach "creationism," but fails to protect those who choose to teach evolution or any other non-creation science theory, or who refuse to teach creation science.

If the Louisiana Legislature's purpose was solely to maximize the comprehensiveness and effectiveness of science instruction, it would have encouraged the teaching of all scientific theories about the origins of humankind.[8] But under the Act's requirements, teachers who were once free to teach any and all facets of this subject are now unable to do so. Moreover, the Act fails even to ensure that creation science will be taught, but instead requires the teaching of this theory only when the theory of evolution is taught. Thus we agree with the Court of Appeals' conclusion that the Act does not serve to protect academic freedom, but has the distinctly different purpose of discrediting "evolution by counterbalancing its teaching at every turn with the teaching of creationism...."

B

Stone v. Graham invalidated the State's requirement that the Ten Commandments be posted in public classrooms. "The Ten Commandments are undeniably a sacred text in the Jewish and Christian faiths, and no legislative recitation of a supposed secular purpose can blind us to that fact." 449 U.S., at 41, 101 S.Ct., at 194 (footnote omitted). As a result, the contention that the law was designed to provide instruction on a "fundamental legal code" was "not sufficient to avoid conflict with the First Amendment." *Ibid.* Similarly *Abington School Dist. v. Schempp* held unconstitutional a statute "requiring the selection and reading at the opening of the school day of verses from the Holy Bible and the recitation of the Lord's Prayer by the students in unison," despite the proffer of such secular purposes as the "promotion of moral values, the

---

8. The dissent concludes that the Act's purpose was to protect the academic freedom of students, and not that of teachers. Such a view is not at odds with our conclusion that if the Act's purpose was to provide comprehensive scientific education (a concern shared by students and teachers, as well as parents), that purpose was not advanced by the statute's provisions.

Moreover, it is astonishing that the dissent, to prove its assertion, relies on a section of the legislation that was eventually deleted by the legislature. The dissent contends that this deleted section—which was explicitly rejected by the Louisiana Legislature—reveals the legislature's "obviously intended meaning of the statutory terms 'academic freedom.'" Quite to the contrary, Boudreaux, the main expert relied on by the sponsor of the Act, cautioned the legislature that the words "academic freedom" meant "freedom to teach science." His testimony was given at the time the legislature was deciding whether to delete this section of the Act.

contradiction to the materialistic trends of our times, the perpetuation of our institutions and the teaching of literature."

As in *Stone* and *Abington,* we need not be blind in this case to the legislature's preeminent religious purpose in enacting this statute. There is a historic and contemporaneous link between the teachings of certain religious denominations and the teaching of evolution. It was this link that concerned the Court in *Epperson v. Arkansas,* 393 U.S. 97, 89 S.Ct. 266, 21 L.Ed.2d 228 (1968), which also involved a facial challenge to a statute regulating the teaching of evolution. In that case, the Court reviewed an Arkansas statute that made it unlawful for an instructor to teach evolution or to use a textbook that referred to this scientific theory. Although the Arkansas antievolution law did not explicitly state its predominant religious purpose, the Court could not ignore that "[t]he statute was a product of the upsurge of 'fundamentalist' religious fervor" that has long viewed this particular scientific theory as contradicting the literal interpretation of the Bible. After reviewing the history of antievolution statutes, the Court determined that "there can be no doubt that the motivation for the [Arkansas] law was the same [as other anti-evolution statutes]: to suppress the teaching of a theory which, it was thought, 'denied' the divine creation of man." The Court found that there can be no legitimate state interest in protecting particular religions from scientific views "distasteful to them," and concluded "that the First Amendment does not permit the State to require that teaching and learning must be tailored to the principles or prohibitions of any religious sect or dogma."

These same historic and contemporaneous antagonisms between the teachings of certain religious denominations and the teaching of evolution are present in this case. The preeminent purpose of the Louisiana Legislature was clearly to advance the religious viewpoint that a supernatural being created humankind. The term "creation science" was defined as embracing this particular religious doctrine by those responsible for the passage of the Creationism Act. Senator Keith's leading expert on creation science, Edward Boudreaux, testified at the legislative hearings that the theory of creation science included belief in the existence of a supernatural creator. Senator Keith also cited testimony from other experts to support the creation-science view that "a creator [was] responsible for the universe and everything in it."[13] The legislative history therefore reveals that the term "creation science," as contemplated by the legislature that adopted this Act, embodies the religious belief that a supernatural creator was responsible for the creation of humankind.

Furthermore, it is not happenstance that the legislature required the teaching of a theory that coincided with this religious view. The legislative history documents that the Act's primary purpose was to change the science curriculum of public schools in order to provide

---

13. * * * Besides Senator Keith, several of the most vocal legislators also revealed their religious motives for supporting the bill in the official legislative history. * * *

persuasive advantage to a particular religious doctrine that rejects the factual basis of evolution in its entirety. The sponsor of the Creationism Act, Senator Keith, explained during the legislative hearings that his disdain for the theory of evolution resulted from the support that evolution supplied to views contrary to his own religious beliefs. According to Senator Keith, the theory of evolution was consonant with the "cardinal principle[s] of religious humanism, secular humanism, theological liberalism, aetheistism [sic]." The state senator repeatedly stated that scientific evidence supporting his religious views should be included in the public school curriculum to redress the fact that the theory of evolution incidentally coincided with what he characterized as religious beliefs antithetical to his own. The legislation therefore sought to alter the science curriculum to reflect endorsement of a religious view that is antagonistic to the theory of evolution.

* * * [T]he Creationism Act is designed *either* to promote the theory of creation science which embodies a particular religious tenet by requiring that creation science be taught whenever evolution is taught *or* to prohibit the teaching of a scientific theory disfavored by certain religious sects by forbidding the teaching of evolution when creation science is not also taught. The Establishment Clause, however, "forbids *alike* the preference of a religious doctrine *or* the prohibition of theory which is deemed antagonistic to a particular dogma." [*Epperson*] at 106–107, 89 S.Ct., at 271 (emphasis added). Because the primary purpose of the Creationism Act is to advance a particular religious belief, the Act endorses religion in violation of the First Amendment.

We do not imply that a legislature could never require that scientific critiques of prevailing scientific theories be taught. Indeed, the Court acknowledged in *Stone* that its decision forbidding the posting of the Ten Commandments did not mean that no use could ever be made of the Ten Commandments, or that the Ten Commandments played an exclusively religious role in the history of Western Civilization. In a similar way, teaching a variety of scientific theories about the origins of humankind to schoolchildren might be validly done with the clear secular intent of enhancing the effectiveness of science instruction. But because the primary purpose of the Creationism Act is to endorse a particular religious doctrine, the Act furthers religion in violation of the Establishment Clause.

IV

* * *

* * * Appellants contend that affidavits made by two scientists, two theologians, and an education administrator raise a genuine issue of material fact and that summary judgment was therefore barred. The affidavits define creation science as "origin through abrupt appearance in complex form" and allege that such a viewpoint constitutes a true scientific theory.

We agree with the lower courts that these affidavits do not raise a genuine issue of material fact. * * * [T]he postenactment testimony of outside experts is of little use in determining the Louisiana Legislature's purpose in enacting this statute. The Louisiana Legislature did hear and rely on scientific experts in passing the bill, but none of the persons making the affidavits produced by the appellants participated in or contributed to the enactment of the law or its implementation. The District Court, in its discretion, properly concluded that a Monday-morning "battle of the experts" over possible technical meanings of terms in the statute would not illuminate the contemporaneous purpose of the Louisiana Legislature when it made the law. * * *

V

The Louisiana Creationism Act advances a religious doctrine by requiring either the banishment of the theory of evolution from public school classrooms or the presentation of a religious viewpoint that rejects evolution in its entirety. The Act violates the Establishment Clause of the First Amendment because it seeks to employ the symbolic and financial support of government to achieve a religious purpose. The judgment of the Court of Appeals therefore is *Affirmed.*

JUSTICE POWELL, with whom JUSTICE O'CONNOR joins, concurring.

I write separately to note certain aspects of the legislative history, and to emphasize that nothing in the Court's opinion diminishes the traditionally broad discretion accorded state and local school officials in the selection of the public school curriculum.

I

* * *

A

"The starting point in every case involving construction of a statute is the language itself." *Blue Chip Stamps v. Manor Drug Stores,* 421 U.S. 723, 756, 95 S.Ct. 1917, 1935, 44 L.Ed.2d 539 (1975) (Powell, J., concurring). The Balanced Treatment for Creation–Science and Evolution–Science Act (Act or Balanced Treatment Act), provides in part:

"[P]ublic schools within [the] state shall give balanced treatment to creation-science and to evolution-science. Balanced treatment of these two models shall be given in classroom lectures taken as a whole for each course, in textbook materials taken as a whole for each course, in library materials taken as a whole for the sciences and taken as a whole for the humanities, and in other educational programs in public schools, to the extent that such lectures, textbooks, library materials, or educational programs deal in any way with the subject of the origin of man, life, the earth, or the universe. When creation or evolution is taught, each shall be taught as a theory, rather than as proven scientific fact." § 17:286.4(A). "Balanced treatment" means "providing whatever information and instruction in both creation and evolution models the classroom teacher determines is necessary and appropriate to provide insight into both theories in view of the textbooks and other instructional materials available for use in his classroom." § 17:286.3(1). "Creation-science" is defined as "the scientific evidences for creation and inferences from those scientific evidences." § 17:286.3(2). "Evolution-science" means "the scientific evidences for evolution and inferences from those scientific evidences." § 17:286.3(3).

Although the Act requires the teaching of the scientific evidences of both creation and evolution whenever either is taught, it does not define either term. "A fundamental canon of statutory construction is that, unless otherwise defined, words will be interpreted as taking their ordinary, contemporary, common meaning." *Perrin v. United States,* 444 U.S. 37, 42, 100 S.Ct. 311, 314, 62 L.Ed.2d 199 (1979). The "doctrine or theory of creation" is commonly defined as "holding that matter, the various forms of life, and the world were created by a transcendent God out of nothing." Webster's Third New International Dictionary 532 (unabridged 1981). "Evolution" is defined as "the theory that the various types of animals and plants have their origin in other preexisting types, the distinguishable differences being due to modifications in successive generations." *Id.,* 463 U.S., at 789, 103 S.Ct., at 3335. Thus, the Balanced Treatment Act mandates that public schools present the scientific evidence to support a theory of divine creation whenever they present the scientific evidence to support the theory of evolution. "[C]oncepts concerning God or a supreme being of some sort are manifestly religious.... These concepts do not shed that religiosity merely because they are presented as a philosophy or as a science." *Malnak v. Yogi,* 440 F.Supp. 1284, 1322 (D.N.J.1977), aff'd *per curiam,* 592 F.2d 197 (C.A.3 1979). From the face of the statute, a purpose to advance a religious belief is apparent.

A religious purpose alone is not enough to invalidate an act of a state legislature. The religious purpose must predominate. The Act contains a statement of purpose: to "protec[t] academic freedom." This statement is puzzling. Of course, the "academic freedom" of teachers to present information in public schools, and students to receive it, is broad. But it necessarily is circumscribed by the Establishment Clause. "Academic freedom" does not encompass the right of a legislature to structure the public school curriculum in order to advance a particular religious belief. Nevertheless, I read this statement in the Act as rendering the purpose of the statute at least ambiguous. Accordingly, I proceed to review the legislative history of the Act.

B

In June 1980, Senator Bill Keith introduced Senate Bill 956 in the Louisiana Legislature. The stated purpose of the bill was to "assure academic freedom by requiring the teaching of the theory of creation ex nihilo in all public schools where the theory of evolution is taught." The bill defined the "theory of creation ex nihilo" as "the belief that the origin of the elements, the galaxy, the solar system, of life, of all the species of plants and animals, the origin of man, and the origin of all things and their processes and relationships were created ex nihilo and fixed by God." * * *

While a Senate committee was studying scientific creationism, Senator Keith introduced a second draft of the bill, requiring balanced treatment of "evolution-science" and "creation-science." Although the Keith bill prohibited "instruction in any religious doctrine or materials," it defined "creation-science" to include

> "the scientific evidences and related inferences that indicate (a) sudden creation of the universe, energy, and life from nothing; (b) the insufficiency of mutation and natural selection in bringing about development of all living kinds from a single organism; (c) changes only within fixed limits or originally created kinds of plants and animals; (d) separate ancestry for man and apes; (e) explanation of the earth's geology by catastrophism, including the occurrence of a worldwide flood; and (f) a relatively recent inception of the earth and living kinds."

Significantly, the model Act on which the Keith bill relied was also the basis for a similar statute in Arkansas. See *McLean v. Arkansas Board of Education,* 529 F.Supp. 1255 (E.D.Ark.1982). The District Court in *McLean* carefully examined this model Act, particularly the section defining creation science, and concluded that "[b]oth [its] concepts and wording ... convey an inescapable religiosity." The court found that "[t]he ideas of [this section] are not merely similar to the literal interpretation of Genesis; they are identical and parallel to no other story of creation."

On May 28, the Louisiana Senate committee amended the Keith bill to delete the illustrative list of scientific evidences. According to the legislator who proposed the amendment, it was "not intended to try to gut [the bill] in any way, or defeat the purpose [for] which Senator Keith introduced [it]," and was not viewed as working "any violence to the bill." Instead, the concern was "whether this should be an all inclusive list."

The legislature then held hearings on the amended bill that became the Balanced Treatment Act under review. The principal creation scientist to testify in support of the Act was Dr. Edward Boudreaux. He did not elaborate on the nature of creation science except to indicate that the "scientific evidences" of the theory are "the objective information of science [that] point[s] to conditions of a creator." He further testified that the recognized creation scientists in the United States, who "numbe[r] something like a thousand [and] who hold doctorate and masters degrees in all areas of science," are affiliated with either or both the Institute for Creation Research and the Creation Research Society. Information on both of these organizations is part of the legislative history, and a review of their goals and activities sheds light on the nature of creation science as it was presented to, and understood by, the Louisiana Legislature.

The Institute for Creation Research is an affiliate of the Christian Heritage College in San Diego, California. The Institute was established to address the "urgent need for our nation to return to belief in a personal, omnipotent Creator, who has a purpose for His creation and to whom all people must eventually give account." A goal of the Institute is "a revival of belief in special creation as the true explanation of the origin of the world." Therefore, the Institute currently is working on the "development of new methods for teaching scientific creationism in public schools." The Creation Research Society (CRS) is located in Ann Arbor, Michigan. A member must subscribe to the following statement of belief: "The Bible is the written word of God, and because it is inspired throughout, all of its assertions are historically and scientifically true." To study creation science at the CRS, a member must accept "that the account of origins in Genesis is a factual presentation of simple historical truth."[3]

C

When, as here, "both courts below are unable to discern an arguably valid secular purpose, this Court normally should hesitate to find one." *Wallace v. Jaffree,* 472 U.S., at 66, 105 S.Ct., at 2494 (POWELL, J., concurring). My examination of the language and the legislative history of the Balanced Treatment Act confirms that the intent of the Louisiana Legislature was to promote a particular religious belief. * * *

Here, it is clear that religious belief is the Balanced Treatment Act's "reason for existence." The tenets of creation science parallel the Genesis story of creation, and this is a religious belief. "[N]o legislative recitation of a supposed secular purpose can blind us to that fact." *Stone v. Graham.* Although the Act as finally enacted does not contain explicit reference to its religious purpose, there is no indication in the legislative history that the deletion of "creation ex nihilo" and the four primary tenets of the theory was intended to alter the purpose of teaching creation science. Instead, the statements of purpose of the sources of creation science in the United States make clear that their purpose is to promote a religious belief. I find no persuasive evidence in the legislative history that the legislature's purpose was any different. The fact that the Louisiana Legislature purported to add information to the school curric-

---

3. The District Court in *McLean* noted three other elements of the CRS statement of belief to which members must subscribe:

" '[i] All basic types of living things, including man, were made by direct creative acts of God during Creation Week as described in Genesis. Whatever biological changes have occurred since Creation have accomplished only changes within the original created kinds. [ii] The great Flood described in Genesis, commonly referred to as the Noachian Deluge, was an historical event, world-wide in its extent and effect. [iii] Finally, we are an organization of Christian men of science, who accept Jesus Christ as our Lord and Savior. The account of the special creation of Adam and Eve as one man and one woman, and their subsequent Fall into sin, is the basis for our belief in the necessity of a Savior for all mankind. Therefore, salvation can come only thru (sic) accepting Jesus Christ as our Savior.' "

ulum rather than detract from it as in *Epperson* does not affect my analysis. Both legislatures acted with the unconstitutional purpose of structuring the public school curriculum to make it compatible with a particular religious belief: the "divine creation of man."

That the statute is limited to the scientific evidences supporting the theory does not render its purpose secular. * * * Whatever the academic merit of particular subjects or theories, the Establishment Clause limits the discretion of state officials to pick and choose among them for the purpose of promoting a particular religious belief. The language of the statute and its legislative history convince me that the Louisiana Legislature exercised its discretion for this purpose in this case.

II

* * * In the context of a challenge under the Establishment Clause, interference with the decisions of [school] * * * authorities is warranted only when the purpose for their decisions is clearly religious.

* * *

As a matter of history, schoolchildren can and should properly be informed of all aspects of this Nation's religious heritage. I would see no constitutional problem if schoolchildren were taught the nature of the Founding Father's religious beliefs and how these beliefs affected the attitudes of the times and the structure of our government. Courses in comparative religion of course are customary and constitutionally appropriate. In fact, since religion permeates our history, a familiarity with the nature of religious beliefs is necessary to understand many historical as well as contemporary events. In addition, it is worth noting that the Establishment Clause does not prohibit *per se* the educational use of religious documents in public school education. Although this Court has recognized that the Bible is "an instrument of religion," *Abington School District v. Schempp*, it also has made clear that the Bible "may constitutionally be used in an appropriate study of history, civilization, ethics, comparative religion, or the like." *Stone v. Graham* (citing *Abington School District v. Schempp*). The book is, in fact, "the world's all-time best seller" with undoubted literary and historic value apart from its religious content. The Establishment Clause is properly understood to prohibit the use of the Bible and other religious documents in public school education only when the purpose of the use is to advance a particular religious belief.

III

In sum, I find that the language and the legislative history of the Balanced Treatment Act unquestionably demonstrate that its purpose is to advance a particular religious belief. Although the discretion of state and local authorities over public school curricula is broad, "the First Amendment does not permit the State to require that teaching and learning must be tailored to the principles or prohibitions of any religious sect or dogma." *Epperson v. Arkansas,* 393 U.S., at 106, 89 S.Ct., at 271. Accordingly, I concur in the opinion of the Court and its judgment that the Balanced Treatment Act violates the Establishment Clause of the Constitution.

JUSTICE WHITE, concurring in the judgment.

As it comes to us, this is not a difficult case. Based on the historical setting and plain language of the Act both courts construed the statutory words "creation science" to refer to a religious belief, which the Act required to be taught if evolution was taught. In other words, the teaching of evolution was conditioned on the teaching of a religious belief. Both courts concluded that the state legislature's primary purpose was to advance religion and that the statute was therefore unconstitutional under the Establishment Clause.

We usually defer to courts of appeals on the meaning of a state statute, especially when a district court has the same view. Of course, we have the power to disagree, and the lower courts in a particular case may be plainly wrong. But if the meaning ascribed to a state statute by a court of appeals is a rational construction of the statute, we normally accept it. * * *

* * * Even if as an original matter I might have arrived at a different conclusion based on a reading of the statute and the record before us, I cannot say that the two courts below are so plainly wrong that they should be reversed. * * *

If the Court of Appeals' construction [of the Act] is to be accepted, so is its conclusion that under our prior cases the Balanced Treatment Act is unconstitutional because its primary purpose is to further a religious belief by imposing certain requirements on the school curriculum. Unless, therefore, we are to reconsider the Court's decisions interpreting the Establishment Clause, I agree that the judgment of the Court of Appeals must be affirmed.

JUSTICE SCALIA, with whom the CHIEF JUSTICE joins, dissenting.

Even if I agreed with the questionable premise that legislation can be invalidated under the Establishment Clause on the basis of its motivation alone, without regard to its effects, I would still find no justification for today's decision. The Louisiana legislators who passed the "Balanced Treatment for Creation–Science and Evolution–Science Act" (Balanced Treatment Act), each of whom had sworn to support the Constitution, were well aware of the potential Establishment Clause problems and considered that aspect of the legislation with great care. After seven hearings and several months of study, resulting in substantial revision of the original proposal, they approved the Act overwhelmingly and specifically articulated the secular purpose they meant it to serve. Although the record contains abundant evidence of the sincerity of that purpose (the only issue pertinent to this case), the Court today holds, essentially on the basis of "its visceral knowledge regarding what *must* have motivated the legislators," 778 F.2d 225, 227 (5th Cir.1985) (Gee, J., dissenting) (emphasis added), that the members of the Louisiana Legislature knowingly violated their oaths and then lied about it. I dissent. Had requirements of the Balanced Treatment Act that are not apparent on its face been clarified by an interpretation of the Louisiana Supreme Court, or by the manner of its implementation, the Act might well be found unconstitutional; but the question of its constitutionality cannot rightly be disposed of on the gallop, by impugning the motives of its supporters.

* * *

Notes and Questions

1. *What About Balance?* Why didn't the state of Louisiana win based on its argument that the teaching of creation science would provide a balance to the teaching of evolution where evolution is taught? What does the state's position assume? Are creation science and evolution the only theories regarding human origins? Why was creation science chosen as the alternative to provide balance when evolution is taught? Would the program have been acceptable if multiple theories of human origins that are at least scientifically plausible were taught— for example the idea that we were put here by aliens, etc ... ? Is evolution different from these other theories because virtually all mainstream scientists assert it occurred and disagree only about how it occurred, while these other theories are scientifically suspect? Does it matter that the alternative theories, such as creationism, often begin with a premise about human origins and then work to prove that theory, rather than the traditional scientific method which first asserts a hypothesis and then works to prove or disprove that hypothesis?

2. *Intelligent Design Theory and Creationism.* Creationism is a broad umbrella for a variety of religiously affected or inspired theories of human origins. A newer theory called intelligent design theory, whose proponents distinguish the theory from creationism, is more scientifically oriented. *See* ROBERT T. PENNOCK, TOWER OF BABEL: THE EVIDENCE AGAINST THE NEW CREATIONISM (1999) (providing an excellent discussion of the relationship, and differences, between creationism and intelligent design theory, and calling the scientific validity of both into question). Should the fact that intelligent design theory is more scientifically informed than creationism make a difference if a legislature passed a statute similar to Louisiana's, but substituted intelligent design theory for creationism? Does the fact that even intelligent design theory may presume its initial hypothesis to be correct—i.e. the theory of human evolution is flawed and G-d or some intelligent force had a role in human or other organism development—and work back from there invalidate it as a proper topic for a public school science class? Would it make a difference to your analysis if many religious schools taught traditional evolutionary theory in their science classes? Why would it make a difference?

3. *Exempting Religious Students.* Should religious students be exempted (with their parents' approval) from the evolution sections of public school science classes? Courts have generally approved of such exemptions, but they are not necessarily required under the Free Exercise Clause, the most relevant clause regarding religious exemptions. In *Employment Division v. Smith*, 494 U.S. 872, 110 S.Ct. 1595, 108 L.Ed.2d 876 (1990)(*See infra.* Chapter 6), the Court held that government entities may, but need not, give exemptions to "generally applicable" laws/rules under the Free Exercise Clause. Should a school give religious exemptions to students excusing them from the evolution components of the

science curriculum? Wouldn't failure to exempt such students place them in the position of being coerced to learn what they may perceive as an antireligious theory? Would it endorse irreligion over religion?

4. *Favoring Christianity*? Was the Louisiana law especially problematic because it promoted the Judeo–Christian account of human origins over other religiously based accounts such as the Hindu or Native American accounts? Could a school include all of these accounts in a science class? What about in a history class? A Comparative religion class? A literature class? What else would you want to know to answer this question? Would the school need to include secular accounts other than evolution in order to include the religious accounts, or would such a curriculum be found unconstitutional regardless of the inclusion of secular accounts?

Chapter Three

PUBLIC DISPLAYS, PUBLIC FORUMS, AND EQUAL ACCESS

A. INTRODUCTION

The issue of public displays of religious objects on government property has received a good deal of attention in court opinions and in the scholarly literature. The same is true for the issue of access by religiously affected entities to government facilities where other entities are allowed access; an issue commonly referred to as "equal access." Both of these issues can raise not only religion clause questions, but also questions under the Free Speech Clause. This is so when a private religious entity seeks to express itself in, or gain access to, government property that has been generally opened to a variety of private speakers or groups. In the context of public displays of religious symbols the public/private speech dichotomy becomes quite important. When government seeks to erect a religious symbol the case is generally analyzed under the Establishment Clause, but where a private entity seeks to erect a religious display it is important to determine whether the display is in a public forum. If so, important free speech concerns are raised. Of course, when private individuals or entities display religious symbols on private property there is generally no constitutional issue.

This Chapter will explore both the religious symbolism and equal access issues. Public displays of religious symbols on government property will be addressed first. This will be followed by a discussion of equal access to government facilities. There are some common themes that run through both issues. As you read the material in this Chapter see if you can determine what themes the two issues have in common.

B. RELIGIOUS SYMBOLISM AND PUBLIC DISPLAYS

As noted above, the issues surrounding the display of religious symbols on government property are heavily dependent on the public/private distinction. In other words, there is a significant difference between government displays and privately sponsored displays, at least where the latter occur in a public forum. Government sponsored displays raise questions about purpose and effect. The same is true of privately sponsored displays that are placed on government property when there is no public forum. The following section addresses situations where government entities sponsor religious displays and situations where government entities endorse private religious displays by allowing those displays access to government property that is not generally available for other displays. This will be followed by a section addressing private displays on public property that has been opened to a variety of expressive activities.

1.   Government Sponsored or Endorsed Displays

In *Lynch v. Donnelly*, 465 U.S. 668, 104 S.Ct. 1355, 79 L.Ed.2d 604 (1984), the Court considered whether a crèche (a nativity scene) that was placed in a park in Pawtucket, Rhode Island, as part of a larger Christmas display that included such things as a Santa Claus house and plastic reindeer, violated the Establishment Clause. The city owned the display and clearly supported and sponsored its erection in the park. Thus, this was a case involving a government supported display. The Court held the display was constitutional, ostensibly applying the *Lemon* test, which was then the prevailing test for Establishment Clause claims. In applying that test the Court utilized analysis similar to that it had used in *Marsh v. Chambers*, 463 U.S. 783, 103 S.Ct. 3330, 77 L.Ed.2d 1019 (1983) (*See supra.* at Chapter Two). The Court noted the long history of various forms of government interaction with religion, such as legislative chaplains. It also acknowledged the religious meaning of the crèche, yet held that holiday displays like that in Pawtucket are part of a long tradition connected to the winter holiday season and that Christmas has a secular aspect in addition to its religious aspects.

Significantly, the Court noted the importance of the broader context of the display, which included "a Santa Claus house, reindeer pulling a sleigh, candy-striped poles, a Christmas tree, carolers, cutout figures of a clown, an elephant, and a teddy bear, hundreds of colored lights, [and] a large banner that [read] 'Seasons Greetings * * *.' " It also noted the display's connection to the secular/commercial aspects of the holiday. In this context the display as a whole represented the secular aspects of Christmas. Thus, while the crèche was a religious symbol, it did not foster a government establishment of religion in the context of the broader display and the holiday season, because that context demonstrated both a secular purpose and a primary effect that neither advanced nor inhibited religion. The Court also found no entanglement because of the low cost of the display and held that political divisiveness, which was an element of entanglement at that time, was insufficient by itself to support an Establishment Clause claim.

The dissenting opinions pointed out that the government sponsored crèche would not have survived scrutiny had the Court applied the *Lemon* test in the manner it had in other cases under the Establishment

Clause. Those opinions also pointed out the obvious fact that placing a patently religious symbol representing an event central to Christian theology in the context of a broader display of items connected to the Christmas holiday is likely to favor the dominant Christian tradition, and thus could not be saved by relying on the commercialized aspects of the holiday. Such government action favoring one religion would violate the *Lemon* test. Moreover, the dissents argued that by minimizing the religious import of the crèche in the context of the display the Court both degraded the religious meaning of the symbol and the holiday, and failed to address the exclusionary message the display sent to non-Christians.

Perhaps the most important opinion in the *Lynch* case was Justice O'Connor's concurring opinion. That opinion gave birth to what has become known as the "endorsement test." While many people have questioned Justice O'Connor's application of that test in *Lynch*, the test itself has become highly influential, especially in cases involving government supported or endorsed religious symbols. Justice O'Connor wrote:

> The Establishment Clause prohibits government from making adherence to a religion relevant in any way to a person's standing in the political community. Government can run afoul of that prohibition in two principal ways. One is excessive entanglement with religious institutions, which may interfere with the independence of the institutions, give the institutions access to government or governmental powers not fully shared by nonadherents of the religion, and foster the creation of political constituencies defined along religious lines. (Citation omitted). The second and more direct infringement is government endorsement or disapproval of religion. Endorsement sends a message to nonadherents that they are outsiders, not full members of the political community, and an accompanying message to adherents that they are insiders, favored members of the political community. Disapproval sends the opposite message. *Schempp*.

> Our prior cases have used the three-part test articulated in *Lemon*, as a guide to detecting these two forms of unconstitutional government action. It has never been entirely clear, however, how the three parts of the test relate to the principles enshrined in the Establishment Clause. Focusing on institutional entanglement and on endorsement or disapproval of religion clarifies the *Lemon* test as an analytical device.

* * *

The central issue in this case is whether Pawtucket has endorsed Christianity by its display of the crèche. To answer that question, we must examine both what Pawtucket intended to communicate in displaying the crèche and what message the City's display actually conveyed. The purpose and effect prongs of the

Lemon test represent these two aspects of the meaning of the City's action.

* * *

The purpose prong of the *Lemon* test asks whether government's actual purpose is to endorse or disapprove of religion. The effect prong asks whether, irrespective of government's actual purpose, the practice under review in fact conveys a message of endorsement or disapproval. An affirmative answer to either question should render the challenged practice invalid.

* * *

Applying that formulation to this case, I would find that Pawtucket did not intend to convey any message of endorsement of Christianity or disapproval of nonChristian religions. The evident purpose of including the crèche in the larger display was not promotion of the religious content of the crèche but celebration of the public holiday through its traditional symbols. Celebration of public holidays, which have cultural significance even if they also have religious aspects, is a legitimate secular purpose.

* * *

Focusing on the evil of government endorsement or disapproval of religion makes clear that the effect prong of the *Lemon* test is properly interpreted not to require invalidation of a government practice merely because it in fact causes, even as a primary effect, advancement or inhibition of religion. * * * What is crucial is that a government practice not have the effect of communicating a message of government endorsement or disapproval of religion. It is only practices having that effect, whether intentionally or unintentionally, that make religion relevant, in reality or public perception, to status in the political community.

Pawtucket's display of its crèche, I believe, does not communicate a message that the government intends to endorse the Christian beliefs represented by the crèche. Although the religious and indeed sectarian significance of the crèche, as the district court found, is not neutralized by the setting, the overall holiday setting changes what viewers may fairly understand to be the purpose of the display—as a typical museum setting, though not neutralizing the religious content of a religious painting, negates any message of endorsement of that content. * * *

Every government practice must be judged in its unique circumstances to determine whether it constitutes an endorsement or disapproval of religion. In making that determination, courts must keep in mind both the fundamental place held by the Establishment Clause in our constitutional scheme and the myriad, subtle ways in which Establishment Clause values can be eroded. Government practices that purport to celebrate or acknowledge events with religious significance must be subjected to careful judicial scrutiny.

Lynch, 465 U.S. at 687–94 (O'Connor, J., concurring). Justice O'Connor found no endorsement under the facts in *Lynch*. How is this possible given the points made by the dissenting Justices? Regardless of her specific application of the test in *Lynch*, it soon began to appear in other significant opinions.

COUNTY OF ALLEGHENY v. AMERICAN CIVIL LIBERTIES UNION GREATER PITTSBURGH CHAPTER

Supreme Court of the United States, 1989.
492 U.S. 573, 109 S.Ct. 3086, 106 L.Ed.2d 472.

JUSTICE BLACKMUN announced the judgment of the Court and delivered the opinion of the Court with respect to Parts III–A, IV, and V, an opinion with respect to Parts I and II, in which JUSTICE STEVENS and JUSTICE O'CONNOR join, an opinion with respect to Part III–B, in which JUSTICE STEVENS joins, an opinion with respect to Part VII, in which JUSTICE O'CONNOR joins, and an opinion with respect to Part VI.

This litigation concerns the constitutionality of two recurring holiday displays located on public property in downtown Pittsburgh. The first is a crèche placed on the Grand Staircase of the Allegheny County Courthouse. The second is a Chanukah menorah placed just outside the City–County Building, next to a Christmas tree and a sign saluting liberty. The Court of Appeals for the Third Circuit ruled that each display violates the Establishment Clause of the First Amendment because each has the impermissible effect of endorsing religion. We agree that the crèche display has that unconstitutional effect but reverse the Court of Appeals' judgment regarding the menorah display.

I

A

The county courthouse is owned by Allegheny County and is its seat of government. It houses the offices of the county commissioners, controller, treasurer, sheriff, and clerk of court. Civil and criminal trials are held there. The "main," "most beautiful," and "most public" part of the courthouse is its Grand Staircase, set into one arch and surrounded by others, with arched windows serving as a backdrop.

Since 1981, the county has permitted the Holy Name Society, a Roman Catholic group, to display a crèche in the county courthouse during the Christmas holiday season. Christmas, we note perhaps needlessly, is the holiday when Christians celebrate the birth of Jesus of Nazareth, whom they believe to be the Messiah. Western churches have celebrated Christmas Day on December 25 since the fourth century. As observed in this Nation, Christmas has a secular, as well as a religious, dimension.

The crèche in the county courthouse, like other crèches, is a visual representation of the scene in the manger in Bethlehem shortly after the birth of Jesus, as described in the Gospels of Luke and Matthew. The crèche includes figures of the infant Jesus, Mary, Joseph, farm animals, shepherds, and wise men, all placed in or before a wooden representation of a manger, which has at its crest an angel bearing a banner that proclaims "Gloria in Excelsis Deo!"

During the 1986–1987 holiday season, the crèche was on display on the Grand Staircase from November 26 to January 9. It had a wooden fence on three sides and bore a plaque stating: "This Display Donated by the Holy Name Society." Sometime during the week of December 2, the county placed red and white poinsettia plants around the fence. The county also placed a small evergreen tree, decorated with a red bow, behind each of the two endposts of the fence. These trees stood alongside the manger backdrop and were slightly shorter than it was. The angel thus was at the apex of the crèche display. Altogether, the crèche, the fence, the poinsettias, and the trees occupied a substantial amount of space on the Grand Staircase. No figures of Santa Claus or other decorations appeared on the Grand Staircase. * * *

The county uses the crèche as the setting for its annual Christmas-carole program. During the 1986 season, the county invited high school choirs and other musical groups to perform during weekday lunch hours from December 3 through December 23. The county dedicated this program to world peace and to the families of prisoners-of-war and of persons missing in action in Southeast Asia.

* * *

B

The City–County Building is separate and a block removed from the county courthouse and, as the name implies, is jointly owned by the city of Pittsburgh and Allegheny County. The city's portion of the building houses the city's principal offices, including the mayor's. The city is responsible for the building's Grant Street entrance which has three rounded arches supported by columns.

For a number of years, the city has had a large Christmas tree under the middle arch outside the Grant Street entrance. Following this practice, city employees on November 17, 1986, erected a 45–foot tree under the middle arch and decorated it with lights and ornaments. A few days later, the city placed at the foot of the tree a sign bearing the mayor's name and entitled "Salute to Liberty." Beneath the title, the sign stated:

"During this holiday season, the city of Pittsburgh salutes liberty. Let these festive lights remind us that we are the keepers of the flame of liberty and our legacy of freedom."

At least since 1982, the city has expanded its Grant Street holiday display to include a symbolic representation of Chanukah, an 8–day

Jewish holiday that begins on the 25th day of the Jewish lunar month of Kislev. The 25th of Kislev usually occurs in December, and thus Chanukah is the annual Jewish holiday that falls closest to Christmas Day each year. In 1986, Chanukah began at sundown on December 26.

According to Jewish tradition, on the 25th of Kislev in 164 B.C.E. (before the common era (165 B.C.)), the Maccabees rededicated the Temple of Jerusalem after recapturing it from the Greeks, or, more accurately, from the Greek-influenced Seleucid Empire, in the course of a political rebellion. Chanukah is the holiday which celebrates that event. The early history of the celebration of Chanukah is unclear; it appears that the holiday's central ritual—the lighting of lamps—was well established long before a single explanation of that ritual took hold.

The Talmud[13] explains the lamplighting ritual as a commemoration of an event that occurred during the rededication of the Temple. The Temple housed a seven-branch menorah, which was to be kept burning continuously. When the Maccabees rededicated the Temple, they had only enough oil to last for one day. But, according to the Talmud, the oil miraculously lasted for eight days (the length of time it took to obtain additional oil). To celebrate and publicly proclaim this miracle, the Talmud prescribes that it is a mitzvah (*i.e.,* a religious deed or commandment), for Jews to place a lamp with eight lights just outside the entrance to their homes or in a front window during the eight days of Chanukah. Where practicality or safety from persecution so requires, the lamp may be placed in a window or inside the home. The Talmud also ordains certain blessings to be recited each night of Chanukah before lighting the lamp. * * *

* * *

Chanukah, like Christmas, is a cultural event as well as a religious holiday. Indeed, the Chanukah story always has had a political or national, as well as a religious, dimension: it tells of national heroism in addition to divine intervention. Also, Chanukah, like Christmas, is a winter holiday; according to some historians, it was associated in ancient times with the winter solstice. Just as some Americans celebrate Christmas without regard to its religious significance, some nonreligious American Jews celebrate Chanukah as an expression of ethnic identity, and "as a cultural or national event, rather than as a specifically religious event."[29]

13. The Talmud (specifically the Babylonian Talmud) is a collection of rabbinic commentary on Jewish law that was compiled before the sixth century.

29. The Court of Appeals in this litigation plainly erred when it asserted that Chanukah "is not ... a holiday with secular aspects." This assertion contradicts uncontroverted record evidence presented by respondents' own expert witness:

"There are also those Jews within the Jewish community who are non-theistic.... [T]hey base their celebration [of Chanukah] on something other than religion."

In response to further questioning, the expert added that the celebration of Chanukah as a cultural event "certainly exists." Thus, on this record, Chanukah unquestionably has "secular aspects," although it is also a religious holiday.

The cultural significance of Chanukah varies with the setting in which the holiday is celebrated. * * * In this country, the tradition of giving Chanukah gelt has taken on greater importance because of the temporal proximity of Chanukah to Christmas. Indeed, some have suggested that the proximity of Christmas accounts for the social prominence of Chanukah in this country. Whatever the reason, Chanukah is observed by American Jews to an extent greater than its religious importance would indicate: in the hierarchy of Jewish holidays, Chanukah ranks fairly low in religious significance. This socially heightened status of Chanukah reflects its cultural or secular dimension.

On December 22 of the 1986 holiday season, the city placed at the Grant Street entrance to the City–County Building an 18–foot Chanukah menorah of an abstract tree-and-branch design. The menorah was placed next to the city's 45–foot Christmas tree, against one of the columns that supports the arch into which the tree was set. The menorah is owned by Chabad, a Jewish group, but is stored, erected, and removed each year by the city. * * *

II

This litigation began on December 10, 1986, when respondents, the Greater Pittsburgh Chapter of the American Civil Liberties Union and seven local residents, filed suit against the county and the city, seeking permanently to enjoin the county from displaying the crèche in the county courthouse and the city from displaying the menorah in front of the City–County Building. * * * Respondents claim that the displays of the crèche and the menorah each violate the Establishment Clause of the First Amendment * * *.

* * *

III

A

This Nation is heir to a history and tradition of religious diversity that dates from the settlement of the North American Continent. Sectarian differences among various Christian denominations were central to the origins of our Republic. Since then, adherents of religions too numerous to name have made the United States their home, as have those whose beliefs expressly exclude religion.

Precisely because of the religious diversity that is our national heritage, the Founders added to the Constitution a Bill of Rights, the very first words of which declare: "Congress shall make no law respecting an establishment of religion, or prohibiting the free exercise thereof. . . . " Perhaps in the early days of the Republic these words were understood to protect only the diversity within Christianity, but today they are recognized as guaranteeing religious liberty and equality to "the infidel, the atheist, or the adherent of a non-Christian faith such as Islam or Judaism." *Wallace v. Jaffree.* It is settled law that no government official in this Nation may violate these fundamental constitutional rights regarding matters of conscience.

In the course of adjudicating specific cases, this Court has come to understand the Establishment Clause to mean that government may not promote or affiliate itself with any religious doctrine or organization, may not discriminate among persons on the basis of their religious beliefs and practices, may not delegate a governmental power to a religious institution, and may not involve itself too deeply in such an institution's affairs. Although "the myriad, subtle ways in which Establishment Clause values can be eroded," are not susceptible to a single verbal formulation, this Court has attempted to encapsulate the essential precepts of the Establishment Clause. * * * [Justice Blackmun quotes from *Everson* here].

In *Lemon v. Kurtzman*, the Court sought to refine these principles by focusing on three "tests" for determining whether a government practice violates the Establishment Clause. Under the *Lemon* analysis, a statute or practice which touches upon religion, if it is to be permissible under the Establishment Clause, must have a secular purpose; it must neither advance nor inhibit religion in its principal or primary effect; and it must not foster an excessive entanglement with religion. This trilogy of tests has been applied regularly in the Court's later Establishment Clause cases.

Our subsequent decisions further have refined the definition of governmental action that unconstitutionally advances religion. In recent years, we have paid particularly close attention to whether the challenged governmental practice either has the purpose or effect of "endorsing" religion, a concern that has long had a place in our Establishment Clause jurisprudence. * * *

Of course, the word "endorsement" is not self-defining. Rather, it derives its meaning from other words that this Court has found useful over the years in interpreting the Establishment Clause. Thus, it has been noted that the prohibition against governmental endorsement of religion "preclude[s] government from conveying or attempting to convey a message that religion or a particular religious belief is *favored* or *preferred*." *Wallace v. Jaffree*, 472 U.S., at 70, 105 S.Ct., at 2497 (O'Connor, J., concurring in judgment) (emphasis added). * * * Moreover, the term "endorsement" is closely linked to the term "promotion," and this Court long since has held that government "may not ... promote one religion or religious theory against another or even against the militant opposite," *Epperson v. Arkansas*.

Whether the key word is "endorsement," "favoritism," or "promotion," the essential principle remains the same. The Establishment Clause, at the very least, prohibits government from appearing to take a position on questions of religious belief or from "making adherence to a religion relevant in any way to a person's standing in the political community." *Lynch v. Donnelly*, 465 U.S., at 687, 104 S.Ct., at 1366 (O'Connor, J., concurring).

B

We have had occasion in the past to apply Establishment Clause principles to the government's display of objects with religious significance. In *Stone v. Graham*, we held that the display of a copy of the Ten Commandments on the walls of public classrooms violates the Establishment Clause. Closer to the facts of this litigation is *Lynch v. Donnelly*, in which we considered whether the city of Pawtucket, R.I., had violated the Establishment Clause by including a crèche in its annual Christmas display, located in a private park within the downtown shopping district. By a 5–to–4 decision in that difficult case, the Court upheld inclusion of the crèche in the Pawtucket display, holding, *inter alia,* that the inclusion of the crèche did not have the impermissible effect of advancing or promoting religion.

The rationale of the majority opinion in *Lynch* is none too clear: the opinion contains two strands, neither of which provides guidance for decision in subsequent cases. First, the opinion states that the inclusion of the crèche in the display was "no more an advancement or endorsement of religion" than other "endorsements" this Court has approved in the past, but the opinion offers no discernible measure for distinguishing between permissible and impermissible endorsements. Second, the opinion observes that any benefit the government's display of the crèche gave to religion was no more than "indirect, remote, and incidental," without saying how or why.

Although Justice O'Connor joined the majority opinion in *Lynch*, she wrote a concurrence that differs in significant respects from the majority opinion. The main difference is that the concurrence provides a sound analytical framework for evaluating governmental use of religious symbols.

First and foremost, the concurrence squarely rejects any notion that this Court will tolerate some government endorsement of religion. Rather, the concurrence recognizes any endorsement of religion as "invalid," because it "sends a message to nonadherents that they are outsiders, not full members of the political community, and an accompanying message to adherents that they are insiders, favored members of the political community."

Second, the concurrence articulates a method for determining whether the government's use of an object with religious meaning has the effect of endorsing religion. The effect of the display depends upon the message that the government's practice communicates: the question is "what viewers may fairly understand to be the purpose of the display." That inquiry, of necessity, turns upon the context in which the contested object appears: "[A] typical museum setting, though not neutralizing the religious content of a religious painting, negates any message of endorsement of that content." The concurrence thus emphasizes that the constitutionality of the crèche in that case depended upon its "particular physical setting," and further observes: "Every government practice must be judged in its unique circumstances to determine whether it [endorses] religion."

* * *

The four *Lynch* dissenters agreed with the concurrence that the controlling question was "whether Pawtucket ha[d] run afoul of the Establishment Clause by endorsing religion through its display of the crèche." *Lynch*, at 698, n. 3, 104 S.Ct., at 1372, n.3 (Brennan, J., dissenting). The dissenters also agreed with the general proposition that the context in which the government uses a religious symbol is relevant for determining the answer to that question. * * *

Thus, despite divergence at the bottom line, the five Justices in concurrence and dissent in *Lynch* agreed upon the relevant constitutional principles: the government's use of religious symbolism is unconstitutional if it has the effect of endorsing religious beliefs, and the effect of the government's use of religious symbolism depends upon its context. These general principles are sound, and have been adopted by the Court in subsequent cases. * * * Accordingly, our present task is to determine whether the display of the crèche and the menorah, in their respective "particular physical settings," has the effect of endorsing or disapproving religious beliefs.

IV

We turn first to the county's crèche display. There is no doubt, of course, that the crèche itself is capable of communicating a religious message. Indeed, the crèche in this lawsuit uses words, as well as the picture of the Nativity scene, to make its religious meaning unmistakably clear. "Glory to God in the Highest!" says the angel in the crèche— Glory to God because of the birth of Jesus. This praise to God in Christian terms is indisputably religious—indeed sectarian—just as it is when said in the Gospel or in a church service.

Under the Court's holding in *Lynch*, the effect of a crèche display turns on its setting. Here, unlike in *Lynch*, nothing in the context of the display detracts from the crèche's religious message. * * *

* * *

Furthermore, the crèche sits on the Grand Staircase, the "main" and "most beautiful part" of the building that is the seat of county government. No viewer could reasonably think that it occupies this location without the support and approval of the government.[50] Thus, by permitting the "display of the crèche in this particular physical setting," *Lynch*, 465 U.S., at 692, 104 S.Ct., at 1369 (O'Connor, J., concurring),

---

50. The Grand Staircase does not appear to be the kind of location in which all were free to place their displays for weeks at a time, so that the presence of the crèche in that location for over six weeks would then not serve to associate the government with the crèche. Even if the Grand Staircase occasionally was used for displays other than the crèche, it remains true that any display located there fairly may be understood to express views that receive the support and endorsement of the government. * * * In this respect, the crèche here does not raise [a] * * * "public forum" issue.

the county sends an unmistakable message that it supports and promotes the Christian praise to God that is the crèche's religious message.

The fact that the crèche bears a sign disclosing its ownership by a Roman Catholic organization does not alter this conclusion. On the contrary, the sign simply demonstrates that the government is endorsing the religious message of that organization, rather than communicating a message of its own. But the Establishment Clause does not limit only the religious content of the government's own communications. It also prohibits the government's support and promotion of religious communications by religious organizations. Indeed, the very concept of "endorsement" conveys the sense of promoting someone else's message. * * *

Finally, the county argues that it is sufficient to validate the display of the crèche on the Grand Staircase that the display celebrates Christmas, and Christmas is a national holiday. This argument obviously proves too much. It would allow the celebration of the Eucharist inside a courthouse on Christmas Eve. * * * The government may acknowledge Christmas as a cultural phenomenon, but under the First Amendment it may not observe it as a Christian holy day by suggesting that people praise God for the birth of Jesus.

In sum, *Lynch* teaches that government may celebrate Christmas in some manner and form, but not in a way that endorses Christian doctrine. Here, Allegheny County has transgressed this line. It has chosen to celebrate Christmas in a way that has the effect of endorsing a patently Christian message: Glory to God for the birth of Jesus Christ. Under *Lynch,* and the rest of our cases, nothing more is required to demonstrate a violation of the Establishment Clause. The display of the crèche in this context, therefore, must be permanently enjoined.

V

Justice Kennedy and the three Justices who join him would find the display of the crèche consistent with the Establishment Clause. He argues that this conclusion necessarily follows from the Court's decision in *Marsh v. Chambers*, which sustained the constitutionality of legislative prayer. He also asserts that the crèche, even in this setting, poses "no realistic risk" of "represent[ing] an effort to proselytize," having repudiated the Court's endorsement inquiry in favor of a "proselytization" approach. The Court's analysis of the crèche, he contends, "reflects an unjustified hostility toward religion."

* * *

A

* * *

Justice Kennedy's reading of *Marsh* would gut the core of the Establishment Clause, as this Court understands it. The history of this Nation, it is perhaps sad to say, contains numerous examples of official acts that endorsed Christianity specifically. Some of these examples date back to the Founding of the Republic, but this heritage of official discrimination against non-Christians has no place in the jurisprudence of the Establishment Clause. Whatever else the Establishment Clause may mean * * * , it certainly means at the very least that government may not demonstrate a preference for one particular sect or creed (including a preference for Christianity over other religions). * * * There have been breaches of this command throughout this Nation's history, but they cannot diminish in any way the force of the command. Cf. Laycock, *supra,* n. 39, at 923.

C

Although Justice Kennedy repeatedly accuses the Court of harboring a "latent hostility" or "callous indifference" toward religion, nothing could be further from the truth, and the accusations could be said to be as offensive as they are absurd. Justice Kennedy apparently has misperceived a respect for religious pluralism, a respect commanded by the Constitution, as hostility or indifference to religion. No misperception could be more antithetical to the values embodied in the Establishment Clause.

Justice Kennedy's accusations are shot from a weapon triggered by the following proposition: if government may celebrate the secular aspects of Christmas, then it must be allowed to celebrate the religious aspects as well because, otherwise, the government would be discriminating against citizens who celebrate Christmas as a religious, and not just a secular, holiday. This proposition, however, is flawed at its foundation. The government does not discriminate against any citizen on the basis of the citizen's religious faith if the government is secular in its functions and operations. On the contrary, the Constitution mandates that the government remain secular, rather than affiliate itself with religious beliefs or institutions, precisely in order to avoid discriminating among citizens on the basis of their religious faiths.

A secular state, it must be remembered, is not the same as an atheistic or antireligious state. A secular state establishes neither atheism nor religion as its official creed. * * *

* * *

VI

The display of the Chanukah menorah in front of the City–County Building may well present a closer constitutional question. The menorah, one must recognize, is a religious symbol: it serves to commemorate the miracle of the oil as described in the Talmud. But the menorah's message is not exclusively religious. The menorah is the primary visual symbol for a holiday that, like Christmas, has both religious and secular dimensions.

Moreover, the menorah here stands next to a Christmas tree and a sign saluting liberty. While no challenge has been made here to the display of the tree and the sign, their presence is obviously relevant in determining the effect of the menorah's display. The necessary result of placing a menorah next to a Christmas tree is to create an "overall holiday setting" that represents both Christmas and Chanukah—two holidays, not one.

The mere fact that Pittsburgh displays symbols of both Christmas and Chanukah does not end the constitutional inquiry. If the city celebrates both Christmas and Chanukah as religious holidays, then it violates the Establishment Clause. The simultaneous endorsement of Judaism and Christianity is no less constitutionally infirm than the endorsement of Christianity alone.

Conversely, if the city celebrates both Christmas and Chanukah as secular holidays, then its conduct is beyond the reach of the Establishment Clause. Because government may celebrate Christmas as a secular holiday, it follows that government may also acknowledge Chanukah as a secular holiday. Simply put, it would be a form of discrimination against Jews to allow Pittsburgh to celebrate Christmas as a cultural tradition while simultaneously disallowing the city's acknowledgment of Chanukah as a contemporaneous cultural tradition.

Accordingly, the relevant question for Establishment Clause purposes is whether the combined display of the tree, the sign, and the menorah has the effect of endorsing both Christian and Jewish faiths, or rather simply recognizes that both Christmas and Chanukah are part of the same winter-holiday season, which has attained a secular status in our society. Of the two interpretations of this particular display, the latter seems far more plausible and is also in line with *Lynch*.[64]

The Christmas tree, unlike the menorah, is not itself a religious symbol. Although Christmas trees once carried religious connotations, today they typify the secular celebration of Christmas. Numerous Americans place Christmas trees in their homes without subscribing to Christian religious beliefs, and when the city's tree stands alone in front of the City–County Building, it is not considered an endorsement of Christian faith. Indeed, a 40–foot Christmas tree was one of the objects that validated the crèche in *Lynch*. The widely accepted view of the Christmas tree as the preeminent secular symbol of the Christmas holiday season serves to emphasize the secular component of the message communicated by other elements of an accompanying holiday display, including the Chanukah menorah.

The tree, moreover, is clearly the predominant element in the city's display. The 45–foot tree occupies the central position beneath the middle archway in front of the Grant Street entrance to the City–County Building; the 18–foot menorah is positioned to one side. Given this configuration, it is much more sensible to interpret the meaning of the menorah in light of the tree, rather than vice versa. In the shadow of the

---

64. * * * The conclusion that Pittsburgh's combined Christmas–Chanukah display cannot be interpreted as endorsing Judaism alone does not mean, however, that it is implausible, as a general matter, for a city like Pittsburgh to endorse a minority faith. The display of a menorah alone might well have that effect.

tree, the menorah is readily understood as simply a recognition that Christmas is not the only traditional way of observing the winter-holiday season. In these circumstances, then, the combination of the tree and the menorah communicates, not a simultaneous endorsement of both the Christian and Jewish faiths, but instead, a secular celebration of Christmas coupled with an acknowledgment of Chanukah as a contemporaneous alternative tradition.

Although the city has used a symbol with religious meaning as its representation of Chanukah, this is not a case in which the city has reasonable alternatives that are less religious in nature. It is difficult to imagine a predominantly secular symbol of Chanukah that the city could place next to its Christmas tree. An 18–foot dreidel would look out of place and might be interpreted by some as mocking the celebration of Chanukah. * * *

The mayor's sign further diminishes the possibility that the tree and the menorah will be interpreted as a dual endorsement of Christianity and Judaism. The sign states that during the holiday season the city salutes liberty. * * * While no sign can disclaim an overwhelming message of endorsement, an "explanatory plaque" may confirm that in particular contexts the government's association with a religious symbol does not represent the government's sponsorship of religious beliefs. Here, the mayor's sign serves to confirm what the context already reveals: that the display of the menorah is not an endorsement of religious faith but simply a recognition of cultural diversity.

Given all these considerations, it is not "sufficiently likely" that residents of Pittsburgh will perceive the combined display of the tree, the sign, and the menorah as an "endorsement" or "disapproval ... of their individual religious choices." While an adjudication of the display's effect must take into account the perspective of one who is neither Christian nor Jewish, as well as of those who adhere to either of these religions, the constitutionality of its effect must also be judged according to the standard of a "reasonable observer." When measured against this standard, the menorah need not be excluded from this particular display. The Christmas tree alone in the Pittsburgh location does not endorse Christian belief; and, on the facts before us, the addition of the menorah "cannot fairly be understood to" result in the simultaneous endorsement of Christian and Jewish faiths.[69]

* * *

VII

Lynch v. Donnelly confirms, and in no way repudiates, the long-standing constitutional principle that government may not engage in a practice that has the effect of promoting or endorsing religious beliefs.

---

69. [This footnote has been relocated] This is not to say that the combined display of a Christmas tree and a menorah is constitutional wherever it may be located on government property. For example, when located in a public school, such a display might raise additional constitutional considerations.

The display of the crèche in the county courthouse has this unconstitutional effect. The display of the menorah in front of the City–County Building, however, does not have this effect, given its "particular physical setting."

The judgment of the Court of Appeals is affirmed in part and reversed in part, and the cases are remanded for further proceedings.

JUSTICE O'CONNOR, with whom JUSTICE BRENNAN and JUSTICE STEVENS join as to Part II, concurring in part and concurring in the judgment.

I

Judicial review of government action under the Establishment Clause is a delicate task. The Court has avoided drawing lines which entirely sweep away all government recognition and acknowledgment of the role of religion in the lives of our citizens for to do so would exhibit not neutrality but hostility to religion. Instead the courts have made case-specific examinations of the challenged government action and have attempted to do so with the aid of the standards described by Justice Blackmun in Part III–A of the Court's opinion. Unfortunately, even the development of articulable standards and guidelines has not always resulted in agreement among the Members of this Court on the results in individual cases. And so it is again today.

The constitutionality of the two displays at issue in these cases turns on how we interpret and apply the holding in *Lynch v. Donnelly* * * *.

* * *

I joined the majority opinion in *Lynch* because, as I read that opinion, it was consistent with the analysis set forth in my separate concurrence, which stressed that "[e]very government practice must be judged in its *unique circumstances* to determine whether it constitutes an endorsement or disapproval of religion." Indeed, by referring repeatedly to "inclusion of the crèche" in the larger holiday display, the *Lynch* majority recognized that the crèche had to be viewed in light of the total display of which it was a part. Moreover, I joined the Court's discussion in Part II of *Lynch* concerning government acknowledgments of religion in American life because, in my view, acknowledgments such as the legislative prayers upheld in *Marsh v. Chambers*, and the printing of "In God We Trust" on our coins serve the secular purposes of "solemnizing public occasions, expressing confidence in the future and encouraging the recognition of what is worthy of appreciation in society." * * * At the same time, it is clear that "[g]overnment practices that purport to celebrate or acknowledge events with religious significance must be subjected to careful judicial scrutiny."

In my concurrence in *Lynch,* I suggested a clarification of our Establishment Clause doctrine to reinforce the concept that the Establishment Clause "prohibits government from making adherence to a religion relevant in any way to a person's standing in the political community." The government violates this prohibition if it endorses or disapproves of religion. "Endorsement sends a message to nonadherents that they are outsiders, not full members of the political community, and an accompanying message to adherents that they are insiders, favored members of the political community." Disapproval of religion conveys the opposite message. Thus, in my view, the central issue in *Lynch* was whether the city of Pawtucket had endorsed Christianity by displaying a crèche as part of a larger exhibit of traditional secular symbols of the Christmas holiday season.

* * *

For the reasons stated in Part IV of the Court's opinion in these cases, I agree that the crèche displayed on the Grand Staircase of the Allegheny County Courthouse, the seat of county government, conveys a message to nonadherents of Christianity that they are not full members of the political community, and a corresponding message to Christians that they are favored members of the political community. In contrast to the crèche in *Lynch,* which was displayed in a private park in the city's commercial district as part of a broader display of traditional secular symbols of the holiday season, this crèche stands alone in the county courthouse. The display of religious symbols in public areas of core government buildings runs a special risk of "mak[ing] religion relevant, in reality or public perception, to status in the political community." * * * The Court correctly concludes that placement of the central religious symbol of the Christmas holiday season at the Allegheny County Courthouse has the unconstitutional effect of conveying a government endorsement of Christianity.

II

In his separate opinion, Justice Kennedy asserts that the endorsement test "is flawed in its fundamentals and unworkable in practice." In my view, neither criticism is persuasive. As a theoretical matter, the endorsement test captures the essential command of the Establishment Clause, namely, that government must not make a person's religious beliefs relevant to his or her standing in the political community by conveying a message "that religion or a particular religious belief is favored or preferred." *Wallace v. Jaffree,* 472 U.S. 38, 70, 105 S.Ct. 2479, 2497, 86 L.Ed.2d 29 (1985) (O'Connor, J., concurring in judgment) * * * . We live in a pluralistic society. Our citizens come from diverse religious traditions or adhere to no particular religious beliefs at all. If government is to be neutral in matters of religion, rather than showing either favoritism or disapproval towards citizens based on their personal religious choices, government cannot endorse the religious practices and beliefs of some citizens without sending a clear message to nonadherents that they are outsiders or less than full members of the political community.

* * *

Under the endorsement test, the "history and ubiquity" of a practice is relevant not because it creates an "artificial exception" from that test. On the contrary, the "history and ubiquity" of a practice is relevant because it provides part of the context in which a reasonable observer evaluates whether a challenged governmental practice conveys a message of endorsement of religion. * * * The question under endorsement analysis, in short, is whether a reasonable observer would view such longstanding practices as a disapproval of his or her particular religious choices, in light of the fact that they serve a secular purpose rather than a sectarian one and have largely lost their religious significance over time. Although the endorsement test requires careful and often difficult line-drawing and is highly context specific, no alternative test has been suggested that captures the essential mandate of the Establishment Clause as well as the endorsement test does, and it warrants continued application and refinement.

Contrary to Justice Kennedy's assertions, neither the endorsement test nor its application in these cases reflects "an unjustified hostility toward religion." Instead, the endorsement standard recognizes that the religious liberty so precious to the citizens who make up our diverse country is protected, not impeded, when government avoids endorsing religion or favoring particular beliefs over others. Clearly, the government can *acknowledge* the role of religion in our society in numerous ways that do not amount to an endorsement. * * *

III

For reasons which differ somewhat from those set forth in Part VI of Justice Blackmun's opinion, I also conclude that the city of Pittsburgh's combined holiday display of a Chanukah menorah, a Christmas tree, and a sign saluting liberty does not have the effect of conveying an endorsement of religion. I agree with Justice Blackmun, that the Christmas tree, whatever its origins, is not regarded today as a religious symbol. * * * A Christmas tree displayed in front of city hall, in my view, cannot fairly be understood as conveying government endorsement of Christianity. Although Justice Blackmun's opinion acknowledges that a Christmas tree alone conveys no endorsement of Christian beliefs, it formulates the question posed by Pittsburgh's combined display of the tree and the menorah as whether the display "has the effect of endorsing *both* Christian and Jewish faiths, or rather simply recognizes that both Christmas and Chanukah are part of the same winter-holiday season, which has attained a secular status in our society."

That formulation of the question disregards the fact that the Christmas tree is a predominantly secular symbol and, more significantly, obscures the religious nature of the menorah and the holiday of Chanukah. The opinion is correct to recognize that the religious holiday of Chanukah has historical and cultural as well as religious dimensions, and that there may be certain "secular aspects" to the holiday. But that is not to conclude, however, * * * that Chanukah has become a "secular holiday" in our society. * * * Chanukah is a religious holiday with strong historical components particularly important to the Jewish people. Moreover, the menorah is the central religious symbol and ritual object of that religious holiday. * * * In my view, the relevant question for Establishment Clause purposes is whether the city of Pittsburgh's display of the menorah, the religious symbol of a religious holiday, next to a Christmas tree and a sign saluting liberty sends a message of government endorsement of Judaism or whether it sends a message of pluralism and freedom to choose one's own beliefs.

* * * One need not characterize Chanukah as a "secular" holiday or strain to argue that the menorah has a "secular" dimension, in order to conclude that the city of Pittsburgh's combined display does not convey a message of endorsement of Judaism or of religion in general.

In setting up its holiday display, which included the lighted tree and the menorah, the city of Pittsburgh stressed the theme of liberty and pluralism by accompanying the exhibit with a sign bearing the following message: " 'During this holiday season, the city of Pittsburgh salutes liberty. Let these festive lights remind us that we are the keepers of the flame of liberty and our legacy of freedom.' " This sign indicates that the city intended to convey its own distinctive message of pluralism and freedom. By accompanying its display of a Christmas tree—a secular symbol of the Christmas holiday season—with a salute to liberty, and by adding a religious symbol from a Jewish holiday also celebrated at roughly the same time of year, I conclude that the city did not endorse Judaism or religion in general, but rather conveyed a message of pluralism and freedom of belief during the holiday season. * * *

* * *

In sum, I conclude that the city of Pittsburgh's combined holiday display had neither the purpose nor the effect of endorsing religion, but that Allegheny County's crèche display had such an effect. Accordingly, I join Parts I, II, III–A, IV, V, and VII of the Court's opinion and concur in the judgment.

JUSTICE BRENNAN, with whom JUSTICE MARSHALL and JUSTICE STEVENS join, concurring in part and dissenting in part.

I have previously explained at some length my views on the relationship between the Establishment Clause and government-sponsored celebrations of the Christmas holiday. I continue to believe that the display of an object that "retains a specifically Christian [or other] religious meaning," is incompatible with the separation of church and state demanded by our Constitution. I therefore agree with the Court that Allegheny County's display of a crèche at the county courthouse signals an endorsement of the Christian faith in violation of the Establishment Clause, and join Parts III–A, IV, and V of the Court's opinion. I cannot agree, however, that the city's display of a 45–foot Christmas tree and an 18–foot Chanukah menorah at the entrance to the building housing the mayor's office shows no favoritism towards Christianity, Judaism, or both. Indeed, I should have thought that the answer as to the first display supplied the answer to the second.

* * *

* * * [The Court's] decision as to the menorah rests on three premises: the Christmas tree is a secular symbol; Chanukah is a holiday with secular dimensions, symbolized by the menorah; and the government may promote pluralism by sponsoring or condoning displays having strong religious associations on its property. None of these is sound.

I

The first step toward Justice Blackmun's conclusion is the claim that, despite its religious origins, the Christmas tree is a secular symbol. * * *

Justice O'Connor accepts this view of the Christmas tree * * *.

Thus, while acknowledging the religious origins of the Christmas tree, Justices Blackmun and O'Connor dismiss their significance. In my view, this attempt to take the "Christmas" out of the Christmas tree is unconvincing. That the tree may, without controversy, be deemed a secular symbol if found alone, does not mean that it will be so seen when combined with other symbols or objects. * * *

* * * While conceding that the "menorah standing alone at city hall may well send" a message of endorsement of the Jewish faith, [Justice O'Connor] nevertheless concludes: "By accompanying its display of a Christmas tree—a secular symbol of the Christmas holiday season—with a salute to liberty, and by adding a religious symbol from a Jewish holiday also celebrated at roughly the same time of year, I conclude that the city did not endorse Judaism or religion in general, but rather conveyed a message of pluralism and freedom of belief during the holiday season." But the "pluralism" to which Justice O'Connor refers is *religious* pluralism, and the "freedom of belief" she emphasizes is freedom of *religious* belief. The display of the tree and the menorah will symbolize such pluralism and freedom only if more than one religion is represented; if only Judaism is represented, the scene is about Judaism, not about pluralism. Thus, the pluralistic message Justice O'Connor stresses *depends on* the tree's possessing some religious significance.

In asserting that the Christmas tree, regardless of its surroundings, is a purely secular symbol, Justices Blackmun and O'Connor ignore the precept they otherwise so enthusiastically embrace: that context is all important in determining the message conveyed by particular objects. * * *

* * *

Justice Blackmun believes that it is the tree that changes the message of the menorah, rather than the menorah that alters our view of the tree. * * * The distinguishing characteristic, it appears, is the size of the tree. The tree, we are told, is much taller—2 1/2 times taller, in fact—than the menorah, and is located directly under one of the building's archways, whereas the menorah "is positioned to one side . . . [i]n the shadow of the tree."

As a factual matter, it seems to me that the sight of an 18–foot menorah would be far more eye catching than that of a rather conventionally sized Christmas tree. It also seems to me likely that the symbol with the more singular message will predominate over one lacking such a clear meaning. Given the homogenized message that Justice Blackmun associates with the Christmas tree, I would expect that the menorah, with its concededly religious character, would tend to dominate the tree. And, though Justice Blackmun shunts the point to a footnote at the end of his opinion, it is highly relevant that the menorah was lit during a religious ceremony complete with traditional religious blessings. * * * With such an openly religious introduction, it is most likely that the religious aspects of the menorah would be front and center in this display.

I would not, however, presume to say that my interpretation of the tree's significance is the "correct" one, or the one shared by most visitors to the City–County Building. I do not know how we can decide whether it was the tree that stripped the religious connotations from the menorah, or the menorah that laid bare the religious origins of the tree. Both are reasonable interpretations of the scene the city presented, and thus both, I think, should satisfy Justice Blackmun's requirement that the display "be judged according to the standard of a 'reasonable observer.' " I shudder to think that the only "reasonable observer" is one who shares the particular views on perspective, spacing, and accent expressed in Justice Blackmun's opinion, thus making analysis under the Establishment Clause look more like an exam in Art 101 than an inquiry into constitutional law.

II

The second premise on which today's decision rests is the notion that Chanukah is a partly secular holiday, for which the menorah can serve as a secular symbol. It is no surprise and no anomaly that Chanukah has historical and societal roots that range beyond the purely religious. I would venture that most, if not all, major religious holidays have beginnings and enjoy histories studded with figures, events, and practices that are not strictly religious. It does not seem to me that the mere fact that Chanukah shares this kind of background makes it a secular holiday in any meaningful sense. The menorah is indisputably a religious symbol, used ritually in a celebration that has deep religious significance. That, in my view, is all that need be said. Whatever secular practices the holiday of Chanukah has taken on in its contemporary observance are beside the point.

Indeed, at the very outset of his discussion of the menorah display, Justice Blackmun recognizes that the menorah is a religious symbol. That should have been the end of the case. But, as did the Court in

Lynch, Justice Blackmun, "by focusing on the holiday 'context' in which the [menorah] appeared, seeks to explain away the clear religious import of the [menorah]. . . . " 465 U.S., at 705, 104 S.Ct., at 1376 (Brennan, J., dissenting). By the end of the opinion, the menorah has become but a coequal symbol, with the Christmas tree, of "the winter-holiday season." Pittsburgh's secularization of an inherently religious symbol, aided and abetted here by Justice Blackmun's opinion, recalls the effort in *Lynch* to render the crèche a secular symbol. As I said then: "To suggest, as the Court does, that such a symbol is merely 'traditional' and therefore no different from Santa's house or reindeer is not only offensive to those for whom the crèche has profound significance, but insulting to those who insist for religious or personal reasons that the story of Christ is in no sense a part of 'history' nor an unavoidable element of our national 'heritage.' " 465 U.S., at 711–712, 104 S.Ct., at 1379. * * *

* * *

III

Justice Blackmun, in his acceptance of the city's message of "diversity," even more so, Justice O'Connor, in her approval of the "message of pluralism and freedom to choose one's own beliefs," appear to believe that, where seasonal displays are concerned, more is better. Whereas a display might be constitutionally problematic if it showcased the holiday of just one religion, those problems vaporize as soon as more than one religion is included. I know of no principle under the Establishment Clause, however, that permits us to conclude that governmental promotion of religion is acceptable so long as one religion is not favored. We have, on the contrary, interpreted that Clause to require neutrality, not just among religions, but between religion and nonreligion.

* * *

The uncritical acceptance of a message of religious pluralism also ignores the extent to which even that message may offend. Many religious faiths are hostile to each other, and indeed, refuse even to participate in ecumenical services designed to demonstrate the very pluralism Justices Blackmun and O'Connor extol. To lump the ritual objects and holidays of religions together without regard to their attitudes toward such inclusiveness, or to decide which religions should be excluded because of the possibility of offense, is not a benign or beneficent celebration of pluralism: it is instead an interference in religious matters precluded by the Establishment Clause.

The government-sponsored display of the menorah alongside a Christmas tree also works a distortion of the Jewish religious calendar. * * * It is the proximity of Christmas that undoubtedly accounts for the city's decision to participate in the celebration of Chanukah, rather than the far more significant Jewish holidays of Rosh Hashanah and Yom Kippur. Contrary to the impression the city and Justices Blackmun and O'Connor seem to create, with their emphasis on "the winter-holiday season," December is not the holiday season for Judaism. Thus, the city's erection alongside the Christmas tree of the symbol of a relatively minor Jewish religious holiday, far from conveying "the city's secular recognition of different traditions for celebrating the winter-holiday season," or "a message of pluralism and freedom of belief," has the effect of promoting a Christianized version of Judaism. The holiday calendar they appear willing to accept revolves exclusively around a Christian holiday. And those religions that have no holiday at all during the period between Thanksgiving and New Year's Day will not benefit, even in a second-class manner, from the city's once-a-year tribute to "liberty" and "freedom of belief." This is not "pluralism" as I understand it.

JUSTICE STEVENS, with whom JUSTICE BRENNAN and JUSTICE MARSHALL join, concurring in part and dissenting in part.

Governmental recognition of not one but two religions distinguishes these cases from our prior Establishment Clause cases. It is, therefore, appropriate to reexamine the text and context of the Clause to determine its impact on this novel situation.

* * *

* * * [The Establishment] Clause as ratified proscribes federal legislation establishing a number of religions as well as a single national church.

Treatment of a symbol of a particular tradition demonstrates one's attitude toward that tradition. Thus the prominent display of religious symbols on government property falls within the compass of the First Amendment, even though interference with personal choices about supporting a church, by means of governmental tithing, was the primary concern in 1791. Whether the vice in such a display is characterized as "coercion," or "endorsement," or merely as state action with the purpose and effect of providing support for specific faiths, it is common ground that this symbolic governmental speech "respecting an establishment of religion" may violate the Constitution.

In my opinion the Establishment Clause should be construed to create a strong presumption against the display of religious symbols on public property. There is always a risk that such symbols will offend nonmembers of the faith being advertised as well as adherents who consider the particular advertisement disrespectful. Some devout Christians believe that the crèche should be placed only in reverential settings, such as a church or perhaps a private home; they do not countenance its use as an aid to commercialization of Christ's birthday. In this very suit, members of the Jewish faith firmly opposed the use to which the menorah was put by the particular sect that sponsored the display at Pittsburgh's City–County Building. Even though "[p]assersby who disagree with the message conveyed by these displays are free to ignore them, or even to turn their backs," displays of this kind inevitably have a greater tendency to emphasize sincere and deeply felt differences among individuals than to achieve an ecumenical goal. The Establishment Clause does not allow public bodies to foment such disagreement.

* * *

* * * Accordingly, I concur in the Court's judgment regarding the crèche for substantially the same reasons discussed in Justice Brennan's opinion, which I join, as well as Part IV of Justice Blackmun's opinion and Part I of Justice O'Connor's opinion.

I cannot agree with the Court's conclusion that the display at Pittsburgh's City–County Building was constitutional. Standing alone in front of a governmental headquarters, a lighted, 45–foot evergreen tree might convey holiday greetings linked too tenuously to Christianity to have constitutional moment. Juxtaposition of this tree with an 18–foot menorah does not make the latter secular * * * . Rather, the presence of the Chanukah menorah, unquestionably a religious symbol, gives religious significance to the Christmas tree. The overall display thus manifests governmental approval of the Jewish and Christian religions. Although it conceivably might be interpreted as sending "a message of pluralism and freedom to choose one's own beliefs," the message is not sufficiently clear to overcome the strong presumption that the display, respecting two religions to the exclusion of all others, is the very kind of double establishment that the First Amendment was designed to outlaw. I would, therefore, affirm the judgment of the Court of Appeals in its entirety.

JUSTICE KENNEDY, with whom THE CHIEF JUSTICE, JUSTICE WHITE, and JUSTICE SCALIA join, concurring in the judgment in part and dissenting in part.

The majority holds that the County of Allegheny violated the Establishment Clause by displaying a crèche in the county courthouse, because the "principal or primary effect" of the display is to advance religion within the meaning of *Lemon v. Kurtzman*. This view of the Establishment Clause reflects an unjustified hostility toward religion, a hostility inconsistent with our history and our precedents, and I dissent from this holding. The crèche display is constitutional, and, for the same reasons, the display of a menorah by the city of Pittsburgh is permissible as well. On this latter point, I concur in the result, but not the reasoning, of Part VI of Justice Blackmun's opinion.

I

In keeping with the usual fashion of recent years, the majority applies the *Lemon* test to judge the constitutionality of the holiday displays here in question. I am content for present purposes to remain within the *Lemon* framework, but do not wish to be seen as advocating, let alone adopting, that test as our primary guide in this difficult area. Persuasive criticism of *Lemon* has emerged. * * * Substantial revision of our Establishment Clause doctrine may be in order; but it is unnecessary to undertake that task today, for even the *Lemon* test, when applied with proper sensitivity to our traditions and our case law, supports the conclusion that both the crèche and the menorah are permissible displays in the context of the holiday season.

The only *Lemon* factor implicated in these cases directs us to inquire whether the "principal or primary effect" of the challenged government practice is "one that neither advances nor inhibits religion." The requirement of neutrality inherent in that formulation has sometimes been stated in categorical terms. * * * We have stated that government "must be neutral in matters of religious theory, doctrine, and practice" and "may not aid, foster, or promote one religion or religious theory against another or even against the militant opposite." *Epperson v. Arkansas.* * * *

These statements must not give the impression of a formalism that does not exist. * * * Government policies of accommodation, acknowledgment, and support for religion are an accepted part of our political and cultural heritage. * * *

* * *

A categorical approach would install federal courts as jealous guardians of an absolute "wall of separation," sending a clear message of disapproval. In this century, as the modern administrative state expands to touch the lives of its citizens in such diverse ways and redirects their financial choices through programs of its own, it is difficult to maintain the fiction that requiring government to avoid all assistance to religion can in fairness be viewed as serving the goal of neutrality.

* * *

The ability of the organized community to recognize and accommodate religion in a society with a pervasive public sector requires diligent observance of the border between accommodation and establishment. Our cases disclose two limiting principles: government may not coerce anyone to support or participate in any religion or its exercise; and it may not, in the guise of avoiding hostility or callous indifference, give direct benefits to religion in such a degree that it in fact "establishes a [state] religion or religious faith, or tends to do so." *Lynch v. Donnelly,* 465 U.S., at 678, 104 S.Ct., at 1361. These two principles, while distinct, are not unrelated, for it would be difficult indeed to establish a religion without some measure of more or less subtle coercion, be it in the form of taxation to supply the substantial benefits that would sustain a state-established faith, direct compulsion to observance, or governmental exhortation to religiosity that amounts in fact to proselytizing.

It is no surprise that without exception we have invalidated actions that further the interests of religion through the coercive power of government. * * * The freedom to worship as one pleases without government interference or oppression is the great object of both the Establishment and the Free Exercise Clauses. Barring all attempts to aid religion through government coercion goes far toward attainment of this object.

* * * [S]ome of our recent cases reject the view that coercion is the sole touchstone of an Establishment Clause violation. That may be true if by "coercion" is meant *direct* coercion in the classic sense of an establishment of religion that the Framers knew. But coercion need not be a direct tax in aid of religion or a test oath. Symbolic recognition or accommodation of religious faith may violate the Clause in an extreme case. I doubt not, for example, that the Clause forbids a city to permit the permanent erection of a large Latin cross on the roof of city hall. This is not because government speech about religion is *per se* suspect, as the majority would have it, but because such an obtrusive year-round religious display would place the government's weight behind an obvious effort to proselytize on behalf of a particular religion. * * *

* * * Absent coercion, the risk of infringement of religious liberty by passive or symbolic accommodation is minimal. Our cases reflect this reality by requiring a showing that the symbolic recognition or accommodation advances religion to such a degree that it actually "establishes a religion or religious faith, or tends to do so." *Lynch*.

* * *

II

These principles are not difficult to apply to the facts of the cases before us. In permitting the displays on government property of the menorah and the crèche, the city and county sought to do no more than "celebrate the season," and to acknowledge, along with many of their citizens, the historical background and the religious, as well as secular, nature of the Chanukah and Christmas holidays. This interest falls well within the tradition of government accommodation and acknowledgment of religion that has marked our history from the beginning. * * *

* * * The Religion Clauses do not require government to acknowledge these holidays or their religious component; but our strong tradition of government accommodation and acknowledgment permits government to do so.

There is no suggestion here that the government's power to coerce has been used to further the interests of Christianity or Judaism in any way. No one was compelled to observe or participate in any religious ceremony or activity. Neither the city nor the county contributed significant amounts of tax money to serve the cause of one religious faith. The crèche and the menorah are purely passive symbols of religious holidays. Passersby who disagree with the message conveyed by these displays are free to ignore them, or even to turn their backs, just as they are free to do when they disagree with any other form of government speech.

* * *

III

* * * Since the majority does not state its intent to overrule *Lynch*, I find its refusal to apply the reasoning of that decision quite confusing.

Even if *Lynch* did not control, I would not commit this Court to the test applied by the majority today. The notion that cases arising under the Establishment Clause should be decided by an inquiry into whether a " 'reasonable observer' " may " 'fairly understand' " government action to " 'sen[d] a message to nonadherents that they are outsiders, not full members of the political community,' " is a recent, and in my view most unwelcome, addition to our tangled Establishment Clause jurisprudence. * * * I submit that the endorsement test is flawed in its fundamentals and unworkable in practice. The uncritical adoption of this standard is every bit as troubling as the bizarre result it produces in the cases before us.

* * *

A

* * *

Either the endorsement test must invalidate scores of traditional practices recognizing the place religion holds in our culture, or it must be twisted and stretched to avoid inconsistency with practices we know to have been permitted in the past, while condemning similar practices with no greater endorsement effect simply by reason of their lack of historical antecedent. Neither result is acceptable.

* * *

IV

* * *

A further contradiction arises from the majority's approach, for the Court also assumes the difficult and inappropriate task of saying what every religious symbol means. * * * Even if the majority is quite right about the history of the menorah, it hardly follows that this same history informed the observers' view of the symbol and the reason for its presence. This Court is ill-equipped to sit as a national theology board, and I question both the wisdom and the constitutionality of its doing so. * * *

* * *

Notes and Questions

1. *What is a Religious Object or Symbol?* When one is dealing with an obviously religious object or symbol such as a crèche or cross, this is not a major issue. In other situations the threshold question of what qualifies as a religious object is important. For example, the court suggests that Christmas trees, Santas, and the like are not religious objects—and for that matter Christmas is a public holiday as well as a religious one. Yet, to many non-Christians (and probably to many Christians), these objects clearly represent a Christian holiday—even if it is a holiday that many who are secular also celebrate. Observant

Jews, Muslims, Buddhists, Hindus, etc . . . do not celebrate Christmas in any of its forms. Eastern Orthodox and Greek Orthodox Christians do not celebrate Christmas on December 25th, Jehovah's Witnesses do not "celebrate" Christmas in the public sense of the word, and of course many Atheists do not celebrate Christmas. For many religious minorities Christmas (and thus the symbols of Christmas) is a clearly Christian holiday, whether it is religiously Christian, culturally Christian, or both. *See generally*, STEPHEN M. FELDMAN, PLEASE DON'T WISH ME A MERRY CHRISTMAS: A CRITICAL HISTORY OF THE SEPARATION OF CHURCH AND STATE (NYU Press 1997). If this is so, does the inclusion of symbols of the secular/commercial aspects of Christmas, such as Santas and reindeer, make the context of the crèche more or less sectarian?

2.   *Religious Objects as Legal Subjects.* Many of the cases in this area involve the meaning of religious objects. While the endorsement test explicitly considers this issue, the issue is also relevant under the general purpose and effects analysis of the *Lemon* test. If the government erects a religious object such as a crèche without more, there would seem to be a clear violation of the Establishment Clause. Thus, in order to uphold such government action courts must minimize the religious impact of the objects to satisfy the legal demands of the Establishment Clause. In minimizing the religious impact of religious objects courts turn them into legal subjects, and the effect of this can be to degrade the religious significance of the object for believers or ignore the religious message sent by the object to those who do not share the faith reflected by the governmentally sponsored object (almost always Christianity). This is what the *Lynch* dissent suggests the Majority implicitly did in that case.

3.   *Menorahs and Christmas Trees.* There is no doubt that a Menorah is a religious object, and as the Court points out the Menorah is used in the religious rituals surrounding the holiday of Chanukah. Given this fact, does it seem odd that the Court would hold that the placement of a Menorah next to a Christmas tree and a sign saluting liberty does not endorse religion? How might a Muslim or an Atheist view the government sponsorship of a Christmas Tree (which arguably has some religious message), a symbol of a Christian holiday, along with the Menorah, a Jewish religious object? What message might the sign saluting liberty send to such observers in this context? The entire scene?

4.   *Endorsement*? The endorsement test is focused upon what a reasonable observer would perceive the government action in question to mean in light of its context and a presumed knowledge of the relevant history of the location and the display. *See Capitol Square Review Bd. v. Pinette, infra.* this Chapter (O'Connor, J., concurring); *Id.* (Stevens, J., dissenting). Would a reasonable observer of the display in *Lynch* or the display upheld in *Allegheny* perceive that Christianity (or Christianity and Judaism in the latter case) is being favored or that non-Christians are less favored members of the political community? Would it make a difference if the reasonable observer is presumed to be a reasonable member of a religious minority group that does not share the faith(s) reflected in the display? Is there any way to understand the message sent to religious outsiders without viewing the display from their perspective? Could any display symbolizing the beliefs or traditions of the religious majority survive such analysis? Could displays reflecting the beliefs and traditions of religious minorities survive such analysis? Would it be fair to allow the latter but not the former? The former but not the latter? To allow both?

The Ten Commandments Cases

In *Stone v. Graham*, 449 U.S. 39, 101 S.Ct. 192, 66 L.Ed.2d 199 (1980)(per curiam), the Supreme Court struck down a Kentucky statute requiring the posting of the Ten Commandments in public schools. The brief opinion, which is well summarized in the cases excerpted in this section, held that the law violated both the purpose and effects prongs of the *Lemon* test. This was not the end of the Ten Commandments debate, however. Issues regarding the posting of the Ten Commandments in various forms have arisen in the years since *Stone v. Graham*, and there has been a flurry of such cases in recent years. As with most symbolism cases, context and history have been quite important to the outcomes in these cases. Following are two cases recently decided by different panels of the Federal Court of Appeals for the Eleventh Circuit. One case upholds the use of the Ten Commandments on a small court seal, and the other strikes down the erection of a large granite monument of the Ten Commandments in the Rotunda of the Alabama state courthouse. Despite the differing outcomes, the cases are arguably consistent with each other. As you read the cases, see if you can determine why. Following these cases will be a brief summary of several other recent cases involving the Ten Commandments.

KING v. RICHMOND COUNTY, GEORGIA

United States Court of Appeals, Eleventh Circuit, 2003.
331 F.3d 1271.

KRAVITCH, CIRCUIT JUDGE:

The question presented is whether the use of a court clerk's seal violates the Establishment Clause of the First Amendment when the seal contains an outline of the Ten Commandments, a sword, and the name of the court and is used solely to authenticate documents. We conclude that it does not.

I. BACKGROUND

Since 1852, a Georgia statute has required clerks of the state superior courts to have a "substantial seal of office" with the name of the county and court inscribed thereon. In conformance with the statute, the Clerk of the Superior Court of Richmond County has maintained an official seal (the "Seal") for more than 130 years. Records found in the Richmond County clerk's office indicate that the Seal has been used on documents at least since 1872.

The Seal is circular, with the words "SUPERIOR COURT RICH-MOND COUNTY, GA" inscribed around the perimeter. The center of the Seal contains a depiction of a hilt and tip of a sword, the center of which is overlaid by two rectangular tablets with rounded tops. Roman numerals I though V are listed vertically on the left tablet; the right lists numerals VI to X. The Seal is placed on documents in one of three ways: with ink from a rubber stamp, by embossment into paper, or by embossment into a gold seal on paper. The ink-stamped version of the seal is approximately one-and-a-half inches in diameter, with the center portion depicting the tablets measuring approximately one inch. The embossed version is smaller, approximately one-and-a-fourth inches in diameter, with the center portion measuring less than three-fourths of an inch.

The Seal's only function is to authenticate legal documents. In one of the forms described above, the Seal is affixed to all certified copies of court documents and real-estate records, witness subpoenas, certifications of juror service, notary certificates of appointment, and attorney licenses. Approximately 24,000 documents bore the Seal in 1999. The Seal does not appear on the office of the clerk's letterhead or on its website, nor is it displayed in the clerk's office, in the courtroom, or anywhere else in the Richmond County Courthouse. The office of the clerk's letterhead and envelopes bear the seal of the state of Georgia instead.

* * *

Appellants Reverend Daniel King, E. Ronald Garnett, and Shirley Fencl filed suit in federal district court under 42 U.S.C. § 1983, contending that the Seal violates the Establishment Clause of the First Amendment. * * * According to the complaint, the Seal "prominently displays the Ten Commandments, a sacred text in the Judeo–Christian religious traditions," in violation of the Establishment Clause * * * . In response, the Appellees conceded that the pictograph in the center of the Seal resembles depictions of the Ten Commandments, but argued that the use of the Seal is not unconstitutional under any of the Supreme Court's Establishment Clause tests.

After a summary bench trial, the District Court concluded that although the tablets depicted on the Seal represented the Ten Commandments, and that a reasonable observer could view them as such, there was no Establishment Clause violation. The District Court found, and both parties agreed, that the Seal had been in use for more than 130 years but that there was no evidence of the purpose for the Seal's design or when it was adopted by the clerk of the superior court.

* * *

On appeal, Appellants argue that the District Court erred in finding that the Seal did not violate the Establishment Clause because (1) the Seal has a religious purpose and (2) the use of the Seal has the primary effect of endorsing religion. * * * .

* * *

III. ANALYSIS

The issue presented is whether the use of the Seal violates the Establishment Clause of the First Amendment. * * *

In religious-symbols cases, the Supreme Court has applied the analysis outlined in *Lemon v. Kurtzman*. Under the *Lemon* analysis, a governmental practice violates the Establishment Clause if it does not have a secular purpose, if its primary effect is to advance or inhibit religion, or if it fosters excessive government entanglement with religion.

Despite the Supreme Court's reliance on these three "tests," it has emphasized that there is no bright-line rule for evaluating Establishment Clause challenges and that each challenge calls for line-drawing based on a fact-specific, case-by-case analysis. In recent years, the Court has "paid particularly close attention" to whether the challenged governmental practice has either "the purpose or effect of 'endorsing religion.'" *County of Allegheny*, 492 U.S. at 592, 109 S.Ct. 3086. Even though some Justices and commentators have strongly criticized *Lemon*, both the Supreme Court and this circuit continue to use *Lemon*'s three-pronged analysis.

Here, Appellants argue that the use of the Seal violates the purpose and effect prongs of the *Lemon* analysis; they do not contend that use of the Seal implicates excessive government entanglement with religion. Accordingly, for Appellants to prevail, they must show that, given the particular facts of this case, the use of the Seal violates either the purpose test or the effect test of *Lemon*.

A. Purpose Prong

* * * According to Appellants, our analysis of this prong could begin and end with *Stone v. Graham*, 449 U.S. 39, 101 S.Ct. 192, 66 L.Ed.2d 199 (1980) (per curiam). Although informative, *Stone* does not foreclose our inquiry.

In *Stone*, the Supreme Court invalidated a Kentucky statute that required the posting of the text of the Ten Commandments on the wall of every public-school classroom. Describing the Ten Commandments as an "undeniably sacred text," the Court found that the "pre-eminent purpose for posting the Ten Commandments on schoolroom walls is plainly religious in nature." *Stone*, however, does not stand for the proposition that there can never be a permissible secular use of the Ten Commandments. The opinion distinguishes Kentucky's posting the text of the Ten Commandments on schoolroom walls from constitutionally appropriate uses of the Commandments and other parts of the Bible in a public-school curriculum * * * . Accordingly, because governmental use of the Ten Commandments is not a per se violation of the purpose prong, we must continue our inquiry and determine whether the Seal's depiction of the Ten Commandments and sword has a secular purpose.

* * * Appellees argue that the first prong of *Lemon* is satisfied because state law requires the superior court's clerk to have a seal. Appellees' assertion, however, misperceives the true inquiry. Under the purpose test, the relevant inquiry is not whether there was a secular purpose for creating and using a legal seal; it is to determine the government's purpose for adopting this particular seal, one that depicts the Ten Commandments and sword.

As stated previously, the District Court found, and both parties concede, that there was no evidence regarding the original purpose for adopting the design of the Seal and that the Seal has existed in its current form since at least 1872. The District Court hypothesized that, because approximately thirty-five percent of Georgia's population in 1872 was illiterate, the then-clerk of the court may have chosen the Ten Commandments and the sword as pictographs that were easily recognizable symbols of the law. Additionally, the District Court found that a pictograph of the Ten Commandments was, in addition to being a religious symbol, a secular symbol for the rule of law. Nevertheless, the court admitted that the purpose for adopting this particular seal design has been "lost in the mists of history."

This case, therefore, presents the issue of how to apply the purpose test when there is no evidence of the government's intent for adopting a particular practice. No decision from the Supreme Court or the Eleventh Circuit addresses this issue directly, but precedents do give some guidance. * * * [I]t seems that the government always has the obligation to propose a secular justification for the challenged practice. This does not mean, however, that the government fails the purpose prong in cases in which there is no available evidence of the original intent for adopting a practice.

When there is no evidence of the original purpose for adopting a practice, the government may propose possible secular justifications for the challenged practice. In *Mueller v. Allen*, the Supreme Court explained that it was reluctant to attribute an unconstitutional motive to the government where a "plausible secular purpose" may be discerned from the statute. The fact that the government articulates a possible legitimate secular purpose for the practice, however, does not mean that it has satisfied the purpose prong. Although courts should be "deferential to a State's articulation of a secular purpose," *Edwards v. Aguillard*, the party challenging the governmental practice can prevail under the purpose prong if it can show that the government's articulated secular purpose is insincere or a "sham." *Id.* * * * . Therefore, once the government proposes a possible secular purpose for the challenged practice, the party challenging the practice has the opportunity to rebut the stated secular purpose with evidence showing that the articulated purpose is insincere or a sham.

Applying this approach to the present case, Appellees have articulated a plausible secular purpose for the design of the Seal. They claim that, in the context of authenticating legal documents, using a pictograph of the Ten Commandments intertwined with the sword helps viewers recognize the legal validity of documents. The District Court's findings support Appellees' proposed justification. The court found that during the 1870s the outline of the Ten Commandments presumably would have enabled illiterate citizens to recognize the legal validity of documents displaying the Seal. Appellees' proffered secular justification satisfies the initial burden under the purpose prong. * * * [The court did not find that appellant demonstrated this secular purpose was a "sham"].

Of course, this analysis applies only when there is no evidence of governmental intent for adopting a practice. When evidence shows that endorsement or promotion of religion was a primary purpose for the challenged practice, the inquiry ends, as the practice violates the Establishment Clause.

B. Effect Prong

The second inquiry of the *Lemon* test, the effect prong, is whether the "principal or primary effect" of a challenged law or conduct is "to advance or inhibit religion." *Lynch*. The Court has explained the effect prong to mean that, even when evidence of religious purpose is lacking, the Establishment Clause prohibits the government from "appearing to take a position on questions of religious belief or from 'making adherence to a religion relevant in any way to a person's standing in the political community.' " *County of Allegheny* (quoting *Lynch,* 465 U.S. at 687, 104 S.Ct. 1355 (O'Connor, J., concurring)). Two of the Court's most recent religious-symbols cases give guidance in applying *Lemon* 's effect prong.

1. Prior Precedent

a. Lynch v. Donnelly

In *Lynch v. Donnelly*, the Supreme Court held that the City of Pawtucket, Rhode Island did not violate the Establishment Clause when it displayed a crèche as part of its annual Christmas display. In addition to the crèche, which is a representation of the Nativity scene, the display included a Santa Clause house, reindeer, candy-striped poles, a Christmas tree, carolers, hundreds of colored lights, and a large banner with the words "Seasons Greetings."

Rejecting a strict wall-of-separation theory of the Establishment Clause, the Court cited numerous examples of "the Government's acknowledgment of our religious heritage and governmental sponsorship of that heritage," to demonstrate that the Constitution does not prevent government from ever using religious symbols or references to divinity. The Court explained, "In every Establishment Clause case, we must reconcile the inescapable tension between the objective of preventing unnecessary intrusion of either the church or the state upon the other, and the reality that, as the Court has so often noted, total separation of the two is not possible." The Court continued, "In each case, the inquiry calls for line drawing; no fixed, *per se* rule can be framed."

Repeating the three "useful" "inquiries" of the *Lemon* test, the Court emphasized that the constitutionality of the government's use of a predominantly religious symbol depends on the context in which it appears. Hence, the Court instructed that in deciding the constitutionality of Pawtucket's display, the "focus of our inquiry must be on the crèche *in the context* of the Christmas season." * * *

* * * [T]he Court applied *Lemon* 's effect test and concluded that the use of the nativity scene, at least in the context of a Christmas display that included both religious and nonreligious symbols, did not have the primary effect of advancing or endorsing religion.

In a concurring opinion that has influenced subsequent religious-symbols cases, Justice O'Connor framed the central issue in the case as "whether Pawtucket has endorsed Christianity by its display of the crèche." "To answer that question, we must examine both what Pawtucket intended to communicate in displaying the crèche and what message the City's display actually conveyed. The purpose and effect prongs of the Lemon test represent these two aspects of the meaning of the City's action." According to the concurrence, "[t]he meaning of a statement to its audience depends both on the intention of the speaker and on the 'objective' meaning of the statement in the community." Thus, the test has both a subjective and an objective component. A governmental statement or action fails *Lemon* 's purpose prong if, despite the existence of a stated secular purpose, the "government intends to convey a message of endorsement or disapproval of religion." The effect prong asks whether, irrespective of government's actual purposes, the practice under review in fact would convey a message of endorsement or disapproval to an informed, reasonable observer.

* * * Because governmental celebrations of the holiday season are so common, Justice O'Connor concluded that a reasonable person would not perceive a crèche that is accompanied by purely secular symbols of the season to be a governmental endorsement of religion.

b.   County of Allegheny v. American Civil Liberties Union

A more recent religious-symbols case is *County of Allegheny v. ACLU, Greater Pittsburgh Chapter*. That case involved two holiday displays located on public property. The first was a crèche displayed on the Grand Staircase of the county courthouse during the Christmas season. The crèche "include[d] figures of the infant Jesus, Mary, Joseph, farm animals, shepherds, and wise men, all placed in or before a wooden representation of a manger, which ha[d] at its crest an angel bearing a banner that proclaim[ed] 'Gloria in Excelsis Deo!' " * * *

The second holiday display was located at the entrance to the main office building for the city and county. The display contained an 18–foot–tall Chanukah menorah standing next to a 45–foot–tall evergreen Christmas tree. A sign referred to the display as a "Salute to Liberty." * * *

A splintered Court held that the crèche display violated the Establishment Clause but that the use of the menorah did not. Justice Kennedy, joined by Chief Justice Rehnquist and Justices White and Scalia, believed that both displays were constitutional; Justice Brennan, joined by Justices Marshall and Stevens, would have found both to be unconstitutional. Only Justices Blackmun and O'Connor believed that the menorah display was constitutional and that the crèche display was not, but, as they were the "swing votes" in the case, their view prevailed.

In holding the crèche display unconstitutional, the Court focused on the display's effect. The Court began its analysis by explaining that "[u]nder the Court's holding in *Lynch*, the effect of a crèche turns on its setting" and that, unlike the display in *Lynch*, the crèche in this case stood alone as "the single element of the display on the Grand Staircase." * * * Furthermore, because the crèche sat on the Grand Staircase, which was "the 'main' and 'most beautiful part' of the building that is the seat of county government," the Court reasoned that "[n]o viewer could reasonably think that it occupie[d] this location without the support and approval of government." * * * In short, the Court assessed the crèche's "endorsement effect" by analyzing the display's overall context and the display's likely impact on reasonable viewers.

* * *

The Court did not agree on the reason for upholding the menorah display * * *. Justices Blackmun and O'Connor, the swing votes, focused their individual opinions on the importance of context when applying the effect prong, just as the Court had done in its opinion regarding the crèche display.

Supreme Court precedent in the most recent religious-symbols cases makes one thing clear: when applying *Lemon*'s effect test, the constitutionality of the government's use of a predominantly religious symbol depends upon the context in which it appears. * * * [W]e therefore must inquire whether observers would reasonably believe that the government's use of a predominantly religious symbol sends a message of governmental endorsement of religion. Courts must evaluate challenged governmental practices on a case-by-case basis, judging each practice in its unique circumstances and in its particular physical setting.

2. *Application of the Effect Prong*

* * * As the Supreme Court has recognized, the Ten Commandments are "undeniably a sacred text in the Jewish and Christian faiths.... " *Stone*, 449 U.S. at 41, 101 S.Ct. 192. In many contexts, governmental use of the text of the Ten Commandments would convey a message of endorsement and thereby violate the Establishment Clause.

Yet, as the Supreme Court explained in *Lynch,* it is improper to "[f]ocus exclusively on the religious component of any activity," as doing so "would inevitably lead to its invalidation under the Establishment Clause." *Lynch,* 465 U.S. at 680, 104 S.Ct. 1355. * * * The issue under the effect prong in this case is whether, given the context in which the Seal is used and the Seal's overall appearance, the pictograph representing the Ten Commandments conveys a message of religious endorsement.

Although the Ten Commandments are a predominantly religious symbol, they also possess a secular dimension. As *Stone* pointed out, the first four Commandments concern an individual's relationship with God and "the religious duties of believers: worshiping the Lord God alone, avoiding idolatry, not using the Lord's name in vain, and observing the Sabbath Day." * * * The final six commandments, however, deal with honoring one's parents, killing or murder, adultery, stealing, bearing false witness, and covetousness; all of these prescribe rules of conduct for dealing with other people. Much of our private and public law derives from these final six commandments. For this reason, although primarily having a religious connotation, the Ten Commandments can, in certain contexts, have a secular significance.

The proper inquiry in this case is which of these two messages the Seal is most likely to communicate to a reasonable observer. In making this determination, we have considered four factors.

a.   Limited Context

First, the Seal is solely limited to the very narrow context of authenticating legal documents. There is a tight nexus between a legitimate secular purpose for using the pictograph of the Ten Commandments and sword (using recognizable symbols of secular law, ones that suggest the force of law) and the context in which the Seal is used (authentication of legal documents). Even when the government's motives are permissible, if there is not a tight nexus between the secular purpose for using a symbol and the context in which the symbol appears, a reasonable observer may suspect that the true reason for adopting the symbol was to endorse religion. In this case, a reasonable observer has no reason to harbor such suspicions, as the use of this recognizable legal symbol promotes the secular purpose of enabling individuals to recognize the legal validity of documents.

* * * Courts have held the use of religious symbols to be unconstitutional when the symbols have appeared in contexts in which the links between the symbols and their supposed secular purposes are not readily apparent. Here, however, the Seal has not proliferated to contexts unrelated to document authentication. As stated previously, with the exception of the embossing instruments themselves, no representations of the Ten Commandments or other religious symbols appear in the office of the court clerk; the Seal is not displayed in the superior court's courtroom or anywhere else in the courthouse; and the Seal is not used on official stationery or envelopes. Rather, the seal of the state of Georgia appears on the office's official stationery. The clerk of the court has confined the use of the Seal to the very limited context of authenticating legal documents, where reasonable observers would logically perceive it as a symbol of the force of law.

b.   Use of Other Symbols in the Seal

Second, the outline of the Ten Commandments is not the only symbol in the Seal; the Seal also has a depiction of a sword intertwined with the tablets. The presence of this additional symbol increases the probability that observers will associate the Seal with secular law rather than with religion.

* * *

Given the strong symbolic associations between the sword and the power of law, a reasonable observer is likely to understand the Seal's depiction of the Ten Commandments intertwined with the sword as a symbol of the secular legal system. Like the secular decorations surrounding the crèche in *Lynch* or the other lawgivers who accompany Moses and the Ten Commandments on the south wall frieze of the Supreme Court building, the Seal's sword and the words "SUPERIOR COURT RICHMOND COUNTY, GA" contextualize the Ten Commandments pictograph.

c.   Size and Placement of the Seal

Third, the Seal is relatively small, and because it is generally placed near the bottom or on the last page of legal documents, it is also discreet. In assessing the effect that a symbol has on a reasonable observer, courts often analyze the size and placement of the challenged practice. For example, in *Allegheny County,* the Supreme Court noted the crèche display's special placement in the Grand Staircase, "the 'main' and 'most beautiful' part of the building that is the seat of county government." In *Stone,* the Court observed that the text of the Ten Commandments appeared on the wall of "each public elementary and secondary school classroom in the Commonwealth," where "[i]f the posted copies of the Ten Commandments [were] to have any effect at all, it [would] be to induce the schoolchildren to read, meditate upon," and perhaps "venerate and obey" the Commandments.

Two circuit courts of appeals have dealt with Ten Commandments monuments that were located or that were to be located on the grounds of state capitols. *Adland v. Russ,* 307 F.3d 471 (6th Cir.2002); *Ind. Civil Liberties Union v. O'Bannon,* 259 F.3d 766 (7th Cir.2001). In both cases, the monuments were "prominently located" at "the heart of state government" and displayed the text of the Ten Commandments in "large lettering." *Adland,* 307 F.3d at 486; *see also Ind. Civil Liberties Union,* 259 F.3d at 772–73. Although the monument in *Adland* also contained text from other sources of secular law, the Ten Commandments "occup[ied] the bulk of the surface area and accordingly plainly dominate[d] the monument." *Adland* * * *. The *Adland* court found that a reasonable observer would infer religious endorsement, because the "Ten Commandments monument physically dominate[d] the 'historical and cultural display' in the Capitol garden area" and its "sheer dimensions ... dwarf[ed] all the other memorials" in the area.

All of these cases found the use of the religious symbols to be unconstitutional, and all but the *Stone* opinion specifically analyzed the effect that the symbols would have on a reasonable observer. All of the cases involved displays that were large or "in your face" and occupied a place of prominence or special honor, often dominating the other objects surrounding them. In contrast, the pictograph of the tablets and sword is at most only one inch in diameter and is not the focal point of any governmental display in an important public building. Consequently, the Seal's size and placement make it less likely that a reasonable observer would believe that the government intended to send a message of religious endorsement.

When assessing the effect that a governmental practice would have on a reasonable observer, we recognize that it would be improper to rely solely on any single factor. The fact that a symbol is small or inconspicuous, alone, is not dispositive. The caselaw shows that exclusively religious symbols, such as a cross, will almost always render a governmental seal unconstitutional, no matter how small the religious symbol is. Size and placement are, however, factors to consider in the overall effect-prong analysis.

d.   Fact that Seal Does Not Contain the Ten Commandments' Text

Finally, unlike the depiction of the Ten Commandments in the *Stone* case, the text of the Commandments does not appear on the Seal. This distinction is material under the effect test. Because the words "Lord thy God" and the purely religious mandates (commandments one through four) do not appear on the Seal, a reasonable observer is less likely to focus on the religious aspects of the Ten Commandments. Unlike the textual posting in *Stone,* the Seal does not "induce [observers] to read, meditate upon, perhaps to venerate and obey, the Commandments." * * *[T]he use of Roman numerals rather than text on the tablets—together with the other factors already discussed—allows a reasonable observer to infer that the government is using the Ten Commandments to symbolize the force of law.

Although none of the above factors, standing alone, would be sufficient to satisfy the effect test, in this case the combination of these four factors favors Appellees' position. Furthermore, we note that the Seal has been in use for at least 130 years, a fact that arguably supports Appellees under the effect test. Like all holdings interpreting the Establishment Clause, our holding applies only to the particular facts of this case. Just as there is no per se rule that a crèche is constitutional when placed in a display celebrating the holiday season, there is no per se rule that the use of the Ten Commandments will be constitutional when used in the context of the legal system.

IV.   Conclusion

Because the use of the Seal does not have the purpose or primary effect of endorsing religion, we AFFIRM the District Court.

EDMONDSON, CHIEF JUDGE, concurring in the judgment:

I concur in today's judgment of the Court. I agree that the pertinent seal does *not* violate the Establishment Clause. I write separately because I am uncomfortable with the characterization and the manner of application of some of the precedents discussed as the Court explains its decision. I, however, readily agree that no precedent comes close to compelling the conclusion that Defendants violate the Federal Constitution by use of the seal.

GLASSROTH v. MOORE

United States Court of Appeals, Eleventh Circuit, 2003.
335 F.3d 1282.

CARNES, CIRCUIT JUDGE:

The Chief Justice of the Alabama Supreme Court installed a two-and-one-half ton monument to the Ten Commandments as the centerpiece of the rotunda in the Alabama State Judicial Building. He did so in order to remind all Alabama citizens of, among other things, his belief in the sovereignty of the Judeo–Christian God over both the state and the church. And he rejected a request to permit a monument displaying a historically significant speech in the same space on the grounds that "[t]he placement of a speech of any man alongside the revealed law of God would tend in consequence to diminish the very purpose of the Ten Commandments monument." *Glassroth v. Moore,* 229 F.Supp.2d 1290, 1297 (M.D.Ala.2002).

The monument and its placement in the rotunda create the impression of being in the presence of something holy and sacred * * *. Three attorneys who do not consider the monument appropriate at all and who do not share the Chief Justice's religious beliefs brought two separate lawsuits to have the monument taken out. Agreeing with them that it violated the Establishment Clause of the First Amendment, the district court ordered the monument removed. The Chief Justice appealed. We affirm.

I.

Because "[i]n religious-symbols cases, context is the touchstone," *King v. Richmond County,* 331 F.3d 1271 (11th Cir.2003), we set out the relevant facts in some detail * * * .

Chief Justice Moore began his judicial career as a judge on the Circuit Court of Etowah County, Alabama. After taking office he hung a hand-carved, wooden plaque depicting the Ten Commandments behind the bench in his courtroom and routinely invited clergy to lead prayer at jury organizing sessions. Those actions generated two high-profile lawsuits in 1995 based on the Establishment Clause, one filed by a nonprofit organization seeking an injunction and the other brought by the State of Alabama seeking a declaratory judgment that then-Judge Moore's actions were not unconstitutional. Both suits were dismissed on justiciability grounds.

During his campaign for the Chief Justice position in the November 2000 election, then-Judge Moore's campaign committee, capitalizing on name recognition from the lawsuits, decided to refer to him as the "Ten Commandments Judge." Although the Chief Justice says he never described himself that way, he did not disagree with his campaign committee's decision. As a result, most of his campaign materials, including billboards, television and radio commercials, telephone scripts, and mailings, described him as the "Ten Commandments Judge" or otherwise referred to the Ten Commandments. The central platform of his campaign was a promise "to restore the moral foundation of law."

After he was elected, Chief Justice Moore fulfilled his campaign promise by installing the Ten Commandments monument in the rotunda of the Alabama State Judicial Building. That building houses the Alabama Supreme Court, the Court of Criminal Appeals, the Court of Civil Appeals, the state law library, and the state's Administrative Office of the Courts. The Chief Justice, as administrative head of the Alabama judicial system and as lessee of the Judicial Building, has final authority over the decoration of the rotunda and whether to put any displays in the building. Chief Justice Moore placed the monument in the rotunda of the Judicial Building without the advance approval or even knowledge of any one of the other eight justices of the Alabama Supreme Court. * * * He did not use any government funds in creating or installing the monument.

Thousands of people enter the Judicial Building each year. In addition to attorneys, parties, judges, and employees, every fourth grader in the state is brought on a tour of the building as part of a field trip to the state capital. No one who enters the building through the main entrance can miss the monument. It is in the rotunda, directly across from the main entrance, in front of a plate-glass window with a courtyard and waterfall behind it. After entering the building, members of the public must pass through the rotunda to access the public elevator or stairs, to enter the law library, or to use the public restrooms. A person walking to the elevator, stairs, or restroom will pass within ten to twenty feet of the monument. The Chief Justice chose the location of the monument so that everyone visiting the Judicial Building would see it.

The 5280–pound granite monument is "approximately three feet wide by three feet deep by four feet tall." Two tablets with rounded tops are carved into the sloping top of the monument. Excerpts from *Exodus* 20:2–17 of the King James Version of the Holy Bible, the Ten Commandments, are chiseled into the tablets. The left one reads:

I am the Lord thy God

THOU SHALT HAVE NO OTHER GODS BEFORE ME

THOU SHALT NOT MAKE UNTO THEE ANY GRAVEN IMAGE

THOU SHALT NOT TAKE THE NAME OF THE LORD THY GOD IN VAIN

REMEMBER THE SABBATH DAY, TO KEEP IT HOLY

The right one reads:

Honour thy father and thy mother

THOU SHALT NOT KILL

THOU SHALT NOT COMMIT ADULTERY

THOU SHALT NOT STEAL

THOU SHALT NOT BEAR FALSE WITNESS

THOU SHALT NOT COVET

Below the Ten Commandments, each side of the monument contains one large-sized and several smaller-sized quotations. The quotations are excerpted from various historical documents and authorities. * * * The quotations from secular sources were placed below the Ten Commandments because of Chief Justice Moore's belief that the words of mere men could not be placed on the same plane as the Word of God.

"Due to the slope of the monument's top and the religious appearance of the tablets, the tablets call to mind an open Bible resting on a lectern." The appearance and location of the monument itself give one "the sense of being in the presence of something not just valued and revered (such as an historical document) but also holy and sacred." Employees and visitors to the building consider it an appropriate and inviting place for prayer.

The monument was installed after the close of business during the evening of July 31, 2001. The Chief Justice has explained that it was done at night to avoid interrupting the normal business of the building. The installation of the monument that night was filmed by Coral Ridge Ministries, an evangelical Christian media outreach organization. The organization used its exclusive footage of the installation to raise funds for its own purpose and for Chief Justice Moore's legal defense, which it has underwritten.

At the public unveiling of the monument the day after its installation, Chief Justice Moore delivered a speech commemorating the event, and in that speech he talked about why he had placed the monument, which he described as one "depicting the moral foundation of our law," where he did. He explained that the location of the monument was "fitting and proper" because:

> this monument will serve to remind the appellate courts and judges of the circuit and district courts of this state, the members of the bar who appear before them, as well as the people who visit the Alabama Judicial Building, of the truth stated in the preamble of the Alabama Constitution, that in order to establish justice, we must invoke "the favor and guidance of Almighty God."

During that speech, the Chief Justice criticized government officials who "forbid teaching your children that they are created in the image of Almighty God" and who "purport all the while that it is a government and not God who gave us our rights," because they have "turned away from those absolute standards which form the basis of our morality and the moral foundation of our law" and "divorced the Constitution and the Bill of Rights from these principles." Recalling his campaign "pledge to restore the moral foundation of law," he noted that "[i]t is axiomatic that to restore morality, we must first recognize the source of that morality," and that "our forefathers recognized the sovereignty of God." He noted during the speech that no government funds had been expended on the monument.

The Chief Justice described various acknowledgments of God throughout this country's history, some of which, he pointed out, are inscribed on the monument. He proclaimed that the unveiling of the monument that day "mark[ed] the restoration of the moral foundation of law to our people and the return to the knowledge of God in our land." In closing, he told the audience that they would "find no documents surrounding the Ten Commandments because they stand alone as an acknowledgment of that God that's contained in our pledge, contained in our motto, and contained in our oath."

During the trial the Chief Justice testified candidly about why he had placed the monument in the rotunda. The following exchanges between him and one of the plaintiffs' attorneys establish that purpose:

Q [W]as your purpose in putting the Ten Commandments monument in the Supreme Court rotunda to acknowledge GOD's law and GOD's sovereignty? . . .

A Yes.

Q . . . Do you agree that the monument, the Ten Commandments monument, reflects the sovereignty of GOD over the affairs of men?

A Yes.

Q And the monument is also intended to acknowledge GOD's overruling power over the affairs of men, would that be correct? . . .

A Yes.

Q . . . [W]hen you say "GOD" you mean GOD of the Holy Scripture?

A Yes.

The rotunda is open to the public, but it is not a public forum where citizens can place their own displays. Chief Justice Moore has denied the two requests that have been made to place other displays in the rotunda. He did so because he believed that those displays would have been inconsistent with the rotunda's theme of the moral foundation of law. An Alabama State Representative asked the Chief Justice if a monument containing the Rev. Dr. Martin Luther King Jr.'s famous "I Have a Dream" speech could be placed in the rotunda. The Chief Justice denied the request in a letter, stating that, "The placement of a speech of any man alongside the revealed law of God would tend in consequence to diminish the very purpose of the Ten Commandments monument." He also denied an atheist group's request to display a symbol of atheism in the rotunda.

The Chief Justice did add two smaller displays to the rotunda at some point after the Ten Commandments monument was installed. The first, a plaque entitled "Moral Foundation of Law," contains a quotation from the Rev. Dr. Martin Luther King Jr.'s letter from the Birmingham jail speaking of just laws and "the moral law or law of God," and a quotation from Frederick Douglass speaking of slavery as hiding man "from the laws of God." That plaque, which the Chief Justice paid for with his own money, measures forty-two inches by thirty-two inches. The second display is a brass plaque that contains the Bill of Rights. That plaque, measuring thirty inches by thirty-six inches, had been found in a box in the building. The Chief Justice added both plaques because he thought that they "comported with the 'moral foundation of law theme.' " The two plaques are inconspicuous compared to the Ten Commandments monument. Each is not only much smaller than the monument, but also is located seventy-five feet from it. A person standing in front of the monument cannot see either plaque. Nothing about their location or appearance indicates that they are connected to the monument.

The three plaintiffs are practicing attorneys in the Alabama courts. As a result of their professional obligations, each of them has entered, and will in the future have to enter, the Judicial Building. Because of its location, they necessarily come in contact with the monument. The monument offends each of them and makes them feel like "outsiders." Because of the monument, two of the plaintiffs have chosen to visit the Judicial Building less often and enjoy the rotunda less when they are there. One of those two has avoided the building to the extent of purchasing law books and online research services instead of using the library, and hiring a messenger to file documents in the courts located in the Judicial Building.

II.

* * * [T]he three plaintiffs sued Chief Justice Moore in his official capacity as administrative head of Alabama's judicial system, claiming that his actions violated the Establishment Clause of the First Amendment as applied to the states through the Due Process Clause of the Fourteenth Amendment. * * * .

After a seven-day bench trial, the district court concluded that Chief Justice Moore's actions violated the Establishment Clause because his purpose in displaying the monument was non-secular and because the monument's primary effect is to advance religion. * * *.

III.

As this Court recently explained, Establishment Clause challenges are not decided by bright-line rules, but on a case-by-case basis with the result turning on the specific facts. *King v. Richmond County,* 331 F.3d 1271 (11th Cir.2003). As we have already noted, the facts set out in this opinion are taken largely from the district court's findings. The Chief Justice attacks those findings on several bases.

A.

First, he contends that the district court judge should not have made any factfindings based upon his viewing of the monument and its surrounds. The judge unquestionably made important factfindings as a result of what he saw when he viewed the monument and the rotunda in which it is located. That was error, the Chief Justice argues * * *.

* * *

* * * "[I]t is a cardinal rule of appellate review that a party may not challenge as error a ruling or other trial proceeding invited by that party." Counsel for Chief Justice Moore urged the district court judge to undertake a view [of the monument]. * * *

* * *

* * * So eager was he to have the district court judge conduct the view* * *that counsel for the Chief Justice volunteered his help in arranging parking for the district court judge at the Judicial Building. Any conceivable error was not just invited error, but invited error with a parking space.

* * *

C.

* * * [T]he Chief Justice argues that the district court judge should not have relied upon his subjective impressions from viewing the monument and its surrounding space. Recall that this same party's counsel had urged the district court judge to undertake a view in order to find the "social facts" about how a reasonable person would see the monument and its surroundings. When the district court described how the monument and its presentation in the rotunda gave one a "sense of being in the presence of something not just valued and revered (such as an historical document) but also holy and sacred," the court was articulating findings about the impression the monument made on the viewer, and would make on a reasonable person viewing it. It was required to do that in order to apply the reasonable person test.

* * *

IV.

[The court held that the plaintiffs had standing to challenge the installation of the monument].

V.

Because of this country's "history and tradition of religious diversity that dates from the settlement of the North American Continent," the Founders included in the Bill of Rights an Establishment Clause which prohibits any law "respecting an establishment of religion." *County of Allegheny v. ACLU.* In the more than two centuries since that clause became part of our Constitution, the Supreme Court has arrived at an understanding of its general meaning, which is that "government may not promote or affiliate itself with any religious doctrine or organization, may not discriminate among persons on the basis of their religious beliefs and practices, may not delegate a governmental power to a religious institution, and may not involve itself too deeply in such an institution's affairs." *Id.* at 590–91, 109 S.Ct. at 3099 (footnotes omitted). Some aspects of the Chief Justice's position in this case are aimed directly at that understanding. Take, for example, the one we address next.

A.

* * * Chief Justice Moore * * * apparently recognizes that the religion clauses of the First Amendment apply to all laws, not just those enacted by Congress. Even with that concession, his position is still plenty bold. He argues that because of its "no law" language, the First Amendment proscribes only laws, which should be defined as "a rule of civil conduct ... commanding what is right and prohibiting what is wrong." Any governmental action promoting religion in general or a particular religion is free from constitutional scrutiny, he insists, so long as it does not command or prohibit conduct. The monument does neither, but instead is what he calls "a decorative reminder of the moral foundation of American law."

The breadth of the Chief Justice's position is illustrated by his counsel's concession at oral argument that if we adopted his position, the Chief Justice would be free to adorn the walls of the Alabama Supreme Court's courtroom with sectarian religious murals and have decidedly religious quotations painted above the bench. Every government building could be topped with a cross, or a menorah, or a statue of Buddha, depending upon the views of the officials with authority over the premises. A crèche could occupy the place of honor in the lobby or rotunda of every municipal, county, state, and federal building. Proselytizing religious messages could be played over the public address system in every government building at the whim of the official in charge of the premises.

However appealing those prospects may be to some, the position Chief Justice Moore takes is foreclosed by Supreme Court precedent. *County of Allegheny*, which held unconstitutional the placement of a crèche in the lobby of a courthouse, stands foursquare against the notion that the Establishment Clause permits government to promote religion so long as it does not command or prohibit conduct. To the same effect is the decision in *Lee v. Weisman*, where the Supreme Court explained that, "[a] school official, the principal, decided that an invocation and a benediction should be given; this is a choice attributable to the State, and from a constitutional perspective it is as if a state statute decreed that the prayers must occur." * * *

B.

Another of the Chief Justice's broad-based attacks on the application of the Establishment Clause to his conduct involves the definition of religion. He insists that for First Amendment purposes religion is "the duty which we owe to our Creator, and the manner of discharging it";

nothing more, nothing less. The Chief Justice argues that the Ten Commandments, as he has presented them in the monument, do not involve the duties individuals owe the Creator, and therefore they are not religious; instead, he says, they represent the moral foundation of secular duties that individuals owe to society.

The Supreme Court has instructed us that for First Amendment purposes religion includes non-Christian faiths and those that do not profess belief in the Judeo–Christian God; indeed, it includes the lack of any faith. Chief Justice Moore's proffered definition of religion is inconsistent with the Supreme Court's because his presupposes a belief in God. We understand that the Chief Justice disagrees with the Supreme Court's definition of religion, but we are bound by it.

As for the other essential premise of Chief Justice Moore's argument—that the Ten Commandments monument depicts only the moral foundation of secular duties—the Supreme Court has instructed us that "[t]he Ten Commandments are undeniably a sacred text in the Jewish and Christian faiths, and no legislative recitation of a supposed secular purpose can blind us to that fact." *Stone v. Graham.* The *Stone* decision did not hold that all government uses of the Ten Commandments are impermissible; they may be used, for example, in a secular study of history, civilization, or comparative religion. Use of the Ten Commandments for a secular purpose, however, does not change their inherently religious nature, and a particular governmental use of them is permissible under the Establishment Clause only if it withstands scrutiny under the prevailing legal test. As we discuss next, the use to which Chief Justice Moore, acting as a government official, has put the Ten Commandments in this case fails that test.

C.

For a practice to survive an Establishment Clause inquiry, it must pass the three-step test laid out in *Lemon v. Kurtzman.* The *Lemon* test requires that the challenged practice have a valid secular purpose, not have the effect of advancing or inhibiting religion, and not foster excessive government entanglement with religion.

We follow the tradition in this area by beginning with the almost obligatory observation that the *Lemon* test is often maligned. * * * But it is even more often applied.

What the Supreme Court said ten years ago remains true today: "*Lemon,* however frightening it might be to some, has not been overruled." *Lamb's Chapel.* * * *

* * *

Chief Justice Moore testified candidly that his purpose in placing the monument in the Judicial Building was to acknowledge the law and sovereignty of the God of the Holy Scriptures, and that it was intended to acknowledge "God's overruling power over the affairs of men." In his unveiling speech, the Chief Justice described his purpose as being to remind all who enter the building that "we must invoke the favor and guidance of Almighty God." And he said that the monument marked "the return to the knowledge of God in our land." He refused a request to give a famous speech equal position and prominence because, he said, placing "a speech of any man alongside the revealed law of God would tend to diminish the very purpose of the Ten Commandments monument."

Against the weight of all this evidence, Chief Justice Moore's insistence in his briefs and argument, and in part of his testimony, that the Ten Commandments as presented in his monument have a purely secular application is unconvincing. That argument is akin to the state's contention in *Stone* that the fine print about secular purpose on the Ten Commandments posters in that case gave them a constitutionally permissible purpose. At the bottom of each poster was a statement that: "The secular application of the Ten Commandments is clearly seen in its adoption as the fundamental legal code of Western Civilization and the common law of the United States." The Supreme Court said, "[u]nder this Court's rulings, however, such an 'avowed' secular purpose is not sufficient to avoid conflict with the First Amendment." The same is true here.

Under our circuit law, the purpose inquiry is a factual one, and on appeal we are obligated to accept the district court's findings of fact unless they are clearly erroneous * * * . * * * [E]ven if we were free to review the determination *de novo*, having examined the record ourselves, we agree with the district court that it is "self-evident" that Chief Justice Moore's purpose in displaying the monument was non-secular. Given all of the evidence, including the Chief Justice's own words, we cannot see how a court could reach any other conclusion.

* * * [I]n the interest of completeness, we will also review the district court's additional holding that the monument had the primary effect of advancing religion.

The effect prong asks whether . . . the practice under review in fact would convey a message of endorsement or disapproval to an informed, reasonable observer." The district court concluded that a reasonable observer would view the monument's primary effect as an endorsement of religion. It based that conclusion on: the appearance of the monument itself; its location and setting in the rotunda; the selection and location of the quotations on its sides; and the inclusion on its face of the text of the Ten Commandments, which is an "undeniably . . . sacred text," *Stone*, all of which contributed to "the ineffable but still overwhelming holy aura of the monument." The court also considered: the fact that the Chief Justice campaigned as the "Ten Commandments Judge"; his statements at the monument's unveiling; and the fact that the rotunda is not a public forum for speech. The court concluded that a reasonable observer "would find nothing on the monument to de-emphasize its religious nature, and would feel as though the State of Alabama is advancing or endorsing, favoring or preferring, Christianity."

* * * Having reviewed the matter *de novo,* and aided by the district court's meticulous findings of fact, we reach the same conclusion the district court did * * * . The monument fails two of *Lemon*'s three prongs. It violates the Establishment Clause.

D.

Chief Justice Moore contends that even if it cannot clear the *Lemon* test, the monument is saved by the Supreme Court's decision in *Marsh v. Chambers.* In that case, the Supreme Court considered a challenge to the Nebraska Legislature's practice of employing a chaplain to lead it in prayer at the beginning of each session. * * * The Supreme Court, without applying *Lemon,* reversed on the ground that the challenged practice was "deeply embedded in the history and tradition of this country."

* * * The Court concluded that "[i]n light of the unambiguous and unbroken history of more than 200 years, there can be no doubt that the practice of opening legislative sessions with prayer has become part of the fabric of our society."

Turning back to this case, there is no evidence of an "unambiguous and unbroken history" of displaying religious symbols in judicial buildings. Chief Justice Moore insists, though, that *Marsh* must be read much more broadly, that the issue turns on "whether the monument's acknowledgments of God as the source of law and liberty in America parallel similar acknowledgments of God at the time of America's founding." That there were some government acknowledgments of God at the time of this country's founding and indeed are some today, however, does not justify under the Establishment Clause a 5280–pound granite monument placed in the central place of honor in a state's judicial building. The Supreme Court has warned that a broad reading of *Marsh* "would gut the core of the Establishment Clause" and has stated that "*Marsh* plainly does not stand for the sweeping proposition . . . that all accepted practices 200 years old and their equivalents are constitutional today." *Allegheny County.*

Chief Justice Moore has pointed to no evidence that the Ten Commandments in any form were publically displayed in any state or federal courthouse, much less that the practice of displaying them was widespread at the time the Bill of Rights was proposed and adopted. * * * [W]e do not believe that *Marsh* saves the Ten Commandments monument in this case from the proscriptions of the Establishment Clause.

E.

The result we reach in this case is not inconsistent with our recent decision in *King.* In that case, we applied the *Lemon* test and concluded that the Seal of the Richmond County Superior Court did not violate the Establishment Clause despite its inclusion of a depiction of the Ten Commandments. The Seal included an image of two tablets, the first with Roman numerals I through V and the second with numerals VI through X. The Seal had been in use for more than one hundred thirty years, and there was no evidence about why the pictograph of the Commandments was originally included. The county proffered a plausible secular purpose, which was that the Commandments allowed illiterate Georgians to recognize the Seal as a symbol of law, and in the absence of any showing that the proffered secular purpose was implausible, we concluded that the County had satisfied the purpose prong of the *Lemon* test.

On the effect prong, we noted in *King* that the constitutionality of a government's use of a predominantly religious symbol depends on the context in which it appears, and we concluded that given the context in which the pictograph of the Ten Commandments appeared on the Seal, a reasonable observer would not believe that the Seal was an endorsement of religion. Alongside the tablets on the Seal was a sword, which is a symbol of the legal system, and we reasoned that the depiction of the Ten Commandments on that Seal must be taken in context. * * *

In *King,* we also gave weight to the small size of the tablets * * * . Finally we noted that the tablets did not include the text of the Ten Commandments, and that a reasonable observer would therefore be less likely to focus on the religious aspects of the Commandments.

The distinctions between that case and this one are clear. In *King,* there was no evidence of a non-secular purpose; in this case, there is an abundance of evidence, including parts of the Chief Justice's own testimony, that his purpose in installing the monument was not secular. In *King,* the image was in the context of another symbol of law; in this case the monument sits prominently and alone in the rotunda of the Judicial Building. In *King,* the image was approximately one-inch in size and not a focal point; in this case the monument is an unavoidable two- and-one-half ton centerpiece of the rotunda. Finally, there was no text of the Commandments on the Seal in *King;* in this case the monument contains text from the King James version of the Bible.[3]

* * *

3. "The clearest command of the Establishment Clause is that one religious denomination cannot be officially preferred over another." *Larson v. Valente,* 456 U.S. 228, 244, 102 S.Ct. 1673, 1683, 72 L.Ed.2d 33 (1982). Several amici in this case have pointed out that Chief Justice Moore chose the excerpts of the Ten Commandments from the King James Version of the Bible, which is a Protestant version. Jewish, Catholic, Lutheran, and Eastern Orthodox faiths use different parts of their holy texts as the authoritative Ten Commandments. "In some cases the differences among them might seem trivial or semantic, but lurking behind the disparate accounts are deep theological disputes." Steven Lubet, *The Ten Commandments in Alabama,* 15 Const. Comment. 471, 474–76 & n. 18 (1998) * * * .

To give but one example, the Hebrew translation of the Sixth Commandment prohibits only murder, not all killings as the King James Version does (and in the Lutherans and Catholic versions it is the Fifth Commandment, not the Sixth). The point is that choosing which version of the Ten Commandments to display can have religious endorsement implications under the Establishment Clause.

F.

* * * Our decision is necessarily limited to the case before us. It implies nothing about different cases involving other facts. We do not say, for example, that all recognitions of God by government are per se impermissible. Several Supreme Court Justices have said that some acknowledgments of religion such as the declaration of Thanksgiving as a government holiday, our national motto "In God We Trust," its presence on our money, and the practice of opening court sessions with "God save the United States and this honorable Court" are not endorsements of religion. * * *

VI

Finally, we turn to a position of Chief Justice Moore's that aims beyond First Amendment law to target a core principle of the rule of law in this country. He contends that the district court's order and injunction in this case contravene the right and authority he claims under his oath of office to follow the state and federal constitutions "as he best understands them, not as understood by others." He asserts that "courts are bound by the Constitution, not by another court's interpretation of that instrument," and insists that he, as Chief Justice is "not a ministerial officer; nor is he answerable to a higher judicial authority in the performance of his duties as administrative head of the state judicial system."

The Chief Justice's brief reminds us that he is "the highest officer of one of the three branches of government in the State of Alabama," and claims that because of his important position, "Chief Justice Moore possesses discretionary power to determine whether a court order commanding him to exercise of [sic] his duties as administrative head is consistent with his oath of office to support the federal and state constitution." Article VI, clause 3, of the U.S. Constitution states: "The Senators and Representatives before mentioned, and the Members of the several State Legislatures, and all executive and judicial Officers, both of the United States and of the several States, shall be bound by Oath or Affirmation, to support this Constitution...." Article XVI, section 279 of the Alabama Constitution requires state officials to take a similar oath or affirmation to support the federal and state constitutions. Chief Justice Moore's argument takes his obligation and turns it into a license. To say the least, there is nothing in law or logic to support his theory.

The clear implication of Chief Justice Moore's argument is that no government official who heads one of the three branches of any state or of the federal government, and takes an oath of office to defend the Constitution, as all of them do, is subject to the order of any court, at least not of any federal court below the Supreme Court. In the regime he champions, each high government official can decide whether the Constitution requires or permits a federal court order and can act accordingly. That, of course, is the same position taken by those southern governors who attempted to defy federal court orders during an earlier era.

Any notion of high government officials being above the law did not save those governors from having to obey federal court orders, and it will not save this chief justice from having to comply with the court order in this case. What a different federal district court judge wrote forty years ago, in connection with the threat of another high state official to defy a federal court order, remains true today:

> In the final analysis, the concept of law and order, the very essence of a republican form of government, embraces the notion that when the judicial process of a state or federal court, acting within the sphere of its competence, has been exhausted and has resulted in a final judgment, all persons affected thereby are obliged to obey it.

United States v. Wallace, 218 F.Supp. 290, 292 (N.D.Ala.1963) (enjoining Governor George C. Wallace from interfering with the court-ordered desegregation of the University of Alabama) * * *.

The rule of law does require that every person obey judicial orders when all available means of appealing them have been exhausted. The chief justice of a state supreme court, of all people, should be expected to abide by that principle. We do expect that if he is unable to have the district court's order overturned through the usual appellate processes, when the time comes Chief Justice Moore will obey that order. If necessary, the court order will be enforced. The rule of law will prevail.

* * *

EDMONDSON, CHIEF JUDGE, concurs in the result.

Recent Ten Commandments Cases in Other Circuits

In addition to the above cases from the 11th Circuit, in recent years the 3rd, 5th, 6th, 7th, 8th and 10th Circuits have each decided cases involving Ten Commandments displays. The 6th, 7th and 8th Circuit decisions have a good deal in common. In *Adland v. Russ*, 307 F.3d 471 (6th Cir.2002), the 6th Circuit struck down a Kentucky legislative resolution requiring a Ten Commandments monument that had been in storage be relocated to the grounds of the state capitol as part of a "historical and cultural display" in which "the Ten Commandments monument physically dominat[ed]" the display. The monument was donated to the state in 1971 by the Fraternal Order of Eagles, and was displayed at the Capitol until 1980 when it was placed in storage during construction on the grounds around the Capitol. The resolution, which also included quotes from various historical sources referencing God or the bible, required that the monument be put back on the Capitol grounds. The court held that the resolution did not have a secular legislative purpose and that the placement of the monument on the Capitol pursuant to the resolution would be an endorsement of religion. Significantly, the court noted that government displays of the Ten Commandments do not automatically violate the Constitution. A display that was not dominated by the Ten Commandments and that included a variety of other legal or historical documents, thus providing an appropriately secular context, might be constitutional. Judge Batchelder dissented, arguing that the case was not yet ripe.

In *Books v. City of Elkhart, Indiana*, 235 F.3d 292 (7th Cir.2000), the 7th Circuit likewise addressed a situation involving a Ten Commandments monument that was placed on government property after having been donated by the Fraternal Order of Eagles. The monument was donated to the City of Elkhart in 1958, and was located on the grounds in front of the city municipal building. The case includes an interesting historical discussion about the evolution of the program through which the Fraternal Order of Eagles donated such monuments to government entities around the country. The court reiterated the holding in *Stone v. Graham*, that the Ten Commandments are unmistakably a religious symbol. It then held that the context of the display, including the religious nature of the speeches given when it was erected in 1958, demonstrated that there was no secular purpose for the display. The court rejected the secular purpose espoused by the city "on the eve of" the litigation. Moreover, the court held that the primary effect of the monument was to endorse religion, and the fact that the monument had stood on prominent city property for so long did not alter this fact precisely because the monument stood permanently on the grounds of the seat of government in prominent view and nothing in the context of the monument detracted from its religious message to nonadherents. Judge Manion concurred in part and dissented in part, disagreeing with the majority's analysis under the *Lemon* test.

Similarly, in *ACLU Nebraska Foundation v. City of Plattsmouth*, 358 F.3d 1020 (8th Cir. 2004), a panel of the U.S. Court of Appeals for the 8th Circuit held it was unconstitutional for the city of Plattsmouth, Nebraska, to display a Ten Commandments monument donated by the Fraternal Order of Eagles in 1965, in a city park. The court held that the monument violated both the purpose and effects prongs of the *Lemon* test. Under 8th Circuit precedent, the endorsement "test" is a gloss on the effects prong of *Lemon*, and thus a finding that the monument had an impermissible effect also demonstrated that the monument endorsed religion. Unlike the situation in *Books*, there was no record of the facts surrounding the donation or erection of the monument in the city of Plattsmouth. There was, however, evidence that the city maintained the monument and that the city reinstalled the monument after it had been toppled in 2001. The court found that given the inherently religious nature of the Ten Commandments the city could not have had a secular purpose for initially installing and maintaining the monument. The court also held that the primary effect of the monument was to endorse religion. the court considered the broader context of the monument, which included the fact that it was the only monument in its general area in the park and that it was the only monument with a religious theme in the park. The court rejected the city's argument that the display was constitutional under *Marsh v. Chambers, see supra.* Chapter Two, because unlike legislative prayer, government display of Ten Commandments monuments is not a longstanding and ubiquitous practice.

The court also rejected the argument that the monument was a "historical" monument (*see Freethought Society*, below). Judge Arnold concurred with the court's analysis and holding under *Lemon*, but would also have held (unlike the court) that the display discriminated in favor of Christianity and Judaism in violation of the Supreme Court's decision in *Larson v. Valente*, 456 U.S. 228, 102 S.Ct. 1673, 72 L.Ed.2d 33 (1982). Judge Bowman dissented from the court's analysis under *Lemon*, and would have upheld the display of the monument as consistent with the Establishment Clause.

The 5th Circuit reached a contrary result under similar, but not identical, facts. In *Van Orden v. Perry*, 351 F.3d 173 (5th Cir.2003), the court upheld the display of a Ten Commandments monument donated by the Fraternal Order of Eagles in 1961. The monument was displayed on the grounds between the Texas state capitol and the state supreme court building. The decision uses the context of the monument to distinguish it from the 7th Circuit's decision in *Books*, pointing out that the history of the Texas monument does not have the religious connotations that the Elkhart monument had, and implying that the location of the monument on the Texas capitol grounds was not as prominent. The court failed to cite to *Adland*, or for that matter *Stone v. Graham*. The court, without citation or serious explanation, held that the Ten Commandments can have a secular meaning as well as a religious meaning, which seems at odds with the Supreme Court's holding in *Stone*. This helped the court to find that the monument had both a secular purpose and effect, and that it did not endorse religion. The court's holding was bolstered by the fact that there are numerous monuments on the capitol grounds, and by the argument that the monument is "historical" (see *Freethought Society* below). The context argument makes some sense given the history and location of the monument, but what can be charitably called the court's selective citation—i.e. failing to cite to a relevant Supreme Court case, and failure to even mention *Adland*, which was available when the court issued its decision—leaves some doubt about the court's holding that the Ten Commandments can have a separable secular meaning in the context of a large monument depicting them in detail without other legal texts or figures.

Freethought Society of Greater Philadelphia v. Chester County, 334 F.3d 247 (3d Cir. 2003), presented a different factual context for the display of the Ten Commandments. In this case the Ten Commandments were on a plaque that was placed near the old entrance of the county courthouse. The plaque was placed on the courthouse in 1920 and had been there for 82 years. The courthouse, but not the plaque, had been put on the National Register of Historic Places. The entrance at which the plaque was located was closed in 2001 in favor of an entrance that was part of a newer addition to the building. The entrance was moved for security and efficiency reasons. The evidence suggested that the city had made little effort to maintain or call attention to the plaque since it was dedicated in 1920. There were a few smaller plaques and signs in the same general area as the Ten Commandments plaque. The long history and relatively isolated location of the plaque were highly relevant to the court's decision.

The court analyzed both the purpose and effect of the plaque. In analyzing the purpose, the court held that it had to analyze the city's purpose for not removing the plaque in 2001. The city's stated purpose in 2001 was the historical preservation of the building. The court found that historical preservation was an adequate secular purpose given the longstanding history of the plaque and building, and the fact that the city had done nothing to call attention to the plaque. It also relied on the argument that the city commissioners viewed the Ten Commandments as a "foundational legal document," and that this augmented their secular purpose of historic preservation. Is the "foundational legal document" argument accurate? *See Glassroth v. Moore, supra.* this Chapter. The court also applied the endorsement test to gauge the effects of the plaque, and held that the plaque was not an unconstitutional endorsement of religion. In applying the endorsement test the court "adopted" Justice O'Connor's view that the reasonable observer under that test is "presumed to have an understanding of the general history of the community in which it is displayed * * * ." Thus, the reasonable observer in Chester County would know that the plaque had been there for over 80 years, was not erected by recent administrations, and that the city did not call attention to the plaque. Also relevant to the reasonable observer would be the current context of the display, which was no longer at the main entrance. Would it have made a difference if the plaque was at the main entrance? Wouldn't this effect the overall context in such a way as to weaken the city's historical argument?

The 10th Circuit in *Summum v. City of Ogden*, 297 F.3d 995 (10th Cir.2002),* addressed the Ten Commandment monument issue in a different context. The city of Ogden, Utah had erected a Ten Commandments monument on the lawn outside the city municipal building. The monument had been donated in 1966, by—you guessed it—the Fraternal Order of Eagles. In this case, however, the Summum religious group asked to erect its own monument near the Ten Commandments monument. When the city declined, Summum sued arguing both that the Ten Commandments monument violated the Establishment Clause and that the denial of their request to erect their own monument constituted viewpoint discrimination under the Free Speech Clause. On appeal, Summum conceded the Establishment Clause issue because of an earlier 10th Circuit decision that seemed to directly undermine its Establishment Clause claim. Interestingly, the 10th Circuit suggested in a footnote that this concession may have been unnecessary. *Id.* at 1000 n.3. Thus, the case was decided on free speech grounds.

* In *Anderson v. Salt Lake City Corp.*, 475 F.2d 29 (10th Cir. 1973), the 10th Circuit upheld the display of a Ten Commandments monument donated by the Fraternal Order of Eagles. The court held the monument had both a secular purpose and effect. In *Summum*, the 10th Circuit calls the validity of its decision in Anderson into question, but does not specifically address the Establishment Clause issue.

The city argued that the Ten Commandments monument was the city's own speech and not that of the Fraternal Order of the Eagles, and thus it was not engaging in viewpoint discrimination by maintaining the Ten Commandments monument and denying the request to erect the other monument. How do you think the city's argument would effect a challenge under the Establishment Clause if such a challenge had been decided by the court? The court disagreed, citing evidence that the monument did not clearly constitute the city's own speech and thus the denial of requests to erect monuments by other religious groups constituted viewpoint discrimination favoring the Christian or Judeo–Christian viewpoint or disfavoring other religious viewpoints. In an unusually ironic move, the city attempted to defend itself against the claim of viewpoint discrimination by arguing that it had a compelling interest to exclude the Summum monument in order to avoid an Establishment Clause violation. The court acknowledged that it was unclear whether viewpoint discrimination could be overcome by meeting strict scrutiny, *see Good News Club v. Milford Central Schools*, *infra.* this Chapter, but analyzed the city's compelling interest argument anyway.

The irony of the city's position—i.e. that despite its erection of the Ten Commandments monument it would be violating the Establishment Clause by allowing the other monument—was not lost on the court. The court rejected the city's claim that the Ten Commandments monument was different because the city had the right to erect monuments that reflected the general values of its citizens (can you see why?), and held that the city did not have a compelling interest for excluding the Summum monument from what the court had implicitly found to be a limited public forum. Whether such a forum existed under the facts, and whether the Ten Commandments monument really constituted the Eagles' speech rather than the city's, are questionable, but since the court was not faced with the Establishment Clause question (except as a defense to viewpoint discrimination) the implications of the free speech holding for future Ten Commandments cases is unclear.

Notes and Questions

1. *Context Matters.* One consistent theme throughout the Ten Commandments cases, and in fact all the public symbolism cases, is that the context of the display is important. Context is significant both under the endorsement test and the *Lemon* test. The context is both physical—i.e. where a display is located and how it interacts with its surroundings, and for lack of a better term, vocal—i.e. what message is being sent by the officials who erected the display. The latter concern goes both to the purpose and effect of a display as was demonstrated in the *Moore* case. If a large granite Ten Commandments monument was placed on the lawn outside a state courthouse in plain view of all who approached the building, but the monument also contained engravings of other historical legal documents such as the Magna Carta, Justinian's Code, the Code of Hammurabi, and the Declaration of Independence, would the monument be unconstitutional? What more would you want to know before you answer this question? What if the other engravings were much smaller and less noticeable than the Ten

Commandments? What if they were roughly as large as the Ten Commandments, but placed at angles that are harder to see on approach to the building? What if they were as large as the Ten Commandments and as noticeable? Would it make a difference if all the historical documents chosen made religious references or references to G-d? Would it make a difference if religious speeches were given at the dedication of the monument and none of the other documents were mentioned?

2. *Historical Monuments.* In the *Chester County* case, the plaque had been there for 82 years with no complaints and the building was listed on a historical registry—both significant factors in the outcome. Yet, in *Books*, the monument had been in its location for 40 years when the challenge was brought, and the court held that the monument was unconstitutional. How do you account for the differing results? Is the difference that one had been in place for 82 years and the other for 40 years? Is it that one involved a large stone monument that was still highly visible to those visiting the municipal building when the challenge was brought, and the other a relatively small plaque that was not as visible because the entrance to the courthouse had been moved? If so, how do you distinguish the *Van Orden* decision, where an identical stone monument had been in place for roughly 40 years? Or are *Books* and *Van Orden* irreconcilable? Would the *Chester County* case have been decided differently despite the age of the monument if the entrance had not been moved? Is the fact that a monument or plaque has historical significance enough to make its display *per se* constitutional?

3. *Lemon* or Endorsement? Courts seem to apply both the *Lemon* and endorsement tests to Ten Commandments displays. Most courts acknowledge that the endorsement test is a way of judging both purpose and effect under the *Lemon* test as Justice O'Connor had originally suggested in her *Lynch* concurrence. Which test works better in this area, the traditional *Lemon* test, or the endorsement test whether integrated with *Lemon* or not? Why do courts apply both tests? In *Stone v. Graham*, the Supreme Court applied only the *Lemon* test because the endorsement test had not yet been proposed by Justice O'Connor (its originator on the Court), but subsequent symbolism cases such as *Allegheny* have utilized the concept of endorsement.

4. *The Public/Private Distinction.* What would happen if a private group placed a monument in a public forum? Would it make a difference if the monument was permanent? Does the *Summum* case adequately address the permanent display issue? If that court had addressed it, how should it have proceeded?

2.   Privately Sponsored Displays on Government Property

The above cases address government sponsored displays, but what about privately sponsored displays on government property? The latter issue involves significant free speech concerns in addition to the Establishment Clause concerns. One reason for this is that some government property or activities are considered public forums for speech purposes, and in such a forum all private speakers including religious speakers may express themselves. A variation of the public forum is the limited or designated public forum in which the government entity has opened a forum for free expression for a limited period of time or for a designated purpose/group of speakers (the government may not designate a group of speakers based on their viewpoint—i.e. a school may designate a forum for students, or even just for seniors, but may not designate a forum just for Christian students or liberal students). This introduction provides only a simplistic overview of the public forum issue. That issue, and its interaction with religion clause issues will be addressed in greater detail in the cases set forth throughout the rest of this chapter.

CAPITOL SQUARE REVIEW AND ADVISORY BOARD v. PINETTE

Supreme Court of the United States, 1995.
515 U.S. 753, 115 S.Ct. 2440, 132 L.Ed.2d 650.

JUSTICE SCALIA announced the judgment of the Court and delivered the opinion of the Court with respect to Parts I, II, and III, and an opinion with respect to Part IV, in which the CHIEF JUSTICE, JUSTICE KENNEDY, and JUSTICE THOMAS join.

The Establishment Clause of the First Amendment, made binding upon the States through the Fourteenth Amendment, provides that government "shall make no law respecting an establishment of religion." The question in this case is whether a State violates the Establishment Clause when, pursuant to a religiously neutral state policy, it permits a private party to display an unattended religious symbol in a traditional public forum located next to its seat of government.

I

Capitol Square is a 10–acre, state-owned plaza surrounding the statehouse in Columbus, Ohio. For over a century the square has been used for public speeches, gatherings, and festivals advocating and celebrating a variety of causes, both secular and religious. Ohio Admin.Code Ann. § 128–4–02(A) makes the square available "for use by the public ... for free discussion of public questions, or for activities of a broad public purpose," and Ohio Rev.Code Ann. § 105.41, gives the Capitol Square Review and Advisory Board (Board) responsibility for regulating public access. To use the square, a group must simply fill out an official application form and meet several criteria, which concern primarily safety, sanitation, and non-interference with other uses of the square, and which are neutral as to the speech content of the proposed event.

It has been the Board's policy "to allow a broad range of speakers and other gatherings of people to conduct events on the Capitol Square." Such diverse groups as homosexual rights organizations, the Ku Klux Klan, and the United Way have held rallies. The Board has also permitted a variety of unattended displays on Capitol Square: a state-sponsored lighted tree during the Christmas season, a privately sponsored menorah during Chanukah, a display showing the progress of a United Way fundraising campaign, and booths and exhibits during an arts festival. Although there was some dispute in this litigation regarding the frequency of unattended displays, the District Court found, with ample justification, that there was no policy against them.

In November 1993, after reversing an initial decision to ban unattended holiday displays from the square during December 1993, the Board authorized the State to put up its annual Christmas tree. On November 29, 1993, the Board granted a rabbi's application to erect a menorah. That same day, the Board received an application from respondent Donnie Carr, an officer of the Ohio Ku Klux Klan, to place a cross on the square from December 8, 1993, to December 24, 1993. The Board denied that application on December 3, informing the Klan by letter that the decision to deny "was made upon the advice of counsel, in a good faith attempt to comply with the Ohio and United States Constitutions, as they have been interpreted in relevant decisions by the Federal and State Courts."

Two weeks later, having been unsuccessful in its effort to obtain administrative relief from the Board's decision, the Ohio Klan, through its leader Vincent Pinette, filed the present suit in the United States District Court for the Southern District of Ohio, seeking an injunction requiring the Board to issue the requested permit. The Board defended on the ground that the permit would violate the Establishment Clause. The District Court determined that Capitol Square was a traditional public forum open to all without any policy against freestanding displays; that the Klan's cross was entirely private expression entitled to full First Amendment protection; and that the Board had failed to show that the display of the cross could reasonably be construed as endorsement of Christianity by the State. The District Court issued the injunction and * * * the Board permitted the Klan to erect its cross. The Board then received, and granted, several additional applications to erect crosses on Capitol Square during December 1993 and January 1994.

On appeal by the Board, the United States Court of Appeals for the Sixth Circuit affirmed the District Court's judgment. That decision agrees with a ruling by the Eleventh Circuit, but disagrees with decisions of the Second and Fourth Circuits. We granted certiorari.

II

First, a preliminary matter: Respondents contend that we should treat this as a case in which freedom of speech (the Klan's right to present the message of the cross display) was denied because of the State's disagreement with that message's political content, rather than because of the State's desire to distance itself from sectarian religion. They suggest * * * that Ohio's genuine reason for disallowing the display was disapproval of the political views of the Ku Klux Klan. Whatever the fact may be, the case was not presented and decided that way. The record facts before us and the opinions below address only the Establishment Clause issue; that is the question upon which we granted certiorari; and that is the sole question before us to decide.

Respondents' religious display in Capitol Square was private expression. Our precedent establishes that private religious speech, far from being a First Amendment orphan, is as fully protected under the Free

Speech Clause as secular private expression. Indeed, in Anglo–American history, at least, government suppression of speech has so commonly been directed *precisely* at religious speech that a free-speech clause without religion would be Hamlet without the prince. Accordingly, we have not excluded from free-speech protections religious proselytizing, or even acts of worship. Petitioners do not dispute that respondents, in displaying their cross, were engaging in constitutionally protected expression. They do contend that the constitutional protection does not extend to the length of permitting that expression to be made on Capitol Square.

It is undeniable, of course, that speech which is constitutionally protected against state suppression is not thereby accorded a guaranteed forum on all property owned by the State. The right to use government property for one's private expression depends upon whether the property has by law or tradition been given the status of a public forum, or rather has been reserved for specific official uses. If the former, a State's right to limit protected expressive activity is sharply circumscribed: It may impose reasonable, content-neutral time, place, and manner restrictions (a ban on all unattended displays, which did not exist here, might be one such), but it may regulate expressive *content* only if such a restriction is necessary, and narrowly drawn, to serve a compelling state interest. These strict standards apply here, since the District Court and the Court of Appeals found that Capitol Square was a traditional public forum.

Petitioners do not claim that their denial of respondents' application was based upon a content-neutral time, place, or manner restriction. To the contrary, they concede—indeed it is the essence of their case—that the Board rejected the display precisely because its content was religious. Petitioners advance a single justification for closing Capitol Square to respondents' cross: the State's interest in avoiding official endorsement of Christianity, as required by the Establishment Clause.

III

There is no doubt that compliance with the Establishment Clause is a state interest sufficiently compelling to justify content-based restrictions on speech. Whether that interest is implicated here, however, is a different question. And we do not write on a blank slate in answering it. We have twice previously addressed the combination of private religious expression, a forum available for public use, content-based regulation, and a State's interest in complying with the Establishment Clause. Both times, we have struck down the restriction on religious content. *Lamb's Chapel; Widmar.*

In *Lamb's Chapel,* a school district allowed private groups to use school facilities during off-hours for a variety of civic, social, and recreational purposes, excluding, however, religious purposes. We held that even if school property during off-hours was not a public forum, the school district violated an applicant's free-speech rights by denying it use of the facilities solely because of the religious viewpoint of the program it wished to present. We rejected the district's compelling-state-interest Establishment Clause defense (the same made here) because the school property was open to a wide variety of uses, the district was not directly sponsoring the religious group's activity, and "any benefit to religion or to the Church would have been no more than incidental." The *Lamb's Chapel* reasoning applies *a fortiori* here, where the property at issue is not a school but a full-fledged public forum.

Lamb's Chapel followed naturally from our decision in *Widmar* * * * . [In *Widmar*] [w]e stated categorically that "an open forum in a public university does not confer any imprimatur of state approval on religious sects or practices."

Quite obviously, the factors that we considered determinative in *Lamb's Chapel* and *Widmar* exist here as well. The State did not sponsor respondents' expression, the expression was made on government property that had been opened to the public for speech, and permission was requested through the same application process and on the same terms required of other private groups.

IV

Petitioners argue that one feature of the present case distinguishes it from *Lamb's Chapel* and *Widmar*: the forum's proximity to the seat of government, which, they contend, may produce the perception that the cross bears the State's approval. They urge us to apply the so-called "endorsement test," and to find that, because an observer might mistake private expression for officially endorsed religious expression, the State's content-based restriction is constitutional.

We must note, to begin with, that it is not really an "endorsement test" of any sort, much less the "endorsement test" which appears in our more recent Establishment Clause jurisprudence, that petitioners urge upon us. "Endorsement" connotes an expression or demonstration of approval or support. The New Shorter Oxford English Dictionary 818 (1993); Webster's New Dictionary 845 (2d ed. 1950). Our cases have accordingly equated "endorsement" with "promotion" or "favoritism." *Allegheny*. We find it peculiar to say that government "promotes" or "favors" a religious display by giving it the same access to a public forum that all other displays enjoy. And as a matter of Establishment Clause jurisprudence, we have consistently held that it is no violation for government to enact neutral policies that happen to benefit religion. Where we have tested for endorsement of religion, the subject of the test was either expression *by the government itself, Lynch,* or else government action alleged to *discriminate in favor* of private religious expression or activity, *Board of Ed. of Kiryas Joel Village School Dist. v. Grumet,* 512 U.S. 687, 708–710, 114 S.Ct. 2481, 2493–2494, 129 L.Ed.2d 546 (1994); *Allegheny*. The test petitioners propose, which would attribute to a neutrally behaving government *private* religious expression, has no antecedent in our jurisprudence, and would better be called a "transferred endorsement" test.

Petitioners rely heavily on *Allegheny* and *Lynch,* but each is easily distinguished. In *Allegheny* we held that the display of a privately sponsored crèche on the "Grand Staircase" of the Allegheny County Courthouse violated the Establishment Clause. That staircase was not, however, open to all on an equal basis, so the county was *favoring* sectarian religious expression. We expressly distinguished that site from the kind of public forum at issue here * * * . In *Lynch* we held that a city's display of a crèche did not violate the Establishment Clause because, in context, the display did not endorse religion. The opinion does assume, as petitioners contend, that the *government's* use of religious symbols is unconstitutional if it effectively endorses sectarian religious belief. But the case neither holds nor even remotely assumes that the government's neutral treatment of *private* religious expression can be unconstitutional.

Petitioners argue that absence of perceived endorsement was material in *Lamb's Chapel* and *Widmar.* We did state in *Lamb's Chapel* that there was "no realistic danger that the community would think that the District was endorsing religion or any particular creed." But that conclusion was not the result of empirical investigation; it followed directly, we thought, from the fact that the forum was open and the religious activity privately sponsored. It is significant that we referred only to what would be thought by "the community"—not by outsiders or individual members of the community uninformed about the school's practice. Surely some of the latter, hearing of religious ceremonies on school premises, and not knowing of the premises' availability and use for all sorts of other private activities, *might* leap to the erroneous conclusion of state endorsement. But, we in effect said, given an open forum and private sponsorship, erroneous conclusions do not count. Once we determined that the benefit to religious groups from the public forum was incidental and shared by other groups, we categorically rejected the State's Establishment Clause defense.

What distinguishes *Allegheny* and the dictum in *Lynch* from *Widmar* and *Lamb's Chapel* is the difference between government speech and private speech. "[T]here is a crucial difference between *government* speech endorsing religion, which the Establishment Clause forbids, and *private* speech endorsing religion, which the Free Speech and Free Exercise Clauses protect." *Mergens,* 496 U.S., at 250, 110 S.Ct., at 2372 (opinion of O'Connor, J.). Petitioners assert, in effect, that distinction disappears when the private speech is conducted too close to the symbols of government. But that, of course, must be merely a subpart of a more general principle: that the distinction disappears whenever private speech can be mistaken for government speech. That proposition cannot be accepted, at least where, as here, the government has not fostered or encouraged the mistake.

Of course, giving sectarian religious speech preferential access to a forum close to the seat of government (or anywhere else for that matter) would violate the Establishment Clause (as well as the Free Speech Clause, since it would involve content discrimination). And one can conceive of a case in which a governmental entity manipulates its administration of a public forum close to the seat of government (or within a government building) in such a manner that only certain religious groups take advantage of it, creating an impression of endorsement *that is in fact accurate.* But those situations, which involve governmental *favoritism,* do not exist here. * * *

The contrary view, most strongly espoused by Justice Stevens, but endorsed by Justice Souter and Justice O'Connor as well, exiles private religious speech to a realm of less-protected expression heretofore inhabited only by sexually explicit displays and commercial speech. It will be a sad day when this Court casts piety in with pornography, and finds the First Amendment more hospitable to private expletives, than to private prayers. This would be merely bizarre were religious speech simply *as* protected by the Constitution as other forms of private speech; but it is outright perverse when one considers that private religious expression receives *preferential* treatment under the Free Exercise Clause. It is no answer to say that the Establishment Clause tempers religious speech. By its terms that Clause applies only to the words and acts of *government.* It was never meant, and has never been read by this Court, to serve as an impediment to purely *private* religious speech connected to the State only through its occurrence in a public forum.

Since petitioners' "transferred endorsement" principle cannot possibly be restricted to squares in front of state capitols, the Establishment Clause regime that it would usher in is most unappealing. * * * Policymakers would find themselves in a vise between the Establishment Clause on one side and the Free Speech and Free Exercise Clauses on the other. Every proposed act of private, religious expression in a public forum would force officials to weigh a host of imponderables. How close to government is too close? What kind of building, and in what context, symbolizes state authority? If the State guessed wrong in one direction, it would be guilty of an Establishment Clause violation; if in the other, it would be liable for suppressing free exercise or free speech (a risk not run when the State restrains only its *own* expression).

The "transferred endorsement" test would also disrupt the settled principle that policies providing incidental benefits to religion do not contravene the Establishment Clause. * * * It has radical implications for our public policy to suggest that neutral laws are invalid whenever hypothetical observers may—*even reasonably*—confuse an incidental benefit to religion with state endorsement.

If Ohio is concerned about misperceptions, nothing prevents it from requiring all private displays in the Square to be identified as such. That would be a content-neutral "manner" restriction that is assuredly constitutional. But the State may not, on the claim of misperception of official endorsement, ban all private religious speech from the public square, or discriminate against it by requiring religious speech alone to disclaim public sponsorship.[4]

---

4. For this reason, among others, we do not inquire into the adequacy of the identification that was attached to the cross ultimately erected in this case. The difficulties

Religious expression cannot violate the Establishment Clause where it (1) is purely private and (2) occurs in a traditional or designated public forum, publicly announced and open to all on equal terms. Those conditions are satisfied here, and therefore the State may not bar respondents' cross from Capitol Square.

The judgment of the Court of Appeals is *Affirmed.*

JUSTICE THOMAS, concurring.

I join the Court's conclusion that petitioners' exclusion of the Ku Klux Klan's cross cannot be justified on Establishment Clause grounds. But the fact that the legal issue before us involves the Establishment Clause should not lead anyone to think that a cross erected by the Ku Klux Klan is a purely religious symbol. The erection of such a cross is a political act, not a Christian one.

There is little doubt that the Klan's main objective is to establish a racist white government in the United States. In Klan ceremony, the cross is a symbol of white supremacy and a tool for the intimidation and harassment of racial minorities, Catholics, Jews, Communists, and any other groups hated by the Klan. The cross is associated with the Klan not because of religious worship, but because of the Klan's practice of cross burning. * * * .

To be sure, the cross appears to serve as a religious symbol of Christianity for some Klan members. * * * But to the extent that the Klan had a message to communicate in Capitol Square, it was primarily a political one. * * *

* * * In my mind, this suggests that this case may not have truly involved the Establishment Clause, although I agree with the Court's disposition because of the manner in which the case has come before us. In the end, there may be much less here than meets the eye.

JUSTICE O'CONNOR, with whom JUSTICE SOUTER and JUSTICE BREYER join, concurring in part and concurring in the judgment.

I join Parts I, II, and III of the Court's opinion and concur in the judgment. Despite the messages of bigotry and racism that may be conveyed along with religious connotations by the display of a Ku Klux Klan cross, at bottom this case must be understood as it has been presented to us—as a case about private religious expression and wheth-

posed by such an inquiry, however, are yet another reason to reject the principle of "transferred endorsement." The only principled line for adequacy of identification would be identification that is legible at whatever distance the cross is visible. Otherwise, the uninformed viewer who does not have time or inclination to come closer to read the sign might be misled, just as (under current law) the uninformed viewer who does not have time or inclination to inquire whether speech in Capitol Square is publicly endorsed speech might be misled. Needless to say, such a rule would place considerable constraint upon religious speech, not to mention that it would be ridiculous. But if one rejects that criterion, courts would have to decide (on what basis we cannot imagine) how large an identifying sign is large enough. Our Religion Clause jurisprudence is complex enough without the addition of this highly litigable feature.

er the State's relationship to it violates the Establishment Clause. In my view, "the endorsement test asks the right question about governmental practices challenged on Establishment Clause grounds, including challenged practices involving the display of religious symbols," *County of Allegheny v. American Civil Liberties Union, Greater Pittsburgh Chapter*, 492 U.S. 573, 628, 109 S.Ct. 3086, 3120, 106 L.Ed.2d 472 (1989) (O'Connor, J., concurring in part and concurring in judgment), even where a neutral state policy toward private religious speech in a public forum is at issue. Accordingly, I see no necessity to carve out, as the plurality opinion would today, an exception to the endorsement test for the public forum context.

* * * I conclude on the facts of this case that there is "no realistic danger that the community would think that the [State] was endorsing religion or any particular creed," *Lamb's Chapel v. Center Moriches Union Free School Dist.*, by granting respondents a permit to erect their temporary cross on Capitol Square. I write separately, however, to emphasize that, because it seeks to identify those situations in which government makes " 'adherence to a religion relevant . . . to a person's standing in the political community,' " the endorsement test necessarily focuses upon the perception of a reasonable, informed observer.

I

* * *

While the plurality would limit application of the endorsement test to "expression *by the government itself*, . . . or else government action alleged to *discriminate in favor* of private religious expression or activity," I believe that an impermissible message of endorsement can be sent in a variety of contexts, not all of which involve direct government speech or outright favoritism. * * * [W]e have on several occasions employed an endorsement perspective in Establishment Clause cases where private religious conduct has intersected with a neutral governmental policy providing some benefit in a manner that parallels the instant case. * * *

* * *

None of this is to suggest that I would be likely to come to a different result from the plurality where truly private speech is allowed on equal terms in a vigorous public forum that the government has administered properly. * * *

* * *

Our agreement as to the outcome of this case, however, cannot mask the fact that I part company with the plurality on a fundamental point: I disagree that "[i]t has radical implications for our public policy to suggest that neutral laws are invalid whenever hypothetical observers may—*even reasonably*—confuse an incidental benefit to religion with state endorsement." On the contrary, when the reasonable observer would view a government practice as endorsing religion, I believe that it is our *duty* to hold the practice invalid. The plurality today takes an exceedingly narrow view of the Establishment Clause that is out of step both with the Court's prior cases and with well-established notions of what the Constitution requires. * * * [T]he Establishment Clause forbids a State to hide behind the application of formally neutral criteria and remain studiously oblivious to the effects of its actions. * * *

Where the government's operation of a public forum has the effect of endorsing religion, even if the governmental actor neither intends nor actively encourages that result, the Establishment Clause is violated. This is so not because of " 'transferred endorsement,' " or mistaken attribution of private speech to the State, but because the State's own actions (operating the forum in a particular manner and permitting the religious expression to take place therein), and their relationship to the private speech at issue, *actually convey* a message of endorsement. At some point, for example, a private religious group may so dominate a public forum that a formal policy of equal access is transformed into a demonstration of approval. * * *

* * *

II

* * * Today, Justice Stevens reaches a different conclusion regarding whether the Board's decision to allow respondents' display on Capitol Square constituted an impermissible endorsement of the cross' religious message. Yet I believe it is important to note that we have not simply arrived at divergent results after conducting the same analysis. Our fundamental point of departure, it appears, concerns the knowledge that is properly attributed to the test's "reasonable observer [who] evaluates whether a challenged governmental practice conveys a message of endorsement of religion." In my view, proper application of the endorsement test requires that the reasonable observer be deemed more informed than the casual passerby postulated by Justice Stevens.

* * * [T]he endorsement inquiry is not about the perceptions of particular individuals or saving isolated nonadherents from the discomfort of viewing symbols of a faith to which they do not subscribe. * * * [O]ur Establishment Clause jurisprudence must seek to identify the point at which the government becomes responsible, whether due to favoritism toward or disregard for the evident effect of religious speech, for the injection of religion into the political life of the citizenry.

I therefore disagree that the endorsement test should focus on the actual perception of individual observers, who naturally have differing degrees of knowledge. Under such an approach, a religious display is necessarily precluded so long as some passersby would perceive a governmental endorsement thereof. In my view, however, the endorsement test creates a more collective standard to gauge "the 'objective' meaning of the [government's] statement in the community," *Lynch, supra,* at 690, 104 S.Ct., at 1368 (O'Connor, J., concurring). * * *

It is for this reason that the reasonable observer in the endorsement inquiry must be deemed aware of the history and context of the community and forum in which the religious display appears. * * *

* * * The reasonable observer would recognize the distinction between speech the government supports and speech that it merely allows in a place that traditionally has been open to a range of private speakers accompanied, if necessary, by an appropriate disclaimer.

* * *

III

* * *

I agree that "compliance with the Establishment Clause is a state interest sufficiently compelling to justify content-based restrictions on speech." The Establishment Clause "prohibits government from appearing to take a position on questions of religious belief or from 'making adherence to a religion relevant in any way to a person's standing in the political community.' " *Allegheny* * * * . Because I believe that, under the circumstances at issue here, allowing the Klan cross, along with an adequate disclaimer, to be displayed on Capitol Square presents no danger of doing so, I conclude that the State has not presented a compelling justification for denying respondents their permit.

JUSTICE SOUTER, with whom JUSTICE O'CONNOR and JUSTICE BREYER join, concurring in part and concurring in the judgment.

I concur in Parts I, II, and III of the Court's opinion. I also want to note specifically my agreement with the Court's suggestion that the State of Ohio could ban all unattended private displays in Capitol Square if it so desired. The fact that the capitol lawn has been the site of public protests and gatherings, and is the location of any number of the government's own unattended displays, such as statues, does not disable the State from closing the square to all privately owned, unattended structures. * * *

Otherwise, however, I limit my concurrence to the judgment. Although I agree in the end that, in the circumstances of this case, petitioners erred in denying the Klan's application for a permit to erect a cross on Capitol Square, my analysis of the Establishment Clause issue differs from Justice Scalia's, and I vote to affirm in large part because of the possibility of affixing a sign to the cross adequately disclaiming any government sponsorship or endorsement of it.

The plurality's opinion declines to apply the endorsement test to the Board's action, in favor of a *per se* rule: religious expression cannot violate the Establishment Clause where it (1) is private and (2) occurs in a public forum, even if a reasonable observer would see the expression as indicating state endorsement. This *per se* rule would be an exception to the endorsement test, not previously recognized and out of square with our precedents.

I

My disagreement with the plurality on the law may receive some focus from attention to a matter of straight fact that we see alike: in some circumstances an intelligent observer may mistake private, unattended religious displays in a public forum for government speech endorsing religion. * * *

* * * Capitol Square, for example, is the site of a number of unattended displays owned or sponsored by the government, some permanent (statues), some temporary (such as the Christmas tree and a "Seasons Greetings" banner), and some in between (flags, which are, presumably, taken down and put up from time to time). Given the domination of the square by the government's own displays, one would not be a dimwit as a matter of law to think that an unattended religious display there was endorsed by the government, even though the square has also been the site of three privately sponsored, unattended displays over the years * * *, and even though the square meets the legal definition of a public forum and has been used "[f]or over a century" as the site of "speeches, gatherings, and festivals." * * *

* * *

II

* * *

* * * Unless we are to retreat entirely to government intent and abandon consideration of effects, it makes no sense to recognize a public perception of endorsement as a harm only in that subclass of cases in which the government owns the display. * * *

* * *

* * * As long as the governmental entity does not "manipulat[e]" the forum in such a way as to exclude all other speech, the plurality's opinion would seem to invite * * * government encouragement, even when the result will be the domination of the forum by religious displays and religious speakers. By allowing government to encourage what it cannot do on its own, the proposed *per se* rule would tempt a public body to contract out its establishment of religion, by encouraging the private enterprise of the religious to exhibit what the government could not display itself.

* * *

III

As for the specifics of this case, one must admit that a number of facts known to the Board, or reasonably anticipated, weighed in favor of upholding its denial of the permit. For example, the Latin cross the Klan sought to erect is the principal symbol of Christianity around the world, and display of the cross alone could not reasonably be taken to have any secular point. It was displayed immediately in front of the Ohio Statehouse, with the government's flags flying nearby, and the government's statues close at hand. For much of the time the cross was supposed to stand on the square, it would have been the only private display on the public plot * * *. There was nothing else on the statehouse lawn that would have suggested a forum open to any and all private, unattended religious displays.

* * * [T]he Board was understandably concerned about a possible Establishment Clause violation if it had granted the permit. But a flat denial of the Klan's application was not the Board's only option to protect against an appearance of endorsement, and the Board was required to find its most "narrowly drawn" alternative. Either of two possibilities would have been better suited to this situation. In support of the Klan's application, its representative stated in a letter to the Board that the cross would be accompanied by a disclaimer, legible "from a distance," explaining that the cross was erected by private individuals " 'without government support.' " The letter said that "the contents of the sign" were "open to negotiation." The Board, then, could have granted the application subject to the condition that the Klan attach a disclaimer sufficiently large and clear to preclude any reasonable inference that the cross was there to "demonstrat[e] the government's allegiance to, or endorsement of, the Christian faith." *Allegheny*. In the alternative, the Board could have instituted a policy of restricting all private, unattended displays to one area of the square, with a permanent sign marking the area as a forum for private speech carrying no endorsement from the State.

With such alternatives available, the Board cannot claim that its flat denial was a narrowly tailored response to the Klan's permit application * * * . For these reasons, I concur in the judgment.

JUSTICE STEVENS, dissenting.

The Establishment Clause should be construed to create a strong presumption against the installation of unattended religious symbols on public property. Although the State of Ohio has allowed Capitol Square, the area around the seat of its government, to be used as a public forum, and although it has occasionally allowed private groups to erect other sectarian displays there, neither fact provides a sufficient basis for rebutting that presumption. On the contrary, the sequence of sectarian displays disclosed by the record in this case illustrates the importance of rebuilding the "wall of separation between church and State" that Jefferson envisioned.

I

At issue in this case is an unadorned Latin cross, which the Ku Klux Klan placed, and left unattended, on the lawn in front of the Ohio State Capitol. * * * The record indicates that the "Grand Titan of the Knights of the Ku Klux Klan for the Realm of Ohio" applied for a permit to place a cross in front of the state capitol because " 'the Jews' " were placing a "symbol for the Jewish belief" in the square. Some observers, unaware of who had sponsored the cross, or unfamiliar with the history of the Klan and its reaction to the menorah, might interpret the Klan's cross as an inspirational symbol of the crucifixion and resurrection of Jesus Christ. More knowledgeable observers might regard it, given the context, as an anti-semitic symbol of bigotry and disrespect for a particular religious sect. Under the first interpretation, the cross is plainly a religious symbol. Under the second, an icon of intolerance expressing an anticlerical message should also be treated as a religious symbol because the Establishment Clause must prohibit official sponsorship of irreligious as well as religious messages. This principle is no less binding if the antireligious message is also a bigoted message.

* * *

II

The plurality does not disagree with the proposition that the State may not espouse a religious message. It concludes, however, that the State has not sent such a message; it has merely allowed others to do so on its property. Thus, the State has provided an "incidental benefit" to religion by allowing private parties access to a traditional public forum. In my judgment, neither precedent nor respect for the values protected by the Establishment Clause justifies that conclusion.

The Establishment Clause, "at the very least, prohibits government from appearing to take a position on questions of religious belief or from 'making adherence to a religion relevant in any way to a person's standing in the political community.'" *County of Allegheny v. American Civil Liberties Union*, quoting *Lynch v. Donnelly* (O'Connor, J., concurring). At least when religious symbols are involved, the question whether the State is "appearing to take a position" is best judged from the standpoint of a "reasonable observer." It is especially important to take account of the perspective of a reasonable observer who may not share the particular religious belief it expresses. A paramount purpose of the Establishment Clause is to protect such a person from being made to feel like an outsider in matters of faith, and a stranger in the political community. If a reasonable person could perceive a government endorsement of religion from a private display, then the State may not allow its property to be used as a forum for that display. No less stringent rule can adequately protect nonadherents from a well-grounded perception that their sovereign supports a faith to which they do not subscribe.[5]

---

5. * * * With respect, I think [Justice O'Connor's] enhanced tort-law standard is singularly out of place in the Establishment Clause context. It strips of constitutional protection every reasonable person whose knowledge happens to fall below some " 'ideal' " standard. Instead of protecting only the " 'ideal' " observer, then, I would extend protection to the universe of reason-able persons and ask whether some viewers of the religious display would be likely to perceive a government endorsement. Justice O'Connor's argument that "[t]here is always *someone*" who will feel excluded by any particular governmental action, ignores the requirement that such an apprehension be objectively reasonable. * * *

In determining whether the State's maintenance of the Klan's cross in front of the statehouse conveyed a forbidden message of endorsement, we should be mindful of the power of a symbol standing alone and unexplained. Even on private property, signs and symbols are generally understood to express the owner's views. The location of the sign is a significant component of the message it conveys.

* * *

That the State may have granted a variety of groups permission to engage in uncensored expressive activities in front of the capitol building does not, in my opinion, qualify or contradict the normal inference of endorsement that the reasonable observer would draw from the unattended, freestanding sign or symbol. Indeed, parades and demonstrations at or near the seat of government are often exercises of the right of the people to petition their government for a redress of grievances—exercises in which the government is the recipient of the message rather than the messenger. * * *

* * *

* * * [O]ur "public forum" cases do not foreclose public entities from enforcing prohibitions against all unattended displays in public parks, or possibly even limiting the use of such displays to the communication of non-controversial messages. Such a limitation would not inhibit any of the traditional forms of expression that have been given full constitutional protection in public fora.

* * * [T]he endorsement inquiry under the Establishment Clause follows from the State's power to exclude unattended private displays from public property. Just as the Constitution recognizes the State's interest in preventing its property from being used as a conduit for ideas it does not wish to give the appearance of ratifying, the Establishment Clause prohibits government from allowing, and thus endorsing, unattended displays that take a position on a religious issue. If the State allows such stationary displays in front of its seat of government, viewers will reasonably assume that it approves of them. * * *

When the message is religious in character, it is a message the State can neither send nor reinforce without violating the Establishment Clause. Accordingly, I would hold that the Constitution generally forbids the placement of a symbol of a religious character in, on, or before a seat of government.

III

* * *

The existence of a "public forum" in itself cannot dispel the message of endorsement. A contrary argument would assume an "ultrareasonable observer" who understands the vagaries of this Court's First Amendment jurisprudence. I think it presumptuous to consider such knowledge a precondition of Establishment Clause protection. Many (probably most) reasonable people do not know the difference between a "public forum," a "limited public forum," and a "non-public forum." They *do* know the difference between a state capitol and a church. Reasonable people have differing degrees of knowledge; that does not make them " 'obtuse;' " nor does it make them unworthy of constitutional protection. It merely makes them human. For a religious display to violate the Establishment Clause, I think it is enough that *some* reasonable observers would attribute a religious message to the State.

* * *

IV

Conspicuously absent from the plurality's opinion is any mention of the values served by the Establishment Clause. * * *

The wrestling over the Klan cross in Capitol Square is far removed from the persecution that motivated William Penn to set sail for America, and the issue resolved in *Everson* is quite different from the controversy over symbols that gave rise to this litigation. Nevertheless, the views expressed by both the majority and the dissenters in that landmark case counsel caution before approving the order of a federal judge commanding a State to authorize the placement of freestanding religious symbols in front of the seat of its government. The Court's decision today is unprecedented. It entangles two sovereigns in the propagation of religion, and it disserves the principle of tolerance that underlies the prohibition against state action "respecting an establishment of religion."

I respectfully dissent.

JUSTICE GINSBURG, dissenting.

We confront here * * * a large Latin cross that stood alone and unattended in close proximity to Ohio's Statehouse. Near the stationary cross were the government's flags and the government's statues. No human speaker was present to disassociate the religious symbol from the State. No other private display was in sight. No plainly visible sign informed the public that the cross belonged to the Klan and that Ohio's government did not endorse the display's message.

If the aim of the Establishment Clause is genuinely to uncouple government from church, a State may not permit, and a court may not order, a display of this character. Justice Souter, in the final paragraphs of his opinion, suggests two arrangements that might have distanced the State from "the principal symbol of Christianity around the world:" a sufficiently large and clear disclaimer, or an area reserved for unattended displays carrying no endorsement from the State, a space plainly and permanently so marked. Neither arrangement is even arguably present in this case. * * *

Whether a court order allowing display of a cross, but demanding a sturdier disclaimer, could withstand Establishment Clause analysis is a question more difficult than the one this case poses. I would reserve that question for another day and case. But I would not let the prospect of what might have been permissible control today's decision on the constitutionality of the display the District Court's order in fact authorized.

Notes and Questions

1. *"Transferred Endorsement."* Justice Scalia suggests that Justice O'Connor's approach, which would allow a plaintiff to prevail on a claim where government endorses private speech on government property, is not endorsement but rather "transferred endorsement." He argues the government can not be liable for private speech in a public forum, and he suggests that the Court has never accepted the "transferred endorsement" test. Is this accurate? Justice O'Connor responds in her concurrence by suggesting that the very nature of "endorsement" acknowledges that the government can endorse the speech of private actors. The question is whether in a given context a reasonable observer would believe the government has done so. Justice Scalia points out, however, that what constitutes a "reasonable observer" under the endorsement test is a disputed issue among the Justices who would apply that test. Justice Stevens and Justice O'Connor disagree about what characteristics the reasonable observer possesses. Could it be possible that government can never endorse private speech in a public forum (except where a religious organization(s) is given preferred access to that forum, which would violate both the Establishment and Free Speech Clauses)? Consider the following situation: a government entity in a small town dominated by one large church annually sets up a display like that in *Lynch* on the grounds outside the municipal building, and directly abutting those grounds is a small public park that is acknowledged to be a public forum for speech purposes, but the only displays that have ever been placed in the park were Christian—including a cross, a crèche, a "Jesus loves you" banner, and a church picnic sign. There are a significant number of religious minorities in the town, but they are comparatively small in number and from a variety of sects and religions. The government has never made an effort to keep others from posting in the park, but members of the town council have made the local church (of which they are all members) aware of the forum, and the council members are aware that religious minorities have been offended by the town's display and the displays in the park and are afraid to complain publically. Would the displays in the park be endorsed by the city government? What if the public forum was on the grounds directly in front of the municipal building? Would it make a difference if, as in Capitol Square, the cross was placed in the public forum by an overtly bigoted group such that the cross sends a message of hate and intimidation to some citizens in addition to its religious message?

2. *Disclaimers.* Several Justices suggest that whether a private display in a public forum is constitutional should be effected by the existence and sufficiency of a disclaimer. Should such a disclaimer be placed next to each religious display? What message would it send if disclaimers are only placed near religious displays? Or should the disclaimer be placed in clear view of the forum as a whole? And if so, how big should it be? Is it likely that a reasonable Atheist, Muslim or Jewish citizen would perceive an endorsement when passing by the state capitol and seeing a large white cross on the lawn? Would a disclaimer that could not be read from the relevant distance make a difference? Would knowledge of such a disclaimer? Does it matter that the cross may also send a message of hate because it was sponsored by a well known hate group? Does this increase or decrease the effectiveness of any disclaimer?

3. *Content/Viewpoint Discrimination.* The Court points out that to exclude religious speech generally from a public forum would be content discrimination, and to exclude specific religious views would be viewpoint discrimination. The Court also acknowledges that the Establishment Clause provides a potential compelling interest to overcome such claims if the government action is narrowly tailored to support the government's interest in not violating the Establishment Clause (*but see, Good News Club v. Milford Central Schools, infra* this Chapter, for a discussion of whether or not this is true in cases of viewpoint discrimination). Yet, if government can not endorse private speech in a public forum could there ever be a valid Establishment Clause defense to claims of content or viewpoint discrimination?

4. *Government Funding Programs.* In *Rosenberger v. Rector and Visitors of the University of Virginia*, 515 U.S. 819, 115 S.Ct. 2510, 132 L.Ed.2d 700 (1995), a case decided the same term as Capitol Square, the Court held that it was unconstitutional for the University of Virginia to deny funding to a student publication that had requested such funding under a program through which the university provided funding for other student publications and organizations. The student publication in question was overtly religious and was meant to both proselytize and spread the sponsoring organization's religious views through its exploration of the issues addressed in the publication. The Court, over a strong dissent by Justice Souter joined by three other Justices, held that the university's funding regime was analogous to a public forum, and thus since the funding regime was neutral toward religion—i.e. it did not on its face favor religious over irreligious organizations or one religion over others—the exclusion of overtly religious viewpoints was viewpoint discrimination. Like the state of Ohio in *Capitol Square*, the University of Virginia did not have an adequate interest under the Establishment Clause to overcome the claim of viewpoint discrimination. Therefore, the university could not deny the funding to the religious publication because of that publication's religious viewpoint. *Rosenberger* is relevant in the "equal access" context discussed in the next section. Interestingly, it has also become relevant in the funding context, *see infra.* at Chapter Four, because it stands for the proposition that government can not deny funding to religiously affected individuals/organizations under a program that is neutral toward religion because of the religious viewpoints of those individuals/organizations. The funding context raises additional questions, but you will see in Chapter Four that the Court has moved toward a formal neutrality approach in funding cases, and thus the reasoning from *Rosenberger* has become more germane in that context.

C. ACCESS TO GOVERNMENT FACILITIES AND PROGRAMS

The public forum question arises in another context: the use of government owned facilities by religious organizations. These are often called "equal access" cases. The most common context for equal access disputes involve the use of public school buildings. These cases generally fall into two broadly defined categories. The first is the use of school buildings by non-student groups. Thus, if the school opens its building after school hours to the Elk Lodge and other non-school related organizations must it allow a religious organization or church to hold a meeting there? The second involves non-curriculum related student groups. If a school allows non-curriculum related student groups such as the key club or boy scouts and girl scouts to meet on school property, must the school allow religious clubs to meet as well, and if so, are there any limitations applicable to such clubs that are not applicable to others?

The Court first confronted the equal access issue in the religion clause context in *Widmar v. Vincent*, 454 U.S. 263, 102 S.Ct. 269, 70 L.Ed.2d 440 (1981), which involved access to facilities at a public university by a religious student group. In *Widmar*, the Court held that the religious group could not be denied access to university facilities simply because it was a religious group, when non-religious, non-curriculum related groups were allowed access. Thus, if the University opened its facilities to non-curriculum related student groups it could not exclude religious groups based on the religious nature of the organizations or their meetings. The mature age of college students and the intellectually diverse nature of universities were both relevant to the Court's decision. This left open the question of equal access to primary and secondary school buildings, and the lower courts disagreed on whether such access was permitted.

In response, Congress passed the Equal Access Act, 20 U.S.C. § 4071, which requires that public secondary schools provide equal access to religious, political and philosophical organizations if such schools maintain a "limited open forum," a concept similar to a limited public forum. This essentially means that the schools allow non-curriculum related student groups to meet. The law includes other requirements when religious clubs meet, such as the requirement that school teachers and administrators should only attend meetings in a custodial capacity (i.e. they should not be sponsoring or otherwise endorsing the group.) The Equal Access Act was upheld against an Establishment Clause challenge in *Board of Education of the Westside Community Schools v. Mergens*, 496 U.S. 226, 110 S.Ct. 2356, 110 L.Ed.2d 191 (1990). In that case the Court relied on, among other factors, the fact that the Act applied to secondary school students who were less impressionable than younger students and less likely to perceive a non-curriculum related student group in a "limited open forum" as being school sponsored or endorsed. Of course, this left open the question of access by religious student groups to primary schools.

The following two cases address access by a non-student related religious organization to school facilities after school hours, and access by a non-curriculum related student group designed primarily for elementary school students to a school building housing an elementary school (it also housed a secondary school), respectively. What themes do the two cases have in common? How does the impressionability of younger students play out in the Court's decision in *Good News Club v. Milford Central School* (the elementary school case)?

LAMB'S CHAPEL v. CENTER MORICHES UNION FREE SCHOOL DISTRICT

Supreme Court of the United States, 1993.
508 U.S. 384, 113 S.Ct. 2141, 124 L.Ed.2d 352.

JUSTICE WHITE delivered the opinion of the Court.

New York Educ. Law § 414 (McKinney 1988 and Supp.1993) authorizes local school boards to adopt reasonable regulations for the use of school property for 10 specified purposes when the property is not in use for school purposes. Among the permitted uses is the holding of "social, civic and recreational meetings and entertainments, and other uses pertaining to the welfare of the community; but such meetings, entertainment and uses shall be non-exclusive and shall be open to the general public." The list of permitted uses does not include meetings for religious purposes, and a New York appellate court * * *, ruled that local boards could not allow student bible clubs to meet on school property because "[r]eligious purposes are not included in the enumerated purposes for which a school may be used under section 414." * * *

Pursuant to § 414's empowerment of local school districts, the Board of Center Moriches Union Free School District (District) has issued rules and regulations with respect to the use of school property when not in use for school purposes. The rules allow only 2 of the 10 purposes authorized by § 414: social, civic, or recreational uses (Rule 10) and use by political organizations if secured in compliance with § 414 (Rule 8). Rule 7, however, consistent with the judicial interpretation of state law, provides that "[t]he school premises shall not be used by any group for religious purposes."

The issue in this case is whether, against this background of state law, it violates the Free Speech Clause of the First Amendment, made applicable to the States by the Fourteenth Amendment, to deny a church access to school premises to exhibit for public viewing and for assertedly religious purposes, a film series dealing with family and child-rearing issues faced by parents today.

I

Petitioners (Church) are Lamb's Chapel, an evangelical church in the community of Center Moriches, and its pastor John Steigerwald. Twice the Church applied to the District for permission to use school facilities to show a six-part film series containing lectures by Doctor James Dobson. A brochure provided on request of the District identified Dr. Dobson as a licensed psychologist, former associate clinical professor of pediatrics at the University of Southern California, best-selling author, and radio commentator. The brochure stated that the film series would discuss Dr. Dobson's views on the undermining influences of the media that could only be counterbalanced by returning to traditional, Christian family values instilled at an early stage. The brochure went on to describe the contents of each of the six parts of the series. The District denied the first application, saying that "[t]his film does appear to be church related and therefore your request must be refused." The second application for permission to use school premises for showing the film series, which described it as a "Family oriented movie—from a Christian perspective," was denied using identical language.

The Church brought suit in the District Court, challenging the denial as a violation of the Freedom of Speech and Assembly Clauses, the Free Exercise Clause, and the Establishment Clause of the First Amendment, as well as the Equal Protection Clause of the Fourteenth Amendment. * * * The District Court granted summary judgment for respondents, rejecting all the Church's claims. With respect to the free-speech claim under the First Amendment, the District Court characterized the District's facilities as a "limited public forum." The court noted that the enumerated purposes for which § 414 allowed access to school facilities did not include religious worship or instruction, that Rule 7 explicitly proscribes using school facilities for religious purposes, and that the Church had conceded that its showing of the film series would be for religious purposes. The District Court stated that once a limited public forum is opened to a particular type of speech, selectively denying access to other activities of the same genre is forbidden. Noting that the District had not opened its facilities to organizations similar to Lamb's Chapel for religious purposes, the District Court held that the denial in this case was viewpoint neutral and, hence, not a violation of the Freedom of Speech Clause. * * *.

The Court of Appeals affirmed the judgment of the District Court "in all respects." * * * The court observed that exclusions in [a limited public] forum need only be reasonable and viewpoint neutral, and ruled that denying access to the Church for the purpose of showing its film did not violate this standard. Because the holding below was questionable under our decisions, we granted the petition for certiorari, which in principal part challenged the holding below as contrary to the Free Speech Clause of the First Amendment.[4]

II

There is no question that the District, like the private owner of property, may legally preserve the property under its control for the use to which it is dedicated. It is also common ground that the District need not have permitted after-hours use of its property for any of the uses permitted by N.Y. Educ. Law § 414. The District, however, did open its property for 2 of the 10 uses permitted by § 414. * * *

With respect to public property that is not a designated public forum open for indiscriminate public use for communicative purposes, we have

---

4. The petition also presses the claim by the Church, rejected by both courts below, that the rejection of its application to exhibit its film series violated the Establishment Clause because it and Rule 7's categorical refusal to permit District property to be used for religious purposes demonstrate hostility to religion. Because we reverse on another ground, we need not decide what merit this submission might have.

said that "[c]ontrol over access to a nonpublic forum can be based on subject matter and speaker identity so long as the distinctions drawn are reasonable in light of the purpose served by the forum and are viewpoint neutral." *Cornelius,* 473 U.S., at 806, 105 S.Ct., at 3451, citing *Perry Education Assn., supra,* 460 U.S., at 49, 103 S.Ct., at 957. The Court of Appeals appeared to recognize that the total ban on using District property for religious purposes could survive First Amendment challenge only if excluding this category of speech was reasonable and viewpoint neutral. The court's conclusion in this case was that Rule 7 met this test. We cannot agree with this holding, for Rule 7 was unconstitutionally applied in this case.

The Court of Appeals thought that the application of Rule 7 in this case was viewpoint neutral because it had been, and would be, applied in the same way to all uses of school property for religious purposes. That all religions and all uses for religious purposes are treated alike under Rule 7, however, does not answer the critical question whether it discriminates on the basis of viewpoint to permit school property to be used for the presentation of all views about family issues and child rearing except those dealing with the subject matter from a religious standpoint.

There is no suggestion from the courts below or from the District or the State that a lecture or film about child rearing and family values would not be a use for social or civic purposes otherwise permitted by Rule 10. That subject matter is not one that the District has placed off limits to any and all speakers. Nor is there any indication in the record before us that the application to exhibit the particular film series involved here was, or would have been, denied for any reason other than the fact that the presentation would have been from a religious perspective. In our view, denial on that basis was plainly invalid under our holding in *Cornelius,* that

> "[a]lthough a speaker may be excluded from a non-public forum if he wishes to address a topic not encompassed within the purpose of the forum ... or if he is not a member of the class of speakers for whose especial benefit the forum was created ... , the government violates the First Amendment when it denies access to a speaker solely to suppress the point of view he espouses on an otherwise includible subject."

The film series involved here no doubt dealt with a subject otherwise permissible under Rule 10, and its exhibition was denied solely because the series dealt with the subject from a religious standpoint. The principle that has emerged from our cases "is that the First Amendment forbids the government to regulate speech in ways that favor some viewpoints or ideas at the expense of others." *City Council of Los Angeles v. Taxpayers for Vincent,* 466 U.S. 789, 804, 104 S.Ct. 2118, 2128, 80 L.Ed.2d 772 (1984). That principle applies in the circumstances of this case * * * .

The District, as a respondent, would save its judgment below on the ground that to permit its property to be used for religious purposes would be an establishment of religion forbidden by the First Amendment. This Court suggested in *Widmar v. Vincent*, that the interest of the State in avoiding an Establishment Clause violation "may be [a] compelling" one justifying an abridgment of free speech otherwise protected by the First Amendment; but the Court went on to hold that permitting use of university property for religious purposes under the open access policy involved there would not be incompatible with the Court's Establishment Clause cases.

We have no more trouble than did the *Widmar* Court in disposing of the claimed defense on the ground that the posited fears of an Establishment Clause violation are unfounded. The showing of this film series would not have been during school hours, would not have been sponsored by the school, and would have been open to the public, not just to church members. The District property had repeatedly been used by a wide variety of private organizations. Under these circumstances, as in *Widmar,* there would have been no realistic danger that the community would think that the District was endorsing religion or any particular creed, and any benefit to religion or to the Church would have been no more than incidental. As in *Widmar*, permitting District property to be used to exhibit the film series involved in this case would not have been an establishment of religion under the three-part test articulated in *Lemon v. Kurtzman*: The challenged governmental action has a secular purpose, does not have the principal or primary effect of advancing or inhibiting religion, and does not foster an excessive entanglement with religion.

* * *

For the reasons stated in this opinion, the judgment of the Court of Appeals is *Reversed.*

JUSTICE KENNEDY, concurring in part and concurring in the judgment.

Given the issues presented as well as the apparent unanimity of our conclusion that this overt, viewpoint-based discrimination contradicts the Speech Clause of the First Amendment and that there has been no substantial showing of a potential Establishment Clause violation, I agree with Justice Scalia that the Court's citation of *Lemon v. Kurtzman,* is unsettling and unnecessary. The same can be said of the Court's use of the phrase "endorsing religion," which, as I have indicated elsewhere, cannot suffice as a rule of decision consistent with our precedents and our traditions in this part of our jurisprudence. With these observations, I concur in part and concur in the judgment.

JUSTICE SCALIA, with whom JUSTICE THOMAS joins, concurring in the judgment.

I join the Court's conclusion that the District's refusal to allow use of school facilities for petitioners' film viewing, while generally opening the schools for community activities, violates petitioners' First Amendment free-speech rights (as does N.Y.Educ.Law § 414 (McKinney 1988 and Supp.1993)), to the extent it compelled the District's denial. I also agree with the Court that allowing Lamb's Chapel to use school facilities poses "no realistic danger" of a violation of the Establishment Clause, but I cannot accept most of its reasoning in this regard. The Court explains that the showing of petitioners' film on school property after school hours would not cause the community to "think that the District was endorsing religion or any particular creed," and further notes that access to school property would not violate the three-part test articulated in *Lemon v. Kurtzman*.

As to the Court's invocation of the *Lemon* test: Like some ghoul in a late-night horror movie that repeatedly sits up in its grave and shuffles abroad, after being repeatedly killed and buried, *Lemon* stalks our Establishment Clause jurisprudence once again, frightening the little children and school attorneys of Center Moriches Union Free School District. * * * Over the years, however, no fewer than five of the currently sitting Justices have, in their own opinions, personally driven pencils through the creature's heart (the author of today's opinion repeatedly), and a sixth has joined an opinion doing so.

* * *

For my part, I agree with the long list of constitutional scholars who have criticized *Lemon* and bemoaned the strange Establishment Clause geometry of crooked lines and wavering shapes its intermittent use has produced. I will decline to apply *Lemon*—whether it validates or invalidates the government action in question—and therefore cannot join the opinion of the Court today.

I cannot join for yet another reason: the Court's statement that the proposed use of the school's facilities is constitutional because (among other things) it would not signal endorsement of religion in general. What a strange notion, that a Constitution which *itself* gives "religion in general" preferential treatment (I refer to the Free Exercise Clause) forbids endorsement of religion in general. * * *

* * *

For the reasons given by the Court, I agree that the Free Speech Clause of the First Amendment forbids what respondents have done here. As for the asserted Establishment Clause justification, I would hold, simply and clearly, that giving Lamb's Chapel nondiscriminatory access to school facilities cannot violate that provision because it does not signify state or local embrace of a particular religious sect.

GOOD NEWS CLUB v. MILFORD CENTRAL SCHOOL

Supreme Court of the United States, 2001.
533 U.S. 98, 121 S.Ct. 2093, 150 L.Ed.2d 151.

JUSTICE THOMAS delivered the opinion of the Court.

This case presents two questions. The first question is whether Milford Central School violated the free speech rights of the Good News

Club when it excluded the Club from meeting after hours at the school. The second question is whether any such violation is justified by Milford's concern that permitting the Club's activities would violate the Establishment Clause. We conclude that Milford's restriction violates the Club's free speech rights and that no Establishment Clause concern justifies that violation.

I

The State of New York authorizes local school boards to adopt regulations governing the use of their school facilities. In particular, N.Y. Educ. Law § 414 (McKinney 2000) enumerates several purposes for which local boards may open their schools to public use. In 1992, respondent Milford Central School (Milford) enacted a community use policy adopting seven of § 414's purposes for which its building could be used after school. Two of the stated purposes are relevant here. First, district residents may use the school for "instruction in any branch of education, learning or the arts." Second, the school is available for "social, civic and recreational meetings and entertainment events, and other uses pertaining to the welfare of the community, provided that such uses shall be nonexclusive and shall be opened to the general public."

Stephen and Darleen Fournier reside within Milford's district and therefore are eligible to use the school's facilities as long as their proposed use is approved by the school. Together they are sponsors of the local Good News Club, a private Christian organization for children ages 6 to 12. Pursuant to Milford's policy, in September 1996 the Fourniers submitted a request to Dr. Robert McGruder, interim superintendent of the district, in which they sought permission to hold the Club's weekly afterschool meetings in the school cafeteria. The next month, McGruder formally denied the Fourniers' request on the ground that the proposed use—to have "a fun time of singing songs, hearing a Bible lesson and memorizing scripture,"—was "the equivalent of religious worship." According to McGruder, the community use policy, which prohibits use "by any individual or organization for religious purposes," foreclosed the Club's activities.

In response to a letter submitted by the Club's counsel, Milford's attorney requested information to clarify the nature of the Club's activities. The Club sent a set of materials used or distributed at the meetings and the following description of its meeting:

> "The Club opens its session with Ms. Fournier taking attendance. As she calls a child's name, if the child recites a Bible verse the child receives a treat. After attendance, the Club sings songs. Next Club members engage in games that involve, *inter alia,* learning Bible verses. Ms. Fournier then relates a Bible story and explains how it applies to Club members' lives. The Club closes with prayer. Finally, Ms. Fournier distributes treats and the Bible verses for memorization."

McGruder and Milford's attorney reviewed the materials and concluded that "the kinds of activities proposed to be engaged in by the Good News Club were not a discussion of secular subjects such as child rearing, development of character and development of morals from a religious perspective, but were in fact the equivalent of religious instruction itself." In February 1997, the Milford Board of Education adopted a resolution rejecting the Club's request to use Milford's facilities "for the purpose of conducting religious instruction and Bible study."

In March 1997, petitioners, the Good News Club, Ms. Fournier, and her daughter Andrea Fournier (collectively, the Club), filed an action * * * against Milford in the United States District Court for the Northern District of New York. * * *

* * *

There is a conflict among the Courts of Appeals on the question whether speech can be excluded from a limited public forum on the basis of the religious nature of the speech. * * * We granted certiorari to resolve this conflict.

II

The standards that we apply to determine whether a State has unconstitutionally excluded a private speaker from use of a public forum depend on the nature of the forum. If the forum is a traditional or open public forum, the State's restrictions on speech are subject to stricter scrutiny than are restrictions in a limited public forum. We have previously declined to decide whether a school district's opening of its facilities pursuant to N.Y. Educ. Law § 414 creates a limited or a traditional public forum. See *Lamb's Chapel*. Because the parties have agreed that Milford created a limited public forum when it opened its facilities in 1992, we need not resolve the issue here. Instead, we simply will assume that Milford operates a limited public forum.

When the State establishes a limited public forum, the State is not required to and does not allow persons to engage in every type of speech. The State may be justified "in reserving [its forum] for certain groups or for the discussion of certain topics." *Rosenberger v. Rector and Visitors of Univ. of Va.,* 515 U.S. 819, 829, 115 S.Ct. 2510, 132 L.Ed.2d 700 (1995) * * *. The State's power to restrict speech, however, is not without limits. The restriction must not discriminate against speech on the basis of viewpoint, and the restriction must be "reasonable in light of the purpose served by the forum," *Cornelius*.

III

Applying this test, we first address whether the exclusion constituted viewpoint discrimination. We are guided in our analysis by two of our prior opinions, *Lamb's Chapel* and *Rosenberger*. In *Lamb's Chapel*, we held that a school district violated the Free Speech Clause of the First Amendment when it excluded a private group from presenting films at the school based solely on the films' discussions of family values from a religious perspective. Likewise, in *Rosenberger,* we held that a university's refusal to fund a student publication because the publication addressed issues from a religious perspective violated the Free Speech Clause. Concluding that Milford's exclusion of the Good News Club based on its religious nature is indistinguishable from the exclusions in these cases, we hold that the exclusion constitutes viewpoint discrimination. * * *

Milford has opened its limited public forum to activities that serve a variety of purposes, including events "pertaining to the welfare of the community." Milford interprets its policy to permit discussions of subjects such as child rearing, and of "the development of character and morals from a religious perspective." For example, this policy would allow someone to use Aesop's Fables to teach children moral values. Additionally, a group could sponsor a debate on whether there should be a constitutional amendment to permit prayer in public schools, and the Boy Scouts could meet "to influence a boy's character, development and spiritual growth." In short, any group that "promote[s] the moral and character development of children" is eligible to use the school building.

Just as there is no question that teaching morals and character development to children is a permissible purpose under Milford's policy, it is clear that the Club teaches morals and character development to children. * * * Nonetheless, because Milford found the Club's activities to be religious in nature—"the equivalent of religious instruction itself,"—it excluded the Club from use of its facilities.

Applying Lamb's Chapel, we find it quite clear that Milford engaged in viewpoint discrimination when it excluded the Club from the after-school forum. In *Lamb's Chapel,* the local New York school district similarly had adopted § 414's "social, civic or recreational use" category as a permitted use in its limited public forum. The district also prohibited use "by any group for religious purposes." Citing this prohibition, the school district excluded a church that wanted to present films teaching family values from a Christian perspective. We held that, because the films "no doubt dealt with a subject otherwise permissible" under the rule, the teaching of family values, the district's exclusion of the church was unconstitutional viewpoint discrimination.

Like the church in *Lamb's Chapel,* the Club seeks to address a subject otherwise permitted under the rule, the teaching of morals and character, from a religious standpoint. * * * The only apparent difference between the activity of Lamb's Chapel and the activities of the Good News Club is that the Club chooses to teach moral lessons from a Christian perspective through live storytelling and prayer, whereas Lamb's Chapel taught lessons through films. This distinction is inconsequential. Both modes of speech use a religious viewpoint. Thus, the exclusion of the Good News Club's activities, like the exclusion of Lamb's Chapel's films, constitutes unconstitutional viewpoint discrimination.

Our opinion in *Rosenberger* also is dispositive. In *Rosenberger,* a student organization at the University of Virginia was denied funding for printing expenses because its publication, Wide Awake, offered a Christian viewpoint. Just as the Club emphasizes the role of Christianity in students' morals and character, Wide Awake " 'challenge[d] Christians to live, in word and deed, according to the faith they proclaim and . . . encourage[d] students to consider what a personal relationship with Jesus Christ means.' " Because the university "select[ed] for disfavored treatment those student journalistic efforts with religious editorial viewpoints," we held that the denial of funding was unconstitutional. * * *

Despite our holdings in *Lamb's Chapel* and *Rosenberger,* the Court of Appeals, like Milford, believed that its characterization of the Club's activities as religious in nature warranted treating the Club's activities as different in kind from the other activities permitted by the school. The "Christian viewpoint" is unique, according to the court, because it contains an "additional layer" that other kinds of viewpoints do not. That is, the Club "is focused on teaching children how to cultivate their relationship with God through Jesus Christ," which it characterized as "quintessentially religious." With these observations, the court concluded that, because the Club's activities "fall outside the bounds of pure 'moral and character development,' " the exclusion did not constitute viewpoint discrimination.

We disagree that something that is "quintessentially religious" or "decidedly religious in nature" cannot also be characterized properly as the teaching of morals and character development from a particular viewpoint. What matters for purposes of the Free Speech Clause is that we can see no logical difference in kind between the invocation of Christianity by the Club and the invocation of teamwork, loyalty, or patriotism by other associations to provide a foundation for their lessons. * * * [W]e reaffirm our holdings in *Lamb's Chapel* and *Rosenberger* that speech discussing otherwise permissible subjects cannot be excluded from a limited public forum on the ground that the subject is discussed from a religious viewpoint. Thus, we conclude that Milford's exclusion of the Club from use of the school, pursuant to its community use policy, constitutes impermissible viewpoint discrimination.[4]

4. Despite Milford's insistence that the Club's activities constitute "religious worship," the Court of Appeals made no such determination. It did compare the Club's activities to "religious worship," but ultimately it concluded merely that the Club's activities "fall outside the bounds of pure 'moral and character development,' " In any event, we conclude that the Club's activities do not constitute mere religious worship, divorced from any teaching of moral values.

Justice Souter's recitation of the Club's activities is accurate. But in our view, religion is used by the Club in the same fashion that it was used by Lamb's Chapel and by the students in *Rosenberger*: Religion is the viewpoint from which ideas are conveyed. We did not find the *Rosenberger* students' attempt to cultivate a personal relationship with Christ to bar their claim that religion was a viewpoint. And we see no reason to treat the Club's use of religion as something other than a viewpoint merely because of any evangelical message it conveys. According to Justice Souter, the Club's activities constitute "an evangelical service of worship." Regardless of the label Justice Souter wishes to use, what matters is the substance of the Club's activities, which we conclude are materially indistinguishable from the activities in *Lamb's Chapel* and *Rosenberger*.

IV

Milford argues that, even if its restriction constitutes viewpoint discrimination, its interest in not violating the Establishment Clause outweighs the Club's interest in gaining equal access to the school's facilities. * * * We disagree.

We have said that a state interest in avoiding an Establishment Clause violation "may be characterized as compelling," and therefore may justify content-based discrimination. However, it is not clear whether a State's interest in avoiding an Establishment Clause violation would justify viewpoint discrimination. We need not, however, confront the issue in this case, because we conclude that the school has no valid Establishment Clause interest.

We rejected Establishment Clause defenses similar to Milford's in two previous free speech cases, *Lamb's Chapel* and *Widmar*. In particular, in *Lamb's Chapel*, we explained that "[t]he showing of th[e] film series would not have been during school hours, would not have been sponsored by the school, and would have been open to the public, not just to church members." Accordingly, we found that "there would have been no realistic danger that the community would think that the District was endorsing religion or any particular creed." Likewise, in *Widmar*, where the university's forum was already available to other groups, this Court concluded that there was no Establishment Clause problem.

The Establishment Clause defense fares no better in this case. As in *Lamb's Chapel*, the Club's meetings were held after school hours, not sponsored by the school, and open to any student who obtained parental consent, not just to Club members. As in *Widmar*, Milford made its forum available to other organizations. * * * Thus, Milford's reliance on the Establishment Clause is unavailing.

Milford attempts to distinguish *Lamb's Chapel* and *Widmar* by emphasizing that Milford's policy involves elementary school children. According to Milford, children will perceive that the school is endorsing the Club and will feel coercive pressure to participate, because the Club's activities take place on school grounds, even though they occur during nonschool hours. This argument is unpersuasive.

First, we have held that "a significant factor in upholding governmental programs in the face of Establishment Clause attack is their *neutrality* towards religion." *Rosenberger,* 515 U.S., at 839, 115 S.Ct. 2510 (emphasis added). Milford's implication that granting access to the Club would do damage to the neutrality principle defies logic. For the "guarantee of neutrality is respected, not offended, when the government, following neutral criteria and evenhanded policies, extends benefits to recipients whose ideologies and viewpoints, including religious ones, are broad and diverse." *Rosenberger, supra,* at 839, 115 S.Ct. 2510. The Good News Club seeks nothing more than to be treated neutrally and given access to speak about the same topics as are other groups. Because allowing the Club to speak on school grounds would ensure neutrality, not threaten it, Milford faces an uphill battle in arguing that the Establishment Clause compels it to exclude the Good News Club.

Second, to the extent we consider whether the community would feel coercive pressure to engage in the Club's activities, the relevant community would be the parents, not the elementary school children. It is the parents who choose whether their children will attend the Good News Club meetings. Because the children cannot attend without their parents' permission, they cannot be coerced into engaging in the Good News Club's religious activities. Milford does not suggest that the parents of elementary school children would be confused about whether the school was endorsing religion. * * *

Third, whatever significance we may have assigned in the Establishment Clause context to the suggestion that elementary school children are more impressionable than adults, we have never extended our Establishment Clause jurisprudence to foreclose private religious conduct during nonschool hours merely because it takes place on school premises where elementary school children may be present.

None of the cases discussed by Milford persuades us that our Establishment Clause jurisprudence has gone this far. For example, Milford cites *Lee v. Weisman* for the proposition that "there are heightened concerns with protecting freedom of conscience from subtle coercive pressure in the elementary and secondary public schools." In *Lee,* however, we concluded that attendance at the graduation exercise was obligatory. We did not place independent significance on the fact that the graduation exercise might take place on school premises. Here, where the school facilities are being used for a nonschool function and there is no government sponsorship of the Club's activities, *Lee* is inapposite.

Fourth, even if we were to consider the possible misperceptions by schoolchildren in deciding whether Milford's permitting the Club's activities would violate the Establishment Clause, the facts of this case simply do not support Milford's conclusion. There is no evidence that young children are permitted to loiter outside classrooms after the schoolday has ended. Surely even young children are aware of events for which their parents must sign permission forms. The meetings were held in a combined high school resource room and middle school special education room, not in an elementary school classroom. The instructors are not schoolteachers. And the children in the group are not all the same age as in the normal classroom setting; their ages range from 6 to 12. In sum, these circumstances simply do not support the theory that small children would perceive endorsement here.

Finally, even if we were to inquire into the minds of schoolchildren in this case, we cannot say the danger that children would misperceive the endorsement of religion is any greater than the danger that they would perceive a hostility toward the religious viewpoint if the Club were excluded from the public forum. This concern is particularly acute given the reality that Milford's building is not used only for elementary school children. Students, from kindergarten through the 12th grade, all attend school in the same building. * * * Any bystander could conceivably be aware of the school's use policy and its exclusion of the Good News Club, and could suffer as much from viewpoint discrimination as elementary school children could suffer from perceived endorsement.

We cannot operate, as Milford would have us do, under the assumption that any risk that small children would perceive endorsement should counsel in favor of excluding the Club's religious activity. We decline to employ Establishment Clause jurisprudence using a modified heckler's veto, in which a group's religious activity can be proscribed on the basis of what the youngest members of the audience might misperceive. There are countervailing constitutional concerns related to rights of other individuals in the community. In this case, those countervailing concerns are the free speech rights of the Club and its members. And, we have already found that those rights have been violated, not merely perceived to have been violated, by the school's actions toward the Club.

We are not convinced that there is any significance in this case to the possibility that elementary school children may witness the Good News Club's activities on school premises, and therefore we can find no reason to depart from our holdings in *Lamb's Chapel* and *Widmar*. Accordingly, we conclude that permitting the Club to meet on the school's premises would not have violated the Establishment Clause.

V

When Milford denied the Good News Club access to the school's limited public forum on the ground that the Club was religious in nature, it discriminated against the Club because of its religious viewpoint in violation of the Free Speech Clause of the First Amendment. Because Milford has not raised a valid Establishment Clause claim, we do not address the question whether such a claim could excuse Milford's viewpoint discrimination.

The judgment of the Court of Appeals is reversed, and the case is remanded for further proceedings consistent with this opinion.

JUSTICE SCALIA, concurring.

I join the Court's opinion but write separately to explain further my views on two issues.

I

First, I join Part IV of the Court's opinion, regarding the Establishment Clause issue, with the understanding that its consideration of coercive pressure, and perceptions of endorsement, "to the extent" that the law makes such factors relevant, is consistent with the belief (which I hold) that in this case that extent is zero. As to coercive pressure: Physical coercion is not at issue here; and so-called "peer pressure," if it can even be considered coercion, is, when it arises from private activities, one of the attendant consequences of a freedom of association that is constitutionally protected. What is at play here is not coercion, but the compulsion of ideas—and the private right to exert and receive that compulsion (or to have one's children receive it) is *protected* by the Free Speech and Free Exercise Clauses, not banned by the Establishment Clause. A priest has as much liberty to proselytize as a patriot.

As to endorsement, I have previously written that "[r]eligious expression cannot violate the Establishment Clause where it (1) is purely private and (2) occurs in a traditional or designated public forum, publicly announced and open to all on equal terms." *Capitol Square Review and Advisory Bd. v. Pinette.* The same is true of private speech that occurs in a limited public forum, publicly announced, whose boundaries are not drawn to favor religious groups but instead permit a cross-section of uses. In that context, which is this case, "erroneous conclusions [about endorsement] do not count."

II

Second, since we have rejected the only reason that respondent gave for excluding the Club's speech from a forum that clearly included it * * * , I do not suppose it matters whether the exclusion is characterized as viewpoint or subject-matter discrimination. * * * [R]espondent would seem to fail First Amendment scrutiny regardless of how its action is characterized. Even subject-matter limits must at least be "reasonable in light of the purpose served by the forum," *Cornelius.* But I agree, in any event, that respondent did discriminate on the basis of viewpoint.

* * *

With these words of explanation, I join the opinion of the Court.

JUSTICE BREYER, concurring in part.

I agree with the Court's conclusion and join its opinion to the extent that they are consistent with the following three observations. First, the government's "neutrality" in respect to religion is one, but only one, of the considerations relevant to deciding whether a public school's policy violates the Establishment Clause. As this Court previously has indicated, a child's perception that the school has endorsed a particular religion or religion in general may also prove critically important. Today's opinion does not purport to change that legal principle.

Second, the critical Establishment Clause question here may well prove to be whether a child, participating in the Good News Club's activities, could reasonably perceive the school's permission for the Club to use its facilities as an endorsement of religion. The time of day, the age of the children, the nature of the meetings, and other specific circumstances are relevant in helping to determine whether, in fact, the Club "so dominate[s]" the "forum" that, in the children's minds, "a formal policy of equal access is transformed into a demonstration of approval." *Capitol Square Review and Advisory Bd.* (O'Connor, J., concurring in part and concurring in judgment).

Third, the Court cannot fully answer the Establishment Clause question this case raises, given its procedural posture. The specific legal action that brought this case to the Court of Appeals was the District Court's decision to grant Milford Central School's motion for summary judgment. * * * We now hold that the school was not entitled to summary judgment, either in respect to the Free Speech or the Establishment Clause issue. Our holding must mean that, *viewing the disputed facts* (including facts about the children's perceptions) *favorably to the Club* (the nonmoving party), the school has not shown an Establishment Clause violation.

To deny one party's motion for summary judgment, however, is not to grant summary judgment for the other side. There may be disputed "genuine issue[s]" of "material fact," particularly about how a reasonable child participant would understand the school's role. Indeed, the Court itself points to facts not in evidence, identifies facts in evidence which may, depending on other facts not in evidence, be of legal significance, and makes assumptions about other facts. The Court's invocation of what is missing from the record and its assumptions about what is present in the record only confirm that both parties, if they so desire, should have a fair opportunity to fill the evidentiary gap in light of today's opinion.

JUSTICE STEVENS, dissenting.

The Milford Central School has invited the public to use its facilities for educational and recreational purposes, but not for "religious purposes." Speech for "religious purposes" may reasonably be understood to encompass three different categories. First, there is religious speech that is simply speech about a particular topic from a religious point of view. * * * Second, there is religious speech that amounts to worship, or its equivalent. * * * Third, there is an intermediate category that is aimed principally at proselytizing or inculcating belief in a particular religious faith.

A public entity may not generally exclude even religious worship from an open public forum. Similarly, a public entity that creates a limited public forum for the discussion of certain specified topics may not exclude a speaker simply because she approaches those topics from a religious point of view. * * *

* * * The novel question that this case presents concerns the constitutionality of a public school's attempt to limit the scope of a public forum it has created. More specifically, the question is whether a school can, consistently with the First Amendment, create a limited public forum that admits the first type of religious speech without allowing the other two.

Distinguishing speech from a religious viewpoint, on the one hand, from religious proselytizing, on the other, is comparable to distinguishing meetings to discuss political issues from meetings whose principal purpose is to recruit new members to join a political organization. If a school decides to authorize afterschool discussions of current events in its classrooms, it may not exclude people from expressing their views simply because it dislikes their particular political opinions. But must it therefore allow organized political groups—for example, the Democratic Party, the Libertarian Party, or the Ku Klux Klan—to hold meetings, the principal purpose of which is not to discuss the current-events topic from their own unique point of view but rather to recruit others to join their respective groups? I think not. Such recruiting meetings may introduce divisiveness and tend to separate young children into cliques that undermine the school's educational mission.

School officials may reasonably believe that evangelical meetings designed to convert children to a particular religious faith pose the same risk. And, just as a school may allow meetings to discuss current events from a political perspective without also allowing organized political recruitment, so too can a school allow discussion of topics such as moral development from a religious (or nonreligious) perspective without thereby opening its forum to religious proselytizing or worship. * * *

The particular limitation of the forum at issue in this case is one that prohibits the use of the school's facilities for "religious purposes." It is clear that, by "religious purposes," the school district did not intend to exclude all speech from a religious point of view. Instead, it sought only to exclude religious speech whose principal goal is to "promote the gospel." In other words, the school sought to allow the first type of religious speech while excluding the second and third types. As long as this is done in an evenhanded manner, I see no constitutional violation in such an effort.[10]

This case is undoubtedly close. Nonetheless, regardless of whether the Good News Club's activities amount to "worship," it does seem clear, based on the facts in the record, that the school district correctly classified those activities as falling within the third category of religious speech and therefore beyond the scope of the school's limited public forum. In short, I am persuaded that the school district could (and did) permissibly exclude from its limited public forum proselytizing religious speech that does not rise to the level of actual worship. I would therefore affirm the judgment of the Court of Appeals.

* * *

Accordingly, I respectfully dissent.

JUSTICE SOUTER, with whom JUSTICE GINSBURG joins, dissenting.

The majority rules on two issues. First, it decides that the Court of Appeals failed to apply the rule in *Lamb's Chapel*, which held that the government may not discriminate on the basis of viewpoint in operating a limited public forum. The majority applies that rule and concludes that

10. The school district, for example, could not, consistently with its present policy, allow school facilities to be used by a group that affirmatively attempted to inculcate nonbelief in God or in the view that morality is wholly unrelated to belief in God. Nothing in the record, however, indicates that any such group was allowed to use school facilities.

Milford violated *Lamb's Chapel* in denying Good News the use of the school. The majority then goes on to determine that it would not violate the Establishment Clause of the First Amendment for the Milford School District to allow the Good News Club to hold its intended gatherings of public school children in Milford's elementary school. The majority is mistaken on both points. The Court of Appeals unmistakably distinguished this case from *Lamb's Chapel* * * *. As for the applicability of the Establishment Clause to the Good News Club's intended use of Milford's school, the majority commits error even in reaching the issue, which was addressed neither by the Court of Appeals nor by the District Court. I respectfully dissent.

I

* * *

This case, like *Lamb's Chapel,* properly raises no issue about the reasonableness of Milford's criteria for restricting the scope of its designated public forum. Milford has opened school property for, among other things, "instruction in any branch of education, learning or the arts" and for "social, civic and recreational meetings and entertainment events and other uses pertaining to the welfare of the community, provided that such uses shall be nonexclusive and shall be opened to the general public." But Milford has done this subject to the restriction that "[s]chool premises shall not be used ... for religious purposes." As the District Court stated, Good News did "not object to the reasonableness of [Milford]'s policy that prohibits the use of [its] facilities for religious purposes."

The sole question before the District Court was, therefore, whether, in refusing to allow Good News's intended use, Milford was misapplying its unchallenged restriction in a way that amounted to imposing a viewpoint-based restriction on what could be said or done by a group entitled to use the forum for an educational, civic, or other permitted purpose. The question was whether Good News was being disqualified when it merely sought to use the school property the same way that the Milford Boy and Girl Scouts and the 4–H Club did. The District Court held on the basis of undisputed facts that Good News's activity was essentially unlike the presentation of views on secular issues from a religious standpoint held to be protected in *Lamb's Chapel*, and was instead activity precluded by Milford's unchallenged policy against religious use, even under the narrowest definition of that term.

The Court of Appeals understood the issue the same way. The Court of Appeals also realized that the *Lamb's Chapel* criterion was the appropriate measure: "The activities of the Good News Club do not involve merely a religious perspective on the secular subject of morality." The appeals court agreed with the District Court that the undisputed facts in this case differ from those in *Lamb's Chapel,* as night from day. A sampling of those facts shows why both courts were correct.

Good News's classes open and close with prayer. In a sample lesson considered by the District Court, children are instructed that "[t]he Bible tells us how we can have our sins forgiven by receiving the Lord Jesus Christ. It tells us how to live to please Him.... If you have received the Lord Jesus as your Saviour from sin, you belong to God's special group—His family." The lesson plan instructs the teacher to "lead a child to Christ," and, when reading a Bible verse, to "[e]mphasize that this verse is from the Bible, God's Word," and is "important—and true—because God said it." The lesson further exhorts the teacher to "[b]e sure to give an opportunity for the 'unsaved' children in your class to respond to the Gospel" and cautions against "neglect[ing] this responsibility."

While Good News's program utilizes songs and games, the heart of the meeting is the "challenge" and "invitation," which are repeated at various times throughout the lesson. During the challenge, "saved" children who "already believe in the Lord Jesus as their Savior" are challenged to " 'stop and ask God for the strength and the want ... to obey Him.' " They are instructed that

> "[i]f you know Jesus as your Savior, you need to place God first in your life. And if you don't know Jesus as Savior and if you would like to, then we will—we will pray with you separately, individually.... And the challenge would be, those of you who know Jesus as Savior, you can rely on God's strength to obey Him."

During the invitation, the teacher "invites" the "unsaved" children " 'to trust the Lord Jesus to be your Savior from sin,' " and " 'receiv[e] [him] as your Savior from sin.' " The children are then instructed that "[i]f you believe what God's Word says about your sin and how Jesus died and rose again for you, you can have His forever life today. Please bow your heads and close your eyes. If you have never believed on the Lord Jesus as your Savior and would like to do that, please show me by raising your hand. If you raised your hand to show me you want to believe on the Lord Jesus, please meet me so I can show you from God's Word how you can receive His everlasting life."

It is beyond question that Good News intends to use the public school premises not for the mere discussion of a subject from a particular, Christian point of view, but for an evangelical service of worship calling children to commit themselves in an act of Christian conversion. The majority avoids this reality only by resorting to the bland and general characterization of Good News's activity as "teaching of morals and character, from a religious standpoint." If the majority's statement ignores reality, as it surely does, then today's holding may be understood only in equally generic terms. Otherwise, indeed, this case would stand for the remarkable proposition that any public school opened for civic meetings must be opened for use as a church, synagogue, or mosque.

II

I also respectfully dissent from the majority's refusal to remand on all other issues, insisting instead on acting as a court of first instance in reviewing Milford's claim that it would violate the Establishment Clause to grant Good News's application. Milford raised this claim to demonstrate a compelling interest for saying no to Good News, even on the erroneous assumption that *Lamb's Chapel's* public forum analysis would otherwise require Milford to say yes. Whereas the District Court and Court of Appeals resolved this case entirely on the ground that Milford's actions did not offend the First Amendment's Speech Clause, the majority now sees fit to rule on the application of the Establishment Clause, in derogation of this Court's proper role as a court of review.

* * *

This Court has accepted the independent obligation to obey the Establishment Clause as sufficiently compelling to satisfy strict scrutiny under the First Amendment. Milford's actions would offend the Establishment Clause if they carried the message of endorsing religion under the circumstances, as viewed by a reasonable observer. The majority concludes that such an endorsement effect is out of the question in Milford's case, because the context here is "materially indistinguishable" from the facts in *Lamb's Chapel* and *Widmar*. In fact, the majority is in no position to say that, for the principal grounds on which we based our Establishment Clause holdings in those cases are clearly absent here.

* * *

What we know about this case looks very little like *Widmar* or *Lamb's Chapel*. The cohort addressed by Good News is not university students with relative maturity, or even high school pupils, but elementary school children as young as six.[4] The Establishment Clause cases have consistently recognized the particular impressionability of schoolchildren, and the special protection required for those in the elementary grades in the school forum. We have held the difference between college students and grade school pupils to be a "distinction [that] warrants a difference in constitutional results," *Edwards v. Aguillard*.

Nor is Milford's limited forum anything like the sites for wide-ranging intellectual exchange that were home to the challenged activities in *Widmar* and *Lamb's Chapel*. In *Widmar*, the nature of the university campus and the sheer number of activities offered precluded the reasonable college observer from seeing government endorsement in any one of them, and so did the time and variety of community use in the *Lamb's Chapel* case.

The timing and format of Good News's gatherings, on the other hand, may well affirmatively suggest the *imprimatur* of officialdom in the minds of the young children. The club is open solely to elementary

---

4. It is certainly correct that parents are required to give permission for their children to attend Good News's classes, * * * and correct that those parents would likely not be confused as to the sponsorship of Good News's classes. But the proper focus of concern in assessing effects includes the elementary school pupils who are invited to meetings, who see peers heading into classrooms for religious instruction as other classes end, and who are addressed by the "challenge" and "invitation."

* * *

students (not the entire community, as in *Lamb's Chapel*), only four outside groups have been identified as meeting in the school, and Good News is, seemingly, the only one whose instruction follows immediately on the conclusion of the official schoolday. Although school is out at 2:56 p.m., Good News apparently requested use of the school beginning at 2:30 on Tuesdays "during the school year," so that instruction could begin promptly at 3:00, at which time children who are compelled by law to attend school surely remain in the building. Good News's religious meeting follows regular school activities so closely that the Good News instructor must wait to begin until "the room is clear," and "people are out of the room," before starting proceedings in the classroom located next to the regular third- and fourth-grade rooms. In fact, the temporal and physical continuity of Good News's meetings with the regular school routine seems to be the whole point of using the school. When meetings were held in a community church, 8 or 10 children attended; after the school became the site, the number went up three-fold.

Even on the summary judgment record, then, a record lacking whatever supplementation the trial process might have led to, and devoid of such insight as the trial and appellate judges might have contributed in addressing the Establishment Clause, we can say this: there is a good case that Good News's exercises blur the line between public classroom instruction and private religious indoctrination, leaving a reasonable elementary school pupil unable to appreciate that the former instruction is the business of the school while the latter evangelism is not. Thus, the facts we know (or think we know) point away from the majority's conclusion * * *.

Notes and Questions

1. *How Many Groups Does a Forum Make?* Under the Court's reasoning how many non-school or non-curriculum related student groups must a school allow before a forum is opened? The answer would appear to be one, but what if a school makes known that its buildings are open for non-school or non-curriculum related use, the school would allow any group to use the facilities, but only a religious group takes advantage of the forum? This would seem to be constitutional under the Court's reasoning, but what if several groups took advantage and all were religious? What if they were all affiliated with one religion? One sect?

2. *Limited Public and Limited Open Forums.* The notion of a "limited" forum in the free speech (limited public forum) and the Equal Access Act (limited open forum) context makes sense, doesn't it? Essentially the forum is limited to student related groups, but it is public or open because any non-curriculum related student group—except perhaps those posing a danger to others, such as groups that practice weapons use at meetings—can have access to the forum. What about hate groups? Could the school open its forum to all non-curriculum related student groups except a Ku Klux Klan related group? What would happen if the school denied access to a student group focused on gay rights issues, but allowed Evangelical Christian groups to meet? What if one of the Evangelical groups focuses on anti-gay messages, the school's access policy denies access to groups that teach hatred against members of protected classes defined

by state law, and state law includes sexual orientation as a protected class? Which would be illegal/unconstitutional: 1. the exclusion of the Evangelical group?; 2. the inclusion of the Evangelical group?; or 3. the access policy to the extent that it prohibits access by groups that teach hatred?

3. *Closing a Forum.* One of the obvious implications of a public or open forum is that there can be non-public or closed forums. As the cases in this section, and *Santa Fe v. Doe*, Chapter Two *supra.*, suggest, when a government forum is not public it is far more likely that any speech that occurs there will be endorsed or sponsored by government. This raises the obvious question as to what would occur when a government decides to close a limited public forum. By its very nature a limited public (or a designated public forum) is capable of being closed when its purpose is no longer served. Thus, courts have made clear that a school that uses an auditorium or a classroom for an open student discussion on a given issue or on any issue does not by doing so turn that auditorium or classroom into a traditional public forum that is open to free speech by students at all times. Of course, as stated in *Capitol Square Review Board v. Pinette*, this can not be done in a traditional public forum such as a public park or sidewalk, except for limited time, place, and manner restrictions. *See also, Frisby v. Schultz*, 487 U.S. 474, 108 S.Ct. 2495, 101 L.Ed.2d 420 (1988). Yet, what would happen if a school decided to close a forum (or repeal an equal access policy) that had been open to a variety of non-curriculum related student groups, including religious groups, because a club for Atheist or homosexual students decided to use the forum? Cf. Boyd County High School Gay Straight Alliance v. Board of Education of Boyd County, 258 F.Supp.2d 667 (E.D.Ky.2003); East High Gay/Straight Alliance v. Bd. of Education of Salt Lake City School Dist., 81 F.Supp.2d 1166 (D.Utah 1999). What if a school that made its facilities available to a variety of non-student organizations after school hours, including religious organizations such as churches, decided to close its facilities when a Wiccan group asks to use the facilities? A Muslim group? A Jewish group? A Seventh Day Adventist group?

4. *Age and Impressionability.* The *Widmar* decision noted that college students are less likely to mistake a religious clubs meeting on university premises as government sponsored or endorsed than are younger students, and in *Mergens*, the court noted that secondary school students were mature enough to understand that a non-curriculum related student group meeting on school premises during non-instructional time was not favored by the school. Yet, the *Good News Club* decision applies the equal access approach to elementary schools and gives little serious attention to the issue of impressionability and perceived endorsement, instead suggesting that excluding the religious group might send a message of disfavor to the students in the religious club. Isn't this question begging? If young children are more likely to perceive endorsement of religion, shouldn't this fact be carefully addressed in the Court's opinion? Does the viewpoint discrimination claim affect this analysis? If so, isn't the court simply creating an irrebutable formalistic rule that denial of equal access is unconstitutional viewpoint discrimination? After all, the Court is saying that excluding religious clubs from meeting on school premises when other non-curriculum related student groups meet is inherently viewpoint discrimination, yet impressionability and any perceived endorsement are not an adequate defense (i.e. the most likely argument under the Establishment Clause will not work). Is there anything wrong with this approach? Does it make sense from a free speech perspective? Does it also make sense from a religion clause perspective? What role, if any, should a proselytizing focus and/or outside sponsorship of the club play in your answer to the preceding questions?

Chapter Four

GOVERNMENT AID TO RELIGION OR RELIGIOUS INSTITUTIONS

A. INTRODUCTION

The early history of government "aid" cases was discussed in Chapter One. For purposes of the present discussion government "aid" can be defined as financial or other beneficial support provided by a government entity or entities, not including the issues discussed in Chapters Two and Three. The most common genre of aid cases involve government grants, subsidies, tax exemptions, or other types of funding. This area of law has undergone major changes in recent years. The Court has moved from an approach that relied heavily on separationist principles (balanced with pragmatic concerns) to one that relies more on notions of formal neutrality. The earlier regime led to a confusing web of decisions, but there are significant problems with the Court's current approach as well. The problems with the Court's current approach will be addressed *infra.* at Section C and Chapter Five. As you read the materials in this chapter, consider which approach you favor and why. Also consider which approach is a better interpretation of the Establishment Clause, and which approach is most consistent with the cases in Chapter One. You may find that a given approach works better in some contexts than in others.

B. THE LEMON TEST: FROM *LEMON* TO *AGOSTINI*

This section explores the evolution of the doctrine applicable to aid cases from the seminal *Lemon v. Kurtzman* case in 1971, which gave rise to the *Lemon* test, to the Court's more recent decision in *Agostini v. Felton*, which altered the traditional three pronged *Lemon* test. It is important to stress that the *Lemon* test was not created out of thin air in *Lemon*. The first two prongs of the *Lemon* test were set forth in cases such as *Abington Township v. Schempp, supra.* Chapter One, and the third prong in cases such as *Walz v. Tax Commissioners. Id.*

LEMON v. KURTZMAN*

Supreme Court of the United States, 1971.
403 U.S. 602, 91 S.Ct. 2105, 29 L.Ed.2d 745.

MR. CHIEF JUSTICE BURGER delivered the opinion of the Court.

These two appeals raise questions as to Pennsylvania and Rhode Island statutes providing state aid to church-related elementary and secondary schools. Both statutes are challenged as violative of the Establishment and Free Exercise Clauses of the First Amendment and the Due Process Clause of the Fourteenth Amendment.

Pennsylvania has adopted a statutory program that provides financial support to nonpublic elementary and secondary schools by way of reimbursement for the cost of teachers' salaries, textbooks, and instructional materials in specified secular subjects. Rhode Island has adopted a statute under which the State pays directly to teachers in nonpublic elementary schools a supplement of 15% of their annual salary. Under each statute state aid has been given to church-related educational institutions. We hold that both statutes are unconstitutional.

I

THE RHODE ISLAND STATUTE

The Rhode Island Salary Supplement Act * * * rests on the legislative finding that the quality of education available in nonpublic elementary schools has been jeopardized by the rapidly rising salaries needed to attract competent and dedicated teachers. The Act authorizes state officials to supplement the salaries of teachers of secular subjects in nonpublic elementary schools by paying directly to a teacher an amount not in excess of 15% of his current annual salary. As supplemented, however, a nonpublic school teacher's salary cannot exceed the maximum paid to teachers in the State's public schools, and the recipient must be certified by the state board of education in substantially the same manner as public school teachers.

In order to be eligible for the Rhode Island salary supplement, the recipient must teach in a nonpublic school at which the average per-pupil expenditure on secular education is less than the average in the State's public schools during a specified period. Appellant State Commissioner of Education also requires eligible schools to submit financial data. If this information indicates a per-pupil expenditure in excess of

---

*[Author's note] This opinion actually addresses three cases: *Lemon v. Kurtzman*, case No. 89 (the Pennsylvania case), *Earley v. DiCenso*, case No. 569, and *Robinson v. DiCenso*, case No. 570 (the Rhode Island cases). Additionally, *Tilton v. Richardson*, 403 U.S. 672, 91 S.Ct. 2091, 29 L.Ed.2d 790 (1971), which involved Title I of the Higher Education Facilities Act of 1963, was decided the same day as the *Lemon* trilogy. The opinions of two Justices addressed both *Lemon* and *Tilton*. Thus, Justice Brennan's concurring opinion, and Justice White's opinion concurring as to the Pennsylvania case and dissenting as to the Rhode Island cases, both of which are omitted here, also addressed *Tilton*.

the statutory limitation, the records of the school in question must be examined in order to assess how much of the expenditure is attributable to secular education and how much to religious activity.

The Act also requires that teachers eligible for salary supplements must teach only those subjects that are offered in the State's public schools. They must use 'only teaching materials which are used in the public schools.' Finally, any teacher applying for a salary supplement must first agree in writing 'not to teach a course in religion for so long as or during such time as he or she receives any salary supplements' under the Act.

Appellees are citizens and taxpayers of Rhode Island. They brought this suit to have the Rhode Island Salary Supplement Act declared unconstitutional and its operation enjoined on the ground that it violates the Establishment and Free Exercise Clauses of the First Amendment. * * *

* * *

THE PENNSYLVANIA STATUTE

Pennsylvania has adopted a program that has some but not all of the features of the Rhode Island program. The Pennsylvania Nonpublic Elementary and Secondary Education Act was passed in 1968 in response to a crisis that the Pennsylvania Legislature found existed in the State's nonpublic schools due to rapidly rising costs. The statute affirmatively reflects the legislative conclusion that the State's educational goals could appropriately be fulfilled by government support of 'those purely secular educational objectives achieved through nonpublic education * * *.'

The statute authorizes appellee state Superintendent of Public Instruction to 'purchase' specified 'secular educational services' from nonpublic schools. Under the 'contracts' authorized by the statute, the State directly reimburses nonpublic schools solely for their actual expenditures for teachers' salaries, textbooks, and instructional materials. A school seeking reimbursement must maintain prescribed accounting procedures that identify the 'separate' cost of the 'secular educational service.' These accounts are subject to state audit. The funds for this program were originally derived from a new tax on horse and harness racing, but the Act is now financed by a portion of the state tax on cigarettes.

There are several significant statutory restrictions on state aid. Reimbursement is limited to courses 'presented in the curricula of the public schools.' It is further limited 'solely' to courses in the following 'secular' subjects: mathematics, modern foreign languages, physical science, and physical education. Textbooks and instructional materials included in the program must be approved by the state Superintendent of Public Instruction. Finally, the statute prohibits reimbursement for any course that contains 'any subject matter expressing religious teaching, or the morals or forms of worship of any sect.'

The Act went into effect on July 1, 1968, and the first reimbursement payments to schools were made on September 2, 1969. It appears that some $5 million has been expended annually under the Act. The State has now entered into contracts with some 1,181 nonpublic elementary and secondary schools with a student population of some 535,215 pupils—more than 20% of the total number of students in the State. More than 96% of these pupils attend church-related schools, and most of these schools are affiliated with the Roman Catholic church.

Appellants brought this action in the District Court to challenge the constitutionality of the Pennsylvania statute. The organizational plaintiffs-appellants are associations of persons resident in Pennsylvania declaring belief in the separation of church and state; individual plaintiffs-appellants are citizens and taxpayers of Pennsylvania. Appellant Lemon, in addition to being a citizen and a taxpayer, is a parent of a child attending public school in Pennsylvania. * * *

* * *

[Three judge district court panels were created pursuant to federal statute in each of the cases. The district court in the Rhode Island case found the statute in question unconstitutional. The district court in the Pennsylvania case upheld the statute].

II

In Everson v. Board of Education, this Court upheld a state statute that reimbursed the parents of parochial school children for bus transportation expenses. There Mr. Justice Black, writing for the majority, suggested that the decision carried to 'the verge' of forbidden territory under the Religion Clauses. Candor compels acknowledgment, moreover, that we can only dimly perceive the lines of demarcation in this extraordinarily sensitive area of constitutional law.

The language of the Religion Clauses of the First Amendment is at best opaque, particularly when compared with other portions of the Amendment. Its authors did not simply prohibit the establishment of a state church or a state religion, an area history shows they regarded as very important and fraught with great dangers. Instead they commanded that there should be 'no law respecting an establishment of religion.' A law may be one 'respecting' the forbidden objective while falling short of its total realization. A law 'respecting' the proscribed result, that is, the establishment of religion, is not always easily identifiable as one violative of the Clause. A given law might not establish a state religion but nevertheless be one 'respecting' that end in the sense of being a step that could lead to such establishment and hence offend the First Amendment.

In the absence of precisely stated constitutional prohibitions, we must draw lines with reference to the three main evils against which the Establishment Clause was intended to afford protection: 'sponsorship, financial support, and active involvement of the sovereign in religious activity.' Walz v. Tax Commission, 397 U.S. 664, 668, 90 S.Ct. 1409, 1411, 25 L.Ed.2d 697 (1970).

Every analysis in this area must begin with consideration of the cumulative criteria developed by the Court over many years. Three such tests may be gleaned from our cases. First, the statute must have a secular legislative purpose; second, its principal or primary effect must be one that neither advances nor inhibits religion, Board of Education v. Allen, 392 U.S. 236, 243, 88 S.Ct. 1923, 1926, 20 L.Ed.2d 1060 (1968); finally, the statute must not foster 'an excessive government entanglement with religion.' Walz.

Inquiry into the legislative purposes of the Pennsylvania and Rhode Island statutes affords no basis for a conclusion that the legislative intent was to advance religion. On the contrary, the statutes themselves clearly state that they are intended to enhance the quality of the secular education in all schools covered by the compulsory attendance laws. * * * [W]e find nothing here that undermines the stated legislative intent; it must therefore be accorded appropriate deference.

* * * The legislatures of Rhode Island and Pennsylvania have concluded that secular and religious education are identifiable and separable. In the abstract we have no quarrel with this conclusion.

The two legislatures, however, have also recognized that church-related elementary and secondary schools have a significant religious mission and that a substantial portion of their activities is religiously oriented. They have therefore sought to create statutory restrictions designed to guarantee the separation between secular and religious educational functions and to ensure that State financial aid supports only the former. All these provisions are precautions taken in candid recognition that these programs approached, even if they did not intrude upon, the forbidden areas under the Religion Clauses. We need not decide whether these legislative precautions restrict the principal or primary effect of the programs to the point where they do not offend the Religion Clauses, for we conclude that the cumulative impact of the entire relationship arising under the statutes in each State involves excessive entanglement between government and religion.

III

In Walz, the Court upheld state tax exemptions for real property owned by religious organizations and used for religious worship. That holding, however, tended to confine rather than enlarge the area of permissible state involvement with religious institutions by calling for close scrutiny of the degree of entanglement involved in the relationship. The objective is to prevent, as far as possible, the intrusion of either into the precincts of the other.

Our prior holdings do not call for total separation between church and state; total separation is not possible in an absolute sense. Some relationship between government and religious organizations is inevitable. Fire inspections, building and zoning regulations, and state requirements under compulsory school-attendance laws are examples of necessary and permissible contacts. Indeed, under the statutory exemption before us in Walz, the State had a continuing burden to ascertain that the exempt property was in fact being used for religious worship. Judicial caveats against entanglement must recognize that the line of separation, far from being a 'wall,' is a blurred, indistinct, and variable barrier depending on all the circumstances of a particular relationship.

This is not to suggest, however, that we are to engage in a legalistic minuet in which precise rules and forms must govern. * * * Here we examine the form of the relationship for the light that it casts on the substance.

In order to determine whether the government entanglement with religion is excessive, we must examine the character and purposes of the institutions that are benefitted, the nature of the aid that the State provides, and the resulting relationship between the government and the religious authority. * * * Here we find that both statutes foster an impermissible degree of entanglement.

(a) Rhode Island program

The District Court made extensive findings on the grave potential for excessive entanglement that inheres in the religious character and purpose of the Roman Catholic elementary schools of Rhode Island, to date the sole beneficiaries of the Rhode Island Salary Supplement Act.

The church schools involved in the program are located close to parish churches. This understandably permits convenient access for religious exercises since instruction in faith and morals is part of the total educational process. The school buildings contain identifying religious symbols such as crosses on the exterior and crucifixes, and religious paintings and statues either in the classrooms or hallways. Although only approximately 30 minutes a day are devoted to direct religious instruction, there are religiously oriented extracurricular activities. Approximately two-thirds of the teachers in these schools are nuns of various religious orders. Their dedicated efforts provide an atmosphere in which religious instruction and religious vocations are natural and proper parts of life in such schools. * * *

* * * In short, parochial schools involve substantial religious activity and purpose.

The substantial religious character of these church-related schools gives rise to entangling church-state relationships of the kind the Religion Clauses sought to avoid. Although the District Court found that concern for religious values did not inevitably or necessarily intrude into the content of secular subjects, the considerable religious activities of these schools led the legislature to provide for careful governmental controls and surveillance by state authorities in order to ensure that state aid supports only secular education.

The dangers and corresponding entanglements are enhanced by the particular form of aid that the Rhode Island Act provides. Our decisions from Everson to Allen have permitted the States to provide church-related schools with secular, neutral, or nonideological services, facilities, or materials. Bus transportation, school lunches, public health services, and secular textbooks supplied in common to all students were not thought to offend the Establishment Clause. * * *

* * * [T]eachers have a substantially different ideological character from books. In terms of potential for involving some aspect of faith or morals in secular subjects, a textbook's content is ascertainable, but a teacher's handling of a subject is not. We cannot ignore the danger that a teacher under religious control and discipline poses to the separation of the religious from the purely secular aspects of precollege education. The conflict of functions inheres in the situation.

* * *

Several teachers testified * * * that they did not inject religion into their secular classes. And the District Court found that religious values did not necessarily affect the content of the secular instruction. But what has been recounted suggests the potential if not actual hazards of this form of state aid. The teacher is employed by a religious organization, subject to the direction and discipline of religious authorities, and works in a system dedicated to rearing children in a particular faith. These controls are not lessened by the fact that most of the lay teachers are of the Catholic faith. Inevitably some of a teacher's responsibilities hover on the border between secular and religious orientation.

We need not and do not assume that teachers in parochial schools will be guilty of bad faith or any conscious design to evade the limitations imposed by the statute and the First Amendment. We simply recognize that a dedicated religious person, teaching in a school affiliated with his or her faith and operated to inculcate its tenets, will inevitably experience great difficulty in remaining religiously neutral. Doctrines and faith are not inculcated or advanced by neutrals. With the best of intentions such a teacher would find it hard to make a total separation between secular teaching and religious doctrine. What would appear to some to be essential to good citizenship might well for others border on or constitute instruction in religion. Further difficulties are inherent in the combination of religious discipline and the possibility of disagreement between teacher and religious authorities over the meaning of the statutory restrictions.

We do not assume, however, that parochial school teachers will be unsuccessful in their attempts to segregate their religious beliefs from their secular educational responsibilities. But the potential for impermissible fostering of religion is present. The Rhode Island Legislature has not, and could not, provide state aid on the basis of a mere assumption that secular teachers under religious discipline can avoid conflicts. The State must be certain, given the Religion Clauses, that subsidized teachers do not inculcate religion—indeed the State here has undertaken to do so. * * *

A comprehensive, discriminating, and continuing state surveillance will inevitably be required to ensure that these restrictions are obeyed and the First Amendment otherwise respected. Unlike a book, a teacher cannot be inspected once so as to determine the extent and intent of his or her personal beliefs and subjective acceptance of the limitations imposed by the First Amendment. These prophylactic contacts will involve excessive and enduring entanglement between state and church.

There is another area of entanglement in the Rhode Island program that gives concern. The statute excludes teachers employed by nonpublic schools whose average per-pupil expenditures on secular education equal or exceed the comparable figures for public schools. In the event that the total expenditures of an otherwise eligible school exceed this norm, the program requires the government to examine the school's records in order to determine how much of the total expenditures is attributable to secular education and how much to religious activity. This kind of state inspection and evaluation of the religious content of a religious organization is fraught with the sort of entanglement that the Constitution forbids. It is a relationship pregnant with dangers of excessive government direction of church schools and hence of churches. * * * [W]e cannot ignore here the danger that pervasive modern governmental power will ultimately intrude on religion and thus conflict with the Religion Clauses.

(b) Pennsylvania program

The Pennsylvania statute also provides state aid to church-related schools for teachers' salaries. The complaint describes an educational system that is very similar to the one existing in Rhode Island. According to the allegations, the church-related elementary and secondary schools are controlled by religious organizations, have the purpose of propagating and promoting a particular religious faith, and conduct their operations to fulfill that purpose. Since this complaint was dismissed for failure to state a claim for relief, we must accept these allegations as true for purposes of our review.

As we noted earlier, the very restrictions and surveillance necessary to ensure that teachers play a strictly non-ideological role give rise to entanglements between church and state. The Pennsylvania statute, like that of Rhode Island, fosters this kind of relationship. * * *

The Pennsylvania statute, moreover, has the further defect of providing state financial aid directly to the church-related schools. This factor distinguishes both Everson and Allen, for in both those cases the Court was careful to point out that state aid was provided to the student and his parents—not to the church-related school. In Walz, the Court warned of the dangers of direct payments to religious organizations:

'Obviously a direct money subsidy would be a relationship pregnant with involvement and, as with most governmental grant programs, could encompass sustained and detailed administrative relationships for enforcement of statutory or administrative standards * * *.'

The history of government grants of a continuing cash subsidy indicates that such programs have almost always been accompanied by varying measures of control and surveillance. The government cash grants before us now provide no basis for predicting that comprehensive measures of surveillance and controls will not follow. In particular the government's post-audit power to inspect and evaluate a church-related school's financial records and to determine which expenditures are religious and which are secular creates an intimate and continuing relationship between church and state.

IV

A broader base of entanglement of yet a different character is presented by the divisive political potential of these state programs. In a community where such a large number of pupils are served by church-related schools, it can be assumed that state assistance will entail considerable political activity. Partisans of parochial schools, understandably concerned with rising costs and sincerely dedicated to both the religious and secular educational missions of their schools, will inevitably champion this cause and promote political action to achieve their goals. Those who oppose state aid, whether for constitutional, religious, or fiscal reasons, will inevitably respond and employ all of the usual political campaign techniques to prevail. Candidates will be forced to declare and voters to choose. It would be unrealistic to ignore the fact that many people confronted with issues of this kind will find their votes aligned with their faith.

Ordinarily political debate and division, however vigorous or even partisan, are normal and healthy manifestations of our democratic system of government, but political division along religious lines was one of the principal evils against which the First Amendment was intended to protect. The potential divisiveness of such conflict is a threat to the normal political process. To have States or communities divide on the issues presented by state aid to parochial schools would tend to confuse and obscure other issues of great urgency. * * * The history of many countries attests to the hazards of religion's intruding into the political arena or of political power intruding into the legitimate and free exercise of religious belief.

Of course, as the Court noted in Walz, '(a)dherents of particular faiths and individual churches frequently take strong positions on public issues.' Walz. We could not expect otherwise, for religious values pervade the fabric of our national life. But in Walz we dealt with a status under state tax laws for the benefit of all religious groups. Here we are confronted with successive and very likely permanent annual appropriations that benefit relatively few religious groups. Political fragmentation and divisiveness on religious lines are thus likely to be intensified.

The potential for political divisiveness related to religious belief and practice is aggravated in these two statutory programs by the need for continuing annual appropriations and the likelihood of larger and larger demands as costs and populations grow. The Rhode Island District Court found that the parochial school system's 'monumental and deepening financial crisis' would 'inescapably' require larger annual appropriations subsidizing greater percentages of the salaries of lay teachers. Although no facts have been developed in this respect in the Pennsylvania case, it appears that such pressures for expanding aid have already required the state legislature to include a portion of the state revenues from cigarette taxes in the program.

V

* * *

* * * We have already noted that modern governmental programs have self-perpetuating and self-expanding propensities. These internal pressures are only enhanced when the schemes involve institutions whose legitimate needs are growing and whose interests have substantial political support. Nor can we fail to see that in constitutional adjudication some steps, which when taken were thought to approach 'the verge,' have become the platform for yet further steps. A certain momentum develops in constitutional theory and it can be a 'downhill thrust' easily set in motion but difficult to retard or stop. Development by momentum is not invariably bad; indeed, it is the way the common law has grown, but it is a force to be recognized and reckoned with. The dangers are increased by the difficulty of perceiving in advance exactly where the 'verge' of the precipice lies. As well as constituting an independent evil against which the Religion Clauses were intended to protect, involvement or entanglement between government and religion serves as a warning signal.

Finally, nothing we have said can be construed to disparage the role of church-related elementary and secondary schools in our national life. Their contribution has been and is enormous. Nor do we ignore their economic plight in a period of rising costs and expanding need. Taxpayers generally have been spared vast sums by the maintenance of these educational institutions by religious organizations, largely by the gifts of faithful adherents.

The merit and benefits of these schools, however, are not the issue before us in these cases. The sole question is whether state aid to these schools can be squared with the dictates of the Religion Clauses. Under our system the choice has been made that government is to be entirely excluded from the area of religious instruction and churches excluded from the affairs of government. The Constitution decrees that religion must be a private matter for the individual, the family, and the institutions of private choice, and that while some involvement and entanglement are inevitable, lines must be drawn.

The judgment of the Rhode Island District Court in No. 569 and No. 570 is affirmed. The judgment of the Pennsylvania District Court in No. 89 is reversed, and the case is remanded for further proceedings consistent with this opinion.

MR. JUSTICE MARSHALL took no part in the consideration or decision of No. 89.

MR. JUSTICE DOUGLAS, whom MR. JUSTICE BLACK joins, concurring.

While I join the opinion of the Court. I have expressed at some length my views as to the rationale of today's decision * * *.

* * *

There is in my view * * * an entanglement here. The surveillance or supervision of the States needed to police grants involved in these three cases, if performed, puts a public investigator into every classroom and entails a pervasive monitoring of these church agencies by the secular authorities. Yet if that surveillance or supervision does not occur the zeal of religious proselytizers promises to carry the day and make a shambles of the Establishment Clause. Moreover, when taxpayers of many faiths are required to contribute money for the propagation of one faith, the Free Exercise Clause is infringed.

The analysis of the constitutional objections to these two state systems of grants to parochial or sectarian schools must start with the admitted and obvious fact that the raison d'etre of parochial schools is the propagation of a religious faith. They also teach secular subjects; but they came into existence in this country because Protestant groups were perverting the public schools by using them to propagate their faith. The Catholics naturally rebelled. If schools were to be used to propagate a particular creed or religion, then Catholic ideals should also be served. Hence the advent of parochial schools.

* * *

If the government closed its eyes to the manner in which these grants are actually used it would be allowing public funds to promote sectarian education. If it did not close its eyes but undertook the surveillance needed, it would, I fear, intermeddle in parochial affairs in a way that would breed only rancor and dissension.

We have announced over and over again that the use of taxpayers' money to support parochial schools violates the First Amendment, applicable to the States by virtue of the Fourteenth.

We said in unequivocal words in Everson v. Board of Education, 'No tax in any amount, large or small, can be levied to support any religious activities or institutions, whatever they may be called, or whatever form they may adopt to teach or practice religion.' We reiterated the same idea in Zorach v. Clauson, and in McGowan v. Maryland, and in Torcaso v. Watkins, 367 U.S. 488, 493, 81 S.Ct. 1680, 1682, 6 L.Ed.2d 982. We repeated the same idea in McCollum v. Board of Education, and added that a State's tax-supported public schools could not be used 'for the dissemination of religious doctrines' nor could a State provide the church 'pupils for their religious classes through use of the state's compulsory public school machinery.'

Yet in spite of this long and consistent history there are those who have the courage to announce that a State may nonetheless finance the secular part of a sectarian school's educational program. That, however, makes a grave constitutional decision turn merely on cost accounting and bookkeeping entries. A history class, a literature class, or a science class in a parochial school is not a separate institute; it is part of the organic whole which the State subsidizes. The funds are used in these cases to pay or help pay the salaries of teachers in parochial schools; and the presence of teachers is critical to the essential purpose of the parochial school, viz., to advance the religious endeavors of the particular church. It matters not that the teacher receiving taxpayers' money only teaches religion a fraction of the time. Nor does it matter that he or she teaches no religion. The school is an organism living on one budget. What the taxpayers give for salaries of those who teach only the humanities or science without any trace of proseletyzing enables the school to use all of its own funds for religious training. * * *

In my view the taxpayers' forced contribution to the parochial schools in the present cases violates the First Amendment.

MR. JUSTICE MARSHALL, who took no part in the consideration or decision of No. 89 [the Pennsylvania case], while intimating no view as to the continuing vitality of *Everson v. Bd. of Education*, concurs in MR. JUSTICE DOUGLAS' opinion covering Nos. 569 and 570 [the Rhode Island cases].

[MR. JUSTICE BRENNAN's concurring opinion in *Lemon* and partial concurrence in *Tilton v. Richardson* is omitted.]

[MR. JUSTICE WHITE's opinion concurring in the judgements in *Lemon* (the Pennsylvania case only) and *Tilton v. Richardson*, and dissenting in the Rhode Island cases, is omitted].

Notes and Questions

1. *Legislative Purpose.* How is secular purpose to be determined when the government entity involved in the alleged Establishment Clause violation is a large group such as a legislature? How can a court determine whether a statute has a secular purpose when numerous legislators vote for a bill that isn't expressly religious on its face? Is it enough to look at statements by a few legislators or those of the bill's sponsors? *See Wallace v. Jaffree, supra.* at Chapter Two. Or is it a mistake to attempt to determine the purpose of a large body of actors, many of whom may have acted for different reasons? *See id.* (Burger, J., dissenting).

2. *Primary Effect.* How "primary" must the religious or antireligious effect of a government action be in order to violate the second prong of the *Lemon* test? Would a law that has the effect of advancing or inhibiting religion, but also has several other effects that have nothing to do with religion, violate the second prong of the *Lemon* test? What if the effect of the law on religion was large, but not nearly as large as the nonreligious impact? What if the effect of the law on

religion was small but was the primary effect of the law? How might a law have a primary effect that "inhibits" religion? Wouldn't any law that affected the religious practices of some group "inhibit" religion? Of course, such an effect might not be a primary effect of the law. How might the impact of a law that has the effect—but not the primary effect—of inhibiting religion, be treated under the Free Exercise Clause? *See infra.* Chapters Six and Seven.

3. *Entanglement.* Entanglement under *Lemon* would seem to include both institutional entanglement, where government and religious institutions are too involved with one another, and divisiveness. How is divisiveness part of the entanglement analysis? Wouldn't it make sense to consider divisiveness as part of the effects element? Institutional entanglement and divisiveness were two of the major concerns the Court attributed to the framers in earlier decisions such as *Everson* and *McCollum.* Would you be surprised to learn that in 1995, the Court removed divisiveness from the factors to be considered in aid cases under *Lemon,* and rolled the institutional entanglement inquiry into the effects prong? *See Agostini v. Felton, infra.* this Chapter. How can courts determine when government and religious institutions are institutionally entangled under *Lemon*? Is it enough to show that there is some cooperative effort between the two? If not, what else must be shown?

4. *Vouchers.* How might a voucher program fare under *Lemon* if over 96% of students receiving vouchers use them at religious schools and the relevant religious schools represent only a small number of faiths or denominations? *See Zelman v. Simmons–Harris, infra.* this Chapter.

The Winding Path of the *Lemon* Test

The tale of the *Lemon* test in the context of government "aid" to religion is a winding one with many twists and turns along the way. As you will learn in the next section, there is not much left of the *Lemon* test in the aid context, even if the Court ostensibly follows the first two prongs of that test. However, the path of *Lemon* did not always portend its demise, even if some scholars accurately, but prematurely, predicted that demise. *See* Michael Stokes Paulsen, *Lemon is Dead,* 43 CASE W. RES. L. REV. 795 (1993). Even though Justice Scalia has noted the *Lemon* test's seemingly supernatural ability to rise from the grave, *see Lamb's Chapel v. Center Moriches Union Free School District,* 508 U.S. 384, 398, 113 S.Ct. 2141, 124 L.Ed.2d 352 (Scalia, J., concurring) (Like some ghoul in a late-night horror movie that repeatedly sits up in its grave and shuffles abroad, after being repeatedly killed and buried, *Lemon* stalks our Establishment Clause jurisprudence once again, frightening the little children and school attorneys of Central Moriches Union Free School District), Paulsen's claim that "*Lemon* is dead" would seem correct, at least in the aid context in 2004. But before exploring *Lemon's* demise it is necessary to explore the "evolution" of the *Lemon* test.

Shortly after the Court decided *Lemon,* it decided *Committee for Public Education v. Nyquist,* 413 U.S. 756, 93 S.Ct. 2955, 37 L.Ed.2d 948 (1973). *Nyquist* involved three New York state programs. One provided grants to private schools for building and equipment maintenance on a per pupil basis, another tuition grants for low income families, and the third a tuition tax credit. The Court struck down all three programs under the effects prong of the *Lemon* test. The thrust of the Court's reasoning was that the aid could be easily diverted to support the religious aspects of a sectarian school even if such a result was not mandated. The state funds provided for maintenance were not restricted to maintenance of equipment and facilities "used exclusively for secular purposes," and thus the program had the primary effect of advancing religion because the funds can be used to subsidize "the religious activities of sectarian [schools]." As for the tuition grants and tax credits, the Court held that they were unconstitutional absent "an effective means" of assuring that any state funds would be exclusively used "for secular, neutral, and nonideological purposes," and equated the two forms of aid for purposes of its analysis. In light of the Court's recent decisions (discussed in the next section) it is interesting to note that the *Nyquist* Court held it was irrelevant that the grants went to parents to reimburse for expenses without any requirement that the government money be spent for tuition or other school expenses, because the "substantive impact" is the same where the grants are "offered" as an incentive for parents to send their children to religious schools.

In *Meek v. Pittenger*, 421 U.S. 349, 95 S.Ct. 1753, 44 L.Ed.2d 217 (1975), and *Wolman v. Walter*, 433 U.S. 229, 97 S.Ct. 2593, 53 L.Ed.2d 714 (1977), the Court struck down programs that allowed the state to loan instructional materials to religious schools (*Meek*), and to students attending those schools (*Wolman*). In *Meek*, the Court held that the equipment "[e]ven though earmarked for secular purposes, 'when it flows to an institution in which religion is so pervasive that a substantial portion of its functions are subsumed in the religious mission,' * * * has the impermissible primary effect of advancing religion." The type of instructional materials involved in the two cases included maps, charts, recordings and periodicals. *Meek* also involved instructional support. In *Wolman*, the state tried to comply with *Meek* by lending the equipment to the students rather than the school, but the equipment was stored at the various schools. The Court rejected the distinction between loans to the schools and loans to the students in this context, because the schools benefitted from the availability of the equipment in any event. One problem with both of these cases was that the Court had upheld the loan of secular textbooks to students in *Board of Education v. Allen*, *see supra*. Chapter One, and while the Court attempted to distinguish the equipment at issue in *Meek* and *Wolman*, many found the distinctions unpersuasive. *Meek* and *Wolman* were overturned in the next principle case, *Mitchell v. Helms*.

In *Aguilar v. Felton*, 473 U.S. 402, 105 S.Ct. 3232, 87 L.Ed.2d 290 (1985), the Court struck down the part of the Secondary Education Act of 1965 that required federally funded remedial education teachers to help students at all public and private schools if those students met certain criteria. The program included religious schools, and instruction generally occurred on school premises. The Court held that the program violated the entanglement prong of the *Lemon* test because "the aid is provided in a pervasively sectarian environment," and the "assistance is provided in the form of teachers," therefore "ongoing inspection is required to ensure the absence of a religious message." Thus, "the scope and duration" of the "program would require a permanent and pervasive state presence in * * * sectarian schools." The Court held that this created entanglement problems because the program could influence religious schools to alter their practices and mission to comply with government requirements, the program requires significant interaction between public school teachers and religious institutions on numerous matters and significant monitoring to assure that religious material is not present in classes held under the program, and the program increases the possibility of "political divisiveness along religious lines." As a result of this case, remedial instruction, which was still mandated under the relevant law, had to be held off of religious school campuses. Students had to be transported to remote locations for the instruction, or the government had to pay for facilities (usually portable classrooms) near the various religious schools. *Aguilar* was overturned in *Agostini v. Felton*, 521 U.S. 203, 117 S.Ct. 1997, 138 L.Ed.2d 391 (1997).

In *School District of Grand Rapids v. Ball*, 473 U.S. 373, 105 S.Ct. 3216, 87 L.Ed.2d 267 (1985), which was decided the same day as *Aguilar*, the Court struck down a state program similar to the program struck down in *Aguilar*, but which also provided for classes which "supplemented the curriculum" at religious schools "with courses not previously offered" at those schools. The Court held that the state program violated the effects prong of *Lemon* because teachers teaching under the state program "may become involved intentionally or inadvertently in inculcating particular religious tenets or beliefs," the state program creates a "symbolic link between government and religion" by suggesting to students that government supports "the religious denomination operating" a given religious school, and the state program has "the effect of directly promoting religion by impermissibly providing a subsidy to the primary religious mission of the institutions affected," i.e. the state provided "direct" aid to the religious institutions. The petitioners argued that the benefits of the program flowed "primarily to the students," but the Court rejected this argument "[w]here, as here, no meaningful distinction can be made between aid to the student and aid to the school." *Ball* was overturned in part in *Agostini v. Felton*.

Mueller v. Allen, 463 U.S. 388, 103 S.Ct. 3062, 77 L.Ed.2d 721 (1983), *Witters v. Washington Dept. of Services for the Blind*, 474 U.S. 481, 106 S.Ct. 748, 88 L.Ed.2d 846 (1986), and *Zobrest v. Catalina Foothills School District*, 509 U.S. 1, 113 S.Ct. 2462, 125 L.Ed.2d 1 (1993), are all cases that stand for the proposition that it is constitutional for government to make aid available to individuals without regard to whether they use that aid at secular or religious schools (or in the case of *Allen*, whether they receive a tax credit for expenses at such school). Interestingly, the *Witters* and *Zobrest* Courts seemed to seriously consider the practical effects of the programs in question unlike recent cases that rely on similar analysis. *See infra. Mitchell v. Helms*; *Zelman v. Simmons–Harris*. These later cases, while relying heavily on all three of the above cases (as well as others) may be more the legacy of *Mueller v. Allen* than the other two cases, as *Mueller* came closer to a pure formal neutrality approach, where facial neutrality and private choice functioned to make a program constitutional even when the bulk of the aid under the program goes to those with children in religious schools.

Mueller v. Allen, involved a challenge to a tax deduction provided by the state of Minnesota for expenses relating to education in primary and secondary schools. Parents could deduct expenses related to education at any primary or secondary school, including religious schools. The deduction could be taken for education related expenses including tuition and transportation costs. Thus, the practical effect of the deduction was that parents with children in private schools would reap most of the benefits of the deduction, and the overwhelming majority of private schools were religious schools. The Court held that the program did not violate the *Lemon* test. The program was not the type "readily subject to challenge under the Establishment Clause, because the government aid (the tax deduction)" neutrally provides state assistance to a broad spectrum of citizens. The fact that the deductions were given to the parents, not the religious schools, was important to the Court's decision. Interestingly, in analyzing the secular purpose of the deduction the Court noted the general public benefits from a strong private school system because such a system diverts students from the public schools, while the parents of private school students still must pay property taxes which benefit the public schools.

Witters and *Zobrest* both involved aid provided to disabled students to enable them to attend school. In *Witters*, a blind student wanted to use vocational rehabilitation aid at a religious college. The aid, which was provided pursuant to a state statute, went directly to the student. Moreover, the student could choose to use the aid at any college or university, whether secular or religious. Thus, the Court held that any benefit to a religious institution under the program would only be incidental, the aid provided pursuant to the program was not likely to further a school's religious mission, and the program created no financial incentive for a student to attend a religious as opposed to a secular school. The fact that the aid went to the student who could use it at a wide range of secular or religious institutions, and the fact that the benefits to such institutions under the program would be minimal, were central to the Court's decision. *Zobrest* extended the rationale of *Witters* to the provision of a sign language interpreter to a deaf student attending a Catholic high school. While the rationale of *Zobrest* closely parallels that in *Witters*—i.e. the aid went to the student who could use it at a wide range of secular or religious schools, the benefits to any religious school under the program would be minimal, and the program "creates no financial incentive for parents to choose a sectarian school"—the Court had to address the fact that the interpreter would be interpreting both secular and religious material because the lower court had held that the interpreter "would act as a conduit" for the religious training of the student. The Court held that it was unlikely that an interpreter would affect the religious content of the messages he was interpreting, and thus the interpreter would be unlike a teacher who decides the content of the message. Moreover, because the federal statute entitled deaf children to an interpreter under circumstances set forth in the statute and the religious school would not have had a duty to supply the interpreter, the religious school "was not relieved of an expense" that it would have had in educating students.

In *Bowen v. Kendrick*, 487 U.S. 589, 108 S.Ct. 2562, 101 L.Ed.2d 520 (1988), the Court upheld the Adolescent Family Life Act against an Establishment Clause challenge. The Act allowed federal grants to agencies that provide services related to teen sexuality and pregnancy. Both public and private agencies (including private religious organizations) were eligible for the grants under the Act. The Act was challenged on its face—i.e. it was challenged as being unconstitutional by itself, rather than as applied to various agencies. Justice Rehnquist, who also authored the opinion for the Court in *Mueller v. Allen*, wrote the majority opinion. The Court held that while the Act in some ways paralleled the views and practices of certain religions, the purpose of the Act was not to promote religion, but rather to address the problems caused by teen pregnancy and sexual behavior. The Court also held that the primary effect of the Act was not to advance religion, because the grants were available to a wide range of agencies and organizations, it was reasonable for Congress to include religious organizations in the Act because they can have an obvious influence on values and family structure, and many of the religious organizations that would receive funds under the program were not "pervasively sectarian." Thus, religion would only benefit incidentally and remotely from the Act. Additionally, the Court held that the monitoring required under the Act did not lead to excessive entanglement. The Court did remand the case for a determination of whether the Act violated the Establishment Clause as applied.

Another line of cases in the government "aid" context involves situations where the government delegates power to a religious entity or where the government uses religion as a factor in structuring government entities. In *Larkin v. Grendel's Den, Inc.*, 459 U.S. 116, 103 S.Ct. 505, 74 L.Ed.2d 297 (1982), the Court struck down a state law that prevented the grant of a liquor license to any establishment within five hundred feet of a church or school that objected. The Court held that the effect of the Act was to give churches the ability to veto liquor licenses, the granting of which is a state function. This power could be used by churches to further their "religious goals." Moreover, the law created a symbolic link between government and religion that could benefit religion. The law also violated the entanglement prong of *Lemon* because the government delegated power to churches under the law.

Relatedly, in *Board of Education of Kiryas Joel v. Grumet*, 512 U.S. 687, 114 S.Ct. 2481, 129 L.Ed.2d 546 (1994), the Court held that the creation of a school district based on boundaries that were consistent with a particular religious sect for the benefit of that sect violated the

Establishment Clause. The case involved the Satmar Hasidim, a devout and insular sect of Orthodox Jews. The Satmar generally sent their children to private religious schools, but those schools could not provide the remedial and special education necessary for disabled students. Thus, the Satmar had to send disabled children to nearby school districts for the special education the children needed and were entitled to under federal and state law. The children who had to attend the public schools were traumatized because the Satmar generally do not interact with those outside their community, and there are significant religious and cultural differences between the Satmar and those outside the Satmar community. Additionally, there were genuine concerns about the ability of the public schools to accommodate the dietary and other religious needs of the Satmar children. To respond to these concerns, the state created a new school district along the boundaries of the Satmar community, Kiryas Joel. The newly formed Kiryas Joel school district only offered a special education curriculum. Satmar children who did not need special education remained in private religious schools. The Court held that the newly created district unconstitutionally fused government and religious functions by granting power to a government entity defined by a shared religion, and that the state did not do so in a manner that would prevent favoritism based on religion. The state was not impartial toward religion when it created the district along religious lines. The Court rejected the argument that the state was simply accommodating the religious needs of its citizens, because the grant of government power to a religiously defined group is not a "permissible accommodation" of religion.

The *Lemon* test was modified—some have suggested "watered down"—in *Agostini v. Felton*, 521 U.S. 203, 117 S.Ct. 1997, 138 L.Ed.2d 391 (1997). *Agostini* involved the same program struck down in *Aguilar*. After *Aguilar,* the special education courses mandated by federal law had to be held off site when the students attended religious schools. This led to a system of portable classrooms, often trailers, being set up near religious schools. The resulting system was unpopular, expensive, and not as efficient as on site remedial education classes. *Agostini* overruled *Aguilar*, and held that remedial education by public school employees under a broad program requiring such education at all schools regardless of whether they are public or private, secular or religious, can be held on site at religious schools just as it is in other schools. *Agostini* also overruled the holding in *Ball* that dealt with the shared time program (this was the part of the program struck down in *Ball* that enabled public school employees to teach remedial courses and courses that supplemented the secular curriculum).

While the result of the *Agostini* decision may have been laudable as a matter of public policy, the decision made some significant changes to the *Lemon* test, both in its structure and application. These changes later enabled the Court to move toward a system of formal neutrality in aid cases. This move will be discussed further in the next section. The cases in that section include further discussion of *Agostini*. For now it is important to note that *Agostini* rolled the third prong of the *Lemon* test into the second. Thus, entanglement became part of the effects test (the political divisiveness aspect of entanglement was eliminated from the test). The Court also recharacterized the effects test in the aid context. Whether government aid has the effect of advancing religion is now determined by analyzing three elements: 1. Does it result in "governmental indoctrination" of religion?; 2. Does it "define its recipients by reference to religion?"; or 3. Does it "create an excessive entanglement" between government and religion? The facial neutrality of the aid program and the mechanism through which the aid is distributed are central to the first two questions.

If the aid may be used at a wide range of providers without regard to their religious affiliation, and the aid is allocated based on the individual choices of the recipients (the remedial education classes only take place at religious schools if parents choose to send their children to such schools), any indoctrination is not the result of government action. Similarly, a program does not "define its recipients by reference to religion" if the aid recipients are defined based on neutral criteria—i.e. the aid goes to the students regardless of which school their parents choose to send them to—because under such circumstances the aid does not create a financial incentive for "religious indoctrination." Specifically, the Court held that a financial incentive for religious indoctrination "is not present * * * where the aid is allocated on the basis of neutral, secular criteria that neither favor nor disfavor religion, and is made available to both religious and secular beneficiaries on a nondiscriminatory basis * * *." The Court also rejected the arguments, accepted in *Aguilar* and *Ball*, that public employees teaching special education at a religious school are likely to include religion in their instruction, that any aid to the educational aspects of a religious school aids religion, and that programs like those involved in these cases foster an unconstitutional "symbolic union" between government and religion. The next section suggests that *Agostini* signaled a major change in the Court's approach to aid cases.

C.   THE MOVE TOWARD FORMAL NEUTRALITY

In recent years the Court has moved toward the principle of formal neutrality. Under a formal neutrality approach the Court analyzes the facial neutrality of a policy along with the way in which funding is allocated (the private choice factor described in the cases below). This shift has been relatively precipitous, yet it is not without support in earlier precedent. Cases such as *Witters*, *Mueller v. Allen*, and *Zobrest* rely heavily on the facial neutrality of an aid program and on whether funds are allocated based on the private choices of individual recipients. Yet those cases—with perhaps the exception of *Mueller v. Allen*— seriously considered the effects of the programs in question. As you will see in *Zelman v. Simmons–Harris*, *infra.*, the Court's current focus on formal neutrality, which gains support from some of these earlier decisions, seems to have strayed from any serious consideration of effects. As you read the following decisions consider whether they are consistent with the Court's earlier decisions in the aid context, and if so, with which ones? It is at least arguable that an earlier Court would have upheld the program involved in *Mitchell v. Helms* (the next principle case), but it is unlikely that the voucher program upheld in *Zelman* would have been upheld prior to the *Agostini* decision (and probably not prior to the decision in *Mitchell v. Helms*). The following cases completed the shift toward a doctrine of formal neutrality in aid cases.

MITCHELL v. HELMS

Supreme Court of the United States, 2000.
530 U.S. 793, 120 S.Ct. 2530, 147 L.Ed.2d 660.

JUSTICE THOMAS announced the judgment of the Court and delivered an opinion, in which the CHIEF JUSTICE, JUSTICE SCALIA, and JUSTICE KENNEDY join.

As part of a longstanding school-aid program known as Chapter 2, the Federal Government distributes funds to state and local governmental agencies, which in turn lend educational materials and equipment to public and private schools, with the enrollment of each participating school determining the amount of aid that it receives. The question is whether Chapter 2, as applied in Jefferson Parish, Louisiana, is a law respecting an establishment of religion, because many of the private schools receiving Chapter 2 aid in that parish are religiously affiliated. We hold that Chapter 2 is not such a law.

I

A

Chapter 2 of the Education Consolidation and Improvement Act of 1981, Pub.L. 97–35, 95 Stat. 469, as amended, 20 U.S.C. §§ 7301–7373, has its origins in the Elementary and Secondary Education Act of 1965 (ESEA), and is a close cousin of the provision of the ESEA that we recently considered in *Agostini v. Felton,* 521 U.S. 203, 117 S.Ct. 1997, 138 L.Ed.2d 391 (1997). Like the provision at issue in *Agostini,* Chapter 2 channels federal funds to local educational agencies (LEA's), which are usually public school districts, via state educational agencies (SEA's), to implement programs to assist children in elementary and secondary schools. Among other things, Chapter 2 provides aid

> "for the acquisition and use of instructional and educational materials, including library services and materials (including media materials), assessments, reference materials, computer software and hardware for instructional use, and other curricular materials." 20 U.S.C. § 7351(b)(2).

LEA's and SEA's must offer assistance to both public and private schools (although any private school must be nonprofit). Participating private schools receive Chapter 2 aid based on the number of children enrolled in each school, and allocations of Chapter 2 funds for those schools must generally be "equal (consistent with the number of children to be served) to expenditures for programs . . . for children enrolled in the public schools of the [LEA]." LEA's must in all cases "assure equitable participation" of the children of private schools "in the purposes and benefits" of Chapter 2. Further, Chapter 2 funds may only "supplement and, to the extent practical, increase the level of funds that would . . . be made available from non-Federal sources." LEA's and SEA's may not operate their programs "so as to supplant funds from non-Federal sources."

Several restrictions apply to aid to private schools. Most significantly, the "services, materials, and equipment" provided to private schools must be "secular, neutral, and nonideological." In addition, private schools may not acquire control of Chapter 2 funds or title to Chapter 2 materials, equipment, or property. A private school receives the materials and equipment listed in § 7351(b)(2) by submitting to the LEA an application detailing which items the school seeks and how it will use them; the LEA, if it approves the application, purchases those items from the school's allocation of funds, and then lends them to that school.

In Jefferson Parish (the Louisiana governmental unit at issue in this case), as in Louisiana as a whole, private schools have primarily used their allocations for nonrecurring expenses, usually materials and equipment. In the 1986–1987 fiscal year, for example, 44% of the money budgeted for private schools in Jefferson Parish was spent by LEA's for acquiring library and media materials, and 48% for instructional equipment. Among the materials and equipment provided have been library books, computers, and computer software, and also slide and movie projectors, overhead projectors, television sets, tape recorders, VCR's, projection screens, laboratory equipment, maps, globes, filmstrips, slides, and cassette recordings.

It appears that, in an average year, about 30% of Chapter 2 funds spent in Jefferson Parish are allocated for private schools. For the 1985–1986 fiscal year, 41 private schools participated in Chapter 2. For the following year, 46 participated, and the participation level has remained relatively constant since then. Of these 46, 34 were Roman Catholic; 7 were otherwise religiously affiliated; and 5 were not religiously affiliated.

B

Respondents filed suit in December 1985, alleging, among other things, that Chapter 2, as applied in Jefferson Parish, violated the Establishment Clause of the First Amendment of the Federal Constitution. The case's tortuous history over the next 15 years indicates well the degree to which our Establishment Clause jurisprudence has shifted in recent times, while nevertheless retaining anomalies with which the lower courts have had to struggle.

* * *

II

* * *

In *Agostini* * * * we brought some clarity to our case law, by overruling two anomalous precedents (one in whole, the other in part) and by consolidating some of our previously disparate considerations under a revised test. Whereas in *Lemon* we had considered whether a statute (1) has a secular purpose, (2) has a primary effect of advancing or inhibiting religion, or (3) creates an excessive entanglement between government and religion, in *Agostini* we modified *Lemon* for purposes of evaluating aid to schools and examined only the first and second factors. We acknowledged that our cases discussing excessive entanglement had applied many of the same considerations as had our cases discussing primary effect, and we therefore recast *Lemon*'s entanglement inquiry as simply one criterion relevant to determining a statute's effect. We also acknowledged that our cases had pared somewhat the factors that could justify a finding of excessive entanglement. We then set out revised criteria for determining the effect of a statute:

> "To summarize, New York City's Title I program does not run afoul of any of three primary criteria we currently use to evaluate whether government aid has the effect of advancing religion: It does not result in governmental indoctrination; define its recipients by reference to religion; or create an excessive entanglement."

In this case, our inquiry under *Agostini*'s purpose and effect test is a narrow one. Because respondents do not challenge the District Court's holding that Chapter 2 has a secular purpose, * * * we will consider only Chapter 2's effect. Further, in determining that effect, we will consider only the first two *Agostini* criteria, since neither respondents nor the Fifth Circuit has questioned the District Court's holding that Chapter 2 does not create an excessive entanglement. Considering Chapter 2 in light of our more recent case law, we conclude that it neither results in religious indoctrination by the government nor defines its recipients by reference to religion. We therefore hold that Chapter 2 is not a "law respecting an establishment of religion." In so holding, we acknowledge [that] * * * *Meek* and *Wolman* are anomalies in our case law. We therefore conclude that they are no longer good law.

A

As we indicated in *Agostini,* and have indicated elsewhere, the question whether governmental aid to religious schools results in governmental indoctrination is ultimately a question whether any religious indoctrination that occurs in those schools could reasonably be attributed to governmental action. We have also indicated that the answer to the question of indoctrination will resolve the question whether a program of educational aid "subsidizes" religion, as our religion cases use that term.

In distinguishing between indoctrination that is attributable to the State and indoctrination that is not, we have consistently turned to the principle of neutrality, upholding aid that is offered to a broad range of groups or persons without regard to their religion. If the religious, irreligious, and areligious are all alike eligible for governmental aid, no one would conclude that any indoctrination that any particular recipient conducts has been done at the behest of the government. For attribution of indoctrination is a relative question. If the government is offering assistance to recipients who provide, so to speak, a broad range of indoctrination, the government itself is not thought responsible for any particular indoctrination. To put the point differently, if the government, seeking to further some legitimate secular purpose, offers aid on the same terms, without regard to religion, to all who adequately further that purpose, then it is fair to say that any aid going to a religious recipient only has the effect of furthering that secular purpose. * * *

As a way of assuring neutrality, we have repeatedly considered whether any governmental aid that goes to a religious institution does so "only as a result of the genuinely independent and private choices of individuals." *Agostini.* * * * For if numerous private choices, rather than the single choice of a government, determine the distribution of aid pursuant to neutral eligibility criteria, then a government cannot, or at least cannot easily, grant special favors that might lead to a religious establishment. Private choice also helps guarantee neutrality by mitigating the preference for pre-existing recipients that is arguably inherent in any governmental aid program, and that could lead to a program inadvertently favoring one religion or favoring religious private schools in general over nonreligious ones.

* * *

Agostini's second primary criterion for determining the effect of governmental aid is closely related to the first. The second criterion requires a court to consider whether an aid program "define[s] its recipients by reference to religion." As we briefly explained in *Agostini,* this second criterion looks to the same set of facts as does our focus, under the first criterion, on neutrality, but the second criterion uses those facts to answer a somewhat different question—whether the criteria for allocating the aid "creat[e] a financial incentive to undertake religious indoctrination." In *Agostini* we set out the following rule for answering this question:

> "This incentive is not present, however, where the aid is allocated on the basis of neutral, secular criteria that neither favor nor disfavor religion, and is made available to both religious and secular beneficiaries on a nondiscriminatory basis. Under such circumstances, the aid is less likely to have the effect of advancing religion."

The cases on which *Agostini* relied for this rule, and *Agostini* itself, make clear the close relationship between this rule, incentives, and private choice. For to say that a program does not create an incentive to choose religious schools is to say that the private choice is truly "independent," *Witters*. When such an incentive does exist, there is a greater risk that one could attribute to the government any indoctrination by the religious schools.

We hasten to add, what should be obvious from the rule itself, that simply because an aid program offers private schools, and thus religious schools, a benefit that they did not previously receive does not mean that the program, by reducing the cost of securing a religious education, creates, under *Agostini*'s second criterion, an "incentive" for parents to choose such an education for their children. For *any* aid will have some such effect.

B

Respondents inexplicably make no effort to address Chapter 2 under the *Agostini* test. Instead, dismissing *Agostini* as factually distinguishable, they offer two rules that they contend should govern our determination of whether Chapter 2 has the effect of advancing religion. They argue first, and chiefly, that "direct, nonincidental" aid to the primary educational mission of religious schools is always impermissible. Second, they argue that provision to religious schools of aid that is divertible to religious use is similarly impermissible. Respondents' arguments are inconsistent with our more recent case law, in particular *Agostini* and *Zobrest,* and we therefore reject them.

1

Although some of our earlier cases, particularly *Ball,* 473 U.S., at 393–394, 105 S.Ct. 3248, did emphasize the distinction between direct and indirect aid, the purpose of this distinction was merely to prevent "subsidization" of religion. * * * [O]ur more recent cases address this purpose not through the direct/indirect distinction but rather through the principle of private choice, as incorporated in the first *Agostini* criterion (*i.e.,* whether any indoctrination could be attributed to the government). If aid to schools, even "direct aid," is neutrally available and, before reaching or benefiting any religious school, first passes through the hands (literally or figuratively) of numerous private citizens who are free to direct the aid elsewhere, the government has not provided any "support of religion," *Witters*. Although the presence of private choice is easier to see when aid literally passes through the hands of individuals—which is why we have mentioned directness in the same breath with private choice—there is no reason why the Establishment Clause requires such a form.

* * *

Of course, we have seen "special Establishment Clause dangers," *Rosenberger,* when *money* is given to religious schools or entities directly rather than, as in *Witters* and *Mueller,* indirectly. But direct payments of money are not at issue in this case, and we refuse to allow a "special" case to create a rule for all cases.

2

Respondents also contend that the Establishment Clause requires that aid to religious schools not be impermissibly religious in nature or be divertible to religious use. We agree with the first part of this argument but not the second. Respondents' "no divertibility" rule is inconsistent with our more recent case law and is unworkable. So long as the governmental aid is not itself "unsuitable for use in the public schools because of religious content," *Allen, supra,* at 245, 88 S.Ct. 1923, and eligibility for aid is determined in a constitutionally permissible manner, any use of that aid to indoctrinate cannot be attributed to the government and is thus not of constitutional concern. * * *

* * *

C

The dissent serves up a smorgasbord of 11 factors that, depending on the facts of each case "in all its particularity," could be relevant to the constitutionality of a school aid program. And those 11 are a bare minimum. We are reassured that there are likely more. Presumably they will be revealed in future cases, as needed, but at least one additional factor is evident from the dissent itself: The dissent resurrects the concern for political divisiveness that once occupied the Court but that post-*Aguilar* cases have rightly disregarded. * * *

One of the dissent's factors deserves special mention: whether a school that receives aid (or whose students receive aid) is pervasively sectarian. The dissent is correct that there was a period when this factor mattered, particularly if the pervasively sectarian school was a primary or secondary school. But that period is one that the Court should regret, and it is thankfully long past.

There are numerous reasons to formally dispense with this factor. First, its relevance in our precedents is in sharp decline. Although our case law has consistently mentioned it even in recent years, we have not struck down an aid program in reliance on this factor since 1985, in *Aguilar* and *Ball*. *Agostini* of course overruled *Aguilar* in full and *Ball* in part * * *. In *Witters,* a year after *Aguilar* and *Ball,* we did not ask whether the Inland Empire School of the Bible was pervasively sectarian. In *Bowen,* a 1988 decision, we refused to find facially invalid an aid program (although one not involving schools) whose recipients had, the District Court found, included pervasively sectarian institutions. * * * Then, in *Zobrest* and *Agostini,* we upheld aid programs to children who attended schools that were not only pervasively sectarian but also were primary and secondary. * * * In disregarding the nature of the school, *Zobrest* and *Agostini* were merely returning to the approach of *Everson* and *Allen,* in which the Court upheld aid programs to students at pervasively sectarian schools.

Second, the religious nature of a recipient should not matter to the constitutional analysis, so long as the recipient adequately furthers the government's secular purpose. If a program offers permissible aid to the religious (including the pervasively sectarian), the areligious, and the irreligious, it is a mystery which view of religion the government has established, and thus a mystery what the constitutional violation would be. The pervasively sectarian recipient has not received any special favor, and it is most bizarre that the Court would, as the dissent seemingly does, reserve special hostility for those who take their religion seriously, who think that their religion should affect the whole of their lives, or who make the mistake of being effective in transmitting their views to children.

Third, the inquiry into the recipient's religious views required by a focus on whether a school is pervasively sectarian is not only unnecessary but also offensive. It is well established, in numerous other contexts, that courts should refrain from trolling through a person's or institution's religious beliefs. Yet that is just what this factor requires, as was evident before the District Court. Although the dissent welcomes such probing, we find it profoundly troubling. In addition, and related, the application of the "pervasively sectarian" factor collides with our decisions that have prohibited governments from discriminating in the distribution of public benefits based upon religious status or sincerity.

Finally, hostility to aid to pervasively sectarian schools has a shameful pedigree that we do not hesitate to disavow. Although the dissent professes concern for "the implied exclusion of the less favored," the exclusion of pervasively sectarian schools from government-aid programs is just that, particularly given the history of such exclusion. Opposition to aid to "sectarian" schools acquired prominence in the 1870's with Congress' consideration (and near passage) of the Blaine Amendment, which would have amended the Constitution to bar any aid to sectarian institutions. Consideration of the amendment arose at a time of pervasive hostility to the Catholic Church and to Catholics in general, and it was an open secret that "sectarian" was code for "Catholic." See generally Green, The Blaine Amendment Reconsidered, 36 Am. J. Legal Hist. 38 (1992). * * *

In short, nothing in the Establishment Clause requires the exclusion of pervasively sectarian schools from otherwise permissible aid programs, and other doctrines of this Court bar it. This doctrine, born of bigotry, should be buried now.

III

Applying the two relevant *Agostini* criteria, we see no basis for concluding that Jefferson Parish's Chapter 2 program "has the effect of advancing religion." Chapter 2 does not result in governmental indoctrination, because it determines eligibility for aid neutrally, allocates that aid based on the private choices of the parents of schoolchildren, and does not provide aid that has an impermissible content. Nor does Chapter 2 define its recipients by reference to religion.

Taking the second criterion first, it is clear that Chapter 2 aid "is allocated on the basis of neutral, secular criteria that neither favor nor disfavor religion, and is made available to both religious and secular beneficiaries on a nondiscriminatory basis." *Agostini.* Aid is allocated based on enrollment: "Private schools receive Chapter 2 materials and equipment based on the per capita number of students at each school," and allocations to private schools must "be equal (consistent with the number of children to be served) to expenditures for programs under this subchapter for children enrolled in the public schools of the [LEA]," 20 U.S.C. § 7372(b). LEA's must provide Chapter 2 materials and equipment for the benefit of children in private schools "[t]o the extent consistent with the number of children in the school district of [an LEA] . . . who are enrolled in private nonprofit elementary and secondary schools." § 7372(a)(1). The allocation criteria therefore create no improper incentive. * * *

Chapter 2 also satisfies the first *Agostini* criterion. The program makes a broad array of schools eligible for aid without regard to their religious affiliations or lack thereof. We therefore have no difficulty concluding that Chapter 2 is neutral with regard to religion. Chapter 2 aid also, like the aid in *Agostini, Zobrest,* and *Witters,* reaches participating schools only "as a consequence of private decisionmaking." *Agostini.* Private decisionmaking controls because of the per capita allocation scheme, and those decisions are independent because of the program's neutrality. It is the students and their parents—not the government—who, through their choice of school, determine who receives Chapter 2 funds. The aid follows the child.

Because Chapter 2 aid is provided pursuant to private choices, it is not problematic that one could fairly describe Chapter 2 as providing "direct" aid. The materials and equipment provided under Chapter 2 are presumably used from time to time by entire classes rather than by individual students (although individual students are likely the chief consumers of library books and, perhaps, of computers and computer software), and students themselves do not need to apply for Chapter 2 aid in order for their schools to receive it, but, as we explained in *Agostini,* these traits are not constitutionally significant or meaningful. Nor, for reasons we have already explained, is it of constitutional significance that the schools themselves, rather than the students, are the bailees of the Chapter 2 aid. The ultimate beneficiaries of Chapter 2 aid are the students who attend the schools that receive that aid, and this is so regardless of whether individual students lug computers to school each day or, as Jefferson Parish has more sensibly provided, the schools receive the computers. * * *

Finally, Chapter 2 satisfies the first *Agostini* criterion because it does not provide to religious schools aid that has an impermissible content. The statute explicitly bars anything of the sort, providing that all Chapter 2 aid for the benefit of children in private schools shall be "secular, neutral, and nonideological," § 7372(a)(1), and the record indicates that the Louisiana SEA and the Jefferson Parish LEA have faithfully enforced this requirement insofar as relevant to this case. The chief aid at issue is computers, computer software, and library books. The computers presumably have no pre-existing content, or at least none that would be impermissible for use in public schools. Respondents do not contend otherwise. Respondents also offer no evidence that religious schools have received software from the government that has an impermissible content.

There is evidence that equipment has been, or at least easily could be, diverted for use in religious classes. * * * [W]e agree with the dissent that there is evidence of actual diversion and that, were the safeguards anything other than anemic, there would almost certainly be more such evidence. In any event, for reasons we discussed in Part II–B–2, the evidence of actual diversion and the weakness of the safeguards against actual diversion are not relevant to the constitutional inquiry, whatever relevance they may have under the statute and regulations.

* * *

IV

In short, Chapter 2 satisfies both the first and second primary criteria of *Agostini*. It therefore does not have the effect of advancing religion. For the same reason, Chapter 2 also "cannot reasonably be viewed as an endorsement of religion," *Agostini*. Accordingly, we hold that Chapter 2 is not a law respecting an establishment of religion. Jefferson Parish need not exclude religious schools from its Chapter 2 program. To the extent that *Meek* and *Wolman* conflict with this holding, we overrule them.

* * *

The judgment of the Fifth Circuit is reversed.

JUSTICE O'CONNOR, with whom JUSTICE BREYER joins, concurring in the judgment.

* * * I believe that *Agostini* * * * controls the constitutional inquiry respecting Title II presented here, and requires the reversal of the Court of Appeals' judgment that the program is unconstitutional as applied in Jefferson Parish, Louisiana. To the extent our decisions in *Meek v. Pittenger*, and *Wolman v. Walter*, are inconsistent with the Court's judgment today, I agree that those decisions should be overruled. I therefore concur in the judgment.

I

I write separately because, in my view, the plurality announces a rule of unprecedented breadth for the evaluation of Establishment Clause challenges to government school aid programs. Reduced to its essentials, the plurality's rule states that government aid to religious schools does not have the effect of advancing religion so long as the aid is offered on a neutral basis and the aid is secular in content. The plurality also rejects the distinction between direct and indirect aid, and holds that the actual diversion of secular aid by a religious school to the advancement of its religious mission is permissible. Although the expansive scope of the plurality's rule is troubling, two specific aspects of the opinion compel me to write separately. First, the plurality's treatment of neutrality comes close to assigning that factor singular importance in the future adjudication of Establishment Clause challenges to government school aid programs. Second, the plurality's approval of actual diversion of government aid to religious indoctrination is in tension with our precedents and, in any event, unnecessary to decide the instant case.

* * *

I agree with Justice Souter that the plurality, by taking such a stance, "appears to take evenhandedness neutrality and in practical terms promote it to a single and sufficient test for the establishment constitutionality of school aid."

I do not quarrel with the plurality's recognition that neutrality is an important reason for upholding government-aid programs against Establishment Clause challenges. Our cases have described neutrality in precisely this manner, and we have emphasized a program's neutrality repeatedly in our decisions approving various forms of school aid. Nevertheless, we have never held that a government-aid program passes constitutional muster *solely* because of the neutral criteria it employs as a basis for distributing aid. For example, in *Agostini,* neutrality was only one of several factors we considered in determining that New York City's Title I program did not have the impermissible effect of advancing religion. Indeed, given that the aid in *Agostini* had secular content and was distributed on the basis of wholly neutral criteria, our consideration of additional factors demonstrates that the plurality's rule does not accurately describe our recent Establishment Clause jurisprudence.

* * * As I have previously explained, neutrality is important, but it is by no means the only "axiom in the history and precedent of the Establishment Clause." *Rosenberger v. Rector and Visitors of Univ. of Va.,* 515 U.S. 819, 846, 115 S.Ct. 2510, 132 L.Ed.2d 700 (1995) (concurring opinion). Thus, I agree with Justice Souter's conclusion that our "most recent use of 'neutrality' to refer to generality or evenhandedness of distribution ... is relevant in judging whether a benefit scheme so characterized should be seen as aiding a sectarian school's religious mission, but this neutrality is not alone sufficient to qualify the aid as constitutional."

I also disagree with the plurality's conclusion that actual diversion of government aid to religious indoctrination is consistent with the Establishment Clause. * * * At least two of the decisions at the heart of today's case demonstrate that we have long been concerned that secular government aid not be diverted to the advancement of religion. In both *Agostini,* our most recent school aid case, and *Board of Ed. of Central School Dist. No. 1 v. Allen,* we rested our approval of the relevant programs in part on the fact that the aid had not been used to advance the religious missions of the recipient schools. * * *

The plurality bases its holding that actual diversion is permissible on *Witters* and *Zobrest*. Those decisions, however, rested on a significant factual premise missing from this case, as well as from the majority of cases thus far considered by the Court involving Establishment Clause challenges to school aid programs. Specifically, we decided *Witters* and *Zobrest* on the understanding that the aid was provided directly to the individual student who, in turn, made the choice of where to put that aid to use. Accordingly, our approval of the aid in both cases relied to a significant extent on the fact that "[a]ny aid ... that ultimately flows to religious institutions does so only as a result of the genuinely independent and private choices of aid recipients." *Witters*; *see Zobrest* ("[A] government-paid interpreter will be present in a sectarian school only as a result of the private decision of individual parents"). This characteristic of both programs made them less like a direct subsidy, which would be impermissible under the Establishment Clause, and more akin to the government issuing a paycheck to an employee who, in turn, donates a portion of that check to a religious institution.

* * * I do not believe that we should treat a per-capita-aid program the same as the true private-choice programs considered in *Witters* and *Zobrest*. First, when the government provides aid directly to the student beneficiary, that student can attend a religious school and yet retain control over whether the secular government aid will be applied toward the religious education. The fact that aid flows to the religious school and is used for the advancement of religion is therefore *wholly* dependent on the student's private decision. * * *

Second, I believe the distinction between a per capita school aid program and a true private-choice program is significant for purposes of endorsement. In terms of public perception, a government program of direct aid to religious schools based on the number of students attending each school differs meaningfully from the government distributing aid directly to individual students who, in turn, decide to use the aid at the same religious schools. In the former example, if the religious school uses the aid to inculcate religion in its students, it is reasonable to say that the government has communicated a message of endorsement. Because the religious indoctrination is supported by government assistance, the reasonable observer would naturally perceive the aid program as *government* support for the advancement of religion. That the amount of aid received by the school is based on the school's enrollment does not separate the government from the endorsement of the religious message. * * * In contrast, when government aid supports a school's religious mission only because of independent decisions made by numerous individuals to guide their secular aid to that school, "[n]o reasonable observer is likely to draw from the facts ... an inference that the State itself is endorsing a religious practice or belief." *Witters* (O'Connor, J., concurring in part and concurring in judgment). * * *

Finally, the distinction between a per-capita-aid program and a true private-choice program is important when considering aid that consists of direct monetary subsidies. This Court has "recognized special Establishment Clause dangers where the government makes direct money payments to sectarian institutions." *Rosenberger* * * *. If, as the plurality contends, a per-capita-aid program is identical in relevant constitutional respects to a true private-choice program, then there is no reason that, under the plurality's reasoning, the government should be precluded from providing direct money payments to religious organizations (including churches) based on the number of persons belonging to each organization. And, because actual diversion is permissible under the plurality's holding, the participating religious organizations (including churches) could use that aid to support religious indoctrination. To be sure, the plurality does not actually hold that its theory extends to direct money payments. That omission, however, is of little comfort. * * *

* * *

II

In *Agostini*, * * * we explained that the general principles used to determine whether government aid violates the Establishment Clause have remained largely unchanged. Thus, we still ask "whether the government acted with the purpose of advancing or inhibiting religion" and "whether the aid has the 'effect' of advancing or inhibiting religion." We also concluded in *Agostini*, however, that the specific criteria used to determine whether government aid has an impermissible effect had changed. Looking to our recently decided cases, we articulated three primary criteria to guide the determination whether a government-aid program impermissibly advances religion: (1) whether the aid results in governmental indoctrination, (2) whether the aid program defines its recipients by reference to religion, and (3) whether the aid creates an excessive entanglement between government and religion. Finally, we noted that the same criteria could be reviewed to determine whether a government-aid program constitutes an endorsement of religion.

Respondents neither question the secular purpose of the Chapter 2 (Title II) program nor contend that it creates an excessive entanglement. Accordingly, for purposes of deciding whether Chapter 2, as applied in Jefferson Parish, Louisiana, violates the Establishment Clause, we need ask only whether the program results in governmental indoctrination or defines its recipients by reference to religion.

Taking the second inquiry first, it is clear that Chapter 2 does not define aid recipients by reference to religion. In *Agostini*, we explained that scrutiny of the manner in which a government-aid program identifies its recipients is important because "the criteria might themselves have the effect of advancing religion by creating a financial incentive to undertake religious indoctrination." We then clarified that this financial incentive is not present "where the aid is allocated on the basis of neutral, secular criteria that neither favor nor disfavor religion, and is made available to both religious and secular beneficiaries on a nondiscriminatory basis." * * * Chapter 2 uses wholly neutral and secular criteria to allocate aid to students enrolled in religious and secular schools alike. As a result, it creates no financial incentive to undertake religious indoctrination.

Agostini next requires us to ask whether Chapter 2 "result[s] in governmental indoctrination." Because this is a more complex inquiry under our case law, it is useful first to review briefly the basis for our decision in *Agostini* that New York City's Title I program did not result in governmental indoctrination. Under that program, public-school teachers provided Title I instruction to eligible students on private school premises during regular school hours. Twelve years earlier, in *Aguilar v. Felton,* 473 U.S. 402, 105 S.Ct. 3232, 87 L.Ed.2d 290 (1985), we had held the same New York City program unconstitutional. In *Ball,* a companion case to *Aguilar,* we also held that a similar program in Grand Rapids, Michigan, violated the Constitution. Our decisions in *Aguilar* and *Ball* were both based on a presumption, drawn in large part from *Meek,* that public-school instructors who teach secular classes on the campuses of religious schools will inevitably inculcate religion in their students.

In *Agostini,* we recognized that "[o]ur more recent cases [had] undermined the assumptions upon which *Ball* and *Aguilar* relied." First, we explained that the Court had since abandoned "the presumption erected in *Meek* and *Ball* that the placement of public employees on parochial school grounds inevitably results in the impermissible effect of state-sponsored indoctrination or constitutes a symbolic union between government and religion." Rather, relying on *Zobrest,* we explained that in the absence of evidence showing that teachers were actually using the Title I aid to inculcate religion, we would presume that the instructors would comply with the program's secular restrictions. * * *

Second, we noted that the Court had "departed from the rule relied on in *Ball* that all government aid that directly assists the educational function of religious schools is invalid." * * * With respect to the specific Title I program at issue, we noted several factors that precluded us from finding an impermissible financing of religious indoctrination: the aid was "provided to students at whatever school they choose to attend," the services were "by law supplemental to the regular curricula" of the benefited schools, "[n]o Title I funds ever reach the coffers of religious schools," and there was no evidence of Title I instructors having "attempted to inculcate religion in students." Relying on the same factors, we also concluded that the New York City program could not "reasonably be viewed as an endorsement of religion." * * *

The Chapter 2 program at issue here bears the same hallmarks of the New York City Title I program that we found important in *Agostini.* First, as explained above, Chapter 2 aid is distributed on the basis of neutral, secular criteria. The aid is available to assist students regardless of whether they attend public or private nonprofit religious schools. Second, the statute requires participating SEA's and LEA's to use and allocate Chapter 2 funds only to supplement the funds otherwise available to a religious school. Chapter 2 funds must in no case be used to supplant funds from non-Federal sources. Third, no Chapter 2 funds ever reach the coffers of a religious school. Like the Title I program considered in *Agostini,* all Chapter 2 funds are controlled by public agencies—the SEA's and LEA's. The LEA's purchase instructional and educational materials and then lend those materials to public and private schools. With respect to lending to private schools under Chapter 2, the statute specifically provides that the relevant public agency must retain title to the materials and equipment. Together with the supplantation restriction, this provision ensures that religious schools reap no financial benefit by virtue of receiving loans of materials and equipment. Finally, the statute provides that all Chapter 2 materials and equipment must be "secular, neutral, and nonideological." That restriction is reinforced by a further statutory prohibition on "the making of any payment . . . for religious worship or instruction." Although respondents claim that Chapter 2 aid has been diverted to religious instruction, that evidence is *de minimis* * * *.

III

* * *

[In response to *Allen*] [r]espondents insist that there is a reasoned basis under the Establishment Clause for the distinction between textbooks and instructional materials and equipment. They claim that the presumption that religious schools will use instructional materials and equipment to inculcate religion is sound because such materials and equipment, unlike textbooks, are reasonably divertible to religious uses. For example, no matter what secular criteria the government employs in selecting a film projector to lend to a religious school, school officials can always divert that projector to religious instruction. Respondents therefore claim that the Establishment Clause prohibits the government from giving or lending aid to religious schools when that aid is reasonably divertible to religious uses. * * *

I would reject respondents' proposed divertibility rule. First, respondents cite no precedent of this Court that would require it. The only possible direct precedential support for such a rule is a single sentence contained in a footnote from our *Wolman* decision. There, the Court described *Allen* as having been "premised on the view that the educational content of textbooks is something that can be ascertained in advance and cannot be diverted to sectarian uses." *Wolman, supra,* at 251, n. 18, 97 S.Ct. 2593. To the extent this simple description of *Allen* is even correct, it certainly does not constitute an actual holding that the Establishment Clause prohibits the government from lending any divertible aid to religious schools. Rather, as explained above, the *Wolman* Court based its holding invalidating the lending of instructional materials and equipment to religious schools on the rationale adopted in *Meek*—that the secular educational function of a religious school is inseparable from its religious mission. Indeed, if anything, the *Wolman* footnote confirms the irrationality of the distinction between textbooks and instructional materials and equipment. * * *

* * *

In any event, even if *Meek* and *Wolman* had articulated the divertibility rationale urged by respondents and Justice Souter, I would still reject it for a more fundamental reason. Stated simply, the theory does not provide a logical distinction between the lending of textbooks [upheld in *Allen*] and the lending of instructional materials and equipment. An educator can use virtually any instructional tool, whether it has ascertainable content or not, to teach a religious message. In this respect, I agree with the plurality that "it is hard to imagine any book that could not, in even moderately skilled hands, serve to illustrate a religious message." * * *

* * *

IV

* * *

* * * When a religious school receives textbooks or instructional materials and equipment lent with secular restrictions, the school's teachers need not refrain from teaching religion altogether. Rather, the instructors need only ensure that any such religious teaching is done without the instructional aids provided by the government. We have always been willing to assume that religious school instructors can abide by such restrictions when the aid consists of textbooks * * *. The same assumption should extend to instructional materials and equipment.

* * *

V

Respondents do not rest, however, on their divertibility argument alone. Rather, they also contend that the evidence respecting the actual administration of Chapter 2 in Jefferson Parish demonstrates that the program violated the Establishment Clause. First, respondents claim that the program's safeguards are insufficient to uncover instances of actual diversion. Second, they contend that the record shows that some religious schools in Jefferson Parish may have used their Chapter 2 aid to support religious education (*i.e.*, that they diverted the aid). Third, respondents highlight violations of Chapter 2's secular content restrictions. And, finally, they note isolated examples of potential violations of Chapter 2's supplantation restriction. * * * The limited evidence amassed by respondents during 4 years of discovery (which began approximately 15 years ago) is at best *de minimis* and therefore insufficient to affect the constitutional inquiry.

* * *

Given the important similarities between the Chapter 2 program here and the Title I program at issue in *Agostini*, respondents' Establishment Clause challenge must fail. As in *Agostini*, the Chapter 2 aid is allocated on the basis of neutral, secular criteria; the aid must be supplementary and cannot supplant non-Federal funds; no Chapter 2 funds ever reach the coffers of religious schools; the aid must be secular; any evidence of actual diversion is *de minimis*; and the program includes adequate safeguards. Regardless of whether these factors are constitutional requirements, they are surely sufficient to find that the program at issue here does not have the impermissible effect of advancing religion. For the same reasons, "this carefully constrained program also cannot reasonably be viewed as an endorsement of religion." *Agostini*. Accordingly, I concur in the judgment.

JUSTICE SOUTER, with whom JUSTICE STEVENS and JUSTICE GINSBURG join, dissenting.

The First Amendment's Establishment Clause prohibits Congress (and, by incorporation, the States) from making any law respecting an establishment of religion. It has been held to prohibit not only the institution of an official church, but any government act favoring religion, a particular religion, or for that matter irreligion. Thus, it bars the use of public funds for religious aid.

The establishment prohibition of government religious funding serves more than one end. It is meant to guarantee the right of individual conscience against compulsion, to protect the integrity of religion against the corrosion of secular support, and to preserve the unity of political society against the implied exclusion of the less favored and the antagonism of controversy over public support for religious causes.

These objectives are always in some jeopardy since the substantive principle of no aid to religion is not the only limitation on government action toward religion. Because the First Amendment also bars any prohibition of individual free exercise of religion, and because religious organizations cannot be isolated from the basic government functions that create the civil environment, it is as much necessary as it is difficult to draw lines between forbidden aid and lawful benefit. For more than 50 years, this Court has been attempting to draw these lines. Owing to the variety of factual circumstances in which the lines must be drawn, not all of the points creating the boundary have enjoyed self-evidence.

So far as the line drawn has addressed government aid to education, a few fundamental generalizations are nonetheless possible. There may be no aid supporting a sectarian school's religious exercise or the discharge of its religious mission, while aid of a secular character with no discernible benefit to such a sectarian objective is allowable. Because the religious and secular spheres largely overlap in the life of many such schools, the Court has tried to identify some facts likely to reveal the relative religious or secular intent or effect of the government benefits in particular circumstances. We have asked whether the government is acting neutrally in distributing its money, and about the form of the aid itself, its path from government to religious institution, its divertibility to religious nurture, its potential for reducing traditional expenditures of religious institutions, and its relative importance to the recipient, among other things.

In all the years of its effort, the Court has isolated no single test of constitutional sufficiency, and the question in every case addresses the substantive principle of no aid: what reasons are there to characterize this benefit as aid to the sectarian school in discharging its religious mission? Particular factual circumstances control, and the answer is a matter of judgment.

In what follows I will flesh out this summary, for this case comes at a time when our judgment requires perspective on how the Establishment Clause has come to be understood and applied. It is not just that a majority today mistakes the significance of facts that have led to conclusions of unconstitutionality in earlier cases, though I believe the Court commits error in failing to recognize the divertibility of funds to the service of religious objectives. What is more important is the view revealed in the plurality opinion, which espouses a new conception of neutrality as a practically sufficient test of constitutionality that would, if adopted by the Court, eliminate enquiry into a law's effects. The plurality position breaks fundamentally with Establishment Clause principle, and with the methodology painstakingly worked out in support of it. I mean to revisit that principle and describe the methodology at some length, lest there be any question about the rupture that the plurality view would cause. From that new view of the law, and from a majority's mistaken application of the old, I respectfully dissent.

I

* * *

A

At least three concerns have been expressed since the founding and run throughout our First Amendment jurisprudence. First, compelling an individual to support religion violates the fundamental principle of freedom of conscience. * * *

Second, government aid corrupts religion. * * *

Third, government establishment of religion is inextricably linked with conflict. * * *

B

These concerns are reflected in the Court's classic summation delivered in *Everson v. Board of Education,* its first opinion directly addressing standards governing aid to religious schools:

"The 'establishment of religion' clause of the First Amendment means at least this: Neither a state nor the Federal Government can set up a church. Neither can pass laws which aid one religion, aid all religions, or prefer one religion over another. Neither can force nor influence a person to go to or to remain away from church against his will or force him to profess a belief or disbelief in any religion. No person can be punished for entertaining or professing religious beliefs or disbeliefs, for church attendance or non-attendance. No tax in any amount, large or small, can be levied to support any religious activities or institutions, whatever they may be called, or whatever form they may adopt to teach or practice religion. Neither a state nor the Federal Government can, openly or secretly, participate in the affairs of any religious organizations or groups and *vice versa*. In the words of Jefferson, the clause against establishment of religion by law was intended to erect 'a wall of separation between church and State.' "

The most directly pertinent doctrinal statements here are these: no government "can pass laws which aid one religion [or] all religions.... No tax in any amount ... can be levied to support any religious activities or institutions ... whatever form they may adopt to teach ... religion." Thus, the principle of "no aid," with which no one in *Everson* disagreed.

Immediately, however, there was the difficulty over what might amount to "aid" or "support." The problem for the *Everson* Court was not merely the imprecision of the words, but the "other language of the [First Amendment that] commands that [government] cannot hamper its citizens in the free exercise of their own religion," with the consequence that government must "be a neutral in its relations with groups of religious believers and non-believers." Since withholding some public benefits from religious groups could be said to "hamper" religious exercise indirectly, and extending other benefits said to aid it, an argument-proof formulation of the no-aid principle was impossible, and the Court wisely chose not to attempt any such thing. * * *

* * *

Today, the substantive principle of no aid to religious mission remains the governing understanding of the Establishment Clause as applied to public benefits inuring to religious schools. * * * The cases have, however, recognized that in actual Establishment Clause litigation over school aid legislation, there is no pure aid to religion and no purely secular welfare benefit; the effects of the laws fall somewhere in between, with the judicial task being to make a realistic allocation between the two possibilities. * * *

II

A

* * * [W]e have used the term [neutrality] in at least three ways in our cases, and an understanding of the term's evolution will help to explain the concept as it is understood today, as well as the limits of its

significance in Establishment Clause analysis. "Neutrality" has been employed as a term to describe the requisite state of government equipoise between the forbidden encouragement and discouragement of religion; to characterize a benefit or aid as secular; and to indicate evenhandedness in distributing it.

As already mentioned, the Court first referred to neutrality in *Everson,* simply stating that government is required "to be a neutral" among religions and between religion and nonreligion. Although "neutral" may have carried a hint of inaction when we indicated that the First Amendment "does not require the state to be [the] adversary" of religious believers, or to cut off general government services from religious organizations, *Everson* provided no explicit definition of the term or further indication of what the government was required to do or not do to be "neutral" toward religion. In practical terms, "neutral" in *Everson* was simply a term for government in its required median position between aiding and handicapping religion. The second major case on aid to religious schools, *Allen,* used "neutrality" to describe an adequate state of balance between government as ally and as adversary to religion. The term was not further defined, and a few subsequent school cases used "neutrality" simply to designate the required relationship to religion, without explaining how to attain it.

The Court began to employ "neutrality" in a sense different from equipoise, however, as it explicated the distinction between "religious" and "secular" benefits to religious schools, the latter being in some circumstances permissible. Even though both *Everson* and *Allen* had anticipated some such distinction, neither case had used the term "neutral" in this way. * * * [T]he Court's premise in *Lemon* [shifted] the use of the word "neutral" from labeling the required position of the government to describing a benefit that was nonreligious. We spoke of "[o]ur decisions from *Everson* to *Allen* [as] permitt[ing] the States to provide church-related schools with secular, neutral, or nonideological services, facilities, or materials," and thereafter, we regularly used "neutral" in this second sense of "secular" or "nonreligious."

The shift from equipoise to secular was not, however, our last redefinition, for the Court again transformed the sense of "neutrality" in the 1980's. Reexamining and reinterpreting *Everson* and *Allen,* we began to use the word "neutral" to mean "evenhanded," in the sense of allocating aid on some common basis to religious and secular recipients. Again, neither *Everson* nor *Allen* explicitly used "neutral" in this manner, but just as the label for equipoise had lent itself to referring to the secular characteristic of what a government might provide, it was readily adaptable to referring to the generality of government services * * *.

* * *

There is, of course, good reason for considering the generality of aid and the evenhandedness of its distribution in making close calls between benefits that in purpose or effect support a school's religious mission and those that do not. This is just what *Everson* did. Even when the disputed practice falls short of *Everson's* paradigms, the breadth of evenhanded distribution is one pointer toward the law's purpose, since on the face of it aid distributed generally and without a religious criterion is less likely to be meant to aid religion than a benefit going only to religious institutions or people. And, depending on the breadth of distribution, looking to evenhandedness is a way of asking whether a benefit can reasonably be seen to aid religion in fact; we do not regard the postal system as aiding religion, even though parochial schools get mail. Given the legitimacy of considering evenhandedness, then, there is no reason to avoid the term "neutrality" to refer to it. But one crucial point must be borne in mind.

In the days when "neutral" was used in *Everson's* sense of equipoise, neutrality was tantamount to constitutionality; the term was conclusory, but when it applied it meant that the government's position was constitutional under the Establishment Clause. This is not so at all, however, under the most recent use of "neutrality" to refer to generality or evenhandedness of distribution. This kind of neutrality is relevant in judging whether a benefit scheme so characterized should be seen as aiding a sectarian school's religious mission, but this neutrality is not alone sufficient to qualify the aid as constitutional. It is to be considered only along with other characteristics of aid, its administration, its recipients, or its potential that have been emphasized over the years as indicators of just how religious the intent and effect of a given aid scheme really is. Thus, the basic principle of establishment scrutiny of aid remains the principle as stated in *Everson,* that there may be no public aid to religion or support for the religious mission of any institution.

B

The insufficiency of evenhandedness neutrality as a stand-alone criterion of constitutional intent or effect has been clear from the beginning of our interpretative efforts, for an obvious reason. Evenhandedness in distributing a benefit approaches the equivalence of constitutionality in this area only when the term refers to such universality of distribution that it makes no sense to think of the benefit as going to any discrete group. Conversely, when evenhandedness refers to distribution to limited groups within society, like groups of schools or schoolchildren, it does make sense to regard the benefit as aid to the recipients.

Hence, if we looked no further than evenhandedness, and failed to ask what activities the aid might support, or in fact did support, religious schools could be blessed with government funding as massive as expenditures made for the benefit of their public school counterparts, and religious missions would thrive on public money. This is why the consideration of less than universal neutrality has never been recognized as dispositive and has always been teamed with attention to other facts bearing on the substantive prohibition of support for a school's religious objective.

At least three main lines of enquiry addressed particularly to school aid have emerged to complement evenhandedness neutrality. First, we have noted that two types of aid recipients heighten Establishment Clause concern: pervasively religious schools and primary and secondary religious schools. Second, we have identified two important characteristics of the method of distributing aid: directness or indirectness of distribution and distribution by genuinely independent choice. Third, we have found relevance in at least five characteristics of the aid itself: its religious content; its cash form; its divertibility or actually diversion to religious support; its supplantation of traditional items of religious school expense; and its substantiality.

[Due to considerations of space Justice Souter's detailed discussion of the above mentioned factors is omitted. Some of the factors are discussed in Justice Souter's dissenting opinion in *Zelman v. Simmons–Harris, infra.*]

* * *

C

This stretch of doctrinal history leaves one point clear beyond peradventure: together with James Madison we have consistently understood the Establishment Clause to impose a substantive prohibition against public aid to religion and, hence, to the religious mission of sectarian schools. Evenhandedness neutrality is one, nondispositive pointer toward an intent and (to a lesser degree) probable effect on the permissible side of the line between forbidden aid and general public welfare benefit. Other pointers are facts about the religious mission and education level of benefited schools and their pupils, the pathway by which a benefit travels from public treasury to educational effect, the form and content of the aid, its adaptability to religious ends, and its effects on school budgets. The object of all enquiries into such matters is the same whatever the particular circumstances: is the benefit intended to aid in providing the religious element of the education and is it likely to do so?

The substance of the law has thus not changed since *Everson*. Emphasis on one sort of fact or another has varied depending on the perceived utility of the enquiry, but all that has been added is repeated explanation of relevant considerations, confirming that our predecessors were right in their prophecies that no simple test would emerge to allow easy application of the establishment principle.

The plurality, however, would reject that lesson. The majority misapplies it.

III

A

* * *

As a break with consistent doctrine the plurality's new criterion is unequaled in the history of Establishment Clause interpretation. Simple on its face, it appears to take evenhandedness neutrality and in practical terms promote it to a single and sufficient test for the establishment constitutionality of school aid. Even on its own terms, its errors are manifold, and attention to at least three of its mistaken assumptions will show the degree to which the plurality's proposal would replace the principle of no aid with a formula for generous religious support.

First, the plurality treats an external observer's attribution of religious support to the government as the sole impermissible effect of a government aid scheme. While perceived state endorsement of religion is undoubtedly a relevant concern under the Establishment Clause, it is certainly not the only one. *Everson* made this clear from the start: secret aid to religion by the government is also barred. State aid not attributed to the government would still violate a taxpayer's liberty of conscience, threaten to corrupt religion, and generate disputes over aid. * * * Under the plurality's rule of neutrality, if a program met the first part of the *Lemon* enquiry, by declining to define a program's recipients by religion, it would automatically satisfy the second, in supposedly having no impermissible effect of aiding religion.[19]

Second, the plurality apparently assumes as a fact that equal amounts of aid to religious and nonreligious schools will have exclusively secular and equal effects, on both external perception and on incentives to attend different schools. But there is no reason to believe that this will be the case; the effects of same-terms aid may not be confined to the secular sphere at all. This is the reason that we have long recognized that unrestricted aid to religious schools will support religious teaching in addition to secular education, a fact that would be true no matter what the supposedly secular purpose of the law might be.

Third, the plurality assumes that per capita distribution rules safeguard the same principles as independent, private choices. But that is clearly not so. We approved university scholarships in *Witters* because we found them close to giving a government employee a paycheck and allowing him to spend it as he chose, but a per capita aid program is a far cry from awarding scholarships to individuals, one of whom makes an independent private choice. Not the least of the significant differences between per capita aid and aid individually determined and directed is the right and genuine opportunity of the recipient to choose not to give the aid. To hold otherwise would be to license the government to donate

---

19. Adopting the plurality's rule would permit practically any government aid to religion so long as it could be supplied on terms ostensibly comparable to the terms under which aid was provided to nonreligious recipients. As a principle of constitutional sufficiency, the manipulability of this rule is breathtaking. A legislature would merely need to state a secular objective in order to legalize massive aid to all religions, one religion, or even one sect, to which its largess could be directed through the easy exercise of crafting facially neutral terms under which to offer aid favoring that religious group. Short of formally replacing the Establishment Clause, a more dependable key to the public fisc or a cleaner break with prior law would be difficult to imagine.

funds to churches based on the number of their members, on the patent fiction of independent private choice.

The plurality's mistaken assumptions explain and underscore its sharp break with the Framers' understanding of establishment and this Court's consistent interpretative course. Under the plurality's regime, little would be left of the right of conscience against compelled support for religion; the more massive the aid the more potent would be the influence of the government on the teaching mission; the more generous the support, the more divisive would be the resentments of those resisting religious support, and those religions without school systems ready to claim their fair share.

B

* * * The facts most obviously relevant to the Chapter 2 scheme in Jefferson Parish are those showing divertibility and actual diversion in the circumstance of pervasively sectarian religious schools. The type of aid, the structure of the program, and the lack of effective safeguards clearly demonstrate the divertibility of the aid. While little is known about its use, owing to the anemic enforcement system in the parish, even the thin record before us reveals that actual diversion occurred.

The aid that the government provided was highly susceptible to unconstitutional use. Much of the equipment provided under Chapter 2 was not of the type provided for individual students, but included "slide projectors, movie projectors, overhead projectors, television sets, tape recorders, projection screens, maps, globes, filmstrips, cassettes, computers," and computer software and peripherals, as well as library books and materials. The videocassette players, overhead projectors, and other instructional aids were of the sort that we have found can easily be used by religious teachers for religious purposes. *Meek*; *Wolman*. The same was true of the computers, which were as readily employable for religious teaching as the other equipment, and presumably as immune to any countervailing safeguard. * * *

* * *

The concern with divertibility thus predicated is underscored by the fact that the religious schools in question here covered the primary and secondary grades, the grades in which the sectarian nature of instruction is characteristically the most pervasive, and in which pupils are the least critical of the schools' religious objectives. * * * The threat to Establishment Clause values was accordingly at its highest in the circumstances of this case. Such precautionary features as there were in the Jefferson Parish scheme were grossly inadequate to counter the threat. To be sure, the disbursement of the aid was subject to statutory admonitions against diversion, and was supposedly subject to a variety of safeguards. But the provisions for onsite monitoring visits, labeling of government property, and government oversight cannot be accepted as sufficient in the face of record evidence that the safeguard provisions proved to be empty phrases in Jefferson Parish.

The plurality has already noted at length the ineffectiveness of the government's monitoring program. Monitors visited a nonpublic school only sporadically, discussed the program with a single contact person, observed nothing more than attempts at recordkeeping, and failed to inform the teachers of the restrictions involved. * * * Government officials themselves admitted that there was no way to tell whether instructional materials had been diverted, and, as the plurality notes, the only screening mechanism in the library book scheme was a review of titles by a single government official. The government did not even have a policy on the consequences of noncompliance.

The risk of immediate diversion of Chapter 2 benefits had its complement in the risk of future diversion, against which the Jefferson Parish program had absolutely no protection. By statute all purchases with Chapter 2 aid were to remain the property of the United States, merely being "lent" to the recipient nonpublic schools. In actuality, however, the record indicates that nothing in the Jefferson Parish program stood in the way of giving the Chapter 2 property outright to the religious schools when it became older. * * *

Providing such governmental aid without effective safeguards against future diversion itself offends the Establishment Clause, and even without evidence of actual diversion, our cases have repeatedly held that a "substantial risk" of it suffices to invalidate a government aid program on establishment grounds. A substantial risk of diversion in this case was more than clear, as the plurality has conceded. The First Amendment was violated.

But the record here goes beyond risk, to instances of actual diversion. What one would expect from such paltry efforts at monitoring and enforcement naturally resulted, and the record strongly suggests that other, undocumented diversions probably occurred as well. * * *

* * *

IV

* * * [T]here is no mistaking the abandonment of doctrine that would occur if the plurality were to become a majority. It is beyond question that the plurality's notion of evenhandedness neutrality as a practical guarantee of the validity of aid to sectarian schools would be the end of the principle of no aid to the schools' religious mission. And if that were not so obvious it would become so after reflecting on the plurality's thoughts about diversion and about giving attention to the pervasiveness of a school's sectarian teaching.

The plurality is candid in pointing out the extent of actual diversion of Chapter 2 aid to religious use in the case before us, and equally candid in saying it does not matter. To the plurality there is nothing wrong with aiding a school's religious mission; the only question is whether religious teaching obtains its tax support under a formally evenhanded criterion of distribution. The principle of no aid to religious teaching has no independent significance.

* * * [I]n rejecting the principle of no aid to a school's religious mission the plurality is attacking the most fundamental assumption underlying the Establishment Clause, that government can in fact operate with neutrality in its relation to religion. I believe that it can, and so respectfully dissent.

ZELMAN v. SIMMONS–HARRIS

Supreme Court of the United States, 2002.
536 U.S. 639, 122 S.Ct. 2460, 153 L.Ed.2d 604.

CHIEF JUSTICE REHNQUIST delivered the opinion of the Court.

The State of Ohio has established a pilot program designed to provide educational choices to families with children who reside in the Cleveland City School District. The question presented is whether this program offends the Establishment Clause of the United States Constitution. We hold that it does not.

There are more than 75,000 children enrolled in the Cleveland City School District. The majority of these children are from low-income and minority families. Few of these families enjoy the means to send their children to any school other than an inner-city public school. For more than a generation, however, Cleveland's public schools have been among the worst performing public schools in the Nation. In 1995, a Federal District Court declared a "crisis of magnitude" and placed the entire Cleveland school district under state control. Shortly thereafter, the state auditor found that Cleveland's public schools were in the midst of a "crisis that is perhaps unprecedented in the history of American education." The district had failed to meet any of the 18 state standards for minimal acceptable performance. Only 1 in 10 ninth graders could pass a basic proficiency examination, and students at all levels performed at a dismal rate compared with students in other Ohio public schools. More than two-thirds of high school students either dropped or failed out before graduation. Of those students who managed to reach their senior year, one of every four still failed to graduate. Of those students who did graduate, few could read, write, or compute at levels comparable to their counterparts in other cities.

It is against this backdrop that Ohio enacted, among other initiatives, its Pilot Project Scholarship Program. The program provides financial assistance to families in any Ohio school district that is or has been "under federal court order requiring supervision and operational management of the district by the state superintendent." Cleveland is the only Ohio school district to fall within that category.

The program provides two basic kinds of assistance to parents of children in a covered district. First, the program provides tuition aid for students in kindergarten through third grade, expanding each year through eighth grade, to attend a participating public or private school of their parent's choosing. Second, the program provides tutorial aid for students who choose to remain enrolled in public school.

The tuition aid portion of the program is designed to provide educational choices to parents who reside in a covered district. Any private school, whether religious or nonreligious, may participate in the program and accept program students so long as the school is located within the boundaries of a covered district and meets statewide educational standards. Participating private schools must agree not to discriminate on the basis of race, religion, or ethnic background, or to "advocate or foster unlawful behavior or teach hatred of any person or group on the basis of race, ethnicity, national origin, or religion." Any public school located in a school district adjacent to the covered district may also participate in the program. Adjacent public schools are eligible to receive a $2,250 tuition grant for each program student accepted in addition to the full amount of per-pupil state funding attributable to each additional student. All participating schools, whether public or private, are required to accept students in accordance with rules and procedures established by the state superintendent.

Tuition aid is distributed to parents according to financial need. Families with incomes below 200% of the poverty line are given priority and are eligible to receive 90% of private school tuition up to $2,250. For these lowest-income families, participating private schools may not charge a parental co-payment greater than $250. For all other families, the program pays 75% of tuition costs, up to $1,875, with no co-payment cap. These families receive tuition aid only if the number of available scholarships exceeds the number of low-income children who choose to participate. Where tuition aid is spent depends solely upon where parents who receive tuition aid choose to enroll their child. If parents choose a private school, checks are made payable to the parents who then endorse the checks over to the chosen school.

The tutorial aid portion of the program provides tutorial assistance through grants to any student in a covered district who chooses to remain in public school. Parents arrange for registered tutors to provide assistance to their children and then submit bills for those services to the State for payment. Students from low-income families receive 90% of the amount charged for such assistance up to $360. All other students receive 75% of that amount. The number of tutorial assistance grants offered to students in a covered district must equal the number of tuition aid scholarships provided to students enrolled at participating private or adjacent public schools.

The program has been in operation within the Cleveland City School District since the 1996–1997 school year. In the 1999–2000 school year, 56 private schools participated in the program, 46 (or 82%) of which had a religious affiliation. None of the public schools in districts adjacent to Cleveland have elected to participate. More than 3,700 students participated in the scholarship program, most of whom (96%) enrolled in religiously affiliated schools. Sixty percent of these students were from families at or below the poverty line. In the 1998–1999 school year, approximately 1,400 Cleveland public school students received tutorial aid. This number was expected to double during the 1999–2000 school year.

The program is part of a broader undertaking by the State to enhance the educational options of Cleveland's schoolchildren in response to the 1995 takeover. That undertaking includes programs governing community and magnet schools. Community schools are funded under state law but are run by their own school boards, not by local school districts. These schools enjoy academic independence to hire their own teachers and to determine their own curriculum. They can have no religious affiliation and are required to accept students by lottery. During the 1999–2000 school year, there were 10 start-up community schools in the Cleveland City School District with more than 1,900 students enrolled. For each child enrolled in a community school, the school receives state funding of $4,518, twice the funding a participating program school may receive.

Magnet schools are public schools operated by a local school board that emphasize a particular subject area, teaching method, or service to students. For each student enrolled in a magnet school, the school district receives $7,746, including state funding of $4,167, the same amount received per student enrolled at a traditional public school. As of 1999, parents in Cleveland were able to choose from among 23 magnet schools, which together enrolled more than 13,000 students in kindergarten through eighth grade. These schools provide specialized teaching methods, such as Montessori, or a particularized curriculum focus, such as foreign language, computers, or the arts.

* * *

In July 1999, respondents filed this action in United States District Court, seeking to enjoin the * * * program on the ground that it violated the Establishment Clause of the United States Constitution. * * * In December 1999, the District Court granted summary judgment for respondents. In December 2000, a divided panel of the Court of Appeals affirmed the judgment of the District Court, finding that the program had the "primary effect" of advancing religion in violation of the Establishment Clause. The Court of Appeals stayed its mandate pending disposition in this Court. We granted certiorari, and now reverse the Court of Appeals.

The Establishment Clause of the First Amendment, applied to the States through the Fourteenth Amendment, prevents a State from enacting laws that have the "purpose" or "effect" of advancing or inhibiting religion. There is no dispute that the program challenged here was enacted for the valid secular purpose of providing educational assistance to poor children in a demonstrably failing public school system. Thus, the question presented is whether the Ohio program nonetheless has the forbidden "effect" of advancing or inhibiting religion.

To answer that question, our decisions have drawn a consistent distinction between government programs that provide aid directly to religious schools, and programs of true private choice, in which government aid reaches religious schools only as a result of the genuine and independent choices of private individuals. While our jurisprudence with respect to the constitutionality of direct aid programs has "changed significantly" over the past two decades, our jurisprudence with respect to true private choice programs has remained consistent and unbroken. Three times we have confronted Establishment Clause challenges to neutral government programs that provide aid directly to a broad class of individuals, who, in turn, direct the aid to religious schools or institutions of their own choosing. Three times we have rejected such challenges.

In *Mueller,* we rejected an Establishment Clause challenge to a Minnesota program authorizing tax deductions for various educational expenses, including private school tuition costs, even though the great majority of the program's beneficiaries (96%) were parents of children in religious schools. We began by focusing on the class of beneficiaries, finding that because the class included "*all* parents," including parents with "children [who] attend nonsectarian private schools or sectarian private schools," the program was "not readily subject to challenge under the Establishment Clause." Then, viewing the program as a whole, we emphasized the principle of private choice, noting that public funds were made available to religious schools "only as a result of numerous, private choices of individual parents of school-age children." This, we said, ensured that " 'no imprimatur of state approval' can be deemed to have been conferred on any particular religion, or on religion generally." We thus found it irrelevant to the constitutional inquiry that the vast majority of beneficiaries were parents of children in religious schools * * *.

That the program was one of true private choice, with no evidence that the State deliberately skewed incentives toward religious schools, was sufficient for the program to survive scrutiny under the Establishment Clause.

In *Witters,* we used identical reasoning to reject an Establishment Clause challenge to a vocational scholarship program that provided tuition aid to a student studying at a religious institution to become a pastor. Looking at the program as a whole, we observed that "[a]ny aid . . . that ultimately flows to religious institutions does so only as a result of the genuinely independent and private choices of aid recipients." We further remarked that, as in *Mueller,* "[the] program is made available generally without regard to the sectarian-nonsectarian, or public-nonpublic nature of the institution benefited." * * *

Five Members of the Court, in separate opinions, emphasized the general rule from *Mueller* that the amount of government aid channeled to religious institutions by individual aid recipients was not relevant to the constitutional inquiry. Our holding thus rested not on whether few or many recipients chose to expend government aid at a religious school but, rather, on whether recipients generally were empowered to direct the aid to schools or institutions of their own choosing.

Finally, in *Zobrest,* we applied *Mueller* and *Witters* to reject an Establishment Clause challenge to a federal program that permitted sign-language interpreters to assist deaf children enrolled in religious schools. Reviewing our earlier decisions, we stated that "government programs that neutrally provide benefits to a broad class of citizens defined without reference to religion are not readily subject to an Establishment Clause challenge." * * *

We further observed that "[b]y according parents freedom to select a school of their choice, the statute ensures that a government-paid interpreter will be present in a sectarian school only as a result of the private decision of individual parents." Our focus again was on neutrality and the principle of private choice, not on the number of program beneficiaries attending religious schools. Because the program ensured that parents were the ones to select a religious school as the best learning environment for their handicapped child, the circuit between government and religion was broken, and the Establishment Clause was not implicated.

Mueller, Witters, and *Zobrest* thus make clear that where a government aid program is neutral with respect to religion, and provides assistance directly to a broad class of citizens who, in turn, direct government aid to religious schools wholly as a result of their own genuine and independent private choice, the program is not readily subject to challenge under the Establishment Clause. A program that shares these features permits government aid to reach religious institutions only by way of the deliberate choices of numerous individual recipients. The incidental advancement of a religious mission, or the perceived endorsement of a religious message, is reasonably attributable to the individual recipient, not to the government, whose role ends with the disbursement of benefits. * * *

* * * It is precisely for these reasons that we have never found a program of true private choice to offend the Establishment Clause.

We believe that the program challenged here is a program of true private choice, consistent with *Mueller, Witters,* and *Zobrest,* and thus constitutional. As was true in those cases, the Ohio program is neutral in all respects toward religion. It is part of a general and multifaceted undertaking by the State of Ohio to provide educational opportunities to the children of a failed school district. It confers educational assistance directly to a broad class of individuals defined without reference to religion, *i.e.,* any parent of a school-age child who resides in the Cleveland City School District. The program permits the participation of *all* schools within the district, religious or nonreligious. Adjacent public schools also may participate and have a financial incentive to do so. Program benefits are available to participating families on neutral terms, with no reference to religion. The only preference stated anywhere in the program is a preference for low-income families, who receive greater assistance and are given priority for admission at participating schools.

There are no "financial incentive[s]" that "ske[w]" the program toward religious schools. Such incentives "[are] not present ... where the aid is allocated on the basis of neutral, secular criteria that neither favor nor disfavor religion, and is made available to both religious and secular beneficiaries on a nondiscriminatory basis." *Agostini*. The program here in fact creates financial *dis*incentives for religious schools, with private schools receiving only half the government assistance given to community schools and one-third the assistance given to magnet schools. Adjacent public schools, should any choose to accept program students, are also eligible to receive two to three times the state funding of a private religious school. Families too have a financial disincentive to choose a private religious school over other schools. Parents that choose to participate in the scholarship program and then to enroll their children in a private school (religious or nonreligious) must copay a portion of the school's tuition. Families that choose a community school, magnet school, or traditional public school pay nothing. Although such features of the program are not necessary to its constitutionality, they clearly dispel the claim that the program "creates ... financial incentive[s] for parents to choose a sectarian school." *Zobrest*.

Respondents suggest that even without a financial incentive for parents to choose a religious school, the program creates a "public perception that the State is endorsing religious practices and beliefs." But we have repeatedly recognized that no reasonable observer would think a neutral program of private choice, where state aid reaches religious schools solely as a result of the numerous independent decisions of private individuals, carries with it the *imprimatur* of government endorsement. The argument is particularly misplaced here since "the reasonable observer in the endorsement inquiry must be deemed aware" of the "history and context" underlying a challenged program. *Good News Club v. Milford Central School.* * * * Any objective observer familiar with the full history and context of the Ohio program would reasonably view it as one aspect of a broader undertaking to assist poor children in failed schools, not as an endorsement of religious schooling in general.

There also is no evidence that the program fails to provide genuine opportunities for Cleveland parents to select secular educational options for their school-age children. Cleveland schoolchildren enjoy a range of educational choices: They may remain in public school as before, remain in public school with publicly funded tutoring aid, obtain a scholarship and choose a religious school, obtain a scholarship and choose a nonreligious private school, enroll in a community school, or enroll in a magnet school. That 46 of the 56 private schools now participating in the program are religious schools does not condemn it as a violation of the Establishment Clause. The Establishment Clause question is whether Ohio is coercing parents into sending their children to religious schools, and that question must be answered by evaluating *all* options Ohio provides Cleveland schoolchildren, only one of which is to obtain a program scholarship and then choose a religious school.

Justice Souter speculates that because more private religious schools currently participate in the program, the program itself must somehow discourage the participation of private nonreligious schools. But Cleveland's preponderance of religiously affiliated private schools certainly did not arise as a result of the program; it is a phenomenon common to many American cities. Indeed, by all accounts the program has captured a remarkable cross-section of private schools, religious and nonreligious. It is true that 82% of Cleveland's participating private schools are religious schools, but it is also true that 81% of private schools in Ohio are religious schools. To attribute constitutional significance to this figure, moreover, would lead to the absurd result that a neutral school-choice program might be permissible in some parts of Ohio, such as Columbus, where a lower percentage of private schools are religious schools, but not in inner-city Cleveland, where Ohio has deemed such programs most sorely needed, but where the preponderance of religious schools happens to be greater. * * *

Respondents and Justice Souter claim that even if we do not focus on the number of participating schools that are religious schools, we should attach constitutional significance to the fact that 96% of scholarship recipients have enrolled in religious schools. They claim that this alone proves parents lack genuine choice, even if no parent has ever said so. We need not consider this argument in detail, since it was flatly rejected in *Mueller,* where we found it irrelevant that 96% of parents taking deductions for tuition expenses paid tuition at religious schools. * * * The constitutionality of a neutral educational aid program simply does not turn on whether and why, in a particular area, at a particular time, most private schools are run by religious organizations, or most recipients choose to use the aid at a religious school. * * *

This point is aptly illustrated here. The 96% figure upon which respondents and Justice Souter rely discounts entirely (1) the more than 1,900 Cleveland children enrolled in alternative community schools, (2) the more than 13,000 children enrolled in alternative magnet schools, and (3) the more than 1,400 children enrolled in traditional public schools with tutorial assistance. Including some or all of these children in the denominator of children enrolled in nontraditional schools during the 1999–2000 school year drops the percentage enrolled in religious schools from 96% to under 20%. The 96% figure also represents but a snapshot of one particular school year. In the 1997–1998 school year, by contrast, only 78% of scholarship recipients attended religious schools. The difference was attributable to two private nonreligious schools that had accepted 15% of all scholarship students electing instead to register as community schools, in light of larger per-pupil funding for community schools and the uncertain future of the scholarship program generated by this litigation. Many of the students enrolled in these schools as scholarship students remained enrolled as community school students, thus demonstrating the arbitrariness of counting one type of school but not the other to assess primary effect. * * *

Respondents finally claim that we should look to *Committee for Public Ed. & Religious Liberty v. Nyquist*, 413 U.S. 756, 93 S.Ct. 2955, 37 L.Ed.2d 948 (1973), to decide these cases. We disagree for two reasons. First, the program in *Nyquist* was quite different from the program challenged here. *Nyquist* involved a New York program that gave a package of benefits exclusively to private schools and the parents of private school enrollees. Although the program was enacted for ostensibly secular purposes, we found that its "function" was "*unmistakably* to provide desired financial support for nonpublic, sectarian institutions." Its genesis, we said, was that private religious schools faced "increasingly grave fiscal problems." The program thus provided direct money grants to religious schools. It provided tax benefits "unrelated to the amount of money actually expended by any parent on tuition," ensuring a windfall to parents of children in religious schools. It similarly provided tuition reimbursements designed explicitly to "offe[r] . . . an incentive to parents to send their children to sectarian schools." Indeed, the program flatly prohibited the participation of any public school, or parent of any public school enrollee. Ohio's program shares none of these features.

Second, were there any doubt that the program challenged in *Nyquist* is far removed from the program challenged here, we expressly reserved judgment with respect to "a case involving some form of public assistance (*e.g.*, scholarships) made available generally without regard to the sectarian-nonsectarian, or public-nonpublic nature of the institution benefited." That, of course, is the very question now before us * * *. To the extent the scope of *Nyquist* has remained an open question in light of * * * later decisions, we now hold that *Nyquist* does not govern neutral educational assistance programs that, like the program here, offer aid directly to a broad class of individual recipients defined without regard to religion.

In sum, the Ohio program is entirely neutral with respect to religion. It provides benefits directly to a wide spectrum of individuals, defined only by financial need and residence in a particular school district. It permits such individuals to exercise genuine choice among options public and private, secular and religious. The program is therefore a program of true private choice. In keeping with an unbroken line of decisions rejecting challenges to similar programs, we hold that the program does not offend the Establishment Clause.

The judgment of the Court of Appeals is reversed.

JUSTICE O'CONNOR, concurring.

The Court holds that Ohio's Pilot Project Scholarship Program, survives respondents' Establishment Clause challenge. While I join the Court's opinion, I write separately for two reasons. First, although the Court takes an important step, I do not believe that today's decision, when considered in light of other longstanding government programs that impact religious organizations and our prior Establishment Clause jurisprudence, marks a dramatic break from the past. Second, given the emphasis the Court places on verifying that parents of voucher students in religious schools have exercised "true private choice," I think it is worth elaborating on the Court's conclusion that this inquiry should consider all reasonable educational alternatives to religious schools that are available to parents. To do otherwise is to ignore how the educational system in Cleveland actually functions.

I

These cases are different from prior indirect aid cases in part because a significant portion of the funds appropriated for the voucher program reach religious schools without restrictions on the use of these funds. The share of public resources that reach religious schools is not, however, as significant as respondents suggest. Data from the 1999–2000 school year indicate that 82 percent of schools participating in the voucher program were religious and that 96 percent of participating students enrolled in religious schools (46 of 56 private schools in the program are religiously-affiliated; 3,637 of 3,765 voucher students attend religious private schools), but these data are incomplete. These statistics do not take into account all of the reasonable educational choices that may be available to students in Cleveland public schools. When one considers the option to attend community schools, the percentage of students enrolled in religious schools falls to 62.1 percent. If magnet schools are included in the mix, this percentage falls to 16.5 percent.

Even these numbers do not paint a complete picture. The Cleveland program provides voucher applicants from low-income families with up to $2,250 in tuition assistance and provides the remaining applicants with up to $1,875 in tuition assistance. In contrast, the State provides community schools $4,518 per pupil and magnet schools, on average, $7,097 per pupil. Even if one assumes that all voucher students came from low-income families and that each voucher student used up the entire $2,250 voucher, at most $8.2 million of public funds flowed to religious schools under the voucher program in 1999–2000. Although just over one-half as many students attended community schools as religious private schools on the state fisc, the State spent over $1 million more— $9.4 million—on students in community schools than on students in religious private schools because per-pupil aid to community schools is more than double the per-pupil aid to private schools under the voucher program. Moreover, the amount spent on religious private schools is minor compared to the $114.8 million the State spent on students in the Cleveland magnet schools.

* * *

II

Nor does today's decision signal a major departure from this Court's prior Establishment Clause jurisprudence. A central tool in our analysis of cases in this area has been the *Lemon* test. As originally formulated, a statute passed this test only if it had "a secular legislative purpose," if its "principal or primary effect" was one that "neither advance[d] nor inhibit [ed] religion," and if it did "not foster an excessive government entanglement with religion." In *Agostini*, we folded the entanglement inquiry into the primary effect inquiry. This made sense because both inquiries rely on the same evidence, and the degree of entanglement has implications for whether a statute advances or inhibits religion. The test today is basically the same as that set forth in *School Dist. of Abington Township v. Schempp* * * *, over 40 years ago.

The Court's opinion in these cases focuses on a narrow question related to the *Lemon* test: how to apply the primary effects prong in indirect aid cases? Specifically, it clarifies the basic inquiry when trying to determine whether a program that distributes aid to beneficiaries, rather than directly to service providers, has the primary effect of advancing or inhibiting religion, or as I have put it, of "endors[ing] or disapprov[ing] ... religion." Courts are instructed to consider two factors: first, whether the program administers aid in a neutral fashion, without differentiation based on the religious status of beneficiaries or providers of services; second, and more importantly, whether beneficiaries of indirect aid have a genuine choice among religious and nonreligious organizations when determining the organization to which they will direct that aid. If the answer to either query is "no," the program should be struck down under the Establishment Clause.

* * *

III

There is little question in my mind that the Cleveland voucher program is neutral as between religious schools and nonreligious schools. Justice Souter rejects the Court's notion of neutrality, proposing that the neutrality of a program should be gauged not by the opportunities it presents but rather by its effects. In particular, a "neutrality test ... [should] focus on a category of aid that may be directed to religious as well as secular schools, and ask whether the scheme favors a religious direction." Justice Souter doubts that the Cleveland program is neutral under this view. He surmises that the cap on tuition that voucher schools may charge low-income students encourages these students to attend religious rather than nonreligious private voucher schools. But Justice Souter's notion of neutrality is inconsistent with that in our case law. As we put it in *Agostini,* government aid must be "made available to both religious and secular beneficiaries on a nondiscriminatory basis."

I do not agree that the nonreligious schools have failed to provide Cleveland parents reasonable alternatives to religious schools in the voucher program. For nonreligious schools to qualify as genuine options for parents, they need not be superior to religious schools in every respect. They need only be adequate substitutes for religious schools in the eyes of parents. The District Court record demonstrates that nonreligious schools were able to compete effectively with Catholic and other religious schools in the Cleveland voucher program. The best evidence of this is that many parents with vouchers selected nonreligious private schools over religious alternatives and an even larger number of parents send their children to community and magnet schools rather than seeking vouchers at all. Moreover, there is no record evidence that any voucher-eligible student was turned away from a nonreligious private school in the voucher program, let alone a community or magnet school.

* * *

Justice Souter * * * claims that, of the 10 community schools operating in Cleveland during the 1999–2000 school year, 4 were unavailable to students with vouchers and 4 others reported poor test scores. But that analysis unreasonably limits the choices available to Cleveland parents. It is undisputed that Cleveland's 24 magnet schools are reasonable alternatives to voucher schools. And of the four community schools Justice Souter claims are unavailable to voucher students, he is correct only about one. Justice Souter rejects the three other community schools (Horizon Science Academy, Cleveland Alternative Learning, and International Preparatory School) because they did not offer primary school classes, were targeted towards poor students or students with disciplinary or academic problems, or were not in operation for a year. But a community school need not offer primary school classes to be an alternative to religious middle schools, and catering to impoverished or otherwise challenged students may make a school more attractive to certain inner-city parents. * * *

Of the six community schools that Justice Souter admits as alternatives to the voucher program in 1999–2000, he notes that four (the Broadway, Cathedral, Chapelside, and Lincoln Park campuses of the Hope Academy) reported lower test scores than public schools during the school year *after* the District Court's grant of summary judgment to respondents, according to report cards prepared by the Ohio Department of Education. These report cards underestimate the value of the four Hope Academy schools. Before they entered the community school program, two of them participated in the voucher program. Although they received far less state funding in that capacity, they had among the highest rates of parental satisfaction of all voucher schools, religious or nonreligious. This is particularly impressive given that a Harvard University study found that the Hope Academy schools attracted the "poorest and most educationally disadvantaged students." Moreover, Justice Souter's evaluation of the Hope Academy schools assumes that the only relevant measure of school quality is academic performance. It is reasonable to suppose, however, that parents in the inner city also choose schools that provide discipline and a safe environment for their children. On these dimensions some of the schools that Justice Souter derides have performed quite ably.

* * * [T]he goal of the Court's Establishment Clause jurisprudence is to determine whether, after the Cleveland voucher program was enacted, parents were free to direct state educational aid in either a nonreligious or religious direction. That inquiry requires an evaluation of all reasonable educational options Ohio provides the Cleveland school system, regardless of whether they are formally made available in the same section of the Ohio Code as the voucher program.

Based on the reasoning in the Court's opinion, which is consistent with the realities of the Cleveland educational system, I am persuaded that the Cleveland voucher program affords parents of eligible children genuine nonreligious options and is consistent with the Establishment Clause.

JUSTICE THOMAS, concurring.

Frederick Douglass once said that "[e]ducation . . . means emancipation. It means light and liberty. It means the uplifting of the soul of man into the glorious light of truth, the light by which men can only be made free." Today many of our inner-city public schools deny emancipation to urban minority students. Despite this Court's observation nearly 50 years ago in *Brown v. Board of Education,* that "it is doubtful that any child may reasonably be expected to succeed in life if he is denied the opportunity of an education," urban children have been forced into a system that continually fails them. These cases present an example of such failures. Besieged by escalating financial problems and declining academic achievement, the Cleveland City School District was in the midst of an academic emergency when Ohio enacted its scholarship program.

The dissents and respondents wish to invoke the Establishment Clause of the First Amendment, as incorporated through the Fourteenth, to constrain a State's neutral efforts to provide greater educational opportunity for underprivileged minority students. Today's decision properly upholds the program as constitutional, and I join it in full.

I

* * * I agree with the Court that Ohio's program easily passes muster under our stringent test, but, as a matter of first principles, I question whether this test should be applied to the States.

The Establishment Clause of the First Amendment states that "Congress shall make no law respecting an establishment of religion." On its face, this provision places no limit on the States with regard to religion. The Establishment Clause originally protected States, and by extension their citizens, from the imposition of an established religion by the Federal Government. Whether and how this Clause should constrain state action under the Fourteenth Amendment is a more difficult question.

The Fourteenth Amendment fundamentally restructured the relationship between individuals and the States and ensured that States would not deprive citizens of liberty without due process of law. * * *

When rights are incorporated against the States through the Fourteenth Amendment they should advance, not constrain, individual liberty.

Consequently, in the context of the Establishment Clause, it may well be that state action should be evaluated on different terms than similar action by the Federal Government. "States, while bound to observe strict neutrality, should be freer to experiment with involvement [in religion]—on a neutral basis—than the Federal Government." *Walz v. Tax Comm'n of City of New York,* 397 U.S. 664, 699, 90 S.Ct. 1409, 25 L.Ed.2d 697 (1970) (Harlan, J., concurring). Thus, while the Federal Government may "make no law respecting an establishment of religion," the States may pass laws that include or touch on religious matters so long as these laws do not impede free exercise rights or any other individual religious liberty interest. * * *

Whatever the textual and historical merits of incorporating the Establishment Clause, I can accept that the Fourteenth Amendment protects religious liberty rights. But I cannot accept its use to oppose neutral programs of school choice through the incorporation of the Establishment Clause. There would be a tragic irony in converting the Fourteenth Amendment's guarantee of individual liberty into a prohibition on the exercise of educational choice.

II

The wisdom of allowing States greater latitude in dealing with matters of religion and education can be easily appreciated in this context. Respondents advocate using the Fourteenth Amendment to handcuff the State's ability to experiment with education. But without education one can hardly exercise the civic, political, and personal freedoms conferred by the Fourteenth Amendment. Faced with a severe educational crisis, the State of Ohio enacted wide-ranging educational reform that allows voluntary participation of private and religious schools in educating poor urban children otherwise condemned to failing public schools. The program does not force any individual to submit to religious indoctrination or education. It simply gives parents a greater choice as to where and in what manner to educate their children. This is a choice that those with greater means have routinely exercised.

* * *

While the romanticized ideal of universal public education resonates with the cognoscenti who oppose vouchers, poor urban families just want the best education for their children, who will certainly need it to function in our high-tech and advanced society. * * * An individual's life prospects increase dramatically with each successfully completed phase of education. * * *

* * *

Ten States have enacted some form of publicly funded private school choice as one means of raising the quality of education provided to underprivileged urban children. These programs address the root of the problem with failing urban public schools that disproportionately affect minority students. Society's other solution to these educational failures is often to provide racial preferences in higher education. Such preferences, however, run afoul of the Fourteenth Amendment's prohibition against distinctions based on race. By contrast, school choice programs that involve religious schools appear unconstitutional only to those who would twist the Fourteenth Amendment against itself by expansively incorporating the Establishment Clause. Converting the Fourteenth Amendment from a guarantee of opportunity to an obstacle against education reform distorts our constitutional values and disserves those in the greatest need.

As Frederick Douglass poignantly noted "no greater benefit can be bestowed upon a long benighted people, than giving to them, as we are here earnestly this day endeavoring to do, the means of an education."

JUSTICE STEVENS, dissenting.

Is a law that authorizes the use of public funds to pay for the indoctrination of thousands of grammar school children in particular religious faiths a "law respecting an establishment of religion" within the meaning of the First Amendment? In answering that question, I think we should ignore three factual matters that are discussed at length by my colleagues.

First, the severe educational crisis that confronted the Cleveland City School District when Ohio enacted its voucher program is not a matter that should affect our appraisal of its constitutionality. In the 1999–2000 school year, that program provided relief to less than five percent of the students enrolled in the district's schools. The solution to the disastrous conditions that prevented over 90 percent of the student body from meeting basic proficiency standards obviously required massive improvements unrelated to the voucher program. Of course, the emergency may have given some families a powerful motivation to leave the public school system and accept religious indoctrination that they would otherwise have avoided, but that is not a valid reason for upholding the program.

Second, the wide range of choices that have been made available to students *within the public school system* has no bearing on the question whether the State may pay the tuition for students who wish to reject public education entirely and attend private schools that will provide them with a sectarian education. The fact that the vast majority of the voucher recipients who have entirely rejected public education receive religious indoctrination at state expense does, however, support the claim that the law is one "respecting an establishment of religion." The State may choose to divide up its public schools into a dozen different options and label them magnet schools, community schools, or whatever else it decides to call them, but the State is still required to provide a public education and it is the State's decision to fund private school education over and above its traditional obligation that is at issue in these cases.

Third, the voluntary character of the private choice to prefer a parochial education over an education in the public school system seems to me quite irrelevant to the question whether the government's choice to pay for religious indoctrination is constitutionally permissible. Today, however, the Court seems to have decided that the mere fact that a family that cannot afford a private education wants its children educated in a parochial school is a sufficient justification for this use of public funds.

For the reasons stated by Justice Souter and Justice Breyer, I am convinced that the Court's decision is profoundly misguided. Admittedly, in reaching that conclusion I have been influenced by my understanding of the impact of religious strife on the decisions of our forbears to migrate to this continent, and on the decisions of neighbors in the Balkans, Northern Ireland, and the Middle East to mistrust one another. Whenever we remove a brick from the wall that was designed to separate religion and government, we increase the risk of religious strife and weaken the foundation of our democracy.

I respectfully dissent.

JUSTICE SOUTER, with whom JUSTICE STEVENS, JUSTICE GINSBURG, and JUSTICE BREYER join, dissenting.

The Court's majority holds that the Establishment Clause is no bar to Ohio's payment of tuition at private religious elementary and middle schools under a scheme that systematically provides tax money to support the schools' religious missions. The occasion for the legislation thus upheld is the condition of public education in the city of Cleveland. The record indicates that the schools are failing to serve their objective, and the vouchers in issue here are said to be needed to provide adequate alternatives to them. If there were an excuse for giving short shrift to the Establishment Clause, it would probably apply here. But there is no excuse. Constitutional limitations are placed on government to preserve constitutional values in hard cases, like these. * * * I therefore respectfully dissent.

* * *

* * * [T]he majority holds that the Establishment Clause is not offended by Ohio's Pilot Project Scholarship Program, under which students may be eligible to receive as much as $2,250 in the form of tuition vouchers transferable to religious schools. In the city of Cleveland the overwhelming proportion of large appropriations for voucher money must be spent on religious schools if it is to be spent at all, and will be spent in amounts that cover almost all of tuition. The money will thus pay for eligible students' instruction not only in secular subjects but in religion as well, in schools that can fairly be characterized as founded to teach religious doctrine and to imbue teaching in all subjects with a religious dimension. Public tax money will pay at a systemic level for teaching the covenant with Israel and Mosaic law in Jewish schools, the primacy of the Apostle Peter and the Papacy in Catholic schools, the

truth of reformed Christianity in Protestant schools, and the revelation to the Prophet in Muslim schools, to speak only of major religious groupings in the Republic.

How can a Court consistently leave *Everson* on the books and approve the Ohio vouchers? The answer is that it cannot. It is only by ignoring *Everson* that the majority can claim to rest on traditional law in its invocation of neutral aid provisions and private choice to sanction the Ohio law. It is, moreover, only by ignoring the meaning of neutrality and private choice themselves that the majority can even pretend to rest today's decision on those criteria.

I

The majority's statements of Establishment Clause doctrine cannot be appreciated without some historical perspective on the Court's announced limitations on government aid to religious education, and its repeated repudiation of limits previously set. * * *

Viewed with the necessary generality, the cases can be categorized in three groups. In the period from 1947 to 1968, the basic principle of no aid to religion through school benefits was unquestioned. Thereafter for some 15 years, the Court termed its efforts as attempts to draw a line against aid that would be divertible to support the religious, as distinct from the secular, activity of an institutional beneficiary. Then, starting in 1983, concern with divertibility was gradually lost in favor of approving aid in amounts unlikely to afford substantial benefits to religious schools, when offered evenhandedly without regard to a recipient's religious character, and when channeled to a religious institution only by the genuinely free choice of some private individual. Now, the three stages are succeeded by a fourth, in which the substantial character of government aid is held to have no constitutional significance, and the espoused criteria of neutrality in offering aid, and private choice in directing it, are shown to be nothing but examples of verbal formalism.

A

Everson v. Board of Ed. of Ewing inaugurated the modern development of Establishment Clause doctrine * * *. Although the Court split, no Justice disagreed with the basic doctrinal principle already quoted, that "[n]o tax in any amount . . . can be levied to support any religious activities or institutions, . . . whatever form they may adopt to teach . . . religion." Nor did any Member of the Court deny the tension between the New Jersey program and the aims of the Establishment Clause. The majority upheld the state law on the strength of rights of religious-school students under the Free Exercise Clause, which was thought to entitle them to free public transportation when offered as a "general government servic[e]" to all schoolchildren. Despite the indirect benefit to religious education, the transportation was simply treated like "ordinary police and fire protection, connections for sewage disposal, public highways and sidewalks," and, most significantly, "state-paid policemen, detailed to protect children going to and from church schools from the very real hazards of traffic." The dissenters, however, found the benefit to religion too pronounced to survive the general principle of no establishment, no aid, and they described it as running counter to every objective served by the establishment ban * * *.

The difficulty of drawing a line that preserved the basic principle of no aid was no less obvious some 20 years later in *Board of Ed. of Central School Dist. No. 1 v. Allen,* which upheld a New York law authorizing local school boards to lend textbooks in secular subjects to children attending religious schools, a result not self-evident from *Everson's* "general government services" rationale. The Court relied instead on the theory that the in-kind aid could only be used for secular educational purposes, and found it relevant that "no funds or books are furnished [directly] to parochial schools, and the financial benefit is to parents and children, not to schools." * * *

Transcending even the sharp disagreement [between the majority and the dissent], however, was "the consistency in the way the Justices went about deciding the case.... Neither side rested on any facile application of the 'test' or any simplistic reliance on the generality or evenhandedness of the state law. Disagreement concentrated on the true intent inferrable behind the law, the feasibility of distinguishing in fact between religious and secular teaching in church schools, and the reality or sham of lending books to pupils instead of supplying books to schools.... [T]he stress was on the practical significance of the actual benefits received by the schools."

B

Allen recognized the reality that "religious schools pursue two goals, religious instruction and secular education," * * * if state aid could be restricted to serve the second, it might be permissible under the Establishment Clause. But in the retrenchment that followed, the Court saw that the two educational functions were so intertwined in religious primary and secondary schools that aid to secular education could not readily be segregated, and the intrusive monitoring required to enforce the line itself raised Establishment Clause concerns about the entanglement of church and state. To avoid the entanglement, the Court's focus in the post-*Allen* cases was on the principle of divertibility, on discerning when ostensibly secular government aid to religious schools was susceptible to religious uses. The greater the risk of diversion to religion (and the monitoring necessary to avoid it), the less legitimate the aid scheme was under the no-aid principle. * * *

The fact that the Court's suspicion of divertibility reflected a concern with the substance of the no-aid principle is apparent in its rejection of stratagems invented to dodge it. In *Committee for Public Ed. & Religious Liberty v. Nyquist,* 413 U.S. 756, 93 S.Ct. 2955, 37 L.Ed.2d 948 (1973), for example, the Court struck down a New York program of tuition grants for poor parents and tax deductions for more affluent ones who sent their children to private schools. The *Nyquist* Court dismissed warranties of a "statistical guarantee," that the scheme provided at most 15% of the total cost of an education at a religious school, which could presumably be matched to a secular 15% of a child's education at the school. And it rejected the idea that the path of state aid to religious schools might be dispositive: "far from providing a *per se* immunity from examination of the substance of the State's program, the fact that aid is disbursed to parents rather than to the schools is only one among many factors to be considered." The point was that "the effect of the aid is unmistakably to provide desired financial support for nonpublic, sectarian institutions." *Nyquist* thus held that aid to parents through tax deductions was no different from forbidden direct aid to religious schools for religious uses. The focus remained on what the public money bought when it reached the end point of its disbursement.

C

Like all criteria requiring judicial assessment of risk, divertibility is an invitation to argument, but the object of the arguments provoked has always been a realistic assessment of facts aimed at respecting the principle of no aid. In *Mueller v. Allen*, however, that object began to fade, for *Mueller* started down the road from realism to formalism.

The aid in *Mueller* was in substance indistinguishable from that in *Nyquist,* and both were substantively difficult to distinguish from aid directly to religious schools. But the Court upheld the Minnesota tax deductions in *Mueller,* emphasizing their neutral availability for religious and secular educational expenses and the role of private choice in taking them. The Court relied on the same two principles in *Witters,* approving one student's use of a vocational training subsidy for the blind at a religious college, characterizing it as aid to individuals from which religious schools could derive no "large" benefit: "the full benefits of the program [are not] limited, in large part or in whole, to students at sectarian institutions."

School Dist. of Grand Rapids v. Ball, overruled in part by *Agostini,* clarified that the notions of evenhandedness neutrality and private choice in *Mueller* did not apply to cases involving direct aid to religious schools, which were still subject to the divertibility test. But in *Agostini,* where the substance of the aid was identical to that in *Ball,* public employees teaching remedial secular classes in private schools, the Court rejected the 30–year–old presumption of divertibility, and instead found it sufficient that the aid "supplement[ed]" but did not "supplant" existing educational services. * * *

In the 12 years between *Ball* and *Agostini,* the Court decided not only *Witters,* but two other cases emphasizing the form of neutrality and private choice over the substance of aid to religious uses, but always in circumstances where any aid to religion was isolated and insubstantial. *Zobrest,* like *Witters,* involved one student's choice to spend funds from a general public program at a religious school (to pay for a sign-language interpreter). * * * *Rosenberger v. Rector and Visitors of Univ. of Va.,* 515

U.S. 819, 115 S.Ct. 2510, 132 L.Ed.2d 700 (1995), like *Zobrest* and *Witters,* involved an individual and insubstantial use of neutrally available public funds for a religious purpose (to print an evangelical magazine).

To be sure, the aid in *Agostini* was systemic and arguably substantial, but, as I have said, the majority there chose to view it as a bare "supplement." And this was how the controlling opinion described the systemic aid in our most recent case, *Mitchell v. Helms,* as aid going merely to a "portion" of the religious schools' budgets. The plurality in that case did not feel so uncomfortable about jettisoning substance entirely in favor of form, finding it sufficient that the aid was neutral and that there was virtual private choice, since any aid "first passes through the hands (literally or figuratively) of numerous private citizens who are free to direct the aid elsewhere." But that was only the plurality view.

Hence it seems fair to say that it was not until today that substantiality of aid has clearly been rejected as irrelevant by a majority of this Court, just as it has not been until today that a majority, not a plurality, has held purely formal criteria to suffice for scrutinizing aid that ends up in the coffers of religious schools. Today's cases are notable for their stark illustration of the inadequacy of the majority's chosen formal analysis.

II

Although it has taken half a century since *Everson* to reach the majority's twin standards of neutrality and free choice, the facts show that, in the majority's hands, even these criteria cannot convincingly legitimize the Ohio scheme.

A

Consider first the criterion of neutrality. As recently as two Terms ago, a majority of the Court recognized that neutrality conceived of as evenhandedness toward aid recipients had never been treated as alone sufficient to satisfy the Establishment Clause, *Mitchell* (O'Connor, J., concurring in judgment); *id.* (Souter, J., dissenting). But at least in its limited significance, formal neutrality seemed to serve some purpose. Today, however, the majority employs the neutrality criterion in a way that renders it impossible to understand.

Neutrality in this sense refers, of course, to evenhandedness in setting eligibility as between potential religious and secular recipients of public money.[6] Thus, for example, the aid scheme in *Witters* provided an

---

6. Justice O'Connor apparently no longer distinguishes between this notion of evenhandedness neutrality and the free-exercise neutrality in *Everson.* Compare *ante,* at 2476 (concurring opinion), with *Mitchell,* 530 U.S., at 839, 120 S.Ct. 2530 (opinion concurring in judgment) ("Even if we at one time used the term 'neutrality' in a descriptive sense to refer to those aid programs characterized by the requisite equipoise between support of religion and antagonism to religion, Justice Souter's discussion convincingly demonstrates that the evolution in the meaning of the term

eligible recipient with a scholarship to be used at any institution within a practically unlimited universe of schools; it did not tend to provide more or less aid depending on which one the scholarship recipient chose, and there was no indication that the maximum scholarship amount would be insufficient at secular schools. * * *

In order to apply the neutrality test, then, it makes sense to focus on a category of aid that may be directed to religious as well as secular schools, and ask whether the scheme favors a religious direction. Here, one would ask whether the voucher provisions, allowing for as much as $2,250 toward private school tuition (or a grant to a public school in an adjacent district), were written in a way that skewed the scheme toward benefiting religious schools.

This, however, is not what the majority asks. The majority looks not to the provisions for tuition vouchers, but to every provision for educational opportunity * * *. The majority then finds confirmation that "participation of *all* schools" satisfies neutrality by noting that the better part of total state educational expenditure goes to public schools, thus showing there is no favor of religion.

The illogic is patent. If regular, public schools (which can get no voucher payments) "participate" in a voucher scheme with schools that can, and public expenditure is still predominantly on public schools, then the majority's reasoning would find neutrality in a scheme of vouchers available for private tuition in districts with no secular private schools at all. "Neutrality" as the majority employs the term is, literally, verbal and nothing more. This, indeed, is the only way the majority can gloss over the very nonneutral feature of the total scheme covering "*all* schools": public tutors may receive from the State no more than $324 per child to support extra tutoring (that is, the State's 90% of a total amount of $360), whereas the tuition voucher schools (which turn out to be mostly religious) can receive up to $2,250.[7]

Why the majority does not simply accept the fact that the challenge here is to the more generous voucher scheme and judge its neutrality in relation to religious use of voucher money seems very odd. It seems odd, that is, until one recognizes that comparable schools for applying the criterion of neutrality are also the comparable schools for applying the

---

in our jurisprudence is cause to hesitate before equating the neutrality of recent decisions with the neutrality of old").

7. The majority's argument that public school students within the program "direct almost twice as much state funding to their chosen school as do program students who receive a scholarship and attend a private school," was decisively rejected in *Committee for Public Ed. & Religious Liberty v. Nyquist*:

"We do not agree with the suggestion . . . that tuition grants are an analogous endeavor to provide comparable benefits to all parents of schoolchildren whether en-

rolled in public or nonpublic schools. . . . The grants to parents of private school children are given in addition to the right that they have to send their children to public schools 'totally at state expense.' And in any event, the argument proves too much, for it would also provide a basis for approving through tuition grants the *complete subsidization* of all religious schools on the ground that such action is necessary if the State is fully to equalize the position of parents who elect such schools—a result wholly at variance with the Establishment Clause."

other majority criterion, whether the immediate recipients of voucher aid have a genuinely free choice of religious and secular schools to receive the voucher money. And in applying this second criterion, the consideration of "*all* schools" is ostensibly helpful to the majority position.

B

The majority addresses the issue of choice the same way it addresses neutrality, by asking whether recipients or potential recipients of voucher aid have a choice of public schools among secular alternatives to religious schools. Again, however, the majority asks the wrong question and misapplies the criterion. The majority has confused choice in spending scholarships with choice from the entire menu of possible educational placements, most of them open to anyone willing to attend a public school. I say "confused" because the majority's new use of the choice criterion, which it frames negatively as "whether Ohio is coercing parents into sending their children to religious schools," ignores the reason for having a private choice enquiry in the first place. Cases since *Mueller* have found private choice relevant under a rule that aid to religious schools can be permissible so long as it first passes through the hands of students or parents. The majority's view that all educational choices are comparable for purposes of choice thus ignores the whole point of the choice test: it is a criterion for deciding whether indirect aid to a religious school is legitimate because it passes through private hands that can spend or use the aid in a secular school. The question is whether the private hand is genuinely free to send the money in either a secular direction or a religious one. The majority now has transformed this question about private choice in channeling aid into a question about selecting from examples of state spending (on education) including direct spending on magnet and community public schools that goes through no private hands and could never reach a religious school under any circumstance. When the choice test is transformed from where to spend the money to where to go to school, it is cut loose from its very purpose.

Defining choice as choice in spending the money or channeling the aid is, moreover, necessary if the choice criterion is to function as a limiting principle at all. If "choice" is present whenever there is any educational alternative to the religious school to which vouchers can be endorsed, then there will always be a choice and the voucher can always be constitutional, even in a system in which there is not a single private secular school as an alternative to the religious school. And because it is unlikely that any participating private religious school will enroll more pupils than the generally available public system, it will be easy to generate numbers suggesting that aid to religion is not the significant intent or effect of the voucher scheme.

That is, in fact, just the kind of rhetorical argument that the majority accepts in these cases. In addition to secular private schools (129 students), the majority considers public schools with tuition assistance (roughly 1,400 students), magnet schools (13,000 students), and community schools (1,900 students), and concludes that fewer than 20% of pupils receive state vouchers to attend religious schools. (In fact, the numbers would seem even more favorable to the majority's argument if enrollment in traditional public schools without tutoring were considered, an alternative the majority thinks relevant to the private choice enquiry). Justice O'Connor focuses on how much money is spent on each educational option and notes that at most $8.2 million is spent on vouchers for students attending religious schools, which is only 6% of the State's expenditure if one includes separate funding for Cleveland's community ($9.4 million) and magnet ($114.8 million) public schools. The variations show how results may shift when a judge can pick and choose the alternatives to use in the comparisons, and they also show what dependably comfortable results the choice criterion will yield if the identification of relevant choices is wide open. * * *

Confining the relevant choices to spending choices, on the other hand, is not vulnerable to comparable criticism. Although leaving the selection of alternatives for choice wide open, as the majority would, virtually guarantees the availability of a "choice" that will satisfy the criterion, limiting the choices to spending choices will not guarantee a negative result in every case. There may, after all, be cases in which a voucher recipient will have a real choice, with enough secular private school desks in relation to the number of religious ones, and a voucher amount high enough to meet secular private school tuition levels. But, even to the extent that choice-to-spend does tend to limit the number of religious funding options that pass muster, the choice criterion has to be understood this way in order, as I have said, for it to function as a limiting principle. Otherwise there is surely no point in requiring the choice to be a true or real or genuine one.

It is not, of course, that I think even a genuine choice criterion is up to the task of the Establishment Clause when substantial state funds go to religious teaching * * *. The point is simply that if the majority wishes to claim that choice is a criterion, it must define choice in a way that can function as a criterion with a practical capacity to screen something out.

If, contrary to the majority, we ask the right question about genuine choice to use the vouchers, the answer shows that something is influencing choices in a way that aims the money in a religious direction: of 56 private schools in the district participating in the voucher program (only 53 of which accepted voucher students in 1999–2000), 46 of them are religious; 96.6% of all voucher recipients go to religious schools, only 3.4% to nonreligious ones. Unfortunately for the majority position, there is no explanation for this that suggests the religious direction results simply from free choices by parents. One answer to these statistics, for example, which would be consistent with the genuine choice claimed to be operating, might be that 96.6% of families choosing to avail themselves of vouchers choose to educate their children in schools of their own religion. This would not, in my view, render the scheme constitutional, but it would speak to the majority's choice criterion. Evidence shows, however, that almost two out of three families using vouchers to send their children to religious schools did not embrace the religion of those schools. The families made it clear they had not chosen the schools because they wished their children to be proselytized in a religion not their own, or in any religion, but because of educational opportunity.[12]

Even so, the fact that some 2,270 students chose to apply their vouchers to schools of other religions, might be consistent with true choice if the students "chose" their religious schools over a wide array of private nonreligious options, or if it could be shown generally that Ohio's program had no effect on educational choices and thus no impermissible effect of advancing religious education. But both possibilities are contrary to fact. First, even if all existing nonreligious private schools in Cleveland were willing to accept large numbers of voucher students, only a few more than the 129 currently enrolled in such schools would be able to attend, as the total enrollment at all nonreligious private schools in Cleveland for kindergarten through eighth grade is only 510 children, and there is no indication that these schools have many open seats.[13] Second, the $2,500 cap that the program places on tuition for participating low-income pupils has the effect of curtailing the participation of nonreligious schools: "nonreligious schools with higher tuition (about $4,000) stated that they could afford to accommodate just a few voucher students." By comparison, the average tuition at participating Catholic schools in Cleveland in 1999–2000 was $1,592, almost $1,000 below the cap.

Of course, the obvious fix would be to increase the value of vouchers so that existing nonreligious private and non-Catholic religious schools would be able to enroll more voucher students, and to provide incentives

12. When parents were surveyed as to their motives for enrolling their children in the voucher program, 96.4% cited a better education than available in the public schools, and 95% said their children's safety. When asked specifically in one study to identify the most important factor in selecting among participating private schools, 60% of parents mentioned academic quality, teacher quality, or the substance of what is taught (presumably secular); only 15% mentioned the religious affiliation of the school as even a consideration.

13. Justice O'Connor points out that "there is no record evidence that any voucher-eligible student was turned away from a nonreligious private school in the voucher program." But there is equally no evidence to support her assertion that "many parents with vouchers selected nonreligious private schools over religious alternatives," and in fact the evidence is to the contrary, as only 129 students used vouchers at private nonreligious schools.

Justice O'Connor argues that nonreligious private schools can compete with Catholic and other religious schools below the $2,500 tuition cap. The record does not support this assertion, as only three secular private schools in Cleveland enroll more than eight voucher students. Nor is it true, as she suggests, that our national statistics are spurious because secular schools cater to a different market from Catholic or other religious schools: while there is a spectrum of nonreligious private schools, there is likely a commensurate range of low-end and high-end religious schools. My point is that at each level, the religious schools have a comparative cost advantage due to church subsidies, donations of the faithful, and the like. The majority says that nonreligious private schools in Cleveland derive similar benefits from "third-party contributions," but the one affidavit in the record that backs up this assertion with data concerns a private school for "emotionally disabled and developmentally delayed children" that received 11% of its budget from the United Way organization * * *.

for educators to create new such schools given that few presently exist. Private choice, if as robust as that available to the seminarian in *Witters,* would then be "true private choice" under the majority's criterion. But it is simply unrealistic to presume that parents of elementary and middle schoolchildren in Cleveland will have a range of secular and religious choices even arguably comparable to the statewide program for vocational and higher education in *Witters.* And to get to that hypothetical point would require that such massive financial support be made available to religion as to disserve every objective of the Establishment Clause even more than the present scheme does.

There is, in any case, no way to interpret the 96.6% of current voucher money going to religious schools as reflecting a free and genuine choice by the families that apply for vouchers. The 96.6% reflects, instead, the fact that too few nonreligious school desks are available and few but religious schools can afford to accept more than a handful of voucher students. And contrary to the majority's assertion, public schools in adjacent districts hardly have a financial incentive to participate in the Ohio voucher program, and none has.[17] For the overwhelming number of children in the voucher scheme, the only alternative to the public schools is religious. And it is entirely irrelevant that the State did not deliberately design the network of private schools for the sake of channeling money into religious institutions. The criterion is one of genuinely free choice on the part of the private individuals who choose, and a Hobson's choice is not a choice, whatever the reason for being Hobsonian.

III

I do not dissent merely because the majority has misapplied its own law, for even if I assumed *arguendo* that the majority's formal criteria were satisfied on the facts, today's conclusion would be profoundly at odds with the Constitution. Proof of this is clear on two levels. The first is circumstantial, in the now discarded symptom of violation, the substantial dimension of the aid. The second is direct, in the defiance of every objective supposed to be served by the bar against establishment.

A

The scale of the aid to religious schools approved today is unprecedented, both in the number of dollars and in the proportion of systemic school expenditure supported. Each measure has received attention in previous cases. On one hand, the sheer quantity of aid, when delivered to a class of religious primary and secondary schools, was suspect on the theory that the greater the aid, the greater its proportion to a religious school's existing expenditures, and the greater the likelihood that public

---

17. As the Court points out, an out-of-district public school that participates will receive a $2,250 voucher for each Cleveland student on top of its normal state funding. The basic state funding, though, is a drop in the bucket as compared to the cost of educating that student, as much of the cost (at least in relatively affluent areas with presumptively better academic standards) is paid by local income and property taxes. * * *

money was supporting religious as well as secular instruction. * * * Conversely, the more "attenuated [the] financial benefit ... that eventually flows to parochial schools," the more the Court has been willing to find a form of state aid permissible. *Mueller*.[18]

On the other hand, the Court has found the gross amount unhelpful for Establishment Clause analysis when the aid afforded a benefit solely to one individual, however substantial as to him, but only an incidental benefit to the religious school at which the individual chose to spend the State's money. When neither the design nor the implementation of an aid scheme channels a series of individual students' subsidies toward religious recipients, the relevant beneficiaries for establishment purposes, the Establishment Clause is unlikely to be implicated. * * *

The Cleveland voucher program has cost Ohio taxpayers $33 million since its implementation in 1996 ($28 million in voucher payments, $5 million in administrative costs), and its cost was expected to exceed $8 million in the 2001–2002 school year. These tax-raised funds are on top of the textbooks, reading and math tutors, laboratory equipment, and the like that Ohio provides to private schools, worth roughly $600 per child.

The gross amounts of public money contributed are symptomatic of the scope of what the taxpayers' money buys for a broad class of religious-school students. In paying for practically the full amount of tuition for thousands of qualifying students, the scholarships purchase everything that tuition purchases, be it instruction in math or indoctrination in faith. * * *

B

* * *

* * * [A] condition of receiving government money under the program is that participating religious schools may not "discriminate on the basis of ... religion," which means the school may not give admission preferences to children who are members of the patron faith; children of a parish are generally consigned to the same admission lotteries as nonbelievers. This indeed was the exact object of a 1999 amendment repealing the portion of a predecessor statute that had allowed an admission preference for "[c]hildren ... whose parents are affiliated with any organization that provides financial support to the school, at the discretion of the school." Nor is the State's religious antidiscrimination restriction limited to student admission policies: by its terms, a participating religious school may well be forbidden to choose a member of its own clergy to serve as teacher or principal over a layperson of a different religion claiming equal qualification for the job. Indeed, a separate condition that "[t]he school ... not ... teach hatred of any

---

18. The majority relies on *Mueller, Agostini,* and *Mitchell* to dispute the relevance of the large number of students that use vouchers to attend religious schools, but the reliance is inapt because each of those cases involved insubstantial benefits to the religious schools, regardless of the number of students that benefitted.

person or group on the basis of ... religion," could be understood (or subsequently broadened) to prohibit religions from teaching traditionally legitimate articles of faith as to the error, sinfulness, or ignorance of others,[24] if they want government money for their schools.

For perspective on this foot-in-the-door of religious regulation, it is well to remember that the money has barely begun to flow. Prior examples of aid, whether grants through individuals or in-kind assistance, were never significant enough to alter the basic fiscal structure of religious schools; state aid was welcome, but not indispensable. But given the figures already involved here, there is no question that religious schools in Ohio are on the way to becoming bigger businesses with budgets enhanced to fit their new stream of tax-raised income. * * *

When government aid goes up, so does reliance on it; the only thing likely to go down is independence. If Justice Douglas in *Allen* was concerned with state agencies, influenced by powerful religious groups, choosing the textbooks that parochial schools would use, 392 U.S., at 265, 88 S.Ct. 1923 (dissenting opinion), how much more is there reason to wonder when dependence will become great enough to give the State of Ohio an effective veto over basic decisions on the content of curriculums? A day will come when religious schools will learn what political leverage can do, just as Ohio's politicians are now getting a lesson in the leverage exercised by religion.

Increased voucher spending is not, however, the sole portent of growing regulation of religious practice in the school, for state mandates to moderate religious teaching may well be the most obvious response to the third concern behind the ban on establishment, its inextricable link with social conflict. As appropriations for religious subsidy rise, competition for the money will tap sectarian religion's capacity for discord. * * *

Justice Breyer has addressed this issue in his own dissenting opinion, which I join, and here it is enough to say that the intensity of the expectable friction can be gauged by realizing that the scramble for money will energize not only contending sectarians, but taxpayers who take their liberty of conscience seriously. Religious teaching at taxpayer expense simply cannot be cordoned from taxpayer politics, and every major religion currently espouses social positions that provoke intense opposition. Not all taxpaying Protestant citizens, for example, will be

---

24. See, *e.g.*, Christian New Testament (2 Corinthians 6:14) (King James Version) ("Be ye not unequally yoked together with unbelievers: for what fellowship hath righteousness with unrighteousness? and what communion hath light with darkness?"); The Book of Mormon (2 Nephi 9:24) ("And if they will not repent and believe in his name, and be baptized in his name, and endure to the end, they must be damned; for the Lord God, the Holy One of Israel, has spoken it"); Pentateuch (Deut.29:18) (The New Jewish Publication Society Translation) (for one who converts to another faith, "[t]he LORD will never forgive him; rather will the LORD's anger and passion rage against that man, till every sanction recorded in this book comes down upon him, and the LORD blots out his name from under heaven"); The Koran 334 (The Cow Ch. 2:1) (N. Dawood transl. 4th rev. ed. 1974) ("As for the unbelievers, whether you forewarn them or not, they will not have faith. Allah has set a seal upon their hearts and ears; their sight is dimmed and a grievous punishment awaits them").

content to underwrite the teaching of the Roman Catholic Church condemning the death penalty. Nor will all of America's Muslims acquiesce in paying for the endorsement of the religious Zionism taught in many religious Jewish schools, which combines "a nationalistic sentiment" in support of Israel with a "deeply religious" element. Nor will every secular taxpayer be content to support Muslim views on differential treatment of the sexes, or, for that matter, to fund the espousal of a wife's obligation of obedience to her husband, presumably taught in any schools adopting the articles of faith of the Southern Baptist Convention. Views like these, and innumerable others, have been safe in the sectarian pulpits and classrooms of this Nation not only because the Free Exercise Clause protects them directly, but because the ban on supporting religious establishment has protected free exercise, by keeping it relatively private. With the arrival of vouchers in religious schools, that privacy will go, and along with it will go confidence that religious disagreement will stay moderate.

* * *

* * * *Everson's* statement is still the touchstone of sound law, even though the reality is that in the matter of educational aid the Establishment Clause has largely been read away. True, the majority has not approved vouchers for religious schools alone, or aid earmarked for religious instruction. But no scheme so clumsy will ever get before us, and in the cases that we may see, like these, the Establishment Clause is largely silenced. * * * I hope that a future Court will reconsider today's dramatic departure from basic Establishment Clause principle.

JUSTICE BREYER, with whom JUSTICE STEVENS and JUSTICE SOUTER join, dissenting.

I join Justice Souter's opinion, and I agree substantially with Justice Stevens. I write separately, however, to emphasize the risk that publicly financed voucher programs pose in terms of religiously based social conflict. I do so because I believe that the Establishment Clause concern for protecting the Nation's social fabric from religious conflict poses an overriding obstacle to the implementation of this well-intentioned school voucher program. And by explaining the nature of the concern, I hope to demonstrate why, in my view, "parental choice" cannot significantly alleviate the constitutional problem.

I

The First Amendment begins with a prohibition, that "Congress shall make no law respecting an establishment of religion," and a guarantee, that the government shall not prohibit "the free exercise thereof." These Clauses embody an understanding, reached in the 17th century after decades of religious war, that liberty and social stability demand a religious tolerance that respects the religious views of all citizens, permits those citizens to "worship God in their own way," and allows all families to "teach their children and to form their characters" as they wish. The Clauses reflect the Framers' vision of an American

Nation free of the religious strife that had long plagued the nations of Europe. Whatever the Framers might have thought about particular 18th century school funding practices, they undeniably intended an interpretation of the Religion Clauses that would implement this basic First Amendment objective.

In part for this reason, the Court's 20th century Establishment Clause cases—both those limiting the practice of religion in public schools and those limiting the public funding of private religious education—focused directly upon social conflict, potentially created when government becomes involved in religious education. * * *

* * *

When it decided these 20th century Establishment Clause cases, the Court did not deny that an earlier American society might have found a less clear-cut church/state separation compatible with social tranquility. * * *

The 20th century Court was fully aware, however, that immigration and growth had changed American society dramatically since its early years. By 1850, 1.6 million Catholics lived in America, and by 1900 that number rose to 12 million. There were similar percentage increases in the Jewish population. Not surprisingly, with this increase in numbers, members of non-Protestant religions, particularly Catholics, began to resist the Protestant domination of the public schools. Scholars report that by the mid–19th century religious conflict over matters such as Bible reading "grew intense," as Catholics resisted and Protestants fought back to preserve their domination. In some States "Catholic students suffered beatings or expulsions for refusing to read from the Protestant Bible, and crowds ... rioted over whether Catholic children could be released from the classroom during Bible reading."

The 20th century Court was also aware that political efforts to right the wrong of discrimination against religious minorities in primary education had failed; in fact they had exacerbated religious conflict. * * *

These historical circumstances suggest that the Court, applying the Establishment Clause through the Fourteenth Amendment to 20th century American society, faced an interpretive dilemma that was in part practical. The Court appreciated the religious diversity of contemporary American society. It realized that the status quo favored some religions at the expense of others. And it understood the Establishment Clause to prohibit (among other things) any such favoritism. Yet *how* did the Clause achieve that objective? Did it simply require the government to give each religion an equal chance to introduce religion into the primary schools—a kind of "equal opportunity" approach to the interpretation of the Establishment Clause? Or, did that Clause avoid government favoritism of some religions by insisting upon "separation"—that the government achieve equal treatment by removing itself from the business of providing religious education for children? This interpretive choice arose in respect both to religious activities in public schools and government aid to private education.

In both areas the Court concluded that the Establishment Clause required "separation," in part because an "equal opportunity" approach was not workable. With respect to religious activities in the public schools, how could the Clause require public primary and secondary school teachers, when reading prayers or the Bible, *only* to treat all religions alike? In many places there were too many religions, too diverse a set of religious practices, too many whose spiritual beliefs denied the virtue of formal religious training. This diversity made it difficult, if not impossible, to devise meaningful forms of "equal treatment" by providing an "equal opportunity" for all to introduce their own religious practices into the public schools.

With respect to government aid to private education, did not history show that efforts to obtain equivalent funding for the private education of children whose parents did not hold popular religious beliefs only exacerbated religious strife? As Justice Rutledge recognized:

"Public money devoted to payment of religious costs, educational or other, brings the quest for more. It brings too the struggle of sect against sect for the larger share or for any. Here one [religious sect] by numbers [of adherents] alone will benefit most, there another. This is precisely the history of societies which have had an established religion and dissident groups." *Everson v. Board of Ed. of Ewing* (dissenting opinion).

* * *

II

The principle underlying these cases—avoiding religiously based social conflict—remains of great concern. As religiously diverse as America had become when the Court decided its major 20th century Establishment Clause cases, we are exponentially more diverse today. America boasts more than 55 different religious groups and subgroups with a significant number of members. Major religions include, among others, Protestants, Catholics, Jews, Muslims, Buddhists, Hindus, and Sikhs. And several of these major religions contain different subsidiary sects with different religious beliefs. * * *

Under these modern-day circumstances, how is the "equal opportunity" principle to work—without risking the "struggle of sect against sect" against which Justice Rutledge warned? School voucher programs finance the religious education of the young. And, if widely adopted, they may well provide billions of dollars that will do so. Why will different religions not become concerned about, and seek to influence, the criteria used to channel this money to religious schools? Why will they not want to examine the implementation of the programs that provide this money—to determine, for example, whether implementation has biased a program toward or against particular sects, or whether recipient religious schools are adequately fulfilling a program's criteria? If so, just how is the State to resolve the resulting controversies without provoking legitimate fears of the kinds of religious favoritism that, in so religiously diverse a Nation, threaten social dissension?

Consider the voucher program here at issue. That program insists that the religious school accept students of all religions. Does that criterion treat fairly groups whose religion forbids them to do so? The program also insists that no participating school "advocate or foster unlawful behavior or teach hatred of any person or group on the basis of race, ethnicity, national origin, or religion." And it requires the State to "revoke the registration of any school if, after a hearing, the superintendent determines that the school is in violation" of the program's rules. As one *amicus* argues, "it is difficult to imagine a more divisive activity" than the appointment of state officials as referees to determine whether a particular religious doctrine "teaches hatred or advocates lawlessness."

* * *

III

I concede that the Establishment Clause currently permits States to channel various forms of assistance to religious schools, for example, transportation costs for students, computers, and secular texts. * * * Yet the consequence has not been great turmoil.

School voucher programs differ, however, in both *kind* and *degree* from aid programs upheld in the past. They differ in kind because they direct financing to a core function of the church: the teaching of religious truths to young children. For that reason the constitutional demand for "separation" is of particular constitutional concern.

* * *

Vouchers also differ in *degree*. The aid programs recently upheld by the Court involved limited amounts of aid to religion. But the majority's analysis here appears to permit a considerable shift of taxpayer dollars from public secular schools to private religious schools. That fact, combined with the use to which these dollars will be put, exacerbates the conflict problem. * * *

IV

I do not believe that the "parental choice" aspect of the voucher program sufficiently offsets the concerns I have mentioned. Parental choice cannot help the taxpayer who does not want to finance the religious education of children. It will not always help the parent who may see little real choice between inadequate nonsectarian public education and adequate education at a school whose religious teachings are contrary to his own. It will not satisfy religious minorities unable to participate because they are too few in number to support the creation of their own private schools. It will not satisfy groups whose religious beliefs preclude them from participating in a government-sponsored program, and who may well feel ignored as government funds primarily support the education of children in the doctrines of the dominant religions. * * *

V

The Court, in effect, turns the clock back. It adopts, under the name of "neutrality," an interpretation of the Establishment Clause that this Court rejected more than half a century ago. In its view, the parental choice that offers each religious group a kind of equal opportunity to secure government funding overcomes the Establishment Clause concern for social concord. An earlier Court found that "equal opportunity" principle insufficient; it read the Clause as insisting upon greater separation of church and state, at least in respect to primary education. See *Nyquist,* 413 U.S., at 783, 93 S.Ct. 2955. In a society composed of many different religious creeds, I fear that this present departure from the Court's earlier understanding risks creating a form of religiously based conflict potentially harmful to the Nation's social fabric. Because I believe the Establishment Clause was written in part to avoid this kind of conflict, and for reasons set forth by Justice Souter and Justice Stevens, I respectfully dissent.

Notes and Questions

1. *Neutrality.* The plurality in *Mitchell* and the majority in *Zelman* rely on the notion of neutrality. Is the neutrality principle reflected in these decisions neutral? Is there any way to show that a program is neutral under the Establishment Clause? Is the facial neutrality of a law and the fact that money at least figuratively passes through private hands before reaching a religious institution enough to demonstrate that a program is neutral? Consider the facts set forth in Justice Souter's dissent in *Zelman.* In what sense is the result in *Zelman* neutral? Would members of a religious group that has no private school in the Cleveland area ("religious outsiders") find the voucher program neutral when their neighbors who share (or do not object to) the faith taught at participating religious schools send their kids to such schools, thus giving those children a chance to overcome the terrible state of the public school system without compromising their religious values, while the religious "outsiders" can only give their children that option at the expense of their deeply held religious beliefs and values? Would the opposite situation be any more neutral?—i.e. where religious parents must pay both property taxes and private school tuition (or the time and expense of home schooling) in order to send their kids to a school that does not undermine their religious beliefs and values, while secular and other religious parents are comfortable with the local public schools. *See* Frank S. Ravitch, *A Funny Thing Happened on the Way to Neutrality: Broad Principles, Formalism, and the Establishment Clause,* 38 GA. L. REV. 489 (suggesting that neutrality does not exist under the Establishment Clause, and that the Court's shift toward formal neutrality in recent cases is problematic because it relies on a non-existent concept as both the means and ends of Establishment Clause analysis); *see also,* STEVEN D. SMITH, FOREORDAINED FAILURE: THE QUEST FOR A CONSTITUTIONAL PRINCIPLE OF RELIGIOUS FREEDOM 96–97 (1995)("[T]he quest for neutrality * * * is an attempt to grasp at an illusion").

2. *Baselines of Neutrality.* Some have suggested that neutrality is a function of the baseline one chooses for the concept. Thus, the Court has chosen a baseline of "formal neutrality" or "evenhandedness neutrality." One of the most persuasive advocates of the baselines notion would actually advise against the formal neutrality approach, instead opting for a substantive neutrality approach. Douglas Laycock, *Formal, Substantive, and Disaggregated Neutrality Toward Religion*, 39 DePaul L. Rev. 993 (1990)(analyzing formal and substantive neutrality, and rejecting formal neutrality). Yet, is the baseline notion of neutrality helpful beyond defining what the Court considers neutral at a given time—i.e. if the baseline for neutrality is not itself neutral how can the resulting definition of neutrality be neutral? This brings us back to square one and the question of whether neutrality can exist under the Establishment Clause. Steven D. Smith, *The Restoration of Tolerance*, 78 Cal. L. Rev. 305, 319–24 (1990) (critiquing the argument that neutrality requires a baseline, and rejecting neutrality as an empty ideal). What do you think about the concept of neutrality as used by the plurality in *Mitchell* and the majority in *Zelman*? What do you think of earlier Courts' use of neutrality? You will see the neutrality issue explored further in some of the articles excerpted in Chapter Five, *infra*.

3. *Effects.* Under the Court's current approach is there really anything beyond formal neutrality in aid cases? Does the Court seriously consider the effects of a government program? The *Zelman* Court holds that secular purpose is still relevant and that direct aid may be more problematic than the aid evaluated in that case, but when would either really be an issue in an aid case? How likely is it that a legislature would not have a plausible secular purpose for an aid program created to improve educational opportunities or to help those in need? Moreover, since government can now write the check directly to a religious organization so long as the amount of the check is determined by how many private individuals choose to enroll in or take advantage of a program offered by a religious entity, is there really a clear distinction between direct and indirect aid? For example, it appears that it would be constitutional under *Zelman* for a government entity to give a grant to a religious institution based on the number of eligible students enrolled (multiplied by the voucher or other relevant amount). Thus, unless a government entity was incredibly sloppy, it should simply tie the funding amount to those who "choose" to enroll in a program. In the end, it seems that the current test boils down to formal neutrality plus a private "circuit breaker," regardless of the empirical effect of a given program. Neither the purpose analysis or direct/indirect aid distinction would appear to be relevant unless a government entity were especially sloppy (or blatant in designing or applying the program to benefit or hurt religious entities). After *Zelman*, the "effects" test would seem to focus little on effects when "indirect" aid is involved. Given all this is Justice O'Connor's support for the Court's reasoning in *Zelman* consistent with the reasoning in her concurring opinion in *Mitchell*?

4. *What About Lemon/Agostini?* Is the test in *Zelman* consistent with the *Lemon/Agostini* test? Is it inconsistent? How would formal neutrality and private choice function under the *Lemon/Agostini* test? Both factors are relevant under that test. The question is how relevant. Is *Zelman*, as the Court suggests, simply a logical step from the reasoning in cases like *Witters*, *Kendrick*, and *Zobrest*, or is there something different about the facts in *Zelman* and/or the legal analysis?

5. *Charitable Choice.* What does *Zelman* mean for "charitable choice" programs? These are programs that provide government funding to charitable entities, including religious ones, to provide charitable services. Some religious charities proselytize in the course of their charitable work, while others do not.

Under traditional doctrines it was relatively clear that government could not fund such proselytizing even indirectly, but what about after *Zelman*? The question takes on greater importance because the Bush Administration has sought to expand charitable choice funding (including funding to religious entities that proselytize) to a large number of programs. "Charitable choice" was first initiated as part of a welfare reform act in 1996, but was limited to certain programs. Long before 1996 religious organizations could receive funding for their charitable enterprises, but those organizations were not able to require beneficiaries of the charities to engage in religious practices and the charitable entities that received such funding were generally separated from general church operations.

Charitable choice programs have an obvious secular purpose—to help those in need. After *Zelman*, most of the programs will likely tie funding to the number of recipients that are served. If not, charitable choice programs might implicate the question of whether the direct/indirect aid distinction still has any practical meaning after *Zelman* and *Mitchell*. Assuming, however, that funding is tied to the number of recipients of charitable services, the *Zelman* test would seem to apply. Virtually any charitable choice program will be facially neutral because the programs do not generally distinguish between religious and nonreligious providers or between providers from various religions. So the question will likely come down to whether the recipients actually have a choice in going to a particular provider. This question is hard to answer because in some cases there will be a clear choice between a variety of providers, but in others a person in need of a charitable benefit may only have one place to go in a given area and that provider may be sectarian, or a person in need may have a few places to go all of which are sectarian. What would happen under *Zelman* in such situations? While the *Zelman* majority seemed relatively unconcerned about the practical effects of the program under its holding, the situation there was different in at least one respect—the children could go to public school. Someone who is starving or needs shelter may have little or no choice about where to go for help, particularly in smaller communities. Thus, the question may not be easy to answer. What do you think the result should be in such cases? Why?

6. *Blaine Amendments*. In the 19th Century and early part of the Twentieth Century numerous so called "Blaine Amendments" were introduced around the country. Their purpose was to amend state constitutions (or in some cases to use legislation) to prevent any public funds from going to religious schools. The term "Blaine Amendment" refers to Senator James Blaine who proposed such an amendment to the U.S. Constitution. That proposed amendment was defeated by two votes in the Senate (it passed in the House). Several of the state amendments were passed before Blaine proposed his amendment, but because the movement for passing such state constitutional amendments was inspired in part by the defeat of Senator Blaine's amendment, they are commonly referred to as "Blaine Amendments." While at first glance the Blaine amendments might seem to have been an attempt to promote separation of church and state, they were frequently the product of anti-Catholic bias and an attempt to keep any public funds from reaching the evolving Catholic School system (of course, some who supported the amendments were genuinely influenced by a belief in separationism). *See* PHILIP HAMBURGER, SEPARATION OF CHURCH AND STATE (Harvard Univ. Press 2002) at 297–98, 324–25, 338–42; Douglas Laycock, *The Underlying Unity of Separation and Neutrality*, 46 EMORY L.J. 43, 50–52 (1997). Similarly, states that entered the Union after 1876 were required to maintain a public school system "free from sectarian control." *McCollum*, 333 U.S. at 220 (Frankfurter,

J., concurring). Should such amendments be upheld given this history? Does the fact that today they may be understood as promoting separation rather than anti-Catholic bigotry change anything? How might someone challenge such an amendment if she was denied funding under a generally applicable state funding program because she intended to use it at a religious institution? For religious training—i.e. to become a minister, rabbi, priest, etc . . . ? *See Locke v. Davey*, ___ U.S. ___, 124 S.Ct. 1307, 158 L.Ed.2d 1 (2004), infra at Section D.

7. *"Fund Only Public Schools" Amendments and Statutes.* How should a state constitutional amendment that denies funding for any private school regardless of whether such school is religious be treated after *Zelman*? Several states have such constitutional amendments or similar legislation? Could such a law ever be problematic under the *Zelman* approach? It would seem not since such laws are inherently neutral on their face because they do not distinguish between religious and nonreligious private schools. Therefore, unless the law had a legislative history that reflected animus against religion or a specific religious group, or was applied in a way that disfavored such groups, there would seem to be no Establishment Clause problem. There could theoretically be a problem under the Free Exercise Clause, but because such laws are generally applicable (to religious and nonreligious entities alike) they do not likely violate the Free Exercise Clause. *See infra.* at Chapter Six. What effect would such laws have on religious parents who do not want to educate their children in the public schools because they find some of the teachings in those schools offensive to their beliefs? Would the formal neutrality approach reflected in *Zelman* and recent Free Exercise Clause cases, *see infra* at Chapter Six, take such effects into consideration?

8. *Education Policy.* None of the above discussion goes to the relevant merits of vouchers as an educational policy. Do you think vouchers are good educational policy after reading the various opinions in *Zelman*? What more would you want to know before answering this question? If vouchers were unconstitutional would it matter whether they were good educational policy? Should such concerns have an impact on a court's consideration of constitutional questions? Do you think such concerns do impact court decisions whether they should do so or not?

D. MUST GOVERNMENT FUND RELIGIOUS PURSUITS IF IT CREATES A GENERAL FUNDING PROGRAM?

The question of whether government must fund those engaged in religious pursuits or those who wish to attend religious schools when it creates a general funding program open to private individuals naturally arises after the Court's decision in *Zelman*. This question is even more significant given the number of state "Blaine Amendments" as discussed in the notes above. These amendments prohibit the states that have adopted them from providing funding to support sectarian education. If it is constitutional to fund vouchers that are used at religious schools because the program providing for such vouchers is neutral on its face— i.e. it doesn't distinguish between religions or between religious and nonreligious institutions—and because private individuals choose where to use the vouchers, could a state create a voucher or other funding program and specifically exclude only religious training or religious institutions without running afoul of the neutrality principle? Now that the "neutrality" principle from *Zelman* governs "indirect aid" cases, would such an exclusion discriminate based on religious viewpoint (thus violating the Establishment, Free Speech and Free Exercise Clauses)? Would a state constitutional provision prohibiting funding of religious education be an adequate defense in this context? The following case, which was decided by the United States Supreme Court in 2004, addresses some, but not all, of these questions.

LOCKE v. DAVEY

Supreme Court of the United States, 2004.
___ U.S. ___, 124 S.Ct. 1307, 158 L.Ed.2d 1.

Chief Justice REHNQUIST delivered the opinion of the Court.

The State of Washington established the Promise Scholarship Program to assist academically gifted students with postsecondary education expenses. In accordance with the State Constitution, students may not use the scholarship at an institution where they are pursuing a degree in devotional theology. We hold that such an exclusion from an otherwise inclusive aid program does not violate the Free Exercise Clause of the First Amendment.

The Washington State Legislature found that "[s]tudents who work hard ... and successfully complete high school with high academic marks may not have the financial ability to attend college because they cannot obtain financial aid or the financial aid is insufficient." In 1999, to assist these high-achieving students, the legislature created the Promise Scholarship Program, which provides a scholarship, renewable for one year, to eligible students for postsecondary education expenses. Students may spend their funds on any education-related expense, including room and board. The scholarships are funded through the State's general fund, and their amount varies each year depending on the annual appropriation, which is evenly prorated among the eligible students. The scholarship was worth $1,125 for academic year 1999–2000 and $1,542 for 2000–2001.

To be eligible for the scholarship, a student must meet academic, income, and enrollment requirements. A student must graduate from a Washington public or private high school and either graduate in the top 15% of his graduating class, or attain on the first attempt a cumulative score of 1,200 or better on the Scholastic Assessment Test I or a score of 27 or better on the American College Test. The student's family income must be less than 135% or the State's median. Finally, the student must enroll "at least half time in an eligible postsecondary institution in the state of Washington," and may not pursue a degree in theology at that institution while receiving the scholarship. Private institutions, including those religiously affiliated, qualify as "eligible postsecondary institution[s]" if they are accredited by a nationally recognized accrediting body. A "degree in theology" is not defined in the statute, but, as both parties concede, the statute simply codifies the State's constitutional prohibition on providing funds to students to pursue degrees that are "devotional in nature or designed to induce religious faith."

A student who applies for the scholarship and meets the academic and income requirements is notified that he is eligible for the scholarship if he meets the enrollment requirements. Once the student enrolls at an eligible institution, the institution must certify that the student is enrolled at least half time and that the student is not pursuing a degree in devotional theology. The institution, rather than the State, determines whether the student's major is devotional. * * *

Respondent, Joshua Davey, was awarded a Promise Scholarship, and chose to attend Northwest College. Northwest is a private, Christian college affiliated with the Assemblies of God denomination, and is an eligible institution under the Promise Scholarship Program. Davey had "planned for many years to attend a Bible college and to prepare [himself] through that college training for a lifetime of ministry, specifically as a church pastor." To that end when he enrolled in Northwest College, he decided to pursue a double major in pastoral ministries and business management/administration. There is no dispute that the pastoral ministries degree is devotional and therefore excluded under the Promise Scholarship Program.

At the beginning of the 1999–2000 academic year, Davey met with Northwest's director of financial aid. He learned for the first time at this meeting that he could not use his scholarship to pursue a devotional theology degree. He was informed that to receive the funds appropriated for his use, he must certify in writing that he was not pursuing such a degree at Northwest.[1] He refused to sign the form and did not receive any scholarship funds.

Davey then brought an action under 42 U.S.C. § 1983 against various state officials (hereinafter State) in the District Court for the Western District of Washington to enjoin the State from refusing to award the scholarship solely because a student is pursuing a devotional theology degree, and for damages. He argued the denial of his scholarship based on his decision to pursue a theology degree violated, *inter alia*, the Free Exercise, Establishment, and Free Speech Clauses of the First Amendment, as incorporated by the Fourteenth Amendment * * *. The District Court rejected Davey's constitutional claims and granted summary judgment in favor of the State.

A divided panel of the United States Court of Appeals for the Ninth Circuit reversed. The court concluded that the State had singled out religion for unfavorable treatment and thus under our decision in *Church of Lukumi Babalu Aye, Inc. v Hialeah*, 508 U.S. 520, 113 S.Ct. 2217, 124 L.Ed.2d 472 (1993), the State's exclusion of theology majors must be narrowly tailored to achieve a compelling state interest. Finding that the State's own antiestablishment concerns were not compelling,

---

1. The State does not require students to certify anything or sign any forms.

the court declared Washington's Promise Scholarship Program unconstitutional. We granted certiorari, and now reverse.

The Religion Clauses of the First Amendment provide: "Congress shall make no law respecting an establishment of religion, or prohibiting the free exercise thereof." These two Clauses, the Establishment Clause and the Free Exercise Clause, are frequently in tension. Yet we have long said that "there is room for play in the joints" between them. In other words, there are some state actions permitted by the Establishment Clause but not required by the Free Exercise Clause.

This case involves that "play in the joints" described above. Under our Establishment Clause precedent, the link between government funds and religious training is broken by the independent and private choice of recipients. See *Zelman v. Simmons–Harris* * * *. As such, there is no doubt that the State could, consistent with the Federal Constitution, permit Promise Scholars to pursue a degree in devotional theology, see *Witters*, and the State does not contend otherwise. The question before us, however, is whether Washington, pursuant to its own constitution,[2] which has been authoritatively interpreted as prohibiting even indirectly funding religious instruction that will prepare students for the ministry, can deny them such funding without violating the Free Exercise Clause.

Davey urges us to answer that question in the negative. He contends that under the rule we enunciated in *Church of Lukumi Babalu Aye, Inc. v. Hialeah, supra,* the program is presumptively unconstitutional because it is not facially neutral with respect to religion.[3] We reject his claim of presumptive unconstitutionality, however; to do otherwise would extend the *Lukumi* line of cases well beyond not only their facts but their reasoning. In *Lukumi*, the city of Hialeah made it a crime to engage in certain kinds of animal slaughter. We found that the law sought to suppress ritualistic animal sacrifices of the Santeria religion. In the present case, the State's disfavor of religion (if it can be called that) is of a far milder kind. It imposes neither criminal nor civil sanctions on any type of religious service or rite. It does not deny to ministers the right to participate in the political affairs of the communi-

2. The relevant provision of the Washington Constitution, Art. I, § 11, states:

"Religious Freedom. Absolute freedom of conscience in all matters of religious sentiment, belief and worship, shall be guaranteed to every individual, and no one shall be molested or disturbed in person or property on account of religion; but the liberty of conscience hereby secured shall not be so construed as to excuse acts of licentiousness or justify practices inconsistent with the peace and safety of the state. No public money or property shall be appropriated for or applied to any religious worship, exercise or instruction, or the support of any religious establishment."

3. Davey, relying on *Rosenberger v. Rector and Visitors of Univ. of Va.,* 515 U.S. 819, 115 S.Ct. 2510, 132 L.Ed.2d 700 (1995), contends that the Promise Scholarship Program is an unconstitutional viewpoint restriction on speech. But the Promise Scholarship Program is not a forum for speech. The purpose of the Promise Scholarship Program is to assist students from low- and middle-income families with the cost of postsecondary education, not to " 'encourage a diversity of views from private speakers.' " *United States v. American Library Assn., Inc.,* 539 U.S. 194, 206, 123 S.Ct. 2297, 156 L.Ed.2d 221 (2003) (plurality opinion) (quoting *Rosenberger, supra,* at 834). Our cases dealing with speech forums are simply inapplicable. * * *

ty. And it does not require students to choose between their religious beliefs and receiving a government benefit.[4] The State has merely chosen not to fund a distinct category of instruction.

Justice Scalia argues, however, that generally available benefits are part of the "baseline against which burdens on religion are measured." Because the Promise Scholarship Program funds training for all secular professions, Justice Scalia contends the State must also fund training for religious professions. But training for religious professions and training for secular professions are not fungible. Training someone to lead a congregation is an essentially religious endeavor. Indeed, majoring in devotional theology is akin to a religious calling as well as an academic pursuit. See *Calvary Bible Presbyterian Church v. Board of Regents*, 72 Wash.2d 912, 919, 436 P.2d 189, 193 (1967) (holding public funds may not be expended for "that category of instruction that resembles worship and manifests a devotion to religion and religious principles in thought, feeling, belief, and conduct") * * *. And the subject of religion is one in which both the United States and state constitutions embody distinct views—in favor of free exercise, but opposed to establishment—that find no counterpart with respect to other callings or professions. That a State would deal differently with religious education for the ministry than with education for other callings is a product of these views, not evidence of hostility toward religion.

Even though the differently worded Washington Constitution draws a more stringent line than that drawn by the United States Constitution, the interest it seeks to further is scarcely novel. In fact, we can think of few areas in which a State's antiestablishment interests come more into play. Since the founding of our country, there have been popular uprisings against procuring taxpayer funds to support church leaders, which was one of the hallmarks of an "established" religion. See R. Butts, The American Tradition in Religion and Education 15–17, 19–20, 26–37 (1950); F. Lambert, The Founding Fathers and the Place of Religion in America 188 (2003) ("In defending their religious liberty against overreaching clergy, Americans in all regions found that Radical Whig ideas best framed their argument that state-supported clergy undermined liberty of conscience and should be opposed"); see also J. Madison, Memorial and Remonstrate Against Religious Assessments, reprinted in *Everson v. Board of Ed. of Ewing*, 330 U.S. 1, 65, 68, 67 S.Ct. 504, 91 L.Ed. 711 (1947) (appendix to dissent to Rutledge, J.) (noting the dangers to civil liberties from supporting clergy with public funds).

Most States that sought to avoid an establishment of religion around the time of the founding placed in their constitutions formal prohibitions against using tax funds to support the ministry. The plain text of these constitutional provisions prohibited *any* tax dollars from supporting the clergy. We have found nothing to indicate, as Justice Scalia contends,

---

4. Promise Scholars may still use their scholarship to pursue a secular degree at a different institution from where they are studying devotional theology.

that these provisions would not have applied so long as the State equally supported other professions or if the amount at stake was *de minimis*. That early state constitutions saw no problem in explicitly excluding *only* the ministry from receiving state dollars reinforces our conclusion that religious instruction is of a different ilk.[7]

Far from evincing the hostility toward religion which was manifest in *Lukumi*, we believe that the entirety of the Promise Scholarship Program goes a long way toward including religion in its benefits. The program permits students to attend pervasively religious schools, so long as they are accredited. As Northwest advertises, its "concept of education is distinctly Christian in the evangelical sense." It prepares *all* of its students, "through instruction, through modeling, [and] through [its] classes, to use . . . the Bible as their guide, as the truth," no matter their chosen profession. And under the Promise Scholarship Program's current guidelines, students are still eligible to take devotional theology courses. Davey notes all students at Northwest are required to take at least four devotional courses, "Exploring the Bible," "Principles of Spiritual Development," "Evangelism in the Christian Life," and "Christian Doctrine," and some students may have additional religious requirements as part of their majors.

In short, we find neither in the history or text of Article I, § 11 of the Washington Constitution, nor in the operation of the Promise Scholarship Program, anything that suggests animus towards religion. Given the historic and substantial state interest at issue, we therefore cannot conclude that the denial of funding for vocational religious instruction alone is inherently constitutionally suspect.

Without a presumption of unconstitutionality, Davey's claim must fail. The State's interest in not funding the pursuit of devotional degrees is substantial and the exclusion of such funding places a relatively minor burden on Promise Scholars. If any room exists between the two Religion Clauses, it must be here. We need not venture further into this difficult area in order to uphold the Promise Scholarship Program as currently operated by the State of Washington.

The judgment of the Court of Appeals is therefore *Reversed.*

Justice SCALIA, with whom Justice THOMAS joins, dissenting.

---

7. The *amici* contend that Washington's Constitution was born of religious bigotry because it contains a so-called "Blaine Amendment," which has been linked with anti-Catholicism. As the State notes and Davey does not dispute, however, the provision in question is not a Blaine Amendment. The enabling Act of 1889, which authorized the drafting of the Washington Constitution, required the state constitution to include a provision "for the establishment and maintenance of systems of public schools, which shall be . . . free from sectarian control." This provision was included in Article IX, § 4, of the Washington Constitution ("All schools maintained and supported wholly or in part by the public funds shall be forever free from sectarian control or influence"), and is not at issue in this case. Neither Davey nor *amici* have established a credible connection between the Blaine Amendment and Article I, § 11, the relevant constitutional provision. Accordingly, the Blaine Amendment's history is simply not before us.

In *Church of Lukumi Babalu Aye, Inc. v. Hialeah*, 508 U.S. 520, 113 S.Ct. 2217, 124 L.Ed.2d 472 (1993), the majority opinion held that "[a] law burdening religious practice that is not neutral ... must undergo the most rigorous of scrutiny," and that "the minimum requirement of neutrality is that a law not discriminate on its face." The concurrence of two Justices stated that "[w]hen a law discriminates against religion as such, ... it automatically will fail strict scrutiny." *Id.*, at 579 (Blackmun, J., joined by O'Connor, J., concurring in judgment). And the concurrence of a third Justice endorsed the "noncontroversial principle" that "formal neutrality" is a "necessary conditio[n] for free-exercise constitutionality." *Id.*, at 563 (Souter, J., concurring in part and concurring in judgment). These opinions are irreconcilable with today's decision, which sustains a public benefits program that facially discriminates against religion.

I

We articulated the principle that governs this case more than 50 years ago in *Everson v. Board of Ed. of Ewing*, 330 U.S. 1, 67 S.Ct. 504, 91 L.Ed. 711 (1947): "New Jersey cannot hamper its citizens in the free exercise of their own religion. Consequently, it cannot exclude individual Catholics, Lutherans, Mohammedans, Baptists, Jews, Methodists, Non-believers, Presbyterians, or the members of any other faith, because of their faith, or lack of it, from receiving the benefits of public welfare legislation." *Id.*, at 16 (emphasis deleted).

When the State makes a public benefit generally available, that benefit becomes part of the baseline against which burdens on religion are measured; and when the State withholds that benefit from some individuals solely on the basis of religion, it violates the Free Exercise Clause no less than if it had imposed a special tax.

That is precisely what the State of Washington has done here. It has created a generally available public benefit, whose receipt is conditioned only on academic performance, income, and attendance at an accredited school. It has then carved out a solitary course of study for exclusion: theology. No field of study but religion is singled out for disfavor in this fashion. Davey is not asking for a special benefit to which others are not entitled. He seeks only *equal* treatment—the right to direct his scholarship to his chosen course of study, a right every other Promise Scholar enjoys.

The Court's reference to historical "popular uprisings against procuring taxpayer funds to support church leaders," is therefore quite misplaced. That history involved not the inclusion of religious ministers in public benefits programs like the one at issue here, but laws that singled them out for financial aid. * * * One can concede the Framers' hostility to funding the clergy *specifically*, but that says nothing about whether the clergy had to be excluded from benefits the State made available to all. No one would seriously contend, for example, that the

Framers would have barred ministers from using public roads on their way to church.

The Court does not dispute that the Free Exercise Clause places some constraints on public benefits programs, but finds none here, based on a principle of " 'play in the joints.' " I use the term "principle" loosely, for that is not so much a legal principle as a refusal to apply *any* principle when faced with competing constitutional directives. There is nothing anomalous about constitutional commands that abut. A municipality hiring public contractors may not discriminate *against* blacks or *in favor of* them; it cannot discriminate a little bit each way and then plead "play in the joints" when haled into court. If the Religion Clauses demand neutrality, we must enforce them, in hard cases as well as easy ones.

Even if "play in the joints" were a valid legal principle, surely it would apply only when it was a close call whether complying with one of the Religion Clauses would violate the other. But that is not the case here. * * *

In any case, the State already has all the play in the joints it needs. There are any number of ways it could respect both its unusually sensitive concern for the conscience of its taxpayers *and* the Federal Free Exercise Clause. It could make the scholarships redeemable only at public universities (where it sets the curriculum), or only for select courses of study. Either option would replace a program that facially discriminates against religion with one that just happens not to subsidize it. The State could also simply abandon the scholarship program altogether. If that seems a dear price to pay for freedom of conscience, it is only because the State has defined that freedom so broadly that it would be offended by a program with such an incidental, indirect religious effect.

What is the nature of the State's asserted interest here? It cannot be protecting the pocketbooks of its citizens; given the tiny fraction of Promise Scholars who would pursue theology degrees, the amount of any citizen's tax bill at stake is *de minimis*. It cannot be preventing mistaken appearance of endorsement; where a State merely declines to penalize students for selecting a religious major, "[n]o reasonable observer is likely to draw ... an inference that the State itself is endorsing a religious practice or belief." Nor can Washington's exclusion be defended as a means of assuring that the State will neither favor nor disfavor Davey in his religious calling. Davey will throughout his life contribute to the public fisc through sales taxes on personal purchases, property taxes on his home, and so on; and nothing in the Court's opinion turns on whether Davey winds up a net winner or loser in the State's tax-and-spend scheme.

No, the interest to which the Court defers is not fear of a conceivable Establishment Clause violation, budget constraints, avoidance of endorsement, or substantive neutrality—none of these. It is a pure philosophical preference: the State's opinion that it would violate taxpayers' freedom of conscience *not* to discriminate against candidates for the ministry. This sort of protection of "freedom of conscience" has no logical limit and can justify the singling out of religion for exclusion from public programs in virtually any context. The Court never says whether it deems this interest compelling (the opinion is devoid of any mention of standard of review) but, self-evidently, it is not.

II

The Court makes no serious attempt to defend the program's neutrality, and instead identifies two features thought to render its discrimination less offensive. The first is the lightness of Davey's burden. The Court offers no authority for approving facial discrimination against religion simply because its material consequences are not severe. I might understand such a test if we were still in the business of reviewing facially neutral laws that merely happen to burden some individual's religious exercise, but we are not. See *Employment Div., Dept. of Human Resources of Ore. v. Smith,* 494 U.S. 872, 885, 110 S.Ct. 1595, 108 L.Ed.2d 876 (1990). Discrimination *on the face of a statute* is something else. The indignity of being singled out for special burdens on the basis of one's religious calling is so profound that the concrete harm produced can never be dismissed as insubstantial. The Court has not required proof of "substantial" concrete harm with other forms of discrimination, and it should not do so here.

Even if there were some threshold quantum-of-harm requirement, surely Davey has satisfied it. The First Amendment, after all, guarantees *free* exercise of religion, and when the State exacts a financial penalty of almost $3,000 for religious exercise—whether by tax or by forfeiture of an otherwise available benefit—religious practice is anything *but* free. The Court's only response is that "Promise Scholars may still use their scholarship to pursue a secular degree at a different institution from where they are studying devotional theology." But part of what makes a Promise Scholarship attractive is that the recipient can apply it to his *preferred* course of study at his *preferred* accredited institution. That is part of the "benefit" the State confers. The Court distinguishes our precedents only by swapping the benefit to which Davey was actually entitled (a scholarship for his chosen course of study) with another, less valuable one (a scholarship for any course of study *but* his chosen one). On such reasoning, any facially discriminatory benefits program can be redeemed simply by redefining what it guarantees.

The other reason the Court thinks this particular facial discrimination less offensive is that the scholarship program was not motivated by animus toward religion. The Court does not explain why the legislature's motive natters, and I fail to see why it should. If a State deprives a citizen of trial by jury or passes an *ex post facto* law, we do not pause to investigate whether it was actually trying to accomplish the evil the Constitution prohibits. It is sufficient that the citizen's rights have been infringed. * * *

The Court has not approached other forms of discrimination this way. When we declared racial segregation unconstitutional, we did not ask whether the State had originally adopted the regime, not out of "animus" against blacks, but because of a well-meaning but misguided belief that the races would be better off apart. * * * We do sometimes look to legislative intent to smoke out more subtle instances of discrimination, but we do so as a *supplement* to the core guarantee of facially equal treatment, not as a replacement for it.

There is no need to rely on analogies, however, because we have rejected the Court's methodology in this very context. In *McDaniel v. Paty,* 435 U.S. 618, 98 S.Ct. 1322, 55 L.Ed.2d 593 (1978), we considered a Tennessee statute that disqualified clergy from participation in the state constitutional convention. That statute, like the one here, was based upon a state constitutional provision—a clause in the 1796 Tennessee Constitution that disqualified clergy from sitting in the legislature. The State defended the statute as an attempt to be faithful to its constitutional separation of church and state, and we accepted that claimed benevolent purpose as bona fide. Nonetheless, because it did not justify facial discrimination against religion, we invalidated the restriction.

It may be that Washington's original purpose in excluding the clergy from public benefits was benign, and the same might be true of its purpose in maintaining the exclusion today. But those singled out for disfavor can be forgiven for suspecting more invidious forces at work. Let there be no doubt: This case is about discrimination against a religious minority. Most citizens of this country identify themselves as professing some religious belief, but the State's policy poses no obstacle to practitioners of only a tepid, civic version of faith. Those the statutory exclusion actually affects—those whose belief in their religion is so strong that they dedicate their study and their lives to its ministry—are a far narrower set. One need not delve too far into modern popular culture to perceive a trendy disdain for deep religious conviction. In an era when the Court is so quick to come to the aid of other disfavored groups, *see, e.g., Romer v. Evans,* 517 U.S. 620, 635, 116 S.Ct. 1620, 134 L.Ed.2d 855 (1996), its indifference in this case, which involves a form of discrimination to which the Constitution actually speaks, is exceptional.

* * *

Today's holding is limited to training the clergy, but its logic is readily extendible, and there are plenty of directions to go. What next? Will we deny priests and nuns their prescription-drug benefits on the ground that taxpayers' freedom of conscience forbids medicating the clergy at public expense? This may seem fanciful, but recall that France has proposed banning religious attire from schools, invoking interests in secularism no less benign than those the Court embraces today. When the public's freedom of conscience is invoked to justify denial of equal treatment, benevolent motives shade into indifference and ultimately into repression. Having accepted the justification in this case, the Court is less well equipped to fend it off in the future. I respectfully dissent.

Justice THOMAS, dissenting,

Because the parties agree that a "degree in theology" means a degree that is "devotional in nature or designed to induce religious faith," I assume that this is so for purposes of deciding this case. With this understanding, I join Justice Scalia's dissenting opinion. I write separately to note that, in my view, the study of theology does not necessarily implicate religious devotion or faith. The contested statute denies Promise Scholarships to students who pursue "a degree in theology." But the statute itself does not define "theology." And the usual definition of the term "theology" is not limited to devotional studies. "Theology" is defined as "[t]he study of the nature of God and religious truth" and the "rational inquiry into religious questions." American Heritage Dictionary 1794 (4th ed.2000). * * * These definitions include the study of theology from a secular perspective as well as from a religious one.

Assuming that the State denies Promise Scholarships only to students who pursue a degree in devotional theology, I believe that Justice Scalia's application of our precedents is correct. Because neither party contests the validity of these precedents, I join Justice Scalia's dissent.

Notes and Questions

1. *The Scope of Locke.* After *Zelman*, the question remained whether government *must* fund religious pursuits or entities when it creates a general funding program that is neutral on its face and provides private choice to recipients. As the *Locke* Majority notes, the holding in *Zelman* is permissive—i.e. government can open such programs to those who will use the funds at religious entities—not mandatory. Did *Locke* answer this question? What if the state denied Mr. Davey the right to use his scholarship at religious institutions in general? It would seem the Majority decision in *Locke* does not answer this question, and indeed may provide support for both sides in such a case.

2. *Discrimination Versus Subsidy.* The *Locke* Majority characterizes the state's decision to refuse to fund a degree in devotional theology as a subsidy decision. It points out that the state allows its scholarship funds to be used at religious institutions and by religion majors (not majoring in devotional theology) at any eligible institution. Thus, the state simply decided not to pay for something that it could pay for, devotional theology training, because of state constitutional (and perhaps political) concerns. The dissent characterizes this as discrimination against religion. How does the dissent define discrimination under these facts? Under the dissent's approach would the state have a duty to fund core religious training and institutions if it makes general funding available for similar non-religious training and institutions? Is this consistent with the Court's earlier decisions? If so, which ones?

3. *Locke as a Limiting Principle.* The holding in *Locke* provides a limiting principle on the *Zelman* rationale. Government may, but need not, fund devotional theology training pursuant to a facially neutral funding program. Is this much of a limiting principle? Would the Court allow a state to deny funding to anyone who sought to use that funding to major in religion? Consider the fact that the state could allow students to use the funding to major in anything but

law. Why might this be allowed, but the denial of funding for religion majors not allowed? Or does *Locke* suggest there is no difference?

4. *State Versus Federal Constitutional Claims.* The Supremacy Clause, U.S. Const. Art. VI, makes the U.S. Constitution the supreme law of the land. Thus, when state constitutional provisions lead to results that violate a provision of the U.S. Constitution, the state constitutional claim must yield. View it as a game of rock, paper, scissors, where the U.S. Constitution always wins. The best way to avoid losing is to stay out of the game. In fact, most state constitutional provisions and laws do not conflict with provisions of the U.S. Constitution, but when they do, the smart money is on the U.S. Constitution. Ordinarily, the U.S. Constitution can be seen as creating a floor below which states can not go—i.e. state's can not provide less protection than they are required to under the U.S. Constitution. Yet, state constitutions may provide more protection than the Federal Constitution. This is where the state of Washington's argument comes into play. The state argued that its state establishment clause provides greater protection against state establishment of religion than the federal Establishment Clause, and that in denying Davey funding under the program it was simply fulfilling its duty under its own constitution. But because Davey asserted claims under the U.S. Constitution the state constitutional claims could not trump a valid claim under First Amendment to the U.S. Constitution. Thus, the dispute between the majority and dissent in *Locke* over the duty to subsidize question is significant. If the majority is correct Davey's First Amendment rights haven't been violated, and therefore Washington is free to act pursuant to its state constitution. If the dissent is correct, Davey has asserted a valid claim under the Federal Free Exercise Clause and the state may not justify such an interference with Davey's federal constitutional rights based on the state constitution. Rock, paper, scissors. The dispute between the majority and dissent is heavily focused on whether the state was playing the game.

Chapter Five

PERSPECTIVES ON THE ESTABLISHMENT CLAUSE

A. INTRODUCTION

In the preceding four chapters you read cases and materials exploring a number of major issues that arise under the Establishment Clause. As you saw, there has been significant disagreement over the meaning and purpose of the Establishment Clause among the Justices and among lower court judges. There is a rich literature exploring these issues from a variety of perspectives. Unfortunately, there is no way to capture the richness of this literature while keeping the readings in this book manageable. Yet exposure to this literature is essential to your understanding of the Establishment Clause because the debate over the clause's meaning and purpose continues. This is not a field in which the labels "doctrine" and "theory" can be seen as separate. The trend in the field has consistently shown that today's theory can be the basis for tomorrow's doctrine (and sometimes tomorrow's doctrine reaches back to yesterday's theory).

In this Chapter, and in Chapter Seven dealing with the Free Exercise Clause, you will have a chance to explore significant concepts and theories. Much of the material in this Chapter was written by leading scholars in the field. All of the material has something to say about the meaning of the Establishment Clause. Choosing the material was a hard job because it was necessary to leave out a large number of great articles. The choices were made based on subject matter, inclusion of earlier work in the selected articles, and in some cases on timeliness. All of the material has been edited with most footnotes omitted. As you read the material you might find answers to some of the questions that arose in earlier readings. You might also find yourself asking new questions or questioning old positions.

B. SEPARATION, ACCOMMODATION, AND NEUTRALITY

The following materials explore whether the relationship between government and religion should be based on principles of separation, accommodation, and/or neutrality. More importantly, it addresses the meaning of these concepts and the interaction between them. As you will see, there is great disagreement among the authors regarding the meaning, and even the existence, of some of these concepts. Yet it is interesting to see that many of the scholars who disagree about the governing principles or the nature of those principles may agree on results, while those who agree on the governing principles may disagree about their meaning and application. Several of the articles reference the Free Exercise Clause, which you will study in Chapters Six and Seven. It is important to be aware that the debate over the meaning of the Establishment Clause can have repercussions in the Free Exercise Clause context and vice versa. While you have not yet studied the Free Exercise Clause in detail, the articles excerpted here provide enough context for you to understand the relevant aspects of that clause.

It is important to remember that the following articles are simply a sampling of the debate regarding the concepts of separation, accommodation, and neutrality. Each article provides a lens on the issues, and each draws from earlier scholarship in the field. You should not assume, however, that they cover the full range of ideas in this area. The articles are not in chronological order. They are roughly ordered based on overlapping substance. Even this ordering was hard, however, because there are numerous ways in which articles interact with each other.

The first three articles in this section address the meaning of "neutrality" and the role of the concept of separation (if any) in defining "neutrality." The last two articles in this section address the interaction between separation and accommodation of religion, and in the process demonstrate two very different views of the concept of separation (each of these views may be contrasted with the views of that concept set forth in the first three articles). As you read the following material ask yourself which positions you agree with and why. Also ask yourself at what level the authors disagree with each other if they disagree at all.

DOUGLAS LAYCOCK, *THE UNDERLYING UNITY OF SEPARATION AND NEUTRALITY*

46 EMORY L.J. 43 (1997).

I. INTRODUCTION

This Article began as an oral comment on Professor Carl Esbeck's article in this Journal,[1] but it has grown into much more. It also comments on Professor Ira Lupu's recent article on the death of separa-

---

1. Carl H. Esbeck, *A Constitutional Case for Governmental Cooperation with* *Faith–Based Social Service Providers*, 46 EMORY L.J. 1 (1997).

tionism,[2] which posits a theoretical model quite similar to Professor Esbeck's, and it offers a synthesis of the Supreme Court's cases that is quite different from that of Professors Esbeck and Lupu. They view separation and neutrality as inconsistent theories, with neutrality gradually replacing separation in the Supreme Court's decisions. I do not believe that the Supreme Court has ever understood separation to be inconsistent with neutrality, although a minority of the Court may have come to see such a conflict in recent cases. I believe that the Supreme Court has thought itself committed to both separation and neutrality, and that separation and neutrality are two aspects of a consistent understanding of religious liberty.

Professor Esbeck posits two fundamentally different theories of religious liberty. He offers the theory of separationism, which he attributes to the Supreme Court and which he describes as dominant. He also offers the theory of neutrality, which he attributes to recent religious speech cases, and which he describes as "separationism's major competitor." He says the neutrality theory offers "a theory centered on the unleashing of personal liberty to the end that, with minimal governmental interference, individuals make their own religious choices."

* * *

* * * Professor Esbeck posits competing theories of religious liberty and asks which of these theories would permit government funding of secular services delivered by religious providers. I am more interested in how the competing theories relate to each other.

Indeed, I agree with almost everything Professor Esbeck says except the way he structures and labels his theories. I agree with his claim that charitable choice is constitutional in most of its applications. I agree that the Supreme Court has brought two conflicting theories to the Establishment Clause. And I agree that the way to resolve the conflict between these theories is to recognize that an underlying purpose of religious liberty is to minimize government influence on religious choices. I have called this underlying purpose "substantive neutrality" * * *.[19]

II. Two Ways of Thinking About Two Theories

Professor Esbeck's labels for the two conflicting theories in the Supreme Court are "separationism" and "neutrality." I think that these are the wrong labels, and that it is both a theoretical and tactical mistake to contrast these labels so sharply. To frame the universe of possibilities in this way is to make the Court's doctrine seem more hostile than it is to Professor Esbeck's substantive position. It concedes the rhetorical benefits of the separationist label to those who do indeed believe that separation requires discrimination against religion; it sug-

---

2. Ira C. Lupu, *The Lingering Death of Separationism*, 62 Geo. Wash. L. Rev. 230 (1994).

19. Douglas Laycock, *Formal, Substantive, and Disaggregated Neutrality Toward Religion*, 39 DePaul L. Rev. 993 (1990).

gests that neutrality requires repudiation of the separation of church and state. Neither the Court nor the American people are likely to accept such a repudiation, nor should they. Separation has important benefits that neither Professor Esbeck nor I are willing to abandon.

The central meaning of separation is to separate the authority of the church from the authority of the state, so that "no religion can invoke government's coercive power and no government can coerce any religious act or belief." This separation is essential to the religious liberty of the numerically dominant faith, if any, and to the religious liberty of dissenters and nonbelievers.

I believe that the Court's view of separation is similar, although less fully articulated. In the Court's view, separation is and always has been a means of maximizing religious liberty, of minimizing government interference with religion, and thus, of implementing neutrality among faiths and between faith and disbelief. The Court may have been mistaken in some of its applications of separation, but it has never said that separation was fundamentally distinct from neutrality or religious choice.

My disagreement with Professor Esbeck is also a disagreement with Professor Lupu, who has offered a similar analysis of how neutrality is replacing separation as the core concept of religious liberty. In Professor Lupu's view, "separationism has a doctrine of secular privilege at its heart; the public arena is for secular argument only." "The separationist premise of thoroughly privatized religion is symbolically threatened even if sectarian forces merely occupy public space." There are advocates, and even Justices, who sometimes seem to understand separation in this way. That is why I once called separation a "misleading metaphor" * * *.

As I have argued elsewhere, there is little basis for that version of separation in constitutional text, history, or structure. So-called separationism that would privilege secular beliefs and bar religious arguments from public debates mistakes freedom of speech and the working of democracy for establishment. It distorts constitutional provisions that protect the people from the government into provisions that protect the government from the people. And separation that subordinates or marginalizes religion is hard to reconcile with the historical fact that evangelical Christians demanded the Establishment Clause as well as the Free Exercise Clause.

I will say more about history later, but the principal point of this Article is doctrinal. Professors Esbeck and Lupu describe a certain view of separation, but that view has never commanded a majority of the Supreme Court. The conflict in the Supreme Court has not been over separation versus neutrality. A better set of labels for the two competing theories in the Court's cases would be the "no-aid" theory and the "nondiscrimination" theory. * * * The no-aid theory would forbid any government conduct that aids religion, and it would most especially and most stringently forbid financial aid. What I am calling the nondiscrimination theory would forbid government to discriminate either in favor of religion or against religion.

Each of these theories is said by its supporters to be consistent with neutrality; the disagreement is over the baseline from which to measure neutrality. It is fair to say that the Court has rarely discussed its choice of baseline, and that Justices of all persuasions have sometimes appeared inconsistent in their choice of baseline. But the implicit baselines of the two theories are readily identifiable. In the no-aid theory, the baseline is government inactivity, because doing nothing neither helps nor hurts religion. Any government aid to religion is a departure from that baseline, and thus a departure from neutrality. In the nondiscrimination theory, the baseline is the government's treatment of analogous secular activities; a government that pays for medical care should pay equally whether the care is provided in a religious or a secular hospital. In this theory, any discrimination against religion is a departure from neutrality.

III.   No Answer from History

The no-aid theory has a narrower version, or a core application, which we might call the "no-funding principle": government should not fund religious functions. The no-funding principle looms large in the American tradition of religious liberty because of two historical controversies of great importance: church finance in the eighteenth century and school finance in the nineteenth century. But neither of these controversies is a reliable guide to the choice between the no-aid theory and the nondiscrimination theory.

Financing of churches was the central church-state issue of the 1780s, and was the immediate background to the adoption of the Establishment Clause in 1791. The single most famous American statement on disestablishment, James Madison's Memorial and Remonstrance Against Religious Assessments, was written in opposition to the general assessment bill in the Virginia legislature, which would have provided tax support for teachers of the Christian religion. If history settles anything in this area, it is that a general assessment would be unconstitutional.

But nothing like the general assessment has been seriously proposed since repeal of the Massachusetts establishment in 1833. The general assessment was a tax solely for the support of clergy in the performance of their religious functions. The reason for supporting religious functions was not that they fell within the neutrally drawn boundaries of some larger category of activities to be supported by the state. Rather, religion was to be singled out for special support because the state deemed it to be of special value.

The essence of the general assessment was massive discrimination in favor of religious viewpoints. * * * When government funded almost nothing, the baseline of government inactivity was the same as the baseline of analogous secular activities. As applied to the general assessment, the no-aid theory and the nondiscrimination theory were fully consistent. But the two theories are not consistent, and the choice of baselines matters dramatically, when government spends three-eighths of gross domestic product. * * *

The other great controversy that gave prominence to the no-funding principle was the nineteenth century dispute over common schools. Over a period of decades, and amidst great controversy, Americans built up the public schools and withdrew funding from religious schools. Thirty-two states adopted constitutional provisions expressly prohibiting public funding of religious schools. This controversy was the source of the legal tradition that treats school funding as an especially important issue in the separation of church and state.

The nineteenth century resolution of the school funding controversy arguably represents a political judgment on the constitutional questions raised by such funding. But there are difficulties with relying on that political judgment, even with respect to schools. It is especially danger-ous to abstract from that judgment a bright-line rule that applies to all contexts and overrides competing principles of religious neutrality and even freedom of speech. It is dangerous to reason from premises derived from an old dispute without recognizing and examining the source of the premises.

One difficulty with reasoning from nineteenth century rejection of funding for religious schools is that rejection was not part of the background of the First Amendment. And although the movement against funding religious schools amended many state constitutions, it conspicuously failed in its attempt to amend the federal Constitution.

Perhaps more important, the nineteenth century movement was based in part on premises that were utterly inconsistent with the First Amendment. Although there were legitimate arguments to be made on both sides, the nineteenth century opposition to funding religious schools drew heavily on anti-Catholicism. * * *

* * *

In contrast to the general assessment debate, the nineteenth centu-ry debate over school finance did present the choice between the no-aid theory and the nondiscrimination theory. Indeed, it presented the choice between the two competing baselines in substantially its modern form. Yet these nineteenth century debates did not produce a principled resolution to a difficult problem. Badly tainted by anti-Catholicism, these debates produced instead a nativist Protestant victory over Catholic immigrants. There was only a pretense of neutrality; the end result sustained a Protestant establishment in the public schools at public expense, with no relief for religious minorities. Major Jewish groups responded with their long effort to secularize the public schools. Catho-lics continued their long effort to build and finance private schools. Anti–Catholicism continued; the most extreme achievement of the attack on

Catholic schools was Oregon's law to close all private schools, struck down in 1925.[50]

* * *

The relevance of the nineteenth century Protestant–Catholic conflict is principally as a warning not to beg questions. Americans today should not unwittingly reason from a premise rooted in nineteenth century anti-Catholicism. We must think these questions out afresh, with no inherited presuppositions.

IV. The Two Theories in the Supreme Court

A. *The Conflicting Theories Struggling to Coexist*

The long controversy over financial aid to religious schools has associated separation with the no-aid theory. But that is not the only or necessary meaning of separation, and it has not been the dominant meaning of separation in the Supreme Court's cases. The Court rejected any strong version of the no-aid theory in Everson v. Board of Education, the case that Professor Esbeck cites as the beginning of separationist doctrine. Indeed, the essence of both the no-aid and the nondiscrimination theories is succinctly laid out in two paragraphs of the Court's opinion in Everson:

> Neither a state nor the Federal government can . . . aid one religion, (or) aid all religions. . . . No tax in any amount, large or small, can be levied to support any religious activities or institutions, whatever they may be called, or whatever form they may adopt to teach or practice religion. . . .

> New Jersey cannot . . . contribute tax-raised funds to the support of an institution which teaches the tenets and faith of any church. On the other hand, . . . New Jersey cannot hamper its citizens in the free exercise of their own religion. Consequently, it cannot exclude individual Catholics, Lutherans, Mohammedans, Baptists, Jews, Methodists, Non-believers, Presbyterians, or the members of any other faith, because of their faith, or lack of it, from receiving the benefits of public welfare legislation.

The tension between these two approaches has continued ever since. The Court unanimously supported separation, and even unanimously believed that government should not aid religion, but it voted five to four on what these principles meant for the facts of Everson. The majority held that nondiscriminatory payments for transportation to religious and public schools are not aid to religion. The dissenters thought that free transportation to religious schools is a form of aid, and that even nondiscriminatory aid is an establishment.

The majority in Everson rejected the no-aid theory on the facts, but it did not reject that theory universally, nor did it adopt the nondiscrimination theory universally. Both theories have had continuing influence.

50. Pierce v. Society of Sisters, 268 U.S. 510 (1925).

The influence of the no-aid theory is most apparent in the context of financial support for religious schools. * * * Of course this is no accident; the special doctrinal and political sensitivity of schools is partly a function of battles to control the minds of children and partly the legacy of the bitter nineteenth century conflicts over public funding of Catholic schools.

But even in this context, the no-aid theory never fully prevailed. The no-aid theory was rejected in all of the much-criticized distinctions that permitted money to flow, even to religious elementary schools, over the objection of no-aid advocates. As Professor Esbeck summarizes these distinctions, the Court has forbidden only direct aid to pervasively sectarian institutions. Indirect aid is permitted, as is direct aid to institutions that are sectarian but not pervasively so. Even direct aid to "pervasively sectarian" institutions may be permitted if it is directed to secular functions and cannot be diverted to religious functions. The Court's explanations of its "pervasively sectarian" category are inconsistent and incoherent; in practice, the category seems to be a synonym for elementary and secondary education.

* * *

Professor Esbeck poses the choice as separation versus neutrality, but the Court has rarely, if ever, posed the choice that way. The Lemon test, the very symbol of strict separation, itself began as an elaboration of neutrality. * * * The Lemon test's most explicit formulation of the neutrality requirement is in the second prong, which requires that government action have a primary effect "that neither advances nor inhibits religion." But the Lemon test disaggregated the inquiry into neutrality, asking about effects that advance religion and separately asking about effects that inhibit religion.

Disaggregating the inquiry made it easy for advocates of the no-aid position to implicitly use government inactivity as the baseline. It was easy to compare the funding of religious schools to doing nothing, and considered in light of that comparison, funding clearly seemed to "advance" religion. The disaggregated inquiry did not require the Court to compare the "advancing" effects of aid to the "inhibiting" effects of funding secular schools but not religious schools, so the Court did not have to decide which was the greater departure from neutrality. And anyway, the Court never took the "inhibiting" prong of Lemon seriously in the context of school finance. The Court summarily rejected claims that refusing to fund religious schools discriminates against those who wish to attend them, and it also rejected arguments that funding should be permitted under the Establishment Clause because it serves free exercise values.

There were many possible reasons for the Justices' inclination to the no-aid baseline in the context of aid to religious schools. Indeed, when historical context is also considered, the surprise is not that the Court so often adopted the no-aid baseline, but that even in the context of schools it sometimes adopted the analogous-secular-funding baseline, permitting nondiscriminatory funding of transportation, textbooks, and some services.

The no-aid baseline seemed natural because it had seemed politically settled for all of the Justices' lives that the state could not finance religious schools. Moreover, all of the Justices had lived their formative years well before the dramatic reduction of Protestant–Catholic conflict in the 1960s. But the story runs deeper than that. The historian John T. McGreevy has recently documented a shift in the nature of anti-Catholicism in the period leading up to Everson. The 1920s saw a resurgence of the Ku Klux Klan and of the obviously bigoted anti-Catholicism associated with it; few intellectuals were willing to publicly associate themselves with that. But that wave faded, to be replaced by a wave of open and respectable anti-Catholicism among the American intellectual elite. * * *[T]hese intellectuals saw Catholicism as inimical to democracy and conducive to fascism or other forms of authoritarian government. * * *

* * * McGreevy was able to document that this intellectual anti-Catholic movement attracted the favorable attention of Justices Black, Frankfurter, Rutledge, and Burton, and with the intellectual attitude so pervasive, many of the other Justices and the elite lawyers who would later become Justices were likely to have been exposed to it directly or indirectly.

Everson was written in 1947, before Blanshard's book but well into the period of intellectual anti-Catholicism. These anti-Catholic attitudes plainly did not control the result in Everson, but they influenced the dissent and they may have influenced the majority's no-aid rhetoric. It is at least clear that the dominant intellectual response to Everson was to endorse its no-aid rhetoric and to condemn the holding.

Respectable anti-Catholicism faded in the 1950s and all but collapsed in the 1960s in the wake of the Kennedy presidency and Vatican II. But even at the time of Lemon, some Justices were influenced by residual anti-Catholicism and by a deep suspicion of Catholic schools. This appears most clearly in Justice Douglas's citation of an anti-Catholic hate tract in his concurring opinion in Lemon,[89] and in Justice Black's dissenting opinion in Board of Education v. Allen. The Court's opinion in Lemon is more subtle and arguably open to more charitable interpretations, but it relied on what it considered to be inherent risks in religious schools despite the absence of a record in Lemon itself and despite contrary fact-finding by the district court in the companion case.

Funding for religious schools was still a Catholic issue in 1971, and the Court's assumptions about religious schools were assumptions about Catholic schools. Most Protestants still opposed funding for religious schools; this included evangelical Protestants, who had not yet sought funding for their own schools. While Lemon was pending in the Supreme Court, eleven state conventions of Southern Baptists passed resolutions

---

89. Lemon v. Kurtzman, 403 U.S. 602, 635 n. 20 (1971) (Douglas, J., concurring). For illustrative quotations from the tract, see Douglas Laycock, *Civil Rights and Civil Liberties*, 54 Chi.-Kent L. Rev. 390, 418–21 (1977).

opposing financial aid to private schools. * * * At the time of Lemon, the evangelical claim that public schools were secular and hostile to religion was little developed beyond criticism of the school prayer decisions, and there was substantial dissent even from that: the Southern Baptist Convention adhered to its separationist tradition and opposed the school prayer amendment. The evangelical movement is bitterly unhappy with Lemon today, but at the time, it was on the other side.

Two important denominations dissented from the dominant Protestant position: the Missouri Synod Lutherans and the Christian Reformed Church, each with well-developed systems of religious schools. These denominations supported financial aid in the 1960s and led in developing the argument against secularized public schools. Protestant, Jewish, and independent schools were active defendants in Lemon, and Protestant and Orthodox Jewish organizations filed or joined in briefs supporting financial aid to schools, but these efforts did little to change the impression that the case was essentially about aid to Catholic schools. * * * At oral argument both sides reportedly emphasized that the legislation was needed to rescue the financially troubled Catholic schools in Pennsylvania. In the companion case, the Court focused on the characteristics of Roman Catholic schools in Rhode Island, which taught 95% of the private school students in the state.

* * *

With the case posed in this way, it was easier to see funding as a subsidy for one church than as a means of achieving neutrality across a wide range of views. Viewing the program as a subsidy for one church made it harder to take the view of later conservatives that opposition to funding reflected hostility to religion in general.

The analogous-secular-activity baseline was also partially obscured by the facts of cases, which never squarely presented the discrimination argument. When government funds only public schools, it discriminates between public schools and private schools and only incidentally between secular schools and religious schools. Discrimination between public and private institutions is rarely if ever unconstitutional; the Court is always suspicious of claims of a constitutional right to government money.

Finally, the Court in 1971 was at the height of its battle "to achieve the greatest possible degree of actual desegregation" in public schools; it affirmed a busing order for the first time in the same Term as Lemon. The prospect of subsidized private schools threatened to aggravate the difficulties of desegregation by expanding the avenues for white flight. * * * The Justices may or may not have known that desegregation in Mississippi had produced a nine-fold increase in the number of non-Catholic private schools * * *. Those who organized the Lemon litigation argued these dangers; they named an African–American man, Alton Lemon, as the lead plaintiff, and devoted ten pages of their brief to a segregation claim. No Justice ruled on that claim, but every Justice took note of the issue, and it is hard to believe that no Justice was influenced by it.

All these factors tended to obscure the possibility of choosing the government's treatment of analogous secular activity as the baseline. Thus, throughout the 1970s and into the 1980s, the Court more often than not restricted financial aid to religious schools, usually without attention to its implicit choice of baseline. But despite these factors, the Court never invalidated all forms of aid, it never abandoned talk of neutrality, and it never repudiated the nondiscrimination theory.

Professors Esbeck, Lupu, and Monsma all attribute the birth of the neutrality theory to Widmar v. Vincent in 1981 [See supra. at Chapter Three]. * * *

The Court did not adopt a neutrality theory in Widmar and a separation theory in Lemon. The Court did indeed have two different theories, but it thought that they were variants of a single theory and that each variant was consistent with neutrality and also with separation. Each variant applied in its own sphere. There was the no-aid (or no-advancing) variant of Lemon, with its core application to financial aid to religious schools, and the nondiscrimination variant of Widmar, with its core application to religious speech. The Court thought that Lemon and Widmar were entirely consistent.

The problem with treating these cases as consistent is that the separate spheres are illusory. Advocates can logically expand each variant from its point of origin until it covers the universe of cases. The no-aid theory can be applied to religious speech, and some lower courts and commentators have done so. When a religious group meets on campus, it gets free use of a room, free heating or air conditioning, free lighting, a convenient meeting place for its members, and access to a larger potential audience. These may all be said to advance religion, and if no one inquires into the inhibiting effects of allowing groups to meet on campus only so long as they refrain from discussing religion, letting religious groups meet on campus looks like aid forbidden by the no-aid theory.

Similarly, the nondiscrimination theory can be applied to financial aid to religious schools, and advocates for such aid have attempted to do so. The state will spend large sums to educate children in secular public schools, but only if they forfeit their constitutional right to attend religious schools. This is certainly discrimination between two sets of schools that differ sharply in their approach to religion. The nondiscrimination theory could be applied here, and if it were, the Court would have to overrule all the cases invalidating aid to religious schools. State subsidies to both public and private schools would neutrally fund education that satisfies the compulsory education laws, without regard to whether that education is provided in a religious or secular environment. The Court would not have to hold that the Constitution requires public funding for religious schools; it could say that the existing discrimination is really between public schools and private schools, not between secular schools and religious schools. But if government chose to end that discrimination and fund private schools, the nondiscrimination theory would permit such funding and would require that it not discriminate between religious private schools and secular private schools.

* * *

It is thus impossible to create a coherent theory out of what the Court has done since Lemon. There are two theories, and they are inconsistent, as Professor Esbeck argues. But for most of the last half century, the Court did not recognize the inconsistency. It is a mistake to apply the separationist label only to the no-aid half of what the Court did under Lemon, or to apply the neutrality label only to the nondiscrimination half. To concede that charitable choice cannot be reconciled with separation is to create unnecessary doctrinal difficulty; it is to sever connections with a long and honorable tradition and to endanger the benefits of separation. Supporters of charitable choice need not oppose or repudiate the separation of church and state.

B.   The Theories in Open Conflict

* * *

After Rosenberger v. [Rector and Visitors of the Univ. of Virginia, *see supra.* at Chapters Three and Four], it is very difficult to imagine that the no-aid and nondiscrimination theories can be reconciled by drawing careful boundaries between their separate spheres. The boundaries have been erased and the Court will have to choose, however much it hopes to avoid the choice. The Court split five to four in Rosenberger, and the majority hedged the opinion with unpersuasive distinctions and reservations. But forced to choose, the Court applied the nondiscrimination theory to the funding of religious speech by a pervasively religious organization.

Charitable choice presents a far easier case than Rosenberger for application of the nondiscrimination theory. Charitable choice is easier both doctrinally and politically, because when government contracts with religious providers to deliver social services, it gets full secular value for its money. The government gets to specify the social service, and the government gets that service delivered. The secular benefit is far more tangible than in Rosenberger, and there is little doubt that the secular benefit is fully equal to the government's cost.

The social service context also makes charitable choice far easier than school vouchers or other forms of support for religious education. As already noted, religious education has its own unique history of bitter religious conflict in this country. There was arguably a political resolution of the constitutional question, and judicial doctrine reflects that history. An especially strong suspicion of government funding for religious education is deeply embedded in the case law and in the beliefs and motivations of the organizations that litigate these issues.

Apart from education cases, there are no Supreme Court cases restricting government financing of church-affiliated social services. Bradfield v. Roberts is the case most nearly on point, unanimously upholding payments for medical services.[146] Bowen v. Kendrick[147] is the nearest modern equivalent, narrowly upholding government grants to religious institutions to teach sexual responsibility to adolescents. The Court may have found Kendrick difficult in part because it involved a form of education—indeed, education on a topic where the government's secular message closely paralleled well-known religious teachings. I know of no modern cases challenging government payments to church hospitals, feeding programs, or other noneducational social services. * * *

Charitable choice does not appear to be different in principle from these and other longstanding contracts with religious social service agencies. The recently enacted provisions for charitable choice regularize, and make more visible, a practice that some states and cities have long followed without significant challenge. If charitable choice is challenged, I expect the Court to apply the nondiscrimination theory and to uphold the statute.

V.   UNITING THE TWO THEORIES: SUBSTANTIVE NEUTRALITY

I have argued that the no-aid and nondiscrimination theories each attempt to implement both neutrality and separation. I have also argued that the attempt to confine the no-aid and nondiscrimination theories to separate spheres has collapsed; we must find some deeper criterion for choosing between them. This criterion must be found in the underlying purposes that unite neutrality and separation. * * *

* * *

When Professor Esbeck favors separation on some issues, and neutrality on other issues, we have additional evidence that these two theories are not as opposed as he claims. Something unites them, as I have said. This something eventually appears in his article: The "goal is the minimization of the government's influence over personal choices concerning religious beliefs and practices."[158]

I have been urging that standard for ten years, in almost those words. Minimizing government influence maximizes religious liberty by maximizing the autonomy of religious choice. Minimizing government influence is consistent with neutrality; a government without influence over religion neither encourages nor discourages religion; it neither advances nor inhibits religion. Minimizing government influence is consistent with the central meaning of separation—it maximally separates government power and influence from religious belief and practice. Minimizing government influence implements separation in terms of a coherent purpose—not institutional separation as a goal in itself, and not separation as a euphemism for whatever is worst for religion, but separation as minimizing government influence over religious belief or disbelief, practice or nonpractice.

---

146. 175 U.S. 291 (1899).

147. 487 U.S. 589 (1988).* * *

158. Esbeck, *supra* note 1, at 25, *accord, id.* at 26 n.100.

The goal of minimizing government influence on religious choices provides a criterion for choosing between the baseline of government inactivity and the baseline of how government treats analogous secular activity. Recall that this choice of baseline defines the difference between the no-aid version of neutrality and the nondiscrimination version of neutrality. The same choice of baseline appears in a somewhat different guise in the debate over regulatory exemptions. Those who support exemptions argue from a government-inactivity baseline: compared to doing nothing, government regulation burdens religion. Those who oppose exemptions argue for an analogous-secular-activity baseline: if secular peyote use is regulated and religious peyote use is not, this looks like discrimination.

Uniform selection of government inactivity as the baseline would produce a regime of no financial aid (money would be aid) and of regulatory exemptions (regulation would be a burden). This approximates the traditional position of the ACLU and Americans United [for Separation of Church and State]. Uniform selection of analogous secular activity as the baseline would produce a regime of nondiscriminatory financial aid and no regulatory exemptions. * * * I have called [this] formal neutrality.

Minimizing government influence on religion, which I have called substantive neutrality, is its own baseline, dictating variable choices between the two baselines discussed so far. Substantive neutrality sometimes invokes government's treatment of analogous secular activity as the baseline, requiring that religious and secular activity get the same treatment. Equal funding for religious and secular hospitals is an example. But sometimes substantive neutrality requires that religion get better treatment than similar secular activities, as in most claims to religious exemptions from regulation. And sometimes, substantive neutrality requires that religion be treated in ways that are arguably worse than the treatment available to similar secular activities. Most obviously, government cannot celebrate religion or lead religious exercises. In these contexts, when religion must be treated better or worse than analogous secular activities, substantive neutrality invokes government inactivity as the baseline. Prosecution makes religion worse off, and celebration makes it better off, than if government did nothing.

How do we know when to use which baseline? How does minimizing government influence generate a more fundamental baseline that unifies these arguably contrasting results? Minimizing government influence requires that we minimize government incentives to change religious behavior in either direction. Thus, the underlying criterion for choosing among baselines depends on the incentives that government creates.

If government says it will pay for your soup kitchen if and only if you secularize it, that is a powerful incentive to secularize. If government is paying for soup kitchens, it ought to pay no matter who runs them, and it ought to pay without requiring religious providers to surrender their religious identity. In this context, the baseline of analogous secular activity is substantively neutral: if government will pay both religious and secular providers, it creates no incentive for either to change.

* * *

In the regulatory context, substantive neutrality generally requires the baseline of government inactivity. If government says it will send you to jail if you consume peyote in a worship service, that is a powerful disincentive to religious behavior. But an exemption for religious behavior rarely encourages people to join the exempted church. When religious exemptions do encourage religious behavior (when claims for religious exemptions are self-interested in a secular sense), claims to exemption present special difficulties and require special solutions. But when the claim to religious exemption is not contaminated by secular self-interest, exemption minimizes government influence on religion. The formal neutrality of punishing religious behavior under secular norms does not serve substantive neutrality.

Similarly, if government were free to praise or condemn religion, celebrate religious holidays, or lead prayers or worship services, government could potentially have enormous influence on religious belief and liturgy. Government is large and highly visible; for better or worse, it would model one form of religious speech or observance as compared to others. The closest approximation to substantive neutrality is for government to be silent on religious matters, and to leave private and public fora open to the enormous variety of religious views and forms of worship represented in the American people.

* * *

VI. CONCLUSION

Professor Esbeck and I agree that a significant doctrinal shift appears to be in progress. But the shift is not accurately described as the abandonment of separation and the adoption of neutrality. The Court was not against neutrality in the past, and the majority need not be against separation today.

A more precise statement would be that the Court has sometimes measured neutrality from a baseline of government inactivity, and sometimes from a baseline of how government treats analogous secular activities. With increasing frequency, and in increasingly sensitive contexts, the Court is choosing the baseline of analogous secular activity. Professor Esbeck emphasizes the funding cases, but there has been a similar shift with respect to regulatory exemptions, tax exemptions, and resolution of internal church disputes. Sometimes the Court attends to the choice of baseline; sometimes the shift appears to be intuitive and unreflective. * * *

Neither choice is right in every context. Sometimes one baseline best serves religious liberty, sometimes the other, depending on the incentives created. Unelaborated talk of neutrality tends toward formal neutrality, because it diverts attention from the substantive components of religious liberty. Substantive neutrality, understood as minimizing government influence on religious belief or practice, better captures both the individual's substantive right and the government's obligation of neutrality.

Separation is consistent with substantive neutrality. Separation can be a misleading metaphor; it requires definition and integration with other components of the religious liberty tradition. But it is too much a part of that tradition to be repudiated, and properly understood, it captures essential elements of that tradition. Separation helps explain why government cannot try to influence religious belief with its own religious speech, and why the Court's unelaborated neutrality talk has led to error on the question of regulatory exemptions.

The no-aid theory has an historical and political claim to the separationist label, but in the Supreme Court's cases, the no-aid theory was always forced to coexist with the nondiscrimination theory. And nondiscriminatory funding maximally separates government influence from religious choices. In the debate over charitable choice, both sides can claim parts of the separationist tradition. * * *

JOHN H. GARVEY, *WHAT'S NEXT AFTER SEPARATIONISM?*

46 Emory L.J. 75(1997).

Professor Carl Esbeck argues in his article that the traditional theory of separationism is giving way to a theory of equality (or more accurately, protection for religious choice). The argument is very astute, and I agree with much of it. I will give my own perspective on the same two points.

I. Separationism

A. *Indirect Aid*

Separationism is a theory about cause and effect. Lemon v. Kurtzman states the rule: the government must not cause religious effects. The distinction between direct and indirect aid is one way of implementing this rule. Indirect aid (e.g., vouchers, tax deductions) does not cause trouble for the government because there is an intervening cause: the individual who receives the aid can spend it in a number of different places. Hart and Honoré illustrate this way of thinking in their book Causation in the Law:

> If a guest sits down at a table laid with knife and fork and plunges the knife into his hostess's breast, her death is not in any context . . . thought of as caused by, or the effect or result of the waiter's action in laying the table. . . .

The Supreme Court in Witters v. Washington Department of Services for the Blind adopted a similar paradigm:

Any aid provided under Washington's program that ultimately flows to religious institutions does so only as a result of the genuinely independent and private choices of aid recipients.

Suppose now that the government gives the individual recipient aid that can only be used at a religious institution. In this case the outcome has been different. Joel Feinberg explains the distinction in his book Doing & Deserving:

> If the murder occurred in a prison dining hall ... where knives are never set on tables and diners may be expected to get violent, then the laying of the table would be the abnormal event of great explanatory power, and the provision of opportunity "the cause." The pertinent principle here is that the more expectable human behavior is, whether voluntary or not, the less likely it is to "negative causal connection."

The Court has reached a similar conclusion in cases about tuition grants that can only be used at private schools. * * * [T]he rule about indirect aid is this: It is permissible if given on equal terms to people who can spend it at religious and other institutions.

B.   Direct Aid: Separate Secular Services

The Court has sometimes approved even direct aid to religious institutions under the rule of separation. Once again the question has been whether the government causes religious effects. It does not, the Court has said, when the recipient can separate its religious and secular services, and the aid goes strictly to the secular side. This requires an effort on both sides—by the recipient and by the government—to keep money out of religious pockets. The recipient must divide its programs and activities into secular ones and religious ones. Think of the institution as a pool table with pockets on each side. You can see the effect of this rule on the campuses of religious colleges: some buildings are swept clean of religious icons, some courses are taught in a way that makes no mention of religion. The end result of this process is to put religion off in one place all by itself—like the divinity schools at Harvard, Chicago, and Duke. This is, to my mind, the most pernicious effect of the rule of separation. To obtain government aid, religious institutions will abandon or "privatize" their mission in much of what they do.

As for the government, we must keep an eye on the aid to see which pocket it goes into. This is often just a matter of accounting rules. For example, in Roemer v. Board of Public Works, a college aid case, the Court held that a state could give noncategorical grants to private (including religious) colleges, provided the schools segregated the funds, agreed not to spend the money for sectarian purposes, and accounted for the funds at the end of the year. The government has its accountants watch the ball to ensure it goes into a secular pocket.

A variation on this solution is to provide aid in kind (books, tests, diagnostic services), so it cannot be converted to religious use. This type of aid will fit only in the secular pocket, so we need not watch it.

Although I have been using school aid cases as examples, this way of thinking is also evident in the two direct-aid social services cases that the Court has decided. In Bowen v. Kendrick, the more recent decision, the Court upheld a facial challenge to the Adolescent Family Life Act (AFLA). AFLA permitted religious institutions to get federal grants to run programs for the care and prevention of teenage pregnancy. You can imagine the local office of Catholic Social Services doing this. Of course, the counselors at Catholic Social Services might say that the Bible, for a variety of good reasons, frowns on sex before marriage. The Court assumed that if that happened, aid would have gone into the wrong pocket. As I said, however, the suit was a challenge to AFLA on its face, and the Court said that "nothing in our prior cases warrants the presumption ... that religiously affiliated AFLA grantees are not capable of carrying out their functions under the AFLA in a lawful, secular manner."

It is possible to read the Court's opinion in Bradfield v. Roberts in the same way. That case was a challenge on its face to a law appropriating money to Providence Hospital in the District of Columbia, a hospital run by the Sisters of Charity of Emmitsburg, Maryland. The Court upheld the grant saying, "(t)here is no allegation that its hospital work is confined to members of that church or that in its management the hospital has been conducted so as to violate its charter in the smallest degree."

I. EQUALITY

A. *What Is Wrong with Causing Religious Effects?*

Separationism was the rule in Establishment Clause cases for three or four decades, but I think Professor Esbeck is right to suggest that its reign is ending. In fact, I would say that the end of separationism has been coming about since Ronald Reagan's first term. In his article, The Lingering Death of Separationism, Professor Ira Lupu gives several examples of this trend:[20]

1. New History: Since 1947, the official history of the Establishment Clause has been the one Justices Black and Rutledge wrote in Everson v. Board of Education. Everson stressed the role of Madison and Jefferson in Virginia's break with the Anglican church. But today we are more aware of the role that Congregationalists in New England and evangelicals in the North and South played in the early constitutional debates. Justice Rehnquist legitimized this history in 1985 in his dissent in Wallace v. Jaffree.

2. Justiciability Retreat: In the 1960s Flast v. Cohen created a special standing rule designed to encourage Establishment Clause claims. In 1982 the Court denied standing to a separationist organization

---

20. Ira C. Lupu, *The Lingering Death of Separationism*, 62 GEO. WASH. L. REV. 230 (1994).

challenging the federal government's transfer of some land to a Christian school for its ministry.

3.   New Symbols: In 1983 and 1984, the Court approved legislative prayer and a municipal nativity scene. This has not meant a regime of laissez-faire, but it is inconsistent with strict separationism.

4.   School Aid: The low point undoubtedly came in Aguilar v. Felton and Grand Rapids v. Ball, but since 1983 the Court has allowed aid to parochial schools in Mueller v. Allen and Zobrest v. Catalina Foothills School District. In addition, I think the Court essentially approved vouchers in Witters.

Why is this happening? One part of the answer is that the world has changed. Professor Lupu explains:

> Separationism thrived best when white Anglo–Saxon Protestants of low-level religious intensity constituted the bulk of our cultural elite. For members of this group, separationism reflected an attractive mix of privatized (hence unobtrusive) religion, opposition to a public subsidy of the educational mission of the Roman Catholic Church, and support for the mission of socializing Americans in what this elite perceived as the common American culture.[32]

Since then, the cultural elite has grown more diverse, America has had a spiritual awakening, and the public schools have lost our confidence.

Another part of the answer is that separationism rests on doubtful axioms. * * * In nearly all of these cases we are talking about aid that causes religious side effects. The aid is designed to improve math skills or cure hepatitis, but may incidentally help religion because it is given to religious providers. We assume that it is bad for the government to cause religious side effects. But why is it bad? Consider an analogy to equal protection. The Equal Protection Clause * * * holds that the government should not give aid to schools, hospitals, or lunch counters that engage in racial discrimination. The reason is that aid designed to improve math skills or cure hepatitis at segregated institutions will have the unpleasant side effect of promoting discrimination as well. But there is a difference between the two cases. Religion is not intrinsically evil like race discrimination; quite the contrary. When government aid causes religious side effects, such side effects are not inherently bad, like bigotry. In the case of religion, the harm occurs one step further removed. When government aid goes to religion we might then see:

1.   Bad secondary effects on the political system. Some people will form religious parties and fight (like "special interest groups") for subsidies. Others will form antireligious parties and fight (like "public interest groups") against aid for principles they oppose.

---

32.   Lupu, *supra* note 20, at 231.

2.   Bad secondary effects on religion. Madison argued in his Memorial and Remonstrance that aid has a debilitating effect. Religion that does not have to feed itself gets fat and lazy.

But we do not have additional effects like these every time government aid causes religious side effects. Suppose that in Bradfield the federal government not only built the isolation ward but also paid $500,000 to run it for a year. And suppose that the Sisters of Charity who staffed it offered prayers and spiritual comfort to patients who wanted them. This would violate the principle of separation because the nuns have not split apart their secular and religious activities. Therefore, we cannot be sure which ones the federal money is going to pay for. But as long as the nuns must provide what Jesse Choper calls "full secular value" we are unlikely to have churches lining up for government subsidies and ministers retiring on government pensions. To get a $500,000 grant a recipient has to spend at least that much running a hospital. That is not a very attractive proposition for an institution seeking a handout.

Here is a second doubtful axiom behind the rule of separation. We assume that if government and religion are kept separate, religious groups can raise their own money, live their own lives, provide their own services, etc. In an eighteenth-century world of minimalist government this may have been so. * * * [We are not] in the same place we were during the eighteenth century. The theory of separation must take account of that.

Here is a third and final point about the assumptions of separationism. Suppose that Congress appropriated $100 million for refurbishing local art galleries throughout the country. To qualify for funding, however, a gallery would have to promise to remove from public display any homoerotic sculpture, paintings, or photographs. This would be challenged, and I think held invalid, as an unconstitutional condition on the exercise of First Amendment rights. The government, we would say, cannot penalize those who take a particular point of view by withholding aid that is available to all other institutions in the same class. It is not a sufficient response to say that the disqualified gallery can still exhibit any art it wishes and raise money privately for its own refurbishing. And yet this is exactly what the theory of separation requires us to say about aid to religious institutions. If Congress gives money for math education, schools cannot qualify for this funding if they offer religion classes.

B.   Equal Aid

If separationism is on the way out, what will replace it? Principles of equality or neutrality will surely play an important part in any eventual solution.

This is certainly true of many cases about religious expression. In a handful of recent cases the Court has applied the First Amendment rule of content neutrality to religious speech. Most involved the use of public forums. * * * The only doubt I have about this area is that the free speech rule about traditional public forums, enforced in Pinette, is in some tension with the Establishment Clause rule about holiday displays. * * *

This rule of content neutrality rests on assumptions that are unique to the Free Speech Clause: that truth will prevail over falsehood in a fair fight and that public discussions should be uninhibited because people need information to vote intelligently. For this reason we cannot assume that the principle of neutrality automatically carries over to aid cases. Whether it is a related or an independent development, though, there is a discernible trend toward a rule of neutrality in aid cases too. The principle has been around for a while. It appeared in 1970 in Walz v. Tax Commission. The Court extended the principle to schools in 1983 in Mueller v. Allen. Walz and Mueller involved tax exemptions and deductions. In 1986 in Witters, the Court applied the rule to an outright grant. One way to explain the result, which appeals to separationists, is to say that the grant was indirect. But another way to see it is that the state made funds available to all blind people and expressed no preference about where they should spend it. This is equal treatment of all institutions. The Court said something similar in Zobrest in 1993.

* * *

I do not want to suggest that the idea of neutrality, if applied sensitively, will solve all Establishment Clause problems. I think this is unlikely. In free speech law, for example, the rule of content neutrality figures prominently in public forum cases; but we also have rules about prior restraints, overbreadth, commercial speech, libel, obscenity, and so on, and they are not all particular applications of a more general neutrality principle. The same is true here. The religious speech cases I mentioned * * * were all public forum cases, but religious speech problems can arise in other contexts where neutrality is not the answer. There is a sense in which regulatory exemptions are not neutral, but they are consistent with the Establishment Clause. And the rules of neutrality that we do use in Establishment Clause cases may differ from one another: the first two aid cases (Walz, Mueller) held that equal treatment was permitted; the free speech rule of neutrality is mandatory.

* * * I think * * * separationism is falling out of favor. And I also think that a principle of equality or neutrality will play an important part in filling the gap that it leaves.

FRANK S. RAVITCH, *A FUNNY THING HAPPENED ON THE WAY TO NEUTRALITY: BROAD PRINCIPLES, FORMALISM, AND THE ESTABLISHMENT CLAUSE*

38 Ga. L. Rev. 489 (2004).

I. Introduction

In recent years the landscape of Establishment Clause jurisprudence has changed dramatically. Landmark decisions such as *Zelman v. Sim-*

mons–Harris, and *Good News Club v. Milford Central School*, have placed significant emphasis on the concept of neutrality, specifically formal neutrality. Yet what if neutrality under the Establishment Clause is a myth—an unattainable dream? This Article explores the implications of this question, suggests that the answer raises serious concerns about the Court's approach, and points toward an alternative way of addressing Establishment Clause issues.

Interpreting the Establishment Clause has never been easy. There are many reasons for this, but a major factor is the interaction between the broad principles said to undergird the Establishment Clause and the myriad of factual contexts to which those principles must be applied. One obvious concern is the failure of the Justices of the U.S. Supreme Court to agree on underlying principles. Justices have long had disagreements about the meaning of principles such as separation and neutrality even when they agree on which principles apply. Some of these disagreements have been about the nature of the principles themselves, and others have been about their application to specific facts and contexts. Scholars have had similar disagreements over the nature of broad principles such as neutrality and separation, as well as their application. In recent years the Supreme Court has moved toward the principle of neutrality, specifically formal neutrality—at least in cases of government aid to religious institutions, religious access to government property and funding, and of course in the Free Exercise Clause context.

This Article asserts that neutrality, whether formal or substantive, does not exist. Other scholars have recognized this, and still others suggest that the concept is inherently dependant upon the baseline one chooses to use in describing it. The nature of neutrality has always been problematic, but over the last three terms the Court has made neutrality a concept of singular importance, whereas earlier Courts had other principles driving their decisions. * * *

Claims of neutrality cannot be proven. There is no independent neutral truth or baseline to which they can be tethered. Thus, any baseline to which we attach neutrality is not neutral; claims of neutrality built on these baselines are by their nature not neutral. This reasoning might seem circular—i.e., since there is no independent state of neutrality from which to derive neutral rules or applications of rules, there can be no neutral results and no means by which one can prove that a given baseline is neutral. * * * [T]he Court has used varying concepts of neutrality. In several cases Justices in the majority and dissenting opinions claimed to be relying on principles of neutrality yet reached opposite conclusions. Still, for all the problems the concept of neutrality caused in terms of doctrinal coherence, the fact that the Court generally viewed it as a broad and nebulous principle forced the Justices to rely on other principles in forming their views. * * *

* * * [T]he current Court's version of neutrality is particularly problematic because of its intensively formalistic nature and the fact that it appears to minimize the effects of government programs. Estab-

lishment Clause jurisprudence has traditionally been fact-sensitive, but the Court's formal neutrality approach lacks the tools to deal with the many situations to which it will invariably be applied. The more flexible *Lemon* test was much maligned because of the questionable distinctions drawn by the Court. Thirty years from now, the Court's apparent move toward a formal neutrality test might be viewed in the same way. Formalism does not necessarily beget clarity, and in the end—when the issues that arise are complex and fact specific a more formalistic test may lead to less clarity in the long-run. Such a test must either be contorted to fit the diversity of situations to which it will be applied, or it will ignore context and function somewhat like a bull in a china shop. * * *

* * *

If indeed there is no such thing as neutrality in Establishment Clause cases, and the current Court's concept of formal neutrality is flawed, where can we turn for a less flawed Establishment Clause jurisprudence? Alternatives proposed by scholars and others include: separationism, accommodation, equality, liberty, non-preferentialism, and some hybrid of these principles with neutrality. I do not mean to imply that these concepts do not make their own claims to neutrality but rather that they have been identified as broad principles in their own right. This Article will argue that most of these concepts have something to contribute to Religion Clause Jurisprudence, but no single principle is adequate across the varied contexts of religion clause cases. Indeed, some of these principles are little more than malleable constructions. The Article will propose a new test, the "facilitation test," which is based on several narrow principles.

* * *

II. NEUTRALITY DOES NOT EXIST

Steven Smith has explained:

... [T]he quest for neutrality, despite its understandable appeal and the tenacity with which it has been pursued, is an attempt to grasp at an illusion. Upon reflection, this failure should not be surprising. The impossibility of a truly "neutral" theory of religious freedom is analogous to the impossibility, recognized by modern philosophers, of finding some outside Archimedean point ... from which to look down on and describe reality. Descriptions of reality are always undertaken from a point within reality. In the same way, theories of religious freedom are always offered from the viewpoint of one of the competing positions that generate the need for such a theory; there is no neutral vantage point that can permit the theorist or judge to transcend these competing positions. Hence, insofar as a genuine and satisfactory theory of religious freedom would need to be "neutral" in this sense, rather than one that privileges one of the competing positions from the outset, a theory of religious freedom is as illusory as the ideal of neutrality it seeks to embody.[52]

Other scholars have also acknowledged the illusive and malleable nature of neutrality. Yet the Supreme Court has often used the term neutrality in its Religion Clause jurisprudence and has recently placed a great deal of emphasis on neutrality in a number of cases. The Court's use of the term until recently was largely symbolic—not in the sense that William Marshall's fascinating work has used that term—but rather in the sense that the Court was trying to send a message that its consideration of the issues was balanced. The Court did not use neutrality as the "be all" or "end all" concept in actually deciding cases. Rather, it also had to rely on other principles because neutrality is so malleable * * *. If there is no such thing as neutrality—or at least neutrality as more than a buzz-word—this seems a logical state of affairs. The Court suggests that it is acting neutrally, but can only define this neutrality by reference to other principles (which are not neutral).

The current Court, however, has begun to rely on neutrality more directly. Neutrality is no longer a background principle that the Court sees no need to consistently define. Rather it is an actuating principle that the Court apparently believes must be given a formalistic definition which can be rigidly applied. As will be seen, the Court connects its formal neutrality with what appear to be arguments for formal equality between religion and "non-religion." * * * This is particularly problematic because the Court does not explain why its formal neutrality is neutral given the competing views of neutrality, yet it uses terms such as "entirely neutral," "neutral in all respects," and "a program of true private choice." By relying on the term "neutrality" in this direct, yet unsubstantiated manner, the Court gives it extra power.

* * *

Lurking underneath the Court's "formal neutrality" doctrine is the notion that religion has no special status, and thus there is no need to differentiate between religion and non-religion if the government is acting "neutrally." A corollary to this notion is the argument that by treating religion differently, one is being hostile to religion. Thus, it is discrimination and hostility to religion if religious organizations are not given access to the same benefits as secular organizations, and at the same time there is nothing wrong with failing to provide religious exemptions to "generally applicable" laws even if those laws interfere with core religious practices. There would be significant problems with the Court's implicit presumptions even if neutrality were a real and attainable concept, but if neutrality is nothing more than an empty

---

52. *Smith,* FOREORDAINED FAILURE, supra note 13, at 96–97; *See also* Smith, *Symbols, Perceptions, and Doctrinal Illusions, supra* note 13, at 314 (the "pervasive commitment to neutrality has not yet generated any clear and convincing account of what neutrality actually entails. It has become increasingly clear, rather, that neutrality is a 'coat of many colors' ").

construction as this article asserts, the Court's other presumptions are even more problematic.

To understand the Rehnquist Court's notion of neutrality, it is useful to explore several of the cases where the Court has used neutrality analysis in varying contexts. * * * [T]his article will evaluate the Court's recent decision * * * in *Zelman v. Simmons–Harris* * * *. [That case] represent[s] a major area where the Court has used a version of its neutrality concept. * * * [T]he government aid to religious schools * * *. There are a number of other cases where the Court has used its formal neutrality principle [the sections discussing these cases have been deleted]. * * *

A.   *What Is Neutrality?*

The answer to the question—"What is neutrality?"—is central to the discussion of neutrality's place in religion clause jurisprudence. Thus, the answer that neutrality in the religion clause context is a myth may seem wholly unsatisfying. Yet can there be some use for a concept that is impossible to achieve? Neutrality is nothing more than a variable social construction, and formal neutrality nothing more than a rigid judicial construction. Even though each construction relies on a baseline that is not provably neutral, each has a value because people take solace in the notion of neutrality. Even if objectivity does not exist, there may be value in the *perception* of objectivity.

This sounds a bit odd at first, but it actually tracks much of what the pre-Rehnquist Court did with the concept of neutrality. Neutrality was mentioned quite a bit in numerous contexts, and sometimes the Court used a vague adjective to describe it such as "benevolent neutrality." Yet the Court never relied exclusively on the principle, supplementing it with separationism or accommodationism. For those who did not dig too deeply, there was always the reassuring tone of neutrality. For those who did dig, it was apparent that the Court could not substantiate its claim to neutrality, it had the other principles to fall back on and one could support or attack those other principles without focusing on whether they were neutral * * *. * * *

I do not defend the earlier Courts' use of the term. It was in a sense false advertising, because there is no way to prove that separationism or accommodationism is inherently more neutral than other principles. Yet the implicit message that was at least potentially infused in these earlier decisions—we know that neutrality is just a lofty principle and we are only using it to describe the outcome in this case *vis a vis* the alternatives—is less troubling than claims that both the mode of analysis and the results *are* neutral, while the alternatives are not. The latter is the message of the Rehnquist Court. The current Court has converted neutrality from a lofty goal to both the means and ends of religion clause analysis. Thus the question "What is neutrality?" takes on greater import.

The Court's struggle with neutrality reminds me of a conversation I recently had with my five-year-old daughter who was excited when she realized that her tooth was loose and would soon fall out. She realized that I might be the tooth fairy, and she asked if the tooth fairy is real or if I was the tooth fairy. Not wanting to burst her bubble or lie, I responded that the tooth fairy would leave her a present when she lost her tooth. She responded that she knows I am the tooth fairy but that she wants the tooth fairy to visit and leave her a present anyway.

This is akin to the struggle for neutrality. Like the tooth fairy, neutrality is just a myth, but like children who want the tooth fairy to visit, we want it to be real or at least for something to stand in for it to make us believe it is real. Unlike my five-year-old daughter, however, the Rehnquist Court has strenuously argued in essence that the tooth fairy is real, and when confronted with the question of why, the answer seems to be, "because we said so." The nuance of the stand-in concept— neutrality not as a real thing but a lofty principle that we try to emulate—seems lost.

Of course, even though neutrality as a lofty principle is less problematic than formal neutrality because it is not used to reach or empower outcomes, it is no more neutral. Thus, it is useful to look at another conception of neutrality that is far more nuanced and sophisticated. This conception of neutrality is one that recognizes there is no agreement about what neutrality is. I am referring to Douglas Laycock's construction of substantive neutrality. Laycock is not alone in arguing for substantive neutrality. Scholars, as well as Justices of the Supreme Court, have argued for some form of substantive neutrality. Professor Laycock's substantive neutrality has a lot to recommend it. In fact, it has had a strong influence on the facilitation approach I propose below. Still, as I hope to show, his approach has a lot of substantive value, but no neutrality. This might seem a bit nitpicky because as will be seen, the approach has a lot to offer. But while Professor Laycock may have made a wise choice among potential baselines, his choice and the resulting baseline are no more neutral than the Court's formal neutrality.

Professor Laycock's formulation of substantive neutrality is reflected in the following quote:

> My basic formulation of substantive neutrality is this: the religion clauses require government to minimize the extent to which it either encourages or discourages belief or disbelief, practice or nonpractice, observance or nonobservance. If I have to stand or fall on a single formulation of neutrality, I will stand or fall on that one. But I must elaborate on what I mean by minimizing encouragement or discouragement. I mean that religion is to be left as wholly to private choice as anything can be. It should proceed as unaffected by government as possible. Government should not interfere with our beliefs about religion either by coercion or by persuasion. Religion may flourish or whither; it may change or stay the same. What happens to religion is

up to the people acting severally and voluntarily; it is not up to the people acting collectively through government.[96]

Professor Laycock refers to the above as a formulation of neutrality, but while it is immensely valuable is it neutral? Professor Laycock suggests that neutrality depends on the baseline one sets in defining it, and that there are varying baselines. This article asserts that as a result a problem arises because there is no super-baseline to determine whether a given baseline is neutral. Yet the very term neutrality asserts an epistemic (in the sense that it suggests some theory or way to know something is neutral) and arguably a teleological claim. A given baseline might be a useful paradigm for Establishment Clause jurisprudence, but unless one can demonstrate the neutrality of the baseline itself, the baseline can not support claims of neutrality.

The *Zelman* case is a good example through which to view this. If the Court in *Zelman* had held that vouchers are unconstitutional when given for attendance at religious schools, but that districts can maintain vouchers for secular private schools and of course can maintain the secularized public schools without any voucher program, would the result encourage secularism? Would such a limitation advance private choice or would it place burdens only on the private choice of religious individuals because they must choose between a secular education free of charge and their values? Yet, under the Court's holding which allows vouchers to be used at religious schools, there is a powerful argument that religion, and particularly more dominant and well funded religions, will benefit from an infusion of government funds, and that private choice will be skewed toward sending one's children to schools with whose faith mission one disagrees simply to keep them on a level playing field with other children in the area who may face no such conflict.

* * *

Yet, as will be seen, this does not destroy the force of Laycock's principle. Significantly, the fact that divorcing Laycock's substantive principle from neutrality does not undermine that principle demonstrates the lack of import the neutrality concept has. As between formal neutrality and substantive neutrality, substantive neutrality is the better option, not because it is more neutral—neither option is neutral—but because it is still useful even when divorced from its neutrality claim. The Court's formal neutrality hinges too much on neutrality as a real concept, or at least on formal equality as neutrality, and while a more sophisticated and consistently applied version of the equality principle could have independent value, the formal-equality-as-formal-neutrality version has little to offer since its claim to neutrality cannot be proven.

Issues surrounding governmental interaction with religious entities has become increasingly complex over the last hundred years or so as government, both state and federal, has grown and gotten involved in

---

96. Douglas Laycock, *Formal, Substantive, and Disaggregated Neutrality Toward* *Religion*, 39 DePaul L. Rev. 993, 1001–02 (1990).

many areas of life where there was traditionally little or no government participation or regulation. It is hard for government to act "neutrally" when its actions or failure to act in the same situation can have massive repercussions. This creates problems for any "neutrality" test that must be applied to this massive web of government action and inaction. At the theoretical level such a test can not make make an absolute claim to neutrality because there is no principle of super-neutrality to demonstrate a tests' neutrality; contested perspectives necessarily enter the process of developing such a test. It would solve the problem if one could prove neutrality by looking at the effects of a court's approach, but as the above examples demonstrate, this is impossible to do without presuming that a certain baseline is neutral and using the presumed baseline to justify the neutrality of outcomes.

* * *

B.   Zelman v. Simmons–Harris

Zelman is a significant case for several reasons. It is the first United States Supreme Court case to uphold a government-funded educational voucher program and thus is quite significant from the education policy perspective as well as the law and religion perspective. Additionally, a majority of the Court affirmed the notion that, so long as a program is neutral on its face and functions through "true private choice," the program is constitutional. * * * [W]hile the majority opinion purports to consider whether private individuals who channelled government money to religious schools had real choices, the opinion expands the pool of "choices" to include public magnet and charter schools. This leaves open the possibility that the comparison group could be further expanded to include all public schools, at least in districts that have open enrollment or public school choice programs. * * * [I]t is hard to believe earlier Courts would have so expanded the comparison groups or found no primary effect benefitting religion given the data regarding the Cleveland voucher program * * *. * * *

The *Zelman* Court ostensibly followed the *Agostini/Lemon* test. Yet, the Court's application of the "effects" prong of that test is the key. As a preliminary matter *Zelman* did not present a secular purpose issue because the goal of providing a better education to students in the Cleveland School District was an adequate secular purpose. Indeed, at least in government aid and equal access cases, it is hard to imagine a situation where there would not be an adequate secular purpose. Thus, the case centered on the effects of the program, as have several other funding cases.

Yet there is a significant catch. In order for an indirect aid program to satisfy the *Zelman* test, the program must be neutral on its face and the money must flow through individuals who have "true private choice" regarding where to direct the aid. If a program is neutral on its face between religious and nonreligious entities it is highly unlikely it would ever fail the secular purpose test. Further, there is no significant distinction between direct and indirect aid, since so long as the government entity drafting the program relates the aid that flows to religious institutions to the number of individuals who choose to use the private service, it does not matter that the check is written from the government directly to the religious institution. Thus, as Justice O'Connor argued in her concurring opinion in *Mitchell v. Helms*, neutrality is assigned singular importance. It is not a stretch to say that, at least in cases of government aid to religious institutions the test is one of facial neutrality plus a private "circuit breaker"—i.e. the money ostensibly flows to the religious institution because of the choices of private individuals. Significantly, the "circuit breaker" element is connected to the Court's broader neutrality analysis. It is the private individual "choice" that makes a facially neutral program "entirely neutral."

This begs the question, however, of what constitutes "true private choice" under the Court's analysis. The Court's answer to this question is significant, because it involves a statistical sleight of hand that could potentially make all public schools the relevant comparison group to religious schools for purposes of government aid programs, even in areas with no secular private schools or where such private schools cannot afford to take voucher students, so long as secular private schools would be included in the program if they existed. This makes the Court's new test an exercise in almost pure formalism. If a program is neutral on its face—that is, it does not specify religious entities as beneficiaries—and there is some government or nonreligious private entity that the recipients could conceivable choose to go to for service, the test is met because the program is neutral on its face and provides "true private choice," even if virtually all funding going to private organizations goes to religious organizations.

If this really were neutral, and neutrality was an appropriate actuating principle under the Establishment Clause, the Court's approach would be perfectly acceptable. Conversely, if the Court's approach is not neutral, calling it neutral should give it no further power and it should be adequately supported by some other principle. In fact, if the Court's approach is not neutral, having the Court pronounce its neutrality is especially dangerous, because the Court would simply be placing the label of neutrality on analysis that is neither neutral nor likely to lead to "neutral" results and using the label to validate its approach. The Court could call its undergirding principle "Ralph" and it would have the same descriptive accuracy. In fact, "Ralph" might be more descriptively accurate because one would still have to determine what the essence of Ralphness is, and the nature of the term does not suggest that it has any extra power or reality until it is defined.

This might seem a bit tongue-in-cheek (and it is, to a point), but it demonstrates the serious problems with claims to neutrality. Since there is no neutral foundation or baseline that can be used to prove that something is "truly" neutral, neutrality is nothing more than a buzzword and a dangerous one at that, because it implies that the supposedly neutral approach should be taken more seriously because it is actually neutral. Legal tests and definitions of neutrality do not make an approach neutral—they are simply tests or definitions and neutrality is nothing but extra baggage. As was explained above, this does not mean that conceptions of neutrality—such as Douglas Laycock's substantive neutrality—are not useful tools, but it does mean that they are not neutral and should gain no additional validity from the use of that term.

This suggests that the Court's formal neutrality approach is especially dangerous, because the formalistic approach leaves little room for introspection, and its very nature makes it less likely to account for nuances or context. Supporting such a rigid regime with a concept that can not be proven is particularly perilous, since once the formalistic test controls outcomes, there will be little opportunity to adapt to varied circumstances without sacrificing the clarity such formalistic tests are intended to create. Thus, courts applying the test must either rigidly apply a test that has never adequately justified itself because it is based on a non-existent principle, attempt to modify the test in its application to varied circumstances without the help of a useful guiding principle, or in the case of the Supreme Court, abandon *stare decisis* and either overturn the decisions giving rise to the approach or apply the approach in a manner that goes against its underlying purpose.

A response to this line of reasoning might be that none of this is relevant if the Court's approach is "truly" neutral. I will respond to this argument next. My response will proceed in three parts. First, I will look at whether the individual beneficiaries of the program in *Zelman* had "true private choice." Second, I will examine whether the notion of a private circuit breaker can make a government funding program "neutral" where that program ultimately gives a disproportionate amount of public money meant for private entities to religious institutions. As will be seen the answer to this question is related to the first question, even if one accepts the notion that neutrality exists and that it consists of treating both religious and nonreligious individuals and institutions the same. Finally, I will explore whether the "facial neutrality" of a law— the fact that a law does not distinguish between potential recipients within the broad class of recipients eligible for aid—has anything to do with neutrality as an actuating principle for Establishment Clause jurisprudence.

In *Zelman*, the Court found that the parents of the students in the Cleveland School District, the private "circuit-breakers" in this case, had real individual choice regarding where to send their children. In finding this "true" choice, the Court went beyond the private school options the parents had and included several public school options. Thus, government run programs became part of the field of options the Court considered. Arguably, a program would be neutral and parents would have "true" choices even if one hundred percent of the money going to private entities went to religious entities or if the only private choices parents had were religious. This would seemingly be so even if the resulting government funded regime put nonreligious private programs at a competitive disadvantage and led to religious institutions funded by a single sect taking over a market for services.

One argument in favor of so expanding the comparison group is that government is so pervasive that to exclude government-run programs—which are by their nature secular—from the comparison group would be to put religion at a disadvantage in the marketplace of ideas and programs. Yet this argument is something of a red herring. For example, religious groups have not generally had equal access to compete to run police or fire services, nor would one have thought (prior to *Zelman*) that religious organizations could compete to take over road services or state run children and family services. Moreover, religious organizations could not administer a public school or a charter school that relies on public funds for its existence. The relevant comparison group in the context of a voucher program is thus private schools. Such schools are the only relevant entities that are not government-run, wholly reliant on government funds, or subject to pervasive government regulation and oversight.

The relevant statistics regarding private schools in the Cleveland area were skewed such that the bulk of the money passing through the voucher program into private hands went to religious schools, and parents who participated in the voucher aspect of the Cleveland program had few nonreligious options. More than 3,700 hundred students participated in the voucher program, and of those ninety six percent enrolled in religious schools. Forty-six of the fifty-six private schools participating in the program were religious schools. Moreover, the nonreligious private schools were generally small and had fewer seats for voucher students. These figures are not unusual because religious schools make up a significantly larger proportion of private schools nationally than nonreligious schools.

* * * Let us assume for the moment that the Court's statistical slight of hand was a valid comparison of apples to apples, and thus in addition to the 3,765 voucher students in the program, we can consider the 1,400 students who stayed in public school and received subsidized tutorial aid, the 1,900 students enrolled in publically-funded community schools, and the 13,000 enrolled in public magnet schools. The percentage of students attending religious schools drops to below twenty percent when the reference group shifts from 3,765 students to 20,000 students. In fact, if we were to include the entire Cleveland schools system in the comparison group using the *Zelman* majority's approximate figure of 75,000, the percentage going to religious schools under the voucher program would be approximately 4.85%. The 75,000 figure would represent all the "choices" parents in the Cleveland District had (or could have assuming open enrollment at all Cleveland public schools).

Yet if parents choose to take advantage of the voucher program because of dissatisfaction with all public school options (including community schools), the inability to get into a magnet school or failure to win a lottery slot at a community school, the parent may have little choice but to send his or her children to religious schools or forego the voucher option entirely. If parents in the area do not subscribe to the faith of any participating religious school, as is likely for nonbelievers and many religious minorities, they can make the same "choice" as their neighbors who participate in the voucher program and who do subscribe to one of the represented faiths, only by sending their children to a religious school that may indoctrinate them in a faith with which the family disagrees or at the very least does not believe in. This choice hardly seems neutral. Nor does the Court's assurance that the program is neutral because it provides everyone with "true private choice" and does not discriminate on its face, provide much solace to a parent who desperately wants to provide the best education possible for her children but who is afraid that her children will be confronted daily with lessons and choices that are alien to the families' faith.

This is the problem with neutrality. One person's neutrality is another's discrimination or favoritism, and if a court proclaims something to be neutral there is no way of proving the proclamation to be true. The Rehnquist Court relies on "true private choice" and facial neutrality as the basis for demonstrating that a program is "entirely neutral." It is easy, however, to dispute the availability of "true private choice," and the facial neutrality of a program does not mean that the program is neutral or even that it was not designed to discriminate against religious minorities or to favor dominant religious groups in a given area.

Even if the Court was correct in concluding that parents had a choice of multiple, equally viable nonreligious options, the program is not neutral. The overwhelming amount of money flowing into private (i.e. not *initially* dependant on government for survival) hands flows to religious schools as does the overwhelming number of students. Unless the Court explains how the existence of "true private choice" under such circumstances is neutral, especially in light of the inequity in same-sect options between the denominational "haves" and "have nots," there is no reason to take the Court's word for it. The Court's reasoning is circular neutrality equals private choice and facial neutrality because, if a program is facially neutral and provides private choice it is neutral. The neutrality claim remains unsubstantiated. Without the claim to neutrality, however, the Court is left having to justify why religion is indistinct as a matter of constitutional law and why excluding only religion from the voucher program would exhibit hostility to religion. The claim that the program is neutral allows the Court to evade significant doctrinal and conceptual problems.

* * * This Article asserts that if there were a real range of choices available to parents within the voucher option, as was the case with the programs in *Zobrest*[183] and *Witters*,[184] the program would be constitutional, not because the private choice makes an otherwise biased program

---

183. *Zobrest*, 509 U.S. 1.   **184.** *Witters*, 474 U.S. 481.

neutral, but rather because the effects of such a program do not give religion a disproportionate and substantial benefit.

* * *

III. Principles and Tests

The notion that there is tension between the broad principles traditionally used in Establishment Clause cases and the results in those cases is not new. Moreover, the relationship between broad principles and the tests used under the Establishment Clause has been well explored. Without reinventing the wheel, it is useful to explore the principles often used in Establishment Clause cases and the notion that it would be far better to rely either on a variety of narrow principles or upon doctrinal tests that may or may not be anchored to any specific principle.

While the concept of neutrality has always been lurking in religion clause jurisprudence, other principles such as separation and accommodation have also played an important part. Moreover, these principles did not automatically conflict with earlier Courts' more ethereal concept of neutrality. In fact, separation was initially framed as furthering neutrality. The current development of neutrality as both the overarching broad principle and the test for deciding cases is far different from the earlier notion of neutrality as an overarching but ethereal principle that needed something more, such as separationism, to make it function. In this earlier context, the formal equality of religion was relevant, but it was not equated with neutrality in the way it is in *Zelman* and *Mitchell*.

This section will assert that none of the other broad principles traditionally discussed in the religion clause context work as broad principles. Thus, separation, accommodation, equality, and liberty all may be valuable in some contexts, but some of these concepts are too vague to be of great use beyond platitudes and buzzwords while others suffer some of the same problems as neutrality. * * *

Once the various principles are explored, the Article proposes that something similar to Douglas Laycock's substantive neutrality, tweaked with aspects of separationism and accommodationism, should prevail as a guiding principle for Establishment Clause purposes, but divorced from the term neutrality and wary of any such claim. The proposed principle will act as a narrow principle rather than as a broad one in applying the test proposed later in this article.

* * *

A. *Separationism*

* * * The historical argument for strict separationism is rather weak when one considers all the variables involved in gleaning the intent of the many framers and ratifying conventions, as well as the interpretations and practices of early government entities in the U.S. Yet, for the same reasons the case is not any stronger for the competing theories as a historical matter. If we look to the broad intent of the framers and interpret historical practices and principles in light of today's diverse society and massive government, the argument for separation may be stronger. This has been called soft-originalism in other contexts.

This article does not attempt to take sides in this historical debate, because even if we accept that separationism is at some level a guiding principle—as this article does—it is, like neutrality, a principle in search of a baseline. The difference is that separation need not make the same type of claim that neutrality does. Separation can be a broad or limited concept depending on how we define it. There can be degrees of separation. Neutrality on the other hand is not provably neutral regardless of how broadly or narrowly we define it.

Scholars and the Court have long recognized that "strict separation" is impossible, because at least at the margins there is bound to be some interaction between religion and government. Strict separation would amount to establishing a purely secular state, where secularism is at least implicitly encouraged and favored and religion banished from the public square and public life. Moreover, it would be impossible or at the very least highly impractical, to maintain.

Another possibility is to use a narrow concept, such as prohibiting direct aid to religious institutions as a limit. Thus, separation would be defined by a context and a test, not by some broad notion of absolute separation. The current Court has rejected or muddied (depending on one's perspective) the long-standing prohibition on direct aid to religious institutions. At the very least, the prohibition against direct aid has little of the force it used to have since the circuit breaker concept of "true individual choice" has been interpreted to allow the government to write the check directly to a religious entity so long as the amount of the check is determined by the number of people who decide to enroll. Even if it were revived, the direct aid version of separation only applies in the context of government aid programs, and even then it is more a formalistic test than a guiding principle.

Another possibility is to use separation as a guiding principle in some contexts, but not others. Thus, separation would be used in the school prayer context, the public school curriculum context, and perhaps the direct aid context, but not in equal access or indirect aid cases. This is not too far from the current situation. The current situation, though, is more a result of the positions of the swing voters on the Court, none of whom take a consistent separationist position, than of a dedication to separation on these issues.

Depending on which baseline one picks for separation in given contexts, it could function as a narrow test, a broad principle that urges as much separation between the government and religion as possible, or somewhere in between. Separation is less problematic than neutrality because some degree of separation may be achieved. Separation by itself, however, is problematic at the practical level because one must still choose where and how to implement it, and short of a draconian absolute separation which is hard to implement, troubling from a policy perspective, and contrary to the historical idea of the religion clauses, separation is a malleable concept that may function best if implemented as a narrow principle. The test set forth later in this article is guided in part by the benefits of keeping some form of separation in the religion clause equation * * *.

B. Accommodationism

Like separation, accommodation can arguably function both at the level of a broad principle and as a narrow principle, or as a facet of a doctrinal test. Accommodationist arguments are most common under the Free Exercise Clause. In that context, accommodationism would support exemptions from laws of general applicability. However, accommodationism can also be used in the Establishment Clause context. * * *

* * * [E]ven where accommodationism functions as a background principle, as it arguably did in *Lynch v. Donnelly*, and *County of Allegheny v. ACLU*, the results can be troubling both for devoutly religious people and for nonbelievers. In those cases, Christmas was declared to be essentially a general or commercial holiday with religious roots, at least to the extent that it is "celebrated" in public life, and in *Lynch* the religious impact of a crèche—the depiction of the birth of Jesus—while acknowledged, was deemed sufficiently minimized because it was included with secular symbols of the "holiday season." In *Allegheny* the religious impact of a Menorah was somehow offset by its location near a Christmas tree and a sign saluting liberty. The reasoning and results in these cases have been decried by many scholars, both secular and religious, and I need not rehash the rich arguments here. The salient points are that these holdings trivialize a sacred holiday for devout Christians by trying to accommodate public recognition of it without crossing the line into government support of a particular religion, and at the same time insult non-Christians by suggesting that Christ's Mass is somehow our holiday too, even if we don't celebrate it. * * *

Accommodationism does not work well by itself in the Establishment Clause context. This is not because it isn't feasible—nonpreferentialism is feasible—but because short of moving toward nonpreferentialism, accommodationism requires distinctions to be made that allow government to engage in or foster religious activities while somehow denouncing the religious nature or impact of those activities. An example is turning religious symbols or rituals into a form of ceremonial deism in order to accommodate them without acknowledging that government is sponsoring or performing a religious function.

To the extent that accommodationism is connected to notions of formal equality between religion and non-religion, it may be a more plausible approach than neutrality. However, it would not by itself solve the * * * concern that the formal equality approach ignores the disparities between more dominant and minority religions thus giving dominant religions in given areas a competitive edge and a preferred status. Still, accommodationism has a role to play under the Establishment Clause, and a potentially important role to play in the Free Exercise Clause context. Yet, over reliance on accommodationism under the Establishment Clause might force the big square peg of religion into narrow round holes in order to maintain some minimal level of separation. As will be seen, however, a narrow view of accommodationism together with a narrow view of separationism, may serve as a useful animating principle.

C. Religious Liberty

Michael McConnell and others have made powerful arguments that religious liberty is the guiding principle under the religion clauses. Of course, this does not answer the obvious question: What is religious liberty? The problem is that religious liberty is more like neutrality than separation or accommodation.

The concept of religious liberty must struggle with its underlying epistemic claim: that there is some way of knowing what religious liberty is. Yet every school of thought that has addressed the religion clauses claims to be promoting religious liberty at some level, and some view their approach as synonymous with religious liberty. Thus, religious liberty must either be tied to some baseline or viewed simply as an aspiration to be fulfilled by the doctrine or theory *du jour*. Yet, whatever baseline or results one argues are consistent with religious liberty, there can be a competing baseline.

For example, lets take what should be the easiest situation for promoting the religious liberty principle, Free Exercise Clause Exemptions. It is arguable that the reasoning and results in *Goldman v. Weinberger*, *Lyng v. Northwest Indian Cemetery Protection Ass'n.*, and *Employment Division v. Smith*, to name just a few cases, are inconsistent with religious liberty. The reasoning is by now standard (and I would argue valid). That is, laws of "general applicability" sometimes interfere with religious practice, and in fact, are more likely to interfere with the religious practices of those who are not in the religious mainstream. This is attenuated by the fact that the dominant religion in the United States is heavily faith based (although that is a highly oversimplified description), and that many minority religions are practice oriented. These practices are not preferences in most contexts, but rather central to the faiths of the practitioners. Thus, laws of general applicability should not be allowed to interfere with these practices without a compelling governmental interest and narrow tailoring. To find otherwise is to interfere with a central aspect of religious liberty.

Yet there is an easy response that also claims to be consistent with religious liberty: that the Free Exercise Clause absolutely protects religious faith and belief. Still, laws of general applicability do not require religious exemptions, even though this might be helpful to some religious practitioners. Everyone has the same level of protection of religious liberty, but unfortunately, some religions or religious practices will be more impacted by laws of general applicability than others, and there is no absolute right to religious liberty that trumps the interest in maintaining social order. Each of the above approaches could claim that it is consistent with the principle of religious liberty.

* * *

At its broadest, religious liberty is more a platitude than a principle. When we try to define it we are faced with competing and contestable notions of what religious liberty is, and thus the concept can not rely on a provable baseline of "liberty," but rather must rely on other concepts or doctrinal tests to fill the gap. Through accommodation, the principle of religious liberty operates best in the Free Exercise Clause context, but even there, competing views of religious liberty preclude one baseline of religious liberty from being "the" correct view.

I like the lofty goal of religious liberty. It sounds good. But then again, it is my concept of religious liberty that I like, and I doubt that others, such as Justice Scalia, share my concept of religious liberty. I have no means, though, to prove that my view of religious liberty is any more correct than his view. I can argue based on other principles or history that his view of religious liberty is wrong, but I can not prove that it is any less or any more "religious liberty" than my view without some super-baseline of religious liberty (or perhaps an absolutely decisive historical record, which does not exist here).

D. Equality

Like Religious Liberty, an approach to religion clause analysis grounded in the quest for equality sounds good. If it could be delivered, all religions would be treated equally and religion would be treated equally with nonreligion. Scholars who have advocated an equality-based approach to the religion clauses are not naive enough to think that such a state of perfect equality could exist, just as scholars who have advocated a neutrality-based approach are not naive enough to think that perfect and incontestable neutrality could exist. Yet, as with neutrality, one person's equality is another's hostility. Do we measure equality by government purpose? By the facial equality of government action? By the effects of government action? Is treating similarly situated groups the same equality, even if doing so has a disparate impact based on social factors? Is treating differently situated groups the same equality?

Various equality based approaches have attempted to answer these questions, and some are quite impressive in their intellectual rigor and potentially of great use. Yet, they all rest on creaky theoretical claims. As with Laycock's substantive neutrality, which as we saw is quite valuable but not provably neutral, equality-based approaches may be valuable, but whether they foster equality, and what equality is, remain open questions. This makes the "equality" garnered by the application of such principles contestable even among those who accept a given approach, and of course there are a variety of "equality based approaches." * * *

The important point here is that equality, like religious liberty, can function as a broad amorphous principle that is never clearly definable or reachable, but it can not do the work of answering questions in a variety of contexts without the help of some other narrow principle. To the extent the Court has tied formal equality to formal neutrality in its more recent cases, the results have hardly been equal for many religious minorities and nonbelievers. If the Court is relying on another principle such as majoritarianism or nonpreferentialism some of the results in recent religion clause cases may make more sense (even if they are disagreeable), but using neutrality and equality in the way the Court recently has only masks the fact that it is relying on other principles.

* * * [T]he broad notion of equality does have a role to play in religion clause jurisprudence. That role is the opposite of the role equality plays in the Court's formal neutrality approach. Equality comes into play because we should consider the results of even facially neutral government actions (including those that utilize private intermediaries) in order to determine whether those actions give substantial benefits to some religions over others or to religion over non-religion.

* * *

IV. THE FACILITATION TEST

It should be clear by now that this Article does not advocate reliance on specific broad principles, especially for purposes of developing legal doctrine, but various principles can inform the development of useful doctrine. For this to happen, the principles must be honestly confronted. This requires acknowledgment that some principles are simply social or judicial constructions that have no claim to accuracy or truth. Thus, narrower principles that do not suggest universal truth, and which are readily subject to degrees of implementation without undermining their meaning are more useful in developing legal tests.

At the base though, the tests themselves are central to the practical meaning of the religion clauses, even if that meaning has become quite confused as a result of the application of such tests. * * * Yet how a given test is applied may be more important than the choice of tests, and each of these choices can be affected by the principles one believes undergird the Establishment Clause (or subconsciously assume undergird that clause).

This interplay between principles and tests is important and complex, but where does it leave us if we accept the idea that most broad principles are impossible to pin down and that there is no super-principle that enables us to choose correctly between competing narrow principles because there is no way to gauge "correctness" in this context? Ironically, it leaves us with doctrinal tests that must necessarily be divorced from any one principle because of the impossibility of absolutely realizing that principle but which can be informed by multiple principles once we realize and acknowledge the limitations inherent in those principles. Thus, this Article proposes a test for Establishment Clause cases that I assert can work in the varied Establishment Clause contexts such as school prayer, government display of religious symbols, government aid, and access to government facilities and programs. The test does not work because it fits any one broad principle, but because it is informed by a number of principles that ebb and flow in their import depending on the context.

As will be seen, the test is informed by notions of liberty, equality, separation, and accommodation. None of these principles serves as the overarching principle. This is where Douglas Laycock's version of substantive neutrality comes into play, minus any claim to neutrality. His approach gels aspects of liberty, equality, separation, and accommodation, because each of these principles has a role to play in minimizing government encouragement or discouragement of religion. Yet in a massive regulatory state how one minimizes government encouragement of religion without discouraging religion is a complex problem. The facilitation test is an attempt to avoid government encouragement of religion without unduly discouraging religion.

The test is essentially this: Government action that substantially facilitates or discourages religion violates the Establishment Clause. The definition of "government action" and substantial facilitation or discouragement of religion are essential to understanding this test. Before addressing these two issues, it is useful to note that the test is very much focused on the effects of government action, and as will be seen, purpose is only relevant when there is relatively clear evidence of an intent to favor or discriminate against religion. Focusing on effects is certainly not a new idea. The "effects" prong of the *Lemon* test is a good example, and the endorsement test also focuses on effects, at least in theory. Additionally, a number of scholars have proposed effects oriented tests, often based on the *Lemon* "effects" prong.

For purposes of this test, "government action" consists of any program, activity, or decision supported by government entities or officials in their official capacity. Whether the actions or decisions of private individuals can cut off the government's role in facilitating religion depends on the nature of the government action and the role of the private individual or individuals. This is a clear rejection of the formalistic "true private choice" doctrine espoused in *Zelman* and *Mitchell*, but it allows for private choice to play a role in the analysis. * * *

Defining substantial facilitation or discouragement of religion is both hard and easy. Facilitation is not the same thing as support. One can provide attenuated support for something without facilitating it. Facilitation is about furthering the religious activities of a program or entity, or about furthering religious practice or the stature of a given religion or of religion generally. Thus, facilitation does not rely on bright line distinctions such as direct or indirect aid, because it is the effect of the aid that determines whether it facilitates religion under the test. While it is more likely that direct aid to a religious organization will facilitate religion than indirect aid (although indirect aid can facilitate religion as well), it is not automatically so.

Discouragement of religion is highly relevant in the Free Exercise Clause context, but for present purposes, the key is that discouragement relates more to religious adherents than to religious organizations. Thus, for example, government can not facilitate the religious work of religious organizations, nor can it prevent individuals from using public funds at religious institutions under truly broad and open government programs. These two concepts would dramatically conflict with each other were it not for the substantiality requirement.

Substantial facilitation is more than simply giving some minor support to a religious institution—it is not a strict separationist concept. It is a balancing approach that looks to the real-world impact of government action. * * * Thus, in some contexts such as government sponsored prayer it is always violated, while in the context of government aid programs the total amount of aid going to religious entities matters, as does the proportion of program funds that go to religious entities. There is a vast difference between *Zobrest* and *Zelman* under the facilitation test. * * *

The facilitation test will not provide bright-line answers in some contexts, but it might in others. Bright-line answers, however, are not the primary goal of the facilitation test. Rather, reasonable consistency is the most that can be expected. Reasonable consistency is possible under the test even in aid cases where context has the largest impact on its application. The goal is to provide reasonable consistency while remaining sensitive to the variety of principles that are at play in religion clause cases. * * *

It is essential to point out here that this is the first attempt to frame the test. Thus, this Article provides a sketch of the test at best. While the test is not perfect, it has the potential to be useful as an alternative to the current formalistic approach without sacrificing a reasonable level of consistency. The test attempts to effectuate various principles, especially separationism and accommodationism, and through its application the false antinomy between these principles will hopefully be reduced. * * * [The section of the article in which the test is applied to a variety of situations has been deleted].

CONCLUSION

This Article has set forth the inherent problems with the principle of neutrality in Establishment Clause cases. The principle sounds good in theory, but there is no neutral baseline from which we can gauge claims of neutrality. Thus neutrality is an empty concept. Yet, the Court has been increasingly gravitating toward neutrality, specifically formal neutrality, as the centerpiece of its Establishment Clause doctrine. While this shift has not taken place in every context to which the Establishment Clause can be applied, it has become dominant in government aid and equal access cases. This move is dangerous, not because of its results, but because the Court has gone from using neutrality as a broad and vague principle that needs other principles such as separation or accommodation in order to function, to using it as both the means and ends of Establishment Clause analysis. It is deeply troubling that the Court has placed such great weight on such weak footing.

As an alternative to the neutrality principle, this Article recommends looking beneath broad principles to narrower ones, which may be applied separately or in tandem to issues under the Establishment Clause. Relying on Douglas Laycock's concept of substantive neutrality, divorced from any claim to neutrality, this Article has proposed a test that is focused upon whether government activity facilitates or discourages religion. The test is not formalistic like the current Court's formal neutrality approach, but it is better able to address the highly complex and contextually bound issues that arise under the Establishment Clause.

STEPHEN L. CARTER, *REFLECTIONS ON THE SEPARATION OF CHURCH AND STATE*

44 ARIZ. L. REV. 293 (2002).*
Copyright 2002, Arizona Board of Regents, Stephen L. Carter.

I.

I call my lecture "reflections" on the separation of church and state in part because I have no strong assertions to make about it. Indeed, I will confess to those here present that after two decades of laboring in the salubrious vineyards of constitutional law, about half of that spent as what I suppose one would call a specialist on religion, I continue to find the concept of separation of church and state baffling, utterly baffling. I do not mean by this admission to suggest that I am an opponent of it; quite the contrary, I am fairly sure that I favor it. The problem is that I have only the dimmest idea what the words mean, and therefore have but the haziest notion of what it is that I favor; and I rather suspect that a fair number of those who use the words, including some eminent jurists, share my confusion.

I suppose many people would describe the separation of church and state as a mandate of the First Amendment; others would suggest that it is a fundamental principle of liberal democracy; yet I can find no serious reason to believe that either of these postulates is true; or, rather, if true, neither one is sufficiently unambiguous to admit of serious dialogue. In other words, when we use the phrase "separation of church and state," I suspect that few of us can really guess what the other is talking about. And this has been true all through the nation's history. Roger Williams and Thomas Jefferson, had they been contemporaries, could have had an entirely incoherent conversation on the doctrine, because they understood it so differently. * * *

* [Professor Carter is the William Nelson Cromwell Professor of Law at Yale * * *. The article excerpted here is from a lecture delivered by Professor Carter on Feb. 8, 2002, at the James E. Rogers College of Law, University of Arizona, Tucson, Arizona.]

* * * I am skeptical of the proposition that the separation of church and state is or could ever be a doctrine of constitutional law. I fear that the image of the wall confuses more than it clarifies * * *. But my discontent goes deeper. The serious historian will readily admit that the metaphorical separation of church and state, whatever precise meaning we might choose to assign to it today, has its origins in Protestant theology, for it was the Protestants who laid before an unenlightened Europe the model of the two great powers, the temporal and the spiritual, and the theological argument for placing the capacities in the hands of separate earthly masters.

It is vital that we in our legalist ahistoricism not forget that the Protestant separatists believed in dividing church from state, not God from state. The purpose of the separation was not to protect the state from religious believers but to protect the church in its work of salvation from the corruption of the state. Both earthly capacities were understood to fall under the rule of the one God, and, indeed, the traditional Christian teaching on obedience to constituted authority rests on this assumption. * * *

* * *

The early Protestant theorists of church and state were inspired, as John Noonan has lately reminded us, by the prophets of Israel, for it is in the often lengthy biblical passages rehearsing the arguments between the rulers and the prophets that we find what appear to be the first historical instances of outsiders daring to accuse the sovereign of acting against the will of God. Prior to that time, as far as we can tell, rulers were themselves thought to be divine or semi-divine. The idea that the king could do something contrary to the will of God denied the monarch's divinity, and that denial carried within it the seeds of the separatist revolution that would in time sweep the globe.

The Puritans certainly understood the problem, which was why they took marriage away from the priests. In Protestant New England, it was actually against the law for a member of the clergy to officiate at a wedding. The justice of the peace, an individual with no clerical function, was required to perform the ceremony. In this way, the Puritans "separated" the church from the state. But let us be clear about their motive. In separating the two great powers, they were seeking to purify the church, not the state. Their beloved church, they feared, was at risk when it exercised authority over matters that the Bible did not command it to run.

These early American separationists—often called "pietistic" by the historians—separated church and state for theological reasons. Yet, even as they insisted that the two great powers remain rigorously demarcated, these pietistic separationists never imagined that either power was to be separated from the authority of the one true God: on the contrary, they saw divine edict as the source of the sovereign's right to rule, and of the state's right to exist.

To be sure, other strands of separationism exist in American thought: there were, for example, the Enlightenment separationists, who thought the state would be better off were it separated from the church. But—without laboring the point here—we probably overplay the differences. The Enlightenment thinkers did not believe religion was dangerous, or that it was a pollutant in the pure waters of politics. Rather, they worried about the danger that the church, if merged with the state, would be tempted to coerce individuals into beliefs that the Bible required them to accept voluntarily or not at all. Recent history had taught them this lesson * * *.

In any event, I wish to talk about the pietists. I am interested, in particular, in how we might enrich our understanding of the separation of church and state by envisioning it as first laid down, as a means to protect the church, not the state. Although the lecture is intended as speculative, I will, I hope, have some points to make about the way we might improve our constitutional law of religion as well.

II.

The separationist metaphor was popularized in the New World by Roger Williams, the Baptist preacher (among other things) who founded Rhode Island, first as a refuge for those seeking religious freedom from Puritan Massachusetts, although it later became the site of religious discriminations of its own. Williams coined the metaphor of the garden and the wilderness to describe the relationship between the church and the society it inhabited. For Williams, the garden was the place of God's people, the community of people of faith, who gathered together to determine what the Lord required of them, nurturing and building their religious understanding in relative tranquility. Outside the garden was the unevangelized world, what Williams called the wilderness. And between the two, separating the wilderness from the garden, was a high hedge wall, constructed to protect the people of the garden in their work of religious nurture. The hedge wall existed to keep the wilderness out, not to keep the people of the garden hemmed in. It was the vital work of the garden, not the less vital work of the wilderness, that the wall was built in order to protect. * * * [T]he Supreme Court was wrong, and has been consistently wrong, in attributing American authorship of the idea of a wall of separation to Thomas Jefferson rather than to Williams.

But even if Roger Williams, the seventeenth century Baptist, believed that the wall of separation existed to protect the church from the state rather than the other way around, is it not possible that the Enlightened eighteenth century gentlemen who drafted the Constitution were worried more about the influence the church might gain over the state?

Well, no.

In the first place, the familiar contention that the Framers were dominated by deists or other secularists rather than by traditional religious believers has not stood up well to historical analysis. And, although it is commonly suggested that the Framers sought to keep religion out of public life because they worried about the sectarian warfare sweeping Europe, that suggestion, too, is on shaky historical footing. The last arguably religious war on the European continent was the Thirty Years War, which ended in the middle of the seventeenth century—well over a hundred years before the drafting of the Constitution. * * * The Founders were wise enough to understand that it was people, not religions, that made wars; and so their Constitution made it tougher for people to get together to do mischievous things, whatever their motivations might have been.

The notion that the Founding Generation was particularly afraid of the influence of religion over the state is nonsense—pardonable nonsense, but nonsense all the same. It does not stand up well to the evidence. * * *

* * * At the moment of revolution, every Southern state had an established Anglican church, and, as the historian William Lee Miller has pointed out, "an Anglican clergyman took an oath to support the king, the supreme head of the church, as part of his ordination." As the war neared, most of the clergy evidently did as the oath prescribed.

Yet that is not the point of the story. The point is that the clergy took sides in the war, and that both parties wanted them to. Far from fearing the incursion of the religious voice into politics, even on the most vital issues of the day, the Founding Generation welcomed it. As a matter of fact, they relied on it.

III.

This history is only prologue. I do not mean to suggest that an account of past controversy creates in us a binding obligation to the political science of an earlier generation. I believe, of course, that we owe to traditions prior to our own a healthy degree of respect, and even deference, and, certainly, that we should not view them through the eyes of ahistorical critique. But we may have better ideas. Let us investigate whether that is true.

If the separation of church and state is a rule of constitutional law, then it must emerge, through a process of interpretation, from the Constitution itself, and must then admit of workable definition. The Supreme Court has identified the First Amendment as the source of the metaphor, locating it, in particular, in what nearly everybody calls the Establishment Clause.

I put the point that way because the text of the First Amendment, on its face, does not admit of the two-religion-clause interpretation. Let us simply look at the language, elegant and gracious if perhaps needlessly involute:

Congress shall make no law respecting an establishment of religion, or prohibiting the free exercise thereof; . . .

The First Amendment is made up of a series of three clauses, separated by semi-colons. We have, thus, the religion clause, the speech and press clause, and the assembly and petition clause.

The religion clause is the first to which we come when we read over the amendment. The religion clause on its face appears to address a single subject. The two-clause reading given it by all courts and most commentators is not the one that emerges most readily from the text. After all, if the clause is meant to be in two segments, each referring substantively to a different area of constitutional law, why on earth does it end with the word "thereof" ? The minimum we must grant to the authors is that this final tantalizing word, "thereof," must refer to the word "religion," as in the phrase "establishment of religion," which suggests—one might even say requires—that the word be given the same definition in both parts of the clause. That is, even if we grant the shaky proposition that the religion clause is actually two clauses, there is no plausible interpretation on which the word "religion," mentioned once and then marked with a pregnant "thereof," can mean two different things.

Why does this matter? It matters because the tendency of courts and commentators has been to give a very narrow reading of the word religion in what we are bold to label the "Establishment Clause," and a much broader reading in what we insist on calling the "Free Exercise Clause." Contrary to the evident structure of the text, we use the word religion to refer to two very different things. * * *

Very well. How is all of this semantic inquiry related to the problem of the separation of church and state? At the outset of this lecture, you will recall, I expressed doubt on the proposition that the separation of church and state is, or can be transformed into, a doctrine of substantive constitutional law. But let us assume, contra my skepticism, that it can. What is its source? Where in the document do we find the text to which we will attach it?

Let us look back at the "Establishment Clause," as it is called. There, after all, is the provision in which the separationist metaphor is located by its most ardent constitutional advocates. But what a peculiar place the clause turns out to be! "Congress shall make no law respecting an establishment of religion." Let us be realistic. Surely the clause means what it says, and no more than that. At the moment of the founding, the majority of the states had official, state-supported, established churches, and all but two required religious tests for public office. The states were not giving these powers away. On the contrary, they wanted to protect their own established churches from interference by the new national government, and also wanted to prevent that national government from establishing a church of its own. My Yale colleague Akhil Reed Amar has argued persuasively that we should therefore read the "Establishment Clause" as a states'-rights provision, as an allocation between the national and local sovereignties of the authority to create or to endorse an official church.[15]

If Professor Amar is right, then the Supreme Court's subsequent proclamation that the clause is "incorporated" against the states through the agency of the Fourteenth Amendment begins to lose its luster, to say nothing of its coherence. If the purpose of the "Establishment Clause" was to keep the national government from interfering in what was properly a local responsibility, the only sensible meaning of incorporation would be that it now prevents the state government from interfering with local communities as they decide whether to establish their own churches. In other words, if the clause is truly to be applied against the states, then the state of Arizona would not be able to prevent Tucson from establishing an official church, and the state of Connecticut would not be able to prevent New Haven from reviving the old established Congregational Church as its formal public faith.

I am not suggesting that this is a desirable result. I mention it only because I think it quite wrong historically, and quite unpersuasive textually, to look to the "Establishment Clause" as the source of a prohibition on creation of these things called "establishments," which leads in turn to the long line of unfathomable federal court cases telling us which government programs amount to forbidden "establishments" and which do not. Without that line of cases, however, we have no wall of separation; or none, at least, located in the first half of the first clause of the First Amendment.

IV.

So if the wall of separation is to be constructed on a foundation of the constitutional text, perhaps we might find its support in the second half of the first clause of the First Amendment, that is, the so-called "Free Exercise Clause." * * *

I am hardly the first to suggest that the separation of church and state is better understood as a means for protecting religious liberty than as a way of preventing forbidden religious establishments. As a matter of fact, much of the serious theory of the religion clause in recent years points in that direction. Yet, as I continue along this speculative path of reasoning, I hope to reach the same end—the proper location and thus the proper understanding of the separation of church and state—by a slightly different route than the one scholars have tended to follow.

Let us consider, first, one of the great constitutional rulings of the twentieth century, the Supreme Court's 1943 decision in West Virginia Board of Education v. Barnette. There the Justices ruled that objecting children whose parents were Jehovah's Witnesses could not be compelled, contrary to the dictates of their faith, to recite the Pledge of Allegiance. The case is nominally about free speech, and often cited as an

---

15. *See* Akhil Reed Amar, The Bill of Rights: Creation and Reconstruction 32–45 (1998).

early example of the protection of religious liberty, but what is most remarkable is the breadth of Justice Jackson's language for the Court:

> If there is any fixed star in our constitutional constellation, it is that no official, high or petty, can prescribe what shall be orthodox in politics, nationalism, religion, or other matters of opinion or force citizens to confess by word or act their faith therein. If there are any circumstances which permit an exception, they do not now occur to us.[18]

According to Justice Jackson, it is the prescription—the compulsory recital of a creed—that leads to the constitutional problem. The difficulty, in other words, is not that the state likes the Pledge of Allegiance and is willing to make its preferences clear; the difficulty is that the dissenters are coerced into acting as though they agree, and punished if they do not.

This, surely, is what the separation of church and state is (or should be) most keenly about. The high hedge wall protects the garden from the wilderness precisely in order to allow the people of the garden to nurture the faith without the interference of the state. And one can imagine few more intrusive state acts than requiring that the people of the garden recite an official creed that is inconsistent with what their religion teaches.

* * *

What has all this to do with separationism? Just this: Barnette is justly celebrated as a judicial recognition of the primacy of individual conscience. What Pierce [v. Society of Sisters] adds to the mix is a celebration of the places where conscience is formed. Indeed, it is a striking weakness of contemporary liberal theory that so much attention is paid to protecting the individual in the exercise of the convictions he may possess, but so little is paid to how he comes to possess them. The separation of church and state, as understood by Williams, would propose that the principal place in which conscience is formed is the delicate space of the garden. The wall of separation must protect that space from state interference.

It has become a commonplace of liberal theory to argue for the importance of educating the young in the faculty of critical rationality, so that, as they grow, they may choose for themselves which convictions to adopt. Some theorists today would prefer a somewhat thicker liberalism, in which basic tenets of liberal thought—tolerance seems to top most lists—would be taught. There is a surface attractiveness to both these ideas, for it is terribly tempting, once one knows the great truths, to reach out and seize the institutions of the state in order to inculcate those truths in the young, and thus to make the political sphere safe for generations to come. Tempting, yes—but also dangerous, and not different in kind from the idea that we ought to have classroom prayer because the students who pray will be better off for having done so.

---

18.   [319 U.S.] at 642.

Organized classroom prayer, too, tends to break down the wall of separation, not because it is an "establishment" of religion (which it isn't) but because it represents a profound interference with the freedom of the family to create for its children the garden it prefers. Teaching tolerance, teaching prayer: Each argument begins with the same error; each ends with the same mischief.

The mischief is coercion. But let us be clear where the coercion problem lies. The parents are always free to coerce their children: You must go to school. You must do your homework. You must go to the party. The school, moreover, is always free to coerce the children in the parents' name: You must serve your detention. The coercion that brings the problem, then, is not of the student qua student; it is of the student as a representative of the family. It is the religious liberty of the family that matters, the liberty to decide for itself on the particular moral world—the garden—that it wants the children to inherit. If the garden is the sphere in which conscience is nurtured, parents are the nurturers who stand watch on the high hedge wall. And it may be that the particular wilderness against which they wish to build walls is the very wilderness the state wants the children to inhabit.

Thus the separation of church and state, as guardian of religious liberty, means that the school should not be permitted to force the children to adhere to a creed contrary to the moral or religious teaching of the family. If the state uses its schools as a tool to wean the children away from the parents' religion—as many states tried actively to do at the height of anti-Catholic nativism in the nineteenth century—the state is breaching the wall. So far, courts have for the most part overlooked their duty to protect the garden that the parents try to build. But it is time for a change. If we protect the nurturing in the garden of values and ideas very different from the mainstream, we will create a steady supply of challenges to the status quo, of radical dissenters who might lead us in new directions, of fools and knaves, certainly, but of martyrs in just causes, too. The civil rights movement and the abolition movement were church-led revolutions, and they were accomplished because the garden was largely left alone: raised to ideas radically different from the wisdom of the moment, the leaders of those movements, as well as the rank-and-file, put their faith into practice and changed the nation.

Religions have always been characterized by the attempt to project themselves into the future. Indeed, some have argued that a religion should not qualify for the name until it has managed to survive over several generations. Anyone can have a belief about God; but it takes the nurturing of the belief over time to transform it into a religion. Many religions take the view that it is a requirement of the faith that the children be trained in it. Christianity, my own tradition, carries a strong norm, and perhaps a duty, of teaching the young. Indeed, there is every reason to think that the religious training of the young was of first importance in Christian families from earliest times. * * *

To believe in true religious liberty, one must accept a broad ability of the people of the garden to pass on their faith to their children. The fact that the state might think it has a better idea than the people of the garden do (today, critical rationality and tolerance; a century and a half ago, Americanism) is actually a rather meager justification for breaching the wall. And, as to the claim, commonly pressed, that the school curriculum will not interfere with religion as properly understood—well, the dissenters in the garden, struggling to raise their children, are entitled to their improper understanding. If the state is free to breach the wall simply because it has better ideas, then one supposes that the people of the garden must try to protect themselves by getting their hands on those same levers; after all, they, too, believe that they possess better ideas.

The wall of separation of church and state was developed to prevent this competition. If the garden is protected by the hedge wall, then the mere fact that a powerful group of outsiders believes its own ideas to be more important to the education of children than the ideas of the parents and their religious communities is not a sufficient reason to supersede the family's authority to build its moral world. Otherwise, Barnette is simply wrong. If the high hedge wall does not prevent state interference as children are raised in the garden, then there is no reason for the courts to get involved if the state chooses to coerce adherence to the nationalist creed contained in the Pledge of Allegiance. * * *

V.

But now the reflection has brought us face-to-face with an interesting problem. It is easy, as we have seen, to understand how an enriched appreciation of religious liberty would handle the classroom prayer cases. The question is whether it should matter that the prayers in question are noticeably religious. The Pledge of Allegiance, by way of distinction, is not. Lest one point to the language "under God" as evidence of religiosity, it is useful to bear in mind that in 1943, when Barnette was decided, those words were not yet part of the text. They were added later, in the early years of the Cold War, to distinguish the United States from what used to be called "Godless communism." Consequently, if we consider the Barnette case (as I am speculating that we should) as an exemplar of judicial protection of the sphere in which conscience is nurtured, we cannot make the contours of that sphere depend upon whether the recitation that is coerced happens to be religious. It is the coercion, not its religiousness, that the separation of church and state forbids.

* * *

Abolitionist preaching [frequently used] argumentation * * * resting on the same simple truth as the separation of church and state itself: that the state can be wrong, and the believer may consult the will of God to understand when this is so. Were church and state not separated, the contention that the state is wrong for God's reasons would be difficult if not impossible to articulate, as the state might therefore claim to speak for God. Even Kant understood this point, and addressed it at some length in his essay "Religion within the Bounds of Mere Reason." According to Kant, the idea of divinely inspired Scripture implies that the text holds a message, and that implication in turn suggests the need for a trained interpreter to work out what the message is. The interpreter must be guided by his reason, applied in a way that is consistent with the teaching of the faith. Thus, Kant argued, from the point of view of religious faith, the state cannot be allowed to enact dogma and creeds, because the state is the voice of the people, the laity; and official enactment of a creed would amount to the laity telling the clergy what the Scriptures meant—exactly the reverse of what revealed religion requires.

But the space in which the clergy will explain Scripture to the laity must therefore be protected absolutely from interference by the state. And it is the same sphere—the same garden—which we have already been pondering. The people of the garden (or, rather, the many gardens) must be free to teach the young that obedience to God is a higher value than obedience to the state; and that the state is wrong when it enacts laws requiring what God forbids. If the state is allowed to use its schools, or other tools, to shape the young contrary to the designs of the garden, this freedom is infringed, and radical argumentation of the sort featured in abolitionist preaching becomes impossible.

* * *

VI.

In my rush to speculate about matters not often associated with religious liberty, I have so far neglected a variety of questions that plainly belong in the conversation. The Supreme Court, after all, has supplied us with a voluminous jurisprudence on a way of approaching religious liberty, and if much of the law is quite bad, it is at least possessed of the virtue of consistency. And what is most interesting about our bad constitutional law of religious liberty is where the Court has made its error. For the stumbling block, in nearly every case, is at the same precise point: the fruitless effort to pour content into the "free exercise clause" without violating the "establishment clause." Because the Justices seem to see the two parts of the religion clause as being at war with each other, it is inevitable that the law the Court produces will be in key respects mistaken.

The mistaken idea that the First Amendment protects some important value other than states rights through its ban on establishments had led the Court, and not a few of the commentators, to worry about giving too much to believers who seek to invoke the clause's protection for their free exercise of religion. The problem is this: if a group of believers, as will surely occur, seeks exemption from generally applicable laws on the ground that the group's religion will not allow them to comply, a grant of a special privilege to ignore the law—what the courts call an accommodation—would seem, on its face, a special favor. Because the Court has decided that the First Amendment prohibits, through the "establishment clause," special favors for religious groups, the protection sought is, unfortunately, not the Court's to grant. This line of reasoning has led to a long line of rather shaky decisions, in which, to put the matter simply, the Justices have pointed religious dissenters to politics to seek protection from generally applicable laws—even though if a political solution were likely, judicial sanctuary would not have been sought in the first place * * * [see Chapters Six and Seven for further exploration of Free Exercise Clause exemptions].

If the wall of separation is conceptualized in the way I have suggested, as a metaphor for keeping the state's nose out of the affairs of the church rather than the other way around, it is plain that some level of accommodation will be necessary. In no other way can we truly nurture the diverse gardens our democracy needs and the First Amendment demands. So, for example, when a woman hired by the attorney general of Georgia had her job offer yanked away because she had married another woman in a religious ceremony, contrary to the public policy of the state, one need have no particular view of same-sex marriage, or even on gay rights, to see that the state has crossed the wall of separation: for what goes on within the four walls of the house of worship is, absent some sort of life-threatening emergency, simply not the state's business. Similarly, when a preacher decides, for better or worse, that the time has come to endorse a political candidate from the pulpit, the Internal Revenue Service should launch no investigation into the tax-deductible status of the church in question, because, again, the state that believes in the wall of separation must take no account whatever of words spoken by the clergy within the performance of their duties.

Does all this speculation seem to give an awful lot of special rights to religionists? Of course it does. But if we do not want to grant those rights, we surely should stop talking about the separation of church and state. If we treat religion like everything else, we are not separating church and state, we are combining them, by reducing the sphere of religion to one far smaller than the authors of the metaphor imagined. Indeed, if we do not want to honor religious liberty by providing the litigative tools for religionists to use to protect the moral worlds they wish to build, we should cease any pretense that we believe in separating church and state; for in that case, what we really want is for the state to knock down the wall and win the day.

VII.

In our enthusiasm for the anti-establishment side of the separation of church and state—the side that neither has nor can have any coherent doctrine behind it—we tend to neglect the pro-religious liberty side, the real concern of the pioneers of the metaphor. I think that is probably why we guard free exercise so poorly. We choose to place the energy of radical judicial intervention on the side of limiting government speech;

whereas the greatest threats to liberty lie not in the government's speech but in its action. The posting of the Ten Commandments on the wall of a courtroom might be, for many Americans, offensive; but not allowing a grade school student in New Jersey to read his favorite story to the class, merely because the story comes from the Bible, is an offense to religious liberty.[39] The cross that the Ku Klux Klan erected in Capitol Square in Columbus, Ohio, might, for many of the citizens, be a reminder of what they hated or feared;[40] but, if a school can coerce students into reciting as true what the faith of their fathers believes to be false, the state becomes, for those parents, a hated and feared source of religious oppression.

How, then, to resolve our establishment dilemmas? We might be far better off it we tried to find answers in politics. The Supreme Court, to its credit, did much of the spadework forty years ago when it banned organized classroom prayer led by a teacher. The Justices created a conversational climate in which it is possible—if we are interested—to discuss exactly what is wrong with the observances that had been part of the school day for a century and a half before Engel and Abington, and perhaps to find a rule of reason, based somewhere in the need to compromise that lies at the heart of democracy at its best. Surely finding compromises would be a better solution than the endless partisan posturing by ideologues of the left and right, which leads to the endless stream of litigation, and the endless supply of ever-more-confusing court decisions that purport to tell us what counts, and what does not, as an establishment of religion.

On the free exercise side of the ledger, on the other hand, we would do well to find greater judicial scrutiny, not less. We cannot protect religious liberty—the only concern of the authors of the religion clause—if we do not protect the places where religious belief is nurtured. And that should be the primary work of the courts under the religion clause. Alas, as we have seen, it is work at which the courts have failed badly.

Instead, the law tries to reduce religion in scope, making it just like everything else. If religion is just a form of speech or belief, then it is unjust to reserve for religious speakers or believers privileges not granted to other speakers or believers. But the fact that the religion clause is included in the First Amendment suggests that, at least to the Founders, religion was not a species of the other important aspects of conscience that the Amendment was written to protect. Religion is not like everything else, and is damaged in the attempt to draw comparisons. The judge who seeks a definition, even for the purpose of enforcing the First Amendment's protections, has already proposed to reduce religion to a merely human scale. Kierkegaard was surely right: when we make of our faith a thing to be defended, we also shrink it to a defensible size, and thus remove a part of its power.

* * *

39. *See* C. H. v. Oliva, 226 F.3d 198 (3d Cir.2000).

40. *See* Capitol Square Review and Advisory Bd. v. Pinette, 515 U.S. 753 (1995).

The war to define the meaning of separationism continues apace, with both sides sharpening their rhetoric, and neither showing any sign of backing down, or, indeed, of a serious interest in compromise. So we battle on, two nations, mutually unintelligible, each deeply suspicious of the other, and each one rightly certain that the other is trying to manipulate the rules of the game. I see no solution, and, indeed, no end; perhaps we democrats (small d) must learn to live with the tension. But let us remember what Camus wrote of Sisyphus: The struggle itself toward the heights is enough to fill a man's heart.

* * *

I began these remarks as a reflection. I explained at the beginning that I bring to the task of interpreting the metaphor of separation of church and state far less certainty than I would prefer, especially after studying the subject for so many years. Yet it does seem to me that our constitutional law of religion is dead wrong on three counts:

1) Despite what courts and commentators say, the First Amendment contains only one religion clause, not two, and the text will not admit of an interpretation that tries to assign two different meanings to the word religion, which appears only once.

2) The separation of church and state, if it is to be a rule of constitutional law at all, should be understood as a tool for furthering religious liberty, not hampering it, for the wall protects the garden, not the wilderness.

3) The liberty that must be protected is not simply the liberty of conscience, but the liberty of those fragile spaces in which conscience is nurtured. If the wall turns out not to guard the people of the garden in their work, then the wall does no service to the cause in which the metaphor was invented.

* * *

STEVEN G. GEY, *WHY IS RELIGION SPECIAL?: RECONSIDERING THE ACCOMMODATION OF RELIGION UNDER THE RELIGION CLAUSES OF THE FIRST AMENDMENT*

52 U. PITT. L. REV. 75 (1990).

It is difficult to begin an article on the religion clauses of the first amendment without repeating critical phrases already used by others to describe the present status of establishment and free exercise clause jurisprudence. * * * Almost everyone, including most of the present membership of the Supreme Court, is dissatisfied with the current state of constitutional law regarding church and state. Despite this widespread dissatisfaction, certain basic principles of religion clause jurisprudence are now accepted by most Justices and commentators.

Almost all religion clause commentary, both on the Court and in the law reviews, is based on the premise that the religion clauses have dual functions: to protect the state from religion, and to protect religion (and religious adherents) from the state. Broadly stated, these goals ultimately conflict. The Court and most academic commentators have determined that the goal of protecting religion from the state requires the state to "accommodate" religious practice by granting to religious practitioners dispensations not available to others. Such dispensations conflict with a rigorous enforcement of the alternative principle that the state should refrain from aiding or favoring religion in any way.

This conflict between the two functions of the religion clauses has become more pronounced as the accommodation principle has outgrown its origins in free exercise clause jurisprudence, where it was first used to protect individual religious practitioners from legal obligations inconsistent with their religious beliefs. * * * Accommodationist notions have recently become increasingly prominent in establishment clause decisions, in which the principle is used to justify the weakening of restrictions in areas such as financial aid to religious institutions.

At first glance, the growth and transformation of the accommodation principle seems ironic. In its original narrow form, it was offered as a means of protecting religious minorities from legal duties inconsistent with their faiths. In its new broad form, the accommodation principle has become a justification for enacting into law the religious preferences of the political majority.

Several of the current Supreme Court Justices are willing to adopt a broad version of the accommodation principle as the cornerstone of the establishment clause. Members of this faction willingly embrace the necessary implication that the accommodation principle permits the state explicitly to favor religious belief over nonbelief. Under the broad version of the accommodation principle, state action favoring religion is limited only by a prohibition on the establishment of one sect as the state church, and by a restriction on the government's ability to coerce individuals to participate in religious activities.

* * *

I. THE BIRTH AND GROWTH OF THE ACCOMMODATION PRINCIPLE

* * *

The perceived conflict between the establishment and free exercise clauses has pervaded religion clause jurisprudence since Everson. * * * The principle of neutrality, which was Justice Black's focus in the Everson decision, was gradually replaced in later decisions by a principle of accommodation, under which religious adherents receive consideration not afforded to the nonreligious. The Court sometimes casts the accommodation principle in permissive terms, usually in cases where government grants a statutory accommodation of religion. In other cases, the Court makes the accommodation mandatory. In sum, "this Court has long recognized that the government may (and sometimes must) accommodate religious practices and that it may do so without violating the Establishment Clause."[17]

The accommodation principle is not absolute. The Court has acknowledged that "judicial deference to all legislation that purports to facilitate the free exercise of religion would completely vitiate the Establishment Clause." The line, however, between a permissible accommodation and an impermissible establishment sometimes turns on variations in statutes that are at best minute and at worst trivial.

Zorach v. Clauson, the Court's earliest explicit articulation of the accommodation principle, illustrates how the principle sometimes leads the Court to focus on trivial distinctions between virtually identical cases. Zorach upheld a "release time" program in public schools. Under this program, students were released for certain periods during the school day to attend classes in religious instruction or devotional exercises. Four years prior to Zorach, the Court had struck down a similar program in McCollum v. Board of Education. The McCollum and Zorach programs were identical in all relevant respects except one: in McCollum the religion classes were held on the school premises and in Zorach the religion classes were held off the school premises. In both cases, however, the state substantially aided religious organizations by using its mandatory school attendance laws to channel students to religious studies. * * *

* * * Justice Douglas justified the majority's decision by referring to the accommodation principle:

> When the state encourages religious instruction or cooperates with religious authorities by adjusting the schedule of public events to sectarian needs, it follows the best of our traditions. For it then respects the religious nature of our people and accommodates the public service to their spiritual needs.

Douglas did not view the accommodation principle as inconsistent with the constitutionally mandated separation of church and state. "The constitutional standard is the separation of Church and State," Douglas concluded. "The problem, like many problems in constitutional law, is one of degree." Since Zorach, the Court has searched in vain for a coherent method of defining the degree of constitutionally mandated separation of church and state. In this atmosphere, seemingly nonessential details often are imbued with constitutional significance.

A. The Accommodation Principle and Free Exercise Rights of Religious Individuals

Zorach v. Clauson was an establishment clause case. The Court rejected the plaintiffs' establishment clause argument on the ground that the school system did nothing more than accommodate students' variegated religious practices. This was the genesis of the modern accommodation principle. The next stage of growth would take place in

17. Hobbie, 480 U.S. at 144–45.

free exercise cases. In Zorach, the accommodation principle was permissive in nature; it merely provided the state with a justification for action the state wanted to take. In the free exercise cases, the principle became mandatory; the Court used the accommodation principle to force states to reformulate religion-neutral programs to protect religious practices implicated by those programs.

* * *

The discrimination against nonpractitioners [as a result of mandatory exemptions] required by the accommodation principle takes two forms* * *. First, the principle requires government to shift certain social burdens from practitioners to nonpractitioners. * * * This form of discrimination * * * [takes] a more onerous form in statutes requiring nonpractitioners within a company to work on disfavored days in order to accommodate the religious practices of Sabbatarian co-workers.

The accommodation principle requires a second form of discrimination by creating a category of social benefits to which nonpractitioners have no access. * * *

* * * [T]he Court has never extended the accommodation principle to protect nonreligious first amendment concerns. Indeed, not only are state and federal governments not obligated to accommodate nonreligious practices that are closely connected to the exercise of first amendment rights such as free speech, but in some circumstances government agencies may even penalize the exercise of these rights.

* * *

B. The Accommodation Principle and the Free Exercise Rights of Religious Organizations

Ironically, the Court's expansion of the accommodation principle to cover religiously mandated secular activity has been used in some situations to undermine the very free exercise values on which the principle was founded. Wisconsin v. Yoder is one example of the Court's treatment of this conflict between individual religious freedom and a religious organization's need to maintain theological supremacy and consistency. In Yoder the Court gave the Old Amish Order religious authorities a free exercise right to take Amish children out of school after the eighth grade, in violation of a state policy that children remain in school at least until the age of sixteen. The majority viewed the issue of religious liberty in light of the Old Amish Order's asserted interest in mandating uniform behavior among children born into Amish families. The constitutionally relevant issue was the impact of state mandatory education laws on the community as a whole.

Only Justice Douglas recognized the inevitable conflict between the religious imperatives of the organized faith and the freedom of conscience of individual youngsters. As Douglas noted, the Court's ruling gave Amish parents a constitutional right to ''impose the parents' notions of religious duty upon their children.'' Even more significantly, the ruling in Yoder gave the broader religious community the right to perpetuate its faith by imposing significant disadvantages upon those who might consider rejecting the faith. * * * The accommodation principle frequently requires courts to distinguish between conflicting claims of religious liberty. In Yoder, the Court decided that the accommodation principle gives constitutional priority to the imperatives of religion in its collective, organized form when the interests of the religious collective conflict with the interests of a dissenting (or potentially dissenting) individual member.

As in Yoder, religious mandates regarding the secular activities of the faithful tend to be imposed by ecclesiastical representatives of organized religious sects. The theological primacy ascribed to ecclesiastical authorities in an organized religion often requires them to dictate a uniform standard of conduct for the faith's adherents. Moreover, in any system based on the presumption of an absolute truth, dissent and skepticism can be tolerated only up to the point that it calls into question the unquestionable eternal verities of the faith. The religious imperatives perceived by the authorities of a particular faith will always include the need to inculcate sacred values and reject the profane. But inculcation of unquestionable sacred values is a form of indoctrination, and indoctrination is always an assault on freedom of conscience. On some occasions, therefore, the imperatives of the ecclesiastical authorities will conflict with an individual's freedom to dissent from religious authority. * * *

* * *

* * * [T]he Court favors free exercise in the form of the theological integrity of religious organizations over free exercise in the form of personal freedom of conscience and belief.

* * *

C.   Limitations on the Accommodation
Principle in Free Exercise Cases

The accommodation principle in the free exercise context is now very broad. It now protects both secular behavior that is mandated by religious belief and specifically spiritual activities such as worship and prayer. In some circumstances the principle also protects the integrity of religious doctrine itself, as articulated and applied by religious organizations established by the doctrine, even when protection of the organization results in religious discrimination against individual non-practitioners. Nevertheless, the accommodation principle is not absolute. The Court has rejected absolute statutory preferences for religious practitioners, and has restricted the scope of mandated accommodation in situations where religious behavior runs afoul of a fundamental social policy.

In Employment Division, Department of Human Resources v. Smith [see infra. at Chapters Six and Seven], a five-member majority of the Court proposed a general rule for limiting the application of the accommodation principle in free exercise cases. This rule holds that the free exercise clause does not require the state to exempt religious practitioners from compliance with an "across-the-board criminal prohibition on a particular form of conduct," even if the prohibited conduct is mandated by a bona fide religious faith. According to Justice Scalia's majority opinion in Smith, the Court's previous accommodation holdings * * * did not apply to cases involving generally applicable criminal laws. According to Justice Scalia, those earlier accommodation cases held only that "where the State has in place a system of individual exemptions, it may not refuse to extend that system to cases of 'religious hardship' without compelling reason."

At first glance, Smith seems to significantly diminish the importance of the accommodation principle in free exercise cases. Actually, Justice Scalia's opinion merely states explicitly what has been obvious all along in the Court's free exercise accommodation cases: The accommodation principle has never been applied consistently to protect religious minorities from social obligations imposed upon them by laws passed by the political representatives of the religious majority. This inconsistent application can be explained in part by the insurmountable problems incumbent in any attempt to define which religious mandates require accommodation. * * * Smith seems to leave the Court's free exercise accommodation principle exactly where it found it. Smith does not overrule any decision in which the Court ruled in favor of accommodation * * *.

The importance of the Smith decision is not that it alters significantly the Court's free exercise jurisprudence, but rather that it illustrates the continuing evolution of the accommodation principle. Justice Scalia's opinion in Smith does not hold that accommodation of religion is constitutionally suspect. Rather, it endorses accommodation, and asserts simply that decisions concerning accommodation should be made by the political branches rather than by the courts. This politicized version of the accommodation principle evidences the Court's retreat from the concept of strict separation that has provided the theoretical background for modern religion clause jurisprudence since the Court unanimously endorsed the concept in Everson v. Board of Education. * * * The next section addresses this expansion of the accommodation principle into establishment clause jurisprudence.

D. The Accommodation Principle in Establishment Clause Cases

As noted above, the accommodation principle was originally articulated in Zorach v. Clauson, an establishment clause case upholding a public school program that released students for a portion of the school day to attend religious education classes. A frequently quoted statement from Justice Douglas's majority opinion in Zorach encapsulates the central premise of the accommodation principle: "We are a religious people whose institutions presuppose a Supreme Being." The institutional support of religion upheld in Zorach reflected this presupposition. Douglas noted that in implementing the school release time programs the public school systems did nothing more "than accommodate their schedules to a program of outside religious instruction." Holding this form of accommodation unconstitutional, Douglas believed, would position the state and religion as "aliens to each other—hostile, suspicious, and even unfriendly."

The Court has followed a meandering path since Zorach in applying the accommodation principle to establishment clause problems. Most Justices have hesitated to pursue a rigorous application of the accommodation principle in the establishment clause context because it would eviscerate the notion of separation of church and state, which a working majority on the Court has considered central to the establishment clause ever since this notion was originally articulated in Everson. Yet even the most anti-establishmentarian Justices continue to endorse and routinely invoke the accommodation principle. This internal ambivalence gives modern establishment clause jurisprudence a schizoid quality. The ambivalence exhibited by the Court's present majority has prevented the Court from abandoning completely its adherence to separation of church and state as a value in establishment clause theory. The internal contradictions between the values of separation and accommodation, however, make the continued dominance of the separation value in establishment clause doctrine highly uncertain.

* * * Although the overall movement away from separation and toward accommodation has been slower and more erratic in establishment clause than in free exercise clause cases, it is nevertheless undeniable that establishment clause theory has moved in this direction. Moreover, three present members of the Court, Chief Justice Rehnquist and Justices Scalia and Kennedy, have explicitly urged the Court to adopt the accommodation principle as the primary objective of the establishment clause. Although the strong accommodationists are still a minority on the Court, they have already achieved significant success in at least one area of frequent establishment clause litigation: government financial support of religious organizations. Finally, the Court has incorporated the accommodation principle into the "endorsement of religion" standard now applied in all establishment cases. * * *

1. Accommodation and Financial Support of Religion

Cases involving government financial support of religious organizations are important because, historically, they have been perceived as touching on one of the three central concerns of the establishment clause. Even James Madison became "unrelentingly absolute" when he addressed the issue of government funding of religion. Yet after much wavering and backtracking, the Supreme Court has settled on a standard that permits government to furnish financial support to religious organizations as long as the support is conveyed "incidentally." In the Court's establishment clause lexicon, aid is "incidental" if the government submerges it within a program that provides similar subsidies to nonreligious groups, or distributes the funds through a conduit (such as the parents of parochial school students). The accommodation principle thus has been insinuated into one of the most important corners of the establishment clause. The traditional separationist arguments have prevailed only as a justification for controlling the manner in which the accommodation is carried out; they are no longer capable of preventing the provision of aid altogether.

The Court continues to prohibit unrestricted direct grants of government funds to religious organizations such as parochial schools. The prohibition on direct aid, however, is inconsistent with the willingness of a majority of the Court to approve an increasingly broad array of programs that provide state aid to religion "incidentally." The development of the "incidental aid" concept represents the doctrinal compromise that the Court's present majority has made between the mutually contradictory notions of accommodation and separation. This compromise illustrates the subtle influence that the accommodation principle has had even among the members of the Court who are reluctant to apply the accommodation principle directly in establishment clause cases.

* * *

Because a majority of the Court continues to resist taking the final step in approving direct, above-board financial aid, the Supreme Court's opinions in this area are a miasma of contradictory signals; as a result, the doctrine is robbed of any coherent theoretical substance. The mechanics of an aid program have become more important in determining the program's constitutionality than is the actual economic effect of the program on religious institutions.

Moreover, the members of the Court who favor a markedly more pronounced interrelationship of church and state—Chief Justice Rehnquist, Justice Scalia, and Justice Kennedy [today this group would include Justice Thomas]—increasingly use the illogic and inconsistency of the Court's present doctrine to bolster their argument that the accommodation principle should govern all aspects of religion clause jurisprudence. Two recent cases indicate how far the Court has already come toward the accommodationist position, and provide an outline of the approach the accommodationist Justices will take in future funding cases.

Chief Justice Rehnquist's majority opinion in Bowen v. Kendrick illustrates the extent to which existing doctrine, developed in cases such as Walz, has already integrated the accommodation principle into establishment clause jurisprudence. In Bowen, the accommodationist Justices provided the core of a 5–4 majority upholding the Adolescent Family Life Act ("AFLA"). The portions of the Act challenged provided "care services" for pregnant adolescents, and "prevention services" for the prevention of adolescent sexual relations. The Act expressly directed that the programs utilizing these funds involve religious groups as well as other community organizations. Moreover, religious organizations were primary grant recipients under the program. * * *

The Court upheld the AFLA "on its face." Applying the first part of the Lemon test, the Court agreed with the district court's ruling that the Act was supported by a legitimate secular purpose in preventing problems associated with teenage sex. But the Supreme Court reversed the district court's ruling that the AFLA had violated the other two parts of the Lemon test. Chief Justice Rehnquist identified and dispelled two arguments relating to the secular effect portion of the Lemon standard. The first argument was that the AFLA impermissibly endorsed religion by expressly enlisting the involvement of religious groups in the program. The second argument was that the state impermissibly funded religious teaching by permitting religious organizations to obtain grants under the program.

To respond to these arguments, Rehnquist referred to the accommodation principle and the breadth-of-benefits analysis, and analogized to a series of previous decisions permitting religious organizations to receive governmental funding. Rehnquist asserted that nothing in the Court's establishment clause jurisprudence prevents Congressional recognition of "the important part that religion or religious organizations may play in resolving certain secular problems." Rehnquist then noted that the statute applied to a broad range of community organizations other than religious groups, and that the benefit to religion was therefore incidental. Finally, Rehnquist argued that the statute was "neutral with respect to the grantee's status as a sectarian or purely secular institution." He concluded by citing a number of decisions upholding tax exemptions to churches, governmental grants to parochial schools, and grants to religiously affiliated colleges and universities. As long as the recipient institution is not pervasively sectarian, Rehnquist held, the institution's religious affiliation alone is an insufficient basis for prohibiting government aid in the pursuit of secular ends.

Justice Blackmun's dissent objected both to the majority opinion's narrow definition of "pervasively sectarian," and to the application of the term to the defendants in Kendrick. But Justice Blackmun and the other three dissenters complained about a problem they helped to create. Justice Blackmun inadvertently demonstrated the problem in his objection that "on a continuum of 'sectarianism' running from parochial schools at one end to the colleges funded by the statutes upheld in Tilton, Hunt, and Roemer at the other, the AFLA grantees described by the District Court clearly are much closer to the former than to the latter." The problem is not, however, as Justice Blackmun believes, that the majority has improperly located the Kendrick grantees on the continuum of sectarianism. Rather, the existence of the continuum itself is the problem. Given the proposition on which the continuum is premised—that some degree of governmental aid to religious institutions is permissible—Blackmun has no coherent way of explaining why he has located the Kendrick defendants more accurately than Rehnquist.

Once the decision whether to permit government funding of a religiously affiliated institution is deemed to turn on where the Court places the recipient institution on an ill-defined continuum of religiosity, the separationists have lost the battle over the establishment clause. Having approved the funding of some religious operations, the separationists on the Court have necessarily abandoned the argument that religious organizations are different in kind from nonreligious organizations. The dissenters are relegated to the much more difficult argument that some religious organizations must be denied government funding because the religious aspects of their operations are different in significant degree from the religious aspects of other religious organizations. Arguments based on differences in degree pose more difficulty not only in theory but in practice, because every other Justice can make equally defensible arguments in favor of drawing the line a little further along the continuum.

Chief Justice Rehnquist's majority opinion in Kendrick demonstrates that the accommodationist Justices currently possess numerous conceptual tools with which to pursue their efforts to reduce the constitutional limitations on government aid to religion. Nevertheless, Justice Kennedy's short concurring opinion in Kendrick, in which Justice Scalia joined, indicates that the accommodationist Justices would prefer to go even further. Justice Kennedy suggested that the lenient version of the "pervasively sectarian" standard applied by Chief Justice Rehnquist is insufficiently deferential to religion. He would remove altogether the restriction on government aid to pervasively sectarian institutions, as long as the benefits under the statute were "distributed . . . to religious and non-religious applicants alike."

Direct state aid to pervasively sectarian institutions would constitute the final step in the march toward an accommodationist establishment clause. * * *

Justice Scalia's dissenting opinion in Texas Monthly v. Bullock[141] represents the theoretical aspect of the accommodationist effort. Texas Monthly involved a constitutional challenge to a Texas statute exempting from the state's sales tax, "periodicals that are published or distributed by a religious faith and that consist wholly of writings sacred to a religious faith." The Court held that the statute violated both the secular purpose and secular effects prongs of the Lemon test by singling out religious publications for preferential treatment. * * *

* * * Justice Scalia's [dissenting] opinion is premised on a wholesale theoretical reinterpretation of the Court's early opinions upholding government aid to religious institutions. Scalia took the results reached in these cases, enlarged upon the "incidental aid" concept, emphasized the accommodation language in Justice Burger's majority opinion in Walz, and formulated a new establishment clause theory explicitly based on the accommodation principle.

141. 109 S.Ct. 890, 907 (1989) (Scalia, J., dissenting joined by Rehnquist, C.J. and Kennedy, J.).

As the Scalia opinion demonstrates, the battle over the meaning of the establishment clause in financial aid cases is largely a battle over the meaning of Walz. * * *

* * * According to Scalia, Walz explicitly endorsed state action favoring religion, and therefore must be interpreted as "just one of a long line of cases in which we have recognized that 'the government may (and sometimes must) accommodate religious practices and that it may do so without violating the Establishment Clause.' " * * * In Walz, the secular purpose for tax exemptions to religious organizations was not the general, wholly secular social benefits that these organizations provide, but was rather the legislature's desire to avoid hostility to religion and to "accommodate the public service to the people's spiritual needs." Likewise, even though tax deductions and direct subsidies for religious organizations "may have the same economic effect," tax deductions do not violate the secular effect prong of the Lemon test because the state is simply providing an "indirect economic benefit" to religion by abstaining from requiring religion to financially support the state.

By "reformulating" the Lemon test to make it conform to the accommodation principle, and by asserting that the accommodation principle is the foundation of the religion clauses, Justice Scalia brings to light the controversial central premise of the accommodation principle: that religion is different—that is, better than—other forms of human belief and expression. Justice Scalia discusses this premise in the final portion of his Texas Monthly opinion, in which he asserts that religious publications should be given favored treatment under the free press clause. Specifically, Scalia contends that the free press clause's requirement that regulation of periodicals be content-neutral may not be applied to religious publications.

If the purpose of accommodating religion can support action that might otherwise violate the Establishment Clause, I see no reason why it does not also support action that might otherwise violate the Press Clause or the Speech Clause. To hold otherwise would be to narrow the accommodation principle enormously, leaving it applicable to only nonexpressive religious worship. . . . Such accommodation is unavoidably content-based—because the Freedom of Religion clause is content-based.

Thus "reformulated," the establishment clause standard no longer prevents favoritism toward religion. Indeed, the new standard requires favoritism toward religion. The Court's task under the accomodationist establishment clause is simply to draw the line between mandatory and permissible favoritism toward religion.

I emphasize once again that a majority of the Court does not support this radical new establishment clause standard. The standard has, however, been adopted expressly by three of the four youngest members of the Court, and other members of the Court do not strongly resist every aspect of the Scalia/Rehnquist/Kennedy position [Justice Thomas has since joined the Court and shares this position]. Moreover, the majority's acceptance of Justice O'Connor's "endorsement of religion" test in establishment clause cases represents a further movement by the majority toward the accomodationist position. * * *

2. Accommodation and the "Endorsement of Religion" Test

The proposition that the accomodation principle should govern all establishment clause cases does not yet command the support of a majority on the Court. The nominally separationist majority, however, has itself reduced establishment clause restrictions on government financial aid to religious organizations by permitting various forms of "incidental" aid in order to accommodate religion. This section describes one way in which the accommodation principle has influenced the positions taken by Justices who continue to resist its express adoption in establishment clause cases. Specifically, this section argues that the "endorsement of religion" test increasingly favored by the present majority incorporates a number of accomodationist presumptions. It is actually a half-step toward the accommodation principle, and can easily be adapted by the accomodationists as a mechanism for the complete abandonment of separationist theories.

Justice O'Connor first proposed that the Court focus its establishment clause doctrine on the issue of government endorsement of religion in her concurring opinion in Lynch v. Donnelly. She modified the test slightly in Wallace v. Jaffree [see supra. at Chapters Two and Three]. * * *

At its worst, O'Connor's endorsement test invites duplicitous governmental favoritism toward religion. According to Justice O'Connor, the government may encourage silent prayer in school, but only if it does not mention the word "prayer" in the statutory authorization. The government may legally mandate that employers give religious employees favorable treatment, but only if a few exceptions are thrown in for the sake of symbolic neutrality. The government may permit a religious organization's business enterprises to discriminate against workers who refuse to join the faith, but only if the business is incorporated under a state's nonprofit statutes. The government may grant tax exemptions specifically to religious organizations (which are numerous), as long as the exemption is extended to "atheistic organizations" (which are virtually nonexistent). And the government may use its property to erect religious iconography, but only if the religious symbols are framed by two plastic reindeer. * * *

An accommodationist majority would have little trouble incorporating the accommodation principle into the brittle framework defined by these precedents. For the moment, however, it is the separationists who have adopted the endorsement test. * * *

The inconsistent results reached under the endorsement test prove that the test is so malleable that it can mean anything; the results depend on the policy presumptions that are plugged into the objective observer's calculus. * * *

II.   The Case for the Accommodation Principle

Arguments for adopting the accommodation principle to govern all religion clause cases can be divided into three broad categories: the original intent argument, the political pluralism argument, and the "special status" argument. The first argument is the most traditional. This argument asserts that the accommodation principle is required in order to enforce the original intent of the framers of the first amendment. Justice Rehnquist's dissenting opinion in Wallace v. Jaffree provides a good synopsis of the original intent argument. The second argument contends that the accommodation principle is a legitimate consequence of the participation of religious groups and individuals in the political process. This argument is contained in opinions by Justices Frankfurter and Kennedy * * *. The third argument is that the accommodation principle is justified by the "special status" of religion in American society and in the constitutional scheme. This argument is implicit in Justice Douglas's notion that the United States is a religious nation "whose institutions presuppose a Supreme Being" * * *.

* * * [N]either of the first two arguments adequately explains or justifies the accommodation principle. * * * [E]ach of the first two arguments must rely ultimately on the third argument in favor of the accommodation principle. This section concludes that the special status argument for the accommodation principle rests on an unjustifiably broad definition of religion—a definition that seeks to protect both behavioral and theological aspects of the religious experience. * * *

A.   The Original Intent Argument

There are as many different ways to read the original intent of the framers as there are judges and constitutional theorists. For example, the Court's modern establishment clause jurisprudence originated with several opinions ascribing to the framers a strict separationist point of view. I am concerned here with the very different original intent argument of the modern accommodationists. The originalist argument for the accommodation principle asserts that the framers intended to permit nonpreferential establishments of religion—i.e., governmental favoritism toward religion in general that stops short of favoritism toward one particular sect. Then–Justice Rehnquist's dissent in Wallace v. Jaffree [see supra. at Chapter Two] is the most complete exposition of this position by a present member of the Court. * * *

This section is not another attempt to dispute the accuracy of Justice Rehnquist's portrayal of the framers' intent. That argument has been made very well elsewhere.[210] This section addresses the somewhat different question of whether the original intent position is sufficient to support a broadly defined accommodation principle. The indeterminacy

---

210.   The literature is voluminous, but three examples deserve special attention. *See* T. Curry, The First Freedoms: Church and State in America to the Passage of the First Amendment (1986); L. Levy, The Estab-lishment Clause (1986); Laycock, *"Nonpreferential" Aid to Religion: A False Claim About Original Intent*, 27 Wm. & Mary L. Rev. 875 (1986).

of historical materials forecloses an absolute refutation of the Rehnquist position. Substantial contrary evidence can be mustered against his contentions, but the ultimate decision on constitutional meaning will depend on emphases and interpretations largely derived from the interpreter's contemporary views of the issues. This section contends simply that Justice Rehnquist may be wrong, and that the accommodation principle must therefore be based on something in addition to the framers' intent, and specifically the "special status" argument * * *.

* * *

2. *Rehnquist's Originalism*

The problems inherent in the application of originalism to the religion clauses can be illustrated by a short critique of then-Justice Rehnquist's argument in Jaffree that nonpreferential aid to religion is constitutionally permissible. Rehnquist's Jaffree opinion begins by addressing Jefferson's "wall of separation" metaphor, the bete noire of the accommodationists. According to Rehnquist, the adoption of this "misleading metaphor" has been the root of the Court's problems in the establishment clause area, but in order to attack the metaphor and the strict separationist views it reflects, Rehnquist must effectively remove Jefferson from the pantheon of the framers. Thus, Rehnquist asserts that it is wrong to look to Jefferson for evidence of the meaning of the establishment clause. This proposition is a bit disconcerting, for Jefferson was one of the country's foremost early crusaders for disestablishment of religion. He was the author of the antiestablishment Virginia Bill for Religious Freedom, and was James Madison's close friend and collaborator. Furthermore, at the time Jefferson used the "wall of separation" metaphor in the letter to the Danbury Baptist Association, he was president of the United States.

Yet Rehnquist asserts that Jefferson's role in framing the debate over disestablishment during the country's early years is largely irrelevant because Jefferson "was of course in France at the time the constitutional Amendments known as the Bill of Rights were passed by Congress and ratified by the States." Rehnquist ignores the fact that Jefferson was president at the time he wrote the letter to the Danbury Baptists (in contrast to the strong emphasis Rehnquist places on other post-ratification presidential actions), and dismisses Jefferson's letter as "a short note of courtesy," despite Jefferson's own view of the Danbury letter as a major statement of his theory of the establishment clause of the first amendment.

Having dismissed Jefferson's views, Rehnquist then turns to the problem posed by the separationist views of James Madison. Although Rehnquist admits that Madison "did play as large a part as anyone in the drafting of the Bill of Rights," Rehnquist attempts to diminish Madison's separationist views by arguing that they were merely political tools that must be considered in the context of the political battle over ratification of the Constitution. By emphasizing the political context of ratification, Rehnquist subordinates Madison's stated views to the external factors to which Madison was responding. Rehnquist is thus able to move back and forth in time, collecting bits of support from actions taking place over several years and involving several historical actors, some of whom had no direct role in the drafting and ratifying of the Bill of Rights. Rehnquist turns the search for an original intent into the search for an original Zeitgeist, which cannot be identified precisely with any particular person or any particular time.

* * *

* * * Rehnquist notes that in the early years of the republic the federal government was involved with religion in many ways, ranging from endorsement of religion in the Northwest Ordinance to presidential proclamations of Thanksgiving. Even this aspect of history, however, is ambiguous. For example, when Congress reenacted the Northwest Ordinance in 1789, it retained the section endorsing religion, but eliminated a provision in the 1787 Ordinance that set aside a plot in each township "perpetually for the purposes of religion." Furthermore, although Thanksgiving proclamations were issued by Presidents Washington, Adams, and Madison, President Jefferson specifically refused to do so on the ground that such a proclamation would be unconstitutional.

The ambiguity and internal contradictions evident in the historical record do not indicate that Justice Rehnquist's Jaffree dissent is intellectually dishonest or intentionally misleading. The indeterminacy of the historical record, however, does indicate that Rehnquist's accommodationist interpretation of the establishment clause must rest on something more than the historical evidence alone; it is also based on the Chief Justice's judgment about which historical materials should be emphasized, which materials should be dismissed, and how ambiguities should be interpreted and resolved. Chief Justice Rehnquist's policy preferences lead him to make perfectly reasonable observations about the substantial role of religion in early American political society, but they also lead him to assert the less reasonable proposition that James Madison was not a strict separationist, and the even more untenable notion that Thomas Jefferson's views on church and state have little if any bearing on the meaning of the first amendment. At most, Rehnquist's originalist arguments prove that history provides support for two alternative traditions concerning the role of religion in our political culture: one separationist and one accommodationist. Although history helps to define the choices between these alternative traditions, it cannot make this choice for us.

B.   The Political Pluralism Argument

The second argument supporting the application of the accommodation principle in religion clause cases is based on the more general constitutional principle of political pluralism. This section will first analyze the mainstream version of the pluralism argument in favor of the accommodation principle. This version asserts that the political process is capable of reconciling competing claims of religious entitlement to political favoritism, as long as the Court requires that programs favoring religion be open to all sects. * * *

1. Mainstream Pluralism

All forms of political pluralism arguments are variations on the theme of judicial restraint. All such arguments maintain that in the absence of special circumstances, the courts should respect the decisions made by the political branches of government. The Court has accepted the political pluralism argument in interpreting certain substantive rights provisions of the Constitution. For example, the Court generally rejects equal protection challenges to economic regulations passed by the political branches, unless the regulation disadvantages a discrete social group that cannot protect itself politically. A majority of the Court, however, has consistently refused to adopt this deferential standard in religion clause cases. The Court has ruled instead that sheer political power cannot be used to impose the majority's religious faith upon "the infidel, the atheist, or the adherent of a non-Christian faith such as Islam or Judaism." Even Justice O'Connor's endorsement test, which is potentially very deferential to majoritarian favoritism toward religion, is phrased in terms that protect religious minorities from suffering the consequences of their political weakness.

* * *

* * * If the Court chose to defer to political action on religious matters, and refused to set ground rules against the promulgation of religious principles by political dictate, the Court would install a majoritarian ethos that would constitutionally certify any set of principles the politically powerful majority chose to enact. This religious majoritarianism would more likely than not breed indifference or even hostility toward nonadherents (not to mention nonbelievers).

* * *

* * * [T]he bottom line of pluralism, that the majority can do whatever it wants short of installing one particular national religion, permits the religious majority to run roughshod over religious dissenters. This consequence is unpalatable to the proponents of the accommodation principle. The accommodationists implicitly concede that the broad version of the accommodation principle cannot successfully be defended solely as a legitimate exercise of political power. Rather, they support the accommodation of religion by reference to a more basic recognition, that religion is the cornerstone of our entire culture. Even religious minorities and nonbelievers are subsumed within the benign and universal religious culture. Thus, like the originalist arguments proffered by Chief Justice Rehnquist and others, mainstream pluralism arguments in support of the accommodation principle ultimately rest on the special status of religion.

* * *

C. The Special Status Argument

The ancillary constitutional values of original intent and democratic pluralism are not sufficient to justify the accommodation principle. Original intent is inconclusive, and pluralism (if applied consistently) eliminates virtually all constitutional limits on the majority's ability to write its religious beliefs into law. The final argument in favor of the accommodation principle is implicit in each of the previous arguments: The accommodation principle should govern adjudication of religion clause issues because religion is afforded special status by the first amendment itself.

The most cogent presentation of the special status argument is contained in Professor Michael McConnell's 1985 article "Accommodation of Religion."[311] Professor McConnell's examination of the special status of religion leads him to * * * [conclude that]: Government has the power to accommodate religion in any manner as long as the government stops short of establishing one particular church or alliance of churches, and as long as the accommodation does not coerce nonadherents into joining a particular faith or participating unwillingly in a religious observance. McConnell's defense of the accommodation principle, however, explicitly redefines the government as a sectarian entity. "The underlying theme is that individual choice in religion is a public value; the state itself is religiously pluralistic—not secular."

This transformation of the state from a secular entity to a sectarian one is an inevitable consequence of McConnell's argument that religion has special status under the Constitution. * * * Professor McConnell begins his analysis by redefining the tension between the two religion clauses. Professor McConnell believes that the true tension is not between the establishment and free exercise clauses, but rather between the ideal of separation, which has guided the Court since Everson, and the facilitation of religious liberty, which McConnell believes is the "central value and animating purpose" of the religion clauses. The Court's present treatment of religious issues is incoherent, McConnell argues, because the Court misconstrues the objective of the religion clauses.* * * Therefore, the relevant question in religion clause cases is not whether government may aid religion, but "when may the government treat religion differently and when must it do so?"

The lynchpin of McConnell's analysis is that religious beliefs and practices are different in kind from all other forms of beliefs and practices. If religion were merely one "element in the mix of beliefs and associations in the community," then McConnell's emphasis on religious liberty would not be sufficient to justify the accommodation principle. * * * According to McConnell, religion is philosophically superior to nonreligious beliefs and associations because "the liberal state . . . cannot reject in principle the possibility that a religion may be true; and if true, religious claims are of a higher order than anything in statecraft." * * *

---

311. McConnell, *Accommodation of Religion*, 1985 SUP. CT. REV. 1.

Aside from the state's inability to question the commands of a superior celestial authority, McConnell gives other, more earthly reasons for accommodating religion, that relate directly to the political well-being of the government itself. * * * Professor McConnell accepts the premises of the liberal state and does not believe religion is inconsistent with those premises. However * * * McConnell believes that "the liberal state cannot itself ultimately be the source ... of the people's values." McConnell therefore concludes that some external source must be found to instill in the population a "commitment to order and morality," and to satisfy a "need for internalized constraints and natural sentiments of justice" among the citizenry. * * *

* * * According to McConnell, "mediating" institutions such as churches are politically crucial in the American constitutional system because "they are the principal means by which the citizens in a liberal polity learn to transcend their individual interests and opinions and to develop civic responsibility." Therefore, although the state is prohibited from interfering with the "higher authority" represented by religion, the state may use the authority of religion to discipline and train its citizens (and incidentally, to bolster and perpetuate the state's own authority). * * *

McConnell's deemphasis of religion's spiritual aspect, and the politicization of the church as an institution, dictate that the accommodation mandated under his view of the first amendment be very broad indeed. First, McConnell would require government to accommodate religious practices as well as beliefs. Whenever the state requires individuals to behave in one manner and the individual's religion requires the opposite, the state must give way. McConnell seems to consider this almost as a matter of jurisdiction. That is, accommodation is required because the state lacks jurisdiction over the higher authority—religion. * * * McConnell would also extend the free exercise clause accommodation principle to religious institutions, in the form of protection for institutional autonomy.

* * * McConnell would use the accommodation principle in establishment clause cases to uphold virtually all forms of governmental favoritism to religion that do not give one particular faith advantages denied to another. He bluntly acknowledges that such "religious accommodations often, perhaps always, impose some costs on others. Sometimes these costs are not inconsiderable." These "not inconsiderable" costs, however, do not have constitutional significance if they are not religious in nature. Legislatures granting favorable treatment to religion are not required "to treat religious conviction as if it had no greater weight or dignity under the Constitution than economics or similar interests."

* * * As McConnell acknowledges, the debate over the legitimacy of the accommodation principle turns on the correctness of his assessment that religion deserves "special status." * * *

III.   What is Religion and Why is it Special?

There are three elements to the argument that religion should be granted special status under the Constitution. The first element of the argument is that constitutional protection of religion must extend beyond the protection offered to nonreligious expression because the first amendment itself singles out religion from other forms of expression. The second element of the special status argument is that, for constitutional purposes, the term "religion" should be construed very broadly— broadly enough to include not only religious beliefs and expression, but also behavior that is dictated or influenced by the practitioner's religious faith. The final element of the special status argument is that religious ideas and institutions make positive contributions to democratic self-governance that are not made by nonreligious ideas and institutions, and that this difference justifies special constitutional dispensations to religion. * * *

A.   Religious Expression, Nonreligious Expression, and the Text of the First Amendment

The first element of the special status argument is derived from textualist and originalist methods of constitutional interpretation. It asserts that religion must have some special status in constitutional law because the text of the first amendment distinguishes religion from other forms of expression; the phrasing of the amendment reflects the framers' intent that religion be given special consideration under the Constitution. * * *

There are several flaws in these claims that the particular phrasing of the first amendment mandates that religious expression be given greater protection than nonreligious expression. First, when the proponents of the accommodation principle emphasize the first amendment's preferential "identification of religion," they necessarily refer only to the free exercise clause, to which they subordinate the establishment clause. They must do so, because the establishment clause also singles out religion in a manner that directly contradicts the accommodation principle. A literal reading of the establishment clause would prohibit the state from advancing religion in any way, and would therefore preclude the accommodation of religion. The accommodationist and separationist interpretations are each defensible readings of the first amendment, but neither reading follows inevitably from the simple fact that religion is mentioned in the constitutional text.

Second, even if one focuses exclusively on the identification of religion in the free exercise clause, the text of the first amendment does not necessarily favor religion over other forms of expression. It is equally plausible to read the free exercise clause as merely one component of the first amendment's broad protection of all forms of expression, including political, artistic, literary, scientific, and religious expression. Under this interpretation the free exercise of religion is protected to the same extent as other forms of expression, but is not singled out for favored treatment. * * *

* * *

Third, interpreting the first amendment as providing broad protection to all forms of expression without regard to their religious nature is consistent with the sketchy historical evidence of the process by which the First Congress arrived at the final phrasing of the first amendment. * * *

It is impossible to discern the definitive meaning of the constitutional terminology either from the text itself or from the incomplete evidence we have of the framers' intent. It is, however, certainly a plausible reading of the first amendment text and the circumstances of its adoption to interpret the specifically enumerated rights in the text as illustrations of a multifaceted right of conscience, the expression of which is generally protected from governmental intrusion or control. This interpretation has the advantage of saving the establishment clause from the trivial role it has been assigned under an accommodationist theory. Instead of merely protecting against the establishment of one particular faith, the establishment clause once again becomes a barrier to the use of political power for religious ends. * * *

B. The Accommodation Principle and the Definition of Religion

The accommodation principle is premised on the proposition that religious beliefs, expressions and practices are by nature different from nonreligious beliefs, expressions and practices. Deciding whether to apply the accommodation principle to any set of beliefs, expressions, or practices presents a definitional dilemma, namely, what is religion?

This definitional dilemma has two aspects. The first is the problem of theological definition, which requires an analysis of the structure of beliefs, which, in turn, are the basis for the requested accommodation. The following questions arise in the course of this analysis: What kinds of ideas are "religious"? For example, is any comprehensive moral doctrine "religious" or must the moral doctrine be derived from an extra-human metaphysical authority to satisfy the criteria for religion? May agnosticism or atheism ever qualify as a religion? Must religion exist within a structured set of beliefs and practices that establishes a spiritual hierarchy? If so, will a pantheistic religion ever qualify? Is religion social? Will the accommodation principle protect an undoubtedly devout individual whose idiosyncratic beliefs are not certified by recognized ecclesiastical authorities and do not include common religious indicia such as a catechism and liturgy?

The second aspect of the definitional dilemma concerns the relationship between the accommodation principle and the religiously mandated behavior of adherents. Specifically, the courts must identify which religious obligations and duties are so significant to the religious life of the believer that they should be protected under the free exercise clause. The most important question in confronting the problem of religious behavior is whether the accommodation principle protects only primary religious behavior and absolute religious duties and obligations, or whether it also protects the behavioral implications of religious belief that do not rise to the level of absolute theological obligations. Stated in practical terms, does the accommodation principle protect only the core aspects of religion such as the expression of religious ideas in prayer or worship, or does the principle also protect the manifold consequences that flow from the application of those ideas to a believer's daily life?

The proponents of the accommodation principle have asserted that the second aspect of the definitional dilemma should be resolved in favor of broad protection of religious behavior. * * * Indeed, proponents of the accommodation principle are logically compelled to insist upon the protection of a broad range of religious behavior, because protection of the core elements of religious faith would provide little more protection than is currently offered under the free speech clause.

The breadth of the accommodationist position on protecting religiously motivated behavior necessarily limits the extent to which accommodationists can extend the protections offered by the accommodation principle to religious minorities and nonbelievers. By insisting on protecting a broad range of religious behavior, proponents of the accommodation principle must restrict the scope of the principle in other ways, such as by denying the theological legitimacy of nontraditional or unfamiliar faiths. * * *

IV. THE NATURE OF RELIGION AND ITS ROLE IN THE MODERN STATE

The previous section reveals the inconsistency at the heart of the accommodation principle. The accommodation principle is premised on the notion that religion and religious ideas are "special" and, therefore, are deserving of heightened protection under the Constitution. The primary objective of the accommodation principle is to protect both behavior motivated by religion and the belief and expression of religious ideas. These themes cannot be reconciled without introducing into religion clause jurisprudence a preference for traditional forms of religious belief and practice. Attempts to define the essence of religion broadly enough to encompass the full range of arguably religious beliefs render the protection of behavior motivated by religion impossible because, under such broad definitions, virtually all behavior would be constitutionally protected. Each attempt to define religion broadly within an accommodationist perspective arbitrarily narrows the definition of religion to protect only the more traditional or nonthreatening forms of religious belief and practice.

In this section I argue that these two themes of the accommodation principle conflict, and that each of the themes is fundamentally flawed. In the first subsection below I offer a much narrower definition of "religion" than those discussed in the previous section. In the second subsection I apply this narrow definition to specific problems raised by the religion clauses. In particular, I argue that the narrow definition illustrates the need to reinforce strong establishment clause prohibitions on the use of state agencies to advance religious goals. I also definitively rebut claims that the state may not pursue a secular agenda in education and social welfare when that agenda conflicts with the doctrines of particular religious sects. * * * In the third subsection, I argue that a broader definition is unnecessary to protect religious liberty because (a) religious ideas and expression are adequately protected under a broadly construed free speech doctrine, and (b) there is no constitutional justification for using the free exercise clause to prefer religiously motivated behavior over nonreligious behavior.

A. A Narrow Definition of Religion

In this section, I propose to adopt and expand upon a narrow definition of religion suggested recently by Professor Stanley Ingber. Professor Ingber argues that religion "consists of a 'unified system of beliefs and practices relative to sacred things.' "[433] Although Ingber notes that the sacred aspects of religion are not necessarily bound within theistic concepts, "religious duties must be based in the 'otherworldly' or the transcendent . . . a transcendentreality." The extra-human nature of religious obligation "makes secular law which interferes with divinely ordained responsibilities suspect. Human beings may not undo an obligation not of human making." In sum, religion involves the subordination of the individual will to the unchallengeable dictates of an extra-human, transcendent force or reality. This definition is helpful because it focuses on the three key aspects of religion: (1) religious principles are derived from a source beyond human control; (2) religious principles are immutable and absolutely authoritative; and (3) religious principles are not based on logic or reason, and, therefore, may not be proved or disproved.

* * * The three elements of the narrow definition focus attention solely on the particular facets of religion that are significant for constitutional purposes.

The first element of the narrow definition is necessary because without some reference to an external authority, a claim of religious duty or obligation becomes indistinguishable from a purely solipsistic individual desire. Unless "religion" means "all strong human desire," the definition of religion must locate the source of an asserted religious obligation outside the individual. * * *

The second element of the definition is also required in order to formulate a sensible limitation on constitutional entitlements. Religious principles that are neither immutable nor absolutely authoritative would not lead to a conflict between secular and religious obligations because, by definition, mutable and non-absolute religious obligations can be

---

433. [Ingber, *Religion or Ideology: A Needed Clarification of the Religion Clauses*, 41 STAN. L. REV. 233, 285 (1989)] (quoting E. DURKHEIM, THE ELEMENTARY FORMS OF THE RELIGIOUS LIFE 62 (J. Swain trans. 1965)).

modified or ignored by the adherent in order to comply with secular duties. * * *

The third element of the narrow definition is necessary because of the evolution in the philosophy of religion. At least since Immanuel Kant's publication of the Critique of Pure Reason, theistic forms of religion have been unable to rely upon the traditional logical proofs of God's existence. This transformation in the nature of theistic religion rendered God unknowable and placed theistic religion on the same foundation with nontheistic religion—a manifestation of human faith alone. * * * The significant fact is that a theology based on belief rather than on reason creates a far more precarious basis for political action, certainly far too unstable a foundation to serve as the basis for the coercive application of religious principles to everyone in society.

Although the narrow definition is initially compelling as a matter of abstract theory, the definition is problematic when considered within the context of present religion clause doctrine, which includes at least a weak form of the accommodation principle. When the narrow definition is incorporated into current jurisprudence and applied to nontraditional or new forms of religious doctrine, where most free exercise litigation occurs, it seems to present some of the same difficulties that the broader definitions present. In particular, the definition seems to be grossly underinclusive. * * *

* * *

I argue that Professor Ingber's narrow definition of religion is helpful for religion clause analysis not because it provides a mechanism for rationally distinguishing the entitlements of different groups under the accommodation principle, but because it undercuts the very premises of the accommodation principle by identifying the characteristics that make religion an inappropriate basis for political and constitutional favoritism.

B.   The Narrow Definition and the Application of the Accommodation Principle in Establishment Clause Cases

As Professor McConnell acknowledged, the question "Why is Religion Different?" is the key to the establishment clause debate. The narrow definition of religion provides a conceptual framework within which that question may be answered. The narrow definition of religion helps to explain why a strongly separationist interpretation of the establishment clause remains compelling. Proponents of the accommodation principle necessarily contend just the opposite. * * *

The narrow definition of religion * * * focus[es] establishment clause analysis on the nature of religious principles and on their relationship to democratic self-governance. Recall the three key aspects of religion identified by the narrow definition: religion's guiding principles are derived from a source beyond human control; religious principles are immutable and absolutely authoritative; religious principles are not based on logic or reason, and therefore may not be proved or disproved. Each of these three characteristics is incompatible with any democratic theory of the modern state.

Indeed, one could summarize the basic attributes of modern democratic theory by stating the converse of the first and second elements of religion. First, popular control of government and law is the essence of democracy in any form. By definition, democratic theory views all government actions as reflections of temporal human authority. This authority may be channeled through representative agencies and mediated by constitutional processes, but a democratic government's ultimate claim to legitimacy must be that those subject to the dictates of the system acquiesce to the system's exercise of power. Conversely, when a government places its imprimatur on principles derived from an extra-human source, or uses its resources to cultivate allegiance to an extra-human authority, it implicitly places certain political questions beyond human control. Democracy depends on the perpetuation of a healthy anti-authoritarian mindset among the citizenry; religion cultivates deference to some authority or power that cannot be questioned or changed, or even fully comprehended by the human mind.

Likewise, whereas religion asserts that its principles are immutable and absolutely authoritative, democratic theory asserts just the opposite. The sine qua non of any democratic state is that everything political is open to question; not only specific policies and programs, but the very structure of the state itself must always be subject to challenge. Democracies are by nature inhospitable to political or intellectual stasis or certainty. Religion is fundamentally incompatible with this intellectual cornerstone of the modern democratic state. The irreconcilable distinction between democracy and religion is that, although there can be no sacrosanct principles or unquestioned truths in a democracy, no religion can exist without sacrosanct principles and unquestioned truths.

The third characteristic identified by the narrow definition of religion reinforces these tendencies. Because religious principles are essentially nonrational and unprovable, they are insulated from many ordinary forms of political critique. Because religion concedes at the outset that it reaches policy conclusions by other means, empirical and utilitarian challenges to these policies are foreclosed. For example, it is fruitless to dispute the veracity of creationism within the intellectual framework of the scientific method if adherents of creationism believe in the inviolability of the story of creation set forth in Genesis. It is also impossible to critique the inegalitarian implications of social or economic policies if the state may respond that it is obligated by God to enact into law the untestable commands and principles of theological doctrine.

* * *

* * * My point is simply that some form of rational, critical analysis is the centerpiece of any democratic project to achieve political and social change. Such a project depends on its participants' ability to observe sociopolitical phenomena, to arrange the knowledge they obtain in a coherent way, to analyze the implications of a given set of social arrangements, to detect the unstated biases and hidden tendencies of a given system or policy, and to devise a manner of successfully challenging any undesirable aspects that have been noted during the critical process.

* * * [R]eligion is fundamentally incompatible with the critical rationality on which democracy depends. In a proper democracy, political truth is developed, not discovered, and it may change over time as the individual components of political truth lose their usefulness or become counterproductive to the larger social undertaking. In a religious context, on the other hand, truth is discovered, not developed, and its essential verities cannot be challenged or disproved. The adherent's disapproval of received truth in a religious scheme is an indication of the adherent's inadequate faith or devotion, rather than an indication of flaws in the governing religious concepts. A democratic system should be structured in a way that encourages the development and application of critical reason. A government that places itself in the service of nonrational and unquestionable religious principles, therefore, loses its claim to democratic legitimacy.

* * *

I should emphasize that none of the above is a criticism of religion itself, the views of particular religious faiths, or the internal operation of religious orders. The arguments above relate only to extending the influence of religion and religious organizations into the political sphere. The very characteristics that define modern religion—its reliance on faith in what is unknowable, unprovable, but absolutely true—provide a recipe for oppression when transferred to the political sphere and enshrined into law. Faith ultimately may be rewarded, but it should not be rewarded with political power.

In sum, the narrow definition of religion is appealing in two respects regarding establishment clause issues. First, it places the establishment clause in its proper context, as an expression of the Enlightenment movement away from political theory's prior reliance on political certainty and immutable hierarchy, and toward a concept of the political structure that is fluid and (at least in theory) responsive to democratically determined decisions about the temporal needs of society. In other words, the establishment clause removed from political discourse the final resort to the Almighty that had previously characterized determinations of political truth, and simultaneously severed the state's tie with an unelected and very powerful clergy. The establishment clause is itself a value choice in favor of collective relativism and uncertainty about everlasting political truth. Religious values (and the expression of such values) that conflict with these themes of rationality and skepticism are protected, but because of their undemocratic nature, these values cannot be written into law, nor may the state use the adherence to these values as the basis for granting specific legal or political advantages.

The narrow definition of religion is also appealing because it leaves government free to pursue any social or regulatory goal that does not specifically endorse or deny the transcendental essence of religion. Thus, public schools may use reading materials that provide role models premised on gender equality because social theories advocating gender equality do not implicate the basic transcendental verities of religion. For the same reason, the state may teach the value of rationalism and critical thought in the humanities, and favor logically coherent theories in the sciences because those actions do not concern the fundamental questions which form the heart of the religious project.

C.   The Narrow Definition and the Application of the Accommodation Principle in Free Exercise Clause Cases

The above discussion indicates that a proper interpretation of the first amendment precludes the extension of a broad form of the accommodation principle into establishment clause jurisprudence. Under this interpretation of the establishment clause, a democratic government may not subscribe to the dictates of a higher authority than that of the secular democratic process itself, nor may the government be the agency of such an authority. Application of the above analysis to the free exercise clause reveals that the accommodation principle also should be excised from free exercise jurisprudence.

* * *

CONCLUSION[*]

This article has traced the lineage of the accommodation of religion under the first amendment's religion clauses. All nine Supreme Court Justices now endorse the application of the accommodation principle in some free exercise clause cases. Three Supreme Court Justices have argued that a much broader version of the principle should be applied in establishment clause cases, as well. Among legal academics, fondness for increasing the influence of religion in politics has expanded beyond its usual precincts on the political right. Well-known constitutional theorists associated with the left have now taken up the call for reinvigorating the political system through religiously inspired civic virtue.

Despite the accommodation principle's widespread support, the principle continues to pose disturbing problems for first amendment theory. First, the accommodation principle has never been applied consistently and never will be. If religion is defined broadly enough to cover beliefs and practices that seem to an honest observer at least partially "religious," then accommodation would threaten virtually all governmental operations. To avoid this problem, the courts simply limit the definition of religion to beliefs and practices with which they feel comfortable. The overt discrimination against nonbelievers and non-practicing believers required by the accommodation principle is, therefore, compounded by discrimination against those who exhibit nontraditional or idiosyncratic religious beliefs. Second, the weak accommodation principle presently accepted by a majority of the Court creates an unavoidable doctrinal contradiction in first amendment theory. Governmental favoritism toward religion in the free exercise context, which all the Justices now favor, is inconsistent with the continuing refusal by the Court's present majority to permit favoritism toward religion in more traditional establishment clause contexts.

These two problems with the accommodation principle pale beside the larger problem at the core of the principle. * * * The essence of the accommodation principle requires that democratic control over certain aspects of public policy be subordinated to a higher force that is beyond human control.

An alliance between church and state has several appealing features. The infusion of religious principles into politics would anchor an often capricious and fractious democratic political process in the comforting certainties of everlasting truth. The certainties of religion would in turn certify our own sense of specialness, and would give the population the satisfaction of answering to a higher calling in its public affairs than is possible through secular politics. But the undoubted benefits that accrue from the alliance of church and state would come with a high cost. Religion is incompatible with individual traits that all healthy democracies should encourage, such as anti-authoritarianism, intellectual skepticism, and nonconformity. Moreover, religion rejects the fundamental democratic notion that society can define its own objectives and then successfully achieve them. * * *

Notes and Questions

1. *Separation.* After reading the articles it should be apparent that the principle of separation has many possible meanings, and that in fact, the Court has shifted back and forth between some of these various notions of separation without expressly acknowledging that it is doing so. Thus, Professor Laycock suggests separation can be understood as a concept that is narrower than the Court's early strict separationist rhetoric would suggest and that it works with substantive neutrality to create a useful base for interpreting the Establishment Clause. Dean Garvey agrees that strict separationism is completely unworkable and that a very limited form of separationism may survive, but "evenhandedness" neutrality will likely take over as the governing standard. Professor Ravitch agrees with Professor Laycock that a limited form of separationism is useful in interpreting the Establishment Clause, but disagrees that neutrality can exist in this area, and thus the limited form of separationism must work in unison with other narrow principles rather than notions of neutrality. Professor Carter argues that separation works best as a limitation on the state interfering with religious beliefs and practices. Conversely, Professor Gey argues for a strict separationist approach. What is separation of church and state, and does it still govern in the religion clause context? If so, should it be defined in the same way in all situations? Is strict separation possible? Desirable? What are the benefits of strict separation versus the benefits of more limited notions of separation? Can the principle of separation be limited in any non-arbitrary fashion?

2. *Accommodation.* Professor Gey suggests that the principle of accommodation does not work well in the Establishment Clause context. Professor Carter,

and implicitly Dean Garvey, see accommodation as an important aspect of religious liberty. Who makes the stronger argument and why? What about Professor Ravitch's suggestion that accommodation works best in the Free Exercise Clause context and can only have limited effect under the Establishment Clause? Professor Gey suggests that accommodation is not the best approach under the Free Exercise Clause and that it would be hard to limit the concept in the Establishment Clause context. Do you agree with him on either or both points?

3. *Neutrality*. This may be the toughest of the concepts. All the authors agree that the Court has used varying concepts of neutrality in its decisions, and all the authors except for Professor Ravitch seem to believe that neutrality is a useful concept in the Establishment Clause context. Yet the question remains as to what would constitute neutrality under the Establishment Clause. Which author do you agree with regarding this issue? Ironically, Professor Ravitch seems to agree with Professor Laycock that minimizing government encouragement or discouragement of religion is a good approach to Establishment Clause questions, but he disagrees that this approach, which Professor Laycock calls substantive neutrality, is neutral. Professor Laycock, and implicitly Dean Garvey ("evenhandedness" neutrality) and Professor Gey (separation), suggest that defining neutrality depends on the baseline one sets for the concept, but the three would seem to set the baseline in different places. Professor Ravitch disagrees that there can be a baseline for neutrality, arguing that any baseline used would not itself be neutral. Which position do you agree with? If you agree that there can be baselines for neutrality, which baseline do you agree with?

4. *Principles and Tests*. The authors seem to disagree not only regarding the governing principles for interpreting the Establishment Clause, but also regarding the tests that should be applied. Interestingly, some authors that apparently disagree about the underlying principles would appear to agree about the appropriate tests, at least as a general matter. Thus, it would seem that Professor Carter and Dean Garvey may agree on the governing test in a number of contexts, as would Professor Laycock and Professor Ravitch. In fact, Professor Gey might agree with the latter two on at least some aspects of the relevant test. How can this be if they disagree on the underlying principles? Would it be possible to use a principle without a test in applying the Establishment Clause? Tests without a principle? The debate over principles and tests in the Establishment Clause context is a longstanding one. For an interesting discussion of the problem of creating tests under the Clause, see Kent Greenawalt, *Quo Vadis: The Status and Prospects of "Tests" Under the Religion Clauses*, 1995 SUP. CT. REV. 323 (1995).

C. OTHER VIEWS OF THE ESTABLISHMENT CLAUSE

The two articles that follow do not fit neatly into the above debate, yet each has something to say about that debate. There are many articles that could have been included in this section but the two that are included here offer relatively "unique" perspectives on the Establishment Clause. Each of these perspectives has in turn been questioned. Unlike the articles in the first section, the two articles in this section do not have a natural connection to each other (except that they both deal with the Establishment Clause).

Bill Marshall's article, *"We Know It When We See It" The Supreme Court Establishment*, is an interesting attempt to make sense of the conflicts within Establishment Clause jurisprudence (at least those that existed in the mid–1980's when the article was written). Professor Marshall uses a semiotic approach to these cases, which views Establishment Clause doctrine through its symbolic meaning. His approach also lends itself to cases that have been decided since the article was written, and the article is written in such a way that the reader can extrapolate his analysis to these later cases. Marshall's article is followed by Carl Esbeck's recent article, *The Establishment Clause as a Structural Restraint on Governmental Power*, which argues that the Establishment Clause is best understood as a structural clause that restrains government power and not as an individual rights clause. Professor Esbeck takes on the traditional notion that the Establishment Clause is meant to protect individual rights, but he suggests that when the Establishment Clause is understood as a structural restraint on government power the results in many of the Court's cases would not change, even if some of the reasoning would. Of course, he suggests the results in other cases would necessarily change.

As you read these articles, consider whether you agree or disagree with the assumptions underlying them and why. Also consider whether the articles suggest anything about the assumptions contained in the other articles in this chapter and/or about each other. Whether you agree or disagree with these articles, they both demonstrate that traditional views of the religion clauses may sometimes benefit from new perspectives, even if those perspectives are contestable. Every addition to the debate over the meaning of the Establishment Clause adds something to our understanding of that Clause.

WILLIAM P. MARSHALL, *"WE KNOW IT WHEN WE SEE IT" THE SUPREME COURT ESTABLISHMENT*

59 S. Cal. L. Rev. 495 (1986).
Reprinted with permission of the Southern California Law Review.

From the outset it has been painfully clear that logical consistency and establishment clause jurisprudence were to have little in common. In its first application of the establishment clause to the states in Everson v. Board of Education, the Court dramatically pronounced that "[n]o tax in any amount, large or small, can be levied to support any religious activities...." As if this was not enough, the Court underlined this proposition by stating that the establishment clause was intended to erect "a wall of separation" between church and state. Having thus enunciated the governing principle, the Court blithely proceeded to uphold a tax supported program providing aid to parochial education—a feat which the dissenting Justice Jackson compared to Byron's Julia who, " 'whispering 'I will ne'er consent,'—consented."

Not much has changed since then. In the forty years since Everson, the Court has reached results in establishment cases that are legendary in their inconsistencies. * * * [T]he entire body of law consists of an unparalleled exercise in the fine art of distinguishing cases.

The Court's inconsistency pervades more than just the results of the cases; the Court has also waivered constantly in its depiction of the underlying theory of the establishment clause. At times the Court has indicated the clause mandates a wall of separation between church and state. At other times, the Court has stated that neutrality is required. In still other instances, the Court has spoken of accommodation.

Finally, there is contradiction and confusion in the standards to be applied to establishment cases. In 1971 the Court in Lemon v. Kurtzman announced a three-part inquiry to be used in evaluating establishment clause challenges. Specifically, the Court required that in order to pass establishment clause scrutiny a challenged enactment must (1) have a secular purpose, (2) have a primary effect that neither advances nor inhibits religion, and (3) not foster excessive government entanglement with religion. Since that time the Court has reiterated this test in all establishment cases save one.[14] However, the role of this test in resolving the establishment inquiry is ambiguous. At times the Court has described the test as a helpful signpost, at other times the Court has suggested that it can be discarded in certain circumstances, at still other times the Court has held that it must be rigorously applied.

It is, then, no wonder that establishment jurisprudence has been universally criticized. The Court itself has acknowledged its own "considerable internal inconsistency," candidly admitting that it has "sacrifice[d] clarity and predictability for flexibility," and commentators have found the area hopelessly confused.

* * *

Despite the harshness of this criticism, however, there is a substantial argument to be made that the difficulty in achieving an intelligible establishment doctrine rests primarily with the issue itself and only to a lesser extent with the Court's deficiencies. Inherent inconsistencies and tensions exist within the establishment inquiry itself which serve to make its interpretation highly problematic. * * *

This Article is an attempt to provide a "general direction" to the establishment inquiry. Part of the Article is descriptive. It examines the factors that lead to the confusion within establishment analysis and shows how the presence of these factors leads to a jurisprudence that is primarily "symbolic" and not "substantive," that is, concerned less with the substantive goal of limiting certain types of government involvements and supports of religion than with eliminating the perception of improper government action. Further, I will show how this symbolic understanding of establishment, now gradually becoming explicit in the cases, serves to reconcile the otherwise unintelligible pattern of Supreme Court decisions. The remainder of the Article is normative. I will argue that despite its problem of inherent subjectivity, a symbolic understand-

---

14. See Marsh [v. Chambers], 463 U.S. 783 [(1983)]. * * *

ing of establishment may appropriately provide a cohesive framework under which establishment jurisprudence may be remodeled.

* * *

I.   THE INHERENT CONFUSION WITHIN ESTABLISHMENT: THE DIFFICULTY IN RECONCILING PRINCIPLES WITH RESULTS

There is a central difficulty in establishment: The application of substantive establishment policies to situations giving rise to establishment issues does not explain the given results; in instances where the offense to these principles seems particularly strong, the practices may be upheld, while in circumstances where the offense is weak or negligible, the practices may be struck down. This observation is not merely applicable to the decisions of the Court, although, as will be seen, the Court's failure to recognize this phenomenon has led to increased obfuscation. The observation also pertains to the positions of the commentators and reflects the general common-sense understanding of the establishment issue.

That the enforcement of establishment goals does not explain the results of the cases is readily demonstrable. Let us start with some consistently identified goals of the establishment clause—the prohibition of state financial aid to religious organizations, of state sponsorship of religious organizations, of the state's providing religion with favorable treatment, and of state entanglement with religious organizations and apply these goals to a relatively common practice, the granting of a property tax exemption to religious organizations. This particular practice was addressed by the Supreme Court in Walz v. Tax Commission, which upheld the constitutionality of the tax exemption.

Yet, with respect to the purported establishment goal of prohibiting financial aid, it is indisputable that of all the provisions ever reviewed by the Supreme Court (much less the ones actually upheld), there was no program which provided as significant a financial aid to religion as the property exemption challenged in Walz. Indeed, I would suggest that if religious leaders could choose to uphold either tax exemptions, prayer in schools, or aid to parochial education, the vote for exemptions would be virtually unanimous.

It is also quite apparent that despite the Court's protestations on this point, tax exemptions constitute state sponsorship of religion. The exemption subsidy of the religious organization was based on the state's approbation of the organization's activity in promoting the community's "moral and mental" improvement. This approbation is of particular significance, since it was not required that the religious organization justify its contribution to the community by any secular-based criteria such as charitable works or community involvement. Religion was supported as religion and received favorable treatment on that ground alone.

* * * Nonetheless, the Walz court upheld the exemptions 8–1, and although commentators have occasionally balked at the decision, the result in the case has not been criticized seriously.

Tax exemptions are not alone in illustrating that offenses to the goals of establishment are unavoidable. * * *

* * *

II.   THE CONFLICTS OF ESTABLISHMENT

The foregoing illustrates the difficulty with deciding establishment issues by reference to particular substantive goals. The analysis simply does not work. Certain governmental actions which should be found unconstitutional from a policy standpoint, are indisputably permissible. The question is why.

The answer, it is submitted, rests with the proposition that inherent tensions within the establishment issue undermine logical consistency. These tensions may be identified as the conflicts between the establishment clause and (1) principles of free exercise and speech, (2) the nation's cultural heritage, and (3) competing establishment values. As will be shown, it is the manifestation of these conflicts which leads to the chaos within the establishment issue.

A.   Free Exercise and Speech

The first conflict is between establishment and freedom of religious exercise and speech. The establishment clause's tension with the free exercise clause, in particular, is unique and well-documented. The first amendment's religion clause states: "Congress shall make no law respecting an establishment of religion, or prohibiting the free exercise thereof." Literally, then, the first amendment may be read as simultaneously requiring that religion be accorded no special treatment (the establishment clause) and that it be accorded deferential treatment (the free exercise clause). Even without a literal interpretation of these clauses, conflicting value decisions regarding state and religion are quite apparent. On the one hand there is the government's positive goal of non-promotion of religion; on the other is a positive value in the exercise of religion generally. The government, then, is forbidden by the Constitution to aid affirmatively the exercise of a right guaranteed by the Constitution.

The difficulties created by these competing values are reflected in the case law. * * *

* * *

* * * [T]he more vitality ascribed to the free exercise clause, the more establishment values are undermined. Conversely, the greater adherence to establishment values, the greater is the potential inhibition of free exercise. In the Court's own words, the result of absolute adherence to the policies expressed in either constitutional provision leads to an inevitable "clash."

The conflict of establishment with free speech is also extraordinarily troublesome. A state's interest in separating religious activity from public schools, for example, may lead it to forbid voluntary prayer groups from convening on school grounds. * * * Yet, if nonreligious groups are permitted to meet on school grounds, then the state's regulation denying access to the religious group is a restriction imposed solely on the grounds of the content of that group's speech. As such, the restriction violates the principle of "content neutrality" that has become "a cornerstone of contemporary First Amendment [speech] jurisprudence." Again the discrepancy is evident. "[T]he [speech clause] means that government has no power to restrict expression because of its message, its ideas, its subject matter, or its content," while the establishment clause indicates that at times some speech should be inhibited precisely because of its message, subject matter, or content.

As with free exercise, conflict is apparent. The commitment to government abstinence in accommodating religion cannot be absolute without concurrent harm to the values of another constitutional provision.

B.   Cultural Heritage

A second conflict in establishment doctrine exists in relation to what can only be described as an accomplished fact. Analytic consistency and/or academic principles aside, there are religious acknowledgments, symbols, and accommodations in the public culture that are beyond first amendment purview. This phenomenon will be termed "culture heritage" although it is not suggested by the use of the term "culture" that these practices have no religious component. The conflict with establishment principles occurs, rather, precisely because the religious component exists.* * * National holidays such as Thanksgiving and Christmas, even if partially "secularized," have strong religious bases. * * * Our mottos and emblems are replete with religious references. Our regulatory programs are pervaded with religious exceptions.

Religion is simply a fact of public life. As the Court has noted with ample citation, "[t]here is an unbroken history of official acknowledgment by all three branches of government of the role of religion in American life from at least 1789." * * *

In Court doctrine the reflection of religion's permanent status in our public culture was most frankly stated by Justice Douglas in his oft quoted phrase "we are a religious people whose institutions presuppose a Supreme Being." But Court deference to this aspect of cultural heritage runs far deeper than a lone quotation. Respect for the "de facto establishment" has created doctrinal havoc from the beginning of the Court's venture into the establishment area. The decisions invalidating school prayer and release-time programs in the public schools ignored logical consistency by treating such traditions as military and legislative chaplaincies and the national motto as if they were constitutionally inviolate. In later cases, when these or other "de facto" establishments eventually reached it, the Court distinguished, distorted, or failed to apply establishment doctrine in order to save the challenged practice.

In short, while history and accepted practice cannot legitimize an otherwise unconstitutional activity—because if it did, the vestiges of the most invidious discrimination might be immune from constitutional attack—religion is apparently exceptional. * * *

The point is clear. There are certain religious symbols and practices that the establishment clause leaves untouched. Establishment doctrine must reconcile anti-establishment principles with a "de facto establishment" reality.

C. Competing Establishment Values

A third area of establishment tension occurs ironically because various policies ascribed to the establishment clause are at times in conflict with themselves. For example, the Court's interpretation that the establishment clause prevents inhibition of religion as well as its advancement creates a tension similar to that of the free exercise clause. * * *

A similar tension occurs, as Walz indicates, between the principles of nonentanglement and nonaid. Again the conflict is easily observed. If a regulatory or tax program is applied to a religious organization, the result may involve governmental monitoring and entanglement with the institution's religious function. On the other hand, an exemption from a particular program may benefit the religious institution and, therefore, also raise establishment concerns.

Still another form of the establishment tension is created by the exclusion of religion from government. At one level there is a definitional concern—are ideas or concepts which implicate, refute, or conflict with religious ideas themselves religious precepts? In the school prayer cases, for example, the Court's mandate that religion must be removed from education is laden with theological implications, particularly in its application to the teaching of morality and values. Indeed, some have suggested that in the teaching of morality, the public schools have displaced the function previously accomplished by organized religion. * * *

* * *

* * * Both the vast infusion of new sects into this country since the eighteenth century and the modern trends in philosophy and theology have greatly expanded the meaning of religion. The problem of defining religion has, therefore, become increasingly common. * * *

Unfortunately, despite this difficulty, many establishment decisions depend on this definition: Is the teaching of Yoga, religion? Is any allusion to God in our public schools, no matter how vague, religion? Is the exclusion of the teaching of evolution from the public schools religion? Is the exclusion of school prayer? Given the force of Supreme Court decisions, the irony is that the definition of religion may ultimately be the greatest establishment; that is, the Supreme Court's approbation—what is or is not religion—may be far more of an establishment than any of the legislative programs struck down as improper aid to religion.

The final irony in the process is that the more broadly religion is defined, the more establishment problems are implicated. To the extent that religion is defined to include general affirmations or negations on issues relating to theological concerns, the removal of a particular practice from government (such as the teaching of evolution or the recital of prayer in public schools) increases establishment scrutiny. On the other hand, the more stringent the Court is in its definition of religion, the more the traditional or culturally accepted concepts of religion will be favored over new or culturally unfamiliar approaches, and the more the Court may be accused of creating its own denominational preference.

Again, as we have seen with free exercise and cultural heritage, conflict is unavoidable. For every goal there are countervailing considerations within the constitutional inquiry. Establishment principles are simply not susceptible to consistent implementation.

III.   THE SYMBOLIC UNDERSTANDING OF ESTABLISHMENT

A. *Introduction*

If establishment is a phenomenon which occurs without consistent reference to substantive goals, how is it determined? The answer has only gradually been articulated in the cases, but it seems to be what the Court has been aiming for all along. It is a concern that government action not symbolize an endorsement of, or an improper relationship with, religion.

A brief semantic digression is necessary at this point. The term "symbol" is one of the hardest terms for linguists and social scientists to define. Indeed, many recent works in semiotics have mainly involved the authors' disagreements on definitional terms.

The manner in which the term is used here, however, is based on the definition employed by Raymond Firth. He states that: "The essence of symbolism lies in the recognition of one thing as standing for (representing) another, the relation between them normally being that of concrete to abstract, particular to general." In the establishment inquiry, "the concrete" is the challenged government action, and "the abstract" is the issue whether that action denotes improper endorsement. No particular governmental activity, therefore, is critical in and of itself. It is the message denoted by the governmental activity that is critical. For example, assume a state provides direct financial payment to a minister. The establishment harm is not in the payment. It is in what the payment symbolizes. For example, for many, financial payment to a minister employed by a public school will symbolize improper state endorsement of religion, while payment to a minister in the military will not.

It should be stressed, moreover, that the term "symbol" applies to more than artifacts such as medals, crosses, crowns, or flags; those objects referred to as "referential" symbols. Activities and practices (for our purposes, government actions) are also symbols, and in semiotic theory they are referred to as "condensation" symbols. Our financial payment to a minister is an example of a condensation symbol. Similarly, the Court and commentators have treated state aid to parochial education as a symbol. Indeed, the entire relation of religion to politics has been described as a "condensation symbol."

B.   Precedential Foundations of a Symbolic Understanding

1.   The Emergence of a Symbolic Understanding in Recent Cases.

That establishment issues are laden with symbolic overtones is not a new revelation. Its symbolic aspects have been noted occasionally by both Court and commentators. Still, it was not until the 1984 decision in Lynch v. Donnelly, or more accurately, in two of the separate opinions submitted in the case, that a symbolic understanding of establishment was utilized as the governing decisional inquiry. In Lynch, the Court was faced with the constitutionality of a city's use of a nativity scene in its Christmas display. Writing for the majority, the Chief Justice upheld the city's action. Of more particular interest to the present inquiry are the concurrence of Justice O'Connor and the dissent of Justice Brennan. * * *

* * *

For Justice O'Connor and Justice Brennan * * * the issue appeared to be characterized in symbolic terms. To Justice O'Connor, establishment was defined in two parts. The first was a question of entanglement: Did the challenged action improperly entangle the realm of government in the realm of religion? The second part was a question of endorsement or disappproval: Did the government action convey a message of entanglement to the community? She explained: "Endorsement sends a message to nonadherents that they are outsiders, not full members of the political community, and an accompanying message to adherents that they are insiders, favored members of the political community. Disapproval sends the opposite message."

* * *

Justice Brennan was also concerned with the meaning attached to the crèche by members of the community. Applying the second prong of the Lemon test (primary effect), he argued as follows:

> The "primary effect" of including a nativity scene in the City's display is, as the District Court found, to place the government's imprimatur of approval on the particular religious beliefs exemplified by the crèche. Those who believe in the message of the nativity receive the unique and exclusive benefit of public recognition and approval of their views. For many, the City's decision to include the crèche as part of its extensive and costly efforts to celebrate Christ-

mas can only mean that the prestige of the government has been conferred on the beliefs associated with the créche, thereby providing "a significant symbolic benefit to religion. . . ." The effect on minority religious groups, as well as on those who may reject all religion, is to convey the message that their views are not similarly worthy of public recognition nor entitled to public support.

Both the O'Connor and Brennan opinions, then, are essentially paradigms of symbolic interpretation. * * * It is not the city's action but what that action stands for that is critical. For Brennan, however, symbolic interpretation is not the sole governing inquiry. It is but one of a number of possible impermissible effects to be examined under Lemon. Nonetheless, the reliance of O'Connor and Brennan on symbolic interpretation is significant in setting a foundation for a more comprehensive understanding of establishment.

* * *

2. The Implicit Symbolic Understanding: Reconstructing Establishment Jurisprudence as Symbolic Interpretation.

The role of symbolism as establishment did not begin with Lynch v. Donnelly and it is useful to examine how comprehensively a symbolic understanding may serve to explain establishment jurisprudence in situations where its application has not been explicitly recognized. Even prior to Lynch the recognition of symbolic concerns had occasionally surfaced in opinions of the Court. * * *

Symbolic interpretation is evidenced in the case law in more than simply the Court's sporadic use of relevant terms. In fact, a review of some of the earlier cases in light of Lynch establishes that many otherwise obscure holdings can be reconciled by symbolic interpretation. * * *

* * *

A further example which indicates the presence of a symbolic theme in establishment jurisprudence is the much maligned first prong of the Lemon test—improper purpose. Although inquiry into legislative purpose is not confined to establishment cases, establishment is unique in that the absence of proper purpose alone, irrespective of effect, will lead to a finding of unconstitutionality. Taken to its logical conclusion, this suggests that laws which respect free exercise rights, including those patterned after the results in the Court's free exercise cases, are unconstitutional. It would also suggest that laws which prohibit abortion or murder could be held unconstitutional on establishment grounds if improper religious purpose is shown. As we have seen, however, logical conclusions have seldom played a part in establishment decisions, and the Court has yet to find such laws vulnerable on establishment grounds. In fact, the Supreme Court has not found an improper purpose in such relatively obvious cases as Sunday closing laws and state sponsored nativity displays.

The secular purpose prong, however, has had some vitality when there has been symbolic endorsement of religion, even when the actual benefit to religion was negligible at best. No case better demonstrates this than Epperson v. Arkansas. At issue was an Arkansas statute prohibiting the teaching of evolution in public schools. How this law would have any actual effect on the establishment of a religion is far from clear. A student attending a public school in Arkansas would be exposed to nothing religious in nature. The law did not require the teaching of religious tenets and, on its face, did not convey any religious idea. The law only required the exclusion of a particular subject from the school's curriculum. Thus, as Justice Black pointed out, the statute could be viewed as an item of simple curriculum regulation. * * *

Nonetheless, Epperson is not intuitively a hard case. There is no question as to Arkansas' motive in enacting the anti-evolution law, and there is no question as to its symbolic message. The message is favoritism of a particular theological position.

* * *

Finally, in demonstrating the extent to which a symbolic understanding best describes the establishment cases, I submit that the most significant establishment cases, the school prayer decisions, are best understood in symbolic terms.

The first of these decisions, Engel v. Vitale, involved a challenge to the so-called Regents' Prayer in the New York public school system. The prayer was brief. It stated simply: "Almighty God, we acknowledge our dependence upon Thee, and we beg Thy blessings upon us, our parents, our teachers and our Country." In the second case decided the following year, Abington School District v. Schempp, the Court struck down the practice of Bible readings in the public schools.

The narrow holding in Engel prohibited a state from composing prayer. This holding, of course, does not explain Abington School District * * *. Rather, the explanation for the school prayer decisions must lie elsewhere. Thus, more notable, in this respect, are the grounds upon which the Court did not rely.

First, the Court did not find that the prayers in either Engel or Abington School District had any actual effect of promoting a belief of any kind. * * *

Second, the Court did not find that the prayer infringed upon any student's existing beliefs. * * *

Third, there was no finding of compulsion or coercion in the sense of a forced allegiance to the "beliefs" expressed in the prayer. * * *

* * *

Fifth, the decisions may be explained as protecting the religious sensibilities of those exposed to the prayer. Obviously, some persons are offended by prayer (at least the plaintiffs were); yet protection of religious sensibilities is not and cannot be a proper establishment clause goal. If some person, or even a significant segment of society, were offended by a movie considered to be blasphemous, the state certainly could not censor the picture. Nor could it prohibit people from engaging in prayer in public forums, no matter how offensive the prayer might be to others. * * *

The touchstone, of course, is not that some are offended by the religious view being propagated, but that it is the state doing the propagation. * * *

This analysis, however, ultimately does no more than restate the original question. Given that some governmental support and involvement with religion is inevitable, why does the state's action in these particular circumstances rise to a level of unconstitutionality? The only conclusion is that, without justifying the school prayer decisions for their cognizable effect, the Court engaged in a symbolic exercise. It concluded that school prayer, unlike other government-led religious practices, sends a message of improper endorsement. Indeed, as we shall see, in so holding, the Court manufactured its own symbol—public schools as a symbol of separation.

IV.   EXAMINING THE SYMBOLIC APPROACH

A.   *The Symbolic Inquiry*

Because a symbolic understanding of establishment is useful in explaining the holdings and distinctions of the Supreme Court does not necessarily make it the correct model for deciding future cases. Indeed, at this point, the approach may be seen as particularly subject to criticism since many of its results seem so arbitrary and subjective. Nonetheless, there are significant factors which suggest that fashioning an establishment jurisprudence based upon symbolic understanding is appropriate. First, a symbolic theory is accurately descriptive. Symbolism plays a prominent role in both religion and government, and the relationship between the two has been described as having a "heavily charged symbolic atmosphere."

Second, an approach which concentrates on the form of statechurch involvement rather than on specific harms is also descriptive of the seemingly nonintelligible pattern of establishment violations. Firth explains that in symbolic theory generally, "the relation between symbol and referent [(the meaning of the symbol) is] often apparently arbitrary." This is also true in establishment. Because symbolic endorsement of religion may occur without consistency, programs with only minimally favorable religious effects may create establishment problems, while programs with highly substantial effects may not. Referring to our initial examples, a symbolic theory could account for the reason why significant aids to religion, such as tax exemptions or military chaplains, are clearly less troublesome than are more trivial aids * * *.

Third, a symbolic approach absorbs the tensions within establishment noted previously (free exercise, cultural heritage, and conflicting establishment policies) in a manner in which a more "objective" jurisprudence cannot. The question posed by the symbolic injury is whether the challenged government action is perceived as improperly endorsing religion. Whether the challenged activity will symbolize improper endorsement depends upon other interpretations that can be ascribed to it. If the challenged governmental action, no matter how offensive to substantive establishment goals, is seen as reflecting concerns of free exercise, cultural heritage, or competing establishment policies, it will not convey the forbidden message. On the other hand, a constitutional violation occurs when the government activity is perceived as going beyond that supportable by reference to a competing interest. How this works is demonstrated in Justice O'Connor's opinion in Lynch v. Donnelly. Lynch is a case in which establishment concerns are pitted against a "given" of our cultural heritage—Christmas. For Justice O'Connor, the question in Lynch was whether the city's display did something more than simply acknowledge the holiday. If the display represented more than such acknowledgment, it would be deemed establishment and would be impermissable. If it did not, then it would be permissible. In short, an adjustment for "cultural heritage" was built into the establishment equation and became a part of the relevant frame of reference from which endorsement or non-endorsement would be perceived.

* * *

Undoubtedly O'Connor's specific application of the symbolic analysis in Lynch is subject to criticism. Justice Brennan, for example, found * * * the créche symbolized more than just the acknowledgment of the religious holiday, and was therefore unconstitutional. Yet regardless of result, the approach taken by O'Connor (and Brennan) is appropriate. * * *

B.   The Problem With Perception

As is by now surely obvious, there is an essential weakness in the symbolic approach, despite any mitigating factors. As has been explained, a symbol has no natural meaning independent of its "interpretive community"—the meaning of a symbol depends on the nature of its audience. Thus, as our discussion of Lynch shows, a symbolic theory is potentially highly individualistic and subject to extraordinary manipulation. A government action is (or is not) an establishment because it is perceived or explained as such by the decisionmaker. The symbolic theory's critical dependence on who is interpreting the "symbol" is particularly troublesome since, in a pluralistic culture, there is often no shared consensus of symbolic meaning. The Star of Bethlehem, for example, may have religious significance for Christians but not for others. Is it therefore a religious symbol? What if non-Christians view the star as a religious symbol of Christianity even if Christians do not? Whose view should predominate?

Equally problematic is the interpretation of when a government action symbolizes endorsement. As with the meaning of a symbol, how endorsement is perceived depends largely upon one's initial outlook. For example, the "perception" of whether a parochial aid program is an endorsement depends largely upon whether one views the aid as an indicia of governmental support for religious education or a program designed to "equalize the treatment of those parents and students who desire a religious education with those who prefer a secular education."

Finally, the possibility that government practices may through time become "secularized" further compounds the issue. Many persons who would question the result in Lynch, for example, have apparently accepted the national celebration of Christmas as permissible. For them, apparently, Christmas is primarily a secular event while the nativity scene is primarily religious. But who decides what is secular and what is religious? Strong Christians are likely to view the holiday as having religious content equally as strong as, if not stronger than, a crèche. To them description of the holiday as a folk event is certainly as demeaning of their religious principles as a similar depiction is of the crèche. Similarly, Christmas is not a secular occurrence to many non-Christians, and public celebration of the holiday is as offensive and alienating as the display of a crèche. Perhaps a greater segment of the population might find the crèche to be more religious than the holiday; but even so, should the majority rule? In any event, how should the threshold of "secularization" be determined? Whose perspective (and perception) should govern?

The approaches advanced by the Court thus far have not been satisfactory. In Grand Rapids School District, Justice Brennan suggested that the perspective of the students attending the non-religious school was the key to determining whether the aid program was an endorsement. Why this group should be the constitutional determinant is not clear. Presumably, parents who pay tuition for private school education and taxes for public school education might have a different perception than Justice Brennan. Similarly, public school officials, whose support of parochial aid is based on the decreased cost in public education created by the religious school alternative, might also have a different perception. Brennan's choice of perspective, in short, may simply be a choice in desired result.

* * *

O'Connor's "objective observer" test, though laudable in its effort to provide an objective standard, is also deficient. Although she suggests that her test may be evidentiary, she, like Brennan, advances nothing more than her subjective determination of endorsement. More fundamentally, there are insoluble difficulties within the test itself. First, the test attempts to objectify that which avoids objectification. Her test incorrectly assumes that the symbolic inquiry is reducible to a rational construct, while the interpretation of symbols, and perhaps religion itself, is inherently irrational. Objectifying the inquiry in this manner is, as the idiom suggests, to place a square peg in a round hole.

O'Connor's analogy between the "objective observer" and the "average person," who in the obscenity context must determine whether according to "contemporary community standards the work taken as a whole appeals to the prurient interest," is more accurately drawn, since the "obscenity" test does not raise questions of rational decisionmaking but is instead a question of a community's irrational response to a particular stimulus. Nonetheless, the test remains incomprehensible. Is the objective observer (or average person) a religious person, an agnostic, a separationist, a person sharing the predominate religious sensibility of the community, or one holding a minority view? Is there any "correct" perception?

Finally, as with obscenity, the "externalizing" of the inquiry will be difficult, if not impossible. A judge charged with applying an objective observer standard must understand and evaluate a symbol on the basis of an objective paradigm different from his or her own. However, as has been persuasively argued, it is far more likely that such a person will assume the objective observer to be him or herself rather than employ an external standard. A satisfactory objective construct, then, is simply not achievable.

V.   TOWARDS A WORKABLE SYMBOLIC UNDERSTANDING: THE CONTEXTS OF ESTABLISHMENT

The conclusion derived from the foregoing is, at the least, unsettling. If establishment is essentially a problem of symbolic perception, and symbolic perception is not susceptible to definitive or objective interpretation, then establishment becomes a vacuous concept. Establishment is no more than what the Justices perceive it to be.

Before abandoning all hope, however, it is appropriate to examine whether an establishment understanding might reach beyond individual reaction. Is it possible to maintain a structure which will serve to limit the range of subjective decision making and, therefore, promote predictability and clarity within the jurisprudence? In an absolute sense, the answer is no. Reliance on individualized interpretation is inherent in the inquiry. On the other hand, doctrinal barriers to pure subjective response may be constructed which will render the inquiry far more definitive than a "we know it when we see it" approach.

The key to this process is to limit the scope of the establishment inquiry. As we have seen, perception of endorsement may depend largely on the initial perspective of the viewer. An accommodationist is likely to have a different perception of what constitutes government endorsement of religion than a separationist would. Thus, if the Court can agree upon the appropriate initial perspective to employ in establishment cases, the range of individualized interpretations will be profoundly limited.

Perspective, moreover, is not the only variable that may be limited. The meaning ascribed to symbols is often a function of the context in which the particular symbol arises. For example, prayer in a state assembly creates a different symbolism than prayer in a public school. Regardless of one's views on the constitutionality of these practices, the overall symbolic "statement" raised in each is vastly different. Accordingly, if the establishment inquiry were broken down from its current monolithic structure into subcategories reflecting the effect of context on symbolic meaning, subjectivity may be further limited. In this regard, I suggest that there are three identifiable contexts already present in the case law: (1) the public schools; (2) government regulations and practices; and (3) aid to parochial education.

The critical inquiry is to determine which perspective the Court should apply in each of the three contexts when ascertaining the message "sent by the challenged government action." While no approach is flawless, examining the developments in symbolic understanding that have already occurred in the jurisprudence is of principle importance. The cases already decided should be re-examined to see whether an appropriate symbolic perspective has already been outlined in each specific context.

At this point, I am sure it will be protested that this is no more than an appeal for stare decisis. Why should this venerable doctrine, easily discarded in other instances, be of special interest here—particularly when, as we have seen, the entire area of law has been roundly criticized? A number of reasons exist.

First, taking the existing jurisprudences seriously reflects an understanding that legal principles, even when based on symbolic concerns, are capable of generating into an intelligible framework for decisionmaking. Professor Carol Rose has traced precisely this process in showing how symbolic acts of possession have led to common law rules of ownership in property law. While acknowledging that the meaning of symbols is never independent of its subjective audience, she nonetheless demonstrates how the interpretive process may through time and legal precedent lead to a commonly understood set of symbols from which an enforceable set of rules may be derived. The reliance on individual perception that may be dominant in the early stages of legal development then is eventually minimized by the legal process' creation of its own structure of symbolic understanding. Indeed, as we shall see, this structure is already largely in place in the establishment jurisprudence.

Second, and closely related to the first, deference to previous decisions is appropriate because the jurisprudence itself has symbolic value. Court decisions are themselves a part of society's expectations and, in the words of one writer, become "ingrained within the minds of the American people." The symbolic effect of a particular action, therefore, may be as much a function of how the action relates to a previous Court decision as it is a function of how it is interpreted in its own right. * * *

Third, from a purely legalistic viewpoint, the policies normally associated with stare decisis are particularly appropriate when the analysis is so highly subjective. A strict requirement of stare decisis limits the range of decisionmaking. Given the particularly subjective nature of a symbolic approach, a tight rein on decisionmaking should be required in order to minimize wholly subjective decisions. Stare decisis, in effect, inserts an objective component into the otherwise subjective analysis.

Fourth, adherence to stare decisis promotes substantive establishment policy. Unfortunately, litigation surrounding religious issues gives rise to the deepest concerns in church-state relations, i.e., bickering along religious lines and political divisiveness. * * * To the extent that stare decisis discourages litigation, it is beneficial for substantive establishment purposes. This, of course, does not mean that establishment issues should not be litigated or that a Court decision will automatically quiet a controversial area. * * *

Finally, in what undoubtedly is a bootstrap argument, strict adherence to precedent should be maintained because the current case law, while not perfect and undoubtedly debatable, is essentially a moderate position which presents a workable solution. If establishment cases are divided into the three specific and distinct contexts present in the case law ((1) the public schools, (2) governmental practices and regulatory programs, and (3) aid to parochial education) a relatively clear and defensible jurisprudence emerges. * * *

A. The Public Schools

The Court has been its most consistent and forceful in the context of the public schools. In every public school case, except one, where establishment has been alleged, the Court has struck down the challenged practice. The Court's "perspective" in this context has been that of the ardent separationist. This approach is soundly based. Symbolic concerns in the public school context are particularly sensitive because of the peculiar role public education plays in the development of national culture and values. This sensitivity is not due solely to the purported impressionability of school-aged children. It also exists because public schools embody what Professor Ronald Garet calls society's "moral vision, a dream that society dreams of itself." As such, the public schools are likely to produce particularly heated debates from all segments of society as to what that "dream" should be. Thus, adoption of another's "moral vision" may be quickly perceived as endorsement, unless the government's justifications are strongly apparent.

More importantly, the countervailing tensions to establishment principles are not sufficiently implicated in the public schools to legitimize any governmental support of religion. * * *

* * *

* * * There are no cases which have had the symbolic impact of the school prayer decisions. First, because the decisions embraced the entire nation, the symbolic effect on us all was unavoidable. Second, the symbolic effect was particularly profound because the public schools are both the most visible and the most important vehicle in setting our national goals and values. Third, the decisions' effect has permeated our national understanding of the role of the church and the state far beyond the limits of the public school building. As Professor Kurland predicted,

the cases have "come to be recognized as one of the bulwarks of American freedom." In short, separation in the public schools has become the governing symbol. Any governmental action benefitting religion in the public schools, then, should be upheld only under extraordinarily narrow circumstances.

B.   Governmental Practices and Regulations

Cases involving governmental practices and regulations have apparently employed precisely the opposite perspective. In this area, the Court has upheld every practice reviewed with some colorable claim to historical acceptance. * * * Indeed, deference to religion is so extensive that the Court has construed statutes in two cases in a manner creating exemptions which benefit religious organizations.[284] The Court's perspective in this context, then, has been that of an accommodationist. Some government support of, or involvement with, religion, and some culturally-based, public acknowledgments of religion, are permissible. The constitutional question under this perspective is: When does the support or involvement become "excessive" in relation to the conflicting interest from which it purports to derive justification?

This accommodationist approach is understandable given the strength of the countervailing tensions to establishment policy in this area. In situations where governmental practices having a cultural heritage basis, such as when Sunday closing laws, legislative chaplaincy, or Christmas displays are at issue, the cultural heritage conflict virtually defines the issue. This is especially true once the position, or, more accurately, the reality, that all religious vestiges cannot be removed from government is accepted. The question becomes simply, to what extent will such practices be tolerated? By definition, this is an accommodationist approach, and, as any fair reading of the cases demonstrates, it is the question of the extent of accommodation, not of purpose and effect, that the Court has been asking.

Similarly, when the issues concern governmental regulations purportedly favoring religious practices, such as exemptions from tax obligations and military service, the challenged enactment may be supported by cultural heritage concerns. But other justifications may support these exemptions even when cultural heritage does not. For example, exemptions from the relatively modern regulatory requirements of labor law and charitable solicitation law are supported by the policy of avoiding church-state entanglement, even when not constitutionally compelled. * * *

---

284. Larson, 456 U.S. 228 (no church need register under state charitable solicitation act); NLRB v. Catholic Bishop, 440 U.S. 490 (1979) (statute granting the NLRB jurisdiction over nonreligious schools did not apply to church-operated schools); see also Saint Martin Evangelical Lutheran Church v. South Dakota, 451 U.S. 772 (1981) (federal unemployment tax construed to exempt schools that are part of a religious institution's corporate structure).

C. Aid to Parochial Education

The final context, parochial aid, is most problematic. Because the parochial aid cases are so inconsistent, they do not suggest any overall perspective other than rejection of both the separationist and accommodationist alternatives. Recognition of the symbolic aspects of parochial aid, however, is evident in the jurisprudence. For example, the one consistently applied rule that no state aid may be directly applied to the school's religious function, is a purely symbolic distinction. Since any state aid dollar given to a school's non-sectarian function is available for sectarian purposes, the direct payment limitation serves only to alter the message associated with the state aid, not its actual effect.

Such an emphasis on form makes sense only if we examine the factors affecting symbolic interpretation in the parochial school area. Parochial aid raises a number of concerns which we have encountered throughout the establishment issue. First, there is a fundamental conflict with free exercise, since the right to send a child to parochial school is itself grounded on free exercise concerns. Indeed, because the school's purpose is religious inculcation, the aid purportedly "required" by the Constitution in allowing the schools to serve as alternatives to secular education more effectively promotes religion than do any of the relatively limited financial assistance programs provided by government. Second, as Everson v. Board of Education indicates, establishment principles in the parochial aid area may also conflict with themselves. Denying benefits available to all others may exhibit impermissible hostility. On the other hand, establishment issues are unusually sensitive even in the public schools because of "the symbolic role of elementary and secondary education . . . in our society." Thus, the symbolic effect of any state aid to a religious school is particularly pronounced.

Integrating these factors leads to a perspective that may be termed "qualified neutrality," a position somewhere between an accommodationist and a separationist approach. Some aid to parochial eduation is permissible, subject to two conditions. First, it must be neutral; the aid must be no greater than that provided all students, including those attending public schools. Second, its form must not be, in one writer's words, "conspicuous," meaning, for lack of a better definition, symbolically charged in some way.

Admittedly, this standard is far from scientific. Determining what forms of aid are "conspicuous" is subject to a wide variety of responses, and many of them are likely to be mutually inconsistent. * * *

* * *

* * * [I]t is not my purpose to argue in favor of any particular formulation—all may potentially provide a definition for the qualified neutrality approach. What I do advocate is that once the Court defines what forms of aid survive constitutional inquiry, the Court should remain consistent in its decision. Hopefully, through the development of a series of constructs, a stable jurisprudence will be created.

This is not to say that employing a symbolic method of interpretation will solve all establishment problems. In parochial education, as in any other area, particular perceptions may vary even after a general perspective is adopted. However, once a symbolic method of analysis is employed, the Court will be able to avoid the rhetoric of suggesting that no religious purpose or effect exists, when the contrary is clearly true. More importantly, the Court will be able to analyze the establishment issue for what it is—symbolic interpretation of governmental action. Thus focused, a workable jurisprudence can be developed. Obviously, symbolic understanding does not eliminate the difficult problem of line drawing so prevalent in the establishment area. It does, however, provide some structure from which difficult distinctions may be made.

CONCLUSION

* * * Establishment exists when a governmental action symbolizes improper state endorsement of religion. This phenomenon occurs without consistency and is ultimately subjective since symbolic interpretation depends upon the inclinations of those who perceive the symbol.

Once this is recognized, however, it is not appropriate to abandon all efforts to make establishment a more predictable doctrine, for the stakes are too high. The lack of predictability in establishment analysis unfortunately has become establishment's own worst enemy. Increased litigation and confusion has led to the bickering and divisiveness the antiestablishment mandate was intended to inhibit.

In this Article I have suggested that the subjectivity involved in symbolic interpretation may be limited in three significant respects. First, the establishment inquiry should be divided into three separate categories: public schools, parochial schools, and governmental practices and regulations. This reflects the reality that similar actions convey different meanings depending on the context in which they arise. Second, the Court should employ a general perspective in each separate context in order to minimize differences in doctrinal disagreements. Third, as a part of the analysis of both context and perspective, the establishment inquiry requires increased adherence to stare decisis. Stability is critical for the furtherance of substantive establishment goals.

One final note should be emphasized. Understanding establishment to be a conflict over symbols and not actual effects does not minimize its importance. * * * As Professor Kurland has noted, "the issues of government and religion that come before our courts may seem picayune to many of us. Indeed, they may be more important as symbols than for pragmatic reasons. But, as Holmes also told us, 'We live by symbols....'"

CARL H. ESBECK, *THE ESTABLISHMENT CLAUSE AS A STRUCTURAL RESTRAINT ON GOVERNMENTAL POWER*

84 Iowa L. Rev. 1 (1998).
Reprinted with permission of the Iowa Law Review.

I. Introduction

This Article inquires into whether the singular purpose of the Establishment Clause is to secure individual rights, as is conventionally believed, or whether its role is more properly understood as a structural restraint on governmental power. If the Clause is indeed structural in nature, then its task is to negate from the purview of civil governance all matters "respecting an establishment of religion." Conceptualizing the role of the Establishment Clause as either rights-securing or structural has profound consequences for the nation's constitutional settlement concerning the interrelationship of government and religion.

The distinction between rights and structure within the overall Constitution is commonplace. For government to avoid violating a right is a matter of constitutional duty owed to each individual within its jurisdiction. On the other hand, for government to avoid exceeding a structural restraint is a matter of limiting its activities and laws to the scope of its powers. While individual rights can be waived, structural restraints cannot. The distinction manifests itself in subtle but often useful ways that can prove definitive. A structural clause, to be sure, can have a laudable effect on individual rights by constraining the branches of government to act only within the scope of their delegated powers. Nevertheless, the immediate object of the Constitution's structure is the management of power: a dividing, dispersing, and balancing of the various prerogatives of national sovereignty. * * * Structural clauses are helpfully thought of as power-conferring and power-limiting, so long as it is understood that many such clauses serve both functions.

This Article will show that the Supreme Court's case law is more easily understood when the Establishment Clause is conceptualized as a structural restraint on the government's power to act on certain matters pertaining to religion. In 1947, the Supreme Court handed down Everson v. Board of Education, which made the Clause applicable to the actions of state and local governments via the incorporation doctrine. Since Everson, the Court has sub silentio given the Establishment Clause a far different application than if its object were to guarantee individual religious rights. The Court has done this (seemingly intuitively rather than by grand design) by applying the Establishment Clause as if it works as a structural restraint on government. As a separate and secondary point, the argument in this Article is that the Court has been correct in doing so, albeit other mistakes have been made along the way.

* * *

The Supreme Court's view of the Establishment Clause as structural can be most easily glimpsed by the manner in which the Court carved out an exception to the law of standing. The Court generally requires "injury in fact" of a rights claimant in order to have standing to sue. Contrariwise, the Court denies standing when the claimant can show no more than a "generalized grievance," meaning that the plaintiff's asserted interest is no more than that shared by most everyone desiring to live under a government that itself obeys the law. In cases pleading a no-establishment claim, however, the Court dispensed with the requirement that the plaintiff show concrete "injury in fact," lest laws putatively unconstitutional are, nonetheless, insusceptible to challenge in the courts. This relaxation of standing would be unnecessary if the Court regarded the Establishment Clause as only securing individual rights, for the violation of a rights clause will in due season produce a complainant with a concrete injury. * * *

An examination of the nature of the remedies the Supreme Court awards in successful Establishment Clause cases reinforces the foregoing observation concerning standing. Remedies tailored to relieving plaintiffs of injuries actually suffered are indicative of an individual rights clause. This is not the pattern in no-establishment cases, where courts have enjoined government from acting in an entire field of concerns deemed to be in the exclusive province of religion. The class-wide and impersonal nature of these injunctions suggests a clause whose function is negating the power of government, not the offering of relief tailored to the injuries of the complainants actually before the court.

* * *

Another reason for viewing the Supreme Court's application of the Establishment Clause as structural is that it solves the "two-definitions puzzle." The Court has implicitly adopted two definitions of religion, one for the Establishment Clause and another for the Free Exercise Clause. This is puzzling because the word "religion" appears only once in the text of the First Amendment, applicable to both Clauses.

* * *

Jurists critically examining the two-definitions approach have found it an unsatisfactory hermeneutic. However, the Court's approach is not objectionable—indeed, it seems naturally to follow—when the Establishment Clause is conceptualized as structural. The logic is tied to the difference in tasks between a structural clause and a rights clause. For a rights clause to succeed in the task of securing personal religious liberty, the political majority must be compelled to adjust its police power objectives to the needs of the religious minority or religious nonconformist. Thus, the Free Exercise Clause's meaning of "religion" is necessarily broad to account for the vast differences in human belief, the Framers fully appreciating that human hearts vary widely in spiritual matters.

In contrast, the task of a structural clause is to manage sovereign power. America's religious pluralism virtually guarantees that legislation, even when nondiscriminatory in both text and purpose, will have disparate effects across the spectrum of religions dotting the land. When these unintended effects occur, the resulting burden on some religions but not others cannot force an invalidation of the law due to the legislation exceeding the government's power, that is, exceeding a structural restraint. This follows because intrinsic to the structure of a written constitution is that the powers delegated to (and withheld from) government remain fixed or constant. Hence, a structural clause cannot be seen as varying case-by-case in the scope of its delegation (or negation) to adjust for the individual needs of religious nonconformists. If the Establishment Clause is structural, then any such definition of "religion" would have to remain fixed and thereby help demarcate the boundary at which the government's power comes to an end and the purview of religion begins.

Moreover, any definition for no-establishment purposes has to be narrow in order not to overturn social welfare and moral-based legislation. The case law confirms that this is indeed how the Clause has been applied. The Supreme Court has said that legislation does not violate the Establishment Clause just because the law has a disparate effect (beneficial or detrimental) on particular religions. To the Court, it is sufficient that the legislation has, inter alia, a secular purpose, with the question of what is secular being answered using a narrow, fixed definition of "religion." In summary, the difference in function of the two Religion Clauses—free exercise is a right and no-establishment is a structural restraint—is what causes the Supreme Court to have a broad, flexible definition of religion for the Free Exercise Clause and a narrow, fixed definition for the Establishment Clause.

An important consequence of attributing structural characteristics to the Establishment Clause is that it acknowledges the existence of a competency centered in religion that is on a plane with that of civil government. Stated differently, the Establishment Clause presupposes a constitutional model consisting of two spheres of competence: government and religion. The subject matters that the Clause sets apart from the sphere of civil government—and thereby leaves to the sphere of religion—are those topics "respecting an establishment of religion," e.g., ecclesiastical governance, the resolution of doctrine, the composing of prayers, and the teaching of religion. ·

The Court's reluctance to openly acknowledge that it views the Establishment Clause as structural has caused legal doctrine to appear muddled, thereby making the Court's holdings uncommonly vulnerable to criticism. More importantly, to continue to ignore the differences in juridical tasks between a rights-securing clause and a power-limiting clause is to obscure the search for the proper scope of the Establishment Clause. For example, courts are increasingly confronted with supposed "collisions" of the Establishment Clause with other Clauses in the First Amendment that force them to subordinate one Clause to give the other full play. This makes no sense. Putting the Establishment Clause at war with the Free Exercise and Free Speech Clauses suggests that the Framers drafted a constitutional Amendment that contradicts itself. A major cause of this imagined "tension" is the uncritical assumption that the Establishment Clause is rights-based. If the object of that Clause really was to secure a freedom from religion (and the Free Exercise Clause doubtlessly secures some right to exercise religion) then of course the two Clauses would frequently be found on a collision course. These "battles of the Clauses" would not occur if the Establishment Clause were openly acknowledged as structural.

* * *

II.   THE ARCHITECTURE OF THE ESTABLISHMENT CLAUSE

From the time of its ratification by the states, the Establishment Clause worked as a dual restraint on national sovereignty. The use of the double-edged word "respecting" in the Clause had the effect of denying to the new central government the power to make laws in two dimensions: a state (or vertical) restraint and a national (or horizontal) restraint. Keeping distinct these two dimensions is important because only the horizontal restraint survives today.

The vertical restraint on the power of the new central government was that Congress could not enact legislation operable at the state level on certain matters pertaining to ("respecting") religion. Because "making ... law respecting an establishment" was a power denied to Congress, the new central government was without competence to abolish state religious establishments. Likewise, the national government was without power to undo state laws that had earlier disestablished a church. * * *

The vertical restraint was born of federalism, a concern that the new national government be kept from intermeddling in a matter that was considered the sole prerogative of each state. There was more to this restraint, however, than a continued vesting of power in the states to deal with the nettlesome matter of religion. It was also a public proclamation of sorts. The First Congress was laying to rest latent but widespread fears about the new central government by declaring the popular sentiment: although there were state-by-state disagreements concerning official support for religion, the national government was one of limited delegated powers and hence had no say in the matter. Accordingly, the resolution of these thorny disagreements was left to each state, which in 1789–1791 were experimenting with a variety of arrangements concerning religion. * * *

The horizontal restraint put in place by the Establishment Clause was that Congress could not enact legislation operable at the national level pertaining to "an establishment of religion." In 1789–1791, a minimalist understanding of "an establishment" was a church ordained by law, much like the Church of England familiar to members of the First Congress. Thus, the most straightforward application of the national-level restraint was that Congress had no authority to set up a national church, or even to support financially the full spectrum of American religions on a nonpreferential basis.

Religious pluralism, albeit a Protestant pluralism, was widespread in America even in 1791, so there was no more prospect then than now of Congress actually establishing a national church. However, absent the Establishment Clause, the possibility of Congress adopting laws within its purview that overly involved the national government with religion could not be ruled out entirely. So adoption of the horizontal restraint was not an empty gesture, but a hedge against possible future abuses.

The meaning of laws "respecting an establishment" surely included a ban at the national level on the sort of legal supports that were closely attendant to a national church. In the popular understanding of the day, an established church was associated with tax assessments explicitly earmarked for the support of religion, a parliamentary role in the appointment of bishops, magisterial enforcement of church discipline, licensure of non-conformist preachers or their meeting houses, and the imposition of test oaths and creeds for civil office holders. * * *

These resentments were likely thought within the scope of the Establishment Clause's national-level restraint, or so it would originally appear. However, the new national government was small and preoccupied with trade, westward expansion, and complicated foreign relations (even foreign invasions), and thus the scope of this horizontal restraint faced few tests in the new Republic. The actions of the first generation of federal officials bound by the Clause demonstrate that certainly all did not believe themselves disabled when it came to "mak[ing] ... law [operable at the national level] respecting ... religion." Both Congress and Presidents took actions which, at least by present standards, appear establishmentarian.* * * These actions throw into confusion the original scope of the national-level restraint in the Establishment Clause.

In order to reconcile words with deeds, some have suggested that the Framers had in mind a near absolutist restraint on national power by the phrase "respecting an establishment," but that there soon followed a gap between lofty principle and actual practice. Others have noted that these departures were few and thus should not be taken as setting a general rule. Still others suggest that Congress's most problematic deeds were in the territories and federal "enclaves" over which congressional power was untempered by state federalism. Finally, concerning events such as Thanksgiving proclamations or chaplaincy prayer, there may have been a failure to distinguish between sentiments the culture found most agreeable and the promotion of religion, specifically Protestant Christianity. It would have been natural for many to have thought a few such pieties were religiously neutral, those common to Protestantism generally, in a society where Catholics and Jews were marginalized and other religions effectively nonexistent. So it could be argued that any lack of sensitivity to religious diversity in the early Republic should not set a precedent. Others counter that the most straightforward explanation is that to its authors in the First Congress "an establishment" had little scope beyond prohibiting a national church.

These competing ways of interpreting official acts during America's early nationhood have led to considerable debate, the results of which are inconclusive. The resolution of that debate, however, does not affect the argument of this Article: namely, from its inception the Establishment Clause—whatever the intended scope of its national-level restraint—had the role of a structural clause rather than a rights-based clause.

Although scholars debate which laws were barred to national action by the Establishment Clause, there is greater agreement concerning the nature of past harms that supporters of the Clause sought to prevent. That is, there is more agreement when the focus is not on the offenses peculiar to the period of 1789–1791, but on the broader concern over the harms that had made the interaction of political society and religion difficult as Western civilization emerged from the Middle Ages. Those harms were two-fold: the political tyranny and civil-sectarian divisions that accompany the establishment of a single church, and the loss of integrity in religion (and its ecclesiastical organizations) when it becomes dependent on governmental support. * * *

* * *

During the nineteenth century, the progressive opinion in state governments regarded religion as an institution that should be supported voluntarily and thus not subject to the heavy hand of governmental involvement. Religion was deregulated from ecclesiastical control as well, and—no longer controlled by elites—became classless and thereafter spread mightily among common people. Although religion had been disestablished, state leaders were not taking a stand against religion. Indeed, the free exercise of religion warranted, in their view, specific state constitutional protection. * * * By midcentury, the meaning of "establishment" at the state-law level, especially state constitutional law, had evolved into notions of individual freedom and equality among sects. Formal institutional ties between religion and the state governments had been severed and many mutual dependencies were dissolved. Yet state and local governments remained highly subject to the influence of religion—albeit indirectly so and from the ground up.

Until the first third of the twentieth century, the state-level restraint and the national-level restraint were still securely tucked away in the interstices of the Establishment Clause. However, the slow but steady acceptance of greater institutional separation of religion and government at the state level was uncritically projected onto the federal Establishment Clause and assumed to be the meaning of "an establishment" at the national level as well. Thus, the understanding of "establishment" in the First Amendment was expanded following the pattern that had already occurred in many states. The practical effect of this development was quite limited, however, because the national-level restraint in the Clause was rarely brought into contention during the first half of this century. * * * Most legislation that really touched people where they lived was that of states and municipalities. Thus, citizens practiced their religion and were affected, if at all, by local school boards, local city councils, and local judges. For citizens who took religion seriously, these local officials were also their like-minded neighbors and often fellow parishioners.

This is where matters stood approaching the middle of this century. * * *

III.   THE INCORPORATION DEBATE

The state-level (or vertical) restraint dropped out of the Establishment Clause when the Clause was incorporated through the "liberty" provision in the Due Process Clause of the Fourteenth Amendment. The Supreme Court accomplished this, without debate or even seeming appreciation of what it was doing, when it ignored the federalist limitation in the framework of the Clause. Despite the criticism that ensued immediately after Everson was handed down, sixteen years passed before one of the Court's Justices even sought to mount a serious defense of the incorporation of the Establishment Clause. Ignoring federalism in the Clause was an act of sheer judicial will which is still ' debated by academicians today.

Unlike the impact on federalism, the restraint in the Establishment Clause operable at the national (or horizontal) level survived the incorporation process, indeed, did so without being watered down. The horizontal restraint's survival was not a foregone conclusion. The Due Process Clause incorporates only "libert[ies]" that are deemed by the Court to be fundamental rights. Accordingly, in order to make a power-limiting clause suitable for absorption into the Fourteenth Amendment, the Court had to strain in order to squeeze a structural clause into a "liberty" mold. The critics again objected, this time to the Court's ham-handed treatment of the fundamental-rights principle as if a power-limiting clause was inter-changeable with a rights-based clause such as freedom of speech or free exercise of religion.

The national-level restraint did not merely survive incorporation through the Due Process Clause at full strength, its field of operation vastly expanded. The original task of the Establishment Clause—to separate the competencies of the new national government from matters within the competency of religion—had grown. Added to its tasks was that of separating the comparable acts of state and local governments from religion. Accordingly, following Everson, what has been called here the "national-level restraint," most commentators termed "separation of church and state" (or simply "separationism"). Implied in separationism is a model of dual jurisdictions: a structural clause separates two competencies and thereby orders relations between religion (including ecclesiastical organizations) and government (national, state, and local).

* * *

* * * Everson's expansion of the scope of the no-establishment principle to state and local concerns was profound because separationism is not neutral as to either political theory (the nature and role of the state) or ecclesiology (the nature and role of the church). Rather, an Establishment Clause that parses society into dual competencies necessarily embodies a substantive choice. Inherent within this choice is a value-laden judgment that certain areas of the human condition best lie within the purview of religion, that other areas of life properly lie within the power of civil government, and that still others are shared by religion and government or remain with the people.

This Article does not argue for a reversal of the Supreme Court's incorporation decision in Everson. For purposes of my argument, reversal is neither required nor is it obviously desirable. The Court, in any event, has shown no interest in rolling back incorporation. Rather, the aim of this Article is more modest: to undo the doctrinal confusion that results when the no-establishment restraint is mistakenly regarded as a rights-based clause. Notwithstanding its awkward incorporation as a "liberty" through the Due Process Clause, the Establishment Clause still retains its original character as a structural limit on power. When its structural nature is forgotten, confusion soon follows.

America is paradoxical: it is both modern and religious. When the Establishment Clause was made applicable to state and local governments in Everson, all the ingredients for controversy were present. History was not to disappoint. From 1947 to the present, America's factions, contending as they do over the role of religion in public life, have sought to enlist the federal courts to play a central part in their skirmishes. The wider culture war soon followed, turning the Establishment Clause into a major killing field for Americans doing battle over the meaning of America.

* * *

V. Twin Aims: To Avoid Government Inducing Religious Faction Into the Body Politic and Government Undermining Religion

Since the Everson decision in 1947, the Justices of the Supreme Court have proposed all manner of verbal formulae in their attempts to give greater specificity to the scope of the Establishment Clause. Most prominent are the two-prong purpose-effect test first set down by Justice Clark in School District of Abington Township v. Schempp, with later accretion of an "entanglement" prong by Chief Justice Burger writing in Lemon v. Kurtzman, and the "no endorsement" test first propounded by Justice O'Connor in Lynch v. Donnelly. Both the Lemon and "no endorsement" tests conceptualize the Establishment Clause as having two tasks, that is, as restraining the government from projecting its power in either of two directions.

The first of these tasks is the obvious one of preventing government from singling out religion for special promotion or official sponsorship. The Clause's second task is far more curious to the modern jurist. The

Supreme Court's premise is that certain forms of governmental support for religion are ultimately bad for religion. * * *

It does not surprise us moderns when the Supreme Court announces that certain governmental attempts to advance religion will result in harm to the body politic (the civitas) in the form of religious factionalism within the republic. The Court's collateral proposition, however, that certain forms of governmental aid can be corrupting or otherwise harmful to religious faith (religare) or religious organizations (the ekklesia), is—at least to the novice—counterintuitive. This latter proposition is that religion is not only free from governmental interference, but also free from those forms of governmental aid that in practice work to undermine its integrity.

Consider how the Court's premise—that certain attempts by the government to aid religion will end up undermining religion—works in practice. Assume Riverside Church is offered a federal grant to expand its clerical staff and construct an addition to its house of worship, thereby increasing the number of parishioners it can serve. The Parish Council, following protracted and careful consideration, votes unanimously to accept the money. The Council promptly embarks on a new hiring and building program. If challenged as unconstitutional, should a court deny the grant out of a constitutional requirement to protect Riverside Church from the untoward consequences that accompany government support of religious ministries? Although advantageous in the short term, perhaps taking the money will over time prove harmful to Riverside Church in terms of loss of autonomy or timidity in its critique of the government's latest policy initiative. On the other hand, should not each religion or local church be able to judge for itself whether taking the grant compromises its message or mission? How does the Establishment Clause divine which public benefit programs will bring injury to a religious community such as Riverside Church that, having carefully deliberated the matter, believes itself more helped than hindered by the proffered grant?

Commentators have puzzled over the Supreme Court's invocation of the Establishment Clause to protect religious organizations from their own decisions to seek governmental aid. This puzzlement is based on a two-fold assumption: the task of safeguarding religion from harmful government actions is that of the Free Exercise Clause, whereas the task of the Establishment Clause is to keep government from supporting the cause of religion. However, when the Establishment Clause is viewed as a structural restraint the juridical task of confining government to the civil sphere also keeps government from being involved with inherently religious matters. This in turn prevents government invasion into the sphere reserved for religion, including government-proposed forms of financial aid that may ultimately compromise religion. Moreover, this protection of religion from seemingly benign assistance is one of the Establishment Clause's twin objectives, not just an incidental effect of the Clause's operation.

A structuralist view of the Establishment Clause thus explains how the no-establishment principle comes to protect religion even from a government's well-meaning attempt to support it, solving yet another doctrinal riddle. It makes sense that within the constitutional scheme for the Establishment Clause, one of its two tasks is to protect religion from government. * * * At times various religions will, of course, make decisions that result in harm to themselves. That is not the concern of the Establishment Clause. Rather, the aim of the Clause is for government to avoid activities that harm the integrity of religion (religare) or religious organizations (the ekklesia).

The Clause thereby has the ironic twist, on more than just a few occasions, of protecting religion from its own bad choices. In the illustration, the Establishment Clause would prohibit the federal grant to Riverside Church, and the rationale, inter alia, is that aid of that nature would be detrimental to religious organizations. But how is it that the no-establishment principle presumes to tell the church what is best for the church?

A.   Voluntaristic Religion

* * * Developments in political theory on these shores [the U.S.] took a unique turn resulting in religious voluntarism: the juridical stance that beliefs and practices that are inherent to religious faith are not to be the intentional object of governmental influence. Government could, of course, continue to legislate about morality, but it was to refrain from matters inherently religious. That uncommon turn of events is today reflected in the strictures laid down by the Establishment Clause. It accounts for why the government is restrained from involvement with prayer, devotional Bible reading, the teaching of religious doctrine, veneration of the Ten Commandments, and similar practices that are inherently religious.

Voluntarism is not merely the absence of official coercion. It is also the absence of the government's influence concerning inherently religious beliefs and practices. Official coercion of religiously informed conscience can (and often will) result in individual religious injury. Such injury or harm is a matter to be addressed by the Free Exercise Clause. But government can act in ways that shape people's religious choices, albeit its acts fall short of coercion. For example, a public school teacher who, at the close of each school day in December, urges her students to "remember to keep Christ in Christmas," does not force anyone to do anything and erects no official barriers to the religious observance (or nonobservance) of her students. Yet, it is these more furtive influences that undermine religious voluntarism and therefore are prohibited. The Supreme Court accomplishes this task through the restraint on government built into the Establishment Clause.

* * *

From the perspective of constitutional law, then, religions of integrity ("worthy of respect") are those religions subscribed to and held wholly apart from the government's influence. * * * The Court's position is a religious proposition that overlaps with a secular one. This constitutional settlement was born, in part, of the untoward experience that "any religion that had relied upon the support of government to spread its faith" lost the people's respect. Religious persecution has brought eventual ruin to the cause of the dominant faith.

Looking back over half a century of public life, James Madison observed that the improvement of religion following disestablishment in Virginia and elsewhere in the South was proof that the experiment with voluntarism was good for religion * * *.

* * *

Although formal alliances between government and church yielded grudgingly in America, genuine religious faith is now presumed (from the perspective of the First Amendment) to be a matter of personal inquiry and persuasion rather than official privilege or juridical status. Influenced as it was by the common cause of Protestant pietists and devotees of the Enlightenment, the constitutional settlement now lodged in the Establishment Clause leaves religious communities to attract members by force of their doctrine and appeal of their beneficence, not by the imprimatur of officialdom. Most certainly, then, the government should not become an agent for achieving religious propagation. The Establishment Clause, applied by a Supreme Court that presumes voluntarism, now restrains government when its actions involve the civic arm in inherently religious matters. And the Clause does so, in part, to protect religion—that is, voluntaristic religion.

B. A Limited State

A natural correlative to the first principle—voluntarism—is that religions that point to a transcendent authority help check the power of the modern nation-state. This is because such religions refuse to recognize the state's sovereignty as absolute. Transcendent religions posit another sovereignty—a God (or gods)—that is (are) beyond, before, and superior to the state. Indeed, theistic religion posits a Sovereignty that sits in judgment over the state, its ambitions to temporal power, and its pretensions of infallibility. It is for this reason that at crucial points in Western history the institutional church had a "pivotal role in guarding against political absolutism."

* * * Transcendent religion is indeed too powerful to allow politics to control it, and thus the Constitution disestablished it. The complete opposite—the privatization of religion—is equally in error. With privatization, politics has the field to itself and becomes paramount. This is the twentieth century error on both the right and the left, Fascism and Communism, respectively. By being the guardian of absolute truths, religion, to its followers, relativitizes all else. By asserting absolutes, which is what religion does, the contingency of truths that are of lessee order (political truths) are blocked from their totalitarian impulse. Those members of society holding the most raw power—those with control of

government's machinery—cannot, via their raw power, become absolute. Relativizing the political operates to expand that social space that is nongovernmental, and in turn to give breathing room to individuals, families, neighborhoods, schools, and other mediating groups.

* * *

Out of concern for religion, the Establishment Clause has a role in preventing those forms of governmental sponsorship that may turn churches into mere franchises for implementing the current social agenda of the state. In turn, democracy has a stake in the Establishment Clause protecting religion from its own bad choices, to the end that religion—at least religion that intends transcendence and calls its followers to ultimate allegiance—thereby has the vitality to limit the state.

C. Civil Religion

In addition to voluntarism and the notion of a limited state is the hazard of cultural religion. Cultural religion is the confusion of genuine religious faith with one's pride in tradition, love of country, and the badge of having entered into full acceptance as a citizen of a nation. It is the elevation of certain ceremonies, holidays, and other habits of a nation, all good in themselves, to the level of the sacred. Concomitantly, certain sacraments and holy days of the church come to be regarded as rites of passage in proper civic life. In this blurring of the line between religion and civic culture, it is genuine religion, observed Justice Brennan, that is the likely loser * * *. Cultural religion, then, is the conflating of religious piety with sentimentality for the nation. In its extreme, sociologists term this phenomenon "civil religion," which comes about when the predominant religion is so closely merged with national self-identity that patriotism and nationalism march hand in hand with spirituality. * * *

As the author of Schempp, Justice Clark faced a firestorm of criticism from short-sighted religionists. His response was that the critics ought not to be dismayed but relieved, for it is religion that "gets hurt when there is a confusion of patriotism with genuine religion."[297] Thus, Justice Clark defended Schempp not in terms of the result being good for nonreligious people or those of minority faiths, but as being good for mainline religions that hope to retain their integrity.

Civil religion is used to rationalize away as not "inherently religious" what are otherwise clear violations of the Establishment Clause. For example, the Court has passed off prayers by legislative chaplains and governmental displays depicting the birth of Jesus Christ as practices that are not religious. Civil religion is the culprit and authentic religion the inevitable victim.

The chaplaincy and Christmas-display cases were decided over dissents by Justices that saw the long-term consequence of mistaking religion for agreeable traditions. In Marsh v. Chambers, a case challeng-

297. Tom C. Clark, *Religion and the Law*, 15 S.C. L. REV. 855, 863–64 (1963).

ing the constitutionality of using prayer to open state legislative sessions, Justice Brennan said that one of the purposes of the Establishment Clause "is to prevent the trivialization and degradation of religion by too close an attachment to the organs of government." * * *

Vibrant religion often defines itself in opposition to culture. Indeed, sociologists have observed that in certain respects religion needs to be in tension with or resistant to the prevailing course of culture. When a religion assumes the role of a political party or takes up the reins of civil power, it loses its energizing distinctiveness and apartness. * * *

To become wholly comfortable with the culture is to threaten the long-term survival of the religion. A right ordering of government and religion can avoid a civil religion that anesthetizes individuals from the felt urgency of making religious decisions. In short, the Establishment Clause works on behalf of voluntary religion.

D. A Captive Church

The final reason government-religion separation is good for religion is that it forstalls a loss of control by churches over their schools and social welfare ministries. A church that receives government sponsorship is vulnerable to having its ministries redirected to ends dictated by government policy and enforced by regulatory controls attached to the state funding. * * *

* * *

This is not to say that all (or even most) governmental funding to faith-based institutions violates the Establishment Clause. It is to say that the program, its attendant oversight, and the nature of the aid must be designed to prevent this intrusion by government into religion's sphere.

Religious ministries are often motivated by unselfish love of neighbor, not a desire to serve the policy aims of government. Churches should be moved by the promptings of their faith and ennobling self-sacrifice, not political initiatives by government. Once the church is responding more to state policy goals than to the teachings of its own lights, spontaneity is dulled and the fervor and allegiance of its workers wane. In turn, as the Court has observed, those outside the religion respond with disrespect and derision * * *.

* * *

When religious groups enter into partnerships with government, the relationship, unless properly structured, is inherently unequal. Government will attempt to dominate the terms of the "cooperation." Churches always have the option of turning away the money if they think the regulations become too intrusive. But pulling out of a program is not always feasible if a ministry has come to depend on the government funding.

* * *

Constitutional structure, among its other virtues, separates the two centers of authority and protects the integrity of both. When the Establishment Clause is viewed as structural, it then makes sense that one of its tasks is to protect the integrity of religion. As discussed in this Part, the no-establishment principle does so to the benefit of voluntaristic religion and to the benefit of limited government. * * *

VI. THE CONSEQUENCES OF REGARDING THE CLAUSE AS STRUCTURAL

Openly applying the Establishment Clause as a structural, rather than a rights-based, clause would bring about a shift in how judges and litigants conceptualize problems involving government-religion relations. The question explored in this Part is whether the Supreme Court's controlling cases come out any differently as a consequence of this new paradigm. Given that the principal argument of this Article is that in several instances the modern Court has sub silentio applied the Establishment Clause as structural, it would be expected that the number of overall changes in final results (as opposed to expressed rationale) would not be great. That indeed turns out to be the case. However, the ones that would change are important. Moreover, because the Court's First Amendment doctrine has at times placed the Establishment Clause in conflict with the Free Exercise and Free Speech Clauses, a most welcomed analytical change flowing from a structuralist view is that the Court would avoid these imagined "tensions" * * *. * * *

A. *Weighing the Importance of Religious Practices*

For reasons of simplicity, it is best to start with some rules of law that would not change under a structuralist view. The Supreme Court has held that matters of religious belief or practice need not be "central" to a claimant's faith to be protected by the First Amendment. Indeed, the Court has said that judges have no authority to weigh the relative importance of religious words, practices, and events, neither against other practices of the same denomination nor against competing governmental interests. As a parallel principle, the Court has held that claimants may disagree with coreligionists or be unsure or wavering, and still have their causes taken up for free exercise protection. Additionally, in order not to wrongly attach juridical significance to an individual's sectarian affiliation, the Court has said that legislative classifications are not to turn on denominational membership. The foregoing rules are part of a larger admonition by the Court that, whenever possible, governmental officials should eschew detailed inquiries into religious doctrine and avoid probing the significance of religious words, practices, and events. A shift to a structuralist view would not change these rules of law. The only change would be that the foundation for these rules would be explicitly attributed to the Establishment Clause.

* * *

Under the current case law, government cannot penalize sacrilege, blasphemy, or other activity that does no more than speak ill of another's religion. Additionally, government cannot compel an individual, upon pain of material penalty, inconvenience, or loss of public benefit or advantage, to profess a religious belief or to observe an inherently religious practice. Once again, these rules of law, long promulgated by the Court, would not change under a structuralist view. There would be no doubt, however, that the basis for these rules is the Establishment Clause rather than the Free Exercise Clause.

B.   Regulatory Burdens on Religious Organizations

A structuralist perspective would resolve the conflict in the Supreme Court's cases dealing with generally applicable regulatory legislation, the burden of which falls on, among others, religious organizations. Given that a structuralist view reserves a sphere of autonomy for religious groups, regulatory burdens that touch on matters in the religious domain (doctrine, polity, clerics, church membership) violate no-establishment. This is so, not as a matter of group or associational rights, but as a matter of government exceeding its jurisdiction as limited by the Establishment Clause. * * *

The Establishment Clause is never violated merely because a law, neutral in purpose, has an unintended impact on a particular church or religious practice. * * * That is how a structural clause operates: it gives class-wide relief to all religious organizations, in contrast with the victim-specific relief of a rights-based clause. * * *

Under a structuralist perspective, then, legislators imposing regulatory burdens on the private sector must take care not to intrude on religious organizations' sphere of autonomy. The Supreme Court has reached this result in its parochial school cases when adverse effects befell these schools as a result of unemployment compensation taxes and mandatory collective bargaining laws. However, the Court's rationale avoided dealing frontally with the issue of Congress exceeding its power. These cases would come out the same under a structuralist application but with ecclesiastical autonomy protected without any timidity in stating that such a result is required by the Establishment Clause.

* * *

C.   Exemptions for Religious Organizations

The current Supreme Court rule is that the government may refrain from imposing a regulatory burden on religion, even as it imposes the burden on others similarly situated. Hence, this type of classification between religion and nonreligion (or even irreligion) is permitted. A structuralist perspective would not change that result. Indeed, it would strengthen the rule by giving the cases a more secure foundation in the power restraints of the Establishment Clause.

* * *

Some have argued that exemptions from regulatory burdens for religious organizations violate the no-establishment principle by advancing religion. The argument belies a view of the Establishment Clause either as requiring government to affirmatively work against religion or as granting an individual right to be free from religion. This makes no sense. Extension of this line of reasoning culminates in the argument that by protecting the free exercise of religion the government is advancing religion, thereby violating the no-establishment principle. That "logic" leads to the Free Exercise Clause being violative of the Establishment Clause! An accurate statement of the Court's rule is that the government cannot intentionally discriminate against religion. The rule is not one of blind equality as between religion and nonreligion * * *. To spare religious organizations regulatory burdens on their ecclesiastical endeavors, effectively "leaving the church where the government found it," is to facilitate the boundary-keeping role of the Establishment Clause. That role is not one-sided. Half of the reason for the boundary-drawing is to keep the state out of the church.

D.   *Speech of Religious Content*

During the 1980s and 1990s, in an unbroken line of victories for freedom of speech, the Supreme Court held that the religious expression of individuals and religious organizations was entitled to the same high protection accorded nonreligious expression (e.g., speech of political, artistic, or educational content). Although the Free Exercise Clause grants no preference to private religious expression, the Free Speech Clause calls for equal treatment. * * * [T]he Court [framed] the issue in such a way that Establishment Clause compliance could, in theory at least, supply a "compelling interest" for subjugating the Free Speech Clause. A structuralist perspective would reach the same result-namely equal access for religious expression-but reject framing the issue as a "clash between the Clauses."

* * *

This "battle of the Clauses" goes away when the Establishment Clause is conceptualized as a structural restraint. If the speaker is private rather than governmental, then the Free Speech Clause supplies a right of equal access to the forum, and the expression cannot be suppressed simply because it is religious. There is never any "tension" with the Establishment Clause, real or apparent, for that Clause is a restraint on government rather than on private actors. * * *

There will be cases, of course, in which it is a close call whether the speech of a private individual is adopted by the government as its own. If the facts are such that the speaker is private but the government is doing something to place its power or prestige behind the message, then the no-establishment restraint still applies. The remedy, however, should not aim to suppress the private speech as such, but instead to enjoin only those governmental actions that are uniquely endorsing the private religious message.

The rules are altogether different when the religious speech is not private but fairly attributed to government or its officials. The government itself has no free speech rights. Rather, government has a duty to see to it that its actions conform to the restraints on its power set down in the Establishment Clause. In accord with this boundary-keeping role, the Supreme Court has held that government may neither confess inherently religious beliefs nor advocate that individuals profess such beliefs or observe such practices. Government may acknowledge the role of religion in society and teach about its contributions to, for example, history, literature, music, and the visual arts. However, the limit imposed by the Establishment Clause is exceeded when the government's expression places its imprimatur on a religion or on an inherently religious belief or practice. A structuralist view would not change the result in any of these cases.

E. Governmental Aid to Religion

Governmental aid to religion takes both direct and indirect forms. The Supreme Court has analyzed these two forms somewhat differently. With indirect aid, the government confers a benefit on private individuals who in turn exercise personal choice in using their governmental benefit at similarly situated organizations, whether public or private, religious or nonreligious. If some individuals choose to "spend" their benefit at a provider of services that also happens to be religious in character, arguably religion is thereby advanced. Nevertheless, when this occurs, the Court has determined that the Establishment Clause is not violated.

The rationale for this rule is two-fold. First, the constitutionally salient cause of any indirect benefit to religion is the self-determination of numerous individuals, not a choice by the government. Merely enabling private choice—where individuals may freely choose or not choose services from a religious provider—logically cannot be a governmental establishment of religion. Second, the indirect nature of the aid reduces government-religion interaction and government's oversight and regulation of faith-based service providers. This enhances the institutional separation of government and religious organizations that is desirable from the perspective of the boundary-keeping task of the Establishment Clause. Under a structuralist application, these indirect funding cases would not change.

Governmental programs that provide direct aid to the private sector are, in the Court's view, a different matter. A structuralist perspective would facilitate a change in this case law, as well as much needed clarification and simplification. Direct-aid programs, funded out of general revenues, must have a secular purpose, typically the improvement of education, health care, or social welfare. The question is whether faith-based organizations can fully participate in such programs on an equal basis with other providers, or if they must be barred from participation because they are religious.

Neutrality between religion and nonreligion calls for equal treatment of all providers. Indeed, it would seem that the Free Exercise

Clause prohibits government from designing programs of aid that intentionally discriminate on the basis of religion. By that measure, a rule of equal treatment of faith-based schools, as well as health care and social service providers, requires that these religious organizations be fully eligible for direct programs of aid. Conversely, the no-aid view held by some separationists would have the Establishment Clause bar religious organizations from participating in these direct-funding programs.

Once again no-aid separationists frame the issue such that two First Amendment Clauses are in apparent conflict. The resulting "tension" between free exercise and no-establishment principles, they propose, is to be relieved by tipping the balance in the direction of no-aid. Again, this makes no sense. It is not consistent with the First Amendment's text because neither Clause has primacy over the other. Moreover, such conflicts are not inherent to the Religion Clauses and thereby logically unavoidable. From a structuralist view, there is no "battle of the Clauses," as will be shown below.

The Supreme Court has steered an uneven course between the command of neutrality and the command of no-aid. Looking only at the results in its cases, the Court has consistently permitted states to administer neutral programs of direct aid for institutions of higher education, including assistance to those colleges that are church-affiliated. Additionally, although the cases are few, the Court has rebuffed challenges to neutral programs of direct aid to health care and social services. The results in these cases would not change under a structuralist perspective, provided that any regulatory oversight that came with the governmental funding did not undermine the religious integrity of the faith-based provider.

Concerning programs of direct aid to primary and secondary education, the Court's case law is far more complex and uneven. Unlike colleges and social welfare agencies, faith-based primary and secondary schools are regarded as "pervasively sectarian" by the Court. Where the program of aid was targeted at private schools alone, including private religious schools, the legislation was nonneutral and the Court struck it down as violative of the Establishment Clause. Where the program was directed toward helping all primary and secondary schools, public and private, religious and nonreligious, the program satisfied the neutrality requirement.

Whether satisfying the neutrality requirement, without more, is sufficient to comply with the Establishment Clause is the question upon which the Court remains sharply divided. * * *

* * *

A structuralist view would permit neutral programs of direct aid for all service providers, including faith-based providers. * * * The no-aid view of separationism argues that political divisiveness along denominational or creedal lines will result unless all aid is denied to religious providers. Typically the point is buttressed by reference to European religious wars, which were known to the founding generation, as well as by warnings that point to modern-day Northern Ireland, Bosnia, or India. These are indeed events and internecine conflicts worthy of avoidance, and the fear of sectarian factions within the civitas has received frequent mention in the Court's opinions. But no-aid separationists overlook an obvious distinction between these instances of denominational factionalism and their no-aid solution. The religious wars of medieval Europe were wars for religious monopoly—each side sought to defeat the other in order to impose its own religious hegemony. Neutrality in the design of financial aid programs has no such goal. Indeed, the goal is just the opposite. If a program of aid is truly neutral, then each individual's religious choices are maximized while the government's influence over those choices is minimized. Religious choice is not held up as the ultimate constitutional value in itself; rather, the value is in each person being free to pursue the dictates of his or her own worldview. The result is cultural pluralism, the opposite of religious hegemony. As citizens take control of those life choices that implicate deeply held beliefs, neutrality in programs of aid leads to a reduction in factionalism along denominational or creedal lines, and the unity of the civitas is enhanced.

It is not political division in the body politic that a structuralist view was designed to avoid. Nor is it division over moral questions. Such political and moral divisions are inevitable, and vigorous debate—including debate over religion as such, and its moral and political implications-is protected by the Free Speech Clause. To wield the Establishment Clause as a censor's pen suppressing any such outbreaks in debate, as no-aid separationists do, puts the Free Speech Clause in conflict with the Establishment Clause. Rather, it is the government's official actions causing factional strife along denominational lines that are subject to examination for having caused Establishment Clause harm, not the resulting private actions of citizens reflecting such divisions or debate.

The harm to the body politic, or civitas, addressed by a structuralist perspective is that which results when a government fails to act with a secular purpose. When the government acts, it may not have as its object the awarding (or burdening) of an inherently religious belief or practice, nor may it have as its object the awarding (or burdening) of a religious group. "If politics cannot explicitly favor in its governmental outputs one sect over another, the incentives to organize politically along explicit religious lines are diminished."

There will always be religious factions, of course, within any open society. This is not the concern of the Establishment Clause. The aim of the Clause is for government to avoid inducing new religious factions or heightening old ones. True, there are situations where no matter what decision the government makes, old wounds will be inflamed. In such cases, the path of neutrality promises the least factionalism within the body politic. With neutrality, the government is least involved in influencing the religious choices of its citizens.

This fracturing of the civitas is a polity-wide harm, a generalized grievance as opposed to an individualized injury. * * * [The] remedy limits government by restraining its use of sovereign power in a way that is discriminatory, that is, in a way that supports or awards creedal or ideological hegemony. Neutrality in the design of government aid programs promises to reduce division within the civitas that is the result of governmental bias for one worldview over others. Contrariwise, continued adherence to the no-aid view promises only to increase ideological tyranny within the civitas. Citizens know when a worldview alien to their own is being imposed, and they will resist.

* * *

No-aid separationism was plausible when government was small, taxes were low, and most education and social welfare was privately funded. It was plausible when America was more homogeneous, more Protestant, and more Northern European in national origin. In the present age of the affirmative state, when government monopolizes most of the available resources for education and social services, private funding as the sole source of aid for independent schools and welfare services is no longer a sustainable alternative. Not only has the no-aid view led to an inequitable division of limited resources, but the lack of evenhandedness has stifled the parental role in choosing and directing the education of children. The same is true with social services, where lack of neutrality in funding hampers the poor and needy from choosing the service provider that will best meet their needs for job training, child care, rehabilitation from drug dependencies, and other social services.

In addition to protecting the civitas, the structuralist view is concerned with avoiding harm to religare/ekklesia. From the perspective of neutrality, when government provides benefits such as education, health care, or social welfare to promote the public good, there should be no exclusionary criteria requiring faith-based providers to engage in self-censorship, or to otherwise water down their religious identity as a condition of program participation. If neutrality is to succeed, faith-based providers must not be forced to shed or disguise their religious character and suppress their spiritual voice, all to appear "secular enough" to be eligible for the needed funding. Unless the ekklesia is protected along with the civitas, the goal of pluralism will be frustrated, and the state-sanctioned dominance of a single worldview will continue.

The structuralist view has the added advantage over a strict rule of no-aid in that it eliminates unnecessary "tensions" among the Clauses of the First Amendment. By not discriminating in favor of secular providers over faith-based providers of education, health care, and social services, the Free Exercise Clause is not brought into conflict with the Establishment Clause. The structuralist perspective would also do away with the Supreme Court's cases denying direct aid to "pervasively sectarian" providers while allowing aid to nonpervasively sectarian organizations. In singling out "pervasively sectarian" organizations, the Court has set up an aid/no-aid test that violates two of the Court's other principles of law, namely, its rule against government favoring one religious organization over another, and its rule against delving into the nature of religious doctrine and practices. By abandoning the "pervasively sectarian" category and allowing neutral programs of aid, the Court's case law would no longer be conflicted.

VII.   LOCATING THE BOUNDARY BETWEEN RELIGION AND GOVERNMENT

What remains in question is not so much the existence of a "wall of separation" as it is the question of where civil and religious authorities say the boundary between religion and government lies and what people can do on the ecclesiastical side of the boundary free from governmental interference, as well as free from government's over-involvement. This Part marshals the cases that indicate where the Supreme Court has located that boundary. First, however, the unnecessary confusion concerning the place of the Free Exercise Clause needs to be addressed.

A.   *Differentiating the Free Exercise and Establishment Clauses*

As a structural restraint, the purpose of the Establishment Clause is not to safeguard individual religious rights. That is the role of the Free Exercise Clause, indeed its singular role. Even in archetypal no-establishment cases as those concerning religion in public schools, such as Engel v. Vitale and McCollum v. Board of Education, the Court has applied the Establishment Clause not to relieve individual complainants of religious coercion or religious harm, but to keep in proper relationship two centers of authority: government and religion. This is why in popular discourse it is said that the Establishment Clause is about "church-state relations" or the "separation of church and state." It is in this primary role—when invoked to keep the spheres of government and religion in the right relationship to each other—that the Establishment Clause broke free from older European patterns and made its most unique and celebrated contribution to the American constitutional settlement.

The Establishment Clause can be a means of redress for personal harms, but only when the injury is other than religious in nature, such as economic harm or damage to property, constraints on academic inquiry by teachers and students, or restraints on free-thinking atheists. Even in these situations, however, the no-establishment principle is not transformed into an individual rights clause with the assigned task of protecting, respectively, property, academic freedom, and freedom from religion. Rather, these injuries are remedied only consequentially to the Establishment Clause as it fulfills its structuralist role.

* * *

The literature is often uneven when using the terms "religious freedom," "religious liberty," and "religious rights." This Article equates all three, and the terms are used in the sense of an individual right that protects against personal religious burdens or harms. Such a right is secured by the Free Exercise Clause. Moreover, the redressing of personal harm to an individual's religious belief or practice is the Free Exercise Clause's only function. This makes sense because the Clause is, by its terms, about prohibiting the free exercise of religion rather than unbelief. The Free Exercise Clause says nothing about other injuries such as protecting against encumbrances on the use of one's property (Thornton) or removing hindrances to academic inquiry (Epperson). Nor does the Free Exercise Clause prohibit the forced taking of oaths by free-thinking atheists (Torcaso). The latter is true because to suffer a personal religious harm an individual must first profess a religion. It follows that the Free Exercise Clause is not an all-purpose conscience Clause. It protects religiously informed belief and practice, nothing more. People can incur injuries other than religious harms* * *. These are individual harms, to be sure, but not religious harms. They are left to be remedied, if at all, as a by-product of the Establishment Clause's ordering of the respective competencies of government and religion.

In the hands of the Supreme Court, then, the task of the Establishment Clause is independent of the Free Exercise Clause. Neither Clause is subordinate or instrumental to the other. This is not to say that the Establishment Clause has nothing to do with religious liberty writ large. By delimiting and qualifying governmental sovereignty, structure often redounds to further secure individual rights. Conversely, although rights clauses have as their immediate purpose the protection of individual freedom, they have a consequential impact on governmental power. But this happy symmetry between structure and rights is no reason to conflate the two. The object of a structural clause is to set compensating checks on the powers of a modern nation-state, checks that must be honored whether or not individual complainants suffer concrete "injury in fact." Because the Establishment Clause is a structural clause rather than a rights clause, it is vital that it be understood as such and be so applied.

B.   A Matter of Boundary Keeping

Proper relations between religion and government (or "church and state") are codified in the words "make no law respecting an establishment of religion." A structuralist view casts this Clause in the role of boundary keeper. In setting out to locate that boundary, it is a useful reminder that the "keeper's" task is to restrain government, not private individuals, not churches, and not religion.

Identification of the precise topics that fall within the meaning of the words "make no law respecting an establishment of religion"—hence subject matter placed beyond the reach of governmental authority—necessarily entails substantive choices. That boundary has been disputed for over two thousand years, so it would be naive to suppose that there is an easy formula for determining "what is Caesar's and what is God's." * * *

On the other hand, the difficulty should not be exaggerated. * * * In the vast number of cases, a ready reference to the Western tradition as received on this side of the Atlantic will yield a result on which there is an understanding of what is right. It is the hard cases that get most of the attention, thereby leaving the impression that the overall task of boundary keeping is hopelessly conflicted. Moreover, that factions are forever struggling over the location of the boundary actually confirms the central point—it is presumed that there are two spheres of competency and, hence, a religious sphere in which the state is not sovereign.

The Supreme Court has not left lower courts, legislators, and litigants without guidance on this all-important question. The cases indicate that government does not exceed the restraints of the Establishment Clause unless it is acting on topics that are "inherently religious." The Supreme Court has found that prayer, devotional Bible reading, veneration of the Ten Commandments, classes in confessional religion, and the biblical story of creation taught as science are all inherently religious. Hence, by virtue of the Establishment Clause, these topics are off limits as objects of legislation or any other purposeful government action. Closely related to these case-by-case designations of what is inherently religious and what is "arguably non-religious" is the rule that the Establishment Clause is not violated when a governmental restriction (or social welfare program) merely reflects a moral judgment, shared by some religions, about conduct thought harmful (or beneficial) to society. Accordingly, overlap between a law's purpose and the mores and ethics of a well-known religion does not, without more, render the law one "respecting an establishment of religion." * * *

The Supreme Court has successfully avoided two mistakes when drawing the line between government and religion. First, the Court has not identified churches and other religious institutions (e.g., educational, charitable, and mission organizations) and then assumed that religion is actually confined to those institutions. Churches and their affiliated ministries (ekklesia) do not monopolize religion (religare). * * * Hence, Establishment Clause violations can occur notwithstanding the complete absence of any involvement by churches, mission societies, religious schools, and the like.

Second, the Court has not set out to separate government from all that could be said to be religious. Rather, the separation is of government from matters inherently religious. A separation of government from all that is religion or religious would result in a secular public square, one hostile to the public face of religion. The Founders intended no such regime. * * *

* * *

"Inherently religious," * * * means those exclusively religious activities of worship and the propagation or inculcation of the sort of tenets that comprise confessional statements or creeds common to many religions. The term includes, as well, the supernatural claims of churches, mosques, synagogues, temples, and other houses of worship, using those words not to identify buildings, but to describe the confessional community (the ekklesia) around which a religion (religare) identifies and defines itself, conducts its collective worship, divines and teaches doctrine, and propagates the faith to children and adult converts. A structuralist view places these matters—being in the exclusive sphere of religion—beyond the government's jurisdiction.

VIII. CONCLUSION

None of the foregoing claims that the Supreme Court has resolved all of the problems in defining the boundary between religion and government by relegating the no-establishment restraint to governmental actions on matters inherently religious. There will always be boundary disputes, for the task of determining what is "inherently religious" is not substantively neutral. In the main, the Court's decisions have favored the government-religion settlement advanced by the allied efforts of the Enlightenment rationalists and Protestant pietists. Accordingly, those who disagree with this constitutional settlement will be aggrieved. The validity of these grievances is beyond the scope of this Article. It suffices here to candidly acknowledge that a structuralist view is not substantively neutral; indeed, substantive neutrality is impossible because every theory of government-religion relations necessarily takes a position on the nature and contemporary value of organized religion and the purpose and direction of modern government. One positive bias of the structuralist view is that it places a great deal of importance on the autonomy of the religious community (the ekklesia). A second affirmative bias is that the view minimizes government's role in influencing the spiritual impulse of humankind (religare) by leaving members of the political community (the civitas) free to make these choices for themselves.

It is tempting to label the accommodationists and liberal secularists as partisans in the culture war and to characterize the Supreme Court's fixing the government-religion boundary where it does as symbolizing the DMZ between these warring factions. In candor, however, the Supreme Court's position is not a neutral zone either. Its first line of defense is that the Court's government-religion boundary is the original constitutional settlement. It is not to be tampered with by latter-day judge-made law. In the end, however, if the Court's government-religion boundary is to have staying power it has to be defended not because it is neutral or noncontroversial, but because it is good. Indeed, it is a threefold good: it maximizes individual religious choice, protects the institutional integrity of the ekklesia, and minimizes government-induced religious factionalism within the civitas.

Under the structuralist settlement, then, the Establishment Clause is not a silver bullet for winning (or ending) the culture war. Although the government-religion boundary policed by the no-establishment principle keeps government from taking sides on confessional and other inherently religious matters, moral and ethical questions are still proper objects of legislation. Whose morality will dominate the Republic at any point in time, and hence gets to be reflected in the positive law of the nation, is not pre-determined by the Establishment Clause. That determination is left for the making based on who has the more persuasive argument in the market-place of ideas, as well as the better organizational acumen to promote it.

Notes and Questions

1. *Symbolism and the Establishment Clause.* Professor Marshall is able to weave together some consistency in Establishment Clause decisions by looking at their symbolic meaning. Do you agree with his analysis? Would it be better to use a standard based on symbolism such as the more nuanced version of the endorsement test proposed by Professor Marshall? What would the advantages of such an approach be? What would the disadvantages be, if any? Various situations that may give rise to claims under the Establishment Clause can have different symbolic meaning for those in the religious minority and for dissenters than it does for those in the religious majority. How should this be factored in to the issue? What about the symbolic impact on the religious majority of decisions prohibiting majoritarian practices that offend religious minorities? How would you balance these concerns?

2. *The Endorsement Test.* Professor Marshall suggests that a modified version of Justice O'Connor's endorsement test would work well as a symbolic approach to the Establishment Clause. His proposed modifications make sense, don't they? Who should the reasonable observer be when evaluating whether a government practice violates the endorsement test? Professor Marshall's approach would suggest that it should be someone who at least considers the views of religious minorities or dissenters. How can this be done? Through expert testimony, or simply through the testimony of those challenging the relevant practices?

3. *The Establishment Clause as a Structural Restraint.* Professor Esbeck argues that the Establishment Clause can best be understood as a restraint on government power rather than an individual rights provision. Is this consistent with the Court's interpretation of that clause? Even if it is not, does it make sense as a practical matter? As a matter of history and constitutional structure? What would Professor Esbeck's reading mean for religious minorities and dissenters? It seems that they would be protected from government sponsored religious exercises and the like, but might be forced to fund massive social service and educational programs that primarily benefit more established and larger religious groups. Is this a problem that can or should be addressed by the Establishment Clause? What would Professor Esbeck's approach mean for a unified reading of the religion clauses such as that advocated by Professor Carter, since it is apparent that the Free Exercise Clause is an individual rights clause? In other words, can the two clauses represent a unified theory if their underlying natures are different? Professor Esbeck suggests that reading the Establishment Clause as a structural restraint minimizes any tension with the Free Exercise Clause. He is correct, isn't he? Yet it is apparent that while his reading would minimize the tension, it would preclude treating the two clauses as one as Professor Carter does? Is this a strength or weakness in Professor Esbeck's approach? Could it be both?

4. *The Distinction Between Prayer and Funding.* As noted above, Professor Esbeck argues that organized religious activity by government entities would violate the Establishment Clause under the structural approach, but government funding of activities carried out by religious organizations under a broad funding

regime open to religious and non-religious entities alike would be consistent with the structural understanding of the Establishment Clause. Assume a religious entity receives a large amount of funding under a local government program for charitable activities, and that entity uses the funding to help those in need while spreading the faith. Those who accept the faith are likewise encouraged to spread the faith. What happens when a taxpayer of a different faith objects to funding the training of those who will ultimately proselytize her and her family, even if the religious entity receiving the funding does a good job of providing food and shelter to those in need? Of course, if the Establishment Clause is not an individual rights clause there is no basis for complaint assuming the funding was dispersed fairly—i.e., not on the basis of religion. Is this problematic or is it simply a necessary byproduct of a funding regime that does not discriminate on the basis of religion? Would treating the Establishment Clause as an individual rights clause necessarily change this result? Should it?

Chapter Six

THE FREE EXERCISE CLAUSE

A. WHAT IS RELIGION?

The question "what is religion?" is relevant in both the Free Exercise Clause and Establishment Clause contexts, but it is especially relevant to the Free Exercise Clause because whether one's free exercise of religion is interfered with by state action necessarily requires that religion be defined at some point. This creates a problem for any court that tries to define religion, because the act of trying to define religion could itself embroil the judiciary in religious issues that the religion clauses suggest are off limits to government. Yet, as has often been said, courts must decide cases that are properly brought before them, and thus the courts have had to address the question of what counts as religion for religion clause purposes.

The modern Court has directly addressed this issue in the two cases discussed below, but it has mentioned the issue in a number of other cases. Additionally, in *Davis v. Beason*, 133 U.S., 333, 342, 10 S.Ct. 299, 33 L.Ed. 637 (1890), the Court defined religion in terms far narrower than the modern Court:

> The term 'religion' has reference to one's views of his relations to his Creator, and to the obligations they impose of reverence for his being and character, and of obedience to his will. It is often confounded with the *cultus* or form of worship of a particular sect, but is distinguishable from the latter.

More recent decisions have defined religion far more broadly than the *Davis* Court. In *United States v. Seeger*, 380 U.S. 163, 165–66, 85 S.Ct. 850, 13 L.Ed.2d 733 (1965), a case involving three conscientious objectors to the Vietnam War, the Court provided the following definition:

> * * * whether a given belief that is sincere and meaningful occupies a place in the life of its possessor parallel to that filled by the orthodox belief in God of one who clearly qualifies for the exemption. Where such beliefs have parallel positions in the lives of

their respective holders we cannot say that one 'is in relation to a Supreme being' and the other is not.

The reference to 'in relation to a Supreme being' refers to a provision of the Universal Military Training and Service Act, which the Court had to interpret to decide the case. The limited definition in that Act was challenged on First Amendment grounds. In relation to the broad definition set forth above, the Court added that "the claim of the registrant that his belief is an essential part of a religious faith must be given great weight," but "while the 'truth' of a belief is not open to question, there remains the significant question whether it is 'truly held.'" *Id.* at 184–85.

In *Seeger*, all three of the objectors, their last names are Seeger, Jakobson and Peter, were found to meet this test. Seeger stated "that his was a 'belief in and devotion to goodness and virtue for their own sakes, and a religious faith in a purely ethical creed.'" Jakobson stated that "he believed in a 'supreme being' who was the 'Creator of Man' in the sense of being 'ultimately responsible for the existence of' man and who was 'the Supreme Reality' of which 'the existence of man is the result.'" Peter stated that his beliefs could be called a belief in a Supreme Being, but that "[t]hese just do not happen to be the words I use." None of the three claimed to be members of any organized religion; although Seeger acknowledged agreement with a number of Quaker tenets. Yet all three acknowledged that their beliefs could be considered religious in the broad sense of that term.

How far the *Seeger* Court's definition would extend when a claimant espoused a deeply held belief system that was not "religious" in any sense remained an open question. The Court was clear, however, that the definition did not include those "whose beliefs are based on a 'merely personal moral code.'" Five years later, the Court had the chance to answer this question.

In *Welsh v. United States*, 398 U.S. 333, 90 S.Ct. 1792, 26 L.Ed.2d 308 (1970), the Court held that a person was entitled to a conscientious objector exemption based on deep and sincere, but purely ethical and moral beliefs, where those beliefs, though not religious, were held with the same strength as "more traditional religious convictions." Welsh had insisted that his beliefs were not religious beliefs, but the Court nonetheless held in his favor because "very few registrants are fully aware of the broad scope of the word 'religious'" as used in the relevant provision, "and accordingly a registrant's statement that his beliefs are nonreligious is a highly unreliable guide for those charged with administering the exemption." The Court acknowledged, as it had in *Seeger*, that a person's statement that his belief *is* religious is entitled to "great weight."

Relatedly, in *United States v. Ballard*, 322 U.S. 78, 64 S.Ct. 882, 88 L.Ed. 1148 (1944), the Court held that it is not constitutional for government to put people "to the proof of their religious doctrines or beliefs." The Court continued: "Local boards and courts * * * are not free to reject beliefs because they consider them 'incomprehensible.'

Their task is to decide whether the beliefs professed by a registrant are sincerely held and whether they are, in his own scheme of things, religious." Thus, government may not require anyone to prove his or her beliefs, but rather may only inquire whether the beliefs are sincerely held. Of course, government entities may make sure that the belief meets the *Seeger–Welsh* test—i.e. that it is more than simply a personal moral belief which is not held with the same strength as "more traditional religious convictions."

You obviously get the picture by now that the definition of religion is very broad, but that can't be the end of the discussion, can it? What about the Establishment Clause? The *Seeger–Welsh* approach makes sense in the Free Exercise Clause context, where a narrow definition of religion might inhibit the Free Exercise of religion of those who do not hold traditional religious beliefs, but a broad definition of religion under the Establishment Clause might lead to anomalous results. For example, a belief in science and proof by the scientific method might qualify as "religious" under the *Seeger–Welsh* approach. In fact, some have argued that the public schools teach a creed of "secular humanism," which is akin to a religious doctrine. Volumes have been written on this issue, but for present purposes it is enough to point out that the definition of religion in the Establishment Clause context would appear to be narrower. The exact confines are unclear, but most cases involve some connection to a deity or supernatural forces. Of course, the establishment of Atheism—government endorsing the idea that there is no God—would also qualify. This would, of course, still be connected to questions regarding a deity. Additionally, both *Seeger* and *Welsh* were decided more than thirty years ago and involved conscientious objectors. Both cases are still good law, but the Court has not directly revisited the issue since *Welsh* was decided in 1970, and it is unclear whether the current Court would define religion in the same way, or even whether it would consider it proper to attempt to define religion.

B. FREE EXERCISE CLAUSE EXEMPTIONS: THE EARLY CASES—FROM *REYNOLDS* TO *BRAUNFELD*

The first five chapters were devoted to the Establishment Clause, and it may seem odd to spend only two chapters on the Free Exercise Clause. As you will learn, however, the Court has limited the impact of that clause in all but a few contexts. The issue of exemptions from generally applicable laws—perhaps the most important issue under the Free Exercise Clause, and certainly the most controversial—has had a winding history. Interestingly, a major decision by the Court in 1990 drew heavily on interpretations of the Free Exercise Clause developed in the Nineteenth Century. We will begin there.

This section will trace some of the Court's major decisions between 1879 and 1961. As you will see later, the doctrine developed during this time period is quite similar to the current doctrine. *Reynolds v. United States*, 98 U.S. (8 Otto) 145, 25 L.Ed. 244 (1878) and *Davis v. Beason*, 133 U.S. 333, 10 S.Ct. 299, 33 L.Ed. 637 (1890), both involved challenges by Mormons (members of the Church of Jesus Christ of Latter Day Saints) to anti-polygamy laws. *Reynolds* held that criminalization of polygamy was constitutional even though it interfered with a religious practice, and *Davis* upheld criminal sanctions for falsely swearing an oath mandated by federal law that required one wishing to vote to affirm that they were not a member of any group that advocated polygamy. Both Courts held that the Free Exercise Clause protects beliefs but does not protect religious practices from regulation by government when those practices are contrary to public values and mores (today the Court would simply say when such practices are contrary to "laws of general applicability").

The Rehnquist Court has relied on both *Reynolds* and *Davis*, but it has not seriously discussed the history behind those cases or the laws they upheld. Both cases were decided at a time of overwhelming bigotry against Mormons, and both opinions contain language that essentially chastises the Mormon faith for condoning polygamy, suggesting that it was against "Christian" values. Of course, even then most Mormons did not practice polygamy, but it was allowed under Mormon theology. After these decisions, and further pressure from the government when Utah was seeking statehood, Mormon leaders renounced polygamy. Whatever one thinks of polygamy, this was not exactly an auspicious start for the "free exercise" of religion.

In 1943, the Supreme Court decided *West Virginia State Bd. of Education v. Barnette*, 319 U.S. 624, 63 S.Ct. 1178, 87 L.Ed. 1628 (1943), in which the Court held that public school students who objected to the flag salute because of their Jehovah's Witness faith, could not be compelled to do so. The Court did not rely heavily on the Free Exercise Clause in deciding the case, but rather it relied primarily on the Free Speech Clause. Still, the case established that religious conduct can sometimes be protected as an exercise of speech. *Barnette* was cited in some subsequent Free Exercise Clause cases as well. *See infra.* this Chapter. Three years prior to *Barnette*, in *Cantwell v. Connecticut*, 310 U.S. 296, 60 S.Ct. 900, 84 L.Ed. 1213 (1940), the Court overturned the convictions of Jehovah's Witnesses who had solicited religious contributions without first obtaining a license as required by state law. *Cantwell* incorporated the Free Exercise Clause through the Fourteenth Amendment, but the case relied on the Free Speech Clause in addition to the Free Exercise Clause. *See also, Murdock v. Pennsylvania*, 319 U.S. 105, 63 S.Ct. 870, 87 L.Ed. 1292 (1943) (license tax applied to Jehovah's Witness street preachers unconstitutional).

Despite the apparent momentum toward increased protection for religious practices that seemed to come about in the 1940's, the Court decided a Free Exercise Clause case in 1961 that further complicated the situation. In *Braunfeld v. Brown*, 366 U.S. 599, 81 S.Ct. 1144, 6 L.Ed.2d 563 (1961), the Court upheld a state Sunday closing law which was challenged by an Orthodox Jewish store owner who was required to close on Saturday for religious reasons. The Sunday closing law could effectively put Saturday Sabbatarians out of business by forcing them to close all weekend. The Court used a formalistic approach similar to that of the *Reynolds* and *Davis* Courts. However, rather than relying on the formalistic distinction between religious belief and religious practice relied upon in those cases, the *Braunfeld* Court drew a formalistic distinction between direct burdens on religious conduct and indirect burdens. Thus, a law that forces someone to salute the flag in violation of her religious beliefs would be a direct violation. Yet Sunday closing laws that cause economic hardship for Saturday Sabbatarians were an indirect burden because such laws did not force the stores to open on Saturday, but rather only to close on Sunday. The belief/practice dichotomy (and its direct/indirect burden cousin) will be discussed further later in this chapter.

In 1961, the Court also decided *Torcaso v. Watkins*, 367 U.S. 488, 81 S.Ct. 1680, 6 L.Ed.2d 982 (1961). *Torcaso* held unconstitutional a provision in the Maryland state constitution requiring state officials to swear that they believe in God. It is unclear how much the *Torcaso* Court relied on the Free Exercise Clause as opposed to the Establishment Clause as the Court used precedents under both clauses in invalidating the Maryland provision. It seems that such a requirement violates the Establishment Clause by preferring theistic religions over nontheistic religions and nonreligion (or monotheistic religions over other religions). Moreover, the provision could violate the Free Exercise Clause because it forces people to give up their right to hold public office unless they swear to beliefs they may not hold. Because state law was involved the Court did not rely on the Religious Test Clause of Article VI, which most likely only applies to the federal government. Thus, by the early 1960's there were a mixture of results under the Free Exercise Clause, with the majority of cases favoring the absolute protection of beliefs but not practices, at least when those practices conflict with generally applicable laws. All of that was about to change, at least temporarily.

C.   FREE EXERCISE CLAUSE EXEMPTIONS AND THE COMPELLING INTEREST TEST

As a practical matter, the early Free Exercise Clause cases did little to protect the free exercise of those whose religious practices conflicted with the established legal regime. Of course, since those religious groups with a large number of adherents in a given area were more likely to have their religious concerns considered by government actors, the Free Exercise Clause was more likely to protect those who least needed constitutional protection of their free exercise rights. The question naturally arose as to whether this was consistent with the language and purpose of the Free Exercise Clause. The Court began to address these concerns in the next principle case, *Sherbert v. Verner*. *Sherbert* was decided at roughly the same time as the early school prayer cases and reflected a similar concern for the rights of religious minorities. As you read *Sherbert* consider whether it is consistent with earlier Free Exercise Clause cases and which approach (that in *Sherbert* or that in the earlier cases) you think is better given the language and asserted purposes of the Free Exercise Clause.

SHERBERT v. VERNER

Supreme Court of the United States, 1963.
374 U.S. 398, 83 S.Ct. 1790, 10 L.Ed.2d 965.

MR. JUSTICE BRENNAN delivered the opinion of the Court.

Appellant, a member of the Seventh-day Adventist Church was discharged by her South Carolina employer because she would not work on Saturday, the Sabbath Day of her faith.[1] When she was unable to obtain other employment because from conscientious scruples she would not take Saturday work,[2] she filed a claim for unemployment compensation benefits under the South Carolina Unemployment Compensation Act. That law provides that, to be eligible for benefits, a claimant must be 'able to work and * * * is available for work'; and, further, that a claimant is ineligible for benefits '(i)f * * * he has failed, without good cause * * * to accept available suitable work when offered him by the employment office or the employer * * *.' The appellee Employment Security Commission, in administrative proceedings under the statute, found that appellant's restriction upon her availability for Saturday work brought her within the provision disqualifying for benefits insured workers who fail, without good cause, to accept 'suitable work when offered * * * by the employment office or the employer * * *.' The Commission's finding was sustained by the Court of Common Pleas for Spartanburg County. That court's judgment was in turn affirmed by the South Carolina Supreme Court * * *. We noted probable jurisdiction of appellant's appeal. We reverse the judgment of the South Carolina Supreme Court and remand for further proceedings not inconsistent with this opinion.

I.

The door of the Free Exercise Clause stands tightly closed against any governmental regulation of religious beliefs as such. Government

---

1. Appellant became a member of the Seventh-day Adventist Church in 1957, at a time when her employer, a textile-mill operator, permitted her to work a five-day week. It was not until 1959 that the work week was changed to six days, including Saturday, for all three shifts in the employer's mill. No question has been raised in this case concerning the sincerity of appellant's religious beliefs. Nor is there any doubt that the prohibition against Saturday labor is a basic tenet of the Seventh-day Adventist creed, based upon that religion's interpretation of the Holy Bible.

2. After her discharge, appellant sought employment with three other mills in the Spartanburg area, but found no suitable five-day work available at any of the mills. In filing her claim with the Commission, she expressed a willingness to accept employment at other mills, or even in another industry, so long as Saturday work was not required. The record indicates that of the 150 or more Seventh-day Adventists in the Spartanburg area, only appellant and one other have been unable to find suitable non-Saturday employment.

may neither compel affirmation of a repugnant belief; nor penalize or discriminate against individuals or groups because they hold religious views abhorrent to the authorities; nor employ the taxing power to inhibit the dissemination of particular religious views. On the other hand, the Court has rejected challenges under the Free Exercise Clause to governmental regulation of certain overt acts prompted by religious beliefs or principles, for 'even when the action is in accord with one's religious convictions, (it) is not totally free from legislative restrictions.' Braunfeld. The conduct or actions so regulated have invariably posed some substantial threat to public safety, peace or order.

Plainly enough, appellant's conscientious objection to Saturday work constitutes no conduct prompted by religious principles of a kind within the reach of state legislation. If, therefore the decision of the South Carolina Supreme Court is to withstand appellant's constitutional challenge, it must be either because her disqualification as a beneficiary represents no infringement by the State of her constitutional rights of free exercise, or because any incidental burden on the free exercise of appellant's religion may be justified by a 'compelling state interest in the regulation of a subject within the State's constitutional power to regulate * * *.' NAACP v. Button, 371 U.S. 415, 438, 83 S.Ct. 328, 341, 9 L.Ed.2d 405.

II.

We turn first to the question whether the disqualification for benefits imposes any burden on the free exercise of appellant's religion. We think it is clear that it does. In a sense the consequences of such a disqualification to religious principles and practices may be only an indirect result of welfare legislation within the State's general competence to enact; it is true that no criminal sanctions directly compel appellant to work a six-day week. But this is only the beginning, not the end, of our inquiry. For '(i)f the purpose or effect of a law is to impede the observance of one or all religions or is to discriminate invidiously between religions, that law is constitutionally invalid even though the burden may be characterized as being only indirect.' Braunfeld. Here not only is it apparent that appellant's declared ineligibility for benefits derives solely from the practice of her religion, but the pressure upon her to forego that practice is unmistakable. The ruling forces her to choose between following the precepts of her religion and forfeiting benefits, on the one hand, and abandoning one of the precepts of her religion in order to accept work, on the other hand. Governmental imposition of such a choice puts the same kind of burden upon the free exercise of religion as would a fine imposed against appellant for her Saturday worship.

Nor may the South Carolina court's construction of the statute be saved from constitutional infirmity on the ground that unemployment compensation benefits are not appellant's 'right' but merely a 'privilege.' It is too late in the day to doubt that the liberties of religion and expression may be infringed by the denial of or placing of conditions upon a benefit or privilege. * * * In Speiser v. Randall, 357 U.S. 513, 78 S.Ct. 1332, 2 L.Ed.2d 1460, we emphasized that conditions upon public benefits cannot be sustained if they so operate, whatever their purpose, as to inhibit or deter the exercise of First Amendment freedoms. We there struck down a condition which limited the availability of a tax exemption to those members of the exempted class who affirmed their loyalty to the state government granting the exemption. While the State was surely under no obligation to afford such an exemption, we held that the imposition of such a condition upon even a gratuitous benefit inevitably deterred or discouraged the exercise of First Amendment rights of expression and thereby threatened to 'produce a result which the State could not command directly.' 'To deny an exemption to claimants who engage in certain forms of speech is in effect to penalize them for such speech.' Likewise, to condition the availability of benefits upon this appellant's willingness to violate a cardinal principle of her religious faith effectively penalizes the free exercise of her constitutional liberties.

Significantly South Carolina expressly saves the Sunday worshipper from having to make the kind of choice which we here hold infringes the Sabbatarian's religious liberty. When in times of 'national emergency' the textile plants are authorized by the State Commissioner of Labor to operate on Sunday, 'no employee shall be required to work on Sunday * * * who is conscientiously opposed to Sunday work; and if any employee should refuse to work on Sunday on account of conscientious * * * objections he or she shall not jeopardize his or her seniority by such refusal or be discriminated against in any other manner.' S.C.Code, § 64–4. No question of the disqualification of a Sunday worshipper for benefits is likely to arise, since we cannot suppose that an employer will discharge him in violation of this statute. The unconstitutionality of the disqualification of the Sabbatarian is thus compounded by the religious discrimination which South Carolina's general statutory scheme necessarily effects.

III.

We must next consider whether some compelling state interest enforced in the eligibility provisions of the South Carolina statute justifies the substantial infringement of appellant's First Amendment right. It is basic that no showing merely of a rational relationship to some colorable state interest would suffice; in this highly sensitive constitutional area, '(o)nly the gravest abuses, endangering paramount interest, give occasion for permissible limitation.' No such abuse or danger has been advanced in the present case. The appellees suggest no more than a possibility that the filing of fraudulent claims by unscrupulous claimants feigning religious objections to Saturday work might not only dilute the unemployment compensation fund but also hinder the scheduling by employers of necessary Saturday work. But that possibility is not apposite here because no such objection appears to have been made before the South Carolina Supreme Court, and we are unwilling to assess the importance of an asserted state interest without the views of the state court. Nor, if the contention had been made below, would the record appear to sustain it; there is no proof whatever to warrant such fears of malingering or deceit as those which the respondents now advance. * * * For even if the possibility of spurious claims did threaten to dilute the fund and disrupt the scheduling of work, it would plainly be incumbent upon the appellees to demonstrate that no alternative forms of regulation would combat such abuses without infringing First Amendment rights.

In these respects, then, the state interest asserted in the present case is wholly dissimilar to the interests which were found to justify the less direct burden upon religious practices in Braunfeld. The Court recognized that the Sunday closing law which that decision sustained undoubtedly served 'to make the practice of (the Orthodox Jewish merchants') religious beliefs more expensive.' But the statute was nevertheless saved by a countervailing factor which finds no equivalent in the instant case—a strong state interest in providing one uniform day of rest for all workers. That secular objective could be achieved, the Court found, only by declaring Sunday to be that day of rest. Requiring exemptions for Sabbatarians, while theoretically possible, appeared to present an administrative problem of such magnitude, or to afford the exempted class so great a competitive advantage, that such a requirement would have rendered the entire statutory scheme unworkable. In the present case no such justifications underlie the determination of the state court that appellant's religion makes her ineligible to receive benefits.

IV.

In holding as we do, plainly we are not fostering the 'establishment' of the Seventh-day Adventist religion in South Carolina, for the extension of unemployment benefits to Sabbatarians in common with Sunday worshippers reflects nothing more than the governmental obligation of neutrality in the face of religious differences, and does not represent that involvement of religious with secular institutions which it is the object of the Establishment Clause to forestall. Nor does the recognition of the appellant's right to unemployment benefits under the state statute serve to abridge any other person's religious liberties. Nor do we, by our decision today, declare the existence of a constitutional right to unemployment benefits on the part of all persons whose religious convictions are the cause of their unemployment. This is not a case in which an employee's religious convictions serve to make him a nonproductive member of society. Finally, nothing we say today constrains the States to adopt any particular form or scheme of unemployment compensation. Our holding today is only that South Carolina may not constitutionally apply the eligibility provisions so as to constrain a worker to abandon his religious convictions respecting the day of rest. This holding but reaffirms a principle that we announced a decade and a half ago, namely that no State may 'exclude individual Catholics, Lutherans, Mohammedans, Baptists, Jews, Methodists, Non-believers, Presbyterians, or the members of any other faith, because of their faith, or lack of it, from receiving the benefits of public welfare legislation.' Everson.

* * *

The judgment of the South Carolina Supreme Court is reversed and the case is remanded for further proceedings not inconsistent with this opinion. It is so ordered.

Reversed and remanded.

Mr. Justice Douglas, concurring.

The case we have for decision seems to me to be of small dimensions, though profoundly important. The question is whether the South Carolina law which denies unemployment compensation to a Seventh-day Adventist, who, because of her religion, has declined to work on her Sabbath, is a law 'prohibiting the free exercise' of religion as those words are used in the First Amendment. It seems obvious to me that this law does run afoul of that clause.

Religious scruples of Moslems require them to attend a mosque on Friday and to pray five times daily. Religious scruples of a Sikh require him to carry a regular or a symbolic sword. Religious scruples of a Jehovah's Witness teach him to be a colporteur, going from door to door, from town to town, distributing his religious pamphlets. Religious scruples of a Quaker compel him to refrain from swearing and to affirm instead. Religious scruples of a Buddhist may require him to refrain from partaking of any flesh, even of fish.

The examples could be multiplied, including those of the Seventh-day Adventist whose Sabbath is Saturday and who is advised not to eat some meats.

These suffice, however, to show that many people hold beliefs alien to the majority of our society—beliefs that are protected by the First Amendment but which could easily be trod upon under the guise of 'police' or 'health' regulations reflecting the majority's views.

Some have thought that a majority of a community can, through state action, compel a minority to observe their particular religious scruples so long as the majority's rule can be said to perform some valid secular function. That was the essence of the Court's decision in the Sunday Blue Law Cases, a ruling from which I then dissented and still dissent.

That ruling of the Court travels part of the distance that South Carolina asks us to go now. She asks us to hold that when it comes to a day of rest a Sabbatarian must conform with the scruples of the majority in order to obtain unemployment benefits.

The result turns not on the degree of injury, which may indeed be nonexistent by ordinary standards. The harm is the interference with the individual's scruples or conscience—an important area of privacy which the First Amendment fences off from government. * * *

This case is resolvable not in terms of what an individual can demand of government, but solely in terms of what government may not do to an individual in violation of his religious scruples. The fact that government cannot exact from me a surrender of one iota of my religious scruples does not, of course, mean that I can demand of government a sum of money, the better to exercise them. For the Free Exercise Clause is written in terms of what the government cannot do to the individual, not in terms of what the individual can exact from the government.

Those considerations, however, are not relevant here. If appellant is otherwise qualified for unemployment benefits, payments will be made to her not as a Seventh-day Adventist, but as an unemployed worker. Conceivably these payments will indirectly benefit her church, but no more so than does the salary of any public employee. * * *

MR. JUSTICE STEWART, concurring in the result.

Although fully agreeing with the result which the Court reaches in this case, I cannot join the Court's opinion. This case presents a double-barreled dilemma, which in all candor I think the Court's opinion has not succeeded in papering over. The dilemma ought to be resolved.

I.

Twenty-three years ago in Cantwell v. Connecticut, the Court said that both the Establishment Clause and the Free Exercise Clause of the First Amendment were made wholly applicable to the States by the Fourteenth Amendment. In the intervening years several cases involving claims of state abridgment of individual religious freedom have been decided here * * *. During the same period 'cases dealing with the specific problems arising under the 'Establishment' Clause which have reached this Court are few in number.' The most recent are last Term's Engel, and this Term's Schempp and Murray cases.

I am convinced that no liberty is more essential to the continued vitality of the free society which our Constitution guarantees than is the religious liberty protected by the Free Exercise Clause explicit in the First Amendment and imbedded in the Fourteenth. And I regret that on occasion, and specifically in Braunfeld, the Court has shown what has seemed to me a distressing insensitivity to the appropriate demands of this constitutional guarantee. By contrast I think that the Court's approach to the Establishment Clause has on occasion, and specifically in Engel, Schempp and Murray, been not only insensitive, but positively wooden, and that the Court has accorded to the Establishment Clause a meaning which neither the words, the history, nor the intention of the authors of that specific constitutional provision even remotely suggests.

But my views as to the correctness of the Court's decisions in these cases are beside the point here. The point is that the decisions are on the books. And the result is that there are many situations where legitimate claims under the Free Exercise Clause will run into head-on collision with the Court's insensitive and sterile construction of the Establishment Clause. The controversy now before us is clearly such a case.

Because the appellant refuses to accept available jobs which would require her to work on Saturdays, South Carolina has declined to pay unemployment compensation benefits to her. Her refusal to work on Saturdays is based on the tenets of her religious faith. The Court says that South Carolina cannot under these circumstances declare her to be not 'available for work' within the meaning of its statute because to do so would violate her constitutional right to the free exercise of her religion.

Yet what this Court has said about the Establishment Clause must inevitably lead to a diametrically opposite result. If the appellant's refusal to work on Saturdays were based on indolence, or on a compulsive desire to watch the Saturday television programs, no one would say that South Carolina could not hold that she was not 'available for work' within the meaning of its statute. That being so, the Establishment Clause as construed by this Court not only permits but affirmatively requires South Carolina equally to deny the appellant's claim for unemployment compensation when her refusal to work on Saturdays is based upon her religious creed. * * *

To require South Carolina to so administer its laws as to pay public money to the appellant under the circumstances of this case is thus clearly to require the State to violate the Establishment Clause as construed by this Court. This poses no problem for me, because I think the Court's mechanistic concept of the Establishment Clause is historically unsound and constitutionally wrong. I think the process of constitutional decision in the area of the relationships between government and religion demands considerably more than the invocation of broad-brushed rhetoric * * *. * * *

* * *

* * * With all respect, I think it is the Court's duty to face up to the dilemma posed by the conflict between the Free Exercise Clause of the Constitution and the Establishment Clause as interpreted by the Court. It is a duty, I submit, which we owe to the people, the States, and the Nation, and a duty which we owe to ourselves. For so long as the resounding but fallacious fundamentalist rhetoric of some of our Establishment Clause opinions remains on our books, to be disregarded at will as in the present case, or to be undiscriminatingly invoked as in the Schempp case, so long will the possibility of consistent and perceptive decision in this most difficult and delicate area of constitutional law be impeded and impaired. And so long, I fear, will the guarantee of true religious freedom in our pluralistic society be uncertain and insecure.

II.

My second difference with the Court's opinion is that I cannot agree that today's decision can stand consistently with Braunfeld. The Court says that there was a "less direct burden upon religious practices" in that case than in this. With all respect, I think the Court is mistaken, simply as a matter of fact. The Braunfeld case involved a state criminal statute. The undisputed effect of that statute,* * * was that "Plaintiff, Abraham Braunfeld, will be unable to continue in his business if he may not stay open on Sunday and he will thereby lose his capital investment." In other words, "the issue in this case—and we do not understand either appellees or the Court to contend otherwise—is whether a State may put an individual to a choice between his business and his religion."

The impact upon the appellant's religious freedom in the present case is considerably less onerous. We deal here not with a criminal statute, but with the particularized administration of South Carolina's Unemployment Compensation Act. Even upon the unlikely assumption that the appellant could not find suitable non-Saturday employment, the appellant at the worst would be denied a maximum of 22 weeks of compensation payments. I agree with the Court that the possibility of that denial is enough to infringe upon the appellant's constitutional right to the free exercise of her religion. But it is clear to me that in order to reach this conclusion the court must explicitly reject the reasoning of Braunfeld. I think the Braunfeld case was wrongly decided and should be overruled, and accordingly I concur in the result reached by the Court in the case before us.

MR. JUSTICE HARLAN, whom MR. JUSTICE WHITE joins, dissenting.

Today's decision is disturbing both in its rejection of existing precedent and in its implications for the future. The significance of the decision can best be understood after an examination of the state law applied in this case.

South Carolina's Unemployment Compensation Law was enacted in 1936 in response to the grave social and economic problems that arose during the depression of that period. * * *

Thus the purpose of the legislature was to tide people over, and to avoid social and economic chaos, during periods when work was unavailable. But at the same time there was clearly no intent to provide relief for those who for purely personal reasons were or became unavailable for work. * * *

The South Carolina Supreme Court has uniformly applied this law in conformity with its clearly expressed purpose. It has consistently held that one is not 'available for work' if his unemployment has resulted not from the inability of industry to provide a job but rather from personal circumstances, no matter how compelling. * * *

In the present case all that the state court has done is to apply these accepted principles. Since virtually all of the mills in the Spartanburg area were operating on a six-day week, the appellant was 'unavailable for work,' and thus ineligible for benefits, when personal considerations prevented her from accepting employment on a full-time basis in the industry and locality in which she had worked. The fact that these personal considerations sprang from her religious convictions was wholly without relevance to the state court's application of the law. Thus in no proper sense can it be said that the State discriminated against the appellant on the basis of her religious beliefs or that she was denied benefits because she was a Seventh-day Adventist. She was denied benefits just as any other claimant would be denied benefits who was not 'available for work' for personal reasons.

With this background, this Court's decision comes into clearer focus. What the Court is holding is that if the State chooses to condition unemployment compensation on the applicant's availability for work, it is constitutionally compelled to carve out an exception—and to provide benefits—for those whose unavailability is due to their religious convictions. Such a holding has particular significance in two respects.

First, despite the Court's protestations to the contrary, the decision necessarily overrules Braunfeld, which held that it did not offend the 'Free Exercise' Clause of the Constitution for a State to forbid a Sabbatarian to do business on Sunday. The secular purpose of the statute before us today is even clearer than that involved in Braunfeld. And just as in Braunfeld—where exceptions to the Sunday closing laws for Sabbatarians would have been inconsistent with the purpose to achieve a uniform day of rest and would have required case-by-case inquiry into religious beliefs—so here, an exception to the rules of eligibility based on religious convictions would necessitate judicial examination of those convictions and would be at odds with the limited purpose of the statute to smooth out the economy during periods of industrial instability. Finally, the indirect financial burden of the present law is far less than that involved in Braunfeld. Forcing a store owner to close his business on Sunday may well have the effect of depriving him of a satisfactory livelihood if his religious convictions require him to close on Saturday as well. Here we are dealing only with temporary benefits, amounting to a fraction of regular weekly wages and running for not more than 22 weeks. Clearly, any differences between this case and Braunfeld cut against the present appellant.

Second, the implications of the present decision are far more troublesome than its apparently narrow dimensions would indicate at first glance. The meaning of today's holding, as already noted, is that the State must furnish unemployment benefits to one who is unavailable for work if the unavailability stems from the exercise of religious convictions. The State, in other words, must single out for financial assistance those whose behavior is religiously motivated, even though it denies such assistance to others whose identical behavior (in this case, inability to work no Saturdays) is not religiously motivated.

It has been suggested that such singling out of religious conduct for special treatment may violate the constitutional limitations on state action. My own view, however, is that at least under the circumstances of this case it would be a permissible accommodation of religion for the State, if it chose to do so, to create an exception to its eligibility requirements for persons like the appellant. The constitutional obligation of 'neutrality,' is not so narrow a channel that the slightest deviation from an absolutely straight course leads to condemnation. There are too many instances in which no such course can be charted, too many areas in which the pervasive activities of the State justify some special provision for religion to prevent it from being submerged by an all-embracing secularism. The State violates its obligation of neutrality when, for example, it mandates a daily religious exercise in its public schools, with all the attendant pressures on the school children that such an exercise entails. But there is, I believe, enough flexibility in the Constitution to permit a legislative judgment accommodating an unemployment compensation law to the exercise of religious beliefs such as appellant's.

For very much the same reasons, however, I cannot subscribe to the conclusion that the State is constitutionally compelled to carve out an exception to its general rule of eligibility in the present case. Those situations in which the Constitution may require special treatment on account of religion are, in my view, few and far between, and this view is amply supported by the course of constitutional litigation in this area. Such compulsion in the present case is particularly inappropriate in light of the indirect, remote, and insubstantial effect of the decision below on the exercise of appellant's religion and in light of the direct financial assistance to religion that today's decision requires.

For these reasons I respectfully dissent from the opinion and judgment of the Court.

Notes and Questions

1. *Is Sherbert Consistent With Braunfeld?* Justice Brennan's majority opinion attempts to reconcile the result in *Sherbert* with that in *Braunfeld* (the Sunday closing case). Are the two opinions consistent? The concurring opinions of Justices Douglas and Stewart and the dissenting opinion of Justice Harlan all suggest that *Braunfeld* should be overruled and that *Sherbert* is inconsistent with *Braunfeld* (the dissent suggests that *Sherbert* overruled *Braunfeld* without so acknowledging). The plaintiff in *Braunfeld* was forced to close his business on Sunday under threat of criminal sanctions. This could potentially force him out of business because as an Orthodox Jew he could not do business from sundown on Friday until after sundown on Saturday. Thus, his business would have to be closed both weekend days—the best sales days of the week—because of a law that was obviously based on the Christian religious calender. Does the state's interest in a "uniform day of rest" that just happens to be the day adhered to by the majority religion seem any more compelling than South Carolina's asserted interest in a uniform set of unemployment benefit standards? Doesn't the potential damage to Braunfeld's business and the possibility of criminal sanctions if he disobeys the law seem more deserving of accommodation than the denial of 22 weeks of unemployment benefits to Sherbert? One need not think *Sherbert* was wrongly decided to question the Court's treatment of *Braunfeld* in that case. It does seem, however, that the Court should have overturned *Braunfeld* in light of its holding in *Sherbert*. As you will see below, *Braunfeld* comes closer to the current Court's approach to Free Exercise Clause exemptions than *Sherbert* does.

2. *The Compelling Interest Test. Sherbert* holds that government must have a compelling interest before it can interfere with one's free exercise of religion, even through a law of general applicability. Such an interest—for example an interest in protecting the lives of citizens—would alleviate the government's duty to provide an exemption to a law that interferes with religious practices. Therefore, in the absence of such an interest, the government would be required to create an exemption for religious practices that are infringed by a law. This makes sense since most laws of general applicability will be designed to consider the religious needs of the more dominant religions in a given area but may interfere with religious practices of other groups. The interference might be direct such as the effects on Catholics and Jews of a law that prohibits the consumption of alcohol (there was a religious exemption during prohibition), or it might be more indirect such as the choice that was thrust upon Sherbert to either work on the Sabbath or lose potential jobs and unemployment benefits. Yet, as sensible as this may seem, is it consistent with prior precedent? It would seem that *Sherbert* could draw on cases such as *Barnette* for support, but most of those cases also involved free speech or other issues. The most directly on point cases—those dealing with exemptions to generally applicable laws—such as *Reynolds* and *Braunfeld* would seem to go against the holding in *Sherbert.* This leaves the question of which approach is more consistent with the Free Exercise Clause. Under the *Sherbert* approach, the Free Exercise Clause could potentially provide substantial protection for all religious groups, while the alternative approach would allow government to more uniformly enforce some laws, and would provide more protection for those groups dominant enough to have their needs reflected when laws are drafted so that those laws either include exemptions for their religious practices or don't interfere with those practices in the first place. Which approach do you think is more consistent with the Free Exercise Clause, and why?

3. *Counter-majoritarian Concerns.* The Court seems concerned with the negative impact that laws can have on religious practices unless exemptions are provided when needed. The decision acknowledges the heavy toll that laws of general applicability can have on minority religious practices. Implicit in the decision is a concern about an unintended tyranny of the majority through laws that don't conflict with mainstream religious values but do conflict with the religious practices of religious minorities, and a view of the Free Exercise Clause that stresses its counter-majoritarian implications. Therefore, exemptions to generally applicable laws can be mandated under that clause.

4. *The Sherbert Dissent and Smith.* Interestingly, it is the *Sherbert* dissent that may be the closest to the Court's current approach. *See Employment Division v. Smith, infra.* this Chapter. As you read the cases that follow, consider whether *Sherbert* ever lived up to its potential as a tool to protect the interests of those whose religious practices are threatened by generally applicable laws and whether the *Sherbert* approach retains any vitality today.

The Compelling Interest Test Applied

As you will learn below, the compelling interest test had relatively little effect outside the unemployment context. Still, there was a period where it appeared the test would be used broadly and the test was regularly applied in the unemployment context. In *Wisconsin v. Yoder,* 406 U.S. 205, 92 S.Ct. 1526, 32 L.Ed.2d 15 (1972), the Court held that members of the Amish faith must be exempted from a state compulsory school attendance law. Amish parents whose children did not meet the requirement that they attend school until the age of sixteen were convicted of violating the law and given small fines (most Amish children remained in school only through eighth grade). The Supreme Court held that the failure to exempt the Amish from the generally applicable law violated their rights under the Free Exercise Clause, and thus the convictions must be overturned. There was no evidence that the law was designed to discriminate against the Amish or that it was applied any differently to Amish children than it was to non-Amish children.

The Court held that the burden on the Amish was quite serious because the attendance law compelled them "under threat of criminal sanction, to perform, acts undeniably at odds with fundamental tenets of their religious beliefs." The Court pointed out that the Amish would have to comply with the Wisconsin law if they wished to remain in the state. The Amish held a deep belief in separating themselves from the secular world, and thus forcing their children to attend high school might tend to assimilate the children more into secular culture because of the things they would be exposed to and the pressures they might face. Moreover, the Amish in Wisconsin were self sufficient without much influence from the outside world, and part of the reason for this was that their children were trained in the relevant trades from an early age. Thus, the compulsory attendance law placed a substantial burden on the Amish religion.

After finding a substantial burden, the Court proceeded to the next stage of the analysis, whether the government was able to justify the burden on the Amish. The Court appeared to apply the compelling interest test to require the exemption, but was a bit more cryptic. Specifically, the Court held that "only those interests of the highest order and those not otherwise served can overbalance legitimate claims to the free exercise of religion." The state interests asserted—developing well educated citizens who would be able to participate in a democratic society and training students to be self-reliant—were not adequate to meet this standard.

The Court discussed in some depth the Amish way of life—their work ethic, their stable society, and their general compliance with other laws. The Court's discussion of these issues when compared with its treatment of non-Christian religious minorities in other Free Exercise Clause exemption cases (see sections D and E of this chapter) has drawn the criticism that it glorifies traits deemed good when considered under traditional Protestant values while treating as "other" the values, beliefs, and practices of less similar groups. See STEPHEN M. FELDMAN, PLEASE DON'T WISH ME A MERRY CHRISTMAS: A CRITICAL HISTORY OF THE SEPARATION OF CHURCH AND STATE (NYU Press 1997) at 246–47.

Another aspect of the decision that has drawn a great deal of attention is the Court's treatment of the rights of the individual Amish children as opposed to the rights of the parents. Justice Douglas directly raised this concern in his dissenting opinion, but the Court held that the right of parents to direct "the religious upbringing and education of their children" was well settled, and that the parents had the right to make such choices in the absence of an explicit objection by the children. There was no evidence that any child explicitly objected to being removed from school after the eighth grade, and thus the Court held that any such harm to the children would be speculative under the facts presented. Interestingly, the Court suggested that the Amish were protected precisely because their belief in separating themselves from the rest of society was religiously based and thus those parents with non-religious reasons for removing their children from school would not be eligible for an exemption under the Free Exercise Clause. Justice Douglas argued in dissent that the Amish children may not have objected precisely because the parents made the choice to prevent the children from being unnecessarily exposed to outside influences, and therefore the children should be consulted to see whether they wanted to attend school. The reason all of this has become so important is that in 1990 (in a case you will read later), the Court held that there is no duty to provide exemptions from "generally applicable" laws, and in the process had to distinguish *Yoder*, which would appear to state that sometimes the government must do so. The Court created the concept of hybrid rights (where the free exercise right combines with another constitutional right to require an exemption), and distinguished *Yoder* by claiming that the Court did not rely solely on the Free Exercise Clause, but also on the parents' right to direct the education of their children. Is this a fair description of *Yoder*? Think about this as you read the materials in Section E later in this chapter.

In addition to *Yoder*, the Court decided a string of unemployment cases where it appeared to apply the compelling interest test. In *Thomas v. Review Board of Indiana Employ. Sec. Div.*, 450 U.S. 707, 101 S.Ct. 1425, 67 L.Ed.2d 624 (1981), the Court held that a Jehovah's witness could not be denied unemployment benefits when he quit his job after he was told he would have to work on armaments, which he said violated his faith. Not all Jehovah's Witnesses shared Thomas' view regarding manufacturing armaments, but the Court accepted the sincerity of his belief. The Court held:

> "Where the state conditions receipt of an important benefit upon conduct proscribed by a religious faith, or where it denies such a benefit because of conduct mandated by religious belief, thereby putting substantial pressure on an adherent to modify his behavior and violate his beliefs, a burden on religion exists."

The Court acknowledged that the compulsion in the case was "indirect," but held that "the infringement upon free exercise is nonetheless substantial." The Court further held that the state did not have a compelling interest and thus an exemption was required. The *Thomas* Court also echoed *Sherbert* in holding that such an exemption does not violate the Establishment Clause.

Similarly, in *Hobbie v. Unemployment Appeals Commission*, 480 U.S. 136, 107 S.Ct. 1046, 94 L.Ed.2d 190 (1987), the Court applied the compelling interest test to require an exemption for a Seventh–Day Adventist employee who was denied unemployment benefits after being fired because she refused to work on Friday night and Saturday due to her religious beliefs. The state of Florida had argued that a lower standard should be applied in light of a subsequent decision (*see Bowen v. Roy*, discussed *infra.*), but the court applied the compelling interest test and held that Florida did not meet that test. Likewise, in *Frazee v. Illinois Dept. of Employment Sec.*, 489 U.S. 829, 109 S.Ct. 1514, 103 L.Ed.2d 914 (1989), the Court held that Illinois violated Frazee's rights under the Free Exercise Clause when it denied him unemployment benefits because he refused to accept a job that required Sunday work. He believed that as a Christian he could not work on Sunday.

D. THE RETREAT FROM THE COMPELLING IN-TEREST TEST

In the mid–1980's, the Court began to seriously erode the impact of the compelling interest test. In a string of cases, including the next case, the Court minimized how compelling an interest needs to be to meet the compelling interest test, carved out exceptions to the application of the test based on the context (i.e. the accommodation was sought by someone in the military, a prisoner, etc. . . .), or both. In most of the cases the Court gave a great deal of deference to the government decision makers; an approach that is somewhat inconsistent with the *Sherbert* Court's. With the possible exception of *Yoder*, the compelling interest test showed more promise than it ever delivered. This trend culminated in the Court's decision in *Employment Division, Dept. Of Human Resources of Oregon v. Smith*, 494 U.S. 872, 110 S.Ct. 1595, 108 L.Ed.2d 876 (1990), which essentially eliminated the compelling interest test when a party is seeking an exemption from a generally applicable law. *Smith* will be discussed in greater detail in section E of this chapter.

Some of the cases that were part of this trend will be discussed after the next principle case. That case illustrates a situation where the Court failed to apply the compelling interest test, and instead gave great deference to government officials' judgement because of the institutional context (the military) of the case.

GOLDMAN v. WEINBERGER

Supreme Court of the United States, 1986.
475 U.S. 503, 106 S.Ct. 1310, 89 L.Ed.2d 478.

JUSTICE REHNQUIST delivered the opinion of the Court.

Petitioner S. Simcha Goldman contends that the Free Exercise Clause of the First Amendment to the United States Constitution permits him to wear a yarmulke while in uniform, notwithstanding an

Air Force regulation mandating uniform dress for Air Force personnel. The District Court for the District of Columbia permanently enjoined the Air Force from enforcing its regulation against petitioner and from penalizing him for wearing his yarmulke. The Court of Appeals for the District of Columbia Circuit reversed on the ground that the Air Force's strong interest in discipline justified the strict enforcement of its uniform dress requirements. We granted certiorari because of the importance of the question, and now affirm.

Petitioner Goldman is an Orthodox Jew and ordained rabbi. In 1973, he was accepted into the Armed Forces Health Professions Scholarship Program and placed on inactive reserve status in the Air Force while he studied clinical psychology at Loyola University of Chicago. During his three years in the scholarship program, he received a monthly stipend and an allowance for tuition, books, and fees. After completing his Ph.D. in psychology, petitioner entered active service in the United States Air Force as a commissioned officer, in accordance with a requirement that participants in the scholarship program serve one year of active duty for each year of subsidized education. Petitioner was stationed at March Air Force Base in Riverside, California, and served as a clinical psychologist at the mental health clinic on the base.

Until 1981, petitioner was not prevented from wearing his yarmulke on the base. He avoided controversy by remaining close to his duty station in the health clinic and by wearing his service cap over the yarmulke when out of doors. But in April 1981, after he testified as a defense witness at a court-martial wearing his yarmulke but not his service cap, opposing counsel lodged a complaint with Colonel Joseph Gregory, the Hospital Commander, arguing that petitioner's practice of wearing his yarmulke was a violation of Air Force Regulation (AFR) 35–10. This regulation states in pertinent part that "[h]eadgear will not be worn ... [w]hile indoors except by armed security police in the performance of their duties."

Colonel Gregory informed petitioner that wearing a yarmulke while on duty does indeed violate AFR 35–10, and ordered him not to violate this regulation outside the hospital. Although virtually all of petitioner's time on the base was spent in the hospital, he refused. Later, after petitioner's attorney protested to the Air Force General Counsel, Colonel Gregory revised his order to prohibit petitioner from wearing the yarmulke even in the hospital. Petitioner's request to report for duty in civilian clothing pending legal resolution of the issue was denied. The next day he received a formal letter of reprimand, and was warned that failure to obey AFR 35–10 could subject him to a court-martial. Colonel Gregory also withdrew a recommendation that petitioner's application to extend the term of his active service be approved, and substituted a negative recommendation.

Petitioner then sued respondent Secretary of Defense and others, claiming that the application of AFR 35–10 to prevent him from wearing his yarmulke infringed upon his First Amendment freedom to exercise his religious beliefs. * * *

Petitioner argues that AFR 35–10, as applied to him, prohibits religiously motivated conduct and should therefore be analyzed under the standard enunciated in *Sherbert v. Verner*. But we have repeatedly held that "the military is, by necessity, a specialized society separate from civilian society." * * * "[T]he military must insist upon a respect for duty and a discipline without counterpart in civilian life," in order to prepare for and perform its vital role.

Our review of military regulations challenged on First Amendment grounds is far more deferential than constitutional review of similar laws or regulations designed for civilian society. The military need not encourage debate or tolerate protest to the extent that such tolerance is required of the civilian state by the First Amendment; to accomplish its mission the military must foster instinctive obedience, unity, commitment, and esprit de corps. The essence of military service "is the subordination of the desires and interests of the individual to the needs of the service."

These aspects of military life do not, of course, render entirely nugatory in the military context the guarantees of the First Amendment. But "within the military community there is simply not the same [individual] autonomy as there is in the larger civilian community." In the context of the present case, when evaluating whether military needs justify a particular restriction on religiously motivated conduct, courts must give great deference to the professional judgment of military authorities concerning the relative importance of a particular military interest. Not only are courts " 'ill-equipped to determine the impact upon discipline that any particular intrusion upon military authority might have,' " but the military authorities have been charged by the Executive and Legislative Branches with carrying out our Nation's military policy. "[J]udicial deference ... is at its apogee when legislative action under the congressional authority to raise and support armies and make rules and regulations for their governance is challenged."

The considered professional judgment of the Air Force is that the traditional outfitting of personnel in standardized uniforms encourages the subordination of personal preferences and identities in favor of the overall group mission. Uniforms encourage a sense of hierarchical unity by tending to eliminate outward individual distinctions except for those of rank. The Air Force considers them as vital during peacetime as during war because its personnel must be ready to provide an effective defense on a moment's notice; the necessary habits of discipline and unity must be developed in advance of trouble. * * *

To this end, the Air Force promulgated AFR 35–10, a 190–page document, which states that "Air Force members will wear the Air Force uniform while performing their military duties, except when authorized to wear civilian clothes on duty." The rest of the document describes in minute detail all of the various items of apparel that must be worn as part of the Air Force uniform. It authorizes a few individualized options with respect to certain pieces of jewelry and hairstyle, but even these are subject to severe limitations. In general, authorized headgear may be worn only out of doors. Indoors, "[h]eadgear [may] not be worn ... except by armed security police in the performance of their duties." A narrow exception to this rule exists for headgear worn during indoor religious ceremonies. In addition, military commanders may in their discretion permit visible religious headgear and other such apparel in designated living quarters and nonvisible items generally.

Petitioner Goldman contends that the Free Exercise Clause of the First Amendment requires the Air Force to make an exception to its uniform dress requirements for religious apparel unless the accouterments create a "clear danger" of undermining discipline and esprit de corps. He asserts that in general, visible but "unobtrusive" apparel will not create such a danger and must therefore be accommodated. He argues that the Air Force failed to prove that a specific exception for his practice of wearing an unobtrusive yarmulke would threaten discipline. He contends that the Air Force's assertion to the contrary is mere *ipse dixit,* with no support from actual experience or a scientific study in the record, and is contradicted by expert testimony that religious exceptions to AFR 35–10 are in fact desirable and will increase morale by making the Air Force a more humane place.

But whether or not expert witnesses may feel that religious exceptions to AFR 35–10 are desirable is quite beside the point. The desirability of dress regulations in the military is decided by the appropriate military officials, and they are under no constitutional mandate to abandon their considered professional judgment. Quite obviously, to the extent the regulations do not permit the wearing of religious apparel such as a yarmulke, a practice described by petitioner as silent devotion akin to prayer, military life may be more objectionable for petitioner and probably others. But the First Amendment does not require the military to accommodate such practices in the face of its view that they would detract from the uniformity sought by the dress regulations. The Air Force has drawn the line essentially between religious apparel that is visible and that which is not, and we hold that those portions of the regulations challenged here reasonably and evenhandedly regulate dress in the interest of the military's perceived need for uniformity. The First Amendment therefore does not prohibit them from being applied to petitioner even though their effect is to restrict the wearing of the headgear required by his religious beliefs.

The judgment of the Court of Appeals is *Affirmed.*

JUSTICE STEVENS, with whom JUSTICE WHITE and JUSTICE POWELL join, concurring.

Captain Goldman presents an especially attractive case for an exception from the uniform regulations that are applicable to all other Air Force personnel. His devotion to his faith is readily apparent. The yarmulke is a familiar and accepted sight. In addition to its religious significance for the wearer, the yarmulke may evoke the deepest respect and admiration—the symbol of a distinguished tradition and an eloquent rebuke to the ugliness of anti-Semitism. Captain Goldman's military duties are performed in a setting in which a modest departure from the uniform regulation creates almost no danger of impairment of the Air Force's military mission. Moreover, on the record before us, there is reason to believe that the policy of strict enforcement against Captain Goldman had a retaliatory motive—he had worn his yarmulke while testifying on behalf of a defendant in a court-martial proceeding. Nevertheless, as the case has been argued, I believe we must test the validity of the Air Force's rule not merely as it applies to Captain Goldman but also as it applies to all service personnel who have sincere religious beliefs that may conflict with one or more military commands.

Justice Brennan is unmoved by the Government's concern that "while a yarmulke might not seem obtrusive to a Jew, neither does a turban to a Sikh, a saffron robe to a Satchidananda Ashram–Integral Yogi, nor do dreadlocks to a Rastafarian." He correctly points out that "turbans, saffron robes, and dreadlocks are not before us in this case," and then suggests that other cases may be fairly decided by reference to a reasonable standard based on "functional utility, health and safety considerations, and the goal of a polished, professional appearance." As the Court has explained, this approach attaches no weight to the separate interest in uniformity itself. Because professionals in the military service attach great importance to that plausible interest, it is one that we must recognize as legitimate and rational even though personal experience or admiration for the performance of the "rag-tag band of soldiers" that won us our freedom in the Revolutionary War might persuade us that the Government has exaggerated the importance of that interest.

The interest in uniformity, however, has a dimension that is of still greater importance for me. It is the interest in uniform treatment for the members of all religious faiths. The very strength of Captain Goldman's claim creates the danger that a similar claim on behalf of a Sikh or a Rastafarian might readily be dismissed as "so extreme, so unusual, or so faddish an image that public confidence in his ability to perform his duties will be destroyed." If exceptions from dress code regulations are to be granted on the basis of a multifactored test such as that proposed by Justice Brennan, inevitably the decisionmaker's evaluation of the character and the sincerity of the requester's faith—as well as the probable reaction of the majority to the favored treatment of a member of that faith—will play a critical part in the decision. For the difference between a turban or a dreadlock on the one hand, and a yarmulke on the other, is not merely a difference in "appearance"—it is also the difference between a Sikh or a Rastafarian, on the one hand, and an Orthodox Jew on the other. The Air Force has no business drawing distinctions between such persons when it is enforcing commands of universal application.

As the Court demonstrates, the rule that is challenged in this case is based on a neutral, completely objective standard—visibility. It was not motivated by hostility against, or any special respect for, any religious faith. An exception for yarmulkes would represent a fundamental departure from the true principle of uniformity that supports that rule. For that reason, I join the Court's opinion and its judgment.

JUSTICE BRENNAN, with whom JUSTICE MARSHALL joins, dissenting.

Simcha Goldman invokes this Court's protection of his First Amendment right to fulfill one of the traditional religious obligations of a male Orthodox Jew—to cover his head before an omnipresent God. The Court's response to Goldman's request is to abdicate its role as principal expositor of the Constitution and protector of individual liberties in favor of credulous deference to unsupported assertions of military necessity. I dissent.

I

In ruling that the paramount interests of the Air Force override Dr. Goldman's free exercise claim, the Court overlooks the sincere and serious nature of his constitutional claim. It suggests that the desirability of certain dress regulations, rather than a First Amendment right, is at issue. The Court declares that in selecting dress regulations, "military officials . . . are under no constitutional mandate to abandon their considered professional judgment." If Dr. Goldman wanted to wear a hat to keep his head warm or to cover a bald spot I would join the majority. Mere personal preferences in dress are not constitutionally protected. The First Amendment, however, restrains the Government's ability to prevent an Orthodox Jewish serviceman from, or punish him for, wearing a yarmulke.[2]

The Court also attempts, unsuccessfully, to minimize the burden that was placed on Dr. Goldman's rights. The fact that "the regulations do not permit the wearing of . . . a yarmulke," does not simply render military life for observant Orthodox Jews "objectionable." It sets up an almost absolute bar to the fulfillment of a religious duty. Dr. Goldman spent most of his time in uniform indoors, where the dress code forbade him even to cover his head with his service cap. Consequently, he was asked to violate the tenets of his faith virtually every minute of every work-day.

II

A

Dr. Goldman has asserted a substantial First Amendment claim, which is entitled to meaningful review by this Court. The Court, however, evades its responsibility by eliminating, in all but name only, judicial

---

2. The yarmulke worn by Dr. Goldman was a dark-colored skullcap measuring approximately 5 1/2 inches in diameter.

review of military regulations that interfere with the fundamental constitutional rights of service personnel.

Our cases have acknowledged that in order to protect our treasured liberties, the military must be able to command service members to sacrifice a great many of the individual freedoms they enjoyed in the civilian community and to endure certain limitations on the freedoms they retain. Notwithstanding this acknowledgment, we have steadfastly maintained that " 'our citizens in uniform may not be stripped of basic rights simply because they have doffed their civilian clothes.' " * * *

Today the Court eschews its constitutionally mandated role. It adopts for review of military decisions affecting First Amendment rights a subrational-basis standard—absolute, uncritical "deference to the professional judgment of military authorities." If a branch of the military declares one of its rules sufficiently important to outweigh a service person's constitutional rights, it seems that the Court will accept that conclusion, no matter how absurd or unsupported it may be.

A deferential standard of review, however, need not, and should not, mean that the Court must credit arguments that defy common sense. When a military service burdens the free exercise rights of its members in the name of necessity, it must provide, as an initial matter and at a minimum, a *credible* explanation of how the contested practice is likely to interfere with the proffered military interest.[3] Unabashed *ipse dixit* cannot outweigh a constitutional right.

In the present case, the Air Force asserts that its interests in discipline and uniformity would be undermined by an exception to the dress code permitting observant male Orthodox Jews to wear yarmulkes. The Court simply restates these assertions without offering any explanation how the exception Dr. Goldman requests reasonably could interfere with the Air Force's interests. Had the Court given actual consideration to Goldman's claim, it would have been compelled to decide in his favor.

B

1

The Government maintains in its brief that discipline is jeopardized whenever exceptions to military regulations are granted. Service personnel must be trained to obey even the most arbitrary command reflexively. Non–Jewish personnel will perceive the wearing of a yarmulke by an Orthodox Jew as an unauthorized departure from the rules and will begin to question the principle of unswerving obedience. Thus shall our fighting forces slip down the treacherous slope toward unkempt appearance, anarchy, and, ultimately, defeat at the hands of our enemies.

---

3. I continue to believe that Government restraints on First Amendment rights, including limitations placed on military personnel, may be justified only upon showing a compelling state interest which is precisely furthered by a narrowly tailored regulation. I think that any special needs of the military can be accommodated in the compelling-interest prong of the test. My point here is simply that even under a more deferential test Dr. Goldman should prevail.

The contention that the discipline of the Armed Forces will be subverted if Orthodox Jews are allowed to wear yarmulkes with their uniforms surpasses belief. It lacks support in the record of this case, and the Air Force offers no basis for it as a general proposition. While the perilous slope permits the services arbitrarily to refuse exceptions requested to satisfy mere personal preferences, before the Air Force may burden free exercise rights it must advance, at the *very least,* a rational reason for doing so.

* * *

2

The Government also argues that the services have an important interest in uniform dress, because such dress establishes the preeminence of group identity, thus fostering esprit de corps and loyalty to the service that transcends individual bonds. In its brief, the Government characterizes the yarmulke as an assertion of individuality and as a badge of religious and ethnic identity, strongly suggesting that, as such, it could drive a wedge of divisiveness between members of the services.

First, the purported interests of the Air Force in complete uniformity of dress and in elimination of individuality or visible identification with any group other than itself are belied by the service's own regulations. The dress code expressly abjures the need for total uniformity:

> * * * "(2) Appearance in uniform is an important part of this image.... Neither the Air Force nor the public expects absolute uniformity of appearance. Each member has the right, within limits, to express individuality through his or her appearance. However, the image of a disciplined service member who can be relied on to do his or her job excludes the extreme, the unusual, and the fad."

It cannot be seriously contended that a serviceman in a yarmulke presents so extreme, so unusual, or so faddish an image that public confidence in his ability to perform his duties will be destroyed. Under the Air Force's own standards, then, Dr. Goldman should have and could have been granted an exception to wear his yarmulke.

* * *

Moreover, the services allow, and rightly so, other manifestations of religious diversity. It is clear to all service personnel that some members attend Jewish services, some Christian, some Islamic, and some yet other religious services. Barracks mates see Mormons wearing temple garments, Orthodox Jews wearing tzitzit, and Catholics wearing crosses and scapulars. That they come from different faiths and ethnic backgrounds is not a secret that can or should be kept from them.

I find totally implausible the suggestion that the overarching group identity of the Air Force would be threatened if Orthodox Jews were allowed to wear yarmulkes with their uniforms. To the contrary, a yarmulke worn with a United States military uniform is an eloquent reminder that the shared and proud identity of United States serviceman embraces and unites religious and ethnic pluralism.

Finally, the Air Force argues that while Dr. Goldman describes his yarmulke as an "unobtrusive" addition to his uniform, obtrusiveness is a purely relative, standardless judgment. The Government notes that while a yarmulke might not seem obtrusive to a Jew, neither does a turban to a Sikh, a saffron robe to a Satchidananda Ashram–Integral Yogi, nor dreadlocks to a Rastafarian. If the Court were to require the Air Force to permit yarmulkes, the service must also allow all of these other forms of dress and grooming.

The Government dangles before the Court a classic parade of horribles, the specter of a brightly-colored, "rag-tag band of soldiers." Although turbans, saffron robes, and dreadlocks are not before us in this case and must each be evaluated against the reasons a service branch offers for prohibiting personnel from wearing them while in uniform, a reviewing court could legitimately give deference to dress and grooming rules that have a *reasoned* basis in, for example, functional utility, health and safety considerations, and the goal of a polished, professional appearance. It is the lack of any reasoned basis for prohibiting yarmulkes that is so striking here.

Furthermore, contrary to its intimations, the Air Force has available to it a familiar standard for determining whether a particular style of yarmulke is consistent with a polished, professional military appearance—the "neat and conservative" standard by which the service judges jewelry. No rational reason exists why yarmulkes cannot be judged by the same criterion. Indeed, at argument Dr. Goldman declared himself willing to wear whatever style and color yarmulke the Air Force believes best comports with its uniform.

3

Department of Defense Directive 1300.17 (June 18, 1985) grants commanding officers the discretion to permit service personnel to wear religious items and apparel that are not visible with the uniform, such as crosses, temple garments, and scapulars. Justice Stevens favors this "visibility test" because he believes that it does not involve the Air Force in drawing distinctions among faiths. He rejects functional utility, health, and safety considerations, and similar grounds as criteria for religious exceptions to the dress code, because he fears that these standards will allow some servicepersons to satisfy their religious dress and grooming obligations, while preventing others from fulfilling theirs. But, the visible/not visible standard has that same effect. Furthermore, it restricts the free exercise rights of a larger number of servicepersons. The visibility test permits *only* individuals whose outer garments and grooming are indistinguishable from those of mainstream Christians to fulfill their religious duties. In my view, the Constitution requires the selection of criteria that permit the greatest possible number of persons to practice their faiths freely.

Implicit in Justice Stevens' concurrence, and in the Government's arguments, is what might be characterized as a fairness concern. It would be unfair to allow Orthodox Jews to wear yarmulkes, while prohibiting members of other minority faiths with visible dress and grooming requirements from wearing their saffron robes, dreadlocks, turbans, and so forth. While I appreciate and share this concern for the feelings and the free exercise rights of members of these other faiths, I am baffled by this formulation of the problem. What puzzles me is the implication that a neutral standard that could result in the disparate treatment of Orthodox Jews and, for example, Sikhs is *more* troublesome or unfair than the existing neutral standard that does result in the different treatment of Christians, on the one hand, and Orthodox Jews and Sikhs on the other. *Both* standards are constitutionally suspect; before either can be sustained, it must be shown to be a narrowly tailored means of promoting important military interests.

I am also perplexed by the related notion that for purposes of constitutional analysis religious faiths may be divided into two categories—those with visible dress and grooming requirements and those without. This dual category approach seems to incorporate an assumption that fairness, the First Amendment, and, perhaps, equal protection, require all faiths belonging to the same category to be treated alike, but permit a faith in one category to be treated differently from a faith belonging to the other category. The practical effect of this categorization is that, under the guise of neutrality and evenhandedness, majority religions are favored over distinctive minority faiths. This dual category analysis is fundamentally flawed and leads to a result that the First Amendment was intended to prevent. Under the Constitution there is only *one* relevant category—*all* faiths. Burdens placed on the free exercise rights of members of one faith must be justified independently of burdens placed on the rights of members of another religion. It is not enough to say that Jews cannot wear yarmulkes simply because Rastafarians might not be able to wear dreadlocks.

Unless the visible/not visible standard for evaluating requests for religious exceptions to the dress code promotes a significant military interest, it is constitutionally impermissible. * * * [M]ore directly, Government agencies are not free to define their own interests in uniform treatment of different faiths. That function has been assigned to the First Amendment. The First Amendment requires that burdens on free exercise rights be justified by independent and important interests that promote the function of the agency. The only independent military interest furthered by the visibility standard is uniformity of dress. * * *

The Air Force has failed utterly to furnish a credible explanation why an exception to the dress code permitting Orthodox Jews to wear neat and conservative yarmulkes while in uniform is likely to interfere with its interest in discipline and uniformity. * * * Under any meaningful level of judicial review, Simcha Goldman should prevail.

III

Through our Bill of Rights, we pledged ourselves to attain a level of human freedom and dignity that had no parallel in history. Our constitutional commitment to religious freedom and to acceptance of religious pluralism is one of our greatest achievements in that noble endeavor. * * *

Guardianship of this precious liberty is not the exclusive domain of federal courts. It is the responsibility as well of the States and of the other branches of the Federal Government. Our military services have a distinguished record of providing for many of the religious needs of their personnel. But that they have satisfied much of their constitutional obligation does not remove their actions from judicial scrutiny. Our Nation has preserved freedom of religion, not through trusting to the good faith of individual agencies of government alone, but through the constitutionally mandated vigilant oversight and checking authority of the judiciary.

It is not the province of the federal courts to second-guess the professional judgments of the military services, but we are bound by the Constitution to assure ourselves that there exists a rational foundation for assertions of military necessity when they interfere with the free exercise of religion. * * * Definitions of necessity are influenced by decisionmakers' experiences and values. As a consequence, in pluralistic societies such as ours, institutions dominated by a majority are inevitably, if inadvertently, insensitive to the needs and values of minorities when these needs and values differ from those of the majority. The military, with its strong ethic of conformity and unquestioning obedience, may be particularly impervious to minority needs and values. A critical function of the Religion Clauses of the First Amendment is to protect the rights of members of minority religions against quiet erosion by majoritarian social institutions that dismiss minority beliefs and practices as unimportant, because unfamiliar. It is the constitutional role of this Court to ensure that this purpose of the First Amendment be realized.

The Court and the military services have presented patriotic Orthodox Jews with a painful dilemma—the choice between fulfilling a religious obligation and serving their country. Should the draft be reinstated, compulsion will replace choice. Although the pain the services inflict on Orthodox Jewish servicemen is clearly the result of insensitivity rather than design, it is unworthy of our military because it is unnecessary. The Court and the military have refused these servicemen their constitutional rights; we must hope that Congress will correct this wrong.

JUSTICE BLACKMUN, dissenting.

I would reverse the judgment of the Court of Appeals, but for reasons somewhat different from those respectively enunciated by Justice Brennan and Justice O'Connor. I feel that the Air Force is justified in considering not only the costs of allowing Captain Goldman to cover his head indoors, but also the cumulative costs of accommodating constitutionally indistinguishable requests for religious exemptions. Because, however, the Government has failed to make any meaningful showing that either set of costs is significant, I dissent from the Court's rejection of Goldman's claim.

The Government concedes that Goldman wears his yarmulke out of sincere religious conviction. For Goldman, as for many other Jews, "a yarmulke is an expression of respect for God ... intended to keep the wearer aware of God's presence." If the Free Exercise Clause of the First Amendment means anything, it must mean that an individual's desire to follow his or her faith is not simply another personal preference, to be accommodated by government when convenience allows. Indeed, this Court has read the Clause, I believe correctly, to require that "only those interests of the highest order and those not otherwise served can overbalance legitimate claims to the free exercise of religion." *Wisconsin v. Yoder.* * * *

Nor may free exercise rights be compromised simply because the military says they must be. * * * Except as otherwise required by "interests of the highest order," soldiers as well as civilians are entitled to follow the dictates of their faiths.

In my view, this case does not require us to determine the extent to which the ordinary test for inroads on religious freedom must be modified in the military context, because the Air Force has failed to produce even a minimally credible explanation for its refusal to allow Goldman to keep his head covered indoors. I agree with the Court that deference is due the considered judgment of military professionals that, as a general matter, standardized dress serves to promote discipline and esprit de corps. But Goldman's modest supplement to the Air Force uniform clearly poses by itself no threat to the Nation's military readiness. Indeed, the District Court specifically found that Goldman has worn a yarmulke on base for years without any adverse effect on his performance, any disruption of operations at the base, or any complaints from other personnel.

* * * [The argument has been made that t]o allow noncombat personnel to wear yarmulkes but not turbans or dreadlocks because the latter seem more obtrusive * * * would be to discriminate in favor of this country's more established, mainstream religions, the practices of which are more familiar to the average observer. Not only would conventional faiths receive special treatment under such an approach; they would receive special treatment precisely *because* they are conventional. * * *

The problem with this argument, it seems to me, is not doctrinal but empirical. The Air Force simply has not shown any reason to fear that a significant number of enlisted personnel and officers would request religious exemptions that could not be denied on neutral grounds such as safety, let alone that granting these requests would noticeably impair the overall image of the service. * * *

In these circumstances, deference seems unwarranted. Reasoned military judgments, of course, are entitled to respect, but the military has failed to show that this particular judgment with respect to Captain Goldman is a reasoned one. If, in the future, the Air Force is besieged with requests for religious exemptions from the dress code, and those requests cannot be distinguished on functional grounds from Goldman's, the service may be able to argue credibly that circumstances warrant a flat rule against any visible religious apparel. That, however, would be a case different from the one at hand.

JUSTICE O'CONNOR, with whom JUSTICE MARSHALL joins, dissenting.

The issue posed in this case is whether, consistent with the Free Exercise Clause of the First Amendment, the Air Force may prohibit Captain Goldman, an Orthodox Jewish psychologist, from wearing a yarmulke while he is in uniform on duty inside a military hospital.

The Court rejects Captain Goldman's claim without even the slightest attempt to weigh his asserted right to the free exercise of his religion against the interest of the Air Force in uniformity of dress within the military hospital. No test for free exercise claims in the military context is even articulated, much less applied. It is entirely sufficient for the Court if the military perceives a need for uniformity.

* * *

I believe that the Court should attempt to articulate and apply an appropriate standard for a free exercise claim in the military context, and should examine Captain Goldman's claim in light of that standard.

Like the Court today in this case involving the military, the Court in the past has had some difficulty, even in the civilian context, in articulating a clear standard for evaluating free exercise claims that result from the application of general state laws burdening religious conduct. * * *

* * * One can, however, glean at least two consistent themes from this Court's precedents. First, when the government attempts to deny a Free Exercise claim, it must show that an unusually important interest is at stake, whether that interest is denominated "compelling," "of the highest order," or "overriding." Second, the government must show that granting the requested exemption will do substantial harm to that interest, whether by showing that the means adopted is the "least restrictive" or "essential," or that the interest will not "otherwise be served." These two requirements are entirely sensible in the context of the assertion of a free exercise claim. First, because the government is attempting to override an interest specifically protected by the Bill of Rights, the government must show that the opposing interest it asserts is of especial importance before there is any chance that its claim can prevail. Second, since the Bill of Rights is expressly designed to protect the individual against the aggregated and sometimes intolerant powers of the state, the government must show that the interest asserted will in fact be substantially harmed by granting the type of exemption requested by the individual.

There is no reason why these general principles should not apply in the military, as well as the civilian, context. * * * Furthermore, the test that one can glean from this Court's decisions in the civilian context is sufficiently flexible to take into account the special importance of defending our Nation without abandoning completely the freedoms that make it worth defending.

The first question that the Court should face here, therefore, is whether the interest that the Government asserts against the religiously based claim of the individual is of unusual importance. It is perfectly appropriate at this step of the analysis to take account of the special role of the military. The mission of our Armed Services is to protect our Nation from those who would destroy all our freedoms. I agree that, in order to fulfill that mission, the military is entitled to take some freedoms from its members. * * * The need for military discipline and esprit de corps is unquestionably an especially important governmental interest.

But the mere presence of such an interest cannot, as the majority implicitly believes, end the analysis of whether a refusal by the Government to honor the free exercise of an individual's religion is constitutionally acceptable. * * * The second question in the analysis of a free exercise claim under this Court's precedents must also be reached here: will granting an exemption of the type requested by the individual do substantial harm to the especially important governmental interest?

I have no doubt that there are many instances in which the unique fragility of military discipline and esprit de corps necessitates rigidity by the Government when similar rigidity to preserve an assertedly analogous interest would not pass constitutional muster in the civilian sphere. Nonetheless, as Justice Brennan persuasively argues, the Government can present no sufficiently convincing proof in *this* case to support an assertion that granting an exemption of the type requested here would do substantial harm to military discipline and esprit de corps.

First, the Government's asserted need for absolute uniformity is contradicted by the Government's own exceptions to its rule. * * *

Furthermore, the Government does not assert, and could not plausibly argue, that petitioner's decision to wear his yarmulke while indoors at the hospital presents a threat to health or safety. And finally, the District Court found as fact that in this particular case * * *, "[f]rom September 1977 to May 7, 1981, *no objection* was raised to Goldman's wearing of his yarmulke while in uniform."

In the rare instances where the military has not consistently or plausibly justified its asserted need for rigidity of enforcement, and where the individual seeking the exemption establishes that the assertion by the military of a threat to discipline or esprit de corps is in his or her case completely unfounded, I would hold that the Government's policy of uniformity must yield to the individual's assertion of the right of free exercise of religion. On the facts of this case, therefore, I would require the Government to accommodate the sincere religious belief of Captain Goldman. * * *

I respectfully dissent.

Notes and Questions

1. *Rational Basis or Compelling Interest.* The Court obviously did not apply the compelling interest test in *Goldman*, but the deference it gave to military officials suggests that the standard applicable to such claims is rational basis or even sub-rational basis, especially if one considers the dissenting opinions' response to the military's reasons for denying Goldman an exemption. One can obviously distinguish *Goldman* from *Sherbert* on the basis that *Goldman* took place in the military setting, but interestingly, a number of cases that were not decided in the military setting (or other institutional settings, *see* Note 4 below) utilized reasoning similar to the *Goldman* Court's; although the level of deference given to government officials may not have been quite as unflinching as in *Goldman*.

2. *Minimizing Central Religious Practices.* Justice Rehnquist's opinion for the Court suggests that Captain Goldman's wearing of the yarmulka is merely a preference, and as the dissents suggest the decision seems consistent with this inaccurate assumption. Thus, Justice Rehnquist wrote, "[t]he considered professional judgment of the Air Force is that the traditional outfitting of personnel in standardized uniforms encourages the subordination of personal preferences and identities in favor of the overall group mission." Justice Brennan responded in his dissenting opinion, "[m]ere personal preferences in dress are not constitutionally protected. The First Amendment, however, restrains the Government's ability to prevent an Orthodox Jewish serviceman from, or punish him for, wearing a yarmulke." As the dissent points out, Captain Goldman would have had to resign his commission and all the indicia thereof if he was not allowed to wear a yarmulka. Thus, the wearing of a yarmulka was not a preference, but rather a central religious command for Captain Goldman. Cases like *Sherbert* and *Yoder* suggested that the centrality of a religious practice was relevant to the Court's analysis under the Free Exercise Clause. Does *Goldman* suggest that the Court has retreated from that position, or is the result simply a matter of the military context? *See Employment Division v. Smith, infra.* this Chapter at section E (the Court explicitly repudiated reliance on the centrality of a religious practice).

3. *The Military Setting.* The Court places a great deal of importance on the military setting of the case. The Court holds that military authorities need to be given a great deal of leeway given the nature of military service, and essentially applies a sub-rational basis test. Even Justice Brennan agrees that the military must be given more leeway than civilian authorities. Yet, the majority doesn't seem to give any deference to Captain Goldman's free exercise interests while giving, as Justice Brennan suggests, almost total deference to the militaries' stated reasons no matter how implausible those reasons seem and given the facts pointed out by the dissenting opinions. However, doesn't Justice Rehnquist have a point when he suggests that if mandatory exemptions from military dress regulations were available other religious groups would also seek exemptions? Thus, a Rastafarian might seek to wear dreadlocks, or a Sikh a turban and a sword. How could the military give an exemption to one religious group without creating the proverbial "slippery slope?" Of course, the answer to this question

could be provided under the compelling interest test that the Court does not apply. Another option would be to use the rational basis approach as Justice Brennan suggests. Under that approach the military could be given greater leeway and would have a wider range of interests that would satisfy the test, but if the military is unable to demonstrate an interest even with the great leeway given, it would have to provide an exemption.

As Justice Brennan points out, the military recognized that soldiers may demonstrate some individuality and provided for exemptions from the dress code, which suggests that complete uniformity was not imperative so long as the key "neat and conservative" standard of military dress was adhered to. A yarmulka would seem to meet this standard. Whether other religious garb meets the standard would need to be decided by military authorities and perhaps the courts. Do you think the military would meet even the rational basis test given the evidence in the case? Are you comfortable with the possible disparities in treatment between religions under Justice Breman's approach, where an Orthodox Jew or Muslim might be accommodated, but a Rastafarian or Sikh might not? Isn't that already the result under the Court's approach in *Goldman*, since Christians are free to wear rosaries or crosses even if they deviate from uniform military dress standards, while other religions are not accommodated in the existing regulations? Or are other religions accommodated to the same degree because they can also wear religious necklaces anytime? Is the regulation at issue in *Goldman* simply the result of the military setting its uniformity standard with the needs of most Christian soldiers in mind (or at least implicitly considered), while not considering the religious needs of others? Without an exemption can Orthodox Jews join the military without risking immediate dismissal? What about a Jewish Chaplain?

4. *Other Institutional Settings.* As *Goldman* makes clear, the Court gives great deference to military authorities, even when their policies have the effect of interfering with religious practice. Another area where the Court has traditionally given great deference to government authorities is in the prison setting. In the prison context, the Court has generally deferred to "the legitimate penological interests of prison authorities." *See, e.g. O'Lone v. Shabazz*, 482 U.S. 342, 107 S.Ct. 2400, 96 L.Ed.2d 282 (1987). As in the military context, this is virtually a sub-rational basis standard. In *O'Lone*, Muslim prisoners in New Jersey had requested that they be allowed to attend a Friday afternoon Muslim prayer service that is an important religious observance in the Muslim faith. The problem was that the complaining prisoners had been assigned to work details outside prison buildings, the services were held indoors, and prison standards required that prisoners working outside not be allowed to return inside during the work day. Prison officials argued that there were security risks inherent in giving the prisoners exemptions, that the requirements simulated work conditions outside the prison, that an exemption would place undue pressure on guards who must decide when to allow a prisoner to return, and that granting the exemptions would foster "affinity groups" that would be detrimental to the prison environment. The Court accepted the judgement of prison officials on these issues with little exploration of their reasonableness, and also held that prison officials are not required to use alternative means to serve their "legitimate penological interests" in order to accommodate the prisoner's religious practice. The Court's held: "We take this opportunity to reaffirm our refusal * * * 'to substitute our judgement on [difficult] and sensitive matters of institutional administration' for [that of prison officials] * * *."

The Move Away From the Compelling Interest Test

Goldman is not the only decision in the 1980's that seemed to abandon or limit the *Sherbert* doctrine. The cases can be broken into two rough categories: 1. Those applying the compelling interest test and upholding the state action; and 2. Those not applying the compelling interest test. The first group includes *United States v. Lee*, 455 U.S. 252, 102 S.Ct. 1051, 71 L.Ed.2d 127 (1982), *Bob Jones University v. United States*, 461 U.S. 574, 103 S.Ct. 2017, 76 L.Ed.2d 157 (1983), and *Hernandez v. Commissioner*, 490 U.S. 680, 109 S.Ct. 2136, 104 L.Ed.2d 766 (1989). In *Lee*, the Court held that an Amish employer was not entitled to an exemption from participation in the social security system. The Court held that the state can support a limitation on a citizen's free exercise of religion by demonstrating that the government action is "essential to accomplish an overriding governmental interest." The Court further held that the government's interest in the integrity of the social security system was an overriding governmental interest, and that the social security system would be at serious risk if government were required to create "myriad exceptions" based on a "wide variety of religious beliefs." The Court acknowledged that Lee's beliefs were sincere.

In *Bob Jones University*, the Court likewise found a compelling governmental interest sufficient to justify a limitation on the free exercise of religion. In that case the Court upheld a ruling by the Internal Revenue Service that denied tax exemptions to Universities (and other schools) that discriminate on the basis of race. The University prohibited interracial romantic relationships based on its interpretation of the bible. The Court held that the government's interest in eliminating racial discrimination was a "fundamental, overriding interest," that outweighed the burden on the University's free exercise based on the denial of a tax exemption. Moreover, the Court held that there were no less restrictive means to achieve the government's interest in eradicating racial discrimination in this context. Of course, this case is different from *Lee* in one important respect, namely, that the failure to exempt in *Lee* compelled him to participate in a system he said violated his religious beliefs while the denial of the tax exemption does not compel the University to change its policy; although it may encourage the University to do so.

Hernandez, like *Bob Jones University*, involved the denial of a tax deduction by the Internal Revenue Service. In *Hernandez*, the Church of Scientology argued that its members should be allowed to deduct as a charitable contribution fees for training sessions. The Court held that even if the denial of the exemptions was a substantial burden on the members' free exercise rights (the Court openly acknowledged its doubt that this was so under the facts), the government's interest in a "sound tax system, free of myriad exceptions" was adequate to overcome that burden. Do you think the test applied in these cases is the same as the compelling interest test in other contexts such as under the Equal Protection Clause or the Free Speech Clause?

Despite applying the compelling interest test in the above cases, the Court, in a series of cases, developed an elaborate range of reasons for not applying the compelling interest test. One of these reasons is the nature of certain institutional settings such as the military or prisons as reflected in *Goldman* and *O'Lone* (discussed *supra.*). Several other cases that did not apply the compelling interest test to cases involving exemptions under the Free Exercise Clause were decided in the 1980's. Most notable among these cases are *Bowen v. Roy*, 476 U.S. 693, 106 S.Ct. 2147, 90 L.Ed.2d 735 (1986), and *Lyng v. Northwest Indian Cemetery Protective Assn.*, 485 U.S. 439, 108 S.Ct. 1319, 99 L.Ed.2d 534 (1988).

In *Bowen*, the Plurality led by Chief Justice Burger applied essentially a rational basis standard to a claim by a native American challenging the AFDC requirement that recipients provide their social security numbers. Interestingly, a majority of the Court would have applied the compelling interest test, but the five Justices who would have done so disagreed about its application under the facts in the case. Roy also challenged the government's use of social security numbers in administering the AFDC program. Roy's reason for objecting to the social security requirement was his sincere religious belief that the requirement would harm his daughter's spirit by representing her as a number. The plurality did not apply the compelling interest test, rather Justice Burger wrote that when the burden on free exercise is "indirect" a lower standard applies:

> "Absent proof of an intent to discriminate against particular religious beliefs or against religion in general, the Government meets its burden when it demonstrates that a challenged requirement for governmental benefits, neutral and uniform in its application, is a reasonable means of promoting a legitimate public interest."

The standard is essentially a rational basis standard, and the plurality held that it was met in this case because requiring social security numbers helps prevent fraud, a "legitimate public interest." The plurality also distinguished the benefit context from other contexts. Justice Burger wrote that "government regulation that indirectly * * * calls for a choice between securing a government benefit and adherence to religious beliefs" is different from situations where government "criminalizes religiously inspired conduct" or "inescapably compels" conduct that is religiously objectionable. The plurality attempted to limit *Sherbert*, which would seem to conflict with its analysis, to the unemployment context where the legal regime created a series of individualized exemptions and thus denial of a religious exemption would be discriminatory. The plurality suggested that it is this discrimination that justifies the compelling interest standard in the unemployment context. Justice O'Connor responded to the plurality's use of the rational basis standard in the Free Exercise Clause exemption context as follows: "Such a test has no basis in precedent and relegates a serious First Amendment value to the barest level of minimal scrutiny that the Equal Protection Clause already provides." Is she correct about this? If so, can the plurality's approach be justified?

As to Roy's other claim, a Majority of the Court held that the government's internal administrative use of Roy's daughter's social security number did not interfere with anyone's free exercise rights, and that Roy was essentially asking that the government change its internal behavior. The Court held that no one has the right to make the government behave in a way that would further his or her religious beliefs. Thus, the Court suggested there is a difference between challenging government action that operates directly on an individual believer and internal government action that does not act directly on an individual. Is this a plausible distinction given the nature of Roy's free exercise claim?

In *Lyng*, the Court allowed the United States Forestry Service to build a road through land that was sacred to three Native American Tribes. The tribes used the land for religious purposes. The land was owned by the U.S. government at the time the case was brought. Before moving on, consider how this may have come to pass. Ironically, Justice O'Connor wrote the majority opinion. The Court noted that the road would "virtually destroy the Indians' ability to practice their religion," but nonetheless held that a compelling interest was not necessary because the effect on the tribes' free exercise rights was an incidental effect of a government program, and that such incidental effects do not require a compelling governmental interest to justify them even if they "make it more difficult to practice certain religions," so long as they do not "coerce individuals into acting contrary to their religious beliefs." The Court held that the road building project did not force the tribal members to choose between a government benefit and sacrificing their religious beliefs. Nor did the road project coerce them or impose a penalty on them for practicing their religion according to the Court. Rather, the Court held that the situation was more akin to the issue in *Bowen* where the Court held that the government had no duty to conform *its own* conduct to an individual or individuals' religious beliefs. Thus, the claims of the Native Americans did not "divest the government of the right to use what is, after all, its land." Can this be correct? On the one hand it makes sense that the government should be able to use its property in any way it sees fit, but on the other hand by doing so it will be destroying the tribes' ability to practice their religion. Is the answer to simply hope the government will choose to accommodate in such situations? Should the fact that the complainants are Native American tribes whose land was often taken by force or subterfuge relevant? Would you want to know the history of this particular land and these particular tribes before answering that question?

Another situation in which the Court did not apply the compelling interest test was when the Court found that a particular burden on religion was not adequate to require application of the test. Such cases are potentially consistent with *Sherbert*. Do you see why? In *Tony and Susan Alamo Foundation v. Secretary of Labor*, 471 U.S. 290, 105 S.Ct. 1953, 85 L.Ed.2d 278 (1985), the Court held that a non-profit religious foundation was not entitled to an exemption from the minimum wage requirements of the Fair Labor Standards Act. The foundation's activities were primarily carried out by workers (called "associates") who received benefits such as food, shelter, and clothing for their work rather than wages. The organization argued that the receipt of wages by its "associates" would be a violation of the associates' religious convictions. The Court held that the minimum wage requirements were applicable to the organization and did not place a significant burden on the associates' religious convictions, because the law does not require the payment of cash. The "associates" could be paid in the form of increased benefits of the type they already received, which would be consistent with their religious convictions. Thus, "application of the Act [would not] interfere with the associates' rights to freely exercise their religion."

Similarly, in *Jimmy Swaggart Ministries v. Board of Equalization*, 493 U.S. 378, 110 S.Ct. 688, 107 L.Ed.2d 796 (1990), the court held that a religious ministry was not entitled to an exemption from the California sales tax when it sold religious materials. The Court held that the tax was neutral because it applied to all "sales and uses" of "tangible property" in the state of California, whether religious or not. The tax was not aimed specifically at the sale of religious material and in fact was imposed on those purchasing the materials rather than directly on the ministries. The Court held that the burden imposed on the ministries by the tax was not "constitutionally significant," and therefore the compelling interest test was not applicable.

The above cases demonstrate that in the years after *Yoder* the compelling interest test was frequently not applied and when it was applied it was applied with significantly less stringency than it had been in *Sherbert*. The exception to this trend seemed to be in unemployment cases. Yet *Sherbert* and *Yoder* were still good law and they were applied by lower courts in a number of situations. The Supreme Court, however, appeared to be retreating from the compelling interest test, and this retreat was soon to be a nearly complete one.

E. LAWS OF GENERAL APPLICABILITY AND THE RETREAT FROM THE COMPELLING INTEREST TEST

As the above discussion demonstrates, the Court carved out numerous exceptions to the *Sherbert/Yoder* approach and over time the interests needed to satisfy the test when it was applied became less "compelling." Claims for exemption based on the Free Exercise Clause were rarely successful outside the unemployment benefit context, and scholars have noted that such claims were *never* successful before the U.S. Supreme Court when brought by non-Christians. Mark Tushnet,*"Of Church and State and the Supreme Court": Kurland Revisited*, 1989 S. CT. REV. 373; *See also* STEPHEN M. FELDMAN, PLEASE DON'T WISH ME A MERRY CHRISTMAS: A CRITICAL HISTORY OF THE SEPARATION OF CHURCH AND STATE (NYU Press 1997) at 246–47. Yet the Court still ostensibly used the compelling interest test when none of the many exceptions to the test applied. The compelling interest test, however, was soon to meet its official end in exemption cases (outside a few limited contexts).

EMPLOYMENT DIVISION, DEPT. OF HUMAN RESOURCES OF OREGON v. SMITH

Supreme Court of the United States, 1990.
494 U.S. 872, 110 S.Ct. 1595, 108 L.Ed.2d 876.

JUSTICE SCALIA delivered the opinion of the Court.

This case requires us to decide whether the Free Exercise Clause of the First Amendment permits the State of Oregon to include religiously inspired peyote use within the reach of its general criminal prohibition on use of that drug, and thus permits the State to deny unemployment benefits to persons dismissed from their jobs because of such religiously inspired use.

I

Oregon law prohibits the knowing or intentional possession of a "controlled substance" unless the substance has been prescribed by a medical practitioner. The law defines "controlled substance" as a drug classified in Schedules I through V of the Federal Controlled Substances Act * * * as modified by the State Board of Pharmacy. Persons who violate this provision by possessing a controlled substance listed on Schedule I are "guilty of a Class B felony." As compiled by the State Board of Pharmacy under its statutory authority, Schedule I contains the drug peyote, a hallucinogen derived from the plant *Lophophora williamsii Lemaire*.

Respondents Alfred Smith and Galen Black (hereinafter respondents) were fired from their jobs with a private drug rehabilitation organization because they ingested peyote for sacramental purposes at a ceremony of the Native American Church, of which both are members. When respondents applied to petitioner Employment Division (hereinafter petitioner) for unemployment compensation, they were determined to be ineligible for benefits because they had been discharged for work-related "misconduct." The Oregon Court of Appeals reversed that determination, holding that the denial of benefits violated respondents' free exercise rights under the First Amendment.

On appeal to the Oregon Supreme Court, petitioner argued that the denial of benefits was permissible because respondents' consumption of peyote was a crime under Oregon law. The Oregon Supreme Court reasoned, however, that the criminality of respondents' peyote use was irrelevant to resolution of their constitutional claim—since the purpose of the "misconduct" provision under which respondents had been disqualified was not to enforce the State's criminal laws but to preserve the financial integrity of the compensation fund, and since that purpose was inadequate to justify the burden that disqualification imposed on respondents' religious practice. Citing our decisions in *Sherbert v. Verner*, and

Thomas v. Review Bd., Indiana Employment Security Div., 450 U.S. 707, 101 S.Ct. 1425, 67 L.Ed.2d 624 (1981), the court concluded that respondents were entitled to payment of unemployment benefits. We granted certiorari.

Before this Court in 1987, petitioner continued to maintain that the illegality of respondents' peyote consumption was relevant to their constitutional claim. We agreed, concluding that "if a State has prohibited through its criminal laws certain kinds of religiously motivated conduct without violating the First Amendment, it certainly follows that it may impose the lesser burden of denying unemployment compensation benefits to persons who engage in that conduct." *Employment Div., Dept. of Human Resources of Oregon v. Smith,* 485 U.S. 660, 670, 108 S.Ct. 1444, 1450, 99 L.Ed.2d 753 (1988) (*Smith I*). We noted, however, that the Oregon Supreme Court had not decided whether respondents' sacramental use of peyote was in fact proscribed by Oregon's controlled substance law, and that this issue was a matter of dispute between the parties. Being "uncertain about the legality of the religious use of peyote in Oregon," we determined that it would not be "appropriate for us to decide whether the practice is protected by the Federal Constitution." Accordingly, we vacated the judgment of the Oregon Supreme Court and remanded for further proceedings.

On remand, the Oregon Supreme Court held that respondents' religiously inspired use of peyote fell within the prohibition of the Oregon statute, which "makes no exception for the sacramental use" of the drug. It then considered whether that prohibition was valid under the Free Exercise Clause, and concluded that it was not. The court therefore reaffirmed its previous ruling that the State could not deny unemployment benefits to respondents for having engaged in that practice.

We again granted certiorari.

II

Respondents' claim for relief rests on our decisions in *Sherbert v. Verner, Thomas v. Review Bd. of Indiana Employment Security Div.,* and *Hobbie v. Unemployment Appeals Comm'n of Florida,* 480 U.S. 136, 107 S.Ct. 1046, 94 L.Ed.2d 190 (1987), in which we held that a State could not condition the availability of unemployment insurance on an individual's willingness to forgo conduct required by his religion. As we observed in *Smith I,* however, the conduct at issue in those cases was not prohibited by law. We held that distinction to be critical, for "if Oregon does prohibit the religious use of peyote, and if that prohibition is consistent with the Federal Constitution, there is no federal right to engage in that conduct in Oregon," and "the State is free to withhold unemployment compensation from respondents for engaging in work-related misconduct, despite its religious motivation." Now that the Oregon Supreme Court has confirmed that Oregon does prohibit the religious use of peyote, we proceed to consider whether that prohibition is permissible under the Free Exercise Clause.

A

The Free Exercise Clause of the First Amendment, which has been made applicable to the States by incorporation into the Fourteenth Amendment, provides that "Congress shall make no law respecting an establishment of religion, or *prohibiting the free exercise thereof....*" The free exercise of religion means, first and foremost, the right to believe and profess whatever religious doctrine one desires. Thus, the First Amendment obviously excludes all "governmental regulation of religious *beliefs* as such." *Sherbert.* The government may not compel affirmation of religious belief, punish the expression of religious doctrines it believes to be false, impose special disabilities on the basis of religious views or religious status, or lend its power to one or the other side in controversies over religious authority or dogma.

But the "exercise of religion" often involves not only belief and profession but the performance of (or abstention from) physical acts: assembling with others for a worship service, participating in sacramental use of bread and wine, proselytizing, abstaining from certain foods or certain modes of transportation. It would be true, we think (though no case of ours has involved the point), that a State would be "prohibiting the free exercise [of religion]" if it sought to ban such acts or abstentions only when they are engaged in for religious reasons, or only because of the religious belief that they display. It would doubtless be unconstitutional, for example, to ban the casting of "statues that are to be used for worship purposes," or to prohibit bowing down before a golden calf.

Respondents in the present case, however, seek to carry the meaning of "prohibiting the free exercise [of religion]" one large step further. They contend that their religious motivation for using peyote places them beyond the reach of a criminal law that is not specifically directed at their religious practice, and that is concededly constitutional as applied to those who use the drug for other reasons. They assert, in other words, that "prohibiting the free exercise [of religion]" includes requiring any individual to observe a generally applicable law that requires (or forbids) the performance of an act that his religious belief forbids (or requires). As a textual matter, we do not think the words must be given that meaning. * * *

* * * We have never held that an individual's religious beliefs excuse him from compliance with an otherwise valid law prohibiting conduct that the State is free to regulate. On the contrary, the record of more than a century of our free exercise jurisprudence contradicts that proposition. As described succinctly by Justice Frankfurter in *Minersville School Dist. Bd. of Ed. v. Gobitis,* 310 U.S. 586, 594–595, 60 S.Ct. 1010, 1012–1013, 84 L.Ed. 1375 (1940): "Conscientious scruples have not, in the course of the long struggle for religious toleration, relieved the individual from obedience to a general law not aimed at the pro-

motion or restriction of religious beliefs. The mere possession of religious convictions which contradict the relevant concerns of a political society does not relieve the citizen from the discharge of political responsibilities (footnote omitted)." We first had occasion to assert that principle in *Reynolds v. United States,* 98 U.S. 145, 25 L.Ed. 244 (1879), where we rejected the claim that criminal laws against polygamy could not be constitutionally applied to those whose religion commanded the practice. "Laws," we said, "are made for the government of actions, and while they cannot interfere with mere religious belief and opinions, they may with practices. . . . Can a man excuse his practices to the contrary because of his religious belief? To permit this would be to make the professed doctrines of religious belief superior to the law of the land, and in effect to permit every citizen to become a law unto himself."

Subsequent decisions have consistently held that the right of free exercise does not relieve an individual of the obligation to comply with a "valid and neutral law of general applicability on the ground that the law proscribes (or prescribes) conduct that his religion prescribes (or proscribes)." * * *

Our most recent decision involving a neutral, generally applicable regulatory law that compelled activity forbidden by an individual's religion was *United States v. Lee,* 455 U.S., at 258–261, 102 S.Ct., at 1055–1057. There, an Amish employer, on behalf of himself and his employees, sought exemption from collection and payment of Social Security taxes on the ground that the Amish faith prohibited participation in governmental support programs. We rejected the claim that an exemption was constitutionally required. There would be no way, we observed, to distinguish the Amish believer's objection to Social Security taxes from the religious objections that others might have to the collection or use of other taxes. "If, for example, a religious adherent believes war is a sin, and if a certain percentage of the federal budget can be identified as devoted to war-related activities, such individuals would have a similarly valid claim to be exempt from paying that percentage of the income tax. The tax system could not function if denominations were allowed to challenge the tax system because tax payments were spent in a manner that violates their religious belief."

The only decisions in which we have held that the First Amendment bars application of a neutral, generally applicable law to religiously motivated action have involved not the Free Exercise Clause alone, but the Free Exercise Clause in conjunction with other constitutional protections, such as freedom of speech and of the press, see *Cantwell v. Connecticut* (invalidating a licensing system for religious and charitable solicitations under which the administrator had discretion to deny a license to any cause he deemed nonreligious); *Murdock v. Pennsylvania* (invalidating a flat tax on solicitation as applied to the dissemination of religious ideas); *Follett v. McCormick* (same), or the right of parents, acknowledged in *Pierce v. Society of Sisters*, to direct the education of their children, see *Wisconsin v. Yoder* (invalidating compulsory school-attendance laws as applied to Amish parents who refused on religious grounds to send their children to school). Some of our cases prohibiting compelled expression, decided exclusively upon free speech grounds, have also involved freedom of religion. And it is easy to envision a case in which a challenge on freedom of association grounds would likewise be reinforced by Free Exercise Clause concerns.

The present case does not present such a hybrid situation, but a free exercise claim unconnected with any communicative activity or parental right. Respondents urge us to hold, quite simply, that when otherwise prohibitable conduct is accompanied by religious convictions, not only the convictions but the conduct itself must be free from governmental regulation. We have never held that, and decline to do so now. There being no contention that Oregon's drug law represents an attempt to regulate religious beliefs, the communication of religious beliefs, or the raising of one's children in those beliefs, the rule to which we have adhered ever since *Reynolds* plainly controls. "Our cases do not at their farthest reach support the proposition that a stance of conscientious opposition relieves an objector from any colliding duty fixed by a democratic government." *Gillette v. United States.*

B

Respondents argue that even though exemption from generally applicable criminal laws need not automatically be extended to religiously motivated actors, at least the claim for a religious exemption must be evaluated under the balancing test set forth in *Sherbert v. Verner.* Under the *Sherbert* test, governmental actions that substantially burden a religious practice must be justified by a compelling governmental interest. Applying that test we have, on three occasions, invalidated state unemployment compensation rules that conditioned the availability of benefits upon an applicant's willingness to work under conditions forbidden by his religion. We have never invalidated any governmental action on the basis of the *Sherbert* test except the denial of unemployment compensation. Although we have sometimes purported to apply the *Sherbert* test in contexts other than that, we have always found the test satisfied. In recent years we have abstained from applying the *Sherbert* test (outside the unemployment compensation field) at all. In *Bowen v. Roy,* 476 U.S. 693, 106 S.Ct. 2147, 90 L.Ed.2d 735 (1986), we declined to apply *Sherbert* analysis to a federal statutory scheme that required benefit applicants and recipients to provide their Social Security numbers. The plaintiffs in that case asserted that it would violate their religious beliefs to obtain and provide a Social Security number for their daughter. We held the statute's application to the plaintiffs valid regardless of whether it was necessary to effectuate a compelling interest. In *Lyng v. Northwest Indian Cemetery Protective Assn.,* 485 U.S. 439, 108 S.Ct. 1319, 99 L.Ed.2d 534 (1988), we declined to apply *Sherbert* analysis to the Government's logging and road construction activities on lands used for religious purposes by several Native American Tribes, even though it was undisputed that the activities "could have devastating effects on traditional Indian religious practices." In *Goldman v. Wein-*

berger, we rejected application of the *Sherbert* test to military dress regulations that forbade the wearing of yarmulkes. In *O'Lone v. Estate of Shabazz*, 482 U.S. 342, 107 S.Ct. 2400, 96 L.Ed.2d 282 (1987), we sustained, without mentioning the *Sherbert* test, a prison's refusal to excuse inmates from work requirements to attend worship services.

Even if we were inclined to breathe into *Sherbert* some life beyond the unemployment compensation field, we would not apply it to require exemptions from a generally applicable criminal law. The *Sherbert* test, it must be recalled, was developed in a context that lent itself to individualized governmental assessment of the reasons for the relevant conduct. As a plurality of the Court noted in *Roy*, a distinctive feature of unemployment compensation programs is that their eligibility criteria invite consideration of the particular circumstances behind an applicant's unemployment: "The statutory conditions [in *Sherbert* and *Thomas*] provided that a person was not eligible for unemployment compensation benefits if, 'without good cause,' he had quit work or refused available work. The 'good cause' standard created a mechanism for individualized exemptions." As the plurality pointed out in *Roy,* our decisions in the unemployment cases stand for the proposition that where the State has in place a system of individual exemptions, it may not refuse to extend that system to cases of "religious hardship" without compelling reason.

Whether or not the decisions are that limited, they at least have nothing to do with an across-the-board criminal prohibition on a particular form of conduct. Although, as noted earlier, we have sometimes used the *Sherbert* test to analyze free exercise challenges to such laws, we have never applied the test to invalidate one. We conclude today that the sounder approach, and the approach in accord with the vast majority of our precedents, is to hold the test inapplicable to such challenges. The government's ability to enforce generally applicable prohibitions of socially harmful conduct, like its ability to carry out other aspects of public policy, "cannot depend on measuring the effects of a governmental action on a religious objector's spiritual development." *Lyng.* To make an individual's obligation to obey such a law contingent upon the law's coincidence with his religious beliefs, except where the State's interest is "compelling"—permitting him, by virtue of his beliefs, "to become a law unto himself,"—contradicts both constitutional tradition and common sense.

The "compelling government interest" requirement seems benign, because it is familiar from other fields. But using it as the standard that must be met before the government may accord different treatment on the basis of race, or before the government may regulate the content of speech, is not remotely comparable to using it for the purpose asserted here. What it produces in those other fields—equality of treatment and an unrestricted flow of contending speech—are constitutional norms; what it would produce here—a private right to ignore generally applicable laws—is a constitutional anomaly.[3]

Nor is it possible to limit the impact of respondents' proposal by requiring a "compelling state interest" only when the conduct prohibited is "central" to the individual's religion. It is no more appropriate for judges to determine the "centrality" of religious beliefs before applying a "compelling interest" test in the free exercise field, than it would be for them to determine the "importance" of ideas before applying the "compelling interest" test in the free speech field. What principle of law or logic can be brought to bear to contradict a believer's assertion that a particular act is "central" to his personal faith? Judging the centrality of different religious practices is akin to the unacceptable "business of evaluating the relative merits of differing religious claims." As we reaffirmed only last Term, "[i]t is not within the judicial ken to question the centrality of particular beliefs or practices to a faith, or the validity of particular litigants' interpretations of those creeds." *Hernandez v. Commissioner,* 490 U.S., at 699, 109 S.Ct., at 2148. Repeatedly and in many different contexts, we have warned that courts must not presume to determine the place of a particular belief in a religion or the plausibility of a religious claim.

If the "compelling interest" test is to be applied at all, then, it must be applied across the board, to all actions thought to be religiously commanded. Moreover, if "compelling interest" really means what it says (and watering it down here would subvert its rigor in the other fields where it is applied), many laws will not meet the test. Any society adopting such a system would be courting anarchy, but that danger increases in direct proportion to the society's diversity of religious beliefs, and its determination to coerce or suppress none of them. Precisely because "we are a cosmopolitan nation made up of people of almost every conceivable religious preference," and precisely because we value and protect that religious divergence, we cannot afford the luxury of deeming *presumptively invalid,* as applied to the religious objector, every regulation of conduct that does not protect an interest of the highest order. The rule respondents favor would open the prospect of constitutionally required religious exemptions from civic obligations of

---

3. Justice O'Connor suggests that "[t]here is nothing talismanic about neutral laws of general applicability," and that all laws burdening religious practices should be subject to compelling-interest scrutiny because "the First Amendment unequivocally makes freedom of religion, like freedom from race discrimination and freedom of speech, a 'constitutional nor[m],' not an 'anomaly.'" But this comparison with other fields supports, rather than undermines, the conclusion we draw today. Just as we subject to the most exacting scrutiny laws that make classifications based on race, or on the content of speech, so too we strictly scrutinize governmental classifications based on religion. But we have held that race-neutral laws that have the *effect* of disproportionately disadvantaging a particular racial group do not thereby become subject to compelling-interest analysis under the Equal Protection Clause; and we have held that generally applicable laws unconcerned with regulating speech that have the *effect* of interfering with speech do not thereby become subject to compelling-interest analysis under the First Amendment. Our conclusion that generally applicable, religion-neutral laws that have the effect of burdening a particular religious practice need not be justified by a compelling governmental interest is the only approach compatible with these precedents.

almost every conceivable kind—ranging from compulsory military service, to the payment of taxes; to health and safety regulation such as manslaughter and child neglect laws, compulsory vaccination laws, drug laws, and traffic laws; to social welfare legislation such as minimum wage laws, child labor laws, animal cruelty laws, environmental protection laws, and laws providing for equality of opportunity for the races. The First Amendment's protection of religious liberty does not require this.

Values that are protected against government interference through enshrinement in the Bill of Rights are not thereby banished from the political process. Just as a society that believes in the negative protection accorded to the press by the First Amendment is likely to enact laws that affirmatively foster the dissemination of the printed word, so also a society that believes in the negative protection accorded to religious belief can be expected to be solicitous of that value in its legislation as well. It is therefore not surprising that a number of States have made an exception to their drug laws for sacramental peyote use. But to say that a nondiscriminatory religious-practice exemption is permitted, or even that it is desirable, is not to say that it is constitutionally required, and that the appropriate occasions for its creation can be discerned by the courts. It may fairly be said that leaving accommodation to the political process will place at a relative disadvantage those religious practices that are not widely engaged in; but that unavoidable consequence of democratic government must be preferred to a system in which each conscience is a law unto itself or in which judges weigh the social importance of all laws against the centrality of all religious beliefs.

* * *

Because respondents' ingestion of peyote was prohibited under Oregon law, and because that prohibition is constitutional, Oregon may, consistent with the Free Exercise Clause, deny respondents unemployment compensation when their dismissal results from use of the drug. The decision of the Oregon Supreme Court is accordingly reversed.

JUSTICE O'CONNOR, with whom JUSTICE BRENNAN, JUSTICE MARSHALL, and JUSTICE BLACKMUN join as to Parts I and II, concurring in the judgment.*

Although I agree with the result the Court reaches in this case, I cannot join its opinion. In my view, today's holding dramatically departs from well-settled First Amendment jurisprudence, appears unnecessary to resolve the question presented, and is incompatible with our Nation's fundamental commitment to individual religious liberty.

* * *

II

The Court today extracts from our long history of free exercise precedents the single categorical rule that "if prohibiting the exercise of

---

* Although Justice Brennan, Justice Marshall, and Justice Blackmun join Parts I and II of this opinion, they do not concur in the judgment.

religion ... is ... merely the incidental effect of a generally applicable and otherwise valid provision, the First Amendment has not been offended." Indeed, the Court holds that where the law is a generally applicable criminal prohibition, our usual free exercise jurisprudence does not even apply. To reach this sweeping result, however, the Court must not only give a strained reading of the First Amendment but must also disregard our consistent application of free exercise doctrine to cases involving generally applicable regulations that burden religious conduct.

A

* * * As the Court recognizes * * * the "free *exercise*" of religion often, if not invariably, requires the performance of (or abstention from) certain acts. "[B]elief and action cannot be neatly confined in logic-tight compartments." *Yoder.* Because the First Amendment does not distinguish between religious belief and religious conduct, conduct motivated by sincere religious belief, like the belief itself, must be at least presumptively protected by the Free Exercise Clause.

The Court today, however, interprets the Clause to permit the government to prohibit, without justification, conduct mandated by an individual's religious beliefs, so long as that prohibition is generally applicable. But a law that prohibits certain conduct—conduct that happens to be an act of worship for someone—manifestly does prohibit that person's free exercise of his religion. A person who is barred from engaging in religiously motivated conduct is barred from freely exercising his religion. Moreover, that person is barred from freely exercising his religion regardless of whether the law prohibits the conduct only when engaged in for religious reasons, only by members of that religion, or by all persons. It is difficult to deny that a law that prohibits religiously motivated conduct, even if the law is generally applicable, does not at least implicate First Amendment concerns.

The Court responds that generally applicable laws are "one large step" removed from laws aimed at specific religious practices. The First Amendment, however, does not distinguish between laws that are generally applicable and laws that target particular religious practices. Indeed, few States would be so naive as to enact a law directly prohibiting or burdening a religious practice as such. Our free exercise cases have all concerned generally applicable laws that had the effect of significantly burdening a religious practice. If the First Amendment is to have any vitality, it ought not be construed to cover only the extreme and hypothetical situation in which a State directly targets a religious practice. * * *

To say that a person's right to free exercise has been burdened, of course, does not mean that he has an absolute right to engage in the conduct. Under our established First Amendment jurisprudence, we have recognized that the freedom to act, unlike the freedom to believe, cannot be absolute. Instead, we have respected both the First Amendment's express textual mandate and the governmental interest in regulation of conduct by requiring the government to justify any substantial burden on religiously motivated conduct by a compelling state interest and by means narrowly tailored to achieve that interest. The compelling interest test effectuates the First Amendment's command that religious liberty is an independent liberty, that it occupies a preferred position, and that the Court will not permit encroachments upon this liberty, whether direct or indirect, unless required by clear and compelling governmental interests "of the highest order," *Yoder.* * * *

The Court attempts to support its narrow reading of the Clause by claiming that "[w]e have never held that an individual's religious beliefs excuse him from compliance with an otherwise valid law prohibiting conduct that the State is free to regulate." But as the Court later notes, as it must, in cases such as *Cantwell* and *Yoder* we have in fact interpreted the Free Exercise Clause to forbid application of a generally applicable prohibition to religiously motivated conduct. Indeed, in *Yoder* we expressly rejected the interpretation the Court now adopts:

> "[O]ur decisions have rejected the idea that religiously grounded conduct is always outside the protection of the Free Exercise Clause. It is true that activities of individuals, even when religiously based, are often subject to regulation by the States in the exercise of their undoubted power to promote the health, safety, and general welfare, or the Federal Government in the exercise of its delegated powers. But to agree that religiously grounded conduct must often be subject to the broad police power of the State is not to deny that there are areas of conduct protected by the Free Exercise Clause of the First Amendment and thus beyond the power of the State to control, *even under regulations of general applicability....*

> " ... A regulation neutral on its face may, in its application, nonetheless offend the constitutional requirement for government neutrality if it unduly burdens the free exercise of religion."

The Court endeavors to escape from our decisions in *Cantwell* and *Yoder* by labeling them "hybrid" decisions, but there is no denying that both cases expressly relied on the Free Exercise Clause, and that we have consistently regarded those cases as part of the mainstream of our free exercise jurisprudence. Moreover, in each of the other cases cited by the Court to support its categorical rule, we rejected the particular constitutional claims before us only after carefully weighing the competing interests. That we rejected the free exercise claims in those cases hardly calls into question the applicability of First Amendment doctrine in the first place. Indeed, it is surely unusual to judge the vitality of a constitutional doctrine by looking to the win-loss record of the plaintiffs who happen to come before us.

B

Respondents, of course, do not contend that their conduct is automatically immune from all governmental regulation simply because it is motivated by their sincere religious beliefs. The Court's rejection of that argument, might therefore be regarded as merely harmless dictum. Rather, respondents invoke our traditional compelling interest test to argue that the Free Exercise Clause requires the State to grant them a limited exemption from its general criminal prohibition against the possession of peyote. The Court today, however, denies them even the opportunity to make that argument, concluding that "the sounder approach, and the approach in accord with the vast majority of our precedents, is to hold the [compelling interest] test inapplicable to" challenges to general criminal prohibitions.

In my view, however, the essence of a free exercise claim is relief from a burden imposed by government on religious practices or beliefs, whether the burden is imposed directly through laws that prohibit or compel specific religious practices, or indirectly through laws that, in effect, make abandonment of one's own religion or conformity to the religious beliefs of others the price of an equal place in the civil community. * * * A State that makes criminal an individual's religiously motivated conduct burdens that individual's free exercise of religion in the severest manner possible, for it "results in the choice to the individual of either abandoning his religious principle or facing criminal prosecution." *Braunfeld.* I would have thought it beyond argument that such laws implicate free exercise concerns.

Indeed, we have never distinguished between cases in which a State conditions receipt of a benefit on conduct prohibited by religious beliefs and cases in which a State affirmatively prohibits such conduct. The *Sherbert* compelling interest test applies in both kinds of cases. * * * A neutral criminal law prohibiting conduct that a State may legitimately regulate is, if anything, *more* burdensome than a neutral civil statute placing legitimate conditions on the award of a state benefit.

* * * To me, the sounder approach—the approach more consistent with our role as judges to decide each case on its individual merits—is to apply [the compelling interest] test in each case to determine whether the burden on the specific plaintiffs before us is constitutionally significant and whether the particular criminal interest asserted by the State before us is compelling. Even if, as an empirical matter, a government's criminal laws might usually serve a compelling interest in health, safety, or public order, the First Amendment at least requires a case-by-case determination of the question, sensitive to the facts of each particular claim. Given the range of conduct that a State might legitimately make criminal, we cannot assume, merely because a law carries criminal sanctions and is generally applicable, that the First Amendment *never* requires the State to grant a limited exemption for religiously motivated conduct.

* * *

* * * [The cases] cited by the Court for the proposition that we have rejected application of the *Sherbert* test outside the unemployment compensation field, are distinguishable because they arose in the narrow, specialized contexts in which we have not traditionally required the

government to justify a burden on religious conduct by articulating a compelling interest. See *Goldman* ("Our review of military regulations challenged on First Amendment grounds is far more deferential than constitutional review of similar laws or regulations designed for civilian society"); *O'Lone v. Estate of Shabazz*, 482 U.S. 342, 349, 107 S.Ct. 2400, 2404, 96 L.Ed.2d 282 (1987) ("[P]rison regulations alleged to infringe constitutional rights are judged under a 'reasonableness' test less restrictive than that ordinarily applied to alleged infringements of fundamental constitutional rights") (citation omitted). That we did not apply the compelling interest test in these cases says nothing about whether the test should continue to apply in paradigm free exercise cases such as the one presented here.

The Court today gives no convincing reason to depart from settled First Amendment jurisprudence. There is nothing talismanic about neutral laws of general applicability or general criminal prohibitions, for laws neutral toward religion can coerce a person to violate his religious conscience or intrude upon his religious duties just as effectively as laws aimed at religion. Although the Court suggests that the compelling interest test, as applied to generally applicable laws, would result in a "constitutional anomaly," the First Amendment unequivocally makes freedom of religion, like freedom from race discrimination and freedom of speech, a "constitutional nor[m]," not an "anomaly." Nor would application of our established free exercise doctrine to this case necessarily be incompatible with our equal protection cases. We have in any event recognized that the Free Exercise Clause protects values distinct from those protected by the Equal Protection Clause. As the language of the Clause itself makes clear, an individual's free exercise of religion is a preferred constitutional activity. A law that makes criminal such an activity therefore triggers constitutional concern—and heightened judicial scrutiny—even if it does not target the particular religious conduct at issue. Our free speech cases similarly recognize that neutral regulations that affect free speech values are subject to a balancing, rather than categorical, approach. The Court's parade of horribles, not only fails as a reason for discarding the compelling interest test, it instead demonstrates just the opposite: that courts have been quite capable of applying our free exercise jurisprudence to strike sensible balances between religious liberty and competing state interests.

Finally, the Court today suggests that the disfavoring of minority religions is an "unavoidable consequence" under our system of government and that accommodation of such religions must be left to the political process. In my view, however, the First Amendment was enacted precisely to protect the rights of those whose religious practices are not shared by the majority and may be viewed with hostility. The history of our free exercise doctrine amply demonstrates the harsh impact majoritarian rule has had on unpopular or emerging religious groups such as the Jehovah's Witnesses and the Amish. Indeed, the words of Justice Jackson in *West Virginia State Bd. of Ed. v. Barnette* (overruling

Minersville School Dist. v. Gobitis, 310 U.S. 586, 60 S.Ct. 1010, 84 L.Ed. 1375 (1940)) are apt:

"The very purpose of a Bill of Rights was to withdraw certain subjects from the vicissitudes of political controversy, to place them beyond the reach of majorities and officials and to establish them as legal principles to be applied by the courts. One's right to life, liberty, and property, to free speech, a free press, freedom of worship and assembly, and other fundamental rights may not be submitted to vote; they depend on the outcome of no elections."

* * * The compelling interest test reflects the First Amendment's mandate of preserving religious liberty to the fullest extent possible in a pluralistic society. For the Court to deem this command a "luxury," is to denigrate "[t]he very purpose of a Bill of Rights."

III

The Court's holding today not only misreads settled First Amendment precedent; it appears to be unnecessary to this case. I would reach the same result applying our established free exercise jurisprudence.

A

There is no dispute that Oregon's criminal prohibition of peyote places a severe burden on the ability of respondents to freely exercise their religion. Peyote is a sacrament of the Native American Church and is regarded as vital to respondents' ability to practice their religion. As we noted in *Smith I,* the Oregon Supreme Court concluded that "the Native American Church is a recognized religion, that peyote is a sacrament of that church, and that respondent's beliefs were sincerely held." Under Oregon law, as construed by that State's highest court, members of the Native American Church must choose between carrying out the ritual embodying their religious beliefs and avoidance of criminal prosecution. That choice is, in my view, more than sufficient to trigger First Amendment scrutiny.

There is also no dispute that Oregon has a significant interest in enforcing laws that control the possession and use of controlled substances by its citizens. As we recently noted, drug abuse is "one of the greatest problems affecting the health and welfare of our population" and thus "one of the most serious problems confronting our society today." *Treasury Employees v. Von Raab,* 489 U.S. 656, 668, 674, 109 S.Ct. 1384, 1395, 103 L.Ed.2d 685 (1989). Indeed, under federal law (incorporated by Oregon law in relevant part), peyote is specifically regulated as a Schedule I controlled substance, which means that Congress has found that it has a high potential for abuse, that there is no currently accepted medical use, and that there is a lack of accepted safety for use of the drug under medical supervision. In light of our recent decisions holding that the governmental interests in the collection of income tax, a comprehensive Social Security system, and military conscription, are compelling, respondents do not seriously dispute that

Oregon has a compelling interest in prohibiting the possession of peyote by its citizens.

B

Thus, the critical question in this case is whether exempting respondents from the State's general criminal prohibition "will unduly interfere with fulfillment of the governmental interest." *Lee* * * *. Although the question is close, I would conclude that uniform application of Oregon's criminal prohibition is "essential to accomplish" * * * its overriding interest in preventing the physical harm caused by the use of a Schedule I controlled substance. Oregon's criminal prohibition represents that State's judgment that the possession and use of controlled substances, even by only one person, is inherently harmful and dangerous. Because the health effects caused by the use of controlled substances exist regardless of the motivation of the user, the use of such substances, even for religious purposes, violates the very purpose of the laws that prohibit them. Moreover, in view of the societal interest in preventing trafficking in controlled substances, uniform application of the criminal prohibition at issue is essential to the effectiveness of Oregon's stated interest in preventing any possession of peyote.

For these reasons, I believe that granting a selective exemption in this case would seriously impair Oregon's compelling interest in prohibiting possession of peyote by its citizens. Under such circumstances, the Free Exercise Clause does not require the State to accommodate respondents' religiously motivated conduct. * * *

Respondents contend that any incompatibility is belied by the fact that the Federal Government and several States provide exemptions for the religious use of peyote. But other governments may surely choose to grant an exemption without Oregon, with its specific asserted interest in uniform application of its drug laws, being *required* to do so by the First Amendment. Respondents also note that the sacramental use of peyote is central to the tenets of the Native American Church, but I agree with the Court, that because " '[i]t is not within the judicial ken to question the centrality of particular beliefs or practices to a faith,' " our determination of the constitutionality of Oregon's general criminal prohibition cannot, and should not, turn on the centrality of the particular religious practice at issue. This does not mean, of course, that courts may not make factual findings as to whether a claimant holds a sincerely held religious belief that conflicts with, and thus is burdened by, the challenged law. The distinction between questions of centrality and questions of sincerity and burden is admittedly fine, but it is one that is an established part of our free exercise doctrine, and one that courts are capable of making.

I would therefore adhere to our established free exercise jurisprudence and hold that the State in this case has a compelling interest in regulating peyote use by its citizens and that accommodating respondents' religiously motivated conduct "will unduly interfere with fulfillment of the governmental interest." *Lee.* Accordingly, I concur in the judgment of the Court.

JUSTICE BLACKMUN, with whom JUSTICE BRENNAN and JUSTICE MARSHALL join, dissenting.

This Court over the years painstakingly has developed a consistent and exacting standard to test the constitutionality of a state statute that burdens the free exercise of religion. Such a statute may stand only if the law in general, and the State's refusal to allow a religious exemption in particular, are justified by a compelling interest that cannot be served by less restrictive means.

Until today, I thought this was a settled and inviolate principle of this Court's First Amendment jurisprudence. The majority, however, perfunctorily dismisses it as a "constitutional anomaly." As carefully detailed in Justice O'Connor's concurring opinion, the majority is able to arrive at this view only by mischaracterizing this Court's precedents. The Court discards leading free exercise cases * * * as "hybrid." The Court views traditional free exercise analysis as somehow inapplicable to criminal prohibitions (as opposed to conditions on the receipt of benefits), and to state laws of general applicability (as opposed, presumably, to laws that expressly single out religious practices). The Court cites cases in which, due to various exceptional circumstances, we found strict scrutiny inapposite, to hint that the Court has repudiated that standard altogether. In short, it effectuates a wholesale overturning of settled law concerning the Religion Clauses of our Constitution. One hopes that the Court is aware of the consequences, and that its result is not a product of overreaction to the serious problems the country's drug crisis has generated.

This distorted view of our precedents leads the majority to conclude that strict scrutiny of a state law burdening the free exercise of religion is a "luxury" that a well-ordered society cannot afford, and that the repression of minority religions is an "unavoidable consequence of democratic government." I do not believe the Founders thought their dearly bought freedom from religious persecution a "luxury," but an essential element of liberty—and they could not have thought religious intolerance "unavoidable," for they drafted the Religion Clauses precisely in order to avoid that intolerance.

For these reasons, I agree with Justice O'Connor's analysis of the applicable free exercise doctrine, and I join parts I and II of her opinion. As she points out, "the critical question in this case is whether exempting respondents from the State's general criminal prohibition 'will unduly interfere with fulfillment of the governmental interest.'" I do disagree, however, with her specific answer to that question.

I

In weighing the clear interest of respondents Smith and Black (hereinafter respondents) in the free exercise of their religion against Oregon's asserted interest in enforcing its drug laws, it is important to articulate in precise terms the state interest involved. It is not the State's broad interest in fighting the critical "war on drugs" that must be weighed against respondents' claim, but the State's narrow interest in refusing to make an exception for the religious, ceremonial use of peyote. Failure to reduce the competing interests to the same plane of generality tends to distort the weighing process in the State's favor.

The State's interest in enforcing its prohibition, in order to be sufficiently compelling to outweigh a free exercise claim, cannot be merely abstract or symbolic. The State cannot plausibly assert that unbending application of a criminal prohibition is essential to fulfill any compelling interest, if it does not, in fact, attempt to enforce that prohibition. In this case, the State actually has not evinced any concrete interest in enforcing its drug laws against religious users of peyote. Oregon has never sought to prosecute respondents, and does not claim that it has made significant enforcement efforts against other religious users of peyote. The State's asserted interest thus amounts only to the symbolic preservation of an unenforced prohibition. * * *

Similarly, this Court's prior decisions have not allowed a government to rely on mere speculation about potential harms, but have demanded evidentiary support for a refusal to allow a religious exception. In this case, the State's justification for refusing to recognize an exception to its criminal laws for religious peyote use is entirely speculative.

The State proclaims an interest in protecting the health and safety of its citizens from the dangers of unlawful drugs. It offers, however, no evidence that the religious use of peyote has ever harmed anyone.[4] The factual findings of other courts cast doubt on the State's assumption that religious use of peyote is harmful.

The fact that peyote is classified as a Schedule I controlled substance does not, by itself, show that any and all uses of peyote, in any circumstance, are inherently harmful and dangerous. The Federal Government, which created the classifications of unlawful drugs from which Oregon's drug laws are derived, apparently does not find peyote so dangerous as to preclude an exemption for religious use.[5] Moreover, other Schedule I drugs have lawful uses.

4. This dearth of evidence is not surprising, since the State never asserted this health and safety interest before the Oregon courts; thus, there was no opportunity for factfinding concerning the alleged dangers of peyote use. What has now become the State's principal argument for its view that the criminal prohibition is enforceable against religious use of peyote rests on no evidentiary foundation at all.

5. See 21 CFR § 1307.31 (1989) ("The listing of peyote as a controlled substance in Schedule I does not apply to the nondrug use of peyote in bona fide religious ceremonies of the Native American Church, and members of the Native American Church so using peyote are exempt from registration. Any person who manufactures peyote for or distributes peyote to the Native American Church, however, is required to obtain registration annually and to comply with all other requirements of law"); see *Olsen v. Drug Enforcement Admin.*, 279 U.S.App. D.C. 1, 6–7, 878 F.2d 1458, 1463–1464 (1989) (explaining DEA's rationale for the exception).

Moreover, 23 States, including many that have significant Native American populations, have statutory or judicially crafted exemptions in their drug laws for religious

The carefully circumscribed ritual context in which respondents used peyote is far removed from the irresponsible and unrestricted recreational use of unlawful drugs.[6] The Native American Church's internal restrictions on, and supervision of, its members' use of peyote substantially obviate the State's health and safety concerns. See *Olsen,* at 10, 878 F.2d, at 1467 (" 'The Administrator [of the Drug Enforcement Administration (DEA)] finds that ... the Native American Church's use of peyote is isolated to specific ceremonial occasions,' " and so " 'an accommodation can be made for a religious organization which uses peyote in circumscribed ceremonies' " (quoting DEA Final Order)); *id.,* at 7, 878 F.2d, at 1464 ("[F]or members of the Native American Church, use of peyote outside the ritual is sacrilegious") * * *.

Moreover, just as in *Yoder,* the values and interests of those seeking a religious exemption in this case are congruent, to a great degree, with those the State seeks to promote through its drug laws. Not only does the church's doctrine forbid nonreligious use of peyote; it also generally advocates self-reliance, familial responsibility, and abstinence from alcohol. There is considerable evidence that the spiritual and social support provided by the church has been effective in combating the tragic effects of alcoholism on the Native American population. * * * Far from promoting the lawless and irresponsible use of drugs, Native American Church members' spiritual code exemplifies values that Oregon's drug laws are presumably intended to foster.

The State also seeks to support its refusal to make an exception for religious use of peyote by invoking its interest in abolishing drug trafficking. There is, however, practically no illegal traffic in peyote. Also, the availability of peyote for religious use, even if Oregon were to allow an exemption from its criminal laws, would still be strictly controlled by federal regulations, and by the State of Texas, the only State in which peyote grows in significant quantities. Peyote simply is not a popular drug; its distribution for use in religious rituals has nothing to do with the vast and violent traffic in illegal narcotics that plagues this country.

Finally, the State argues that granting an exception for religious peyote use would erode its interest in the uniform, fair, and certain enforcement of its drug laws. The State fears that, if it grants an exemption for religious peyote use, a flood of other claims to religious exemptions will follow. It would then be placed in a dilemma, it says, between allowing a patchwork of exemptions that would hinder its law

use of peyote. Although this does not prove that Oregon must have such an exception too, it is significant that these States, and the Federal Government, all find their (presumably compelling) interests in controlling the use of dangerous drugs compatible with an exemption for religious use of peyote.

6. In this respect, respondents' use of peyote seems closely analogous to the sacramental use of wine by the Roman Catholic Church. During Prohibition, the Federal Government exempted such use of wine from its general ban on possession and use of alcohol. However compelling the Government's then general interest in prohibiting the use of alcohol may have been, it could not plausibly have asserted an interest sufficiently compelling to outweigh Catholics' right to take communion.

enforcement efforts, and risking a violation of the Establishment Clause by arbitrarily limiting its religious exemptions. This argument, however, could be made in almost any free exercise case. This Court, however, consistently has rejected similar arguments in past free exercise cases, and it should do so here as well.

The State's apprehension of a flood of other religious claims is purely speculative. Almost half the States, and the Federal Government, have maintained an exemption for religious peyote use for many years, and apparently have not found themselves overwhelmed by claims to other religious exemptions.[8] Allowing an exemption for religious peyote use would not necessarily oblige the State to grant a similar exemption to other religious groups. The unusual circumstances that make the religious use of peyote compatible with the State's interests in health and safety and in preventing drug trafficking would not apply to other religious claims. Some religions, for example, might not restrict drug use to a limited ceremonial context, as does the Native American Church. See, *e.g.,* *Olsen,* 279 U.S.App.D.C., at 7, 878 F.2d, at 1464 ("[T]he Ethiopian Zion Coptic Church ... teaches that marijuana is properly smoked 'continually all day' "). Some religious claims, involve drugs such as marijuana and heroin, in which there is significant illegal traffic, with its attendant greed and violence, so that it would be difficult to grant a religious exemption without seriously compromising law enforcement efforts. That the State might grant an exemption for religious peyote use, but deny other religious claims arising in different circumstances, would not violate the Establishment Clause. Though the State must treat all religions equally, and not favor one over another, this obligation is fulfilled by the uniform application of the "compelling interest" *test* to all free exercise claims, not by reaching uniform *results* as to all claims. A showing that religious peyote use does not unduly interfere with the State's interests is "one that probably few other religious groups or sects could make," this does not mean that an exemption limited to peyote use is tantamount to an establishment of religion.

II

Finally, although I agree with Justice O'Connor that courts should refrain from delving into questions whether, as a matter of religious doctrine, a particular practice is "central" to the religion, I do not think this means that the courts must turn a blind eye to the severe impact of a State's restrictions on the adherents of a minority religion.

Respondents believe, and their sincerity has *never* been at issue, that the peyote plant embodies their deity, and eating it is an act of worship and communion. Without peyote, they could not enact the essential ritual of their religion. See Brief for Association on American Indian Affairs et al. as *Amici Curiae* 5–6 ("To the members, peyote is consecrated with powers to heal body, mind and spirit. It is a teacher; it teaches

---

8. Over the years, various sects have raised free exercise claims regarding drug use. In no reported case, except those involving claims of religious peyote use, has the claimant prevailed.

the way to spiritual life through living in harmony and balance with the forces of the Creation. The rituals are an integral part of the life process. They embody a form of worship in which the sacrament Peyote is the means for communicating with the Great Spirit").

If Oregon can constitutionally prosecute them for this act of worship, they, like the Amish, may be "forced to migrate to some other and more tolerant region." *Yoder.* This potentially devastating impact must be viewed in light of the federal policy—reached in reaction to many years of religious persecution and intolerance—of protecting the religious freedom of Native Americans. See American Indian Religious Freedom Act, 92 Stat. 469, 42 U.S.C. § 1996 (1982 ed.) * * *. Congress recognized that certain substances, such as peyote, "have religious significance because they are sacred, they have power, they heal, they are necessary to the exercise of the rites of the religion, they are necessary to the cultural integrity of the tribe, and, therefore, religious survival." H.R.Rep. No. 95–1308, p. 2 (1978) * * *.

The American Indian Religious Freedom Act, in itself, may not create rights enforceable against government action restricting religious freedom, but this Court must scrupulously apply its free exercise analysis to the religious claims of Native Americans, however unorthodox they may be. Otherwise, both the First Amendment and the stated policy of Congress will offer to Native Americans merely an unfulfilled and hollow promise.

III

For these reasons, I conclude that Oregon's interest in enforcing its drug laws against religious use of peyote is not sufficiently compelling to outweigh respondents' right to the free exercise of their religion. Since the State could not constitutionally enforce its criminal prohibition against respondents, the interests underlying the State's drug laws cannot justify its denial of unemployment benefits. Absent such justification, the State's regulatory interest in denying benefits for religiously motivated "misconduct," is indistinguishable from the state interests this Court has rejected in *Frazee, Hobbie, Thomas,* and *Sherbert.* The State of Oregon cannot, consistently with the Free Exercise Clause, deny respondents unemployment benefits.

I dissent.

Notes and Questions

1. *Laws of General Applicability.* The Court holds that there is no constitutional requirement that government entities create exemptions to "generally applicable" laws to accommodate even core religious practices. Yet the question naturally arises as to whether the "general applicability" of a law should be determined in the free exercise context or in a more general context—i.e. is a law that has significant negative impact on religious practices "generally applicable" for free exercise purposes? The Court answers yes. Thus the test is a highly formalistic one: is a law generally applicable on its face without regard to any

disparate impact it has on religious practices? If the answer is yes, there is no constitutional duty to create an exemption and no inquiry into the centrality or importance of the religious practice interfered with. This looks very much like the pre-*Sherbert* approach initially used in *Reynolds v. United States, supra.* Under that approach there is a dichotomy between belief and practice, with the former being absolutely protected but the latter receiving no protection when it conflicts with legal requirements. If this is so, what exactly does the Free Exercise Clause protect against beyond bare animus toward religion or a particular religion? If intentional discrimination is the only thing covered by the Free Exercise Clause, does the clause protect the free exercise of religion in any serious way? Consider that many minority religions that won't be considered in the drafting of "generally applicable laws," and therefore will often find it harder to gain exemptions to such laws, are more practice oriented than the more dominant Christian traditions in the United States (although it is a vast oversimplification to refer to the latter as belief rather than practice based). Does this suggest that the Free Exercise Clause protects those who need protection the least while providing little practical protection for those whose religious practices may be significantly affected by government action? Does the fact that government entities *may* give exemptions if they choose to alter your answer?

2. *Hybrid Cases.* The Court explains that its rule regarding laws of general applicability does not apply in certain hybrid cases. According to the Court, hybrid cases are those where the free exercise right combines with another right such as free speech or parental rights. This enables the Court to distinguish cases such as *Barnette* and *Yoder*, because the Court argues those cases really involved hybrid claims and therefore do not govern the outcome of cases where only a claim for an exemption under the Free Exercise Clause is sought. This makes sense in the context of *Barnette*, which obviously involved both free exercise and free expression issues, but what about *Yoder*? Wasn't the Court's decision in *Yoder* based on analysis under the Free Exercise Clause? Were the parental rights really central to that case as they were in *Pierce v. Society of Sisters*? Even if the Court is correct about *Yoder*, what purpose does the hybrid analysis serve? If neither the free exercise or other asserted claim is adequate on its own, why should the combination of two inadequate claims be successful? If the other asserted right (free speech, parenting, etc . . .) is adequate on its own what purpose does the free exercise claim serve? Is it possible the Court used the hybrid claim notion simply to distinguish precedent that went against the Court's decision in *Smith*? Even though it seems the *Smith* Court meant to use the hybrid claim idea to support its limitation of the *Sherbert* approach, can one now use the hybrid claim notion to expand the number of situations where *Smith* doesn't apply by expanding the types of claims that may be hybridized with free exercise claims? The likelihood of this approach being regularly successful appears weak. Steven H. Aden & Lee J. Strang, *When a "Rule" Doesn't Rule: The Failure of the Oregon Employment Division v. Smith "Hybrid Rights Exception,"* 108 PENN ST. L. REV. 573 (2003). Another possible argument for lessening the impact of *Smith* is to use the Court's suggestion that religious exemptions may be required under the Free Exercise Clause when a government entity creates nonreligious exemptions to laws of general applicability. *Tenafly Eruv Association, Inc. v. Borough of Tenafly*, 309 F.3d 144 (3d Cir. 2002).

3. *Unemployment Cases.* The Court suggests that the compelling interest test is generally limited to unemployment cases (and possibly hybrid cases). In fact, other than *Yoder*, all the cases where parties have prevailed on a claim under the compelling interest test were unemployment cases. *See also Bowen v.*

Roy, 476 U.S. 693, 106 S.Ct. 2147, 90 L.Ed.2d 735 (1986) (plurality opinion). Given this fact, is the Court's reading of *Sherbert* accurate? Did the *Sherbert* Court really intend its reasoning to be limited to unemployment cases? The Court points out that the test is well adapted for unemployment cases because unemployment systems have a built in exemption regime and thus lend themselves well to religious exemptions. This makes the failure to exempt in unemployment cases less explainable absent a compelling interest. Is this a reason to limit the compelling interest test to the unemployment context? If not, why do you think the Court does so? If so, why didn't the *Sherbert* or *Hobbie* Courts so limit the test? What about *Yoder*?

4. *Religious Practice Versus Religious Belief.* The *Smith* Court draws the same distinction between religious belief and religious practice that was drawn by the *Reynolds* and *Davis* Courts in the late 1800's. Once this distinction is drawn if religious practices violate a "law of general applicability" the result is predetermined unless an exception such as "hybrid rights" applies. Yet many religious groups do not draw the artificial distinction between belief and practice drawn by the Court. The distinction reflects some of the tendencies of dualistic models. By creating a formalistic black and white distinction (belief versus practice), the Court ignores a reality long recognized by many religious people and scholars—i.e. that the line between belief and practice is not always clear and that regulating practices may also regulate central beliefs. For example, under *Smith* it would be possible for every state in the country to pass a uniform animal slaughtering law that would require all animals slaughtered for consumption to be killed by lethal injection. This would mean that observant Jews would have no way to get Kosher meat within the United States, a central aspect of traditional Jewish belief and practice (at least for those who eat meat), because the Kosher slaughtering of animals requires a different procedure. Would this regulate belief or practice? If you think this couldn't happen imagine if the hypothetical involved an even smaller religious minority and a less well known religious requirement. Some scholars have argued that the Court's approach is Christocentric—that it reflects a mainstream Christian view of religion and assures only those who hold that view or similar views will have comparable free exercise rights. *See* Stephen M. Feldman, Please Don't Wish Me a Merry Christmas: A Critical History of the Separation of Church and State at 248–49 (NYU Press 1999). Is this true after *Smith*? If so, how can the Court avoid such a result without opening many "generally applicable" laws to challenges by religious individuals?

The Response to *Smith*

The response to *Smith* by scholars and Congress was primarily negative. Numerous articles penned by legal scholars and practitioners attacked the *Smith* decision on a variety of fronts (you will read some of these articles, as well as some that defend *Smith*, in Chapter Seven). An unprecedented coalition of religious and civil liberties organizations banded together and lobbied Congress for a law providing increased protection for the free exercise of religion. Congress responded by passing the Religious Freedom Restoration Act of 1993, 42 U.S.C. §§ 2000bb-*et seq.* (RFRA), which required that government entities could not "substantially burden" one's free exercise of religion (whether through a generally applicable law or not) without demonstrating that the burden is the "least restrictive means" of furthering a "compelling governmental interest." Additionally, several states passed their own RFRA's. In *City of Boerne v. Flores*, 521 U.S. 507, 117 S.Ct. 2157, 138 L.Ed.2d 624 (1997), the Court struck down the federal RFRA as applied to state and local governments because it exceeded Congress' authority under § 5 of the Fourteenth Amendment. RFRA appears to be constitutional as applied to the federal government, but separation of powers problems may remain. Additionally, state RFRA's are constitutional so long as they are consistent with the relevant state constitution.

More recently, Congress passed the Religious Land Use And Institutionalized Persons Act, 42 U.S.C. §§ 2000cc-*et seq.* (RLUIPA). The Act was designed to be more limited in scope than RFRA, protecting religious land use (primarily zoning situations) and religious freedom for institutionalized persons such as prisoners. The Act applied the same standard as that applied under RFRA: government action that places a substantial burden on religious activity in the land use and prison contexts requires a "compelling governmental interested" and the "least restrictive means" necessary to further that interest. Congress passed the Act pursuant to its spending, commerce, and § 5 (of the Fourteenth Amendment) powers. Several lower courts have already held that the provisions applicable to prisoners are unconstitutional because they exceed Congress' authority, but the land use provisions have enjoyed greater success. Marci A. Hamilton, *Federalism and the Public Good: the True Story Behind the Religious Land Use and Institutionalized Persons Act*, 78 Ind. L. J. 311, 352–52 (2003). At least one court, however, has held the land use provisions of the law to be unconstitutional as well. *Elsinore Christian Center v. City of Lake Elsinore*, 291 F.Supp.2d 1083 (C.D.Cal.2003). The future of RLUIPA as of the early part of 2004 is unclear. The law may very well be unconstitutional or it may be that only part of the law is unconstitutional. Even if RLUIPA is constitutional it must be remembered that it only provides protection in the land use and institutionalized persons contexts.

F. INTENTIONAL DISCRIMINATION AND FREE EXERCISE RIGHTS

The Free Exercise Clause does protect against government action *aimed* at interfering with the free exercise of religion. Thus, government may not pass a law that targets a specific religion(s) or religion generally for inferior treatment. The following case, decided three years after *Smith*, makes this explicit. The case also makes clear that a law need not specify the infringement of religious exercise as one of its goals in order to be unconstitutional, so long as there is adequate evidence that the law was intended to discriminate against a religious entity or individual. This reasoning raises significant questions given the Court's recent holdings that government funding may be used at religious institutions under facially neutral programs that allow for private choice. *See supra* Chapter Four.

CHURCH OF THE LUKUMI BABALU AYE, INC. v. CITY OF HIALEAH

Supreme Court of the United States, 1993.
508 U.S. 520, 113 S.Ct. 2217, 124 L.Ed.2d 472.

JUSTICE KENNEDY delivered the opinion of the Court, except as to Part II–A–2.*

The principle that government may not enact laws that suppress religious belief or practice is so well understood that few violations are recorded in our opinions. Concerned that this fundamental nonpersecution principle of the First Amendment was implicated here, however, we granted certiorari.

Our review confirms that the laws in question were enacted by officials who did not understand, failed to perceive, or chose to ignore the fact that their official actions violated the Nation's essential commitment to religious freedom. The challenged laws had an impermissible object; and in all events the principle of general applicability was violated because the secular ends asserted in defense of the laws were pursued only with respect to conduct motivated by religious beliefs. We invalidate the challenged enactments and reverse the judgment of the Court of Appeals.

I

A

This case involves practices of the Santeria religion, which originated in the 19th century. When hundreds of thousands of members of the Yoruba people were brought as slaves from western Africa to Cuba, their traditional African religion absorbed significant elements of Roman Catholicism. The resulting syncretion, or fusion, is Santeria, "the way of the saints." The Cuban Yoruba express their devotion to spirits, called *orishas,* through the iconography of Catholic saints, Catholic symbols are often present at Santeria rites, and Santeria devotees attend the Catholic sacraments.

The Santeria faith teaches that every individual has a destiny from God, a destiny fulfilled with the aid and energy of the *orishas.* The basis of the Santeria religion is the nurture of a personal relation with the *orishas,* and one of the principal forms of devotion is an animal sacrifice. The sacrifice of animals as part of religious rituals has ancient roots. Animal sacrifice is mentioned throughout the Old Testament, and it played an important role in the practice of Judaism before destruction of the second Temple in Jerusalem. In modern Islam, there is an annual sacrifice commemorating Abraham's sacrifice of a ram in the stead of his son.

---

* The Chief Justice, Justice Scalia, and Justice Thomas join all but Part II–A–2 of this opinion. Justice White joins all but Part II–A of this opinion. Justice Souter joins only Parts I, III, and IV of this opinion.

According to Santeria teaching, the *orishas* are powerful but not immortal. They depend for survival on the sacrifice. Sacrifices are performed at birth, marriage, and death rites, for the cure of the sick, for the initiation of new members and priests, and during an annual celebration. Animals sacrificed in Santeria rituals include chickens, pigeons, doves, ducks, guinea pigs, goats, sheep, and turtles. The animals are killed by the cutting of the carotid arteries in the neck. The sacrificed animal is cooked and eaten, except after healing and death rituals.

Santeria adherents faced widespread persecution in Cuba, so the religion and its rituals were practiced in secret. The open practice of Santeria and its rites remains infrequent. The religion was brought to this Nation most often by exiles from the Cuban revolution. The District Court estimated that there are at least 50,000 practitioners in South Florida today.

B

Petitioner Church of the Lukumi Babalu Aye, Inc. (Church), is a not-for-profit corporation organized under Florida law in 1973. The Church and its congregants practice the Santeria religion. The president of the Church is petitioner Ernesto Pichardo, who is also the Church's priest and holds the religious title of *Italero,* the second highest in the Santeria faith. In April 1987, the Church leased land in the City of Hialeah, Florida, and announced plans to establish a house of worship as well as a school, cultural center, and museum. Pichardo indicated that the Church's goal was to bring the practice of the Santeria faith, including its ritual of animal sacrifice, into the open. * * *

The prospect of a Santeria church in their midst was distressing to many members of the Hialeah community, and the announcement of the plans to open a Santeria church in Hialeah prompted the city council to hold an emergency public session on June 9, 1987. * * *

* * * First, the city council adopted Resolution 87–66, which noted the "concern" expressed by residents of the city "that certain religions may propose to engage in practices which are inconsistent with public morals, peace or safety," and declared that "[t]he City reiterates its commitment to a prohibition against any and all acts of any and all religious groups which are inconsistent with public morals, peace or safety." Next, the council approved an emergency ordinance, which incorporated in full, except as to penalty, Florida's animal cruelty laws. Among other things, the incorporated state law subjected to criminal punishment "[w]hoever ... unnecessarily or cruelly ... kills any animal."

The city council desired to undertake further legislative action, but Florida law prohibited a municipality from enacting legislation relating to animal cruelty that conflicted with state law. To obtain clarification, Hialeah's city attorney requested an opinion from the attorney general of Florida as to whether [the Florida statute] prohibited "a religious group from sacrificing an animal in a religious ritual or practice" and whether the city could enact ordinances "making religious animal sacrifice unlawful." The attorney * * * concluded that the "ritual sacrifice of animals for purposes other than food consumption" was not a "necessary" killing and so was prohibited * * *. The attorney general appeared to define "unnecessary" as "done without any useful motive, in a spirit of wanton cruelty or for the mere pleasure of destruction without being in any sense beneficial or useful to the person killing the animal." He advised that religious animal sacrifice was against state law, so that a city ordinance prohibiting it would not be in conflict.

The city council responded at first with a hortatory enactment * * * that noted its residents' "great concern regarding the possibility of public ritualistic animal sacrifices" and the state-law prohibition. The resolution declared the city policy "to oppose the ritual sacrifices of animals" within Hialeah and announced that any person or organization practicing animal sacrifice "will be prosecuted."

In September 1987, the city council adopted three substantive ordinances addressing the issue of religious animal sacrifice. Ordinance 87–52 defined "sacrifice" as "to unnecessarily kill, torment, torture, or mutilate an animal in a public or private ritual or ceremony not for the primary purpose of food consumption," and prohibited owning or possessing an animal "intending to use such animal for food purposes." It restricted application of this prohibition, however, to any individual or group that "kills, slaughters or sacrifices animals for any type of ritual, regardless of whether or not the flesh or blood of the animal is to be consumed." The ordinance contained an exemption for slaughtering by "licensed establishment[s]" of animals "specifically raised for food purposes." Declaring, moreover, that the city council "has determined that the sacrificing of animals within the city limits is contrary to the public health, safety, welfare and morals of the community," the city council adopted Ordinance 87–71. That ordinance defined sacrifice as had Ordinance 87–52, and then provided that "[i]t shall be unlawful for any person, persons, corporations or associations to sacrifice any animal within the corporate limits of the City of Hialeah, Florida." The final Ordinance, 87–72, defined "slaughter" as "the killing of animals for food" and prohibited slaughter outside of areas zoned for slaughterhouse use. The ordinance provided an exemption, however, for the slaughter or processing for sale of "small numbers of hogs and/or cattle per week in accordance with an exemption provided by state law." All ordinances and resolutions passed the city council by unanimous vote. Violations of each of the four ordinances were punishable by fines not exceeding $500 or imprisonment not exceeding 60 days, or both.

Following enactment of these ordinances, the Church and Pichardo filed this action pursuant to 42 U.S.C. § 1983 in the United States District Court for the Southern District of Florida. * * *

II

* * * The city does not argue that Santeria is not a "religion" within the meaning of the First Amendment. Nor could it. Although the

practice of animal sacrifice may seem abhorrent to some, "religious beliefs need not be acceptable, logical, consistent, or comprehensible to others in order to merit First Amendment protection." *Thomas v. Review Bd.* Given the historical association between animal sacrifice and religious worship, petitioners' assertion that animal sacrifice is an integral part of their religion "cannot be deemed bizarre or incredible." *Frazee v. Illinois Dept. of Employment Security.* Neither the city nor the courts below, moreover, have questioned the sincerity of petitioners' professed desire to conduct animal sacrifices for religious reasons. We must consider petitioners' First Amendment claim.

In addressing the constitutional protection for free exercise of religion, our cases establish the general proposition that a law that is neutral and of general applicability need not be justified by a compelling governmental interest even if the law has the incidental effect of burdening a particular religious practice. Neutrality and general applicability are interrelated, and, as becomes apparent in this case, failure to satisfy one requirement is a likely indication that the other has not been satisfied. A law failing to satisfy these requirements must be justified by a compelling governmental interest and must be narrowly tailored to advance that interest. These ordinances fail to satisfy the *Smith* requirements. We begin by discussing neutrality.

A

In our Establishment Clause cases we have often stated the principle that the First Amendment forbids an official purpose to disapprove of a particular religion or of religion in general. These cases, however, for the most part have addressed governmental efforts to benefit religion or particular religions, and so have dealt with a question different, at least in its formulation and emphasis, from the issue here. Petitioners allege an attempt to disfavor their religion because of the religious ceremonies it commands, and the Free Exercise Clause is dispositive in our analysis.

At a minimum, the protections of the Free Exercise Clause pertain if the law at issue discriminates against some or all religious beliefs or regulates or prohibits conduct because it is undertaken for religious reasons. Indeed, it was "historical instances of religious persecution and intolerance that gave concern to those who drafted the Free Exercise Clause." *Bowen v. Roy,* 476 U.S. 693, 703, 106 S.Ct. 2147, 2154, 90 L.Ed.2d 735 (1986) (opinion of Burger, C.J.). These principles, though not often at issue in our Free Exercise Clause cases, have played a role in some. In *McDaniel v. Paty,* for example, we invalidated a State law that disqualified members of the clergy from holding certain public offices, because it "impose[d] special disabilities on the basis of . . . religious status." On the same principle, in *Fowler v. Rhode Island,* we found that a municipal ordinance was applied in an unconstitutional manner when interpreted to prohibit preaching in a public park by a Jehovah's Witness but to permit preaching during the course of a Catholic mass or Protestant church service.

1

Although a law targeting religious beliefs as such is never permissible * * * if the object of a law is to infringe upon or restrict practices because of their religious motivation, the law is not neutral; and it is invalid unless it is justified by a compelling interest and is narrowly tailored to advance that interest. There are, of course, many ways of demonstrating that the object or purpose of a law is the suppression of religion or religious conduct. To determine the object of a law, we must begin with its text, for the minimum requirement of neutrality is that a law not discriminate on its face. A law lacks facial neutrality if it refers to a religious practice without a secular meaning discernable from the language or context. Petitioners contend that three of the ordinances fail this test of facial neutrality because they use the words "sacrifice" and "ritual," words with strong religious connotations. We agree that these words are consistent with the claim of facial discrimination, but the argument is not conclusive. The words "sacrifice" and "ritual" have a religious origin, but current use admits also of secular meanings. The ordinances, furthermore, define "sacrifice" in secular terms, without referring to religious practices.

We reject the contention advanced by the city, that our inquiry must end with the text of the laws at issue. Facial neutrality is not determinative. The Free Exercise Clause, like the Establishment Clause, extends beyond facial discrimination. The Clause "forbids subtle departures from neutrality," *Gillette v. United States*, and "covert suppression of particular religious beliefs," *Bowen v. Roy* (opinion of Burger, C.J.). Official action that targets religious conduct for distinctive treatment cannot be shielded by mere compliance with the requirement of facial neutrality. The Free Exercise Clause protects against governmental hostility which is masked, as well as overt. "The Court must survey meticulously the circumstances of governmental categories to eliminate, as it were, religious gerrymanders." *Walz v. Tax Comm'n* (Harlan, J., concurring).

The record in this case compels the conclusion that suppression of the central element of the Santeria worship service was the object of the ordinances. First, though use of the words "sacrifice" and "ritual" does not compel a finding of improper targeting of the Santeria religion, the choice of these words is support for our conclusion. There are further respects in which the text of the city council's enactments discloses the improper attempt to target Santeria. Resolution 87–66 * * * recited that "residents and citizens of the City of Hialeah have expressed their concern that certain religions may propose to engage in practices which are inconsistent with public morals, peace or safety," and "reiterate[d]" the city's commitment to prohibit "any and all [such] acts of any and all religious groups." No one suggests, and on this record it cannot be maintained, that city officials had in mind a religion other than Santeria.

It becomes evident that these ordinances target Santeria sacrifice when the ordinances' operation is considered. Apart from the text, the effect of a law in its real operation is strong evidence of its object. To be sure, adverse impact will not always lead to a finding of impermissible targeting. For example, a social harm may have been a legitimate concern of government for reasons quite apart from discrimination. The subject at hand does implicate, of course, multiple concerns unrelated to religious animosity, for example, the suffering or mistreatment visited upon the sacrificed animals and health hazards from improper disposal. But the ordinances when considered together disclose an object remote from these legitimate concerns. The design of these laws accomplishes instead a "religious gerrymander," an impermissible attempt to target petitioners and their religious practices.

It is a necessary conclusion that almost the only conduct subject to Ordinances 87-40, 87-52, and 87-71 is the religious exercise of Santeria church members. The texts show that they were drafted in tandem to achieve this result. We begin with Ordinance 87-71. It prohibits the sacrifice of animals, but defines sacrifice as "to unnecessarily kill ... an animal in a public or private ritual or ceremony not for the primary purpose of food consumption." The definition excludes almost all killings of animals except for religious sacrifice, and the primary purpose requirement narrows the proscribed category even further, in particular by exempting kosher slaughter. We need not discuss whether this differential treatment of two religions is itself an independent constitutional violation. It suffices to recite this feature of the law as support for our conclusion that Santeria alone was the exclusive legislative concern. The net result of the gerrymander is that few if any killings of animals are prohibited other than Santeria sacrifice, which is proscribed because it occurs during a ritual or ceremony and its primary purpose is to make an offering to the *orishas,* not food consumption. Indeed, careful drafting ensured that, although Santeria sacrifice is prohibited, killings that are no more necessary or humane in almost all other circumstances are unpunished.

Operating in similar fashion is Ordinance 87-52, which prohibits the "possess[ion], sacrifice, or slaughter" of an animal with the "inten[t] to use such animal for food purposes." This prohibition, extending to the keeping of an animal as well as the killing itself, applies if the animal is killed in "any type of ritual" and there is an intent to use the animal for food, whether or not it is in fact consumed for food. The ordinance exempts, however, "any licensed [food] establishment" with regard to "any animals which are specifically raised for food purposes," if the activity is permitted by zoning and other laws. This exception, too, seems intended to cover kosher slaughter. Again, the burden of the ordinance, in practical terms, falls on Santeria adherents but almost no others: If the killing is—unlike most Santeria sacrifices—unaccompanied by the intent to use the animal for food, then it is not prohibited by Ordinance 87-52; if the killing is specifically for food but does not occur during the course of "any type of ritual," it again falls outside the prohibition; and if the killing is for food and occurs during the course of a ritual, it is still exempted if it occurs in a properly zoned and licensed establishment and involves animals "specifically raised for food purposes." A pattern of exemptions parallels the pattern of narrow prohibitions. Each contributes to the gerrymander.

Ordinance 87–40 incorporates the Florida animal cruelty statute. Its prohibition is broad on its face, punishing "[w]hoever ... unnecessarily ... kills any animal." The city claims that this ordinance is the epitome of a neutral prohibition. The problem, however, is the interpretation given to the ordinance by respondent and the Florida attorney general. Killings for religious reasons are deemed unnecessary, whereas most other killings fall outside the prohibition. The city, on what seems to be a *per se* basis, deems hunting, slaughter of animals for food, eradication of insects and pests, and euthanasia as necessary. There is no indication in the record that respondent has concluded that hunting or fishing for sport is unnecessary. Indeed, one of the few reported Florida cases decided under § 828.12 concludes that the use of live rabbits to train greyhounds is not unnecessary. Further, because it requires an evaluation of the particular justification for the killing, this ordinance represents a system of "individualized governmental assessment of the reasons for the relevant conduct," *Smith*. As we noted in *Smith*, in circumstances in which individualized exemptions from a general requirement are available, the government "may not refuse to extend that system to cases of 'religious hardship' without compelling reason." Respondent's application of the ordinance's test of necessity devalues religious reasons for killing by judging them to be of lesser import than nonreligious reasons. Thus, religious practice is being singled out for discriminatory treatment.

We also find significant evidence of the ordinances' improper targeting of Santeria sacrifice in the fact that they proscribe more religious conduct than is necessary to achieve their stated ends. It is not unreasonable to infer, at least when there are no persuasive indications to the contrary, that a law which visits "gratuitous restrictions" on religious conduct, seeks not to effectuate the stated governmental interests, but to suppress the conduct because of its religious motivation.

The legitimate governmental interests in protecting the public health and preventing cruelty to animals could be addressed by restrictions stopping far short of a flat prohibition of all Santeria sacrificial practice. If improper disposal, not the sacrifice itself, is the harm to be prevented, the city could have imposed a general regulation on the disposal of organic garbage. It did not do so. Indeed, counsel for the city conceded at oral argument that, under the ordinances, Santeria sacrifices would be illegal even if they occurred in licensed, inspected, and zoned slaughterhouses. Thus, these broad ordinances prohibit Santeria sacrifice even when it does not threaten the city's interest in the public health. * * *

Under similar analysis, narrower regulation would achieve the city's interest in preventing cruelty to animals. With regard to the city's interest in ensuring the adequate care of animals, regulation of conditions and treatment, regardless of why an animal is kept, is the logical response to the city's concern, not a prohibition on possession for the purpose of sacrifice. The same is true for the city's interest in prohibiting cruel methods of killing. * * *

Ordinance 87–72—unlike the three other ordinances—does appear to apply to substantial nonreligious conduct and not to be overbroad. For our purposes here, however, the four substantive ordinances may be treated as a group for neutrality purposes. Ordinance 87–72 was passed the same day as Ordinance 87–71 and was enacted, as were the three others, in direct response to the opening of the Church. It would be implausible to suggest that the three other ordinances, but not Ordinance 87–72, had as their object the suppression of religion. We need not decide whether the Ordinance 87–72 could survive constitutional scrutiny if it existed separately; it must be invalidated because it functions, with the rest of the enactments in question, to suppress Santeria religious worship.

2

In determining if the object of a law is a neutral one under the Free Exercise Clause, we can also find guidance in our equal protection cases. As Justice Harlan noted in the related context of the Establishment Clause, "[n]eutrality in its application requires an equal protection mode of analysis." *Walz v. Tax Comm'n of New York City* (concurring opinion). Here, as in equal protection cases, we may determine the city council's object from both direct and circumstantial evidence. Relevant evidence includes, among other things, the historical background of the decision under challenge, the specific series of events leading to the enactment or official policy in question, and the legislative or administrative history, including contemporaneous statements made by members of the decisionmaking body. These objective factors bear on the question of discriminatory object.

That the ordinances were enacted " 'because of,' not merely 'in spite of,' " their suppression of Santeria religious practice, is revealed by the events preceding their enactment. Although respondent claimed at oral argument that it had experienced significant problems resulting from the sacrifice of animals within the city before the announced opening of the Church, the city council made no attempt to address the supposed problem before its meeting in June 1987, just weeks after the Church announced plans to open. The minutes and taped excerpts of the June 9 session, both of which are in the record, evidence significant hostility exhibited by residents, members of the city council, and other city officials toward the Santeria religion and its practice of animal sacrifice. The public crowd that attended the June 9 meetings interrupted statements by council members critical of Santeria with cheers and the brief comments of Pichardo with taunts. When Councilman Martinez, a supporter of the ordinances, stated that in prerevolution Cuba "people were put in jail for practicing this religion," the audience applauded.

Other statements by members of the city council were in a similar vein. * * *

Various Hialeah city officials made comparable comments. The chaplain of the Hialeah Police Department told the city council that Santeria was a sin, "foolishness," "an abomination to the Lord," and the worship of "demons." He advised the city council: "We need to be helping people and sharing with them the truth that is found in Jesus Christ." He concluded: "I would exhort you ... not to permit this Church to exist." The city attorney commented that Resolution 87–66 indicated: "This community will not tolerate religious practices which are abhorrent to its citizens...." * * * This history discloses the object of the ordinances to target animal sacrifice by Santeria worshipers because of its religious motivation.

3

In sum, the neutrality inquiry leads to one conclusion: The ordinances had as their object the suppression of religion. The pattern we have recited discloses animosity to Santeria adherents and their religious practices; the ordinances by their own terms target this religious exercise; the texts of the ordinances were gerrymandered with care to proscribe religious killings of animals but to exclude almost all secular killings; and the ordinances suppress much more religious conduct than is necessary in order to achieve the legitimate ends asserted in their defense. These ordinances are not neutral, and the court below committed clear error in failing to reach this conclusion.

B

We turn next to a second requirement of the Free Exercise Clause, the rule that laws burdening religious practice must be of general applicability. All laws are selective to some extent, but categories of selection are of paramount concern when a law has the incidental effect of burdening religious practice. The Free Exercise Clause "protect[s] religious observers against unequal treatment," *Hobbie* (Stevens, J., concurring in judgment), and inequality results when a legislature decides that the governmental interests it seeks to advance are worthy of being pursued only against conduct with a religious motivation.

The principle that government, in pursuit of legitimate interests, cannot in a selective manner impose burdens only on conduct motivated by religious belief is essential to the protection of the rights guaranteed by the Free Exercise Clause. * * * In this case we need not define with precision the standard used to evaluate whether a prohibition is of general application, for these ordinances fall well below the minimum standard necessary to protect First Amendment rights.

Respondent claims that Ordinances 87–40, 87–52, and 87–71 advance two interests: protecting the public health and preventing cruelty to animals. The ordinances are underinclusive for those ends. They fail to prohibit nonreligious conduct that endangers these interests in a similar or greater degree than Santeria sacrifice does. The underinclusion is substantial, not inconsequential. Despite the city's proffered interest in preventing cruelty to animals, the ordinances are drafted with care to forbid few killings but those occasioned by religious sacrifice. Many types of animal deaths or kills for nonreligious reasons are either not prohibited or approved by express provision. For example, fishing—which occurs in Hialeah—is legal. Extermination of mice and rats within a home is also permitted. Florida law incorporated by Ordinance 87–40 sanctions euthanasia of "stray, neglected, abandoned, or unwanted animals;" destruction of animals judicially removed from their owners "for humanitarian reasons" or when the animal "is of no commercial value;" the infliction of pain or suffering "in the interest of medical science;" the placing of poison in one's yard or enclosure; and the use of a live animal "to pursue or take wildlife or to participate in any hunting," and "to hunt wild hogs."

The city concedes that "neither the State of Florida nor the City has enacted a generally applicable ban on the killing of animals." It asserts, however, that animal sacrifice is "different" from the animal killings that are permitted by law. According to the city, it is "self-evident" that killing animals for food is "important"; the eradication of insects and pests is "obviously justified"; and the euthanasia of excess animals "makes sense." These *ipse dixits* do not explain why religion alone must bear the burden of the ordinances, when many of these secular killings fall within the city's interest in preventing the cruel treatment of animals.

The ordinances are also underinclusive with regard to the city's interest in public health, which is threatened by the disposal of animal carcasses in open public places and the consumption of uninspected meat. Neither interest is pursued by respondent with regard to conduct that is not motivated by religious conviction. The health risks posed by the improper disposal of animal carcasses are the same whether Santeria sacrifice or some nonreligious killing preceded it. The city does not, however, prohibit hunters from bringing their kill to their houses, nor does it regulate disposal after their activity. Despite substantial testimony at trial that the same public health hazards result from improper disposal of garbage by restaurants, restaurants are outside the scope of the ordinances. Improper disposal is a general problem that causes substantial health risks, but which respondent addresses only when it results from religious exercise.

The ordinances are underinclusive as well with regard to the health risk posed by consumption of uninspected meat. Under the city's ordinances, hunters may eat their kill and fishermen may eat their catch without undergoing governmental inspection. Likewise, state law requires inspection of meat that is sold but exempts meat from animals raised for the use of the owner and "members of his household and nonpaying guests and employees." The asserted interest in inspected meat is not pursued in contexts similar to that of religious animal sacrifice.

Ordinance 87–72, which prohibits the slaughter of animals outside of areas zoned for slaughterhouses, is underinclusive on its face. The ordinance includes an exemption for "any person, group, or organization" that "slaughters or processes for sale, small numbers of hogs and/or cattle per week in accordance with an exemption provided by state law." Respondent has not explained why commercial operations that slaughter "small numbers" of hogs and cattle do not implicate its professed desire to prevent cruelty to animals and preserve the public health. Although the city has classified Santeria sacrifice as slaughter, subjecting it to this ordinance, it does not regulate other killings for food in like manner.

We conclude, in sum, that each of Hialeah's ordinances pursues the city's governmental interests only against conduct motivated by religious belief. The ordinances "ha[ve] every appearance of a prohibition that society is prepared to impose upon [Santeria worshippers] but not upon itself." *Florida Star v. B.J.F.,* 491 U.S. 524, 542, 109 S.Ct. 2603, 2614, 105 L.Ed.2d 443 (1989) (Scalia, J., concurring in part and concurring in judgment). This precise evil is what the requirement of general applicability is designed to prevent.

III

A law burdening religious practice that is not neutral or not of general application must undergo the most rigorous of scrutiny. To satisfy the commands of the First Amendment, a law restrictive of religious practice must advance " 'interests of the highest order' " and must be narrowly tailored in pursuit of those interests. The compelling interest standard that we apply once a law fails to meet the *Smith* requirements is not "water[ed] ... down" but "really means what it says." *Smith,* 494 U.S., at 888, 110 S.Ct., at 1605. A law that targets religious conduct for distinctive treatment or advances legitimate governmental interests only against conduct with a religious motivation will survive strict scrutiny only in rare cases. It follows from what we have already said that these ordinances cannot withstand this scrutiny.

First, even were the governmental interests compelling, the ordinances are not drawn in narrow terms to accomplish those interests. As we have discussed, all four ordinances are overbroad or underinclusive in substantial respects. The proffered objectives are not pursued with respect to analogous non-religious conduct, and those interests could be achieved by narrower ordinances that burdened religion to a far lesser degree. The absence of narrow tailoring suffices to establish the invalidity of the ordinances.

Respondent has not demonstrated, moreover, that, in the context of these ordinances, its governmental interests are compelling. Where government restricts only conduct protected by the First Amendment and fails to enact feasible measures to restrict other conduct producing substantial harm or alleged harm of the same sort, the interest given in justification of the restriction is not compelling. It is established in our strict scrutiny jurisprudence that "a law cannot be regarded as protecting an interest 'of the highest order' ... when it leaves appreciable damage to that supposedly vital interest unprohibited." *Florida Star v. B.J.F.* (citation omitted). As we show above, the ordinances are underinclusive to a substantial extent with respect to each of the interests that respondent has asserted, and it is only conduct motivated by religious conviction that bears the weight of the governmental restrictions. There can be no serious claim that those interests justify the ordinances.

IV

The Free Exercise Clause commits government itself to religious tolerance, and upon even slight suspicion that proposals for state intervention stem from animosity to religion or distrust of its practices, all officials must pause to remember their own high duty to the Constitution and to the rights it secures. Those in office must be resolute in resisting importunate demands and must ensure that the sole reasons for imposing the burdens of law and regulation are secular. Legislators may not devise mechanisms, overt or disguised, designed to persecute or oppress a religion or its practices. The laws here in question were enacted contrary to these constitutional principles, and they are void.

Reversed.

JUSTICE SCALIA, with whom the CHIEF JUSTICE joins, concurring in part and concurring in the judgment.

The Court analyzes the "neutrality" and the "general applicability" of the Hialeah ordinances in separate sections (Parts II–A and II–B, respectively), and allocates various invalidating factors to one or the other of those sections. If it were necessary to make a clear distinction between the two terms, I would draw a line somewhat different from the Court's. But I think it is not necessary, and would frankly acknowledge that the terms are not only "interrelated," but substantially overlap.

The terms "neutrality" and "general applicability" are not to be found within the First Amendment itself, of course, but are used in *Smith*, and earlier cases to describe those characteristics which cause a law that prohibits an activity a particular individual wishes to engage in for religious reasons nonetheless not to constitute a "law ... prohibiting the free exercise" of religion within the meaning of the First Amendment. In my view, the defect of lack of neutrality applies primarily to those laws that *by their terms* impose disabilities on the basis of religion * * *; whereas the defect of lack of general applicability applies primarily to those laws which, though neutral in their terms, through their design, construction, or enforcement target the practices of a particular religion for discriminatory treatment. But certainly a law that is not of general applicability (in the sense I have described) can be considered "nonneutral"; and certainly no law that is nonneutral (in the relevant sense) can be thought to be of general applicability. Because I agree with most of the invalidating factors set forth in Part II of the Court's opinion, and because it seems to me a matter of no consequence under which rubric ("neutrality," Part II–A, or "general applicability," Part II–B) each invalidating factor is discussed, I join the judgment of the Court and all of its opinion except section 2 of Part II–A.

I do not join that section because it departs from the opinion's general focus on the object of the *laws* at issue to consider the subjective motivation of the *lawmakers, i.e.,* whether the Hialeah City Council actually *intended* to disfavor the religion of Santeria. As I have noted elsewhere, it is virtually impossible to determine the singular "motive" of a collective legislative body, and this Court has a long tradition of refraining from such inquiries.

Perhaps there are contexts in which determination of legislative motive *must* be undertaken. But I do not think that is true of analysis under the First Amendment (or the Fourteenth, to the extent it incorporates the First). The First Amendment does not refer to the purposes for which legislators enact laws, but to the effects of the laws enacted: "Congress shall make no law ... prohibiting the free exercise [of religion]. . . ." This does not put us in the business of invalidating laws by reason of the evil motives of their authors. Had the Hialeah City Council set out resolutely to suppress the practices of Santeria, but ineptly adopted ordinances that failed to do so, I do not see how those laws could be said to "prohibi[t] the free exercise" of religion. Nor, in my view, does it matter that a legislature consists entirely of the pure-hearted, if the law it enacts in fact singles out a religious practice for special burdens. * * *

JUSTICE SOUTER, concurring in part and concurring in the judgment.

This case turns on a principle about which there is no disagreement, that the Free Exercise Clause bars government action aimed at suppressing religious belief or practice. The Court holds that Hialeah's animal-sacrifice laws violate that principle, and I concur in that holding without reservation.

Because prohibiting religious exercise is the object of the laws at hand, this case does not present the more difficult issue addressed in our last free-exercise case, *Smith*, which announced the rule that a "neutral, generally applicable" law does not run afoul of the Free Exercise Clause even when it prohibits religious exercise in effect. The Court today refers to that rule in dicta, and despite my general agreement with the Court's opinion I do not join Part II, where the dicta appear, for I have doubts about whether the *Smith* rule merits adherence. I write separately to explain why the *Smith* rule is not germane to this case and to express my view that, in a case presenting the issue, the Court should re-examine the rule *Smith* declared.

According to *Smith*, if prohibiting the exercise of religion results from enforcing a "neutral, generally applicable" law, the Free Exercise Clause has not been offended. I call this the *Smith* rule to distinguish it from the noncontroversial principle, also expressed in *Smith* though established long before, that the Free Exercise Clause is offended when prohibiting religious exercise results from a law that is not neutral or generally applicable. It is this noncontroversial principle, that the Free Exercise Clause requires neutrality and general applicability, that is at issue here. * * *

* * *

* * * A law that is religion neutral on its face or in its purpose may lack neutrality in its effect by forbidding something that religion requires or requiring something that religion forbids. A secular law, applicable to all, that prohibits consumption of alcohol, for example, will affect members of religions that require the use of wine differently from members of other religions and nonbelievers, disproportionately burdening the practice of, say, Catholicism or Judaism. Without an exemption for sacramental wine, Prohibition may fail the test of religion neutrality.

It does not necessarily follow from that observation, of course, that the First Amendment requires an exemption from Prohibition; that depends on the meaning of neutrality as the Free Exercise Clause embraces it. The point here is the unremarkable one that our common notion of neutrality is broad enough to cover not merely what might be called formal neutrality, which as a free-exercise requirement would only bar laws with an object to discriminate against religion, but also what might be called substantive neutrality, which, in addition to demanding a secular object, would generally require government to accommodate religious differences by exempting religious practices from formally neutral laws. If the Free Exercise Clause secures only protection against deliberate discrimination, a formal requirement will exhaust the Clause's neutrality command; if the Free Exercise Clause, rather, safeguards a right to engage in religious activity free from unnecessary governmental interference, the Clause requires substantive, as well as formal, neutrality.[3]

Though *Smith* used the term "neutrality" without a modifier, the rule it announced plainly assumes that free-exercise neutrality is of the formal sort. Distinguishing between laws whose "object" is to prohibit religious exercise and those that prohibit religious exercise as an "incidental effect," *Smith* placed only the former within the reaches of the Free Exercise Clause; the latter, laws that satisfy formal neutrality, *Smith* would subject to no free-exercise scrutiny at all, even when they prohibit religious exercise in application. The four Justices who rejected the *Smith* rule, by contrast, read the Free Exercise Clause as embracing what I have termed substantive neutrality. The enforcement of a law "neutral on its face," they said, may "nonetheless offend [the Free Exercise Clause's] requirement for government neutrality if it unduly burdens the free exercise of religion." The rule these Justices saw as flowing from free-exercise neutrality, in contrast to the *Smith* rule,

---

3. One might further distinguish between formal neutrality and facial neutrality. While facial neutrality would permit discovery of a law's object or purpose only by analysis of the law's words, structure, and operation, formal neutrality would permit enquiry also into the intentions of those who enacted the law. For present purposes, the distinction between formal and facial neutrality is less important than the distinction between those conceptions of neutrality and substantive neutrality.

"requir[es] the government to justify *any* substantial burden on religiously motivated conduct by a compelling state interest and by means narrowly tailored to achieve that interest."

The proposition for which the *Smith* rule stands, then, is that formal neutrality, along with general applicability, are sufficient conditions for constitutionality under the Free Exercise Clause. That proposition is not at issue in this case, however, for Hialeah's animal-sacrifice ordinances are not neutral under any definition, any more than they are generally applicable. This case, rather, involves the noncontroversial principle repeated in *Smith,* that formal neutrality and general applicability are necessary conditions for free-exercise constitutionality. * * * In applying that principle the Court does not tread on troublesome ground.

* * * The question whether the protections of the Free Exercise Clause also pertain if the law at issue, though nondiscriminatory in its object, has the effect nonetheless of placing a burden on religious exercise is not before the Court today, and the Court's intimations on the matter are therefore dicta.

* * *

II

In being so readily susceptible to resolution by applying the Free Exercise Clause's "fundamental nonpersecution principle," this is far from a representative free-exercise case. While, as the Court observes, the Hialeah City Council has provided a rare example of a law actually aimed at suppressing religious exercise, *Smith* was typical of our free-exercise cases, involving as it did a formally neutral, generally applicable law. The rule *Smith* announced, however, was decidedly untypical of the cases involving the same type of law. Because *Smith* left those prior cases standing, we are left with a free-exercise jurisprudence in tension with itself, a tension that should be addressed, and that may legitimately be addressed, by reexamining the *Smith* rule in the next case that would turn upon its application.

A

In developing standards to judge the enforceability of formally neutral, generally applicable laws against the mandates of the Free Exercise Clause, the Court has addressed the concepts of neutrality and general applicability by indicating, in language hard to read as not foreclosing the *Smith* rule, that the Free Exercise Clause embraces more than mere formal neutrality, and that formal neutrality and general applicability are not sufficient conditions for free-exercise constitutionality * * *.

Not long before the *Smith* decision, indeed, the Court specifically rejected the argument that "neutral and uniform" requirements for governmental benefits need satisfy only a reasonableness standard, in part because "[s]uch a test has no basis in precedent." *Hobbie.* Rather, we have said, "[o]ur cases have established that '[t]he free exercise inquiry asks whether government has placed a substantial burden on the observation of a central religious belief or practice and, if so, whether a compelling governmental interest justifies the burden.' " *Swaggart Ministries,* 493 U.S., at 384–385, 110 S.Ct., at 692–693 (quoting *Hernandez v. Commissioner,* 490 U.S. 680, 699, 109 S.Ct. 2136, 2148, 104 L.Ed.2d 766 (1989)).

Thus we have applied the same rigorous scrutiny to burdens on religious exercise resulting from the enforcement of formally neutral, generally applicable laws as we have applied to burdens caused by laws that single out religious exercise: " 'only those interests of the highest order and those not otherwise served can overbalance legitimate claims to the free exercise of religion.' " *McDaniel v. Paty* (plurality opinion) (quoting *Yoder*). * * *

Though *Smith* sought to distinguish the free-exercise cases in which the Court mandated exemptions from secular laws of general application, I am not persuaded. *Wisconsin v. Yoder,* and *Cantwell v. Connecticut,* according to *Smith,* were not true free-exercise cases but "hybrid[s]" involving "the Free Exercise Clause in conjunction with other constitutional protections, such as freedom of speech and of the press, or the right of parents ... to direct the education of their children." Neither opinion, however, leaves any doubt that "fundamental claims of religious freedom [were] at stake." And the distinction *Smith* draws strikes me as ultimately untenable. If a hybrid claim is simply one in which another constitutional right is implicated, then the hybrid exception would probably be so vast as to swallow the *Smith* rule, and, indeed, the hybrid exception would cover the situation exemplified by *Smith,* since free speech and associational rights are certainly implicated in the peyote ritual. But if a hybrid claim is one in which a litigant would actually obtain an exemption from a formally neutral, generally applicable law under another constitutional provision, then there would have been no reason for the Court in what *Smith* calls the hybrid cases to have mentioned the Free Exercise Clause at all.

Smith sought to confine the remaining free-exercise exemption victories, which involved unemployment compensation systems, "stand[ing] for the proposition that where the State has in place a system of individual exemptions, it may not refuse to extend that system to cases of 'religious hardship' without compelling reason." But prior to *Smith* the Court had already refused to accept that explanation of the unemployment compensation cases. * * * *Smith* also distinguished the unemployment compensation cases on the ground that they did not involve "an across-the-board criminal prohibition on a particular form of conduct." But even Chief Justice Burger's plurality opinion in *Bowen v. Roy,* on which *Smith* drew for its analysis of the unemployment compensation cases, would have applied its reasonableness test only to "denial of government benefits" and not to "governmental action or legislation that criminalizes religiously inspired activity or inescapably compels conduct that some find objectionable for religious reasons," *Bowen* (opinion of Burger, C.J., joined by Powell and Rehnquist, JJ.); to the latter category of governmental action, it would have applied the test employed in *Yoder,* which involved an across-the-board criminal prohibition and which Chief Justice Burger's opinion treated as an ordinary free-exercise case.

* * *

Since holding in 1940 that the Free Exercise Clause applies to the States, the Court repeatedly has stated that the Clause sets strict limits on the government's power to burden religious exercise, whether it is a law's object to do so or its unanticipated effect. *Smith* responded to these statements by suggesting that the Court did not really mean what it said, detecting in at least the most recent opinions a lack of commitment to the compelling-interest test in the context of formally neutral laws. But even if the Court's commitment were that palid, it would argue only for moderating the language of the test, not for eliminating constitutional scrutiny altogether. In any event, I would have trouble concluding that the Court has not meant what it has said in more than a dozen cases over several decades, particularly when in the same period it repeatedly applied the compelling-interest test to require exemptions, even in a case decided the year before *Smith.* See *Frazee v. Illinois Dept. of Employment Security,* 489 U.S. 829, 109 S.Ct. 1514, 103 L.Ed.2d 914 (1989). In sum, it seems to me difficult to escape the conclusion that, whatever *Smith's* virtues, they do not include a comfortable fit with settled law.

B

The *Smith* rule, in my view, may be reexamined consistently with principles of *stare decisis.** * *

* * *

* * * One important further consideration warrants mention here, however, because it demands the reexamination I have in mind. *Smith* presents not the usual question of whether to follow a constitutional rule, but the question of which constitutional rule to follow, for *Smith* refrained from overruling prior free-exercise cases that contain a free-exercise rule fundamentally at odds with the rule *Smith* declared. *Smith,* indeed, announced its rule by relying squarely upon the precedent of prior cases. Since that precedent is nonetheless at odds with the *Smith* rule, as I have discussed above, the result is an intolerable tension in free-exercise law which may be resolved, consistently with principles of *stare decisis,* in a case in which the tension is presented and its resolution pivotal.

While the tension on which I rely exists within the body of our extant case law, a rereading of that case law will not, of course, mark the limits of any enquiry directed to reexamining the *Smith* rule, which should be reviewed in light not only of the precedent on which it was rested but also of the text of the Free Exercise Clause and its origins. As for text, *Smith* did not assert that the plain language of the Free Exercise Clause compelled its rule, but only that the rule was "a permissible reading" of the Clause. Suffice it to say that a respectable argument may be made that the pre-*Smith* law comes closer to fulfilling the language of the Free Exercise Clause than the rule *Smith* announced. "[T]he Free Exercise Clause . . . , by its terms, gives special protection to the exercise of religion," *Thomas v. Review Bd.*, specifying an activity and then flatly protecting it against government prohibition. The Clause draws no distinction between laws whose object is to prohibit religious exercise and laws with that effect, on its face seemingly applying to both.

Nor did *Smith* consider the original meaning of the Free Exercise Clause, though overlooking the opportunity was no unique transgression. Save in a handful of passing remarks, the Court has not explored the history of the Clause since its early attempts in 1879 and 1890, attempts that recent scholarship makes clear were incomplete. See generally McConnell, The Origins and Historical Understanding of Free Exercise of Religion, 103 Harv.L.Rev. 1409 (1990). The curious absence of history from our free-exercise decisions creates a stark contrast with our cases under the Establishment Clause, where historical analysis has been so prominent.

This is not the place to explore the history that a century of free-exercise opinions have overlooked, and it is enough to note that, when the opportunity to reexamine *Smith* presents itself, we may consider recent scholarship raising serious questions about the *Smith* rule's consonance with the original understanding and purpose of the Free Exercise Clause. There appears to be a strong argument from the Clause's development in the First Congress, from its origins in the post-Revolution state constitutions and pre-Revolution colonial charters, and from the philosophy of rights to which the Framers adhered, that the Clause was originally understood to preserve a right to engage in activities necessary to fulfill one's duty to one's God, unless those activities threatened the rights of others or the serious needs of the State. If, as this scholarship suggests, the Free Exercise Clause's original "purpose [was] to secure religious liberty in the individual by prohibiting any invasions thereof by civil authority," *Schempp*, then there would be powerful reason to interpret the Clause to accord with its natural reading, as applying to all laws prohibiting religious exercise in fact, not just those aimed at its prohibition, and to hold the neutrality needed to implement such a purpose to be the substantive neutrality of our pre-*Smith* cases, not the formal neutrality sufficient for constitutionality under *Smith*.[8]

---

8. The Court today observes that "historical instances of religious persecution and intolerance . . . gave concern to those who drafted the Free Exercise Clause." That is no doubt true, and of course it supports the proposition for which it was summoned, that the Free Exercise Clause forbids religious persecution. But the Court's remark merits this observation: the fact that the Framers were concerned about victims of religious persecution by no means demonstrates that the Framers in-

The scholarship on the original understanding of the Free Exercise Clause is, to be sure, not uniform. And there are differences of opinion as to the weight appropriately accorded original meaning. But whether or not one considers the original designs of the Clause binding, the interpretive significance of those designs surely ranks in the hierarchy of issues to be explored in resolving the tension inherent in free-exercise law as it stands today.

III

The extent to which the Free Exercise Clause requires government to refrain from impeding religious exercise defines nothing less than the respective relationships in our constitutional democracy of the individual to government and to God. "Neutral, generally applicable" laws, drafted as they are from the perspective of the non-adherent, have the unavoidable potential of putting the believer to a choice between God and government. Our cases now present competing answers to the question when government, while pursuing secular ends, may compel disobedience to what one believes religion commands. The case before us is rightly decided without resolving the existing tension, which remains for another day when it may be squarely faced.

JUSTICE BLACKMUN, with whom JUSTICE O'CONNOR joins, concurring in the judgment.

The Court holds today that the city of Hialeah violated the First and Fourteenth Amendments when it passed a set of restrictive ordinances explicitly directed at petitioners' religious practice. With this holding I agree. I write separately to emphasize that the First Amendment's protection of religion extends beyond those rare occasions on which the government explicitly targets religion (or a particular religion) for disfavored treatment, as is done in this case. In my view, a statute that burdens the free exercise of religion "may stand only if the law in general, and the State's refusal to allow a religious exemption in particular, are justified by a compelling interest that cannot be served by less restrictive means." The Court, however, applies a different test. It applies the test announced in *Smith,* under which "a law that is neutral and of general applicability need not be justified by a compelling governmental interest even if the law has the incidental effect of burdening a particular religious practice." I continue to believe that *Smith* was wrongly decided, because it ignored the value of religious freedom as an affirmative individual liberty and treated the Free Exercise Clause as no more than an antidiscrimination principle. Thus, while I agree with the result the Court reaches in this case, I arrive at that result by a different route.

* * *

tended the Free Exercise Clause to forbid only persecution, the inference the *Smith* rule requires. On the contrary, the eradication of persecution would mean precious little to a member of a formerly persecuted sect who was nevertheless prevented from practicing his religion by the enforcement of "neutral, generally applicable" laws. * * *

When a law discriminates against religion as such, as do the ordinances in this case, it automatically will fail strict scrutiny under *Sherbert v. Verner.* This is true because a law that targets religious practice for disfavored treatment both burdens the free exercise of religion and, by definition, is not precisely tailored to a compelling governmental interest.

Thus, unlike the majority, I do not believe that "[a] law burdening religious practice that is not neutral or not of general application must undergo the most rigorous of scrutiny." In my view, regulation that targets religion in this way, *ipso facto,* fails strict scrutiny. It is for this reason that a statute that explicitly restricts religious practices violates the First Amendment. Otherwise, however, "[t]he First Amendment ... does not distinguish between laws that are generally applicable and laws that target particular religious practices." *Smith* (opinion concurring in judgment).

It is only in the rare case that a state or local legislature will enact a law directly burdening religious practice as such. Because respondent here does single out religion in this way, the present case is an easy one to decide.

A harder case would be presented if petitioners were requesting an exemption from a generally applicable anticruelty law. The result in the case before the Court today, and the fact that every Member of the Court concurs in that result, does not necessarily reflect this Court's views of the strength of a State's interest in prohibiting cruelty to animals. This case does not present, and I therefore decline to reach, the question whether the Free Exercise Clause would require a religious exemption from a law that sincerely pursued the goal of protecting animals from cruel treatment. * * *

Notes and Questions

1. *Was the Free Exercise Clause Necessary?* The holding in *Lukumi Babalu Aye* makes sense at a number of levels. It would seem an obvious violation of the Free Exercise Clause when government targets biased laws at a particular religious sect. Yet, what does the Free Exercise Clause really add here? It could also be argued that the Hialeah ordinances violated the Establishment Clause by discouraging the Santerian religion and/or favoring locally recognized religions over Santeria. Moreover, the Cities' conduct might also violate the Equal Protection Clause. After *Smith,* it seems that intentional discrimination, and maybe hybrid claims and/or pattern of exemption situations, are the only circumstances where the Free Exercise Clause is useful. Does this make the Clause superfluous? Is this one of the reasons that some of the concurring Justices in *Lukumi Babalu Aye* urged that *Smith* should be overturned?

2. *The Reynolds Paradox. Smith* relied heavily on *Reynolds v. United States* as discussed earlier in this Chapter. Yet that case involved a law and social situation not all that different from the one in *Lukumi Babalu Aye,* albeit on a broader scale. The anti-polygamy laws were aimed at Mormons because of a public perception that polygamy was alien and repugnant to civilized society and prevailing social norms, just as the Hialeah ordinances were aimed at Santeria

because of a public perception that Santeria was alien and animal sacrifice repugnant to civilized society and prevailing social norms. Moreover, even in the absence of polygamy there was a great deal of anti-Mormon sentiment in the United States when *Reynolds* was decided, just as there was a great deal of animosity toward Santeria in the city of Hialeah. Is it possible that *Reynolds* represents a case of intentional discrimination under the *Lukumi Babalu Aye* standard? *See* Keith E. Sealing, *Polygamists Out of the Closet: Statutory and State Constitutional Prohibitions Against Polygamy are Unconstitutional Under the Free Exercise Clause*, 17 GA. ST. UNIV. L. REV. 691, 710–20 (2001) (suggesting the answer is yes). If so, what does this say about the belief/practice dichotomy it used? Couldn't *Reynolds* simply be a case of the right standard under the wrong facts—i.e. the belief/practice dichotomy is an appropriate standard in *Smith*, where there was no claim of intentional discrimination, but not in *Reynolds* where the law was targeted at Mormons?

3. *Strict Scrutiny*? What test did the Court apply to the Hialeah ordinances? Can you envision a situation where a government entity might meet that standard under facts showing an intent to discriminate against a religious entity or entities? How does the *Lukumi Babalu Aye* standard compare with the *Sherbert* standard as applied in later cases?

4. *Denial of Funding Available Under a "Neutral" Government Program.* As you read in Chapter Four, government funding may be used at religious entities so long as the funding is provided under a facially neutral program and individuals receiving the funding have a choice where to use that funding. In *Locke v. Davey*, supra at Chapter Four, the Court held that denial of scholarship funding for devotional theology training did not violate a student's rights under the Free Exercise Clause. Given the reasoning in *Lukumi Babalu Aye,* does this make sense once the Court allowed such funding under the Establishment Clause? If the Court held that Davey's free exercise rights were violated, the Supremacy Clause would have prevented the state's establishment clause from supplying a compelling governmental interest to justify the "discrimination." Might this still be possible given the limited holding in *Locke*, if a state denies funding for any use at a religious institution under a general funding program that utilizes private choice?

Chapter Seven

PERSPECTIVES ON THE FREE EXERCISE CLAUSE

A. INTRODUCTION

As the materials in Chapter Six suggest, the Free Exercise Clause has been interpreted in a variety of ways over the years. This is especially true in the context of exemptions under that Clause. Numerous scholars have written about the Free Exercise Clause. The purpose of this Chapter is to introduce you to some of the various perspectives on that clause. It would be impossible to adequately capture the rich discourse in this area in one chapter, but the material in this chapter should provide you with a taste of some of the major arguments that have arisen. All of the articles in this chapter were written by leading scholars in the field. It was hard to decide what material to include, and I had to leave out a number of excellent articles that would also merit inclusion were it not for considerations of space. Each article included in this Chapter provides an important perspective in the Free Exercise Clause debate. Please note that each of the articles has been edited and most of the footnotes deleted.

B. THE MEANING OF THE FREE EXERCISE CLAUSE

As with the Establishment Clause there has been disagreement over the meaning of the Free Exercise Clause. Does the Free Exercise Clause require government to create exemptions to laws of general applicability? Does it simply protect against intentional discrimination aimed at religious institutions or religious believers? As you read in Chapter Six, the Court has generally rejected claims for exemptions under the Free Exercise Clause, especially when religious minorities have brought those claims. Yet, at least as a matter of doctrine, the Court has shifted its position in interpreting the Free Exercise Clause. The pre-*Sherbert* cases used a different approach than that used in *Sherbert* and *Yoder*, and *Smith* (despite the Court's protestations otherwise) essentially rejected the *Sherbert/Yoder* approach. What explains these shifts in doctrine and why did the doctrinal shifts make little difference in outcomes (i.e. religious minorities generally lost before and after the institution of the "compelling interest test")? In order to address these questions it is useful to think about what the Free Exercise Clause means. Needless to say, there is significant disagreement over the meaning of that clause. The following readings are meant to give you a variety of suggestions relating to the meaning of the Free Exercise Clause. It might be useful for you to consider whether the various approaches discussed below would favor the reasoning of the *Sherbert* Court, the *Smith* Court, or neither (in a few cases the authors address this), and which approach you think best comports with the meaning of the Free Exercise Clause.

1.   The Accommodationist Perspective

One approach to Free Exercise Clause analysis would require government to accommodate religious practitioners through exemptions unless government has a truly compelling reason not to do so. The accomodationist approach in its various forms has been championed by a number of leading scholars and by the Court in *Sherbert*. The leading proponent of this approach is Professor Michael W. McConnell (now a judge on the United States Court of Appeals for the 10th Circuit). In a string of well regarded articles Professor McConnell made the case for the accommodationist perspective in both the free exercise and establishment contexts, although his approach has garnered more support in the Free Exercise Clause area. The article excerpted below is a bit more recent than his classic articles on this subject (although it is by no means his most recent), and it provides a post-*Smith* discussion of his approach. This is followed by an excerpt from an article by another leading scholar in the field, Ira Lupu, which is based on a talk he gave at a symposium for the BYU Law Review in 1993. Professor Lupu's piece is a very accessible discussion of the results of *Smith*, and his commentary on that case suggests that he would favor a more accommodationist perspective.

MICHAEL W. McCONNELL, *RELIGIOUS FREEDOM AT A CROSSROADS*

59 U. Chi. L. Rev. 115 (1992).

The Religion Clause jurisprudence of the Warren and Burger Courts is coming to an end—a victim, if not of its own internal contradictions, then of changes of personnel on the Court. To this we might happily say "good riddance," for a more confused and often counterproductive mode of interpreting the First Amendment would have been difficult to devise. * * *

The old jurisprudence failed to distinguish between government action that promotes the free exercise of diverse faiths and government action that promotes the majority's understanding of proper religion—treating both with suspicion. The Court's conception of the First Amendment more closely resembled freedom from religion (except in its most private manifestations) than freedom of religion. The animating principle was not pluralism and diversity, but maintenance of a scrupulous secularism in all aspects of public life touched by government. This approach successfully warded off the dangers of majoritarian religion, but it exacerbated the equal and opposite danger of majoritarian indifference or intolerance toward religion. There is reason to believe this period is coming to an end.

There is no guarantee, however, that the Rehnquist Court's approach to the Religion Clauses will be a great improvement. Initial decisions suggest that the Rehnquist Court may replace the reflexive secularism of the Warren and Burger Courts with an equally inappropriate statism. Just when the Court appears to be shedding its inordinate distrust of religion, it appears to be embracing an inordinate faith in government.

Already the new Court has adopted an interpretation of the Free Exercise Clause that permits the state to interfere with religious practices—even to make the central ceremonies of some ancient faiths illegal or impossible—without any substantial justification, so long as the regulation does not facially discriminate against religion. * * * [T]he debate over the Religion Clauses is all too often framed as if there were but two choices: more religion in public life or less; tearing down the wall of separation between church and state or building it up again. * * *

This Article presents another way. In Section I, I criticize the Religion Clause jurisprudence of the Warren and Burger Courts and its influence today. In Section II, I explain why the emerging Religion Clause jurisprudence of the Rehnquist Court appears to be moving in the wrong direction. Finally, in Section III, I suggest how a proper jurisprudence of the Religion Clauses should look. My position is that the Religion Clauses do not create a secular public sphere, as was often thought in the past; nor do they sanction government discretion to foster broadly acceptable civil religion in public life. Rather, the purpose of the Religion Clauses is to protect the religious lives of the people from unnecessary intrusions of government, whether promoting or hindering religion. It is to foster a regime of religious pluralism, as distinguished from both majoritarianism and secularism. It is to preserve what Madison called the "full and equal rights" of religious believers and communities to define their own way of life, so long as they do not interfere with the rights of others, and to participate fully and equally with their fellow citizens in public life without being forced to shed their religious convictions and character.

I. THE OLD JURISPRUDENCE AND ITS INFLUENCE TODAY

A. *Inconsistency and Confusion*

Any serious interpretation of the Religion Clauses must explain the relation between the two constituent parts, the Free Exercise Clause and the Establishment Clause, which are joined together in the single command: "Congress shall make no law respecting an establishment of religion, or prohibiting the free exercise thereof." The Free Exercise Clause forbids Congress (and, after incorporation through the Fourteenth Amendment, any government) to discriminate against religion, and may require affirmative accommodation of free exercise in some contexts. The Establishment Clause, however, has been interpreted to forbid the government to aid or advance religion. In a world in which the government aids or advances many different causes and institutions, this means that the government must discriminate against religion in the distribution of benefits. Thus the Establishment Clause is said to require what the Free Exercise Clause forbids.

The doctrinal confusion is compounded when we take into account the remainder of the First Amendment, which protects the freedoms of speech, press, petition, and assembly. The central feature of the constitutional law of speech and press is a prohibition on "content-based" discrimination, except in the most compelling of circumstances. Yet the distinction between religion and nonreligious ideologies and institutions—a distinction seemingly demanded by the very text of the Religion Clauses—is based on the content of ideas and beliefs. The content-neutral thrust of the Free Speech Clause thus coexists uneasily with the special status of religion under the Free Exercise and Establishment Clauses.

The Court has tended to address these problems one clause at a time, building up inconsistencies often without seeming to notice them. * * *

* * *

B. Hostility or Indifference Toward Religion

But analytical confusion was the least of the problems with the Religion Clause jurisprudence of the Warren and Burger Courts. More significant was the Court's tendency to press relentlessly in the direction of a more secular society. The Court's opinions seemed to view religion as an unreasoned, aggressive, exclusionary, and divisive force that must be confined to the private sphere. When religions stuck to the private functions of "spiritual comfort, guidance, and inspiration," the Court extended the protection of the Constitution. But the Court was ever conscious that religion "can also serve powerfully to divide societies and to exclude those whose beliefs are not in accord with particular religions." The Court's more important mission was to protect democratic society from religion.

This set the Religion Clauses apart from the remainder of the Bill of Rights, which protects various nongovernmental activities from the power of democratic majorities. Only the Religion Clauses have been interpreted to protect democratic society from the power of the private citizen, even from the supposed power of minority religions. * * * The explanation presumably lies not in the logic of the Bill of Rights but in the Court's perception of religion. Before examining the details of legal doctrine, then, let us look at how the Court talks about religion.

Justice Hugo Black provides a starting point, since his opinions were so extremely influential in the early development of Establishment Clause doctrine. Black referred to the Catholics who advocated the loan of textbooks to religious schools as "powerful sectarian religious propagandists," and to their religious views as "preferences and prejudices."[31] He accused them of "looking toward complete domination and supremacy of their particular brand of religion."[32] This was a strange way to talk about people who sought equal rights for all families to direct the upbringing of their children.

The bigotry of Justice Black's language is particularly striking in light of its historical context. The reason Roman Catholics and Orthodox Jews created separate schools in the nineteenth century, while Protestants did not, was that the public schools were imbued with Protestant (and not infrequently anti-Catholic and anti-Jewish) religious and moral teaching. Opposition to parochial school aid at that time was part and parcel of nativist, anti-Catholic politics. * * * Only in the mid-twentieth century, when overt anti-Catholicism had subsided, were legislatures in Protestant-majority states willing to consider sharing a modest portion of the resources available for education. * * *

The language in recent Supreme Court opinions is more guarded, but continues to evince suspicion of religion. * * *

* * *

This understanding of religion is not merely the idiosyncratic viewpoint of a transitory majority of the Court. It represents a specific and powerful philosophical position, most clearly articulated by John Dewey. Dewey, the leading philosophical influence on American secular liberalism, was a determined critic of traditional religion. He claimed that there was "nothing left worth preserving in the notions of unseen powers, controlling human destiny to which obedience, reverence and worship are due." Unlike the scientific method, which is "open and public" and based on "continued and rigorous inquiry," religion is "a body of definite beliefs that need only to be taught and learned as true." Religion, he said, is based on the "servile acceptance of imposed dogma." This did not mean that Dewey and his followers were skeptical toward all moral teaching, or that the government should remain "neutral" toward conflicting points of view. To the contrary, Dewey contended that the public schools have an "ethical responsibility" to inculcate social values derived from scientific and democratic principles.

Dewey's point of view maintains a hold on mainstream thinking about religion and constitutional law, both in the academy and in the courts. * * *

---

31. *Allen*, 392 U.S. at 251 (Black dissenting).   **32.** *Id.*

If the Court's education decisions sometimes reflected hostility toward religion, other decisions more often displayed indifference or incomprehension. In Estate of Thornton v Caldor, Inc., for example, the Court held it unconstitutional for a state to require employers to accommodate work schedules to their employees' days of Sabbath observance. In a concurring opinion, Justice O'Connor explained that

> [a]ll employees, regardless of their religious orientation, would value the benefit which the statute bestows on Sabbath observers-the right to select the day of the week in which to refrain from labor. Yet Connecticut requires private employers to confer this valued and desirable benefit only on those employees who adhere to a particular religious belief.[53]

It would come as some surprise to a devout Jew to find that he has "selected the day of the week in which to refrain from labor," since the Jewish people have been under the impression for some 3,000 years that this choice was made by God. Jewish observers do not seek the right to "select the day" in which to refrain from labor, but only the right to obey laws over which they have no control. Sabbath observers are not "favored" over co-workers, any more than injured workers are "favored" when given disability leave. The law simply alleviates for them a conflict of loyalties not faced by their secular co-workers. Justice O'Connor's error was to reduce the dictates of religious conscience to the status of mere choice. Some people like to go sailing on Saturdays; some observe the Sabbath. How could the State consider the one "choice" more worthy of respect than the other? In Stephen Carter's apt phrase, this is to "treat religion as a hobby."

In Lyng v Northwest Indian Cemetery Protective Ass'n, the Supreme Court considered whether the Forest Service constitutionally could construct a logging road in a National Forest through the ancient sites of worship of the Yurok, Karok, and Talowa Indians of Northern California. This road, the Court conceded, would "virtually destroy" the Indians' ability "to practice their religion." The Supreme Court nonetheless upheld the project without inquiring whether its purpose was "compelling" or even important. The Court explained that "government simply could not operate if it were required to satisfy every citizen's religious needs and desires." One might think that the government would have to give some substantial justification to destroy a religion. But the Court responded that free exercise rights "do not divest the Government of its right to use what is, after all, its land." There is, admittedly, no evidence of hostility to religion in the opinion * * * But how could the opinion be read any other way?

These decisions do not give the impression that the Justices consider religion a particularly important aspect of life. Freedom of worship may be worthwhile in the abstract, but it is outweighed by virtually any secular interest. In its attitude toward religion, the Court may typify the gulf between a largely secularized professional and academic elite and

53. [*Estate of Thornton v. Caldor,* 472   U.S.] at 711 (O'Connor concurring).

most ordinary citizens, for whom religion commonly remains a central aspect of life. How many of the Justices and their clerks have had personal experience with serious religion—religion understood as more than ceremony, as the guiding principle of life? How many have close friends or associates who have had such experiences? For those who have lived their lives among academics and professionals, it may be difficult to understand why believers attach so much importance to things that seem so inconsequential.

C. Legal Doctrine

The formal legal doctrines espoused by the Warren and Burger Courts reinforced their lack of sympathy for religion. This may seem not to be true of the Free Exercise Clause doctrine, under which the Warren and Burger Courts forbade the enforcement of laws burdening the exercise of religion unless necessary to achieve a compelling governmental interest. The compelling interest test is, after all, the most exacting level of constitutional scrutiny. But in the years between the test's formal appearance in 1963 and its formal abandonment in 1990, the Supreme Court rejected all but one claim for free exercise exemption outside the field of unemployment compensation. In every other case decided on the merits, the Court found either that the claimant's exercise of religion was not burdened or that the government's interest was compelling. The doctrine was supportive, but its enforcement was half-hearted or worse.

In its Establishment Clause doctrine, the Court upheld the values of religious liberty in a few important cases, most notably the school prayer cases of the early 1960s. But the formal Establishment Clause doctrine, the Lemon test, has an inherent tendency to devalue religious exercise.
* * *

* * *

* * * [T]o accommodate the Native Americans in Lyng would violate all three prongs of the Lemon test. Yet the purposes of the Religion Clauses are advanced, not frustrated, when the government administers its property in such a way as to avoid devastating injury to the religious lives of its people. If Lemon stands in the way, then Lemon is the problem.

* * *

Despite their differences, the two sides on the Warren and Burger Courts shared a conception that everything touched by government must be secular. One side was deeply suspicious of religion, especially Catholicism, and concluded that quarantine was the only way to stave off theocracy. The other side was willing to accept a certain role for religion in public life, so long as religious institutions sacrificed their distinctively religious character. Whichever side might prevail in a particular case— the results swung back and forth between the two—the decisions consistently favored the secular over the religious. The Justices simply did not conceive of a world in which the governmental role was confined to finance, and the content of education left to the free choices of individual families. The Court thus placed the welfare-regulatory state on a collision course with religious freedom. As the sphere of government expanded, the field of religious pluralism had to shrink.

II. THE EMERGING JURISPRUDENCE OF THE REHNQUIST COURT

The Religion Clause jurisprudence of the Warren and Burger era was thus characterized by a hostility or indifference to religion, manifested in a weak application of free exercise doctrine and an aggressive application of an establishment doctrine systematically weighted in favor of the secular and against genuine religious pluralism. Far from protecting religious freedom against the vagaries of democratic politics, the Religion Clauses during this period became an additional instrument for promoting the politically dominant ideology of secular liberalism.

The ideology of secular liberalism, while still strong among the American elite, has lost its position of unquestioned dominance. On the left, a postmodernist intellectual current has cast doubt on the idea that secular liberalism should enjoy a privileged position and has opened the possibility for treating religion as one of many competing conceptions of reality. It is no longer intellectually credible to maintain that secular liberalism is simply the "neutral" position. On the right, the resurgence of conservative religious movements among both Protestants and Catholics—and to a lesser extent among Jews—has made religion a more salient force in the political culture. If taken to extremes, this religious resurgence might well support measures inconsistent with the pluralist religious ideals of the First Amendment. Calls for a "Christian America" and the return of organized prayers in the schools give genuine—if often exaggerated—cause for alarm. But appropriately channeled, this shift in popular attitudes could provide a corrective for the secularist biases of the previous judicial era.

It is too early to tell how the Rehnquist Court ultimately will treat the Religion Clauses. The new Court seems prepared to repudiate the approach of the old, and in important areas * * * has ameliorated unfortunate features of Warren and Burger Court Establishment Clause doctrine. But these improvements on establishment issues have come at a heavy price: the radical reduction of free exercise rights. Moreover, even where the results seem correct, the Rehnquist Court has failed to articulate a coherent vision of what it is attempting to accomplish. The positive developments, without exception, have involved the Court's decision not to overturn actions taken by the political branches. Thus, it is possible that the Court has mistaken the real vices of the old jurisprudence as ones of excessive judicial activism rather than of favoring the secular over the religious.

One of the anomalies of the Warren and Burger approach was its expansive reading of both the Free Exercise and Establishment Clauses (though in the case of free exercise this expansive reading was largely an illusion). If the government attempted to regulate a religious activity, it might be held to violate the Free Exercise Clause; if it carved out a religious exemption, this might be held an establishment. The government seemed destined to lose, no matter what policy it adopted toward religion. * * *

The initial response of the Rehnquist Court has been to shrink the scope of both Religion Clauses and thereby to restore a significant degree of governmental discretion. This response can be seen as part of a general jurisprudential shift in favor of greater judicial restraint, which in other constitutional areas may be a welcome corrective. But judicial restraint, for its own sake, is not a faithful mode of interpreting the Religion Clauses. There is a crucial difference between the discovery of "rights" not expressly or implicitly protected by the Constitution, where the dangers of judicial legislation and the need for judicial restraint are greatest, and the enforcement of rights firmly based on the text and tradition of the Constitution.

The original theory of the First Amendment was not deferential to government in matters of religion. Daniel Carroll, one of two non-Protestant members of the First Congress, captured the spirit during the deliberations over what would become the Religion Clauses of the First Amendment. "The rights of conscience," he said, "will little bear the gentlest touch of governmental hand." The Religion Clauses were born of distrust of government in matters of religion, based on experience. Those groups most vocal in demanding protection for religious freedom—the Quakers, the Presbyterians, and above all the Baptists—were precisely those groups whose practices were out of keeping with the majoritarian culture and who had borne the brunt of governmental hostility and indifference. It is a mistake to read the Religion Clauses as a triumph for the forces of Enlightenment secularism. Proponents of religious freedom were the least secular and most "enthusiastic" of the sects. But it is equally mistaken to treat the Religion Clauses as acquiescing in governmental interference with religion. The advocates of the Religion Clauses valued their religious convictions too much to allow them to be subjected to governmental power. The overriding objective of the Religion Clauses was to render the new federal government irrelevant to the religious lives of the people.

This objective has been vastly complicated by the emergence of the welfare-regulatory state. During the early days of the Republic, the reach of the federal government was strictly limited, and the matters within its jurisdiction—chiefly foreign and military affairs and commerce—had little effect on religion. Recall that Madison and the other Federalists initially argued that a Bill of Rights was not necessary because the powers of the federal government were so limited that it could pose no danger to our liberties. With some exceptions, if the federal government simply took no actions directed at religion, the objectives of the Religion Clauses would be fulfilled. As the powers of the federal government expanded and the coverage of the First Amendment was extended to the states, however, this ceased to be true. The government now fosters a vast sector of publicly-supported, privately-administered social welfare programs, and the allocation of resources in this sector inevitably affects religion. * * * Where once the government could treat religious institutions with benign neglect, the welfare-regulatory state requires a substantive policy toward religion that will preserve the conditions of religious freedom without hobbling the activist state. Unfortunately, neither the free exercise nor the establishment jurisprudence that seems to be emerging in the Rehnquist Court addresses that central problem.

A. Free Exercise

The Rehnquist Court's tendency to defer to majoritarian decision-making is most clearly evident in its reversal of free exercise doctrine. As noted above, the Warren and Burger Courts held governmental action invalid when it imposed a burden on the exercise of a sincerely held religious belief without compelling justification. This meant that the government sometimes had to make accommodations or exceptions to laws that burdened the exercise of religion. In 1990, in Employment Division v Smith, the Rehnquist Court held that "the right of free exercise does not relieve an individual of the obligation to comply with a 'valid and neutral law of general applicability on the ground that the law proscribes (or prescribes) conduct that his religion prescribes (or proscribes).' " If the law is "generally applicable," the government need not show that it serves an important (let alone compelling) purpose, even if its effect—as in Smith itself—is to make the practice of a religion virtually impossible. Thus Smith holds that the state may forbid the central religious practice of a centuries-old religion now called the Native American Church—the sacramental ingestion of peyote—even though there was no evidence that this practice had deleterious consequences for the practitioners or for anyone else.

I have criticized the Smith decision elsewhere at length,[107] and I will not repeat those arguments. Nonetheless, a few observations on Smith will illustrate why I am concerned that the Rehnquist Court may be as mistaken in its way as were the Warren and Burger Courts. First and foremost, the Smith decision gives social policy, determined by the State, primacy over the rights of religious communities to order their affairs according to their own convictions. Smith describes this effect as an "unavoidable consequence of democratic government." * * * Under Smith, the state is more powerful, the forces of homogenization are more powerful, and the ability of churches to maintain their distinctive ways of life depends upon their skill at self-protection in the halls of Congress.

Second, as the Smith opinion candidly acknowledges, its interpretation will place "those religious practices that are not widely engaged in" at a "relative disadvantage." Some religions are close to the center of prevailing culture in America. Their practices rarely, if ever, will conflict with an "otherwise valid law," because, in a democracy, the laws will

107. Michael W. McConnell, *Free Exercise Revisionism and the Smith Decision*, 57 U. Chi. L. Rev. 1109 (1990).

reflect the beliefs and preferences of the median groups. Religious groups whose practices and beliefs are outside the mainstream are most likely to need exceptions and accommodations. * * * Moreover, only some of the religious groups in need of exceptions and accommodations will win the ear of the legislature. Those groups whose beliefs are least foreign and least offensive to the mainstream, and those with the largest numbers and greatest visibility, will be better able to protect themselves than will the smaller, more unpopular groups. Smith thus not only increases the power of the state over religion, it introduces a bias in favor of mainstream over nonmainstream religions. That bias may not displease those who believe in the wisdom and virtue of majoritarian culture, but it is not consistent with the original theory of the Religion Clauses.

Third, the Smith Court treated the claim for a free exercise exemption as essentially a request for a special benefit. In an earlier opinion, Justice Scalia, the author of Smith, characterized free exercise exemptions as "intentional governmental advancement" of religion. This misstates the issue. The Native American Church was not asking government for "advancement"; it was asking to be left alone. When the government criminalizes the religious ritual of a church, it "prohibits" the free exercise of religion in the most direct and literal sense of the word. If the courts cannot distinguish the failure to "prohibit" from the decision to "advance," it is no wonder that their decisions are so confused. To conceive of free exercise exemptions as requests for special benefits implicitly assumes that the state has the natural authority to regulate the church, and that choosing not to do so is a favor. That is not the inalienable right to freedom of religion conceived by those who wrote and ratified the First Amendment.

Finally, Smith converts a constitutionally explicit liberty into a nondiscrimination requirement, in violation of the most straight-forward interpretation of the First Amendment text. If the Constitution guaranteed the "right to own cattle," who would interpret it to allow the government to ban the ownership of all animals, so long as cattle are not "singled out"? The freedom of citizens to exercise their faith should not depend on the vagaries of democratic politics, even if expressed through laws of general applicability.

B.   Establishment

The Rehnquist Court's greatest contributions to Establishment Clause doctrine have been its dismantling of some of Lemon's mistakes. * * *

* * *

6.   Establishment implications of Smith.

The Rehnquist Court, with its respect for legal formalism, is unlikely to repeat the Warren and Burger Courts' mistake of reading the Religion Clauses as inconsistent principles, especially since the author of Smith, Justice Scalia, is the most systematic thinker on the Court. Scalia is not likely to remain content with a jurisprudence in which the Court, in his words, has "not yet come close to reconciling Lemon and our Free Exercise cases." Since Smith now represents the Court's interpretation of the Free Exercise Clause, it is to be expected that the Court will soon reinterpret the Establishment Clause in a manner consistent with Smith. What would that be?

The most logical step would be to read both clauses as embodying a formal neutrality toward religion. Under Smith, the Free Exercise Clause precludes government action that is "directed at," or "singles out," religion for unfavorable treatment. The Establishment Clause analog would be to preclude government action that singles out religion for favorable treatment. This position has long been advocated by Justice Scalia's sometime University of Chicago colleague, Philip Kurland. Kurland contends that the two Religion Clauses should be "read as a single precept that government cannot utilize religion as a standard for action or inaction because these clauses prohibit classification in terms of religion either to confer a benefit or to impose a burden." Until 1990, the Supreme Court had rejected this position as to both Clauses. In Smith, the Court adopted this position as to the Free Exercise Clause. Perhaps its extension to the Establishment Clause will be the next shoe to drop.

Logical though this move might be, it is highly unlikely. The formal neutrality position would make unconstitutional all legislation that explicitly exempts religious institutions or individuals from generally applicable burdens or obligations. Yet the theory of Smith is that exemptions are a form of beneficent legislation, left to the discretion of the political branches. The problem with requiring exemptions under the Free Exercise Clause is not that exemptions violate the principle of neutrality, but that enforcement under the Constitution would give judges too much discretion: "it is horrible to contemplate that federal judges will regularly balance against the importance of general laws the significance of religious practice." Noting that "a number of States have made an exception to their drug laws for sacramental peyote use," the Court commented: "to say that a nondiscriminatory religious-practice exemption is permitted, or even that it is desirable, is not to say that it is constitutionally required."

Smith thus rejects the formal neutrality position under the Establishment Clause. This is not surprising. One of the positive developments in the Supreme Court over the past ten years has been its growing acceptance of the legitimacy of accommodation of religion. The Court has accepted special treatment of religion where it facilitates the free exercise of religion, even if it is not constitutionally compelled under the Free Exercise Clause. The conservatives on the Court have been the most enthusiastic supporters of this development. It would be most peculiar if the conservative wing of the Court were to repudiate the doctrine of accommodation now that it has achieved wide acceptance.

If Smith does not augur adoption of the formal neutrality interpretation, what does it mean for the Establishment Clause? The answer is not obvious. Other than his suggestion to eliminate the purpose prong of the Lemon test, Justice Scalia has not set forth a comprehensive theory of the Establishment Clause, even in his numerous separate dissents and concurrences. But while Scalia has not offered a comprehensive theory, his opinions do show a clear pattern. In each of them, Scalia suggests a modification of the Lemon test that is one step more deferential to the government than the Lemon test requires. In Edwards, he proposed eliminating the purpose prong. In Kendrick, he joined an opinion by Justice Kennedy suggesting elimination of the rule that direct government funding may not go to pervasively sectarian organizations. In Texas Monthly, he argued that tax exemptions could be skewed in favor of religious organizations. In each case, he left in place the often unprincipled doctrinal categories of the Lemon test, modifying them only to the extent of easing the standard. This pattern suggests that Justice Scalia is more concerned about cabining the judicial role in cases involving religion than in developing a comprehensive substantive theory.

But as discussed above, deference to majoritarian decision-making is out of keeping with the spirit of the Religion Clauses. The great danger of revising Establishment Clause doctrine in light of Smith is replicating Smith's vices of excessive deference to governmental decisionmaking and bias in favor of mainstream religion. These vices may be preferable to the secularist bias of the Warren and Burger Courts, but not by much.

III.   A RELIGION CLAUSE JURISPRUDENCE FOR A PLURALISTIC NATION

A jurisprudence of the Religion Clauses must begin with a proper understanding of the ideals of the Clauses and the evils against which they are directed. We can then formulate legal doctrine. The great mistake of the Warren and Burger Courts was to embrace the ideal of the secular state, with its corresponding tendencies toward indifference or hostility to religion. The mistake of the emerging jurisprudence of the Rehnquist Court is to defer to majoritarian decisionmaking. A better understanding of the ideal of the Religion Clauses, both normatively and historically, is that they guarantee a pluralistic republic in which citizens are free to exercise their religious differences without hindrance from the state (unless necessary to important purposes of civil government), whether that hindrance is for or against religion.

The great evil against which the Religion Clauses are directed is government—induced homogeneity—the tendency of government action to discourage or suppress the expression of differences in matters of religion. As Madison explained to the First Congress, "the people feared one sect might obtain a preeminence, or two combine together, and establish a religion to which they would compel others to conform." As such authorities of the day as Thomas Jefferson and Adam Smith argued, government-enforced uniformity in religion produced both "indolence" within the church and oppression outside the church. Diversity allows each religion to "flourish according to the zeal of its adherents and the appeal of its dogma," without creating the danger that any particular religion will dominate the others. At some times in our history, and even in some isolated regions of the country today, the great threat to religious pluralism has been a triumphalist majority religion. The more serious threat to religious pluralism today is a combination of indifference to the plight of religious minorities and a preference for the secular in public affairs. This translates into an unwillingness to enforce the Free Exercise Clause when it matters, and a hypertrophic view of the Establishment Clause.

When scrutinizing a law or governmental practice under the Religion Clauses, the courts should ask the following question: is the purpose or probable effect to increase religious uniformity, either by inhibiting religious practice (a Free Exercise Clause violation) or by forcing or inducing a contrary religious practice (an Establishment Clause violation), without sufficient justification? The baseline for these judgments is the hypothetical world in which individuals make decisions about religion on the basis of their own religious conscience, without the influence of government. The underlying principle is that governmental action should have the minimum possible effect on religion, consistent with achievement of the government's legitimate purposes.

Virtually everything government does has some effect on religion, however indirect. No doctrinal formulation can eliminate the difficult questions of judgment in determining when the government's purpose is sufficiently important, when its chosen means are sufficiently tailored, or when the effect of the action on religious practice is sufficiently minor or indirect. But we can be clear about the ideal toward which a jurisprudence of the Religion Clauses should be directed.

A.   A Pluralist Approach to the Free Exercise Clause

In free exercise cases, the pluralist approach would be something like the approach of the Warren and Burger Courts—albeit with more vigorous and consistent enforcement. This is not to say that the "compelling interest test" was without problems. The test was excessively abstract and failed to define its key operative concepts. It provided little guidance to legislatures or lower courts about what burdens on religious practice triggered heightened scrutiny, or about how to evaluate the governmental interest. The first requirement for scholarship in this field, should Smith be overturned, is the development of more precise definitions of the elusive concepts of "burden" and "compelling governmental interest."

Apart from the question of generally applicable laws, at issue in Smith, there are two other currents of change in free exercise jurisprudence, one from the right and one from the left. From the right comes the movement to resuscitate the right-privilege distinction by limiting the Free Exercise Clause to outright "prohibitions" of religious practice.

From the left comes the movement to transform the free exercise right into a right of personal autonomy or self-definition. Both should be confronted and resisted.

1. "Prohibitions" of religious practice and conditions on government aid.

In Lyng, the Court emphasized that the "the crucial word in the constitutional text is 'prohibit.'" From this, the Court concluded that the Free Exercise Clause does not limit how the government controls its property, even when, as in Lyng, the government owns holy sites indispensable for religious worship. Thus the Forest Service could build a road over an American Indian holy site and "virtually destroy" the religion. By the same reasoning, the Free Exercise Clause would not limit the government's exercise of other nonregulatory powers, even if the government's action or inaction made the exercise of religion difficult or impossible. The Free Exercise Clause would apply only when the government made religious practice unlawful (and even then, under Smith, the Clause would not apply if the prohibition were generally applicable and not directed at religion). Presumably, the government could draft men and women into the Army and send them to distant lands, and then refuse to provide for their religious worship needs; it could incarcerate prisoners without providing chapels or chaplains. The government could require all citizens to pay taxes to support welfare or educational programs, but then condition the benefits from the programs on rules which conflict with religious principles. These would not be "prohibitions" and so would not be coerced.

Lyng thus raises the central question surrounding the enforcement of constitutional rights under a welfare state: are the conditions which the government attaches to the use and distribution of resources subject to the same constitutional limitations as direct governmental legislation? Specifically, does the word "prohibit" in the First Amendment limit the Free Exercise Clause to "negative" legislation—direct prohibitions—aimed at religion? I am not persuaded that a 1791 audience necessarily would have understood the term "prohibitions" so narrowly; but even if it would have, we cannot fulfill the purposes of the Free Exercise Clause under modern conditions without adapting to the vastly expanded role that government now plays in our lives. Like every other constitutional protection, the Free Exercise Clause should be understood to be violated by unconstitutional conditions as well as by direct restraints.

2. Free exercise and the rights of conscience.

On the other hand, some would expand the scope of the Free Exercise Clause by treating the free exercise right as a right of personal autonomy or self-definition. Rather than understanding religion as a matter over which we have no control—the demands of a transcendent authority—it has become common to regard religion as valuable and important only because it is what we choose. In the words of Justice Stevens, "religious beliefs worthy of respect are the product of free and voluntary choice by the faithful." This treats religion as an individualistic choice rather than as the irresistible conviction of the authority of God.

The most obvious manifestation of this shift is the move to extend free exercise protections to any and all claims arising from "conscience," understood as the reflective judgment of the individual. David A. J. Richards perhaps best exemplifies this move: he argues that constitutional protections for religious freedom are ultimately based on "respect for the person as an independent source of value." Relying on this premise, Richards argues that it is illegitimate to distinguish between the free exercise of religion and the free exercise of any other personal belief or value. Free exercise becomes an undifferentiated right of personal autonomy.

* * * [I]f we are to understand the theory and principle of the Religion Clauses, we must know what differentiates "religion" from everything else. The essence of "religion" is that it acknowledges a normative authority independent of the judgment of the individual or of the society as a whole. Thus, the Virginia Declaration of Rights defined religion as the "duty which we owe to our Creator, and the manner of discharging it." Madison said that the law protects religious freedom because the duties arising from spiritual authority are "precedent both in order of time and degree of obligation, to the claims of Civil Society." The Free Exercise Clause does not protect autonomy; it protects obligation.

Of course, the Free Exercise Clause protects religious "choice" in the sense that it recognizes the individual believer as the only legitimate judge of the dictates of conscience; authentic religion may not be coerced by human authority. But the theological concept of "soul liberty," from which this principle derives, is not predicated on any belief in the intrinsic worthiness of individual judgment (which, after the fall and before the acceptance of God's grace, is unregenerate). The concept is based on the view that the relations between God and Man are outside the authority of the state.

Thus, in early challenges to Sunday closing laws under state free exercise clauses, courts consistently rejected claims that it violated the right of conscience for the state to designate Sunday as the day of rest, even though plaintiffs persuasively argued that determining which day is the Sabbath is a matter of religious conviction and conscience. But the same courts distinguished cases in which the plaintiff's own religious doctrine required him to work on Sunday. The distinction is subtle but important: free exercise does not give believers the right to choose for themselves to override the socially-prescribed decision; it allows them to obey spiritual rather than temporal authority.

A modern version of this debate is taking place over the claim of a free exercise right to obtain an abortion.[256] In the Utah case now

---

256. See, for example, Ronald Dworkin, *Unenumerated Rights: Whether and How* *Roe Should Be Overruled*, 59 U. Chi. L. Rev. 381, 419 (1992) (arguing that the Free Ex-

underway,[257] plaintiffs claim that the decision whether to have an abortion is an issue of religiously-informed conscience, and that the state's prohibition of abortions is therefore a violation of free exercise. But plaintiffs do not allege that the law prevents them from complying with the dictates of their own religious persuasion, since their religions do not purport to lay down any such dictates. The plaintiffs assert the right to choose for themselves as autonomous individuals, not the right to conform their conduct to religious law.

This claim must be distinguished from a claim that, under some circumstances, the pregnant woman's religion requires her to get an abortion. (Orthodox Jews, for example, believe that an abortion is mandatory if necessary to save the mother's life.) The latter claim, if sincere, is a legitimate free exercise claim, which the government must accommodate unless it has a sufficiently compelling interest in preventing abortion. The Free Exercise Clause does not protect the freedom of self-determination (with respect to abortion, working on Sunday, or anything else); it does protect the freedom to act in accordance with the dictates of religion, as the believer understands them.

B. A Pluralist Approach to the Establishment Clause

* * * Unlike the Lemon test, a pluralistic approach would not ask whether the purpose or effect of the challenged action is to "advance religion," but whether it is to foster religious uniformity or otherwise distort the process of reaching and practicing religious convictions. A governmental policy that gives free rein to individual decisions (secular and religious) does not offend the Establishment Clause, even if the effect is to increase the number of religious choices. The concern of the Establishment Clause is with governmental actions that constrain individual decisionmaking with respect to religion, by favoring one religion over others, or by favoring religion over nonreligion.

The modern welfare-regulatory state wields three forms of power that potentially threaten religious pluralism: the power to regulate religious institutions and conduct, the power to discriminate in distributing state resources, and control over institutions of culture and education. Each of these powers can, and frequently does, promote homogeneity of all kinds, and especially with regard to religion. Too often, however, the Court has interpreted the Establishment Clause to oppose pluralism rather than to foster it by treating as unconstitutional (1) efforts by the political branches to reduce the degree to which the regulatory power of the state interferes with the practice of religion, (2) decisions to include religious individuals and institutions within public programs on an equal and nondiscriminatory basis, and (3) manifestations of religion within the publicly-controlled cultural and educational sector, even in contexts where competitive secular ideologies are given an equal place. Thus, instead of protecting religious freedom from the

---

ercise Clause protects the right to choose an abortion).

257. *Jane L. v Bangerter*, 91–C–345 G (D Utah).

incursions of the welfare-regulatory state, the Establishment Clause all too often was interpreted to exacerbate the problem.

In these areas, the Supreme Court is moving in a generally positive direction, and it may not be long before the Establishment Clause is no longer a serious obstacle to either accommodation of religious exercise or the equal treatment of religious institutions. * * *

* * *

CONCLUSION

The religious freedom cases under the First Amendment have been distorted by the false choice between secularism and majoritarianism, neither of which faithfully reflects the pluralistic philosophy of the Religion Clauses. Instead, the Free Exercise and Establishment Clauses should protect against government-induced uniformity in matters of religion. In the modern welfare-regulatory state, this means that the state must not favor religion over nonreligion, nonreligion over religion, or one religion over another in distributing financial resources; that the state must create exceptions to laws of general applicability when these laws threaten the religious convictions or practices of religious institutions or individuals; and that the state should eschew both religious favoritism and secular bias in its own participation in the formation of public culture. This interpretation will tolerate a more prominent place for religion in the public sphere, but will simultaneously guarantee religious freedom for faiths both large and small.

IRA C. LUPU, *EMPLOYMENT DIVISION V. SMITH AND THE DECLINE OF SUPREME COURT–CENTRISM*

1993 B.Y.U. L. Rev. 259 (1993).

* * *

I.   THE CONSEQUENCES AND FUTURE OF SMITH

Like many others, I believe that Employment Division v. Smith is substantively wrong and institutionally irresponsible. For example, Justice Scalia, the author of Smith, claims to be an originalist. Smith shows no signs, however, of any such orientation; the Court's opinion totally ignores both the text and history of the Free Exercise Clause. In addition, Smith offends institutional and process norms as well. Relying on overruled or doctrinally discredited decisions of the Supreme Court, as did the Smith majority, is ordinarily frowned upon in legal circles, as is the practice of deciding major constitutional questions without giving the parties an opportunity to brief and argue them. Understandably, then, criticism of Smith on those grounds has become commonplace.

What is less obvious and perhaps more intriguing, however, is why Smith matters. If, as has been repeatedly argued, free exercise law on the decision's eve was already quite hostile to religious liberty, what explains the powerful reaction?

A. Cognition and Coase

Smith's sweeping terms plowed through the cognitive dissonance that had become pervasive among followers of free exercise trends. Before Smith, a long line of Supreme Court decisions rejecting free exercise claims could each be satisfactorily explained to most Americans by simply referencing the appropriate buzz words—an Indians case, a military case, a Muslims-in-prison case, a tax-system-integrity case, and several cases concerning churches that many suspected had a fraudulent air about them. The average American could learn of all these cases and still believe that the Free Exercise Clause would protect him or her, even if it did not protect others. This sort of thinking is always good for tyranny and bad for liberty. By ending the stream of decisions designed to appear as special exceptions—that is, by emphasizing a new general principle rather than focusing on the facts of the case—Smith raised consciousness of what had been occurring in the field.

* * * It may have been easy for some conservatives to think that the Bill of Rights is divisible; that is, that the Court in the 1980s would cut back on perceived excesses of its predecessors on questions of privacy, criminal procedure, freedom of expression, or nonestablishment, but that it would not similarly undermine prevailing law on the Free Exercise Clause. That hope, of course, was sheer fantasy; statism tends to swallow the entire Bill of Rights, rather than the particular provisions those in political power do not favor.

* * * [I]f one focuses on the dynamics of litigation and settlement, the argument that Smith only clarified, rather than altered, the law is vastly overstated. Prior to Smith, prospective and actual litigants on both sides of free exercise questions had to consider the distinct possibility that a free exercise claim would successfully exempt a particular group or practice from an otherwise generally applicable law. Indeed, although the Supreme Court grew increasingly inhospitable to free exercise claims over time, such attacks occasionally prevailed in the lower courts, state and federal. Appraising the probability of success in light of these emerging developments presumably affected both a litigator's decision whether or not to bring suit in a particular circumstance, and his or her decision as to the terms and appropriateness of compromise. Pre–Smith free exercise law inevitably cast a significant shadow over the bargains struck by parties to religious liberty disputes.

Smith has altered that shadow. The lower courts have ignored the Supreme Court's emphasis upon criminal laws of general applicability, and they have been quite willing to extend the reasoning of Smith to the fullest extent possible. We all understand that Smith transfers power away from religion and toward the state * * *. As the Mormon experience amply demonstrates, clarification of this sort tends to be little more than a process of change coerced by state oppression or insensitivity.

Of course, those versed in law and economics might say I'm making too much of the argument that pre-Smith law influenced free exercise litigation strategies and settlements, partly because the free exercise entitlement was relatively weak before Smith, and partly because their general view is that the initial assignment of entitlements frequently does not matter. In the hypothetical world described by the Coase Theorem,[23] in which zero transaction costs are assumed, the parties are expected to bargain to an efficient result, regardless of the law's allocation of rights.

With regard to disputes over religion, however, this assumption is highly implausible. However irrational the challenged religious commitments may seem, communities of believers are deeply invested in them. The idea that such commitments can be bargained away without incurring substantial transaction costs, measured by the religious community's willingness to allocate resources in resistance to the state's encroachments upon its religious belief and practice, is absurd. When people believe that God has commanded some practice, and institutions have crystallized around that belief, fidelity to it cannot be negotiated away without costly convulsions.

Under these conditions, it will be very difficult for disputing parties to find common ground for compromise. One would therefore expect the substantive content of the law, rather than the parties' mutual understanding of their respective interests, to be the primary variable in the way disputes are settled. I suspect that the change in free exercise law that Smith represents will have a dramatic affect on the range of suits brought and settlements reached, as well as on the results of actual litigation, all to the detriment of religious liberty.

B. The Importance of Church of the Lukumi in the Future of Free Exercise: Moderating the Effects of Smith

Perhaps the pessimism of this analysis can be escaped by focusing upon what Smith leaves open, rather than upon the damage it may already have done. At the Symposium [from which this article arose], Professor [Douglas] Laycock contended that the Church of the Lukumi case presented little opportunity for substantive gains for free exercise. At best, he said, a disaster for religious liberty might be avoided if the Justices accept his argument [Professor Laycock argued the *Church of Lukumi Balabalu Aye* case to the Supreme Court, *see supra* at Chapter Six] that the City of Hialeah engaged in an unconstitutional religious gerrymander when it enacted various ordinances prohibiting certain forms of ritual slaughter.

With all respect to Professor Laycock's modesty in refusing to proclaim the possibility of an important victory, I believe Church of the Lukumi proved to be much more significant than he suggested. First and foremost, the Court unanimously agreed that this was a religious gerrymander, and that such acts are presumptively unconstitutional. By holding that the Constitution prohibits religious gerrymanders structured to the detriment of a particular faith, the Court has reaffirmed

---

23. R.H. Coase, *The Problem of Social Cost, 3 J.L. & Econ. 1 (1960).*

Larson v. Valente[29] and constructed an outer boundary beyond which the deterioration of free exercise protection will not pass. Although the Court's opinion is entirely true to the equal protection character of Smith, the right of religious minorities to be free from state discrimination, both overt and covert, is of both theoretical and practical significance. Furthermore, any constitutional victory of an unusual, numerically small religion constitutes a significant sign that the Free Exercise Clause still carries some punch.

Second, Church of the Lukumi provides important information about the views of Justices Souter and Thomas, each of whom replaced a dissenting Justice in Smith. The Court opinion in Church of the Lukumi expressly reaffirmed Smith's underlying principle of formal free exercise neutrality. Justice Thomas joined in this portion of the opinion, thus indicating his agreement with the basic principle in Smith. By sharp contrast, Justice Souter * * * wrote a concurring opinion arguing that Smith may have been wrongly decided and should be reexamined. Thus, the two against Smith (Justices Brennan and Marshall) have become Thomas for and Souter against, and the latter brings obvious fervor to the enterprise. The Smith lineup also reveals that the Court is now divided 6–3 in favor of retaining Smith, with one of the six (Justice White) about to be replaced by a nominee whose views on free exercise may be more sympathetic * * *.

Third, Church of the Lukumi reveals Justice Kennedy firmly committed to his vote in Smith. Among the Smith majority, he alone had shown an inclination to depart from tendencies reflected in his earlier Religion Clause opinions. Because the Hialeah ordinances were so obviously gerrymandered against the practitioners of Santería, however, Justice Kennedy might have ruled for the Church while remaining silent on his more general views of free exercise exemptions from facially neutral, generally applicable laws. That he did not do so suggests he was determined to reassure his conservative colleagues that he would not abandon them here as he had on abortion and graduation prayer.

C.   The "Hybrid Rights" Claim: Smith's Open Door

Nothing in Church of the Lukumi expands, narrows, or clarifies Smith's pronouncement concerning so-called hybrid right claims. These claims are based upon the conjunction of free exercise and other constitutionally significant rights, like free speech or parental control over the rearing of children. Whatever the theoretical explanation for greater receptivity to "free exercise plus" than "free exercise pure," a great many free exercise claims might be recast to take advantage of this construct. Although I doubt that Smith itself might be so transformed, free exercise claims frequently involve expression, association, or parental concern for the religious upbringing of their children. The last of these, of course, is the most important; it is the foundation of Wisconsin

---

29.   456 U.S. 228 (1982) (holding that the state may not legislate reporting requirements for religious fund raising that are designed to regulate "street religion" like the Unification Church while exempting mainstream religion). * * *

v. Yoder, and because it depends upon the judge-made right of parental control as a boost to the textual right of free exercise, it is the most controversial member of the hybrid rights set. In addition, a great many free exercise claims involve the parent-child-state triangle, so Yoder's fate is of crucial significance to the development of the law in the field.

Creative lawyering might thus preserve the force of many potential claims. At the very least, pressing hybrid claims wherever plausible will presumably result in either an explanation and reaffirmation of "free exercise plus," or an ultimate admission by the Court that the theory was no more than an unprincipled attempt to pretend that Yoder survived Smith.

D.   The Changing Court and the Future of Smith

Of course, as Justice White's resignation brought home, the Justices that decided Smith will not be around forever. * * * The most a foe of Smith might hope for is a new Justice who takes the Bill of Rights seriously and believes in some version of the Warren Court's commitment to strenuous enforcement of those rights.

If this were to happen, we would be reminded that the set of constitutional rights we enjoy are ultimately indivisible. It is very difficult to sustain the position that the Free Exercise Clause should be actively enforced by courts, but that the Speech Clause, the Press Clause, and the criminal procedure provisions in the Fourth, Fifth, and Sixth Amendments should not. Nor can one legitimately advocate free exercise activism while at the same time arguing that the Fourteenth Amendment's guarantees of equality, procedural fairness, and (as construed) privacy should not be similarly enforced.

Ultimately, this is a roundabout way of asserting that the Free Exercise Clause may be reinvigorated only if Justices with constitutional philosophies akin to those of Thurgood Marshall or William Brennan are appointed. Of course, not everyone who is unhappy with Smith would be prepared to accept a Warren Court civil libertarian-type in exchange for Smith's overruling. * * *

II.   THE MOVE AWAY FROM THE SUPREME COURT

Whatever the future course of free exercise adjudication in the Supreme Court, Smith has already resulted in a flood of activity with the potential to alter the course of religious liberty in American law. The energies flowing in Smith's wake are academic, judicial, and political. As is evidenced by this Symposium, legal scholars have turned substantial attention to the problems and issues raised by Smith. * * * [S]ome state courts have begun to develop state constitutional law in response to the gap created by Smith. And, on the legislative front, the United States Congress continues to consider the Religious Freedom Restoration Act [*see supra* at Chapter Six] and the very recently introduced amendments to the American Indian Religious Freedom Act. I want to comment briefly on each of these phenomena, because I believe that in combination they may eventually lead to and sustain a deep and powerful structure of religious liberty law that is largely independent of the Supreme Court's view of the First Amendment's religion clauses.

A. Academic Commentary

With respect to the academic commentary, my point is simple. Criticizing Smith is no longer original or useful; we have all become repetitive in our criticisms, and by now, our audiences are either persuaded or turned off. What remains before us is the hard work of reconstruction, made more difficult by the chaotic and unsatisfactory state of free exercise law as it stood on the eve of Smith. In other words, it will not do to complain about Smith without offering concrete and detailed proposals for how free exercise principles should be shaped in the future. If such efforts are fruitful, the "new" era of free exercise may turn out to be far more coherent and substantively adequate than anything that has come before.

B. State Law and Religious Liberty

State courts may play a vital role in providing a solid foundation for future protection of religious liberty. Prior to Smith, state supreme courts—even those with a strong religious liberty clause in their respective state constitutions—were quite reluctant to tie their views of the subject to state law. Rather, pursuant to their own versions of "the devil made me do it," they tended to integrate state law with federal law and explicitly follow the federal law wherever it led.

The consequences of this refusal to articulate independent state constitutional law are serious. On the road to Smith, federal law became increasingly less protective of religious liberty. By ignoring the possibility of independent state law protection for religion, state courts became both dependent on the U.S. Supreme Court and vulnerable to the erosion of religious liberty that resulted from the backsliding force of federal law. Because state courts failed to rely upon their state constitutions to fill the widening gap between federal law and an adequate conception of religious freedom, state law initially provided no insulation against Smith's blistering effect on free exercise norms.

Fortunately * * * state courts have begun to rely upon state constitutions in an effort to resurrect some aspects of religious liberty. In addition to the substantive advance this represents, such state court behavior advances process values as well. It permits the development of constitutional norms of religious freedom without the brooding omnipresence of a single, authoritative national tribunal or the lesser (but significant) presence of a single set of national rules and standards. If and when Smith is overturned by the Supreme Court, federal law may have a number of well-developed judicial models, tested in the crucible of real adjudicative systems, from which to borrow and learn.

[The Section of this article discussing RFRA has been deleted in light of *Boerne, see supra* at Chapter Six].

III. Conclusion

In Smith's wake, the responsibility for creatively elaborating norms of religious liberty rests substantially with law-shaping and law-making institutions other than the Supreme Court. The law that may serve this purpose will, for the most part, be the corpus juris outside of federal constitutional law.

As has always been the case, however, the future of free exercise may well rest more upon sociological than legal considerations. The law cannot create the atmosphere of religious tolerance and mutual respect upon which religious liberty ultimately depends. Recall Judge Learned Hand's general view of the extent to which judicial review can preserve liberty:

> [A] society so riven that the spirit of moderation is gone, no court can save ... a society where that spirit flourishes, no court need save ... [and] in a society which evades its responsibility by thrusting upon the courts the nurture of that spirit, that spirit in the end will perish.[69]

Employment Division v. Smith cannot destroy religious liberty in a society that truly respects it; nor, by the same token, can an overruling of Smith save that liberty in a society which does not. The future of free exercise rests with a citizenry committed to the enterprise. Given the dramatic differences among religions, the all-too-frequent nexus between religion and violence, the psychologically threatening character of any religion not one's own, and the history of religious intolerance in our country, it requires a triumph of hope over experience to be confident that religious exercise will remain free in the third century of our Bill of Rights. To the extent law matters on such questions, however, liberating our commitment to religious freedom from the imperialistic grip of the Supreme Court and federal constitutional law may be the course of action most likely to produce salutary results.

2. The Equality Perspective and the Role of Religious Minorities

The material in Chapter Six demonstrates that the Court has been less than welcoming to exemption claims brought by religious minorities (including claims by members of a number of Christian sects). This was so even when the Court developed a doctrine—the compelling interest test—that would seem to support claims by religious minorities. Yet there have been hints in a number of decisions that the Free Exercise Clause is meant to give members of all religions an equal right to practice and worship as they please. A number of scholars have addressed "equality" based perspectives on the Free Exercise Clause. The following article by Professors Christopher L. Eisgruber and Lawrence G. Sager argues for an approach to the Free Exercise Clause that is based on the concept of "equal regard." Eisgruber and Sager's approach

---

69. Learned Hand, *The Contribution of an Independent Judiciary to Civilization, in* THE SPIRIT OF LIBERTY 172, 181 (Irving Dilliard ed., 1952).

is a major contribution to the field, and it provides an alternative to the accommodationist approach, but would still provide a great deal of protection to religious practitioners. The second article in this section is by Professor Stephen M. Feldman, a leading scholar focused on the role of "religious outsiders." Professor Feldman analyzes the Free Exercise Clause from the perspective of religious minorities, and suggests that the Court's decisions have consistently privileged the Protestant perspective on religion at the expense of religious groups whose beliefs and practices differ from the Protestant norm. He points out that religious minorities were able to achieve success in some Establishment Clause cases by identifying with the Protestant norm, but he argues this strategy can not work in Free Exercise Clause cases.

CHRISTOPHER L. EISGRUBER & LAWRENCE G. SAGER, *THE VULNERABILITY OF CONSCIENCE: THE CONSTITUTIONAL BASIS FOR PROTECTING RELIGIOUS CONDUCT*

61 U. CHI. L. REV. 1245 (1994).

I. INTRODUCTION: THE PROBLEMATIC STATUS OF RELIGIOUS EXEMPTIONS

In Employment Division, Department of Human Resources of Oregon v Smith, the Supreme Court held that members of the Native American Church were not constitutionally entitled to ingest peyote as part of their religion's sacrament in the face of an Oregon law outlawing the use of peyote. Many aspects of the Smith decision have been sharply criticized, but none so much as the general view of religious exemptions announced by Justice Scalia's opinion for the Court. Justice Scalia distinguished freedom of religious belief from behavior driven by religious belief, and further distinguished laws directed at religion from general laws that merely collide with behavior driven by religious belief. That work done, Justice Scalia had a simple and flat response to the constitutional claimants in Smith: religious believers have no constitutional license to disregard otherwise-valid general laws that conflict with the dictates of their religion.

Smith sharply divided the Court on the question of extant doctrine as to the constitutional status of religious exemptions. Four of the justices—Justice O'Connor, who concurred in the outcome only, and the three dissenting justices—were outraged at what they saw as the Court's startling and unwarranted departure from settled doctrine. In their view, it had become a commonplace of constitutional doctrine that only governmental interests of "the highest order" could justify a state's interference with religiously driven behavior. Justice Scalia and his colleagues in the majority saw matters very differently; for them, the idea that religious motivation could exempt one from the reach of an otherwise valid general law was wholly novel and out of step with constitutional law and the rule of law generally.

Actually, neither of these characterizations of constitutional law ante-Smith was fair or convincing. Doctrine governing religious exemptions was in a shambles. In a small but durable line of cases involving the entitlement to unemployment benefits of persons whose religious scruples prevented them from working on Saturday (Sherbert v Verner and its progeny) or from manufacturing armaments, the Court had consistently held that the state could put people to a choice between their consciences and material disadvantage only if its reasons for doing so were markedly weighty. But only in one case outside of Sherbert v Verner and its unemployment benefits progeny had the Court actually appeared to act on that principle: in Wisconsin v Yoder, it held that Wisconsin's stake in requiring all children to pursue a recognized program of education until the age of sixteen was not sufficient to justify the state's interference with the religiously motivated commitment of the Amish to integrate children into their working society at the age of fourteen. Everywhere else there were strong indications that the Court could not in fact live with the broad dictum of Sherbert.

In Reynolds v United States, it should be remembered, the Court rejected not only the claim of the Mormons to a constitutional right to practice polygamy; it also rejected as unthinkable the idea of each religious believer creating a microenvironment of law molded to her separate beliefs. The cases that mediated between Reynolds and Sherbert half a century later—notably West Virginia State Board of Education v Barnette and Cantwell v Connecticut—were certainly more sympathetic to religion generally, but they were so fully wrapped with issues of free expression as to deflect rather than answer the concern that animated the Court in Reynolds.

In the Court's more modern experience, the Sherbert line and Yoder emerge as exceptions rather than the rule: in some cases since Yoder and outside the unemployment benefits area, the Court has paid lip service to the Sherbert rule, but in each of these cases it has found the compelling state interest test of Sherbert satisfied. While in other constitutional areas the compelling state interest test is fairly characterized as " 'strict' in theory and fatal in fact," in the religion cases the test is strict in theory but feeble in fact. Furthermore, even before Smith, the Court had begun to find reasons for rejecting the Sherbert formulation altogether in particular exemption contexts.

A candid assessment of the corpus of case law confronting the Court in Smith would have emphasized disarray, not order. And Smith itself, unhappily, did nothing to improve the situation. Neither the majority nor the dissenting positions in Smith offered a view of the exemption problem that can at once explain the distinct status of religion in our constitutional tradition, offer a workable and attractive approach to the exemption issue, and make more or less good sense out of the scattered pattern of precedent.

What is needed is a fresh start. We need to abandon the idea that it is the unique value of religious practices that sometimes entitles them to constitutional attention. What properly motivates constitutional solicitude for religious practices is their distinct vulnerability to discrimination, not their distinct value; and what is called for, in turn, is protection against discrimination, not privilege against legitimate governmental concerns. When we have replaced value with vulnerability, and the paradigm of privilege with that of protection, then it will be possible both to make sense of our constitutional past in this area and to chart an appealing constitutional future.

That is the project of this Article. We hope to demonstrate that the privilege view of religious exemptions is normatively unjustified and unattractive in its practical implications, while the protection view is both justified and attractive in its consequences.

Groups will figure at several points in our discussion. The predominance of groups in religious practice is important to the understanding of both privilege and protection. Religious groups are in some respects uncontroversially secure from the reach of state command. For example, however committed we may be to gender and racial equality, most of us do not imagine that the state can tell a religious group that it must be indifferent to gender or race in its choice of spiritual leaders. This aspect of our constitutional tradition may seem to support the idea that religion is constitutionally privileged. Yet religion has no monopoly on barriers limiting the reach of state authority. We do not imagine that the state could insist on gender or racial neutrality in an individual's choice of her psychiatrist, lawyer, or intimate friends. What makes religious practice distinct for these purposes is not its value, but rather its structure: religion often involves the extensive, communal enactment of behavior and relationships of the sort that ordinarily take place in far more cloistered, personal contexts.

While the group aspect of religious practice thus may produce false signs of constitutional privilege, it is a genuine element in the cultural dynamic that produces the need for constitutional protection. The solidarity and insularity of group membership and belief sustain the insistence of many religions on one right God and one right way to homage and salvation—upon one right and insular epistemology. It is the group identity of the faithful that mobilizes pity, distrust, or even hatred for those who are not believers.

Although we will ultimately return to offer some brief reflections on the relationship between religion and group rights, our path to those conjectures will travel almost entirely through territory dedicated to the problem of exemptions for religiously motivated conduct. * * *

II.   TWO MODALITIES OF CONSTITUTIONAL JUSTICE: PRIVILEGE AND PROTECTION

The vigorous pursuit of political justice in modern constitutional law has two great paradigms: the right of free expression and the right of African Americans to equal protection. These two traditions have dominated our modern constitutional sensibility, and discourse about the propriety of vigorous judicial intervention on behalf of other values often proceeds by way of comparison to them. There is a structural difference between these two pillars of constitutional justice, and understanding that difference illuminates the claim that religion makes on our constitutional judgments.

We have in mind the difference between the Constitution's privileging persons or practices and the Constitution's protecting such persons or practices. Speech is a practice that is privileged in our constitutional tradition, indeed privileged to a high degree. The state is often barred from restricting speech because of its content, even when there is reason to suppose that important concerns would be advanced if the speech in question were suppressed. In contrast, African Americans are not privileged, but rather protected. Constitutional law struggles to abolish caste and its residue, to secure for African Americans treatment as full and equal citizens of our national community.

In our constitutional tradition, a claimant who locates her behavior within the core of protected speech activity acquires the privilege of immunity from the reach of governmental authority, even under circumstances that would otherwise offer strong grounds for the exercise of that authority against her. She may act in a fashion that increases the likelihood that injuries to the property or persons of others may take place; she may act in a fashion that is itself injurious to others; she may even and especially act in a fashion that is injurious to the national interest as it is presently conceived. Her behavior is privileged, as against other behavior that shares these abstract features, and as against the interests of those persons who may be injured by that behavior.

A claimant who argues for exemption from the reach of state authority on grounds of racial equality stands in a different posture. She is insisting on parity, not advantage: she demands that the state behave in a fashion fully consistent with her status as an equal citizen, as opposed to treating her as a member of a subordinate class who by virtue of that membership does not enjoy the same concern and respect. She invokes the Constitution against subordination. She is asking for something that is in principle the due of every member of our political community. Her racial status is constitutionally distinct in the sense that it marks her as vulnerable to injustice, to treatment as other than an equal; her claim is for protection from that injustice.

Speech and racial equality are thus both treated distinctly and favorably by virtue of their inclusion in the agenda of judicial enforcement of the Constitution, while other claims of political justice—most prominently those diverse claims we lump into the broad category of "economic rights"—are excluded. But only speech is privileged by the substance of the norms upon which the constitutional judiciary draws when it acts. Put another way, privilege and protection refer not to the fact of constitutional (or judicial) priority, but to the grounds for such priority. A claim for constitutional privilege requires a showing of virtue or precedence, while a claim for constitutional protection requires a showing of vulnerability or victimization. The distinction between privilege and protection is therefore ultimately a distinction in constitutional objective. From the recognition of victimization, and of vulnerability to future victimization, flows the constitutional objective of protection; while from the recognition of virtue or precedence flows the constitutional objective of privilege.

The distinction between privilege and protection in constitutional justice cannot always be read from the surface of the rules employed by courts to protect constitutional principles: the compelling state interest test, for example, figures in both speech and racial equality doctrine. But beneath the facial rules of constitutional law, at the level of constitutional justice, the justification for distinct constitutional treatment and the appropriate scope of that treatment are different if the claim is one of privilege or one of protection.

In our constitutional jurisprudence there is no privileging of persons; indeed, opposing caste or subordination is one of the most robust projects of modern constitutional law. One might think that the converse is also true: because protection flows from a concern about vulnerability or victimization, it might seem that only persons or groups, rather than activities, may be the object of constitutional protection. But as religion itself vividly illustrates, individual and group identity can be defined by shared commitments and practices. More to the immediate point, persons and groups can be vulnerable to victimization by virtue of their shared commitments and practices. The bitter divisions of humanity along religious lines, and the global persecution of religious minorities throughout most of recorded history, make the victims of religious intolerance the ultimate and tragic exemplars of vulnerability.

Nevertheless, most modern commentary has proceeded on the assumption that the constitutional status of religious exemptions rises or falls on the degree to which religious practices are constitutionally privileged—privileged in the way, for example, that speech is privileged. If religiously motivated people are to be exempt from the application of laws that they would otherwise be required to obey, it is assumed, this must be because religion is esteemed by the Constitution in a way that most other human commitments, however intense or laudable, are not.

Indeed, though sharply divided in all other respects, the majority and minority factions in Smith tacitly agreed that arguments about religious exemptions should turn on concerns of privilege. * * *

* * *

III. THE CASE AGAINST THE PRIVILEGING VIEW OF RELIGIOUS EXEMPTIONS

A. *The Privileging of Religion Made More*
Precise: Unimpaired Flourishing

The underlying logic of the privileging view of religious exemptions is this: It is a matter of constitutional regret whenever government prevents or discourages persons from honoring their religious commitments; accordingly, government should act so as to avoid placing religious believers at a substantial disadvantage by virtue of their efforts to conform their conduct to their beliefs. This is the principle of unimpaired flourishing.

The principle of unimpaired flourishing is at the heart of the minority Justices' view in Smith, where it sponsored Justice O'Connor's ringing announcement that only governmental interests "of the highest order" could justify interference with religiously motivated conduct. It is also common to the discourse of those commentators who argue for generous religious exemptions. Michael McConnell, for example, holds that "[t]he purpose of free exercise exemptions is to ensure that incentives to practice a religion are not adversely affected by government action."

Unimpaired flourishing is sometimes offered as a principle of equity, as though it functions merely to make those who respond to the strong demands of their religious beliefs no worse off than others. But unimpaired flourishing is different than that: it privileges religious commitments over other deep commitments that persons have. Members of our political community are not generally entitled to governmental arrangements that enable them to honor their important commitments without being placed at a substantial disadvantage. * * *

We may believe that some personal commitments deserve special support, of course, like a parent's decision to remain at home with a newborn child for the first several months. This means we believe that child care under these circumstances should be privileged as against other commitments (as a matter of sound legislative judgment rather than constitutional dictate). Thus unimpaired flourishing, transposed to this context, would require fully paid parental leave. That is just the point. Unimpaired flourishing is a privileging principle—providing certain parents a benefit because they decide to remain home for a socially preferred reason, rather than for some other reason—even though it only leaves its beneficiary no worse off by virtue of engaging in the privileged conduct.

We have selected unimpaired flourishing to represent the privilege view of religious freedom because it captures the normative essence of the positions advanced by the most thoughtful partisans of a robust view of religious exemptions. In our discussion, however, little will turn on this precise formulation. Most if not all privilege views have this in common with unimpaired flourishing: they regard state interference with the observance of religious commandments as a constitutional vice that the state must avoid whenever it can do so without imperiling its most basic goals and obligations. * * *

B.   Unimpaired Flourishing Applied

* * *

* * * Religious belief need not be founded in reason, guided by reason, or governed in any way by the reasonable. Accordingly, the demands that religions place on the faithful, and the demands that the

faithful can in turn place on society in the name of unimpaired flourishing, are potentially extravagant.

Religious belief can direct parents to withhold medical assistance from their children, or adults to withhold such assistance from one another or to refuse such assistance for themselves. It can direct believers to maintain great caches of weapons against Armageddon; * * * Religion can demand sacrifices that range from vows of abject poverty, to the regular undertaking of expensive pilgrimages, to the ritual slaughter of species protected on grounds of civility or threatened extinction. It can underwrite employment practices that secular judgment would regard as grossly exploitative and dictate the subordination of women, persons in particular racial or ethnic groups, or homosexuals. To be at peace with their religious consciences, the faithful may require that public streets be closed to vehicular traffic on the Sabbath; that particular sites be preserved and freely accessible for their holy worship; and even that the basic institutions of their society be pervasively arranged in conformity with their religious precepts.

The potential of religious beliefs to be arbitrarily demanding, to be greedy in their demands on both the individual and the society committed to the unimpaired flourishing of its religiously faithful, is compounded by the possible all-or-nothing quality of religious dictates. * * * The principle of unimpaired flourishing, as a result, commends a vision of a world that is unrecognizable, unattractive, and ultimately incoherent. In this world, the faithful would be licensed to do as their faith requires, with little regard for the consequences as seen from the vantage of secular society. * * * In this world, the faithful whose beliefs so required would receive disproportionate authority over decisions about the use of collective authority. The chaotic picture that emerges is ultimately incoherent in this sense: the demands of one faith would ultimately extend so far as to come into sharp conflict with the requirements of other religions, and some mechanism, presumably secular, would have to arbitrate.

But, of course, no proponent of the constitutional privileging of religion actually means to take us into this ungainly world. Significantly, almost all judges and commentators who urge something like the principle of unimpaired flourishing nevertheless want collective authority in the United States to remain pretty much as it is; they merely want to find a haven for religiously motivated conduct at the margins of state authority. This produces incoherence of a much more immediate and troubling sort: proponents of unimpaired flourishing are in the unhappy position of offering an unexplainably selective, comparatively modest, practical agenda for reform, on the basis of a sweeping and deeply radical principle of political justice. The result is an analytical scramble. Various limitations are offered, often in combination. Religiously motivated acts that harm others, it is sometimes suggested, may be curtailed by state law, but the state may not interfere with religious believers on paternalistic grounds. * * *

These attempts to rescue unimpaired flourishing from its own logic are unsatisfying. If religious motivation signifies legal immunity only at the margins of state authority, there is good reason to suppose that in these cases we are actually responding to well-founded—if inarticulate—doubts about state authority in general rather than to the needs of religion in particular. On this account, if we valued liberty in general to the appropriate degree, there would be no need for the additional feature of religious motivation to enter the story. This may well be the best way to understand Yoder. Parents who have a systematic, reflective, and durable scheme for educating their children may be entitled to substitute their curricular judgment for the state's—at least at the margin. If so, then Yoder may have been correctly decided; if not, then the religious basis of the Amish approach to education ought not matter.

Indeed, important constitutional benefits depend upon our willingness to recognize this connection between specifically religious interests and more general principles of privilege. Religious groups perform a valuable service in a freedom-loving society: they push at the margins of liberty. But that service is best realized when the regime of law refuses to privilege religion, so that the systematic but idiosyncratic impulses of organized religion act on behalf of us all when they help to maintain or expand the ambit of constitutionally secure choice.

Tests that purport to balance secular and religious needs against each other are at best fronts for more substantive but obscure intuitions about how particular claims for religious exemptions ought to come out. What exactly can such tests for religious exemption mean? Are they meant to be restatements of an overall utilitarian calculus of the form: do we improve utility overall if we pursue Legal Rule A over Legal Rule B, or vice versa? If not, what possible meaning can they have? One is left with nothing but a fictive interest group deal in which religions get "something" but not "too much." And if, on the other hand, utilitarian calculus is indeed the core of the proposed balance, this approach seems at once to have read the principle of unimpaired flourishing entirely out of the equation and to have reduced the issue of exemptions to one of social policy that legislatures are best able to determine.

Beset by these difficulties, judges and commentators who favor some form of constitutional privilege for religion have taken refuge in the compelling state interest test. The compelling state interest test is normally applied in constitutional contexts where practically all instances of collective behavior with the triggering feature are expected to be unconstitutional, but extraordinary cases can be imagined that would have the triggering feature but not fail constitutional scrutiny. Though seldom applied literally, and hence an imperfect guide to what actually distinguishes the extraordinary case, the compelling state interest test, with its strong presumption against validity, seems a reasonably useful banner under which to conduct analyses in cases of this sort. Explicit racial distinctions that disfavor racial minorities provide the classic example.

But in many religious exemption cases, the presumptive invalidity implicit in the compelling state interest test is misplaced. There is a substantial range of religiously motivated conduct—readily observable in contemporary national experience—that quite clearly must yield to conflicting secular laws. This has tacitly been recognized by the all-but-total failure of Sherbert's dictum to travel outside the unemployment benefits situation. As we have noted, the Supreme Court has paid lip service to that standard in some non-Sherbert exemption cases, but found the test satisfied in all except Yoder. That experience could merely reflect the distortions of a small sample, of course, were it not for the fact that the courts of appeals have similarly applied the test in words only, and so found a diverse set of garden-variety legislative interests powerful enough to overwhelm the claims of religious exemption. Under these circumstances, the compelling state interest test becomes just another balancing test, obscuring rather than clarifying analysis. Its invocation here threatens to dilute the meaning of the test in its other, more proper, applications.

C.   The Normative difficulties of Unimpaired Flourishing

1.   The sectarian defect.

In a liberal democracy, the claim that one particular set of practices or one particular set of commitments ought to be privileged (as we have used that term) bears a substantial burden of justification. As we shall see, the background circumstances—that religion is singled out for distinct and emphatic treatment in the text of the Constitution, that many of the colonists fled religious persecution under circumstances that would have made religious liberty vital, that there are various features of religious liberty in our working constitutional tradition that seem at once important and well settled—do not in themselves support the proposition that religion ought to be privileged. An attractive and full account of religion's place in our constitutional tradition can proceed from protection rather than privilege. justification for the privileging of religion must proceed on normative grounds.

* * *

2.   Two nonsectarian strategies.

There are, however, two arguments for the constitutional privileging of religion that do not suffer from this sectarian defect. The first appeals to persons within our political community to recognize—from the outside, in effect—the anguished state of the religious believer who is under state fiat to behave in a way that flatly contradicts the demands of her religion. The second suggests that organized religion enables our society to maintain an important place for the moral, non-self-regarding aspects of life.

One version of the first argument asks us to consider the potential stakes for the religious believer of disobeying her God's commandments. They may be such that it is an understatement to speak of them as

matters of life and death; they may be no less than eternal paradise or damnation. We cannot be expected to act as though those are the stakes, of course, but we can appreciate the unhappy state of someone who regards them as the stakes. This seems an unpromising way to put the case. It asks us to assume—in a way that seems especially inappropriate when it comes to matters spiritual—that self-interest rather than conscience is the stronger human drive. It expects us to treat the religious believer's very long-term (possibly abstract, metaphorical) self-interested reasons for obedience as motivationally more powerful than other persons' immediate self-interest and driving passions—the deeply devoted artist, the parent with a hungry child, or the lover overwrought with love, who are driven to disobey the law. Furthermore, it asks us either to treat all religions as having the structure of eternal reward/punishment because some do, or to parse among religions on this peculiar ground.
* * *

The better version of this first argument for privileging religion emphasizes mortal conscience rather than eternal consequences. It encourages us to see that the religious believer is in the grip of conscience—a motivation that is at once powerful and laudable—and to regard that circumstance as grounds for excusing her from obedience to laws that force her to choose between her conscience and her well-being at the hands of the state. But while conscience is the better motivational grounds for privileging religion, there remain persuasive objections to the claim. Again, religious conscience is just one of many very strong motivations in human life, and there is no particular reason to suppose that it is likely to matter more in the run of religious lives generally than will other very powerful forces in the lives of both the nonreligious and the religious.

This is not to trivialize religious interests. We have no trouble agreeing with Douglas Laycock when he argues that it would be an error to maintain that "(a) soldier who believes he must cover his head before an omnipresent God is constitutionally indistinguishable from a soldier who wants to wear a Budweiser gimme cap." Likewise, we agree with Michael McConnell that a Saturday work schedule imposes qualitatively different burdens on those who "like to go sailing on Saturdays" and those who "observe the Sabbath" on that day. But these comparisons largely beg the question. Of course, burdens upon religious practice differ from burdens upon tastes in fashion and recreation. Do they also differ from the considerably more weighty burdens imposed by secular commitments to one's family, or by secular moral obligations, or by physical disabilities?

Consider two cases:

(1) Goldman is an army officer. His faith requires him to wear a yarmulke. The yarmulke is inconsistent with the Army uniform. The Army insists that Goldman must resign his commission or comply with the uniform regulation. The Army relies entirely on its interest in uniform appearance; it does not contend that Goldman's obli-

gation to wear the yarmulke will in any other way impair his performance.

(2) Collar is an army officer. He has a rare skin disorder on his neck that prevents him from wearing a tie. Army uniform regulations require that all officers wear ties on certain occasions. The Army insists that Collar must resign his commission or comply with the regulation. The Army relies entirely on its interest in uniform appearance; it does not contend that Collar's disability will in any other way impair his performance.

Should we regard Goldman's interests as more weighty than Collar's? Does the Army have a constitutional obligation to accommodate Goldman's religious burden if it accommodates Collar's disability, or vice-versa? To maintain that the Constitution privileges religion, we would have to uncover some ground for constitutionally favoring Goldman's interests over Collar's, a ground that is not impermissibly sectarian or partisan; and that is precisely what is lacking in the case for privileging religion.

The second nonsectarian argument for the constitutional privileging of religion appeals to our desire as a society to remain alive to the moral, non-self-regarding aspects of life, and sees organized religion as a taproot of this vital aspect of human flourishing. But while religion sponsors the highest forms of community, compassion, love, and sacrifice, one need only look around the world, or probe our own history, to recognize that it also sponsors discord, hate, intolerance, and violence. Religion is enormously varied in the demands it places on the faithful. As we observed earlier, religious faith or belief need not be founded in reason, guided by reason, or governed in any way by the reasonable. Religious commandments can be understood as inspired by beneficent forces that are beyond human comprehension or verification, or by the result of the spite, play, accident, or caprice of entities or forces that do not necessarily hold human welfare paramount. The only limitations are those of the human imagination or the range of divine circumstance (depending on whether one looks from within or without religious beliefs): the bounds of the former are very broad indeed, and the logic of the latter implies the absence of any bounds whatsoever. We mention all this because, while the commitment to forces outside and above ourselves seems an attractive human capacity and impulse, the substance of the commitment matters, and there is no warranty on the laudability of religious commitments.

* * * If we believe in a given case that the polity's decision to enact a law was sound, the claim that a conscientious defiance of this same law is virtuous requires some moral gymnastics. There are situations in which our own ambivalence or distaste toward the necessary makes it possible to hold these two views simultaneously. * * *

Religions, of course, are by no means the only sources of moral reflection and impulse; nor are moral reflection and impulse the only forms of elevated human activity. These are not small quibbles to be worked out empirically. They go very much to the heart of the objection to privileging religion. A plural democratic society like ours must develop constitutional principles that recognize that a citizen's ability to contribute to the regime does not depend upon membership in any particular religion, or, indeed, upon religiosity at all. To hold otherwise would simply be another way to insist upon the truth of a particular religion, or to deny the truth of secular ethics. Of course, it might be true, as a contingent empirical matter, that religious faith correlates well with civic virtue, even if there is no theoretically necessary relationship between the two. But that sort of contingent empirical connection between religious belief and constitutional objectives is not an appropriate ground for privileging religion.

Once we have agreed that society must respect the virtue of individuals without regard to their religious beliefs, the claim that religion so breeds virtue that it is constitutionally privileged becomes indefensibly partisan among conflicting views of what is valuable in life and how that which is valuable is best realized. We use the term partisan here, rather than sectarian as before, because there is a difference between the argument that God's commands are prior to those of the state and the arguments we are considering now. The nonsectarian arguments are available to a person from outside religious belief, unlike the sectarian claim for obeisance. But they are nevertheless inconsistent with our constitutional tradition, which contemplates a modern, pluralistic society, whose members find their identities, shape their values, and live the most valuable moments of their lives in a grand diversity of relationships, affiliations, activities, and passions that share a constitutional presumption of legitimacy.

To observe that the burden or nobility of religious belief offers no grounds for constitutionally privileging religion is not to deny the capacity of legislative bodies to accommodate religious beliefs or even help religious institutions to prosper, where good reasons exist for so doing. Some scholars mistakenly find traces of constitutional privilege implicit in the very idea of religious accommodation. * * * Nonsectarian judgment comfortably supports the conclusion that for some people under some circumstances the demands of religious belief are "special and important" in the same sense that disabilities are "special and important": both can have profound effects upon individual well-being. But it does not follow that either religious beliefs or disabilities are "intrinsically valuable." Likewise, policy makers might legitimately take into account the instrumental value of religious institutions as aids to moral development in a democratic society. But, at most, this argument simply indicates that we should think carefully before reading the Establishment Clause to fetter legislative discretion to advance religion where it is judged to have nonsectarian social utility.

3. Generalized versions of the claim for privileging: If you can't beat 'em . . . .

Thus far, our objections to privileging religion have shared a common theme: they have emphasized the sectarian or partisan character of the arguments on behalf of religion. This raises the possibility that a constitutional privilege for religion could be rehabilitated if it were generalized to include a wider range of human commitments and thus avoid the complaints of sectarianism or partisanship. The idea would be to privilege all acts of conscience, not merely those that are rooted in a conventionally religious system of belief.

The difficulty with this approach becomes clear when we try to give content to the idea of conscientious commitment. * * * On the one hand, if we try to contain the idea of conscience within relatively narrow bounds, we will encounter our old difficulties of explaining why a particular form of commitment should be treated differently from comparably gripping life projects. On the other hand, if we broaden conscience to include a great swath of the deep commitments people hold, we face the fantastic idea that it is a matter of constitutional regret whenever an otherwise valid law collides with the commitments of an individual or group.

Our best account of a general privileging of conscience would understand the key term, conscience, as follows: An important mark of a well-formed person is an internal gyroscope that pulls her toward doing the right thing and away from doing the wrong thing. As right and wrong are understood here, self-interest—in an immediate, material, short-term sense—is only coincidentally congruent with rectitude. The tug of this gyroscope toward the right thing is consciously experienced, but in many forms: as raw impulse, as deep but unlocated conviction, or as fully articulate and located within a scheme of belief. The provenance or bona des of this tug is similarly and associatedly diverse: if it is consciously acknowledged at all, it may range from the command of a deity, to the interpreted understanding of a covenant, to a mystic and intuitively driven sense, to a constructed and coherent, but free-standing system of moral judgment. Under some circumstances—chronic and life shaping, or acute and focused—this pull toward rectitude becomes a central, dominating feature of a person's motivation and self-identity. When these circumstances obtain, and a person acts on them, she is performing an act of conscience. Acts of conscience, on this account, are what should be constitutionally privileged.

We have tried in this account to offer a generous conceptual platform on which to found the privileging of conscience, but the problems of justifying such a privilege remain. As with religion more narrowly, we have to separate the general appeal of people being motivated by conscience from the content of their conscientious motivations. * * *

As to the substance of acts of conscience, it by no means follows from the internal phenomenology of conscience, which has rectitude at its core, that we should be optimistic that conscientious impulses will lead persons to do good things. Both good and evil can emanate from conscience * * *. Again, it must be remembered that conscience is being offered here to license the defiance of otherwise valid laws. Perhaps the claim is essentially one of deep sympathy for the person caught between the demands of her conscience and the demands of her state. But we must still justify constitutionalizing sympathy for the strong pull of conscience over the pulls of love, passionately demanding life projects, and the infinitely creative demands of strong psychological compulsion.

Of course, as we note below, settled and attractive constitutional doctrine does in fact privilege a broad variety of conduct that is relevant to conscientious commitments. Issues of conscience play an important role in decisions about family, friendship, belief, and expression, and these decisions receive constitutional privileging through doctrines like privacy, autonomy, and speech. * * *

* * * The religious-exemption issue we have been considering begins at precisely the point where the general shield of private behavior leaves off. If we elide religion with these other matters already more or less uncontroversially shielded by the Constitution, then we need new language to address the question of what we have heretofore been calling religious exemptions. We gain nothing here, and may in fact cause conceptual mischief elsewhere: using religion or even conscience to redescribe values like privacy or autonomy may badly unsettle our understandings of the Establishment Clause.

D. The Failed Argument from Text and History

Often, proponents of a privileging view claim that a simple textual or historical argument distinguishes burdens upon religion from even serious impositions upon secular well-being. This argument sets normative concerns aside and claims a legislated privilege, even in the face of normative difficulties. The Constitution is thus read like a tax code or a treaty, the meaning of which is historically located, recoverable, and articulate to the question of privilege. But neither the text nor the history of the founding (even were we to concede that the founding is the only or most relevant historical period) enables us to choose between privileging and protecting accounts of religious liberty. We believe this state of affairs reflects more general truths. The text of the Constitution is seldom if ever dispositive of interesting constitutional questions. Neither is the history. It is conceptually impossible that the complex social and legal events surrounding the founding could answer hard questions without a normative view to guide the interpretive enterprise. As we and others have argued elsewhere, the project of constitutional interpretation involves the pragmatic pursuit of political justice, not the positivist recovery of fixed historical meaning.

* * *

E. Misreadings of the Status of Religion in Our Constitutional Tradition

1. Uncontroverted elements of (religious) liberty.

Much of the appeal of unimpaired flourishing or other privileging views of religious freedom comes from the observation that our constitutional tradition does seem to exempt religious belief and certain aspects of religious practice from the reach of state authority. This much seems common ground: Persons are entitled to their religious beliefs and cannot on account of those beliefs be punished or deprived of benefits otherwise their due; further, important aspects of religious practice—for example, the choice by a religious group of their compensated spiritual leaders—are largely beyond the reach of the collective authority of the state. What may seem to follow is that religion is systematically valued both in our constitutional tradition and in our best understanding of political justice in a way that should carry over to the question of exemption from otherwise valid general laws. On this account, it seems arbitrary and wrong to deny religion in the exemption context the special status it is acknowledged to enjoy elsewhere.

But this is a misreading of the common ground where religious belief and certain elements of religious practice are beyond the reach of collective authority. The best explanation for each of these attractive limits on state authority does not involve privileging religion. We can see this if we consider each in turn a little more closely.

Consider first the observation that persons are, in a deep sense, entitled to hold their particular religious beliefs. No one may be punished for her religious beliefs; or made to affirm other beliefs; or denied the opportunity to discuss and publish her beliefs; or prevented from associating with others to reflect upon, celebrate, and consummate their beliefs in (otherwise benign) ceremonies of affirmation or worship. All this is true, and sits high in the pantheon of constitutional truths; but none of it is distinct to religious belief. * * *

Our freedom of belief extends to political, aesthetic, and moral matters, to matters that are areligious and antireligious. It is certainly true, for example, that belief in an orthodox deity cannot be made a condition of public office; but neither can belief in the virtues of religion generally, or belief in the falsity of religion, or belief in the virtues of maintaining an open mind to religion, or belief that religion is worth worrying about, or belief in the justness of capital punishment or the redistribution of wealth * * *. It bears emphasis * * * that these beliefs are privileged not on analogy to religious beliefs, or on the view that they occupy the same role in the lives of the persons who hold them as do religious beliefs, but on the simple and sufficient ground that they are beliefs, and that our political community deeply respects the capacity of its members to arrive at and champion their individual understandings of the world.

Consider next the observation that important religious practices have a distinct status in our understanding of constitutional justice, as illustrated, for example, by the widely held view that it would be constitutionally inappropriate to apply Title VII prohibitions of race and sex discrimination to the employment of religious leaders such as priests, pastors, or rabbis. Here, the story is a little more complex, but ends in much the same way as did our observations about freedom of belief. We have in our constitutional tradition—in clear spirit, and if not in clear letter, only because the occasions to spell the point out have not often arisen—an important, morally indispensable sense of the private and the public. Thus, the state can tell us whom we must accommodate at our lunch counters, but not at our dinner tables. The question is not one of "state action," but of state authority, and it does not turn on an obtuse, clunky view that private and public can be mechanically or sweepingly distinguished. But the distinction exists, and it may ultimately be the most important source of liberty there is. * * *

Often, private behavior takes place in private places and in private ways: classically, in the home * * *. Public behavior finds its most common venues in more widely accessible spaces. * * *

Often, but not always. Organized religious activity projects distinctly private behavior into public space and involves distinctly private relationships that are bound by contract and compensated by dollars. * * * The state cannot prescribe a nondiscriminatory protocol for a group's choice of the person who is to bear this private responsibility to its members any more than the state could prescribe such a protocol for the selection of a psychiatrist, or of a neighbor in whom to confide one's hopes and concerns. The aspects of religious practice that are uncontroversially secure from the reach of some state commands are so secure because they are private in general and recognizable ways, not because they are religious.

There are, of course, aspects of all these relationships—priest/parishioner, psychiatrist/patient, friend/friend—that are appropriately vulnerable to state regulation. A religious group may be restrained from making a child its leader under circumstances threatening to the child's well-being, or enslaving or otherwise coercing the service of its adult religious guide, or beating or starving her in the name of ecstatic insight.

The controversial aspect of religious exemptions begins at precisely the point where the general shield of private behavior leaves off. In the present state of constitutional law, persons are not entitled to consume banned drugs like peyote alone in the privacy of their homes, or with good friends who join them in a search for enlightenment through altered states of consciousness; willing partners are not entitled to enter into polygamous or polyandrous marriages * * *.

  2. The Sherbert Quartet.

Sherbert and the short but durable line of cases that follow its lead are widely perceived as supporting the privileging view of religious freedom. In each of these cases, the Court held that a religiously motivated person was constitutionally entitled to retain her eligibility for state unemployment insurance, notwithstanding her observation of the Sabbath or scrupled refusal to work in the manufacture of armaments. Sherbert was the first case to assert that laws interfering with religiously motivated conduct must be analyzed under the compelling state interest test. While that promise is largely unfulfilled in other contexts, Sherbert itself has never been directly questioned by the Court and enjoys widespread support in critical commentary. On the privileging account, Sherbert is taken at its most literal and expansive word: most of us, most of the time, must take laws as we find them, but when we act in response to the dictates of our religion, the laws must yield to us unless they are crucial to very important state interests.

In Smith, justices on both sides of the exemption issue seemed to agree—at least tacitly—that Sherbert must be understood as privileging religion in this way. The four justices who resisted the majority approach to religious exemptions rested their case squarely on Sherbert; and Justice Scalia, writing for the majority, struggled unconvincingly to confine a privileging view of Sherbert to the unique circumstances of the unemployment insurance cases. Commentators on the exemption problem largely replicate the binary structure of disagreement among the justices in Smith: either Sherbert is right and religiously motivated conduct prevails against all but the most compelling of state interests, or Sherbert is wrong, and religiously motivated conduct is not so privileged, bringing serious constitutional scrutiny to an effective close.

Neglected on all sides is an understanding of Sherbert that depends on the protection of minority religious believers rather than the privileging of religiously motivated conduct. Government need not sympathize with religious interests to accommodate them. That much is clear from our attitude toward physical disabilities: we certainly do not consider disabilities beneficial to society, but we believe it wrong to hold the disabled responsible for their condition and believe that the government should do something to make their lives easier. Likewise, even those who consider religiousness a matter for regret might nevertheless support accommodation because it makes religious individuals happier. Of course, the existence of individual interests in accommodation does not by itself generate a constitutional claim. What transforms religious accommodation from a mere policy concern to a constitutional issue is the vulnerability of religion to prejudice and persecution.

Seen through the lens of protection, the Sherbert Quartet ceases to be an anomaly in the jurisprudence of religious freedom and the Constitution more generally, and stands as precedent for a more reasonable and nuanced view of the exemptions issue. In Sherbert itself, South Carolina's violation of norms sounding in protection was transparent, and was an explicit and important element in the Court's opinion. Ms. Sherbert was a Sabbatarian, whose unavailability for work on Saturdays was treated by the state as making her ineligible for the receipt of unemployment benefits. But South Carolina had a Sunday closing law, so that mainstream religious believers were not put to the painful choice between fidelity to the commands of their religion and eligibility for important state benefits in hard times. Writing for the Court, Justice Brennan emphasized this disparity in circumstance:

> Significantly South Carolina expressly saves the Sunday worshipper from having to make the kind of choice which we here hold infringes the Sabbatarian's religious liberty. (Justice Brennan here quoted the South Carolina statute favoring Sunday worshippers.) No question

of the disqualification of a Sunday worshipper for benefits is likely to arise, since we cannot suppose that an employer will discharge him in violation of the statute. The unconstitutionality of the disqualification of the Sabbatarian is thus compounded by the religious discrimination which South Carolina's general statutory scheme necessarily effects.

The choice of Sunday as a uniform day of rest is itself constitutionally provocative, but we are concerned now with a different point. South Carolina's election of Sunday, placed side-by-side with its refusal to accommodate the needs of Sherbert and other Sabbatarians to decline Saturday employment, gives one overwhelming reasons to suppose that the state has disadvantaged a vulnerable group.

* * *

The protection rationale can fully explain the unique results in the Sherbert line of cases. It can also explain the robust use of the compelling state interest test in those cases: when we explore protection in more detail below, we will encounter good reason to regard that test as apt to Sherbert and certain other religion cases, but not well-suited to exemption cases in general. For the moment, though, we are concerned only to demonstrate that one can be sympathetic to the Court's general treatment of the unemployment benefits cases without embracing the privileging of religion.

IV. THE PROTECTION OF MINORITY BELIEF AS A RATIONALE FOR RELIGIOUS EXEMPTIONS

A. A New Approach: Equal Regard

We advocate a new approach to religious exemptions, founded on protection rather than privilege. Protection can explain and justify the distinct status of religion in our constitutional tradition, offer a workable and attractive approach to religious exemptions, and—surprisingly— make some sense out of the patchwork of precedent regarding religious exemptions.

History provides ample evidence that religious distinctions inspire the worst sorts of political oppression. Post–Reformation religious strife and the religious persecution from which many colonial settlers fled come immediately to our minds. But we should not imagine that we need to look that far; within the memory of many adults, anti-Catholicism and anti-Semitism were rampant in many parts of the United States. The sad history of religious intolerance and the unfortunate sociological truths upon which it rests invite and demand the constitutional protection of minority religious beliefs.

In place of the mistaken claim that religion is uniquely valued by the Constitution, an approach based on protection depends upon the special vulnerability of minority religious beliefs to hostility or indifference. Where privilege sponsored the principle of unimpaired flourishing, protection offers the principle of equal regard. Equal regard requires simply that government treat the deep, religiously inspired concerns of minority religious believers with the same regard as that enjoyed by the deep concerns of citizens generally.

Equal regard needs to be on the active agenda of the judiciary because of the confluence of two circumstances. First, for many religious believers, being able to conform their conduct to the dictates of their beliefs is a matter of deep concern. Second, the religious provenance of these strong behavioral impulses makes them highly vulnerable to discrimination by official decision makers. Both of these propositions are widely acknowledged and do not require detailed support here. But the second bears elaboration.

Religious commandments are not necessarily founded on or limited by reasons accessible to nonbelievers; often they are understood to depend on at or covenant and to implicate forces or beings beyond human challenge or comprehension. Religion is often the hub of tightly knit communities, whose habits, rituals, and values are deeply alien to outsiders. At best, this is likely to produce a chronic interfaith "tone deafness," in which the persons of one faith do not easily empathize with the concerns of persons in other faiths. * * *

The axis of antagonism—even with its broad range from indifference to hostility—does not fully capture the subtle pattern of religious vulnerability. From the perspective of some faiths, it is desirable to convert nonbelievers rather than to injure them. Such messianic faiths may have the welfare of the nonbelievers genuinely and fully in mind as they zealously seek converts to the true faith; they may even have the welfare of the nonbelievers fully in mind as they seek to shape the legal regime to discourage or prevent the nonbelievers from pursuing their own beliefs. Even when conversion is not their aim, dominant faiths (or clusters of faiths) that recognize the value and concerns of others may nevertheless use political power to favor themselves. For example, Christians might seek to benefit their faith by prescribing prayers in public schools or by shutting down businesses on Sundays. Proponents might regard these partisan favors as rewards for the virtuous or as inducements to nonbelievers—or simply as nondiscriminatory benefits available to all wise enough to recognize the propriety of the Christian way of life.

These nonantagonist variations may be "kinder, gentler" forms of discrimination, but they remain stark failures of equal regard. The possibility of nonantagonistic disregard of minority concerns makes religious discrimination particularly subtle and complex. This will be important to bear in mind as we turn to the task of sketching a jurisprudence of equal regard.

B.   The General Methodology of a Jurisprudence of Equal Regard

* * * Wherever else it may lead, equal regard prohibits the state from singling out the practices of minority religions for distinct and disfavored treatment. Cases like Church of the Lukumi Babalu Aye v City of Hialeah are thus easy under an equal regard regime. * * * When

the state fails—whether through hate, habit, a misguided impulse to lead others to the true way, or an indifference born of a lack of empathy—to treat the deep concerns of minority believers with the same solicitude as those of mainstream citizens, the judiciary ought to intervene. The problem is crafting a constitutional jurisprudence that is suited to this task.

Let us consider the general pattern of claims for religious exemptions where the law is not overtly or facially hostile to a particular religious faith. Such claims can arise in many circumstances, but two recurring prototypes are instructive. In the first, the state has a law of general application in place, but has carved out exemptions for those able to claim personal hardship or some other particularized qualification. These special exemption statutes include laws that designate formal categories of beneficiaries and others that invoke functional categories. An example of a formal special exemption is a law prohibiting the consumption of alcohol but permitting the sacramental ingestion of wine; an example of a functional special exemption is the requirement of "good cause" in unemployment compensation regimes for persons who are unable to accept or continue in a particular job.

In the second prototype for constitutional claims, the challenged state law has no provision for exemptions. * * *

Equal regard requires that the state treat the deep, religiously inspired concerns of minority religious believers with the same regard as that enjoyed by the deep concerns of citizens generally. In either a special exemption or an at rule case, the equal regard exemption claimant must demonstrate (a) that a general law significantly interferes with some actions motivated by her deep religious commitment; and (b) that had her deep, religiously inspired concerns been treated with the same regard as that enjoyed by the fundamental concerns of citizens generally, she would have been exempted from the reach of the general law. Proposition (b), in turn, can be supported by one of two claims. Either (1) the state has failed to appreciate the gravity of her interest in complying with the commands of her faith; or (2) the state has appreciated the gravity of her interest, but nevertheless has played favorites among different belief systems on sectarian grounds. * * *

To appreciate the gravity of a religious believer's interest in complying with the commands of her faith, the state must adopt the perspective of the believer; it is not at liberty to judge that interest. Equal regard bars the state from disparaging religious interests that seem unreasonable from a secular perspective. So, for example, the state may not defend its refusal to accommodate a religious interest in animal sacrifice by arguing that it is silly or disgusting for people to take a deep interest in slaughtering chickens.

This establishes a limited kind of deference to religious perspectives. The state is further obliged to defer to the perspective of a religious believer with regard to the existence of an interest of great weight within the life of a believer. The state is obliged to treat these deep interests as equal in importance and dignity to the deep religious or secular interests of other persons. The state is not obliged, however, to accept a religious believer's judgment about the importance of her religious interests as compared to the legitimate secular interests of the state. This distinction is crucial to the idea of equal regard: outside religion, the deep interests of individuals figure into but do not override the secular concerns of the state * * *. Equal regard insists on parity for religious belief, not privilege. If religious believers could enforce their priorities over the secular concerns of the state, we would be back to unimpaired flourishing in all of its unacceptable extremity.

The state's obligation to avoid sectarian favoritism among the holders of different belief systems bars it from preferring the deep interests of persons of one faith over those of another. The state cannot act on the perception that one faith is true, ennobling, attractive, or somehow congenial, or that another faith is false, debasing, repulsive, or somehow uncongenial. As with the obligation of the state to appreciate the gravity of a religious believer's interests, however, the obligation to avoid favoritism does not prevent the state from acting on its secular interests. So a decision, for example, to bar the importation of a particular animal on the grounds that it is a notorious carrier of a dangerous disease, does not suffer from the vice of favoritism, even though a particular faith regards the animal as sacred and an important part of its religious ceremonies.

To this point, we have been describing the conceptual entailments of equal regard, entailments that address both special exemption and at rule cases. We now need to explore more concrete, hands-on judicial approaches to religious exemption claims. Here the difference between at rule and special exemption cases becomes important.

We can begin with special exemption cases and the curious status of Sherbert and its progeny. Equal regard offers a principled basis for a distinction the Court has long since backed into but has not fully elaborated; namely, the distinction between at rule cases like Smith, and special exemption cases, at least functional special exemption cases, like Sherbert.

State unemployment benefit regimes understandably require that persons be available for work in order to qualify. Inevitably, cases will arise in which putative beneficiaries are unable to accept or continue in a particular job because of special circumstances. Our earlier example of a worker who develops a nasty allergy to the material she must handle in her job is apt here. So each state, we can imagine, must develop a mechanism for determining whether a disabling circumstance is weighty enough to justify the worker's refusal to accept or continue in a job, yet narrow enough to leave the applicant generally available for work.

* * *

* * * [When] the state has defined a functional exemption category: the exemption is available to claimants who meet certain requirements

(in the unemployment cases, persons generally available for work but unable to take a particular job for personal reasons; in the zoning cases, noncommercial educational and civic institutions with a reason for wishing to build in a residential neighborhood) * * * [i]n principle, the exemption embraces religious interests along with secular ones. Once we know that a particular claimant fits the relevant profile but has nevertheless been denied accommodation, we may appropriately insist that the state prove that it has honored the principle of equal regard.

Matters are even simpler if a religious claimant demands the benefit of a formal, rather than functional, exemption. At best, the formal category would be a proxy for an unarticulated functional category. At worst, the category would reflect an objectionable discrimination like that rejected by the Santeria case. If, for example, a state liquor control ordinance were to exempt the sacramental use of liquor by some sects but not others, the Constitution would require generalizing the exemption.

Less easy to resolve are at rule cases, of which Smith is a good example. In Smith, Oregon's prohibition on the use of peyote was a ban, applicable to everyone; there was no exemption procedure and hence no pole of circumstance that presumptively qualified for exemption. The question posed by equal regard is whether the state's refusal to accommodate the sacramental needs of the Native American Church represented a failure to take the deep interests of the members of the church as seriously as well-recognized secular interests or the interests of adherents to mainstream religions. * * *

The compelling state interest test, especially in the demanding form it takes elsewhere in constitutional law, is poorly suited to the job of answering this question. To be sure, the test in its normal form can function as an effective filter for failures of equal regard; by insisting that the state grant religious exemptions except when doing so would compromise interests of "the highest order," we require the state to weigh religious interests very highly. But our earlier observations about the unworkability of the equal-flourishing approach suggest that serious application of the compelling state interest test would be far too fine a filter, one which distorts civil order in unrecognizable and normatively unattractive ways.

A more satisfying judicial implementation of equal regard depends upon making local comparisons designed to measure the degree of accommodation implicit in the statutory scheme as a whole. * * *

Smith and like cases will require exactly this sort of a case-by-case approach, in which evidence of the failure of equal regard is laid on the table and evaluated. In Smith itself, the evidence was cloudy at best. Oregon, like many states, made exceptions to its alcohol laws for the sacramental use of wine, but the social implications of sacramental wine and sacramental peyote may be very different. Nine other states and the federal government have made exceptions for the sacramental use of peyote, however, and we are a sufficiently national culture to see in this fact some evidence that such an exception would be reasonable in Oregon as well. That reasonability, coupled with the latitude mainstream religions enjoy to consummate their sacraments, argues for finding a failure of equal regard. Smith, we believe, could have plausibly come out either way on a case-by-case equal regard inquiry.

* * *

C. *Equal Regard and the Special Case of Secular Claimants*

A special case that fits imperfectly with our analysis thus far is that of secular claims of conscience. To address that case, we need to pause a moment to give content to two very difficult terms. For our purposes, a person is in the grip of conscience when an ethical tug toward doing the right thing becomes a central, dominating feature of her motivation and self-identity. And, for our purposes, the line between secular and religious conscience is roughly this: religious conscience is crucially dependent on schemes of fact and value (epistemologies) that are private in the sense that they do not depend upon their conformity to generally accepted tests of truth or widely shared perceptions of value; secular conscience, in contrast, appeals to a public epistemology that depends on generally accepted tests of truth and widely shared perceptions of value.

Equal regard, of course, is a symmetrical principle, and applies to secular as well as sectarian concerns. But it does not follow that the enforcement of equal regard as it applies to secular conscience is appropriately on the agenda of the judiciary. * * * As a judicially enforced constitutional principle, equal regard must be justified by vulnerability to discrimination.

Although our focus thus far has been on the vulnerability of minority religious faiths to discrimination, secular beliefs that take the form of deep commitments of conscience are also distinctly vulnerable to discrimination. Our society is sufficiently religious to make the irreligious themselves targets of discrimination, either by those offended by atheism or by those who sympathize only with religious claims of conscience. Understandably, it is easier for some to associate a passionate conscientious commitment that is markedly out of step with general sentiments in the society—as a claim for exemption from an otherwise valid law would entail—with an eccentric religious command than with a moral claim purporting to apply to all right-thinking persons. * * *

There is an additional reason for including the enforcement of equal regard toward secular commitments of conscience within the domain of judicial responsibility. Once we have placed the protection of religious conscience within that domain, the constitutional demand that diverse belief systems be treated even-handedly makes it inappropriate for the judiciary to parse among claimants on the basis of their metaphysics. * * *

While the judicial protection of conscience appropriately extends to secular as well as religious claimants, the picture changes in one important respect with the move to secular claimants. The protection of religious conscience requires that the state treat religious belief as a "black box"; for purposes of assessing the impact of a sincerely held scheme of religious belief upon the believer, the ultimate truth or the reasonability of the scheme is beyond the constitutional competence of the state. This is implicit in the requirement of equal regard that the state defer to the perspective of a religious believer as to the existence of an interest of great weight within her life; it is a function of the epistemically distinct, closed logic of religious belief.

With secular claims of conscience, however, the believer and the state in principle share a common epistemic foundation. For that reason, the state may legitimately reflect upon and respond to the reasonability of the secular claimant's conscientious commitments. Reasonability here speaks not so much to the plausibility of a given belief, as to the elevation of that belief to a dominant position with regard to motivation and self-identity.

* * *

D. Equal Regard and Equal Protection

As we flesh out the idea of equal regard, it may seem to resemble a robust jurisprudence of equal protection. Robust in this sense: contemporary equal protection doctrine protects African Americans and women by barring both facial distinctions disfavoring those groups and facially neutral governmental action that is motivated by animus toward those groups; it does not bar facially neutral governmental action that has only a disparate impact on protected groups. Equal regard seems more demanding in this respect than equal protection, and our readers may wonder whether we mean to argue that religion should enjoy special protection, that the Supreme Court has erred in excluding disparate impact from close constitutional scrutiny in equal protection cases, or some third proposition not yet on the table.

Certainly equal regard and equal protection have much in common—not only because both invoke the general norm of equality, but also because, as we observed earlier, the Supreme Court's jurisprudence of racial equality is the most prominent example of the paradigm of protection in constitutional law. * * * Nevertheless, it would be a mistake to conflate equal regard with traditional equal protection doctrine in general or with a new sensitivity to disparate impact in particular.

* * *

[The article suggests one area where the concept of equal regard might inform equal protection law:] The administration of "good cause" exemptions in unemployment compensation regimes is a ready example of how our analysis of equal regard can inform equal protection analysis outside the domain of religious claimants. Given the unique concerns of pregnant women and the social practices that usually render women responsible for child care, women have job selection interests not shared by men; and it is entirely possible that state administrators' unemployment decisions will chronically undervalue the weight or sincerity of these interests. That being so, it may well be the case that constitutional justice would best be served by heightened judicial scrutiny of adverse "good cause" determinations implicating pregnancy and child care. * * *

* * *

E.   Congress to the Rescue?

1.   Legislative help in securing equal regard.

The principle of unimpaired flourishing, as we have seen, describes an unobtainable and undesirable world, and offers neither conceptual nor practical guidance for making the compromises necessary to reach an appropriate degree of accommodation for religious interests. Equal regard is very different. It is normatively attractive, conceptually precise, and describes a liveable world: a world that accommodates the deep, religiously inspired concerns of minority religious believers to the same degree as the deep concerns of citizens generally.

But equal regard is very demanding in the kind of judgment it requires; so demanding that it is unrealistic to expect the constitutional judiciary to effectively police the requirement in all cases. * * * It is no defense if legislators give lip service to notions of religious equality, or hold extensive hearings about the interests of religious interests, or make warm, sympathetic statements about minority religions and the First Amendment; neither the trappings of good intention nor even good intentions themselves suffice. Equal regard tests the balance of concern; it demands that the government accord the religious interests of minority believers the regard they give other deep concerns, religious and secular.

In some cases, where local comparisons are available, equal regard will invite a tractable judicial inquiry. The invidious distinction between Sunday observers and Saturday observers in Sherbert is blatant because the affected interests resemble one another so closely. As comparisons grow more remote, the confidence and competence of the judiciary will begin to falter. * * * Somewhere along the line, the capacity of the judiciary to police equal regard will run out.

* * * [T]he judicial regime we recommend will vindicate equal regard incompletely, and therefore legislative attention will be indispensable to full satisfaction of the principle.

* * *

There are several reasons why legislatures may be better at both the general task of accommodating religious interests and the more specific task of vindicating the constitutional principle of equal regard. With regard to accommodation in general, the explanation for legislative primacy immediately emerges from our analysis. Even if the demands of equal regard have been fully satisfied, legislatures have discretion to enhance the value they place upon accommodating fundamental personal commitments, including religious commitments. The legislature's decision favoring increased accommodation would not be a matter of constitutional duty, although the principle of equal regard would then require the legislature (and authorize the courts) to ensure that the new premium upon accommodation is shared equally.

When it comes to applying equal regard, legislators again have an advantage over judges. Judges must make local comparisons to test whether legislators have fairly weighed individual interests against the interests of the public as a whole. Legislators, however, need not rely upon local comparisons. They may judge the weight of government interests directly, and thereby compare them even across widely disparate policies. * * *

It may seem odd to rely upon the political branches to bring the enforcement of equal regard up to full measure. Isn't this an especially bold case of inviting the fox to guard the chickens? After all, the need for a judicially enforceable constitutional principle of equal regard stems from the fact that elected officials will often violate it because of religious bias. And, indeed, we do believe that this concern about bias makes it impossible for the judiciary to abandon responsibility for exemption claims entirely, as the Smith majority seemed willing to do.

The institutional dynamic is, however, complicated for two reasons. First, political institutions do not speak with one voice. Religious bias may be most likely to prevail in small policy-making bodies that work in poorly lit corners of the public square. * * * But as Madison pointed out in Federalist 10, we have reason to expect better from more cosmopolitan institutions, especially Congress as a whole.

Second, political institutions may react differently to an issue once they see it as a matter of religious liberty. Some may, as one would hope, take the time and care to research the impact of legislation upon religious freedom. Legislators are, however, always busy and sometimes sloppy. Constitutional issues are not generally their chief preoccupation. They may accordingly pass legislation without recognizing the constitutional questions it poses. Cases like Goldman, Lyng, and Smith thus serve an important "signalling" function by alerting legislative defenders of religious liberty to an issue that may have escaped their attention. Litigation under the principle of equal regard would continue to serve that function, even if (as happened in Goldman, Lyng, and Smith) the courts themselves refused relief.

* * *

F.   The Autonomy of Religious Organizations

Principles of protection can, we believe, supply a powerful and attractive basis for constitutional rights exempting religiously motivated conduct from generally applicable laws. The vulnerability of religion, not its virtue or precedence, seems to us the foundation for the Constitution's special solicitude for religious activity. Yet, having journeyed so doggedly in one direction, it now seems appropriate to tack in another. Protection and privilege are not mutually exclusive competitors. What we have said at least twice before bears repeating: religious conduct will often draw to its aid principles of privilege not limited to religion. If we neglect that point, the limits upon equal regard will begin to seem puzzling. We are now in a position, for example, to see how privilege and protection provide overlapping forms of constitutional security for religious organizations.

* * *

* * * As we begin to explore more nuanced issues of church autonomy * * * we will find it necessary to analyze them in terms of both privilege and protection. Churches are often complex and powerful organizations. In addition to choosing members and leaders, they will likely engage in economic activity and may sponsor a variety of institutions, from hospitals to universities to health clubs. The privacy-based rationale for church autonomy does not afford equal protection to all these aspects of organized religious activity. On the one hand, for example, decisions about membership and leadership will enjoy full protection. These actions are closely analogous to more personal choices about guests and friends. Absent a guarantee of autonomy vigorous enough to protect the integrity of such decisions, true communities—be they religious or companionate—cannot come into being.

On the other hand, when churches offer services and products for sale, their revenues and their decisions about wages and prices will be subject to the full range of state economic regulation. Commercial transactions, we suggested earlier, are a quintessentially public mode of interaction. When churches enter the commercial arena, they take advantage of a market made possible by the government and specifically entrusted to its care. Thus, the privacy-based rationale for institutional autonomy provides no reason to exempt religious manufacturers from the minimum wage laws. Nor does it supply any reason to protect religious merchants from the obligation to collect a sales tax in connection with the merchandise they sell.

That does not end the constitutional analysis, of course. It is precisely at this juncture that equal regard comes to bear upon church autonomy. The religious manufacturer and religious vendor may still make a constitutional claim for exemptions by invoking the local comparisons sponsored by the principle of equal regard. But they, unlike the church seeking the freedom to discriminate when choosing its leaders, must depend upon equal regard because privacy principles do not encompass commercial claims.

* * *

CONCLUSION

Cast in the mold of constitutional privilege, the idea of religious liberty is self-contradictory. The problem is not simply that religious liberty at its margins may conflict with other constitutional precepts, or even that under the umbrella of religious liberty we may find subsidiary principles that are at times in conflict. The problem is deeper than either of these familiar observations. At its core, religious liberty is about the toleration—the celebration—of the divergent ways that members of our society come to understand the foundational coordinates of a well-formed life. To single out one of the ways that persons come to understand what is important in life, and grant those who choose that way a license to disregard legal norms that the rest of us are obliged to obey, is to defeat rather than fulfill our commitment to toleration. Yet that favoritism is precisely what the privileging view of religious liberty requires.

Yet, if the defects of the privileging view are patent, so too are the conditions that make constitutional solicitude for religion essential. Religious persecution drove many of the settlers of the colonies from Europe to America and drove some from their newfound homes in America. Religious discrimination is not merely an artifact of constitutional history. Within the memory of many adults, it was a prominent feature of our national landscape, and it would be far too optimistic to think that we have outgrown the human impulse to respond badly to the basic differences of culture, habit, and belief that attach to diverse religious faiths. So while the root infirmity of conferring constitutional privilege on religious belief has been sufficiently well understood to curb the Court's enthusiasm for such a privilege, the impulse to preserve nonmainstream religious belief from hostile or indifferent governmental treatment has had a durable—and deserved—place in constitutional adjudication. The resulting tension has made a hash of the jurisprudence of religious accommodation.

The problem lies not with religious liberty but with the paradigm of constitutional privilege and with the principle of unimpaired flourishing that paradigm sponsors. If we replace privilege with protection and replace unimpaired flourishing with equal regard, we can rebuild the jurisprudence of religious accommodation. We can make sense of what has seemed scattered precedent, and we can make religious liberty compatible with its own roots in toleration—and hence with the whole of our tradition of constitutional liberty.

STEPHEN M. FELDMAN, RELIGIOUS MINORITIES AND THE FIRST AMENDMENT: THE HISTORY, THE DOCTRINE, AND THE FUTURE

6 U. Pa. J. Const. L. 222 (2003).

Introduction

Progressive or liberal constitutional scholars who focus on religious freedom have not been pleased with the Rehnquist Court. For more than a decade, it seems, the Court has been handing down decisions that have twisted the Free Exercise and Establishment Clauses in an unduly conservative direction. Most notably, Employment Division v. Smith radically transformed free exercise doctrine, while Zelman v. Simmons–Harris, the voucher case, consolidated the Court's recent Establishment Clause cases into a modified doctrinal approach. As a consequence, First Amendment protections have apparently shrunken to their smallest since World War II, especially for religious minorities.

This pessimistic assessment of Religion Clause jurisprudence is based on two hypotheses: first, that the Court for several decades, starting in the 1940s, was particularly receptive to the Religion Clause claims of minorities; second, that the Rehnquist Court's doctrinal innovations will turn subsequent Religion Clause cases against minorities in an unprecedented fashion. This Article challenges both these hypotheses. If the postwar cases are examined from a political, cultural, and social perspective, rather than from a doctrinal one, they reveal a surprising level of judicial hostility toward religious outsiders. To a great extent, then, the Rehnquist Court merely has maintained this antagonism and, in all likelihood, will continue to do so in the future. To be sure, the Rehnquist Court has transformed First Amendment doctrine, but these changes are unlikely to produce results substantially different from prior decisions.

In making this argument, this Article contributes to an emerging strand of Religion Clause revisionism in legal scholarship. During the post-World War II era, most scholars have subscribed to a conventional account of the First Amendment. This standard story maintains, first, that the Framers laid down a foundational principle of religious freedom, and second, that the post-World War II Supreme Court—at least before the Rehnquist Court arrived—formulated doctrine to help fulfill that principle, thus affording great protection to religious outsiders. * * *

Nonetheless, a revisionist understanding of religious freedom has recently begun to emerge. According to one strand of this revisionist work, history reveals that, contrary to the Whiggish conventional account of the Religion Clauses, the First Amendment often has failed to provide equal liberty to religious minorities. A second, though related, strand of revisionist work has begun to detail how the meaning and degree of religious freedom has varied through American history according to contingent political, cultural, and social interests. * * *

Revisionist and conventional scholars agree, though, on at least one important point. Before the post-World War II era, the religion clauses were almost toothless in the United States Supreme Court. Few cases made their way to the Court, and in those few cases, the Court typically upheld the governmental actions, whether challenged under either the Establishment or Free Exercise Clause. During and after the war, however, the Court transformed its Religion Clause jurisprudence. In the 1940s, the Court incorporated both religion clauses to apply against state and local actions through the Due Process Clause of the Fourteenth

Amendment. Consequently, many more governmental actions were subject to constitutional attack and an increasing number of cases reached the Court. Equally important, the Court became more receptive to these new Religion Clause claims, occasionally striking down the challenged governmental actions.

From a revisionist standpoint, this jurisprudential transformation presents an interesting twofold problem: how precisely did the Court's approach to these Religion Clause cases change, and what factors contributed to those changes? * * * During the first 150 years of the nation's history, America was, to a great extent, "de facto" Protestant. Freedom of conscience, or the free exercise of religion, was based directly on Protestant doctrine, while official disestablishment arose primarily because of competition among a multitude of Protestant groups. * * *

Yet, starting in the mid-nineteenth century, immigration helped produce an ever-expanding American Catholic community. From 1850 to 1900, the Catholic population grew from 1.7 million to 12 million, and by 1930, that number had doubled. As early as 1920, one in six Americans and one in three church members were Catholic. If measured against the respective Protestant denominations and sects, Catholics had become by the 1950s the largest Christian group in America: while the total number of Protestants still far outnumbered Catholics, Catholics nonetheless exceeded the largest Protestant denomination, the Baptists, by almost two to one. Throughout the rest of the century, the relative proportion of Protestants and Catholics would remain roughly unchanged. The presence of such a large Catholic community in America had serious repercussions, generally increasing Catholic political power and, at different times, generating Protestant backlashes. * * *

* * * The true measure of a nation's commitment to religious freedom, it would seem, lies in its treatment of religious minorities or outgroups. Given the superior size of the American Catholic population vis-à-vis even the largest Protestant denominations and sects—as of 1999, Catholics constituted twenty-eight percent of the total population and outnumbered Southern Baptists by a whopping forty-six million—a history of religious freedom in America that focuses solely on Catholic–Protestant relations is likely to miss an important part of the story. For that reason, while this Article discusses Catholic–Protestant connections, it primarily explores cases involving American Jews, who have always remained a numerically small religious minority, regardless of their various social and political successes (and failures) in this country. * * *

* * *

I. Causes of Change

A. *Catholic–Protestant Relations*

The enhanced American Catholic population strongly contributed to the Court's increased receptiveness toward religious freedom cases during and after World War II. In some parts of the country, the political ramifications of the growing Catholic community became apparent as early as the nineteenth century. By the 1880s, Catholic mayors had been elected in several Northeastern cities, including New York and Boston. During Prohibition in the 1920s, Catholics did not need to seek judicial intervention to protect their sacramental use of wine because Congress had readily created a legislative exception for such use. The expanding Catholic political power, furthermore, affected attitudes toward the separation of church and state. Specifically, Catholic and Protestant attitudes had traditionally diverged on church-state issues: Protestants tended to favor religious (predominantly Protestant) practices in the public schools but opposed governmental aid to nonpublic (predominantly Catholic) schools, while Catholics tended to hold the opposite viewpoints. Protestant political power long had allowed them to impose their preferences, but during the 1920s and 1930s, Catholic political power in a number of states had grown sufficient "to secure enactment of laws subsidizing parochial schools with publicly funded textbooks and bus transportation." Moreover, at least some state courts in heavily Catholic states, such as Wisconsin and Illinois, became receptive to Catholic challenges to Bible reading and religious displays in the public schools.

Needless to say, though, many Protestants did not meekly accept enhanced Catholic political power and assertiveness. In the late 1940s, for instance, several mainstream Protestant denominations joined to form Protestants and Other Americans United ("POAU") for the Separation of Church and State, which was vociferously anti-Catholic and strongly opposed public aid for parochial schools. Indeed, most important, the Supreme Court's judicial enforcement of religious freedom after World War II can be understood, in part, as a Protestant reaction to the perceived Catholic threat within the American democracy. The Supreme Court always remained overwhelmingly Protestant; from the 1940s through the 1970s, no more than one Catholic and one Jew ever sat on the Court at any time. Insofar as Catholic and Protestant values and practices diverged, the separation of church and state became partly a mechanism that Protestants could invoke to prevent or retard the imposition of Catholic views. Unsurprisingly, then, in cases challenging governmental aid to nonpublic schools, which are overwhelmingly Catholic, the Supreme Court struck down the governmental action as unconstitutional nearly twice as often as it upheld the action. * * *

The Supreme Court's protection, whether conscious or unconscious, of Protestant interests and values vis-à-vis Catholics can also help explain First Amendment cases involving religious displays and practices in the public schools. As Catholic political power grew during the twentieth century, Catholics tended to become more confident of their strength and position in America and thus, particularly after World War II, began to increase their support for public school religious displays. Put simply, as Catholics gained more political control over the public schools, they were more willing to have religion in the schools. One does not have to be overly cynical to recognize that the Supreme Court began to question the constitutionality of these public school religious displays and practices only in this postwar political context. In response to the changing Catholic attitudes concerning religion in the public schools, many Protestants—not only Supreme Court Justices—became more wary of public school religious practices and displays for at least two reasons. First, anti-Catholic Protestants would resist any Catholic exertion of power in the public schools, and second, Protestants were increasingly attracted to the idea of a principled strict separation of church and state to be used as a bulwark against Catholic power, particularly in the face of Catholic efforts to gain public support for parochial schools.

Unsurprisingly, some Justices occasionally revealed their Protestant biases in private communications. * * * In their judicial opinions, however, the Justices most often explained their Religion Clause decisions with ringing declarations of principle.

Undoubtedly, the significance of the Protestant–Catholic division for understanding the judicial enforcement of religious freedom should not be overstated. Positions on issues of church and state did not (and still do not) neatly divide with Protestants on one side of the line and Catholics on the other. Nonetheless, the fact remains: the Supreme Court began to enforce the Religion Clauses with vigor only when Catholics became more politically potent. Given the strong Protestant sentiments against Catholicism expressed so often throughout American history, the concurrence of these judicial and social developments does not seem merely coincidental. * * *

B. The American Jewish Community

A second factor contributing to the Court's increasing solicitude for First Amendment claims during the postwar era was a change in American Jewish attitudes and conduct. Throughout most of the nineteenth century, Jews were an exceedingly small minority in this country: numbering approximately 4,500 in 1830; 40,000 in 1845; and still only 150,000 by the Civil War. Starting in the 1880s, though, Eastern European Jews began streaming into the United States. Between 1887 and 1927, the total number of American Jews increased from 229,000 to over 4,228,000. Nonetheless, the American Jewish community never amounted overall to more than a small numerical minority, even at its peak constituting only about three percent of the total American population.

Furthermore, overt antisemitism was common and socially accepted in most quarters of American society, at least through World War II. * * * In a 1944 poll, twenty-four percent of Americans identified Jews as the single national, religious, or racial group that presented the greatest menace or threat to Americans (as a comparison, nine percent identified Japanese, and six percent chose Germans—even though the poll was conducted well before the end of the war). Given such widespread antisemitic sentiments, Jews tended to avoid asserting their rights and interests either in litigation or even in political electioneering. * * *

Jews hoped that the nonconfrontational education of non-Jews might eventually diminish antisemitic behavior and attitudes. To assert legal rights more directly and energetically, it was feared, would likely have been counterproductive, engendering reactionary reprisals.

After World War II, Jews and Jewish organizations—especially the American Jewish Committee ("AJCommittee"), the Anti–Defamation League ("ADL"), and the American Jewish Congress ("AJCongress")—stepped forward to press for religious freedom and equality in the courts. These organizations were buoyed by a reduction of overt antisemitism in America and spurred by a post-Holocaust sense of urgency. * * * Within the leading Jewish organizations, a more "active, rather than reactive, domestic program of law and social action" was thus called for. Consequently, in a substantial number of the most important postwar Religion Clause cases, the leading Jewish organizations either instituted the action or participated as amicus curiae.

With regard to specific cases, however, unanimity over such tactics rarely existed within the Jewish community. Disagreements among the various Jewish organizations and among Jews from different national regions were common. In the words of one AJCommittee and ADL attorney, Jews in the South could aim for little more than being "accepted as honorary Protestants." Even so, for the most part, American Jews became more assertive of their rights to equality and religious freedom during the postwar period. In particular, the AJCongress, with its General Counsel, Leo Pfeffer, most strongly advocated for the strict separation of church and state. * * *

II. SUPREME COURT CASES AND RELIGIOUS OUTSIDERS

The Supreme Court took its first major step toward an increasingly vigorous enforcement of religious freedom when the Court incorporated the Free Exercise and Establishment Clauses against the states. * * *

A. *Establishment Clause Cases*

* * *

Undoubtedly, American Jews—a prototypical religious outgroup—have, to some degree, litigated successfully under the Establishment Clause. By carefully choosing and arguing cases * * * Jewish organizations fruitfully urged the Court to stretch the scope of the Establishment Clause so as to encompass the Jewish positions. The organizations argued that enforcing the strict separation of church and state was a matter of principle, not merely a matter of Jewish interests, and that the Jewish organizations favored religiosity. By imposing strict separationism, the organizations maintained, the First Amendment fostered religion.

Putting this in different words, the Jewish organizations' basic strategy was to assert their Establishment Clause claims without asking for any special treatment. "We're just like other Americans," they seemed to be saying. "We rely on principles, not on our distinctive interests or values." "And don't forget," they added, "we are just as religious as other Americans." Understood in this way, success in the Establishment Clause cases was due in part to the Jewish organizations' ability to advocate for positions that remained reasonably consistent with mainstream Protestant interests and values. Studies in the art of rhetoric support using this sensible strategy. As a general matter, an effective advocate "must choose a characterization that actually resonates with her audience." When addressing an overwhelmingly Protestant Supreme Court, then, Jewish advocates wisely characterized their positions as consistent with Protestant views. Moreover, it is worth reiterating, insofar as Jewish advocates appealed to Protestant interests and values, those interests and values were, at the time, partly shaped by Protestant defensive reactions against perceived Catholic political overreaching.

Despite the wisdom of the two-pronged litigation strategy, it did not lead to unmitigated success. The Jewish organizations lost cases such as Zorach v. Clauson, a 1952 Establishment Clause case that upheld a released time program where the religious instruction occurred off the public school grounds. * * * And more recently, the infamous Lynch v. Donnelly upheld the public exhibition of a crèche as part of an extensive Christmas display.

Furthermore, the Jewish organizations sometimes failed not only in the courtroom but also in the realm of public opinion. The decision in Engel provoked outrage in both the Protestant and Catholic communities. Local school districts defied the ruling, members of Congress called for a constitutional amendment overturning the decision, and newspapers published editorials and letters condemning the Court. Indeed, this backlash at least calls into question my conclusion that the Jewish organizations' success in Establishment Clause cases was partly due to their arguments remaining consistent with Protestant interests and values.

Nonetheless, this conclusion remains relatively easy to sustain with regard to a case like McCollum, which struck down a released time program. * * *

* * *

Hence, the importance for the Jewish organizations to articulate their Establishment Clause claims consistently with Protestant interests and values should not be gainsaid. In fact, in School District of Abington Township v. Schempp * * * the organizations used the * * * two-pronged strategy to successfully challenge Bible reading as well as the recitation of the Lord's prayer in public schools. The amicus brief of the AJCommittee and ADL emphasized "the principle of separation of church and state as expressed in the First Amendment." Moreover, the brief argued that the Jewish organizations' constituencies not only were religious people but that their views regarding religious freedom echoed Christian views. The brief quoted Paul Hutchinson, onetime editor of the Christian Century, in stating that " 'the American adoption of the principle of church and state separation has been a godsend for the churches, Protestant, Roman Catholic and of every sort.' " * * *

B. Free Exercise Clause Cases

While the Jewish organizations developed and used a moderately effective strategy in the Establishment Clause cases, they were not as successful in articulating or implementing a similar approach in free exercise cases. The most common type of free exercise case is probably the exemption claim: a member of a religious group—almost always a minority or outgroup—seeks an exemption (or exception) from a generally applicable law that burdens the exercise of her religion.

Who wins such free exercise cases? As a general matter, most free exercise claimants lose. More specifically, in an empirical study of free exercise cases in the United States courts of appeals, James C. Brent reports that "claimants who belonged to mainstream Catholic and Protestant sects were more likely to win than were claimants who belonged to other religions (38.9% versus 24.5%)."[134] In free exercise exemption cases at the Supreme Court level, the numbers are even more striking: while members of small Christian sects sometimes win and sometimes lose such free exercise claims, non-Christian religious outsiders never win. Brent speculates:

> America is a predominantly Christian nation. It therefore is not unreasonable to suppose that Christians should receive preferential treatment at the hands of the Court. Christians probably are less likely to find that the exercise of their religion is burdened by laws in the first place. Because of the majoritarian process, lawmakers are less likely to adopt laws that place burdens on adherents of Christianity, the majority religion. If, however, Christians do find themselves in court defending the exercise of their religion, the judiciary is likely to be receptive to their claims. Primarily, this is because Christian judges should be more likely to be sympathetic to the plight of fellow Christians. The religious burden may appear more "substantial," or the governmental interests may seem less "compelling" when they burden Christians than when they burden non-Christians. Therefore, mainstream Christians should prevail more often than non-Christians in free exercise cases.[136]

The majority opinion in Wisconsin v. Yoder, which involved the Old Order Amish, illustrates the importance of Christianity for a successful free exercise exemption claim. The Amish impressed the Yoder Court with their "devotion to a life in harmony with nature and the soil, as exemplified by the simple life of the early Christian era that continued in America during much of our early national life." The Court seemed especially receptive to the Amish's claim for a free exercise exemption

---

134. [James C. Brent, *An Agent and Two Principals: U.S. Court of Appeals Responses to Employment Division, Department of Human Resources v. Smith and the Religious Freedom Restoration Act*, 27 Am. Pol. Q. 236 (1999)] at 250–51 * * *.

136. Brent, *supra* * * * at 248.

from a state compulsory education law because they were able to appeal to the Justices' romantic nostalgia for a mythological past—for a simple Christian America. This national and Christian past was one that most of the Justices (as Protestants) could readily understand; its meaning corresponded with the religious and cultural backgrounds of the Justices themselves. At the post-oral argument conference, Chief Justice Warren Burger commented: "This is an ancient religion, not a new cult. . . . Being raised on an Amish farm is equal to or better than vocational school training." Thus, whereas non-Christian religious outsiders have difficulty convincing the Court that their religious convictions are sincere and meaningful, the Yoder majority opinion, written by Burger, quoted the New Testament in reasoning that "the traditional way of life of the Amish is not merely a matter of personal preference, but one of deep religious conviction." Because the Amish were Christians, the Court could easily relate their way of life to Christian society and Christian history. * * *

The Court consequently sympathized with the free exercise exemption claim of the Amish in Yoder far more than the Court has ever done with the claims of non-Christian outsiders, whether Jews, Muslims, or otherwise. For example, in O'Lone v. Estate of Shabazz, the Court held that prison officials did not need to grant a free exercise exemption from regulations that prevented Muslim prisoners from attending certain religious services. Likewise, in Employment Division v. Smith, the Native American respondents sought to consume peyote as part of the supervised rituals of the Native American Church, but the Court held that the state did not need to grant an exception from a criminal law prohibiting peyote use.

The Smith Court also stressed a constitutional distinction between religious beliefs and conduct (or actions)—a distinction that parallels Protestant doctrine. The Free Exercise Clause, according to the Smith Court, precludes all governmental regulations of religious beliefs but does not similarly preclude governmental restrictions on conduct—such as the use of peyote—even if the conduct arises from religious convictions. A governmental prohibition on particular religiously motivated conduct would be unconstitutional only if the government restricted that conduct exactly because of its religious foundation.

The difficulty for Jews and other non-Christian outsiders in free exercise cases can be understood best if one recalls the Jewish organizations' strategy in Establishment Clause cases. Their basic approach was to advocate for positions that remained reasonably consistent with mainstream Protestant interests and values. They argued, in effect, that they were asking for nothing special. This strategy, though, is practically impossible to articulate in the free exercise exemption scenario. In fact, the nature of a free exercise exemption claim forces the claimant to do the exact opposite: to explain to the Court how her religious beliefs or practices differ from the mainstream. It is, after all, this difference that creates a free exercise problem in the first place, since laws of general applicability rarely interfere with mainstream Protestant or Catholic practices or beliefs. The claimant, then, must ask the Court for special treatment to accommodate her religious difference.

Unsurprisingly, the Court on multiple occasions has rejected the free exercise claims of Jewish litigants—litigants who needed to describe their unusual religious practices (unusual, that is, from a Christian perspective). For example, in Goldman v. Weinberger, an Orthodox Jewish Air Force officer, Simcha Goldman, sought a free exercise exemption so that he could wear his yarmulke (skull-cap) in spite of Air Force regulations. Jewish organizations submitted two amicus briefs, one filed by the ADL and one filed by the AJCongress. As was true in Goldman's petitioner's brief, both amicus briefs explained the practice and importance within Judaism of wearing a yarmulke. The ADL brief stated that "[a]s an Orthodox Jew, [Goldman] wore at all times, as he has done throughout his life, a diminutive head-covering known as a 'yarmulke' in fulfillment of a Jewish religious requirement that he keep his head covered at all times." The brief elaborated:

> The religious practice of wearing a yarmulke, a head covering worn by observant Jews, is of ancient origin. References to the practice appear in the Talmud, an authoritative compendium of Jewish law completed by approximately 500 C.E. The practice has been firmly established since the Middle Ages. For example, Maimonides wrote in his classic 12th century philosophical treatise, The Guide to the Perplexed, that "The great men among our Sages would not uncover their heads because they believed that God's glory was round them and over them...." And Rabbi S. R. Hirsch wrote in his 19th century commentary on the Jewish Siddur (prayer book), that "[t]he Jew symbolically expresses [submission to God] by keeping his head covered, and in this subordination to God he finds his own honor."

Because Air Force regulations sometimes prohibited the wearing of a head covering, the briefs argued that Goldman's Jewish, and therefore unusual, practice of wearing a yarmulke required the granting of a free exercise exemption. Significantly, in struggling to make its argument, the petitioner's brief stressed that the case was not a matter of broad principle, or in the brief's words, "a broad constitutional declaration of right." Rather, Goldman's claim "rests on a careful and particularized appraisal of the personal and nonintrusive nature of the religious observance at issue." The brief, that is, practically begs the Court to focus on Goldman's unique situation, due to his Jewish practices. Finally, the AJCongress brief underscored Goldman's dilemma, one faced by most free exercise claimants: "Because petitioner sincerely holds the religious belief that he must keep his head covered at all times, strict enforcement of [the Air Force regulations] forces petitioner—or any other Orthodox Jew—to choose between adhering to his religious beliefs or serving his country in the Air Force. It is 'a cruel choice.'"

The Supreme Court rejected Goldman's claim. Strikingly, whereas the Yoder Court had sympathized readily with the Christian religious tenets of the Amish, the Goldman Court mistakenly characterized the wearing of a yarmulke as a matter of mere "personal preference[]." But as the amicus briefs had detailed, wearing a yarmulke is not a personal preference or choice for an Orthodox Jew. It is a centuries-old custom that has attained the status of religious law. Apparently, the majority of the Goldman Justices—and all of the Justices at this time were Christian—were unable (or unwilling) to comprehend the religious significance of this non-Christian practice.

Two cases decided in 1961 arose from Jewish religious challenges to Sunday closing laws, from Massachusetts and Pennsylvania respectively. Among other assertions, these cases involved claims for free exercise exemptions that would have allowed Jewish-owned businesses to remain open on Sundays. The Massachusetts Sunday law included an impressively long list of exceptions:

> [The Sunday law forbids] under penalty of a fine of up to fifty dollars, the keeping open of shops and the doing of any labor, business or work on Sunday. Works of necessity and charity are excepted as is the operation of certain public utilities. There are also exemptions for the retail sale of drugs, the retail sale of tobacco by certain vendors, the retail sale and making of bread at given hours by certain dealers, and the retail sale of frozen desserts, confectioneries and fruits by various listed sellers. The statutes under attack further permit the Sunday sale of live bait for noncommercial fishing; the sale of meals to be consumed off the premises; the operation and letting of motor vehicles and the sale of items and emergency services necessary thereto; the letting of horses, carriages, boats and bicycles; unpaid work on pleasure boats and about private gardens and grounds if it does not cause unreasonable noise; the running of trains and boats; the printing, sale and delivery of newspapers; the operation of bootblacks before 11 a.m., unless locally prohibited; the wholesale and retail sale of milk, ice and fuel; the wholesale handling and delivery of fish and perishable foodstuffs; the sale at wholesale of dressed poultry; the making of butter and cheese; general interstate truck transportation before 8 a.m. and after 8 p.m. and at all times in cases of emergency; intrastate truck transportation of petroleum products before 6 a.m. and after 10 p.m.; the transportation of livestock and farm items for participation in fairs and sporting events; the sale of fruits and vegetables on the grower's premises; the keeping open of public bathhouses; the digging of clams; the icing and dressing of fish; the sale of works of art at exhibitions; the conducting of private trade expositions between 1 p.m. and 10 p.m. . . . Permission is granted by local option for the Sunday operation after 1 p.m. of amusement parks and beach resorts, including participation in bowling and games of amusement for which prizes are awarded.[155]

---

155. *Gallagher*, 366 U.S. at 619–20.

Incredibly, the list of exceptions continued on (and on) even further, but there was no exemption for Orthodox Jews or others whose religious convictions demanded that they observe the Sabbath on Saturday.

Jewish organizations were pessimistic about challenging even this Massachusetts statute. Somewhat to their surprise, then, the district court struck down the law as violating both religion clauses. "What Massachusetts has done," the judge wrote, "is to furnish special protection to the dominant Christian sects which celebrate Sunday as the Lord's Day, without furnishing such protection in their religious observances to those Christian sects and to Orthodox and Conservative Jews who observe Saturday as the Sabbath, and to the prejudice of the latter group." Such a sensitive statement sparked optimism among the Jewish organizations.

In arguing the free exercise claims before the Supreme Court, the Jewish claimants' briefs as well as an amicus brief * * * explained, by necessity, the specific religious practices of the Orthodox Jewish claimants. For instance, the appellants' brief in the Pennsylvania case quoted extensively from the Hebrew Bible and Jewish scholars as it devoted several pages to its explanation of "the cardinal importance of the Sabbath institution to Orthodox Judaism." Interestingly, the amicus brief first stated, in a similar vein, that "the appellees in the Crown Kosher case and the appellants in Braunfeld v. Gibbons are Orthodox Jews who observe the seventh day of the week as their Sabbath and refrain from all secular business and labor on that day." * * *

* * * [T]he gist of the claimants' arguments was one of religious difference. As the Pennsylvania appellants' brief specified, "there is no real relationship between the Jews' Sabbath and the Christians' Sunday. While the latter arose out of the former, they are not the same either in conception or in manner of observance." For that reason, the claimants requested exemptions from the Sunday laws so that Orthodox Jews could observe their Sabbath without being penalized. As the amicus brief wryly suggested, however, granting an exemption to Orthodox Jews could not interfere any more with the religious character of Sundays than did professional sporting events, which the Massachusetts statute expressly allowed.

The Jewish organizations' optimism, spurred by the lower court's decision in the Massachusetts case, went unrequited. During the post-oral argument conference, Chief Justice Warren indifferently brushed aside potential injuries to religious outsiders: "[S]omebody is always going to be 'hurt.' Orthodox Jews might lose two days." Given such an attitude, the Court unsurprisingly upheld the Sunday laws in both cases and refused to mandate exemptions for the Orthodox Jewish claimants. A plurality opinion in the Massachusetts case reasoned that Sunday laws merely regulate secular activities. As such, they do not force a "choice [on] the individual of either abandoning his religious principle or facing criminal prosecution. . . . [T]he statute at bar does not make unlawful any religious practices."

In sum, these free exercise cases reveal that Jews and other non-Christian religious outsiders have not fared well when seeking free exercise exemptions from generally applicable laws. Even when the Jewish organizations attempted to advocate consistently with the mainstream Christian interests and values, they were rebuked. Unfortunately, the crux of the claimant's free exercise argument is precisely that her religion diverges from the mainstream Christian views. That divergence, then, compels the claimant to request special recognition or treatment, in the form of a free exercise exemption. In effect, the free exercise claimant asks the Court to create an exception from the mainstream or normal understanding of religion and religious freedom, as manifested in the generally applicable laws as well as in previous Supreme Court decisions. In all such cases involving non-Christian outsiders, the Court implicitly concluded that the claimants' religious freedom already was protected adequately. These outsiders, according to the Court, neither required nor were entitled to any further constitutional shelter.

C. Lessons From History

In light of the history of the postwar establishment and free exercise cases, Religion Clause litigants obviously would be wise to frame their claims, whenever possible, as establishment rather than free exercise issues. Indeed, further analysis suggests a deeper point. Regardless of what Religion Clause provision is invoked, one should avoid constructing arguments that accentuate differences from the mainstream. The more that a First Amendment claimant stresses her divergence from mainstream religious views, the less the Supreme Court is likely to rule in her favor. This point, however troubling, is reinforced by a perhaps intuitive social psychology insight: one's membership in significant social groups greatly determines values and perceptions. "[I]ngroup favoritism and outgroup hostility are seen as consequences of the unit formation between self and other ingroup members and the linking of one's identity to them."[168] As soon as a non-Christian Religion Clause claimant stresses her differences from Christianity, she apparently diminishes her likelihood for success before a Christian-dominated Supreme Court.

Of course, in a free exercise case, a claimant would be hard-pressed not to emphasize religious difference, since that difference is precisely the crux of the claim. But in an Establishment Clause case, there might be considerable leeway for strategically presenting one's position. * * *

* * *

---

168. Norman Miller & Marilynn B. Brewer, *Categorization Effects on Ingroup and Outgroup Perception, in* Prejudice, Discrimination, and Racism 209, 213 (John F. Dovidio & Samuel L. Gaertner eds., 1986); see also David G. Myers, Social Psychology 502–04 (2d ed. 1987) (discussing ingroup-outgroup relations); Geneviève Paicheler, The Psychology of Social Influence 151 (Angela St. James-Emler & Nicholas Emler trans., 1988) ("What is perceived to be most salient about a minority is its difference and not the content of its arguments. Its arguments are accorded meaning first in terms of the minority position they occupy, not in terms of what they express."). * * *

III. The Future of Religion Clause Cases

This Part has three Sections. The first examines current Supreme Court doctrine under, in turn, the Establishment Clause and the Free Exercise Clause. The second recommends certain doctrinal innovations designed to benefit religious outsiders. The final Section then relates both the current doctrine and my doctrinal recommendations to the history detailed in Parts I and II.

A. Current Supreme Court Doctrine

In Lemon v. Kurtzman, a 1971 decision, the Court synthesized previous Establishment Clause cases into a three-part test: "First, the statute must have a secular legislative purpose; second, its principal or primary effect must be one that neither advances nor inhibits religion; . . . finally, the statute must not foster 'an excessive government entanglement with religion.' " The Court has since applied the Lemon test many times and, despite criticisms, has never expressly and fully repudiated it.

Different Justices, though, have introduced and applied alternative doctrines. In Lynch v. Donnelly, decided in 1984, a majority of Justices applied the Lemon test to uphold the public display of a crèche as part of a larger Christmas exhibition. Yet, because of dissatisfaction with the Lemon test, Justice O'Connor wrote a persuasive concurrence that advocated the adoption of an endorsement test, consisting of two prongs: first, does the state action create excessive governmental entanglement with religion, and second, does the state action amount to governmental endorsement or disapproval of religion.

* * *

In Zelman v. Simmons–Harris, decided in 2002, the Court appeared to consolidate these various Establishment Clause tests with a conservative twist, thus effectively diminishing First Amendment protections for religious outsiders. The Zelman Court upheld a school voucher program from Cleveland, Ohio, that allowed parents to use public money to help pay for private school education, including at religious or sectarian schools. The majority opinion recited only the first two prongs of the Lemon test, the purpose and effects prongs. Justice Breyer's dissent stressed the third prong, governmental entanglement with religion, by arguing that the voucher program would generate "religiously based social conflict" or divisiveness. The majority, in a footnote, dismissed this concern as irrelevant: "We quite rightly have rejected the claim that some speculative potential for divisiveness bears on the constitutionality of educational aid programs." In fact, Justice O'Connor's concurrence in Zelman maintained that the Court had previously "folded the entanglement inquiry into the primary effect inquiry."

Zelman thus seems to shift the judicial focus to a modified Lemon test, consisting of only two prongs, purpose and effects. Notably, the two leading proponents of alternative doctrines, Justices O'Connor and Kennedy, both joined the Zelman majority opinion, which briefly mentioned endorsement and coercion as if they were mere considerations under the effects prong. Furthermore, and perhaps even more important, the Zelman Court disemboweled the Lemon effects prong. * * *

This transformation of the Establishment Clause doctrine seems designed to favor the religious mainstream to the detriment of religious outsiders. In future cases, the sole genuine judicial inquiry will be into governmental purpose; the effects prong has been rendered nominal. Thus, so long as the government does not appear to purposefully or intentionally favor specific religions or religion in general, the governmental action will be upheld. The fact that the government's action might grossly favor mainstream religions is immaterial under Zelman. And of course, any supposedly neutral governmental program that allows benefits to flow to religious institutions is likely, in reality, to disproportionately favor mainstream religions since the overwhelming majority of people belong to those religions (which is largely why they are called the mainstream). Meanwhile, any governmental action that appears to disproportionately favor an outsider religion will immediately be judicially suspect as purposefully benefitting that religion—because, after all, how else could a legislature funnel benefits to an outsider religion unless it did so intentionally? Thus, quite rightly, Justice Souter's Zelman dissent denounced the majority's approach as a "verbal formalism," a judicial inquiry lacking in any real substance; the Zelman doctrine allows the religious mainstream to direct benefits to itself under the guise of governmental neutrality.

In the area of free exercise, the Court in Sherbert v. Verner, a 1963 decision, articulated a strict scrutiny test that would remain, at least nominally, the presumptive standard in free exercise cases for over twenty-five years. According to this test, a state could justify a burden on an individual's free exercise of religion only by showing that the state action was necessary to achieve a compelling state interest. While this judicial standard seemed rigorous and favorable to free exercise claimants, including religious outsiders, it proved otherwise in application. The Court repeatedly upheld challenged governmental actions by reasoning either that the government had compelling purposes for its conduct or that strict scrutiny was inappropriate under the specific circumstances. In fact, from 1973 until 1990, the Court concluded that a governmental action contravened the Free Exercise Clause only three times.

Nonetheless, in Employment Division v. Smith, decided in 1990, the Court expressly changed the doctrine for evaluating free exercise claims. The Court abandoned the strict scrutiny test for free exercise challenges to laws of general applicability, except for cases, like Sherbert, that involved the denial of unemployment compensation. Apart from that narrow situation, the Court suggested that the "political process" should effectively determine the scope of free exercise rights.

The Smith Court, in other words, moved from the previous free exercise doctrine of presumptively applying strict scrutiny—at least supposedly showing almost no deference to the political process—to a doctrine without any meaningful judicial scrutiny of challenged governmental actions—a standard showing remarkable deference to the legislative process. Thus, as with the Zelman doctrine under the Establishment Clause, the Smith doctrine under the Free Exercise Clause appears to blatantly favor the religious mainstream at the expense of outsiders. Because of the nature of our majoritarian legislative processes, laws of general applicability are unlikely to burden mainstream religions. Legislators are likely either to belong to the mainstream religions or to be fully aware of their practices and beliefs. Out of ignorance or indifference, though, legislators are likely sometimes to enact general laws that incidentally or accidentally burden the exercise of outsider religions. Yet, members of such religions will be unable to get judicial relief under Smith. Instead, they will be left to beseech legislatures in the hope of procuring statutory exemptions. To be sure, such legislative exemptions will sometimes be forthcoming, but they will be due to majoritarian tolerance or whim. From the outsiders' viewpoint, there is a huge difference between tolerance and constitutional right.

B. Recommended Doctrinal Changes

Doctrine can change, as the recent spate of Rehnquist Court innovations in First Amendment jurisprudence illustrates. With the possibility of further change in mind, this section recommends a number of doctrinal modifications in the establishment and free exercise areas that presumably would benefit religious outsiders.

Under the Establishment Clause, religious minorities would welcome a stronger focus on the effects of governmental actions, whether under the guise of a reinvigorated Lemon effects prong or under some other appellation. Legislatures today rarely discriminate purposefully against religious outsiders, yet those same legislatures might unwittingly enact laws that bestow disproportionate benefits on mainstream religions. Such disproportionate benefits are not diminished even if such a law is neutral on its face. And of course, some clever legislators can intentionally design laws that are facially neutral but that will have disproportionate effects. In theory, these duplicitous laws should be struck down under the still-remaining purpose prong from Lemon, but in reality, proving discriminatory legislative purpose or intent is notoriously difficult.

Another possible way to bolster Establishment Clause protections could be developed either through the coercion test or the endorsement test (or a reinvigorated Lemon entanglements prong). Each of these tests requires the Court to evaluate whether a governmental action produces a certain state of affairs—either coercion or endorsement of (or entanglement with) religion—and thus the application of these doctrines depends partly on the perspective that the Court adopts. * * * If the Court were to adopt the view of the reasonable dissenter or outsider, the Court would be more likely to conclude that coercion [or endorsement] was present. After all, as a matter of definition, the reasonable outsider will not share all the interests and values of the mainstream; otherwise, she would be an insider rather than an outsider (or dissenter).

* * *

Turning to free exercise doctrine, the introduction of a series of presumptions favoring the claimant would possibly benefit religious outsiders. These presumptions would be designed to encourage the Justices (and other judges), who are typically political and religious insiders, to sympathize more closely with the plight of outsiders. The need for such presumptions is paramount. As already discussed, legislatures today rarely discriminate purposefully against religious outsiders, yet legislatures might occasionally burden the practices or beliefs of religious outsiders because of ignorance or indifference. If a legislator is unaware of the practices of a particular minority religion, she might support the enactment of a general law that could have disastrous consequences for members of that religion. The fact that the legislator might have harbored no malice at all toward the religion would be little solace to its practitioners. So, for instance, probably few members of Congress who supported the Aid to Families with Dependent Children program or the Food Stamp program even contemplated how a statutory requirement for recipients to supply Social Security numbers might affect or burden religious practices and beliefs. Yet eventually, a Native American complained that the assignment of a social security number would rob his daughter of spiritual power.

Three different presumptions could help account for the likelihood that outsiders will occasionally confront generally applicable laws that burden their religious practices and beliefs. First, any claim of religious conviction should be presumed to be sincere, genuine, and most important, truly religious in nature. This presumption would possibly discourage the Court from finding, as it did in Goldman v. Weinberger, the Air Force yarmulke case, that outsider religious practices are mere personal preferences rather than sincerely religious acts.

Second, though closely related to the first presumption, any free exercise claim based on nonvolitional religious practices should be presumed to be as important, from a religious standpoint, as a claim based on individual choice related to faith or belief. The Court, in the past, has accepted the religious importance of faith-or belief-based claims (which are central to Christianity, especially Protestantism), but has failed to recognize the significance of religious rituals or sacred objects or events. Thus, if implemented, this presumption of religious importance might help the Court recognize the religious significance of claims arising from outsider religions that differ widely from the mainstream, such as in Lyng v. Northwest Indian Cemetery Protective Ass'n, where the Court refused to uphold a free exercise claim even though the governmental actions, building a road and permitting timber harvesting, would desecrate sacred Indian burial grounds.

A third presumption would relate to the weighing of religious interests against governmental interests. A free exercise claimant's religious interests should be presumed to outweigh all countervailing governmental interests unless the government shows that its interests are of overriding (or compelling) importance and cannot be satisfied in any other manner. Quite evidently, this presumption would reinstitute the strict scrutiny or compelling state interest test that the Court at least claimed to apply for many years in free exercise cases. The reason for reintroducing this presumption is powerful: the Court might all too easily permit the sacrifice of outsiders' sincere religious interests for the mere convenience of the government or democratic majorities (the religious mainstream). Certainly, one can understand Gallagher v. Crown Kosher Super Market, the Massachusetts Sunday closing law case, in this vein: the Court refused to order a free exercise exemption for the Orthodox Jewish claimants even though the state had already statutorily granted a seemingly endless list of exceptions from its closing law. If the Court were to adopt this recommended presumption—and truly implement a strict scrutiny test—then the Justices would be doctrinally directed to give outsiders' religious interests their due weight and would be less likely to hand down decisions like Gallagher.

C.   The Likelihood and Significance of Doctrinal Change

Doctrine matters. Religious outsiders, for instance, unquestionably benefited when the Supreme Court incorporated the Establishment and Free Exercise Clauses to apply against state and local governments in the 1940s. Before that time, outsiders could not possibly bring First Amendment challenges, with any hope of success, against state or local governments, no matter how egregious the governmental action (though outsiders could nonetheless invoke state constitutional provisions in state court actions). * * *

* * * [G]iven Parts I and II of this Article, one must ask the following question: in reality, will * * * suggestions for doctrinal changes be likely to help religious outsiders? The discouraging answer: probably not. Two reasons lead to this conclusion. First, the Court is unlikely to change Religion Clause doctrine in the recommended manner. Second, even if the Court were to do so, the modified doctrine might not significantly alter the outcomes of future Religion Clause cases.

Why is the Court unlikely to change Religion Clause doctrine in the recommended manner? As a general matter, a yawning abyss stretches today between the Supreme Court and legal scholars. The Court shows little interest in legal scholarship and, in fact, has occasionally expressed disdain for legal academics. More specific to Religion Clause jurisprudence, though, the historical discussions in Parts I and II of this Article illustrate, if nothing else, that the Justices' religious orientations influence their decisions in First Amendment cases. The successes and failures of American Jews who litigated before the Court starkly illustrate the impact that religion has on First Amendment cases. So long as the Court remains predominantly Christian, its decisions and doctrines are likely to favor Christian (if not Protestant) interests and values. In short, the Rehnquist Court, as constituted, is unlikely to reverse itself in order to structure Religion Clause doctrine to be more favorable to religious outsiders.

To be sure, the Court is more religiously diverse now than it has ever been before. That diversity might, in theory, prompt the Court to be more receptive to the claims of religious outsiders. But still, such a liberal turn seems improbable given that seven of the Justices' backgrounds are from mainstream Christian religions, while only two of the Justices, Breyer and Ginsberg, are non-Christian. Moreover, to some extent, the religious divisions between Protestant and Catholic Justices, like Rehnquist and Scalia, seem to pale in the glow of their conservative political bonds. It is commonplace now to acknowledge that conservative Catholics and fundamentalist Protestants share more in common on certain political and moral issues than do liberal and conservative Protestants. Thus, the majority-block of politically conservative Justices will likely repress any religiously induced inclinations toward the protection of individual rights, whether under the First Amendment or otherwise.

Indeed, the Court's recent Free Exercise and Establishment Clause landmarks suggest the strength of these political forces working in conjunction with the Justices' mainstream religious orientations. If anything, the Court currently leans strongly toward favoring the mainstream to the detriment of religious outsiders. Thus, in Zelman, the Court wrote: "The constitutionality of a neutral educational aid program simply does not turn on whether and why, in a particular area, at a particular time, most private schools are run by religious organizations, or most recipients choose to use the aid at a religious school." The Court, in other words, is not troubled if a facially neutral law effectively funnels public money to schools owned and operated by mainstream religions. Even more starkly, the Smith Court reasoned that the religious diversity of the American people actually threatened potential "anarchy." As such, according to the Court, American diversity not only justified but even necessitated the transition from a strict scrutiny to a deferential test under free exercise * * *.

* * * Moreover, even if the Court surprisingly were to follow the recommended changes, the modified establishment and free exercise doctrines might not substantially alter the outcomes of future Religion Clause cases. Doctrine matters, but in a sense that is less than most lawyers, judges, and law professors care to admit. To be precise, doctrine matters, but doctrine must always be interpreted. Significantly, then, one's political, cultural (religious), and social perspectives necessarily orient the interpretive process. No more so than any other interpreter, a Supreme Court Justice cannot read First Amendment doctrine without being situated in a particular political, cultural (religious), and social context that affects his or her interpretive conclusions. * * *

The Court's doctrinal statements in Religion Clause cases often do not reflect the reality of the decisions. Thus, as Parts I and II demonstrate, the Warren and Burger Courts were not as liberal in establishment and free exercise areas as is commonly believed—and as is suggested by those Courts' doctrinal statements. * * *

Hence, even if the Rehnquist Court were to adopt my recommended doctrines for establishment and free exercise cases—doctrinal approaches that appear favorable to religious outsiders—the Court's decisions still would be strongly influenced by the religious (as well as political) orientations of the Justices and by the religious slant of the claimants' arguments. In short, when the claimants present their arguments so that their religious beliefs and practices appear largely consistent with the American mainstream, they have some reasonable chance of success. If they instead argue so that their religious beliefs and practices appear exceptional or contrary to the mainstream, then the probability of success diminishes, practically to nil.

* * * One final and important point must be added, though. Namely, the Rehnquist Court, despite its purported conservative doctrinal changes in Religion Clause cases, is unlikely to be as conservative—as hostile to Religion Clause claimants—as many progressive scholars and commentators fear.

In fact, the Rehnquist Court's establishment and free exercise decisions are likely, in the end, to closely resemble those of its predecessor Courts. Without doubt, non-Christian outsiders cannot fare any worse before the Supreme Court under the Smith free exercise doctrine than they did under the strict scrutiny test. In addition, under the Establishment Clause, the Zelman doctrine is unlikely to produce outcomes far different from those that would otherwise be reached by the same set of Justices if they were instead applying the traditional Lemon test, the endorsement test, or the coercion test. * * * [T]he differences among the various Establishment Clause doctrines are neither momentous nor forceful enough to consistently overcome the Justices' religious and political orientations. In short, the doctrinal modifications are unlikely to produce different case outcomes.

* * *

Conclusion

Partly because of enhanced Catholic political power, as explained in Parts I and II of this Article, the postwar Protestant-dominated Supreme Court articulated First Amendment principles that could be used as a bulwark against perceived Catholic overreaching. Jews and other non-Christian outsiders became the incidental beneficiaries of these judicial pronouncements. By invoking these supposedly broad principles rather than idiosyncratic Jewish interests and values—as well as by emphasizing the importance of the strict separation of church and state for promoting religiosity—Jewish organizations sometimes successfully urged the Court to stretch the protections of the Establishment Clause.

The Jewish organizations, in other words, found they needed to present Establishment Clause arguments that largely corresponded with the already-in-place mainstream understandings of religion and religious freedom. Unsurprisingly, then, Jews and other religious outsiders consistently lost before the Supreme Court when, under the Free Exercise Clause, they sought exceptions to this same mainstream understanding, as manifested in generally applicable laws and in prior Court decisions.

When the postwar cases are examined from a political, cultural, and social perspective rather than from a doctrinal one, they reveal a significant judicial succor for the religious mainstream and a concomitant aversion toward non-Christian outsiders. The Rehnquist Court, to a great extent, has maintained these sentiments, and in all likelihood, this Supreme Court pattern will continue in the future. To be sure, the Rehnquist Court has turned First Amendment doctrine in a seemingly conservative direction, but these changes are unlikely to produce results substantially different from prior decisions, at least at the level of the Supreme Court.

Ultimately, the Court will continue to vindicate the occasional First Amendment claim that remains consistent with mainstream religious, cultural, and political outlooks. The Court, likewise, will continue to repudiate the more radical claims that would require a judicial departure from mainstream understandings of religion and religious freedom. These are the lessons from history, and the Court's tinkerings with the establishment and free exercise doctrines are unlikely to change that reality.

3.   The Free Exercise Clause and the Role of Government

One issue that could have a major impact on any interpretation of the Free Exercise Clause is the proper role of government vis-a-vis religion. This is a more specific question than how government should treat religion. It focuses on how the nature and/or structure of government might impact what government can and cannot do to protect those whose religious practices come into conflict with the "common good" as expressed through laws. The following essay, written by Professor Scott Idleman, argues that government must subordinate religious concerns when those concerns conflict with government power. His essay is a significant contribution to the field, raising some important questions about how government should address claims for free exercise exemptions. The second article in this section was written by Professor Marci Hamilton, who argued the *Boerne* case (*see supra* Chapter Six) to the United States Supreme Court (and won). In the article Professor Hamilton analyzes opinion at the time of the framers regarding religious exemptions. Her analysis focuses heavily on the perspective of the clergy whose views were highly influential on public opinion at that time. She argues history demonstrates there was a common belief at the time of the framers that exemptions to laws of "general applicability" could not be mandated because religious believers had a duty to work for the "common good." Thus, when religion came into conflict with the general law, the secular authority needed to prevail in the secular realm, and this was consistent with religious duties.

SCOTT C. IDLEMAN, *WHY THE STATE MUST SUBORDINATE RELIGION, IN* LAW & RELIGION: A CRITICAL ANTHOLOGY

(Stephen M. Feldman, ed., NYU Press 2000) 175.

The First Amendment Free Exercise Clause, as Justice Black would have reminded us, is written in absolute terms. "Congress shall make *no law* . . . prohibiting the free exercise [of religion]." In turn, one might surmise that courts would accord it an absolutist reading, particularly given the relative clarity of the clause's language, the primacy normally accorded to clear textual mandates of the Constitution, and the fact that its companion provision—the Establishment Clause—is itself interpreted in precisely this manner. Such has not been the case, however. When defining the protection accorded to religiously based conduct, the judiciary has never adopted an absolutist interpretation, even in cases of intentional prohibition. Rather, the conventional model for judicial analysis has entailed a less determinate balancing of competing interests, in which the value of free exercise is essentially conceptualized in relative, even instrumental, terms.

This essay will argue that, at bottom, this judicial resistance to a strong reading of the Free Exercise Clause has little to do with text or tradition as such, but, rather, with sovereignty. In particular, the state *must* subordinate religion in order to preserve its jurisdictional supremacy and to maintain its grasp on the allegiance of the citizenry. Under this view, the balancing tests thus serve not only as a doctrinal apparatus within which religious liberty claims are formally resolved, but ultimately and more importantly as a protective apparatus by which the government's sovereign character is effectively preserved. The outer boundaries of permissible free exercise, in other words, are fundamentally defined not by the articulated competing interests themselves, but by the state's need to limit the citizenry's observance of laws other than its own.

Initially, a sovereignty-based reading of the judiciary's free exercise interpretations may seem a rather abstract perspective on religious freedom, far removed from the resolution of any particular dispute. But it is clearly of more than theoretical significance. Not only does it explain the resistance to an absolutist interpretation, it suggests that such an interpretation will never be embraced. Even where a rigorous nonabsolutist approach (such as strict scrutiny) is employed in the protection of religious freedom, a sovereignty-based reading further suggests that such an approach will never yield the results that it does in other contexts—a differential that has frequently been noted, often criticized, but rarely explained. Finally, to the extent that interference with the sovereignty of civil government truly marks the outer bounds of protected free exercise, it may provide a new standard, whether or not acknowledged by courts, for predicting outcomes in certain free exercise cases—and, when combined with the conventional model, at the very least provides a more complete picture of free exercise analysis.

I. Conventional Free Exercise Doctrine and Its Inadequacy

A. *The Conventional Model*

Before critiquing and then departing from the conventional model of free exercise analysis, its basic structure and elements must first be considered. Under the Free Exercise Clause, the government may act unconstitutionally in several ways: by discriminating on the basis of religious status, by prohibiting religious belief, by requiring a particular religious belief or practice, or by prohibiting or otherwise regulating religious conduct. While the first three are forbidden absolutely, especially where the government action is intentional, claims alleging the restriction of religious *conduct* are not so absolutely protected but instead are ultimately subjected to a balancing inquiry.

In order to reach this inquiry, a plaintiff asserting a conduct-based free exercise claim must establish five prima facie elements. First, the government action must constitute a "law" within the meaning of the First Amendment. Second, the claimant's conduct must stem from beliefs that are "religious" within the meaning of that amendment. Third, these beliefs must be sincerely held by the claimant. Fourth, the practice must have a constitutionally cognizable relation to the claimant's religion; that is, it must implicate a "central practice" or "core tenet" of the religion, or must otherwise be mandated, or at least motivated, by the claimant's religious beliefs. Finally, and perhaps alternatively, the practice or one's religious life as a whole must be burdened or substantially burdened by the government conduct in question.

Once these five elements are satisfied, the challenged government action will be subjected to one of two levels of scrutiny. Under current doctrine, strict scrutiny obtains if the government action is not neutral or not generally applicable, or if the free exercise claim is asserted in tandem with another constitutional right. In such instances, the evidentiary burden shifts to the government to demonstrate that its action "advance[s] 'interests of the highest order' and . . . [is] narrowly tailored in pursuit of those interests." In all other cases, rational basis scrutiny applies, and the evidentiary burden remains with the claimant to demonstrate that the action is not rationally related to a legitimate government interest.

Regardless of which level of scrutiny is invoked, the fundamental nature of the inquiry concerns whether the government interest and the manner of its implementation outweigh the claimant's interest in religious liberty. Balancing, in other words, pervades the resolution of conduct-based free exercise cases despite the absolutist phrasing of the First Amendment. Prior to the assessment of any given dispute, of course, at least some of the elements—such as the scope of "religion"— will necessarily have been categorically delineated, and this process may itself entail a kind of absolutism. But the essential nature of conventional free exercise analysis involves the balancing of interests, principally that of religious liberty in relation to one or more governmental objectives.

* * * [I]t is important to examine the government interests that the judiciary formally recognizes as sufficient to override an asserted interest in the free exercise of religion. For convenience, these government interests can be divided into three categories: police power interests, administrative interests, and judicial interests.

The most familiar category encompasses the state's so-called police power, and includes matters relating to public health, welfare, safety, and morals. Although these matters are not intrinsically governmental as such, but rather public or societal, their furtherance by force of law reflects a contractual view of the state that recognizes the existence of "manifold restraints to which every person is necessarily subject for the common good." Within rational basis scrutiny, police power interests virtually always are, and by definition should be, legitimate. Presumably this is why the Supreme Court could state, rather matter-of-factly, that providing nothing more than rational basis scrutiny would essentially "leav[e] accommodation [of religious practices] to the political process." As for strict scrutiny, here too the government's police power interests are often (though not always) deemed sufficient—"compelling" in the language of strict scrutiny—despite the supposed rigor of the test.

A second category of government interests concerns the administration of government itself—"the legitimate conduct by government of its own affairs." These include matters such as cost or effectiveness and, like police power interests, have been recognized as legitimate in a variety of settings. Unlike police power interests, however, they are less frequently deemed compelling. And for good reason. As Professor Douglas Laycock has remarked, "There is no government bureaucrat in America who doesn't believe that his program serves a compelling interest in every application,"[27] and the necessary prevalence of administrative interests would empty the term "compelling" of virtually all meaning were it regularly to be so broadly construed.

A third and final category of government interests can be labeled judicial interests. Because the power of final constitutional review in the United States has been vested in (or at least assumed by) the judicial branch of government, constitutional interpretations are necessarily shaped by the institutional values and interests of the bench. Constitutional interpretation, in other words, is ultimately informed not only by text, tradition, original intent or understanding, and a host of other sources and canons, but also by the peculiar considerations of judicial decisionmaking. Such considerations include a sensitivity to the allocation of scarce judicial resources and to docket management; to the

---

27. Douglas Laycock, *Free Exercise and the Religious Freedom Restoration Act*, 62 FORDHAM L. REV. 883, 901 (1994).

limited but important role of courts in the political-constitutional scheme; and to various judicial traditions such as the concept of justiciability and doctrine of stare decisis. While these interests pervade constitutional decision making, they rarely if ever serve explicitly as government interests in the balancing of conduct-based free exercise claims. * * * Nonetheless, there is no particular reason to think that such interests do not also play a role, at some level, in the actual application of free exercise doctrines.

B. The Inadequacy of the Conventional Model

Although the conventional model of free exercise analysis is obviously workable insofar as it can be applied by judges to produce results in particular cases, it is nevertheless inadequate insofar as its relationship to the text of the Free Exercise Clause is strained, its formal doctrines do not capture the reality of judicial application, and it is not explicitly grounded in a coherent theory of religious liberty. These inadequacies are noted and will be explored here because their number and magnitude signal the operation of unarticulated norms, the most important of which, it shall be argued, is the preservation of the supremacy of civil law and thus the sovereignty of civil government.

This section will address four such anomalies within current free exercise doctrine. First, there is simply the avoidance of an absolutist interpretation, despite the interpretive dissonance that such avoidance—in the absence of persuasive justification—generates. Second, within the conventional analytical framework, certain elements are inexplicably distorted in a manner that can severely diminish the likelihood that particular free exercise claims will prevail. Third, and relatedly, a good case can be made that the substantial burden requirement was devised and is employed precisely because it allows courts to discard troublesome free exercise claims that otherwise appear colorable under the terms of the conventional model. Finally, and more generally, there is the rather stark fact that the Supreme Court has never set forth a theory or principle of conduct-based free exercise, despite ample opportunity and warrant to do so.

Although each anomaly may be independently explicable—and some explanations are considered—what this essay shall argue is that collectively they can more easily be explained, and perhaps best explained, by reference to a governmental concern about the maintenance and furtherance of its own sovereignty in relation to religion.

1. The Unexplained Avoidance of an Absolutist Interpretation

The first indication that unarticulated norms are afoot involves the judiciary's reluctance to interpret the clause in an absolutist manner, as its text would appear to command. More specifically, there is a reluctance to justify in logically persuasive terms why such an interpretation should not be adopted. What typically appears in judicial opinion is either total silence, an appeal to historical practice or understanding, or an outright declaration that an absolutist interpretation would simply be intolerable. Silence, of course, is hardly a justification, though it is arguably probative of the lack of an articulable rationale. Likewise, appeals to historical practice or original understanding may lend formal legal backing to a contemporary interpretation, and may even explain genealogically the roots of a nonabsolutist interpretation, but such appeals merely beg the question of present-day justification.

As for the notion that an absolutist interpretation would prove unacceptable, here too there is ultimately a failure of adequate justification. Several norms of unacceptability are invoked. * * * [T]here is the outright appeal to hyperbole: an absolutist interpretation, it is proposed, would literally bring the operations of civil government, indeed civil society, to a screeching halt. Or, there is the curious notion that the judicial extension of absolute protection from religious belief to religious conduct "might leave government powerless to vindicate compelling state interests"—a line of reasoning that appears to overlook the fact that the medium of judicial review, employing strict scrutiny, is precisely where the government *can* vindicate its interests if truly compelling.

The lack of any real substance to these appeals, resting as they do upon the anticipated intuitive or commonsensical assent of readers, is strong circumstantial evidence that the courts are adverting to a deeper but unarticulated normative calculus in their decisionmaking. Of course, intuition and common sense do enjoy a distinguished place in constitutional interpretation, and to deprive judges of recourse to them would do violence to the role of judgment in judicial decisionmaking. * * *

One theory periodically asserted by judges is that an absolutist reading of the Free Exercise Clause would overrun or cancel out the Establishment Clause. * * * But this argument is problematic for several reasons. For one thing, it overlooks the fact that the Free Exercise Clause's companion provision, the Establishment Clause, does operate in a categorical, absolutist fashion, and yet courts have somehow managed to shield the former from the latter's absolutist interpretation. For another thing, it uncritically accepts that there is, or must be, a tension between the two clauses, when in fact such a tension is largely an outgrowth of the judiciary's expansive Establishment Clause jurisprudence. And even if such a tension is unavoidable, it does not explain why a substantially emasculated Establishment Clause (necessary to accommodate a stronger reading of the Free Exercise Clause) would be so devastating from a constitutional standpoint.

* * *

Finally, there is the more compelling (but not often articulated) proposition that one's free exercise cannot be permitted to cause measurable harm to another, and an absolutist interpretation would undermine this limitation. As the Court has remarked, religious "[c]onduct remains subject to regulation for the protection of society." But unless one adopts an extremely broad notion of harm, including harm to oneself, even this principle does not explain the total or across-the-board rejection of an absolutist interpretation. At most, it points towards a rather rigorous level of constitutional scrutiny, with full protection except in those rare cases, such as religiously motivated homicide or battery, where such harm is clearly demonstrated.

2. The Distortion of the Balancing Analysis

Not only do courts fail to justify adequately the use of balancing in lieu of an absolutist reading, they also tend to distort (without justification) the resulting balancing process in favor of the government, thus further suggesting reliance on one or more deeper yet unarticulated principles. When strict scrutiny is employed in free exercise cases, for example, the range of government interests that qualify as "compelling" is generally much broader than in other constitutional contexts, such as free speech or equal protection, where strict scrutiny is also employed. The compelling interest test, in other words, is watered down in such a way that substantially decreases the likelihood that free exercise claimants might prevail. Moreover, when analyzing the degree to which the government's interest is compelling, courts often (though certainly not always) examine the importance of the government program in its entirety or in the abstract, rather than examining the relative importance of the particular element of the program from which an individualized exemption is sought.

Lastly, and regardless of what level of scrutiny is invoked, courts also tend to adopt an "objective" analytical disposition that explicitly downplays the potential free exercise injury, thus keeping the balance from tilting too far in the claimant's favor. * * * Other than a concern about the range of lawsuits that might be brought, however, there is offered no explanation for rejecting a posture that is more neutral, let alone skewed towards the perspectives of claimants.

The first two of these progovernment distortions are especially ironic given that strict scrutiny is supposed to entail a presumption that the government has acted unconstitutionally, thus absolving the judiciary of its normal obligation to uphold a government enactment by any reasonable means. More fundamentally, they are all significant insofar as they reveal that judges must not consider the balancing process adequate, on its own terms, to protect some larger but unarticulated interest. Rather, there is apparently a perceived need to skew the process—to transcend the inherent limits of the asserted government interest and to ignore the potential potency of the free exercise interest—so that, in the end, the former simply will not prevail against the latter.

3. The Use of the Burden Requirement

Of course, before even arriving at this balancing analysis, claimants must first demonstrate that the government has "burdened" or "substantially burdened" their free exercise to a constitutional significant degree. This seems reasonable enough, but as it turns out the burden requirement often serves as a "gatekeeper doctrine[], which function[s] to increase the likelihood of failure at the prima facie stage, and thereby to reduce the number of claims that must be afforded the searching inquiry demanded by the free exercise clause." It is true, of course, that the judiciary must implement some type of adverse treatment requirement, if only to give meaning to the element "prohibit" as found in the Free Exercise Clause. * * * The substantial burden requirement, however, stands out in terms of its indeterminacy and, thus, its judicial manipulability.

These characteristics are significant precisely because they are the product of judicial choice. When devising doctrines and selecting terms, including those used as threshold requirements, courts often have a full range of options from which to choose, and their choice will reflect not only the congruence of the doctrine and its terms with the provision being interpreted, but also the degree of judicial discretion that will be retained. In turn, courts generally devise indeterminate and manipulable threshold requirements when they desire to retain significant discretion over which claims will, and will not, proceed. And underlying this perceived need for discretion is likely a sense that the subsequent analysis—here, some form of balancing test—will produce outcomes that are inconsistent either with the purpose of the constitutional provision or with larger principles of constitutional governance.

The selection and use of the burden requirement, then, are likely not coincidental, but instead reflect a desire to advance certain objectives or protect certain interests that are not sufficiently advanced or protected by the larger doctrinal framework, particularly the balancing process. * * *

4. The Avoidance of a Theory of Religious Freedom

One final dimension of the conventional model that strongly implies the operation of unarticulated norms is the Court's steadfast failure to articulate a meaningful theory or set of principles underlying the Free Exercise Clause and, in turn, animating the Court's interpretation of it. Although from time to time the Court purports to explain the purpose of the clause, generally such explanations are either circular or unilluminating. Indeed, neither the Court's most protective free exercise cases nor its least protective cases ever meaningfully explains why, from the perspective of religious liberty itself, the level of protection recognized is appropriate.

Given the obvious necessity of this undertaking, especially within a legal system that prizes reason and definition, the Court's failure could imply a number of possibilities. First, the articulation of a theory or principle of religious liberty may simply not be possible because the religion clauses by design or circumstance possess no such theory or principle. Yet, even assuming that this thesis is correct, it does not absolve the Court from the obligation to articulate the theoretical grounds under which it is necessarily deciding cases, however fabricated or incoherent they may be. The Court is, after all, resolving disputes, and therefore its members, individually or collectively, must be operating on *some* theoretical principle that is susceptible to formulation and articulation.

Alternatively, the articulation of a theory of religious liberty may simply not be institutionally prudent to the extent that the theory articulated would not be sufficiently defensible in terms of traditional constitutional reasoning or consonance with the views of the people. * * *

Or perhaps the nonarticulation of a theory of religious liberty reflects an avoidance not of theorizing itself, but of the possibility that any such theory might yield claims whose premises or resolutions would be inconsistent with other interests or norms that the judiciary is attempting to advance or protect. One such interest, and the one that shall provide the focus for the remainder of the essay, is that of protecting the supremacy of the state vis-a-vis claims of competing sovereignty. It is to that possibility that the essay now turns.

II.   RELIGION AND THE SOVEREIGNTY OF CIVIL GOVERNMENT

The foregoing analysis indicates that there are disjunctions or analytical shortfalls not only between the text of the Free Exercise Clause and the conventional model of free exercise analysis, but also between that model and the actual judicial analysis of religious freedom cases. Initially, it might be tempting to conclude that these shortfalls are simply a product of inevitable indeterminacy—a necessary residuum of play in the constitutional joints, if you will—and that there is no meaningful pattern to the case law beyond the doctrines applied, let alone a grand theory of religious freedom operating sub silentio. The magnitude and nature of the disjunctions suggest otherwise, however.

The remainder of the essay will argue that these shortfalls may be explained, partly if not largely, by an implicit understanding (judicially enforced) that religious free exercise must often be subordinated to preserve the supremacy of civil law and government. That an absolutist reading is rejected, that the balancing analysis is skewed, that the burden requirement functions as a gatekeeper, and that the judiciary refuses to expound the principle of religious liberty—these are not, in other words, coincidences. Rather, they constitute an awkward but effective means of cabining religion in an effort to maintain the primacy of the state and its legal apparatus.

* * *

A.   The Interest in Sovereignty

In legal circles, both domestic and international, the most revered status is that of sovereign. This status either implies or guarantees a variety of rather useful powers or characteristics, including a jurisdictional realm over which is exercised ultimate, often exclusive authority, and general autonomy or immunity from the jurisdictional authority of other sovereigns. Sovereignty and its attendant powers thus tend to be jealously guarded by their possessors, lest they might find their own sovereignty functionally if not formally diminished. * * *

* * *

From a functional perspective, there exist several forms of extra-allegiance that can undermine one's fidelity to the state. The classical form is lateral, whereby one pledges or retains allegiance to another sovereign political entity. * * * Extra-allegiance may also be internal, whereby one's self-absorption and civic apathy are so acute that one effectively becomes, for all intents and purposes, a dysfunctional or non-citizen. Although this condition by itself cannot be punished, should it manifest itself in, say, a disregard for law by the commission of a felony, one may then be legally disenfranchised. Finally, extra-allegiance may be vertical, whereby one pledges allegiance to a transcendent being or body of principles which very well could conflict with the demands of the state. It is the thesis of this essay that such vertical extra-allegiance, which undergirds many free exercise claims, is effectively dealt with by the judiciary's underenforcement of the Free Exercise Clause.

* * *

B. *Religious Allegiance as a Threat to Sovereignty*

Given this antipathy towards various forms of competitive sovereignty and the extra-allegiance they foster, it would be surprising indeed if government were not to perceive religion—and if judges were not to perceive free exercise claims—with anything but a jaundiced eye. For it is arguably the case that no form of extra-allegiance, other than lateral allegiance to another geopolitical sovereign, is more problematic for the state than religious adherence. Three common characteristics of religion render it so. First, religious faith and beliefs by definition involve the core of individual and social identity and, at least for the devout, cannot easily be suppressed or dislodged. Second, religion typically generates or transmits normative commitments or obligations that periodically conflict with certain duties imposed by the state, but that "generally are not seen as matters of individual choice and evaluation" and "are, instead, understood to be externally imposed upon the faithful." Third and finally, religion quite often claims some degree of transcendent ultimacy or supremacy vis-a-vis temporal institutions, including civil government. When all three characteristics converge, the potential for conflict is obvious, especially where the state itself proves unyielding in its demands.

In such instances, religion essentially poses the threat of a competing sovereign, manifest by the allegiance of its adherents to superior and normatively binding claims. As Sanford Levinson has observed:

> [R]eligion ... makes obvious claims of sovereignty as against other social institutions. A staple of political theory following the development of the notion of political sovereignty by Bodin is that there cannot be two sovereigns within a polity. By definition sovereignty is an exclusive status. Yet anyone who takes (at least Western) religion seriously poses an alternative sovereign against the claims of the State, however much the claims are dissipated by doctrines like the

Talmudic injunction to follow the local law or by Christian doctrines about God and Caesar.[83]

In turn, "[t]heistic religion necessarily implies a limit on the authority of the state because sincere religious faith refuses to recognize the government's sovereignty as ultimate. Theism posits another sovereignty—a God or gods—that is above, beyond, and before the state."[84]

When one considers the Free Exercise Clause's interpretation, the potential significance of this model of competing sovereigns is obvious. If religious adherence by its nature involves vertical extra-allegiance to a transcendent authority, then every free exercise case is at some level a clash of sovereigns and a challenge to the supremacy of the state. Many, in fact, have argued that the clause rests in part on a recognition of this unique conflict of allegiance potentially faced by those who take seriously their religious obligations. If this essay's thesis is accurate, however, one would expect to encounter in the jurisprudence of free exercise *not* solicitude for such citizens and their beliefs, but some measure of apprehension—and ultimately some form of subordination. * * *

C.   *The Explanatory Force of a Sovereignty–Based Reading*

Describing the relationship between religion and government in terms of sovereignty might be nothing more than just another interesting perspective, were it not for two interrelated circumstances: first, the failure of existing doctrines to account for the actual interpretation and implementation of the Free Exercise Clause, and second, the substantial ability of a sovereignty-based reading of free exercise jurisprudence to fill this role. * * *

Consider once again the anomalies mapped out in Part I—the avoidance of an absolutist interpretation, the distortion of the balancing analysis, the use of the burden requirement as a gatekeeper, and the judicial lack of a theory of religious freedom. If one's goal is the maximum feasible protection of religious liberty, or even something less ambitious, it would be difficult to account for each and every such anomaly. As demonstrated, too many factors and outcomes would simply have to be ignored. If one's goal, however, is understood as the preservation of the supremacy of civil government against claims of a higher and competing authority, the utility and overarching logic of these phenomena become much more apparent, to the point perhaps that they no longer appear analogous.

Most obviously, neither an absolutist interpretation nor even a strong balancing analysis is consistent with a conception of civil government that is exclusive in its sovereignty. Absent intentional discrimination against its citizens (which is a violation of the charter of its powers), no true sovereign would need to justify its general lawmaking authority

---

83.   Levinson, [84 MICH. L. REV.] at 1467 (footnote omitted).

84.   Carl H. Esbeck, *A Restatement of the Supreme Court's Law of Religious Freedom:*

Coherence, Conflict, or Chaos?, 70 NOTRE DAME L. REV. 581, 637 (1995) (footnote omitted).

by having to demonstrate that its ends are compelling and its means are necessary before a citizen must obey its laws. To countenance this would be to place the citizen's religious allegiance above his civic allegiance, and to cede the sovereignty of the state to the sovereignty of God or conscience. In order to prevent this, therefore, courts have rejected an absolutist reading, have more recently rejected a strong balancing analysis, and—particularly before rejecting a strong balancing analysis—have employed the burden requirement as a means of avoiding a confrontation between religion and the state. Even the judicial unwillingness to articulate a theory of religious freedom is consistent with a concern about state sovereignty. For any *meaningful* theory of religious freedom * * * would necessarily support and invite claims that would be inconsistent with the supremacy of the state, either in their premises or their desired outcomes.

Other aspects of free exercise jurisprudence are also congruent with a sovereignty-based approach. Two such phenomena, one conceptual and the other empirical, deserve particular mention. First, the judiciary has gone to great lengths to avoid conceptualizing free exercise in terms of the competing sovereignty of religion and the state, let alone conceptualizing the state as the inferior of the two, despite the fact that the clause's principal drafter, James Madison, appeared to conceptualize the relationship in precisely those terms. Rather, the judiciary has essentially characterized the religious practitioner as a kind of intruder or squatter and the state as extant and proprietary. Even the terms used by the courts, such as "claimant" or "accommodation," lend "rhetorical support to the idea that it is the government, and not the citizen, that is somehow being burdened by the other's demands." More generally, the judiciary has conceptualized religion as a thoroughly private matter, not only in the sense that it is nongovernmental, but in the sense that its practice or observance need not be public and that its exclusion from the public sphere, whether as a matter of nonestablishment or otherwise, is entirely appropriate.

Second—and fully consistent with the phenomena of doctrinal distortion and conceptual marginalization—there is the simple empirical fact that most religious liberty claims do not prevail, despite the ultimate importance of religious obligations to individuals and communities. Assuming that many such claims are not in fact foreclosed by formal doctrine when fairly interpreted, this track record can mean one of two things: either the judiciary does not understand this ultimate importance or the judiciary understands it only too well.

The first possibility is that the general failure of free exercise claims reflects nothing more than an inability of judges, steeped as they often are in the ways of the world, to take seriously the claims of the religiously devout. Such inability may reflect either their own diminished religious devoutness or their heightened commitment to empirical, rationalist modes of knowledge and discourse which—in the view of some—do not include religious belief. In either case, the underprotection of religious liberty may be simply a judicial personnel issue, unless one believes that judges as a sociopolitical class will inevitably consist of persons who disproportionately devalue religious adherence.

The other possibility is that judges *do* take seriously the claims of the religious devout and, in turn, that they understand quite well what those claims signify vis-a-vis the authority of civil government (including their own authority). If this is so, then the underprotection of religious liberty is not a judicial personnel issue as such, but rather one of inherent institutional obligation. Judges, by their nature, must protect and reinforce the sovereignty of civil government, even if it means that otherwise legitimate claims of religious free exercise, as well as doctrinal and theoretical integrity, will be sacrificed. The judiciary, in other words, is the ultimate guardian of civil supremacy and, through its reasoning and holdings, the ultimate apologist of the state. * * *

* * * To embrace the proposition that the secular law does not reach, and indeed may be subordinate to, the dictates of religious faith is to cast doubt upon the sovereignty of the government and, in turn, its ability to maintain order and stability and to uphold the rule of law. And the infusion of doubt into the authority of their own government is something that judges simply cannot countenance, regardless of what sacrifices might be incurred by free exercise claimants, of any doctrinal incoherence that might result, and of the judges' preexisting political or philosophical dispositions.

To be sure, this principle has at times been expressed by the Court, most notably in *Reynolds v. United States*, which was essentially the Court's first significant interpretation of the Free Exercise Clause, and in *Employment Division v. Smith*, which is the Court's most recent significant exposition of the clause's meaning and scope. In *Reynolds*, faced with a challenge to a territorial criminalization of plural marriage, the Court asked: "[A]s a law of the organization of society under the exclusive dominion of the United States, it is provided that plural marriages shall not be allowed. Can a man excuse his practices to the contrary because of his religious belief? To permit this would be to make the professed doctrines of religious belief superior to the law of the land, and in effect to permit every citizen to become a law unto himself. Government could exist only in name under such circumstances."[103] Likewise in *Smith* the Court, drawing in part upon *Reynolds*, explained that:

> "[t]he government's ability to enforce generally applicable prohibitions of socially harmful conduct, like its ability to carry out other aspects of public policy, 'cannot depend on measuring the effects of a governmental action on a religious objector's spiritual development.' To make an individual's obligation to obey such a law contingent upon the law's coincidence with his religious beliefs, except where the State's interest is 'compelling'—permitting him, by virtue of his

---

103. *Reynolds*, 98 U.S. (8 Otto) at 166–67; *cf. also* Long v. State, 137 N.E. 49, 50 (Ind.1922).

beliefs, 'to become a law unto himself,'—contradicts both constitutional tradition and common sense."[104]

More generally, a sovereignty-based reading of the Court's First Amendment jurisprudence also helps to explain why the Court, today at least, rejects mandatory accommodation (whereby the Free Exercise Clause is read to mandate governmental accommodation of claimants' religious practices) but permits discretionary accommodation (whereby governments may, in their discretion, provide such accommodation without violating the Establishment Clause). The doctrine of mandatory accommodation conceptually elevates religious liberty above the state, except where the state's fundamental organic purposes, as expressed by compelling interests, cannot otherwise be achieved. * * * The doctrine of discretionary accommodation, by comparison, conceptually places religion subordinate to, and at the mercy of, the state. Whereas mandatory accommodation constitutionalizes the idea that a certain fraction of sovereignty has been withheld from the state, or ceded by the state, discretionary accommodation implies full sovereignty followed by voluntary dispensations of legislative grace.

* * *

There is, in summary, significant explanatory force to a sovereignty-based reading of the Court's constitutional jurisprudence of religion and government, and in particular its interpretation and implementation of the Free Exercise Clause. While such a reading does not explain all variations in the application of the clause—claimants do, for example, periodically prevail against the state—it does serve to round out the incomplete picture portrayed by official doctrine.

Conclusion

The maxim, *imperium in imperio*, invokes the traditional view that two sovereigns cannot rule the same territory. Today, of course, jurisdiction is no longer conceptualized in such Newtonian terms; it can be concurrent or partial, not simply exclusive and exhaustive. But the maxim's relevance to the dynamics between religion and government remains undiminished. Unable to be confined to the realm of unmanifested belief, religion necessarily generates acts of conscience that periodically conflict with the civil law and, given the nature of religious adherence, challenge the state's jurisdictional supremacy.

This essay has argued that the de facto American solution to this conflict, implemented through the process of judicial review, is to subordinate religion by underenforcing the Free Exercise Clause, at times complemented by corollary doctrines of the Establishment Clause. Religion is not subordinated in the sense that it is deliberately oppressed. But it is domesticated, and never is it accorded a degree of sovereignty that renders it truly competitive with, let alone superior to, the state.

---

104. *Smith*, 494 U.S. at 885 (quoting Lyng v. Northwest Indian Cemetery Protective Ass'n, 485 U.S. 439, 451 (1988), and *Reynolds*, 98 U.S. at 167, respectively).

MARCI A. HAMILTON, *RELIGION, THE RULE OF LAW, AND THE GOOD OF THE WHOLE: A VIEW FROM THE CLERGY*

18 J. L. & POLITICS 387 (2002).

I. INTRODUCTION

"The separation of church and state" is a malapropism, in the sense that it awkwardly captures the constitutional arrangement between church and state. While it rightly captures the notion that church and state are to have distinguishable identities, and distinguishable interests, it fails to come to grips with the reality that religion and the state must and do coexist in the lives of the people. This coexistence was not questioned in the latter half of the eighteenth century, leading up to the framing of the Constitution. Nor should it be today. While the debate over the meaning of Thomas Jefferson's phrase "separation of church and state" may continue indefinitely, there can be little question that the Framers, the text of the Constitution, and its realization in American society point to one fact: the two were intended to and do in fact exist together in a dialectical relationship of difference and interaction.

* * *

Yet, how may government and religious entities coexist and interact under the First Amendment? To admit their mutuality does not answer where the Constitution draws the line between their independent though interrelated existences. To answer this question, one must look not only to the Free Exercise and Establishment Clauses, but also to the structures of lawmaking within the Constitution. This Article reasons that when understood together, it is possible to know when law or religion rightfully may claim the upper hand of the believer's allegiance and which branch is best suited to that determination. With the Supreme Court rightly having rejected the theory that the religious demand must always or even generally trump the law, the question left is when government may adjust the law to lighten burdens on religious believers through permissive legislative accommodation.

While "separation" treats church and state as mutual exiles, the question of permissive accommodation foregrounds the inescapable fact that religion and politics do operate together. They always have, and they always will. The Constitution may put the brakes on some results of that collaboration or relationship, but it cannot hope to forbid either the exchange between or the inevitable mutual attraction of the two most authoritative structures of human existence.

So how are we to understand when the legislature may bow to the requests of religious claimants and when not? How may we understand when the religious believer or organization must defer to the law even when it conflicts with religious conduct?

The debate over the superiority of church or state mandate was energized when Professor Michael McConnell argued in an influential

Harvard Law Review article that religious conduct, in general, ought to trump inconsistent law.[4] Using a blend of historical sources and arguments from a strand of evangelical theology, he argued for a constitutional right to avoid laws that conflict with religious conviction, which I will call the mandatory judicial accommodation thesis. Professors Philip Hamburger and Ellis West did an excellent job showing that the history does not support the concept of mandatory accommodation.[6] Even though the Supreme Court, in Employment Div. v. Smith, plainly rejected the mandatory judicial accommodation thesis nearly simultaneously with the publication of Prof. McConnell's article, the article stakes out an important position in the debate.

The question left open by the Supreme Court's 1990 decision in Employment Div. v. Smith-and by the Supreme Court's silence on the topic since Smith-is when accommodation is consistent with the right principles governing church and state's coexistence. In rejecting McConnell's mandatory judicial accommodation thesis, the Court did not reject accommodation altogether. Rather, the Court in Smith embraced the notion of permissive legislative accommodation: even though legislatures are not required to accommodate religious conduct at odds with generally applicable laws, they may consider and enact accommodations when doing so is consistent with the public good. Thus, the Court did not rush to the opposite of McConnell's position—that the rule of law must always trump or is ontologically superior to religious obligation—but rather simultaneously acknowledged the validity of the rule of the law and the social instinct that would avoid unnecessary burdens on religious conduct not at odds with the greater good * * *.

In other words, the Court assumed in this religion-friendly polity that requests for exemption would be frequent and treated seriously. In fact, they are.

The false inference drawn by many regarding Smith was that the Court was prescribing a rampant majoritarianism that would be unfriendly to minority religions. Thus, rejection of the mandatory judicial accommodation thesis plus the move to the political forum was thought to be a dramatic setback for religious liberty, or so the argument went.

Unfortunately, this point was reinforced by the Court's statement that:

> [I]t may fairly be said that leaving accommodation to the political process will place at a relative disadvantage those religious practices that are not widely engaged in; but that unavoidable consequence of democratic government must be preferred to a system in which each

4. Michael W. McConnell, *The Origins and Historical Understanding of Free Exercise of Religion*, 103 HARV. L. REV. 1409 (1990).

6. Philip A. Hamburger, *A Constitutional Right of Religious Exemption: An Historical Perspective*, 60 GEO. WASH. L. REV. 915 (1992) * * *; Ellis West, *The Case Against a Right to Religious–Based Exemptions*, 4 NOTRE DAME J. L. ETHICS & PUB. POL'Y 591, 624 (1989) (rejecting constitutionally compelled exemptions, but not legislative exemptions).

conscience is a law unto itself or in which judges weigh the social importance of all laws against the centrality of all religious beliefs.

This concession on the part of the Court was as empirically wrong as it was unnecessary, and it betrays the actual structure of representation that legitimates legislative accommodation * * *.

Because McConnell argued that the believer cannot fail to do God's bidding, and did not acknowledge a religious obligation to obey duly enacted law, an inescapable, underlying assumption of his thesis was that mandatory exemptions are religion-friendly, or required by anyone who takes religious devotion seriously. That is to say: within the universe of his reasoning, a mandatory exemption regime is pro-religion, with the corollary being that the Smith constitutional architecture is hostile to religion. That is precisely the message McConnell and others took to the public and the academy immediately following Smith.

This view, however, is an oversimplification that depends on a particular theological perspective, as opposed to a belief held by persons of all, or even most, religions. In fact, it does not reflect the view of the majority of religious leaders at the time of the framing, many of whom were instrumental in instituting and explaining to the people the operation of the rule of law as it applies to the actions of religious believers. It is a fact—as true then as it is today—that some of the most influential leaders of United States society on issues of politics are members of the clergy. * * *

From the mid-to the late-eighteenth century, many members of the clergy—in their sermons—helped to establish the relationship between religious conviction and the rule of law. As the shape of an American polity evolved through the Revolution, the Articles of Confederation, and finally the Constitutional Convention, members of the cloth addressed this pivotal issue directly. Unlike Deist Thomas Jefferson, though, they did not presume a stark separation of church and state, but rather mulled over the hard question of the coexistence in any citizen's life of the demands made by the church and by the state.

The accumulated range of answers from later eighteenth-century clerics reveals a sophisticated set of presuppositions about the proper relationship between the church and the state that betray the easy assumption that application of the rule of law is hostile to religious individuals or faith. These views (1) falsify the either-or choice (for or against religion) implied by the mandatory judicial accommodation thesis as sketched by Prof. McConnell; (2) validate the criticisms levied against the McConnell formulation by Philip Hamburger and Ellis West; and most important for purposes of this Article, (3) pave the way for a legislative permissive accommodation that is in harmony with that described in Smith.

The sermons undermine McConnell's implicit presupposition that the application of laws to religious conduct at odds with the law is anti-religious. At the very least, hearkening back to these members of the clergy makes clear that in most circumstances allegiance to the rule of law (passed by a duly elected representative whose power is derived from the people) was considered an obligation of a religious person.

The latter eighteenth century sermons reveal that religious leaders of the day did not envision a society that would permit any person to be a "law unto himself." Their vision was more collective, or at least more community-based. For believers to achieve true liberty they needed to obey the laws enacted by the duly elected legislatures, for the sake of order and the public good. The social compact generated not a deal whereby the believer could in good conscience retreat from society's requirements, but rather a reciprocating compliance. The rule of law sat firmly in a theological vision of mutual reciprocity and obligation.

It is this duty to obey, and duty to the good of the whole, which sets this religious vision apart from the more recent theories that would interpret the Free Exercise Clause as a requirement of "equal treatment" or "equal regard" of atomistic individuals. The vision painted in these sermons is not one wherein religious individuals meld into society, where all must be treated alike, but rather one in which religious individuals bear special obligations to serve the greater good. To state it in other words, the religious individual is under a stronger obligation to society and its laws than the nonbeliever. The claims to mandatory judicial accommodation turn this understanding on its head by treating the religious believer as a weak member of society that must be accorded special treatment in order to sustain belief. In the sermons of the eighteenth century, the greater good was achieved through believers who conformed their conduct to enacted law.

Yet, the obligation imposed was not a faithless or blind obedience. The obedience was due to just laws, which were defined as the creation of governments duly elected by the people and operating in the public good. When laws became tyrannical, the people had reason and justification to depose their rulers, but not the rule of law itself. * * *

This Article is organized into three sections. First, it lays out the various explanations provided by members of the clergy regarding the rule of law and religious conduct in the half century culminating in the Constitution, for the purpose of more fully laying the groundwork for understanding where the Constitution draws the line between legal obligation and religiously motivated conduct. Second, it sketches the legitimate legislature that culminated in the Constitution and that could compel obedience from religious believers, under the views of the religious leaders at the time. Third, it shows how the Supreme Court's contemporary jurisprudence is consistent with this early vision. By permitting accommodation by duly enacted legislators, the Court has placed accommodation decision-making, and therefore religious believers and lawmakers, under the shared horizon of the good of the whole. Thus, the vision painted by the Supreme Court in Smith is consistent with and supported by the predominant religious viewpoint at the time of the framing and before.

II. EIGHTEENTH CENTURY CLERGY AND EXPLANATIONS OF THE RULE OF LAW

* * *

Whether religious believers would be subject to the general laws of the new country was a topic that was frequently on the minds of preachers in the latter half of the eighteenth century. Their sermons, as well as governing documents of the churches, show the religious leaders of eighteenth-century society articulating a fairly cohesive vision for the coexistence of God's law and civil law. I do not intend to overstate the consistency of their claims, because there are dissenting, minority views and not every preacher adopts every tenet discussed here. Nevertheless, there is a generally accepted view that is sufficiently repeated to justify the claim that it was an important and formative element in the social mix.

To be sure, the ideas that the various sermons set forth are consistent with and can even plausibly be traced not only to theology, but also to political philosophy of the time. In particular, many of the sermons reference the work of John Locke. The purpose of this Article is not to show the ultimate repository of any particular idea, however, but rather the sociological reality that religious leaders at the time of the formation of the Constitution conveyed a vision to their members: Congregants were urged by their religious leaders to follow the rule of law on a number of grounds.

The discussion of religion and the rule of law in the pulpit usually proceeded by an acknowledgment of the existence of two concurrent realms, one civil, one religious, each with a rightful pull on the citizen. While the argument for the superiority of God's obligations is made, a point consistent as far as it goes with the mandatory exemption thesis, a number assert that the civil law is in fact a form of God's law, a turn in the argument that undermines the mandatory exemption thesis. Believers were not to focus solely on their private understanding of what God asks of them individually, but rather, as part of their Christian practice, to take into account the good of the whole in their obedience to the law. They also argued, in the larger picture, that obedience to the civil law is necessary for the realization of true liberty and that the freedom of religion does not extend to conduct beyond worship. * * *

A. Church and Civil Government: Concurrent and Distinguishable Realms of Power

In eighteenth century sermons, there was a repeated emphasis on the concurrent and distinguishable realms of power, church and state. Each was to have its rightful, limited claim on human conduct and mutual boundaries.

* * *

The two domains were coterminous and mutually exclusive. Thus, civil government's proper realm ended when it attempted to "establish any religion" by instituting or requiring "articles of faith, creeds, forms of worship or church government [in part because] . . . these things have no relation to the ends of civil society."

To be sure, the clergy did not intend to rubber stamp the rule of any civil government per se, but rather only that government that flows directly or indirectly from the people and that is obligated to the public good. The law that binds is the law derived as follows:

> [R]eason teaches men to join in society, to unite together into a commonwealth under some form or other, to make a body of laws agreeable to the law of nature, and institute one common power to see them observed. It is they who thus united together, viz. the people, who make and alone have right to make the laws that are to take place among them; or which comes to the same thing, appoint those who shall make them, and who shall see them executed. For every man has an equal right to the preservation of his person and property; and so an equal right to establish a law, or to nominate the makers and executors of the laws which are the guardians both of person and property.[31]

* * *

Part of this shared vision does depend on a notion of differentiation between church and state, but it is not a total separation that forces the believer to choose one sphere over the other, but rather a distinction of spheres, each with a legitimate, concurrent, and strong pull on the believer's allegiance. Thus, the free exercise of religion was to be pursued not in isolation but rather in "so far as may be consistent with the civil rights of society." * * *

The one realm reinforced allegiance to the other. The obligation to obey the civil law was treated as part of the Christian's obligation. * * *

B. Reasons to Obey the Civil Law

Far from urging civil disobedience, many eighteenth century sermons exhorted believers to obey the civil law. There are three reasons offered by the clergy to obey the law. First, the law is given by God and therefore the believer must obey. Second, the rule of law serves the good of the whole. Third, which is a subset of the second justification, true or real liberty cannot be achieved in the absence of the rule of law functioning in a system appointed by the people.

* * *

C. Conduct, Even When Religiously Motivated, Is Regulable

One of the most interesting aspects of the sermons, taken as a whole, is that they are consistent in naming the arenas over which the

---

31. [POLITICAL SERMONS OF THE AMERICAN FOUNDING ERA, 1730–1805 (Ellis Sandoz ed., 1991)] at 58 * * *.

church has complete control as they leave the achievement of peace and order to the civil government. * * *

The ecclesiastical domain ended and the civil domain appropriately held sway when the beliefs, faith, worship, and church governance turned into "overt acts of violence [or effect]." So even when overt acts involved the subject areas of ecclesiastical government, the civil authority permissibly dominated. Thus, religious defenses to a wide range of antisocial conduct, such as "murder, theft, adultery, false witness, and injuring our neighbor, either in person, name, or estate" were immoral or irreligious or both.

The sermons of the latter half of the eighteenth century raised and rejected the possibility that religious fervor could justify or excuse a violent crime * * *.

* * *

In other words, actions taken in contravention of public peace and safety, under a civil government chosen by the people, left the perpetrator, even if a religious believer, vulnerable to civil action. * * *

The portrait of society painted by the sermons of the eighteenth century brought Christians from a wide sweep of denominations under a shared horizon of working toward the public good in concert with the government, a task that required obedience to duly enacted law governing actions. Backus captured this worldview when he explained that religious believers had "an unalienable right to act in all religious affairs according to the full persuasion of his own mind, where others are not injured thereby."

* * *

III. THE LEGITIMATE LEGISLATURE

The sermons depicted believers in a joint enterprise with government to pursue the public good through their actions, which included obedience to duly enacted laws. In the absence of a government oriented toward the public good, their vision could not become real.

The exception that proves the rule of the foregoing (and the following) can be found in sermons delivered during the Revolution. The Revolution was sparked by rebellion against "virtual representation," the claim in Britain that the Parliament could represent colonists' views without representation by colonists. For the colonists, virtual representation was not legitimate representation in the interest of the common good, but rather a usurpation of their rightful role in lawmaking that affected them. Accordingly, many members of the clergy counseled their members to refuse to obey the laws handed down by Parliament and to revolt. For these preachers, the years leading up to the Revolution were a time when the true rule of law had been suspended by Britain vis-a-vis the colonies, and therefore obedience to law was not required. The foundation of their charge to obey the law was the legitimate legislature.

* * *

For many of the religious leaders of the eighteenth century, two elements were essential in this formula. First, the government must be chosen by the people. Second, the lawmaker must be capable of serving and striving for the common good, which was the proper goal of the government. In Witherspoon's words, there needed to be "[w]isdom to plan proper measures for the public good [and f]idelity to have nothing but the public interest in view."

The Constitution crafted lawmaking bodies—the Congress and, via the Guarantee Clause, the state legislatures—that satisfy these requirements. They are chosen by the people through constitutional ratification and election. Though the Convention was not driven solely by the views of religious leaders, of course, the system of representation consciously was constructed to make it possible for representatives to strive for the common good.

* * *

Consistent with the views of religious leaders of the time, the Framers believed that "self-rule" is in fact anarchy. Individuals in a system of self-rule, acting without restraints, were thought to be less likely to serve the common good, a fear expressed in not a few of the sermons. Because of this understanding, representatives were placed in a constitutional structure intended to deter their abuses of power and to channel their decision-making toward the common good through checks and balances and the dispersion of power.

The practical argument for representative government is even more compelling today when the multiplicity of technically complex issues facing government makes it impossible for any one constituent and, perhaps, any one legislator to fully comprehend them all. Reality, time constraints, complexity, and multiplicity all counsel in favor of a delegation of decision-making power through a representative form of government.

The Framers readily conceded the practical impossibility and undesirability of self-rule. In like fashion, they also rejected monarchy. They embraced instead a third option, representation.

* * *

The Constitution makes one facet of representation clear: the constituent delegates not merely the right to vote on an issue according to the majority's preferences but rather the power to determine the particulars of public decisions. This delegation entails a transfer to the legislator of the power and responsibility to make the "hard choices." The nature and scope of the delegation of decision-making power from constituent to representative differs greatly from the self-rule concept's tendency to reduce representation to little more than vote aggregation.

The Constitution's representation scheme legitimizes the representative's exercise of personal and moral judgment.

The people have "intrusted" their representatives with the power and obligation to make binding law. While the self-rule paradigm would turn representatives into little more than placeholders for the majority's preference on any particular issue, the Constitution is centered around the necessity of a delegation of decision-making, which is to say the legislature, as constructed, did not create a majoritarian "difficulty," but rather freed government to pursue the common good, regardless of majority preferences.

The representative contemplated by the Constitution is yoked with heavy responsibilities. The legislature is elected to make independent and well-informed judgments in the best interests of the people regardless of whether the people would make those particular judgments themselves. * * *

The delegation of power is not unlimited, it is a delegation of decision-making power and responsibility. The power and right to make law is "delegated [by the people] for a certain period, on certain conditions, under certain limitations, and to a certain number of persons."

Legislators were held to a high standard of performance whereby they were expected to exercise judgment, which included taking into account the struggle of interests occurring around them and the expressed needs and desires of their constituents.

Representatives were not to be utterly detached from the people, in contemplation of an ideal good. Rather, a representative acting according to the Framers' prescriptions must weigh the desires and needs of her present and future constituents in constructing what she views as the best solution. In attempting to achieve a best-world solution the representative properly may depart from particular constituents' views.

For example, the southern mayor who enforced the dictates of the Brown v. Board of Education decision falls into this category, as does the federal legislator representing the Bible Belt who refuses to vote in favor of legislation that would declare the United States a Christian country. Some would argue or assume that representatives are majority-driven, because they seek re-election, but this is an oversimplification. For each vote cast the representative must think, as James Wilson did, whether his constituents will think he did the right thing, not, whether he followed their will in the face of better ideas at hand. Elections test results, not simple allegiance, except for one-issue voters.

This is precisely the point where the Court in Smith departed from the constitutional design. When the Court presumed and accepted that minority religions would be disabled in the legislative process constructed, it rested on a false assumption. The legislative process is constructed so that representatives consider a larger horizon than the simple majoritarianism the Court presumed, and instead creates the very possibility for minorities to get their voice heard and their needs served.

Although the people have no continuing right to instruct after the election, they do have the power publicly to disapprove, ridicule, and refuse to reelect their representatives. Thus, the typical legislator, far from being an isolated, sovereign ruler, is driven to engage in an ongoing dialogue with the people. Moreover, the legislator hears not only the judgment of her present-day constituents, but also the judgment of history imaginatively played out during the course of her representation. The legislator, thus, is accountable both to her geographically designated constituents, as well as to the res publica. This reality belies the simplemindedness of a representation scheme that involves only the aggregation of existing individual preferences and explains the necessary resort by the representative to best world rather than direct representation.

What distinguishes the legislator from a conduit of preferences is judgment, which includes the capacity to make choices between seemingly equally valued prospects and the capacity to include in the ultimate calculation the prioritization of particular issues. Instead, legislators mediate between two poles of a dialectic, one pole being careful consideration of the judgments of citizens and the other being the exercise of independent judgment in the interest of the polity.

* * *

The resort to self-rule in so much of the literature and public discourse, including the Smith decision, falls in the face of the complicated nature of the representative relationship. The relationship is not a simple pairing of governor and governed, ruler and people. The constitutional relationship is complex and so is the job assigned to the representatives. The prevailing theories falsify reality by oversimplifying representation. The representative stands in a vortex of dialectical relationships to a wide variety of phenomena. It is only by acknowledging the complexity of the judgment required that one fully can come to understand the enormous responsibility the Constitution places on the shoulders of representatives. * * *

* * *

Though the Framers did not institute an aptitude test for federal representatives, they acknowledged that the constitutional scheme would only succeed to the extent that at least some virtuous rulers took the helm. Virtue in those representing the people is in fact the fulcrum on which the constitutional system rests. If no virtuous leaders can be found, the scheme cannot succeed. But that does not mean all representatives must be great leaders. Certain that not all representatives would be virtuous, the Framers hoped that enough would be inclined to serve the common good and that the system could check the overreaching of those bad men not so inclined.

* * *

There is no ideal representative, because there are no perfect humans. Ever pragmatic, the Framers were acutely aware that representatives would not be gods but humans. Thus, the legislature operates best that contains a mix of qualities wherein individual representatives can counterbalance each other's strengths and weaknesses (the play of characteristics found at the Convention itself). But there are qualities that are innately valuable to the formation of good judgment, such as education, maturity, common sense, intelligence, empathy, and integrity. The good legislator might also have certain traits of character, courage, vision, and fealty to the rule of law. Each legislator brings with him a peculiar mix of these qualities.

* * *

The federal representative represents many constituencies, including his electorate (the state or district from which he was elected); the national constituency of the people taken as a whole; the factions or interests that knock on his door; the moral or religious zeitgeist; and even the international community. Despite his obligation to take all or some of these factors into account, depending on the issue, none of the entities being represented has the constitutional right or power to direct the representative's judgment. * * *

* * *

Each legislator is limited by his own shortcomings, a reality the Framers assumed into the constitutional structure. The whole, though, may be greater than the sum of its parts, and the virtues of some compensate for the weaknesses of others. Of course, as Madison feared, this formula only works where the more virtuous outnumber and outjudge their weaker cohorts on important issues. When the uneducated and self-serving reach critical mass, the whole may be no better than accumulated evil of the weaker members.

Legislators are also limited by the necessity of compromise in a body of so many. It is literally impossible for each and every representative to achieve his own independently determined legislative goals. The multiplicity of the participants, combined with the fact that they can only act as a whole, forces representatives to prioritize and to vote at times against their best judgment on a particular issue to preserve the right outcome on a more important issue.

The Constitution also poses meaningful barriers on the ability of legislators to follow their independently reached conclusions. The enumerated and limited powers of Article I, the checks and balances from the President and the courts, the countervailing power of the states' dual sovereignty, and the Bill of Rights place obstacles in the path of decisions that would otherwise satisfy the legislator's designs.

The matrix of representative judgment at the federal level, therefore, is exceedingly complex; indeed, so complex that evaluation of the wisdom of any one legislative enactment is often quite difficult and may be impossible, especially in the short run. Those affected certainly can criticize representatives for not serving their particular concerns, but that is no final judgment on whether the "right" result—the good of the whole—was reached. Thus, the legislator's internal tally of whether a particular decision was right or wrong in retrospect is exceedingly difficult to keep during the term of service. It may be years and even decades before the representative, the historian, or the people can assess whether that act was the right act, at the right time, for the right reasons, and for the right people.

But this assumes that the representative is struggling to reach the right answers for the common good. When members of Congress shirk their responsibilities by deferring solely to interest groups, by solely following opinion polls, or by handing the hard choices to the executive branch, the constitutional judgment is swift: failure. The structure of the Constitution requires more of members of Congress than of any other governmental office. In James Wilson's words, the legislators have the "hardest and least profitable task of any who engage in the service of the state."

* * *

The legislative structure was crafted by the Framers to avoid the problems of majoritarianism, or mob rule. Representatives are free of their constituents' instruction as they are simultaneously driven to consider the public good in a fishbowl of public scrutiny within which they operate and seek re-election. * * *

The foregoing discussion describes the legitimate legislature, which ought to be obeyed even by religious believers, under the reasoning of religious leaders at the time of the framing.

IV.   THE RULE OF LAW, THE LEGISLATURE, AND PERMISSIVE ACCOMMODATION

The rivers of ink spilled in criticism of the decision in Employment Division v. Smith are the stuff of which legends are made. The law review articles, the hearings in Congress, and the numerous editorials in newspapers and magazines contributed to a Nile of print. The standard story was apocalyptic, with the Supreme Court—actually, Justice Scalia himself—betraying the Free Exercise Clause and ruining religious liberty. In the words of one of my First Amendment students, which reflect the view of so many upon first reading the opinion, it was "just idiotic."

The focus of ire was on the reasoning that rejected the McConnell thesis on mandatory judicial exemptions under the Free Exercise Clause and declared that generally applicable laws (i.e., those that pass through duly elected legislatures with a neutral purpose) that incidentally burden religious conduct are constitutional.

Smith is to the Free Exercise Clause what Lemon v. Kurtzman is to the Establishment Clause. Both surveyed the entirety of previous jurisprudence to derive the principles that should govern the Clause. Essentially, in Smith, the Court looked back over its jurisprudence and saw what was there to be seen: religious claimants had not done terribly well fighting the rule of law except during the years 1963–90 in a particular arena, unemployment compensation, and in an individual case involving compulsory education law. Even though the Court accurately captured the general trend of the cases, it immediately was attacked as knowing nothing and being anti-liberty, in the press, in the law reviews, and in Congress. Religious organizations, which were informed by leading academics that the Court had just pulled a fast one, united to fight the Court's alleged unjust treatment.

To be sure, the Court did itself no favors by engaging the issue of what standard to apply under the Free Exercise Clause in a case in which the parties never addressed the issue, either in their briefs or during oral argument. If a charge was ever to be made against the Court for acting unilaterally, those are the conditions that foment such a charge. In this case, it was a criticism more procedural than substantive. Truth be told, the Court did not need briefing to lay out its own cases, and the standard under the Free Exercise Clause was certainly well within the purview of the necessary doctrine to determine the outcome of the case. Yet, had the Court heard re-argument on the issue, the hue and cry would have been muted, because everyone would have known the issue was up for consideration. Oral argument would have permitted the Justices to lay the groundwork for reconsideration.

The standard story on Smith has been tightly focused on the Free Exercise Clause, which has been read as a fundamental right of individual and organized religious believers to trump the rule of law. But the Court did not reject simply the mandatory accommodation thesis. That it decidedly did, but it also pointed to another path: legislative permissive accommodation.

It reaffirmed the view of the relationship between legislative government and religious interests first painted by religious leaders of the latter half of the eighteenth century. The first element of the opinion is quite true to the views of religious leaders in the eighteenth century: there was no absolute or general right for believers to trump duly enacted law. To the contrary, they had an obligation to obey as part of serving the common good. Further, legislatures, when acting legitimately, were responsible for serving the general peace, safety, and welfare of society, the common good, as well.

The question left open is whether legislatures could consider exempting religious believers from a particular law burdening their practices under this horizon. The reasoning follows from the co-presence of the rule of law and the role of the legitimate legislature. There is no reason within that universe to reject the concept of legislative accommodation. In fact, it seems to have been an accepted practice at the time. As Professor Hamburger has pointed out: though some "did seek exemption from civil laws, they typically asked, not for a general right of exemption, but merely for exemptions from a small number of specified civil obligations." Even then, only a few were provided in state constitutions.

Legislators were always under an obligation to consider the public good with every decision, and that horizon logically can extend to considerations for exemption. But the legislature never gets out from under the obligation of considering the common good. Thus, any consideration for exemption that focuses solely on the religious claimant without reference to the common good fails to fulfill the constitutional scheme. Where the exemption can be explained by the legislature as consistent with the public good, then the legislature has acted not solely in response to lobbying by religious entities, but rather with the larger good in mind.

It is impossible to invalidate a law where the legislature does not consider the public good solely on that ground, but it is possible to critique the process and to discern the actual purpose of the law by examining the way in which the legislature considered the public good (or not). Where the legislature's focus is solely upon providing a benefit to a particular religious group, and not on the general good, the argument that it is an unconstitutional, bare benefit for religion in violation of the Establishment Clause is quite strong. But where the focus was on the public good and the exemption was found to be a rational means of lightening a government-caused burden on religious conduct (with the exemption well tailored to the burden and therefore not overbroad), then the argument for bare benefit is likely to fail.

The best example of this lies in the exemptions for faith-healing groups from medical neglect laws. It is illegal in most states medically to neglect either a child or a disabled adult, but religious organizations have achieved exemptions in many states. A crucial question to be asked with respect to such exemptions is whether the legislature ever considered the public good or simply acquiesced to a request from a persistent lobbying effort. The same can be asked about child abuse reporting requirements that exempt religious entities from reporting child abuse.

There is an important caveat. No law issued through such a process is automatically immune from constitutional attack. To the extent that any such law offends constitutional boundaries, then the law is unconstitutional and obviously not intended to be obeyed. Conversely, in the absence of constitutional defect, the law is binding in the system of the rule of law.

For example, a law passed by a legislature that plainly considers the public interest still could fail by transgressing the separation of powers or by violating the procedures for amendment set forth in Article V, or by violating the inherent limitations of federalism.

When a religious individual or entity demands exemption—essentially a right to break the law that otherwise applies to others—it is required to account for how its actions affect the common good.

While this particular issue was not addressed directly in the various sermons, it follows from their discussions that where the welfare of society could be served by creating an exception to a general law for a religious believer, the legislature had still fulfilled its fullest function.

Which is to say that the sermons and the Smith Court's reach for permissive legislative accommodation have in common a resort to a theory of civil government that it is to be devoted to the greater good of the whole and that the life of the citizen-religious believer carries with it a responsibility likewise to be dedicated to the good of the whole and to be bound by laws duly enacted under that horizon.

Having been bound by such laws, there is no constitutional prohibition on believers requesting an exemption to ease a burden on religious belief, so long as the resulting law reasonably can be said to serve the common good.

The history following Smith further illuminates how this union of the rule of law and legislative accommodation might work consistently. After the outcry over Smith, various forces went forward in the state and federal legislative processes and achieved exemptions for the religious use of peyote from additional states and the federal government. In fact, the Smith Court had rather unsubtly pointed the way to such accommodation, by citing state laws that already exempted peyote from narcotics laws for religious use. So even though the standard story was and continues to be that the Court had closed the door on religious liberty, the subject matter in Smith itself was treated to widespread legislative exemption and therefore an increase in religious liberty, consistent with legislative responsibility. The reason why? Because such exemptions were found to be consistent with the larger public good. Peyote is not the sort of recreational drug, like heroin, that poses a serious risk of addiction and death, and it generally is used only in religious ceremonies because the experience it provides is not terribly pleasant. Under the horizon of the common good, the peyote exemptions made a great deal of sense.

In current lawmaking practice, there are instances where the public good is not effectively included within the process. Were an exemption to be enacted outside the usual legislative process and instead through a public initiative, which permits laws to be enacted based on a bare majority of the voters, that exemption would illustrate the bare majoritarianism that is rightly decried by Smith's detractors. Such initiatives fall short of the constitutional scheme for representation.

The peyote example also brings to light the error in the majoritarian thesis advanced against Smith and unnecessarily conceded by the Court in Smith. The Native American Church is a small minority church with few members and little political clout. Were representatives simply subject to majoritarian control, the requests for peyote exemption before Smith and after would have fallen on deaf ears. Yet, there were such exemptions both before and after, because legislators are placed in a position of power that permits them to consider claims by minority groups with concern and seriousness. Representatives are free from the instruction of their constituents and, as discussed above, must make decisions in light of how those decisions actually will play out against the backdrop of the common good.

Political scientist Mancur Olson's work in political science is critical here. His work shows that small, cohesive groups with a coherent message do better in the legislative fight than do unorganized, majority groups.[181] The key is in the directed organization of the delivery of a message and in the coherence of the message itself. These conditions are not insuperable obstacles to a quest by any religious organization for an exemption.

While Smith did not find the Court creating an exemption for the particular claimants in that case, it opened the door to greater dialogue between religious and legislative entities, not only about laws that pose burdens on religious entities, but also about the common good. No longer could legislatures pass such determinations off to the courts, which are institutionally incompetent to consider the nexus between any particular exemption and the common good. Instead of the courts haphazardly skewing the common good through individual determinations under the Free Exercise Clause, the legislatures, which are intentionally constructed to consider the larger public good, became the proper forum.

* * * The permissive accommodation formulation makes it impossible for legislatures to send claimants to the courts for individual case-by-case exemptions. At the same time, it forces religious entities to present their requests for exemption in terms of the public good. Far from being a path to majoritarianism, permissive accommodation brings back the uniting horizon of the common good. While not dictated by the views of the framing generation, the dynamic is consistent with its vision and with common sense.

Of course, permissive accommodation is not all good news for those religious believers who would seek an exemption. The legislative process, including executive signing into law, which considers such requests against the backdrop of the common good, will doom some requests. For example, Sikh schoolchildren in California sought to carry knives—or kirpan—in school as part of their religious heritage, which requires a weapon to defend their honor. The issue was considered publicly by the California legislature over several years, which did enact such an exemption, but Governor Pete Wilson vetoed it on the ground that he was "unwilling to authorize the carrying of knives on school grounds and abandon public safety to the resourcefulness of a thousand districts."

Perhaps the most obvious and sensible permissive accommodation was the exemption for the use of sacramental wine during Prohibition. The harms generated by alcohol could not be substantiated in the miniscule amount of wine drunk during communion, and therefore the exemption was consistent with the public policy goals of the general law and of Prohibition (however misguided Prohibition itself was in retrospect), and independently consistent with the general good.

---

181. *See generally* MANCUR OLSON, THE LOGIC OF COLLECTIVE ACTION: PUBLIC GOODS AND the Theory of Groups (1971).

As the Prohibition example illustrates, as the laws change over time, the need for exemption may change. In addition, as society alters its view on the value of any particular set of individuals within the society, exemptions will appear to be inconsistent or consistent with the public good. For example, many state legislatures have granted exemptions for children's medical neglect and abuse to faith healers. As the rights of children have increased incrementally over time, however, children's advocates have become increasingly vocal and have lobbied state legislatures to repeal the neglect and abuse exemptions. The same story is occurring with respect to reporting requirements of child abuse; there was a time when churches were regularly exempted from such reporting. This era of clergy child abuse scandals has brought into sharp relief this special treatment for religious entities. Massachusetts, the site of the most scandalous of the recent revelations of seriatim child abuse, recently added clergy to the list of professionals required to report child abuse.

This is not the article to lay out the parameters for the consideration and adoption of constitutional permissive legislative accommodation. That I leave to further endeavors. Rather, this final Section was intended to illustrate through contemporary examples how the shared common good that motivates the worldview of eighteenth-century religious leaders and the Constitution's legislative process can be understood to be at work today—both in the Court's doctrine and in existing legislative accommodations.

Without doubt, having sketched this much, a huge question looms, and that is: how do we determine the common good? It is a perfectly fair and a perfectly difficult question, but one, like the question of how to draft a constitutional legislative accommodation, that I will leave to a later day. This Article aims only for the more modest goal of uncovering the inherent connection between two seemingly disconnected elements in the Constitution—free exercise and the legislative process.

Conclusion

What makes the United States' constitutional engine run is in no small part the American people's embrace of the rule of law. This embrace was fostered by religious leaders in the eighteenth century, who took it upon themselves to explain how the believer is to live in two kingdoms simultaneously. Believers were, at the same time, to believe and worship God under the church's domain over belief, conscience, and worship and to obey the civil government when it regulated injurious conduct. Government, church, and believers were intended to share the horizon of a common good.

As arguments for the free exercise of religion have moved to a theory of isolationism rather than participation in the public good, this essential feature of the constitutional experiment has been threatened. The Supreme Court in *Employment Div. v. Smith*, however, reinstituted the accountability of religious believers, a move that is in harmony with the views of religious leaders at the time of the framing of the Constitution and that is likely to be essential to preserving this national community as the plurality of religions ever increases.

4. Free Exercise and the Political Process

This section provides the reader with a brief exposure to the debate over the proper role of religious beliefs and justifications in the political process. Much of this debate has centered on the question of whether government officials should have "publically accessible reasons" for their decisions—reasons that those in the public who do not share the officials' religious views can accept or reject without regard to any religious claim. Many leading scholars have engaged in this debate, including such notable scholars as Robert Audi, Kent Greenawalt, and Ronald Thiemann. The article excerpted in this section is by another leading scholar, Professor Michael Perry. The article was chosen because it is a recent contribution that directly, and in some detail, addresses the interaction of this issue with Free Exercise Clause concerns. Please be aware that volumes have been written on the proper motivation and justification (which are not necessarily the same in this context) for political action by political bodies and individual lawmakers, and this section only provides an introduction to this subject in the Free Exercise Clause Context. For a more thorough discussion of this topic it is well worth reading Professor Perry's wonderful new book, MICHAEL J. PERRY, UNDER GOD? RELIGIOUS FAITH AND LIBERAL DEMOCRACY (Cambridge 2003).

MICHAEL J. PERRY, *RELIGION, POLITICS, AND THE CONSTITUTION*

7 J. CONTEMP. LEGAL ISSUES 407 (1996). Copyright 1996, Journal of Contemporary Legal Issues. Reprinted with the permission of the Journal of Contemporary Legal Issues.

If few Americans were religious believers, the issue of the proper role of religion in politics would probably be marginal to American politics, because religion would be marginal to American religious—perhaps even the most religious—citizenries of the world's advanced industrial democracies. According to recent polling data, "[a]n overwhelming 95% of Americans profess belief in God"; moreover, "70% of American adults [are] members of a church or synagogue." If there were, among the vast majority of Americans who are religious believers, a consensus about most religious matters, the issue of the proper role of religion in politics would probably engage far fewer Americans than it does, because few Americans would have to fear being subjected to alien religious tenets. But there is, among American believers, a dissensus about many fundamental religious matters, including many fundamental religious-moral matters. Because the United States is both such a religious country and such a religiously pluralistic country (now more than ever), the issue of the proper role of religion in politics is anything but marginal to American politics. The proper role of religion in politics is a central, recurring issue in the politics of the United States.

In this essay, I present what seems to me to be the most sensible account of the general meaning of the two basic constitutional norms regarding religion: the free exercise norm and the nonestablishment norm. Then, drawing on that discussion, I make an argument about the role it is constitutionally permissible for religious arguments—in particular, religious arguments about the morality of human conduct—to play in the politics of the United States.

The heart of my account of the free exercise and nonestablishment norms is that government may not make judgments about the value or disvalue—the truth value, the moral value, the social value, any kind of value—of religions or religious practices or religious (theological) tenets. The proposition that government should not have the power to make such judgments is the yield of a long history, leading right up to the present, that has taught us that when the politically powerful arrogate to themselves the power to make judgments about the value or disvalue of religions or religious practices or tenets, they usually do harm, sometimes much harm, and little if any good—and that, moreover, it is utterly unnecessary, in terms of achieving the objectives proper to government, which we can subsume under the term "the common good," that the politically powerful have such power. The power to make judgments about the value or disvalue of religion is, in the hands of government—especially in a religiously pluralistic context like our own—a understandably tempting but nonetheless unnecessary and ultimately dangerous power. This lesson of history, which can be affirmed at least as vigorously by those of us who count ourselves religious believers as by those who do not, lies at the very foundation of the American commitment to the free exercise and nonestablishment norms, which together constitute the particular conception of religious freedom that is the subject of this essay.

I. Getting from There to Here

According to the First Amendment to the Constitution of the United States, "Congress shall make no law respecting an establishment of religion, or prohibiting the free exercise thereof; or abridging the freedom of speech, or of the press; or the right of the people peaceably to assemble, and to petition the government for a redress of grievances." Thus, the First Amendment makes two statements concerning religion: that "Congress shall make no law respecting an establishment of religion" and that "Congress shall make no law ... prohibiting the free exercise [of religion]." Yet, the freedom of religion protected by the constitutional caselaw of the United States—the constitutional law developed by the Supreme Court of the United States in the course of resolving conflicts about what the Constitution forbids—is much broader than the language of the First Amendment indicates. It is not just Congress that may not make a law respecting an establishment of religion or prohibiting the free exercise thereof; no branch of the national government—legislative, executive, or judicial—may take action establishing a religion or prohibiting the free exercise thereof. Moreover, it is not just the national government that may not take such action; no state government may do so either. According to the constitutional law of the United States, neither any branch of the national government nor any state government may either establish religion or prohibit the free exercise thereof.

Is there a basis in any part of the Constitution for extending the command of the First Amendment beyond Congress to the other two branches of the national government? Of course, the First Amendment concerns not just religion, but also speech, press, and peaceable assembly. Still, the command of the First Amendment is directed only at Congress—and even then only at congressional legislation. " 'Congress' does not on its face refer to the president, the courts, or the legions that manage the Executive Branch, and 'law' only arguably includes administrative orders or congressional investigations." * * *

* * *

* * * For present purposes * * * it suffices to observe that this aspect of constitutional caselaw has come to be widely and deeply affirmed by "We the people of the United States." Indeed, the proposition that neither the national government nor state government constitutionally may establish religion, prohibit the free exercise thereof, or abridge the freedom of speech or the freedom of the press has come to be a virtual axiom of American political-moral culture. The proposition is so deeply embedded in the American way of life that, as a practical matter, it is irreversible. Moreover, and as I have explained elsewhere, the proposition is, for "We the people" now living, constitutional bedrock. No one who contended that the Supreme Court should overrule the proposition would be taken seriously as a nominee to the Court.

The freedom of religion protected by the constitutional law of the United States, then, is the freedom constituted by two norms: first, that government shall not establish religion (which I will call "the nonestablishment norm") and, second, that government shall not prohibit the free exercise of religion ("the free exercise norm"). There are different conceptions of (and, correspondingly, different institutionalizations of) "freedom of religion." The conception to which the United States is committed, by its fundamental law, is the conception constituted by the free exercise and nonestablishment norms. * * * [T]here is some controversy about precisely what the norms forbid government to do.

II. FREE EXERCISE

What does it mean to say that government may not prohibit the free exercise of religion? The "exercise" of religion comprises many different but related kinds of religious practice, including: public affirmation of religious beliefs; affiliation, based on shared religious beliefs, with a church or other religious group; worship and study animated by religious beliefs; the proselytizing dissemination of religious beliefs or other religious information; and moral choices, or even a whole way of life, guided by religious beliefs. It is implausible to construe the free exercise norm to forbid government to prohibit each and every imaginable religious practice—including, for example, human sacrifice. Indeed, by its very terms the norm forbids government to prohibit, not the exercise of religion, but the "free" exercise of religion. Just as government may not abridge "the freedom of speech" or "the freedom of the press," so too it may not prohibit the "freedom" of religious exercise. It is one thing to argue, as I do in section V of this essay, that the freedom of religious exercise includes more than just freedom from discrimination against religious practice. It is another thing altogether * * * to suggest that the freedom of religious exercise is an unconditional right to do, on the basis of religious belief, whatever one wants. One need not concoct frightening hypotheticals about human sacrifice to dramatize the point. One need only point, for example, to the refusal of Christian Science parents to seek readily available life-saving medical care for their gravely ill child. Just as the freedom of speech is not a license to say whatever one wants wherever one wants whenever one wants and the freedom of the press is not a license to publish whatever one wants wherever one wants whenever one wants, so too the freedom of religious exercise is not a license to do, on the basis of religious belief, whatever one wants wherever one wants whenever one wants. If, then, there are some religious practices that the free exercise norm does not forbid government to prohibit, what does the norm forbid government to do?

Some persons might fear, dislike, or otherwise disvalue a religious practice. According to the free exercise norm, however, government may not "prohibit," may not ban or otherwise impose any regulatory restraint on, one or more religious practices as such—that is, as religious practice, practice embedded in and expressive of one or more religious beliefs. More generally, government may not take any action, impeding a religious practice (or practices), based on the view that the practice is, as religious practice, inferior along one or another dimension of value to another religious or nonreligious practice or to no practice at all. Thus, the free exercise norm is an antidiscrimination provision: It forbids government to take prohibitory action discriminating against religious practice (i.e., disfavoring religious practice as such). Government "would be 'prohibiting the free exercise [of religion]' if it sought to ban [acts or refusals to act] only when they are engaged in for religious reasons, or only because of the religious belief that they display. It would doubtless be unconstitutional, for example, to ban the casting of 'statues that are to be used for worship purposes,' or to prohibit bowing down before a golden calf."

To ban or otherwise impose a regulatory restraint on a religious practice (as such) is one way for government to take prohibitory action discriminating against the practice, but it is not the only way. The free exercise norm, construed in an appropriately generous way, forbids indirect as well as direct restraint. Government may not impede a religious practice (as such) by denying to persons, because they engage in the practice, a benefit it would otherwise confer on them. It simply would make no sense, it would be naive and even foolish, to forbid government to ban "the casting of 'statues that are to be used for worship purposes' " while leaving government free to deny to persons, because they cast such statues, a benefit it would otherwise give to them.

That the free exercise norm is an antidiscrimination provision—that government "prohibits" the free exercise of religion if its prohibitory action disfavors religious practice as such—is not controversial, but that the norm is more than an antidiscrimination provision is controversial. There is disagreement, both on the Supreme Court and off, about whether the norm forbids government to do anything other than take prohibitory action discriminating against religious practice. Does the free exercise norm forbid, in addition to prohibitory action that is discriminatory, at least some governmental action that, although nondiscriminatory, impedes religious practice? Or is it problematic to read the language of the free exercise norm—in particular, the word "prohibit"—to extend even to some nondiscriminatory governmental action impeding religious practice? In order to pursue this inquiry, we should first answer a prior question: What does the nonestablishment norm forbid government to do?

III. NONESTABLISHMENT

What does it mean to say that government may not establish religion; at least, what has it come to mean, in the United States? As I stated at the beginning of this essay, the central point of the free exercise and nonestablishment norms, taken together, is that government may not make judgments about the value or disvalue—the truth value, the moral value, the social value—of religions or religious practices or religious (theological) tenets as such (i.e., as religious). Government has no such power, and government may not arrogate to itself any such power. Whereas the free exercise norm forbids government to take prohibitory action disfavoring one or more religious practices as such, the nonestablishment norm forbids government to favor one or more religions as such; in particular, it forbids government to discriminate in favor of membership in one or more churches or other religious communities or in favor of the practices or tenets of one or more churches. No matter how much some persons might prefer one or more religions, government may not take any action based on the view that the preferred religion or religions are, as religion, better along one or another dimension of value than one or more other religions or than no religion at all. So, for example, government may not take any action based on the view that Christianity, or Roman Catholicism, or the Fifth Street Baptist Church, is, as a religion or a church, closer to the truth than one or more other religions or churches or than no religion at all—or, if not necessarily closer to the truth, at least a more authentic reflection of the religious history and culture of the American people. (One might believe that by reflecting the religious history and culture of a people, laws and other political choices achieve a moral authority they would otherwise lack and help to maintain a useful sense of moral solidarity among the people.) Similarly, no matter how much some persons might prefer one or more religious practices, government may not take any action based on the view that the preferred practice or practices are, as religious practice (practice embedded in and expressive of one or more religious beliefs), better—truer or more efficacious spiritually, for example, or more authentically American—than one or more other religious or nonreligious practices or than no religious practice at all. For example, government may not take any action based on the view that the Lord's Prayer is, as prayer, better than one or more other prayers or than no prayer at all. Finally, no matter how much some persons might prefer one or more religious tenets—that is, one or more tenets about the existence, nature, activity, or will of God— government may not take any action based on the view that the preferred tenet or tenets are truer or more authentically American or otherwise better than one or more competing religious or nonreligious tenets. For example, government may not take any action based on the view that the Roman Catholic doctrine of apostolic succession (which is, whatever else it is, a doctrine that presupposes that God exists and makes a claim about God's activity and/or will) is closer to the truth than one or more competing theological or nontheological doctrines. * * *

Like the free exercise norm, then, the nonestablishment norm is an antidiscrimination provision; but unlike the free exercise norm, which forbids government to engage in prohibitory action that disfavors one or more religious practices as such, the nonestablishment norm forbids government to favor one or more religions as such—including one or more religious practices or tenets. * * * Moreover, the nonestablishment norm, like the free exercise norm, forbids indirect as well as direct action. Government may not give to persons, because they engage in a particular religious practice, a benefit it would otherwise deny to them, if doing so is based on the view that the practice is, as religious practice, better than one or more other religious or nonreligious practices or than no religious practice at all. * * *

IV. WHY NONESTABLISHMENT?

Why is it a good thing that the constitutional law of the United States includes the free exercise norm? Because, as history helps us understand, and as the protection of religious freedom by the international law of human rights suggests, it would be a bad thing, indeed a terrible thing, were government in the United States free to discriminate against one or more religions or religion generally. Acts of governmental discrimination against religion, in the United States and elsewhere, have been and almost surely would continue to be illiberal, if not authoritarian or totalitarian, in their motivation and divisive and sometimes even destabilizing in their consequences. Moreover, a politics free to discriminate against religion is a politics free to secure favors from one or more religions, including the favor of genuflecting before the politically powerful, in return for not discriminating against them. What an ugly state of affairs that would be: some religions discriminated against and some other religions bought off. Finally, there is simply no need for government in the United States to be free to discriminate against religion; nothing of real value is lost by forbidding government to discriminate against religion.

But is it a good thing that the constitutional law of the United States includes not just the free exercise norm, but the nonestablishment norm as well? Note, in that regard, that although the international law of human rights includes provisions that function just like the free exercise norm—in particular, forbidding government to discriminate against religious practice—the international law of human rights does not include anything like a nonestablishment norm. Nor does governmental action that would violate the nonestablishment norm necessarily violate any human right.

Consider, for example, the Constitution of Ireland, which, in the Preamble, affirms a nonsectarian Christianity: "In the name of the Most Holy Trinity, from Whom is all authority and to Whom, as our final end, all actions both of men and States must be referred, we, the people of Eire, humbling acknowledging all our obligations to our Divine Lord, Jesus Christ, Who sustained our fathers through centuries of trial, . . . do hereby adopt, enact, and give to ourselves this Constitution." Given the religious commitments of the vast majority of the people of Ireland, it is not at all surprising that the Irish Constitution affirms Christianity. In so doing, the Irish Constitution violates no human right. Three things are significant here. First, the religious convictions implicit in the Irish Constitution's affirmation of Christianity in no way deny—indeed, they affirm—the idea that every human being, Christian or not, is sacred; they affirm, that is, the very foundation of the idea of human rights. Second, the Irish Constitution's affirmation of Christianity is not meant to insult or demean anyone; it is meant only to express the most fundamental convictions of the vast majority of the people of Ireland. Third, and perhaps most importantly, the Irish Constitution protects the right, which is a human right, to freedom of religion; moreover, it protects this right not just for Christians, who are the vast majority in Ireland, but for all citizens. Article 44 states, in relevant part: "Freedom of conscience and the free profession and practice of religion are . . . guaranteed to every citizen. . . . The State shall not impose any disabilities or make any discrimination on the ground of religious profession, belief or status." * * *

The question arises, therefore, whether, even though it is certainly a good thing—a very good thing—that the constitutional law of the United States includes the free exercise norm, it is also a good thing—and, if so, how good—that it includes the nonestablishment norm. Let's come at the question from the other side: Why might one think it a bad thing that the constitutional law of the United States includes the nonestablishment norm? What need is there for government in the United States to be free to discriminate in favor of one or more religions? What of value is lost, if anything, by forbidding government to discriminate in favor of religion?

It is at least a moderately good thing, in my view, that the constitutional law of the United States includes the nonestablishment norm, because, all things considered, it would be at least a moderately bad thing—and perhaps, from time to time, a very bad thing—were either the national government or state government constitutionally free to discriminate in favor of one or more religions or religious practices or tenets. Were the politically powerful free to discriminate in favor of one or more religions, history suggests that they would almost certainly do little if any good and some, or more than some, harm. That they would do little if any good and at least some harm is especially likely, of course, in a society as religiously pluralistic as the United States.

It bears emphasis, at this point, that one important way to protect freedom of religion is to protect, as the nonestablishment norm does, freedom from governmentally-imposed religion—which is, of course, a freedom of religious believers no less than of religious nonbelievers. An important way to protect the freedom of those of us who count ourselves religious to follow our religious consciences where they lead—especially the freedom of those of us who are not politically powerful—is for the constitutional law of the United States to forbid the politically powerful among us to act, in large ways or small, in obvious ways or subtle, to privilege ("establish") their brand of religion. Thus, the nonestablishment norm is good news not just for the atheists and agnostics among us; it is good news for us all. It is noteworthy, too, that the nonestablishment norm protects not just freedom of religion, but religion itself. One way for government to corrupt religion—to co-opt it, to drain it of its prophetic potential—is to seduce religion to get in bed with government; an important way to protect religion, therefore, is to forbid government to get in bed with religion. "In this framework religion becomes a tool, a means to control behavior, an instrument to revivify the people, a cheap hireling to provide a basis for unity, a means merely to achieve political ends. In the end, religion is the loser. True religion, genuine faith, is defamed, desecrated, and trivialized. This is the lesson of history, yet we are on the verge of repeating the same error. Religious belief has its public dimensions, to be sure, but it is first and foremost a matter of private right. Church-state separation is the great protector of true faith, not its inhibitor."[31]

Moreover—and this is perhaps the crux of the matter—there is simply no practical need for political bureaucracies, even democratic political bureaucracies, to have the power to discriminate in favor of religion. * * *

Would it be a good thing, or at least not such a bad thing, were government free at least to discriminate, not in favor of one or more religions in relation to one or more other religions, but in favor of religion generally? As I explain in s VI, for the constitutional law of the

31. Derek H. Davis, *Assessing the Proposed Religious Equality Amendment*, 37 J. Church & State 493, 507–08 (1995). * * *

United States to adopt the accommodation position is for it to discriminate in favor of religion—specifically, in favor of religious practice—generally. Except for the good arguably achieved by adopting the accommodation position, I am skeptical that there is anything of real value we Americans might reasonably hope to accomplish by discriminating, or by leaving our politicians free to discriminate, in favor of religion generally. Why do we need to enact laws or make political choices that discriminate in favor of religion generally? From a practical standpoint at least, there is no more need to discriminate in favor of religion generally than to discriminate in favor of one or more religions in relation to one or more other religions. * * *

V. Nonestablishment Conflicts

My aim in sections II–III was to give, briefly and somewhat abstractly, an account of what the free exercise and nonestablishment norms, correctly understood, forbid government to do. Of course, what seems to me to be the correct understanding of the norms might not be what seems to the Supreme Court of the United States to be the correct understanding. As it happens, however, what I have said about the free exercise norm—that it is, whatever else it is, an antidiscrimination provision, forbidding government to take prohibitory action disfavoring religious practice as such—accurately represents the position not only of a majority of the members of the Court today, but of the whole Court. (Again, there is disagreement both on the Court and off about whether the free exercise norm is more than an antidiscrimination provision. * * *) Moreover, what I have said about the nonestablishment norm substantially represents the position of the Court today. * * *

* * *

VI. Free Exercise, Nonestablishment, and the Problem of "Accommodation"

To rehearse an earlier point: That the free exercise norm is an antidiscrimination provision—that government "prohibits" the free exercise of religion if its prohibitory action disfavors religious practice as such—is not controversial, but that the norm is more than an antidiscrimination provision is controversial. As I said, there is disagreement, both on the Supreme Court and off, about whether the norm forbids government to do anything other than take prohibitory action discriminating against religious practice. Does the free exercise norm forbid, in addition to prohibitory action that is discriminatory, at least some governmental action that, although nondiscriminatory, impedes religious practice? One position, the "accommodation" position, holds that the free exercise norm not only forbids government to discriminate against religious practice, but also requires government to maximize the space for religious practice by exempting religious practice from an otherwise applicable ban or other regulatory restraint that would interfere substantially with a person's ability to engage in the practice, unless the exemption would seriously compromise an important public interest. So, for example, if a state were to ban the consumption of alcoholic beverages, the state would have to exempt from the ban the consumption of wine in the Christian sacrament of the Eucharist unless the exemption would seriously compromise an important public interest. In that sense, government must sometimes "accommodate" religious practice, by exempting it from an otherwise applicable regulatory restraint, even if the failure to exempt would not constitute discrimination against the practice. According to the accommodation position, government "prohibits" the free exercise of religion not only if its prohibitory action disfavors religious practice as such, but also if it fails to exempt religious practice from a (nondiscriminatory) restraint if the exemption would not seriously compromise an important public interest.

Some constitutional scholars contend for the accommodation position, others contend against it. As the accommodation debate illustrates, the conventional range of reference of the word "prohibit" is broad enough to accommodate either the accommodation position or the rejection of the position. In that sense, the language of the free exercise norm underdetermines the choice between the accommodation position and its rejection. By government shall not "prohibit" the free exercise of religion one might mean only that government shall not take prohibitory action that discriminates against religious practice, that disfavors religious practice as such. Or, instead, one might mean both that government shall not take prohibitory action discriminating against religious practice and that it shall not take action that, though nondiscriminatory, substantially interferes with a person's ability to engage in a religious practice if exempting the practice would not seriously compromise an important public interest. However, that the conventional range of reference of the word "prohibit" underdetermines the choice between the accommodation position and its rejection does not mean that the free exercise norm that has been established as a part of the constitutional law of the United States is not the norm for which the accommodation position argues.

What norm was the free exercise language of the First Amendment ("Congress shall make no law ... prohibiting the free exercise [of religion]") understood to communicate by the "We the people of the United States" over two hundred years ago who, through their representatives, put that language of the First Amendment into the text of the Constitution; that is, what directive did they understand themselves to be issuing—what norm did they mean to establish? Although it is not unequivocal, the historical evidence does seem to support an answer congenial to the accommodation position. As I explained at the beginning of this essay, however, the First Amendment norm that "Congress shall make no law ... prohibiting the free exercise [of religion]" is not the same as the free exercise norm, now a bedrock part of the constitutional law of the United States, that neither any branch of the national government nor any state government shall prohibit the free exercise of religion. Who are the persons who made the free exercise norm a part of the constitutional law of the United States? Even if it is not clear who they are, even if it is controversial who they are, it is quite clear that they are not the same as the "We the people of the United States" over two hundred years ago who, through their representatives, made the First Amendment, including its free exercise language, a part of the Constitution of the United States. If we accept the "incorporation" position sketched earlier in this essay, and if we accept that the norms incorporated and thereby made applicable to the states include the First Amendment's ban on government establishing religion, prohibiting the free exercise thereof, or abridging the freedom of speech or the freedom of the press, then the persons who made the free exercise norm a part of the constitutional law of the United States—the broad free exercise norm that is a limitation on state government as well as on the national government—are the "We the people" in the 1860s who, through their representatives, made the Fourteenth Amendment a part of the Constitution. According to Kurt Lash, the particular free exercise norm that (in Lash's scenario) they made a part of the Constitution supports the accommodation position. * * *

Even if, contra Lash and others, the Fourteenth Amendment was not meant to make the First Amendment applicable to the states, it is, as I said, constitutional bedrock for "We the people of the United States" now living that the First Amendment's ban on government establishing religion, prohibiting the free exercise thereof, or abridging the freedom or speech or the freedom of the press applies to the states. It is not constitutional bedrock, however, that the free exercise norm applicable to the states (and to the national government) supports the accommodation position. (For those for whom historical arguments about "original meaning" or "original understanding" have great authority in constitutional adjudication, it must be noted that such arguments for the accommodation position are controversial.) And, as it happens, a majority of the Supreme Court, in 1990, rejected the accommodation position. In Employment Division, Oregon Department of Human Resources v. Smith, the Court wrote that "if prohibiting the exercise of religion ... is ... merely the incidental effect of a generally applicable and otherwise valid provision," the free exercise norm, without regard to whether the refusal to exempt the religious practice in question serves an important public interest, has not been violated. The five-person majority's rejection (in an opinion by Justice Scalia) of the accommodation position provoked not only the other four persons on the Court; it provoked so many interested persons off the Court that an unprecedented alliance of groups, from the American Civil Liberties Union on the one side to the so-called "religious right" on the other, joined forces to lobby Congress to undo the decision. * * *

The fundamental political-moral rationale for the accommodation position is that the "free exercise of religion" is such an important value that government must not only not discriminate against religious practice but must also do what it can, short of compromising an important public interest, to avoid putting substantial impediments in the way of religious practice. A similar but broader rationale, not limited to religious practice, explains the breadth of the freedom of conscience protected by the international law of human rights: freedom not only from discrimination but also from some nondiscriminatory interference. The International Covenant on Civil and Political Rights, which the United States ratified in 1992, provides, in Article 18, that: "Everyone shall have the right to freedom of thought, conscience, and religion. This right shall include freedom to have or to adopt a religion or belief of his choice, and freedom, either individually or in community with others and in public or private, to manifest his religion or belief in worship, observance, practice and teaching." Article 18 then states: "Freedom to manifest one's religion or beliefs may be subject only to such limitations as are prescribed by law and are necessary to protect public safety, order, health, or morals or the fundamental rights and freedoms of others." Virtually identical provisions inhabit the Universal Declaration of Human Rights (Articles 18 & 29), the Declaration on the Elimination of All Forms of Intolerance and of Discrimination Based on Religion or on Belief (Article 1), the American Convention on Human Rights (Article 12), and the European Convention on Human Rights (Article 9). According to each of these instruments, government must not only not discriminate against religious or other conscientious practice but must also avoid interfering with such practice except to the extent "necessary to protect public safety, order, health, or morals or the fundamental rights and freedoms of others."

Earlier I said that whether it is problematic to construe the word "prohibit" to extend even to some nondiscriminatory governmental action impeding religious practice depends in part on what the nonestablishment norm forbids government to do. Recall that, among other things, the nonestablishment norm forbids government to take action based on the view that one or more religious practices are, as religious practice, better than one or more other religious or nonreligious practices or than no religious practice at all. The principal argument against the accommodation position is that for government to do what the accommodation position requires—favor, by accommodating, religious practice as such—is for government, in violation of the nonestablishment norm, to take action based on the view that, at least as a general matter, religious practices are, as such, better or more valuable than nonreligious practices. Now, it might be ideal if the constitutional law of the United States were revised to protect acts of secular conscience on a par with acts of religious conscience. * * * As it stands, however, the free exercise norm protects, from discrimination, only acts of religious conscience. It is one thing to suggest that the constitutional law of the United States be revised to protect acts of conscience generally. It is another thing altogether, and extreme, to suggest that unless and until the constitutional law of the United States is revised to protect acts of conscience generally, the free exercise norm should be ignored. The free exercise norm, no less than the nonestablishment norm, is a bedrock part of the existing constitutional law of the United States, and as such it operates as a practical limit on what we can reasonably construe the nonestablishment norm to forbid. At the same time, the nonestablishment norm, in conjunction with the international law of human rights, might exert a gravitational pull on our understanding of what the constitutional law of the United States should protect. Eventually, we might come to accept that the constitutional law of the United States should, to some extent, include protection not just for acts of religious conscience, but for acts of conscience generally—and for the processes of conscience formation.

But if the free exercise norm (as a bedrock part of the existing constitutional law of the United States) operates as a practical limit on what we can reasonably construe the nonestablishment norm to forbid, and if, therefore, it is not inconsistent with the nonestablishment norm for constitutional law to protect only acts of religious conscience from discrimination against them, why then shouldn't we take the next step and conclude that it is not inconsistent with the nonestablishment norm for constitutional law to require government to accommodate only acts of religious conscience (with the proviso, of course, that government need not accommodate even an act of religious conscience if to do so would seriously compromise an important public interest)? Is it less extreme to insist that such acts of accommodation violate the nonestablishment norm than to insist that protecting only acts of religious conscience from discrimination against them violates the nonestablishment norm? It is important to keep things in perspective here: According to the accommodationist version of the free exercise norm, no act of religious conscience merits exemption from a truly nondiscriminatory ban or other regulatory restraint if the exemption would compromise an important public interest.

If the accommodationist version of the free exercise norm were morally obnoxious, even one who found the historical argument for the accommodationist version of the norm stronger than the historical argument for the anti-accommodationist version might want to find a respectable way to reject the accommodationist version. But although the broader position represented by the international law of human rights—the position that protects not just acts of religious conscience, but acts of conscience generally—might be morally preferable, it seems to me farfetched to claim that the accommodation position is morally obnoxious. Indeed, one might fairly conclude that in the context of the United States, the accommodationist version of the free exercise norm is morally preferable to the anti-accommodationist version, according to which the free exercise norm is only an antidiscrimination provision. By insisting that the free exercise norm protects religious practice only from prohibitory action disfavoring religious practice as such—by insisting that the norm is only an antidiscrimination provision * * * the Court in Employment Division, Department of Human Resources of Oregon v. Smith "started down a doctrinal path that leads to a constitutional discourse in which contending parties accuse each other of hostility, persecution, and bad faith.... [T]his sort of demonizing debate is precisely what a doctrinal emphasis on motive as a dispositive factor is calculated to elicit.... [I]f one is searching for alternatives, then pre-Smith free exercise jurisprudence—not merely the "compelling interest" balancing test ... but rather the discourse of humility and tolerance exemplified in [Wisconsin v. Yoder]—invites renewed consideration."[79]

* * *

VII. Religion in Politics: Constitutional Perspectives

* * * The stage is now set for us to pursue the inquiry about the role it is constitutionally permissible for religious arguments to play, if any, in the politics of the United States. As I noted in the introduction to this essay, the controversy about the proper role of religious arguments in politics comprises two inquiries: an inquiry about the constitutionally proper role of religious arguments in politics and a related but distinct inquiry about their morally proper role. In the larger work from which this essay is drawn, I pursue the moral inquiry. In the remainder of this essay, I address this question: Given the freedom of religion protected by the constitutional law of the United States—given, in particular, the nonestablishment norm—what role, if any, is it constitutionally permissible for religious arguments to play, in the United States, either in public debate about what political choices to make or as a basis of political choice?

* * *

The political choices with which I am principally concerned in this essay are those that ban or otherwise disfavor one or another sort of human conduct based on the view that it is immoral for human beings (whether all human beings or some human beings) to engage in the conduct. A law banning abortion is a paradigmatic instance of the kind of political choice I have in mind; a law banning homosexual sexual conduct is another.

* * *

By a "religious" argument, I mean an argument that relies on (among other things) a religious belief: an argument that presupposes the truth of a religious belief and includes that belief as one of its essential premises. * * *

Let's begin with this question: Does a legislator or other public official, or even an ordinary citizen, violate the nonestablishment norm by presenting a religious argument in public political debate? For example, does a legislator violate the nonestablishment norm by presenting, in public debate about whether the law should recognize homosexual marriage, a religious argument that homosexual sexual conduct is immoral? An affirmative answer is wildly implausible. Every citizen, without regard to whether she is a legislator or other public official, is

---

79. [Steven D. Smith, *Free Exercise Doctrine and the Discourse of Disrespect*, 65 U. Colo. L. Rev. 519 (1994)] at 575–76. Smith discusses, and applauds, the Court's per-formance in *Wisconsin v. Yoder* (406 U.S. 205 (1972)) at various points in his excellent article.

constitutionally free to present in public political debate whatever arguments about morality, including whatever religious arguments, she wants to present. Indeed, the freedom of speech protected by the constitutional law of the United States is so generous that it extends even to arguments, including secular arguments, that may not, as a constitutional matter, serve as a basis of political choice * * * Thus, whether or not religious arguments may, as a constitutional matter, serve as a basis of political choice, it is clear that citizens and even legislators and other public officials are constitutionally free to present such arguments in public political debate. * * *

Moreover, to disfavor religious arguments relative to secular ones would violate the core meaning—the antidiscrimination meaning—of the free exercise norm. After all, included among the religious practices protected by the free exercise norm are bearing public witness to one's religious beliefs and trying to influence political decisionmaking on the basis of those beliefs. As the Second Vatican Council of the Catholic Church observed in the document Dignitatis Humanae, true freedom of religion includes the freedom of persons and groups "to show the special value of their doctrine in what concerns the organization of society and the inspiration of the whole of human activity." * * * The serious question, then, is not whether legislators or other public officials, much less citizens, violate the nonestablishment norm by presenting religious arguments in public political debate. The serious question, rather, is whether government would violate the nonestablishment norm by basing a political choice—for example, a law banning abortion—on a religious argument.

Recall that among the other things it forbids government to do, the nonestablishment norm forbids government to take any action based on the view that one or more religious tenets are closer to the truth or more authentically American or otherwise better than one or more competing religious or nonreligious tenets. * * * Thus, the nonestablishment norm does forbid government to base political choices on religious arguments in this sense: Government may not base any action—therefore, it may not base any choice, including one about the morality of human conduct—on the view that a religious belief is closer to the truth or otherwise better than one or more competing religious or nonreligious beliefs. (Again, a religious argument is an argument that presupposes the truth of a religious belief and includes that belief as one of its essential premises.) The nonestablishment norm forbids government to base political choices on religious arguments; at least as an ideal matter, the nonestablishment norm requires that if government wants to make a political choice, including one about the morality of human conduct, it does so only on the basis of a secular argument: an argument that relies neither on any religious belief nor on the belief that God does not exist.

* * * [T]he nonestablishment norm also forbids government to base political choices on secular arguments of a certain sort, namely, secular arguments to the effect that one or more religious tenets are more authentically American, or more representative of the sentiments of the

community, or otherwise better, than one or more competing religious or nonreligious tenets. * * * Again, the central point of the free exercise and nonestablishment norms, taken together, is that government may not make judgments about the value or disvalue—the truth value, the moral value, the social value—of religions or of religious practices or tenets (qua religious).

In making a political choice, especially a political choice about the morality of human conduct, legislators and other public officials some-times rely both on a religious argument and on an independent secular argument: a secular argument that, if accepted, supports the choice without help from a religious argument. * * * If government based a political choice about the morality of human conduct at least partly on a plausible secular argument that supports the choice, it would be ex-tremely difficult for a court to discern whether government based the choice solely on the secular argument or, instead, only partly on the secular argument and partly on the religious argument. That govern-ment would have made the choice even in the absence of the religious argument, solely on the basis of the secular argument, is some evidence that the choice was based solely on the secular argument. Such evidence is not conclusive, however * * *. Moreover, counterfactual inquiry by a court into whether government "would have made" a political choice about the morality of human conduct in the absence of a religious argument on which some officials relied is so speculative as to be unusually vulnerable to distortion by a judge's own sympathies and hostilities. Indeed, an individual legislator or other public official, inquir-ing in good faith, might not be able to decide with confidence whether she herself would have made a political choice about the morality of human conduct in the absence of a religious argument on which she relied (or whether she would make it now).

As an ideal matter, the nonestablishment norm is probably best understood, as I have suggested, to forbid government to make any political choice, even one about the morality of human conduct, on the basis of a religious argument. But, given the difficulty emphasized in the preceding paragraph, we should probably conclude that as a practical matter, the nonestablishment norm requires only that government not make political choices of the kind in question here—political choices about the morality of human conduct—unless a plausible secular ratio-nale supports the choice without help from a parallel religious argument. * * * (An important qualification is necessary here. I explain in the larger work from which this essay is drawn why a religious argument in support of the claim that each and every human being is sacred presents a special case: Even if we assume that no secular argument supports the claim that every human being is sacred, government may, under the nonestablishment norm, rely on a religious argument in support of the claim.)

* * *

* * * For government to make a coercive political choice about the morality of human conduct that can be supported only by a religious reason or reasons is for government to impose religion.

Admittedly, that under the nonestablishment norm government may not make a political choice about the morality of human conduct unless a plausible secular rationale supports the choice has less practical significance than one might think, because there will be plausible secular rationales for most such political choices that government might want to make. (In adjudicating the constitutionality, under the nonestablishment norm, of a political choice about the morality of human conduct, the proper issue for a court is not whether a secular rationale is, in the court's own view, persuasive. After all, the judiciary does not have the principal policymaking authority or responsibility. The proper issue for a court is only whether a secular rationale is plausible—that is, whether a legislator or other public official could reasonably find the rationale persuasive.) However, that a political choice about the morality of human conduct does not violate the nonestablishment norm does not mean that the choice does not violate some other constitutional requirement. In my view, a state's denial of legal recognition to homosexual marriage probably violates the antidiscrimination part of the Fourteenth Amendment.

I said that under the nonestablishment norm, government may not make a political choice about the morality of human conduct unless a plausible secular rationale supports the choice. But what about an individual legislator or other public official: What should she do? Should she vote to support a political choice about the morality of human conduct if she is agnostic about whether, or even skeptical that, a plausible secular rationale supports the choice, leaving it up to others, and ultimately to the courts, to decide if such a rationale exists? Fidelity to the spirit of the nonestablishment norm seems to me to require more of her: She should vote to support a political choice about the morality of human conduct only if, in her view, a persuasive secular rationale exists. (I am not suggesting that such a constitutional duty could be, or even should be, judicially enforced. How could a court determine whether or not an individual legislator really believes that there is a persuasive secular rationale? The duty would have to be self-enforced.) * * *

* * * [T]hat an act would not violate any constitutional norm does not entail that the act would be, all things considered, morally appropriate. Similarly, constitutional illegality does not entail moral impropriety; that an act would violate a constitutional norm does not entail that the act would be, apart from its unconstitutionally, morally inappropriate. Indeed, if we conclude that an act that would violate a constitutional norm would not be, apart from its unconstitutionality, morally inappropriate—and especially if we conclude that the act would be morally appropriate—we can proceed to inquire whether the constitutional law of the United States shouldn't be revised by the Supreme Court, or even amended pursuant to Article V of the Constitution, to permit the act.

Beyond the constitutional inquiry, therefore, lies the moral inquiry.

* * *

Notes and Questions

1. *What Does the Free Exercise Clause Do?* After reading the articles in this chapter, what do you think the proper role and function of the Free Exercise Clause should be? If the purpose is accommodation, should it require accommodation or simply permit it? If accommodation is required, how do we determine when it is required? Should the interpretation of the Free Exercise Clause be focused on equality, and if so, what will this require? Can judges (or jurors) who are often raised in a dominant religious tradition ever adequately value the importance of religious practices to those from vastly different religious traditions? What role does the nature of government play in all of this? Is it possible that an equality based approach to the Free Exercise Clause will frequently require accommodation of religious practices?

2. *Reconciling Approaches?* It would appear that Professor Hamilton's historical arguments support Professor Feldman's assertion that the Free Exercise Clause has generally privileged Protestant beliefs. If this is so, whose interpretation of that Clause is better? Professor Idleman's argument would seem to provide support for Professor Hamilton's position based on the nature of government, but Professors Eisgruber and Sager's position would seem to lend support to the idea that the Free Exercise Clause must protect religious minorities as well as the religious mainstream in order to be effective. What role, if any, should the views of the framers of the Fourteenth Amendment—who were concerned with notions of equality—play in this debate? Does your answer depend on whether the framers of the Fourteenth Amendment intended for the Free Exercise Clause to be incorporated through that amendment?

3. *Accommodation.* What do you think of the accommodation approach advocated by Professor McConnell and seemingly supported by Professor Lupu? How does it differ from equality based approaches? How does it answer the concerns raised by Professors Hamilton and Idleman regarding the role of government and the "common good?" Without accommodation it could be argued that the Free Exercise Clause provides little protection for religious minorities, especially non-Christian religious minorities, because they are less likely to be considered in the legislative process for "generally applicable" laws, less likely to be granted permissive accommodations by government entities even when they seek them, and less likely to win an exemption case in court. Does this suggest that the accommodationist perspective provides the best solution to the concerns raised by Professor Feldman? Does your answer depend on how we define "accommodation?" Consider that religious outsiders faired poorly under the Court's "accommodationist" approach in the years after *Sherbert*. Both Professor McConnell and Professor Lupu answer this concern by suggesting that for accommodation to work the Court must strictly apply a compelling interest test. Will this satisfy the concerns raised by Professor Feldman, or will dominant religious values receive preferential treatment even under a strong accommodationist approach?

4. *Religion and Political Decision Making.* Do you agree with Professor Perry that government officials should rely on "publically accessible reasons"— i.e. reasons that those who do not share the officials' religious values can identify with? Is this a requirement or a suggestion under Professor Perry's approach?

Which do you think it should be? Is it proper for government officials to rely on religious beliefs in making their decisions and then use secular arguments to justify the decisions? Should it matter what the real motivations are so long as the decision can be justified in a manner those who do not share a given religious view can accept? Does the strength of the secular justification make a difference in your analysis? Why shouldn't government officials, especially legislators, be able to openly rely on religious views or values?

SECTION TWO: RELIGIOUS LAW
Chapter Eight

THE ROLE OF LAW IN RELIGIOUS TRADITIONS

A. INTRODUCTION

This chapter will explore the role of law in four religions: Judaism, Islam, Buddhism, and Christianity. Of course, each of these religions have given rise to a number of traditions, and thus when this book discusses a specific "religion" it generally does so in the broadest sense. There is simply no way to capture the diverse traditions within each of these religions in a chapter that is meant to be a very basic introduction to the role of law in each religion. Moreover, the complexity of legal thought within each tradition is vast, and thus the discussion here will be nothing more than a basic overview; a Tapas, if you will.

As you read the following material keep in mind that thousands of volumes have been written about the role of law in each of the religious traditions discussed herein. This chapter provides only a basic overview of how each religious tradition views law, the sources of that law, and how its legal system, if any, works. The chapter begins with sections on Judaism and Islam, which each have a strong legal tradition. Next, the role of law in Buddhism is explored. This is followed by a discussion of Catholic Canon Law and a general overview of the role of law in mainstream Protestant traditions. Space does not permit exploration of the role of law in other religious traditions, most notably Hinduism, Seventh Day Adventism, Sikhism, and the Old Amish Order. Those interested in learning more about the role of law in the religions discussed in this book, or in other religious traditions, can visit their university library which should have numerous books on each of these traditions. Such sources can often be obtained through inter-library loan if your law school or university library does not have them.

B. JEWISH LAW: HALAKHA

Jewish Law, or Halakha, is a complex system of religious law that governs both ritual and secular activities. This section can provide only a basic overview of the sources of Jewish Law, its basic methodology, and a few examples of Jewish Law in action. To say that the section provides only an oversimplified view of Jewish Law would be an understatement because of the incredible complexity and breadth of Jewish Law. The term Halakha translated more literally would roughly mean "the path" or "the way." The prefix "ha" (in Hebrew the letter "hey" with the accompanying vowel "a") literally translated means "the," and lakh (or leykh) means roughly "to go."

There are a number of important sources for Halakha. The most important is the Torah (the first Five Books of the bible). The Torah is central to every aspect of an observant Jew's life, and the various rules that arise from it are the core of Jewish Law. Rabbis and Jewish scholars have long recognized that the Torah must be interpreted in some situations in order for its commands to be applied to concrete circumstances. Thus, in addition to the text of the Torah there is an oral tradition (Torah Sheval Peh) that is also central to Jewish Law. This oral tradition is said to date back to the time that G-d gave the Torah at Mt. Sinai (in the book of Exodus). The oral tradition was put in writing in the Talmud and the Mishnah, two exceptionally important texts in Halakha. In addition, there is a long tradition of Rabbinical commentary on the Torah and the Talmud, which has itself taken written form, often with majority and minority positions emerging. There is also customary law and the decisions by Beit Din or Jewish courts. Of course, many if not most modern Jews do not bring claims before Jewish courts, but observant Jews carefully follow and study the sources of Halakha.

The remainder of this section will consist of two articles. The first is a brief article that provides an excellent overview of the sources of Halakha. The second provides more detail regarding the application of Halakha and provides several excellent examples.

EDWARD H. RABIN, *FOREWORD, SYMPOSIUM: THE EVOLUTION AND IMPACT OF JEWISH LAW*

1 U.C. Davis J. Int'l L. & Pol'y 49 (1995).

* * *

Jewish law has an ancient and honorable history. Indeed, the Jewish legal system is no doubt the oldest continuously applied legal system in the world. It has had to adapt to changing circumstances from biblical times to the present. It has co-existed with the legal systems of countries in Asia, Africa, Europe and elsewhere, and has survived the challenges of exile, dispersion, and oppression, as well as those of modernity and assimilation. Although most modern Jews do not govern their legal affairs by Jewish law, some still do. The Jewish legal system still functions in insular communities in Israel, the United States, and elsewhere. Before I go much further, I should define the term "Jewish law."

I. WHAT IS "JEWISH LAW"?

* * *

From biblical times until the 19th Century, most Jews lived in autonomous communities that applied Jewish law to the everyday life of their inhabitants. With the integration and assimilation of Jews into the larger gentile community, and the murder of most European Jews in the Holocaust, the number of Jewish communities that applied Jewish law to their ordinary commercial and legal matters diminished enormously. Today, there are still some communities of Jews which apply Jewish law to their legal disputes and transactions, but the overwhelming majority of modern Jews either do not consciously apply halakha to themselves at all, or restrict their application of halakha to religious, ethical, and family law matters.

Jewish law is a sub-set of halakha, and thus to understand the scope of Jewish law one must understand the term halakha. Halakha literally means "the way" or the correct path, and is derived from the same root as that for the verb meaning "to go." Halakhic material concerns "law" only in a specialized sense. It includes the laws of religion and ritual, as well as the laws governing civil and criminal matters. I shall call "conventional law" the law dealing with civil and criminal matters. "Jewish law," as that term is used in modern academic discourse, is that part of halakha that deals with conventional law.

Traditional halakhic scholars usually did not find it necessary to distinguish law, morality and religion. All derived ultimately from God's word, and hence had to be obeyed. Ethical imperatives, legal commands, ritual requirements were all incumbent upon the observant Jew and, with some significant exceptions, all were equally important. Hence, Judaism as a legal system is profoundly based on a religious world view. Ritual and religious law (the law concerning the duties that men and women owe to God) and civil and criminal law (the duties that people owe to each other) were traditionally studied together. The same modes of legal reasoning and hermeneutics were derived from the same sources and accorded the same sanctity. Although the distinction between the law governing the relations of humans to each other and the law governing a person's relation to God was sometimes significant, this distinction was not central to the study of halakha. Both types of questions would be answered by reference to the same sources and would be approached by identical forms of legal reasoning.

The modern reader unacquainted with Jewish legal thought can understand the intertwining of religious and conventional law by referring to the Ten Commandments. Some of these are religious in scope, governing humankind's relationship to God. For example, the Fourth Commandment "Remember the Sabbath day and keep it holy . . . " is essentially a religious commandment. The Sixth Commandment "Thou shalt not murder" is a conventional legal rule, one that appears in all modern penal codes. The Tenth Commandment "Thou shalt not covet . . . " is an ethical or moral precept, difficult to enforce in a court of law. The entire Ten Commandments, however, are a unit, and it would be artificial to divide them into religious law, conventional law, and ethical aspirations. It was only in the 20th Century that scholars attempted to divide halakha into religious and conventional law and to refer to the conventional law component of halakha as "Jewish law."

Jewish law must be distinguished from the law governing the modern state of Israel. Israeli law is derived from many sources, including British, American, and European law, original Israeli legislation and decisions, and Jewish law. Family law in Israel is largely governed by halakha, but most other areas of law are not. * * *

* * *

To understand the term "Jewish law" fully, one must be familiar with at least the principal sources of Jewish law. Jewish law has continuously developed from biblical times to the present day. Thus, the sources of Jewish law span the entire period of western civilization. In this brief Foreword I can only mention a few highlights.

The two authoritative sources of Jewish law are: (a) the Written Law embodied in the Hebrew Bible and (b) the Oral Law as reduced to writing in various books, including particularly the Mishnah and the Talmud. Most of the legal norms expressly stated in the Hebrew Bible are contained in the Torah—the first five books of the Bible. The Mishnah was reduced to writing approximately in the year 200 C.E. It was an early attempt to restate the Oral Law. The Oral Law (the commentaries that explain and supplement the Written Law) is considered to be divinely inspired, and thus equal in sanctity and dignity to the Torah itself.

There are two Talmuds: the Jerusalem Talmud (the Yerushalmi) and the Babylonian Talmud (the Bavli). The Yerushalmi was completed around 400 C.E. and the Bavli was completed around 500 C.E., although some additional editing took place over the next 100 years. The Bavli has been far more influential than the Yerushalmi, and has been the subject of many more commentaries. In this Foreword, as elsewhere, a reference to the Talmud refers to the Bavli unless the Yerushalmi is specifically indicated. In form, the Talmud consists of an extended discussion of the Mishnah. Thus standard editions of the Talmud consist of a brief excerpt from the Mishnah and then an extended commentary, followed by another excerpt from the Mishnah and another extended commentary. The commentary is called Gemora.

The Talmud contains two types of material: (a) Halakha and (b) Aggadah. Halakhic material consists of discussions of "legal" material. Aggadah consists of non-legal material such as legends, parables, ethical precepts, and history.

Of course, Jewish law did not stop developing with the completion of the Talmud. Commentators and codifiers like Rashi in the 11th Century and Maimonides in the 12th were extremely influential in the development of Jewish law. In the 16th Century, Rabbi Joseph Caro wrote the famous Shulkhan Aruch (Prepared Table) which, together with the commentaries of Rabbi Moshe Isserles, became an authoritative Code of Jewish Law.

Of great importance are the responsa of leading scholars. These are the written responses of rabbis to questions presented to them on matters of halakha. Responsa reflect the societies in which Jews lived, and resemble to some degree the reports of decided cases with which American lawyers are familiar.

* * *

* * * The specific legal rules contained in the Torah are more than 2,000 years old. Since a basic premise of Jewish law is that the Torah is the literal word of God, it might appear that its specific rules could not be changed by mortal beings. Yet these rules have been changed in response to pressing necessity, sometimes by interpretation and sometimes through legal fictions. The Rabbis of the Talmudic period, and later, derived authority for their power to interpret and supplement Torah law from a passage in the Torah itself that authorized the judges in the future to make decisions which the people should follow.[9] How, when, and why various rules developed over time is beyond the scope of this Foreword. However, it is obvious that the conflict between tradition and innovation that so bedevils American law was foreshadowed by Jewish law centuries ago.

* * *

* * * [T]raditional Jewish society considers the study and practice of halakha as the ultimate goal of humans on earth. Of course halakha includes great principles, such as the injunction to "Love thy neighbor as thyself." But it also addresses such prosaic questions as the ownership of a cloth found by two people. The patience, tenacity and thoroughness with which the Talmud explores every legal issue should serve as a model for law students, lawyers and judges in any legal system. The importance that the Talmud attaches to reaching the just result by close legal analysis should inspire every lawyer who ever was ready to surrender to despair when faced with a seemingly insoluble legal problem.

* * *

* * * When American law students study Jewish law they broaden their horizons. They gain a sense of how law develops over a period of more than 2,000 years, and of how it will continue to develop in the future. * * *

9. Deuteronomy 17:11.

SAMUEL J. LEVINE, *AN INTRODUCTION TO LEGISLATION IN JEWISH LAW, WITH REFERENCES TO THE AMERICAN LEGAL SYSTEM*

29 Seton Hall L. Rev. 916 (1999).

Introduction

* * *

This Article primarily examines the roles of legislative and judicial bodies, in the context of a discussion of broader principles of legislation in the Jewish legal system. In recent years, American legal scholars have increasingly looked to Jewish law as a model of an alternative legal system that considers many of the issues present in the American legal system. In relation to the roles of legislative and judicial bodies, the Jewish legal system provides a particularly illuminating contrast to the American legal system, in part because in Jewish law, the same authority, the Sanhedrin, or High Court, serves in both a legislative and judicial capacity.

Interestingly, though, as a result of the express license for the same authority in Jewish law to serve two separate functions, the two functions are rather clearly delineated, each bounded by specific rules and regulations. * * * A secondary aim of this Article is to illustrate some of the conceptual foundations and functionings of the Jewish legal system evident in the various substantive areas of legislation examined, relying in part on the work of contemporary scholars of Jewish law * * *.

* * *

I.   Categories of Legislation

A.   *The Torah*

Professor Menachem Elon has aptly described the "one basic norm and one single supreme value" in Jewish law: "the command of God as embodied in the Torah given to Moses at Sinai." In his Code of Law, the Medieval scholar Maimonides explains that the commandments in the Torah are eternally binding and not subject to abrogation. Indeed, in his discussion of thirteen fundamental principles of Judaism, Maimonides repeatedly emphasizes the immutable authority of the laws in the Five Books of Moses. Therefore, in categorizing legislation in Jewish law, Professor Elon has observed that the Torah is "the supreme legislation of the Jewish legal system. It is the written 'constitution' of Jewish law, having its ultimate source in divine revelation.... [A]ll legislation promulgated after the revelation of the supreme legislation has been subordinate."

Though divine in origin, the Torah requires human interpretation to be understood and applied as a legal text. To facilitate such interpretation, God revealed to Moses at Sinai, together with the Written Torah, an Oral Torah, consisting of revealed interpretations of certain laws as well as hermeneutic rules to be used by legal authorities to derive further interpretations. Both the written text of the Torah and the interpretations carry the authority of supreme legislation, incorporated in the term d'oraita, a Talmudic adjective form of the Aramaic translation of "Torah." Unlike the revealed text and interpretations, however, laws derived through human interpretation are subject to dispute and reversal by later legal authorities. In fact, one of the principal functions of the Sanhedrin [High Court] in each generation was to serve as the ultimate arbiter of the law through its own interpretation of the Torah.

B. Rabbinic Legislation

Although the laws in the Torah can be described as "legislation," because those laws are divinely mandated and therefore not subject to legislative modification, an analysis of legislative principles in Jewish law might instead focus on rabbinic legislation. Aside from its adjudicatory function, the Sanhedrin served in a legislative capacity. Legislation enacted by the Sanhedrin, subordinate to the legislation in the Torah, is termed d'rabbanan, from the Aramaic for "rabbinic."

Like the laws of the Torah, which consist of both positive commandments and negative commandments, rabbinic legislation can also take both positive and negative form. In addition, although all negative legislation in a sense serves to safeguard adherence to the laws in the Torah, conceptually negative rabbinic legislation can be further divided into sub-categories of legislation, relating to both the purpose and the parameters of the legislation.

1. Positive Legislation

As Maimonides explains in his Introduction to the Mishna, one category of rabbinic legislation is takanot, or positive legislation, which includes both laws implemented for a clearly religious or ritual purpose and laws implemented to improve the nature of interpersonal dealings. Because these laws were enacted by the same legal authorities who functioned as arbiters of the laws of the Torah, these authorities were careful to distinguish rabbinic legislation from divine legislation or from interpretations of divine legislation. The most poignant illustration of these distinctions may be the variety of functions that Moses served after the Revelation at Sinai. In listing some examples of positive legislation, Maimonides includes legislation enacted by Moses. Thus, Moses played at least three different and distinct roles in the legal system. First, he transmitted the revealed Written and Oral Torah. Second, he served as a judge and an interpreter of those areas of the law that required interpretation. Finally, he served as a legislator of rabbinic law. Although Moses was unique in the first of these roles, his functioning as both a judge and a legislator provides an analogue for the dual function of the Sanhedrin.

Perhaps the most widely known example of positive rabbinic legislation is the obligation to light the menorah on Chanuka. This legislation was enacted to commemorate the miraculous events of the Nation of

Israel's military victory over the Syrian–Greeks and the subsequent burning of a small amount of oil in the Temple menorah that lasted for eight days. Although the practice of lighting the menorah in the Temple had been divinely mandated, there was no such obligation incumbent upon individuals prior to the events of Chanuka. As these events occurred more than one thousand years after the Revelation at Sinai, it was the legal authorities living at the time of the miracles who enacted rabbinic legislation requiring individuals to light the menorah on Chanuka.

2. Negative Legislation

a. Meat and Milk

The other category of rabbinic legislation that Maimonides lists is gezeirot, negative legislation. This legislation was enacted in order to safeguard many of the laws of the Torah by adding a protective "fence" around those laws. For example, in three separate places, the Torah prohibits cooking a kid in its mother's milk. Through expansive interpretation of these verses, the Talmud understands this prohibition to include not only cooking meat and milk together, but also eating and deriving benefit from meat and milk that are cooked together. At the same time, the Talmud employs hermeneutic principles to limit the prohibition to the meat of certain animals that are similar to goats, excluding other meat such as poultry. Yet, the Talmud adds that rabbinic legislation was enacted prohibiting eating any meat together with milk. This legislation was based on the concern that people would not distinguish between different kinds of meat, and therefore, if permitted to eat poultry and milk together, would believe that they were likewise permitted to eat all meats together with milk. Thus, to protect against a violation of the laws in the Torah, the legal authorities enacted broader subordinate legislation that would help insure adherence to supreme legislation.

b. The Sabbath

A particularly illuminating example of negative rabbinic legislation is found in the various forms of legislation enacted relating to the Sabbath. The Torah prohibits engaging in melakha on the Sabbath. Interpreting the term melakha, the Talmud delineates numerous activities that are prohibited on the Sabbath. These prohibitions have the status of supreme legislation because they are the result of authoritative judicial interpretation of the Torah. In addition to interpreting the Biblical prohibitions, legal authorities enacted negative rabbinic legislation prohibiting other activities in order to safeguard the observance of the Sabbath. According to Maimonides, some of these activities were prohibited because they are similar to activities that are Biblically prohibited, while others, though not inherently similar to Biblical prohibitions, were prohibited out of a concern that such conduct might nevertheless lead to the violation of Biblical prohibitions. Finally, Maimonides lists a third category of rabbinic legislation intended to preserve the unique qualities of the Sabbath by prohibiting conduct not conducive to the spiritual nature of the day.

The laws involving the institution of mukza [see below] illustrate some of the concerns that serve as a basis for these categories. The Talmud relates that among the activities that were rabbinically prohibited on the Sabbath was the moving of objects that had no purpose on the Sabbath. The Talmud describes a structure of rabbinic legislation that classified various objects as mukza, or set aside from use on the Sabbath, either because they had no intrinsic purpose on the Sabbath or because they were specifically set aside not to be used. These objects generally could not be moved on the Sabbath, although the legislation incorporated exceptions that permitted certain types of objects to be moved when a need arose on the Sabbath. For example, writing is among the activities prohibited on the Sabbath; therefore, it is rabbinically prohibited to move a pen, which has the primary function of being used for a Biblically prohibited activity, and thus generally serves no purpose on the Sabbath. However, because, for purposes other than the Sabbath, a pen functions as an intrinsically useful object, it can be moved if a permitted use for it arises on the Sabbath.

A number of reasons are provided by the Talmud and by Maimonides for the legislation of the institution of mukza, corresponding to some of the general rationales Maimonides offers for rabbinic legislation relating to the Sabbath. The Talmud states that the rabbinic prohibition against moving objects that are mukza was enacted as a safeguard against a Biblical law prohibiting carrying objects between private and public domains. By limiting the class of objects permitted to be moved to those which were necessary on the Sabbath, the legislation aimed to decrease the possibility that objects would be improperly carried from a private domain to a public domain. Maimonides suggests that the laws of mukza serve to safeguard many other Biblical prohibitions as well. For example, in preventing the moving of objects that have a primary use for activities prohibited on the Sabbath, the laws decrease the chances that such activities will be performed. Finally, Maimonides adds a third reason for the laws of mukza, explaining that refraining from moving objects that are ordinarily moved on a weekday will highlight the unique spiritual nature of the Sabbath.

Contemporary scholars of Jewish law have likewise distinguished categories of rabbinic legislation relating to the Sabbath and have noted the legal significance of such classifications. An illustration of the legal ramifications that emerge from these classifications involves the case of a minor illness on the Sabbath. With the exception of murder, idolatry, and certain forms of illicit sexual relations, all of the laws in the Torah may and must be violated when necessary to save a life. Thus, if necessary, the laws of the Sabbath are suspended in the face of a life-threatening illness.

However, when there is a minor illness that poses no possible threat to human life, Biblical prohibitions remain intact, and only some forms of rabbinic legislation are suspended. Rabbi Hershel Schachter has observed that the examples of such legislation, provided by the Talmud and later legal authorities, fall under the category of laws enacted not because of an intrinsic similarity to Biblical prohibitions, but out of a concern that permitting certain activities might nevertheless lead to the violation of Biblical laws. In contrast, rabbinic legislation that was enacted as an independent prohibition because of a similarity to a Biblical prohibition remains in effect when there is a minor illness.

II. SCOPE OF RABBINIC LEGISLATION: LICENSE AND LIMITATIONS

Because the Written Torah serves as the supreme and constitutional legislation in Jewish law, rabbinic license to enact additional subordinate legislation must find its source in the Written Torah. Additionally, the scope of rabbinic authority in enacting legislation is subject to limitations, based in the Torah, which serve as a checking device to the discretion of rabbinic legislators.

A. Sources of Authority

In its discussion of the rabbinic command to light the menorah on Chanuka, the Talmud notes that, similar to the observance of Biblical commandments, observance of the lighting of the menorah is preceded by the recitation of a blessing acknowledging God's command. The text of the blessing includes the statement that God "commanded us to kindle the Chanuka lights."

The Talmud suggests two possible sources to support the notion that lighting the menorah, though rabbinically legislated, is in another sense divinely mandated. The first source, on which Maimonides relies in his Code of Law, is the Biblical description of rabbinic judicial authority, stating that:

> When there is a matter of law that you are unable to decide ... you shall go up to the place that God will choose. And you shall approach the ... judge[s] who will be in those days and you shall inquire, and they will you tell you the law. And you shall act according to that which they will tell you ... and you will observe all that which they will teach you. According to [that] which they will tell you, you shall act; do not veer from that which they tell you, to the right or to the left.[53]

The Talmud understands this passage, carrying the warning not to veer from the judge's teachings, to authorize not only rabbinic adjudication but rabbinic legislation as well. Thus, as Maimonides explains, although the lighting of the menorah is in fact an example of subordinate rabbinic legislation, the blessing recited before lighting the menorah acknowledges the divine command to observe rabbinic legislation.

Similarly, the Talmud identifies a Biblical source for the authority of negative rabbinic legislation, such as the protective measures implement-

---

53. Deuteronomy 17:8–11.

ed to prevent violation of the Biblical laws of the Sabbath or Biblical prohibitions against eating meat and milk together. The Talmud interprets the language of the Biblical verse "You shall keep My charge"[56] as a mandate for legal authorities to enact safeguards to Biblical prohibitions.[57]

B. Limitations on Legislative Authority

1. "You shall not add"

The Torah commands, "Every matter which I command to you, you shall take care to observe it; you shall not add to it and you shall not take away from it."[58] Although this verse apparently places broad limitations on any subordinate legislation, the precise parameters of the verse are subject to interpretation, as developed in both the revealed and derived Oral Torah. In particular, it seems clear that the verse cannot preclude all forms of subordinate legislation, in light of other verses in the Torah that license both positive and negative rabbinic legislation. Maimonides explains that the verse specifically prohibits adding to the Torah per se, in the sense of enacting subordinate laws in a form that suggests supreme authority. For example, to protect against the violation of the Biblical prohibition on eating certain forms of meat cooked with milk, legal authorities are authorized to prohibit eating poultry and milk together as well if they explain that the legislation is a rabbinic decree designed to safeguard the Biblical law. They are precluded, however, from enacting such legislation and stating that poultry is included in the category of meat in the Biblical prohibition.

Moreover, the command not to add to the Torah places additional checks on rabbinic legislative discretion, while further emphasizing the distinction between Biblical and rabbinic legislation. The Talmud relates the rule that rabbinic legislation was enacted only if there existed a substantial need for such legislation. A number of scholars have posited that this rule is derived from the prohibition against adding to the Torah. These scholars explain that the prohibition requires tempering the broad rabbinic legislative authority by limiting it to situations of significant necessity. Legislation in the absence of such need is considered an improper and prohibited addition to the laws of the Torah.

Scholars likewise explain that the Talmudic rule against enacting negative legislation to prevent violation of a previously established rabbinic prohibition derives from the same principle. These scholars suggest that the requirement of a substantial need for the enactment of rabbinic legislation precludes such legislation in the absence of a danger of violation of Biblical law. The possibility of the violation of a rabbinic prohibition does not qualify as a need sufficiently substantial to allow for further rabbinic legislation.

---

56. Leviticus 18:30. The Hebrew words used in this verse for both "keep" and "charge" are derived from the root meaning "guard" or "protect."

57. *See* Talmud Bavli, Yevamoth 21a; see also Maimonides, Code of Law, Introduction; Maimonides, Introduction to the Mishna * * * at 40.

58. Deuteronomy 13:1.

Nevertheless, it is important to distinguish the scenario of rabbinic legislation enacted to prevent violation of previously enacted rabbinic law from a scenario in which two separate rabbinic prohibitions act in concert. For example, scholars of Jewish law addressed the question of whether poultry and milk products that have not been cooked together may be eaten together. The Biblical prohibition against eating meat and milk products together applies only to food cooked together and does not include poultry.

However, to safeguard against eating meat and milk products that were cooked together, rabbinic legislation was enacted prohibiting eating meat and milk products that were not cooked together as well. In addition, to safeguard against eating milk products together with those kinds of meat included in the Biblical prohibition, rabbinic legislation was enacted extending the category of meat products to include poultry. Thus, any prohibition involving poultry and milk that were not cooked together would rely on two rabbinic enactments. Still, scholars explain, the prohibition remains intact because it is premised on two separate rabbinic prohibitions, enacted as a result of two independent concerns, acting in concert with one another. Such a dynamic does not constitute a rabbinic prohibition enacted for the purpose of safeguarding a further rabbinic prohibition.

2.   *"You shall not take away"*

Like the command "you shall not add" to the Torah, the Biblical decree "you shall not take away"[71] appears to place broad restrictions on the scope and authority of subordinate legislation. Moreover, the implication of the verse, prohibiting abrogation of Biblical commandments, is consistent with a number of other verses in the Torah that declare the immutability of Biblical commandments. Nevertheless, even this principle is subject to limited exceptions that exemplify the extent of the discretion available to rabbinic legislators.

The Talmud states that, when necessary, the Sanhedrin has the authority to enact legislation mandating the passive violation of a positive Biblical commandment. For example, the Torah commands that on the holiday of Rosh Hashana, it is incumbent on individuals to hear the sound of the shofar, a ram's horn. Depending on the calendar of a specific year, Rosh Hashana may fall on different days of the week, including the Sabbath. Under Biblical law, the obligation to sound the shofar on Rosh Hashana applies on both weekdays and the Sabbath.

However, rabbinic authorities were concerned about the possibility that the obligation to hear the sound of the shofar might lead to violation of the Sabbath. Specifically, as the Talmud explains, individuals in possession of a shofar but not adept at sounding the shofar might come to carry the shofar to someone else, who would sound the shofar for them. Carrying the shofar between public and private domains would constitute a violation of the Sabbath. Therefore, to protect against the

---

71. Deuteronomy 13:1.

active violation of the Sabbath, for years that Rosh Hashana fell on the Sabbath, legal authorities enacted rabbinic legislation mandating passive violation of the positive commandment to sound the shofar.

Scholars have suggested a Biblical source for the rabbinic authority, delineated in the Talmud, to enact legislation involving the passive violation of a Biblical commandment. In the principal passage authorizing rabbinic adjudication and legislation, the Torah states "do not veer from that which they tell you, to the right or to the left." Rabbinic exegesis of this verse understands it to require that the teachings of legal authorities be adhered to "even if it appears they are telling you that your left is your right and your right is your left." Thus, the verse authorizes a ruling that seems to contradict that which is clearly correct. According to some scholars, the verse serves as the source of authority for rabbinic legislation which, in a sense, might seem incorrect or anomalous because it prevents observance of a Biblical law.

Despite the Talmud's conclusion that rabbinic legislation cannot require the active violation of a positive Biblical commandment, under unique circumstances the Talmud extends the command to heed the words of rabbinic authorities to include the temporary suspension of a negative Biblical commandment. The Talmud cites the Biblical example of Elijah, who, to stem the rampant practice of idolatry and return the nation to the proper path, offered a sacrifice on an altar at Mount Carmel, despite a prohibition against bringing a sacrifice outside the Temple in Jerusalem. The Medieval legal scholar Ra'avad explains that the source of authority for the temporary suspension of a negative Biblical commandment is the verse in Psalms stating that when "it is a time to work for God, suspend your Torah."[85]

Based on Talmudic sources such as the Talmudic exegesis of the episode of Elijah on Mount Carmel, Maimonides codifies the principle of rabbinic authority to enact legislation temporarily suspending a Biblical law, when necessary to restore the nation to the proper faith and observance. Maimonides explains the logic behind such authority through a comparison to the work of a doctor. He writes that, as a doctor may amputate an arm or a leg so that an entire organism may live, similarly, in rare occasions, a court may permit the temporary violation of some commandments in order to safeguard communal observance of the law as a whole.

3. Communal Role in Legislation

The Talmud states that rabbinic legislation is legally binding only if is determined that the majority of the nation will be able to abide by the legislation. Therefore, Maimonides explains, if the court enacts legislation with the erroneous belief that most of the nation can abide by the legislation, but later finds this not to be the case, the legislation is null and void and thus may not be enforced.

---

85. Ra'avad * * * Laws of Mamrim 2:9 (citing Psalms 119:126).

III.   LEGISLATION OVER TIME: CHANGED CIRCUMSTANCES

* * *

A.   Biblical Legislation

Because of the immutable authority of the laws in the Torah, Biblical legislation is generally not subject to abrogation or modification. Thus, the Talmud concludes that the commandments in the Torah remain in force even if the apparent rationale for the commandment no longer applies. However, in the rare event that the Torah provides the reason for a particular commandment, the Talmud concludes that the force of the commandment is dependent on the applicability of its rationale. Nevertheless, it should be noted that, in practice, the Talmud appears to discourage reliance on even this limited license for restricting the scope of a commandment based on its express rationale. The Talmud does so out of the concern that an individual may be mistaken in believing that the rationale does not apply in a given situation.

B.   Rabbinic Legislation

1.   General Principles

Unlike the laws of the Torah, rabbinic legislation can be modified by later legal authorities. Such modifications must be consistent with a complex set of rules regulating the discretion of later authorities. Although these rules apply only to the modification of rabbinic legislation and not to Biblical legislation, they appear to be different from but modeled after the Biblical law, like many areas of rabbinic legislation.

The Talmud states that a Sanhedrin generally cannot abrogate the legislation of an earlier Sanhedrin unless the later Sanhedrin is "greater in wisdom and in number." According to Maimonides, this rule applies even when, as a result of changing circumstances, the reason for the initial legislation no longer exists. Moreover, Maimonides holds that even this limited license applies only to positive rabbinic legislation. He writes that negative rabbinic legislation, enacted to safeguard Biblical laws, can never be abrogated by later authorities.

Ra'avad, however, argues that, according to the Talmud, the rule that a later court must be greater than the legislating court applies only when the reason for the legislation still applies. Therefore, although rabbinic legislation remains in force even if the reason for a particular law no longer applies, in such a situation, even a court that is no greater than the legislating court has the authority to repeal the legislation.

2.   Suspension of Rabbinic Legislation Without Further Legislative Action: Fringes on Four–Cornered Linen Garments

Notwithstanding the dispute regarding the criteria and mechanics generally necessary for a court to abrogate rabbinic legislation, scholars have suggested that in certain scenarios, rabbinic legislation loses force even without official legislative action. Rabbi Hershel Schachter has identified a number of laws that apparently fall under this category and are thus patterned after the rule that the applicability of Biblical laws can be limited according to reasons for the laws expressly presented in the Torah. In addition, these scenarios serve as a further illustration of limitations on rabbinic legislative authority.

For example, the Torah commands the placing of fringes on four-cornered garments. The Talmud documents that the proper fulfillment of the command requires that some of the fringes be of a particular color and of wool material. The Talmud also notes that the requirement to affix wool fringes to all garments, including those of linen, is an exception to the Biblical prohibition not to wear a garment composed of a mixture of wool and linen materials. Nevertheless, despite the propriety of placing wool fringes on a linen garment as an exception to the general rule, Talmudic authorities were concerned that such a practice might, at times, lead to the violation of the Biblical prohibition. To prevent such a violation, these authorities enacted rabbinic legislation prohibiting placing fringes on linen garments.

According to a number of scholars, however, just as rabbinic legislation must be formulated in such a manner that it will not appear to be Biblical legislation, rabbinic legislation that suspends a Biblical law must not contradict Biblical law. Instead, Rabbi Schachter explains, the formulation of such legislation must clearly demonstrate the law's status as subordinate legislation enacted for the express purpose of preventing the violation of a particular Biblical law. Thus, the Talmudic legislators were required to state, as part of the legislation prohibiting fringes on linen garments, that the purpose of the legislation was to protect against the Biblical violation of wearing a garment composed of wool and linen.

In later times, though, as a result of persecution and dispersion of the Jewish nation, the identity of the proper color for the fringes was lost. As a result, the commandment continued to be fulfilled, but without the requirement that some fringes be composed either of the unique color or of wool material. As wool was no longer required for the fringes, linen became a suitable replacement, and there was no longer a viable concern that placing fringes on linen garments might lead to a violation of the Biblical prohibition. Thus, Rabbi Schachter explains, parallel to Biblical laws, because the express reason for the rabbinic legislation no longer applied, the legislation itself likewise no longer applied. In this way, Rabbi Schachter explains the suspension of the Talmudic legislation prohibiting placing fringes on linen garments by a Medieval legal authority without the need for further legislative action.

* * *

C. ISLAMIC LAW: SHARI'AH

Islamic law, or Shari'ah, is central to Muslims everywhere. Literally translated, the word Shari'ah means "road to a watering place," but that is really a metaphor for the path to satisfaction of G-d's will and worldly justice. Like Halakha (Jewish law), Shari'ah is a complete legal system that includes both civil and religious law (and concepts). The Quran is the most important document in Shari'ah. For Muslims, it is the embodiment of Allah's revelations to the Prophet Muhammad. The Quran is thus the most important text in Islamic law and in Islam in general. The next most important sources of Islamic law are the sunna, or the practices of the Prophet Muhammad. Many of these practices were committed to writing shortly after Muhammad's death along with his sayings. This written account of Muhammad's practices and sayings is called "hadith." Hadith is a major source of Shari'ah.

Of course, given the immense importance of the Quran and hadith as sources for Islamic law, they must be interpreted to apply to the vast array of situations that arise for any individual or community. Thus, a process of interpretation is necessary. That process is called "fiqh." Fiqh must be consistent with the primary sources of Islamic law, the Quran and hadith, and the practice of fiqh requires careful reasoning from these sources by those with the appropriate knowledge and qualifications. The following article will explain all of this in much greater detail and provide examples. Shari'ah shares a great deal in common with Halakha and also with many other complex legal systems. It is important to remember, however, that like Halakha, Shari'ah is central to the Islamic religion and thus G-d's commands are central to those interpreting and those applying Shari'ah.

M. CHERIF BASSIOUNI & GAMAL M. BADR, THE SHARI'AH: SOURCES, INTERPRETATION, AND RULE-MAKING

1 UCLA J. Islamic & Near E. L. 135 (2002).

I. Introduction

Like other world legal systems, Islamic law has its own distinctive processes of identifying and formulating legal norms. But unlike other legal systems, Islamic law developed in the evolving contexts of Muslim societies and their political regimes * * *.

Islam is holistic. Consequently, Islamic law (the Shari'ah) derives primarily from religious sources, namely the holy book of Islam (the Qur'an) and the sayings and deeds of the Prophet Muhammad (the sunnah). The great majority of these norms, however, fall into two categories, which are unknown to secular legal systems: those pertaining to faith and ritual norms, ibadat; and those that deal with societal relations and individual interactions in society, mu'amalat.

The Qur'an and the sunnah contain the greater number of norms applicable to the areas of criminal law, family law, and inheritance law as compared to other subjects within the mu'amalat category. These norms evolved over time through the work of legal scholars using the methodology of usul al-fiqh (roots of legal knowledge). As discussed below, fiqh and ilm usul al-fiqh are complex and sophisticated juristic techniques developed by jurists to interpret and develop rules of law.

Pre–Islamic society, however, had tribal laws whose formation and application were the product of certain legal reasoning techniques that were subsequently used by the Prophet and his Companions. Among the legacies of pre-Islamic legal techniques of norm-making and norm-application are ijma (consensus), urf (custom), qiyas (analogy), maslaha and istislah (consideration of the public good), istihsan (the best outcome in a given case), and darura (necessity). Even though these techniques were pre-Islamic tribal sources of law and methods of legal reasoning, they continued to be used as part of the Islamic usul al-fiqh, but with the modifications necessitated by the dictates of Islam. This transition occurred in the days of the Prophet when the need for these legal techniques was more strongly felt. Yet they continued to remain in use as part of Islamic law's techniques, though with some periodic mutations when the Muslim world expanded and centers of legal studies and practice came into being in the ever-expanding realm of Islam, or dar al-islam * * *. As these techniques became diversified, they at times led to contradictions and conflicts with respect to the same issues to which they were applied in the wider parts of dar al-islam. Consequently, the need for consistency and predictability required the development of commonly-agreed techniques of norm-identification and legal reasoning in norm-application. These techniques were particularly needed when the ever-expanding world of Islam extended to non-Arabic-speaking societies whose pre-Islamic legal cultures were quite different from those of the Arabic-speaking Muslims of the Arabian Peninsula. This made the understanding and interpretation of the Qur'an and the sunnah more difficult for non-Arab jurists. Thus, rules had to be developed for the proper understanding of the Qur'an and the sunnah, whose authoritative language was Arabic, as were the foundations of usul al-fiqh.

The first jurist to write a treatise on the discipline of usul al-fiqh was al-Shafi'i (d. 204 A.H./819 C.E.), in his seminal Al–Risalah.[4] He was thus referred to as 'the father of Islamic jurisprudence,' although what he really did was to expand on and systematize principles and techniques of legal reasoning previously used by Arab–Muslim jurists in application of the Shari'ah, and in the development of norms which were to be consonant with the Qur'an and the sunnah.

The role of jurists in formulating rules of law is peculiar to Islamic law, and it therefore differs from other legal systems. In other legal systems, the role of jurisprudence is limited to explicating and systematizing the rules of law enacted by a secular authority. In Roman law, that authority was the Senate, which was the legislative branch of government, while in the English common law, judicial decisions set precedents creating new rules of law, but with the added factor of the English Parliament's supreme legal authority.

---

4. Muhammad ibn Idris al-Shafi'i, ISLAM-IC JURISPRUDENCE: SHAFI'I'S RISALAH (Majid Khadduri trans., 1961).

Islamic law may be characterized as a jurist's law, while Roman law is a legislator's law and the common law is essentially a judge's law. Because Islamic law applies equally to the ruler and to the ruled, the existence of an independent meritocracy of legal scholars not beholden to any political body was considered a guarantee of the supremacy of the rule of law, which is distinguishable from a rule of law process that derives from secular legislative authorities. But in time, that community of legal scholars became fragmented and beholden to political authority. Later, that community of scholars also became politicized itself, as scholars saw in the techniques of interpreting the Shari'ah an instrument of power and influence in Muslim societies.

Ilm usul al-fiqh is the legal science or legal technique that combines legal, philosophical, and epistemological dimensions in a methodological framework. This framework is used to identify, interpret, and apply principles, norms, and standards, and in their absence, to identify by certain techniques an applicable norm to situations for which existing norms are unavailable. It includes the identification, appraisal, and ranking of the sources of law in accordance with a certain methodology deemed valid by the consensus of the community of legal scholars. The complexity of the processes of analysis was compounded by a number of factors that pertain to existing gaps, insufficiencies, ambiguities, and contradictions in and among the sources of law. Usul al-fiqh is, to a large extent, a road map of what the law is, how it is to be applied, and where necessary, how law can be discovered. But it is also a method by which all of the above can be justified, and in that respect, there is no external mechanism of checks and balances on whatever has been agreed upon by the community of legal scholars. As a result, the methods of usul al-fiqh became intrinsic in that the method of law-making was also the method by which to justify the law as made. The absence of extrinsic control mechanisms lead to the authority of those making the legal judgments * * *.

Usul al-fiqh is a process of historical accretion that goes through stages of growth and consolidation until it reaches stages of perceived completion where it becomes rigid, then regressive, in relation to the ever-progressing needs of social change. Thus, the writings of scholars identify different historical periods and analyze the development of Islamic law in that context. While this is a correct way of approaching legal history, it sometimes fails to grasp the overall nature of this evolving and complex legal system.

The sources of law, processes, and methodologies used by Islamic jurists in applying and formulating rules of law are discussed in this article. However, such an undertaking is necessarily fraught with the risk of over-simplification of what is an enormous reservoir of legal and historical knowledge. The early dynamics that permeated the legal culture of adhering to the precedence of authority also allowed for alterations, which occurred in large part through the ijtihad (unprecedented doctrinal development) and the fatwa (advisory opinion). Continuity and change coincide in taqlid (rigid following) and ijtihad. In time, both taqlid and ijtihad became part of a continuum of preservation and change. The qadi (judge) was most likely to follow taqlid, or what today would be called strict constructionism, while the jurisconsult (whose qualifications were always very demanding) was the mujtahid. Yet ijtihad was not necessarily the development of new doctrine, as this was the province of the founders of the madhahib (i.e., the four Sunni doctrinal schools, and the Shi'ah doctrinal schools). The processes of change came early in the history of Islamic law by the making of new law on a case-by-case basis through ijtihad and individual fatawa (plural of fatwa). The challenges of norm-making and norm-application are evident throughout the history of Islamic law, evidencing the everlasting tension between law's continuity and change.

II.   The Sources of Islamic Law

The Shari'ah, Islamic law, is based on two sources, the Qur'an and the sunnah (the sayings and deeds of the Prophet Muhammad). The Qur'an is the principal source of the Shari'ah, which is supplemented by the sunnah. While the Qur'an is the controlling source, both constitute the primary sources of Islamic law.

The prescriptions contained in these two primary sources of Islamic law, however, require interpretation. In fact, many of the Prophet's sayings, or hadith (which are part of the sunnah), interpret some of the Qur'an's verses. After the Prophet's death (11 A.H./632 C.E.), the need for the continuing process of interpretation of the Qur'an became more acute. This led to the development of supplemental sources of law to apply whenever the two primary sources were silent on a given question or when they were, or appeared to be, ambiguous or inconsistent. The four Sunni schools recognized and ranked the supplemental sources differently. They also differed as to the contents of these supplementary sources and their applicability in different circumstances and contexts. The complexity of their methodologies, as well as the diversity of their ad hoc applications, denotes the intellectual depth and breadth of Islamic legal science. Thus, legal methodology became the intellectual framework within which the Shari'ah maintained some rigid continuity, while at the same time preserving elasticity for change. Achieving a commonality of the four Sunni schools is impossible, if for no other reason than that the legal method of each one differs from the others. The acceptance of one method leads to certain conclusions that are not necessarily the same as those that may be reached by another method. It is, therefore, only on the level of generalities that one can reach the same conclusion as that of a mainstream approach in ilm usul al-fiqh * * *. It should be noted that usul al-fiqh developed in historical stages, and legal historians have established that these sources were not all recognized in the earlier stages of the Prophet's time and that of the first four caliphs. Furthermore, their order differed in later periods than what is listed below, and their authoritative ranking also differed in the various Sunni and Shi'ah schools:

Principal Sources

1. The Qur'an
2. The sunnah

Supplemental Sources

3. Ijma (consensus of opinion of the learned scholars)
4. Qiyas (analogy by reference to the Qur'an and the sunnah)
5. Istislah or maslaha (consideration of the public good)
6. Istihsan (reasoning based on the best outcome, or equity)
7. Urf (custom and usage, subdivided between general and special)
8. The practices of the first four 'Wise Caliphs' (a form of authoritative precedent)
9. Ijtihad (unprecedented doctrinal development)
10. Treaties and pacts
11. Contracts (the Shari'ah considers a contract the binding law between the parties, so long as it does not violate the Shari'ah)
12. The jurisprudence of judges

Since the Shari'ah is God-given law to humankind, it has to be integral; consequently, doctrinal concepts, legal approaches, techniques of interpretation, and judicial decisions must neither conflict nor contradict. Thus, their differences needed to be reconciled, distinguished, or explained in a way that showed continuity, unless the change was the product of a valid ijtihad exercised by the competent jurisconsult embodied in a fatwa. This complexity gave rise to fiqh (the science of law) and to the development of the science of interpretation of the Shari'ah, ilm usul al-fiqh (the science of the principles of interpretation of the law).

Several schools of jurisprudence developed, known as madhahib (plural of madhhab). The Sunni (now comprising some 90% of the world's estimated 1.3 billion Muslims) have four schools, each one of them since their origin spawning one or more sub-schools. The Shi'ah also developed several schools and sub-schools. There were also other jurisprudential schools that came out of certain religious or political movements throughout the history of Islam, but whose authority was either short-lived or limited to certain sects.

The madhahib all agree on the primacy of the Qur'an and the sunnah, but they rank the secondary and tertiary sources of law differently, and pursue separate analytical approaches and methods to the Shari'ah's interpretation. Ilm usul al-fiqh recognizes this diversity within a holistic framework and seeks to give it cohesion within the integrity of Islam. Yet it is this diversity which, in the course of fifteen centuries, has created such an overwhelming body of jurisprudential thought that only the most learned jurists can grasp it. This phenomenon has in turn created a gulf between those scholars and the vast majority of Muslims, particularly in non-Arabic-speaking Muslim societies. Throughout these fifteen centuries, and across these cultural diversities, the need to revert back to the relatively less complex period of the Prophet's life, followed by the first four caliphs, led to different doctrines of 'Islamic fundamentalism,' some of which are evident in contemporary times.

One of the great doctrinal debates among all schools of jurisprudence, but more so between Sunni and Shi'ah, is whether the Qur'an and the sunnah are to be interpreted literally, on the basis of the intent and purpose of the text, or by combining both depending upon the subject. Whether one approach or the other is followed will determine if the unstated legislative policies of the many different aspects of the Shari'ah shall be deemed relevant to the textual interpretation of the Qur'an and the sunnah. It is probably in that respect that there exists the greatest divergence of views between what is considered to be the three broad categories of thinking and practice. The first is that of the so-called traditionalists, who represent the prevailing religious establishments in the Sunni and Shi'ah worlds. The influence of these two establishments is controlling, in part because of their dominant role in education. * * * Sunni traditionalists are essentially literalists. Nevertheless, their approach includes the recognition that the Prophet and his first four successors, called the 'wise' ones, can be relied upon to interpret the letter of the Qur'an. In the second category are the so-called fundamentalists, who are essentially dogmatic, intransigent, and literalist. They seek the solutions of earlier times as a panacea for complex contemporary problems, some even turning to political activism and violence as ways of propagating their views. The third is a category consisting of a few secular reformists and a few forward-thinking traditionalists, whom the mainstream traditionalists and fundamentalists refer to (in varying degrees of disapproval) as the ilmani. The ilmani seek to achieve the legislative goals of the Shari'ah by recognized jurisprudential techniques, including ijtihad, in light of scientific knowledge. The ilmani also search for the purposes and policies of the Shari'ah in order to address contemporary problems.

Writings by Muslim scholars will usually reflect one or the other of the views represented by these three categories. Consequently a reader, whether Muslim or not Muslim, who is unfamiliar with these categories as well as with the complexities of the Shari'ah, will face difficulties in understanding all of these theories and their applications.

As Islam spread to regions with cultures different from the Arabic one where it was first rooted, the jurisprudence and doctrine of the Shari'ah that developed in these non-Arab societies differed. But, since the Qur'an is God-given and cannot be altered, these jurisprudential and doctrinal differences had to be reconciled, giving rise to a great deal of sophistry and strained arguments. In time, all of this became very complicated and, as stated above, it limited knowledge of fiqh and ilm usul al-fiqh to those who could devote many years to study it. * * *

To understand the Shari'ah in all its complexities requires knowledge of its jurisprudential and scholarly interpretations and applications, not only over time, but also throughout the many regions of the Muslim world that are characterized by different cultures, customs, and mores that have influenced the way those in the Muslim world interpret and apply the Shari'ah. Even though this understandable social phenomenon is obvious, it is negated on the unchallengeable assumption that the Shari'ah is for all times and all places.

Since the Shari'ah has always been described by its scholars as being applicable in any place and at any time, and thus presumably in the same way, it was necessary to explain differences. Hence, an axiom was developed, namely: 'the rules of law are subject to change from time to time and from place to place, but the Shari'ah never changes.'[34] To change the rules, it was necessary to rely on the following supplemental sources: consensus (ijma), analogy (qiyas), public interest (maslaha), and custom (urf) (which with the expansion of the Muslim world became localized, i.e., local as opposed to general custom; maslaha was also localized to those communities in question). During the golden age of Islamic jurisprudence up to the 9th century C.E, and again since the 19th century C.E., jurists made use of those supplemental sources to help the law keep pace with economic and social changes. The only constraint on the use of supplemental sources and the outcomes deriving from their application is that they cannot contravene a norm or outcome derived from one of the two primary sources, namely, the Qur'an and the sunnah. The impact of this constraint, however, is limited because of the relatively small number of norms found in the Qur'an and the authenticated sunnah as compared to the whole body of Islamic law.

A.   The Primary Sources

1.   The Qur'an

A major tenet of Islamic belief is that the Qur'an is the word of God revealed to His prophet and messenger, Muhammad. It is the last divine scripture, because Muhammad's delivered message is the last divine revelation to humankind. The Qur'an was revealed a few verses at a time over a period of 22 years, ending with the death of the Prophet in 632 C.E., whose life is divided into two periods. The first was the Meccan period (610–622 C.E.) when the Prophet was in the city of Mecca before the hijra, and the second was the Medina period (622–632 C.E.), after the Prophet settled in that city, which is to the north of Mecca. The verses of the Qur'an are therefore identified as 'Meccan' or 'Medinese.'

The Muslims in Mecca were a small, scattered, and persecuted minority, and there was no Muslim community that needed legal norms to regulate its affairs. Thus, the verses revealed in Mecca contained principles of the faith and rules of morality, with little or no specific socio-legal provisions. These were revealed mostly during the Medina period, when Medina became a Muslim city-state with the Prophet acting both as religious leader and as a head of state.

---

34. Husayn H. Hassan, AL-MADKHAL LI DIRASAT AL-FIQH AL-ISLAMI (Cairo 1981) at 22–26.

The text of the Qur'an was arranged into 114 chapters (sura) during the lifetime of the Prophet. * * *

What distinguishes the Qur'an from the scriptures of other religions is the fact that its full text was compiled and was confirmed for authenticity by the Prophet before he departed this world. It was originally inscribed on different writing material under the supervision of the Prophet himself. The text was also committed to memory by a large number of the Prophet's Companions and followers. Soon after his death, his first successor, the Caliph Abu Bakr, entrusted a full written copy of the Qur'an to Hafsa, the widow of the Prophet. The third caliph, Uthman, had five copies of that text made in book form and sent a copy to each center of the then expanding Islamic world. The standard Qur'an that exists today is identical to the five copies, in book form, circulated by Uthman in the early 650's C.E., which was barely twenty years after the death of the Prophet. The authenticity of the text of the Qur'an and its conformity to the revelation received by the Prophet are consequently beyond historical doubt.

Being a book of spiritual guidance and not a legal code, it is not surprising to find only 500 verses (many of which overlap in theme and substance) with legal content among the 6,239 verses of the Qur'an. The breakdown of those legal verses is as follows: 70 verses on family and inheritance law, 70 verses on obligations and contract, 30 verses on criminal law, and 20 verses on procedure. As relatively few as they are, the legal provisions derive directly from the Qur'an and are therefore the highest in the hierarchy of legal norms. They are immutable and cannot be contradicted or modified by rules derived from any of the other sources of the Shari'ah. It should be recalled, however, that the second caliph, Umar ibn al-Khattab, suspended the application of the penalty for theft during what came to be known as the 'year of the famine.' He considered someone who stole to feed his family and himself as not subject to that penalty. This demonstrates that in the true spirit of the Shari'ah, there is no strict rigidity in the application of legal norms.

Also, some verses with legal content are subject to interpretation because of the use of words that lend themselves to more than one meaning. One example is the verse dictating the length of the period during which a divorced woman cannot remarry. The word used can mean either 'menstruation' or 'menstrual period' between two menstruations. The four Sunni schools of Islamic law may differ on the interpretation of such words and, therefore, adopt slightly varying rules to determine the obligatory period for a divorced woman to wait before she can remarry.

2. *The Sunnah*

The Arabic word designating the second primary source of Islamic law, sunnah, means an established practice that sets an example to be followed. In the context of the law, sunnah refers to the practice of the Prophet expressed in actions, in oral pronouncements, or in concurrence in action by others. All three forms of sunnah are considered sources of law that are to guide Muslims.

The sunnah derives its authority from the Qur'an itself, where several verses enjoin the believers to obey the Almighty and His messenger. The practice of the Prophet, especially his oral pronouncements, had been committed to memory by many of his followers and by subsequent narrators in latter generations. Unlike the Qur'an, it was not recorded in written form during the lifetime of the Prophet. Indeed, the Prophet is reported to have discouraged his followers from writing down his sayings, lest they be confused with the text of the Qur'an. Thus, the Prophet emphasized the supremacy of the Qur'an over all else.

From this, a whole discipline of Islamic knowledge came into being centering on the analysis of the orally reported sayings of the Prophet (hadith). This discipline flourished during the 3rd century A.H. (9th century C.E.). Several compilations of hadith were produced, of which the two most authoritative and most widely used are those written by Muhammad ibn Isma'il ibn Ibrahim ibn al-Mughira al-Ja'fi, commonly known as al-Bukhari (d. 256 A.H./869 C.E.), and by Muslim ibn al-Hajjaj ibn Muslim al-Qushayri, commonly referred to by his first name, Muslim (d. 261 A.H./874 C.E.).

Scholars of hadith focus their attention on two elements of every reported saying of the Prophet:

1) The content of the saying, which must be logical and not self-contradictory, and must also not disagree with any provision in the Qur'an or in the established, authenticated hadith, and

2) The chain of transmitters, from the time of the Prophet to the time when the hadith compilations were written. Certain qualifications must be met by the narrators who constitute the links in the chain of transmission (isnad):

     a.   They should be known to be of a high ethical standing and therefore trustworthy, and

     b.   Narrators in any two successive links in the chain must have been contemporaries and must have lived at the same place or otherwise proven to have met, for example, during the pilgrimage to Mecca.

The Shi'ah, however, require that the original narrator must be a member of the Prophet's family. In this way, they distinguish themselves from the Sunni.

Sayings attributed to the Prophet that meet the above two criteria are then divided into two categories:

1) Sayings that are reported at every link of the chain of transmission by such a large number of narrators that it would not be possible to assume that they had conspired to tell a lie or to fabricate a pronouncement purported to have been made by the

Prophet. Hadith which fall in this category are considered authentic and authoritative, and

2) Sayings that are reported at every link of the chain by a limited number of narrators, from the Prophet's generation downward. This category of hadith is subjected to close scrutiny.

Only those sayings having a perfect chain of transmission or one giving no reason for doubt are held to be authentic. Further, some of the different rulings on certain issues by the various schools of Islamic jurisprudence can be traced to the fact that some jurists consider a certain oral pronouncement attributed to the Prophet to be authentic and base their ruling on it, while other jurists disregard it because they consider the attribution to the Prophet doubtful.

As stated above, no rules derived from the secondary sources may abrogate or contravene a rule contained in the two primary sources, the Qur'an and the sunnah, though there is an internal hierarchy between the two primary sources, as evidenced by the Prophet's refusal to have the sunnah recorded, as the Qur'an was, during his lifetime. Thus, the sunnah cannot abrogate or amend a rule contained in the Qur'an. * * * There are very few cases in which the sunnah provides for a different rule from the one contained in the Qur'an. The best-known example of this is the prohibition in the sunnah of a will and testament in favor of a legal heir (unless all the other heirs accept it), while the Qur'an puts no restrictions on the right of a testator. A more enlightened approach is to distinguish these differences, and to consider the sunnah as complementary to the Qur'an. Thus, in this view, the absence of any limitation in the Qur'an on a testator's right is not contradicted by the Prophet's limitations, as the latter may be explained as an extension of the former.

B. The Secondary Sources

Whenever the two primary sources do not cover a given situation, or are insufficient to regulate it, jurists had to have recourse to secondary sources of the law. This is necessary because the Shari'ah applies at all times and in all places, and because the need arises to have flexible rules of law.

1. Consensus (Ijma)

The first supplemental source of rules of law is the convergence of opinion on a particular new rule. Authority for this source is to be found in the Qur'an, where several verses condemn those who stray from the path of the believers.[48] The Prophet is also reported to have said: 'My community will never agree on an error.'[49]

48. *See* Qur'an at 4:115 ('If anyone contends with The Apostle even after Guidance has been plainly conveyed to him, and follows a path other than that Becoming to men of Faith, We shall leave him in the path he has chosen, and land him in Hell— What an evil refuge!'); 4:153 ('Verily, this is My Way, Leading straight: follow it: Follow not (other) paths: They will scatter you about From His (great) Path: Thus doth He command you, That ye may be righteous'); 3:15, ('But if they strive To make thee join in worship with Me things of which thou hast no knowledge, obey them not; Yet bear them company In this life with justice (and consideration), and follow the way of those who turn to Me (in love): In the end the return of you all is to Me, and I will tell you the truth (and meaning) of all that ye did').

49. Hassan, *supra* at 161.

But whose convergence of opinion constitutes consensus (ijma)? In the early times immediately following the death of the Prophet, his followers, especially those recognized as more knowledgeable in such matters, were the ones who contributed to the formation of consensus. In later times, up to our own, consensus is formed by the qualified jurists recognized as capable of reaching independent personal opinion based on the sources. These individuals are known in Arabic as mujtahidin, and the process they use is called ijtihad.

There are two variations of consensus, namely:

1) Active consensus, when all the jurists qualified to participate express the same opinion on a particular issue; and

2) Passive consensus, when some qualified jurists express an opinion and the others, being aware of it, do not dissent.

Active consensus is considered a valid source of new rules of law by all four schools of jurisprudence of Sunni Islam. Passive consensus has the approval of only two of the four schools.

It would illuminate the early workings of consensus to mention some examples of it in the early stages of Islamic law. These examples deal with situations not mentioned in the Qur'an or dealt with in the Prophet's practice. Faced with such situations, the early Muslims had to find out what the law said about them. * * * In the first example, the Qur'an provides that each of the parents receive one-sixth of the estate of the deceased. Nothing was said of the grandfather or the grandmother in case the parents of the deceased had died before the deceased. Early Muslims reached a consensus that in the absence of the father or the mother of the deceased, the grandparents receive their respective shares of one-sixth each. The second example is the Qur'an's explicit prohibition of eating 'the flesh of swine.' The question arose as to whether the fat of the swine was also prohibited. A consensus was reached by early Muslims that it was. Finally, the Qur'an provides that all booty obtained in fighting non-believers be divided among the fighters after one-fifth of it is remitted to the public treasury. When Muslim armies conquered territories in Syria and Mesopotamia, the fighters claimed farmland and other real estate as booty. This claim gave rise to doubt in the community. The second caliph, Umar, convened an assembly of elders in Medina to discuss the matter and reach a conclusion. After three days of debate, a consensus was reached to the effect that real estate was not booty, thus limiting it to personal property. The assembly decided by consensus that farmland and other real estate should remain in the possession of the original owners, but that an annual tax should be collected from them. This addition to the resources of the public treasury served the interests of the community better than making the relatively few Muslim fighters rich to the exclusion of other Muslims and to the detriment of the original owners by endowing the fighters with real estate as booty. Legislative bodies subsequently developed the notion of express consensus, which provided that the legislative representatives must have fully benefitted from the opinions of qualified jurists and stated that qualified jurists neither dissent, nor prove inconsistent with the Shari'ah, the enactments of that legislative body.

2. Analogy (Qiyas)

Qiyas is the second supplementary source of rules of law. It is based on the use of reason to conclude that an existing rule applies to a new situation because it is similar to the situation regulated by that rule, or to abstain from applying the existing rule to the new situation that is proven dissimilar.

Authority for analogy is to be found in the Qur'an, where many verses call for logical thinking in matters relating to the existence of God and to the creation of the universe. The sunnah also provides authority for the use of analogy in formulating new rules of law. * * *

* * *

The use of analogy for the formulation of new rules of law requires a determination of the raison d'être behind the existing rule. This is called illa (rationale) in Arabic. It is narrower and more specific than the rationale of the rule of law, called hikma (judgment or wisdom). This rationale alone is not enough to extend an existing rule to a new situation, and its absence is not sufficient to exclude the new situation from the sphere of the existing rule. This role is left to the narrower and more specific illa, of which the presence justifies applying the existing rule to the new situation, and of which the absence leads to the exclusion of the new situation from the scope of the existing rule. In its technique, analogy is a logical syllogism, i.e., a method of reasoning by which a previously unknown conclusion is derived from two known premises. A well-formed syllogism consists of two premises, one called major and the other called minor. Each premise has one term in common with the other premise and one term in common with the conclusion. In legal analogy, the major premise contains the illa of the known rule of law. This is repeated in the minor premise describing the new situation for which a rule is sought. It is the presence of the illa in the minor premise that justifies the application of the existing rule to the new situation. Its absence in the minor premise would lead to the exclusion of the new situation from the scope of the existing rule.

Two examples of the use of analogy illustrate the mechanism of extending an existing rule to an unregulated situation, and in restricting the application of an existing rule to the situation it was originally meant to regulate. The first is the prohibition of alcoholic drinks, clearly proscribed in the Qur'an. When narcotic drugs came to be known in the Islamic world, the question arose as to whether they too were prohibited. By use of the analogical method, the jurists reached the conclusion that they were also prohibited, thus extending the application of the existing rule to a new situation and formulating a new rule by analogy. The argument they used was as follows: Alcohol is prohibited because it is intoxicating (major premise); narcotic drugs are intoxicating (minor premise); narcotic drugs are prohibited (conclusion).

The same method was, and still can be, used for reaching an opposite conclusion, namely excluding a novel situation from the scope of an existing rule. Gold and silver coins could be exchanged only in the exact amount. Any excess was considered prohibited riba (usury). When coinage of the conquered lands and Islamic coinage with lesser content of gold and silver came into circulation, the question arose as to whether the payment of a loan in the same number of gold and silver pieces of different coinage was a full payment of the loan. The jurists reached a determination that the raison d'être of prohibiting riba was excess in real, and not merely numerical, value. Thus, they required that the gold and silver coins exchanging hands should be weighed at the beginning and at the end of the transaction. If the same number of coins paid by the debtor weighed less than the coins he received, additional coins had to be paid to make up the original weight of the coins lent. Since this numerical excess was not real excess in value, such a transaction did not involve riba. The analogical reasoning was as follows: riba is prohibited because it involves an excess in real value (major premise); payment of a debt with a greater number of gold or silver coins of the same weight as the original loan does not involve an excess in real value (minor premise); therefore, such a transaction does not come under the rule prohibiting riba (conclusion). All Sunni schools of jurisprudence use qiyas, in varying degrees, as a source of new rules of law. Only Shi'i Muslim jurists reject the use of analogy as a supplemental source of legal provisions.

3. Custom (Urf)

The law that applied in pre-Islamic Arabia consisted of customary rules derived from the practice of the members of the community in marketplaces and other arenas of social, commercial, interpersonal, and intertribal interaction. Islamic law did not reject out of hand such customary rules and adopted as its own those of them that were not incompatible with the ethical values of the new faith. A prime example of customary rules repealed as being antagonistic to the values of Islam were those permitting usury and resulting in doubling and redoubling of the amount of the original obligation from year to year. * * *

What distinguishes urf (custom) from ijma (consensus) as a source of rules of law is that consensus is the domain of qualified jurists alone, while custom is derived from the established practices of common people in their daily dealings with each other. Therefore, a rule arrived at by consensus applies everywhere, while customary rules can be localized. * * *

All schools of jurisprudence recognize custom as a supplementary source of rules of law. An axiom was coined to express the place of custom among the sources of legal rules 'What is established by custom is like what is stipulated (among contractual parties).' Like all supplementary sources, custom cannot provide authority for any rule that contravenes a mandatory rule provided by a primary source or by some other supplementary source. Custom is there only to fill in gaps in the body of the law that no other source has dealt with in a mandatory way.

* * *

4. The Common Good (Maslaha)

When a new rule is needed to regulate a novel situation and cannot be derived from qiyas, ijma, or urf, resort to maslaha is permissible. It is, in some respects, equivalent to the common law's equity, though it is much broader because it extends beyond the parties to a given conflict. Consideration of the common or public good is based on the fact that the law is intended to protect and promote the legitimate interests of the community and its individual members. In any unprecedented situation calling for a new rule of law, identifying that public interest is the first step towards formulating a new rule that protects and promotes that public good. Maslaha is therefore an expression of public policy.

Islamic jurists came up with a list of five basic values that they called 'the goals of the Shari'ah.' These five values relate to the individual's faith, his life, his intellect, his progeny, and his wealth. Any rule of law that protects and promotes any of these five values is a valid rule of Islamic law, provided that it does not violate or contradict an existing peremptory rule, i.e., one that derives from the Qur'an or the sunnah.

By adopting this concept of the public good, Islamic jurists were able to objectivize and circumscribe a vague ideal otherwise likely to be conceived subjectively, which might have opened the door to personal preferences under the cloak of an insufficiently defined 'common good.' The five values identified by the jurists as the basis for public good and mentioned above relate mainly to the individual. It is presumed that in those five areas the interest of the individual and the interest of the community coincide. In the rare occasions where those two interests are in conflict, the public interest is given greater weight. Accordingly, when the public treasury needed more resources than what was available from taxes provided for in the two principal sources of the Shari'ah, a new rule permitting the imposition of new taxes was formulated, based on consideration of the public good, which takes precedence over the individual's interest in preserving his wealth. Likewise, a new rule was devised excluding from private ownership any mineral resources discovered in privately owned land. It was considered that the community's interest in adding to the resources of the public treasury, and thus permitting better services to the community, took precedence over one individual's interest in becoming exceedingly rich through exclusive ownership of mineral resources found under his land.

While the other sources of rules of law are limited by their very nature in their potential to provide an unlimited number of new rules, the public good is an open-ended source of new rules of law called for by changing social and economic conditions over time. As will be explained in the remaining pages of this chapter, the evolution of Islamic law in modern times, with all its unregulated novel situations, was based mainly on consideration of the public good.

III.   THE PROCESS OF RULE-MAKING

Even before being formally expressed and deliberately applied, a process evolved since the early times for the formulation of new rules of law. Such an emerging process was observable even during the lifetime of the Prophet. Although his rulings are authoritative in themselves and need no further justification, on occasion he invoked analogy or the public good as a basis for his rule-making. The following examples help to illustrate this point.

The Qur'an prohibits a second marriage where the intended wife is the sister of the first wife. The Prophet extended this prohibition, by analogy, to the second marriage of a woman who is the niece of the first wife. The common factor, he explained, was the need to avoid acrimonious relationships between blood relatives. As another example, in a contract involving the sale of goods, the law requires that the object be existent. The Prophet validated the sale of a future crop in the public interest. The rationalization was that by purchasing future crops, traders would ensure sufficient stocks and the farmers would obtain funds to spend on their agricultural activities.

The Prophet also encouraged his companions to use reason in formulating new rules of law * * *.

* * * [An example] of the early process of formulating new rules concerns criminal law. The Qur'an's penalty for murder is expressed in the words 'a soul for a soul.' This was taken to mean that only one culprit could be executed in punishment for a murder he committed. When several individuals participate in murdering a victim, this would mean that some of the wrongdoers would go free. When such an incident took place during Umar's reign, he decided, upon consultation, that all the participants in a murder should receive the death penalty. Otherwise, it was argued, a murderer could avoid the penalty by having one or more co-murderers participate with him in the commission of the crime. In other words, a single perpetrator would receive a higher penalty than if he were acting with others. This would be contrary to the public good.

The process of formulating new rules of law acquired a new vigor as the professional class of jurists increased in numbers and established a presence in the various centers of the expanding Islamic empire. The different groups of jurists evolved into distinctive schools of legal thought (madhahib), each centered on a founding father whose name the school carries. Four such madhahib came to be recognized in Sunni Islam. The Hanafi school, founded by Abu Hanifa al-Nu'man ibn Thabit al-Taymi (80–150 A.H./699–767 C.E.), came into being in Baghdad. Medina saw the establishment of the Maliki school by Abu Abd Allah Malik ibn Anas (97–179 A.H./713–795 C.E.). The Shafi'i school came into being in Baghdad, although its founder, Muhammad ibn Idris al-Shafi'i

(150–204 A.H./767–819 C.E.), moved to Cairo. Baghdad also saw the establishment of the Hanbali school, founded by Ahmad ibn Hanbal al-Shaybani (164–241 A.H./780–855 C.E.).

There was no uniformity of opinion about major legal issues within any one school of legal thought. On a particular issue, a Hanafi jurist may depart from the majority opinion of his school and adopt a position identical to that of the Maliki school, for example. Soon enough, all schools of legal thought began to produce manuals and treatises expounding their opinions on all aspects of the legal system. As mentioned earlier, some of Shafi'i's rulings while teaching in Cairo differed from his rulings while in Baghdad. This was in response to differing local customs and socio-economic conditions.

Generally speaking, the Maliki and Hanbali schools emphasized textual sources of legal norms, preferring to base their rulings on their understanding of Qur'anic verses and of traditions of the Prophet. The other two schools, the Hanafi and the Shafi'i, made more extensive use of analogy and the public good. This remark, however, is correct only in general terms. For example, one of the most influential works on the public good as a source of law was written by a Hanbali jurist, Najm al-Din al-Tufi (657–716 A.H./ 1259–1316 C.E.).

The methodology followed by the Shi'i schools of legal thought differs from that of their Sunni counterparts on two points: (1) the Shi'i jurists reject the use of analogy (qiyas) and do not consider it a source of new rules of law, and (2) they accept only sunnah that is transmitted by members of the Prophet's family. This results in their rejection of much of the body of Prophetic pronouncements and practice used by Sunni jurists. Furthermore, the Shi'ah believe in the infallibility of their historic Imams and, in the absence of the Hidden Imam, of his representative who is the highest recognized cleric and jurist. Any ruling by any of these is accepted by the Shi'ah as being indisputably the law.

IV. THE SHARI'AH'S EVOLUTION

For a better understanding of the development of the Islamic legal system over time, the stages through which it passed can be identified as follows: Early Development, Maturity, Rigidity, Renaissance, and Uncertainty. Most writers, however, use historical periods to arrive at these stages. The difference is that of temporal as opposed to qualitative categorization. Such categorization is the subject of many studies that are based on different methods of historical legal analogies.

* * *

V. AUTHORITY AND CHANGE

Law is the embodiment of moral, ethical, and social values. The authority of law is derived both from its inherent nature and from its enforcement, which is also norm-reinforcing. Authority in Islamic law derives from its divine source and inspiration, and because ultimate accountability for its transgression is by and before the Creator. Power is not that which gives Islamic law its authority, but rather its higher source is what gives it authority. This is why, theoretically, in Islamic law what constitutes law is more important than the power to enforce it. When voluntary compliance fails, society enforces the law, and thus reinforces the law's authority. The interaction between law and its enforcement shapes social values and conditions compliance. However, the theoretical gap between law and enforcement allows greater influence by those who claim to understand the true meaning of the law over those who have the temporal power to enforce it. Thus, religious leaders, particularly those with a political agenda, use this gap to reinforce their positions.

The primary lawgiver is God and the best interpreter of God's will is the Prophet; thus the sunnah is second only to the Qur'an. As discussed above, however, the Qur'an and the sunnah do not cover everything that man can encounter, experience, or otherwise confront in life, thus the need for man-made law to fill the lacunae. Furthermore, these two primary sources appear to be in some matters ambiguous and even inconsistent. There is, therefore, the need to develop a judicial methodology, or more aptly stated in the French legal tradition, a méthode juridique, to interpret textual language, to apply it to different contexts, to reconcile inconsistencies, and to fill lacunae when they might exist. The methodology thus becomes controlling and different methodologies are not necessarily susceptible to being commingled, no matter how similar and without regard to whether the outcome may be similar. The dominance of methodology is reflected in the dogmatic approach reflected in the madhahib. Adherence to a madhhab requires acceptance of its method, including its own logic of choice in the pursuit of legal analysis.

The four Sunni madhahib, like the Shi'ah madhahib, were started by jurisconsults. The madhahib methods each had a man-made beginning whose claim was a best-effort adherence to the divine source of Islamic law. It was an exercise in interpretation, application, and ijtihad. The methods that were introduced later acquired authority as a result of their acceptance by the madhahib followers. In time, the madhhab, its method, and substantive content became authoritative custom; and as with every custom, there is always a single human act that is its origin. Eventually, the madhahib, though not of divine authority, acquired by consensus an almost undisputed legal authority that gave the originator of the madhhab a moral authority that withstood time. But it was the personal authority of the school's founder that compelled this outcome. Indeed, it was the scholarly, intellectually compelling, and convincing logic and arguments of the school's author, along with his recognized piety, that gave him such recognition and such following. Generations of adherents, who more or less rigidly followed that school's teaching, and above all its methodology, brought to it an evermore imposing authority that in time became almost unshakable.

This process may well be analogized to the one that evolved with the Prophet's early dissemination of God's message. It was his piety and the compelling logic and convincing arguments that he advanced which gave him the initial credibility that was needed before people accepted his word that he was God's chosen messenger. The Prophet's known illiteracy contributed to proving the divine origin of the Qur'an. His personal authority brought people to listen to the Revelations, and the credibility of his teachings, starting from the early days of Mecca and then Medina, convinced the many who converted. The jurisconsults who founded the four Sunni madhahib and those of Shi'ah madhahib emulated the Prophet, who is the role-model for all Muslims. In turn they became the role-model of those who followed their school of thought and method.

The madhahib's methods were not, however, without substantive content. The schools were characterized as much by the substantive content of the school founders' teachings as they were by the methods that they developed. The method embodied the logic that permitted the reaching of the substance, but the method also had to be based on substance and was thus characterized by value-content. Substantive content also served to delineate the contours and boundaries of the madhhab's doctrine. Substance provided either internal boundaries demarcating a given issue, or outer boundaries of the school's doctrine.

The followers of the schools contributed to their internal structure and substantive content through a process of accretion by their jurisprudential thoughts and juridical and social applications. It is within the confines of the school's substantive contours and in accordance with the school's methodology that both continuity and change were achieved. Continuity was simply adherence and reiteration, which is called taqlid, while change occurred from within the madhhab through qiyas and ijtihad. Taqlid provided consistency and predictability, while qiyas and ijtihad provided for evolution and change. Taqlid was mostly the province of the qadi (judge) who was, and is still, viewed as a strict constructionist (by analogy to subsequent positivist judicial doctrines). The mujtahid is a jurisconsult whose qualities and scholarly qualifications permitted him to explore beyond the law as it was into what can be viewed as a development going beyond qiyas to reaching newness.

The qadi had to possess certain qualifying requisites in order to reach taqlid, so it follows that the mujtahid had to meet even higher standards of qualification. * * * The qadi's application of the law was limited to the case before him, unlike the mujtahid who, frequently through a fatwa, could exercise ijtihad in a specific case or independently of any specific case or controversy to decide an issue or question heretofore unaddressed or unresolved.

The first caliph to entrust someone else with exercise of the office of judge was Umar. He appointed Abu Darda to be judge with him in Medina, Shurayh to be a judge in the city of Basra, and Abu Musa al-Ash'ari as judge in the city of Kufa. On appointing Abu Musa, Umar wrote him the famous letter containing all the rules that govern the office of judge. He says in it:

Now the office of judge is a definite religious duty and a generally followed practice.

Understand the depositions that are made before you, for it is useless to consider a plea that is not valid.

Consider all the people equal before you in your court and in your attention, so that the noble will not expect you to be partial and the humble will not despair of justice from you.

The claimant must produce evidence; from the defendant, an oath may be exacted.

Compromise is permissible among Muslims, but not any agreement through which something forbidden would be permitted, or something permitted forbidden.

If you gave judgment yesterday, and today upon reconsideration come to the correct opinion, you should not feel prevented by your first judgment from retracting; for justice is primeval, and it is better to retract than to persist in worthlessness.

Use your brain about matters that perplex you and to which neither Qur'an nor sunnah seem to apply. Study similar cases and evaluate the situation through analogy with them.

If a person brings a claim, which he may or may not be able to prove, set a time limit for him. If he brings proof within the time limit, you should allow his claim, otherwise you are permitted to give judgement against him. This is the better way to forestall or clear up any possible doubt.

All Muslims are acceptable as witnesses against each other, except such as have received a punishment provided for by the religious law, such as are proved to have given false witness, and such as are suspected (of partiality) on (the ground of) client status or relationship, for God, praised be He, forgives when sworn testimony is rendered and postpones (punishment) in the face of the evidence.

Avoid fatigue and weariness and annoyance at the litigants.

For establishing justice in the courts of justice, God will grant you a rich reward and give you a good reputation. Farewell.

From such beginnings a whole genre of legal literature came into being focusing on the judge's role and the manner of his carrying out his judicial duties. * * *

Although it was the caliph who appointed judges, the judge was independent in his judicial activities. The ruler was subject to the law just as the people were. Many historical anecdotes illustrate this independence of the judges and the subjection of the ruler to the judge's authority in case of litigation. * * *

In the earlier stage of Islamic history, jurists who were appointed to the office of judge were capable of exercising independent personal reasoning in pursuit of new rules of law for application to unprecedented situations. They were able to exercise ijtihad. With the passage of time and the expansion of the territory where Islamic law applied, it was sometimes no longer possible to find such jurists to fill all the vacant judgeships. It became permissible to appoint as judges jurists who were fully knowledgeable of the rules constituting the current body of law. This allowed them to decide cases to which one of the existing rules applied. Faced with a case requiring ijtihad, the judge could seek the opinion of a mujtahid (also called a mufti), one with the qualifications to issue authoritative legal opinions.

The fatwa has historically been concerned with a given issue, propounded as a question to which the mufti provides an answer. The authoritative nature of the fatwa derived from the higher qualifications of the person making it. The fatwa, however, had to be specific. Importantly, a fatwa is not necessarily based on ijtihad.

Sometimes the boundaries between qiyas and ijtihad were defined by the manner in which the question was posed or the issue framed. Depending upon the answer and the way in which it was framed, one could conclude that the answer was either based on continuity or charted a new course. The mujtahid could transcend the need for a continuity link and arrive at an outcome that was unconnected to the past. Such a process necessarily led in time to restrictions on ijtihad, if for no other reason than the fact that the mujtahid's qualifications became increasingly more difficult to fulfill. Human nature being what it is, the increased knowledge of many made it less possible for the few to emerge and be recognized by a social process of consensus as possessing such superior qualifications for authority over others. This necessarily led to the collectivization of ijtihad through a group of scholars who, as a group, if not individually, possessed the high requisites of the mujtahid. However, even that was curtailed as of the 6th century A.H. (12th century C.E.), probably to avoid the power that the mujtahid could wield.

The historical process of the madhahib described above and the emergence of sub-schools within each madhhab occurred over several centuries. An examination of that evolution reveals many variables that contributed at once to the richness of legal doctrine and to its complexity. Legal change was always mediated by the individual authority of the jurisconsult, who was nonetheless controlled by his social and political milieu and by his temporal and spatial context. Thus, the madhahib's insistence on the characteristics of the mujtahid, mufti, and qadi were not beyond the effects of external factors. In time, an absolutely staggering accretion of doctrinal plurality and ad hoc juristic applications made Islamic law's knowledge the province of the few. * * *

Students of that impressive legal legacy were left with the task of identifying new methods to rank authoritative legal positions and pronouncements. Thus, another complex dimension was added to the science of law, that of hierarchy of legal opinions. Considering the number of sources of law described above, the diversity of views as to their ranking and relationship, and the ranking of their legal opinions (whether deemed to have been arrived at by means of ijtihad, qiyas, or even progressive taqlid), the number of doctrinal variables became even more numerous. * * *

* * *

D. BUDDHIST LAW

The term "Buddhist Law" is in some ways a misnomer. Unlike Halakha and Shari'ah, there is no formalized system of Buddhist law. The teachings of the Buddha include many principles that can guide and order peoples' behavior and interrelations. Buddhist monasteries generally have a system of rules that are followed and enforced which could be considered a legal system. Moreover, the laws of several governments have been heavily influenced by Buddhist principles and such legal systems could be considered "Buddhist law". Two examples set forth below are Thai law and Tibetan law.

To understand Buddhist legal thinking it is essential to think outside the western box of dualism and to take a more holistic view of legal actors, actions, and relationships. Perhaps the best source for studying Buddhist legal concepts is, Rebecca Redwood French's, THE GOLDEN YOKE: THE LEGAL COSMOLOGY OF BUDDHIST TIBET, (Cornell Univ. Press 1995). A brief excerpt from that book is included in this section, but for those interested in Buddhist conceptions of law it is worthwhile to read the entire book. Prior to the excerpt from French's book is an article on the interaction between Buddhist law and Thai law (the article is based on a report to the International Congress on Comparative Law).

Before reading these materials it is worthwhile to learn a bit more about the Buddhist concept of law. Buddhist terminology and manuscripts are usually in Pali, Sanskrit, Vedic (an ancient form of Sanskrit), or local languages such as Thai. I will use either the Pali or Sanskrit terminology unless otherwise mentioned. Central to Buddhist conceptions of law is the tipitaka or tripitaka, roughly translated as "the Three Baskets." The three baskets are the vinaya (roughly meaning rules of conduct, which are most relevant to monks and monasteries); the sutras (the words of the Buddha and his contemporary disciples); and the abhidharma (interpretations of the Buddha's teachings). Early Buddhist "councils" codified, augmented, and modified aspects of the tipitaka …

As Buddhism spread throughout Asia, numerous schools of Buddhism developed, and each school determined which writings were authoritative. One of the earliest examples of the development of different Buddhist schools, and one that is still relevant today, was the split between the Mahayana school and the Hinayana school. A very basic explanation of this split is that the Mahayana school is concerned with the ideal of the Bodhisattva, whose goal is to reach the highest level of enlightenment in order to help others to find the path to enlightenment and happiness. The Hinayana school is more focused on individual enlightenment and the goal of attaining a state of total happiness (also referred to as nirvana). The Mahayana school saw the Hinayana School's focus on self fulfillment without the more universalistic goal of helping others attain enlightenment to be selfish. Each of the schools that has developed has rules (vinaya) that govern the monastic order. Moreover, the teachings of the Buddha and the interpretations of those teachings provide a model upon which Buddhists can base their actions. This is of course law, in the sense that it provides a normative guide to human conduct. Moreover, the teachings of the Buddha include actual cases where the Buddha or his disciples had to decide disputes, and some of the tipitaka specifically addresses common legal issues. For example, the "twenty-five kinds of robbery" derived from the vinaya. The following two excerpts will add to your knowledge of Buddhist legal concepts, but the reader should be aware that this entire section is incredibly basic and provides only a brief glimpse of Buddhist legal thought.

SOMPONG SUCHARITKUL, *THAI LAW AND BUDDHIST LAW*

46 Am. J. Comp. L. 69 (1998).*

I. Preliminary Notions

The purpose of this Report is to examine the inherent links between Buddhist Law and Thai Law, their coexistence, interrelations and mutual influence within the existing legal system and the religious order of Thailand.

Two basic terms used in this Report need to be clarified: Buddhist Law as the law based on the teachings of the Lord Buddha, and Thai Law as the law interpreted and applied in the various Thai Kingdoms throughout the length and breadth of the national history of the Thai people.

A. *Buddhist Law*

Several questions need to be answered in the present context surrounding the notion of Buddhist Law as a religious law. The first question relates to Buddhism itself as a religion. Most Buddhists regard the teachings of the Buddha as their religious guidance and principles to observe. Some consider Buddhism as a philosophy, a practical way of life. Although Buddhism may be different from other religions of the world in that the conception of a supreme being such as God is singularly absent from the central theme of the Buddha's teachings, nonetheless, Buddhism is generally regarded as a religion by historians and missionaries alike.

By nature, Buddhists are modest and moderate. * * * Buddhism * * * advocates moderation and the middle path, majima pada or via media. If Buddhism were not counted as a religion, then billions of

---

* This article is Section I, Topic I.C.3. of, *American Law at the End of the 20th Centu-* *ry: U.S. National Reports to the XVth International Congress of Comparative Law.*

earthlings who are Buddhists would be deemed without religion. On the other hand, it is not untrue that a person holding the Buddhist faith can also learn and appreciate, or tolerate and practice other faiths without violating any Buddhist principle. Taking into account special characteristics of Buddhism, we are persuaded that Buddhism is a religion in human history since 600 B.C. and is likely to remain with us for the foreseeable future.

The next question to be asked in connection with Buddhist Law qua law is whether the religious principles derived from the teachings of the Buddha are truly law in the sense that they are recognized as binding in the Buddhist community and not as mere moral precepts.

The teaching of the Buddha * * * are divided into three main parts * * *. They are (1) the Vinaya; (2) the Sutta (also Suttanta) and (3) the Abhidhamma. The records were kept in Pali, a dialect of Sanskrit, spoken by the Buddha and came to be known as the Pali canons. The Buddha's use of Pali represents a break from the Indian Hindu Brahmin tradition. Buddha was born a Hindu prince and Buddhism has arisen out of Hindu tradition, but since its inception, Buddhism has followed its own independent direction.

Sanskrit was the classical language of the Brahmins in India. Its earliest form was Vedic (circa 1500–200 B.C.) and it is in this language that the ancient scriptures of Hindu laws were recorded. * * * After the Pali Sutras were lost in India, they were rediscovered in Sri Lanka and translated into Sanskrit, returning to India and eventually traveling the northern route going over Tibet and China, through Korea and Japan. There are variables between Sanskrit and the original Pali scripts * * *. It will be seen that in the Thai language, both Sanskrit and Pali renderings are used in the official Thai language. In the Thai Buddhist temples, however, the chanting and prayers are all conducted in Pali, the spoken language of the Buddha, keeping as close as possible to the Teachings of the Elders, or Theravada Buddhism.

The Vinaya is devoted exclusively to the rules and regulations formulated by the Buddha for the monastic conduct, rites and ceremonies to be followed by the Orders of the Bhikkus (monks) and Bhikkunis (female monks). They are divided into five main sections and are comparable, broadly speaking, to the laws and social norms of secular society.

True it is that the Vinaya lacks some of the elements in the modern legal system from the perspective of the Western world. There is no Court of Appeal, no prison wardens, no bailiffs to compel or enforce compliance with the verdict of monastic peers, while the most serious offenses are punishable with a form of capitis diminutio (defrocking or derobing of a monk). The Vinaya is nonetheless law, if only for application within the religious Order, with inevitable repercussion for serious offenses in the secular world. The Buddhist religious Order is a well-organized monastic community, self-disciplined, autonomous and law-abiding.

The Suttapitaka is a collection of Sutras and dialogues of the Buddha with his various disciples, while the Abhidhamma constitutes a more purely philosophical elaboration of the sayings and teachings of the Buddha. They are not law in the sense of the secular law in force in a given society, but constitute nevertheless a code of conduct, a model of peaceful living for the Buddhist community.

Three objects of the highest veneration in Buddhism are the Buddha, the Dhamma and the Sankha, the three constituting the RATA-NATTAYA or the Holy Triple Gem comparable in some respect to the Holy Trinity.

B. Thai Law

What seems to be begging the question with regard to the notion of Thai Law is not so much the "Law" as the "Thai" part, preceding the word "Law." There can be little doubt as to the nature and character of the law in force in the Kingdom of Thailand as it is today more or less clearly delimited. It is questionable whether the notion of Thai Law is wider than the expression the law of Thailand. The answer appears to be clearly in the affirmative. * * *

* * *

Thai and non-Thai scholars alike have been at a loss to ascertain the true sources of earlier Thai law or to allocate with any precision the exact proportion of the material contribution to its development by Brahmin traditions or Hindu Dharmasastras, and Buddhist law drawn from the Tipitaka or the Buddhist Pali canons. * * * The truth of the matter as revealed by legal historians, appears to be that whatever the contents of the applicable law in modern Thailand and in spite of their western civil-law formulation, pre-western codified Thai statutes and legal traditions deserve the closest attention from the perspective of their internal linkages with the teachings of the Buddha which we have been persuaded to acknowledge as the Buddhist Law.

Before an attempt is made to embark on that enquiry, it is necessary to caution that Thai Law is Buddhist Law only in many parts, the remainder of which is partly of pure Thai origin and partly drawn from international mercantile usages prevailing in Southeast and East Asia. A study of Thai Law as Buddhist Law does not preclude some close encounters with Hindu Law through Dharmasastras, the Code Manu for Kings or Manu Laws or the cultural influences of Sanskrit literature which is predominant in the linguistic evolution of Thai alphabets, scripts and transliteration. While the influence of Indian culture on Thai society is more linguistic through the adoption of Sanskrit, the use of Pali by Dheravada Buddhist monks is a clear indication of a broader impact of Buddhist Law in the progressive development of several branches of Thai civil law in the pre-codified period prior to the current century.

II.   Co-Existence and Interdependence Between
Thai Law and Buddhist Law

* * *

Until recently, scholars thought of "Buddhist legal influence" as an empty category, a contradiction in terms. In the last decade, that view has been challenged by researchers in Buddhological circles. Buddhist legal traditions are now recognized as predating Hindu Dharmasastras, as having their own distinct content and as being a major Indian contribution to Thai and Southeast Asian culture in general.

* * *

Coexistence in the sense of mutual independence, noninterference and to an appreciable extent inter-dependence between the Temple and the State is fully implemented in the Thai kingdoms throughout the ages and everywhere since the reception of Buddhism in the Golden Peninsula * * *. Today, coexistence is reflected in the "Tricolor" of the Thai flag: Red for the Nation–State; White for the Religion, buddhism; and Blue for the King, the Monarchy. * * *

Peaceful coexistence means in effect not only that the Temple or the Monastic Order will be left alone to rule itself without interference or intervention on the part of the State, but more importantly the religious order is recognized not only by the public and administrative law as an autonomous entity but also by the Civil and Commercial Code of Thailand, as each Buddhist Temple is so recognized, as a legal entity, capable of rights and obligations under the legal system of Thailand. Indeed the religious order coexists within the legal and constitutional framework of the Kingdom.

Within the monastic communities, a hierarchy of ecclesiastical order has been established, headed by the Supreme Patriarch, and administered by the Mahathera Council of Elders among the Buddhist monks. In Thailand, as in other Southeast Asian countries, the prevailing Buddhist order has been the Dheravada Buddhism or Hinayana, although traces of Mahayana Buddhism could be found among the Chinese, Japanese, Korean and Vietnamese in the realm. The Council of Elders administers the affairs of the Temple, appoints and promotes senior monks to abbots, Chief Abbots and other official clergical positions within the Dheravada Order. The monks are strictly governed by the Vinaya from the Pali canon.

In any given monastery, once every full-moon or half-moon, the Sankha recites the PATIMOKKHA or the 227 verses of Pali scripture specifying each of the precepts or rules of conduct to be observed by every monk without exception. Minor violations could be absolved by fellow monks, whereas grave violations such as theft, murder and breach of celibacy would end in a mandatory sentence by the Council of Elders after due process of religious law, which is derobing or defrocking, i.e., expulsion from monkhood, never to reenter the order again, the equivalent of death or life sentence. There is no appeal or judicial review by the secular legal order.

The temple or monastery grounds which are open to the public are kept free of weaponry and cannot be violated by any measure of constraints or invasion by the civil authority. For all practical purposes, the temples are inviolable and sacrosanct, no armed intrusion is tolerated. The monks cannot be arrested unless and until defrocked, nor can the temples be searched. No search warrant will be issued against a monastery nor a warrant of arrest or summons issued to compel a monk to appear as witness. Temples have become places of refuge or sanctuaries inaccessible to the State officials, while Buddhist monks are entitled to something much more than the English common-law "benefit of clergy." They are beyond suspicion, especially of political offenses or sedition.

* * *

All State functions are officiated by high priests or the Supreme Patriarch with other highly ordained monks of Somdej rank. In some official functions such as the Ceremony of the First Plough (Pitee Raekna), the ceremonial parts are conducted by a senior Brahmin performing Brahministic rites which are Hindu. This is not untypical of State ceremonies in other parts of Southeast Asia. An army going into battle will first receive the blessings of the monks. Also privately, the marriage ceremonies, the births, birthdays or cremations are performed at the temple or at home by Buddhist monks. The Christening of a vehicle, an aircraft, a boat or a car is often done by a monk or a group of Sankha.

III. THE INTERPLAY OF BUDDHIST LAW AND THAI LEGAL PRINCIPLES

In more ways than one, the influences of the teachings of the Buddha on the formulation of Thai legal norms are apparent, while the legal and constitutional structures of the Thai legal system likewise reinforce and enhance respect for Buddhist law both in the implementation of Vinayapitaka for the monastic order and in the dissemination of the Suttapitaka and the Abhidhamma for the lay Buddhist communities in the Kingdom.

A. *Influence of Buddhist Law Within the Thai Legal System*

The Influence of Buddhism in Lanna Thai Law

In the central Thai language, Kotmai means law, but in Lanna Thai, Kotmai has a wider meaning, embracing all "written records in general." * * *

* * * The Eighth World Buddhist Council was held at Wat Ched Yod in 1447, bringing together many learned Lanna monks to review the TIPITAKA and to discuss Buddhist issues. King Trilokraj relied on Lanna monks to give his rule the authority and legitimacy. The Lanna Court continued to use the VINAYA and other teachings of the Buddha to help govern the layman. Laws administered in Lanna Thai had to be supported by the Dhamma. This served to legitimize State legislation and royal edicts by making them sacred and acceptable to the populace.

Because the monks were the scholars of society at that time and acted as official scribes to the kingdom commissioned to document important events and decrees, Vinaya influence was not apparent at the beginning of the Mangrai Dynasty, but by the time twenty court cases were reported in the time of Phya Kuena, the names of the justices composing the bench were known and the particular reference to the Jataka, Vinaya, Phra Sut or Sikha Vinai was cited at the hearings. Buddhist influence in the law by the 14th century was also reflected in the respect shown by the people for the monks. It was the monks who had gone to study Buddhism in Sri Lanka and Pagan who accounted for the emergence of new Pali literature in Lanna and who had most influence on Lanna law. The use of VINAYA in secular Lanna laws is found in many royal edicts.

One scholar believes that the Lanna law was created from the Vinaya in a very unsystematic way: the writing style is at times confusing and unorganized. In the Kosaraj Law 16, probably issued during the reign of the fifteenth ruler of Chiengmai (1546–1547), the first chapter compares secular cases with ecclesiastical cases and provides some evidence of how religion and State mixed together in the formation of Lanna law.

Another example is given in the Mangraithat–Avaharn 25 (twenty-five kinds of Robbery) which is drawn from the Vinaya * * *. Other areas where the Vinaya exercised some direct influence, include adultery, cases of sexual abuse, divorce, quarrel, theft, blackmail and deceit, monastic regulations could easily be adapted to lay life. Agricultural crimes, irrigation, fighting, rent counterfeiting and fine-sharing were not affected.

* * *

IV.   CLOSING CALL

* * *

Without attempting any concluding observation other than echoing and reiterating a call made by those courageous legal historians and scholars who have preceded me on this front, I would like to end this study by expressing a fondest hope that this Report should proffer an open invitation, and a stepping-stone for future generations to venture into this rich and virtually unexplored field.

Several questions rush to mind, all of which seem urgent and intriguing. Clearly, the substantive law of Thailand must be linked to the teachings of the Buddha. Not every part of Thai law is specifically influenced by the Buddhist doctrine, but the civil law, particularly the law of persons, family law, the law of properties and the law of transactions and obligations must be imbued with legal norms based on Buddhist principles. Even penal laws are not uninfluenced by the teachings of the Buddha * * *.

To give an illustration of the closest linkage between the teachings of the Buddha and the legal status of a person under Thai Civil Law, Section 15 of the Civil Code provides that legal personality begins with the birth of a child and its survival as an infant and ends with death. This represents the SAMSARA, the Cycle of Birth and Death in Buddhism.

* * *

Literally, I observe the precept requiring me to refrain from taking life of a living breathing being. In a way this is not inconsistent with the Old Testament Commandment, "THOU SHALT NOT KILL." Only the Buddhist version is older and far more explicit in its recognition of all forms of life, human, animals, marine life, plants, trees and even grasses that breathe.

The question remains whether a fetus en ventre sa màere can be said to be breathing on its own with an independent separate existence prior to its birth and severance of the umbilical chord.

Many other issues are begging the question. Thai Law under the influence of the Buddha's teaching of lessons of tolerance and compassion, admits of the practice of other religions. Thus, Thai law on family relations reflects the recognition and coexistence of a pluralistic society wherein persons of different faiths could be subject to different personal laws, especially with regard to family relations, adoption, betrothal, marriage, divorce and succession. * * *

* * *

EXCERPT FROM: REBECCA REDWOOD FRENCH, THE GOLDEN YOKE: THE LEGAL COSMOLOGY OF BUDDHIST TIBET

(Cornell Univ. Press 1995) at 341–47.

CONCLUSION

A few days before I left Dharamsala for the final time in the late fall of 1986, Kungola Thubten Sang ye arrived before I did at the office where we worked every morning and began, with his usual laborious lumbering, to climb the steps. I met him on the second flight and stayed behind him, taking the steps one at a time after him.

"I had a dream last night," he said and stopped to look down at me. "I had a dream last night that I was reborn in America." I didn't respond. He continued looking at me and said, "In my dream, I was born to an American woman." He turned to continue up the steps. "We must finish early today because I have many more mantras to complete in preparation."

On the morning of my departure * * * hurrying across the plaza * * * I thought of all the problems to be faced in New Delhi shipping the trunks * * *.

As I turned the corner, I saw Kungola. He had been waiting for me most of the morning. I stopped short and then approached. He clasped both my hands between his hands and bowed *his* head. I bowed my head and held it down in deference until after he spoke. "The outside needs to know about these things we have talked about," Kungola said.

My eyes filled with tears as I responded, "I will bring a book back to show you."

Fumbling with some packages he had under his arm, Kungola took from its newspaper wrapping a white silk scarf and put it around my neck as he said, "It is very important that people know about these matters, so you must work hard, I will die before you come back." Unwrapping another package in his hands * * * it revealed several pages of the religious text he had been reciting over the last weeks. "Take these with you." * * * I bowed again and took it with me * * *.

* * *

I have often wondered, while standing in my black suit before a sea of future lawyers, what Thubten Sang ye would think of me now. He would watch me do the ritual verbal dance of an American law professor and notice my erect body posture, my authoritative gestures, and the way I walk back and forth in front of the chalkboard. It seems certain that he would be surprised at the big, bright room and the number and gender of the students, but he would probably not comment on these things.

The lessons of Thubten Sang ye present a puzzle. From the perspective of comparative law, the Tibetans had a secular state system with hierarchically arranged courts administered by judges and clerks. They used logical analysis, followed procedures, recorded decisions in documents, and used long-established law codes. On the other hand, their legal system was so thoroughly Buddhist that none of the typical maxims any American law professor-indeed, any comparativist-would apply to a bureaucratic legal system apply to Tibet. This is the conundrum that confronts me when I look at the picture of Thubten Sang ye which hangs above my desk. I am left, after considering the Tibetan legal system, with several different kinds of questions and a range of implications about legal systems in general.

(1) Buddhism has both radical particularity and cosmological integration as the basis of its world view. This means that the Tibetan legal system treated individuals both as entirely unique—not comparable to one another—and as entirely integrated, part of the same cosmic system. Tibetans used dichotomies and dialectical argumentation, along with mysticism and many other techniques, as tools to deal with a system of radical particular integration. But their different starting point brings into question the use of Western dualistic analysis and models for analyzing legal systems such as Tibet's and perhaps other legal systems as well. Omnipresent dualisms good/bad, nature/culture, primitive/modern, religious/secular, right/left, scholastic/scientific, faith/reason, pub-

lic/private-permeate the investigation, modeling, and presentation of Western material on legal systems. If most of our conceptual tools are based in a dualistic form of thinking, from logic to symbolic analysis, from categorization to normative evaluation, we will move first to separate and categorize, and then to label as good or bad.

My questions, then: How are we to analyze a system that has radical particularity, does not prioritize dualistic thinking, and uses several different types of reasoning at the same time? What happens if we do not make the dualistic move of separating off other societies in terms of complexity and modernity?

(2) Tibetans believed that their legal system was permeated with the moral requirements of the Buddha and that the self-regulation of each individual's mind was the key to all social systems. This is a radically particular view. Although it created difficulties in the effort to adduce internal motivations and mental states from external behavior (a problem recognized by many legal systems, including our own), still they remained certain of the location and source of morality. The Buddha was an immutable standard of right behavior, the source of legitimation. Hundreds of tales of his decisions in untoward circumstances formed an image for Tibetans of the absolutely correct moral actor. A social system was good to the extent that the actors within the system were examining themselves with respect to this standard, reflecting on their own motivations, thinking of present and future lives, and working to reduce their mental afflictions. Punishment was meant to promote a return to inner morality.

Such an analysis of morality raises some fundamental questions about the location of morality and the separation of law and morality in both Western and East Asian jurisprudence. Is our analysis of law and its relationship to morality only more dualistic thinking? What happens when members of a social system are not operating on inner morality and need only fulfill external behavioral requirements? Is *mens rea,* guilty intent, similar to inner morality? Are the eternal standards of the Buddha similar to other universally applied sets of moral norms? What does all this mean for legal socialization within societies?

(3) From the Tibetan example it is apparent that some legal systems and decision making processes result in *neither* general rule formation and application *nor* the regular use of case precedent. They are particularistic (if one can avoid the negative connotation of that word). The importance of legal recording and remembering, of legal replicating and reproducing in a society has to do with understandings of the nature of law, of procedure, of concepts of time, personhood, and conflict. In Tibet, procedure and predictability meant factoring, and factoring did not require following or forming rules, using or setting precedent. Since the Buddha's life and path provided a constant immutable standard, the universal application of a rule to demonstrate legitimacy was unnecessary.

* * *

(4) Tibetans followed not rules but factors in the law; they used sets of factors related to each circumstance to determine the unique situation of the individual involved. The law codes are filled with factors to be considered in a variety of circumstances, together with hortatory admonitions, precatory advice, and ancient sayings. The Tibetan understanding of legal factoring is related to Buddhist logic, rationality, and reasoning. The purpose of logic in Buddhism is to transcend the individual perspective and through study and debate, to understand the tenets of the Buddha's path. Reasoning leads to an enlightened view and an enlightened view is compassionate toward all sentient beings. In short, faith and reason, logic and compassion are all integrated. Logic and rationality within such a system do not mean rule formation, the use of precedent, the logic of consequence or of antecedence.

Perhaps, though, the operation of this system of legal logic isn't really so different from ours. Is the use of precedents a process of rationalization? Is logic another way of saying "the way we think about things"?

(5) For many, the most interesting and unusual aspect of the Tibetan system is its lack of finality and closure. Cases could be reopened right after they were decided, even when the parties had both agreed to the judge or conciliator's decision. Tibetans considered this one of the best aspects of their system: they were free to disagree until they felt chat the dispute had been correctly decided. Judicial decisions had no finality in the way we understand finality; calming the mind and reaching real harmony were necessary before a dispute could actually be over. In Buddhism, this continuing freedom to disagree is part of the infinite potential of the mind to change and choose. At law, it resulted in the nonexclusiveness of forums, a lack of closure of cases, and also a great flexibility in choosing the kind and level of forum and the type of legal procedure to be followed.

For many American lawyers, such a system seems incomprehensible. But is it really? Do our concepts of closure correlate with the reality of our system? To what extent are our doctrines of closure—*stare decisis* and *res judicata*—related to other ideas about stability and predictability in society?

(6) According to Western legal philosophy, the state's ability to punish is one of the most important attributes of a bureaucratic legal system. The Tibetan legal structure had too few government bureaucrats and police to operate in that way on the Plateau. Local sanctions such as ostracism, shaming, loss of prestige due to fighting, loss of religious merit, loss of social prestige, financial loss, and the discomfort of delay were undoubtedly more important than official sentencing. A state bureaucracy without significant ability to punish is a conundrum in our terms, but the Tibetan example proffers universal procedure and local sanction as a large part of the political glue binding a country together, rather than the state's sanctioning power.

Consensus too took a form different from the consensus-building of Japan or majoritarian consent in America. In Tibet, it meant that individuals must actually consent, even in some criminal cases, to every part of the process—from the choice of forum, authority, and procedure to the decision and the penalties imposed. Without consent, the legal process did not function. This is radically particular consent. The consent of each individual to every part of each case comprised the consent of the society. In America we label such a system normatively as weak and see its government as incapable of enforcing the law. Buddhists saw it as the only solution within their religion and the only way to ensure real consent and personal freedom.

* * *

(7) The nature of the relationship between religion and law in Tibet appears to have been much more complex than the simple religious/secular split we employ in the West. All laws in Tibet were understood as religious, but there were two types: religious law for religious practitioners, and religious law for lay persons. There were also, in a sense, two types of secular law in that law for religious institutions passed through the ecclesiastical side of the government, and law for lay persons was administered by the district courts and the Cabinet. But religion permeated the secular legal system in the form of Buddhist standards, logic, factoring, jurisprudential concepts, and reality shifts that moved an argument into otherworldly reasoning. In the West, the religious perspective is often characterized as dogmatic and destructive of the democratic conversation. In the Tibetan refugee community today, Tibetans are not interested in democracy without a charismatic religious figure to guide them.

* * *

(8) Fairness in Tibet meant using Buddhist moral tenets and logic, legal factoring, and the law codes to investigate every aspect that was presented in a case. The judge or conciliator then fashioned a suitable solution that had to be agreed to by all parties. Factoring each situation uniquely was regarded as logical, compassionate, fair, and legitimated by the law codes. Truth, a multivalent term in Tibet, was first the consensus of two parties to a similar view of what happened, not the sparks from clashing sides. Truth was also the ideal and separate standard of the Buddha. Another notion of truth—well-experienced, honest judges conducting cases with proper formal procedural steps resulting in decisions agreeable to the parties—was closer to American ideas of justice and due process. A final understanding of truth, internal truth and morality, we would perhaps label personal honesty.

Some of these notions of fairness and honesty in Tibet seem to have been directly related to procedure. * * *

Final Thoughts on the Cosmology of Law

As a way of understanding these various issues, I have suggested viewing Tibetan law through the interpretive framework of a kaleidoscopic cosmology. This is a fundamentally different starting point for an analysis of law, one that decenters and destabilizes as it coheres and integrates. Derived from the rich source of Buddhist philosophy, Tibetan legal cosmology is based in assumptions about the world as simultaneously both wholly interconnected and completely particular. Everything is in a constant state of flux, impermanence, and cyclical regeneration.

The framework of cosmology is a larger claim than that of legal culture or legal system. In the Tibetan case, legal concepts and practices are not independent units operating in a separate, autonomous unit designated as "the legal system." Neither are they the particular province of a professionalized group, nor a specific set of rules and forums. Instead, they are understood to be entirely connected to and derived from the Tibetan Buddhist world view of the integrated All–One mandala. The framework of legal cosmology is therefore entirely connected to its cultural base, to the interpenetration of culture with law and the embeddedness of law in culture.

Narratives have been the road to unfolding the legal cosmology of the Tibetans. They are the primary presentation form in the book because Tibetans spoke about law in the form of stories with exegesis. But we can hear stories only when we already know the range of possible meanings, the correct formats, and their possible interpretive contexts. Stories can "say something" to us only when we already know what is going on and what we might expect to hear. Rather than oppositional tools to surprise and arrest the reader, narratives here speak in the voice and tone of a Tibetan, evoke the mundanity of daily life in Tibet. From verbatim cases to detailed descriptions and autobiographies, from local hail protection rituals to hearings in the central bureaucracy, each narrative is layered on the last, reconstituted by the next.

This presentation of the Golden Yoke of Tibet will, I hope, be followed by other versions to contest and deepen our insights into this rich treasure house of material, this "bountiful ocean" of Tibetan legal cosmology. Studying with Kungola Thubten Sang ye and sharing this material have brought me full circle to think more deeply about our own unacknowledged assumptions and the possibly contingent nature of what we assume to be essential in *our* cosmology of law.

E. CHRISTIAN LAW

This section will be split into two parts. The first part will address Canon Law, specifically Roman Catholic Canon Law. Significantly, this is not the only form of Christian Canon Law. The Episcopalian Church and the Eastern Orthodox Churches have Canon Law systems as well. A discussion of each of these Canon Law systems would be beyond the scope of this book. Thus the focus on a single Canon Law system.

The second part of this chapter will address Protestantism and the law. While most Protestant sects do not have a system of Canon Law, or for that matter any formalized legal system (aside from those governing internal church matters), it is incorrect to assume—as many people do—that Protestantism is inherently antinomian. In fact, law does have a role to play in many Protestant sects. A detailed discussion of this role or the sects themselves is beyond the scope of this book, but the second part of this chapter will introduce you to some Protestant views of the law.

1. Catholic Canon Law

Roman Catholic Canon Law is not just a code of law; although it is that. *See* THE CODE OF CANON LAW, 1983 (discussed in the article following this introduction). It is an entire system of law with its own courts, cases, judges, and lawyers. Central to the Catholic Canon Law system is the fulfillment of the Church's mission of salvation. The Pope also plays an important role in the Canon Law system (see below).

Canon law is an old legal system dating back to early in the Catholic Church's history, although it is not as old as other religious law such as Halakha and tipitaka. *See supra* Sections B and D. The first "Code" of Canon Law was published in 1917, and the current Code was first published in 1983. Of course, much of the substance and many of the practices in the Canon Law system were in existence long before Canon Law was codified into a single code. The current code is divided into seven Books and contains over 1,700 canons (rules). The code is written in Latin, but it has been translated into a number of languages including English. It should be noted, however, that the official version of the Code is the Latin version.

As with any legal code, the Code of Canon Law must be interpreted and applied to many situations. It has its own practices and terminology and thus there are also a number of treatises on Catholic Canon Law. Of course, canon Lawyers are central to the system. Canon lawyers need not be trained as secular lawyers (although some are). They must, however, be specially trained in the Canon Law. Many Canon lawyers are priests, but many are not. All Canon lawyers must have a strong background in Catholic theology.

Canon law is applied to many issues relevant to Catholics from internal church matters to the regulation of the faithful. Some examples are provided in the article following this introduction. Just as it is incorrect to suggest that Protestantism inherently rejects legal conceptions of religion, it is equally incorrect to assume that the system of Canon Law is the embodiment of the Catholic religion. Natural law and moral law, which are not completely embodied in the Code of Canon Law, also apply, and of course the relationship between Catholics and G-d is a matter of faith that is reflected in, but not created by, the Canon Law. Moreover, there is an entire realm of law relevant to the liturgy that is not part of the Code of Canon Law.

This section provides only the most basic overview of Catholic Canon Law. The following article gives one perspective on Canon Law, along with a lot of excellent background information. It also does an excellent job of explaining the important role of Papal decrees such as Apostolic letters in the Canon Law system, although some of the conclusions it draws about a specific Apostolic letter may be controversial to some. Those interested in learning more about Canon Law might want to read THE CODE OF CANON LAW, 1983, and some of the commentaries and treatises discussing it.

LADISLAS ORSY, S.J., *STABILITY AND DEVELOPMENT IN CANON LAW AND THE CASE OF "DEFINITIVE" TEACHING*

76 NOTRE DAME L. REV. 865 (2001).

The beginning of knowledge is wonder, wonder provoked by a puzzle whose pieces do not seem to fit together. We do have such an on-going puzzle in canon law; it is the prima facie conflict between the demand of stability and the imperative of development.

Stability is an essential quality of any good legal system because a community's laws are an expression of its identity, and there is no identity without permanency. Many times we hear in the United States that we are a country held together by our laws. Although the statement cannot be the full truth, it is obvious that if our laws ever lost their stability, the nation's identity would be imperiled. In a religious community where the source of its identity is in the common memory of a divine revelation, the demand for stability is even stronger. Fidelity to the "Word of God" becomes the principal virtue.

Yet, any good legal system must be open and receptive to developments. No community, secular or religious, can be frozen in time and live; absolute stillness means death. In a political community, the internal energies of the citizenry and the pressing forces of history have their unrelenting impact on the laws and demand changes. Similar forces operate in a religious community: the "gathering" of the believers, ecclesia, is never a static monument; it is a living body animated by internal resources and responding to external influences. * * *

Thus, the demand for stability and the imperative of development are vital forces in any living community; they operate in nations and churches. The question, therefore, is not how the one could be eliminated and the other kept. Nor could it be which of the two should prevail. Both are needed. Our inquiry can be only about their respective roles and a desirable balance between the two that protects the group's identity and leaves enough space for the imperative of growth and expansion.

* * *

I. GENERAL PRINCIPLES

Concepts are the building blocks for principles. My first task, therefore, will be to account for my use of some foundational terms in this inquiry: canon law, stability, and development.

A. *Foundational Concepts*

Canon law in this Essay means norms created by the ecclesiastical legislator, hence of human origin. Admittedly, the official Code of Canon Law also includes norms of divine origin: baptism is necessary for becoming a Christian, the Church has the power to forgive sins, the evangelical message must be proclaimed to all nations, and so forth. Such divine ordinances, however, are not the subject matter of my inquiry.

I focus on the so-called "ecclesiastical laws"—a conventional expression to designate human laws in the Church. What are they? Let us begin our inquiry with Aquinas's definition of human law: an ordinance of reason—by the one in charge of the community—for the sake of the common good—promulgated. These spare words cover a wealth of ideas. Positively, they state that the purpose of the law is the common good, the maker of the law is someone who holds his power in trust and has been mandated to take care of the community, the content of the law is a command measured by reason, and the birth of the law is in a public act through which due information is given to the community. It follows, negatively, that a norm which is not for the good of the social body is not law, a command that is in contravention of the sacred duty of taking care of the people has no binding force, an ordinance that reason cannot approve of is invalid, and a duty ill-defined is as good as non-existent. In sum, from the realm of the law, Aquinas excludes self-serving politics, tyranny, irrationality, and prosecutions that can catch a person unaware. * * *

We have now a "generic" definition of human law. Canon law is one of its "species": it is human law in the Church. * * *

Canon law, therefore, is an ordinance conceived and articulated by reason and faith—enacted by an authority sacramentally established—for the sake of creating a favorable environment in the community for the reception of God's gifts—promulgated.

Positively, the purpose of the canon law is the creation of a favorable environment for the people to receive God's gifts, or the creation of a favorable environment for God to distribute his gifts (we should not forget that human beings have the capacity to put obstacles even to God's gracious actions); the makers of the law are persons sacramentally entrusted and empowered to guide and serve the community; the content of the law is measured by human rationality and intelligence of faith; and the binding force of the law is created through the act of promulgation.

Negatively, this definition excludes from the life of the Church any ordinance that harms the personal dignity of a believer and blocks the development of his or her intelligence and freedom; it denies the legislator any power that is not of evangelical service; it bars any rule that contradicts reason or faith; and it rejects any criminal procedure based on obscure or ambivalent concepts. In sum, in canon law there is no place for any formalism, any lording it over the community, anything irrational or irreligious, or any prosecution without fair warning about the crime.

The other concepts are stability and development. The two differ essentially as standing differs from running. Existentially, however, they are not autonomous qualities in splendid isolation or in continuous conflict but dynamic forces working together for the good of the whole. They contribute jointly to the well-being of the whole body: the one gives it permanency in identity, the other brings it growth and expansion. Their interaction keeps the body in good balance. A conceptual understanding of the two forces may be necessary, but not enough. To grasp what they are, we must watch them in their dynamic interaction.

Stability in the world of the laws creates a sense of security in the subjects. Legal developments offer them opportunity to use their potentials increasingly. Catholic believers see the Church as well-grounded in stability: Christ is its founder, his Spirit is its life-giver. No one can take away the memory of the evangelical message and no one can strangle the forces of divine energy. The same believers, however, often perceive development as problematic: "How can we know," they ask, "true progress from deceptive change? How can we differentiate healthy growth from sickly decline?"

A seasoned answer is available: it comes from Cardinal John Henry Newman. In his Essay on the Development of Christian Doctrine, published in its final form in 1878, he proposed a theory that is as valid today as it was in his days.[6] His interest was primarily in explaining the development of doctrine in the Christian church, but most of what he said is applicable to the development of canon law.

He proposed seven positive criteria for recognizing genuine developments and as many negative marks for identifying destructive changes. For brevity's sake, I pull them together and summarize them under three headings.

The positive signs are the following: First, a healthy development respects the foundations of the institution—its identity remains intact, and the leading principles of its existence and operations are not destroyed. Second, true development shows a harmonious progress from the old to the new—it is the fruit of historical continuity, the roots of the new are in the old, and the once hidden potentials of the old are revealed in the new. Third, the new has a vigor of life—it is filled with energy, and it brings life to its surroundings.

These signs speak even more clearly if we contrast them with their opposites, the signs of decline: First, a false development destabilizes the foundations of an institution—it has a corrosive impact on the community's identity, and it undermines the original principles of its activities. Second, in the transition from the old to the new there is a radical

---

6. The book had many editions and reprints; for an edition with extensive critical apparatus, see JOHN HENRY NEWMAN, AN ESSAY ON THE DEVELOPMENT OF CHRISTIAN DOCTRINE (Charles Harold ed., Longmans, Green & Co. 1949) (1878). In particular, see chapter 5, *Genuine Developments Contrasted with Corruptions*, id. at 155–91.

break—the new does not grow out of the old, and the image of the old cannot be found in the new. Third, the new shows no vigor of life, it exhibits decay—it weakens the institution, and it leads to stagnation, alienation, and loss of quality of life.

Now we have some workable criteria by which to judge what is, or what is not, an authentic development in the realm of doctrine and in the realm of law. Before we go any further, however, we need to understand the basic difference between the "Church teaching" and the "Church acting." While the Church is protected in its judgments about the articles of faith, in matters of practical prudence it can fall short of the highest standard.

B. Prudence in the Church

The Catholic belief is that in matters of doctrine the universal Church is endowed with the charism of fidelity to God's revelation, commonly explained as infallibility. This charism is granted to the whole Church, but the final judge of the authenticity of the revealed message is the college of bishops presided over by the Pope, or the Pope acting (defining) alone using his own full apostolic authority.

It is not, however, and it has never been, the Catholic belief that in practical and temporal matters the Church at large, or its office holders, were given the charism of the highest degree of prudence. The history of the Church proves overwhelmingly that this is indeed the truth. Vatican Council II spoke on the matter: "In its pilgrimage on earth Christ summons the Church to continual reformation, of which it is always in need, in so far as it is an institution of human beings on earth."

When Pope John Paul II offers his apologies for the past "mistakes" of those who acted "in the name of the Church," he therefore obeys the Council and confirms the timeless fragility of the Church in matters of prudence.

This innate fragility affects the official operations of the Church. It affects all who are making, administering, and explaining ecclesiastical laws. This is not to suggest that the laws should not be obeyed, but it is to state that canon law must never be approached with the same reverence that is due to ecclesiastical teaching. The one is about truth eternal, the other is about matters temporal—some of them sacred but still temporal. Human laws in the Church can be supremely prudent— and they can fail to be prudent. Mostly, though, they do not represent the extremes. Instead, they honor God and display our human limitations. This is not to suggest that the officials of the Church can be so imprudent as to lose sight completely of the end of all laws, which is "the salvation of souls," and then mislead the Church away from the path of the Kingdom. It is to say that, in choosing the temporal means toward the organization of the community and its activities, the persons in charge may fail to reach well-balanced, prudential judgments, as it happened, for example, in the cases of the Crusades, the Inquisition, the close alliance with the secular power, and so forth.

This is the context in which any new legislation needs to be assessed.

II. THE CASE OF DEFINITIVE TEACHING

By way of introducing the case of "definitive teaching," let me state firmly that in matters of doctrine stability is essential. The faithful must not lose the memory of the evangelical message; it is the source of their identity. Yet, as a seed is there to be sown, strike roots, and grow into a plant, so the message sown in the mind and heart of the people must strike roots, grow, and produce fruit that is the intelligence of faith. Such development is equally essential. * * *

An oft-quoted traditional rule expresses well the ideal balance between stability and development in matters of belief: "in necessary things unity, in doubtful things liberty, in all things charity." The "necessary things" are what we need to believe because they belong to the very core of the Christian Tradition; we must be one in professing them. In modern, mainly post Vatican I, times, such doctrines are often described as "articles of faith infallibly taught." They are articulated in our creeds, in the "determinations" of the ecumenical councils, and in the papal "definitions." They are also proclaimed and honored in the daily worship of the universal Church.

The "doubtful things" are not teachings that Christians ought to doubt or contest but points of doctrine that—as yet—have not been fully authenticated in any of the legitimate ways as integral parts of the Tradition. They are positions and opinions (usually inherited) that ought to be respected but are in need of scrutiny to discover their significance for the community. For such an inquiry liberty is essential.

Charity, of course, needs no explanation.

A. *The Code of Canon Law, 1983 [1983 reflects the year of the most recent promulgation of the Code of Canon Law]*

The Code of Canon Law, promulgated in 1983, mandated a healthy balance between stability and development. Its Canon 750 (as it was then) stressed the importance of stability.

> All that is contained in the word of God, handed over in writing or by tradition; that is, [all] that is in the one deposit of faith entrusted to the church, and is proclaimed either by the solemn magisterium of the church, or by its ordinary and universal magisterium, which is made manifest by the common assent of the faithful under the guidance of the sacred magisterium; must be believed with divine and Catholic faith; all are bound, therefore, to reject doctrines contrary to it.[15]

Canon 218 asserted the imperative of development and the need for "just freedom" in research.

15. 1983 Code c.750.

Persons dedicated to sacred disciplines enjoy just freedom in research and in manifesting their opinion prudently in matters in which they are experts while paying due respect to the magisterium of the church.[16]

The two canons together stated well the right and duty of the community—to preserve and to let evolve the evangelical doctrine. In case of conflict between the two tasks, an additional norm tipped the scale in the favor of development, as Canon 749, paragraph 3, prescribed: "No doctrine is understood to be infallible unless it is manifestly so proven." In other terms, the researcher must be free to investigate and report on his findings unless it is manifest that he would undermine infallible teaching. In legal language, there is a presumption in favor of the "faith seeking understanding."

B.   The Apostolic Letter, 1998

This balance established by the Code of Canon Law, however, was changed in 1998 with the promulgation of the Apostolic Letter motu proprio Ad tuendam fidem.[19] The Letter introduced into, and imposed on, the Church a new category of teaching, called "definitive," and explained it as not infallible but irreformable. Effectively, if not verbally, it transferred some freely debated doctrines from the field of the "doubtful things" to the field of the "necessary things," where no question must be raised any more about their unchangeable nature. To this effect, the motu proprio added a second paragraph to Canon 750 (the original text has become paragraph one). The added text reads:

Each and every proposition stated definitively by the magisterium of the church concerning the doctrine of the faith or morals, that is, each and every proposition required for the sacred preservation and faithful explanation of the same deposit of faith, must also be firmly embraced and maintained; anyone, therefore, who rejects those propositions which are to be held definitively is opposed to the doctrine of the Catholic Church.

Thus the document places each and every point of teaching that has been declared "definitive" by the papal magisterium into the body of "the doctrine of the Catholic Church," even when such a declaration does not fulfill the stringent criteria of a papal definition—criteria that Vatican Council I articulated with meticulous care after much search and fierce debate.

The Roman Pontiff, when he speaks ex cathedra, that is, when, acting in the office of shepherd and teacher of all Christians, he defines, by virtue of his supreme apostolic authority, a doctrine concerning faith and morals to be held by the universal church, possesses through the divine assistance promised to him in the person of blessed Peter, the infallibility with which the divine Redeemer willed his church to be endowed.

---

16. *Id.* c.218.

19. Pope John Paul II, *Ad tuendam fidem*, 28 Origins 113 (1998). * * *

Vatican Council II confirmed this definition and articulated its limit with some precision: "This infallibility ... extends just as far as the deposit of divine revelation that is to be guarded as sacred and faithfully expounded."

In protecting the stability of doctrine, the Apostolic Letter went beyond the "deposit of revelation" when it declared that "each and everything [doctrine] which is required to safeguard reverently and expound faithfully the same deposit of faith" can be the object of a definitive statement and thus must be embraced and held as irreformable. Several commentators noted that, with the help of the theory of "definitive teaching," papal infallibility has been expanded beyond the Constitutions of Vatican I and II and beyond the limits "canonized" by the Council and by the Code of Canon Law.

To enforce the observance of this new provision, the motu proprio added a clause to Canon 1371, note 1, that institutes "just penalty" for anyone who fails to embrace and hold all and each that are definitively proposed and "obstinately rejects the doctrine mentioned in Canon 750, paragraph 2, and who does not retract after having been admonished." Such persons, although not heretics, are "opposed to the doctrine of the Catholic Church."

C. An Assessment

What is the result of this new legislation? It has created a new balance between stability and development. In the practical order, it has increased—as no law has ever done it before—the "necessary things," the doctrines that must be held, and it has decreased the "doubtful things," teachings that were disputed questions. It has done so not merely by normative directions but also by punitive sanctions. This was a break with the explicit policy of Vatican Council II, which wanted to proclaim the good news but refused to bolster its teaching with the threat of criminal actions. Also to be noted is that the sanction in a given case can be heavy, since the delict is being "opposed to the doctrine of the Catholic Church," which is, presumably, just one notch under the crime of heresy.

The scope of Canon 218's affirming freedom in research is now more narrowly drawn. Canon 749, paragraph 3, stating that nothing should be held infallible unless it is manifestly so proven, has become moot because some doctrines must be held irreformable even if they are not infallible, and persons in no way contesting infallible doctrine may be punished for being "opposed to the doctrine of the Catholic Church."

All this is canon law now. The universal Church has the task of receiving it, not in the sense of legal ratification but in the sense of understanding it and assimilating its content. Such a reception is bound to be a complex and long drawn-out process.

To reject the legislation would not be a Catholic response. Since it comes from an authoritative source, it must be received with obsequium, respect, in the canonical language. Canon 752 is applicable:

Although not assent of faith, religious obsequium [respect, loyalty] of the intellect and the will must be given to a doctrine which the Supreme Pontiff or the college of bishops declares concerning the faith and morals when they exercise the authentic magisterium.

Obsequium, however, cannot determine the doctrinal weight of a document. That is a matter for critical theological judgment. Nor can reverence assess the degree of prudence that prompted the new legislation, for such a judgment can be articulated only from an historical distance.

While this process of reception is getting under way, some comments are possible and in order.

The initial question for any commentator needs to be about the weight of authority behind the Apostolic Letter. By way of exclusion, the Letter does not carry the authenticating marks of infallibility as they were determined by Vatican Council I and confirmed by Vatican Council II, because it is not a solemn ex cathedra pronouncement. It is a papal document of high authority, but not of the highest. Through this motu proprio, the theory of "definitive teaching" has entered the realm of theology, although not with the same force as the definition of infallibility did at Vatican Council I. No theologian can ignore or bypass it. Indeed, to understand its full meaning, studies are already well under way and progressing.

As regards the content of the document and the substance of the issue, it is probably wise, at this point in time, for a commentator not to go beyond some tentative assessment relying on Newman's criteria for authentic development. I think that we are already in a position to raise some good questions and see where they lead us, but not in a situation to articulate well-grounded conclusions.

(1) Does the new legislation confirm the old foundations and promote the vital operations of the institution? The document certainly intends to protect the stability of the doctrinal foundations, but it seems to extend them beyond the traditional limits. It attributes unchangeable permanency to doctrines to which the universal Church has not committed itself infallibly. In consequence, the vital operation of "faith seeking understanding" appears restricted. The new laws impose a hitherto unknown uniformity in doctrinal matters and safeguards it by punitive measures.

(2) Is the new legislation organically rooted in the old? At the very core of the new legislation is the idea of non-infallible but unchangeable teaching. It is difficult to locate the origins of the idea in the Tradition; it has appeared in the last decades only. Neither Vatican I nor Vatican II discussed definitive but non-infallible teaching to any length or in any depth. Nor has there been—as far as we know—previous to the promulgation of the motu proprio any sustained consultation on this issue among the bishops.

(3) Does the new legislation bring a new vigor of life to the Church? The new legislation is not likely to bring new vigor into theological research. The danger is that "definitive" proclamations will hamper the natural and organic evolution of the "intelligence of faith"; the community endowed by Christ with a supernatural instinct of faith cannot play its part in the discovery of truth. Perhaps even more importantly (tragically?), the expanding of the "irreformable" doctrines is bound to slow down the ecumenical movement, a movement that we believe is wanted by God and sustained by his Spirit. Sooner or later the Catholic Church must state with no ambiguity whether or not the acceptance of "definitive teachings" will be considered an absolute condition for its reunion with other Christian churches. If we are part of the ecumenical movement, we must spell out our intentions.

Assessments of greater weight and of more lasting value will come over a longer period of time and from better sources than this Essay. They will come from the living Church, from all and each part of it: the faithful, the episcopate, the theologians. They, God's people, "cannot be mistaken in belief"—as Vatican Council II stated. Throughout this process of "faith seeking understanding," the magisterium must be present in several ways: first by listening to the people and encouraging their efforts, and then as the legitimate authority to pronounce decisive judgments.

Conclusion

One must not be a Hegelian to assert that, in the history of the human family, progress often comes through dialectical movements. A dominant trend is followed by its opposite, and out of their encounter, a new synthesis emerges. Such a pattern may have something to do with our human nature—we cannot comprehend the fullness of reality all at once, because we approach our complex challenges one-sidedly. Then, we realize that the truth is richer than our understanding of it, and we look at the other side and discover a synthesis.

This pattern of history, or this habit of the human mind, operates in the life of the Church as well. There, too, we find a succession of dialectical forces. To find it, it is enough to reflect on the events of the last century. The beginnings of it were marked by strong trends in support of the stability of doctrine and institutions: the "combat" against modernism and the promulgation of the first Code of Canon Law in 1917 are good examples of it. At the end of the pontificate of Pius XII, the Church lived and operated under a strong central administration. The Pope was the supreme teacher and, by and large the world over, the people lived under a strict discipline, imposed and upheld by clear laws and sanctions (not to mention the far-reaching eternal punishments detailed by many moral theologians and tacitly supported by the hierarchy). Many times we heard that no ecumenical council will ever be needed again: the papacy can take care of the Church. Obedience was the principal virtue.

Then came John XXIII, who in 1959, on the feast of the conversion of Saul the Persecutor who became Paul the Apostle, announced his intention to convoke an ecumenical council. With a few quiet words he reversed the forces of history. Returning to the ancient custom of the Church, he wanted to listen to the bishops and invited them to speak freely—to him and to each other. He risked a new balance between stability and development, and he succeeded. * * *

Through an awareness of the dialectics of history, we can come to a better understanding of the Church's history. Today, stability seems to be favored over creativity. But "in the universal body of the faithful," that is, "in the whole people ... from the bishops to the last of the faithful laity," there is an immense source of energy. Sooner or later, its forces are bound to break to the surface and surprise the observers. This seems to be the pattern of history—or, is this the pattern that God uses to lead his people?

2. Protestantism and Law

There is no way to talk about "Protestant Law" in any coherent sense. There are numerous Protestant sects and a variety of views on the appropriate role of law. From the Episcopalian system of Canon Law to the Anabaptist antinomianism, law is perceived in different ways by a variety of sects. This is true not only in regard to the appropriate role of law, but also the substance of that law. Thus, Seventh Day Adventist practice includes fidelity to many of the laws contained in the "Old Testament," while other Protestant sects reject the primacy of such law. Yet contrary to popular stereotypes of Protestant theology many Protestant sects share a belief in the importance of law. It is true that a central tenet of virtually all Protestant sects is the belief that faith is the path to salvation, but this does not mean that faith can't be augmented by works, even if the works themselves are secondary.

The following article provides an excellent, and amazingly succinct, discussion of the role of law in mainstream Protestant theology from the time of the reformation. The article ultimately focuses on the comparison between traditional Protestant conceptions of law, especially criminal law, and Anglo–American criminal law. It is included here primarily for its discussion of the role of law in mainstream Protestant thought. The discussion of criminal law, which is heavily edited here, provides a good example of "Protestant Law" in action, as well as a comparison of traditional Protestant views of criminal law and American views. This section provides only the most basic overview of the role of law in Protestant thought, especially given the diverse perspectives on law among Protestant sects. Volumes have been written on the subject and most law libraries and university libraries contain useful resources for the study of Protestant views on law.

JOHN E. WITTE, JR. & THOMAS C. ARTHUR, *THE THREE USES OF THE LAW: A PROTESTANT SOURCE OF THE PURPOSES OF CRIMINAL PUNISHMENT?*

10 J.L. & Religion 433 (1993/1994).

* * *

* * * In this article, we focus on the interaction of Anglo–American criminal law and Protestant theological doctrine. We argue (1) that the sixteenth-century Protestant theological doctrine of the uses of moral law provided a critical analogue, if not antecedent, to the classic Anglo–American doctrine of the purposes of criminal law and punishment; and (2) that this theological doctrine provides important signposts to the development of a more integrated moral theory of criminal law and punishment in late twentieth century America.

* * *

I. The Theological Doctrine of the Uses of Moral Law

A. *Classic Formulations*

The theological doctrine of the uses of law was forged in the Protestant Reformation.[4] It was a popular doctrine, particularly among Lutheran and Calvinist reformers. Martin Luther, Philip Melanchthon, John Calvin and other Protestant reformers gave the doctrine a considerable place in their monographs and sermons, as well as in their catechisms and confessional writings. It was also a pivotal doctrine, for it provided the reformers with something of a middle way between radical Catholic legalism, on the one hand, and radical Anabaptist antinomianism, on the other. It allowed the reformers to reject the claims of certain Catholics that salvation can be achieved by works of the law as well as the claims of certain Anabaptists that those who are saved have no further need of the law.

The reformers focused their uses doctrine primarily on the natural or moral law—that compendium of moral rights and duties that transcend the positive laws of the state. God, they believed, has written a moral law on the hearts of all persons, rewritten it in the pages of Scripture, and summarized it in the Ten Commandments. A person comes to know the meaning and measure of this moral law both through the counsel of reason and conscience and, more completely, through the commandments of Scripture and the Spirit. Though a person can be saved if he obeys the moral law perfectly, his inherently sinful nature

---

4. Patristic and scholastic theologians had, of course, recognized the idea that the natural or moral law has different functions in the life of the individual and community. The Protestant reformers, however, were the first to develop a systematic theological doctrine of the "uses of the law" (usus legis), which they wove into their doctrines of God and man, sin and salvation. Luther was apparently the first to give prominence to the doctrine. * * *

renders him incapable of such perfect obedience. This human incapacity does not render the moral law useless. The moral law retains three important uses or functions in a person's life, which the reformers variously called: (1) a civil or political use; (2) a theological or spiritual use; and (3) an educational or didactic use.

First, the moral law has a civil use to restrain persons from sinful conduct by threat of divine punishment. "[T]he law is like a halter," Calvin wrote, "to check the raging and otherwise limitlessly ranging lusts of the flesh. . . . Hindered by fright or shame, [persons] dare neither execute what they have conceived in their minds, nor openly breathe forth the rage of their lust." The law thus imposes upon saints and sinners alike what Calvin called a "constrained and forced righteousness" * * *. Threatened by divine sanctions, persons obey the basic commandments of the moral law—to obey authorities, to respect their neighbor's person and property, to remain sexually continent, to speak truthfully of themselves and their neighbors.

Although "such public morality does not merit forgiveness of sin," it benefits sinners and saints alike. On the one hand, it allows for a modicum of peace and stability in this sin-ridden world. "Unless there is some restraint," Calvin writes, "the condition of wild beasts would be better and more desirable than ours. [Natural] liberty would always bring ruin with it if it were not bridled by the moderation" born of the moral law. On the other hand, such public morality enables persons who later become Christians to know at least the rudiments of Christian morality and to fulfill the vocations to which God has called them. "Even the children of God before they are called and while they are destitute of the spirit of sanctification become partly broken in by bearing the yoke of coerced righteousness. Thus, when they are later called, they are not entirely untutored and uninitiated in discipline as if it were something foreign."

Second, the moral law has a theological use to condemn sinful persons for their violations of the law. Such condemnation ensures both the integrity of the law and the humility of the sinner. On the one hand, the violation of the law is avenged, and the integrity, the balance of the law is restored by the condemnation of those who violate it. On the other hand, the violator of the law is appropriately chastened. In Luther's hard words, the law serves as a mirror "to reveal to man his sin, blindness, misery, wickedness, ignorance, hate, contempt of God. . . . When the law is being used correctly, it does nothing but reveal sin, work wrath, accuse, terrify, and reduce consciences to the point of despair." "In short," Calvin writes, "it is as if someone's face were all marked up so that everybody who saw him might laugh at him. Yet he himself is completely unaware of his condition. But if they bring him a mirror, he will be ashamed of himself, and will hide and wash himself when he sees how filthy he is." Such despair, the reformers believed, was a necessary precondition for the sinner both to seek God's help and to have faith in God's grace. * * *

Third, the moral law has an educational use of enhancing the spiritual development of believers, of teaching those who have already been justified "the works that please God." Even the most devout saints, Calvin wrote, still need the law "to learn more thoroughly . . . the Lord's will [and] to be aroused to obedience." The law teaches them not only the "public" or "external" morality that is common to all persons, but also the "private" or "internal" morality that is becoming only of Christians. As a teacher, the law not only coerces them against violence and violation, but also cultivates in them charity and love. It not only punishes harmful acts of murder, theft, and fornication, but also prohibits evil thoughts of hatred, covetousness, and lust. Through the exercise of this private morality, the saints glorify God, exemplify God's law, and impel other sinners to seek God's grace.

This theological doctrine of the three uses of the moral law was rooted in the Protestant theology of salvation. Following St. Paul, the reformers recognized various stages in the spiritual enhancement of the Christian—from predestination to justification to sanctification. The moral law, they believed, plays a part in all three steps of the soteriological process. It coerces sinners so that they can be preserved. It condemns them so that they can be justified. It counsels them so that they can be sanctified. The doctrine was also rooted in the Protestant theology of the person. Following Luther, the reformers emphasized that a person is simul iustus et peccator, at once saint and sinner, spirit and flesh. The moral law caters to both the spiritual and the carnal dimensions of his or her character. The person of the flesh is coerced to develop at least a minimal public or external morality; the person of the spirit is counselled to develop a more holistic private or internal morality.

Although rooted in the intricacies of Protestant theology, the uses doctrine had broad appeal among sixteenth century Protestants. * * *

B. *Later Elaborations*

Contrary to conventional wisdom, the theological doctrine of the three uses of the moral law was not merely an anachronism of the early Reformation that died with the magisterial reformers. The doctrine remained a staple of Protestant dogma after the early Reformation. The classic texts of Luther, Melanchthon, Calvin and others, which expounded the uses doctrine, were constantly reprinted and translated and circulated widely in Protestant circles. The Protestant editions of the Bible, particularly the Geneva Bible, set out the uses doctrine in its marginal glosses on the relevant texts of St. Paul. A steady stream of references to the doctrine can be found in Protestant monographs, sermons, catechisms, and confessional writings from the seventeenth to the twentieth centuries. A number of distinguished Protestant theologians in this century * * * include the doctrine in their theological systems. One could multiply examples to demonstrate the continuity of this uses doctrine in the Protestant tradition—a worthy exercise, given the paucity of studies available. For our purposes of discovering an intellectual analogue or antecedent to Anglo–American theories of criminal punishment, however, we need cite only a few texts to illustrate the wide acceptance of the uses doctrine among Anglican, Calvinist, and Free Church groups in England and America.

Leading Anglican divines of the later Tudor Reformation embraced the uses doctrine. Bishop Hooper, for example, offered a brisk rendition of the doctrine before launching into his famous exposition on the Decalogue:

> Seeing that the works of the law cannot deserve remission of sin, nor save man, and yet God requireth our diligence and obedience unto the law, it is necessary to know the use of the law, and why it is given us. The first use is civil and external, forbidding and punishing the trangression of politic and civil ordinance.... The second use of the law is to inform and instruct man aright, what sin is, to accuse us, to fear us, and damn us.... These two uses of the law appertain as well unto infideles, as to the fideles.... The third use of the law is to shew unto the Christians what works God requireth of them.[28]

* * *

Among early Anglican divines, Heinrich Bullinger's formulations of the uses doctrine enjoyed perhaps the widest authority. Like Luther, Bullinger viewed the theological use as "the chief and proper office of the law"—"a certain looking-glass, wherein we behold our own corruption, frailness, imbecility, imperfection"—and he waxed eloquently on the doctrine for several pages. He also insisted, however, that the moral law has a vital civil use to teach the unregenerate "the first principles and rudiments of righteousness" and an educational use to teach the redeemed "the very and absolute righteousness" that becomes Christians. By the end of the sixteenth century, Bullinger's printed sermon on the topic became a standard classroom text for budding Anglican clergy. Comparable sentiments on the uses doctrine are peppered throughout Richard Hooker's classic eight-volume Laws of Ecclesiastical Polity.

The uses doctrine did not remain confined to the Anglican academy. An early liturgical handbook from Waldegrave, for example, put a crisp distillation of the doctrine in the hands of the parishioner. The "godly order and discipline" born of adherence to the moral law, the handbook reads, "is, as it were, sinews in the body, which knit and join the members together with decent order and comeliness. It is a bridle to stay the wicked from their mischiefs; it is a spur to prick forward such as be slow and negligent: yea, and for all men it is the Father's rod, ever in a readiness to chastise gently the faults committed, and to cause them afterward to live in more godly fear and reverence." The famous prayers of Chaplain Becon, which enjoyed broad circulation in the English and American Anglican churches, are filled with invocations that God allow

28. John Hooper, *A Declaration of the ten holy comaundementes of allmygthye God....* (Parker Society, 1548), reprinted in 1 EARLY WRITINGS OF JOHN HOOPER, D.D. 281–82 (1843).

His commandments to work their three uses in the lives of individuals and the community. * * *

Calvinist groups in England and America—Puritans, Pilgrims, Huguenots, Presbyterians, Congregationalists, Independents, Brownists, and others—embraced the uses doctrine, both in its classic form, and with a distinctive covenantal cast. Classic formulations of the uses doctrine recur repeatedly in Calvinist sermons, catechisms, and theological handbooks from the early seventeenth century onward. A short catechism, prepared by the seventeenth century Scottish lawyer and theologian Samuel Rutherford, for example, has typical language on the theological and educational uses of the moral law:

> Q. What is the use of the law if we can not obteane salvatione by it? A. It encloseth us under condemnation as a citie beseiged with a garrisone of souldiers that we may seek to Christ for mercie. Q. What is the use of the law after we are com to Christ? A. After Christ has made agreement betwixt us and the law, we delight to walk in it for the love of Christ.[36]

* * *

[The catechism] also devoted several pages to exegesis of the Decalogue, which included ample discussion of the civil use of the moral law.

Puritan Calvinists in England and New England cast the uses doctrine in a distinctive covenantal mode. The broad contours of Puritan covenant theology are well known. Like other Protestants, the Puritans recognized a divine covenant or agreement between God and humanity. They recognized two distinct Biblical covenants: the Old Testament covenant of works whereby the chosen people of Israel, through obedience to God's law, are promised eternal salvation and blessings; and the New Testament covenant of grace, whereby the elect through faith in Christ's incarnation and atonement are promised eternal salvation and beatitude. Unlike other Protestants, however, a number of Puritans conceived these covenants largely in legalistic terms—viewing the moral law as a summary of the provisions of the covenant which God made binding on man. These Puritans further conceived that both the covenant of works and the covenant of grace have continued to operate since biblical times. The covenant of works binds the unregenerate—all those who are without faith, and beyond the realm of salvation. The covenant of grace binds the redeemed—all those who are with faith and are fully justified. Both covenants bind the predestined—those who are elected to salvation but still without faith; their compliance with the covenant of works ultimately leads them to enter the covenant of grace.

* * *

The Free Churches, especially those born of the Great Awakening in America, occasionally included their uses doctrine in their literature and

---

36. *Ane Catachisme Conteining The Soume of Christian Religion* by Mr. Samuel Rutherfurd cap 33 (c 1644), *in* Alexander F. Mitchell, CATECHISMS OF THE SECOND REFORMATION 226 (James Nesbit, 1886) (citations and question numbers omitted).

sermons as well. Among their leaders, John Wesley, the father of Methodism, devoted the most attention to the uses doctrine, both in his writings on law, and in his sermons on salvation and sanctification. His formulations resonate rather closely with those of Melanchthon and Luther. * * *

* * *

The uses doctrine was thus well known in English and American Protestant circles, both academic and lay. To be sure, the doctrine was no centerpiece of Protestant dogma: it never won universal assent or uniform articulation, and it always remained in the shadow of the grand Protestant doctrines of man and God, sin and salvation, law and Gospel. Yet the doctrine had ample enough coherence and adherence to provide a common theological touchstone for members of fiercely competing sects. It also provided a common intellectual framework in which to situate a distinctive understanding of the purposes of criminal law and punishment.

II. THE LEGAL DOCTRINE OF THE PURPOSES OF CRIMINAL LAW

The new theological doctrine of the uses of moral law that emerged out of the Reformation had a close conceptual cousin in the new legal doctrine of the purposes of criminal law that came to prevail in early modern England and America. The early Protestant reformers themselves occasionally touched on this legal doctrine in their discussions of ecclesiastical discipline and in their asides on criminal law. * * *

* * *

A long tradition of Anglo–American jurists and moralists, from the early seventeenth century onward, expounded and expanded the legal doctrine of the purposes of criminal law in an array of treatises, pamphlets, and sermons—in some instances, writing under the direct inspiration of Protestant theologians.

The legal doctrine of the purposes of criminal law was similarly formulated but differently focused than its theological cousin. Like the theologians, early modern jurists accepted a general moral theory of government and criminal law. God has created a moral or natural law. He has vested in this moral law three distinctive uses. He imposes divine punishments to ensure that each use is fulfilled. State magistrates are God's vice-regents in the world. They must represent and reflect God's authority and majesty on earth. The laws which they promulgate must encapsulate and elaborate the principles of God's moral law, particularly as it is set out in the Ten Commandments. The provisions of the criminal law, therefore, must perforce parallel the provisions of the moral law. The purposes of criminal punishment must perforce parallel the purposes of divine punishment. * * *

From these premises, the English and American jurists argued that the criminal law serves three uses or purposes in the lives of the criminal and the community. These they variously called: (1) deterrence or prevention; (2) retribution or restitution; and (3) rehabilitation or reformation—the classic purposes of criminal law and punishment that every law student learns still today. The precise definition of these three purposes, and the relative priority and propriety of them, were subjects of endless debate among jurists and judges. Individual jurists, particularly those inspired by later Enlightenment and utilitarian sentiments, championed deterrence theories alone. But all three purposes were widely accepted at English and American criminal law until the end of the nineteenth century. The definition of the deterrent, retributive, and rehabilitative purposes of criminal law bears a striking resemblance to the definition of the civil, theological, and educational uses of the moral law.

* * *

The theological doctrine of the uses of moral law and the legal doctrine of the purposes of criminal law are closely analogous not only in their formulation, but also in their foundation. Like the theologians, the jurists believed that persons and societies are at once sinful and saintly. They thus tailored the criminal law as a whole to both types of persons and the criminal punishment of any individual to both dimensions of his or her character. Also like the theologians, the jurists subsumed and integrated their "uses" doctrine in a more general theory. The theologians subsumed their uses doctrine in a more general theology of salvation. For them, the moral law played an indispensable role in the process from predestination to justification to sanctification. The jurists subsumed their uses doctrine in a moral theory of government. For them, the criminal law played an indispensable role in discharging the divinely ordained tasks of the state to coerce, discipline, and nurture its citizens.

It would be too strong, of course, to say that the Protestant theological doctrine of the three uses of moral law was the source of the modern Anglo–American legal doctrine of the purposes of criminal law. Western writers since Plato have reflected on the purposes of criminal law, and early modern Anglo–American jurists certainly drew on these writings as much as those of Protestant theology. Yet the Protestant theological "uses" doctrine seems to have provided an important source of integration and instruction for the jurists. The uses doctrine was a commonplace of Protestant theology and ethics from the sixteenth century onward—well known to both learned theologians and lay parishioners. Several sixteenth century Protestant writers explicitly linked the theological and legal "uses" doctrines, and their writings were constantly reprinted and studied by later Protestants in England and America. Protestant jurists and Protestant theologians thereafter regularly collaborated in formulating criminal doctrines, and inflicting criminal punishment. The archives we have consulted harbor no "smoking gun"—no classic legal monograph that systematically pours the theological "uses" doctrine into the theory of criminal law though there may well be such evidence in the proceedings and opinions of lay ecclesiastical, marriage and consistory courts that we have yet to explore. But the close analogies between the structure and content of these theological and legal doctrines reflect ample doctrinal cross-fertilization between them.

III.   THE USES DOCTRINE IN CONTEMPORARY CRIMINAL LAW

Even in late twentieth century America, vestiges of this traditional understanding of criminal law and punishment remain evident.

Consistent with traditional formulations, modern American criminal law still includes deterrence, retribution, and rehabilitation among the principal purposes of punishment. Late nineteenth and early twentieth century experiments at reducing the purposes of criminal punishment to deterrence or rehabilitation alone have proved to be unpersuasive in theory and unworkable in practice. * * *

Also consistent with traditional formulations, contemporary criminal law continues to inculcate various "levels of morality" in citizens. The criminal law still proscribes conduct that harms others. * * * Through such prohibitions and punishments, the criminal law supports a basic "public" or "civic" morality. The criminal law also continues to outlaw attempts, polygamy, obscenity, bestiality, sodomy, and similar actions, that, though not directly harmful to other persons, are nonetheless considered morally and socially unacceptable. Through such punishment, the criminal law supports at least a "quasi-private" form of morality. Certain specialized bodies of criminal law, notably juvenile law, go even further and seek to inculcate in certain citizens charity, piety, sobriety, and other purely private virtues. Whether accidental or deliberate, modern criminal law perforce still defines and enforces moral values in American society.

Most contemporary jurists, however, seem to have abandoned at least three of the cardinal premises upon which the traditional Protestant understanding of the purposes of criminal law and punishment was founded. They have thus lost a vital source of unity and integration inherent in the traditional doctrine.

First, most contemporary jurists have abandoned the theory of natural or moral law, which traditionally inspired both the form and the content of criminal law. * * *

Second, most contemporary writers have abandoned the traditional anthropological assumption that human beings and human communities are at once saintly and sinful, simul iustus et peccator. Some stress the inherent goodness of the person and consider crime as aberrational and correctable. * * * Others stress the inherent depravity of the person and consider crime inevitable. * * *

Third, most contemporary writers have abandoned the traditional moral theory of government which helped to integrate the three purposes of criminal law and punishment. Today the state is seen solely as a representative of the people, not a vice-regent of God. Its laws must effectuate the will of the majority, not appropriate the will of God. * * *

* * *

* * * [I]f criminal law is to succeed, ordinary citizens must voluntarily avoid criminal activity as morally abhorrent. As both the Protestant reformers and classical jurists understood, the retributive function of criminal punishment underscores and reinforces the societal condemnation of morally abhorrent behavior, especially when the punishment fits the crime, when serious offenses are met with serious punishments. Conversely, the failure to impose suitable punishments for serious violations undermines and corrodes the moral beliefs of citizens by suggesting that their moral beliefs are wrong, that this conduct must not be so bad after all. By permitting wrongdoers to profit by their wrongs, the failure to punish demoralizes the law-abiding.

To bring to light a Protestant source of modern Anglo–American theories of criminal law and punishment is not to offer a panacea. One cannot readily transpose the moral concepts and criminal institutions of the sixteenth century into contemporary culture. But the Protestant tradition offers important insights even for our day. Protestant writers recognized that a system of criminal law depends upon a transcendent moral source for its structure, content, and efficacy, that any measure of criminal punishment must balance the values of deterrence, retribution, and rehabilitation, and that through punishment the state serves at once as disciplinarian, counselor, and teacher of its citizens. Protestant writers also recognized that criminal law is inherently limited in its capacities, and cannot operate alone. Other social institutions alongside the state, like the family, the school, the church, and other voluntary associations must play complementary roles. Each of these social institutions, too, bears the responsibility of encapsulating and elaborating moral principles. Each of these social institutions, too, must participate in the deterrence and retribution of crime, and the rehabilitation and reformation of the criminal and the community. These time-tested insights provide important signposts along the way to the development a more integrated understanding of criminal law and punishment for contemporary America.

CONCLUSION

This section has provided you with a basic overview of the role of law in several religions. Each of these religions could be the subject of its own law school course, and in fact, many law schools offer courses in Jewish Law, Islamic Law, and/or Canon Law. While the bulk of this book has been devoted to U.S. Constitutional Law, it is important to remember that Law & Religion consists of a great deal more than Church/State law. Hopefully this section has whet your appetite to learn more about religious law or the role of law in a specific religion(s). The information in this section can be viewed as the first extremely small step toward learning more about religious law, an area that has been the subject of voluminous writing.

*

Index

†